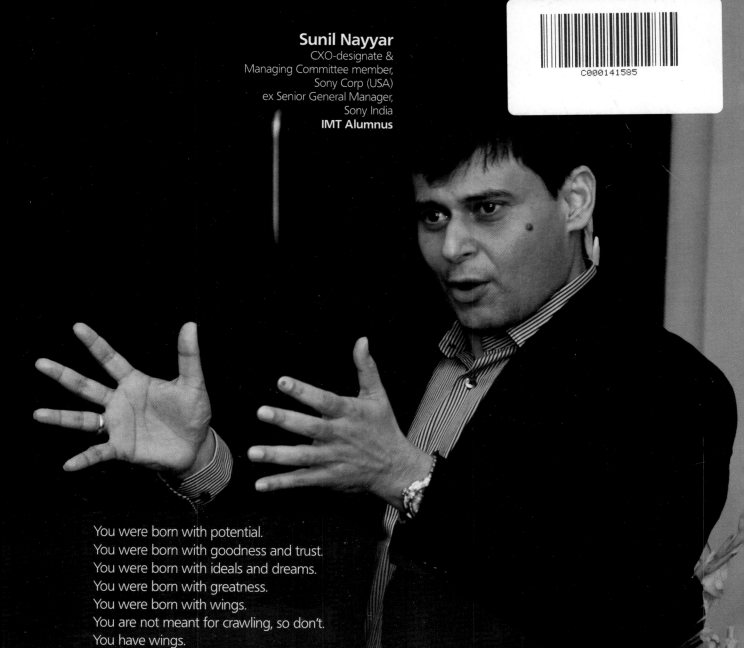

Sunil Nayyar
CXO-designate &
Managing Committee member,
Sony Corp (USA)
ex Senior General Manager,
Sony India
IMT Alumnus

You were born with potential.
You were born with goodness and trust.
You were born with ideals and dreams.
You were born with greatness.
You were born with wings.
You are not meant for crawling, so don't.
You have wings.
Learn to use them and fly.
(Rumi)

www.imt.edu/IMTAdvantage

**Institute of
Management Technology**
Ghaziabad I Nagpur I Dubai I Hyderabad

Nurturing Responsible Leaders

XLRI – Xavier School of Management believes that enduring corporate success can only be built on a foundation of ethics and social consciousness.

Money goes hand in hand with Meaning. Values and Valuations grow in concord.

A multi-dimensional course structure, a diverse selection of colleagues and a collection of responsible academic minds make for a compelling milieu in which to develop potential.

PGDM (HRM)

An organisation is fundamentally its people.
Truer now than any time else.
Master the nuances of HR as an intrinsic part of 21st century corporate strategy.

PGDM (BM)

Ethical, Flexible, Agile, Decisive – The Art & Science of great management.
Tap into the transformative energies & kick-start the journey that makes you.

DOCTORAL PROGRAMS (FPM/EFPM)

The Programs*

The Knowledge Economy is a feeding frenzy for bold, new perspectives.
Get a chance to merge scholarship with creativity to discover an original voice.

PGDM (GMP)

The future won't belong to 'Employees', but to those who take charge.
Discover the leader within and get a second-wind in your career.

PGDM (Global)

Geography is History in the 21st century. The world is flat now. America - China - India, the new axis of commerce.

Log on to
https://xlri.edu

{ **Eligibility, Key Dates, Registration**

Creating a Sustainable Future

* In chronological order

xavier aptitude test (XAT-2016)

conducted by **XLRI (Xavier School of Management)** on behalf of
XAMI (Xavier Association of Management Institutes).

XAT, most comprehensive and oldest MBA entrance examination in India, is conducted on the first Sunday of every Year.

XAT's multidimensional testing framework, is designed to meaningfully assess the aptitude of candidates for future business success.

XAT countries: **India, U.A.E., Nepal**
XAT accreditation at **110+ B-Schools**

Log on to
www.xatonline.net.in/admission

Log on to
www.xatonline.net.in/xatfaqs

- Eligibility
- Test Centres
- Registration

- Exam Schedule
- Exam Structure
- Exam Resources

- • XAT Centre (India)
- **TEXT** Select Participants

IMT
MICA
SPJIMR
GIM

XAMI MEMBERS: •XLRI •XIMB •LIBA •XISS •XIME •XIMR •XIMJ •MCIM •SJCBA •AIMIT •SFIMR

BHARATIYA VIDYA BHAVAN'S

S.P. Jain Institute of Management & Research

Influencing Practice • Promoting Value based Growth

Recent Achievements

SPJIMR crowned global champions at the Unilever Future Leaders' League finals

SPJIMR has been ranked No 3 by Business World & No.5 by MBAUniverse.com

SPJIMR team wins the prestigious TBLA Award

PGDM

2 Year Post Graduate Diploma in Management (Equivalent to MBA)

PGDM (MBA equivalent) is a full time residential programme with the objective to groom graduates as:

> Socially sensitive value driven leaders.

> Having integrated knowledge of selected functions in the global environment.

SPJIMR Advantage
- Excellent Placement Record
- Globally acclaimed Value-based leadership development programme (GMAC Met Fund and Team MBA Award)
- Ranked amongst Top 5 B-schools in India

  Three distinct internship opportunities: Global, Social & Corporate

Eligibility
- Bachelor's degree (10+2+3) or equivalent from a recognised university in India or abroad. Candidates in final year can also apply
- Qualifying Exams: CAT 2015, XAT 2016, GMAT (2013 onwards)
- For PIOs or Foreign Nationals: Graduates with GMAT score above 600.

Placement Highlights of 2015:

Avg. Package: INR 18.2 Lacs	Highest Package: INR 29.5 Lacs

- 80% of the batch has offers of Rs. 15 lacs and more
- The median salary for the batch of 232 students was 17.0 lacs

Some of our prominent recruiters are:

Amazon, Asian Paints, Axis Bank, Colgate-Palmolive, Dell, Flipkart, GE, GSK CH, HSBC, HUL, Mondelez, L'Oreal, Mahindra & Mahindra, Marico, Microsoft, P&G, TAS etc.

For more information visit: http://www.spjmr.org/pgdm

2 year full-time AICTE approved PGDM: 2016-18

The Institute for Financial Management and Research (IFMR) is a not-for-profit academic institution with a history of over four decades of research, consulting, training and management education. IFMR will admit 180 students for the Batch 2016-18.

Excellent placement

Students have been placed in reputed organizations like Accenture, Amba Research, AstraZeneca, Bank of America, Barclays Bank, CapGemini, Cognizant, Deloitte, Genpact, HCL, HDFC Bank, HSBC, ICICI Bank, i-Nautix, Infosys, Irevna, ITC, JP Morgan, L&T, Nomura, Novartis, RBS, SBI Caps, Shell, Syntel, TCS, Vedanta, UBS, etc.

PGDM 14th Batch (2013-15) Salary package

Average: **Rs. 8.0 Lakhs PA**   Highest: **Rs. 12.5 Lakhs PA**

Why PGDM from IFMR?

◆ **Exemplary faculty base**
◆ **Esteemed Board of Governors**
◆ **Focus on industry preparedness**
◆ **Rigorous curriculum**
◆ **Outstanding student community**
◆ **Highly conducive learning environment**

The State-of-the-art Campus in Sri City

IFMR has built its new campus across 40 acres in the midst of global organizations setting up world class manufacturing facilities in Sri City. The campus provides opportunities for self-learning, knowledge building, honing of skills and exploring one's potential to the fullest.

PGDM Program Financing & Scholarships

IFMR also offers
PhD Program
in affiliation with
**University of Madras
and IIT Madras**

- IFMR offers both merit and merit-cum-means scholarships for 15% of the students in every batch.
- Entire cost of PGDM program available as loan
- No collateral security required for Loans provided by certain agencies like Credila (a HDFC subsidiary)
- Needy students to get IFMR scholarships towards interest payment (about Rs. 1.65 Lakhs) for the entire duration of study period
- No financial burden for student or family until student starts earning
- IFMR has been selected by Hindustan Unilever Limited (HUL) as one of the five Business Schools in India to receive the prestigious T. Thomas Scholarship award of Rs. 1 Lakh to be given to the best outgoing student of PGDM.

Selection Process

Selection is based on CAT/XAT/GMAT/GRE/CMAT scores, Written Ability Test (WAT) and PI. The selection Process would be held in Ahmedabad, Bangalore, Bhubaneswar, Bhopal, Chennai, Coimbatore, Delhi, Hyderabad, Jaipur, Kochi, Kolkata, Lucknow, Mumbai, Patna and Ranchi.

Institute for Financial Management and Research

E-mail: pgdm@ifmr.ac.in   Website: **www.ifmr.ac.in**

McGRAW HILL EDUCATION SERIES

How to Prepare for

QUANTITATIVE APTITUDE *for the*

CAT

McGRAW HILL EDUCATION SERIES

6TH
REVISED
EDITION

How to Prepare for

QUANTITATIVE
APTITUDE *for the*
CAT

Arun Sharma
Educational Consultant

McGraw Hill Education (India) Private Limited
NEW DELHI

McGraw Hill Education Offices

New Delhi New York St Louis San Francisco Auckland Bogotá Caracas
Kuala Lumpur Lisbon London Madrid Mexico City Milan Montreal
San Juan Santiago Singapore Sydney Tokyo Toronto

McGraw Hill Education (India) Private Limited

Published by McGraw Hill Education (India) Private Limited,
P-24, Green Park Extension, New Delhi 110 016

How to Prepare for Quantitative Aptitude for the CAT, 6e

Seventh reprint 2015
DAAYCRCVDDQCX

ISBN (13 digits): 978-93-392-0512-6
ISBN (10 digits): 93-392-0512-X

Managing Director: *Kaushik Bellani*
Deputy General Manager—Test Prep and School: *Tanmoy Roychowdhury*
Assistant Sponsoring Editor: *Bhavna Malhotra*
Asst Manager (Developmental Editing): *Anubha Srivastava*
Asst Manager—Production: *Medha Arora*
General Manager—Production: *Rajender P. Ghansela*
Manager—Production: *Reji Kumar*

Typeset at Script Makers, 19, A1-B, DDA Market, Paschim Vihar, New Delhi 110 063 and text and cover printed at Rajkamal Electric Press, Plot No.2, Phase-IV, Kundli, Sonipat.

Cover Designer: K. Anoop

Visit us at: www.mheducation.co.in

Dedicated to my Father (Mr MK Sharma), Mother (Mrs Renu Sharma)
and Brother (Mr Ravi Sharma)
who have instilled in me the courage to have my convictions
and to stand by them

Preface to the Sixth Edition

With the evolution of the CAT in its online avatar, I felt the need to create a comprehensive and updated book that caters to CAT aspirants. Some of its salient features are given below.

1. Questions from this book: Over the past decade, it has been noticed that a minimum of 10–20% questions in CAT and other major management entrance examinations have been directly taken from the questions provided in this book. Furthermore, it has been seen that between 2003 (when the book was first released) to 2013, 80–90% of the questions in CAT and other top management entrance tests were covered in this book.

The CAT having gone online saw no change in this trend. Many questions in each of the test papers that the CAT has administered in its online avatar since 2009 have been covered in this book.

In fact, 2009 onwards, the onset of the CAT online pattern has created a significant shift in terms of the CAT preparation process. This is because, 2009 was the first year where there were multiple CAT papers to study, analyse and base our writing and preparation process on. In subsequent years, with the increase of the CAT window, the number of papers every year has gone up to around 30–40 papers. Thus, I am now richer by the experience of around 150 plus test papers when it comes to understanding what I need to provide to my readers for their preparation. It is on the basis of this rather rich insight that I have based the changes in this edition. (Note: Similar changes have been incorporated in my other books *How to prepare for Verbal Ability and Reading Comprehension for the CAT, How to Prepare for Data Interpretation for the CAT, and How to Prepare for Logical Reasoning for the CAT*).

2. Not too many changes in the pattern: Looking rationally into the paper patterns of the 150 plus CAT papers in the past period, there have not been too many changes with regard to the pattern of the examination as compared to previous years. While the QA in the initial years of Online CAT examination (between 2009–2010) was slightly on the easier side, the standard of the questions from 2011 onwards has become pretty much 'CAT standard'. Hence, the LOD I, LOD II and LOD III scheme of questions followed in this book is even more relevant now than ever before.

In fact, in the near future, the CAT is expected to shift to an adaptive format (like the GMAT) where every test-taker would get a different set of questions. In the adaptive format in the future, question banks of varying difficulty levels would be loaded into the computers and questions would appear for the student one-by-one. The difficulty level of the next question would increase if the previous one has been answered correctly and vice versa.

In order to do this, the examiners would need to build a database of questions which would be parallel to the LOD scheme followed in this book. These factors make this book and the content within all the more relevant for CAT aspirants.

How does Merging Quantitative Aptitude & Data Interpretation change the preparation process?
As you must be aware, the CAT 2011 introduced a new pattern shift by reducing the number of sections from 3 to 2. Before CAT 2011, there used to be three sections containing 20 questions each in the CAT exam namely:

Section 1: Quantitative Aptitude
Section 2: Verbal Ability & Reading Comprehension
Section 3: Data Interpretation & Logical reasoning.
*In the new pattern the number of sections was reduced to **2 sections** containing 30 questions each, namely*
Section 1: Quantitative Aptitude & Data Interpretation
Section 2: Verbal Ability & Logical reasoning.

In many ways, this does not really change your process of preparation. This is because, even though, on the surface the number of sections was changed, the actual number of questions under each category remained the same. In other words, while the three-section CAT used to have 20 questions on Quantitative Aptitude, 20 questions on Verbal Ability and Reading Comprehension, 10-12 questions on Data Interpretation and 8-10 questions on Logical Reasoning, the new two-section examination has 20 questions on Quantitative Aptitude and 10 questions on Data Interpretation merged together under one section, while the 20 questions on Verbal Ability and Reading Comprehension and the 10 questions on Logical reasoning were merged together under the other section.

Thus, the emphasis of your preparation does not really need to change at all. The only change that might occur is in the way you may want to strategise to use the time available to you in each section in order to beat your competition.

3. The need for greater variety in your preparation: Prior to the CAT going online, preparing for QA used to be a battle for Blocks 1, 4, 5 and 6. Even out of these, if someone did Blocks I and V well, he stood a strong chance at QA section.

However, as explained in details in the *introductory note* to the *online CAT*, the new avatar of this exam requires the aspirant to be much more balanced in the context of portion coverage.

4. The tougher level of the CAT exam: As already stated above, the quality of questions asked in the CAT over the past couple of years has become extremely good—requiring an upgradation of your grasp of concepts and understanding of each particular topic to a level not required before. This shift has necessitated that we do more through this book.

5. I have also come to know that many readers use this book for their preparation of other important management entrance exams (like XAT, IIFT, CMAT, MAT, SNAP, etc). So now, I have also included/modified the contents so that aspirants of the above exams need not look for any resource beyond this book for strengthening their hold on the quantitative aptitude section.

Apart from management entrance examinations, the book also has relevance for aspirants of UPSC and state civil services, Bank PO exams, GATE, Engineering Placement exams, etc. In short the scope of this book has considerably widened to cover the entire subject of quantitative aptitude that finds a resonance for all career aspirants.

The book you now hold in your hand has always been written keeping in mind the avowed objective of developing your quantitative intelligence to a point where you can quickly scale the height of preparation in each chapter of the portion.

Key features:

1. **Comprehensive solutions** (wherever relevant) to questions in all LODs of all chapters.
2. Based on an assessment of any logic I have missed in any chapter, I have introduced extra questions for readers in the form of **additional block-wise practice tests**. The questions in these tests have been carefully selected to ensure that I do not miss out on any probable question type.
3. In some chapters, where I felt that there is some deficiency in the number and variety of questions (due to the increased difficulty level of the CAT) based on the concepts of the chapter, we have **introduced new questions into the LODs** of the chapter.
4. At some places, the need was felt to introduce an entire additional exercise on concepts of a chapter. This too has been accomplished in this revision.
5. **The training ground**: Perhaps the biggest differentiator in this book is the introduction of the 'Training Ground' – which is an area through which I teach the readers real time higher-end problem solving. The training ground is a section where I tell you exactly how to think inside the examination hall when faced with questions of varying difficulty levels. Hence, a must read for all management aspirants.

Logic of the Training Ground

The quality of the questions in the Quantitative Aptitude section (especially in CAT & XAT) is of such a high quality level that even if you know the basics of each chapter within a particular block, it might not be enough to reach a point where you might be able to solve the questions from the chapter/block. In order to have a grip on any chapter/block and be able to handle application-based questions in the actual examination, you would need to raise your level of thinking and ideation in that chapter/block to the point where you are able to tackle any twists and turns that can be thrown up by it.

For this edition, the training ground has been introduced into four of the major blocks of chapters of this book – and you can expect a very extensive training ground section especially for Block V and Block VI. (Block V covers the chapters on Functions, Inequalities, Logs and Quadratic & Other Equations, while Block VI covers the chapters on Permutations and Combinations, Probability and Set Theory).

6. An introductory write up on the QA section of the online CAT to give you a holistic view of how to approach the online CAT from the perspective of the examinee.

The book is now totally in sync with the new trend and pattern of the examination.

Ultimately the endeavour is to provide a one-stop solution for CAT and MBA exam aspirants to tackle the QA section of all major management entrance exams—an endeavour I feel I have managed to do pretty well.

Through this book, I am confident of giving you—the reader—an invaluable resource for enhancing your QA section score drastically. Contained in this book is the very best advisory for each and every question type. Your job is simple—to ensure that you follow the process contained in this advisory.

KEY POINTS FOR YOUR PREPARATION

Outline and Strategy

The first aspect I would like to deal with here is to focus on helping you with the formulation of your strategy with respect to the portion to be covered for the Quantitative Aptitude section of the various management entrance exams including the CAT, XAT, CMAT, IIFT, and other examinations.

Let us start by trying to understand some of the key areas in Quantitative Aptitude (QA).

Tackling each portion

My experience shows that very often students look at the vast number of chapters and concepts to be studied for QA and get disheartened. This is especially true for students who do not have a strong traditional background in Mathematics. Indeed if you were to look at it with a chapter-wise approach, you can easily define the course to be studied by dividing it into 20+ chapters—preparation for which is such a long-drawn effort that it ends up draining the student's energy enthusiasm and motivation.

It is in this context and for this precise reason that I have divided this book into six manageable blocks—the approach being rationalising the chapters and grouping them according to the amount of shared concepts these chapters have amongst each other.

The outline as defined in the index to this book would divide your work into 6 major areas to prepare for. For your convenience and strategising I have put down the relative importance of each of these six blocks into perspective:

Block I: Number Systems and Progressions

Importance: **Very High** for CAT, XAT, IIFT, FMS & **High** for MAT, CMAT, SNAP, IRMA, etc.

Block II: Averages and Alligations

Importance: **Low** for QA in CAT, XAT, IIFT, but **High** for Data Interpretation as a lot of questions in DI are based on the concepts of averages and alligations. Also **High** for MAT, CMAT, IRMA, NMIMS, etc.

Block III: Percentages, Ratio, Proportion and Variation, Time and Work, Time, Speed and Distance. (Subsidiary but almost redundant chapters in this block – Interest and Profit & Loss)

Importance: **Moderate to High** for QA in CAT, XAT, IIFT, and **Very High** for Data Interpretation (DI) as DI is almost entirely based on the concept of Percentages and Ratio and Proportions. **Very High** for MAT, CMAT, IRMA, NMIMS, etc.

Note: *The chapter on "Time, Speed and Distance" is extremely important for these exams (especially for the CAT as this chapter has been a constant presence in the CAT for almost a decade.)*

Block IV: Geometry, Mensuration and Coordinate Geometry

Importance: **Very High** for CAT, XAT. **Average** for MAT, CMAT, SNAP, IRMA, IIFT, etc.

Block V: Functions, Inequalities, Logs and Quadratic Equations

Importance: **Very High** for CAT, XAT. **Low** for MAT, CMAT, IRMA, NMIMS, etc.

Block VI: Permutations and Combinations, Probability and Set Theory

Importance: **Very High** for CAT, XAT, IIFT etc. **Average** for MAT, CMAT, IRMA etc.

Based on the experience of the online CAT, the strategic preparation imperative for you should be to do at least four blocks and if possible up to 6 blocks "really well".

What does it mean to prepare a block "really well"? This is something I feel needs emphasis here.

Well what I mean to say is that do not just focus on studying the theory in each of these areas but develop an intuitive knowledge of all problem scenarios which emerge out of each block.

Only then would you be able to reach a situation in the exam—that when the question presents itself to you in the exam—you would have had the logic for the same worked out before hand. This is something that can make a huge difference to your chances in the CAT.

Analysing Your Knowledge Level

The first thing you need to focus on is an analysis of your knowledge level in each of these seven parts. In each of the above areas, first analyse your level of knowledge/ability. In order to do so the typical question you should ask yourself is: For the next 100 questions I face in each of these areas, how many would I be able to handle comfortably?

Think of a number as an answer to this question for each of the six blocks.

Based on your answer, the following analysis would provide you a thumb rule which would tell you how much of a knowledge issue you have:

1. 90+: You know pretty much every question type and variant in the area. You should focus your energies on other aspects rather than knowledge improvement in the area.
2. 80+: Maybe you need to increase your exposure to questions a little bit; around 200–300 more questions in that area would be sufficient.
3. 60–80+: You have a significant knowledge issue in the area. You might need to go back to the basics, but it is less likely to be a theory issue but more of an exposure to questions issue.
4. <60: You need to work on both theory and exposure to questions.

Needless to say, the target and objective for preparations has to be to reach the 90+ range as explained above in any block you intend to do "really well".

Looking beyond Ability (Quick Reflexes)

A common frustrating experience for test-takers while taking the test is to not being able to solve a known question/logic and subsequently, not being able to score marks in questions which they knew.

In order to handle this problem, you would need to work on your reactions and reflexes when faced with QA questions. Once you have solved your knowledge/ability issue in a particular block, your next step is to improve your reactions and reflexes while solving a question. Needless to say you would need to do this block wise.

So obviously the main issue is how to improve reflexes and reactions.

(a) For every block, once you have solved the LODs and the Pre-Assessment/Review tests, the most crucial exercise in this context would be a comprehensive revision and review of each and every question you have solved in that block. Solve every question of every LOD and Pre-Assessment/Review test again and review the logic/process of problem solving used. This need to be done to the point where you almost "recollect" the logic of the question and are able to recognise the same if it is used again in a different context/problem.
(b) A thorough revision on the theory of the block.

1. Improve your ability to select what you know and leave what you do not
In the context of an examination where the required scores for 99 percentile would be 60–70% attempts with 100% accuracy, it is easy to see that perfect knowledge is perhaps not needed in order to crack the CAT. Hence, even if you have around 60–70% knowledge of the questions in an average test, you are perhaps good enough to crack the exam. A good way to test whether you have sufficient knowledge would be to pick up 10–20 test papers and divide your QA section into blocks of 5 questions each. Then test your knowledge by looking at the average number of questions you know. If on an average for every 5 QA test questions that you pick up, if you know more than 3, then the prognosis would be that you have adequate knowledge for cracking the CAT. Thus, while you may want to move towards knowing 5 out of 5 in this context, there are other things that you should focus on—developing your ability to decide on whether you are going to be able to solve a question while reading it for the first time. This would help you stop *fishing* during the test. (*Fishing* can be described as the activity of trying to solve a question without knowing whether you would actually complete the question.)

Your mind should give you a clear indication of whether you would be able to do the last step in a question, before you start doing it. In that sense you should be able to clearly define three types of outcomes when you finish reading a question for the first time:

(a) **I see a clear flowchart** and the steps are manageable—Obviously you need to go on and solve these questions.
(b) **I see a clear flowchart** but the steps are too lengthy—In this case you need to see where you stand in your test-time and attempt-wise.
(c) **I do not see a clear flowchart but I can try as I see a starting point**—This is potentially the most dangerous situation for you in the duration of the test, as once you get sucked into a question, there is a strong tendency to lose track of the time you are using up while trying the question. My advice is that while taking the test you should not even start doing such questions.

(d) **I see no flowchart and no starting point to the question**—Obviously you should leave such questions and in fact if these are limited to around 20–30% of the paper there is no problem and you need not worry about them.

2. Focus on thorough knowledge of 'problem scenarios' rather than theoretical learning

To illustrate this, I would like to start with a few examples.

Consider the following string of 3 questions. Before I come to my main point here, I would like you to start by solving these questions before looking at the explanations provided:

1. A boy starts adding consecutive natural numbers starting from 1. After some time he reaches a total of 1000 when he realises that he has double counted a number. Find the number double counted.
2. A boy starts adding consecutive natural numbers starting from 1. He reaches a total of 575 when he realises that he has missed a number. What can be said about the number missed?
3. Find the 288th term of the series: ABBCCCDDDDEEEEEFFFFFFG....

We can now start to look at each of these 3 questions:

1. Consider the fact that when you add numbers as stated above (1+2+3+4+......) the result is known as a triangular number. Hence, numbers like 1, 1+2=3, 1+2+3=6 and so on are triangular numbers. This question asks us to consider the possibility of making the mistake of double counting a number. So instead of 1+2+3+4 if you were to do by error 1+2+3+3+4 you would realise that the number you would get would be 13 which would be more than 10 (which should have been your correct addition) and less than 15 (the sum of 1 to 5) which is the next triangular number. And the double counted value could be achieved by spotting 10 as the immediately lower value—and the difference between 10 and 13 would give you the required double counted number.

   To carry forward this logic into the given question, we should realise that we are just bothered about finding the last triangular number below 1000—and in trying to work this out is where we really apply our intelligence.

   Before one writes about that though, one fully realises that a lot of readers (especially aspirants with an engineering background at this point are thinking about $n \times (n + 1)/2$. Knowing that process, one chooses to write about the alternate way to think about in this question.

$$1 + 2 + 3 + 4 ... + 10 = 55;$$

   Hence, we can easily see that 11+12+13+14+15+...+20 would equal 155 and the sum of 21 to 30 would equal 255 and so on.

   Thus, in trying to find the last triangular number below 1000 we can just do: 55+155+255+355 = 820 (which is the sum of the first 40 natural numbers) and since we have still not reached close to 1000 we start by adding more numbers as: 820 + 41 + 42 + 43 + 44 = 990 and the difference between 990 and 1000 is 10 which is the required answer.

2. For this question we would just need to carry the learning from the previous question forward and realise that when we miss a number, we actually get a total which is lower than the correct total. Hence, if we want to find the number missed all we need to do is to find the first triangular number greater than 575. This can be got simply by 55+155+255+31+32+33+34 = 595, so the number missed has to be 20.

3. In this question all you would need to notice is that in the series ABBCCCDDDDEEEEEF...

A ends after the first term; B ends after the third (1+2) term; C ends after the sixth (1+2+3) term and so on. So we can infer that what we are looking at is how many numbers need to be added before we get to a number just below 288. So 55 + 155+21+22+23 gives us 276 which pretty much means that the 24th alphabet (i.e. x) would be running in this series when we reach the 288th term.

So looking at the three questions above and the solutions, one wants the reader to only answer one specific question:

How much does knowing the first question and developing your thought ability and your intelligence help you in solving the second and the third one? I hope you see the connection. For your information, the three questions presented above were asked in CAT 2001, CAT 2002 and CAT 2003!!!

CONCLUDING NOTE

You sit in front of your CAT question paper and the first question comes in front of you. If you have identified the logic of the question or seen the question itself earlier, your entire QA preparation is fructified. In fact, every question/logic (that you would face in your test) which you have seen earlier represents a triumph of your preparation process. It is for this very reaction that you prepare for an aptitude exam like the CAT. Any other preparation is quite worthless.

Your battle for CAT would be won if you get a "YES I KNOW THIS PATTERN/LOGIC" reaction to 50–60% of the questions in your test.

Contained in this book is the finest collection questions which you would hope to find anywhere. Remember, each question solved needs to be a learning experience—one that is to be kept in your mind for future problem solving. Adopt this approach with the problems contained in this book and I am quite confident that you would KNOW over 50% of your actual CAT test paper since you have already solved something like that before!!

All The BEST !!!!!!

ARUN SHARMA

Preface to the First Edition

Over the last few years, as a trainer of CAT and other aptitude tests, I have felt the need for a comprehensive book on the subject. Students appearing for the CAT and other aptitude tests usually struggle for appropriate study material to prepare for this vital section of the examination.

This book comes as a humble attempt to fulfil this gap.

Structure of the book

The book is divided into 19 chapters and five test papers. Each chapter is divided into three broad parts:

(a) Theory

(b) Solved examples

(c) Chapter end exercises (LODs I, II & III), with answer key

The questions in the chapter end exercises have been categorised into three levels of difficulty, viz, Level of Difficulty I, Level of Difficulty II and Level of Difficulty III.

Level of Difficulty I (LOD I): These are the basic types of questions pertaining to the chapter. A majority of the MBA entrance tests would test the student with LOD I questions. Tests which ask LOD I questions include MAT, IMT, IRMA, IIFT, NIFT, CET Maharashtra, Bank PO examinations, BBA, BCA, Law, and so on. Besides, there are about 10 questions of LOD I type in the CAT nowadays.

Level of Difficulty II (LOD II): These are questions, which are more advanced than the LOD I questions. These questions test all basic as well as applied concepts in the chapter. *LOD II questions are closest to the difficulty levels of the CAT.* Hence, the objective of LOD II questions should be to:

(a) Clearly understand the concept which underlies the question.

(b) Create a judgment of time required for different mental processes.

(c) Identify the time guzzlers.

(d) Reinforce application of a method in mental processes through the question.

(e) Learn to flowchart complex questions.

Level of Difficulty III (LOD III): LOD III questions build on the previous questions and are a step beyond the LOD II questions. Although they are also normally more difficult than the average CAT question, approximately 5–10 LOD III questions could be asked in the CAT every year. Hence, the learning objectives at LOD III are to:

(a) Learn applications of the basic concepts at the highest level.

(b) Sharpen the flowcharting skills learnt at LOD II.

(c) Use each question as a learning opportunity.

One should not be disheartened if he/she is unable to solve LOD III questions. These questions are extremely tough and uncommon in the CAT and other aptitude tests. Questions in actual tests will appear very simple and elementary if one can solve LOD III questions.

Approach Taken in Writing This Book

In my experience, the 'math skill' of students appearing for CAT can be classified into three levels:

>Level 1: Students who are weak at Mathematics
>Level 2: Students who are average at Mathematics
>Level 3: Students who are strong at Mathematics

This book has been written keeping in mind all the three kinds of students.

From my experience I have given below my perspective of what one should aim for (based on the category that he/she belongs to). It is important to clearly understand the starting level and accordingly define strategy for the QA section.

Level 1: Students who are weak at mathematics: Typically, these are students who were weak at mathematics in school and/or have left mathematics after their 10th or 12th class. They face a mental block in mathematics and have problems in writing equations. They also have severe problems in understanding mathematical language and are unable to convert the mathematical language into mathematical equations. They make mistakes even in interpretation of the most basic statements in mathematics (leave alone the complex statements). Besides, these students also have problems in solving equations. They suffer from the insecurity of knowing that they are unable to solve most problems which they face.

Level 2: Students who are average at mathematics: These students lie between the Level 1 and Level 3 students.

Level 3: Students who are strong at mathematics: These are the students who have got strong, structured and logical thinking ability. They not only understand the basic repetitive statements in mathematics but also complex statements. They are able to create their own flowcharts to arrive at solutions of these complex mathematical situations.

There are two alternative approaches that a student can take in solving this book.

Approach 1: "Start with basic concepts, solved examples then move on to LOD I, then LOD II in the chapter. Do not go into LOD III in the chapter in the first go. Complete all 19 chapters and then re-start with Chapter1 – review the basic concepts, resolve LOD I and LOD II, then move on to LOD III. This approach is advocated for students who are weak to average in mathematics (i.e. students of Level 1 and Level 2).

After completing the theory and practice exercises of the book for a second time, go to the practice sets 1–5 provided at the end of book. Set a time limit of 40 minutes for each set and take the tests. The questions contained in the sets are questions which have appeared in the CAT over the last 5 years (based on memory)."

Approach 2: "Start with the basic concepts, solved examples and then go through the exercises of LOD I, LOD II and LOD III. This is recommended for students who have strong concepts in mathematics (Level 3 students)."

Then go to the 5 practice tests given at the end of the book and take them one by one (time limit of 40 minutes for each test)."

An Important Point
Each of the questions contained in the LOD I, LOD II and LOD III exercises in the chapters have immense learning value. Hence, the approach that one takes while solving the questions should be one of learning. The reader should try to clearly understand the interpretation of each sentence used in the construction of the questions.

In other words the learning in every chapter should not be restricted to the solved examples or the theory contained in the chapter, but should continue through each of the questions contained in the exercises.

In conclusion, this is a book which is unique in approach and coverage. Any CAT aspirant who goes through the questions contained in this book in the manner advised in this book would get a distinct advantage when he/she faces the CAT.

ARUN SHARMA

Acknowledgements

The text and questions contained in this book is the manifestation of a learning process that began for me over 18 years ago. During the intervening period I have come across some wonderful people in the form of relatives, friends or acquaintances from whom I have learnt immensely. While it is not possible to name them individually, I would like to express a deep sense of gratitude towards them.

I would also like to express my heartfelt thanks to my wonderful students due to whom I have had a wonderful opportunity to live a highly fulfilled life. This book would not have been possible in the absence of this opportunity. This work would not have been possible but for the support and encouragement from McGraw-Hill Education, India. My sincere thanks and words of appreciation to them. I would like to make specific mention of Tanmoy Roychowdhury, K.N. Prakash, Niju Sreedharan, Bhavna Malhotra, Anubha Srivastava and Medha Arora.

I would also like to thank my colleagues who have supported me through thick and thin during the last few years. These include Mr Arun Chaturvedi, Mr Shyam Kumar, Mr Ravi Kishore, and Mr Prakash Purti. Besides, a special mention of thanks to Kshitij Gupta, Anadi Upadhyay and Mr Prabhat Ranjan who have worked as hard as me (if not harder) on this book. This book would not have been possible but for their technical inputs and unyielding efforts.

No amount of thanks can ever repay the great debt that I owe my wife Meenakshi (along with my son Shaurya) who have provided me with the constant inspiration over the past few years. In fact, this book would not have been possible but for the direct and indirect support, inspiration and guidance from Meenakshi who has been a constant partner in all my efforts over the past years.

ARUN SHARMA

Online CAT: From the QA Perspective

Welcome to the world of online CAT!

The advent of the online version of the Common Admission Test (CAT) in 2009 and beyond brought with it a whole lot of opinions and views about what has changed in the examination and what should be the ideal preparation pattern. Therefore, one objective in this revised edition of this widely read book is to look at the issues that an aspirant needs to consider while preparing for the online CAT. I would like to discuss this issue in the following parts:

1. *What has changed?* A comprehensive analysis of what are the critical dimensions of the changes that have taken place in the CAT in its online avatar and what it means for the aspirant, both in respect of positive and negative factors, taking into account the following:
   - (a) Changes in the Test-Taking Experience
   - (b) Changes in the Exam pattern
   - (c) Changes in the Marking process
2. *What does all this mean for the Preparation Process?* How it should change in the context of an online examination and how has it remained constant- whether online or paper-and-pen?

While doing so I have taken the help of a varied experiential sample of test-takers from across India and also my own personal experience of taking (and may I add dominating) the CAT. Given below are some of the implications of the online version of the CAT in the context of the Quantitative Aptitude section (which this book is all about).

Note: In this book, whenever I refer to preparation for the Quantitative Aptitude Section, I am referring to the preparation for the approximately 20 questions on Quantitative Aptitude, that are being asked under the Quantitative Aptitude and Data Interpretation sections of the CAT.

I. WHAT HAS CHANGED?

The 'experience' of taking the test

1. Cleaner & More Efficient: Compared to the paper-and-pen based CAT, the online version is much cleaner as the clarity of questions, their visibility, as well as the overall feel of the question solving experience is much better. Consequently, the efficiency (of the thought processes) is much higher, leading to a much superior test-solving experience.

2. Space Management on the Table: In the paper-and-pen version, the aspirant had to typically manage the test paper, admit card, watch, pencils (at least 2), eraser, sharpener as well as the answer sheet on the table. To add to their woes, the paper-and-pen versions of the exam were mostly conducted in schools. Very often the aspirants had to contend with the additional challenge of managing all this paraphernalia on a school boy's small table. In addition, if luck did not run your way and you were made to sit in a classroom meant for juniors, (between classes 3 to 6) you really had a challenge.

Most of these problems have disappeared in the new version. The fact that computer terminals at most colleges and universities are of standard shape and size eliminates the imbalance created due to non-uniformity. Besides, while writing the online version of the CAT, all you need to manage on the table are the mouse, the key board, a pencil and a sheet of paper for rough work; no watches, erasers, sharpeners and most importantly, no test paper and no answer sheet.

3. Moving Questions in the Test: Unlike the paper-and-pen version, where test-takers could scan the whole question paper in one look, in the online CAT, aspirants had to move one question at a time. This had both its advantages and disadvantages in terms of the overall test experience. The obvious disadvantage that most aspirants faced was the fact that since you could not really see the whole paper in one look, you could not make a judgment about the balance, the difficulty level or the portion wise question distribution in the paper. (Although I am referring to the quantitative aptitude section here, this was also true for all the sections in the exam)

Ironically, the biggest advantage for the examinee in terms of the online CAT was exactly the same i.e. since you could not see the paper entirely at one go, the only option while taking the test was to look at the questions one by one.

This turned out to be a huge advantage because of two main reasons mentioned below:

Higher Focus while Solving an Individual Question: Not knowing the exact number of questions from various areas and not being able to estimate the difficulty level of the paper, left individuals with no choice but to focus on the one question that was visible to them on the screen. The result was that achieving the all important 'tunnel vision' while solving a question was much easier. The immediate result of this was that the focus on the `problem at hand' was infinitely more in the online version than in the conventional paper-and-pen format. Thus, ironically, not knowing the pattern of the paper resulted in giving examinees their best chance to solve a question.

The main reason for this was that while solving the question in front of the computer screen the experience of the previous question was totally blanked out. In the paper-and-pen version, students who had a negative experience while solving a question or two carried that negativity to the next question.

Thus the specific advantage of the online version was that "forgetting" a bad experience was relatively easier. The moment you navigated away from the question in front of you, it went away from your mind as well. So much so, that remembering a question that was just two questions back was close to impossible. Naturally the 'carry over' emotions from a previous negative experience were significantly reduced.

The Imperative for Faster Navigation (less time wasted on unsolvable questions):   Since the examinees had not seen the full question paper right at the beginning, the imperative to move to the next question was extremely strong. This resulted in students seeing a higher percentage of the questions in the online test than in the paper-and-pen version.

Author's Note: One of the problems I had noticed in the paper-and-pen version was that most examinees were not able to 'see' the entire paper. i.e. the fraction of the quantitative aptitude section that they were able to process was a fraction of the entire test paper. As a result they used to miss out on a large number of sitters! On an average, out of a 5-page question paper in quantitative aptitude, students were able to process at most upto 2–3 pages. So they would naturally miss out on all easy ones on the pages they did not process. A lot of time would get wasted in questions that they tried and were unable to solve or even if they solved, they were unable to get them correct.

Part of this time mismanagement also occurred due to the fact that they did not have the clock ticking on the screen in front of them. Therefore, they naturally lost track of how much time they had spent in attempting to solve a question. A good percentage of the time the aspirants used to spend in the QA section was spent in trying to solve a question which they were eventually unable to solve.

All this changed for the better in the online version. There was a greater imperative to move to the next question due to the twin facts that you had not seen the entire paper as you were moving from one question to the other, and that the ticking clock was omnipresent in front of your eyes on the screen. As a result, you were aware of the exact amount of time you had spent on a particular question. The net result was that after trying a question for maybe 60 to 90 seconds, in case you did not have a clue about what to do in the same, you moved to the next question. Thus time management improved drastically for the examinee.

I believe this is one of the main reasons why a lot of students who were trying to compare the two versions of the CAT said that the online version was easier. Since the amount of time spent in questions which they were eventually not able to solve, reduced drastically, they got a feeling that they were solving questions all the time as opposed to the paper-and-pen version where aspirants used to have an overall negative experience of the test (as they would end up spending a lot of time in attempting "unsolvable" questions.

---

4. Mark/Unmark Button & the Review Button: A very important feature in the online version was the introduction of the REVIEW button. In the paper-and-pen version, it was extremely difficult to track the number of your attempts and especially so in the context of questions that you were unsure about and/or questions which you wanted to come back to. There was simply no way in which you could keep a track of those and as a result there was effectively 'no second chance' at a question.

This too changed in the online CAT. For every question, apart from the facility to answer it, you also had a MARK button, which would give you easy access to the question at the end of the paper. When you have completed the paper (reached the last question in the paper), you also got access to a review screen that in one visual showed you all the questions you had solved as well as all the questions you had marked with the MARK button. So going back to a specific question in the paper was just the click of the mouse away.

To sum up, the net effect of the online CAT was a superior test-taking experience — something that gives you a chance to be more in control of your test— and thus aim for a higher score assuming that the same set of questions would have been asked in the paper-and-pen version.

What has changed in terms of the exam pattern?

Having seen the specific changes that have occurred in terms of the test-taking experience, let us now examine another crucial aspect.

Changes in Exam Pattern: Obviously for the purpose of this book, the analysis will pertain to the QA portion only. In order to read a similar analysis with respect to the other sections namely, *Verbal Ability & Logical Reasoning* you can refer to my book on these subjects, also published by McGraw Hill. The major changes in the pattern of the Quantitative Aptitude paper can be summarised through the following points:

1. More balanced portion coverage
2. Reduction in number of questions
3. Lack of uniformity
4. Higher percentage cutoffs

1. More Balanced Portion Coverage: As per the scheme followed in this book, the QA portion can be divided into 6 major parts (or blocks as I call them in this book).

The underlying constant that used to exist in the paper-and-pen version (through the entire decade prior to the first online CAT) was the prominence of Block I and Block V. (Block I comprising Number Systems and Progressions and Block V comprising the chapters on Functions, Inequalities, Quadratic and other Equations and Logarithms.)

In each of the years from 1999 to 2008, the QA section required you to get a net score of approximately 30 – 40% of the total marks in order to score a high 90 percentile in this section.

In the light of this fact, the importance of Block I and Block V can be gauged from the table below:

Block	Weightage (as a % of total marks)
Block I	30 – 50%
Block V	15 – 50%
Combined weightage of Blocks I & V	60 – 80%

Add to this, the chapter on Time, Speed and Distance with a minimum weightage of 5–10% and you pretty much had the QA section well covered. In a nutshell, QA for CAT preparation had become "do 10 chapters well".

However, this scenario has changed in the context of the online version of the exam.

The balance of weightage of questions shifted and each of the six blocks have become important. The aspirant of CAT online version saw a weightage distribution of the kind illustrated below.

Block	Total Out of 20 Questions
Block I	3 – 4 questions
Blocks II & III	3 – 5 questions
Block IV	3 – 6 questions
Block V	4 – 5 questions
Block VI	1 – 3 questions

2. Reduction in Number of Questions: The second major change in the QA section is the reduction of questions to 20. From 55 questions in the late nineties to 50 between 2000 to 2003 to 30 & then 25 in the last years of the paper-and-pen version, the number of questions has further gone down to 20 in the online version. Naturally, this reduced the amount of choice the aspirant had for leaving out a question.

For instance in CAT 2003 out of 50 questions, you needed to solve 15 to get to the cut off. This meant that at 100% accuracy you could afford to leave 35 questions. This scenario has now changed drastically as in evident from the following table.

Year	No. of Questions in QA	Number of Marks	Cut off at (approx number of marks)	No. of Questions you could leave @ 100% accuracy	No. of Questions you could leave @ 90% accuracy
CAT 1999	55	55	16–18	37+	32+
CAT 2000–04	50	50	12–14	36+	32+
CAT 2005	30	50	12–14	20+	16+
2006–08	25	100	28–32	17+	14+
Online CAT 2009 & 2010	20	80	40–48	8+	5+
Online CAT 2011–2013 QA & DI Section	20 (QA) + 10 (DI)	80 (QA) + 40 (DI)	68–72	12+	8+

- As you can see, there is very little elbowroom available in the online version now to leave out questions and expect a good percentile score.
- The expectation in the future is that students taking the CAT would have to really use their mathematical intelligence and attempt as many questions as possible in order to get a top percentile in the test.

3. Lack of Uniformity: The third major factor in terms of paper pattern was the lack of uniformity of the test paper. Different students got tests with differing difficulty levels. The papers on the first few days of CAT 2009 were quite simple, but after the third day most papers had a pretty good difficulty level.

An issue that is being discussed widely on the Net is fairness. A lot of voices rose against the CAT committee and the online version of the exam questioning the fairness of the testing process.

The key criticism was: In the context of multiple papers with varying difficulty levels, how would the IIMs judge fairly between students who solved a high percentage of the questions in an easy test versus students who were able to solve a lower number of questions in a more difficult paper? The answer to this is really simple. Since the population size of each paper was significantly large, the IIMs could easily define individual percentiles in each test and ensure fairness to all.

The key point to be noted here is that there are infinite statistical ways through which processes like this can be made fair to everyone. As a future CAT aspirant, however, what you need to worry about is preparing diligently and facing the exam with a positive attitude.

4. Higher Percentage Cutoffs: In the online version, aspirants wasted less time in questions which they thought was unsolvable and moved on to those they could solve. The result— most students were able to raise their scores in this section significantly.

Consequently sectional cut offs which used to be in the range of 30% of the net marks rose to around 40 – 45% of the marks.

Changes in the Marking process

The key change that an analysis of CAT 2009 results showed was that there was an increased emphasis on accuracy. Mistakes were heavily penalised. This was evident from the fact that two students solving the same test paper (December 3 evening slot) scored:

(a) 14 attempts 1 incorrect – score 98.23 percentile
(b) 19 attempts 3 incorrect – score 92.6 percentile

There were innumerable such examples where students solving more questions with higher errors scored significantly lower than students who attempted much less but got most correct.

Hence, the key learning for you while preparing is to focus on improving your accuracy as well as the belief in your process of solving. This is especially true while preparing for the QA section. While solving a QA question, you should be able to know that if your process is correct then so would your answer would also be correct. The need to check the answer to a QA question is something that is only required for minds weak in Quantitative Aptitude. This is where an under-prepared aspirant loses out to the best—in the knowledge of whether what they are solving is correct or not.

Unfortunately, most students I see are more interested in seeing the answer to the question as soon as they solve the same. This is a habit I would strongly discourage you from. The ideal preparation process for you should be:

(a) solve the question,
(b) review your process and tell yourself, "if your process is correct, so is your answer", and
(c) only check your answer after you have reviewed your process.

This is important, because when you are solving a QA question inside the CAT, you would not have the cushion to 'look' at the answer. The only thing you have is the question and the process you use in solving the same. Your mind should be able to tell you whether the answer you have got is correct or not. This is a key difference in solving questions in practice and solving them under exam pressure.

Hence, developing more confidence in your QA problem-solving processes becomes a key ingredient and objective of your preparation process for this section.

II. WHAT DOES ALL THIS MEAN FOR THE PREPARATION PROCESS? HOW HAS IT CHANGED AND HOW HAS IT REMAINED CONSTANT?

Let us look at this aspect in two broad parts:

1. What are the changes that need to happen in the preparation processes for the online CAT vis-a-vis the preparation process for the traditional paper-and-pen version?
2. What are the things and issues that remain constant in the preparation process?

1. For the first question, the specific things that come to my mind are:

   (a) **More Balanced portion coverage needed:** As explained above, in the paper-and-pen version the best approach for Quantitative Aptitude preparation was "do 10 chapters well — really well". In fact, even 4 chapters done well were mostly sufficient to crack this section. However, in the new online version, since the weightage of distribution of questions is much more even, this approach is no longer going to work. Hence, the need to cover all aspects of the portion well and not ignore any particular portion is perhaps the first and the biggest change that needs to be done in the preparation process.

   (b) **Need to cover the basics well, namely, speedily solving LOD I questions and the ability to think through LOD II and LOD III questions:** In the early years (1980s and upto the late 1990s), the CAT used to be essentially a speed test (including the QA section). There were times when the paper used to consist of upto 225+ questions to be solved in 120 minutes. Questions used to be one-liners and could be solved in 1–2 steps. The key differentiation used to be the speed at which the aspirants could solve questions. However, from late 1990s onwards the QA section of the CAT had become a real test of quantitative intelligence. Questions ceased to be one-liners unless you had a very high degree of mathematical understanding and intelligence. The online CAT in its first year tended to be a mix of both these extremes. Papers consisted of between 4–6 one-liners topped up by LOD II and LOD III questions. So while most aspirants found 4–6 very easy questions in each paper, they also had to really use their mathematical strengths to cross 10–12 attempts. In the future, as the IIMs improve the quality of the database of quantitative questions, one can expect the quality of the questions to improve drastically and hence the LOD II and LOD III questions contained in this book would be an extremely important resource to solve for maximising your score in this section in the exam. [In fact after the first 3–4 days of the exam in 2009, examinees taking the test on the subsequent days found the paper to be of really good quality].

   For the future CAT aspirants and the readers of my books, my advice is short and simple. Cover both the flanks—the short cuts and quicker methods to solve the easier LOD I questions *and* improving your mathematical and logical intelligence to cover the higher end questions of LOD II and LOD III level.

   (c) **The need to take computer based tests in order to be able to think on the computer:** Thinking and solving questions from the computer screen is a slightly different experience than solving from a physical book. Thus students and aspirants are advised to experience this change by going for online solving experience. It is in this context that we have tied up with www.mindworkzz.in to give our readers a feel of the online problem solving experience. However, in spite of these seemingly big external changes, my personal opinion is that the changes are mostly external in nature.

2. The essence of preparation of the Quantitative Aptitude section remains the same in a lot many fundamental ways. Some of these that come readily to mind are:

   (a) **The need to develop mental structures for the CAT:** QA preparation has always been associated with the development of the mathematical thinking processes and thought structures for specific mathematical situations. The smart CAT aspirant is able to create mathematical thoughts in his mind to situations that he would encounter in the exam.

   The whole battle for QA preparation in the CAT can be essentially summarised in terms of the quality of pre formed logic that you have to the specific questions that you are going to face in the exam. In other words, your battle in QA section is won if you have during your preparation process, encountered the logic to the question which is in front of you. Hence, the focus of your QA preparation process has to be on creating the logics for as many questions and mathematical situations as possible. You would have well and truly won your battle at the CAT in case you encounter 15 'known' mathematical situations out of the 20 questions in your set. Hence, the **imperative to form "thought algorithms" for standard and non-standard mathematical situations related to various chapters and concepts in the portion remains as strong as ever.** In fact, if anything this imperative is expanded to the entire portion base due to the wider and more balanced portion coverage in the exam.

(b) **The need for thoroughness in your preparation:** This is again something that does not change.

The key point you need to remember is that the CAT still remains a test of your intelligence and an aspirant should focus on this aspect. This book provides plenty of mathematical thinking situations and alternatives related to each and every part of this section that help you hone your skills in the QA section of the examination.

Contents

First Things First

Block I: Numbers

Block III: Arithmetic and Word-based Problems   171–360

FIRST
THINGS
FIRST

DEVELOPING YOUR CALCULATIONS

This special section contains the best available approaches for all kind of calculations that you are likely to face in the CAT or any other aptitude examination...

Chapter 1
Additions and Subtractions (As an Extension of Additions)

Chapter 2
Multiplications

Chapter 3
Divisions, Percentage Calculations and Ratio Comparisons

Chapter 4
Squares and Cubes of Numbers

Developing your ability to calculate well should be one of your major thrust areas for your preparation strategy for Quantitative Aptitude. In fact, most of the times (in most coaching programs and books) this area is totally bypassed leaving the student broadly to develop his/her own methods to calculate faster. Needless to say, your work in trying to develop your ability to calculate would always be greatly superior if you are guided properly with approaches that have been tested and have stood the test of time. The following advisory contained in this special section of the book not just aims to give you the best advice for each and every type of calculation, but also gives you a comprehensive plan to develop your calculation speed—for every conceivable type of calculation.

My focus throughout this special note on calculations is to help you to develop the relevant calculations only, viz., calculations that you are likely to encounter inside the CAT based on the experiences of the past CAT examinations. For this purpose this section has been divided into the following chapters:

Chapter 1: ADDITIONS and SUBTRACTIONS *Ideas for developing your ability to add & subtract well;*

Chapter 2: MULTIPLICATIONS *Ideas for developing your ability to multiply well;*

Chapter 3: DIVISIONS, PERCENTAGE CALCULATIONS and RATIO COMPARISONS *Ideas for developing your ability to divide well as well as to compare ratios more efficiently;*

Chapter 4: SQUARES AND CUBES OF NUMBERS

1
Chapter

Additions and Subtractions (As an Extension of Additions)

IDEAS FOR ADDING AND SUBTRACTING WELL

Addition is perhaps the most critical skill when it comes to developing your calculations. As you would see through the discussions in the remaining chapters of this section of the book, if you have the ability to add well you would be able to handle all the other kinds of calculations with consummate ease.

Skill 1 for addition: The ability to react with the addition of two numbers when you see them.

The first and foremost skill in the development of your addition abilities is the ability to react to 2 two digit numbers when you come across them. You simply have to develop the ability to react with their totals whenever you come across 2 two digit numbers.

For instance, suppose I were to give you two numbers at random—5, 7 and ask you to **STOP!! STOP YOUR MIND BEFORE IT GIVES YOU THE SUM OF THESE TWO NUMBERS!!** What happened? Were you able to stop your mind from saying 12? No! of course not you would say.

TRY AGAIN: 12 + 7 STOP YOUR MIND!! You could not do it again!!

TRY AGAIN: 15+12 STOP!! Could not?

TRY AGAIN: 88+ 73 = ?? STOP!! If you belong to the normal category of what I call "addition disabled aspirants" you did not even start, did you?

TRY AGAIN: 57 + 95 =??

TRY AGAIN: 78+88 =??

What went wrong? You are not used to such big numbers, you would say. Well, if you are serious about your ability to crack aptitude exams, you better make this start to happen in your mind. You would know what I mean if you just try to look at a 5 year old child who has just learnt to add, struggle with a calculation like 12 + 7 on his fingers or his abacus.

His struggle with something like 12 + 7 or even 15 + 12 would be akin to the average aspirant's ability to react to 88+ 78. However, just as you know 15 + 12 is not a special skill so also 88+78 is not a special skill. It is just a function of how much you practice your calculations especially in the domain of 2 digit additions.

So what am I trying to tell you here?

All I am trying to communicate to you is to tell you to work on developing your ability to react to 2 two digit numbers with their addition as soon as these numbers hit your mind. What I am trying to tell you that the moment you make your mind adept at saying something like 74 + 87 = 161 just the way you would do 9 + 6 =15 you would have made a significant movement in your mind's ability to crack aptitude exams.

Why do I say that—you might be justified in asking me at this point of time? In order to answer your question I would like to present the following argument to you:

In numerical questions, a normal student/aspirant would be roughly calculating for approximately 50% of the time that he/she takes to solve a question. This means that half the total time that you would spend in solving questions of basic numeracy or data interpretation would essentially go into calculations. Thus, if the test paper consists of say 30-40% questions on basic numeracy and data interpretation you would be expected to spend somewhere between 36 to 48 minutes on these questions—which would in turn translate to approximately 18 to 24 minutes in calculations inside the test paper.

So the contention is this: If you can improve your calculation speed to 5x, the time you would require to do the same calculations would come down to 1/5th of your original time. In other words, 18 minutes would come down to 3.6 minutes—a saving of 14.4 minutes; 24 minutes would come down to 4.8 minutes—a saving of 19.2 minutes just by improving your calculation speed!!

In an exam like the CAT where you would always run out of time (rather than running out of solvable questions) 19 extra minutes could easily mean anywhere between 15–20 marks (even if you able to solve an additional 6–7 questions in this time).

15–20 extra marks in the prelims exam could very well make the difference between getting a chance to write the mains examination in the same year versus going back to the drawing board and preparing for the prelims for another year!!

Addition being the mother of all calculations has the potential of giving you the extra edge you require to dominate this all important examination.

Over the next few chapters in this section of the book, all I am going to show you is how knowing additions well would have an impact on each and every calculation type that you might encounter in this exam and indeed for all aptitude tests. However, before we go that far you need to develop your ability to add well.

Let us look at the simple calculation of 78 + 88. For eternity you have been constrained to doing this as follows using the carry over method:

$$\begin{array}{r} 1 \\ 7\ 8 \\ +\ 8\ 6 \\ \hline 1\ 6\ 4 \end{array}$$

The problem with this thought is that no matter how many times you practice this process you would still be required to write it down. The other option of doing this same addition is to think on the number line as this:

78 + 86 – how to think of this addition problem

As you can see, the above thinking in an addition situation requires no carry over and after some practice would require no writing at all. It is just an extension of how you are able to naturally react to 5+11 so also you can train your mind to react to 58+63 and react with a two step thought (as 61 → 121—with practice this can be done inside a fraction of a second. It is just a matter of how much you are willing to push your mind for this). Once you can do that your next target is to be able to add multiple 2 digit numbers written randomly on a single page:

Try this: Add the following

In order to do this addition your thinking should go like this:

Alternately you may also do this the other way. The result would be quite the same:

While you are trying to work on this addition you would realize the following about your abilities to add (if you belong to the normal category of aspirants')

1. Something like 121 + 68 would be easier than 189 + 56 because the latter requires you to shift hundreds—something that the former does not require you to do.
2. Something like 48 + 27 would be easier for you to do initially than 136 + 56; and 136 + 56 would be easier than 543 + 48 because your mind would be more comfortable with smaller numbers than you would be with larger numbers.

However as you start practicing your additions, these additions would become automatic for your mind—as they would then fall into the range where your mind can react with the answers. That is the point to which we would want you to target your skill levels for additions.

To put it in other terms, you would need to work on your additions in such a way that 10 numbers written around a circle (as shown above) should be done in around 10-12 seconds in your mind.

Till the time your addition skill levels reach that point, I would want you to work aggressively on your addition ability.

The following 10 × 10 table done at least once daily might be a good way to work on your additions:

	59	68	77	96	84	32	17	69	81	38	TOTALS
48											
54				= 96 + 54 = 150							
67											
89											
56											
73						105					
88											
24											
47											
96											
TOTALS											

Inside the table you would broadly do two things:

(a) For each cell you would add the values in the corresponding row and the corresponding column in order to get the value inside the cell. Thus, the second row and 4th column intersection would give you 54+96=150, the sixth row and the sixth column would add to 73+32 = 105 as shown in the table.

(b) Add the total of the 10 numbers seen in each row after you finish doing the values inside the cells in the total. This would give you the final total of the row. Repeat the same process for the addition of the 10 numbers in the columns.

By this time, I guess you would have realized that we are targeting two broad addition skills—

(i) Your ability to react with the total when you see two 2 digit numbers (like 57+78=135)

(ii) Your ability to add multiple 2 digit numbers if they are given to you consecutively (like 57+78+43+65 +91+38+44+18+64+72=570 in 8–10 seconds)

You might require around 1–2 months of regular practice to get proficient at this. However once you acquire this skill, every conceivable calculation that any aptitude exam can throw at you (or indeed has thrown at you over the past 20 years) would be very much within your zone.

How do you do larger additions?

One you have the skills to handle two digit additions as specified above handling bigger additions should be a cakewalk.

Suppose you were adding:
57436 + 64123 + 44586 + 78304 + 84653 + 5836. In order to do this, first add the thousands. 57 + 64 (=121) + 44 (=165) + 78 (=243) + 84 (=327) + 5 (=332). Thus, you have an interim answer of 332 thousands. At this stage you

know that your answer would be 332000 + a maximum of 6000 (as there are 6 numbers whose last 3 digits you have neglected). If a range of 332000 to 338000 suffices for you in the addition based on the closeness of the options, you would be through with your calculation at this point. In the event that you need to get to a closer answer than this, the next step would involve taking the 100s digit into account.

Thus for the above calculation: 57436+ 64123 +44586+78304+84653 +5836 when you add the hundreds, you get 4+1+5+3+6+8 = 27 hundreds. Your answer gets refined to 334700 and at this point you also know that the upper limit of the addition has to be a maximum of 600 more than 334700 i.e. the answer lies between 334700 to 335300. In case this accuracy level is still not sufficient you may then look at the last 2 digits of the numbers. Our experience tells us that normally that would not be required.

However, in case you still need to add these digits-it would amount to 2 digit additions again. So you would need to add 57**436**+64**123**+44**586**+78**304**+84**653** +58**36** → 36+23 (=59) +86 (=145) + 4 (=149) + 53 (=202) +36 (=238).

Thus, the correct total would be 334700 + 238 = 334938 and while doing this entire calculation we have not gone above 2 digit additions anywhere.

Apart from that, the biggest advantage of the process explained above is that in this process, you could stop the moment you had an answer that was sufficient in the context of the provided options.

🄰 SUBTRACTIONS—JUST AN EXTENSION OF ADDITIONS

The better your additions are, the better you would be able to implement the process explained for subtractions. So, a piece of advice from me—make sure that you have worked on your additions seriously for at least 15 days before you attempt to internalize the process for subtractions that is explained in this chapter.

Throughout school you have always used the conventional carry over method of subtracting. But, I am here to show you that you have an option—something that would be much faster and much more superior to the current process you are using. What is it you would ask me? Well what would you do in case you are trying to subtract 38 from 72?

The conventional process tells us to do this as:

	Carry over 1	
	7	2
−	3	8
	3	4

Well, the alternative and much faster way of thinking about subtractions is shown on the number line below:

Difference between any 2 numbers is equal to the distance between the numbers on the number line

The principle used for doing subtractions this way is that the difference between any two numbers can be seen as the distance between them on the number line.

Thus, imagine you are standing on the number 38 on the number line and you are looking towards 72. To make your calculation easy, your first target has to be to reach a number ending with 2. When you start to move to the right from 38, the first number you see that ends in 2 is the number 42. To move from 38 to 42 you need to cover a distance of +4 (as shown in the figure). Once you are at 42, your next target is to move from 42 to 72. The distance between 42 to 72 is 30.

Thus, the subtraction's value for the numbers 72–38 would be 34.

Consider, the following examples:

Illustration 1 95 − 39

Illustration 2 177 − 83

177–83 = 94

Alternately:

177–83 = 94

Illustration 3 738 − 211

try to reach the first number which ends in 38

738–211 = 527

In this case the first objective is to reach the first number ending in 38 as you start moving to the right of 211. The first such number to the right of 211 being 238, first reach 238 (by adding 27 to 211) and then move from 238 to 738 (adding 500 to 238 to reach 738)

In case you need an intermediate number before reaching 238 you can also think of doing the following:

try to reach the first number which ends in 38

738–211 = 7 + 20 + 500 = 527

Illustration 4 813 − 478

try to reach the first number which ends in 13

Thus, 813–478 = 35 + 300 = 335

Alternately, this thought can also be done as:

try to reach the first number which ends in 13

813–478 = 22 + 13 + 300 = 335

Also, you could have done it as follows:

try to reach the first number which ends in 13

813–478 = 5 + 30 + 300 = 335

Even if we were to get 4 digit numbers, you would still be able to use this process quite easily.

Multiplications

Multiplications are the next calculation which we need to look at—these are obviously crucial because most questions in Mathematics do involve multiplications.

The fundamental view of multiplication is essentially that when we need to add a certain number consecutively—say we want to add the number 17 seven times:

i.e. $17 + 17 + 17 + 17 + 17 + 17 + 17$ it can also be more conveniently done by using 17×7.

Normally in aptitude exams like the CAT, multiplications would be restricted to 2 digits multiplied by 2 digits, 2 digits multiplied by 3 digits and 3 digits multiplied by 3 digits.

So what are the short cuts that are available in Multiplications? Let us take a look at the various options you have in order to multiply.

1. The straight line method of multiplying two numbers (From Vedic Mathematics and also from the Trachtenberg System of Speed Mathematics)

Let us take an example to explain this process:

Suppose you were multiplying two 2 digit numbers like 43×78.

The multiplication would be done in the following manner:

$$\begin{array}{r} 4\ 3 \\ \times\ 7\ 8 \\ \hline \end{array}$$

Step 1: Finding the Unit's digit

The first objective would be to get the unit's digit. In order to do this we just need to multiply the units' digit of both the numbers. Thus, 3×8 would give us 24. Hence, we would write 4 in the units' digit of the answer and carry over the digit 2 to the tens place as follows:

$$\begin{array}{r} 4\ 3 \\ \times\ 7\ 8 \\ \hline 4 \end{array}$$

2 carry over to the tens place

At this point we know that the units' digit is 4 and also that there is a carry over of 2 to the tens place of the answer.

Step 2: Finding the tens' place digit

$$\begin{array}{r} 4\ 3 \\ \times\ 7\ 8 \\ \hline 5\ 4 \end{array}$$

5 carry over to hundreds place

Thought Process:

$4 \times 8 + 3 \times 7 = 32 + 21 = 53$

$53 + 2$ (from carry over) $= 55$

Thus we write 5 in the tens place and carry over 5 to the hundreds place

In the above case, we have multiplied the units digit of the second number with the tens digit of the first number and added the multiplication of the units digit of the first number with the tens digit of the second number. Thus we would get:

8 (units digit of the second number) $\times$ 4 (tens digit of the first number) + 7 (tens digit of the second number) $\times$ 3 (units digit of the first number + 2 (carry over from the units' digit calculation)

$= 32 + 21 + 2 = 55$.

We write down 5 in the tens' digit of the answer and carry over 5 to the hundreds digit of the answer.

Step 3: Finding the hundreds' place digit

$$\begin{array}{r} 4\ 3 \\ \times\ 7\ 8 \\ \hline 3\ 3\ 5\ 4 \end{array}$$

Thought Process:

$$4 \times 7 = 28$$
$$28 + 5 = 33$$

Since, 4 and 7 are the last digits on the left in both the numbers this is the last calculation in this problem and hence we can write 33 for the remaining 2 digits in the answer

Thus, the answer to the question is 3354.

With a little bit of practice you can do these kinds of calculations mentally without having to write the intermediate steps.

Let us consider another example where the number of digits is larger:

Suppose you were trying to find the product of 43578 × 6921

Step 1: Finding the units digit

Units digit: $1 \times 8 = 8$

$$
\begin{array}{r}
4\ 3\ 5\ 7\ 8 \\
\times\ 6\ 9\ 2\ 1 \\
\hline
8
\end{array}
$$

Step 2: Finding the tens digit

$$
\begin{array}{r}
4\ 3\ 5\ 7\ 8 \\
\times\ 6\ 9\ 2\ 1 \\
\hline
3\ 8
\end{array}
$$

Carry over 2

Thought Process:
Tens digit would come by multiplying tens with units and units with tens

$$7 \times 1 + 2 \times 8 = 7 + 16 = 23$$

In order to think about this, we can think of the first pair - by thinking about which number would multiply 1 (units digit of the second number) to make it into tens.

Once, you have spotted the first pair the next pair would get spotted by moving right on the upper number (43578) and moving left on the lower number (6921)

Step 3: Finding the hundreds digit

Let us look at the broken down thought process for this step:

$$
\begin{array}{r}
4\ 3\ 5\ 7\ 8 \\
\times\ 6\ 9\ 2\ 1 \\
\hline
3\ 8
\end{array}
$$

Carry over 2

Thought Process:
Locate the first pair that would give you your hundreds digit.

For this first think of what you need to multiply the digit in the units place of the second number (digit 1) with to get the hundreds digit of the answer.

Since:

Units × Hundreds = Hundreds

We need to pair 1 with 5 in the upper number as shown in the figure.

Once you have identified 5×1 as the first pair of digits, to identify the next pair, move 1 to the right of the upper number and move 1 to the left of the lower number.

Thus, you should be able to get 7×2 as your next pair.

$$
\begin{array}{r}
4\ 3\ 5\ 7\ 8 \\
\times\ 6\ 9\ 2\ 1 \\
\hline
3\ 8
\end{array}
$$

Carry over 2

For the last pair, you can again repeat the above thought-move to the right in the upper number and move to the left in the lower number.

Thus, the final thought for this situation would look like:

$$
\begin{array}{r}
4\ 3\ 5\ 7\ 8 \\
\times\ 6\ 9\ 2\ 1 \\
\hline
3\ 3\ 8
\end{array}
$$

9 carry over to thousands place

Thought Process:
First pair: 5×1
Second pair: 7×2 (move right on upper number and move left on the lower number)
Third pair: 8×9 (move right on upper number and move left on the lower number)
Thus, $5 \times 1 + 7 \times 2 + 8 \times 9 = 91$
$91 + 2$ (carry over) = 93
Hundreds place digit would be 3 and carry over to the thousands place would be 9

Step 4: Finding the thousands digit

We would follow the same process as above. For doing the same first identify the first pair as 3×1 (thousands from the first number multiplied by units from the second number) and then start moving right and moving left on both the numbers to find the other pairs.

$$
\begin{array}{r}
4\ 3\ 5\ 7\ 8 \\
\times\ 6\ 9\ 2\ 1 \\
\hline
3\ 3\ 1\ 8
\end{array}
$$

13 carry over to
ten thousands place

Thought Process:
$3 \times 1 + 5 \times 2 + 7 \times 9 + 8 \times 6 = 124$
thousands × units + hundreds × tens + tens × hundreds + units × thousands

124 + 9 (from the carry over) = 133
put down 3 as the thousands place digit and carry over
13 to the ten thousands place

Step 5: Finding the ten thousands digit

4×1 would be the first pair here followed by 3×2; 5×9 and 7×6 as shown below:

```
    4 3 5 7 8
  × 6 9 2 1
  ─────────────
    0 3 3 3 8
```
11 carry over to
the lacs place

Thought Process:
$4 \times 1 + 3 \times 2 + 5 \times 9 + 7 \times 6 = 97$
$97 + 13$ (from the carry over of the previous step) = 110.
Hence, 0 becomes the digit which would come into the
answer and 11 would be carried over

Step 6: Finding the digit in the lakhs' place

```
    4 3 5 7 8
  × 6 9 2 1
  ─────────────
  6 0 3 3 3 8
```
7 carry over to
the ten lakhs place

Thought Process:
Since we have already used up 4×1 (the left most digit
in the first number multiplied with the right most digit
in the second number, it is no longer possible to use the
digit 1 (units digit of the second number) to form a pair.
Use this as a signal to fix the digit 4 from the first
number and start to write down the pairs by pairing
this digit 4 (ten thousands' digit of the first number)
with the corresponding digit of the second number to
form the lacs digit.
It is evident that ten thousands × tens = lacs.
Thus, the first pair is 4×2.
Note that you could also think of the first pair as 4×2
by realising that since we have used 4×1 as the first
pair for the previous digit we can use the number to
the left of 1 to form 4×2.
Subsequent pairs would be 3×9 and 5×6.
Thus, $4 \times 2 + 3 \times 9 + 5 \times 6 = 8 + 27 + 30 = 65$
$65 + 11$ (carry over) = 76.
Thus, 6 becomes the lacs digit and we get a carry over
of 7.

Step 7: Finding the ten lakh's digit

```
    4 3 5 7 8
  × 6 9 2 1
  ─────────────
  1 6 0 3 3 3 8
```
6 carry over to the next place

Thought Process:
First pair: 4×9
Next pair: 3×6
Thus, $4 \times 9 + 3 \times 6 = 54$
$54 + 7$ (from the carry over) = 61
1 becomes the next digit in the answer and we carry
over 6.

Step 8: Finding the next digit

```
    4 3 5 7 8
  × 6 9 2 1
  ─────────────────
  3 0 1 6 0 3 3 3 8
```

Thought Process:
$4 \times 6 = 24$
$24 + 6$ (from the carry over = 30)
This is the last step because we have multiplied the
left most two digits in the number.

The above process of multiplication- although it looks
extremely attractive and magical – especially for larger
numbers, it's actual usage in the examination context might
actually be quite low. This is because there are better ways
of doing multiplication of 2 to 3 digits and larger multiplications might not be required to be executed in an exam
like the CAT.

However, in order to solve questions where you might be
asked to find the hundreds or even the thousands' digit of
a big multiplication like the one showed above, this might
be your only option.

Let us look at a few more alternative approaches in order
to calculate multiplication problems.

2. Using squares to multiply two numbers

In this approach the usage of the mathematical result $a^2 - b^2 = (a - b)(a + b)$ helps us to find the result of a multiplication.

For instance 18×22 can be done using $20^2 - 2^2 = 400 - 4 = 396$, taking $a = 20$ and $b = 2$

Similarly, $22 \times 28 = 25^2 - 3^2 = 625 - 9 = 616$

$35 \times 47 = 41^2 - 6^2 = 1681 - 36 = 1645$

In case the difference between the two numbers is not
even, we can still use this process by modifying it thus:

$$24 \times 33 = 24 \times 32 + 24 = 28^2 - 4^2 + 24$$
$$= 784 - 16 + 24 = 792$$

However, obviously this process might be ineffective in
the following cases:

(i) If the values of the squares required to calculate an
multiplication are difficult to ascertain (For two digit
numbers, we can bypass this by knowing the short cut
to calculate the squares of 2 digit numbers- **You may
want to look at the methods given in Chapter 4 of
this part to find out the squares of 2 digit numbers
in order to be more effective with these kinds of
calculations.)**

(ii) When one is trying to multiply two numbers which are very far from each other, there might be other processes for multiplying them that might be better than this process. For instance, if you are trying to multiply 24 × 92 trying to do it as $58^2 - 34^2$ obviously would not be a very convenient process.

(iii) Also, in case one moves into trying to multiply larger numbers, obviously this process would fail. For instance 283×305 would definitely not be a convenient calculation if we use this process.

3. Multiplying numbers close to 100 and 1000

A specific method exists for multiplying two numbers which are both close to 100 or 1000 or 10000.

For us, the most important would be to multiply 2 numbers which are close to 100.

The following example will detail this process for you:
Let us say you are trying to multiply 94 × 96.

Step 1: Calculate the difference from 100 for both numbers and write them down (or visualize them) as follows:

$$
\begin{array}{r}
\text{Difference} \\
\text{from 100} \\
9\ 4 \quad -6 \\
\times\ 9\ 6 \quad -4 \\
\end{array}
$$

Step 2: The answer would be calculated in two steps-
(a) The last two digits of the answer would be calculated by multiplying -6×-4 to get 24.

$$
\begin{array}{r}
9\ 4 \quad -6 \\
\times \\
\times\ 9\ 6 \quad -4 \\
\hline
\end{array}
$$

initial digits of the multiplication | last 2 digits would be got by multiplying -6×-4

Note here that we divide the answer into two parts:

Last 2 digits and Initial digits

(In case the numbers were close to 1000 we would divide the calculation into the last three digits and the initial digits)

When we multiply -6×-4 we get 24 and hence we would write that as our last 2 digits in the answer.

We would then reach the following stage of the multiplication:

$$
\begin{array}{r}
9\ 4 \quad -6 \\
\times \\
9\ 6 \quad -4 \\
\hline
\quad |\ 2\ 4 \\
\end{array}
$$

initial digits of the multiplication

The next task is to find the initial digits of the answer:
This can be done by cross adding 94 + (−4) or 96 + (−6) to get the digits as 90 as shown in the figure below:

$$
\begin{array}{r}
\text{Difference} \\
\text{from 100} \\
9\ 4 \quad -6 \\
\times\ 9\ 6 \quad -4 \\
\hline
9\ 0\ |\ 2\ 4 \\
\end{array}
$$

Thought Process:

Add along the diagonal connecting line shown in the figure to get the value of the initial digits of the answer:
Thus we would get 94 + (−4) = 90
or
96 + (−6) = 90
Thus, our initial digits of the answer are 90.

Let us take another example to illustrate a few more points which might arise in such a calculation:
Let us say, you were doing 102 × 103.

$$
\begin{array}{r}
1\ 0\ 2 \quad +2 \\
1\ 0\ 3 \quad +3 \\
\hline
1\ 0\ 5\ |\ 0\ 6 \\
\end{array}
$$

Initial digits Last 2 digits

Thought Process:

In this case, the second part of the answer (the last two digits) turns out to be 2 × 3 = 6. In such a case, since we know that the second part of the answer has to be compulsorily in 2 digits, we would naturally need to take it as 06.
The initial digits of the answer would be got by cross addition:

$$102 + 3 = 103 + 2 = 105$$

Consider: 84 × 88

$$
\begin{array}{r}
8\ 4 \quad -16 \\
8\ 8 \quad -12 \\
\hline
7\ 3\ |\ 9\ 2 \\
\end{array}
$$

Initial digits | Last 2 digits

7392 is the answer

Thought Process:

In this case, the difference from 100 for the two numbers are −12 and −16 respectively.
We multiply them to get the last 2 digits of the number. However, $-12 \times -16 = 192$ which is a 3 digit number.
Hence, retain 92 as the last 2 digits and carry over 1 to the initial digits.
Then while finding the initial digits you would need to add this carry over when you are writing the answer.

Thus, initial digits:

84 + (–12) + 1 (from the carry over) = 72 + 1 = 73

Alternately:

88 + (–16) + 1 (from the carry over) = 72 + 1 = 73

Now consider the situation where one number is above 100 and the other below 100.

For instance:

$$92 \times 104$$

The following figure would show you what to do in this case:

```
    1 0 4    +4
  × 9 2      −8
  ─────────
  9 6 0 0
      − 3 2
  ─────────
  9 5 6 8
```
Initial | Last 2
digits | digits

Thought Process:

The problem in this calculation is that +4 × (–8) = –32 and hence cannot be directly written as the last two digits of the answer.

In this case, first leave the last 2 digits as 00 and find the initial digits of the answer.

Initial digits:

104 + (–8) = 96 = 92 + 4

When you write 96 having kept the last 2 digits of the number as 00, the meaning of the number's value would be 9600.

Now, from this subtract = 4 × (–8) = –32 to get the answer as 9600 – 32 = 9568.

For a multiplication like 994 × 996 the only adjustment you would need to do would be to look at the second part of the answer as a 3- digit number:

The following would make the process clear to you for such cases:

```
    9 9 4    −6
  × 9 9 6    −4
  ─────────
  9 9 0 0 2 4
```
Initial | Last 3
digits | digits

Thought Process:

Last 3 digits = –6 × –4 = 24 → Hence, we write it as 024

Initial digits: Cross addition of 994 + (–4) = 990

Alternately, 996 + (–6) = 990

Thus, the answer would be 990024.

Note:

(i) The above process for multiplication is extremely good in cases when the two numbers are close to any power of 10 (like 100,1000,10000 etc)

However, when the numbers are far away from a power of 10, the process becomes infeasible.

Thus, this process would not be effective at all in the case of 62 × 34.

(ii) For finding squares of numbers between 80 to 120, this process is extremely good and hence you should use this whenever you are faced with the task of finding the square of a number in this range.

For instance, if you are multiplying 91 × 91 you can easily see the answer as 8281.

4. Using additions to multiply

Consider the following view of an option for multiplying

Let us say we are trying to multiply 83 × 32

This can be converted most conveniently into 80 × 30 + 3 × 30 + 2 × 83 = 2400 + 90 + 166 = 2656

This could also have been done as: 83 × 30 + 2 × 83 = 2490 + 166 = 2656

However in the case of 77 × 48 the second conversion shown above might not be so easy to execute- while the first one would be much easier:

70 × 40 + 7 × 40 + 8 × 77 = 70 × 40 + 7 × 40 + 8 × 70 + 8 × 7 = 2800 + 280 + 560 + 56 = 3696.

The advantage of this type of conversion is that at no point of time in the above calculation are you doing anything more than single digit × single digit multiplication.

5. Use of percentages to multiply

Another option that you have can be explained as below:

Let us say you are trying to find 43 × 78.

In order to calculate 43 × 78 first calculate 43% of 78 as follows:

43% of 78 = 10% of 78 + 10% of 78 +10% of 78 +10% of 78 + 1% of 78 + 1% of 78 + 1% of 78 = 7.8 + 7.8 + 7.8 + 7.8 + 0.78 + 0.78 + 0.78 = 33.34

This can be done using: 7 × 4 =28 as the integer part.

For adding the decimals, consider all the decimals as two digit numbers. In the addition if your total is a 2 digit number, write that down in the decimals place of the answer. If the number is a 3 digit number, carry over the hundreds' digit to the integer part of the answer.

Thus, in this case you would get:

80 + 80 + 80 + 80 + 78 + 78 + 78 = 554. This 554 actually means 5.54 in the context that we have written down 0.80 as 80.

Thus, the total is 33.54.

We have found that 43% of 78 is 33.54 and our entire addition has been done in single and 2 digits. We of course realize that 43% of 78 being the same as 0.43 × 78 the digits for 43 × 78 would be the same as the digits for what we have calculated.

Now, the only thing that remains is to put the decimals back where they belong.

There are many ways to think about this- perhaps the easiest being that 43×78 should have 4 as it's units digit and hence the correct answer is 3354.

Of course, this could also have been done by calculating 78% of 43 as $21.5 + 10.75 + 0.43 + 0.43 + 0.43 = 31 + 2.54 = 33.54 \rightarrow$ Hence, the answer is 3354.

You can even handle 2 digit $\times$ 3 digit multiplication through the same process:

Suppose you were multiplying 324×82, instead of doing the multiplication as given, find 324 % of 82.

The question converts to: $3.24 \times 82 = 82 \times 3 + 8.2 + 8.2 + 0.82 + 0.82 + 0.82 + 0.82 = 246 + 16 + 3.68 = 265.68$.

Hence, the answer is 26568.

We would encourage you to try to multiply 2 digits $\times$ 2 digits and 2 digits $\times$ 3 digits and 3 digits $\times$ 3 digits by the methods you find most suitable amongst those given above.

In my view, the use of percentages to multiply is the most powerful tool for carrying out the kinds of multiplications you would come across in Aptitude exams. Once you can master how to think about the decimals digits in these calculations, it has the potential to give you a significant time saving in your examination.

Obviously, when you convert a multiplication into an addition using any of the two processes given above, the speed and efficiency of your calculation would depend largely on your ability to add well. If your 2 digit additions are good (or if you have made your additions of 2 digit numbers good by using the process given in the chapter on additions) you would find the addition processes given here the best.

The simple reason is because this process has the advantage of being the most versatile- in the sense that it is not dependant on particular types of numbers.

Besides, after enough practice you would be able to do 2 digits $\times$ 2 digits and 2 digits $\times$ 3 digits and 3 digits $\times$ 3 digits orally.

Divisions, Percentage Calculations and Ratio Comparisons

3
Chapter

CALCULATING DECIMAL VALUES FOR DIVISION QUESTIONS USING PERCENTAGE CALCULATIONS

I have chosen to club these two together because they are actually parallel to each other—in the sense that for any ratio we can calculate two values—the percentage value and the decimal value. The digits in the decimal value and the percentage value of any ratio would always be the same. Hence, calculating the percentage value of a ratio and the decimal value of the ratio would be the same thing.

How do you calculate the percentage value of a ratio?

PERCENTAGE RULE FOR CALCULATING PERCENTAGE VALUES THROUGH ADDITIONS

Illustrated below is a powerful method of calculating percentages. In my opinion, the ability to calculate percentage through this method depends on your ability to handle 2 digit additions. Unless you develop the skill to add 2 digit additions in your mind, you are always likely to face problems in calculating percentage through the method illustrated below. In fact, trying this method without being strong at 2-digit additions/subtractions (including 2 digits after decimal point) would prove to be a disadvantage in your attempt at calculating percentages fast.

This process, essentially being a commonsense process, is best illustrated through a few examples:

Example What is the percentage value of the ratio: 53/81?

Solution The process involves removing all the 100%, 50%, 10%, 1%, 0.1% and so forth of the denominator from the numerator.

Thus, 53/81 can be rewritten as: $(40.5 + 12.5)/81 = 40.5/81 + 12.5/81 = 50\% + 12.5/81$

$$= 50\% + (8.1 + 4.4)/81 = 50\% + 10\% + 4.4/81$$
$$= 60\% + 4.4/81$$

At this stage you know that the answer to the question lies between 60 – 70% (Since 4.4 is less than 10% of 81)

At this stage, you know that the answer to the calculation will be in the form: $6a.bcde$ ….

All you need to do is find out the value of the missing digits.

In order to do this, calculate the percentage value of 4.4/81 through the normal process of multiplying the numerator by 100.

Thus the % value of $\dfrac{4.4}{81} = \dfrac{4.4 \times 100}{81} = \dfrac{440}{81}$

[**Note:** Use the multiplication by 100, once you have the 10% range. This step reduces the decimal calculations.]

Thus $\dfrac{440}{81} = 5\%$ with a remainder of 35

Our answer is now refined to 65.$bcde$. (1% Range)

Next, in order to find the next digit (first one after the decimal) add a zero to the remainder;

Hence, the value of 'b' will be the quotient of

$b \to 350/81 = 4$ Remainder 26

        Answer: 65.4cde (0.1% Range)

$c \to 260/81 = 3$ Remainder 17

        Answer: 65.43 (0.01% Range)

and so forth.

The advantages of this process are two fold:

(1) You only calculate as long as you need to in order to eliminate the options. Thus, in case there was only a single option between 60–70% in the above question, you could have stopped your calculations right there.

(2) This process allows you to go through with the calculations as long as you need to.

However, remember what I had advised you right at the start: Strong Addition skills are a primary requirement for using this method properly.

To illustrate another example:

What is the percentage value of the ratio $\dfrac{223}{72}$?

223/72 → 300 – 310% Remainder 7
700/72 → 9. Hence 309 – 310%, Remainder 52
520/72 → 7. Hence, 309.7, Remainder 16
160/72 → 2. Hence, 309.72 Remainder 16

Hence, 309.7222 (2 recurs since we enter an infinite loop of 160/72 calculations).

In my view, percentage rule (as I call it) is one of the best ways to calculate percentages since it gives you the flexibility to calculate the percentage value up to as many digits after decimals as you are required to and at the same time allows you to stop the moment you attain the required accuracy range.

Of course I hope you realize that when you get 53/81 = 65.43 % the decimal value of the same would be 0.6543 and for 223/72, the decimal value would be 3.097222.

The kind of exam that the CAT is, I do not think you would not need to calculate ratios beyond 2 digits divided by 2 digits. In other words, if you are trying to calculate 5372/8164, you can take an approximation of this ratio as 53/81 and calculate the percentage value as shown in the process above. The accuracy in the calculation of 53/81 instead of 5372/8164 would be quite sufficient to answer questions on ratio values that the CAT may throw up in Quantitative Aptitude for even in Data Interpretation questions.

🎧 RATIO COMPARISONS

CALCULATION METHODS related to RATIOS

(A) Calculation methods for Ratio comparisons:

There could be four broad cases when you might be required to do ratio comparisons:

The table below clearly illustrates these:

	Numerator	Denominator	Ratio	Calculations
Case 1	Increases	Decreases	Increase	Not required
Case 2	Increases	Increases	May Increase or Decrease	Required
Case 3	Decreases	Increases	Decreases	Not required
Case 4	Decreases	Decreases	May Increase or Decrease	Required

In cases 2 and 4 in the table, calculations will be necessitated. In such a situation, the following processes can be used for ratio comparisons.

1. The Cross Multiplication Method

Two ratios can be compared using the cross multiplication method as follows. Suppose you have to compare

12/15 with 15/19

Then, to test which ratio is higher cross multiply and compare 12×19 and 15×17.

If 12×19 is bigger the Ratio 12/17 will be bigger. If 15×17 is higher, the ratio 15/19 will be higher.

In this case, 15×17 being higher, the Ratio 15/19 is higher.

Note: In real time usage (esp. in D.I.) this method is highly impractical and calculating the product might be more cumbersome than calculating the percentage values.

Thus, this method will not be able to tell you the answer if you have to compare $\dfrac{3743}{5624}$ with $\dfrac{3821}{5783}$

2. Percentage Value Comparison Method

Suppose you have to compare: $\dfrac{173}{212}$ with $\dfrac{181}{241}$

In such a case just by estimating the 10% ranges for each ratio you can clearly see that —
the first ratio is > 80% while the second ratio is < 80%

Hence, the first ratio is obviously greater.

This method is extremely convenient if the two ratios have their values in different 10% ranges.

However, this problem will become slightly more difficult, if the two ratios fall in the same 10% range. Thus, if you had to compare $^{173}/_{212}$ with $^{181}/_{225}$, both the values would give values between 80 – 90%. The next step would be to calculate the 1% range.

The first ratio here is 81 – 82% while the second ratio lies between 80 – 81%

Hence the first ratio is the larger of the two.

Note: For this method to be effective for you, you will first need to master the percentage rule method for calculating the percentage value of a ratio. Hence if you cannot see that 169.6 is 80% of 212 or for that matter that 81% of 212 is 171.72 and 82% is 173.84 you will not be able to use this method effectively. (This is also true for the next method.) However, once you can calculate percentage values of 3 digit ratios to 1% range, there is not much that can stop you in comparing ratios. The CAT and all other aptitude exams normally do not challenge you to calculate further than the 1% range when you are looking at ratio comparisons.

---

3. Numerator Denominator Percentage Change Method

There is another way in which you can compare close ratios like 173/212 and 181/225. For this method, you need to calculate the percentage changes in the numerator and the denominator.

Thus:

$173 \rightarrow 181$ is a % increase of $4 - 5\%$

While $212 \rightarrow 225$ is a % increase of $6 - 7\%$.

In this case, since the denominator is increasing more than the numerator, the second ratio is smaller.

This method is the most powerful method for comparing close ratios—provided you are good with your percentage rule calculations.

(B) Method for calculating the value of a percentage change in the ratio:

PCG (Percentage Change Graphic) gives us a convenient method to calculate the value of the percentage change in a ratio.

Suppose, you have to calculate the percentage change between 2 ratios. This has to be done in two stages as:

$$\text{Original Ratio} \xrightarrow[\text{numerator}]{\text{Effect of}} \text{Intermediate Ratio}$$

$$\xrightarrow[\text{Denominator}]{\text{Effect of}} \text{Final Ratio}$$

Thus if 20/40 becomes 22/50

Effect of numerator = $20 \rightarrow 22(10\%$ increase)

Effect of denominator = $50 \rightarrow 40(25\%$ decrease) (reverse fashion)

Overall effect on the ratio:

$$100 \xrightarrow[\substack{\text{Numerator} \\ \text{Effect}}]{10\% \uparrow} 110 \xrightarrow[\substack{\text{Denominator} \\ \text{Effect}}]{25\% \downarrow} 82.5$$

Hence, overall effect = 17.5% decrease.

4 Chapter · Squares and Cubes of Numbers

SQUARES AND SQUARE ROOTS

When any number is multiplied by itself, it is called as the square of the number.

Thus, $3 \times 3 = 3^2 = 9$

Squares have a very important role to play in mathematics. In the context of preparing for CAT and other similar aptitude exams, it might be a good idea to be able to recollect the squares of 2 digit numbers.

Let us now go through the following table carefully:

Table 4.1

Number	Square	Number	Square	Number	Square
1	1	35	1225	69	4761
2	4	36	1296	70	4900
3	9	37	1369	71	5041
4	16	38	1444	72	5184
5	25	39	1521	73	5329
6	36	40	1600	74	5476
7	49	41	1681	75	5625
8	64	42	1764	76	5776
9	81	43	1849	77	5929
10	100	44	1936	78	6084
11	121	45	2025	79	6241
12	144	46	2116	80	6400
13	169	47	2209	81	6561
14	196	48	2304	82	6724
15	225	49	2401	83	6889
16	256	50	2500	84	7056
17	289	51	2601	85	7225

Contd

Table 4.1 *(Contd)*

Number	Square	Number	Square	Number	Square
18	324	52	2704	86	7396
19	361	53	2809	87	7561
20	400	54	2916	88	7744
21	441	55	3025	89	7921
22	484	56	3136	90	8100
23	529	57	3249	91	8281
24	576	58	3364	92	8464
25	625	59	3481	93	8649
26	676	60	3600	94	8836
27	729	61	3721	95	9025
28	784	62	3844	96	9216
29	841	63	3969	97	9409
30	900	64	4096	98	9604
31	961	65	4225	99	9801
32	1024	66	4356	100	10000
33	1089	67	4489		
34	1156	68	4624		

So, how does one get these numbers onto one's finger tips? Does one memorize these values or is there a simpler way?

Yes indeed! There is a very convenient process when it comes to memorising the squares of the first 100 numbers.

First of all, you are expected to memorise the squares of the first 30 numbers. In my experience, I have normally seen that most students already know this. The problem arises with numbers after 30. You do not need to worry about that. Just follow the following processes and you will know all squares upto 100.

Trick 1: For squares from 51 to 80 – (**Note:** This method depends on your memory of the first thirty squares.)

The process is best explained through an example.

Suppose, you have to get an answer for the value of 67^2. Look at 67 as $(50 + 17)$. The 4 digit answer will have two parts as follows:

First 2 digits   Last 2 digits

The last two digits will be the same as the last two digits of the square of the number 17. (The value 17 is derived by looking at the difference of 67 with respect to 50.)

Since, $17^2 = 289$, you can say that the last two digits of 67^2 will be 89. (i.e. the last 2 digits of 289.) Also, you will need to carry over the '2' in the hundreds place of 289 to the first part of the number.

The first two digits of the answer will be got by adding 17 (which is got from $67 - 50$) and adding the carry over (2 in this case) to the number 25. (Standard number to be used in all cases.) Hence, the first two digits of the answer will be given by $25 + 17 + 2 = 44$.

Hence, the answer is 67^2 = 4489.

Similarly, suppose you have to find 76^2.

Step 1: $76 = 50 + 26$.

Step 2: 26^2 is 676. Hence, the last 2 digits of the answer will be 76 and we will carry over 6.

Step 3: The first two digits of the answer will be $25 + 26 + 6 = 57$.

Hence, the answer is 5776.

This technique will take care of squares from 51 to 80 (if you remember the squares from 1 to 30). You are advised to use this process and see the answers for yourself.

SQUARES FOR NUMBERS FROM 31 TO 50

Such numbers can be treated in the form $(50 - x)$ and the above process modified to get the values of squares from 31 to 50. Again, to explain we will use an example. Suppose you have to find the square of 41.

Step 1: Look at 41 as $(50 - 9)$.

Again, similar to what we did above, realise that the answer has two parts—the first two and the last two digits.

Step 2: The last two digits are got by the last two digits in the value of $(-9)^2 = 81$. Hence, 81 will represent the last two digits of 41^2.

Step 3: The first two digits are derived by $25 - 9 = 16$ (where 25 is a standard number to be used in all cases and -9 comes from the fact that $(50 - 9) = 41$).

Hence, the answer is 1681.

Note: In case there had been a carry over from the last two digits it would have been added to 16 to get the answer.

For example, in finding the value of 36^2 we look at 36 = $(50 - 14)$

Now, $(-14)^2 = 196$. Hence, the last 2 digits of the answer will be 96. The number '1' in the hundreds place will have to be carried over to the first 2 digits of the answer.

The, first two digits will be $25 - 14 + 1 = 12$

Hence, $36^2 = 1296$.

With this process, you are equipped to find the squares of numbers from 31 to 50.

FINDING SQUARES OF NUMBERS BETWEEN 81 TO 100

Suppose you have to find the value of 82^2. The following process will give you the answers.

Step 1: Look at 82 as $(100 - 18)$. The answer will have 4 digits whose values will be got by focusing on getting the value of the last two digits and that of the first two digits.

Step 2: The value of the last two digits will be equal to the last two digits of $(-18)^2$.

Since, $(-18)^2 = 324$, the last two digits of 82^2 will be 24. The '3' in the hundreds place of $(-18)^2$ will be carried over to the other part of the answer (i.e. the first two digits).

Step 3: The first two digits will be got by: $82 + (-18) + 3$ Where 82 is the original number; (-18) is the number obtained by looking at 82 as $(100 - x)$; and 3 is the carry over from $(-18)^2$.

Similarly, 87^2 will give you the following thought process:

$87 = 100 - 13 \rightarrow (-13)^2 = 169$. Hence, 69 are the last two digits of the answer $\rightarrow$ Carry over 1. Consequently, $87 + (-13) + 1 = 75$ will be the first 2 digits of the answer.

Hence, $87^2 = 7569$.

With these three processes you will be able to derive the square of any number up to 100.

Properties of squares:

1. When a perfect square is written as a product of its prime factors each prime factor will appear an even number of times.

2. The difference between the squares of two consecutive natural numbers is always equal to the sum of the natural numbers. Thus, $41^2 - 40^2 = (40 + 41) = 81$.

   This property is very useful when used in the opposite direction—i.e. Given that the difference between the squares of two consecutive integers is 81, you should immediately realise that the numbers should be 40 and 41.

3. The square of a number ending in 1, 5 or 6 also ends in 1, 5 or 6 respectively.

4. The square of any number ending in 5: The last two digits will always be 25. The digits before that in the answer will be got by multiplying the digits leading up to the digit 5 in the number by 1 more than itself.
   Illustration:
   $$85^2 = \_\_\_25.$$
   The missing digits in the above answer will be got by $8 \times (8 + 1) = 8 \times 9 = 72$. Hence, the square of 85 is given by 7225.
   Similarly, $135^2 = \_\_\_25$. The missing digits are $13 \times 14 = 182$. Hence, $135^2 = 18225$.

5. The value of a perfect square has to end in 1, 4, 5, 6, 9 or an even number of zeros. In other words, a perfect square cannot end in 2, 3, 7, or 8 or an odd number of zeros.

6. If the units digit of the square of a number is 1, then the number should end in 1 or 9.

7. If the units digit of the square of a number is 4, then the units digit of the number is 2 or 8.

8. If the units digit of the square of a number is 9, then the units digit of the number is 3 or 7.

9. If the units of the square of a number is 6, then the unit's digit of the number is 4 or 6.

10. The sum of the squares of the first 'n' natural numbers is given by
    $$[(n)\ (n + 1)\ (2n + 1)]/6.$$

11. The square of a number is always non-negative.

12. Normally, by squaring any number we increase the value of the number. The only integers for which this is not true are 0 and 1. (In these cases squaring the number has no effect on the value of the number).

    Further, for values between 0 to 1, squaring the number reduces the value of the number. For example $0.5^2 < 0.5$.

Say, you have to Find the Square Root of a Given Number

Say 7056

Step 1:   Write down the number 7056 as a product of its Prime factors. $7056 = 2 \times 2 \times 2 \times 2 \times 21 \times 21$
$$= 2^4 \times 21^2$$

Step 2:   The required square root is obtained by halving the values of the powers.
Hence, $\sqrt{7056} = 2^2 \times 21^1$

🔊 CUBES AND CUBE ROOTS

When a number is multiplied with itself two times, we get the cube of the number.
   Thus, $x \times x \times x = x^3$

Method to find out the cubes of 2 digit numbers: The answer has to consist of 4 parts, each of which has to be calculated separately.

The first part of the answer will be given by the cube of the ten's digit.

Suppose you have to find the cube of 28.

The first step is to find the cube of 2 and write it down.
$$2^3 = 8.$$

The next three parts of the number will be derived as follows.

Derive the values 32, 128 and 512.

(by creating a G. P. of 4 terms with the first term in this case as 8, and a common ratio got by calculating the ratio of the unit's digit of the number with its tens digit. In this case the ratio is $8/2 = 4$.)

Now, write the 4 terms in a straight line as below. Also, to the middle two terms add double the value.

	8	32	128	512
+		64	256	
	21	9	5	2

(carry over 51)

(8 + 13)   (32 + 64 + 43 =139)   (128 + 256 + 51 = 435)
          Carry over 13   (Carry over 43)

Hence, $28^3 = 21952$

Properties of Cubes

1. When a perfect cube is written in its standard form the values of the powers on each prime factor will be a multiple of 3.

2. In order to find the cube root of a number, first write it in its standard form and then divide all powers by 3.
   Thus, the cube root of $3^6 \times 5^9 \times 17^3 \times 2^6$ is given by $3^2 \times 5^3 \times 17 \times 2^2$

3. The cubes of all numbers (integers and decimals) greater than 1 are greater than the number itself.

4. $0^3 = 0$, $1^3 = 1$ and $-1^3 = -1$. These are the only three instances where the cube of the number is equal to the number itself.

5. The value of the cubes of a number between 0 and 1 is lower than the number itself. Thus, $0.5^3 < 0.5^2 < 0.5$.

6. The cube of a number between 0 and −1 is greater than the number itself. $(-0.2)^3 > -0.2$.

7. The cube of any number less than −1, is always lower than the number. Thus, $(-1.5)^3 < (-1.5)$.

BLOCK I

NUMBERS

Chapter 1
Number
Systems

Chapter 2
Progressions

As already mentioned in the introductory note, Block I constituted the most crucial aspect of the Quantitative Aptitude Section in the paper & pen version of the CAT. Throughout the decade 1999 to 2008, almost 30–50% of the total questions in every CAT paper came from the two chapters given in this block. However, the online CAT has shifted this weightage around, and consequently, the importance of Block I has been reduced to around 20–25% of the total marks in the section.

Thus, although Block I remains an important block for your preparations, it has lost its pre-eminence (as reflected in the strategy—"Do Block I well and you can qualify the QA section").

However, this does not change the need for you to go through this block in great depth.

Thus my advice to you is: *Go through this block in depth and try to gain clarity of concepts as well as exposure to questions for honing your ability to do well in this area.*

...BACK TO SCHOOL

- **Chapters in this Block: Number Systems and Progressions**
- **Block Importance – 20–25%**

The importance of this block can be gauged from the table below:

Year	% of Marks from Block 1	Qualifying Score (approx. score for 96 percentile)
2000	48%	35%
2001	36%	35%
2002	36%	35%
2003 (cancelled)	30%	32%
2003 (retest)	34%	35%
2004	32%	35%
2005	40%	35%
2006	32%	40%
2007	24%	32%
2008	40%	35%
Online CAT 2009–2013	15–30%	60% with no errors

As you can see from the table above, doing well in this block alone could give you a definite edge and take you a long way to qualifying the QA section. Although the online CAT has significantly varied the relative importance to this block, the importance of this block remains high. Besides, there is a good chance that once the IIMs get their act together in the context of the online CAT and its question databases—the pre eminence of this block of chapters might return.

Hence, understanding the concepts involved in these chapters properly and strengthening your problem solving experience could go a long way towards a good score.

Before we move into the individual chapters of this block, let us first organise our thinking by looking at the core concepts that we had learnt in school with respect to these chapters.

Pre-assessment Test

This test consists of 25 questions based on the chapters of BLOCK I (Number Systems and Progressions). Do your best in trying to solve each question.

The time limit to be followed for this test is 30 minutes. However, after the 30 minutes is over continue solving till you have spent enough time and paid sufficient attention to each question. After you finish thinking about each and every question of the test, check your scores. Then go through the SCORE INTERPRETATION ALGORITHM given at the end of the test to understand the way in which you need to approach the chapters inside this block.

1. The number of integers n satisfying $-n + 2 \geq 0$ and $2n \geq 4$ is
   (a) 0   (b) 1
   (c) 2   (d) 3

2. The sum of two integers is 10 and the sum of their reciprocals is 5/12. Then the larger of these integers is
   (a) 2   (b) 4
   (c) 6   (d) 8

3. If x is a positive integer such that $2x + 12$ is perfectly divisible by x, then the number of possible values of x is
   (a) 2   (b) 5
   (c) 6   (d) 12

4. Let K be a positive integer such that $k + 4$ is divisible by 7. Then the smallest positive integer n, greater than 2, such that $k + 2n$ is divisible by 7 equals.
   (a) 9   (b) 7
   (c) 5   (d) 3

5. $2^{73} - 2^{72} - 2^{71}$ is the same as
   (a) 2^{69} (b) 2^{70}
   (c) 2^{71} (d) 2^{72}

6. Three times the first of three consecutive odd integers is 3 more than twice the third. What is the third integer?
   (a) 15   (b) 9
   (c) 11   (d) 5

7. x, y and z are three positive integers such that $x > y > z$. Which of the following is closest to the product xyz?
   (a) $xy(z-1)$ (b) $(x-1)yz$
   (c) $(x-y)xy$ (d) $x(y+1)z$

8. A positive integer is said to be a prime number if it is not divisible by any positive integer other than itself and 1. Let p be a prime number greater than 5, then $(p^2 - 1)$ is
   (a) never divisible by 6.
   (b) always divisible by 6, and may or may not be divisible by 12.
   (c) always divisible by 12, and may or may not be divisible by 24.
   (d) always divisible by 24.

9. Iqbal dealt some cards to Mushtaq and himself from a full pack of playing cards and laid the rest aside. Iqbal then said to Mushtaq "If you give me a certain number of your cards, I will have four times as many cards as you will have. If I give you the same number of cards, I will have thrice as many cards as you will have". Of the given choices, which could represent the number of cards with Iqbal?
   (a) 9   (b) 31
   (c) 12   (d) 35

10. In Sivakasi, each boy's quota of match sticks to fill into boxes is not more than 200 per session. If he reduces the number of sticks per box by 25, he can fill 3 more boxes with the total number of sticks assigned to him. Which of the following is the possible number of sticks assigned to each boy?
    (a) 200   (b) 150
    (c) 125   (d) 175

11. A lord got an order from a garment manufacturer for 480 Denim Shirts. He bought 12 sewing machines and appointed some expert tailors to do the job. However, many didn't report for duty. As a result, each of those who did, had to stitch 32 more shirts than originally planned by Alord, with equal distribution of work. How many tailors had been appointed earlier and how many had not reported for work?
    (a) 12, 4   (b) 10, 3
    (c) 10, 4   (d) None of these

12. How many 3-digit even numbers can you form such that if one of the digits is 5, the following digit must be 7?
    (a) 5   (b) 405
    (c) 365   (d) 495

13. To decide whether a number of n digits is divisible by 7, we can define a process by which its magnitude is reduced as follows: ($i_1, i_2, i_3.....i_n$ are the digits of the number, starting from the most significant digit).

$$i_1i_2...i_n \Rightarrow i_1 \cdot 3^{n-1} + i_2 \cdot 3^{n-2} + ... + I_n 3^0.$$

e.g. $259 \Rightarrow 2.3^2 + 5.3^1 + 9.3^0 = 18 + 15 + 9 = 42$

Ultimately the resulting number will be seven after repeating the above process a certain number of times.

After how many such stages, does the number 203 reduce to 7?
(a) 2   (b) 3
(c) 4   (d) 1

14. A teacher teaching students of third standard gave a simple multiplication exercise to the kids. But one kid reversed the digits of both the numbers and carried out the multiplication and found that the product was exactly the same as the one expected by the teacher. Only one of the following pairs of numbers will fit in the description of the exercise. Which one is that?
(a) 14, 22   (b) 13, 62
(c) 19, 33   (d) 42, 28

15. If 8 + 12 = 2, 7 + 14 = 3 then 10 + 18 =?
(a) 10   (b) 4
(c) 6   (d) 18

16. Find the minimum integral value of n such that the division 55n/124 leaves no remainder.
(a) 124   (b) 123
(c) 31   (d) 62

17. What is the value of k for which the following system of equations has no solution:
$2x - 8y = 3$; and $kx + 4y = 10$.
(a) −2   (b) 1
(c) −1   (d) 2

18. A positive integer is said to be a prime if it is not divisible by any positive integer other than itself and one. Let p be a prime number strictly greater than 3. Then, when $p^2 + 17$ is divided by 12, the remainder is
(a) 6   (b) 1
(c) 0   (d) 8

19. A man sells chocolates that come in boxes. Either full boxes or half a box of chocolates can be bought from him. A customer comes and buys half the number of boxes the seller has plus half a box. A second customer comes and buys half the remaining number of boxes plus half a box. After this, the seller is left with no chocolates box. How many chocolates boxes did the seller have before the first customer came?
(a) 2   (b) 3
(c) 4   (d) 3.5

20. X and Y are playing a game. There are eleven 50 paise coins on the table and each player must pick up at least one coin but not more than five. The person picking up the last coin loses. X starts. How many should he pick up at the start to ensure a win no matter what strategy Y employs?
(a) 4   (b) 3
(c) 2   (d) 5

21. If $a < b$, which of the following is always true?
(a) $a < (a + b) / 2 < b$
(b) $a < ab/2 < b$
(c) $a < b^2 - a^2 < b$
(d) $a < ab < b$

22. The money order commission is calculated as follows. From ₹ X to be sent by money order, subtract 0.01 and divide by 10. Get the quotient and add 1 to it, if the result is Y, the money order commission is ₹ 0.5Y. If a person sends two money orders to Aurangabad and Bhatinda for ₹ 71 and ₹ 48 respectively, the total commission will be
(a) ₹ 7.00   (b) ₹ 6.50
(c) ₹ 6.00   (d) ₹ 7.50

23. The auto fare in Ahmedabad has the following formula based upon the meter reading. The meter reading is rounded up to the next higher multiple of 4. For instance, if the meter reading is 37 paise, it is rounded up to 40 paise. The resultant is multiplied by 12. The final result is rounded off to nearest multiple of 25 paise. If 53 paise is the meter reading what will be the actual fare?
(a) ₹ 6.75   (b) ₹ 6.50
(c) ₹ 6.25   (d) ₹ 7.50

24. Juhi and Bhagyashree were playing simple mathematical puzzles. Juhi wrote a two digit number and asked Bhayashree to guess it. Juhi also indicated that the number is exactly thrice the product of its digits. What was the number that Juhi wrote?
(a) 3 6   (b) 24
(c) 12   (d) 4 8

25. It is desired to extract the maximum power of 3 from 24!, where $n! = n.(n - 1) . (n - 2) \dots 3.2.1$. What will be the exponent of 3?
(a) 8   (b) 9
(c) 11   (d) 10

ANSWER KEY

1. (b)	2. (c)	3. (c)	4. (a)
5. (c)	6. (a)	7. (b)	8. (d)
9. (b)	10. (b)	11. (c)	12. (c)
13. (a)	14. (b)	15. (a)	16. (a)
17. (c)	18. (a)	19. (b)	20. (a)
21. (a)	22. (b)	23. (a)	24. (b)
25. (d)			

Solutions

1. The only value that will satisfy will be 2.
2. ¼ + 1/6 will give you 5/12.

3. The possible values are 1, 2, 3, 4, 6 and 12. (i.e. the factors of 12)

4. k will be a number of the form $7n + 3$. Hence, if you take the value of n as 9, $k + 2n$ will become $7n + 3 + 18 = 7n + 21$. This number will be divisible by 7. The numbers 3, 5 and 7 do not provide us with this solution.

5. $2^{73} - 2^{72} - 2^{71} = 2^{71}(2^2 - 2 - 1) = 2^{71}(1)$. Hence option (c) is correct.

6. Solve through options.

7. The closest value will be option (b), since the percentage change will be lowest when the largest number is reduced by one.

8. This is a property of prime numbers greater than 5.

9. He could have dealt a total of 40 cards, in which case Mushtaq would get 9 cards. On getting one card from Mushtaq, the ratio would become 4:1, while on giving away one card to Mushtaq, the ratio would become 3:1.

10. Looking at the options you realise that the correct answer should be a multiple of 25 and 50 both. The option that satisfies the condition of increasing the number of boxes by 3 is 150. (This is found through trial and error.)

11. Trial and error gives you option 3 as the correct answer.

12. Given that the number must have a 57 in it and should be even at the same time, the only numbers possible are 570, 572, 574, 576 and 578. Also, if there is no 5 in the number, you will get 360 more numbers.

13. 203 becomes $\rightarrow$ $2.3^2 + 0 + 3.3^0 = 21$ $\rightarrow$ $2.3^1 + 1.3^0 = 7$. Hence, clearly two steps are required.

14. Trial and error will give option (b) as the correct answer, since $13 \times 62 = 26 \times 31$

15. The solutions are defined as the sum of digits of the answer. Hence, 10 is correct.

16. There are no common factors between 55 and 124. Hence the answer should be 124.

17. At $k = -1$, the two equations become inconsistent with respect to each other and there will then be no solution to the system of equations.

18. Try with 5, 7, 11. In each case the remainder is 6.

19. Trial and error gives you the answer as 3 Option (b) is correct.

20. Picking up 4 coins will ensure that he wins the game.

21. Option (a) is correct (since the average of any two numbers lies between the numbers.

22. $8/2 + 5/2 = 6.5$.

23. The answer will be $56 \times 12 = 672$ $\rightarrow$ 675. Hence, ₹ 6.75.

24. The given condition is satisfied only for 24.

25. The answer will be given by $8 + 2 = 10$.

(This logic is explained in the Number Systems chapter)

🔊 SCORE INTERPRETATION ALGORITHM FOR PRE-ASSESSMENT TEST OF BLOCK I

(Use a similar process for Blocks II to VI on the basis of your performance).

If You Scored: < 7: (In Unlimited Time)

Step One
Go through the block one **Back to School** Section carefully. Grasp each of the concepts explained in that part carefully. In fact I would recommend that you go back to your Mathematics school books (ICSE/ CBSE) Class 8, 9 and 10 if you feel you need it.

Step Two
Move into the first chapter of the block, viz, Number Systems. When you do so, concentrate on clearly understanding each of the concepts explained in the chapter theory.

Then move onto the LOD 1 exercises. These exercises will provide you with the first level of challenge. Try to solve each and every question provided under LOD 1 of Number systems. While doing so do not think about the time requirement. Once you finish solving LOD 1, revise the questions and their solution processes.

Step Three
After finishing LOD 1 of number systems, move into Chapter 2 of this block—Progressions and repeat the process, viz: chapter theory comprehensively followed by solving LOD 1 questions.

Step Four
Go to the first and second review tests given at the end of the block and solve them. While doing so, first look at the score you get within the mentioned time limit. Then continue to solve the test further without a time limit and try to evaluate the improvement in your unlimited time score.

In case the growth in your score is not significant, go back to the theory of each chapter and review each of the LOD 1 questions for both the chapters.

Step Five
Move to LOD 2 and repeat the process that you followed in LOD 1—first in the chapter of Number Systems, then in the chapter on Progressions. Concentrate on understanding each and every question and its underlying concept.

Step Six
Go to the third to fifth review tests given at the end of the block and solve them. Again, while doing so measure your score within the provided time limit first and then continue to solve the test further without a time limit and try to evaluate the improvement that you have had in your score.

Step Seven
Move to LOD 3 only after you have solved and understood each of the questions in LOD 1 and LOD 2. Repeat the process that you followed in LOD 1—first in the chapter of Number Systems, then with the Chapter on Progressions.

If You Scored: 7–15 (In Unlimited Time)

Although you are better than the person following the instructions above, obviously there is a lot of scope for the development of your score. You will need to work both on your concepts as well as speed. Initially emphasize more on the concept development aspect of your preparations, then move your emphasis onto speed development. The following process is recommended for you:

Step One
Go through the **block one Back to School Section** carefully. Revise each of the concepts explained in that part. Going through your VIIIth, IXth and Xth standard books will be an optional exercise for you. It will be recommended in case you scored in single digits, while if your score is in two digits, I leave the choice to you.

Step Two
Move into the first chapter of the block. Viz Number Systems. When you do so, concentrate on clearly understanding each of the concepts explained in the chapter theory.

Then move onto the LOD 1 exercises. These exercises will provide you with the first level of challenge. Try to solve each and every question provided under LOD 1 of Number Systems. Once you finish solving LOD 1, revise the questions and their solution processes.

Step Three
After finishing LOD 1 of number systems, move into Chapter 2 of this block—Progressions and repeat the process, viz: Chapter theory comprehensively followed by solving LOD 1 questions.

Step Four
Go to the first and second review tests given at the end of the block and solve them. While doing so, first look at the score you get within the time limit mentioned. Then continue to solve the test further without a time limit and try to evaluate the improvement in your score.

Step Five

Move to LOD 2 and repeat the process that you followed in LOD 1—first with the chapter on Number Systems, then with the chapter on Progressions.

Step Six

Go to the third to fifth review tests given at the end of the block and solve it. Again while doing so measure your score within the provided time limit first and then continue to solve the test further without a time limit and try to evaluate the improvement that you have had in your score.

In case the growth in your score is not significant, go back to the theory of both the chapters and re-solve LOD 1 and LOD 2 of both the chapters. While doing so concentrate more on the LOD 2 questions.

Step Seven

Move to LOD 3 and repeat the process that you followed in LOD 1—first with the chapter on Number Systems, then with the Chapter on Progressions.

If You Scored 15+ (In Unlimited Time)

Obviously you are much better than the first two categories of students. Hence unlike them, your focus should be on developing your speed by picking up the shorter processes explained in this book. Besides, you might also need to pick up concepts that might be hazy in your mind. The following process of development is recommended for you:

Step One

Quickly review the concepts given in the block one Back to School Section. Only go deeper into a concept in case you find it new. Going back to school level books is not required for you.

Step Two

Move into the first chapter of the block: Number Systems. Go through the theory explained there carefully. Concentrate specifically on clearly understanding the concepts which are new to you. Work out the short cuts and in fact try to expand your thinking by trying to think of alternative (and expanded) lines of questioning with respect to the concept you are studying.

Then move onto the LOD 1 exercises. Solve each and every question provided under LOD 1 of Number Systems. While doing so, try to think of variations that you can visualize in the same questions and how you would handle them.

Step Three

After finishing LOD 1 of number systems, move into Chapter 2 of this block, (Progressions) and repeat the process, viz: Chapter theory with emphasis on picking up things that you are unaware of, followed by solving LOD 1 questions and thinking about their possible variations.

Step Four

Move to LOD 2 and repeat the process that you followed in LOD 1—first in the chapter of Number Systems, then with the Chapter on Progressions.

Step Five

Go to the first to fifth review tests—given at the end of the block and solve it. While doing so, first look at the score you get within the time limit mentioned. Then continue to solve the test further without a time limit and try to evaluate the improvement in your score.

Step Six

Move to LOD 3 and repeat the process that you followed in LOD 1—first in the chapter of Number Systems, then with the Chapter on Progressions.

🔊 THE NUMBER LINE

Core Concepts

I. The concept of the number line is one of the most crucial concepts in Basic Numeracy.

The number line is a line that starts from zero and goes towards positive infinity when it moves to the right and towards negative infinity when it moves to the left.

The difference between the values of any two points on the number line also gives the distance between the points.

Thus, for example if we look at the distance between the points $+3$ and -2, it will be given by their difference. $3 - (-2) = 3 + 2 = 5$.

II. Types of numbers—

We will be looking at the types of numbers in detail again when we go into the chapter of number systems. Let us first work out in our minds the various types of numbers. While doing so do not fail to notice that most of these number types occur in pairs (i.e. the definition of one of them, defines the other automatically).

Note here that the number line is one of the most critical concepts in understanding and grasping numeracy and indeed mathematics.

Multiples on the Number Line

All tables and multiples of every number can be visualised on the number line. Thus, multiples of 7 on the number line would be seen as follows:

In order to visualize this you can imagine a frog jumping consistently 7 units every time. If it lands on -14, the next landing would be on -7, then on 0, then 7 and finally at 14. This is how you can visualise the table of 7 (in mathematical terms we can also refer to this as $7n$ – meaning the set of numbers which are multiples of 7 or in other words the set of numbers which are divisible by 7).

You can similarly visualise $5n$, $4n$, $8n$ and so on—practically all tables on the number line as above.

What do We Understand by $7n + 1$ and Other such Notations & the Equivalence of $7n + 1$ and $7n - 6$

Look at the following figure closely:

Our $7n$ frog is made to first land on -13 and then asked to keep doing it's stuff (jumping 7 to the right everytime). What is the result? It lands on -6, $+1$, 8, 15 and it's next landing would be on 22, 29 and so forth. These numbers cannot be described as $7n$, but rather they all have a single property which is constant for all numbers.

They can be described as: "One more than a multiple of 7" and in mathematical terms such numbers are also called as $7n + 1$. Alternately these numbers also have the property that they are "6 less than multiples of 7" and in mathematical terms such numbers can also be called as $7n - 6$.

That is why in mathematics, we say that the set of numbers represented by $7n + 1$ is the same as the set of numbers represented by $7n - 6$.

The Implication in Terms of Remainders

This concept can also be talked about in the context of remainders.

When a number which can be described as $7n + 1$ or $7n - 6$ (like the numbers 8, 15, –6, –13, –20, –27, –34, –41...) is divided by 7, the remainder in every case is seen to be 1. For some people reconciling the fact that the remainder when –27 is divided by 7 the remainder is 1, seems difficult on the surface. Note that this needs to be done because about remainders we should know that remainders are always non-negative.

However, the following thinking would give you the remainder in every case:

27/7, remainder is 6.

–27/7, remainder is –6. In the context of dividing by 7, a remainder of –6 means a remainder of 7 – 6 = 1.

Let us look at another example:

What is the remainder when –29 is divided by 8.

First reaction 29/8 → remainder 5, –29/8 → remainder –5, hence actual remainder is 8 – 5 = 3.

The student is advised to practice more such situations and get comfortable in converting positive remainders to negative remainders and vice versa.

Even and Odd Numbers

The meaning of 2n and 2n + 1: $2n$ means a number which is a multiple of the number 2. Since, this can be visualised as a frog starting from the origin and jumping 2 units to the right in every jump, you can also say that this frog represents $2n$.

(**Note**: Multiples of 2, are even numbers. Hence, $2n$ is also used to denote even numbers.)

So, what does $2n + 1$ mean?

Well, simply put, if you place the above frog on the point represented by the number 1 on the number line then the frog will reach points such as 3, 5, 7, 9, 11 …..and so on. This essentially means that the points the frog now reaches are displaced by 1 unit to the right of the $2n$ frog. In mathematical terms, this is represented as $2n + 1$.

In other words, $2n + 1$ also represents numbers which leave a remainder of 1, when divided by 2. (**Note**: This is also the definition of an odd number. Hence, in Mathematics $(2n + 1)$ is used to denote an odd number. Also note that taken together $2n$ and $2n + 1$ denote the entire set of integers. i.e. all integers from $-\infty$ to $+\infty$ on the number line can be denoted by either $2n$ or $2n + 1$. This happens because when we divide any integer by 2, there are only two results possible with respect to the remainder obtained, viz: A remainder of zero $(2n)$ or a remainder of one $(2n + 1)$.

This concept can be expanded to represent integers with respect to any number. Thus, in terms of 3, we can only have three types of integers $3n$, $3n + 1$ or $3n + 2$ (depending on whether the integer leaves a remainder 0, 1 or 2 respectively when divided by 3.) Similarly, with respect to 4, we have 4 possibilities—$4n$, $4n + 1$, $4n + 2$ or $4n + 3$.

Needless to say, from these representations above, the representations $2n$ and $2n + 1$ (which can also be represented as $2n - 1$) have great significance in Mathematics as they represent even and odd numbers respectively. Similarly, we use the concept of $4n$ to check whether a year is a leap year or not.

These representations can be seen on the number line as follows:

Representation of $2n$ and $2n + 1$:

Representation of $3n$, $3n + 1$ and $3n + 2$:

Representation of 4*n*, 4*n* + 1, 4*n* + 2 and 4*n* + 3:

One Particular Number can be a Multiple of more than 1 Number—The Concept of Common Multiples

Of course one of the things you should notice as you go through the above discussion is that individual numbers can indeed be multiples of more than 1 number—and actually often are.

  Thus, for instance the number 14 is a multiple of both 7 and 2—hence 14 can be called as a common multiple of 2 and 7. Obviously, I think you can visualise more such numbers which can be classified as common multiples of 2 and 7?? 28,42,56 and in fact the list is infinite—i.e. the numbers never end. Thus, the common multiples of 2 and 7 can be represented by the infinite set:

$$\{14,28,42,56,70\ldots\ldots\ldots1400\ldots\ldots14000\ldots\ldots140000\ldots\ldots\text{and so on}\}$$

The LCM and It's Significance

From the above list, the number 14 (which is the lowest number in the set of Common multiples of 2 and 7) has a lot of significance in Mathematics. It represents what is commonly known as the **Least Common Multiple (LCM)** of 2 and 7. It is the first number which is a multiple of both 2 and 7 and there are a variety of questions in numeracy which you would come across—not only when you solve questions based on number systems (where the LCM has it's dedicated set of questions), but applications of the LCM are seen even in chapters like Time, Speed Distance, Time and Work etc.

So what did school teach us about the process of finding LCM?
Before you start to review/ relearn that process you first need to know about prime factors of a number.

I hope at this point you recognize the difference between finding factors of a number and prime factors of a number.
Simply put, finding factors of a number means finding the divisors of the number. Thus, for instance the factors of the number 80 would be the numbers 1, 2, 4, 5, 8, 10, 16, 20, 40 and 80. On the other hand finding the prime factors of the same number would mean writing the number 80 as $2^4 \times 5^1$. This form of writing the number is also called the **STANDARD FORM** or the **CANONICAL FORM** of the number.

The school process of writing down the standard form of a number:
Now this is something I would think most of you would remember and recognize:
  Finding the prime factors of the number 80

2	80
2	40
2	20
2	10
5	5
	1

  The prime factors of the number 80 are: $2 \times 2 \times 2 \times 2 \times 5 = 2^4 \times 5^1$.

Exercise for Self-practice

  Write down the standard form of the following numbers.
  (a) 20   (b) 44   (c) 142   (d) 200
  (e) 24   (f) 324   (g) 120   (h) 84
  (i) 371   (j) 143   (k) 339   (l) 147
  (m) 1715

Finding the LCM of two or more numbers: The school process

Step 1: Write down the prime factor form of all the numbers;

Let us say that you have 3 numbers whose standard forms are:

$$2^4 \times 3^2 \times 5^3 \times 7^1$$

$$2^3 \times 3^1 \times 5^2 \times 11^2$$

$$2^4 \times 3^2 \times 5^1 \times 13^1$$

To write down the LCM of these numbers write down all the prime numbers and multiply them with their highest available powers. The resultant number would be the LCM of these numbers.

Thus, in the above case the LCM would be:

$$2^4 \times 3^2 \times 5^3 \times 7^1 \times 11^2 \times 13^1$$

Note: Short cuts to a lot of these processes have been explained in the main chapters of the book.

Divisors (Factors) of a number

As we already mentioned, finding the factors or divisors of a number are one and the same thing. In order to find factors of a number, the key is to spot the factors below the square root of the number. Once you have found them, the factors above the square root would be automatically seen. Consider this for factors of the number 80:

Factors below the square root *of 80 (8.xxx)* *Hence, factors up to and including 8*	
1	
2	
4	
5	
8	

Once you can visualise the list on the left, the factors on the right would be seen automatically.

Factors below the square root *of 80 (8.xxx)* *Hence, factors up to and including 8*	*Factors above the square root*
1	80
2	40
4	20
5	16
8	10

Note that these will be seen automatically the moment you have the list on the left.

Common Divisors Between 2 Numbers

List of Common Divisors

When we write down the factors of two numbers, we can look for the common elements within the two lists.

For instance, the factors of 80 are (1, 2, 4, 5, 8, 10, 16, 20, 40 and 80) while the factors of 144 are (1, 2, 3, 4, 6, 8, 9, 12, 16, 18, 24, 36, 48, 72 and 144)

If you observe the two lists closely you will get the following list of common factors or common divisors between the two:

List of common factors of 80 and 144: (1, 2, 4, 8, 16)

The number 16 being the highest in this list of common factors (or divisors) is also called the Highest Common Factor or the Greatest Common Divisor. In short it is denoted as HCF or GCD. It has a lot of significance in terms of quantitative thinking—as the HCF is used in a multitude of problems and hence being able to spot the HCF of two or more numbers is one of the critical operations in Mathematics. You would be continuously seeing applications of the HCF in problems in the chapter of Number systems and right through the chapters of arithmetic (defined as word based problems in this book).

Rounding off and its use for approximation
One of the important things that we learnt in school was the use of approximation in order to calculate.

Thus, 72×53 can be approximated to 70×50 and hence seen as 3500.

Similarly, the addition of $48 + 53 + 61 + 89$ can be taken as $50 + 50 + 60 + 90 = 250$

Number Types You Should Know

Integers and Decimals: All numbers that do not have a decimal in them are called integers. Thus, $-3, -17, +4, +13, +1473, 0$ etc are all integers.

Obviously, decimal numbers are numbers which have a decimal value attached to them. Thus, $1.3, 14.76, -12.24$ etc are all decimal numbers, since they have certain values after the decimal point.

Before we move ahead, let us pause a brief while, to further understand decimals. As you shall see, the concept of decimals is closely related to the concept of division and divisibility. Suppose, I have 4 pieces of bread which I want to divide equally between two people. It is easy for me to do this, since I can give two whole pieces to each of them.

However, if we alter the situation in such a way, that I now have 5 pieces of bread to distribute equally amongst 2 people. What do I do?

I give two whole pieces each, to each of them. The 5th piece has to be divided equally between the two. I can no longer do this, without in some way breaking the 5th piece into 2 parts. This is the elementary situation that gives rise to the need for decimals in mathematics.

Going back to the situation above, my only option is to divide the 5th piece into two equal parts (which in quants are called as halves).

This concept has huge implications for problem solving especially once you recognise that a half (i.e. a '.5' in the decimal) only comes when you divide a whole into two parts.

Thus, in fact, all standards decimals emerge out of certain fixed divisors.

Hence, for example, the divisor 2, gives rise to the decimal $\cdot 5$.

Similarly the divisor 3 gives rise to the decimals $\cdot 33333$ and $\cdot 66666$, etc.

Prime numbers and Composite numbers   Amongst natural numbers, there are three broad divisions—

Unity   It is representative of the number 1.

Prime numbers   These are numbers which have no divisors/ factors apart from 1 and itself.

Composite numbers   On the other hand, are numbers, which have at least one more divisor apart from 1 and itself.

Note: A brief word about factors/ division—A number X is said to divide Y (or is said to be a divisor or factor of Y) when the division of Y/X leaves no remainder.

All composite numbers have the property that they can be written as a product of their prime factors.

Thus, for instance, the number 40 can be represented as: $40 = 2 \times 2 \times 2 \times 5$ or $40 = 2^3 \times 5^1$

This form of writing is called as the **standard form** of the composite number.

The difference between Rational and Irrational numbers: This difference is one of the critical but unfortunately one of the less well understood differences in elementary Mathematics.

The definition of Rational numbers: Numbers which can be expressed in the form p/q where $q \neq 0$ are called rational numbers.

Obviously, numbers which cannot be represented in the form p/q are called as irrational numbers.

However, one of the less well understood issues in this regard is what does this mean?

The difference becomes clear when the values of decimals are examined in details:

Consider the following numbers.

(1) 4.2,

(2) 4.333....,

(3) 4.1472576345.......

What is the difference between the decimal values of the three numbers above?

To put it simply, the first number has what can be described as a finite decimal value. Such numbers can be expressed in the form p/q easily. Since 4.2 can be first written as 42/10 and then converted to 21/5.

Similarly, numbers like 4.5732 can be represented as 45732/10000. Thus, numbers having a finite terminating decimal value are rational.

Now, let us consider the decimal value: 4.3333........

Such decimal values will continue endlessly, i.e. they have no end. Hence, they are called **infinite decimals** (or non-terminating decimals).

But, we can easily see that the number 4.333.... can be represented as 13/3. Hence, this number is also rational. In fact, all numbers which have infinite decimal values, but have any recurring form within them can be represented in the p/q form.

For example the value of the number: 1.14814814814.... is 93/81.

(What I mean to say is that whenever you have any recurring decimal number, even if the value of 'q' might not be obvious, but it will always exist.)

Thus, we can conclude that all numbers whose decimal values are infinite (non-terminating) but which have a recurring pattern within them are rational numbers.

This leaves us with the third kind of decimal values, viz. **Infinite non-recurring decimal values**. These decimals neither have a recurring pattern, nor do they have an end—they go on endlessly. For such numbers it is not possible to find the value of a denominator 'q' which can be used in order to represent them as p/q. Hence, such numbers are called as irrational numbers.

In day-to-day mathematics, we come across numbers like $\sqrt{3}$, $\sqrt{5}$, $\sqrt[3]{7}$, π, e, etc. which are irrational numbers since they do not have a p/q representation.

Note: $\sqrt{3}$ can also be represented as $3^{1/2}$, just as $\sqrt[3]{7}$ can be represented as $7^{1/3}$.

An Important Tip:

Rational and Irrational numbers do not mix.: This means that in case you get a situation where an irrational number has appeared while solving a question, it will remain till the end of the solution. It can only be removed from the solution if it is multiplied or divided by the same irrational number.

Consider an example: The area of an equilateral triangle is given by the formula $(\sqrt{3}/4) \times a^2$ (where a is the side of the equilateral triangle). Since, $\sqrt{3}$ is an irrational number, it remains in the answer till the end. Hence, the area of an equilateral triangle will always have a $\sqrt{3}$ as part of the answer.

Before we move ahead we need to understand one final thing about recurring decimals.

As I have already mentioned, recurring decimals have the property of being able to be represented in the p/q form. The question that arises is—Is there any process to convert a recurring decimal into a proper fraction?

Yes, there is. In fact, in order to understand how this operates, you first need to understand that there are two kinds of recurring decimals. The process for converting an infinite recurring decimal into a fraction basically varies for both of these types. Let's look at these one by one.

Type 1—Pure recurring decimals: These are recurring decimals where the recurrence starts immediately after the decimal point.

For example:

$$0.5555... = 0.\overline{5}$$

$$3.242424... = 3.\overline{24}$$

$$5.362362... = 5.\overline{362}$$

The process for converting these decimals to fractions can be illustrated as:

$$0.5555 = 5/9$$

$$3.242424 = 3 + (24/99)$$

$$5.362362 = 5 + (362/999)$$

A little bit of introspection will tell you that what we have done is nothing but to put down the recurring part of the decimal as it is and dividing it by a group of 9's. Also the number of 9's in this group equals the number of digits in the recurring part of the decimal.

Thus, in the second case, the fraction is derived by dividing 24 by 99. (24 being the recurring part of the decimal and 99 having 2 nines because the number of digits in 24 is 2.)

Similarly, $0.43576254357625.... = \dfrac{4357625}{9999999}$

Type 2—Impure recurring decimals: Unlike pure recurring decimals, in these decimals, the recurrence occurs after a certain number of digits in the decimal. The process to convert these into a fraction is also best illustrated by an example:

Consider the decimal 0.435424242

$$= 0.435\overline{42}$$

The fractional value of the same will be given by: (43542 – 435)/99000. This can be understood in two steps.

Step 1: Subtract the non-recurring initial part of the decimal (in this case, it is 435) from the number formed by writing down the starting digits of the decimal value upto the digit where the recurring decimals are written for the first time;

Expanding the meaning—

Note: For 0.435424242, subtract 435 from 43542

Step 2: The number thus obtained, has to be divided by a number formed as follows; Write down as many 9's as the number of digits in the recurring part of the decimal. (in this case, since the recurring part '42' has 2 digits, we write down 2 9's.) These nines have to be followed by as many zeroes as the number of digits in the non recurring part of the decimal value. (In this case, the non recurring part of the decimal value is '435'. Since, 435 has 3 digits, attach three zeroes to the two nines to get the number to divide the result of the first step.)

Hence divide 43542 – 435 by 99000 to get the fraction.

Similarly, for 3.436213213 we get $\dfrac{436213 - 436}{999000}$.

Mixed Fractions

A *mixed number* is a whole number plus a fraction. Here are a few mixed numbers:

$$1\frac{1}{2} \quad 1\frac{1}{4} \quad 2\frac{1}{3} \quad 2\frac{2}{7} \quad 5\frac{4}{5}$$

In order to convert a mixed fraction to a proper fraction you do the following conversion process.

$$1\frac{1}{2} = (1 \times 2 + 1)/2 = 3/2$$

$$2\frac{1}{3} = (2 \times 3 + 1)/3 = 7/3$$

Similiarly, $1\frac{1}{4} = 5/4$

$2\frac{2}{7} = 16/7$

$5\frac{4}{5} = 29/5$ and so on.

i.e. multiply the whole number part of the mixed number by the denominator of the fractional part and add the resultant to the numerator of the fractional part to get the numerator of the proper fraction. The denominator of the proper fraction would be the same as the denominator of the mixed fraction.

📶 OPERATIONS ON NUMBERS

Exponents and Powers

Exponents, or powers, are an important part of math as they are necessary to indicate that a number is multiplied by itself for a given number of times.

When a number is multiplied by itself it gives the 'square of the number'.

Thus, $n \times n = n^2$ (for example $3 \times 3 = 3^2$)

If the same number is multiplied by itself twice we get the cube of the number.

Thus, $n \times n \times n = n^3$ (for example $3 \times 3 \times 3 = 3^3$)

$n \times n \times n \times n = n^4$ and so on.

With respect to powers of numbers, there are 5 basic rules which you should know:

For any number 'n' the following rules would apply:

Rule 1: $n^a \times n^b = n^{(a+b)}$. Thus, $4^3 \times 4^5 = 4^8$

Rule 2: $n^a / n^b = n^{a-b}$. Thus, $3^9/3^4 = 3^5$

Rule 3: $(n^a)^b = n^{ab}$. Thus, $(3^2)^4 = 3^8$.

Rule 4: $n^{(-a)} = 1/n^a$. Thus, $3^{-4} = 1/3^4$.

Rule 5: $n^0 = 1$. Thus, $5^0 = 1$.

General Form of Writing 2-3 Digit Numbers

In mathematics many a time we have to use algebraic equations in order to solve questions. In such cases an important concept is the way we represent two or three digit numbers in equation form.

For instance, suppose we have a 2 digit number with the digits 'AB'.

In order to write this in the form of an equation, we have to use:

$10A + B$. This is because in the number 'AB' the digit A is occupying the tens place. Hence, in order to represent the value of the number 'AB' in the form of an equation- we can write $10A + B$.

Thus, the number $29 = 2 \times 10 + 9 \times 1$

Similarly, for a three digit number with the digits A, B and C respectively – the number 'ABC' can be represented as below:

$$ABC = 100\,A + 10\,B + C.$$

Thus, $\qquad 243 = 2 \times 100 + 4 \times 10 + 3 \times 1$

The BODMAS Rule: It is used for the ordering of mathematical operations in a mathematical situation:

In any mathematical situation, the first thing to be considered is Brackets followed by Division, Multiplication, Addition and Subtraction in that order.

Thus $3 \times 5 - 2 = 15 - 2 = 13$

Also, $\qquad 3 \times 5 - 6 \div 3 \qquad = 15 - 2 = 13$

Also, $\qquad 3 \times (5 - 6) \div 3 \quad = 3 \times (-1) \div 3 = -1$.

Operations on Odd and Even numbers

ODDS   *EVENS*

Odd × odd	= Odd	Even × Even	= Even
Odd + odd	= Even	Even + Even	= Even
Odd − odd	= Even	Even − even	= Even
Odd ÷ odd	= odd	Even ÷ even	= Even or odd

Back to School—Block I 17

ODDS & EVENS

Odd × Even	= Even
Odd + Even	= Odd
Odd − Even	= Odd
Even ÷ odd	= Even

Odd ÷ Even → Not divisible

SERIES OF NUMBERS

In many instances in Mathematics we are presented with a series of numbers formed simply when a group of numbers is written together. The following are examples of series:

1. 3, 5, 8, 12, 17…
2. 3, 7, 11, 15, 19…(Such series where the next term is derived by adding a certain fixed value to the previous number are called as Arithmetic Progressions).
3. 5, 10, 20, 40 …..(Such series where the next term is derived by multiplying the previous term by a fixed value are called as Geometric Progressions).
   (**Note**: You will study AP and GP in details in the chapter of progressions which is chapter 2 of this block.)
4. 2, 7, 22, 67 ….
5. 1/3, 1/5, 1/7, 1/9, 1/11…
6. $1/1^2$, $1/2^2$, $1/3^2$, $1/4^2$, $1/5^2$…
7. $1/1^3$, $1/3^3$, $1/5^3$…

Remember the following points at this stage:

1. AP and GP are two specific instances of series. They are studied in details only because they have many applications and have defined rules.
2. Based on the behaviour of their sums, series can be classified as:

Divergent: These are series whose sum to 'n' terms keeps increasing and reaches infinity for infinite terms.

Convergent: Convergent series have the property that their sum tends to approach an upper limit/lower limit as you include more terms in the series. They have the additional property that even when infinite terms of the series are included they will only reach that value and not cross it.

For example consider the series;

$1/1^2 + 1/3^2 + 1/5^2 + 1/7^2 …$

It is evident that subsequent terms of this series keep getting smaller. Hence, their value becomes negligible after a few terms of the series are taken into account.

If taken to infinite terms, the sum of this series will reach a value which it will never cross. Such series are called convergent, because their sum converges to a limit and only reaches that limit for infinite terms.

Note: Questions on finding infinite sums of convergent series are very commonly asked in most aptitude exams including CAT and XAT.

NOTE TO THE READER: NOW THAT YOU ARE THROUGH WITH THE *BACK TO SCHOOL* SECTION, YOU ARE READY TO PROCEED INTO THE CHAPTERS OF THIS BLOCK. HAPPY SOLVING!!

Number Systems

INTRODUCTION

The chapter on Number Systems is amongst the most important chapters in the entire syllabus of Quantitative Aptitude for the CAT examination (and also for other parallel MBA entrance exams).Students are advised to go through this chapter with utmost care understanding each concept and question type on this topic. The CAT has consistently contained anything between 20–40% of the marks based on questions taken from this chapter. Naturally, this chapter becomes one of the most crucial as far as your quest to reach close to the qualification score in the section of Quantitative Aptitude and Data Interpretation is concerned.

Hence, going through this chapter and its concepts properly is imperative for you. It would be a good idea to first go through the basic definitions of all types of numbers. Also closely follow the solved examples based on various concepts discussed in the chapter. Also, the approach and attitude while solving questions on this chapter is to try to maximize your learning experience out of every question. Hence, do not just try to solve the questions but also try to think of alternative processes in order to solve the same question. Refer to hints or solutions only as a last resort.

To start off, the following pictorial representation of the types of numbers will help you improve your quality of comprehension of different types of numbers.

DEFINITION

Natural Numbers   These are the numbers (1, 2, 3, etc.) that are used for counting. In other words, all positive integers are natural numbers.

There are infinite natural numbers and the number 1 is the least natural number.

Examples of natural numbers: 1, 2, 4, 8, 32, 23, 4321 and so on.

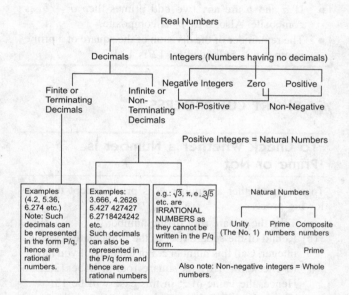

The following numbers are examples of numbers that are not natural: –2, –31, 2.38, 0 and so on.

Based on divisibility, there could be two types of natural numbers: *Prime* and *Composite*.

Prime Numbers   A natural number larger than unity is a prime number if it does not have other divisors except for itself and unity.

***

Note: Unity (i.e. 1) is not a prime number.

***

Some Properties of Prime Numbers

- The lowest prime number is 2.
- 2 is also the only even prime number.
- The lowest odd prime number is 3.

Contd

Some Properties of Prime Numbers
(*Contd*)

- The remainder when a prime number $p \geq 5$ is divided by 6 is 1 or 5. However, if a number on being divided by 6 gives a remainder of 1 or 5 the number need not be prime. Thus, this can be referred to as a necessary but not sufficient condition.
- The remainder of the division of the square of a prime number $p \geq 5$ divided by 24 is 1.
- For prime numbers $p > 3$, $p^2 - 1$ is divisible by 24.
- Prime Numbers between 1 to 100 are: 2, 3, 5, 7, 11, 13, 17, 19, 23, 29, 31, 37, 41, 43, 47, 53, 59, 61, 67, 71, 73, 79, 83, 89, 97.
- Prime Numbers between 100 to 200 are: 101, 103, 107, 109, 113, 127, 131, 137, 139, 149, 151, 157, 163, 167, 173, 179, 181, 191, 193, 197, 199.
- If a and b are any two odd primes then $a^2 - b^2$ is composite. Also, $a^2 + b^2$ is composite.
- The remainder of the division of the square of a prime number $p \geq 5$ divided by 12 is 1.

SHORT CUT PROCESS

To Check Whether a Number is Prime or Not

To check whether a number N is prime, adopt the following process.

(a) Take the square root of the number.
(b) Round of the square root to the immediately lower integer. Call this number z. For example if you have to check for 181, its square root will be 13.____ Hence, the value of z, in this case will be 13.
(c) Check for divisibility of the number N by all prime numbers below z. If there is no prime number below the value of z which divides N then the number N will be prime.

To illustrate :-
The value of $\sqrt{239}$ lies between 15 to 16. Hence, take the value of z as 15.

Prime numbers less than 16 are 2, 3, 5, 7, 11 and 13, 239 is not divisible by any of these. Hence you can conclude that 239 is a prime number.

A Brief Look into why this Works?

Suppose you are asked to find the factors of the number 40.

An untrained mind will find the factors as : 1, 2, 4, 5, 8, 10, 20 and 40.

The same task will be performed by a trained mind as follows:

$$1 \times 40$$
$$2 \times 20$$
$$4 \times 10$$
$$\text{and} \quad 5 \times 8$$

i.e., The discovery of one factor will automatically yield the other factor. In other words, factors will appear in terms of what can be called as factor pairs. The locating of one factor, will automatically pinpoint the other one for you. Thus, in the example above, when you find 5 as a factor of 40, you will automatically get 8 too as a factor.

Now take a look again at the pairs in the example above. If you compare the values in each pair with the square root of 40 (i.e. 6.____) you will find that for each pair the number in the left column is lower than the square root of 40, while the number in the right column is higher than the square root of 40.

This is a property for all numbers and is always true.

Hence, we can now phrase this as: Whenever you have to find the factors of any number N, you will get the factors in pairs (i.e. factor pairs). Further, the factor pairs will be such that in each pair of factors, one of the factors will be lower than the square root of N while the other will be higher than the square root of N.

As a result of this fact one need not make any effort to find the factors of a number above the square root of the number. These come automatically. All you need to do is to find the factors below the square root of the number.

Extending this logic, we can say that if we are not able to find a factor of a number upto the value of its square root, we will not be able to find any factor above the square root and the number under consideration will be a prime number. This is the reason why when we need to check whether a number is prime, we have to check for factors only below the square root.

But, we have said that you need to check for divisibility only with the prime numbers below (and including) the square root of the number.

Let us look at an example to understand why you need to look only at prime numbers below the square root.

Uptil now, we have deduced that in order to check whether a number is prime, we just need to do a factor search below (and including) the square root.

Thus, for example, in order to find whether 181 is a prime number, we need to check with the numbers = 2, 3, 4, 5, 6, 7, 8, 9, 10, 11, 12, and 13.

The first thing you will realise, when you first look at the list above is that all even numbers will get eliminated automatically (since no even number can divide an odd number and of course you will check a number for being prime only if it is odd!)

This will leave you with the numbers 3, 5, 7, 9, 11 and 13 to check 181.

Why do we not need to check with composite numbers below the square root? This will again be understood best if explained in the context of the example above. The only composite number in the list above is 9. You do not need to check with 9, because when you checked N for divisibility with 3 you would get either of two cases:

Case I: If N is divisible by 3: In such a case, N will automatically become non-prime and you can stop your checking. Hence, you will not need to check for the divisibility of the number by 9.

Case II: N is not divisible by 3: If N is not divisible by 3, it is obvious that it will not be divisible by 9. Hence, you will not need to check for the divisibility of the number by 9.

Thus, in either case, checking for divisibility by a composite number (9 in this case) will become useless. This will be true for all composite numbers.

Hence, when we have to check whether a number N is prime or not, we need to only check for its divisibility by prime factors below the square root of N.

Finding Prime Numbers: The Short Cut

Using the logic that we have to look at only the prime numbers below the square root in order to check whether a number is prime, we can actually cut short the time for finding whether a number is prime drastically.

Before I start to explain this, you should perhaps realise that in an examination like the CAT, or any other aptitude test for that matter whenever you would need to be checking for whether a number is prime or not, you would typically be checking 2 digit or maximum 3 digit numbers in the range of 100 to 200.

Also, one would never really need to check with the prime number 5, because divisibility by 5 would automatically be visible and thus, there is no danger of anyone ever declaring a number like 35 to be prime. Hence, in the list of prime numbers below the square root we would never include 5 as a number to check with.

Checking Whether a Number is Prime (For Numbers below 49)

The only number you would need to check for divisibility with is the number 3. Thus, 47 is prime because it is not divisible by 3.

Checking Whether a Number is Prime (For Numbers above 49 and below 121)

Naturally you would need to check this with 3 and 7. But if you remember that 77, 91 and 119 are not prime, you would be able to spot the prime numbers below 121 by just checking for divisibility with the number 3.

Why? Well, the odd numbers between 49 and 121 which are divisible by 7 are 63, 77, 91, 105 and 119. Out of these perhaps 91 and 119 are the only numbers that you can mistakenly declare as prime. 77 and 105 are so obviously

not-prime that you would never be in danger of declaring them prime.

Thus, for numbers between 49 and 121 you can find whether a number is prime or not by just dividing by 3 and checking for its divisibility.

For example:
61 is prime because it is not divisible by 3 and it is neither 91 nor 119.

Checking Whether a Number is Prime (For Numbers above 121 and below 169)

Naturally you would need to check this with 3, 7 and 11. But if you remember that 133, 143 and 161 are not prime, you would be able to spot the prime numbers between 121 to 169 by just checking for divisibility with the number 3.

Why? The same logic as explained above. The odd numbers between 121 and 169 which are divisible by either 7 or 11 are 133, 143, 147, 161 and 165. Out of these 133, 143 and 161 are the only numbers that you can mistakenly declare as prime if you do not check for 7 or 11. The number 147 would be found to be not prime when you check its divisibility by 3 while the number 165 you would never need to check for, for obvious reasons.

Thus, for numbers between 121 and 169 you can find whether a number is prime or not by just dividing by 3 and checking for its divisibility.

For example:
149, is prime because it is not divisible by 3 and it is neither 133, 143 nor 161.

Thus, we have been able to go all the way till 169 with just checking for divisibility with the number 3.

This logic can be represented on the number line as follows:

Integers A set which consists of natural numbers, negative integers $(-1, -2, -3 \ldots -n \ldots)$ and zero is known as the set of integers. The numbers belonging to this set are known as integers.

Integers can be visualised on the number line:

Note: Positive integers are the same thing as natural numbers.

The moment you define integers, you automatically define **decimals**.

Decimals

A *decimal* number is a number with a *decimal point* in it, like these: 1.5, 3.21, 4.173, 5.1 etc

The number to the left of the decimal is an ordinary whole number. The first number to the right of the decimal is the number of tenths (1/10's). The second is the number of hundredths (1/100's) and so on. So, for the number 5.1, this is a shorthand way of writing the mixed number $5\frac{1}{10}$. 3.27 is the same as 3 + 2/10 + 7/100.

A word on where decimals originate from

Consider the situation where there are 5 children and you have to distribute 10 chocolates between them in such a way that all the chocolates should be distributed and each child should get an equal number of chocolates? How would you do it? Well, simple—divide 10 by 5 to get 2 chocolates per child.

Now consider what if you had to do the same thing with 9 chocolates amongst 5 children? In such a case you would not be able to give an integral number of chocolates to each person. You would give 1 chocolate each to all the 5 and the 'remainder' 4 would have to be divided into 5 parts. 4 out of 5 would give rise to the decimal 0.8 and hence you would give 1.8 chocolates to each child. That is how the concept of decimals enters mathematics in the first place.

Taking this concept further, you can realize that the decimal value of any fraction essentially emerges out of the remainder when the numerator of the fraction is divided by the denominator. Also, since we know that each divisor has a few defined remainders possible, there would be a limited set of decimals that each denominator gives rise to.

Thus, for example the divisor 4 gives rise to only 4 remainders (viz. 0,1,2 and 3) and hence it would give rise to exactly 4 decimal values when it divides any integer. These values are:

0 (when the remainder is 0)
.25 (when the remainder is 1)
.50 (when the remainder is 2)
.75 (when the remainder is 3)

There would be similar connotations for all integral divisors—although the key is to know the decimals that the following divisors give you:

Primary list:
2, 3, 4, 5, 6, 7, 8, 9, 10, 11, 12, 15, 16

Secondary list:
18, 20, 24, 25, 30, 40, 50, 60, 80, 90, 120

Composite Numbers It is a natural number that has at least one divisor different from unity and itself.

Every composite number n can be factored into its prime factors. (This is sometimes called the canonical form of a number.)

In mathematical terms: $n = p_1^m \cdot p_2^n \ldots p_k^s$, where p_1, $p_2 \ldots p_k$ are prime numbers called factors and m, $n \ldots k$ are natural numbers.

Thus, $24 = 2^3 \cdot 3$, $84 = 7 \cdot 3 \cdot 2^2$ etc.

This representation of a composite number is known as the standard form of a composite number. It is an extermely useful form of seeing a composite number as we shall see.

Whole Numbers The set of numbers that includes all natural numbers and the number zero are called whole numbers. Whole number are also called as Non-negative integers.

The Concept of the Number Line The number line is a straight line between negative infinity on the left to positive infinity to the right.

The distance between any two points on the number line is got by subtracting the lower value from the higher value. Alternately, we can also start with the lower number and find the required addition to reach the higher number.

For example: The distance between the points 7 and –4 will be 7 – (–4) = 11.

Real Numbers All numbers that can be represented on the number line are called real numbers. Every real number can be approximately replaced with a terminating decimal.

The following operations of addition, subtraction, multiplication and division are valid for both whole numbers and real numbers: [For any real or whole numbers a, b and c].

(a) Commutative property of addition: $a + b = b + a$.
(b) Associative property of addition: $(a + b) + c = a + (b + c)$.
(c) Commutative property of multiplication: $a \cdot b = b \cdot a$.
(d) Associative property of multiplication: $(a \cdot b) \cdot c = a \cdot (b \cdot c)$.
(e) Distributive property of multiplication with respect to addition: $(a + b) c = ac + bc$.
(f) Subtraction and division are defined as the inverse operations to addition and multiplication respectively.

Thus if $a + b = c$, then $c - b = a$ and if $q = a/b$ then $b \cdot q = a$ (where $b \neq 0$).

Division by zero is not possible since there is no number q for which $b \cdot q$ equals a non zero number a.

Rational Numbers A rational number is defined as a number of the form a/b where a and b are integers and $b \neq 0$.

The set of rational numbers encloses the set of integers and fractions. The rules given above for addition, subtraction, multiplication and division also apply on rational numbers.

Rational numbers that are not integral will have decimal values. These values can be of two types:

(a) **Terminating (or finite) decimal fractions:** For example, $17/4 = 4.25$, $21/5 = 4.2$ and so forth.

(b) **Non-terminating decimal fractions:** Amongst non-terminating decimal fractions there are two types of decimal values:

(i) *Non-terminating periodic fractions*: These are non-terminating decimal fractions of the type $x \cdot a_1a_2a_3a_4$ $\ldots a_n a_1 a_2 a_3 a_4 \ldots a_n a_1 a_2 a_3 a_4 \ldots a_n$. For example $\dfrac{16}{3} =$ 5.3333, 15.23232323, 14.287628762 876 … and so on.

(ii) *Non-terminating non-periodic fractions*: These are of the form $x \cdot b_1 b_2 b_3 b_4 \ldots b_n c_1 c_2 c_3 \ldots c_n$. For example: 5.2731687143725186… .

Of the above categories, terminating decimal and non-terminating periodic decimal fractions belong to the set of rational numbers.

Irrational Numbers Fractions, that are non-terminating, non-periodic fractions, are irrational numbers.

Some examples of irrational numbers are $\sqrt{2}$, $\sqrt{3}$ etc. In other words, all square and cube roots of natural numbers that are not squares and cubes of natural numbers are irrational. Other irrational numbers include π, e and so on.

Every positive irrational number has a negative irrational number corresponding to it.

All operations of addition, subtraction, multiplication and division applicable to rational numbers are also applicable to irrational numbers.

As briefly stated in the Back to School section, whenever an expression contains a rational and an irrational number together, the two have to be carried together till the end. In other words, an irrational number once it appears in the solution of a question will continue to appear till the end of the question. This concept is particularly useful in Geometry For example: If you are asked to find the ratio of the area of a circle to that of an equilateral triangle, you can expect to see a $\pi / \sqrt{3}$ in the answer. This is because the area of a circle will always have a π component in it, while that of an equilateral triangle will always have $\sqrt{3}$.

You should realise that once an irrational number appears in the solution of a question, it can only disappear if it is multiplied or divided by the same irrational number.

THE CONCEPT OF GCD (GREATEST COMMON DIVISOR OR HIGHEST COMMON FACTOR)

Consider two natural numbers n, and n_2.

If the numbers n_1 and n_2 are exactly divisible by the same number x, then x is a common divisor of n_1 and n_2.

The highest of all the common divisors of n_1 and n_2 is called as the GCD or the HCF. This is denoted as GCD (n_1, n_2).

Rules for Finding the GCD of Two Numbers n_1 and n_2

(a) Find the standard form of the numbers n_1 and n_2.

(b) Write out all prime factors that are common to the standard forms of the numbers n_1 and n_2.

(c) Raise each of the common prime factors listed above to the lesser of the powers in which it appears in the standard forms of the numbers n_1 and n_2.

(d) The product of the results of the previous step will be the GCD of n_1 and n_2.

Illustration: Find the GCD of 150, 210, 375.

Step 1: Writing down the standard form of numbers

$$150 = 5 \times 5 \times 3 \times 2$$
$$210 = 5 \times 2 \times 7 \times 3$$
$$375 = 5 \times 5 \times 5 \times 3$$

Step 2: Writing Prime factors common to all the three numbers is $5^1 \times 3^1$

Step 3: This will give the same result, i.e. $5^1 \times 3^1$

Step 4: Hence, the HCF will be $5 \times 3 = 15$

For practice, find the HCF of the following:

(a) 78, 39, 195
(b) 440, 140, 390
(c) 198, 121, 1331

SHORTCUT FOR FINDING THE HCF

The above 'school' process of finding the HCF (or the GCD) of a set of numbers is however extremely cumbersome and time taking. Let us take a look at a much faster way of finding the HCF of a set of numbers.

Suppose you were required to find the HCF of 39,78 and 195

Logic The HCF of these numbers would necessarily have to be a factor (divisor) of the difference between any pair of numbers from the above 3. i.e. the HCF has to be a factor of $(78 - 39 = 39)$ as well as of $(195 - 39 = 156)$ and $(195 - 78 = 117)$. Why?

Well the logic is simple if you were to consider the tables of numbers on the number line.

For any two numbers on the number line, a common divisor would be one which divides both. However, for any number to be able to divide both the numbers, it can only do so if it is a factor of the difference between the two numbers. Got it??

Take an example:

Let us say we take the numbers 68 and 119. The difference between them being 51, it is not possible for any number outside the factor list of 51 to divide both 68 and 119. Thus, for example a number like 4, which divides 68 can never divide any number which is 51 away from 68- because 4 is not a factor of 51.

Only factors of 51, i.e. 51,17,3 and 1 *'could'* divide both these numbers simultaneously.

Hence, getting back to the HCF problem we were trying to tackle—take the difference between any two numbers of the set—of course if you want to reduce your calculations in the situation, take the difference between the two closest numbers. In this case that would be the difference between 78 and 39 =39.

The HCF has then to be a factor of this number. In order to find the factors quickly remember to use the fact we learnt in the back to school section of this part of the book—that whenever we have to find the list of factors/ divisors for any number we have to search the factors below the square root and the factors above the square root would be automatically visible)

A factor search of the number 39 yields the following factors:

$$1 \times 39$$
$$3 \times 13$$

Hence, one of these 4 numbers has to be the HCF of the numbers 39,78 and 195. Since we are trying to locate the **Highest** common factor—we would begin our search from the highest number (viz:39)

Check for divisibility by 39 Any one number out of 39 and 78 and also check the number 195 for divisibility by 39. You would find all the three numbers are divisible by 39 and hence 39 can be safely taken to be the correct answer for the HCF of 39,78 and 195.

Suppose the numbers were:

39, 78 and 182?

The HCF would still be a factor of 78–39=39. The probable candidates for the HCF's value would still remain 1,3,13 and 39.

When you check for divisibility of all these numbers by 39, you would realize that 182 is not divisible and hence 39 would not be the HCF in this case.

The next check would be with the number 13. It can be seen that 13 divides 39 (hence would automatically divide 78- no need to check that) and also divides 182. Hence, 13 would be the required HCF of the three numbers.

Typical questions where HCF is used directly

Question 1: The sides of a hexagonal field are 216, 423, 1215, 1422, 2169 and 2223 meters. Find the greatest length of tape that would be able to exactly measure each of these sides without having to use fractions/parts of the tape?

In this question we are required to identify the HCF of the numbers 216,423,1215, 1422, 2169 and 2223.

In order to do that, we first find the smallest difference between any two of these numbers. It can be seen that the

difference between 2223-2169 = 54. Thus, the required HCF would be a factor of the number 54.

The factors of 54 are:

$$1 \times 54$$
$$2 \times 27$$
$$3 \times 18$$
$$6 \times 9$$

One of these 8 numbers has to be the HCF of the 6 numbers. 54 cannot be the HCF because the numbers 423 and 2223 being odd numbers would not be divisible by any even number. Thus, we do not need to check any even numbers in the list.

27 does not divide 423 and hence cannot be the HCF. 18 can be skipped as it is even.
Checking for 9:
9 divides 216,423,1215,1422 and 2169. Hence, it would become the HCF. (Note: we do not need to check 2223 once we know that 2169 is divisible by 9)

Question 2: A nursery has 363,429 and 693 plants respectively of 3 distinct varieties. It is desired to place these plants in straight rows of plants of 1 variety only so that the number of rows required is the minimum. What is the size of each row and how many rows would be required?

The size of each row would be the HCF of 363, 429 and 693. Difference between 363 and 429 =66. Factors of 66 are 66, 33, 22, 11, 6, 3, 2, 1.

66 need not be checked as it is even and 363 is odd. 33 divides 363, hence would automatically divide 429 and also divides 693. Hence, 33 is the correct answer for the size of each row.

For how many rows would be required we need to follow the following process:

Minimum number of rows required = 363/33 + 429/33 + 693/33 = 11 + 13 + 21 = 45 rows.

THE CONCEPT OF LCM (LEAST COMMON MULTIPLE)

Let n_1, and n_2 be two natural numbers distinct from each other. The smallest natural number n that is exactly divisible by n_1 and n_2 is called the Least Common Multiple (LCM) of n_1 and n_2 and is designated as LCM (n_1, n_2).

Rule for Finding the LCM of two Numbers n_1 and n_2

(a) Find the standard form of the numbers n_1 and n_2.
(b) Write out all the prime factors, which are contained in the standard forms of either of the numbers.
(c) Raise each of the prime factors listed above to the highest of the powers in which it appears in the standard forms of the numbers n_1 and n_2.

Contd

Rule for Finding the LCM of two numbers n_1 and n_2 (*Contd*)

(d) The product of results of the previous step will be the LCM of n_1 and n_2.

Illustration: Find the LCM of 150, 210, 375.

Step 1: Writing down the standard form of numbers

$$150 = 5 \times 5 \times 3 \times 2$$
$$210 = 5 \times 2 \times 7 \times 3$$
$$375 = 5 \times 5 \times 5 \times 3$$

Step 2: Write down all the prime factors: that appear at least once in any of the numbers: 5, 3, 2, 7.

Step 3: Raise each of the prime factors to their highest available power (considering each to the numbers).

The LCM = $2^1 \times 3^1 \times 5^3 \times 7^1 = 5250$.

Important Rule:

GCD (n_1, n_2). LCM $(n_1, n_2) = n_1 \cdot n_2$
i.e. The product of the HCF and the LCM equals the product of the numbers.

SHORT CUT FOR FINDING THE LCM

The LCM (least common multiple) again has a much faster way of doing it than what we learnt in school.

The process has to do with the use of co-prime numbers.

Before we look at the process, let us take a fresh look at what co-prime numbers are:

Co-prime numbers are any two numbers which have an HCF of 1, i.e. when two numbers have no common prime factor apart from the number 1, they are called co-prime or relatively prime to each other.

Some Rules for Co-primes

2 Numbers being co-prime

(i) Two consecutive natural numbers are always co-prime (Example 5, 6; 82, 83; 749, 750 and so on)

(ii) Two consecutive odd numbers are always co-prime (Examples: 7, 9; 51, 53; 513, 515 and so on)

(iii) Two prime numbers are always co-prime (Examples: 13, 17; 53, 71 and so on)

(iv) One prime number and another composite number (such that the composite number is not a multiple of the prime number) are always co-prime (Examples: 17, 38; 23, 49 and so on, but note that 17 and 51 are not co-prime)

3 or more numbers being co-prime with each other means that all possible pairs of the numbers would be co-prime with each other.

Thus, 47, 49, 51 and 52 are co-prime since each of the 6 pairs (47,49); (47,51); (47,52); (49,51); (49,52) and (51,52) are co-prime.

Rules for Spotting three Co-prime Numbers

(i) Three consecutive odd numbers are always co-prime (Examples: 15, 17, 19; 51, 53, 55 and so on)

(ii) Three consecutive natural numbers with the first one being odd (Examples: 15, 16, 17; 21, 22, 23; 41, 42, 43 and so on). Note that 22, 23, 24 are not co-prime

(iii) Two consecutive natural numbers along-with the next odd number such that the first no. is even (examples: 22, 23, 25; 52, 53, 55; 68, 69, 71 and so on)

(iv) Three prime numbers (Examples: 17, 23, 29; 13, 31, 43 and so on)

So what do co-prime numbers have to do with LCMs?

By using the logic of co-prime numbers, you can actually bypass the need to take out the prime factors of the set of numbers for which you are trying to find the LCM. How?

The following process will make it clear:

Let us say that you were trying to find the LCM of 9,10,12 and 15.

The LCM can be directly written as: $9 \times 10 \times 2$. The thinking that gives you the value of the LCM is as follows:

Step 1: If you can see a set of 2 or more co-prime numbers in the set of numbers for which you are finding the LCM- write them down by multiplying them.

So in the above situation, since we can see that 9 and 10 are co-prime to each other we can start off writing the LCM by writing 9×10 as the first step.

Step 2: For each of the other numbers, consider what part of them have already been taken into the answer and what part remains outside the answer. In case you see any part of the other numbers such that it is not a part of the value of the LCM you are writing—such a part would need to be taken into the answer of the LCM.

The process will be clear once you see what we do (and how we think) with the remaining 2 numbers in the above problem.

At this point when we have written down 9×10 we already have taken into account the numbers 9 and 10 leaving us to account for 12 and 15.

Thought about 12: 12 is $2 \times 2 \times 3$

9×10 already has a 3 and one 2 in it prime factors. However, the number 12 has two 2's. This means that one of the two 2's of the number 12 is still not accounted for in our answer. Hence, we need to modify the LCM by multiplying the existing 9×10 by a 2. With this change the LCM now becomes:

$$9 \times 10 \times 2$$

Thought about 15: 15 is 5×3

$9 \times 10 \times 2$ already has a 5 and a 3. Hence, there is no need to add anything to the existing answer.

Thus, $9 \times 10 \times 2$ would become the correct answer for the LCM of the numbers 9, 10, 12 and 15.

What if the numbers were: 9, 10, 12 and 25

Step 1: 9 and 10 are co-prime

Hence, the starting value is 9×10

Thought about 12: 12 is $2 \times 2 \times 3$

9×10 already has a 3 and one 2 in it prime factors. However, the number 12 has two 2's. This means that one of the two 2's of the number 12 is still not accounted for in our answer. Hence, we need to modify the LCM by multiplying the existing 9×10 by a 2. With this change the LCM now becomes:

$$9 \times 10 \times 2$$

Thought about 25: 25 is 5×5

$9 \times 10 \times 2$ has only one 5. Hence, we need to add another 5 to the answer.

Thus, $9 \times 10 \times 2 \times 5$ would become the correct answer for the LCM of the numbers 9, 10, 12 and 25.

Rule for Finding out HCF and LCM of Fractions

(A) HCF of two or more fractions is given by:

$$\frac{\text{HCF of Numerators}}{\text{LCM of Denominators}}$$

(B) LCM of two or more fractions is given by:

$$\frac{\text{LCM of Numerators}}{\text{HCF of Denominators}}$$

Typical questions on LCMs

You would be able to see most of the standard questions on LCMs in the practice exercise on HCF and LCM given below.

Rules for HCF: If the HCF of x and y is G, then the HCF of

(i) $x, (x + y)$ is also G

(ii) $x, (x - y)$ is also G

HCF and LCM

PRACTICE EXERCISE

(Typical questions asked in Exams)

1. Find the common factors for the numbers.
   (a) 24 and 64   (b) 42, 294 and 882
   (c) 60, 120 and 220
2. Find the HCF of
   (a) 420 and 1782   (b) 36 and 48
   (c) 54, 72, 198   (d) 62, 186 and 279

3. Find the LCM of
   (a) 13, 23 and 48   (b) 24, 36, 44 and 62
   (c) 22, 33, 45, and 72 (d) 13, 17, 21 and 33
4. Find the series of common multiples of
   (a) 54 and 36   (b) 33, 45 and 60
   [*Hint*: Find the LCM and then create an Arithmetic progression with the first term as the LCM and the common difference also as the LCM.]
5. The LCM of two numbers is 936. If their HCF is 4 and one of the numbers is 72, the other is:
   (a) 42   (b) 52
   (c) 62   (d) None of these
   [Answer: (b). Use $\text{HCF} \times \text{LCM} = $ product of numbers.]
6. Two alarm clocks ring their alarms at regular intervals of 50 seconds and 48 seconds. If they first beep together at 12 noon, at what time will they beep again for the first time?
   (a) 12:10 P.M.   (b) 12:12 P.M.
   (c) 12:11 P.M.   (d) None of these
   [Answer: (d). The LCM of 50 and 48 being 1200, the two clocks will ring again after 1200 seconds.]
7. 4 Bells toll together at 9:00 A.M. They toll after 7, 8, 11 and 12 seconds respectively. How many times will they toll together again in the next 3 hours?
   (a) 3   (b) 4
   (c) 5   (d) 6
   [Answer: (c). The LCM of 7, 8, 11 and 12 is 1848. Hence, the answer will be got by the quotient of the ratio $(10800)/(1848) \rightarrow 5$.]
8. On Ashok Marg three consecutive traffic lights change after 36, 42 and 72 seconds respectively. If the lights are first switched on at 9:00 A.M. sharp, at what time will they change simultaneously?
   (a) 9 : 08 : 04   (b) 9 : 08 : 24
   (c) 9 : 08 : 44   (d) None of these
   [Answer (b). The LCM of 36,42 and 72 is 504. Hence, the lights will change simultaneously after 8 minutes and 24 seconds.]
9. The HCF of 2472, 1284 and a third number 'N' is 12. If their LCM is $2^3 \times 3^2 \times 5^1 \times 103 \times 107$, then the number '$N$' is:
   (a) $2^2 \times 3^2 \times 7^1$ (b) $2^2 \times 3^3 \times 103$
   (c) $2^2 \times 3^2 \times 5^1$ (d) None of these
   [Answer: (c)]
10. Two equilateral triangles have the sides of lengths 34 and 85 respectively.
    (a) The greatest length of tape that can measure both of them exactly is:
    [Answer: HCF of 34 and 85 is 17.]
    (b) How many such equal parts can be measured?
    [Answer: $\frac{34}{17} \times 3 + \frac{85}{17} \times 3 = 2 \times 3 + 5 \times 3 = 21$]

11. Two numbers are in the ratio 17:13. If their HCF is 15, what are the numbers?
(Answer: 17×15 and 13×15 i.e. 255 and 195 respectively.) [Note : This can be done when the numbers are co-prime.]

12. A forester wants to plant 44 apple trees, 66 banana trees and 110 mango trees in equal rows (in terms of number of trees). Also, he wants to make distinct rows of trees (i.e. only one type of tree in one row). The number of rows (minimum) that are required are:

    (a) 2   (b) 3
    (c) 10   (d) 11
    [Answer: (c) $44/22 + 66/22 + 110/22$ (Since 22 is the HCF)]

13. Three runners running around a circular track can complete one revolution in 2, 4 and 5.5 hours respectively. When will they meet at the starting point?

    (a) 22   (b) 33
    (c) 11   (d) 44
    (The answer will be the LCM of 2, 4 and 11/2. This will give you 44 as the answer).

14. The HCF and LCM of two numbers are 33 and 264 respectively. When the first number is divided by 2, the quotient is 33. The other number is?

    (a) 66   (b) 132
    (c) 198   (d) 99
    [Answer: $33 \times 264 = 66 \times n$. Hence, $n = 132$]

15. The greatest number which will divide: 4003, 4126 and 4249:

    (a) 43   (b) 41
    (c) 45   (d) None of these
    The answer will be the HCF of the three numbers. (1 in this case)

16. Which of the following represents the largest 4 digit number which can be added to 7249 in order to make the derived number divisible by each of 12, 14, 21, 33, and 54.

    (a) 9123   (b) 9383
    (c) 8727   (d) None of these
    [Answer: The LCM of the numbers 12, 14, 21, 33 and 54 is 8316. Hence, in order for the condition to be satisfied we need to get the number as:
    $$7249 + n = 8316 \times 2$$
    Hence, $n = 9383$.]

17. Find the greatest number of 5 digits, that will give us a remainder of 5, when divided by 8 and 9 respectively.

    (a) 99931   (b) 99941
    (c) 99725   (d) None of these
    [Answer: The LCM of 8 and 9 is 72. The largest 5 digit multiple of 72 is 99936. Hence, the required answer is 99941.]

18. The least perfect square number which is divisible by 3, 4, 6, 8, 10 and 11 is:
    Solution: The number should have at least one 3, three 2's, one 5 and one 11 for it to be divisible by 3, 4, 6, 8, 10 and 11.
    Further, each of the prime factors should be having an even power in order to be a perfect square. Thus, the correct answer will be: $3 \times 3 \times 2 \times 2 \times 2 \times 2 \times 5 \times 5 \times 11 \times 11$

19. Find the greatest number of four digits which when divided by 10, 11, 15 and 22 leaves 3, 4, 8 and 15 as remainders respectively.

    (a) 9907   (b) 9903
    (c) 9893   (d) None of these
    [Answer: First find the greatest 4 digit multiple of the LCM of 10, 11, 15 and 22. (In this case it is 9900). Then, subtract 7 from it to give the answer.]

20. Find the HCF of $(3^{125} - 1)$ and $(3^{35} - 1)$.
    [Answer: The solution of this question is based on the rule that:
    The HCF of $(a^m - 1)$ and $(a^n - 1)$ is given by $(a^{\text{HCF of } m, n} - 1)$
    Thus, in this question the answer is: $(3^5 - 1)$. Since 5 is the HCF of 35 and 125.]

21. What will be the least possible number of the planks, if three pieces of timber 42 m, 49 m and 63 m long have to be divided into planks of the same length?

    (a) 7   (b) 8
    (c) 22   (d) None of these

22. Find the greatest number, which will divide 215, 167 and 135 so as to leave the same remainder in each case.

    (a) 64   (b) 32
    (c) 24   (d) 16

23. Find the L.C.M of 2.5, 0.5 and 0.175

    (a) 2.5   (b) 5
    (c) 7.5   (d) 17.5

24. The L.C.M of 4.5; 0.009; and 0.18 = ?

    (a) 4.5   (b) 45
    (c) 0.225   (d) 2.25

25. The L.C.M of two numbers is 1890 and their H.C.F is 30. If one of them is 270, the other will be

    (a) 210   (b) 220
    (c) 310   (d) 320

26. What is the smallest number which when increased by 6 is divisible by 36, 63 and 108?

    (a) 750   (b) 752
    (c) 754   (d) 756

27. The smallest square number, which is exactly divisible by 2, 3, 4, – 9, 6, 18, 36 and 60, is

    (a) 900   (b) 1600
    (c) 3600   (d) None of these

28. The H.C.F of two numbers is 11, and their L.C.M is 616. If one of the numbers is 88, find the other.

(a) 77   (b) 87

(c) 97   (d) None of these

29. What is the greatest possible rate at which a man can walk 51 km and 85 km in an exact number of minutes?

(a) 11 km/min   (b) 13 km/min

(c) 17 km/min   (d) None of these

30. The HCF and LCM of two numbers are 12 and 144 respectively. If one of the numbers is 36, the other number is

(a) 4   (b) 48

(c) 72   (d) 432

ANSWER KEY

21. (c)	22. (d)	23. (d)	24. (a)	25. (a)
26. (a)	27. (a)	28. (a)	29. (c)	30. (b)

Solutions

4. (a) The first common multiple is also the LCM. The LCM of 36 and 54 would be 108. The next common multiple would be 216, 324 and so on. Thus, the required series would be 108, 216, 324, 432, 540, 648….

   (b) The LCM of 33, 45 and 60 = $60 \times 3 \times 11$ = 1980. Thus, the required series is: 1980, 3960, 5940…

5. LCM × HCF = $936 \times 4 = N_1 \times N_2 \rightarrow$
   $936 \times 4 = 72 \times N_2 \rightarrow N_2 = 13 \times 4 = 52$. Option (b) is correct.

6. The first bell toll will be after the time elapsed is the LCM of 50 and 48. The LCM of 50 and 48 is $50 \times 24 = 1200$. Hence, the first time they would toll together after 12 noon would be exactly 1200 seconds or 20 minutes later. Option (d) is correct.

7. The LCM of 7, 8, 11 and 12 is given by $12 \times 11 \times 2 \times 7 = 264 \times 7 = 1848$. 1848 seconds is 30 minutes 48 seconds. Hence, the 4 bells would toll together every 30 minutes 48 seconds.

   The number of times they would toll together in the next 3 hours would be given by the quotient of the division:

   $3 \times 60 \times 60 / 1848 \rightarrow 5$ times

   Alternately, by thinking of 1848 seconds as 30 minutes 48 seconds you can also solve the same question by thinking as follows:

Since the sixth ring is after 3 PM, we can say that the bells would toll 5 times in the next 3 hours

9. $2472 = 2^3 \times 103 \times 3$; $1284 = 2^2 \times 107 \times 3$. Since the HCF is 12, the number must have a component of $2^2 \times 3^1$ at the very least in it. Also, since the LCM is $2^3 \times 3^2 \times 5^1 \times 103 \times 107$ we can see that the minimum requirement in the required number has to be $3^2 \times 5^1$. Combining these two requirements we get that the number should have $2^2 \times 3^2 \times 5^1$ at the minimum and the power of 2 could also be 2^3 while we could also have either one of 103^1 and/or 107^1 as a part of the required number.

   Thus, for instance, the number could also be $2^3 \times 3^2 \times 5^1 \times 103^1 \times 107^1$. The question has asked us— what *'could'* the number be?

   Option (c) gives us a possible value of the number and is hence the correct answer.

21. The least possible number of planks would occur when we divide each plank into a length equal to the HCF of 42, 49 and 63. The HCF of these numbers is clearly 7- and this should be the size of each plank. Number of planks in this case would be: $42/7 + 49/7 + 63/7 = 6 + 7 + 9 = 22$ planks. Hence, option (c) is correct.

22. Trial and error would give us that the number 16 would leave the same remainder of 7 in all the three cases. Hence, option (d) is correct.

23. The numbers are 5/2, ½ and 175/1000 = 7/40. The LCM of three fractions is given by the formula:

    LCM of numerators/HCF of denominators = (LCM of 5, 1 and 7)/(HCF of 2 and 40) = 35/2 = 17.5

24. Use the same process as for question 23 for the numbers: 9/2; 9/1000 and 9/50.

    (LCM of 9, 9, 9)/ (HCF of 2, 100, 50) = 9/2 = 4.5

25. $1890 \times 30 = 270 \times N_2 \rightarrow N_2 = 210$. Hence, option (a) is correct.

26. The LCM of 36, 63 and 108 is 756. Hence, the required number is 750. Option (a) is correct.

27. The LCM of the given numbers is 180. Hence, all multiples of 180 would be divisible by all of these numbers. Checking the series 180, 360, 540, 720, 900 we can see that 900 is the first perfect square in the list. Option (a) is correct.

28. Using the property HCF × LCM = product of the numbers, we get:

    $616 \times 11 = 88 \times N_2 \rightarrow N_2 = 77$. Option (a) is correct.

29. The answer would be given by the HCF of 51 and 85 – which is 17. Hence, option (c) is correct.

30. Using the property HCF × LCM = product of the numbers, we get:

    $12 \times 144 = 36 \times N_2 \rightarrow N_2 = 48$. Option (b) is correct.

DIVISIBILITY

A number x is said to be divisible by another number 'y' if it is completely divisible by y (i.e. it should leave no remainder).

In general it can be said that any integer I, when divided by a natural number N, there exist a unique pair of numbers Q and R which are called the quotient and Remainder respectively.

Thus, $I = QN + R$.

For any integer I and any natural number n there is a unique pair of numbers a and b such that:

$$I = QN + R$$

Where Q is an integer and N is a natural number or zero and $0 \geq R < N$ (i.e. remainder has to be a whole number less than N.)

If the remainder is zero we say that the number I is divisible by N.

When $R \neq 0$, we say that the number I is divisible by N with a remainder.

Thus, 25/8 can be written as: $25 = 3 \times 8 + 1$ (3 is the quotient and 1 is the remainder)

While, $-25/7$ will be written as $-25 = 7 \times (-4) + 3$ (-4 is the quotient and 3 is the remainder)

Note: An integer $b \neq 0$ is said to divide an integer a if there exists another integer c such that:

$$a = bc$$

It is important to explain at this point a couple of concepts with respect to the situation, when we divide a negative number by a natural number N.

Suppose, we divide -32 by 7. Contrary to what you might expect, the remainder in this case is $+3$ (and not -4). This is because the remainder is always non negative.

Thus, $-32/7$ gives quotient as -5 and remainder as $+3$.

The relationship between the remainder and the decimal:

1. Suppose we divide 42 by 5. The result has a quotient of 8 and remainder of 2.

   But $42/5 = 8.4$. As you can see, the answer has an integer part and a decimal part. The integer part being 8 (equals the quotient), the decimal part is 0.4 (and is given by 2/5).

   Since, we have also seen that for any divisor N, the set of remainders obeys the inequality $0 \leq R < N$, we should realise that any divisor N, will yield exactly N possible remainders. (For example If the divisor is 3, we have 3 possible remainders 0, 1 and 2. Further, when 3 is the divisor we can have only 3 possible decimal values .00, .333 & 0.666 corresponding to remainders of 0, 1 or 2. I would

want you to remember this concept when you study the fraction to percentage conversion table in the chapter on percentages.

2. In the case of -42 being divided by 5, the value is -8.4. In this case the interpretation should be thus: The integer part is -9 (which is also the quotient of this division) and the decimal part is 0.6 (corresponding to 3/5) Notice that since the remainder cannot be negative, the decimal too cannot be negative.

Theorems of Divisibility

(a) If a is divisible by b then ac is also divisible by b.

(b) If a is divisible by b and b is divisible by c then a is divisible by c.

(c) If a and b are natural numbers such that a is divisible by b and b is divisible by a then $a = b$.

(d) If n is divisible by d and m is divisible by d then $(m + n)$ and $(m - n)$ are both divisible by d. This has an important implication. Suppose 28 and 742 are both divisible by 7. Then $(742 + 28)$ as well as $(742 - 28)$ are divisible by 7. (and in fact so is $+28 - 742$).

(e) If a is divisible by b and c is divisible by d then ac is divisible by bd.

(f) The highest power of a prime number p, which divides $n!$ exactly is given by

$$[n/p] + [n/p^2] + [n/p^3] + \ldots$$

where $[x]$ denotes the greatest integer less than or equal to x.

As we have already seen earlier –

Any composite number can be written down as a product of its prime factors. (Also called standard form)

Thus, for example the number 1240 can be written as $2^3 \times 31^1 \times 5^1$.

The standard form of any number has a huge amount of information stored in it. The best way to understand the information stored in the standard form of a number is to look at concrete examples. As a reader I want you to understand each of the processes defined below and use them to solve similar questions given in the exercise that follows and beyond:

1. **Using the standard form of a number to find the sum and the number of factors of the number:**

   (a) **Sum of factors of a number:**

   Suppose, we have to find the sum of factors and the number of factors of 240.

   $$240 = 2^4 \times 3^1 \times 5^1$$

   The sum of factors will be given by:

$$(2^0 + 2^1 + 2^2 + 2^3 + 2^4)(3^0 + 3^1)(5^0 + 5^1)$$
$$= 31 \times 4 \times 6 = 744$$

Note: This is a standard process, wherein you create the same number of brackets as the number of distinct prime factors the number contains and then each bracket is filled with the sum of all the powers of the respective prime number starting from 0 to the highest power of that prime number contained in the standard form.

Thus, for 240, we create 3 brackets—one each for 2, 3 and 5. Further in the bracket corresponding to 2 we write $(2^0 + 2^1 + 2^2 + 2^3 + 2^4)$.

Hence, for example for the number $40 = 2^3 \times 5^1$, the sum of factors will be given by: $(2^0 + 2^1 + 2^2 + 2^3)$ $(5^0 + 5^1)$ {2 brackets since 40 has 2 distinct prime factors 2 and 5}

(b) **Number of factors of the number:**

Let us explore the sum of factors of 40 in a different context.

$$(2^0 + 2^1 + 2^2 + 2^3)(5^0 + 5^1)$$
$$= 2^0 \times 5^0 + 2^0 \times 5^1 + 2^1 \times 5^0 + 2^1 \times 5^1 + 2^2 \times 5^0 + 2^2$$
$$\times 5^1 + 2^3 \times 5^0 + 2^3 \times 5^1$$
$$= 1 + 5 + 2 + 10 + 4 + 20 + 8 + 40 = 90$$

A clear look at the numbers above will make you realize that it is nothing but the addition of the factors of 40

Hence, we realise that the number of terms in the expansion of $(2^0 + 2^1 + 2^2 + 2^3)(5^0 + 5^1)$ will give us the number of factors of 40. Hence, 40 has $4 \times 2 = 8$ factors.

Note: The moment you realise that $40 = 2^3 \times 5^1$ the answer for the number of factors can be got by $(3 + 1)(1 + 1) = 8$

2. **Sum and Number of even and odd factors of a number.**

Suppose, you are trying to find out the number of factors of a number represented in the standard form by: $2^3 \times 3^4 \times 5^2 \times 7^3$

As you are already aware the answer to the question is $(3 + 1)(4 + 1)(2 + 1)(3 + 1)$ and is based on the logic that the number of terms will be the same as the number of terms in the expansion: $(2^0 + 2^1 + 2^2 + 2^3)$ $(3^0 + 3^1 + 3^2 + 3^3 + 3^4)(5^0 + 5^1 + 5^2)(7^0 + 7^1 + 7^2 + 7^3)$. Now, suppose you have to find out the sum of the even factors of this number. The only change you need to do in this respect will be evident below. The answer will be given by:

$(2^1 + 2^2 + 2^3)(3^0 + 3^1 + 3^2 + 3^3 + 3^4)(5^0 + 5^1 + 5^2)$ $(7^0 + 7^1 + 7^2 + 7^3)$

Note: We have eliminated 2^0 from the original answer. By eliminating 2^0 from the expression for the sum of all factors you are ensuring that you have only even numbers in the expansion of the expression.

Consequently, the number of even factors will be given by: $(3)(4 + 1)(2 + 1)(3 + 1)$

i.e. Since 2^0 is eliminated, we do not add 1 in the bracket corresponding to 2.

Let us now try to expand our thinking to try to think about the number of odd factors for a number.

In this case, we just have to do the opposite of what we did for even numbers. The following step will make it clear:

Odd factors of the number whose standard form is : $2^3 \times 3^4 \times 5^2 \times 7^3$

Sum of odd factors = $(2^0)(3^0 + 3^1 + 3^2 + 3^3 + 3^4)$ $(5^0 + 5^1 + 5^2)(7^0 + 7^1 + 7^2 + 7^3)$

i.e.: Ignore all powers of 2. The result of the expansion of the above expression will be the complete set of odd factors of the number. Consequently, the number of odd factors for the number will be given by the number of terms in the expansion of the above expression.

Thus, the number of odd factors for the number $2^3 \times 3^4 \times 5^2 \times 7^3 = 1 \times (4 + 1)(2 + 1)(3 + 1)$.

3. **Sum and number of factors satisfying other conditions for any composite number**

These are best explained through examples:

(i) Find the sum and the number of factors of 1200 such that the factors are divisible by 15.

Solution : $1200 = 2^4 \times 5^2 \times 3^1$.

For a factor to be divisible by 15 it should compulsorily have 3^1 and 5^1 in it. Thus, sum of factors divisible by $15 = (2^0 + 2^1 + 2^2 + 2^3 + 2^4) \times (5^1 + 5^2)$ (3^1) and consequently the number of factors will be given by $5 \times 2 \times 1 = 10$.

(What we have done is ensure that in every individual term of the expansion, there is a minimum of $3^1 \times 5^1$. This is done by removing powers of 3 and 5 which are below 1.)

Task for the student: Physically verify the answers to the question above and try to convert the logic into a mental algorithm.

NOTE FROM THE AUTHOR—The need for thought algorithms:

I have often observed that the key difference between understanding a concept and actually applying it under examination pressure, is the presence or absence of a mental thought algorithm which clarifies the concept to you in your mind. The thought algorithm is a personal representation of a concept—and any concept that you read/understand in this book (or elsewhere) will remain an external concept till it remains in someone else's words. The moment the thought becomes internalised the concept becomes yours to apply and use.

Practice Exercise on Factors

For the number 2450 find.
1. The sum and number of all factors.
2. The sum and number of even factors.
3. The sum and number of odd factors.
4. The sum and number of factors divisible by 5
5. The sum and number of factors divisible by 35.
6. The sum and number of factors divisible by 245.

For the number 7200 find.
7. The sum and number of all factors.
8. The sum and number of even factors.
9. The sum and number of odd factors.
10. The sum and number of factors divisible by 25.
11. The sum and number of factors divisible by 40.
12. The sum and number of factors divisible by 150.
13. The sum and number of factors not divisible by 75.
14. The sum and number of factors not divisible by 24.
15. Find the number of divisors of 1728.
    (a) 18　　(b) 30
    (c) 28　　(d) 20
16. Find the number of divisors of 1080 excluding the divisors, which are perfect squares.
    (a) 28　　(b) 29
    (c) 30　　(d) 31
17. Find the number of divisors of 544 excluding 1 and 544.
    (a) 12　　(b) 18
    (c) 11　　(d) 10
18. Find the number of divisors 544 which are greater than 3.
    (a) 15　　(b) 10
    (c) 12　　(d) None of these.
19. Find the sum of divisors of 544 excluding 1 and 544.
    (a) 1089　　(b) 545
    (c) 589　　(d) 1134
20. Find the sum of divisors of 544 which are perfect squares.
    (a) 32　　(b) 64
    (c) 42　　(d) 21
21. Find the sum of odd divisors of 544.
    (a) 18　　(b) 34
    (c) 68　　(d) 36
22. Find the sum of even divisors of 4096.
    (a) 8192　　(b) 6144
    (c) 8190　　(d) 6142
23. Find the sum the sums of divisors of 144 and 160.
    (a) 589　　(b) 781
    (c) 735　　(d) None of these
24. Find the sum of the sum of even divisors of 96 and the sum of odd divisors of 3600.
    (a) 639　　(b) 735
    (c) 651　　(d) 589

ANSWER KEY

15. (c)	16. (a)	17. (d)	18. (b)	19. (c)
20. (d)	21. (a)	22. (c)	23. (b)	24. (c)

Solutions

Solutions to Questions 1 to 6:

$2450 = 50 \times 49 = 2^1 \times 5^2 \times 7^2$

1. Sum and number of all factors:
   Sum of factors $= (2^0 + 2^1)(5^0 + 5^1 + 5^2)(7^0 + 7^1 + 7^2)$
   Number of factors $= 2 \times 3 \times 3 = 18$
2. Sum of all even factors:
   $(2^1)(5^0 + 5^1 + 5^2)(7^0 + 7^1 + 7^2)$
   Number of even factors $= 1 \times 3 \times 3 = 9$
3. Sum of all odd factors:
   $(2^0)(5^0 + 5^1 + 5^2)(7^0 + 7^1 + 7^2)$
   Number of odd factors $= 1 \times 3 \times 3 = 9$
4. Sum of factors divisible by 5:
   $(2^0 + 2^1)(5^1 + 5^2)(7^0 + 7^1 + 7^2)$
   Number of factors divisible by $5 = 2 \times 2 \times 3 = 12$
5. Sum of factors divisible by 35:
   $(2^0 + 2^1)(5^1 + 5^2)(7^1 + 7^2)$
   Number of factors divisible by $35 = 2 \times 2 \times 2 = 8$
6. Sum of all factors divisible by 245:
   $(2^0 + 2^1)(5^1 + 5^2)(7^2)$
   Number of factors divisible by $245 = 2 \times 2 \times 1 = 4$

Solutions to Questions 7 to 14:

$7200 = 72 \times 100 = 12 \times 6 \times 100 = 2^5 \times 3^2 \times 5^2$

7. **Sum and number of all factors:**
   Sum of factors $= (2^0 + 2^1 + 2^2 + 2^3 + 2^4 + 2^5)(3^0 + 3^1 + 3^2)(5^0 + 5^1 + 5^2)$
   Number of factors $= 6 \times 3 \times 3 = 54$
8. **Sum and number of even factors:**
   Sum of even factors $= (2^1 + 2^2 + 2^3 + 2^4 + 2^5)(3^0 + 3^1 + 3^2)(5^0 + 5^1 + 5^2)$
   Number of even factors $= 5 \times 3 \times 3 = 45$
9. **Sum and number of odd factors:**
   Sum of odd factors $= (2^0)(3^0 + 3^1 + 3^2)(5^0 + 5^1 + 5^2)$
   Number of odd factors $= 1 \times 3 \times 3 = 9$

10. **Sum and number of factors divisible by 25:**

    Sum of factors divisible by 25 = $(2^0 + 2^1 + 2^2 + 2^3 + 2^4 + 2^5)(3^0 + 3^1 + 3^2)(5^2)$

    Number of factors divisible by 25 = $6 \times 3 \times 1 = 18$

11. **Sum and number of factors divisible by 40:**

    Sum of factors divisible by 40 = $(2^3 + 2^4 + 2^5)(3^0 + 3^1 + 3^2)(5^1 + 5^2)$

    Number of factors = $3 \times 3 \times 2 = 18$

12. **Sum and number of factors divisible by 150:**

    Sum of factors divisible by 150 = $(2^1 + 2^2 + 2^3 + 2^4 + 2^5)(3^1 + 3^2)(5^2)$

    Number of factors divisible by 150 = $5 \times 2 \times 1 = 10$

13. **Sum and number of factors not divisible by 75:**

    Sum of factors not divisible by 75 = Sum of all factors – Sum of factors divisible by 75 =

    $(2^0 + 2^1 + 2^2 + 2^3 + 2^4 + 2^5)(3^0 + 3^1 + 3^2)(5^0 + 5^1 + 5^2) - (2^0 + 2^1 + 2^2 + 2^3 + 2^4 + 2^5)(3^1 + 3^2)(5^2)$

    Number of factors not divisible by 75 = Number of factors of 7200 – Number of factors of 7200 which are divisible by 75 = $6 \times 3 \times 3 - 6 \times 2 \times 1 = 54 - 12 = 42$

14. **Sum and number of factors not divisible by 24:**

    Sum of factors not divisible by 24 = Sum of all factors – Sum of factors divisible by 24 =

    $(2^0 + 2^1 + 2^2 + 2^3 + 2^4 + 2^5)(3^0 + 3^1 + 3^2)(5^0 + 5^1 + 5^2) - (2^3 + 2^4 + 2^5)(3^1 + 3^2)(5^0 + 5^1 + 5^2)$

    Number of factors not divisible by 24 = Number of factors of 7200 – Number of factors of 7200 which are divisible by 24 = $6 \times 3 \times 3 - 3 \times 2 \times 3 = 54 - 18 = 36$

15. **Number of divisors of 1728**

    $1728 = 4 \times 432 = 16 \times 108 = 64 \times 27 = 2^6 \times 3^3$

    Number of factors = $7 \times 4 = 28$. Option (a) is correct.

16. $1080 = 108 \times 10 = 27 \times 4 \times 10 = 3^3 \times 2^3 \times 5^1$

    Number of factors = $4 \times 4 \times 2 = 32$.

    In order to see the number of factors of 1080 which are perfect squares we need to visualize the structure for writing down the sum of perfect square factors of 1080.

    This would be given by:

    Sum of all perfect square factors of 1080 = $(2^0 + 2^2)(3^0 + 3^2)(5^0)$.

    From the above structure it is clear that the number of perfect square factors is going to be $2 \times 2 \times 1 = 4$

    Thus, the number of factors of 1080 which are not perfect squares are equal to $32 - 4 = 28$.

    Option (a) is correct.

17. $544 = 17^1 \times 2^5$. Hence, the total number of factors of 544 is $2 \times 6 = 12$. But we have to count factors excluding 1 and 544. Thus, we need to remove 2 factors from this. The required answer is $12 - 2 = 10$. Option (d) is correct.

18. Using the fact that 544 has a total of 12 factors and the numbers 1 and 2 are the two factors which are lower than 3, we would get a total of 10 factors greater than 3. Option (b) is correct.

19. The required answer would be given by: Sum of all factors of $544 - 1 - 544 = (2^0 + 2^1 + 2^2 + 2^3 + 2^4 + 2^5)(17^0 + 17^1) - 545 = 63 \times 18 - 545 = 589$. Option (c) is correct.

20. Sum of divisors of 544 which are perfect square is: $(2^0 + 2^2 + 2^4)(17^0) = 21$. Option (d) is correct.

21. Sum of odd divisors of 544 = $(2^0)(17^0 + 17^1) = 18$. Option (a) is correct.

22. $4096 = 2^{12}$.

    Sum of even divisors = $(2^1 + 2^2 + 2^3 + 2^4 + 2^5 + 2^6 + 2^7 + 2^8 + 2^9 + 2^{10} + 2^{11} + 2^{12}) = 2^{13} - 2 = 8190$

23. $144 = 2^4 \times 3^2 \rightarrow$ Sum of divisors of 144 = $(2^0 + 2^1 + 2^2 + 2^3 + 2^4)(3^0 + 3^1 + 3^2) = 31 \times 13 = 403$

    $160 = 2^5 \times 5^1 \rightarrow$ Sum of divisors of 160 = $(2^0 + 2^1 + 2^2 + 2^3 + 2^4 + 2^5)(5^0 + 5^1) = 63 \times 6 = 378$.

    Sum of the two = $403 + 378 = 781$.

24. $96 = 2^5 \times 3^1$. Sum of even divisors of 96 = $(2^1 + 2^2 + 2^3 + 2^4 + 2^5)(3^0 + 3^1) = 62 \times 4 = 248$

    $3600 = 2^4 \times 5^2 \times 3^2$. Sum of odd divisors of 3600 = $(2^0)(3^0 + 3^1 + 3^2)(5^0 + 5^1 + 5^2) = 13 \times 31 = 403$

    Sum of the two = $248 + 403 = 651$.

    Option (c) is correct.

NUMBER OF ZEROES IN AN EXPRESSION

Suppose you have to find the number of zeroes in a product: $24 \times 32 \times 17 \times 23 \times 19 = (2^3 \times 3^1) \times (2^5) \times 17^1 \times 23 \times 19$.

As you can notice, this product will have no zeroes because it has no 5 in it.

However, if you have an expression like: $8 \times 15 \times 23 \times 17 \times 25 \times 22$

The above expression can be rewritten in the standard form as:

$$2^3 \times 3^1 \times 5^1 \times 23 \times 17 \times 5^2 \times 2^1 \times 11^1$$

Zeroes are formed by a combination of 2×5. Hence, the number of zeroes will depend on the number of pairs of 2's and 5's that can be formed.

In the above product, there are four twos and three fives. Hence, we shall be able to form only three pairs of (2×5). Hence, there will be 3 zeroes in the product.

Finding the Number of Zeroes in a Factorial Value

Suppose you had to find the number of zeroes in 6!.

$6! = 6 \times 5 \times 4 \times 3 \times 2 \times 1 = (3 \times 2) \times (5) \times (2 \times 2) \times (3) \times (2) \times (1)$.

The above expression will have only one pair of 5×2, since there is only one 5 and an abundance of 2's.

It is clear that in any factorial value, the number of 5's will always be lesser than the number of 2's. Hence, all we need to do is to count the number of 5's. The process for this is explained in Solved Examples 1.1 to 1.3.

Exercise for Self-practice

Find the number of zeroes in the following cases:
1. 47!
2. 58!
3. $13 \times 15 \times 22 \times 125 \times 44 \times 35 \times 11$
4. $12 \times 15 \times 5 \times 24 \times 13 \times 17$
5. 173!
6. $144! \times 5 \times 15 \times 22 \times 11 \times 44 \times 135$
7. 148!
8. 1093!
9. 1132!
10. $1142! \times 348! \times 17!$

Solutions

1. 47/5 → Quotient 9. 9/5 → Quotient → 1. 9 + 1 = 10 zeroes.
2. 58/5 → Quotient 11. 11/5 → Quotient → 2. 11 + 2 = 13 zeroes.
3. The given expression has five 5's and three 2's. Thus, there would be three zeroes in the expression.
4. The given expression has two 5's and five 2's. Thus, there would be two zeroes in the expression.
5. 173/5 → Quotient 34. 34/5 → Quotient 6. 6/5 → Quotient 1. 34 + 6 + 1 = 41 zeroes.
6. 144! Would have 28 + 5 + 1 = 34 zeroes and the remaining part of the expression would have three zeroes. A total of 34 + 3 = 37 zeroes.
7. 148/5 → Quotient 29. 29/5 → Quotient 5. 5/5 → Quotient 1. 29 + 5 + 1 = 35 zeroes.
8. 1093/5 → Quotient 218. 218/5 → Quotient 43. 43/5 → Quotient 8. 8/5 → Quotient 1. 218 + 43 + 8 + 1 = 270 zeroes.
9. 1132/5 → Quotient 226. 226/5 → Quotient 45. 45/5 → Quotient 9. 9/5 → Quotient 1. 226 + 45 + 9 + 1 = 281 zeroes.
10. 1142/5 → Quotient 228. 228/5 → Quotient 45. 45/5 → Quotient 9. 9/5 → Quotient 1. 228 + 45 + 9 + 1 = 284 zeroes.
    348/5 → Quotient 69. 69/5 → Quotient 13. 13/5 → Quotient 2. 69 + 13 + 2 = 84 zeroes.
    17/5 → Quotient 3 → 3 zeroes.

Thus, the total number of zeroes in the expression is: 284 + 84 + 3 = 371 zeroes.

A special implication: Suppose you were to find the number of zeroes in the value of the following factorial values:

45!, 46!, 47!, 48!, 49!

What do you notice? The number of zeroes in each of the cases will be equal to 10. Why does this happen? It is not difficult to understand that the number of fives in any of these factorials is equal to 10. The number of zeroes will only change at 50! (It will become 12).

In fact, this will be true for all factorial values between two consecutive products of 5.

Thus, 50!, 51!, 52!, 53! And 54! will have 12 zeroes (since they all have 12 fives).

Similarly, 55!, 56!, 57!, 58! And 59! will each have 13 zeroes.

Apart from this fact, did you notice another thing? That while there are 10 zeroes in 49! there are directly 12 zeroes in 50!. This means that there is no value of a factorial which will give 11 zeroes. This occurs because to get 50! we multiply the value of 49! by 50. When you do so, the result is that we introduce two 5's in the product. Hence, the number of zeroes jumps by two (since we never had any paucity of twos.)

Note: at 124! you will get $24 + 4 \Rightarrow 28$ zeroes.

At 125! you will get $25 + 5 + 1 = 31$ zeroes. (A jump of 3 zeroes.)

Exercise for Self-practice

1. n! has 23 zeroes. What is the maximum possible value of n?
2. n! has 13 zeroes. The highest and least values of n are?
3. Find the number of zeroes in the product $1^1 \times 2^2 \times 3^3 \times 4^4 \times 5^5 \times 6^6 \times \dots \times 49^{49}$
4. Find the number of zeroes in:
   $100^1 \times 99^2 \times 98^3 \times 97^4 \times \dots \times 1^{100}$
5. Find the number of zeroes in:
   $1^{1!} \times 2^{2!} \times 3^{3!} \times 4^{4!} \times 5^{5!} \times \dots 10^{10!}$
6. Find the number of zeroes in the value of:
   $2^2 \times 5^4 \times 4^6 \times 10^8 \times 6^{10} \times 15^{12} \times 8^{14} \times 20^{16} \times 10^{18} \times 25^{20}$
7. What is the number of zeroes in the following:
   (a) $3200 + 1000 + 40000 + 32000 + 15000000$
   (b) $3200 \times 1000 \times 40000 \times 32000 \times 16000000$

Solutions

1. This can never happen because at 99! number of zeroes is 22 and at 100! the number of zeroes is 24.
2. 59 and 55 respectively.
3. The fives will be less than the twos. Hence, we need to count only the fives.

Thus : $5^5 \times 10^{10} \times 15^{15} \times 20^{20} \times 25^{25} \times 30^{30} \times 35^{35} \times 40^{40} \times 45^{45}$

gives us: $5 + 10 + 15 + 20 + 25 + 25 + 30 + 35 + 40 + 45$ fives. Thus, the product has 250 zeroes.

4. Again the key here is to count the number of fives. This can get done by:

$100^1 \times 95^6 \times 90^{11} \times 85^{16} \times 80^{21} \times 75^{26} \times \ldots\ldots 5^{96}$

$(1 + 6 + 11 + 16 + 21 + 26 + 31 + 36 + 41 + 46 + \ldots\ldots + 96) + (1 + 26 + 51 + 76)$

$= 20 \times 48.5 + 4 \times 38.5$ (Using sum of A.P. explained in the next chapter.)

$= 970 + 154 = 1124.$

5. The answer will be the number of 5's. Hence, it will be 5! + 10!

6. The number of fives is again lesser than the number of twos.

The number of 5's will be given by the power of 5 in the product:

$$5^4 \times 10^8 \times 15^{12} \times 20^{16} \times 10^{18} \times 25^{20}$$
$$= 4 + 8 + 12 + 16 + 18 + 40 = 98.$$

7. A. The number of zeroes in the sum will be two, since:

```
       3200
       1000
      40000
      32000
   15076200
   ---------
   15152400
```

Thus, in such cases the number of zeroes will be the least number of zeroes amongst the numbers.

Exception: 3200 + 1800 = 5000 (three zeroes, not two).

B. The number of zeroes will be:

$$2 + 3 + 4 + 3 + 6 = 18.$$

An extension of the process for finding the number of zeroes.

Consider the following questions:

1. Find the highest power of 5 which is contained in the value of 127!

2. When 127! is divided by 5^n the result is an integer. Find the highest possible value for n.

3. Find the number of zeroes in 127!

In each of the above cases, the value of the answer will be given by:

$$[127/5] + [127/25] + [127/125]$$
$$= 25 + 5 + 1 = 31$$

This process can be extended to questions related to other prime numbers. For example:

Find the highest power of:

1. 3 which completely divides 38!

Solution: $[38/3] + [38/3^2] + [38/3^3] = 12 + 4 + 1 = 17$

2. 7 which is contained in 57!

$[57/7] + [57/7^2] = 8 + 1 = 9.$

This process changes when the divisor is not a prime number. You are first advised to go through worked out problems 1.4, 1.5, 1.6 and 1.19.

Now try to solve the following exercise:

1. Find the highest power of 7 which divides 81!

2. Find the highest power of 42 which divides 122!

3. Find the highest power of 84 which divides 342!

4. Find the highest power of 175 which divides 344!

5. Find the highest power of 360 which divides 520!

Solutions

1. $81/7 \rightarrow$ Quotient 11. $11/7 \rightarrow$ Quotient 1. Highest power of 7 in 81! = 11 + 1 =12.

2. In order to check for the highest power of 42, we need to realize that 42 is $2 \times 3 \times 7$. In 122! The least power between 2,3 and 7 would obviously be for 7. Thus, we need to find the number of 7's in 122! (or in other words- the highest power of 7 in 122!).

This can be done by:

$122/7 \rightarrow$ Quotient 17. $17/7 \rightarrow$ Quotient 2. Highest power of 7 in 122! = 17 + 2 = 19.

3. $84 = 2 \times 2 \times 3 \times 7$. This means we need to think of which amongst 2^2, 3 and 7 would appear the least number of times in 342! It is evident that there would be more 2^2s and 3's than 7's in any factorial value (Because if you write any factorial $1 \times 2 \times 3 \times 4 \times 5 \times 6 \times 7 \times 8 \times 9 \times 10 \times 11 \times 12 \times 13 \times \mathbf{14} \times 15\ldots$ you can clearly see that before a 7 or it's multiple appears in the multiplication, there are at least two 2's and one 3 which appear beforehand.)

Hence, in order to solve this question we just need to find the power of 7 in 342!

This can be done as:

$342/7 \rightarrow$ Quotient 48. $48/7 \rightarrow$ Quotient 6. $6/7 \rightarrow$ Quotient 0. Highest power of 7 in 342! = 48 + 6 = 54.

4. $175 = 5 \times 5 \times 7$. This means we need to think of which amongst 5^2 and 7 would appear the least number of times in 175! In this case it is not immediately evident that whether there would be more 5^2s or more 7's in any factorial value (Because if you write any factorial $1 \times 2 \times 3 \times 4 \times 5 \times 6 \times \mathbf{7} \times 8 \times 9 \times 10 \times 11 \times 12 \times 13 \times 14 \times 15\ldots$you can clearly see that although the 5's appear more frequently than the 7's it is not evident that we would have at least two fives before the 7 appears.) Hence, in this question we would need to check for both the number of 5^2s and the number of 7's.

Number of 7's in 344!

344/7 → Quotient 49. 49/7 → Quotient 7. 7/7 → Quotient 1. Highest power of 7 in 344! = 49 + 7 + 1 = 57.

In order to find the number of 5^2s in 344! We first need to find the number of 5's in 344!

344/5 → Quotient 68. 68/5 → Quotient 13. 13/5 → Quotient 2. Number of 5's in 344! = 68 + 13 + 2 = 83.

83 fives would obviously mean [83/2] = 41 5^2s

Thus, there are 41 5^2s and 57 7's in 344!

Since, the number of 5^2s are lower, they would determine the highest power of 175 that would divide 344!

The answer is 41.

5. $360 = 5 \times 2 \times 2 \times 2 \times 3 \times 3$. This means we need to think of which amongst $2^3, 3^2$ and 5 would appear the least number of times in 520! In this case it is not immediately evident which of these three would appear least number of times. Hence, in this question we would need to check for all three – 2^3 3^2s and 5s.

Number of 5's in 520!

520/5 → Quotient 104. 104/5 → Quotient 20. 20/5 → Quotient 4. Highest power of 5 in 520! = 104 + 20 + 4 = 128.

In order to find the number of 3^2s in 520! we first need to find the number of 3's in 520!

520/3 → Quotient 173. 173/3 → Quotient 57. 57/3 → Quotient 19. 19/3 → Quotient 6. 6/3 → Quotient 2. 2/3 → Quotient 0. Number of 3's in 520! = 173 + 57 + 19 + 6 + 2 = 257.

257 threes would obviously mean [257/2] = 128 3^2s.

In order to find the number of 2^3s in 520! we first need to find the number of 2's in 520!

520/2 → Quotient 260. 260/2 → Quotient 130. 130/2 → Quotient 65. 65/2 → Quotient 32. 32/2 → Quotient 16. 16/2 → Quotient 8. 8/2 → Quotient 4. 4/2 → Quotient 2. 2/2 → Quotient 1. 1/2 → Quotient 0.

Number of 2's in 520! = 260 + 130 + 65 + 32 + 16 + 8 + 4 + 2 + 1 = 518. 518 twos would obviously mean [518/3] = 172 2^3s.

Thus, there are 128 3^2s, 128 5's and 172 2^3's in 520!

The highest power of 360 that would divide 520! would be the least of 128, 128 and 172.

The answer is 128.

Exercise for Self-practice

1. Find the maximum value of n such that 157! is perfectly divisible by 10^n.

2. Find the maximum value of n such that 157! is perfectly divisible by 12^n.
   (a) 77   (b) 76
   (c) 75   (d) 78

3. Find the maximum value of n such that 157! is perfectly divisible by 18^n.
   (a) 37   (b) 38
   (c) 39   (d) 40

4. Find the maximum value of n such that 50! is perfectly divisible by 2520^n.
   (a) 6   (b) 8
   (c) 7   (d) None of these

5. Find the maximum value of n such that 50! is perfectly divisible by 12600^n.
   (a) 7   (b) 6
   (c) 8   (d) None of these

6. Find the maximum value of n such that 77! is perfectly divisible by 720^n.
   (a) 35   (b) 18
   (c) 17   (d) 36

7. Find the maximum value of n such that $42 \times 57 \times 92 \times 91 \times 52 \times 62 \times 63 \times 64 \times 65 \times 66 \times 67$ is perfectly divisible by 42^n.
   (a) 4   (b) 3
   (c) 5   (d) 6

8. Find the maximum value of n such that $570 \times 60 \times 30 \times 90 \times 100 \times 500 \times 700 \times 343 \times 720 \times 81$ is perfectly divisible by 30^n.
   (a) 12   (b) 11
   (c) 14   (d) 13

9. Find the maximum value of n such that $77 \times 42 \times 37 \times 57 \times 30 \times 90 \times 70 \times 2400 \times 2402 \times 243 \times 343$ is perfectly divisible by 21^n.
   (a) 9   (b) 11
   (c) 10   (d) 6

Find the number of consecutive zeroes at the end of the following numbers.

10. 72!
    (a) 17   (b) 9
    (c) 8   (d) 16

11. 77! × 42!
    (a) 24   (b) 9
    (c) 27   (d) 18

12. 100! + 200!
    (a) 73   (b) 24
    (c) 11   (d) 22

13. $57 \times 60 \times 30 \times 15625 \times 4096 \times 625 \times 875 \times 975$
    (a) 6   (b) 16
    (c) 17   (d) 15

(a) 37   (b) 38
(c) 16   (d) −1.15

14. $1! \times 2! \times 3! \times 4! \times 5! \times \text{-------} \times 50!$
    - (a) 235
    - (b) 12
    - (c) 262
    - (d) 105
15. $1^1 \times 2^2 \times 3^3 \times 4^4 \times 5^5 \times 6^6 \times 7^7 \times 8^8 \times 9^9 \times 10^{10}$.
    - (a) 25
    - (b) 15
    - (c) 10
    - (d) 20
16. $100! \times 200!$
    - (a) 49
    - (b) 73
    - (c) 132
    - (d) 33

ANSWER KEY

1. (b)	2. (c)	3. (a)	4. (b)	5. (b)
6. (c)	7. (b)	8. (b)	9. (d)	10. (d)
11. (c)	12. (b)	13. (d)	14. (c)	15. (b)
16. (b)				

Solutions

1. $[157/5] = 31$. $[31/5] = 6$. $[6/5] = 1$. $31 + 6 + 1 = 38$. Option (b) is correct.
2. No of 2's in $157! = [157/2] + [157/4] + [157/8]... + [157/128] = 78 + 39 + 19 + 9 + 4 + 2 + 1 = 152$. Hence, the number of 2^2s would be $[152/2] = 76$. Number of 3's in $157! = 52 + 17 + 5 + 1 = 75$. The answer would be given by the lower of these values. Hence, 75 (Option c) is correct.
3. From the above solution: Number of 2's in $157! = 152$. Number of 3^2s in $157! = [75/2] = 37$. Hence, option (a) is correct.
4. $2520 = 7 \times 3^2 \times 2^3 \times 5$. The value of n would be given by the value of the number of 7s in 50! This value is equal to $[50/7] + [50/49] = 7 + 1 = 8$. Option (b) is correct.
5. $12600 = 7 \times 3^2 \times 2^3 \times 5^2$. The value of 'n' would depend on which of number of 7s and number of 5^2s is lower in 50!. Number of 7's in $50! = 8$. Note here that if we check for 7's we do not need to check for 3^2s as there would be at least two 3's before a 7 comes in every factorial's value. Similarly, there would always be at least three 2's before a 7 comes in any factorial's value. Thus, the number of 3^2s and the number of 2^3s can never be lower than the number of 7s in any factorial's value. Number of 5s in $50! = 10 + 2 = 12$. Hence, the number of 5^2s in $50! = [12/2] = 6$. 6 will be the answer as the number of 5^2s is lower than the number of 7's. Option (b) is correct.
6. $720 = 2^4 \times 5^1 \times 3^2$. In 77! there would be $38 + 19 + 9 + 4 + 2 + 1 = 73$ twos → hence $[73/4] = 18$ 2^4s.

In 77! there would be $25 + 8 + 2 = 35$ threes → hence $[35/2] = 17$ 3^2s. In 77! there would be $15 + 3 = 18$ fives. Since 17 is the least of these values, option (c) is correct.
7. In the expression given, there are three 7's and more than three 2's and 3's. Thus, Option (b) is correct.
8. Checking for the number of 2's, 3's and 5's in the given expression you can see that the minimum is for the number of 3's (there are 11 of them while there are 12 5's and more than 11 2's) Hence, option (b) is correct.
9. The number of 7's in the number is 6, while there are six 3's too. Option (d) is correct.
10. The number of zeroes would depend on the number of 5's in the value of the factorial. $72! \rightarrow 14 + 2 = 16$. Option (d) is correct.
11. The number of zeroes would depend on the number of 5's in the value of the factorial. $77! \times 42! \rightarrow 15 + 3 = 18$ (for 77!) and $8 + 1 = 9$ (for 42!). Thus, the total number of zeroes in the given expression would be $18 + 9 = 27$. Option (c) is correct.
12. The number of zeroes would depend on the number of 5's in the value of the factorial. 100! would end in $20 + 4 = 24$ zeroes. 200! Would end in $40 + 8 + 1 = 49$ zeroes. When you add the two numbers (one with 24 zeroes and the other with 49 zeroes at it's end), the resultant total would end in 24 zeroes. Option (b) is correct.
13. The given expression has fifteen 2's and seventeen 5's. The number of zeroes would be 15 as the number of 2's is lower in this case. Option (d) is correct.
14. 1! to 4! would have no zeroes while 5! to 9! All the values would have 1 zero. Thus, a total of 5 zeroes till 9!. Going further 10! to 14! would have two zeroes each – so a total of 10 zeroes would come out of the product of $10! \times 11! \times 12! \times 13! \times 14!$. Continuing this line of thought further we get: Number of zeroes between $15! \times 16!... \times 19! = 3 + 3 + 3 + 3 + 3 = 3 \times 5 = 15$. Number of zeroes between $20! \times 21!... \times 24! = 4 \times 5 = 20$. Number of zeroes between $25! \times 26!... \times 29! = 6 \times 5 = 30$. Number of zeroes between $30! \times 31!... \times 34! = 7 \times 5 = 35$. Number of zeroes between $35! \times 36!... \times 39! = 8 \times 5 = 40$. Number of zeroes between $40! \times 41!... \times 44! = 9 \times 5 = 45$. Number of zeroes between $45! \times 46!... \times 49! = 10 \times 5 = 50$.

Number of zeroes for 50! = 12

Thus, the total number of zeroes for the expression $1! \times 2! \times 3! .... \times 50! = 5 + 10 + 15 + 20 + 30 + 35 + 40 + 45 + 50 + 12 = 262$ zeroes. Option (c) is correct.

15. The number of 5's is `15 while the number of 2's is much more. Option (b) is correct.

16. The number of zeroes would depend on the number of 5's in the value of the factorial.

    100! would end in $20 + 4 = 24$ zeroes

    200! Would end in $40 + 8 + 1 = 49$ zeroes.

    When you multiply the two numbers (one with 24 zeroes and the other with 49 zeroes at it's end), the resultant total would end in $24 + 49 = 73$ zeroes. Option (b) is correct.

Co-Prime or Relatively Prime Numbers Two or more numbers that do not have a common factor are known as co-prime or relatively prime. In other words, these numbers have a highest common factor of unity.

If two numbers m and n are relatively prime and the natural number x is divisible by both m and n independently then the number x is also divisible by mn.

Key Concept 1: The spotting of two numbers as co-prime has a very important implication in the context of the two numbers being in the denominators of fractions.

The concept is again best understood through an example:

Suppose, you are doing an operation of the following format – $M/8 + N/9$ where M & N are integers.

What are the chances of the result being an integer, if M is not divisible by 8 and N is not divisible by 9? A little bit of thought will make you realise that the chances are zero. The reason for this is that 8 and 9 are co-prime and the decimals of co-prime numbers never match each other. **Note:** this will not be the case in the case of:

$$M/3 + N/27.$$

In this case even if 3 and 27 are not dividing M and N respectively, there is a possibility of the values of M and N being such that you have an integral answer.

For instance: $5/3 + 36/27 = 81/27 = 3$

The result will never be integral if the two denominators are co-prime.

Note: This holds true even for expressions of the nature $A/7 – B/6$ etc.

This has huge implications for problem solving especially in the case of solving linear equations related to word based problems. Students are advised to try to use these throughout Blocks I, II and III of this book.

Example: Find all five-digit numbers of the form $34 x 5Y$ that are divisible by 36.

Solution: 36 is a product of two co-primes 4 and 9. Hence, if $34 x 5y$ is divisible by 4 and 9, it will also be divisible by 36. Hence, for divisibility by 4, we have that the value of y can be 2 or 6. Also, if y is 2 the number becomes $34 x 52$. For this to be divisible by 9, the addition of $3 + 4 + x + 5 + 2$ should be divisible by 9. For this x can be 4.

Hence the number 34452 is divisible by 36.

Also for $y = 6$, the number $34 x 56$ will be divisible by 36 when the addition of the digits is divisible by 9. This will happen when x is 0 or 9. Hence, the numbers 34056 and 34956 will be divisible by 36.

Exercise for Self-practice

Find all numbers of the form $56x3y$ that are divisible by 36.
Find all numbers of the form $72xy$ that are divisible by 45.
Find all numbers of the form $135xy$ that are divisible by 45.
Find all numbers of the form $517xy$ that are divisible by 89.

Divisibility Rules

Divisibility by 2 or 5: A number is divisible by 2 or 5 if the last digit is divisible by 2 or 5.

Divisibility by 3 (or 9): All such numbers the sum of whose digits are divisible by 3 (or 9) are divisible by 3 (or 9).

Divisibility by 4: A number is divisible by 4 if the last 2 digits are divisible by 4.

Divisibility by 6: A number is divisible by 6 if it is simultaneously divisible by 2 and 3.

Divisibility by 8: A number is divisible by 8 if the last 3 digits of the number are divisible by 8.

Divisibility by 11: A number is divisible by 11 if the difference of the sum of the digits in the odd places and the sum of the digits in the even places is zero or is divisible by 11.

Divisibility by 12: All numbers divisible by 3 and 4 are divisible by 12.

Divisibility by 7, 11 or 13: The integer n is divisible by 7, 11 or 13 if and only if the difference of the number of its thousands and the remainder of its division by 1000 is divisible by 7, 11 or 13.

For Example: 473312 is divisible by 7 since the difference between $473 – 312 = 161$ is divisible by 7.

Even Numbers: All integers that are divisible by 2 are even numbers. They are also denoted by $2n$.

Example: 2, 4, 6, 12, 122, –2, –4, –12.
Also note that zero is an even number.
2 is the lowest positive even number.

Odd Numbers: All integers that are not divisible by 2 are odd numbers. Odd number leave a remainder of 1 on being divided by 2. They are denoted by $2n + 1$ or $2n - 1$. Lowest positive odd number is 1.

Example: $-1, -3, -7, -35, 3, 11$, etc.

Complex Numbers: The arithmetic combination of real numbers and imaginary numbers are called complex numbers.

Alternately: All numbers of the form $a + ib$, where $i = \sqrt{-1}$ are called complex number.

Twin Primes: A pair of prime numbers are said to be twin prime when they differ by 2.

Example: 3 and 5 are Twin Primes, so also are 11 and 13.

Perfect Numbers: A number n is said to be a perfect number if the sum of all the divisors of n (including n) is equal to $2n$.

Example: $6 = 1 \times 2 \times 3$ sum of the divisors $= 1 + 2 + 3 + 6 = 12 = 2 \times 6$

$$28 = 1, 2, 4, 7, 14, 28, = 56 = 2 \times 28$$

Task for student: Find all perfect numbers below 1000.

Mixed Numbers: A number that has both an integral and a fractional part is known as a mixed number.

Triangular Numbers: A number which can be represented as the sum of consecutive natural numbers starting with 1 are called as triangular numbers.

e.g.: $1 + 2 + 3 + 4 = 10$. So, 10 is a triangular number.

Certain Rules

1. Of n consecutive whole numbers $a, a + 1 \ldots a + n - 1$, one and only one is divisible by n.
2. *Mixed numbers:* A number that has both the integral and fractional part is known as mixed number.
3. If a number n can be represented as the product of two numbers p and q, that is, $n = p \cdot q$, then we say that the number n is divisible by p and by q and each of the numbers p and q is a divisor of the number n. Also, each factor of p and q would be a divisor of n.
4. Any number n can be represented in the decimal system of numbers as
$N = a_k \times 10^k + a_{k-1} \times 10^{k-1} + \ldots + a_i \times 10 + a_0$
   Example: 2738 can be written as: $2 \times 10^3 + 7 \times 10^2 + 3 \times 10^1 + 8 \times 10^0$.
5. 3^n will always have an even number of tens. (Example: 2 in 27,8 in 81,24 in 243,72 in 729 and so on.)

Contd

Certain Rules (*Contd*)

6. A sum of 5 consecutive whole numbers will always be divisible by 5.
7. The difference between 2 two digit numbers: $(xy) - (yx)$ will be divisible by 9
8. The square of an odd number when divided by 8 will always leave a remainder of 1.
9. The product of 3 consecutive natural numbers is divisible by 6.
10. The product of 3 consecutive natural numbers the first of which is even is divisible by 24.
11. Products:
    Odd $\times$ odd = odd
    Odd $\times$ even = even
    Even $\times$ even = even
12. All numbers not divisible by 3 have the property that their square will have a remainder of 1 when divided by 3.
13. $(a^2 + b^2)/(b^2 + c^2) = (a^2/b^2)$ if $a/b = b/c$.
14. The product of any r consecutive integers (numbers) is divisible by $r!$
15. If m and n are two integers then $(m + n)!$ is divisible by $m!n!$
16. Difference between any number and the number obtained by writing the digits in reverse order is divisible by 9. (for any number of digits)
17. Any number written in the form $10^n - 1$ is divisible by 3 and 9.
18. If a numerical expression contains no parentheses, first the operations of the third stage (involution or raising a number to a power) are performed, then the operations of the second stage (multiplication and division) and, finally, the operations of the first stage (addition and subtraction) are performed. In this case the operations of one and the same stage are performed in the sequence indicated by the notation. If an expression contains parentheses, then the operation indicated in the parentheses are to be performed first and then all the remaining operations. In this case operations of the numbers in parentheses as well as standing without parentheses are performed in the order indicated above.
   If a fractional expression is evaluated, then the operations indicated in the numerator and denominator of the function are performed and the first result is divided by the second.
19. $(a)^n/(a + 1)$ leaves a remainder of
    a if n is odd
    1 if n is even
20. $(a + 1)^n/a$ will always give a remainder of 1.
21. For any natural number n, n^5 has the same units digit as n has.

Contd

22. For any natural number: $n^3 - n$ is divisible by 6.
23. The remainder of $\dfrac{1 \times 2 \times 3 \times 4 \times \cdots (n-1)}{n}$ gives a remainder of $(n-1)$

THE REMAINDER THEOREM

Consider the following question:

$$17 \times 23.$$

Suppose you have to find the remainder of this expression when divided by 12.

We can write this as:

$$17 \times 23 = (12 + 5) \times (12 + 11)$$

Which when expanded gives us:

$$12 \times 12 + 12 \times 11 + 5 \times 12 + 5 \times 11$$

You will realise that, when this expression is divided by 12, the remainder will only depend on the last term above:

Thus, $\dfrac{12 \times 12 + 12 \times 11 + 5 \times 12 + 5 \times 11}{12}$ gives the same

remainder as $\dfrac{5 \times 11}{12}$

Hence, 7.

This is the remainder when 17×23 is divided by 12.

Learning Point: In order to find the remainder of 17×23 when divided by 12, you need to look at the individual remainders of 17 and 23 when divided by 12. The respective remainders (5 and 11) will give you the remainder of the original expression when divided by 12. Mathematically, this can be written as:

The remainder of the expression $[A \times B \times C + D \times E]/M$, will be the same as the remainder of the expression $[A_R \times B_R \times C_R + D_R \times E_R]/M$.

Where A_R is the remainder when A is divided by M,

B_R is the remainder when B is divided by M,

C_R is the remainder when C is divided by M

D_R is the remainder when D is divided by M and

E_R is the remainder when E is divided by M,

We call this transformation as the remainder theorem transformation and denote it by the sign $\xrightarrow{R}$

Thus, the remainder of

$1421 \times 1423 \times 1425$ when divided by 12 can be given as:

$$\dfrac{1421 \times 1423 \times 1425}{12} \xrightarrow{R} \dfrac{5 \times 7 \times 9}{12} = \dfrac{35 \times 9}{12}$$

$$\xrightarrow{R} \dfrac{11 \times 9}{12}.$$

$$\xrightarrow{R} \text{ gives us a remainder of 3.}$$

In the above question, we have used a series of remainder theorem transformations (denoted by $\xrightarrow{R}$) and equality transformations to transform a difficult looking expression into a simple expression.

Try to solve the following questions on Remainder theorem:

Find the remainder in each of the following cases:

1. $17 \times 23 \times 126 \times 38$ divided by 8.
2. $243 \times 245 \times 247 \times 249 \times 251$ divided by 12.
3. $\dfrac{173 \times 261}{13} + \dfrac{248 \times 249 \times 250}{15}.$
4. $\dfrac{1021 \times 2021 \times 3021}{14}.$
5. $\dfrac{37 \times 43 \times 51}{7} + \dfrac{137 \times 143 \times 151}{9}.$

USING NEGATIVE REMAINDERS

Consider the following question:

Find the remainder when: 14×15 is divided by 8.

The obvious approach in this case would be

$$\dfrac{14 \times 15}{8} \xrightarrow{R} \dfrac{6 \times 7}{8} = \dfrac{42}{8} \xrightarrow{R} 2 \text{ (Answer).}$$

However there is another option by which you can solve the same question:

When 14 is divided by 8, the remainder is normally seen as $+ 6$. However, there might be times when using the negative value of the remainder might give us more convenience. Which is why you should know the following process:

Concept Note: Remainders by definition are always non-negative. Hence, even when we divide a number like $- 27$ by 5 we say that the remainder is 3 (and not $- 2$). However, looking at the negative value of the remainder—it has its own advantages in Mathematics as it results in reducing calculations.

Thus, when a number like 13 is divided by 8, the remainder being 5, the negative remainder is $- 3$.

Note: It is in this context that we mention numbers like 13, 21, 29, etc. as $8n + 5$ or $8n - 3$ numbers.

Thus $\dfrac{14 \times 15}{8}$ will give us $\dfrac{-2 \times -1}{8} \; R \to 2.$

Consider the advantage this process will give you in the following question:

$$\dfrac{51 \times 52}{53} \xrightarrow{R} \dfrac{-2 \times -1}{53} \xrightarrow{R} 2.$$

(The alternative will involve long calculations. Hence, the principle is that you should use negative remainders wherever you can. They can make life much simpler!!!)

What if the Answer Comes Out Negative

For instance, $\dfrac{62 \times 63 \times 64}{66} \xrightarrow{R} \dfrac{-4 \times -3 \times -2}{66} \; R \rightarrow \dfrac{-24}{66}$.

But, we know that a remainder of –24, equals a remainder of 42 when divided by 66. Hence, the answer is 42.

Of course nothing stops you from using positive and negative remainders at the same time in order to solve the same question –

Thus $\dfrac{17 \times 19}{9} \xrightarrow{R} \dfrac{(-1) \times (1)}{9} \; R \rightarrow -1 \; R \rightarrow 8$.

Dealing with large powers There are two tools which are effective in order to deal with large powers –

(A) If you can express the expression in the form $\dfrac{(ax+1)^n}{a}$, the remainder will become 1 directly. In such a case, no matter how large the value of the power n is, the remainder is 1.

For instance, $\dfrac{\left(37^{12635}\right)}{9} \xrightarrow{R} \dfrac{\left(1^{12635}\right)}{9} \xrightarrow{R} 1$.

In such a case the value of the power does not matter.

(B) $\dfrac{(ax-1)^n}{a}$. In such a case using –1 as the remainder it will be evident that the remainder will be +1 if n is even and it will be –1 (Hence $a - 1$) when n is odd.

e.g.: $\dfrac{31^{127}}{8} \xrightarrow{R} \dfrac{(-1)^{127}}{8} \xrightarrow{R} \dfrac{(-1)}{8} \xrightarrow{R} 7$

ANOTHER IMPORTANT POINT

Suppose you were asked to find the remainder of 14 divided by 4. It is clearly visible that the answer should be 2.

But consider the following process:

$14/4 = 7/2 \xrightarrow{R} 1$ (The answer has changed!!)

What has happened?
We have transformed 14/4 into 7/2 by dividing the numerator and the denominator by 2. The result is that the original remainder 2 is also divided by 2 giving us 1 as the remainder. In order to take care of this problem, we need to reverse the effect of the division of the remainder by 2. This is done by multiplying the final remainder by 2 to get the correct answer.

Note: In any question on remainder theorem, you should try to cancel out parts of the numerator and denominator as much as you can, since it directly reduces the calculations required.

AN APPLICATION OF REMAINDER THEOREM

Finding the last two digits of an expression:

Suppose you had to find the last 2 digits of the expression:

$$22 \times 31 \times 44 \times 27 \times 37 \times 43$$

The remainder the above expression will give when it is divided by 100 is the answer to the above question.

Hence, to answer the question above find the remainder of the expression when it is divided by 100.

Solution: $\dfrac{22 \times 31 \times 44 \times 27 \times 37 \times 43}{100}$

$= \dfrac{22 \times 31 \times 11 \times 27 \times 37 \times 43}{25}$ (on dividing by 4)

$\xrightarrow{R} \dfrac{22 \times 6 \times 11 \times 2 \times 12 \times 18}{25} = \dfrac{132 \times 22 \times 216}{25}$

$\xrightarrow{R} \dfrac{7 \times 22 \times 16}{25}$

$= \dfrac{154 \times 16}{25} \xrightarrow{R} \dfrac{4 \times 16}{25} \xrightarrow{R} 14$

Thus the remainder being 14, (after division by 4). The actual remainder should be 56.

[Don't forget to multiply by 4 !!]

Hence, the last 2 digits of the answer will be 56.

Using negative remainders here would have helped further.

Note: Similarly finding the last three digits of an expression means finding the remainder when the expression is divided by 1000.

Exercise for Self-practice

1. Find the remainder when 73 + 75 + 78 + 57 + 197 is divided by 34.
   (a) 32
   (b) 4
   (c) 15
   (d) 28

2. Find the remainder when 73 × 75 × 78 × 57 × 197 is divided by 34.
   (a) 22
   (b) 30
   (c) 15
   (d) 28

3. Find the remainder when 73 × 75 × 78 × 57 × 197 × 37 is divided by 34.
   (a) 32
   (b) 30
   (c) 15
   (d) 28

4. Find the remainder when 43^{197} is divided by 7.
   (a) 2
   (b) 4
   (c) 6
   (d) 1

5. Find the remainder when 51^{203} is divided by 7.
   (a) 4   (b) 2
   (c) 1   (d) 6

6. Find the remainder when 59^{28} is divided by 7.
   (a) 2   (b) 4
   (c) 6   (d) 1

7. Find the remainder when 67^{99} is divided by 7.
   (a) 2   (b) 4
   (c) 6   (d) 1

8. Find the remainder when 75^{80} is divided by 7.
   (a) 4   (b) 3
   (c) 2   (d) 6

9. Find the remainder when 41^{77} is divided by 7.
   (a) 2   (b) 1
   (c) 6   (d) 4

10. Find the remainder when 21^{875} is divided by 17.
   (a) 8   (b) 13
   (c) 16   (d) 9

11. Find the remainder when 54^{124} is divided by 17.
   (a) 4   (b) 5
   (c) 13   (d) 15

12. Find the remainder when 83^{261} is divided by 17.
   (a) 13   (b) 9
   (c) 8   (d) 2

13. Find the remainder when 25^{102} is divided by 17.
   (a) 13   (b) 15
   (c) 4   (d) 2

ANSWER KEY

1. (b)   2. (a)   3. (a)   4. (d)   5. (a)
6. (b)   7. (d)   8. (a)   9. (c)   10. (b)
11. (a)   12. (d)   13. (c)

Solutions

1. The remainder would be given by: $(5 + 7 + 10 + 23 + 27)/34 = 72/34 \rightarrow$ remainder = 4. Option (b) is correct.

2. The remainder would be given by: $(5 \times 7 \times 10 \times 23 \times 27)/34 \rightarrow 35 \times 230 \times 27/34 \rightarrow 1 \times 26 \times 27/34 = 702/34 \rightarrow$ remainder = 22. Option (a) is correct.

3. The remainder would be given by: $(5 \times 7 \times 10 \times 23 \times 27 \times 3)/34 \rightarrow 35 \times 230 \times 27 \times 3/34 \rightarrow 1 \times 26 \times 81/34 \rightarrow 26 \times 13/34 = 338/34 \rightarrow$ remainder = 32. Option (a) is correct.

4. $43^{197}/7 \rightarrow 1^{197}/7 \rightarrow$ remainder =1. Option (d) is correct.

5. $51^{203}/7 \rightarrow 2^{203}/7 = (2^3)^{67} \times 2^2/7 = 8^{67} \times 4/7 \rightarrow$ remainder = 4. Option (a) is correct.

6. $59^{28}/7 \rightarrow 3^{28}/7 = (3^6)^4 \times 3^4/7 = 729^6 \times 81/7 \rightarrow$ remainder = 4. Option (b) is correct.

7. $67^{99}/7 \rightarrow 4^{99}/7 = (4^3)^{33}/7 = 64^{33}/7 \rightarrow$ remainder = 1. Option (d) is correct.

8. $75^{80}/7 \rightarrow 5^{80}/7 = (5^6)^{13} \times 5^2/7 \rightarrow 1^{13} \times 25/7 \rightarrow$ remainder = 4. Option (a) is correct.

9. $41^{77}/7 \rightarrow 6^{77}/7 \rightarrow$ remainder = 6 (as the expression is in the form $a^n/(a + 1)$. Option (c) is correct.

10. $21^{875}/17 \rightarrow 4^{875}/17 = (4^4)^n \times 4^3/17 = 256^n \times 64/17 \rightarrow 1^n \times 13/17 \rightarrow$ remainder =13. Option (b) is correct.

11. $54^{124}/17 \rightarrow 3^{124}/17$. At this point, like in each of the other questions solved above, we need to plan the power of 3 which would give us a convenient remainder of either 1 or –1. As we start to look for remainders that powers of 3 would have when divided by 17, we get that at the power 3^6 the remainder is 15. If we convert this to –2 we will get that at the fourth power of 3^6, we should get a 16/17 situation (as $-2 \times -2 \times -2 \times -2 = 16$). This means that at a power of 3^{24} we are getting a remainder of 16 or –1. Naturally then if we double the power to 3^{48}, the remainder would be 1.
With this thinking we can restart solving the problem: $3^{124}/17 = 3^{48} \times 3^{48} \times 3^{24} \times 3^4/17 \rightarrow 1 \times 1 \times 16 \times 81/17 \rightarrow 16 \times 13/17 = 208/17 \rightarrow$ remainder = 4. Option (a) is correct.
(Note that if we are dividing a number by 17 and if we see the remainder as 15, we can logically say that the remainder is –2 – even though negative remainders are not allowed in mathematics)

12. Using the logic developed in Question 11 above, we have $83^{261}/17 \rightarrow 15^{261}/17 \rightarrow (-2)^{261}/17 \rightarrow (-2^4)^{65} \times (-2)/17 \rightarrow 16^{65} \times (-2)/17 \rightarrow (-1) \times (-2)/17 \rightarrow$ remainder = 2. Option (d) is correct.

13. $25^{102}/17 \rightarrow 8^{102}/17 = 2^{306}/17 = (2^4)^{76} \times 2^2/17 \rightarrow 16^{76} \times 4/17 \rightarrow 1 \times 4/17 \rightarrow$ remainder = 4. Option (c) is correct.

🔊 BASE SYSTEM

All the work that we carry out with numbers is called as the decimal system. In other words we work in the decimal system. Why is it called decimal?? It is because there are 10 digits in the system 0–9.

However, depending on the number of digits contained in the base system other number systems are also possible. Thus a number system with base 2 is called the binary number system and will have only two digits 0 and 1. Some of the most commonly used systems are: Binary (base 2), Octal (base 8), Hexadecimal (base 16).

Binary system has 2 digits : 0, 1. Octal has 8 digits : – 0, 1, 2, 3, ⋯ 7.

Hexadecimal has 16 digits – 0, 1, 2, ⋯ 9, A, B, C, D, E, F. Where A has a value 10, $B = 11$ and so on.

Before coming to the questions asked under this category, let us first look at a few issues with regard to converting numbers between different base systems.

1. Conversion from any base system into decimal:

Suppose you have to write the decimal equivalent of the base 8 number 146_8.

In such a case, follow the following structure for conversion:

$$146_8 = 1 \times 8^2 + 4 \times 8^1 + 6 \times 8^0$$
$$= 64 + 32 + 6 = 102.$$

Note: If you remember the process, for writing the value of any random number, say 146, in our decimal system (base 10) we use: $1 \times 10^2 + 4 \times 10^1 + 6 \times 10^0$. All you need to change, in case you are trying to write the value of the number in base 8, is that you replace 10 with 8 in every power.

Try to write the decimal equivalents of the following numbers:

143_5, 143_6, 143_7, 143_8, 143_9
1256_7, 1256_8, 1256_9.

2. Conversion of a number in decimals into any base:

Suppose you have to find out the value of the decimal number 347 in base 6. The following process is to be adopted:

Step 1: Find the highest power of the base (6 in this case) that is contained in 347. In this case you will realise that the value of $6^3 = 216$ is contained in 347, while the value of $6^4 = 1296$ is not contained in 347. Hence, we realise that the highest power of 6 contained in 347 is 3. This should make you realise that the number has to be constructed by using the powers 6^0, 6^1, 6^2, 6^3 respectively. Hence, a 4-digit number.

Structure of number: – – – –

Step 2: We now need to investigate how many times each of the powers of 6 is contained in 347. For this we first start with the highest power as found above. Thus we can see that 6^3 (216) is contained in 347 once. Hence our number now becomes:

1 – – –

That is, we now know that the first digit of the number is 1. Besides, when we have written the number 1 in this place, we have accounted for a value of 216 out of 347. This leaves us with 131 to account for.

We now need to look for the number of times 6^2 is contained in 131. We can easily see that $6^2 = 36$ is contained in 131 three times. Thus, we write 3 as the next digit of our number which will now look like:

1 3 – –

In other words we now know that the first two digits of the number are 13. Besides, when we have written the number 3 in this place, we have accounted for a value of 108 out of 131 which was left to be accounted for. This leaves us with 131–108 = 23 to account for.

We now need to look for the number of times 6^1 is contained in 23. We can easily see that $6^1 = 6$ is contained in 23

three times. Thus, we write 3 as the next digit of our number which will now look like:

1 3 3 –

In other words we now know that the first three digits of the number are 133. Besides, when we have written the number 3 in this place, we have accounted for a value of 18 out of the 23 which was left to be accounted for. This leaves us with 23 – 18 = 5 to account for.

The last digit of the number corresponds to $6^0 = 1$. In order to make a value of 5 in this place we will obviously need to use this power of 6, 5 times thus giving us the final digit as 5. Hence, our number is:

1 3 3 5.

A few points you should know about base systems:

(1) In single digits there is no difference between the value of the number—whichever base we take. For example, the equality $5_6 = 5_7 = 5_8 = 5_9 = 5_{10}$.

(2) Suppose you have a number in base x. When you convert this number into its decimal value, the value should be such that when it is divided by x, the remainder should be equal to the units digit of the number in base x.

In other words, 342_8 will be a number of the form $8n + 2$ in base 10. You can use this principle for checking your conversion calculations.

The following table gives a list of decimal values and their binary, octal and hexadecimal equivalents:

Decimal	Binary	Octal	Hexadecimal
0	0	0	0
1	1	1	1
2	10	2	2
3	11	3	3
4	100	4	4
5	101	5	5
6	110	6	6
7	111	7	7
8	1000	10	8
9	1001	11	9
10	1010	12	A
11	1011	13	B

Illustrations

1. The number of x digit numbers in nth base system will be
   (a) n^x (b) $n^x - 1$
   (c) $n^x - n$ (d) $n^x - n^{(x-1)}$

Solution Base $\to n$, digit $\to x$

So, required number of numbers = $n^x - n^{(x-1)}$

2. The number of 2 digit numbers in binary system is
   (a) 2   (b) 90
   (c) 10   (d) 4

Solution By using the formula, we get the required number of numbers = $2^2 - 2^1 = 2$

$\Rightarrow$ Option (a)

3. The number of 5 digit numbers in binary system is
    (a) 48
    (b) 16
    (c) 32
    (d) 20

Solution Required number of numbers = $2^5 - 2^4 = 32 - 16 = 16$

$\Rightarrow$ Option (b)

4. I celebrate my birthday on 12th January on earth. On which date would I have to celebrate my birthday if I were on a planet where binary system is being used for counting. (The number of days, months and years are same on both the planets.)
    (a) 11th Jan
    (b) 111th Jan
    (c) 110th Jan
    (d) 1100th Jan

Solution On earth (decimal system is used). 12th Jan $\Rightarrow$ 12th Jan

The 12th day on the planet where binary system is being used will be called

$(12)_{10} = (?)_2$

$= \dfrac{1}{2^3} \dfrac{1}{2^2} \dfrac{0}{2^1} \dfrac{0}{2^0}$

i.e., 1100th day on that planet

So, 12th January on earth = 1100th January on that planet

$\Rightarrow$ Option (d)

5. My year of birth is 1982. What would the year have been instead of 1982 if base 12 were used (for counting) instead of decimal system?
    (a) 1182
    (b) 1022
    (c) 2082
    (d) 1192

Solution The required answer will equal to $(1982)_{10} = (?)_{12}$.

$= \dfrac{1}{12^3} \dfrac{1}{12^2} \dfrac{9}{12^1} \dfrac{2}{12^0} \rightarrow$

$1 \times 12^3 + 1 \times 12^2 + 9 \times 12^1 + 2 \times 9^0 = 1728 + 144 + 108 + 2 = 1982$

Hence, the number $(1192)_{12}$ represents 1982 in our base system.

$\Rightarrow$ Option (d)

6. 203 in base 5 when converted to base 8, becomes
    (a) 61
    (b) 53
    (c) 145
    (d) 65

Solution $(203)_5 = (?)_{10}$

$= 2 \times 5^2 + 0 \times 5^1 + 3 \times 5^0$
$= 50 + 0 + 3 = 53$

Now,

$(53)_{10} = (?)8$

$= \dfrac{6}{8^1} \dfrac{5}{8^0}$

$= (203)_5 = (65)_8$

$\Rightarrow$ Option (d)

7. $(52)_7 + 46_8 = (?)_{10}$
    (a) $(75)_{10}$
    (b) $(50)_{10}$
    (c) $(39)_{39}$
    (d) $(28)_{10}$

Solution $(52)_7 = (5 \times 7^1 + 2 \times 7^0)_{10} = (37)_{10}$

also, $(46)_8 = (4 \times 8^1 + 6 \times 8^0)_{10} = (38)_{10}$

sum $= (75)_{10}$

$\Rightarrow$ Option (a)

8. $(23)_5 + (47)_9 = (?)_8$
    (a) 70
    (b) 35
    (c) 64
    (d) 18

Solution $(23)_5 = (2 \times 5^1 + 3 \times 5^0)_{10} = (13)_{10} = (1 \times 8^1 + 5 \times 8^0)_8 = (15)_8$

also, $(47)_9 = (4 \times 9^1 + 7 \times 9^0)_{10} = (43)_{10}$
$= (5 \times 8^1 + 3 \times 8^0)_8 = (53)_8$

sum $= (13)_{10} + (43)_{10} = (56)_{10} \rightarrow (70)_8$

$\Rightarrow$ Option (a)

9. $(11)_2 + (22)_3 + (33)_4 + (44)_5 + (55)_6 + (66)_7 + (77)_8 + (88)_9 = (?)_{10}$
    (a) 396
    (b) 276
    (c) 250
    (d) 342

Solution $(11)_2 = (1 \times 2^1 + 1 \times 2^0)_{10} = (3)_{10}$

$(22)_3 = (2 \times 3^1 + 2 \times 3^0)_{10} = (8)_{10}$

$(33)_4 = (3 \times 4^1 + 3 \times 4^0)_{10} = (15)_{10}$

$(44)_5 = (4 \times 5^1 + 4 \times 5^0)_{10} = (24)_{10}$

$(55)_6 = (5 \times 6^1 + 5 \times 6^0)_{10} = (35)_{10}$

$(66)_7 = (6 \times 7^1 + 6 \times 7^0)_{10} = (48)_{10}$

$(77)_8 = (7 \times 8^1 + 7 \times 8^0)_{10} = (63)_{10}$

$(88)_9 = (8 \times 9^1 + 8 \times 9^0)_{10} = (80)_{10}$

sum $= (276)_{10}$

$\Rightarrow$ Option (b)

10. $(24)_5 \times (32)_5 = (?)_5$
    (a) 1423
    (b) 1422
    (c) 1420
    (d) 1323

Solution $(24)_5 = 14_{10}$ and $32_5 = 17_{10}$. Hence, the required answer can be got by $14 \times 17 = 238_{10} = 1 \times 5^3 + 4 \times 5^2 + 2 \times 5^1 + 3 \times 5^0 \rightarrow 1423$ as the correct answer.

Alternately, you could multiply directly in base 5 as follows:

$$
\begin{array}{r}
(2\ 4) \\
\times (3\ 2) \\
\hline
(1\ 4\ 2\ 3)
\end{array}
$$

Unit's digit of the answer would correspond to: $4 \times 2 = 8 \rightarrow 13_5$. Hence, we write 3 in the units place and carry over 1.

(Note that in this process when we are doing 4×2 we are effectively multiplying individual digits of one number with individual digits of the other number. In such a case we can write $4 \times 2 = 8$ by assuming that both the numbers are in decimal system as the value of a single digit in any base is equal.)

The tens digit will be got by: $2 \times 2 + 4 \times 3 = 16 + 1 = 17 \rightarrow 32_5$

Hence, we write 2 in the tens place and carry over 3 to the hundreds place.

Where we get $3 \times 2 + 3 = 9 \rightarrow 14$

Hence, the answer is 14.

$\Rightarrow$ Option (a)

11. In base 8, the greatest four digit perfect square is
   (a) 9801   (b) 1024
   (c) 8701   (d) 7601

Solution In base 10, the greatest 4 digit perfect square = 9801

In base 9, the greatest 4 digits perfect square = 8701

In base 8, the greatest 4 digits perfect square = 7601

Alternately, multiply $(77)_8 \times (77)_8$ to get 7601 as the answer.

Unit's Digit

(A) The unit's digit of an expression can be calculated by getting the remainder while the expression is divided by 10.

Thus for example if we have to find the units digit of the expression:

$$17 \times 22 \times 36 \times 54 \times 27 \times 31 \times 63$$

We try to find the remainder –

$$\frac{17 \times 22 \times 36 \times 54 \times 27 \times 31 \times 63}{10}$$

$$\xrightarrow{R} \frac{7 \times 2 \times 6 \times 4 \times 7 \times 3}{10}$$

$$= \frac{14 \times 24 \times 21}{10} \xrightarrow{R} \frac{4 \times 4 \times 1}{10} = \frac{16}{10} \xrightarrow{R} 6.$$

Hence, the required answer is 6.

This could have been directly got by multiplying: $7 \times 2 \times 6 \times 4 \times 7 \times 1 \times 3$ and only accounting for the units' digit.

(B) Unit's digits in the contexts of powers – Study the following table carefully.

Unit's digit when 'N' is raised to a power

Number Ending With	Value of power								
	1	2	3	4	5	6	7	8	9
1	1	1	1	1	1	1	1	1	1
2	2	4	8	6	2	4	8	6	2
3	3	9	7	1	3	9	7	1	3
4	4	6	4	6	4	6	4	6	4
5	5	5	5	5	5	5	5	5	5

Contd

Number Ending With	Value of power								
	1	2	3	4	5	6	7	8	9
6	6	6	6	6	6	6	6	6	6
7	7	9	3	1	7	9	3	1	7
8	8	4	2	6	8	4	2	6	8
9	9	1	9	1	9	1	9	1	9
0	0	0	0	0	0	0	0	0	0

In the table above, if you look at the columns corresponding to the power 5 or 9 you will realize that the unit's digit for all numbers is repeated (i.e. it is 1 for 1, 2 for, 3 for 3….9 for 9.)

This means that whenever we have any number whose unit's digit is 'x' and it is raised to a power of the form $4n + 1$, the value of the unit's digit of the answer will be the same as the original units digit.

Illustrations: $(1273)^{101}$ will give a unit's digit of 3. $(1547)^{25}$ will give a units digit of 7 and so forth.

Thus, the above table can be modified into the form –

Value of Power

Number ending in	If the value of the Power is			
	4n + 1	4n + 2	4n + 3	4n
1	1	1	1	1
2	2	4	8	6
3	3	9	7	1
4	4	6	4	6
5	5	5	5	5
6	6	6	6	6
7	7	9	3	1
8	8	4	2	6
9	9	1	9	1

[Remember, at this point that we had said (in the Back to School section of Part 1) that all natural numbers can be expressed in the form $4n + x$. Hence, with the help of the logic that helps us build this table, we can easily derive the units digit of any number when it is raised to a power.)

A special Case

Question: What will be the unit's digit of $(1273)^{122!}$?

Solution: 122! is a number of the form $4n$. Hence, the answer should be 1. [**Note:** 1 here is derived by thinking of it as 3 (for $4n + 1$), 9 (for $4n + 2$), 7 (for $4n + 3$), 1 (for $4n$)]

Exercise for Self-practice

Find the Units digit in each of the following cases:
1. $2^2 \times 4^4 \times 6^6 \times 8^8$
2. $1^1 \times 2^2 \times 3^3 \times 4^4 \times 5^5 \times 6^6 \dots \times 100^{100}$

3. $17 \times 23 \times 51 \times 32 + 15 \times 17 \times 16 \times 22$
4. $13 \times 17 \times 22 \times 34 + 12 \times 6 \times 4 \times 3 - 13 \times 33$
5. $37^{123} \times 43^{144} \times 57^{226} \times 32^{127} \times 52^{51}$
6. $67 \times 37 \times 43 \times 91 \times 42 \times 33 \times 42$

   (a) 2   (b) 6
   (c) 8   (d) 4

7. $67 \times 35 \times 43 \times 91 \times 47 \times 33 \times 49$

   (a) 1   (b) 9
   (c) 5   (d) 6

8. $67 \times 35 \times 45 \times 91 \times 42 \times 33 \times 81$

   (a) 2   (b) 4
   (c) 0   (d) 8

9. $67 \times 35 \times 45 + 91 \times 42 \times 33 \times 82$

   (a) 8   (b) 7
   (c) 0   (d) 5

10. $(52)^{97} \times (43)^{72}$

   (a) 2   (b) 6
   (c) 8   (d) 4

11. $(55)^{75} \times (93)^{175} \times (107)^{275}$

   (a) 7   (b) 3
   (c) 5   (d) 0

12. $(173)^{45} \times (152)^{77} \times (777)^{999}$

   (a) 2   (b) 4
   (c) 8   (d) 6

13. $81 \times 82 \times 83 \times 84 \times 86 \times 87 \times 88 \times 89$

   (a) 0   (b) 6
   (c) 2   (d) 4

14. $82^{43} \times 83^{44} \times 84^{97} \times 86^{98} \times 87^{105} \times 88^{94}$

   (a) 2   (b) 6
   (c) 4   (d) 8

15. $432 \times 532 + 532 \times 974 + 537 \times 531 + 947 \times 997$

   (a) 5   (b) 6
   (c) 9   (d) 8

ANSWER KEY

6. (d)   7. (c)   8. (c)   9. (b)   10. (a)
11. (c)   12. (c)   13. (b)   14. (b)   15. (d)

Solutions

1. The units digit would be given by the units digit of the multiplication of $4 \times 6 \times 6 \times 6 = 4$
2. 0
3. $7 \times 3 \times 1 \times 2 + 0 \to 2 + 0 = 2$
4. $8 + 4 - 9 \to 3$
5. $3 \times 1 \times 9 \times 8 \times 6 = 6$
6. $7 \times 7 \times 3 \times 1 \times 2 \times 3 \times 2 = 4$
7. Since we have a 5 multiplied with odd numbers, the units digit would naturally be 5.
8. $5 \times 2 \to 0$
9. $5 + 2 \to 7$
10. $2 \times 1 \to 2$
11. $5 \times 7 \times 3 \to 5$
12. $3 \times 2 \times 3 \to 8$
13. $2 \times 3 \times 4 \times 6 \times 7 \times 8 \times 9 \to 6$
14. $8 \times 1 \times 4 \times 6 \times 7 \times 4 \to 6$
15. $4 + 8 + 7 + 9 \to 8$

Space for Notes

⊙ WORKED-OUT PROBLEMS

Problem 1.1 Find the number of zeroes in the factorial of the number 18.

Solution 18! contains 15 and 5, which combined with one even number give zeroes. Also, 10 is also contained in 18!, which will give an additional zero. Hence, 18! contains 3 zeroes and the last digit will always be zero.

Problem 1.2 Find the numbers of zeroes in 27!

Solution $27! = 27 \times 26 \times 25 \times \ldots \times 20 \times \ldots \times 15 \times \ldots \times 10 \times \ldots \times 5 \times \ldots \times 1$.

A zero can be formed by combining any number containing 5 multiplied by any even number. Similarly, everytime a number ending in zero is found in the product, it will add an additional zero. For this problem, note that $25 = 5 \times 5$ will give 2 zeroes and zeroes will also be got by 20, 15, 10 and 5. Hence 27! will have 6 zeroes.

Short-cut method: Number of zeroes is $27! \rightarrow [27/5] + [27/25]$ where $[x]$ indicates the integer just lower than the fraction Hence, $[27/5] = 5$ and $[27/5^2] = 1$, 6 zeroes

Problem 1.3 Find the number of zeroes in 137!

Solution $[137/5] + [137/5^2] + [137/5^3]$
$= 27 + 5 + 1 = 33$ zeroes
(since the restriction on the number of zeroes is due to the number of fives.)

Exercise for Self-practice

Find the number of zeroes in

   (a) 81!   (b) 100!   (c) 51!

Answers

   (a) 19   (b) 24   (c) 12

Problem 1.4 What exact power of 5 divides 87!?
Solution $[87/5] + [87/25] = 17 + 3 = 20$

Problem 1.5 What power of 8 exactly divides 25!?

Solution If 8 were a prime number, the answer should be $[25/8] = 3$. But since 8 is not prime, use the following process.

The prime factors of 8 is $2 \times 2 \times 2$. For divisibility by 8, we need three twos. So, everytime we can find 3 twos, we add one to the power of 8 that divides 25! To count how we get 3 twos, we do the following. All even numbers will give one 'two' at least $[25/2] = 12$

Also, all numbers in 25! divisible by 2^2 will give an additional two $[25/2^2] = 6$

Further, all numbers in 25! divisible by 2^3 will give a third two. Hence $[25!/2^3] = 3$

And all numbers in 25! divisible by 2^4 will give a fourth two. Hence $[25!/2^4] = 1$

Hence, total number of twos in 25! is 22. For a number to be divided by 8, we need three twos. Hence, since 25! has 22 twos, it will be divided by 8 seven times.

Problem 1.6 What power of 15 divides 87! exactly?

Solution $15 = 5 \times 3$. Hence, everytime we can form a pair of one 5 and one 3, we will count one.
87! contains $- [87/5] + [87/5^2] = 17 + 3 = 20$ fives

Also 87! contains $- [87/3] + [87/3^2] + [87/3^3] + [87/3^4]$ $= 29 + \ldots$(more than 20 threes).

Hence, 15 will divide 87! twenty times since the restriction on the power is because of the number of 5s and not the number of 3s.

In fact, it is not very difficult to see that in the case of all factors being prime, we just have to look for the highest prime number to provide the restriction for the power of the denominator.

Hence, in this case we did not need to check for anything but the number of 5s.

Exercise for Self-practice

(a) What power of 30 will exactly divide 128!

Hints: $[128/5] + [128/5^2] + [128/5^3]$

(b) What power of 210 will exactly divide 142!

Problem 1.7 Find the last digit in the expression $(36472)^{123!} \times (34767)^{76!}$.

Solution If we try to formulate a pattern for 2 and its powers and their units digit, we see that the units digit for the powers of 2 goes as: 2, 4, 8, 6, 2, 4, 8, 6, 2, 4, 8, 6 and so on. The number 2 when raised to a power of $4n + 1$ will always give a units digit of 2. This also means that the units digit for 2^{4n} will always end in 6. The power of 36472 is 123! . 123! can be written in the form $4n$. Hence, $(36472)^{123!}$ will end in 6.

The second part of the expression is $(34767)^{76!}$. The units digit depends on the power of 7. If we try to formulate a pattern for 7 and its powers and their units digit, we see that the units digit for the powers of 7 go as: 7 9 3 1 7 9 3 1 and so on. This means that the units digit of the expression 7^{4n} will always be 1.

Since 76! can be written as a multiple of 4 as $4n$, we can conclude that the unit's digit in $(34767)^{76!}$ is 1.

Hence the units digit of $(36472)^{123!} \times (34767)^{76!}$ will be 6.

Counting

Problem 1.8 Find the number of numbers between 100 to 200 if

(i) Both 100 and 200 are counted.

(ii) Only one of 100 and 200 is counted.

(iii) Neither 100 nor 200 is counted.

Solution

(i) Both ends included-Solution: $200 - 100 + 1 = 101$

(ii) One end included-Solution: $200 - 100 = 100$

(iii) Both ends excluded-Solution: $200 - 100 - 1 = 99$.

Problem 1.9 Find the number of even numbers between 122 and 242 if:

(i) Both ends are included.

(ii) Only one end is included.

(iii) Neither end is included.

Solution

(i) Both ends included—Solution: $(242 - 122)/2 = 60 + 1 = 61$

(ii) One end included-Solution: $(242 - 122)/2 = 60$

(iii) Both ends excluded-Solution: $(242 - 122)/2 - 1 = 59$

Exercise for Self-practice

(a) Find the number of numbers between 140 to 259, both included, which are divisible by 7.

(b) Find the number of numbers between 100 to 200, that are divisible by 3.

Problem 1.10 Find the number of numbers between 300 to 400 (both included), that are not divisible by 2, 3, 4, and 5.

Solution Total numbers: 101

Step 1: Not divisible by 2 = All even numbers rejected: 51 Numbers left: 50.

Step 2: Of which: divisible by 3 = first number 300, last number 399. But even numbers have already been removed, hence count out only odd numbers between 300 and 400 divisible by 3. This gives us that:

First number 303, last number 399, common difference 6

So, remove: $[(399 - 303)/6] + 1 = 17$.

∴ $50 - 17 = 33$ numbers left.

We do not need to remove additional terms for divisibility by 4 since this would eliminate only even numbers (which have already been eliminated)

Step 3: Remove from 33 numbers left all odd numbers that are divisible by 5 and not divisible by 3.

Between 300 to 400, the first odd number divisible by 5 is 305 and the last is 395 (since both ends are counted, we have 10 such numbers as: $[(395 - 305)/10 + 1 = 10]$.

However, some of these 10 numbers have already been removed to get to 33 numbers.

Operation left: Of these 10 numbers, 305, 315...395, reduce all numbers that are also divisible by 3. Quick perusal shows that the numbers start with 315 and have common difference 30.

Hence [(Last number − First number)/Difference + 1] = $[(375 - 315)/30 + 1] = 3$

These 3 numbers were already removed from the original 100. Hence, for numbers divisible by 5, we need to remove only those numbers that are odd, divisible by 5 but not by 3. There are 7 such numbers between 300 and 400.

So numbers left are: $33 - 7 = 26$.

Exercise for Self-practice

Find the number of numbers between 100 to 400 which are divisible by either 2, 3, 5 and 7.

Problem 1.11 Find the number of zeroes in the following multiplication: $5 \times 10 \times 15 \times 20 \times 25 \times 30 \times 35 \times 40 \times 45 \times 50$.

Solution The number of zeroes depends on the number of fives and the number of twos. Here, close scrutiny shows that the number of twos is the constraint. The expression can be written as

$5 \times (5 \times 2) \times (5 \times 3) \times (5 \times 2 \times 2) \times (5 \times 5) \times (5 \times 2 \times 3) \times (5 \times 7) \times (5 \times 2 \times 2 \times 2) \times (5 \times 3 \times 3) \times (5 \times 5 \times 2)$

Number of 5s − 12, Number of 2s − 8.
Hence: 8 zeroes.

Problem 1.12 Find the remainder for $[(73 \times 79 \times 81)/11]$.

Solution The remainder for the expression: $[(73 \times 79 \times 81)/11]$ will be the same as the remainder for $[(7 \times 2 \times 4)/11]$

That is, $56/11 \Rightarrow$ remainder $= 1$

Problem 1.13 Find the remainder for $(3^{560}/8)$.

Solution $(3^{560}/8) = [(3^2)^{280}/8] = (9^{280}/8)$

$$= [9.9.9...(280 \text{ times})]/8$$

remainder for above expression = remainder for $[1.1.1...(280 \text{ times})]/8 \Rightarrow$ remainder $= 1$.

Problem 1.14 Find the remainder when $(2222^{5555} + 5555^{2222})/7$.

Solution This is of the form: $[(2222^{5555})/7 + (5555^{2222})/7]$

We now proceed to find the individual remainder of : $(2222^{5555})/7$. Let the remainder be R_1.

When 2222 is divided by 7, it leaves a remainder of 3.

Hence, for remainder purpose $(2222^{5555})/7 \xrightarrow{R} (3^{5555}/7)$
$= (3.3^{5554})/7 = [3(3^2)^{2777}]/7 = [3.(7+2)^{2777}]/7 \xrightarrow{R} (3.2^{2777})/7$
$= (3.2^2 \cdot 2^{2775})/7 = [3.2^2 \cdot (2^3)^{925}]/7$
$= [3.2^2 \cdot (8)^{925}]/7 \xrightarrow{R} (12/7)$ Remainder = 5.

Similarly, $(5555^{2222})/7 \xrightarrow{R} (4^{2222})/7 = [(2^2)^{2222}]/7 =$
$(2)^{4444}/7 = (2.2^{4443})/7 = [2.(2^3)^{1481}]/7 = [2.(8)^{1481}]/7 \xrightarrow{R}$
$[2.(1)^{1481}]/7 \rightarrow 2$ (remainder).

Hence, $(2222^{5555})/7 + (5555^{2222})/7 \xrightarrow{R} (5+2)/7 \Rightarrow$
Remainder = 0

Problem 1.15 Find the GCD and the LCM of the numbers 126, 540 and 630.

Solution The standard forms of the numbers are:
$$126 \rightarrow 3 \times 3 \times 7 \times 2 \rightarrow 3^2 \times 7 \times 2$$
$$540 \rightarrow 3 \times 3 \times 3 \times 2 \times 2 \times 5 \rightarrow 2^2 \times 3^3 \times 5$$
$$630 \rightarrow 3 \times 3 \times 5 \times 2 \times 7 \rightarrow 2 \times 3^2 \times 5 \times 7$$

For GCD we use Intersection of prime factors and the lowest power of all factors that appear in all three numbers. $2 \times 3^2 = 18$.

For LCM $\rightarrow$ Union of prime factors and highest power of all factors that appear in any one of the three numbers $\Rightarrow 2^2 \times 3^3 \times 5 \times 7 = 3780$.

Exercise for Self-practice

Find the GCD and the LCM of the following numbers:
  (i) 360, 8400   (ii) 120, 144
  (iii) 275, 180, 372, 156   (iv) 70, 112
  (v) 75, 114   (vi) 544, 720

Problem 1.16 The ratio of the factorial of a number x to the square of the factorial of another number, which when increased by 50% gives the required number, is 1.25. Find the number x.
  (a) 6   (b) 5
  (c) 9   (d) None of these

Solution Solve through options: Check for the conditions mentioned. When we check for option (a) we get $6! = 720$ and $(4!)^2 = 576$ and we have $6!/(4!)^2 = 1.25$, which is the required ratio.

Hence the answer is **(a)**

Problem 1.17 Three numbers A, B and C are such that the difference between the highest and the second highest two-digit numbers formed by using two of A, B and C is 5. Also, the smallest two two-digit numbers differ by 2. If $B > A > C$ then what is the value of B?
  (a) 1   (b) 6   (c) 7   (d) 8

Solution Since B is the largest digit, option (a) is rejected. Check for option (b).

If B is 6, then the two largest two-digit numbers are 65 and 60 (Since, their difference is 5) and we have $B = 6$, $A = 5$ and $C = 0$.

But with this solution we are unable to meet the second condition. Hence (b) is not the answer. We also realise here that C cannot be 0.

Check for option (c).

B is 7, then the nos. are 76 and 71 or 75 and 70. In both these cases, the smallest two two-digit numbers do not differ by 2.

Hence, the answer is not (c).

Hence, option **(d)** is the answer
[To confirm, put $B = 8$, then the solution $A = 6$ and $C = 1$ satisfies the 2nd condition.]

Problem 1.18 Find the remainder when $2851 \times (2862)^2 \times (2873)^3$ is divided by 23.

Solution We use the remainder theorem to solve the problem. Using the theorem, we see that the following expressions have the same remainder.

$$\Rightarrow \frac{2851 \times (2862)^2 \times (2873)^3}{23}$$

$$\Rightarrow \frac{22 \times 10 \times 10 \times 21 \times 21 \times 21}{23}$$

$$\Rightarrow \frac{22 \times 8 \times 441 \times 21}{23} \qquad \Rightarrow \frac{22 \times 21 \times 8 \times 4}{23}$$

$$\Rightarrow \frac{462 \times 32}{23} \qquad \Rightarrow \frac{2 \times 9}{23} \Rightarrow \text{Remainder is } \mathbf{18.}$$

Problem 1.19 For what maximum value of n will the expression $\dfrac{10200!}{504^n}$ be an integer?

Solution For $\dfrac{10200!}{504^n}$ to be a integer, we need to look at the prime factors of $504 \rightarrow$
$$504 = 3^2 \times 7 \times 8 = 2^3 \times 3^2 \times 7$$

We thus have to look for the number of 7s, the number of 2^3s and the number of 3^2s that are contained in 10200!. The lowest of these will be the constraint value for n.

To find the number of 2^3s we need to find the number of 2s as

$$\left[\frac{10200}{2}\right] + \left[\frac{10200}{4}\right] + \left[\frac{10200}{8}\right] + \left[\frac{10200}{16}\right] + \left[\frac{10200}{32}\right]$$

$$+ \left[\frac{10200}{64}\right] + \left[\frac{10200}{128}\right] + \left[\frac{10200}{256}\right] + \left[\frac{10200}{512}\right] + \left[\frac{10200}{1024}\right]$$

$$+ \left[\frac{10200}{2048}\right] + \left[\frac{10200}{4096}\right] + \left[\frac{10200}{8192}\right]$$

where [ ] is the greatest integer function.

= 5100 + 2550 + 1275 + 637 + 318 + 159 + 79 + 39 + 19 + 9 + 4 + 2 + 1

Number of twos = 10192

Hence, number of 2^3 = 3397

Similarly, we find the number of 3s as

$$\text{Number of threes} = \left[\frac{10200}{3}\right] + \left[\frac{10200}{9}\right] + \left[\frac{10200}{27}\right]$$

$$\left[\frac{10200}{81}\right] + \left[\frac{10200}{243}\right] + \left[\frac{10200}{729}\right] + \left[\frac{10200}{2187}\right]$$

$$+ \left[\frac{10200}{6561}\right]$$

= 3400 + 1133 + 377 + 125 + 41 + 13 + 4 + 1

Number of threes = 5094

∴   Number of 3^2 = 2547

Similarly we find the number of 7s as

$$\left[\frac{10200}{7}\right] + \left[\frac{10200}{49}\right] + \left[\frac{10200}{343}\right] + \left[\frac{10200}{2401}\right]$$

= 1457 + 208 + 29 + 4 = 1698.

Thus, we have, 1698 sevens, 2547 nines and 3397 eights contained in 10200!.

The required value of n will be given by the lowest of these three [The student is expected to explore why this happens]

Hence, answer = **1698**.

Short Cut   We will look only for the number of 7s in this case. *Reason*: 7 > 3 × 2. So, the number of 7s must always be less than the number of 2^3.

And 7 > 2 × 3, so the number of 7s must be less than the number of 3^2.

Recollect that earlier we had talked about the finding of powers when the divisor only had prime factors. There we had seen that we needed to check only for the highest prime as the restriction had to lie there.

In cases of the divisors having composite factors, we have to be slightly careful in estimating the factor that will reflect the restriction. In the above example, we saw a case where even though 7 was the lowest factor (in relation to 8 and 9), the restriction was still placed by 7 rather than by 9 (as would be expected based on the previous process of taking the highest number).

Problem 1.20   Find the units digit of the expression: $78^{5562} \times 56^{256} \times 97^{1250}$.

Solution   We can get the units digits in the expression by looking at the patterns followed by 78, 56 and 97 when they are raised to high powers.

In fact, for the last digit we just need to consider the units digit of each part of the product.

A number (like 78) having 8 as the units digit will yield units digit as

$78^1 \rightarrow 8$	$78^5 \rightarrow 8$	$8^{4n+1} \rightarrow 8$
$78^2 \rightarrow 4$	$78^6 \rightarrow 4$	$8^{4n+2} \rightarrow 4$
$78^3 \rightarrow 2$	$78^7 \rightarrow 2$	Hence 78^{5562} will yield
$78^4 \rightarrow 6$	$78^8 \rightarrow 6$	four as the units digit

Similarly,	$56^1 \rightarrow 6$	$\rightarrow 56^{256}$ will yield 6 as
	$56^2 \rightarrow 6$	the units digit.
	$56^3 \rightarrow 6$	

Similarly,

$97^1 \rightarrow 7$	$7^{4n+1} \rightarrow 7$
$97^2 \rightarrow 9$	$7^{4n+2} \rightarrow 9$
$97^3 \rightarrow 3$	Hence, 97^{1250} will yield a units digit of 9.
$97^4 \rightarrow 1$	

Hence, the required units digit is given by $4 \times 6 \times 9 \rightarrow$ **6 (answer)**.

Problem 1.21   Find the GCD and the LCM of the numbers P and Q where $P = 2^3 \times 5^3 \times 7^2$ and $Q = 3^3 \times 5^4$.

Solution   GCD or HCF is given by the lowest powers of the common factors.

Thus,   GCD = 5^3.

LCM is given by the highest powers of all factors available.

Thus,   LCM = $2^3 \times 3^3 \times 5^4 \times 7^2$

Problem 1.22   A school has 378 girl students and 675 boy students. The school is divided into strictly boys or strictly girls sections. All sections in the school have the same number of students. Given this information, what are the minimum number of sections in the school.

Solution   The answer will be given by the HCF of 378 and 675.

$$378 = 2 \times 3^3 \times 7$$
$$675 = 3^3 \times 5^2$$

Hence, HCF of the two is 3^3 = 27.

Hence, the number of sections is given by: $\dfrac{378}{27} + \dfrac{675}{27}$ = 14 + 25 = **39 sections**.

Problem 1.23   The difference between the number of numbers from 2 to 100 which are not divisible by any other number except 1 and itself and the numbers which are divisible by at least one more number along with 1 and itself.

(a) 25	(b) 50
(c) 49	(d) can't be determine

Solution   From 2 to 100.

The number of numbers which are divisible by 1 and itself only = 25

Also, the number of numbers which are divisible by at least one more number except 1 and itself (i.e composite numbers) 99 – 25 = 74

So, required difference = 74 − 25 = 49
⇒ **Option (c)**

Problem 1.24 If the sum of $(2n +1)$ prime numbers where $n \in N$ is an even number, then one of the prime numbers must be

    (a) 2   (b) 3

    (c) 5   (d) 7

Solution For any $n \in N$, $2n + 1$ is odd.

Also, it is given in the problem that the sum of an odd number of prime numbers = even. Since all prime numbers except 2 are odd, the above condition will only be fulfilled if we have an (odd + odd + even) structure of addition. Since, the sum of the three prime numbers is said to be even, we have to include one even prime number. Hence 2 being the only even prime number must be included.

If we add odd number of prime numbers, not including 2 (two), we will always get an odd number, because

$$\frac{\text{odd} + \text{odd} + \text{odd} + ----- + \text{odd}}{\text{(an odd number of times)}} = \text{odd number}$$

⇒ **Option (a)**

Problem 1.25 What will be the difference between the largest and smallest four digit number made by using distinct single digit prime numbers?

    (a) 1800   (b) 4499

    (c) 4495   (d) 5175

Solution Required largest number → 7532
Required smallest number → 2357
    Difference → 5175
⇒ **Option (d)**

Problem 1.26 The difference between the two three-digit numbers XYZ and ZYX will be equal to

    (a) difference between X and Z i.e. $|x - z|$

    (b) sum of X and z i.e $(X + Z)$

    (c) $9 \times$ difference between X and Z

    (d) $99 \times$ difference between X and Z

Solution From the property of numbers, it is known that on reversing a three digit number, the difference (of both the numbers) will be divisible by 99. Also, it is known that this difference will be equal to $99 \times$ difference between the units and hundreds digits of the three digit number.
⇒ **Option (d)**

Problem 1.27 When the difference between the number 842 and its reverse is divided by 99, the remainder will be

    (a) 0   (b) 1

    (c) 74   (d) 17

Solution From the property (used in the above question) we can say that the difference will be divisible by 99

⇒ Remainder = 0 (zero)
⇒ Option (a)

Problem 1.28 When the difference between the number 783 and its reverse is divided by 99, the quotient will be

    (a) 1   (b) 10

    (c) 3   (d) 4

Solution The quotient will be the difference between extreme digits of 783, i.e. $7 - 3 = 4$ (This again is a property which you should know.)
⇒ **Option (d)**

Problem 1.29 A long Part of wood of same length when cut into equal pieces each of 242 cms, leaves a small piece of length 98 cms. If this Part were cut into equal pieces each of 22 cms, the length of the leftover wood would be

    (a) 76 cm   (b) 12 cm

    (c) 11 cm   (d) 10 cm

Solution As 242 is divisible by 22, so the required length of left wood will be equal to the remainder when 98 is divided by 22:
Hence, 10 [98/22; remainder 10]
⇒ **Option (d)**

Problem 1.30 Find the number of numbers from 1 to 100 which are not divisible by 2.

    (a) 51   (b) 50

    (c) 49   (d) 48

Solution The 1st number from 1 to 100, not divisible by 2 is 1 and the last number from 1 to 100, not divisible by 2 is 99.

Every alternate number (i.e, at the gap of 2) will not be divisible by 2 from 1 to 99. (1, 2, 3, - - - -, 95, 97, 99)

So, the required number of nos $= \dfrac{\text{last no.} - \text{first no.}}{\text{gap (or step)}} + 1$

$$= \frac{99 - 1}{2} + 1 = 50$$

⇒ **Option (b)**

Alternate method

Total number of nos from 1 to 100 = 100   (i)

Now, if we count number of numbers from 1 to 100 which are divisible by 2 and subtract that from the total number of numbers from 1 to 100, as a result we will find the number of numbers from 1 to 100 which are not divisible by 2.

To count the number of nos from 1 to 100 which are divisible by 2:

The 1st number which is divisible by 2 = 2

The last number which is divisible by 2 = 100

            (2, 4, 6, - - - -, 96, 98, 100)

Gap/step between two consecutive numbers = 2

So, the number of numbers which are divisible by 2 = =
$$\frac{\text{last no.} - \text{first no.}}{\text{gap (or step)}} + 1 = \frac{100 - 2}{2} + 1 = 50 \qquad \text{(ii)}$$

So, from (i) & (ii)

Required number of numbers = 100 – 50 = 50

⇒ Option (b)

Problem 1.31 Find the number of numbers from 1 to 100 which are not divisible by any one of 2 & 3.

    (a) 16   (b) 17

    (c) 18   (d) 33

Solution From 1 to 100

Number of numbers not divisible by 2 & 3 = Total number of numbers–number of numbers divisible by either 2 or 3.

Now, total number of numbers = 100   (ii)

For number of numbers divisible by either 2 or 3:

Number of numbers divisible by 2 = $\frac{\text{last no.} - \text{first no.}}{\text{gap (or step)}} + 1$

$$= \frac{100 - 2}{2} + 1 = 50$$

Now, the number of numbers divisible by 3 (but not by 2, as it has already been counted)

1st such no. = 3 and the gap will be 6. Hence 2nd such no. will be 9, 3rd no. would be 15 and the last number would be 99. Hence this series is 3, 9, 15, ..., 93, 99

So, the number of numbers divisible by 3 (but not by 2) =
$$\frac{\text{last such no.} - \text{first such no.}}{\text{gap/step}} + 1 = \frac{99 - 3}{6} + 1 = 17$$

Hence, the number of numbers divisible by either 2 or 3 = 50 + 17 = 67

So, from (i), (ii) & (iii) required number of numbers = 100 – 67 = 33

⇒ Option (d)

Problem 1.32 Find the number of numbers from 1 to 100 which are not divisible by any one of 2, 3, and 5.

    (a) 26   (b) 27

    (c) 29   (d) 32

Solution From the above question, we have found out that From 1 to 100, number of numbers divisible by 2 = 50 (i)

Number of numbers divisible by 3 (but not by 2) = 17 (ii)

Now, we have to find out the number of numbers which are divisible by 5 (but not by 2 and 3). Numbers which are divisible by 5

(5) 10 15 20 (25) 30 (35) 40 45 50 (55) 60 (65) 70 75 80 (85) 90 (95) 100

That is, there are 7 such numbers (iii)

Another way to find out the number of numbers that are divisible by 5 but not 2 and 3 is to first only consider odd multiples of 5.

You will get the series of 10 numbers: 5, 15, 25, 35, 45, 55, 65, 75, 85 and 95

From amongst these we need to exclude multiples of 3. In other words, we need to find the number of common elements between the above series and the series of odd multiples of 3, viz, 3, 9, 15, 21 …. 99.

This situation is the same as finding the number of common elements between the two series for which we need to first observe that the first such number is 15. Then the common terms between these two series will themselves form an arithmetic series and this series will have a common difference which is the LCM of the common differences of the two series. (In this case the common difference of the two series are 10 and 6 respectively and their LCM being 30, the series of common terms between the two series will be 15, 45 and 75.) Thus, there will be 3 terms out of the 10 terms of the series 5, 15, 25…95 which will be divisible by 3 and hence need to be excluded from the count of numbers which are divisible by 5 but not 2 or 3.

Hence, the required answer would be: 100 – 50 – 17 – 7 = 26

⇒ Option (a)

Problem 1.33 Find the number of numbers from 1 to 100 which are not divisible by any one of 2, 3, 5 & 7.

    (a) 22   (b) 24

    (c) 23   (d) 27

Solution From the above question we have seen that from 1 to 100.

number of numbers divisible by 2 = 50 (i)

number of numbers divisible by 3 but not by 2 = 17 (ii)

number of numbers divisible by 5 but not by 2 and 3 = 7 (iii)

number of numbers divisible by 7 but not by 2, 3 & 5;

such nos are 7, 49, 77, 91 = 4 nos (iv)

Required number of numbers = Total number of numbers from 1 to 100 – {(i) + (ii) + (iii) + (iv)}

$$= 100 - (50 + 17 + 7 + 4)$$
$$= 22$$

⇒ Option (a)

Problem 1.34 What will be the remainder when – 34 is divided by 5?

    (a) 1   (b) 4

    (c) 2   (d) – 4

Solution $-34 = 5 \times (-6) + (-4)$

Remainder = –4, but it is wrong because remainder cannot be negative.

So, $-34 = 5 \times (-7) + 1$

⇒ Option (a)

Alternately, when you see a remainder of -4 when the number is divided by 5, the required remainder will be equal to $5 - 4 = 1$.

Problem 1.35 What will be the remainder when -24.8 is divided by 6?

(a) 0.8   (b) 5.2

(c) -0.8 (d) -5.2

Solution $-24.8 = 6 \times (-4) + (-0.8)$

Negative remainder, so not correct $-24.8 = 6 \times (-5) + 5.2$

Positive value of remainder, so correct

$\Rightarrow$ Option (b)

Problem 1.36 If p is divided by q, then the maximum possible difference between the minimum possible and maximum possible remainder can be?

(a) $p - q$ (b) $p - 1$

(c) $q - 1$ (d) None of these

Solution $\dfrac{p}{q}$ minimum possible remainder = 0 (when q exactly divides P)

Maximum possible remainder = $q - 1$

So, required maximum possible difference = $(q - 1) - 0$ = $(q - 1)$

$\Rightarrow$ Option (c)

Problem 1.37 Find the remainder when 2^{256} is divided by 17.

(a) 0   (b) 1

(c) 3   (d) 5

Solution $\dfrac{2^{256}}{17} = \dfrac{(2^4)^{64}}{17} = \dfrac{16^{64}}{17} \Rightarrow R = 1$

$\therefore \dfrac{a^n}{a+1}; R = 1$

when $n \to$ even

$\Rightarrow$ Option (b)

Space for Rough Work

Problem 1.38 Find the difference between the remainders when 7^{84} is divided by 342 & 344.

(a) 0   (b) 1

(c) 3   (d) 5

Solution $\dfrac{7^{84}}{342} = \dfrac{(7^3)^{28}}{342} = \dfrac{343^{28}}{342} \Rightarrow R = 1$

also, $\dfrac{7^{84}}{344} = \dfrac{(7^3)^{28}}{344} = \dfrac{343^{28}}{344} \Rightarrow R = 1$

The required difference between the remainders = $1 - 1 = 0$

$\Rightarrow$ Option (a)

Problem 1.39 What will be the value of x for $\dfrac{(100^{17}-1)+(10^{34}+x)}{9}$; the remainder = 0

(a) 3   (b) 6

(c) 9   (d) 8

Solution $\dfrac{(100^{17}-1)+(10^{34}+x)}{9}$

$100^{17} - 1 = \dfrac{\underset{\text{17 zeroes}}{1000...00} - 1}{} = \dfrac{\underset{\text{16 nines}}{9999...99}}{} \Rightarrow$ divisible by $9 \Rightarrow R = 0$

Since the first part of the expression is giving a remainder of 0, the second part should also give 0 as a remainder if the entire remainder of the expression has to be 0. Hence, we now evaluate the second part of the numerator.

$10^{34} + x = \dfrac{\underset{\text{34 zeroes}}{1000...00} + x}{} = \dfrac{\underset{\text{33 zeroes}}{1000...00x}}{}$

with x at the right most place. In order for this number to be divisible by 9, the sum of digits should be divisible by 9.

$\Rightarrow 1 + 0 + 0 \cdots + 0 + x$ should be divisible by 9.

$\Rightarrow 1 + x$ should be divisible by $9 \Rightarrow x = 8$

$\Rightarrow$ Option (d)

LEVEL OF DIFFICULTY (I)

1. The last digit of the number obtained by multiplying the numbers $81 \times 82 \times 83 \times 84 \times 85 \times 86 \times 87 \times 88 \times 89$ will be
   (a) 0
   (b) 9
   (c) 7
   (d) 2

2. The sum of the digits of a two-digit number is 10, while when the digits are reversed, the number decreases by 54. Find the changed number.
   (a) 28
   (b) 19
   (c) 37
   (d) 46

3. When we multiply a certain two-digit number by the sum of its digits, 405 is achieved. If you multiply the number written in reverse order of the same digits by the sum of the digits, we get 486. Find the number.
   (a) 81
   (b) 45
   (c) 36
   (d) 54

4. The sum of two numbers is 15 and their geometric mean is 20% lower than their arithmetic mean. Find the numbers.
   (a) 11, 4
   (b) 12, 3
   (c) 13, 2
   (d) 10, 5

5. The difference between two numbers is 48 and the difference between the arithmetic mean and the geometric mean is two more than half of 1/3 of 96. Find the numbers.
   (a) 49, 1
   (b) 12, 60
   (c) 50, 2
   (d) 36, 84

6. If $A381$ is divisible by 11, find the value of the smallest natural number A.
   (a) 5
   (b) 6
   (c) 7
   (d) 9

7. If $381A$ is divisible by 9, find the value of smallest natural number A.
   (a) 5
   (b) 5
   (c) 7
   (d) 6

8. What will be the remainder obtained when $(9^6 + 1)$ will be divided by 8?
   (a) 0
   (b) 3
   (c) 7
   (d) 2

9. Find the ratio between the LCM and HCF of 5, 15 and 20.
   (a) 8 : 1
   (b) 14 : 3
   (c) 12 : 2
   (d) 12 : 1

10. Find the LCM of 5/2, 8/9, 11/14.
    (a) 280
    (b) 360
    (c) 420
    (d) None of these

11. If the number A is even, which of the following will be true?
    (a) 3A will always be divisible by 6

    (b) 3A + 5 will always be divisible by 11
    (c) $(A^2 + 3)/4$ will be divisible by 7
    (d) All of these

12. A five-digit number is taken. Sum of the first four digits (excluding the number at the units digit) equals sum of all the five digits. Which of the following will not divide this number necessarily?
    (a) 10
    (b) 2
    (c) 4
    (d) 5

13. A number $15B$ is divisible by 6. Which of these will be true about the positive integer B?
    (a) B will be even
    (b) B will be odd
    (c) B will be divisble by 6
    (d) Both (a) and (c)

14. Two numbers $P = 2^3.3^{10}.5$ and $Q = 2^5.3^1.7^1$ are given. Find the GCD of P and Q.
    (a) 2.3.5.7
    (b) 3.2^2
    (c) $2^2.3^2$
    (d) $2^3.3$

15. Find the units digit of the expression $25^{6251} + 36^{528} + 73^{54}$.
    (a) 4
    (b) 0
    (c) 6
    (d) 5

16. Find the units digit of the expression $55^{725} + 73^{5810} + 22^{853}$.
    (a) 4
    (b) 0
    (c) 6
    (d) 5

17. Find the units digit of the expression $11^1 + 12^2 + 13^3 + 14^4 + 15^5 + 16^6$.
    (a) 1
    (b) 9
    (c) 7
    (d) 0

18. Find the units digit of the expression $11^1.12^2.13^3.14^4.15^5.16^6$.
    (a) 4
    (b) 3
    (c) 7
    (d) 0

19. Find the number of zeroes at the end of 1090!
    (a) 270
    (b) 268
    (c) 269
    (d) 271

20. If 146! is divisible by 5^n, then find the maximum value of n.
    (a) 34
    (b) 35
    (c) 36
    (d) 37

21. Find the number of divisors of 1420.
    (a) 14
    (b) 15
    (c) 13
    (d) 12

22. Find the HCF and LCM of the polynomials $(x^2 - 5x + 6)$ and $(x^2 - 7x + 10)$.
    (a) $(x - 2)$, $(x - 2)(x - 3)(x - 5)$
    (b) $(x - 2)$, $(x - 2)(x - 3)$
    (c) $(x - 3)$, $(x - 2)(x - 3)(x - 5)$
    (d) $(x - 2)$, $(x - 2)(x - 3)(x - 5)^2$

Directions for Questions 23 to 25: Given two different prime numbers P and Q, find the number of divisors of the following:

23. $P.Q$
    (a) 2   (b) 4
    (c) 6   (d) 8

24. P^2Q
    (a) 2   (b) 4
    (c) 6   (d) 8

25. P^3Q^2
    (a) 2   (b) 4
    (c) 6   (d) 12

26. The sides of a pentagonal field (not regular) are 1737 metres, 2160 metres, 2358 metres, 1422 metres and 2214 metres respectively. Find the greatest length of the tape by which the five sides may be measured completely.
    (a) 7   (b) 13
    (c) 11   (d) 9

27. There are 576 boys and 448 girls in a school that are to be divided into equal sections of either boys or girls alone. Find the minimum total number of sections thus formed.
    (a) 24   (b) 32
    (c) 16   (d) 20

28. A milkman has three different qualities of milk. 403 gallons of 1st quality, 465 gallons of 2nd quality and 496 gallons of 3rd quality. Find the least possible number of bottles of equal size in which different milk of different qualities can be filled without mixing.
    (a) 34   (b) 46
    (c) 26   (d) 44

29. What is the greatest number of 4 digits that when divided by any of the numbers 6, 9, 12, 17 leaves a remainder of 1?
    (a) 9997   (b) 9793
    (c) 9895   (d) 9487

30. Find the least number that when divided by 16, 18 and 20 leaves a remainder 4 in each case, but is completely divisible by 7.
    (a) 364   (b) 2254
    (c) 2964   (d) 2884

31. Four bells ring at the intervals of 6, 8, 12 and 18 seconds. They start ringing together at 12'O' clock. After how many seconds will they ring together again?

(a) 72   (b) 84
(c) 60   (d) 48

32. For Question 31, find how many times will they ring together during the next 12 minutes. (including the 12 minute mark)
    (a) 9   (b) 10
    (c) 11   (d) 12

33. The units digit of the expression $125^{813} \times 553^{3703} \times 4532^{828}$ is
    (a) 4   (b) 2
    (c) 0   (d) 5

34. Which of the following is not a perfect square?
    (a) 1,00,856   (b) 3,25,137
    (c) 9,45,729   (d) All of these

35. Which of the following can never be in the ending of a perfect square?
    (a) 6   (b) 00
    (c) x 000 where x is a natural number
    (d) 1

36. The LCM of 5, 8,12, 20 will not be a multiple of
    (a) 3   (b) 9
    (c) 8   (d) 5

37. Find the number of divisors of 720 (including 1 and 720).
    (a) 25   (b) 28
    (c) 29   (d) 30

38. The LCM of $(16 - x^2)$ and $(x^2 + x - 6)$ is
    (a) $(x - 3)(x + 3)(4 - x^2)$
    (b) $4(4 - x^2)(x + 3)$
    (c) $(4 - x^2)(x - 3)$
    (d) None of these

39. GCD of $x^2 - 4$ and $x^2 + x - 6$ is
    (a) $x + 2$ (b) $x - 2$
    (c) $x^2 - 2$ (d) $x^2 + 2$

40. The number A is not divisible by 3. Which of the following will not be divisible by 3?
    (a) $9 \times A$ (b) $2 \times A$
    (c) $18 \times A$ (d) $24 \times A$

41. Find the remainder when the number 9^{100} is divided by 8.
    (a) 1   (b) 2
    (c) 0   (d) 4

42. Find the remainder of 2^{1000} when divided by 3.
    (a) 1   (b) 2
    (c) 4   (d) 6

43. Decompose the number 20 into two terms such that their product is the greatest.
    (a) $x_1 = x_2 = 10$ (b) $x_1 = 5, x_2 = 15$
    (c) $x_1 = 16, x_2 = 4$ (d) $x_1 = 8, x_2 = 12$

44. Find the number of zeroes at the end of 50!
    (a) 13   (b) 11
    (c) 5   (d) 12

45. Which of the following can be a number divisible by 24?
    (a) 4,32,15,604   (b) 25,61,284
    (c) 13,62,480   (d) All of these

46. For a number to be divisible by 88, it should be
    (a) Divisible by 22 and 8
    (b) Divisible by 11 and 8
    (c) Divisible by 11 and thrice by 2
    (d) All of these

47. Find the number of divisors of 10800.
    (a) 57   (b) 60
    (c) 72   (d) 64

48. Find the GCD of the polynomials $(x + 3)^2(x - 2)(x + 1)^2$ and $(x + 1)^3(x + 3)(x + 4)$.
    (a) $(x + 3)^3 (x + 1)^2 (x - 2) (x + 4)$
    (b) $(x + 3)(x - 2)(x + 1)(x + 4)$
    (c) $(x + 3)(x + 1)^2$
    (d) $(x + 1)(x + 3)^2$

49. Find the LCM of $(x + 3)(6x^2 + 5x + 4)$ and $(2x^2 + 7x + 3)(x + 3)$
    (a) $(2x + 1)(x + 3)(3x + 4)$
    (b) $(4x^2 - 1)(x + 3)^2(3x + 4)$
    (c) $(4x^2 - 1)(x + 3)(3x + 4)$
    (d) $(2x - 1)(x + 3)(3x + 4)$

50. The product of three consecutive natural numbers, the first of which is an even number, is always divisible by
    (a) 12   (b) 24
    (c) 6   (d) All of these

51. Some birds settled on the branches of a tree. First, they sat one to a branch and there was one bird too many. Next they sat two to a branch and there was one branch too many. How many branches were there?
    (a) 3   (b) 4
    (c) 5   (d) 6

52. The square of a number greater than 1000 that is not divisible by three, when divided by three, leaves a remainder of
    (a) 1 always   (b) 2 always
    (c) 0   (d) either 1 or 2

53. The value of the expression $(15^3 \cdot 21^2)/(35^2 \cdot 3^4)$ is
    (a) 3   (b) 15
    (c) 21   (d) 12

54. If $A = \left(\dfrac{-3}{4}\right)^3$, $B = \left(\dfrac{-2}{5}\right)^2$, $C = (0.3)^2$, $D = (-1.2)^2$
    then
    (a) $A > B > C > D$ (b) $D > A > B > C$
    (c) $D > B > C > A$ (d) $D > C > A > B$

55. If $2 < x < 4$ and $1 < y < 3$, then find the ratio of the upper limit for $x + y$ and the lower limit of $x - y$.

    (a) 6   (b) 7
    (c) 8   (d) None of these

56. The sum of the squares of the digits constituting a positive two-digit number is 13. If we subtract 9 from that number, we shall get a number written by the same digits in the reverse order. Find the number.
    (a) 12   (b) 32
    (c) 42   (d) 52

57. The product of a natural number by the number written by the same digits in the reverse order is 2430. Find the numbers.
    (a) 54 and 45   (b) 56 and 65
    (c) 53 and 35   (d) 85 and 58

58. Find two natural numbers whose difference is 66 and the least common multiple is 360.
    (a) 120 and 54   (b) 90 and 24
    (c) 180 and 114   (d) 130 and 64

59. Find the pairs of natural numbers whose least common multiple is 78 and the greatest common divisor is 13.
    (a) 58 and 13 or 16 and 29
    (b) 68 and 23 or 36 and 49
    (c) 18 and 73 or 56 and 93
    (d) 78 and 13 or 26 and 39

60. Find two natural numbers whose sum is 85 and the least common multiple is 102.
    (a) 30 and 55   (b) 17 and 68
    (c) 35 and 55   (d) 51 and 34

61. Find the pairs of natural numbers the difference of whose squares is 55.
    (a) 28 and 27 or 8 and 3
    (b) 18 and 17 or 18 and 13
    (c) 8 and 27 or 8 and 33
    (d) 9 and 18 or 8 and 27

62. Which of these is greater?
    (a) 54^4 or 21^{12} (b) $(0.4)^4$ or $(0.8)^3$

63. Is it possible for a common fraction whose numerator is less than the denominator to be equal to a fraction whose numerator is greater than the denominator?
    (a) Yes   (b) No

64. What digits should be put in place of c in $38c$ to make it divisible by
    (1) 2   (2) 3
    (3) 4   (4) 5
    (5) 6   (6) 9
    (7) 10

65. Find the LCM and HCF of the following numbers: (54, 81, 135 and 189), (156, 195) and (1950, 5670 and 3900)

66. The last digit in the expansions of the three digit number $(34x)^{43}$ and $(34x)^{44}$ are 7 and 1 respectively. What can be said about the value of x?

(a) $x = 5$ (b) $x = 3$
(c) $x = 6$ (d) $x = 2$

Directions for Questions 67 and 68: Amitesh buys a pen, a pencil and an eraser for ₹ 41. If the least cost of any of the three items is ₹ 12 and it is known that a pen costs less than a pencil and an eraser costs more than a pencil, answer the following questions:

67. What is the cost of the pen?
     (a) 12   (b) 13
     (c) 14   (d) 15

68. If it is known that the eraser's cost is not divisible by 4, the cost of the pencil could be:
     (a) 12   (b) 13
     (c) 14   (d) 15

69. A naughty boy Amrit watches an innings of Sachin Tendulkar and acts according to the number of runs he sees Sachin scoring. The details of these are given below.

1 run   Place an orange in the basket
2 runs   Place a mango in the basket
3 runs   Place a pear in the basket
4 runs   Remove a pear and a mango from the basket

One fine day, at the start of the match, the basket is empty. The sequence of runs scored by Sachin in that innings are given as 11232411234232341121314. At the end of the above innings, how many more oranges were there compared to mangoes inside the basket? (The Basket was empty initially).
     (a) 4   (b) 5
     (c) 6   (d) 7

70. In the famous Bel Air Apartments in Ranchi, there are three watchmen meant to protect the precious fruits in the campus. However, one day a thief got in without being noticed and stole some precious mangoes. On the way out however, he was confronted by the three watchmen, the first two of whom asked him to part with 1/3ʳᵈ of the fruits and one more. The last asked him to part with 1/5ᵗʰ of the mangoes and 4 more. As a result he had no mangoes left. What was the number of mangoes he had stolen?
     (a) 12   (b) 13
     (c) 15   (d) None of these

71. A hundred and twenty digit number is formed by writing the first x natural numbers in front of each other as 12345678910111213… Find the remainder when this number is divided by 8.
     (a) 6   (b) 7
     (c) 2   (d) 0

72. A test has 80 questions. There is one mark for a correct answer, while there is a negative penalty of $-1/2$ for a wrong answer and $-1/4$ for an unattempted question. What is the number of questions answered correctly, if the student has scored a net total of 34.5 marks?
     (a) 45   (b) 48
     (c) 54   (d) Cannot be determined

73. For Question 72, if it is known that he has left 10 questions unanswered, the number of correct answers are:
     (a) 45   (b) 48
     (c) 54   (d) Cannot be determined

74. Three mangoes, four guavas and five watermelons cost ₹ 750. Ten watermelons, six mangoes and 9 guavas cost ₹1580. What is the cost of six mangoes, ten watermelons and 4 guavas?
     (a) 1280   (b) 1180
     (c) 1080   (d) Cannot be determined

75. From a number M subtract 1. Take the reciprocal of the result to get the value of 'N'. Then which of the following is necessarily true?
     (a) $0 \le M^N \le 2$ (b) $M^N > 3$
     (c) $1 < M^N < 3$ (d) $1 < M^N < 5$

76. The cost of four mangoes, six guavas and sixteen watermelons is ₹ 500, while the cost of seven magoes, nine guavas and nineteen watermelons is ₹ 620. What is the cost of one mango, one guava and one watermelon?
     (a) 120   (b) 40
     (c) 150   (d) Cannot be determined

77. For the question above, what is the cost of a mango?
     (a) 20   (b) 14
     (c) 15   (d) Cannot be determined

78. The following is known about three real numbers, x, y and z.
$-4 \le x \le 4$, $-8 \le y \le 2$ and $-8 \le z \le 2$. Then the range of values that $M = xz/y$ can take is best represented by:
     (a) $-\infty < x < \infty$ (b) $-16 \le x \le 8$
     (c) $-8 \le x \le 8$ (d) $-16 \le x \le 16$

79. A man sold 38 pieces of clothing (combined in the form of shirts, trousers and ties). If he sold at least 11 pieces of each item and he sold more shirts than trousers and more trousers than ties, then the number of ties that he must have sold is:
     (a) Exactly 11   (b) At least 11
     (c) At least 12   (d) Cannot be determined

80. For Question 79, find the number of shirts he must have sold.
     (a) At least 13   (b) At least 14
     (c) At least 15   (d) At most 16.

81. Find the least number which when divided by 12, 15, 18 or 20 leaves in each case a remainder 4.
     (a) 124   (b) 364
     (c) 184   (d) None of these

82. What is the least number by which 2800 should be multiplied so that the product may be a perfect square?
    (a) 2 (b) 7
    (c) 14 (d) None of these

83. The least number of 4 digits which is a perfect square is:
    (a) 1064 (b) 1040
    (c) 1024 (d) 1012

84. The least multiple of 7 which leaves a remainder of 4 when divided by 6, 9, 15 and 18 is
    (a) 94 (b) 184
    (c) 364 (d) 74

85. What is the least 3 digit number that when divided by 2, 3, 4, 5 or 6 leaves a remainder of 1?
    (a) 131 (b) 161
    (c) 121 (d) None of these

86. The highest common factor of 70 and 245 is equal to
    (a) 35 (b) 45
    (c) 55 (d) 65

87. Find the least number, which must be subtracted from 7147 to make it a perfect square.
    (a) 86 (b) 89
    (c) 91 (d) 93

88. Find the least square number which is divisible by 6, 8 and 15
    (a) 2500 (b) 3600
    (c) 4900 (d) 4500

89. Find the least number by which 30492 must be multiplied or divided so as to make it a perfect square.
    (a) 11 (b) 7
    (c) 3 (d) 2

90. The greatest 4-digit number exactly divisible by 88 is
    (a) 8888 (b) 9768
    (c) 9944 (d) 9988

91. By how much is three fourth of 116 greater than four fifth of 45?
    (a) 31 (b) 41
    (c) 46 (d) None of these

92. If 5625 plants are to be arranged in such a way that there are as many rows as there are plants in a row, the number of rows will be:
    (a) 95 (b) 85
    (c) 65 (d) None of these

93. A boy took a seven digit number ending in 9 and raised it to an even power greater than 2000. He then took the number 17 and raised it to a power which leaves the remainder 1 when divided by 4. If he now multiples both the numbers, what will be the unit's digit of the number he so obtains?

94. Two friends were discussing their marks in an examination. While doing so they realized that both the numbers had the same prime factors, although Raveesh got a score which had two more factors than Harish. If their marks are represented by one of the options as given below, which of the following options would correctly represent the number of marks they got?
    (a) 30,60 (b) 20,80
    (c) 40,80 (d) 20,60

95. A number is such that when divided by 3, 5, 6, or 7 it leaves the remainder 1, 3, 4, or 5 respectively. Which is the largest number below 4000 that satisfies this property?
    (a) 3358 (b) 3988
    (c) 3778 (d) 2938

96. A number when divided by 2,3 and 4 leaves a remainder of 1. Find the least number (after 1) that satisfies this requirement.
    (a) 25 (b) 13
    (c) 37 (d) 17

97. A number when divided by 2, 3 and 4 leaves a remainder of 1. Find the second lowest number (not counting 1) that satisfies this requirement.
    (a) 25 (b) 13
    (c) 37 (d) 17

98. A number when divided by 2, 3 and 4 leaves a remainder of 1. Find the highest 2 digit number that satisfies this requirement.
    (a) 91 (b) 93
    (c) 97 (d) 95

99. A number when divided by 2,3 and 4 leaves a remainder of 1. Find the highest 3 digit number that satisfies this requirement.
    (a) 991 (b) 993
    (c) 997 (d) 995

100. A frog is sitting on vertex A of a square $ABCD$. It starts jumping to the immediately adjacent vertex on either side in random fashion and stops when it reaches point C. In how many ways can it reach point C if it makes exactly 7 jumps?
    (a) 1 (b) 3
    (c) 5 (d) 0

101. Three bells ring at intervals of 5 seconds, 6 seconds and 7 seconds respectively. If they toll together for the first time at 9 AM in the morning, after what interval of time will they together ring again for the first time?
    (a) After 30 seconds (b) After 42 seconds
    (c) After 35 seconds (d) After 210 seconds

102. For the question above, how many times would they ring, together in the next 1 hour?

    (a) 7 (b) 9
    (c) 3 (d) Cannot be determined

(a) 17   (b) 18
(c) 19   (d) None of these

103. A garrison has three kinds of soldiers. There are 66 soldiers of the first kind, 110 soldiers of the second kind and 242 soldiers of the third kind. It is desired to be arranging these soldiers in equal rows such that each row contains the same number of soldiers and there is only 1 kind of soldier in each row. What is the maximum number of soldiers who can be placed in each row?
(a) 11   (b) 1
(c) 22   (d) 33

104. For the question above, what are the minimum number of rows that would be required to be formed?
(a) 11   (b) 19
(c) 18   (d) None of these

105. A milkman produces three kinds of milk. On a particular day, he has 170 liters, 102 liters and 374 liters of the three kinds of milk. He wants to bottle them in bottles of equal sizes- so that each of the three varieties of milk would be completed bottled. How many bottle sizes are possible such that the bottle size in terms of liters is an integer?
(a) 1   (b) 2
(c) 4   (d) 34

106. For the above question, what is the size of the largest bottle which can be used?
(a) 1   (b) 2
(c) 17   (d) 34

107. For Question 105, what are the minimum number of bottles that would be required?
(a) 11   (b) 19
(c) 18   (d) None of these

108. Find the number of zeroes at the end of 100!
(a) 20   (b) 23
(c) 24   (d) 25

109. Find the number of zeroes at the end of 122!
(a) 20   (b) 23
(c) 24   (d) 28

110. Find the number of zeroes at the end of 1400!
(a) 347   (b) 336
(c) 349   (d) 348

111. Find the number of zeroes at the end of 380!
(a) 90   (b) 91
(c) 94   (d) 95

112. Find the number of zeroes at the end of 72!
(a) 14   (b) 15
(c) 16   (d) 17

113. The highest power of 3 that completely divides 40! is
(a) 18   (b) 15
(c) 16   (d) 17

114. $53!/3^n$ is an integer. Find the highest possible value of n for this to be true.
(a) 19   (b) 21
(c) 23   (d) 24

115. The highest power of 7 that completely divides 80! is:
(a) 12   (b) 13
(c) 14   (d) 15

116. $115!/7^n$ is an integer. Find the highest possible value of n for this to be true.
(a) 15   (b) 17
(c) 16   (d) 18

117. The highest power of 12 that completely divides 122! is:
(a) 54   (b) 56
(c) 57   (d) 58

118. $155!/20^n$ is an integer. Find the highest possible value of n for this to be true.
(a) 77   (b) 38
(c) 75   (d) 37

119. The minimum value of x so that $x^2/1024$ is an integer is:
(a) 4   (b) 32
(c) 16   (d) 64

120. Find the sum of all 2 digit natural numbers which leave a remainder of 3 when divided by 7.
(a) 650   (b) 663
(c) 676   (d) 702

121. How many numbers between 1 and 200 are exactly divisible by exactly two of 3, 9 and 27?
(a) 14   (b) 15
(c) 16   (d) 17

122. A number N is squared to give a value of S. The minimum value of $N + S$ would happen when N is
(a) −0.3   (b) −0.5
(c) −0.7   (d) None of these

123. $L = x + y$ where x and y are prime numbers. Which of the following statement/s is/are true?
(i) The unit's digit of L cannot be 5
(ii) The units digit of L cannot be 0.
(iii) L cannot be odd.
(a) All three   (b) Only iii
(c) only ii   (d) None

124. XYZ is a 3 digit number such that when we calculate the difference between the two three digit numbers $XYZ − YXZ$ the difference is exactly 90. How many possible values exist for the digits X and Y?
(a) 9   (b) 8
(c) 7   (d) 6

125. What is the sum of all even numbers between 1 and 100 (both included)?

(a) 2450   (b) 2500

(c) 2600   (d) 2550

126. The least number which can be added to 763 so that it is completely divisible by 57 is:

(a) 35   (b) 22

(c) 15   (d) 25

127. The least number which can be subtracted from 763 so that it is completely divisible by 57 is:

(a) 35   (b) 22

(c) 15   (d) 25

128. The least number which can be added to 8441 so that it is completely divisible by 57 is?

(a) 42   (b) 15

(c) 5   (d) 52

129. The least number which can be subtracted from 8441 so that it is completely divisible by 57 is:

(a) 3   (b) 4

(c) 5   (d) 6

130. Find the least number of 5 digits that is exactly divisible by 79

(a) 10003   (b) 10033

(c) 10043   (d) None of these

131. Find the maximum number of 5 digits that is exactly divisible by 79:

(a) 99925   (b) 99935

(c) 99945   (d) 99955

132. The nearest integer to 773 which is exactly divisible by 12 is:

(a) 768   (b) 772

(c) 776   (d) None of these

133. A number when divided by 84 leaves a remainder of 57. What is the remainder when the same number is divided by 12?

(a) 7   (b) 8

(c) 9   (d) Cannot be determined

134. A number when divided by 84 leaves a remainder of 57. What is the remainder when the same number is divided by 11?

(a) 2   (b) 7

(c) 8   (d) Cannot be determined

135. 511 and 667 when divided by the same number, leave the same remainder. How many numbers can be used as the divisor in order to make this occur?

(a) 14   (b) 12

(c) 10   (d) 8

136. How many numbers between 200 and 400 are divisible by 13?

(a) 14   (b) 15

(c) 16   (d) 17

137. A boy was trying to find 5/8th of a number. Unfortunately, he found out 8/5th of the number and realized that the difference between the answer he got and the correct answer is 39. What was the number?

(a) 38   (b) 39

(c) 40   (d) 52

138. The sum of two numbers is equal to thrice their difference. If the smaller of the numbers is 10 find the other number.

(a) 15   (b) 20

(c) 40   (d) None of these

139. $4^{11} + 4^{12} + 4^{13} + 4^{14} + 4^{15}$ is divisible by which of the following?

(a) 11   (b) 31

(c) 341   (d) All of the above

140. The product of two numbers is 7168 and their HCF is 16. How many pairs of numbers are possible such that the above conditions are satisfied?

(a) 2   (b) 3

(c) 4   (d) 6

Space for Rough Work

LEVEL OF DIFFICULTY (II)

1. The arithmetic mean of two numbers is smaller by 24 than the larger of the two numbers and the GM of the same numbers exceeds by 12 the smaller of the numbers. Find the numbers.
   - (a) 6 and 54
   - (b) 8 and 56
   - (c) 12 and 60
   - (d) 7 and 55

2. Find the number of numbers between 200 and 300, both included, which are not divisible by 2, 3, 4 and 5.
   - (a) 27
   - (b) 26
   - (c) 25
   - (d) 28

3. Given x and n are integers, $(15n^3 + 6n^2 + 5n + x)/n$ is not an integer for what condition?
   - (a) n is positive
   - (b) x is divisible by n
   - (c) x is not divisible by n
   - (d) (a) and (c)

4. The unit digit in the expression $36^{234}*33^{512}*39^{180} - 54^{29}*25^{123}*31^{512}$ will be
   - (a) 8
   - (b) 0
   - (c) 6
   - (d) 5

5. The difference of $10^{25} - 7$ and $10^{24} + x$ is divisible by 3 for $x = $?
   - (a) 3
   - (b) 2
   - (c) 4
   - (d) 6

6. Find the value of x in $\sqrt{x + 2\sqrt{x + 2\sqrt{x + 2\sqrt{3x}}}} = x$.
   - (a) 1
   - (b) 3
   - (c) 6
   - (d) 12
   - (e) 9

7. If a number is multiplied by 22 and the same number is added to it, then we get a number that is half the square of that number. Find the number
   - (a) 45
   - (b) 46
   - (c) 47
   - (d) data insufficient

8. $12^{55}/3^{11} + 8^{48}/16^{18}$ will give the digit at units place as
   - (a) 4
   - (b) 6
   - (c) 8
   - (d) 0

9. The mean of $1, 2, 2^2 \ldots. 2^{31}$ lies in between
   - (a) 2^{24} to 2^{25}
   - (b) 2^{25} to 2^{26}
   - (c) 2^{26} to 2^{27}
   - (d) 2^{29} to 2^{30}

10. xy is a number that is divided by ab where $xy < ab$ and gives a result $0.xyxyxy\ldots$ then ab equals
    - (a) 11
    - (b) 33
    - (c) 99
    - (d) 66

11. A number xy is multiplied by another number ab and the result comes as pqr, where $r = 2y$, $q = 2(x + y)$ and $p = 2x$ where $x, y < 5$, $q \neq 0$. The value of ab may be:
    - (a) 11
    - (b) 13
    - (c) 31
    - (d) 22

12. $[x]$ denotes the greatest integer value just below x and $\{x\}$ its fractional value. The sum of $[x]^3$ and $\{x\}^2$ is -7.91. Find x.
    - (a) -2.03
    - (b) -1.97
    - (c) -2.97
    - (d) -1.7

13. $16^5 + 2^{15}$ is divisible by
    - (a) 31
    - (b) 13
    - (c) 27
    - (d) 33

14. If $AB + XY = 1XP$, where $A \neq 0$ and all the letters signify different digits from 0 to 9, then the value of A is:
    - (a) 6
    - (b) 7
    - (c) 9
    - (d) 8

Directions for Questions 15 and 16: Find the possible integral values of x.

15. $|x - 3| + 2|x + 1| = 4$
    - (a) 1
    - (b) -1
    - (c) 3
    - (d) 2

16. $x^2 + |x - 1| = 1$
    - (a) 1
    - (b) -1
    - (c) 0
    - (d) 1 or 0

17. If $4^{n+1} + x$ and $4^{2n} - x$ are divisible by 5, n being an even integer, find the least value of x.
    - (a) 1
    - (b) 2
    - (c) 3
    - (d) 0

18. If the sum of the numbers $(a25)^2$ and a^3 is divisible by 9, then which of the following may be a value for a ?
    - (a) 1
    - (b) 7
    - (c) 9
    - (d) There is no value

19. If $|x - 4| + |y - 4| = 4$, then how many integer values can the set (x, y) have?
    - (a) Infinite
    - (b) 5
    - (c) 16
    - (d) 9

20. $[3^{32}/50]$ gives remainder and $\{.\}$ denotes the fractional part of that. The fractional part is of the form $(0 \cdot bx)$. The value of x could be
    - (a) 2
    - (b) 4
    - (c) 6
    - (d) 8

21. The sum of two numbers is 20 and their geometric mean is 20% lower than their arithmetic mean. Find the ratio of the numbers.
    (a) 4 : 1   (b) 9 : 1
    (c) 1 : 1   (d) 17 : 3

22. The highest power on 990 that will exactly divide 1090! is
    (a) 101   (b) 100
    (c) 108   (d) 109

23. If 146! is divisible by 6^n, then find the maximum value of n.
    (a) 74   (b) 70
    (c) 76   (d) 75

24. The last two digits in the multiplication of $35 \cdot 34 \cdot 33 \cdot 32 \cdot 31 \cdot 30 \cdot 29 \cdot 28 \cdot 27 \cdot 26$ is
    (a) 00   (b) 40
    (c) 30   (d) 10

25. The expression $333^{555} + 555^{333}$ is divisible by
    (a) 2   (b) 3
    (c) 37   (d) All of these

26. $[x]$ denotes the greatest integer value just below x and $\{x\}$ its fractional value. The sum of $[x]^2$ and $\{x\}^1$ is 25.16. Find x.
    (a) 5.16   (b) −4.84
    (c) Both (a) and (b)   (d) 4.84

27. If we add the square of the digit in the tens place of a positive two-digit number to the product of the digits of that number, we shall get 52, and if we add the square of the digit in the units place to the same product of the digits, we shall get 117. Find the two-digit number.
    (a) 18   (b) 39
    (c) 49   (d) 28

28. Find two numbers such that their sum, their product and the differences of their squares are equal.

    (a) $\left(\dfrac{3+\sqrt{3}}{2}\right)$ and $\left(\dfrac{1+\sqrt{2}}{2}\right)$ or $\left(\dfrac{3+\sqrt{2}}{2}\right)$ and $\left(\dfrac{1+\sqrt{2}}{2}\right)$

    (b) $\left(\dfrac{3+\sqrt{7}}{2}\right)$ and $\left(\dfrac{1+\sqrt{7}}{2}\right)$ or $\left(\dfrac{3+\sqrt{6}}{2}\right)$ and $\left(\dfrac{1-\sqrt{6}}{2}\right)$

    (c) $\left(\dfrac{3-\sqrt{5}}{2}\right)$ and $\left(\dfrac{1-\sqrt{5}}{2}\right)$ or $\left(\dfrac{3+\sqrt{5}}{2}\right)$ and $\left(\dfrac{1+\sqrt{5}}{2}\right)$

    (d) All of these

29. The sum of the digits of a three-digit number is 17, and the sum of the squares of its digits is 109. If we subtract 495 from that number, we shall get a number consisting of the same digits written in the reverse order. Find the number.
    (a) 773   (b) 863
    (c) 683   (d) 944

30. Find the number of zeros in the product: $1^1 \times 2^2 \times 3^3 \times 4^4 \times \ldots\ldots 98^{98} \times 99^{99} \times 100^{100}$
    (a) 1200   (b) 1300
    (c) 1050   (d) 1225

31. Find the pairs of natural numbers whose greatest common divisor is 5 and the least common multiple is 105.
    (a) 5 and 105 or 15 and 35
    (b) 6 and 105 or 16 and 35
    (c) 5 and 15 or 15 and 135
    (d) 5 and 20 or 15 and 35

32. The denominator of an irreducible fraction is greater than the numerator by 2. If we reduce the numerator of the reciprocal fraction by 3 and subtract the given fraction from the resulting one, we get 1/15. Find the given fraction.
    (a) $\dfrac{2}{4}$ (b) $\dfrac{3}{5}$
    (c) $\dfrac{5}{7}$ (d) $\dfrac{7}{9}$

33. A two-digit number exceeds by 19 the sum of the squares of its digits and by 44 the double product of its digits. Find the number.
    (a) 72   (b) 62
    (c) 22   (d) 12

34. The sum of the squares of the digits constituting a two-digit positive number is 2.5 times as large as the sum of its digits and is larger by unity than the trebled product of its digits. Find the number.
    (a) 13 and 31   (b) 12 and 21
    (c) 22 and 33   (d) 14 and 41

35. The units digit of a two-digit number is greater than its tens digit by 2, and the product of that number by the sum of its digits is 144. Find the number.
    (a) 14   (b) 24
    (c) 46   (d) 35

36. Find the number of zeroes in the product: $5 \times 10 \times 25 \times 40 \times 50 \times 55 \times 65 \times 125 \times 80$
    (a) 8   (b) 9
    (c) 12   (d) 13

37. The highest power of 45 that will exactly divide 123! is
    (a) 28   (b) 30
    (c) 31   (d) 59

38. Three numbers are such that the second is as much lesser than the third as the first is lesser than the second. If the product of the two smaller numbers

is 85 and the product of two larger numbers is 115 find the middle number.

(a) 9   (b) 8
(c) 12   (d) 10

39. Find the smallest natural number n such that $n!$ is divisible by 990.

(a) 3   (b) 5
(c) 11   (d) 12

40. $\sqrt{x}\sqrt{y} = \sqrt{xy}$ is true only when

(a) $x > 0, y > 0$ (b) $x > 0$ and $y < 0$
(c) $x < 0$ and $y > 0$ (d) All of these

Directions for Questions 41 to 60: Read the instructions below and solve the questions based on this.

In an examination situation, always solve the following type of questions by substituting the given options, to arrive at the solution.

However, as you can see, there are no options given in the questions here since these are meant to be an exercise in equation writing (which I believe is a primary skill required to do well in aptitude exams testing mathematical aptitude). Indeed, if these questions had options for them, they would be rated as LOD 1 questions. But since the option-based solution technique is removed here, I have placed these in the LOD 2 category.

41. Find the two-digit number that meets the following criteria. If the number in the units place exceeds, the number in its tens by 2 and the product of the required number with the sum of its digits is equal to 144.

42. The product of the digits of a two-digit number is twice as large as the sum of its digits. If we subtract 27 from the required number, we get a number consisting of the same digits written in the reverse order. Find the number?

43. The product of the digits of a two-digit number is one-third that number. If we add 18 to the required number, we get a number consisting of the same digits written in the reverse order. Find the number?

44. The sum of the squares of the digits of a two-digit number is 13. If we subtract 9 from that number, we get a number consisting of the same digits written in the reverse order. Find the number?

45. A two-digit number is thrice as large as the sum of its digits, and the square of that sum is equal to the trebled required number. Find the number?

46. Find a two-digit number that exceeds by 12 the sum of the squares of its digits and by 16 the doubled product of its digits.

47. The sum of the squares of the digits constituting a two-digit number is 10, and the product of the required number by the number consisting of the same digits written in the reverse order is 403. Find the 2 numbers that satisfy these conditions?

48. If we divide a two-digit number by the sum of its digits, we get 4 as a quotient and 3 as a remainder. Now, if we divide that two-digit number by the product of its digits, we get 3 as a quotient and 5 as a remainder. Find the two-digit number.

49. There is a natural number that becomes equal to the square of a natural number when 100 is added to it, and to the square of another natural number when 169 is added to it. Find the number?

50. Find two natural numbers whose sum is 85 and whose least common multiple is 102.

51. Find two-three digit numbers whose sum is a multiple of 504 and the quotient is a multiple of 6.

52. The difference between the digits in a two-digit number is equal to 2, and the sum of the squares of the same digits is 52. Find all the possible numbers?

53. If we divide a given two-digit number by the product of its digits, we obtain 3 as a quotient and 9 as a remainder. If we subtract the product of the digits constituting the number, from the square of the sum of its digits, we obtain the given number. Find the number.

54. Find the three-digit number if it is known that the sum of its digits is 17 and the sum of the squares of its digits is 109. If we subtract 495 from this number, we obtain a number consisting of the same digits written in reverse order.

55. The sum of the cubes of the digits constituting a two-digit number is 243 and the product of the sum of its digits by the product of its digits is 162. Find the two two-digit number?

56. The difference between two numbers is 16. What can be said about the total numbers divisible by 7 that can lie in between these two numbers.

57. Arrange the following in descending order:

111^4, 110.109.108.107, 109.110.112.113

58. If $3 \leq x \leq 5$ and $4 \leq y \leq 7$. Find the greatest value of xy and the least value of x/y.

59. Which of these is greater:

(a) 200^{300} or 300^{200} or 400^{150}

(b) 5^{100} and 2^{200}

(c) 10^{20} and 40^{10}

60. The sum of the two numbers is equal to 15 and their arithmetic mean is 25 per cent greater than its geometric mean. Find the numbers.

61. Define a number K such that it is the sum of the squares of the first M natural numbers.(i.e. $K = 1^2 + 2^2 + \ldots + M^2$) where $M < 55$. How many values of M exist such that K is divisible by 4?

(a) 10   (b) 11
(c) 12   (d) None of these

62. *M* is a two digit number which has the property that:
The product of factorials of it's digits > sum of factorials of its digits
How many values of *M* exist?
(a) 56 (b) 64
(c) 63 (d) None of these

63. A natural number when increased by 50% has its number of factors unchanged. However, when the value of the number is reduced by 75%, the number of factors is reduced by 66.66%. One such number could be:
(a) 32 (b) 84
(c) 126 (d) None of these

64. Find the 28383rd term of the series: 123456789101112....
(a) 3 (b) 4
(c) 9 (d) 7

65. If you form a subset of integers chosen from between 1 to 3000, such that no two integers add up to a multiple of nine, what can be the maximum number of elements in the subset. (Include both 1 and 3000.)
(a) 1668 (b) 1332
(c) 1333 (d) 1336

66. The series of numbers $(1, 1/2, 1/3, 1/4 ....1/1972)$ is taken. Now two numbers are taken from this series (the first two) say *x*, *y*. Then the operation $x + y + x.y$ is performed to get a consolidated number. The process is repeated. What will be the value of the set after all the numbers are consolidated into one number.
(a) 1970 (b) 1971
(c) 1972 (d) None of these

67. *K* is a three digit number such that the ratio of the number to the sum of its digits is least. What is the difference between the hundreds and the tens digits of *K*?
(a) 9 (b) 8
(c) 7 (d) None of these

68. In Question 67, what can be said about the difference between the tens and the units digit?
(a) 0 (b) 1
(c) 2 (d) None of these

69. For the above question, for how many values of *K* will the ratio be the highest?
(a) 9 (b) 8
(c) 7 (d) None of these

70. A triangular number is defined as a number which has the property of being expressed as a sum of consecutive natural numbers starting with 1. How many triangular numbers less than 1000, have the property that they are the difference of squares of two consecutive natural numbers?
(a) 20 (b) 21
(c) 22 (d) 23

71. *x* and *y* are two positive integers. Then what will be the sum of the coefficients of the expansion of the expression $(x + y)^{44}$? Answer: 2^{44}
(a) 2^{43} (b) $2^{43} + 1$
(c) 2^{44} (d) $2^{44} - 1$

72. What is the remainder when $9 + 9^2 + 9^3 + ...9^{2n+1}$ is divided by 6?
(a) 1 (b) 2
(c) 3 (d) 4

73. The remainder when the number 123456789101112 ......484950 is divided by 16 is:
(a) 3 (b) 4
(c) 5 (d) 6

74. What is the highest power of 3 available in the expression 58! − 38!?
(a) 17 (b) 18
(c) 19 (d) None of these

75. Find the remainder when the number represented by 22334 raised to the power $(1^2 + 2^2 + ..+ 66^2)$ is divided by 5?
(a) 2 (b) 4
(c) 1 (d) None of these

76. What is the total number of divisors of the number $12^{33} \times 34^{23} \times 2^{70}$?
(a) 4658. (b) 9316
(c) 2744 (d) None of these

77. For Question 76, which of the following will represent the sum of factors of the number (such that only odd factors are counted)?
(a) $\dfrac{(3^{34} - 1)}{2} \times \dfrac{(17^{24} - 1)}{16}$ (b) $(3^{34}-1) \times (17^{24} - 1)$
(c) $\dfrac{(3^{34} - 1)}{33}$ (d) None of these

78. What is the remainder when $(1!)^3 + (2!)^3 + (3!)^3 + (4!)^3 + ...(1152!)^3$ is divided by 1152?
(a) 125 (b) 225
(c) 325 (d) 205

79. A set *S* is formed by including some of the first One thousand natural numbers. *S* contains the maximum number of numbers such that they satisfy the following conditions:
1. No number of the set *S* is prime.
2. When the numbers of the set *S* are selected two at a time, we always see co prime numbers
What is the number of elements in the set S?
(a) 11 (b) 12
(c) 13 (d) 7

Find the last two digits of the following numbers

80. $101 \times 102 \times 103 \times 197 \times 198 \times 199$
(a) 54 (b) 74
(c) 64 (d) 84

81. $65 \times 29 \times 37 \times 63 \times 71 \times 87$
    - (a) 05
    - (b) 95
    - (c) 15
    - (d) 25

82. $65 \times 29 \times 37 \times 63 \times 71 \times 87 \times 85$
    - (a) 25
    - (b) 35
    - (c) 75
    - (d) 85

83. $65 \times 29 \times 37 \times 63 \times 71 \times 87 \times 62$
    - (a) 70
    - (b) 30
    - (c) 10
    - (d) 90

84. $75 \times 35 \times 47 \times 63 \times 71 \times 87 \times 82$
    - (a) 50
    - (b) 70
    - (c) 30
    - (d) 90

85. $(201 \times 202 \times 203 \times 204 \times 246 \times 247 \times 248 \times 249)^2$
    - (a) 36
    - (b) 56
    - (c) 76
    - (d) 16

86. Find the remainder when 7^{99} is divided by 2400.
    - (a) 1
    - (b) 343
    - (c) 49
    - (d) 7

87. Find the remainder when $(10^3 + 9^3)^{752}$ is divided by 12^3.
    - (a) 729
    - (b) 1000
    - (c) 752
    - (d) 1

88. Arun, Bikas and Chetakar have a total of 80 coins among them. Arun triples the number of coins with the others by giving them some coins from his own collection. Next, Bikas repeats the same process. After this Bikas now has 20 coins. Find the number of coins he had at the beginning?
    - (a) 22
    - (b) 20
    - (c) 18
    - (d) 24

89. The super computer at Ram Mohan Roy Seminary takes an input of a number N and a X where X is a factor of the number N. In a particular case N is equal to $83p\ 796161q$ and X is equal to 11 where $0 < p < q$, find the sum of remainders when N is divided by $(p + q)$ and p successively.
    - (a) 6
    - (b) 3
    - (c) 2
    - (d) 9

90. On March 1st 2016, Sherry saved Re.1. Everyday starting from March 2nd 2016, he saved Re.1 more than the previous day. Find the first date after March 1st 2016 at the end of which his total savings will be a perfect square.
    - (a) 17th March 2016
    - (b) 18th April 2016
    - (c) 26th March 2016
    - (d) None of these

91. What is the rightmost digit preceding the zeroes in the value of 20^{53}?
    - (a) 2
    - (b) 8
    - (c) 1
    - (d) 4

92. What is the remainder when $2(8!) - 21(6!)$ divides $14(7!) + 14(13!)$?
    - (a) 1
    - (b) 7!
    - (c) 8!
    - (d) 9!

93. How many integer values of x and y are there such that $4x + 7y = 3$, while $|x| < 500$ and $|y| < 500$?
    - (a) 144
    - (b) 141
    - (c) 143
    - (d) 142

94. If $n = 1 + m$, where m is the product of four consecutive positive integers, then which of the following is/are true?
    - (A) n is odd
    - (B) n is not a multiple of 3
    - (C) n is a perfect square
    - (a) All three
    - (b) A and B only
    - (c) A and C only
    - (d) None of these

95. How many two-digit numbers less than or equal to 50, have the product of the factorials of their digits less than or equal to the sum of the factorials of their digits?
    - (a) 18
    - (b) 16
    - (c) 15
    - (d) None of these

96. A candidate takes a test and attempts all the 100 questions in it. While any correct answer fetches 1 mark, wrong answers are penalised as follows; one-tenth of the questions carry 1/10 negative mark each, one-fifth of the questions carry 1/5 negative marks each and the rest of the questions carry ½ negative mark each. Unattempted questions carry no marks. What is the difference between the maximum and the minimum marks that he can score?
    - (a) 100
    - (b) 120
    - (c) 140
    - (d) None of these

Directions for Questions 97 to 99: A mock test is taken at Mindworkzz. The test paper comprises of questions in three levels of difficulty—LOD1, LOD2 and LOD 3.

The following table gives the details of the positive and negative marks attached to each question type:

Difficulty level	Positive marks for answering the question correctly	Negative marks for answering the question wrongly
LOD 1	4	2
LOD 2	3	1.5
LOD 3	2	1

The test had 200 questions with 80 on LOD 1 and 60 each on LOD 2 and LOD 3.

97. If a student has solved 100 questions exactly and scored 120 marks, the maximum number of incorrect questions that he/she might have marked is:
    - (a) 44
    - (b) 56
    - (c) 60
    - (d) None of these

98. If Amit attempted the least number of questions and got a total of 130 marks, and if it is known that he attempted at least one of every type, then the number of questions he must have attempted is:
    (a) 34
    (b) 35
    (c) 36
    (d) None of these

99. In the above question, what is the least number of questions he might have got incorrect?
    (a) 0
    (b) 1
    (c) 2
    (d) None of these

100. Amitabh has a certain number of toffees, such that if he distributes them amongst ten children he has nine left, if he distributes amongst 9 children he would have 8 left, if he distributes amongst 8 children he would have 7 left … and so on until if he distributes amongst 5 children he should have 4 left. What is the second lowest number of toffees he could have with him?
    (a) 2519
    (b) 7559
    (c) 8249
    (d) 5039

Space for Rough Work

LEVEL OF DIFFICULTY (III)

1. What two-digit number is less than the sum of the square of its digits by 11 and exceeds their doubled product by 5?
   (a) 15, 95   (b) 95
   (c) Both (a) and (b) (d) 15, 95 and 12345

2. Find the lower of the two successive natural numbers if the square of the sum of those numbers exceeds the sum of their squares by 112.
   (a) 6   (b) 7
   (c) 8   (d) 9

3. First we increased the denominator of a positive fraction by 3 and then we decreased it by 5. The sum of the resulting fractions proves to be equal to 19/42. Find the denominator of the fraction if its numerator is 2.
   (a) 7   (b) 8
   (c) 12   (d) 9

4. Find the last two digits of: $15 \times 37 \times 63 \times 51 \times 97 \times 17$.
   (a) 35   (b) 45
   (c) 55   (d) 85

5. Let us consider a fraction whose denominator is smaller than the square of the numerator by unity. If we add 2 to the numerator and the denominator, the fraction will exceed 1/3. If we subtract 3 from the numerator and the denominator, the fraction will be positive but smaller than 1/10. Find the value.
   (a) $\dfrac{3}{8}$ (b) $\dfrac{4}{15}$
   (c) $\dfrac{5}{24}$ (d) $\dfrac{6}{35}$

6. Find the sum of all three-digit numbers that give a remainder of 4 when they are divided by 5.
   (a) 98,270   (b) 99,270
   (c) 1,02,090   (d) 90,270

7. Find the sum of all two-digit numbers that give a remainder of 3 when they are divided by 7.
   (a) 686   (b) 676
   (c) 666   (d) 656

8. Find the sum of all odd three-digit numbers that are divisible by 5.
   (a) 50,500   (b) 50,250
   (c) 50,000   (d) 49,500

9. The product of a two-digit number by a number consisting of the same digits written in the reverse order is equal to 2430. Find the lower number.

10. Find the lowest of three numbers as described: If the cube of the first number exceeds their product by 2, the cube of the second number is smaller than their product by 3, and the cube of the third number exceeds their product by 3.
    (a) $3^{1/3}$ (b) $9^{1/3}$
    (c) 2   (d) Any of these
    (e) None of these

11. How many pairs of natural numbers are there the difference of whose squares is 45?
    (a) 1   (b) 2
    (c) 3   (d) 4

12. Find all two-digit numbers such that the sum of the digits constituting the number is not less than 7; the sum of the squares of the digits is not greater than 30; the number consisting of the same digits written in the reverse order is not larger than half the given number.
    (a) 52   (b) 51
    (c) 49   (d) 53

13. In a four-digit number, the sum of the digits in the thousands, hundreds and tens is equal to 14, and the sum of the digits in the units, tens and hundreds is equal to 15. Among all the numbers satisfying these conditions, find the number the sum of the squares of whose digits is the greatest.
    (a) 2572   (b) 1863
    (c) 2573   (d) None of these

14. In a four-digit number, the sum of the digits in the thousands and tens is equal to 4, the sum of the digits in the hundreds and the units is 15, and the digit of the units exceeds by 7 the digit of the thousands. Among all the numbers satisfying these conditions, find the number the sum of the product of whose digit of the thousands by the digit of the units and the product of the digit of the hundreds by that of the tens assumes the least value.
    (a) 4708   (b) 1738
    (c) 2629   (d) 1812

15. If we divide a two-digit number by a number consisting of the same digits written in the reverse order, we get 4 as a quotient and 15 as a remainder. If we subtract 1 from the given number, we get the sum of the squares of the digits constituting that number. Find the number.
    (a) 71   (b) 83
    (c) 99   (d) None of these

(a) 54   (b) 52
(c) 63   (d) 45

16. Find the two-digit number the quotient of whose division by the product of its digits is equal to 8/3, and the difference between the required number and the number consisting of the same digits written in the reverse order is 18

(a) 86   (b) 42
(c) 75   (d) None of these

17. Find the two-digit number if it is known that the ratio of the required number and the sum of its digits is 8 as also the quotient of the product of its digits and that of the sum is 14/9.

(a) 54   (b) 72
(c) 27   (d) 45

18. If we divide the unknown two-digit number by the number consisting of the same digits written in the reverse order, we get 4 as a quotient and 3 as a remainder. If we divide the required number by the sum of its digits, we get 8 as a quotient and 7 as a remainder. Find the number.

(a) 81   (b) 91
(c) 71   (d) 72

19. The last two-digits in the multiplication $122 \times 123 \times 125 \times 127 \times 129$ will be

(a) 20   (b) 50
(c) 30   (d) 40

20. The remainder obtained when $43^{101} + 23^{101}$ is divided by 66 is:

(a) 2   (b) 10
(c) 5   (d) 0

21. The last three-digits of the multiplication 12345×54321 will be

(a) 865   (b) 745
(c) 845   (d) 945

22. The sum of the digits of a three-digit number is 12. If we subtract 495 from the number consisting of the same digits written in reverse order, we shall get the required number. Find that three-digit number if the sum of all pairwise products of the digits constituting that number is 41.

(a) 156   (b) 237
(c) 197   (d) Both (a) and (b)

23. A three-digit positive integer abc is such that $a^2 + b^2 + c^2 = 74$. a is equal to the doubled sum of the digits in the tens and units places. Find the number if it is known that the difference between that number and the number written by the same digits in the reverse order is 495.

(a) 813   (b) 349
(c) 613   (d) 713

24. Represent the number 1.25 as a product of three positive factors so that the product of the first factor by the square of the second is equal to 5 if we have to get the lowest possible sum of the three factors.

(a) $x_1 = 2.25, x_2 = 5, x_3 = 0.2$
(b) $x_1 = 1.25, x_2 = 4, x_3 = 4.5$
(c) $x_1 = 1.25, x_2 = 2, x_3 = 0.5$
(d) $x_1 = 1.25, x_2 = 4, x_3 = 2$

25. Find a number x such that the sum of that number and its square is the least.

(a) −0.5   (b) 0.5
(c) −1.5   (d) 1.5

26. When $2222^{5555} + 5555^{2222}$ is divided by 7, the remainder is

(a) 0   (b) 2
(c) 4   (d) 5

27. If x is a number of five-digits which when divided by 8, 12, 15 and 20 leaves respectively 5, 9, 12 and 17 as remainders, then find x such that it is the lowest such number.

(a) 10017   (b) 10057
(c) 10097   (d) 10137

28. $3^{2n} - 1$ is divisible by 2^{n+3} for $n =$

(a) 1   (b) 2
(c) 3   (d) None of these

29. $10^n - \left(5 + \sqrt{17}\right)^n$ is divisible by 2^{n+2} for what whole number value of n?

(a) 2   (b) 3
(c) 7   (d) None of these

30. $\dfrac{32^{32^{32}}}{9}$ will leave a remainder:

(a) 4   (b) 7
(c) 1   (d) 2

31. Find the remainder that the number $1989 \cdot 1990 \cdot 1992^3$ gives when divided by 7.

(a) 0   (b) 1
(c) 5   (d) 2

32. Find the remainder of 2^{100} when divided by 3.

(a) 3   (b) 0
(c) 1   (d) 2

33. Find the remainder when the number 3^{1989} is divided by 7.

(a) 1   (b) 5
(c) 6   (d) 4

34. Find the last digit of the number $1^2 + 2^2 + ... + 99^2$.

(a) 0   (b) 1
(c) 2   (d) 3

35. Find gcd $(2^{100} - 1, 2^{120} - 1)$.

(a) $2^{20} - 1$ (b) $2^{40} - 1$
(c) $2^{60} - 1$ (d) $2^{10} - 1$

36. Find the gcd (111...11 hundred ones ; 11...11 sixty ones).

(a) 111…,forty ones   (b) 111…twenty five ones

(c) 111…twenty ones   (d) 111…sixty ones

37. Find the last digit of the number $1^3 + 2^3 + 3^3 + 4^3 \ldots + 99^3$.

   (a) 0   (b) 1

   (c) 2   (d) 5

38. Find the GCD of the numbers $2n + 13$ and $n + 7$.

   (a) 1   (b) 2

   (c) 3   (d) 4

39. $\dfrac{32^{32^{32}}}{7}$

   (a) 4   (b) 2

   (c) 1   (d) 3

40. The remainder when $10^{10} + 10^{100} + 10^{1000} + \ldots + 10^{10000000000}$ is divided by 7 is

   (a) 0   (b) 1

   (c) 2   (d) 5

41. n is a number, such that $2n$ has 28 factors and $3n$ has 30 factors. $6n$ has.

   (a) 35   (b) 32

   (c) 28   (d) None of these

42. Suppose the sum of n consecutive integers is $x + (x + 1) + (x + 2) + (x + 3) + \ldots + (x + (n - 1)) = 1000$, then which of the following cannot be true about the number of terms n

   (a) The number of terms can be 16

   (b) The number of terms can be 5

   (c) The number of terms can be 25

   (d) The number of terms can be 20

43. The remainder when $2^2 + 22^2 + 222^2 + 2222^2 + \ldots\ldots(222\ldots..49\ \text{twos})^2$ is divided by 9 is:

   (a) 2   (b) 5

   (c) 6   (d) 7

44. $N = 202 \times 20002 \times 200000002 \times 20000000000000002 \times 200000000\ldots.2$ (31 zeroes) The sum of digits in this multiplication will be:

   (a) 112   (b) 160

   (c) 144   (d) Cannot be determined

45. Twenty five sets of problems on Data Interpretation–one each for the DI sections of 25 CATALYST tests were prepared by the AMS research team. The DI section of each CATALYST contained 50 questions of which exactly 35 questions were unique, i.e. they had not been used in the DI section of any of the other 24 CATALYSTs. What could be the maximum possible number of questions prepared for the DI sections of all the 25 CATALYSTs put together?

   (a) 1100   (b) 975

   (c) 1070   (d) 1055

46. In the above question, what could be the minimum possible number of questions prepared?

   (a) 890   (b) 875

   (c) 975   (d) None of these

Directions for Questions 47 to 49: At a particular time in the twenty first century there were seven bowlers in the Indian cricket team's list of 16 players short listed to play the next world cup. Statisticians discovered that that if you looked at the number of wickets taken by any of the 7 bowlers of the current Indian cricket team, the number of wickets taken by them had a strange property. The numbers were such that for any team selection of 11 players (having 1 to 7 bowlers) by using the number of wickets taken by each bowler and attaching coefficients of +1, 0, or –1 to each value available and adding the resultant values, any number from 1 to 1093, both included could be formed. If we denote W_1, W_2, W_3, W_4, W_5, W_6 and W_7 as the 7 values in the ascending order what could be the answer to the following questions:

47. Find the value of $W_1 + 2W_2 + 3W_3 + 4W_4 + 5W_5 + 6W_6$.

   (a) 2005   (b) 1995

   (c) 1985   (d) None of these

48. Find the index of the largest power of 3 contained in the product $W_1 W_2 W_3 W_4 W_5 W_6 W_7$.

   (a) 15   (b) 10

   (c) 21   (d) 6

49. If the sum of the seven coefficients is 0, find the smallest number that can be obtained.

   (a) – 1067   (b) – 729

   (c) – 1040   (d) – 1053

Directions for Questions 50 and 51: Answer these questions on the basis of the information given below.

In the ancient game of Honololo the task involves solving a puzzle asked by the chief of the tribe. Anybody answering the puzzle correctly is given the hand of the most beautiful maiden of the tribe. Unfortunately, for the youth of the tribe, solving the puzzle is not a cakewalk since the chief is the greatest mathematician of the tribe.

In one such competition the chief called everyone to attention and announced openly:

"A three-digit number 'mnp' is a perfect square and the number of factors it has is also a perfect square. It is also known that the digits m, n and p are all distinct. Now answer my questions and win the maiden's hand."

50. If ($m + n + p$) is also a perfect square, what is the number of factors of the six-digit number $mnpmnp$?

   (a) 32   (b) 72

   (c) 48   (d) Cannot be determined

51. If the fourth power of the product of the digits of the number mnp is not divisible by 5, what is the number of factors of the nine-digit number, $mnpmnpmnp$?

   (a) 32   (b) 72

   (c) 48   (d) Cannot be determined

52. In a cricket tournament organised by the ICC, a total of 15 teams participated. Australia, as usual won the tournament by scoring the maximum number of points. The tournament is organised as a single round robin tournament—where each team plays with every other team exactly once. 3 points are awarded for a win, 2 points are awarded for a tie/washed out match and 1 point is awarded for a loss. Zimbabwe had the lowest score (in terms of points) at the end of the tournament. Zimbabwe scored a total of 21 points. All the 15 national teams got a distinct score (in terms of points scored). It is also known that at least one match played by the Australian team was tied/washed out. Which of the following is always true for the Australian team?

    (a) It had at least two ties/washouts.
    (b) It had a maximum of 3 losses.
    (c) It had a maximum of 9 wins.
    (d) All of the above.

53. What is the remainder when 128^{1000} is divided by 153?

    (a) 103   (b) 145
    (c) 118   (d) 52

54. Find the remainder when $50^{51^{52}}$ is divided by 11.

    (a) 6   (b) 4
    (c) 7 ·   (d) 3

55. Find the remainder when $32^{33^{34}}$ is divided by 11.

    (a) 5   (b) 4
    (c) 10   (d) 1

56. Find the remainder when $30^{72^{87}}$ is divided by 11.

    (a) 5   (b) 9
    (c) 6   (d) 3

57. Find the remainder when $50^{56^{52}}$ is divided by 11.

    (a) 7   (b) 5
    (c) 9   (d) 10

58. Find the remainder when $33^{34^{35}}$ is divided by 7.

    (a) 5   (b) 4
    (c) 6   (d) 2

59. Let S_m denote the sum of the squares of the first m natural numbers. For how many values of $m < 100$, is S_m a multiple of 4?

    (a) 50   (b) 25
    (c) 36   (d) 24

60. For the above question, for how many values will the sum of cubes of the first m natural numbers be a multiple of 5 (if $m < 50$)?

    (a) 20   (b) 21
    (c) 22   (d) None of these

61. How many integer values of x and y satisfy the expression $4x + 7y = 3$ where $|x| < 1000$ and $|y| < 1000$?

    (a) 284   (b) 285
    (c) 286   (d) None of these

Space for Rough Work

ANSWER KEY

Level of Difficulty (I)

1. (a)	2. (a)	3. (b)	4. (b)
5. (a)	6. (c)	7. (d)	8. (d)
9. (d)	10. (d)	11. (a)	12. (c)
13. (d)	14. (d)	15. (b)	16. (c)
17. (b)	18. (d)	19. (a)	20. (b)
21. (d)	22. (a)	23. (b)	24. (c)
25. (d)	26. (d)	27. (c)	28. (d)
29. (b)	30. (d)	31. (a)	32. (b)
33. (c)	34. (d)	35. (c)	36. (b)
37. (d)	38. (d)	39. (b)	40. (b)
41. (a)	42. (a)	43. (a)	44. (d)
45. (c)	46. (d)	47. (b)	48. (c)
49. (c)	50. (d)	51. (a)	52. (a)
53. (b)	54. (c)	55. (d)	56. (b)
57. (a)	58. (b)	59. (d)	60. (d)
61. (a)	62. (a) $\rightarrow (21)^{12}$ (b) $\rightarrow (0.8)^3$		
63. (b)			

64. 1. → 0, 2, 4, 6, 8
    2. → 1, 4, 7
    3. → 0, 4, 8
    4. → 0, 5
    5. → 4
    6. → 7
    7. → 0

65. LCM → 17010
    HCF → 27
    LCM → 780
    HCF → 29
    LCM → 245700
    HCF → 30

66. (b)	67. (a)	68. (c)	69. (c)
70. (c)	71. (a)	72. (d)	73. (b)
74. (b)	75. (a)	76. (b)	77. (d)
78. (a)	79. (a)	80. (b)	81. (c)
82. (b)	83. (c)	84. (c)	85. (c)
86. (a)	87. (c)	88. (b)	89. (b)
90. (c)	91. (d)	92. (d)	93. (a)
94. (c)	95. (c)	96. (b)	97. (a)
98. (c)	99. (c)	100. (d)	101. (d)
102. (a)	103. (c)	104. (b)	105. (c)
106. (d)	107. (b)	108. (c)	109. (d)
110. (c)	111. (c)	112. (c)	113. (a)
114. (c)	115. (a)	116. (d)	117. (d)
118. (b)	119. (b)	120. (c)	121. (b)
122. (b)	123. (d)	124. (a)	125. (d)
126. (a)	127. (b)	128. (d)	129. (c)
130. (b)	131. (b)	132. (a)	133. (c)
134. (d)	135. (b)	136. (b)	137. (c)
138. (b)	139. (d)	140. (a)	

Level of Difficulty (II)

1. (a)	2. (b)	3. (c)	4. (b)
5. (b)	6. (b)	7. (b)	8. (d)
9. (c)	10. (c)	11. (d)	12. (d)
13. (d)	14. (c)	15. (b)	16. (d)
17. (a)	18. (d)	19. (c)	20. (a)
21. (a)	22. (c)	23. (b)	24. (a)
25. (d)	26. (c)	27. (c)	28. (d)
29. (b)	30. (b)	31. (a)	32. (b)
33. (a)	34. (a)	35. (b)	36. (b)
37. (a)	38. (d)	39. (c)	40. (a)
41. (24)	42. (63)	43. (24)	44. (32)
45. (27)	46. (64)	47. (13, 31)	48. (23)
49. (1056)	50. (51, 34)	51. (144, 864)	52. (46,64)
53. (63)	54. (863)	55. (36, 63)	

56. may be 2 or 3 depending upon the numbers
57. $111^4 > 109.110.112.113 > 110.109.108.107$
58. greatest → 35 least 3/7
59. (a) 200^{300} (b) 5^{100} (c) 10^{20} 60. (12, 3)

61. (c)	62. (a)	63. (b)	64. (a)
65. (d)	66. (c)	67. (b)	68. (a)
69. (a)	70. (b)	71. (c)	72. (c)
73. (d)	74. (a)	75. (b)	76. (d)
77. (a)	78. (b)	79. (b)	80. (c)
81. (b)	82. (c)	83. (d)	84. (a)
85. (c)	86. (b)	87. (d)	88. (b)
89. (d)	90. (d)	91. (a)	92. (b)
93. (c)	94. (a)	95. (a)	96. (c)
97. (b)	98. (a)	99. (a)	100. (d)

Level of Difficulty (III)

1. (a)	2. (b)	3. (d)	4. (a)
5. (b)	6. (b)	7. (b)	8. (d)
9. (d)	10. (a)	11. (c)	12. (a)
13. (d)	14. (b)	15. (d)	16. (d)
17. (b)	18. (c)	19. (b)	20. (d)
21. (b)	22. (d)	23. (a)	24. (c)
25. (a)	26. (d)	27. (d)	28. (d)
29. (d)	30. (a)	31. (d)	32. (c)
33. (c)	34. (a)	35. (a)	36. (c)
37. (a)	38. (a)	39. (a)	40. (d)
41. (a)	42. (d)	43. (c)	44. (b)
45. (d)	46. (a)	47. (a)	48. (c)
49. (c)	50. (d)	51. (d)	52. (b)
53. (d)	54. (a)	55. (c)	56. (a)
57. (b)	58. (d)	59. (d)	60. (d)
61. (b)			

Solutions and Shortcuts

Level of Difficulty (I)

1. The units digit in this case would obviously be '0' because the given expression has a pair of 2 and 5 in it's prime factors.

2. When you read the sentence "when the digits are reversed, the number decreases by 54, you should automatically get two reactions going in your mind.

   (i) The difference between the digits would be $54/9 = 6$.

   (ii) Since the number 'decreases'- the tens digit of the number would be larger than the units digit.

   Also, since we know that the sum of the digits is 10, we get that the digits must be 8 and 2 and the number must be 82. Thus, the changed number is 28.

3. The two numbers should be factors of 405. A factor search will yield the factors. (look only for 2 digit factors of 405 with sum of digits between 1 to 19). Also $405 = 5 \times 3^4$. Hence: 15×27

   45×9 are the only two options.

   From these factors pairs only the second pair gives us the desired result.

   i.e. Number × sum of digits = 405.

   Hence, the answer is 45.

4. You can solve this question by using options. It can be seen that Option (b) 12,3 fits the situation perfectly as their Arithmetic mean = 7.5 and their geometric mean = 6 and the geometric mean is 20% less than the arithmetic mean

5. Two more than half of $1/3^{rd}$ of 96 = 18. Also since we are given that the difference between the AM and GM is 18, it means that the GM must be an integer. From amongst the options, only option (a) gives us a GM which is an integer. Thus, checking for option 1, we get the GM=7 and AM=18.

6. For the number A381 to be divisible by 11, the sum of the even placed digits and the odds placed digits should be either 0 or a multiple of 11. This means that $(A + 8) - (3 + 1)$ should be a multiple of 11 – as it is not possible to make it zero. Thus, the smallest value that A can take (and in fact the only value it can take) is 7. Option (c) is correct.

7. For $381A$ to be divisible by 9, the sum of the digits $3 + 8 + 1 + A$ should be divisible by 9. For that to happen A should be 6. Option (d) is correct.

8. 9^6 when divided by 8, would give a remainder of 1. Hence, the required answer would be 2.

9. LCM of 5, 15 and 20 = 60. HCF of 5, 15 and 20 = 5. The required ratio is 60:5 = 12:1.

10. LCM of 5/2, 8/9 and 11/14 would be given by: (LCM of numerators)/(HCF of denominators)
    = 440/1 = 440

11. Only the first option can be verified to be true in this case. If A is even, 3A would always be divisible by 6 as it would be divisible by both 2 and 3. Options b and c can be seen to be incorrect by assuming the value of A as 4.

12. The essence of this question is in the fact that the last digit of the number is 0. Naturally, the number is necessarily divisible by 2,5 and 10. Only 4 does not necessarily divide it.

13. B would necessarily be even- as the possible values of B for the three digit number 15B to be divisible by 6 are 0 and 6. Also, the condition stated in option (c) is also seen to be true in this case – as both 0 and 6 are divisible by 6. Thus, option (d) is correct.

14. For the GCD take the least powers of all common prime factors.

    Thus, the required answer would be $2^3 \times 3$

15. The units digit would be given by $5 + 6 + 9$ (numbers ending in 5 and 6 would always end in 5 and 6 irrespective of the power and 3^{54} will give a units digit equivalent to 3^{4n+2} which would give us a unit digit of 3^2 i.e.9)

16. The respective units digits for the three parts of the expression would be:

    $5 + 9 + 2 = 16 \rightarrow$ required answer is 6. Option (c) is correct.

17. The respective units digits for the six parts of the expression would be:

    $1 + 4 + 7 + 6 + 5 + 6 = 29 \rightarrow$ required answer is 9. Option (b) is correct.

18. The respective units digits for the six parts of the expression would be:

    $1 \times 4 \times 7 \times 6 \times 5 \times 6 \rightarrow$ required answer is 0. Option (d) is correct.

19. The number of zeroes would be given by adding the quotients when we successively divide 1090 by 5:

    $1090/5 + 218/5 + 43/5 + 8/5 = 218 + 43 + 8 + 1 = 270$. Option (a) is correct.

20. The number of 5's in 146! can be got by [146/5] + [29/5] + [5/5]= 29+5+1 = 35

21. $1420 = 142 \times 10 = 2^2 \times 71^1 \times 5^1$.

    Thus, the number of factors of the number would be $(2 + 1)(1 + 1)(1 + 1) = 3 \times 2 \times 2 = 12$.

    Option (d) is correct.

22. $(x^2 - 5x + 6) = (x - 2)(x - 3)$

    $\& (x^2 - 7x + 10) = (x - 5)(x - 2)$

    Required HCF = $(x - 2)$; required LCM = $(x - 2)(x - 3)(x - 5)$.

    Option (a) is correct.

23. Since both P and Q are prime numbers, the number of factors would be $(1 + 1)(1 + 1) = 4$.

24. Since both P and Q are prime numbers, the number of factors would be $(2 + 1)(1 + 1) = 6$.

25. Since both P and Q are prime numbers, the number of factors would be $(3 + 1)(2 + 1) = 12$.

26. The sides of the pentagon being 1422, 1737, 2160, 2214 and 2358, the least difference between any two numbers is 54. Hence, the correct answer will be a factor of 54.

    Further, since there are some odd numbers in the list, the answer should be an odd factor of 54.

    Hence, check with 27, 9 and 3 in that order. You will get 9 as the HCF.

27. The HCF of 576 and 448 is 32. Hence, each section should have 32 children. The number of sections would be given by: $576/32 + 448/32 = 18 + 14 = 32$. Option (b) is correct.

28. The HCF of the given numbers is 31 and hence the number of bottles required would be:

    $403/31 + 465/31 + 496/31 = 13 + 15 + 16 = 44$. Option (d) is correct.

29. The LCM of the 4 numbers is 612. The highest 4 digit number which would be a common multiple of all these 4 numbers is 9792. Hence, the correct answer is 9793.

30. The LCM of 16, 18 and 20 is 720. The numbers which would give a remainder of 4, when divided by 16, 18 and 20 would be given by the series:

    724, 1444, 2164, 2884 and so on. Checking each of these numbers for divisibility by 7, it can be seen that 2884 is the least number in the series that is divisible by 7 and hence is the correct answer. Option (d) is correct.

31. They will ring together again after a time which would be the LCM of 6, 8, 12 and 18. The required LCM = 72. Hence, they would ring together after 72 seconds. Option (a) is correct.

32. $720/72 = 10$ times. Option (b) is correct.

33. $5 \times 7 \times 6 = 0$. Option (c) is correct.

34. All these numbers can be verified to not be perfect squares. Option (d) is correct.

35. A perfect square can never end in an odd number of zeroes. Option (c) is correct.

36. It is obvious that the LCM of 5,12,18 and 20 would never be a multiple of 9. At the same time it has to be a multiple of each of 3, 8 and 5. Option (b) is correct.

37. $720 = 2^4 \times 3^2 \times 5^1$. Number of factors $= 5 \times 3 \times 2 = 30$. Option (d) is correct.

38. $16 - x^2 = (4 - x)(4 + x)$ and $x^2 + x - 6 = (x + 3)(x - 2)$

    The required LCM $= (4 - x)(4 + x)(x + 3)(x - 2)$. Option (d) is correct.

39. $x^2 - 4 = (x - 2)(x + 2)$ and $x^2 + x - 6 = (x + 3)(x - 2)$ GCD or HCF of these expressions $= (x - 2)$. Option (b) is correct.

40. If A is not divisible by 3, it is obvious that 2A would also not be divisible by 3, as 2A would have no '3' in it.

41. $9^{100}/8 = (8 + 1)^{100}/8 \rightarrow$ Since this is of the form $(a + 1)^n/a$, the Remainder $= 1$. Option (a) is correct.

42. $2^{1000}/3$ is of the form $(a)^{\text{EVEN POWER}}/(a + 1)$. The remainder $= 1$ in this case as the power is even. Option (a) is correct.

43. The condition for the product to be the greatest is if the two terms are equal. Thus, the break up in option (a) would give us the highest product of the two parts. Option (a) is correct.

44. $50/5 = 10$, $10/5 = 2$.

    Thus, the required answer would be $10 + 2 = 12$. Option (d) is correct.

45. Checking each of the options it can be seen that the value in option (c)[viz: 1362480]is divisible by 24.

46. Any number divisible by 88, has to be necessarily divisible by 11, 2, 4, 8, 44 and 22. Thus, each of the first three options is correct.

47. $10800 = 108 \times 100 = 3^3 \times 2^4 \times 5^2$.

    The number of divisors would be: $(3 + 1)(4 + 1)(2 + 1) = 4 \times 5 \times 3 = 60$ divisors. Option (b) is correct.

48. The GCD (also known as HCF) would be got by multiplying the least powers of all common factors of the two polynomials. The common factors are $(x + 3)$ – least power 1, and $(x + 1)$ – least power 2. Thus, the answer would be $(x + 3)(x + 1)^2$. Option (c) is correct.

49. For the LCM of polynomials write down the highest powers of all available factors of all the polynomials. The correct answer would be $(x + 3)(3x + 4)(4x^2 - 1)$

50. Three consecutive natural numbers, starting with an even number would always have at least three 2's as their prime factors and also would have at least one multiple of 3 in them. Thus, 6, 12 and 24 would each divide the product.

51. When the birds sat one on a branch, there was one extra bird. When they sat 2 to a branch one branch was extra.

    To find the number of branches, go through options. Checking option (a), if there were 3 branches, there would be 4 birds. (this would leave one bird without branch as per the question.)

    When 4 birds would sit 2 to a branch there would be 1 branch free (as per the question). Hence, the answer (a) is correct.

52. The number would either be $(3n + 1)^2$ or $(3n + 2)^2$. In the expansion of each of these the only term which would not be divisible by 3 would be the square of

1 and 2 respectively. When divided by 3, both of these give 1 as remainder.

53. The given expression can be written as:
$5^3 \times 3^3 \times 3^2 \times 7^2/5^2 \times 7^2 \times 3^4 = 5^3 \times 3^5 \times 7^2/5^2 \times 7^2 \times 3^4 = 15$. Option (b) is correct.

54. $D = 1.44$, $C = 0.09$, $B = 0.16$, while the value of A is negative.
Thus, $D > B > C > A$ is the required order. Option (c) is correct.

55. The upper limit for $x + y = 4 + 3 = 7$. The lower limit of $x - y = 2 - 3 = -1$. Required ratio $= 7/-1 = -7$.
Option (d) is correct.

56. For the sum of squares of digits to be 13, it is obvious that the digits should be 2 and 3. So the number can only be 23 or 32. Further, the number being referred to has to be 32 since the reduction of 9, reverses the digits.

57. trying the value in the options you get that the product of $54 \times 45 = 2430$. Option (a) is correct.

58. Option (b) can be verified to be true as the LCM of 90 and 24 is indeed 360.

59. The pairs given in option (d) 78 and 13 and 26 and 39 meet both the conditions of LCM of 78 and HCF of 13. Option (d) is correct.

60. Solve using options. Option (d) 51 and 34 satisfies the required conditions.

61. $28^2 - 27^2 = 55$ and so also $8^2 - 3^2 = 55$. Option (a) is correct.

62. (a) $21^{12} = (21^3)^4$
Since $21^3 > 54$, $21^{12} > 54^4$.
(b) $(0.4)^4 = (4/10)^4 = 1024/10000 = 0.1024$.
$(0.8)^3 = (8/10)^3 = 512/1000 = 0.512$
Hence, $(0.8)^3 > (0.4)^4$.

63. This is never possible.

64. 1. $c = 0, 2, 4, 6$ or 8 would make $38c$ as even and hence divisible by 2.
2. $c = 1, 4$ or 7 are possible values to make $38c$ divisible by 3.
3. $c = 0, 4$ or 8 would make the number end in 80, 84 or 88 and would hence be divisible by 4.
4. $c = 0$ or 5 would make the number 380 or 385 – in which case it would be divisible by 5.
5. For the number to become divisible by 6, it should be even and divisible by 3. From the values 1, 4 and 7 which make the number divisible by 3, we only have $c = 4$ making it even. Thus, $c = 4$.
6. For the number to be divisible by 9, $3 + 8 + c$ should be a multiple of 9. $c = 7$ is the only value of c which can make the number divisible by 9.
7. Obviously $c = 0$ is the correct answer.

65. Use the standard process to solve for LCM and HCF.

66. For $34x^{43}$ to be ending in 7, x has to be 3 (as $43 = 4n + 3$). Option (b) is correct.

Solutions for 67 & 68:

The given condition says that Pen<Pencil<Eraser.

Also, since the least cost of the three is ₹12, if we allocate a minimum of 12 to each we use up 36 out of the 41 available. The remaining 5 can be distributed as 0,1,4 or 0,2 and 3 giving possible values of Case 1: 12,13 and 16 or Case 2: 12,14 and 15.

67. In both cases, the cost of the pen is 12.

68. If the cost of the eraser is not divisible by 4, it means that Case 2 holds true. For this case, the cost of the pencil is 14.

69. Amrit would place eight oranges in the basket (as there are eight 1's).
For the mangoes, he would place six mangoes (number of 2's) and remove four mangoes (number of 4's) from the basket. Thus, there would be 2 mangoes and 8 oranges in the basket.
A total of $8 - 2 = 6$ extra oranges in the basket. Option (c) is correct.

70. Solve using trial and error – Option (c) fits the situation as if we start with 15 mangoes, the following structure would take place:
Start with 15 mangoes → First watchman takes $1/3^{rd}$ + 1 more = 5 + 1 = 6 mangoes → 9 mangoes left.
Second watchman takes → $1/3^{rd}$ + 1 more = 3 + 1 = 4 mangoes → 5 mangoes left.
Third watchman takes → $1/5^{th}$ + 4 more = 1 + 4 = 5 mangoes → 0 mangoes left.

71. The last 3 digits of the number would determine the remainder when it is divided by 8. The number upto the 120th digit would be 1234567891011… 646. 646 divided by 8 gives us a remainder of 6.

72. There would be multiple ways of scoring 34.5 marks. Think about this as follows:
If he solves 80 and gets all 80 correct, he would end up scoring 80 marks.
With every question that would go wrong his score would fall down by: 1.5 marks (he would lose the 1 mark he is gaining and further attract a penalty of 0.5 marks).
Also, for every question he does not attempt his score would fall down by: 1.25 marks (he would lose the 1 mark he is gaining and further attract a penalty of 0.25 marks).
Thus, his score would drop @ 1.5 and @1.25 marks for every wrong and every unattempted question respectively.
Also, to get a total of 34.5 marks overall he has to lose 45.5 marks.

There are many possible combinations of non attempts and wrongs through which he can possibly lose 45.5 marks—for example:

17 wrongs (loses 25.5 marks) and 16 non-attempts (loses 20 marks)

12 wrongs (loses 18 marks) and 22 non attempts (loses 27.5 marks)

Hence, we cannot answer this question uniquely and the answer is Option (d).

73. Continuing the thought process for the previous question our thinking would go as follows:

10 questions unanswered → loses 12.5 marks

To lose another 33 marks he needs to get 22 incorrects.

Thus, the number of corrects would be $80 - 10 - 22 = 48$. Option (b) is correct.

74. $3M + 4G + 5W = 750$ (i)

$6M + 9G + 10W = 1580$ (ii)

Adding the two equations we get:

$9M + 13G + 15W = 2330$ (iii)

Dividing this expression by 3 we get:

$3M + 4.33G + 5W = 776.666$ (iv)

(iv) - (i) → $0.33 G = 26.666 → G = 80$

Now, if we look at the equation (i) and multiply it by 2, we get: $6M + 8G + 10W = 1500$. If we subtract the cost of 4 guavas from this we would get:

$6M + 4G + 10W = 1500 - 320 = 1180$

Option (b) is correct.

75. If you try a value of M as 5, N would become ¼. It can be seen that $5^{1/4}$ (which would be the value of M^N) would be around 1.4 and hence, less than 2.

If you try for possible values of M^N by increasing the value of M, you would get $6^{1/5}$, $7^{1/6}$, $8^{1/7}$, $9^{1/8}$ and so on. In each of these cases you can clearly see that the value of M^N would always be getting consecutively smaller than the previous value.

If you tried to go for values of M such that they are lower than 5, you would get the following values for M^N:

$4^{1/3}$, $3^{1/2}$ and the last value would be $2^{1/1}$. In this case, we can clearly see that the value of the expression M^N is increasing. However, it ends at the value of 2 (for $2^{1/1}$) and hence that is the maximum value that M^N can take. Option (a) is correct.

76. $(7M + 9G + 19W) - (4M + 6G + 16W) = 120$. Hence, $1M + 1G + 1W = 40$

77. The cost of a mango cannot be uniquely determined here because we have only 2 equations between 3 variables, and there is no way to eliminate one variable.

78. Since the value of y varies between -8 to 2, it is evident that if we take a very small value for y, say 0.0000000000000000000000001, and we take normal integral values for x and z, the expression

xz/y would become either positive or negative infinity (depending on how you manage the signs of the numbers x, y and z).

79. Ties < Trousers < Shirts. Since each of the three is minimum 11, the total would be a minimum of 33 (for all 3). The remaining 5 need to be distributed amongst ties, trousers and shirts so that they can maintain the inequality Ties < Trousers < Shirts

This can be achieved with 11 ties, and the remaining 27 pieces of clothing distributed between trousers and shirts such that the shirts are greater than the trousers.

This can be done in at least 2 ways: 12 trousers and 15 shirts; 13 trousers and 14 shirts.

If you try to go for 12 ties, the remaining 26 pieces of clothing need to be distributed amongst shirts and trousers such that the shirts are greater than the trousers and both are greater than 12.

With only 26 pieces of clothing to be distributed between shirts and trousers this is not possible. Hence, the number of ties has to be exactly 11. Option (a) is correct.

80. The number of shirts would be at least 14 as the two distributions possible are: 11, 12, 15 and 11, 13, 14. Option (b) is correct.

81. The LCM of 12, 15, 18 and 20 is 180. Thus, the least number would be 184.

Option (c) is correct.

82. $2800 = 20 \times 20 \times 7$. Thus, we need to multiply or divide with 7 in order to make it a perfect square.

83. The answer is given by $\sqrt{1024} = 32$.

This can be experimentally verified as $30^2 = 900$, $31^2 = 961$ and $32^2 = 1024$. Hence, 1024 is the required answer. Option (c) is correct.

84. First find the LCM of 6, 9, 15 and 18. Their LCM $= 18 \times 5 = 90$.

The series of numbers which would leave a remainder of 4 when divided by 6, 9, 15 and 18 would be given by:

LCM + 4; $2 \times$ LCM + 4; $3 \times$ LCM + 4; $4 \times$ LCM + 4; $5 \times$ LCM + 4 and so on .

Thus, this series would be:

94, 184, 274, 364, 454....

The other constraint in the problem is to find a number which also has the property of being divisible by 7. Checking each of the numbers in the series above for their divisibility by 7, we see that 364 is the least value which is also divisible by 7. Option (c) is correct.

85. LCM of 2, 3, 4, 5 and $6 = 6 \times 5 \times 2 = 60$ (Refer to the shortcut process for LCM given in the chapter notes).

Thus, the series 61, 121, 181 etc would give us a remainder 1 when divided by 2, 3, 4, 5 and 6.

The least 3 digit number in this series is 121. Option (c) is correct.

86. $70 = 2 \times 5 \times 7$; $245 = 5 \times 7 \times 7$.

    HCF $= 5 \times 7 = 35$. Option (a) is correct.

87. 7056 is the closest perfect square below 7147. Hence, $7147 - 7056 = 91$ is the required answer. Option (c) is correct.

88. If you check each of the options, you can clearly see that the number 3600 is divisible by each of these numbers. Option (b) is correct.

    Alternately, you can also think about this question as:

    The LCM of 6, 8 and 15 = 120. Thus, we need to look for a perfect square in the series of multiples of 120. 120, 240, 360, 480, 600, 720…., the first number which is a perfect square is: 3600.

89. $30492 = 2^2 \times 3^2 \times 7^1 \times 11^2$.

    For a number to be a perfect square each of the prime factors in the standard form of the number needs to be raised to an even power. Thus, we need to multiply or divide the number by 7 so that we either make it: $2^2 \times 3^2 \times 7^2 \times 11^2$ (if we multiply the number by 7) or

    We make it: $2^2 \times 3^2 \times 11^2$. (if we divide the number by 7).

    Option (b) is correct.

90. $88 \times 113 = 9944$ is the greatest 4 digit number exactly divisible by 88. Option (c) is correct.

91. 3/4th of 116 = ¾ × 116 = 87

    4/5th of 45 = 4/5 × 45 = 36.

    Required difference = 51.

    Option (d) is correct.

92. The correct arrangement would be 75 plants in a row and 75 rows since 5625 is the square of 75.

93. $9^{EVEN\ POWER} \times 7^{4n+1} \rightarrow 1 \times 7 = 7$ as the units digit of the multiplication.

    Option (a) is correct.

94. It can be seen that for 40 and 80 the number of factors are 8 and 10 respectively. Thus option (c) satisfies the condition.

95. In order to solve this question you need to realize that remainders of 1, 3, 4 and 5 in the case of 3, 5, 6 and 7 respectively, means remainders of –2 in each case. In order to find the number which leaves remainder –2 when divided by these numbers you need to first find the LCM of 3, 5, 6 and 7 and subtract 2 from them. Since the LCM is 210, the first such number which satisfies this condition is 208. However, the question has asked us to find the largest such number below 4000. So you need to look at multiples of the LCM and subtract 2. The required number is 3990 – 2 = 3988

96. The number would be given by the (LCM of 2, 3 and 4) +1 → which is 12 + 1 = 13. Option (b) is correct.

97. The number would be given by the 2 × (LCM of 2, 3 and 4) +1 → which is 24 + 1 = 25. Option (a) is correct.

98. In order to solve this you need to find the last 2 digit number in the series got by the logic:

    (LCM of 2, 3, 4) + 1; 2 × (LCM of 2, 3, 4) + 1; 3 × (LCM of 2, 3, 4) + 1 …

    i.e. you need to find the last 2 digit number in the series:

    13, 25, 37, 49….

    In order to do so, you can do one of the following:

    (a) Complete the series by writing the next numbers as:

    61, 73, 85, 97 to see that 97 is the required answer.

    (b) Complete the series by adding a larger multiple of 12 so that you reach closer to 100 faster.

    Thus, if you have seen 13, 25, 37,,,,,, you can straightaway add any multiple of 12 to get a number close to 100 in the series in one jump.

    Thus, if you were to add $12 \times 4 = 48$ to 37 you would reach a value of 85 (and because you have added a multiple of 12 to 37 you can be sure that 85 would also be on the same series.

    Thus, the thinking in this case would go as follows: 13, 25, 37, …, 85, 97. Hence, the number is 97.

    If you look at the two processes above- it would seem that there is not much difference between the two, but the real difference would be seen and felt if you would try to solve a question which might have asked you to find the last 3 digit number in the series. (as you would see in the next question). In such a case, getting to the number would be much faster if you use a multiple of 12 to jump ahead on the series rather than writing each number one by one.

    (c) For the third way of solving this, you can see that all the numbers in the series:

    13, 25, 37… are of the form $12n + 1$. Thus, you are required to find a number which is of the form $12n + 1$ and is just below 100.

    For this purpose, you can try to first see what is the remainder when 100 is divided by 12.

    Since the remainder is 4, you can realize that the number 100 is a number of the form $12n + 4$.

    Obviously then, if 100 is of the form $12n + 4$, the largest $12n + 1$ number just below 100 would occur at a value which would be 3 less than 100. (This occurs because the distance between $12n + 4$ and $12n + 1$ on the number line is 3.)

Thus the answer is $100 - 3 = 97$.

Hence, Option (c) is correct.

99. In order to solve this you need to find the last 3 digit number in the series got by the logic:

    (LCM of 2, 3, 4) +1; 2 × (LCM of 2, 3, 4) +1; 3 × (LCM of 2, 3, 4) + 1 ...

    i.e. you need to find the last 3 digit number in the series:

    13, 25, 37, 49....

    In order to do so, you can do one of the following:

    (a) Try to complete the series by writing the next numbers as:

    61, 73, 85, 97, 109... However, you can easily see that this process would be unnecessarily too long and hence infeasible to solve this question.

    (b) Complete the series by adding a larger multiple of 12 so that you reach closer to 1000 faster.

    This is what we were hinting at in the previous question. If we use a multiple of 12 to write a number which will come later in the series, then we can reach close to 1000 in a few steps. Some of the ways of doing this are shown below:

    (i) 13, 25, 37, ... 997 (we add $12 × 80 = 960$ to 37 to get to $37 + 960 = 997$ which can be seen as the last 3 digit number as the next number would cross 1000).

    (ii) 13, 25, 37, ... (add 600)....637, ...(add 120)... 757,,,,, (add 120),,,, 877, ...(add 120)....**997**. This is the required answer.

    (iii) 13, 25, 37, ...(add 120)....157, ...(add 120)...277......(add 120).....397....(add 120)......517.... (add 120)...637......(add 120)...757,,,,, (add 120),,,, 877, ...(add 120)....**997**. This is the required answer.

    What you need to notice is that all the processes shown above are correct. So while one of them might be more efficient than the other, as far as you ensure that you add a number which is a multiple of 12(the common difference) you would always be correct.

    (c) Of course you can also do this by using remainders. For this, you can see that all the numbers in the series:

    13, 25, 37....are of the form $12n + 1$. Thus, you are required to find a number which is of the form $12n + 1$ and is just below 1000.

    For this purpose, you can try to first see what is the remainder when 1000 is divided by 12.

    Since the remainder is 4, you can realize that the number 1000 is a number of the form $12n + 4$.

    Obviously then, if 1000 is of the form $12n + 4$, the largest $12n + 1$ number just below 1000 would occur at a value which would be 3 less than 1000.

(This occurs because the distance between $12n + 4$ and $12n + 1$ on the number line is 3.)

Thus the answer is $1000 - 3 = 997$.

Hence, Option (c) is correct.

100. The logic of this question is that the frog can never reach point C if it makes an odd number of jumps. Since, the question has asked us to find out in how many ways can the frog reach point C in exactly 7 jumps, the answer would naturally be 0. Option (d) is correct.

101. They would ring together again after a time interval which would be the LCM of 5, 6 and 7. Since the LCM is 210, option (d) is the correct answer.

102. Since they would ring together every 210 seconds, their ringing together would happen at time intervals denoted by the following series- 210, 420, 630, 840, 1050, 1260, 1470, 1680, 1890, 2100, 2310, 2520, 2730, 2940, 3150, 3360, 3570 – a total of 17 times. This answer can also be calculated by taking the quotient of $3600/210 = 17$. Option (a) is correct.

103. The maximum number of soldiers would be given by the HCF of 66, 110 and 242. The HCF of these numbers can be found to be 22 and hence, option (c) is correct.

104. The minimum number of rows would happen when the number of soldiers in each row is the maximum. Since, the HCF is 22 the number of soldiers in each row is 22. Then the total number of rows would be given by:

    $66/22 + 110/22 + 242/22 = 3 + 5 + 11 = 19$ rows. Option (b) is correct.

105. The Number of bottle sizes possible would be given by the number of factors of the HCF of 170, 102 and 374. Since, the HCF of these numbers is 34, the bottle sizes that are possible would be the divisors of 34 which are 1 liter, 2 liters, 17 liters and 34 liters respectively. Thus, a total of 4 bottle sizes are possible. Option (c) is correct.

106. The size of the largest bottle that can be used is obviously 34 liters (HCF of 170, 102 and 374). Option (d) is correct.

107. The minimum number of bottles required would be: $170/34 + 102/34 + 374/34 = 5 + 3 + 11 = 19$. Option (b) is correct.

108. The answer would be given by the quotients of $100/5 + 100/25 = 20 + 4 = 24$. Option (c) is correct.

The logic of how to think about Questions 108 to 118 has been given in the theory in the chapter. Please have a relook at that in case you have doubts about any of the solutions till Question 118.

109. $24 + 4 = 28$. Option (d) is correct.

110. $280 + 56 + 11 + 2 = 349$. Option (c) is correct.

111. $76 + 15 + 3 = 94$. Option (c) is correct.

112. $14 + 2 = 16$. Option (c) is correct.

113. $13 + 4 + 1 = 18$. Option (a) is correct.
114. $17 + 5 + 1 = 23$. Option (c) is correct.
115. $11 + 1 = 12$. Option (a) is correct.
116. $16 + 2 = 18$. Option (d) is correct.
117. The number of 3's in 122! $= 40 + 13 + 4 + 1 = 58$. The number of 2's in 122! $= 61 + 30 + 15 + 7 + 3 + 1 = 117$. The number of 2^2s is hence equal to the quotient of $117/2 = 58$. We have to choose the lower one between 58 and 58. Since both are equal, 58 would be the correct answer. Hence, Option (d) is correct.
118. The power of 20 which would divide 155! would be given by the power of 5's which would divide 155! since $20 = 2^2 \times 5$ and the number of 2^2s in any factorial would always be greater than the number of 5s in the factorial. $31 + 6 + 1 = 38$. Option (b) is correct.
119. $1024 = 2^{10}$. Hence, x has to be a number with power of 2 greater than or equal to 5. Since, we are asked for the minimum value, it must be 5. Thus, option (b) is correct.
120. The two digit numbers that would leave a remainder of 3 when divided by 7 would be the numbers 10, 17, 24, 31, 38, 45, …94. The sum of these numbers would be given by the formula

    (number of numbers × average of the numbers) = There are 13 numbers in the series and their average is 52. Thus, the required answer is $13 \times 52 = 676$. Option (c) is correct.

    (Note the logic used here is that of sum of an Arithmetic Progression and is explained in details in the next chapter).
121. All numbers divisible by 27 would also be divisible by 3 and 9. Numbers divisible by 9 but not by 27 would be divisible by 3 and 9 only and need to be counted to give us our answer.

    The numbers which satisfy the given condition are: 9, 18, 36, 45, 63, 72, 90, 99, 117, 126, 144, 153, 171, 180 and 198. There are 15 such numbers.

    Alternately, you could also think of this as:

    Between 1 to 200 there are 22 multiples of 9. But not all these 22 have to be counted as multiples of 27 need to be excluded from the count. There are 7 multiples of 27 between 1 and 200. Thus, the answer would be given by $22 - 7 = 15$. Option (b) is correct.
122. The required minimum happens when we use (-0.5) as the value of N. $(-0.5)^2 + (-0.5) = 0.25 - 0.5 = -0.25$ is the least possible value for the sum of any number and it's square. Option (b) is correct.
123. Each of the statements are false as we can have the sum of 2 prime numbers ending in 5, 0 and the sum can also be odd. Option (d) is correct.
124. This occurs for values such as: $103 - 013$; $213 - 123$; $324 - 234$ etc where it can be seen that the value of

X is 1 more than Y. The possible pairs of values for X and Y are: 1, 0; 2, 1; 3, 2…9, 8 – a total of nine pairs of values. Option (a) is correct.
125. The required sum would be given by the formula $n(n + 1)$ for the first n even numbers. In this case it would be $50 \times 51 = 2550$. Option (d) is correct.
126. 763/57 leaves a remainder of 22 when it is divided by 57. Thus, if we were to add 35 to this number the number we obtain would be completely divisible by 57. Option (a) is correct.
127. Since, 763/57 leaves a remainder of 22, we would need to subtract 22 from 763 in order to get a number divisible by 57. Option (b) is correct.
128. 8441/57 leaves a remainder of 5. Thus, if we were to add 52 to this number the number we obtain would be completely divisible by 57. Option (d) is correct.
129. Since, 8441/57 leaves a remainder of 5. We would need to subtract 5 from 8441 in order to get a number divisible by 57. Option (c) is correct.
130. 10000 divided by 79 leaves a remainder of 46. Hence, if we were to add 33 to 10000 we would get a number divisible by 79. The correct answer is 10033. Option (b) is correct.
131. 100000 divided by 79 leaves a remainder of 65. Hence, if we were to subtract 65 from 100000 we would get a number divisible by 79. The correct answer is 99935. Option (b) is correct.
132. It can be seen that in the multiples of 12, the number closest to 773 is 768. Option (a) is correct.
133. Since 12 is a divisor of 84, the required remainder would be got by dividing 57 by 12. The required answer is 9. Option (c) is correct
134. Since 11 does not divide 84, there are many possible answers for this question and hence we cannot determine one unique value for the answer. Option (d) is thus correct.
135. The numbers that can do so are going to be factors of the difference between 511 and 667 i.e. 156. The factors of 156 are 1,2,3,4,6, 12,13, 26, 39, 52,78,156. There are 12 such numbers. Option (b) is correct.
136. The multiples of 13 between 200 and 400 would be represented by the series:

    208, 221, 234, 247, 260, 273, 286, 299, 312, 325, 338, 351, 364, 377 and 390

    There are a total of 15 numbers in the above series. Option (b) is correct.

    Note: The above series is an Arithmetic Progression. The process of finding the number of terms in an Arithmetic Progression are defined in the chapter on Progressions.
137. $8n/5 - 5n/8 = 39n/40 = 39$. Solve for n to get the value of $n = 40$. Option (c) is correct.

138. $x + y = 3(x - y) \rightarrow 2x = 4y$. If we take y as 10, we would get the value of x as 20. Option (b) is correct.

139. $4^{11} + 4^{12} + 4^{13} + 4^{14} + 4^{15} = 4^{11}(1 + 4^1 + 4^2 + 4^3 + 4^4) = 4^{11} \times 341$. The factors of 341 are:

    1, 11, 31 and 341. Thus, we can see that the values in each of the three options would divide the expression. $4^{11} + 4^{12} + 4^{13} + 4^{14} + 4^{15}$. Thus, option (d) is correct.

140. Since the numbers have their HCF as 16, both the numbers have to be multiples of 16 (i.e. 2^4).

    $$7168 = 2^{10} \times 7^1$$

    In order to visualise the required possible pairs of numbers we need to look at the prime factors of 7168 in the following fashion:

    $7168 = 2^{10} \times 7^1 = (2^4 \times 2^4) \times 2^2 \times 7^1 = (16 \times 16) \times 2 \times 2 \times 7$ It is then a matter of distributing the 2 extra twos and the 1 extra seven in $2^2 \times 7^1$ between the two numbers given by 16 and 16 inside the bracket. The possible pairs are:

    32×224; 64×112; 16×448. Thus there are 3 distinct pairs of numbers which are multiples of 16 and whose product is 7168. However, out of these the pair 32×224 has it's HCF as 32 and hence does not satisfy the given conditions. Thus there are two pairs of numbers that would satisfy the condition that their HCF is 16 and their product is 7168. Option (a) is correct.

Level of Difficulty (II)

1. If a and b are two numbers, then their Arithmetic mean is given by $(a + b)/2$ while their geometric mean is given by $(ab)^{0.5}$. Using the options to meet the conditions we can see that for the numbers in the first option (6 and 54) the AM being 30, is 24 less than the larger number while the GM being 18, is 12 more than the smaller number. Option (a) is correct.

2. Use the principal of counting given in the theory of the chapter. Start with 101 numbers (i.e. all numbers between 200 and 300 both included) and subtract the number of numbers which are divisible by 2 (viz. $[(300 - 200)/2] + 1 = 51$ numbers), the number of numbers which are divisible by 3 but not by 2 (Note: This would be given by the number of terms in the series 201, 207, ... 297. This series has 17 terms) and the number of numbers which are divisible by 5 but not by 2 and 3. (The numbers are 205, 215, 235, 245, 265, 275, 295. A total of 7 numbers) Thus, the required answer is given by $101 - 51 - 17 - 7 = 26$. Option (b) is correct.

3. Since $15n^3$, $6n^2$ and $5n$ would all be divisible by n, the condition for the expression to not be divisible by n would be if x is not divisible by n. Option (c) is correct.

4. It can be seen that the first expression is larger than the second one. Hence, the required answer would be given by the (units digit of the first expression – units digit of the second expression) = 6 – 0 = 6. Option (b) is correct.

5. Suppose you were to solve the same question for $10^3 - 7$ and $10^2 + x$.

    $$10^3 - 7 = 993 \text{ and } 10^2 + x = 100 + x.$$

    Difference $= 993 - x$

    For $10^4 - 7$ and $10^3 + x$

    The difference would be $9993 - (1000 + x)$

    $$= (8993 - x)$$

    For $10^5 - 7$ and $10^3 + x$

    Difference: $99993 - (10000 + x) = 89993 - x$

    You should realize that the difference for the given question would be 8999 . . . . . 9 3 – x. For this difference to be divisible by 3, x must be 2 (since that is the only option which will give you a sum of digits divisible by 3.)

6. The value of x should be such that the left hand side after completely removing the square root signs should be an integer. For this to happen, first of all the square root of $3x$ should be an integer. Only 3 and 12 from the options satisfy this requirement. If we try to put x as 12, we get the square root of $3x$ as 6. Then the next point at which we need to remove the square root sign would be $12 + 2(6) = 24$ whose square root would be an irrational number. This leaves us with only 1 possible value ($x = 3$). Checking for this value of x we can see that the expression is satisfied as LHS = RHS.

7. If the number is n, we will get that $22n + n = 23n$ is half the square of the number n. Thus, we have

    $$n^2 = 46 n \rightarrow n = 46$$

8. $12^{55}/3^{11} = 3^{44}.4^{55} \rightarrow$ 4 as units place.

    Similarly, $8^{48}/16^{18} = 2^{72} \rightarrow$ 6 as the units place.

    Hence, 0 is the answer.

9. $1 + 2 + 2^2 + \ldots + 2^{31} = 2^{32} - 1$

    Hence, the average will be: $\dfrac{2^{32} - 1}{32} = 2^{27} - 1/2^5$

    which lies between 2^{26} and 2^{27}.

    Hence the answer will be (c).

10. The denominator 99 has the property that the decimals it gives rise to are of the form $0.xyxyxy$. This question is based on this property of 99. Option c is correct.

11. The value of b has to be 2 since, $r = 2y$. Hence, option d is the only choice.

12. For $[x]^3 + \{x\}^2$ to give – 7.91,

    $[x]^3$ should give – 8 (hence, $[x]$ should be –2]

    Further, $\{x\}^2$ should be + 0.09.

Both these conditions are satisfied by –1.7.
Hence option (d) is correct.

13. $16^5 + 2^{15} = 2^{20} + 2^{15} = 2^{15}(2^5 + 1) \rightarrow$ Hence, is divisible by 33.

14. The interpretation of the situation $AB + XY = 1XP$ is that the tens digit in XY is repeated in the value of the solution (i.e. $1XP$). Thus for instance if X was 2, it would mean we are adding a 2 digit number AB to a number in the 20's to get a number in the 120's. This can only happen if AB is in the 90's which means that A is 9.

15. $|x - 3| + 2|x + 1| = 4$ can happen under three broad conditions.
   (a) When $2|x + 1| = 0$, then $|x - 3|$ should be equal to 4.
      Putting $x = -1$, both these conditions are satisfied.
   (b) When $2|x + 1| = 2$, x should be 0, then $|x - 3|$ should also be 2. This does not happen.
   (c) When $2|x + 1| = 4$, x should be $+1$ or -3, in either case $|x - 3|$ which should be zero does not give the desired value.

16. At a value of $x = 0$ we can see that the expression $x^2 + |x - 1| = 1 \rightarrow 0 + 1 = 1$. Hence, $x = 0$ satisfies the given expression. Also at $x = 1$, we get $1 + 0 = 1$. Option (d) is correct.

17. 4^{n+1} represents an odd power of 4 (and hence would end in 4). Similarly, 4^{2n} represents an even power of 4 (and hence would end in 6). Thus, the least number 'x' that would make both $4^{n+1} + x$ and $4^{2n} - x$ divisible by 5 would be for $x = 1$.

18. Check for each value of the options to see that the expression does not become divisible by 9 for any of the initial options. Thus, there is no value that satisfies the divisibility by 9 case.

19. The expression would have solutions based on a structure of:
   $4 + 0; 3 + 1; 2 + 2; 1 + 3$ or $0 + 4$.
   There will be $2*1 = 2$ solutions for $4 + 0$ as in this case x can take the values of 8 and 0, while y can take a value of 4;
   Similarly there would be $2*2 = 4$ solutions for $3 + 1$ as in this case x can take the values of 7 or 1, while y can take a value of 5 or 3;
   Thus, the total number of solutions can be visualised as:
   2 (for $4 + 0$) + 4 (for $3 + 1$) + 4 (for $2 + 2$) + 4 (for $1 + 3$) + 2 (for $0 + 2$) = 16 solutions for the set (x, y) where both x and y are integers.

20. The numerator of $3^{32}/50$ would be a number that would end in 1. Consequently, the decimal of the form $.bx$ would always give us a value of x as 2.

21. If we assume the numbers as 16 and 4 based on 4:1 (in option a), the AM would be 10 and the $GM =$

8 a difference of 20% as stipulated in the question. Option (a) is correct.

22. $990 = 11 \times 3^2 \times 2 \times 5$. The highest power of 990 which would divide 1090! would be the power of 11 available in 990. This is given by $[1090/11] + [1090/121] = 99 + 9 = 108$

23. For finding the highest power of 6 that divides 146!, we need to get the number of 3's that would divide 146!. The same can be got by: $[146/3] + [48/3] + [16/3] + [5/3] = 70$.

24. There would be two fives and more than two twos in the prime factors of the numbers in the multiplication. Thus, we would get a total of 2 zeroes.

25. Both 333^{555} and 555^{333} are divisible by 3,37 and 111. Further, the sum of the two would be an even number and hence divisible by 2. Thus, all the four options divide the given number.

26. Both the values of options a and b satisfy the given expression. As for 5.16, the value of $[x]^2 = 25$ and the value of $\{x\} = 0.16$. Thus, $[x]^2 + \{x\}^1 = 25.16$ Similarly for a value of $x = -4.84$, the value of $[x] = -5$ and hence $[x]^2 = 25$ and the value of $\{x\} = 0.16$. Thus, $[x]^2 + \{x\}^1 = 25.16$

27. The given conditions can be seen to be true for the number 49. Option (c) is correct.

28. Solve this question through options. Also realize that $a \times b = a + b$ only occurs for the situation $2 \times 2 = 2 + 2$. Hence, clearly the answer has to be none of these.

29. 863 satisfies each of the conditions and can be spotted through checking of the options.

30. The number of zeroes would be given by counting the number of 5's. The relevant numbers for counting the number of 5's in the product would be given by: $5^5; 10^{10}, 15^{15}, 20^{20}, 25^{25}...$and so on till 100^{100}
   The number of 5's in these values would be given by: $(5 + 10 + 15 + 20 + 50 + 30 + 35 + 40 + 45 + 100 + 55 + 60 + 65 + 70 + 150 + 80 + 85 + 90 + 95 + 200)$
   This can also be written as:
   $(5 + 10 + 15 + 20 + 25 + 30 + 35 + 40 + 45 + 50 + 55 + 60 + 65 + 70 + 75 + 80 + 85 + 90 + 95 + 100) + (25 + 50 + 75 + 100)$
   $= 1050 + 250 = 1300$

31. Option (a) is correct as the LCM of 5 and 105 is 105 and their HCF is 5. Also for the pair of values, 15 and 35 the HCF is 5 and the LCM is 105.

32. Solve using options. Using option b = 3/5 and performing the given operation we get:
   $2/3 - 3/5 = (10 - 9)/15 = 1/15$. Option (b) is hence correct.

33. Both the conditions are satisfied for option (a) = 72 as the number 72 exceeds the sum of squares of the digits by 19 and also 72 exceeds the doubled product of it's digits by 44.

34. Solve by checking the given options. 31 and 13 are possible values of the number as defined by the problem.

35. The given conditions are satisfied for the number 24.

36. The number of 2's in the given expression is lower than the number of 5's. The number of 2's in the product is 9 and hence that is the number of zeroes.

37. $45 = 3^2 \times 5$. Hence, we need to count the number of 3^2's and 5's that can be made out of 123!.

    Number of 3's = 41 + 13 + 4 + 1 = 59 → Number of 3^2's = 29

    Number of 5's = 24 + 4 = 28.

    The required answer is the lower of the two (viz. 28 and 29). Hence, option (a) 28 is correct.

38. The first sentence means that the numbers are in an arithmetic progression. From the statements and a little bit of visualization, you can see that 8.5, 10 and 11.5 can be the three values we are looking for – and hence the middle value is 10.

39. $990 = 11 \times 3^2 \times 5 \times 2$. For $n!$ to be divisible by 990, the value of $n!$ should have an 11 in it. Since, 11 itself is a prime number, hence the value of n should be at least 11.

40. For the expression to hold true, x and y should both be positive.

41. Since, we are not given options here we should go ahead by looking within the factors of 144 (especially the two digit ones)

    The relevant factors are 72,48, 36, 24, 18 and 12. Thinking this way creates an option for you where there is none available and from this list of numbers you can easily identify 24 as the required answer.

42–46. Write simple equations for each of the questions and solve.

47. Since the sum of squares of the digits of the two digit number is 10, the only possibility of the numbers are 31 and 13.

48. If the number is 'ab' we have the following equations:

    $(10a + b) = 4 (a + b) + 3 \rightarrow 6a - 3b = 3$

    $(10a + b) = 3 (a \times b) + 5$.

    Obviously we would need to solve these two equations in order to get the values of the digits a and b respectively. However, it might not be a very prudent decision to try to follow this process- as it might turn out to be too cumbersome.

    A better approach to think here is:

    From the first statement we know that the number is of the form $4n + 3$. Thus, the number has to be a term in the series 11, 15, 19, 23, 27…

    Also from the second statement we know that the number must be a $3n + 5$ number.

Thus, the numbers could be 11, 14, 17, 20, 23…. Common terms of the above two series would be probable values of the number.

It can be seen that the common terms in the two series are: 11, 23, 35, 47, 59, 71, 83 and 95. One of these numbers has to be the number we are looking for.

If we try these values one by one, we can easily seen that the value of the two digit number should be 23 since → 23/ (2 + 3) → Quotient as 4 and remainder = 3.

Similarly, if we look at the other condition given in the problem we would get the following-

23/6 → quotient as 3 and remainder = 5.

Thus, the value of the missing number would be 23.

49. We can see from the description that the number (say X) must be such that $X + 100$ and $X + 169$ both must be perfect squares. Thus we are looking for two perfect squares which are 69 apart from each other. This would happen for 34^2 and 35^2 since their difference would be $(35 - 34)(35 + 34) = 69$.

50. Since their least common multiple is 102, we need to look for two factors of 102 such that they add up to 85. 51 and 34 can be easily spotted as the numbers.

51. If one number is x, the other should be $6x$ or $12x$ or $18x$ or $24x$ and so on. Also, their sum should be either 504 or 1008 or 1512. (Note: the next multiple of 504 = 2016 cannot be the sum of two three digit numbers.

52. Obviously 46 and 64 are the possible numbers.

53. The key here is to look for numbers which are more than three times but less than four times the product of their digits. Also, the product of the digits should be greater than 9 so as to leave a remainder of 9 when the number is divided by the product of it's digits.

    In the 10s, 20s and 30s there is no number which gives a quotient of 3 when it is divided by the product of it's digits. In the 40s, 43 is the only number which has a quotient of 3 when divided by 12 (product of it's digits). But 43/12 does not give us a remainder of 9 as required.

    In the 50s the number 53 divided by 15 leaves a remainder of 8, while in the 60s, 63 divided by 18 gives us a remainder of 9 as required.

54. The first thing to use while solving this question is to look at the information that the sum of squares of the three digits is 109. A little bit of trial and error shows us that this can only occur if the digits are 8, 6 and 3. Using the other information we get that the number must be 863 since, 863 – 495 = 368.

55. It is obvious that the only condition where the cubes of 3 numbers add up to 243 is when we add the

cubes of 3 and 6. Hence, the numbers possible are 36 and 63.

56. There would definitely be two numbers and in case we take the first number as $7n - 1$, there would be three numbers – (as can be seen when we take the first number as 27 and the other number is 43).

57. Between 111^4, $110 \times 109 \times 108 \times 107$, $109 \times 110 \times 112 \times 113$.

    It can be easily seen that

    $111 \times 111 \times 111 \times 111 > 110 \times 109 \times 108 \times 107$

    also $109 \times 110 \times 112 \times 113 > 109 \times 110 \times 108 \times 107$

    Further the product $111 \times 111 \times 111 \times 111 > 109 \times 110 \times 112 \times 113$ (since, the sum of the parts of the product are equal on the LHS and the RHS and the numbers on the LHS are closer to each other than the numbers on the RHS.

58. Both x and y should be highest for xy to be maximum. Similarly x should be minimum and y should be maximum for x/y to be minimum.

59. $200^{300} = (200^6)^{50}$

    $300^{200} = (300^4)^{50}$

    $400^{150} = (400^3)^{50}$

    Hence 200^{300} is greater.

61. The sum of squares of the first n natural numbers is given by $n(n + 1)(2n + 1)/6$.

    For this number to be divisible by 4, the product of $n(n + 1)(2n + 1)$ should be a multiple of 8. Out of n, $(n + 1)$ and $(2n + 1)$ only one of n or $(n + 1)$ can be even and $(2n + 1)$ would always be odd.

    Thus, either n or $(n + 1)$ should be a multiple of 8. This happens if we use $n = 7, 8, 15, 16, 23, 24, 31, 32, 39, 40, 47, 48$. Hence, 12 such numbers.

62. In the 20s the numbers are: 23 to 29

    In the 30s the numbers are: 32 to 39

    Subsequently the numbers are 42 to 49, 52 to 59, 62 to 69, 72 to 79, 82 to 89 and 92 to 99.

    A total of 63 numbers.

63. You need to solve this question using trial and error.

    For 32 (option 1):

    $32 = 2^5$. Hence 6 factors. On increasing by 50%, $48 = 2^4 \times 3^1$ has 10 factors. Thus the number of factors is increasing when the number is increased by 50% which is not what the question is defining for the number. Hence, 32 is not the correct answer.

    Checking for option (b) 84.

    $84 = 2^2 \times 3^1 \times 7^1 \rightarrow (2 + 1)(1 + 1)(1 + 1) = 12$ factors

    On increasing by 50% $\rightarrow 126 = 2^1 \times 32 \times 7^1 \rightarrow (1 + 1)(2 + 1)(1 + 1) = 12$ factors. (no change in number of factors).

Second Condition: When the value of the number is reduced by 75% $\rightarrow 84$ would become 21 ($3^1 \times 7^1$) and the number of factors would be $2 \times 2 = 4$ – a reduction of 66.66% in the number of factors.

64. There will be 9 single digit numbers using 9 digits, 90 two digit numbers using 180 digits, 900 three digit numbers using 2700 digits. Thus, when the number 999 would be written, a total of 2889 digits would have been used up. Thus, we would need to look for the 25494th digit when we write all 4 digit numbers. Since, 25494/4 = 6373.5 we can conclude that the first 6373 four digit numbers would be used up for writing the first 25492 digits. The second digit of the 6374th four digit number would be the required answer. Since, the 6374th four digit number is 7373, the required digit is 3.

65. In order to solve this question, think of the numbers grouped in groups of 9 as:

    {1, 2, 3, 4, 5, 6, 7, 8, 9} {10, 11, 12.....18} and so on till {2989, 2990...2997} – A total of 333 complete sets. From each set we can take 4 numbers giving us a total of $333 \times 4 = 1332$ numbers.

    Apart from this, we can also take exactly 1 multiple of 9 (any one) and also the last 3 numbers viz 2998, 2999 and 3000. Thus, there would be a total of 1332 + 4 = 1336 numbers.

66. It can be seen that for only 2 numbers (1 and ½) the consolidated number would be $1 + ½ + ½ = 2$

    For 3 numbers, (1, ½ , 1/3) the number would be 3. Thus, for the given series the consolidated number would be 1972.

67. The value of K would be 199 and hence, the required difference is $9 - 1 = 8$

68. $9 - 9 = 0$ would be the difference between the units and the tens digits.

69. The highest ratio would be a ratio of 100 in the numbers, 100, 200, 300, 400, 500, 600, 700, 800 and 900. Thus a total of 9 numbers.

70. Basically every odd triangular number would have this property, that it is the difference of squares of two consecutive natural numbers. Thus, we need to find the number of triangular numbers that are odd. 3, 15, 21, 45, 55, 91, 105, 153, 171, 231, 253, 325, 351, 435, 465, 561, 595, 703, 741, 861, 903 – A total of 21 numbers.

71. The coefficients would be $^{44}C_0$, $^{44}C_1$, $^{44}C_2$ and so on till $^{44}C_{44}$. The sum of these coefficients would be 2^{44} (since the value of $^nC_0 + {}^nC_1 + {}^nC_2 +...{}^nC_n = 2^n$)

72. The remainder of each power of 9 when divided by 6 would be 3. Thus, for (2n+1) powers of 9, there would be an odd number of 3's. Hence, the remainder would be 3.

73. The remainder when a number is divided by 16 is given by the remainder of the last 4 digits divided by 16 (because 10000 is a multiple of 16. This principle is very similar in logic to why we look at last 2 digits for divisibility by 4 and the last 3 digits for divisibility by 8). Thus, the required answer would be the remainder of 4950/16 which is 6.

74. $58! - 38! = 38! (58 \times 57 \times 56 \times 55 \times .... \times 39 - 1) \to 38! (3n - 1)$ since the expression inside the bracket would be a $3n - 1$ kind of number. Thus, the number of 3's would depend only on the number of 3's in $38! \to 12 + 4 + 1 = 17$.

75. The given expression can be seen as $(22334^{\text{ODD POWER}})/5$, since the sum of $1^2 + 2^2 + 3^2 + 4^2 + ... + 66^2$ can be seen to be an odd number. The remainder would always be 4 in such a case.

76. $12^{33} \times 34^{23} \times 2^{70} = 2^{159} \times 3^{33} \times 17^{23}$. The number of factors would be $160 \times 34 \times 24 = 130560$. Thus, option (d) is correct.

77. Option (a) is correct.

78. $1152 = 2 \times 2 \times 2 \times 2 \times 2 \times 2 \times 2 \times 3 \times 3 = 2^7 \times 3^2$. Essentially every number starting from $4!^3$ would be divisible perfectly by 1152 since each number after that would have at least 7 twos and 2 threes.
    Thus, the required remainder is got by the first three terms:
    $(1 + 8 + 216)/1152 = 225/1152$ gives us 225 as the required remainder.

79. We can take only perfect squares of odd numbers and one perfect square of an even number. Thus, for instance we can take numbers like 1, 4, 9, 25, 49, 121, 169, 289, 361, 529, 841 and 961. A total of 12 such numbers can be taken.

80. $(101 \times 102 \times 103 \times 197 \times 198 \times 199)/100 \to [1 \times 2 \times 3 \times (-3) \times (-2) \times (-1)]/100 \to -36$ as remainder $\to$ remainder is 64.

81. $[65 \times 29 \times 37 \times 63 \times 71 \times 87]/100 \to [-35 \times 29 \times 37 \times -37 \times -29 \times -13]/100 \to [35 \times 29 \times 37 \times 37 \times 29 \times 13]/100 = [1015 \times 1369 \times 377]/100 \to 15 \times 69 \times 77/100 \to$ remainder as 95.

82. $[65 \times 29 \times 37 \times 63 \times 71 \times 87 \times 85]/100 \to [-35 \times 29 \times 37 \times -37 \times -29 \times -13 \times -15]/100 \to [35 \times 29 \times 37 \times 37 \times 29 \times 13 \times -15]/100 = [1015 \times 1369 \times 377 \times -15]/100 \to [15 \times 69 \times 77 \times -15]/100 \to$ remainder as 75.

83. $[65 \times 29 \times 37 \times 63 \times 71 \times 87 \times 62]/100 \to [-35 \times 29 \times 37 \times -37 \times -29 \times -13 \times 62]/100 \to [35 \times 29 \times 37 \times 37 \times 29 \times 13 \times 62]/100 = [1015 \times 1369 \times 377 \times 62]/100 \to [15 \times 69 \times 77 \times 62]/100 = [1035 \times 4774]/100 \to 35 \times 74/100 \to$ remainder as 90.

84. $[75 \times 35 \times 47 \times 63 \times 71 \times 87 \times 82]/100 = [3 \times 35 \times 47 \times 63 \times 71 \times 87 \times 41]/2 \to$ remainder $= 1$.
    Hence, required remainder $= 1 \times 50 = 50$.

85. For this question we need to find the remainder of:
    $(201 \times 202 \times 203 \times 204 \times 246 \times 247 \times 248 \times 249) \times (201 \times 202 \times 203 \times 204 \times 246 \times 247 \times 248 \times 249)$ divided by 100.
    $(201 \times 202 \times 203 \times 204 \times 246 \times 247 \times 248 \times 249) \times (201 \times 202 \times 203 \times 204 \times 246 \times 247 \times 248 \times 249)/100 = (201 \times 101 \times 203 \times 102 \times 246 \times 247 \times 248 \times 249) \times (201 \times 202 \times 203 \times 204 \times 246 \times 247 \times 248 \times 249)/25$
    $\to (1 \times 1 \times 3 \times 2 \times -4 \times -3 \times -2 \times -1) \times (1 \times 2 \times 3 \times 4 \times -4 \times -3 \times -2 \times -1)/25 = 144 \times 576/25 \to (19 \times 1)/25 =$ remainder 19.
    $19 \times 4 = 76$ is the actual remainder (since we divided by 4 during the process of finding the remainder.

86. $7^4/2400$ gives us a remainder of 1. Thus, the remainder of $7^{99}/2400$ would depend on the remainder of $7^3/2400 \to$ remainder $= 343$.

87. The numerator can be written as $(1729)^{752}/1728 \to$ remainder as 1.

88. Bikas's movement in terms of the number of coins would be:
    B $\to$ 3B (when Arun triples everyone's coins) $\to$ B.
    Think of this as: When Bikas triples everyone's coins, and is left with 20 it means that the other 3 have 60 coins after their coins are tripled. This means that before the tripling by Bikas, the other three must have had 20 coins—meaning Bikas must have had 60 coins.
    But 60 = 3B $\to$ B = 20.

89. For $83p796161q$ to be a multiple of 11 (here X is 11) we should have the difference between the sum of odd placed digits and even placed digits should be 0 or a multiple of 11.
    $(8 + p + 9 + 1 + 1) - (3 + 7 + 6 + 6 + q) = (19 + p) - (22 + q)$. For this difference to be 0, p should be 3 more than q which cannot occur since $0 < p < q$.
    The only way in which $(19 + p) - (22 + q)$ can be a multiple of 11 is if we target a value of -11 for the expression. One such possibility is if we take p as 1 and q as 9.
    The number would be 8317961619. On successive division by $(p + q) = 10$ and 1 the sum of remainders would be 9.

90. $n(n + 1)/2$ should be a perfect square. The first value of n when this occurs would be for $n = 8$. Thus, on the 8th of March the required condition would come true.

91. We have to find the unit's digit of $2^{53} \to 2^{4n+1} \to 2$ as the units digit.

92. $[7! (14 + 14 \times 13 \times 12 \times 11 \times 10 \times 9 \times 8)]/[7! (16 - 3)] = [(14 + 14 \times 13 \times 12 \times 11 \times 10 \times 9 \times 8)]/[(13)] \to$ remainder 1.

Hence, the original remainder must be 7! (because for the sake of simplification of the numbers in the question we have cut the 7! From the numerator and the denominator in the first step.

93. $x = 6$ and $y = 3$ is one pair of values where the given condition is met.

     After that you should be able to spot that if you were to increase x by 7, y would also increase by 4. The number of such pairs would depend on how many terms are there in the series

     $-498, -491, \ldots -1, 6, 13, 20, \ldots 489, 496$. The series has $994/7 + 1 = 143$ terms and hence there would be 143 pairs of values for (x, y) which would satisfy the equation.

94. All three conditions can be seen to be true.

95. Product of factorials < Sum of factorials would occur for any number that has either 0 or 1 in it.

     The required numbers uptil and including 50 are: 10 to 19, 20, 21, 30, 31, 40, 41, 50. Besides for the number 22, the product of factorials of the digits would be equal to the sum of factorials of the digits. Thus a total of 18 numbers.

96. The maximum marks he can score is: 100 (if he gets all correct).

     The minimum marks he can score would be given by: $10 \times (-0.1) + 20 \times (-0.2) + 70 \times (-0.5) = -40$. The difference between the two values would be $100 - (-40) = 140$ marks.

Logic for Questions 97 to 99:

If a student solved 200 questions and got everything correct he would score a total of 620 marks. By getting a LOD 1 question wrong he would lose $4+2=6$ marks, while by not solving an LOD 1 question he would lose 4 marks.

     Similarly for LOD 2 questions, Loss of marks = 4.5 (for wrong answers) and loss of marks= 3 (for not solved)

     Similarly for LOD 3 questions, Loss of marks = 3 (for wrong answers) and loss of marks = 2 (for not solved)

     Since, he has got 120 marks from 100 questions solved he has to lose 500 marks (from the maximum possible total of 620) by combining to lose marks through 100 questions not solved and some questions wrong.

97. It can be seen through a little bit of trial and error with the options, that if he got 44 questions of LOD 1 correct and 56 questions of LOD 3 wrong he would end up scoring $44 \times 4 - 56 \times 1 = 176 - 56 = 120$. In such a case he would have got the maximum possible incorrects with the given score.

98. $32 \times 4 + 1 \times 3 - 1 \times 1 = 130$ (in this case he has solved 32 corrects from LOD 1, 1 correct from LOD 2 and 1 incorrect from LOD 3). Thus, a total of 34 attempts.

99. In the above case he gets 1 question incorrect. However, he can also get 130 marks by $30 \times 4 + 2 \times 3 + 2 \times 2$ where he gets 30 LOD 1 questions correct, and 2 questions correct each from LOD 2 and LOD 3).

     The least number of incorrects would be 0.

100. The least number would be (LCM of 10, 9, 8, 7, 6 and 5 -1) = 2519. The second least number = $2520 \times 2 - 1 = 5039$.

Hints

Level of Difficulty (III)

1–5. Solve through options.

6. Use AP with first term 104 and last term 999 and common difference 5.

7. Find the first 2 digit number which gives a remainder of 3 when divided by 7 and then find the largest such number (10 and 94 respectively). Use Arithmetic Progression formulae to add the numbers.

8. Use AP with first term 105 and last term 995 and common difference is 10.

10. The cubes of the numbers are $x - 3$, $x + 2$ and $x + 3$. Use options and you will see that (a) is the answer.

11. $(x^2 - y^2) = 45$. i.e. $(x - y)(x + y) = 45$. The factors of 45 possible are, 15, 3; 9, 5 and 45, 1.

     Hence, the numbers are 9 and 6, or 7 and 2 or 23 and 22.

12–18. Use options to check the given conditions.

19. The answer will be 50 since, 125*122 will give 50 as the last two digits.

20. The remainder theorem is to be used.

     $43^{101} + 23^{101} = (43 + 23) (. \ . \ . \ . \ .)$

     Hence, when divided by 66 the remainder will be zero.

21. The unit's digit will be $1 \times 5 = 5$ (no carry over.) The tens digit will be ($4*1 + 5*2$) = 4 (carry over 1). The hundreds digit will be ($3*1 + 4*2 + 5*1$) = $6 + 1$ (carried over) = 7. Hence, answer is 745.

22–25. Use options to solve.

26. Use the rule of indices and remainder theorem.

27. Options are not provided as it is an LOD 3 question. If they were there you should have used options.

28. Use trial and error

29. Use options.

30. Use remainder theorem and look at patterns by applying the rules of indices.

     We get the value as:

$$5 \xrightarrow{\dfrac{32.32.32\ldots\ldots32 \text{ times}}{9}}$$

$$7 \xrightarrow{\dfrac{32.32.32\ldots\ldots31 \text{ times}}{9}}$$

$$4 \xrightarrow{\dfrac{32.32.32\ldots\ldots30 \text{ times}}{9}}$$

$$7 \xrightarrow{\overset{32.32....29 \text{ times}}{9}}$$

→ Looking at the pattern we will get 4 as the final remainder.

31. Use the remainder theorem and get the remainder as:

$1 \times 2 \times 4 \times 4 \times 4/7 = 128/7 \rightarrow 2$ is the remainder.

32.

32. $2^{100}/3 = (2^4)^{25}/3 \rightarrow 1$.

33. Use the remainder theorem and try finding the patterns.

34. Find the last digit of the number got by adding $1^2 + 2^2 + \ldots 9^2$ (you will get 5 here). Then multiply by 10 to get zero as the answer.

35. $(2^{100} - 1)$ and $(2^{120} - 1)$ will yield the GCD as $2^{20} - 1$. (This has been explained in the theory of GCDs).

36. The GCDs of 100 ones and 60 ones will be twenty ones because 20 is the GCD of sixty and Hundred.

39. $\dfrac{32^{32^{32}}}{7} \rightarrow \dfrac{4^{32^{32}}}{7}$

But $4^3/7$ gives us a remainder of 1.

Hence we need to convert $4^{32^{32}}$ into $4^{3n + x}$ (Think why!!)

Here again, we will be more interested in finding the value of x rather than n, since the remainder only depends on the value of x.

[Concept Note: When we start to write as the remainder.

$4^{32^{32}}$ in the form $4^3 \times 4^3 \times 4^3 \ldots\ldots n$ times $\times 4^x$ we are not bothered about how many times we can write 4^3 since it will continuously give us 1 every time as the remainder.

Progressions

2
Chapter

The chapter on progressions essentially yields common-sense based questions in examinations.

Questions in the CAT and other aptitude exams mostly appear from either Arithmetic Progressions (more common) or from Geometric Progressions.

The chapter of progressions is a logical and natural extension of the chapter on Number Systems, since there is such a lot of commonality of logic between the problems associated with these two chapters.

ARITHMETIC PROGRESSIONS

Quantities are said to be in arithmetic progression when they increase or decrease by a common difference.

Thus each of the following series forms an arithmetic progression:

$$3, 7, 11, 15,\ldots$$
$$8, 2, -4, -10,\ldots$$
$$a, a + d, a + 2d, a + 3d,\ldots$$

The common difference is found by subtracting any term of the series from the next term.

That is, common difference of an $AP = (t_N - t_{N-1})$.

In the first of the above examples the common difference is 4; in the second it is −6; in the third it is d.

If we examine the series $a, a + d, a + 2d, a + 3d,\ldots$ we notice that *in any term the coefficient of d is always less by one than the position of that term in the series.*

Thus the rth term of an arithmetic progression is given by $T_r = a + (r - 1)d$.

If n be the number of terms, and if L denotes the last term or the nth term, we have

$$L = a + (n - 1)d$$

To Find the Sum of the given Number of Terms in an Arithmetic Progression

Let a denote the first term d, the common difference, and n the total number of terms. Also, let L denote the last term, and S the required sum; then

$$S = \frac{n(a + L)}{2} \tag{1}$$
$$L = a + (n - 1)d \tag{2}$$
$$S = \frac{n}{2} \times [2a + (n - 1)d] \tag{3}$$

If any two terms of an arithmetical progression be given, the series can be completely determined; for this data results in two simultaneous equations, the solution of which will give the first term and the common difference.

When three quantities are in arithmetic progression, the middle one is said to be the **arithmetic mean** of the other two.

Thus a is the arithmetic mean between $a - d$ and $a + d$. So, when it is required to arbitrarily consider three numbers in AP take $a - d$, a and $a + d$ as the three numbers as this reduces one unknown thereby making the solution easier.

To Find the Arithmetic Mean between any Two given Quantities

Let a and b be two quantities and A be their arithmetic mean. Then since a, A, b, are in AP. We must have

$$b - A = A - a$$

Each being equal to the common difference;

This gives us $\quad A = \dfrac{(a + b)}{2}$

Between two given quantities it is always possible to insert any number of terms such that the whole series thus formed shall be in *AP*. The terms thus inserted are called the **arithmetic means**.

To Insert a given Number of Arithmetic Means between Two given Quantities

Let *a* and *b* be the given quantities and *n* be the number of means.

Including the extremes, the number of terms will then be *n* + 2 so that we have to find a series of *n* + 2 terms in *AP*, of which *a* is the first, and *b* is the last term.

Let *d* be the common difference;

then $\quad\quad b =$ the $(n + 2)$th term

$$= a + (n + 1)d$$

Hence, $\quad\quad d = \dfrac{(b - a)}{(n + 1)}$

and the required means are

$$a + \frac{(b - a)}{n - 1}, a + \frac{2(b - a)}{n + 1}, \cdots a + \frac{n(b - a)}{n + 1}$$

Till now we have studied APs in their mathematical context. This was important for you to understand the basic mathematical construct of A.Ps. However, you need to understand that questions on A.P. are seldom solved on a mathematical basis, (Especially under the time pressure that you are likely to face in the CAT and other aptitude exams). In such situations the mathematical processes for solving progressions based questions are likely to fail or at the very least, be very tedious. Hence, understanding the following logical aspects about Arithmetic Progressions is likely to help you solve questions based on APs in the context of an aptitude exam.

Let us look at these issues one by one:

1. Process for finding the nth term of an A.P.

Suppose you have to find the 17th term of the
A.P. 3, 7, 11.......

The conventional mathematical process for this question would involve using the formula.

$$T_n = a + (n - 1)\, d$$

Thus, for the 17th term we would do

$$T_{17} = 3 + (17 - 1) \times 4 = 3 + 16 \times 4 = 67$$

Most students would mechanically insert the values for *a*, *n* and *d* and get this answer.

However, if you replace the above process with a thought algorithm, you will get the answer much faster.
The algorithm goes like this:

In order to find the 17th term of the above sequence add the common difference to the first term, sixteen times. (**Note:** Sixteen, since it is one less than 17).

Similarly, in order to find the 37th term of the A.P. 3, 11 ..., All you need to do is add the common difference (8 in this case), 36 times.

Thus, the answer is $288 + 3 = 291$.

(**Note:** You ultimately end up doing the same thing, but you are at an advantage since the entire solution process is reactionary.)

2. Average of an A.P. and Corresponding terms of the A.P.

Consider the A.P., 2, 6, 10, 14, 18, 22. If you try to find the average of these six numbers you will get: Average = (2 + 6 + 10 + 14 + 18 + 22)/6 = 12

Notice that 12 is also the average of the first and the last terms of the A.P. In fact, it is also the average of 6 and 18 (which correspond to the second and 5th terms of the A.P.). Further, 12 is also the average of the 3rd and 4th terms of the A.P.

(**Note:** In this A.P. of six terms, the average was the same as the average of the 1st and 6th terms. It was also given by the average of the 2nd and the 5th terms, as well as that of the 3rd and 4th terms.)

We can call each of these pairs as "CORRESPONDING TERMS" in an A.P.

What you need to understand is that every A.P. has an average.

And for any A.P., the average of any pair of corresponding terms will also be the average of the A.P.

If you try to notice the sum of the term numbers of the pair of corresponding terms given above:

1st and 6th (so that 1 + 6 = 7)
2nd and 5th(hence, 2 + 5 =7)
3rd and 4th (hence, 3 + 4 = 7)

***

Note: In each of these cases, the sum of the term numbers for the terms in a corresponding pair is one greater than the number of terms of the A.P.

***

This rule will hold true for all A.P.s.

For example, if an A.P. has 23 terms then for instance, you can predict that the 7th term will have the 17th term as its corresponding term, or for that matter the 9th term will have the 15th term as its corresponding term. (Since 24 is one more than 23 and 7 + 17 = 9 + 15 = 24.)

3. Process for finding the sum of an A.P.

Once you can find a pair of corresponding terms for any A.P., you can easily find the sum of the A.P. by using the property of averages:

i.e.   Sum = Number of terms × Average.

In fact, this is the best process for finding the sum of an A.P. It is much more superior than the process of finding the sum of an A.P. using the expression $\frac{n}{2}(2a+(n-1)d)$.

4. Finding the common difference of an A.P., given 2 terms of an A.P.

Suppose you were given that an A.P. had its 3rd term as 8 and its 8th term as 28. You should visualize this A.P. as
$$-, -, 8, -, -, -, -, 28.$$

From the above figure, you can easily visualize that to move from the third term to the eighth term, (8 to 28) you need to add the common difference five times. The net addition being 20, the common difference should be 4.

Illustration: Find the sum of an A.P. of 17 terms, whose 3rd term is 8 and 8th term is 28.

Solution: Since we know the third term and the eighth term, we can find the common difference as 4 by the process illustrated above.

The total = 17 × Average of the A.P.
Our objective now shifts into the finding of the average of the A.P. In order to do so, we need to identify either the 10th term (which will be the corresponding term for the 8th term) or the 15th term (which will be the corresponding term for the 3rd term.)

Again: Since the 8th term is 28 and $d = 4$, the 10th term becomes $28 + 4 + 4 = 36$.

Thus, the average of the A.P.
$$= \text{Average of 8th and 10th terms}$$
$$= (28 + 36)/2 = 32.$$

Hence, the required answer is sum of the A.P. = 17 × 32 = 544.

The logic that has applied here is that the difference in the term numbers will give you the number of times the common difference is used to get from one to the other term.

For instance, if you know that the difference between the 7th term and 12th term of an AP is –30, you should realize that 5 times the common difference will be equal to –30. (Since 12 – 7 = 5).

Hence, $d = -6$.

Note: Replace this algorithmic thinking in lieu of the mathematical thinking of:
$$12^{th} \text{ term} = a + 11d$$
$$7^{th} \text{ term} = a + 6d$$
$$\text{Hence, difference} = -30 = (a + 11d) - (a + 6d)$$
$$-30 = 5d$$
$$\therefore \qquad\qquad d = -6.$$

---

5. Types of APs: Increasing and Decreasing A.P.s.

Depending on whether 'd' is positive or negative, an A.P. can be increasing or decreasing.

Let us explore these two types of A.P.s further:

(A) Increasing A.P.s:

Every term of an increasing AP is greater than the previous term.

Depending on the value of the first term, we can construct two graphs for sum of an increasing A.P.

Case 1: When the first term of the increasing A.P. is positive. In such a case the sum of the A.P. will show a continuously increasing graph which will look like the one shown in the figure below:

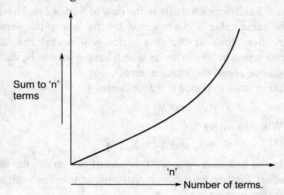

Case 2: When the first term of the increasing A.P. is negative. In such a case, the Sum of the A.P. plotted against the number of terms will give the following figure:

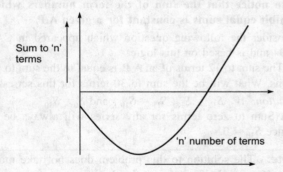

The specific case of the sum to n_1 terms being equal to the sum to n_2 terms.

In the series case 2 above, there is a possibility of the sum to 'n' terms being repeated for 2 values of 'n'. However, this will not necessarily occur.

This issue will get clear through the following example:
Consider the following series:
Series 1: –12, –8, –4, 0, 4, 8, 12
As is evident the sum to 2 terms and the sum to 5 terms in this case is the same. Similarly, the sum to 3 terms is the same as the sum to 4 terms. This can be written as:
$$S_2 = S_5 \text{ and } S_3 = S_4.$$

In other words the sum to n_1 terms is the same as the sum to n_2 terms.

Such situations arise for increasing A.P.'s where the first term is negative. But as we have already stated that this does not happen for all such cases.

Consider the following A.P.s.

Series 2 : –8, –3, +2, + 7, + 12…

Series 3 : –13, –7, –1, + 5, + 11…

Series 4 : –12, –6, 0, 6, 12 …

Series 5 : –15, –9, –3, + 3, 9, 15 …

Series 6 : –20, –12, –4, 4 , 12, …

If you check the series listed above, you will realize that this occurrence happens in the case of Series 1, Series 4, Series 5 and Series 6 while in the case of Series 2 and Series 3 the same value is not repeated for the sum of the Series.

A clear look at the two series will reveal that this phenomenon occurs in series which have what can be called a balance about the number zero.

Another issue to notice is that in Series 4,

$$S_2 = S_3 \text{ and } S_1 = S_4$$

While in series 5

$$S_1 = S_5 \text{ and } S_2 = S_4.$$

In the first case (where '0' is part of the series) the sum is equal for two terms such that one of them is odd and the other is even.

In the second case on the other hand (when '0' is not part of the series) the sum is equal for two terms such that both are odd or both are even.

Also notice that the sum of the term numbers which exhibit equal sums is constant for a given A.P.

Consider the following question which appeared in CAT 2004 and is based on this logic:

The sum to 12 terms of an A.P. is equal to the sum to 18 terms. What will be the sum to 30 terms for this series?

Solution: If $S_{12} = S_{18}$, $S_{11} = S_{19}$ and $S_0 = S_{30}$

But Sum to zero terms for any series will always be 0. Hence $S_{30} = 0$.

Note: The solution to this problem does not take more than 10 seconds if you know this logic

---

(B) Decreasing A.P.s.

Similar to the cases of the increasing A.Ps, we can have two cases for decreasing APs –

Case 1– Decreasing A.P. with first term negative.

Case 2– Decreasing A.P. with first term positive.

I leave it to the reader to understand these cases and deduce that whatever was true for increasing A.Ps with first term negative will also be true for decreasing APs with first term positive.

GEOMETRIC PROGRESSION

Quantities are said to be in Geometric Progression when they increase or decrease by a constant factor.

The constant factor is also called the *common ratio* and it is found by dividing any term by the term immediately preceding it.

If we examine the series a, ar, ar^2, ar^3, ar^4,… *we notice that in any term the index of r is always less by one than the number of the term in the series.*

If n be the number of terms and if l denote the last, or nth term, we have

$$l = ar^{n-1}$$

When three quantities are in geometrical progression, the middle one is called the geometric mean between the other two. While arbitrarily choosing three numbers in GP, we take a/r, a and ar. This makes it easier since we come down to two variables for the three terms.

To Find the Geometric Mean between Two Given Quantities

Let a and b be the two quantities; G the geometric mean. Then since a, G, b are in GP,

$$b/G = G/a$$

Each being equal to the common ratio

$$G^2 = ab$$

Hence $\quad G = \sqrt{ab}$

To Insert a given Number of Geometric Means between Two Given Quantities

Let a and b be the given quantities and n the required number of means to be inserted. In all there will be $n + 2$ terms so that we have to find a series of $n + 2$ terms in GP of which a is the first and b the last.

Let r be the common ratio;

Then $\qquad b = $ the $(n + 2)$th term $= ar^{n+1}$;

$$\therefore \quad r^{(n+1)} = \frac{b}{a}$$

$$\therefore \qquad r = \left(\frac{b}{a}\right)^{\frac{1}{n+1}} \qquad (1)$$

Hence the required number of means are ar, ar^2, … ar^n, where r has the value found in (1).

To Find the Sum of a Number of Terms in a Geometric Progression

Let a be the first term, r the common ratio, n the number of terms, and S_n be the sum to n terms.

If $r > 1$, then

$$S_n = \frac{a(r^n - 1)}{(r - 1)} \qquad (1)$$

If $r < 1$, then

$$S_n = \frac{a(1 - r^n)}{(1 - r)} \qquad (2)$$

Note: It will be convenient to remember both forms given above for S. Number (2) will be used in all cases except when r is positive and greater than **one**.

Sum of an infinite geometric progression when $r < 1$

$$S_\infty = \frac{a}{(1 - r)}$$

Obviously, this formula is used only when the common ratio of the GP is less than one.

Similar to APs, GPs can also be logically viewed. Based on the value of the common ratio and its first term a G.P. might have one of the following structures:

(1) Increasing GPs type 1:
A G.P. with first term positive and common ratio greater than 1. This is the most common type of G.P.

e.g: 3, 6, 12, 24…(A G.P. with first term 3 and common ratio 2)

The plot of the sum of the series with respect to the number of terms in such a case will appear as follows:

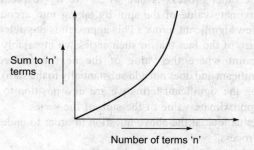

(2) Increasing GPs type 2:
A G.P. with first term negative and common ratio less than 1.

e.g: –8, –4, –2, –1, – ……

As you can see in this GP all terms are greater than their previous terms.

[The following figure will illustrate the relationship between the number of terms and the sum to 'n' terms in this case]

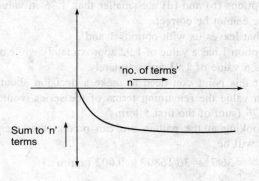

(3) Decreasing G.Ps type 1:
These GPs have their first term positive and common ratio less than 1.

e.g: 12, 6, 3, 1.5, 0.75 …..

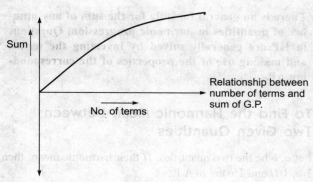

(4) Decreasing GPs type 2:
First term negative and common ratio greater than 1.

e.g: –2, –6, –18 ….

In this case the relationship looks like.

HARMONIC PROGRESSION

Three quantities a, b, c are said to be in Harmonic Progression when $a/c = \dfrac{(a - b)}{(b - c)}$.

In general, if a, b, c, d are in AP then $1/a$, $1/b$, $1/c$ and $1/d$ are all in HP.

Any number of quantities are said to be in harmonic progression when every three consecutive terms are in harmonic progression.

The reciprocals of quantities in harmonic progression are in arithmetic progression. This can be proved as:

By definition, if a, b, c are in harmonic progression,

$$\frac{a}{c} = \frac{(a - b)}{(b - c)}$$

$$\therefore \quad a(b - c) = c(a - b),$$

dividing every term by abc, we get

$$\left[\frac{1}{c} - \frac{1}{b} = \frac{1}{b} - \frac{1}{a}\right]$$

which proves the proposition.

> There is no general formula for the sum of any number of quantities in harmonic progression. Questions in HP are generally solved by inverting the terms, and making use of the properties of the corresponding AP.

To Find the Harmonic Mean between Two Given Quantities

Let a, b be the two quantities, H their harmonic mean; then $1/a$, $1/H$ and $1/b$ are in A.P.;

$$\therefore \quad \frac{1}{H} - \frac{1}{a} = \frac{1}{b} - \frac{1}{H}$$

$$\frac{2}{H} = \frac{1}{a} + \frac{1}{b}$$

i.e. $\qquad \boxed{H = \frac{2ab}{(a+b)}}$

THEOREMS RELATED WITH PROGRESSIONS

If A, G, H are the arithmetic, geometric, and harmonic means between a and b, we have

$$A = \left(\frac{a+b}{2}\right) \qquad (1)$$

$$G = \sqrt{ab} \qquad (2)$$

$$H = \frac{2ab}{(a+b)} \qquad (3)$$

Therefore, $A \times H = \dfrac{(a+b)}{2} \times \dfrac{2ab}{(a+b)} = ab = G^2$

that is, G is the geometric mean between A and H.
From these results we see that

$$A - G = \frac{a+b}{2} - \sqrt{ab} = \frac{(a+b-2\sqrt{ab})}{2}$$

$$= \left[\frac{(\sqrt{a} - \sqrt{b})}{\sqrt{2}}\right]^2$$

which is positive if a and b are positive. Therefore, the arithmetic mean of any two positive quantities is greater than their geometric mean.

Also from the equation $G^2 = AH$, we see that G is intermediate in value between A and H; and it has been proved that $A > G$, therefore $G > H$ and $A > G > H$.

The arithmetic, geometric, and harmonic means between any two positive quantities are in descending order of magnitude.

As we have already seen in the Back to school section of this block there are some number series which have a continuously decreasing value from one term to the next – and such series have the property that they have what can be defined as the sum of infinite terms. Questions on such series are very common in most aptitude exams. Even though they cannot be strictly said to be under the domain of progressions, we choose to deal with them here.

Consider the following question which appeared in CAT 2003.

Find the infinite sum of the series:

$$1 + \frac{4}{7} + \frac{9}{7^2} + \frac{16}{7^3} + \frac{25}{7^4} + \dots\dots$$

(a) 27/14 (b) 21/13
(c) 49/27 (d) 256/147

Solution: Such questions have two alternative widely divergent processes to solve them.

The first relies on mathematics using algebraic solving. Unfortunately this process being overly mathematical requires a lot of writing and hence is not advisable to be used in an aptitude exam.

The other process is one where we try to predict the approximate value of the sum by taking into account the first few significant terms. (This approach is possible to use because of the fact that in such series we invariably reach the point where the value of the next term becomes insignificant and does not add substantially to the sum). After adding the significant terms we are in a position to guess the approximate value of the sum of the series.

Let us look at the above question in order to understand the process.

In the given series the values of the terms are:

First term = 1
Second term = 4/7 = 0.57
Third term = 9/63 = 0.14
Fourth term = 16/343 = 0.04
Fifth term = 25/2401 = 0.01

Addition upto the fifth term is approximately 1.76

Options (b) and (d) are smaller than 1.76 in value and hence cannot be correct.

That leaves us with options 1 and 3

Option 1 has a value of 1.92 approximately while option 3 has a value of 1.81 approximately.

At this point you need to make a decision about how much value the remaining terms of the series would add to 1.76 (sum of the first 5 terms)

Looking at the pattern we can predict that the sixth term will be

$$36/7^5 = 36/16807 = 0.002 \text{ (approx.)}$$

And the seventh term would be $49/7^6 = 49/117649 = 0.0004$ (approx.).

The eighth term will obviously become much smaller.

It can be clearly visualized that the residual terms in the series are highly insignificant. Based on this judgement you realize that the answer will not reach 1.92 and will be restricted to 1.81. Hence the answer will be option 3.

Try using this process to solve other questions of this nature whenever you come across them. (There are a few such questions inserted in the LOD exercises of this chapter)

Useful Results

1. If the same quantity be added to, or subtracted from, all the terms of an AP, the resulting terms will form an *AP*, but with the same common difference as before.

2. If all the terms of an AP be multiplied or divided by the same quantity, the resulting terms will form an AP, but with a new common difference, which will be the multiplication/division of the old common difference. (as the case may be)

3. If all the terms of a GP be multiplied or divided by the same quantity, the resulting terms will form a GP with the same common ratio as before.

4. If $a, b, c, d, ...$ are in GP, they are also in continued proportion, since, by definition,
$$a/b = b/c = c/d = ... = 1/r$$
Conversely, a series of quantities in continued proportion may be represented by $x, xr, xr^2, ...$

5. If you have to assume 3 terms in *AP*, assume them as
$$a - d, a, a + d \quad \text{or} \quad \text{as } a, a + d \text{ and } a + 2d$$
For assuming 4 terms of an AP we use: $a - 3d$, $a - d, a + d$ and $a + 3d$
For assuming 5 terms of an *AP*, take them as:
$$a - 2d, a - d, a, a + d, a + 2d.$$
These are the most convenient in terms of problem solving.

6. For assuming three terms of a GP assume them as
$$a, ar \quad \text{and} \quad ar^2 \quad \text{or} \quad \text{as } a/r, a \text{ and } ar$$

7. To find the sum of the first n natural numbers
Let the sum be denoted by S; then
$$S = 1 + 2 + 3 + ... + n, \text{ is given by}$$
$$S = \frac{n(n+1)}{2}$$

8. To find the sum of the squares of the first n natural numbers
Let the sum be denoted by S; then
$$S = 1^2 + 2^2 + 3^2 + ... + n^2$$

Useful Results (*Contd*)

This is given by : $S = \left\{ \dfrac{n(n+1)(2n+1)}{6} \right\}$

9. To find the sum of the cubes of the first n natural numbers.
Let the sum be denoted by S; then
$$S = 1^3 + 2^3 + 3^3 + ... + n^3$$
$$S = \left[\frac{n(n+1)}{2} \right]^2$$
Thus, the sum of the cubes of the first n natural numbers is equal to the square of the sum of these numbers.

10. To find the sum of the first n odd natural numbers.
$$S = 1 + 3 + 5 + ... + (2n - 1) \rightarrow n^2$$

11. To find the sum of the first n even natural numbers.
$$S = 2 + 4 + 6 + ... + 2n \rightarrow n(n + 1)$$
$$= n^2 + n$$

12. To find the sum of odd numbers $\leq n$ where n is a natural number:

Case A: If n is odd $\rightarrow [(n + 1)/2]^2$
Case B: If n is even $\rightarrow [n/2]^2$

13. To find the sum of even numbers $\leq n$ where n is a natural number:

Case A: If n is even $\rightarrow \{(n/2)[(n/2) + 1]\}$
Case B: If n is odd $\rightarrow [(n - 1)/2][(n + 1)/2]$

14. Number of terms in a count:

- If we are counting in steps of 1 from n_1 to n_2 including both the end points, we get $(n_2 - n_1) + 1$ numbers.
- If we are counting in steps of 1 from n_1 to n_2 including only one end, we get $(n_2 - n_1)$ numbers.
- If we are counting in steps of 1 from n_1 to n_2 excluding both ends, we get $(n_2 - n_1) - 1$ numbers.

Example: Between 16 and 25 both included there are $9 + 1 = 10$ numbers.
Between 100 and 200 both excluded there are $100 - 1 = 99$ numbers.

- If we are counting in steps of 2 from n_1 to n_2 including both the end points, we get $[(n_2 - n_1)/2] + 1$ numbers.
- If we are counting in steps of 2 from n_1 to n_2 including only one end, we get $[(n_2 - n_1)/2]$ numbers.
- If we are counting in steps of 2 from n_1 to n_2 excluding both ends, we get $[(n_2 - n_1)/2] - 1$ numbers.

Contd

Contd

Useful Results (*Contd*)

- If we are counting in steps of 3 from n_1 to n_2 including both the end points, we get $[(n_2 - n_1)/3] + 1$ numbers.
- If we are counting in steps of 3 from n_1 to n_2 including only one end, we get $[(n_2 - n_1)/3]$ numbers.
- If we are counting in steps of 3 from n_1 to n_2, excluding both ends, we get $[(n_2 - n_1)/3] - 1$ numbers.

Example: Number of numbers between 100 and 200 divisible by three.

Solution: The first number is 102 and the last number is 198. Hence, answer $= (96/3) + 1 = 33$ (since both 102 and 198 are included).

Alternately, highest number below 100 that is divisible by 3 is 99, and the lowest number above 200 which is divisible by 3 is 201.

Hence, $201 - 99 = 102 \rightarrow 102/3 = 34 \rightarrow$ Answer $= 34 - 1 = 33$ (Since both ends are not included.)

In General

- If we are counting in steps of x from n_1 to n_2 including both the end points, we get $[(n_2 - n_1)/x] + 1$ numbers.

Contd

Space for Notes

Useful Results (*Contd*)

- If we are counting in steps of "x" from n_1 to n_2 including only one end, we get $(n_2 - n_1)/x$ numbers.
- If we are counting in steps of "x" from n_1 to n_2 excluding both ends, we get $[(n_2 - n_1)/x] - 1$ numbers.

For instance, if we have to find how many terms are there in the series 107, 114, 121, 128 ... 254, then we have

$(254 - 107)/7 + 1 = 147/7 + 1 = 21 + 1 = 22$ terms in the series

Of course, an appropriate adjustment will have to be made when n_2 does not fall into the series. This will be done as follows:

For instance, if we have to find how many terms of the series 107, 114, 121, 128 ... are below 258, then we have by the formula:

$(258 - 107)/7 + 1 = 151/7 + 1 = 21.57 + 1. = 22.57$. This will be adjusted by taking the lower integral value $= 22. \rightarrow$ The number of terms in the series below 258.

The student is advised to try and experiment on these principles to get a clear picture.

🎯 WORKED-OUT PROBLEMS

Problem 2.1   Two persons—Ramu Dhobi and Kalu Mochi have joined Donkey-work Associates. Ramu Dhobi and Kalu Mochi started with an initial salary of ₹ 500 and ₹ 640 respectively with annual increments of ₹ 25 and ₹ 20 each respectively. In which year will Ramu Dhobi start earning more salary than Kalu Mochi?

Solution   The current difference between the salaries of the two is ₹ 140. The annual rate of reduction of this dfference is ₹ 5 per year. At this rate, it will take Ramu Dhobi 28 years to equalise his salary with Kalu Dhobi's salary.

Thus, in the 29th year he will earn more.

This problem should be solved while reading and the thought process should be 140/5 = 28. Hence, answer is 29th year.

Problem 2.2   Find the value of the expression

$$1 - 6 + 2 - 7 + 3 - 8 + \ldots \ldots \text{ to } 100 \text{ terms}$$

    (a) −250   (b) −500

    (c) −450   (d) −300

Solution   The series $(1 - 6 + 2 - 7 + 3 - 8 + \ldots \ldots$ to 100 terms) can be rewritten as:

$\Rightarrow$ (1 + 2 + 3 + … to 50 terms) − (6 + 7 + 8 + … to 50 terms)

Both these are *AP*'s with values of *a* and *d* as →
$a = 1$, $n = 50$ and $d = 1$ and $a = 6$, $n = 50$ and $d = 1$ respectively.

Using the formula for sum of an *AP* we get:

    → $25(2 + 49) - 25(12 + 49)$

    → $25(51 - 61) = -250$

Alternatively, we can do this faster by considering $(1 - 6)$, $(2 - 7)$, and so on as one unit or one term.

$1 - 6 = 2 - 7 = \ldots = -5$. Thus the above series is equivalent to a series of fifty −5's added to each other.

So, $(1 - 6) + (2 - 7) + (3 - 8) + \ldots$ 50 terms $= -5 \times 50$ = **−250**

Problem 2.3   Find the sum of all numbers divisible by 6 in between 100 to 400.

Solution   Here 1st term $= a = 102$ (which is the 1st term greater than 100 that is divisible by 6.)

The last term less than 400, which is divisible by 6 is 396.

The number of terms in the *AP;* 102, 108, 114…396 is given by $[(396 - 102)/6] + 1 = 50$ numbers.

Common difference $= d = 6$

So, $S = 25 (204 + 294) = 12450$

Problem 2.4   If x, y, z are in *GP*, then $1/(1 + \log_{10}x)$, $1/(1 + \log_{10}y)$ and $1/(1 + \log_{10}z)$ will be in:

    (a) AP   (b) GP

    (c) HP   (d) Cannot be said

Solution   Go through the options.

Checking option (a), the three will be in AP if the 2nd expression is the average of the 1st and 3rd expressions. This can be mathematically written as

$$2/(1 + \log_{10}y) = [1/(1 + \log_{10}x)] + [1/(1 + \log_{10}z)]$$

$$= \frac{[1 + (1 + \log_{10}x) + 1 + (1 + \log_{10}z)]}{[(1 + \log_{10}x)(1 + \log_{10}z)]}$$

$$= \frac{[2 + \log_{10}xz]}{(1 + \log_{10}x)\,(1 + \log_{10}z)}$$

Applying our judgement, there seems to be no indication that we are going to get a solution.

Checking option (b)

$$[1/(1 + \log_{10}y)]^2 = [1/(1 + \log_{10}x)]\,[1/(1 + \log_{10}z)]$$

$$= [1/(1 + \log_{10}(x + z) + \log_{10}xz)]$$

Again we are trapped and any solution is not in sight. Checking option (c).

$1/(1 + \log_{10}x)$, $1/(1 + \log_{10}y)$ and $1/(1 + \log_{10}z)$ are in *HP* then $1 + \log_{10}x$, $1 + \log_{10}y$ and $1 + \log_{10}z$ will be in AP.

So, $\log_{10}x$, $\log_{10}y$ and $\log_{10}z$ will also be in AP.

Hence, $2 \log_{10}y = \log_{10}x + \log_{10}z$

$\Rightarrow$ $y^2 = xz$ which is given.

So, **(c)** is the correct option.

Alternatively, you could have solved through the following process.

x, y and z are given as logarithmic functions.

Assume $x = 1$, $y = 10$ and $z = 100$ as x, y, z are in GP

So, $1 + \log_{10}x = 1$, $1 + \log_{10}y = 2$ and $1 + \log_{10}z = 3$

$\Rightarrow$ Thus we find that since 1, 2 and 3 are in AP, we can assume that

    $1 + \log_{10}x$, $1 + \log_{10}y$ and $1 + \log_{10}z$ are in AP

$\Rightarrow$ Hence, by definition of an HP we have that $1/(1 + \log_{10}x)$, $1/(1 + \log_{10}y)$ and $1/(1 + \log_{10}z)$ are in *HP*. Hence, option (c) is the required answer.

Author's Note: In my experience I have always found that the toughest equations and factorisations get solved very easily when there are options, by assuming values in place of the variables in the equation. The values of the variables should be taken in such a manner that the basic restrictions put on the variables should be respected. For example, if an expression in three variables a, b and c is given and it is mentioned that $a + b + c = 0$ then the values that you assume for a, b and c should satisfy this restriction. Hence, you should look at values like 1, 2 and –3 or 2, –1, –1 etc.

This process is especially useful in the case where the question as well as the options both contain expressions. Factorisation and advanced techniques of maths are then not required. This process will be very beneficial for students who are weak at Mathematics.

Problem 2.5 Find t_{10} and S_{10} for the following series:

$$1, 8, 15, \ldots$$

Solution This is an AP with first term 1 and common difference 7.

$$t_{10} = a + (n - 1)\, d = 1 + 9 \times 7 = 64$$

$$S_{10} = \frac{n[2a + (n-1)d]}{2}$$

$$= \frac{10[2(1) + (10 - 1)7]}{2} = 325$$

Alternatively, if the number of terms is small, you can count it directly.

Problem 2.6 Find t_{18} and S_{18} for the following series:

$$2, 8, 32, \ldots$$

Solution This is a GP with first term 2 and common ratio 4.

$$t_{18} = ar^{n-1} = 2.4^{17}$$

$$S_{18} = \frac{a(r^n - 1)}{r - 1} = \frac{2(4^{18} - 1)}{(4 - 1)}$$

Problem 2.7 Is the series 1, 4,… to n terms an *AP*, or a *GP*, or an *HP*, or a series which cannot be determined?

Solution *To determine any progression, we should have at least three terms.*

If the series is an *AP* then the next term of this series will be 7

Again, if the next term is 16, then this will be a *GP* series (1, 4, 16 …)

So, *we cannot determine* the nature of the progression of this series.

Problem 2.8 Find the sum to 200 terms of the series $1 + 4 + 6 + 5 + 11 + 6 + \ldots$

    (a) 30,200   (b) 29,800

    (c) 30,200   (d) None of these

Solution Spot that the above series is a combination of two *APs*.

The 1st *AP* is $(1 + 6 + 11 + \ldots)$ and the 2nd *AP* is $(4 + 5 + 6 + \ldots)$

Since the terms of the two series alternate, $S = (1 + 6 + 11 + \ldots$ to 100 terms$) + (4 + 5 + 6 + \ldots$ to 100 terms$)$

$$= \frac{100[2 \times 1 + 99 \times 5]}{2} + \frac{100[2 \times 4 + 99 \times 1]}{2} \rightarrow \text{(Using the}$$

formula for the sum of an *AP*)

$$= 50[497 + 107] = 50[604] = 30200$$

Alternatively, we can treat every two consecutive terms as one.

So we will have a total of 100 terms of the nature:

$$(1 + 4) + (6 + 5) + (11 + 6) \ldots \rightarrow 5, 11, 17\ldots$$

Now, $a = 5$, $d = 6$ and $n = 100$

Hence the sum of the given series is

$$S = \frac{100}{2} \times [2 \times 5 + 99 \times 6]$$

$$= 50[604] = 30200$$

Problem 2.9 How many terms of the series –12, –9, –6,… must be taken that the sum may be 54?

Solution Here $S = 54$, $a = -12$, $d = 3$, n is unknown and has to be calculated. To do so we use the formula for the sum of an *AP* and get.

$$54 = \frac{[2(-12) + (n-1)3]n}{2}$$

or $108 = -24n - 3n + 3n^2$ or $3n^2 - 27n - 108 = 0$

or $n^2 - 9n - 36 = 0$, or $n^2 - 12n + 3n - 36 = 0$

$$n(n - 12) + 3(n - 12) = 0 \Rightarrow (n + 3)\,(n - 12) = 0$$

The value of n (the number of terms) cannot be negative. Hence –3 is rejected.

So we have $n = 12$

Alternatively, we can directly add up individual terms and keep adding manually till we get a sum of 54. We will observe that this will occur after adding 12 terms. (In this case, as also in all cases where the number of terms is mentally manageable, mentally adding the terms till we get the required sum will turn out to be much faster than the equation based process.

Problem 2.10 Find the sum of n terms of the series $1.2.4 + 2.3.5 + 3.4.6 + \ldots$

    (a) $n(n + 1)(n + 2)$

    (b) $(n(n + 1)/12)(3n^2 + 19n + 26)$

    (c) $((n + 1)(n + 2)(n + 3))/4$

    (d) $(n^2\,(n + 1)(n + 2)(n + 3))/3$

Solution In order to solve such problems in the examination, the option-based approach is the best. Even if you can find out the required expression mathematically, it is advisable to solve through the options as this will end up saving a lot of time for you. Use the options as follows:

If we put $n = 1$, we should get the sum as $1.2.4 = 8$. By substituting $n = 1$ in each of the four options we will get the following values for the sum to 1 term:

Option (a) gives a value of: 6
Option (b) gives a value of: 8
Option (c) gives a value of: 6
Option (d) gives a value of: 8

From this check we can reject the options (a) and (c).

Now put $n = 2$. You can see that up to 2 terms, the expression is $1.2.4 + 2.3.5 = 38$

The correct option should also give 38 if we put $n = 2$ in the expression. Since, (a) and (c) have already been rejected, we only need to check for options (b) and (d).

Option (b) gives a value of 38
Option (d) gives a value of 80.

Hence, we can reject option (d) and get (b) as the answer.

> **Note:** The above process is very effective for solving questions having options. The student should try to keep an eye open for the possibility of solving questions through options. In my opinion, approximately 50–75% of the questions asked in CAT in the QA section can be solved with options (at least partially).

Space for Rough Work

LEVEL OF DIFFICULTY (I)

1. How many terms are there in the AP 20, 25, 30,... 130.
   (a) 22   (b) 23
   (c) 21   (d) 24

2. Bobby was appointed to Mindworkzz in the pay scale of ₹ 7000–500–12,500. Find how many years he will take to reach the maximum of the scale.
   (a) 11 years   (b) 10 years
   (c) 9 years   (d) 8 years

3. Find the 1st term of an AP whose 8th and 12th terms are respectively 39 and 59.
   (a) 5   (b) 6
   (c) 4   (d) 3

4. A number of squares are described whose perimetres are in GP. Then their sides will be in
   (a) AP   (b) GP
   (c) HP   (d) Nothing can be said

5. There is an *AP* 1, 3, 5.... Which term of this AP is 55?
   (a) 27th   (b) 26th
   (c) 25th   (d) 28th

6. How many terms are identical in the two *AP*s 1, 3, 5,... up to 120 terms and 3, 6, 9,... up to 80 terms?
   (a) 38   (b) 39
   (c) 40   (d) 41

7. Find the lowest number in an AP such that the sum of all the terms is 105 and greatest term is 6 times the least.
   (a) 5   (b) 10
   (c) 15   (d) (a), (b) & (c)

8. Find the 15th term of the sequence 20, 15, 10, ...
   (a) –45   (b) –55
   (c) –50   (d) 0

9. A sum of money kept in a bank amounts to ₹ 1240 in 4 years and ₹ 1600 in 10 years at simple Interest. Find the sum.
   (a) ₹ 800   (b) ₹ 900
   (c) ₹ 1150   (d) ₹ 1000

10. A number 15 is divided into three parts which are in *AP* and the sum of their squares is 83. Find the smallest number.
    (a) 5   (b) 3
    (c) 6   (d) 8

11. The sum of the first 16 terms of an *AP* whose first term and third term are 5 and 15 respectively is
    (a) 600   (b) 765
    (c) 640   (d) 680

12. The number of terms of the series 54 + 51 + 48 +... such that the sum is 513 is
    (a) 18   (b) 19
    (c) Both *a* and *b*   (d) 15

13. The least value of *n* for which the sum of the series 5 + 8 + 11... *n* terms is not less than 670 is
    (a) 20   (b) 19
    (c) 22   (d) 21

14. A man receives ₹ 60 for the first week and ₹ 3 more each week than the preceding week. How much does he earn by the 20th week?
    (a) ₹ 1770   (b) ₹ 1620
    (c) ₹ 1890   (d) ₹ 1790

15. How many terms are there in the GP 5, 20, 80, 320,... 20480?
    (a) 6   (b) 5
    (c) 7   (d) 8

16. A boy agrees to work at the rate of one rupee on the first day, two rupees on the second day, four rupees on the third day and so on. How much will the boy get if he starts working on the 1st of February and finishes on the 20th of February?
    (a) 2^{20} (b) $2^{20} - 1$
    (c) $2^{19} - 1$ (d) 2^{19}

17. If the fifth term of a GP is 81 and first term is 16, what will be the 4th term of the GP?
    (a) 36   (b) 18
    (c) 54   (d) 24

18. The seventh term of a GP is 8 times the fourth term. What will be the first term when its fifth term is 48?
    (a) 4   (b) 3
    (c) 5   (d) 2

19. The sum of three numbers in a GP is 14 and the sum of their squares is 84. Find the largest number.
    (a) 8   (b) 6
    (c) 4   (d) 12

20. The first term of an arithmetic progression is unity and the common difference is 4. Which of the following will be a term of this AP?
    (a) 4551   (b) 10091
    (c) 7881   (d) 13531

21. How many natural numbers between 300 to 500 are multiples of 7?
    (a) 29   (b) 28
    (c) 27   (d) 30

22. The sum of the first and the third term of a geometric progression is 20 and the sum of its first three terms is 26. Find the progression.

(a) 2, 6, 18,...   (b) 18, 6, 2,...

(c) Both of these   (d) None of these

23. If a man saves ₹ 4 more each year than he did the year before and if he saves ₹ 20 in the first year, after how many years will his savings be more than ₹ 1000 altogether?

    (a) 19 years   (b) 20 years

    (c) 21years   (d) 18 years

24. A man's salary is ₹ 800 per month in the first year. He has joined in the scale of 800–40–1600. After how many years will his savings be ₹ 64,800?

    (a) 8 years   (b) 7 years

    (c) 6 years   (d) Cannot be determined

25. The 4th and 10th term of a GP are 1/3 and 243 respectively. Find the 2nd term.

    (a) 3   (b) 1

    (c) 1/27   (d) 1/9

26. The 7th and 21st terms of an AP are 6 and −22 respectively. Find the 26th term.

    (a) −34   (b) −32

    (c) −12   (d) −10

27. The sum of 5 numbers in AP is 30 and the sum of their squares is 220. Which of the following is the third term?

    (a) 5   (b) 6

    (c) 8   (d) 9

28. Find the sum of all numbers in between 10–50 excluding all those numbers which are divisible by 8. (include 10 and 50 for counting.)

    (a) 1070   (b) 1220

    (c) 1320   (d) 1160

29. The sum of the first four terms of an AP is 28 and sum of the first eight terms of the same AP is 88. Find the sum of the first 16 terms of the AP?

    (a) 346   (b) 340

    (c) 304   (d) 268

30. Find the general term of the GP with the third term 1 and the seventh term 8.

    (a) $(2^{3/4})^{n-3}$ (b) $(2^{3/2})^{n-3}$

    (c) $(2^{3/4})^{3-n}$ (d) $(2^{3/4})^{2-n}$

31. Find the number of terms of the series 1/81, −1/27, 1/9,... −729.

    (a) 11   (b) 12

    (c) 10   (d) 13

32. Four geometric means are inserted between 1/8 and 128. Find the third geometric mean.

    (a) 4   (b) 16

    (c) 32   (d) 8

33. A and B are two numbers whose AM is 25 and GM is 7. Which of the following may be a value of A?

    (a) 10   (b) 20

    (c) 49   (d) 25

34. Two numbers A and B are such that their GM is 20% lower than their AM. Find the ratio between the numbers.

    (a) 3 : 2   (b) 4 : 1

    (c) 2 : 1   (d) 3 : 1

35. A man saves ₹ 100 in January 2014 and increases his saving by ₹ 50 every month over the previous month. What is the annual saving for the man in the year 2014?

    (a) ₹ 4200   (b) ₹ 4500

    (c) ₹ 4000   (d) ₹ 4100

36. In a nuclear power plant a technician is allowed an interval of maximum 100 minutes. A timer with a bell rings at specific intervals of time such that the minutes when the timer rings are not divisible by 2, 3, 5 and 7. The last alarm rings with a buzzer to give time for decontamination of the technician. How many times will the bell ring within these 100 minutes and what is the value of the last minute when the bell rings for the last time in a 100 minute shift?

    (a) 25 times, 89   (b) 21 times, 97

    (c) 22 times, 97   (d) 19 times, 97

37. How many zeroes will be there at the end of the expression $(2!)^{2!} + (4!)^{4!} + (8!)^{8!} + (9!)^{9!} + (10!)^{10!} + (11!)^{11!}$?

    (a) $(8!)^{8!} + (9!)^{9!} + (10!)^{10!} + (11!)^{11!}$

    (b) 10^{101} (c) $4! + 6! + 8! + 2 (10!)$

    (d) $(0!)^{0!}$

38. The 1st, 8th and 22nd terms of an AP are three consecutive terms of a GP. Find the common ratio of the GP, given that the sum of the first twenty-two terms of the AP is 385.

    (a) Either 1 or1/2   (b) 2

    (c) 1   (d) Either 1 or 2

39. The internal angles of a plane polygon are in AP. The smallest angle is 100° and the common difference is 10°. Find the number of sides of the polygon.

    (a) 8   (b) 9

    (c) Either 8 or 9   (d) None of these

40. After striking a floor a rubber ball rebounds (7/8)th of the height from which it has fallen. Find the total distance that it travels before coming to rest, if it is gently dropped from a height of 420 meters.

    (a) 2940   (b) 6300

    (c) 1080   (d) 3360

41. Each of the series 13 + 15 + 17+.... and 14 + 17 + 20+... is continued to 100 terms. Find how many terms are identical between the two series.

    (a) 35   (b) 34

    (c) 32   (d) 33

42. Jack and Jill were playing mathematical puzzles with each other. Jill drew a square of sides 8 cm and then kept on drawing squares inside the squares by

joining the mid points of the squares. She continued this process indefinitely. Jill asked Jack to determine the sum of the areas of all the squares that she drew. If Jack answered correctly then what would be his answer?

(a) 128   (b) 64
(c) 256   (d) 32

43. How many terms of the series $1 + 3 + 5 + 7 + \ldots\ldots$ amount to 123454321?

(a) 11101   (b) 11011
(c) 10111   (d) 11111

44. A student takes a test consisting of 100 questions with differential marking is told that each question after the first is worth 4 marks more than the preceding question. If the third question of the test is worth 9 marks. What is the maximum score that the student can obtain by attempting 98 questions?

(a) 19698   (b) 19306
(c) 9900   (d) None of these

45. In an infinite geometric progression, each term is equal to 2 times the sum of the terms that follow. If the first term of the series is 8, find the sum of the series?

(a) 12   (b) 32/3
(c) 34/3   (d) Data inadequate

46. What is the maximum sum of the terms in the arithmetic progression 25, 24 ½ , 24, ...?

(a) 637 ½   (b) 625
(c) 662 ½   (d) 650

47. An equilateral triangle is drawn by joining the midpoints of the sides of another equilateral triangle. A third equilateral triangle is drawn inside the second one joining the midpoints of the sides of the second equilateral triangle, and the process continues infinitely. Find the sum of the perimeters of all the equilateral triangles, if the side of the largest equilateral triangle is 24 units.

(a) 288 units (b) 72 units
(c) 36 units   (d) 144 units

48. The sum of the first two terms of an infinite geometric series is 18. Also, each term of the series is seven times the sum of all the terms that follow. Find the first term and the common ratio of the series respectively.

(a) 16, 1/8   (b) 15, 1/5
(c) 12, 1/2   (d) 8, 1/16

49. Find the 33rd term of the sequence: 3, 8, 9, 13, 15, 18, 21, 23...

(a) 93   (b) 99
(c) 105   (d) 83

50. For the above question, find the sum of the series till 33 terms.

(a) 728   (b) 860
(c) 1595   (d) 1583

Space for Rough Work

LEVEL OF DIFFICULTY (II)

1. If a times the ath term of an AP is equal to b times the bth term, find the $(a + b)$th term.
   (a) 0
   (b) $a^2 - b^2$
   (c) $a - b$
   (d) 1

2. A number 20 is divided into four parts that are in AP such that the product of the first and fourth is to the product of the second and third is 2 : 3. Find the largest part.
   (a) 12
   (b) 4
   (c) 8
   (d) 9

3. Find the value of the expression: $1 - 4 + 5 - 8 \ldots$ to 50 terms.
   (a) -150
   (b) -75
   (c) -50
   (d) 75

4. If a clock strikes once at one o'clock, twice at two o'clock and twelve times at 12 o'clock and again once at one o'clock and so on, how many times will the bell be struck in the course of 2 days?
   (a) 156
   (b) 312
   (c) 78
   (d) 288

5. What will be the maximum sum of 44, 42, 40, … ?
   (a) 502
   (b) 504
   (c) 506
   (d) 500

6. Find the sum of the integers between 1 and 200 that are multiples of 7.
   (a) 2742
   (b) 2842
   (c) 2646
   (d) 2546

7. If the mth term of an AP is $1/n$ and nth term is $1/m$, then find the sum to mn terms.
   (a) $(mn - 1)/4$
   (b) $(mn + 1)/4$
   (c) $(mn + 1)/2$
   (d) $(mn - 1)/2$

8. Find the sum of all odd numbers lying between 100 and 200.
   (a) 7500
   (b) 2450
   (c) 2550
   (d) 2650

9. Find the sum of all integers of 3 digits that are divisible by 7.
   (a) 69,336
   (b) 71,336
   (c) 70,336
   (d) 72,336

10. The first and the last terms of an AP are 107 and 253. If there are five terms in this sequence, find the sum of sequence.
    (a) 1080
    (b) 720
    (c) 900
    (d) 620

11. Find the value of $1 - 2 - 3 + 2 - 3 - 4 + \ldots + $ upto 100 terms.
    (a) -694
    (b) -626
    (c) -624
    (d) -549

12. What will be the sum to n terms of the series $8 + 88 + 888 + \ldots$?
    (a) $\dfrac{8(10^n - 9n)}{81}$
    (b) $\dfrac{8(10^{n+1} - 10 - 9n)}{81}$
    (c) $8(10^{n-1} - 10)$
    (d) $8(10^{n+1} - 10)$

13. If a, b, c are in GP, then $\log a$, $\log b$, $\log c$ are in
    (a) AP
    (b) GP
    (c) HP
    (d) None of these

14. After striking the floor, a rubber ball rebounds to 4/5th of the height from which it has fallen. Find the total distance that it travels before coming to rest if it has been gently dropped from a height of 120 metres.
    (a) 540 metres
    (b) 960 metres
    (c) 1080 metres
    (d) 1020 metres

15. If x be the first term, y be the nth term and p be the product of n terms of a GP, then the value of p^2 will be
    (a) $(xy)^{n-1}$
    (b) $(xy)^n$
    (c) $(xy)^{1-n}$
    (d) $(xy)^{n/2}$

16. The sum of an infinite GP whose common ratio is numerically less than 1 is 32 and the sum of the first two terms is 24. What will be the third term?
    (a) 2
    (b) 16
    (c) 8
    (d) 4

17. What will be the value of $x^{1/2}.x^{1/4}.x^{1/8}\ldots$ to infinity.
    (a) x^2
    (b) x
    (c) $x^{3/2}$
    (d) x^3

18. Find the sum to n terms of the series
    $1.2.3 + 2.3.4 + 3.4.5 + \ldots$
    (a) $(n + 1)(n + 2)(n + 3)/3$
    (b) $n(n + 1)(2n + 2)(n + 2)/4$
    (c) $n(n + 1)(n + 2)$
    (d) $n(n + 1)(n + 2)(n + 3)/4$

19. Determine the first term of the geometric progression, the sum of whose first term and third term is 40 and the sum of the second term and fourth term is 80.
    (a) 12
    (b) 16
    (c) 8
    (d) 4

20. Find the second term of an AP if the sum of its first five even terms is equal to 15 and the sum of the first three terms is equal to -3.
    (a) -3
    (b) -2
    (c) -1
    (d) 0

21. The sum of the second and the fifth term of an AP is 8 and that of the third and the seventh term is 14. Find the eleventh term.
    (a) 19   (b) 17
    (c) 15   (d) 16

22. How many terms of an AP must be taken for their sum to be equal to 120 if its third term is 9 and the difference between the seventh and the second term is 20?
    (a) 6   (b) 9
    (c) 7   (d) 8

23. Four numbers are inserted between the numbers 4 and 39 such that an AP results. Find the biggest of these four numbers.
    (a) 31.5   (b) 31
    (c) 32   (d) 30

24. Find the sum of all three-digit natural numbers, which on being divided by 5, leave a remainder equal to 4.
    (a) 57,270   (b) 96,780
    (c) 49,680   (d) 99,270

25. The sum of the first three terms of the arithmetic progression is 30 and the sum of the squares of the first term and the second term of the same progression is 116. Find the seventh term of the progression if its fifth term is known to be exactly divisible by 14.
    (a) 36   (b) 40
    (c) 43   (d) 22

26. A and B set out to meet each other from two places 165 km apart. A travels 15 km the first day, 14 km the second day, 13 km the third day and so on. B travels 10 km the first day, 12 km the second day, 14 km the third day and so on. After how many days will they meet?
    (a) 8 days   (b) 5 days
    (c) 6 days   (d) 7 days

27. If a man saves ₹ 1000 each year and invests at the end of the year at 5% compound interest, how much will the amount be at the end of 15 years?
    (a) ₹ 21,478   (b) ₹ 21,578
    (c) ₹ 22,578   (d) ₹ 22,478

28. If sum to n terms of a series is given by $(n + 8)$, then its second term will be given by
    (a) 10   (b) 9
    (c) 8   (d) 1

29. If A is the sum of the n terms of the series $1 + 1/4 + 1/16 + \ldots$ and B is the sum of $2n$ terms of the series $1 + 1/2 + 1/4 + \ldots$, then find the value of A/B.
    (a) 1/3   (b) 1/2
    (c) 2/3   (d) 3/4

30. A man receives a pension starting with ₹ 100 for the first year. Each year he receives 90% of what he received the previous year. Find the maximum total amount he can receive even if he lives forever.
    (a) ₹ 1100   (b) ₹ 1000
    (c) ₹ 1200   (d) ₹ 900

31. The sum of the series represented as:
    $1/1 \times 5 + 1/5 \times 9 + 1/9 \times 13 \ldots.. + 1/221 \times 225$ is
    (a) 28/221   (b) 56/221
    (c) 56/225   (d) None of these

32. The sum of the series
    $1/(\sqrt{2} + \sqrt{1}) + 1/(\sqrt{2} + \sqrt{3}) + \ldots\ldots\ldots+$
    $1/(\sqrt{120} + \sqrt{121})$ is:
    (a) 10   (b) 11
    (c) 12   (d) None of these

33. Find the infinite sum of the series $1/1 + 1/3 + 1/6 + 1/10 + 1/15 \ldots$
    (a) 2   (b) 2.25
    (c) 3   (d) 4

34. The sum of the series $5 \times 8 + 8 \times 11 + 11 \times 14$ upto n terms will be:
    (a) $(n + 1)[3(n + 1)^2 + 6(n + 1) + 1] - 10$
    (b) $(n + 1)[3(n + 1)^2 + 6(n + 1) + 1] + 10$
    (c) $(n + 1)[3(n + 1) + 6(n + 1)^2 + 1] - 10$
    (d) $(n + 1)[3(n + 1) + 6(n + 1)^2 + 1] + 10$

35. The sum of the series: $\frac{1}{2} + 1/6 + 1/12 + 1/20 + \ldots 1/156 + 1/182$ is:
    (a) 12/13   (b) 13/14
    (c) 14/13   (d) None of these

36. For the above question 35, what is the sum of the series if taken to infinite terms:
    (a) 1.1   (b) 1
    (c) 14/13   (d) None of these

Directions for Questions 37 to 39: Answer these questions based on the following information.

There are 250 integers $a_1, a_2 \ldots\ldots a_{250}$, not all of them necessarily different. Let the greatest integer of these 250 integers be referred to as Max, and the smallest integer be referred to as Min. The integers a_1 through a_{124} form sequence A, and the rest form sequence B. Each member of A is less than or equal to each member of B.

37. All values in A are changed in sign, while those in B remain unchanged. Which of the following statements is true?
    (a) Every member of A is greater than or equal to every member of B.
    (b) Max is in A.

(c) If all numbers originally in A and B had the same sign, then after the change of sign, the largest number of A and B is in A.

(d) None of these

38. Elements of A are in ascending order, and those of B are in descending order. a_{124} and a_{125} are interchanged. Then which of the following statements is true?

(a) A continues to be in ascending order.

(b) B continues to be in descending order.

(c) A continues to be in ascending order and B in descending order.

(d) None of the above

39. Every element of A is made greater than or equal to every element of B by adding to each element of A an integer x. Then, x cannot be less than:

(a) 2^{10}

(b) the smallest value of B

(c) the largest value of B

(d) (Max-Min)

40. Rohit drew a rectangular grid of 529 cells, arranged in 23 Rows and 23 columns, and filled each cell with a number. The numbers with which he filled each cell were such that the numbers of each row taken from left to right formed an arithmetic series and the numbers of each column taken from top to bottom also formed an arithmetic series. The seventh and the seventeenth numbers of the fifth row were 47 and 63 respectively, while the seventh and the seventeenth numbers of the fifteenth row were 53 and 77 respectively. What is the sum of all the numbers in the grid?

(a) 32798　　(b) 65596

(c) 52900　　(d) None of these

41. How many three digit numbers have the property that their digits taken from left to right form an Arithmetic or a Geometric Progression?

(a) 15　　(b) 36

(c) 20　　(d) 42

Directions for Questions 42 and 43: These questions are based on the following data.

At Burger King—a famous fast food centre on Main Street in Pune, burgers are made only on an automatic burger making machine. The machine continuously makes different sorts of burgers by adding different sorts of fillings on a common bread. The machine makes the burgers at the rate of 1 burger per half a minute. The various fillings are added to the burgers in the following manner. The 1st, 5th, 9th, ... burgers are filled with a chicken patty; the 2nd, 9th, 16th, ... burgers with vegetable patty; the 1st, 5th, 9th, ... burgers with mushroom patty; and the rest with plain cheese and tomato fillings.

The machine makes exactly 660 burgers per day.

42. How many burgers per day are made with cheese and tomato as fillings?

(a) 424　　(b) 236

(c) 237　　(d) None of these

43. How many burgers are made with all three fillings Chicken, vegetable and mushroom?

(a) 23　　(b) 24

(c) 25　　(d) 26

44. An arithmetic progression P consists of n terms. From the progression three different progressions $P_1 P_2$ and P_3 are created such that P_1 is obtained by the 1st, 4th ,7th...... terms of P, P_2 has the 2nd, 5th, 8th,...... terms of P and P_3 has the 3rd, 6th, 9th, ... terms of P. It is found that of P_1, P_2 and P_3 two progressions have the property that their average is itself a term of the original Progression P. Which of the following can be a possible value of n?

(a) 20　　(b) 26

(c) 36　　(d) Both (a)and (b)

45. For the above question, if the Common Difference between the terms of P_1 is 6, what is the common difference of P?

(a) 2　　(b) 3

(c) 6　　(d) Cannot be determined

Space for Rough Work

LEVEL OF DIFFICULTY (III)

1. If in any decreasing arithmetic progression, sum of all its terms, except for the first term, is equal to −36, the sum of all its terms, except for the last term, is zero, and the difference of the tenth and the sixth term is equal to − 16, then what will be first term of this series?

   (a) 16   (b) 20

   (b) −16   (d) −20

2. The sum of all terms of the arithmetic progression having ten terms except for the first term, is 99, and except for the sixth term, 89. Find the third term of the progression if the sum of the first and the fifth term is equal to 10.

   (a) 15   (b) 5

   (c) 8   (d) 10

3. Product of the fourth term and the fifth term of an arithmetic progression is 456. Division of the ninth term by the fourth term of the progression gives quotient as 11 and the remainder as 10. Find the first term of the progression.

   (a) − 52   (b) − 42

   (c) − 56   (d) − 66

4. A number of saplings are lying at a place by the side of a straight road. These are to be planted in a straight line at a distance interval of 10 meters between two consecutive saplings. Mithilesh, the country's greatest forester, can carry only one sapling at a time and has to move back to the original point to get the next sapling. In this manner he covers a total distance of 1.32 kms. How many saplings does he plant in the process if he ends at the starting point?

   (a) 15   (b) 14

   (c) 13   (d) 12

5. A geometric progression consists of 500 terms. Sum of the terms occupying the odd places is P_1 and the sum of the terms occupying the even places is P_2. Find the common ratio.

   (a) P_2/P_1 (b) P_1/P_2

   (c) $P_2 + P_1/P_1$ (d) $P_2 + P_1/P_2$

6. The sum of the first ten terms of the geometric progression is S_1 and the sum of the next ten terms (11th through 20th) is S_2. Find the common ratio.

   (a) $(S_1/S_2)^{1/10}$ (b) $-(S_1/S_2)^{1/10}$

   (c) $\pm \sqrt[10]{S_2/S_1}$ (d) $(S_1/S_2)^{1/5}$

7. The first and the third terms of an arithmetic progression are equal, respectively, to the first and the third term of a geometric progression, and the second term of the arithmetic progression exceeds the second term of the geometric progression by 0.25. Calculate the sum of the first five terms of the arithmetic progression if its first term is equal to 2.

   (a) 2.25 or 25   (b) 2.5 or 27.5

   (c) 1.5   (d) 3.25

8. If $(2 + 4 + 6 + \dots 50 \text{ terms})/(1 + 3 + 5 + \dots n \text{ terms}) = 51/2$, then find the value of n.

   (a) 12   (b) 13

   (c) 9   (d) 10

9. $(666\dots n \text{ digits})^2 + (888\dots n \text{ digits})$ is equal to

   (a) $(10^n - 1) \times \dfrac{4}{9}$ (b) $(10^{2n} - 1) \times \dfrac{4}{9}$

   (c) $\dfrac{4(10^n - 10^{n-1} - 1)}{9}$ (d) $\dfrac{4(10^n + 1)}{9}$

10. The interior angles of a polygon are in AP. The smallest angle is 120° and the common difference is 5°. Find the number of sides of the polygon.

    (a) 7   (b) 8

    (c) 9   (d) 10

11. Find the sum to n terms of the series $11 + 103 + 1005 + \dots$

    (a) $\dfrac{10(10^n - 1)}{9} + 1$ (b) $\dfrac{10(10^n - 1)}{9} + n$

    (c) $\dfrac{10(10^n - 1)}{9} + n^2$ (d) $\dfrac{10(10^n + 1)}{11} + n^2$

12. The sum of the first term and the fifth term of an AP is 26 and the product of the second term by the fourth term is 160. Find the sum of the first seven terms of this AP.

    (a) 110   (b) 114

    (c) 112   (d) 116

13. The sum of the third and the ninth term of an AP is 10. Find a possible sum of the first 11 terms of this AP.

    (a) 55   (b) 44

    (c) 66   (d) 48

14. The sum of the squares of the fifth and the eleventh term of an AP is 3 and the product of the second and the fourteenth term is equal it P. Find the product of the first and the fifteenth term of the AP.

    (a) $(58P - 39)/45$ (b) $(98P + 39)/72$

    (c) $(116P - 39)/90$ (d) $(98P + 39)/90$

15. If the ratio of harmonic mean of two numbers to their geometric mean is 12 : 13, find the ratio of the numbers.

    (a) 4/9 or 9/4   (b) 2/3 or 3/2

    (c) 2/5 or 5/2   (d) 3/4 or 4/5

16. Find the sum of the series $1.2 + 2.2^2 + 3.2^3 + \ldots + 100.2^{100}$.
    - (a) $100.2^{101} + 2$
    - (b) $99.2^{100} + 2$
    - (c) $99.2^{101} + 2$
    - (d) None of these

17. The sequence $[x_n]$ is a GP with $x_2/x_4 = 1/4$ and $x_1 + x_4 = 108$. What will be the value of x_3?
    - (a) 42
    - (b) 48
    - (c) 44
    - (d) 56

18. If x, y, z are in GP and a^x, b^y and c^z are equal, then a, b, c are in
    - (a) AP
    - (b) GP
    - (c) HP
    - (d) None of these

19. Find the sum of all possible whole number divisors of 720.
    - (a) 2012
    - (b) 2624
    - (c) 2210
    - (d) 2418

20. Sum to n terms of the series $\log m + \log m^2/n + \log m^3/n^2 + \log m^4/n^3 \ldots$ is
    - (a) $\log \left(\dfrac{m^{n+1}}{n^{n-1}} \right)^{\frac{n}{2}}$
    - (b) $\log \left(\dfrac{n^{n-1}}{m^{n+1}} \right)^{\frac{n}{2}}$
    - (c) $\log \left(\dfrac{m^n}{n^n} \right)^{\frac{n}{2}}$
    - (d) $\log \left(\dfrac{m^{1-n}}{n^{1-m}} \right)^{\frac{n}{2}}$

21. The sum of first 20 and first 50 terms of an AP is 420 and 2550. Find the eleventh term of a GP whose first term is the same as the AP and the common ratio of the GP is equal to the common difference of the AP.
    - (a) 560
    - (b) 512
    - (c) 1024
    - (d) 3072

22. If three positive real numbers x, y, z are in AP such that $xyz = 4$, then what will be the minimum value of y?
    - (a) $2^{1/3}$
    - (b) $2^{2/3}$
    - (c) $2^{1/4}$
    - (d) $2^{3/4}$

23. If a_n be the nth term of an AP and if $a_7 = 15$, then the value of the common difference that would make $a_2 a_7 a_{12}$ greatest is
    - (a) 3
    - (b) 3/2
    - (c) 7
    - (d) 0

24. If $a_1, a_2, a_3 \ldots a_n$ are in AP, where $a_i > 0$, then what will be the value of the expression
    $1/(\sqrt{a_1} + \sqrt{a_2}) + 1/(\sqrt{a_2} + \sqrt{a_3}) + 1/(\sqrt{a_3} + \sqrt{a_4}) + \ldots$ to n terms?
    - (a) $(1-n)/(\sqrt{a_1} + \sqrt{a_n})$
    - (b) $(n-1)/(\sqrt{a_1} + \sqrt{a_n})$
    - (c) $(n-1)/(\sqrt{a_1} - \sqrt{a_n})$
    - (d) $(1-n)/(\sqrt{a_1} + \sqrt{a_n})$

25. If the first two terms of a HP are 2/5 and 12/13 respectively, which of the following terms is the largest term?
    - (a) 4th term
    - (b) 5th term
    - (c) 6th term
    - (d) 7th term

26. One side of a staircase is to be closed in by rectangular planks from the floor to each step. The width of each plank is 9 inches and their height are successively 6 inches, 12 inches, 18 inches and so on. There are 24 planks required in total. Find the area in square feet.
    - (a) 112.5
    - (b) 107
    - (c) 118.5
    - (d) 105

27. The middle points of the sides of a triangle are joined forming a second triangle. Again a third triangle is formed by joining the middle points of this second triangle and this process is repeated infinitely. If the perimetre and area of the outer triangle are P and A respectively, what will be the sum of perimetres of triangles thus formed?
    - (a) $2P$
    - (b) P^2
    - (c) $3P$
    - (d) $p^2/2$

28. In Problem 27, find the sum of areas of all the triangles.
    - (a) $\dfrac{4}{5}A$
    - (b) $\dfrac{4}{3}A$
    - (c) $\dfrac{3}{4}A$
    - (d) $\dfrac{5}{4}A$

29. A square has a side of 40 cm. Another square is formed by joining the mid-points of the sides of the given square and this process is repeated infinitely. Find the perimetre of all the squares thus formed.
    - (a) $160(1 + \sqrt{2})$
    - (b) $160(2 + \sqrt{2})$
    - (c) $160(2 - \sqrt{2})$
    - (d) $160(1 - \sqrt{2})$

30. In problem 29, find the area of all the squares thus formed.
    - (a) 1600
    - (b) 2400
    - (c) 2800
    - (d) 3200

31. The sum of the first n terms of the arithmetic progression is equal to half the sum of the next n terms of the same progression. Find the ratio of the sum of the first $3n$ terms of the progression to the sum of its first n terms.
    - (a) 5
    - (b) 6
    - (c) 7
    - (d) 8

32. In a certain colony of cancerous cells, each cell breaks into two new cells every hour. If there is a single productive cell at the start and this process continues for 9 hours, how many cells will the colony have at the end of 9 hours? It is known that the life of an individual cell is 20 hours.
    - (a) $2^9 - 1$
    - (b) 2^{10}
    - (c) 2^9
    - (d) $2^{10} - 1$

33. Find the sum of all three-digit whole numbers less than 500 that leave a remainder of 2 when they are divided by 3.
    (a) 49637   (b) 39767
    (c) 49634   (d) 39770

34. If a be the arithmetic mean and b, c be the two geometric means between any two positive numbers, then $(b^3 + c^3)/abc$ equals

(a) $(ab)^{1/2}/c$ (b) 1
(c) a^2c/b (d) None of these

35. If p, q, r are three consecutive distinct natural numbers then the expression $(q + r - p)(p + r - q)(p + q - r)$ is
    (a) Positive   (b) Negative
    (c) Non-positive   (d) Non-negative

Space for Rough Work

ANSWER KEY

Level of Difficulty (I)

1. (b)	2. (a)	3. (c)	4. (b)
5. (d)	6. (c)	7. (d)	8. (c)
9. (d)	10. (b)	11. (d)	12. (c)
13. (a)	14. (a)	15. (c)	16. (b)
17. (c)	18. (b)	19. (a)	20. (c)
21. (a)	22. (c)	23. (a)	24. (d)
25. (c)	26. (b)	27. (b)	28. (a)
29. (c)	30. (a)	31. (a)	32. (d)
33. (c)	34. (b)	35. (b)	36. (c)
37. (d)	38. (b)	39. (c)	40. (b)
41. (d)	42. (a)	43. (d)	44. (d)
45. (a)	46. (a)	47. (d)	48. (a)
49. (b)	50. (c)		

Level of Difficulty (II)

1. (a)	2. (c)	3. (b)	4. (b)
5. (c)	6. (b)	7. (c)	8. (a)
9. (c)	10. (c)	11. (b)	12. (b)
13. (a)	14. (c)	15. (b)	16. (d)
17. (b)	18. (d)	19. (c)	20. (c)
21. (a)	22. (d)	23. (c)	24. (d)
25. (b)	26. (c)	27. (b)	28. (d)
29. (c)	30. (b)	31. (c)	32. (a)
33. (a)	34. (a)	35. (b)	36. (b)
37. (d)	38. (a)	39. (d)	40. (a)
41. (d)	42. (a)	43. (b)	44. (d)
45. (a)			

Level of Difficulty (III)

1. (a)	2. (b)	3. (d)	4. (d)
5. (a)	6. (c)	7. (b)	8. (d)
9. (b)	10. (c)	11. (c)	12. (c)
13. (a)	14. (d)	15. (d)	16. (d)
17. (b)	18. (b)	19. (d)	20. (a)
21. (d)	22. (b)	23. (d)	24. (b)
25. (d)	26. (a)	27. (a)	28. (b)
29. (b)	30. (d)	31. (b)	32. (d)
33. (b)	34. (d)	35. (d)	

Hints

Level of Difficulty (II)

2. $a + (a + d) + (a + 2d) + (a + 3d) = 20$
   and $a(a + 3d) = (a + d)(a + 2d)$

4. Calculate the sum of an AP with first term 1, common difference 1 and last term 12. Multiply this sum by 4 for 2 days.

5. The maximum sum will occur when the last term is either 2 or 0.

6. Visualise the AP as 7, 14…196.

9. The AP is 105, 112 …994.

10. The common difference is $\dfrac{146}{5} = 29.2$.

11. See the terms of the series in 33 blocks of 3 each. This will give the AP – 4, –5, – 6…–33. Further, the hundredth term will be 34.

12. Solve through options.

14. The first drop is 120 metres. After this the ball will rise by 96 metres and fall by 96 meters. This process will continue in the form of an infinite GP with common ratio 0.8 and first term 96.
    The required answer will be got by
    $120 + 96 * 1.25 * 2$

15. Take any GP and solve by using values.

18. Solve by using values to check options.

22. The difference between the seventh and third term is given by
    $$(a + 6d) - (a + d)$$

23. $\dfrac{(39 - 4)}{5} = 7$.

27. The required answer will be by adding 20 terms of the GP starting with the first term as 1000 and the common ratio as 1.05.

30. Visualise it as an infinite GP with common ratio 0.9.

Level of Difficulty (III)

1. Difference between the tenth and the sixth term = –16
   or $(a + 9d) - (a + 5d) = -16$
   $\rightarrow d = -4$

2. Sum of the first term and the fifth term = 10
   or $\qquad a + a + 4d = 10$
   or $\qquad a + 2d = 5$ $\qquad\qquad$ (1)
   and, the sum of all terms of the AP except for the 1st term = 99
   or $\qquad 9a + 45d = 99$
   $\qquad\qquad a + 5d = 11$ $\qquad\qquad$ (2)
   Solve (1) and (2) to get the answer.

3. The second statement gives the equation as $a + 8d = 2(a + 3d) + 6$
   or $\qquad\qquad a - 2d = 6$
   Now, use the options to find the value of d, and put these values to check the equation obtained from the first statement.
   i.e. $\qquad (a + 2d)(a + 5d) = 406$

4. To plant the 1st sapling, Mithilesh will cover 20 m; to plant the 2nd sapling he will cover 40 m and so on. But for the last sapling, he will cover only the distance from the starting point to the place where the sapling has to be planted.

5. Assume a series having a few number of terms e.g. 1, 2, 4, 8, 16, 32…
   Now sum of all the terms at the even places = 42 (P_2)
   and sum of all the terms at the odd places = 21 (P_1)
   common ratio of this series = $\dfrac{42}{21} = 2 = P_2/P_1$.

6. Use the same process as illustrated above.
7. Check the options by putting $n = 1, 2, \ldots$ and then equate it with the original equation given in question.
9. For 1 term, the value should be:
$$6^2 + 8 = 44$$
Only option (b) gives 44 for $n = 1$
10. Sum of the AP for n sides = Sum of interior angles of a polygon of n sides.
$$\frac{n}{2} \times (2a + (n-1)d) = (2n-4) \times 90$$
where $a = 120°$ and $d = 5°$.
11. Solve using options to check for the correct answer.
12. $a + (a + 4d) = 26$ and $(a + d)(a + 3d) = 160$
Alternatively, you can try to look at the factors of 160 and create an AP such that it meets the criteria.
Thus, 160 can be written as
$$2 \times 80$$
$$4 \times 40$$
$$8 \times 20$$
$$10 \times 16$$
and so on.
If we consider 8×20, then one possibility is that $d = 6$ and the first and fifth terms are 2 and 26. But $2 + 26 \neq 28$. Hence, this cannot be the correct factors.
Try 10×16. This will give you,
$a = 7$, $d = 3$ and 5th term = 19
and $7 + 19 = 26$ satisfies the condition
13. A possible AP satisfying this condition is
$0, 1, 2, 3, 4, 5, 6, 7, 8, \ldots$
14. Assume the fifth term as $(a + 4d)$, the eleventh term as $(a + 10d)$, the second term as $(a + d)$, the fourteenth term as $(a + 13d)$, the first term as (a) and the fifteenth term as $(a + 14d)$.
Then,   First term × Fifteenth term
$$= a \times (a + 14d) = a^2 + 14ad$$
Also $(a + d)(a + 13d) = P$
and $(a + 4d)^2 + (a + 10d)^2 = 3$
16. The solution (from the options) has got something to do with either 2^{100} or 2^{101} for 100 terms. Hence, for 3 terms recreate the options and crosscheck with the actual sum.
For 3 terms: Sum $= 2 + 8 + 24 = 34$.
(a) $100 \times 2^{101} + 2$ for 100 terms becomes $3 \times 2^4 + 2$ for 3 terms.
$$= 48 + 2 = 50 \neq 34.$$ Hence is not correct.
(b) $99 \times 2^{100} + 2$ for 100 terms becomes $2 \times 2^3 + 2$ for 3 terms.
But this does not give 34. Hence is not correct.
(c) $99 \times 2^{101} + 2 \rightarrow 2 \times 2^4 + 2 = 34$
(d) $100 \times 2^{100} + 2 \rightarrow 3 \times 2^3 + 2 \neq 34$.
Hence, option (c) is correct.

17. $r = 2$ and $a + ar^3 = 108$.
20. Solve by checking options and using principles of logarithms.
21. The sum of the first 20 terms will be
$a + (a + d) + (a + 2d) \ldots + (a + 19d)$
i.e. $20a + 190d = 400$
Similarly, use the sum to fifty terms.
23. For a product $a \times b \times c$ to be maximum, given $a + b + c = $ constant, the condition is $a = b = c$.
27. The length of sides of successive triangles form a GP with common ratio 1/3.
28. The area of successive triangles form an infinite GP with a common ratio 1/4.
29. Common ration $= 1/\sqrt{2}$.
31. Ration of sum of the first $2n$ terms to the first n terms is equal to 3.
Thus,
$$\frac{2n\left(\dfrac{a_1 + a_{2n}}{2}\right)}{n\left(\dfrac{a_1 + a_n}{2}\right)} = 3$$
Solve to get, $2a = (n + 1)d$.
Put values for a and n to get a value for d and check for the conditions given in the question.
33. Visualize the AP and solve using standard formulae.
34. Take any values for the numbers.
Say, the two positive numbers are 1 and 27.
Then, $a = 14$, $b = 3$ and $c = 9$.

Solutions and Shortcuts

Level of Difficulty (I)

1. In order to count the number of terms in the AP, use the short cut:
[(last term − first term)/ common difference] + 1. In this case it would become:
[(130 − 20)/5] +1 = 23. Option (b) is correct.
2. 7000 − 500 − 12500 means that the starting scale is 7000 and there is an increment of 500 every year. Since, the total increment required to reach the top of his scale is 5500, the number of years required would be 5500/500 = 11. Option (a) is correct.
3. Since the 8th and the 12th terms of the AP are given as 39 and 59 respectively, the difference between the two terms would equal 4 times the common difference. Thus we get $4d = 59 - 39 = 20$. This gives us $d = 5$. Also, the 8th term in the AP is represented by $a + 7d$, we get:
$a + 7d = 39 \rightarrow a + 7 \times 5 = 39 \rightarrow a = 4$. Option (c) is correct.
4. If we take the sum of the sides we get the perimeters of the squares. Thus, if the side of the respective squares are $a_1, a_2, a_3, a_4 \ldots$ their perimeters would be $4a_1, 4a_2, 4a_3, 4a_4$. Since the perimeters are in GP, the sides would also be in GP.

5. The number of terms in a series are found by:

$$\frac{\text{Difference between first and last terms}}{\text{Common Difference}} + 1$$

6. The first common term is 3, the next will be 9 (Notice that the second common term is exactly 6 away from the first common term. 6 is also the LCM of 2 and 3 which are the respective common differences of the two series.)

Thus, the common terms will be given by the A.P 3, 9, 15 ....., last term. To find the answer you need to find the last term that will be common to the two series.

The first series is 3, 5, 7 ... 239

While the second series is 3, 6, 9 ..... 240.

Hence, the last common term is 237.

Thus our answer becomes $\frac{237 - 3}{6} + 1 = 40$

7. Trying Option (a),

We get least term 5 and largest term 30 (since the largest term is 6 times the least term).

The average of the A.P becomes (5 + 30)/2 = 17.5

Thus, $17.5 \times n = 105$ gives us:

to get a total of 105 we need $n = 6$ i.e. 6 terms in this A.P. That means the A.P should look like:

5, _ , _ , _, _, 30.

It can be easily seen that the common difference should be 5. The A.P, 5, 10, 15, 20, 25, 30 fits the situation.

The same process used for option (b) gives us the A.P. 10, 35, 60. (10 + 35 + 60 = 105) and in the third option 15, 90 (15 + 90 = 105).

Hence, all the three options are correct.

8. The first term is 20 and the common difference is −5, thus the 15th term is:

$20 + 14 \times (-5) = -50$. Option (c) is correct.

9. The difference between the amounts at the end of 4 years and 10 years will be the simple interest on the initial capital for 6 years.

Hence, 360/6 = 60 =(simple interest.)

Also, the Simple Interest for 4 years when added to the sum gives 1240 as the amount.

Hence, the original sum must be 1000.

10. The three parts are 3, 5 and 7 since $3^2 + 5^2 + 7^2 = 83$. Since, we want the smallest number, the answer would be 3. Option (b) is correct.

11. $a = 5$, $a + 2d = 15$ means $d = 5$. The 16th term would be $a + 15d = 5 + 75 = 80$. The sum of the series would be given by:

$[16/2] \times [5 + 80] = 16 \times 42.5 = 680$. Option (d) is correct.

12. Use trial and error by using various values from the options.

If you find the sum of the series till 18 terms the value is 513. So also for 19 terms the value of the sum would be 513. Option (c) is correct.

13. Solve this question through trial and error by using values of n from the options:

For 19 terms, the series would be 5 + 8 + 11 + ... + 59 which would give us a sum for the series as $19 \times 32 = 608$. The next term (20th term of the series) would be 62. Thus, 608 + 62 = 670 would be the sum to 20 terms. It can thus be concluded that for 20 terms the value of the sum of the series is not less than 670. Option (a) is correct.

14. His total earnings would be 60 + 63 + 66 + ... + 117 = ₹ 1770. Option (a) is correct.

15. The series would be 5, 20, 80, 320, 1280, 5120, 20480. Thus, there are a total of 7 terms in the series. Option (c) is correct.

16. Sum of a G.P. with first term 1 and common ratio 2 and no. of terms 20.

$$\frac{1 \times (2^{20} - 1)}{(2 - 1)} = 2^{20} - 1$$

17. $16r^4 = 81 \rightarrow r^4 = 81/16 \rightarrow r = 3/2$. Thus, 4th term $= ar^3 = 16 \times (3/2)^3 = 54$. Option (c) is correct.

18. In the case of a G.P. the 7th term is derived by multiplying the fourth term thrice by the common ratio. (**Note:** this is very similar to what we had seen in the case of an A.P.)

Since, the seventh term is derived by multiplying the fourth term by 8, the relationship.

$r^3 = 8$ must be true.

Hence, $r = 2$

If the fifth term is 48, the series in reverse from the fifth to the first term will look like:

48, 24, 12, 6, 3. Hence, option (b) is correct.

19. Visualising the squares below 84, we can see that the only way to get the sum of 3 squares as 84 is: $2^2 + 4^2 + 8^2 = 4 + 16 + 64$. The largest number is 8. Option (a) is correct.

20. The series would be given by: 1, 5, 9... which essentially means that all the numbers in the series are of the form $4n + 1$. Only the value in option (c) is a $4n + 1$ number and is hence the correct answer.

21. The series will be 301, 308, ... 497

Hence, Answer = $\frac{196}{7} + 1 = 29$

22. The answer to this question can be seen from the options. Both 2, 6, 18 and 18, 6, 2 satisfy the required conditions- viz: GP with sum of first and third terms as 20. Thus, option (c) is correct.

23. We need the sum of the series 20 + 24 + 28 to cross 1000. Trying out the options, we can see that in 20 years the sum of his savings would be: 20 + 24 +

$28 + \ldots + 96$. The sum of this series would be $20 \times 58 = 1160$. If we remove the 20th year we will get the series for savings for 19 years. The series would be $20 + 24 + 28 + \ldots 92$. Sum of the series would be $1160 - 96 = 1064$. If we remove the 19th year's savings the savings would be $1064 - 92$ which would go below 1000. Thus, after 19 years his savings would cross 1000. Option (a) is correct.

24. The answer to this question cannot be determined because the question is talking about income and asking about savings. You cannot solve this unless you know the value of the expenditure the man incurs over the years. Thus, "Cannot be Determined" is the correct answer.

25. Similar to what we saw in question 18,
    4th term $\times r^6 = $ 10th term.
    The 4th term here is 3^{-1} and the tenth term is 3^5.
    Hence $3^{-1} \times r^6 = 3^5$
    Gives us: $r = 3$.
    Hence, the second term will be given by (fourth term/r^2)
    $^1/_3 \times {}^1/_3 \times {}^1/_3 = {}^1/_{27}$
    [**Note:** To go forward in a G.P. you multiply by the common ratio, to go backward in a G.P. you divide by the common ratio.]

26. $a + 6d = 6$ and $a + 20d = -22$. Solving we get $14d = -28 \rightarrow d = -2$. 26th term = 21st term + 5d = $-22 + 5 \times (-2) = -32$. Option (b) is correct.

27. Since the sum of 5 numbers in AP is 30, their average would be 6. The average of 5 terms in AP is also equal to the value of the 3rd term (logic of the middle term of an AP). Hence, the third term's value would be 6. Option (b) is correct.

28. The answer will be given by:
    $[10 + 11 + 12 + \ldots + 50] - [16 + 24 + \ldots + 48]$
    $= 41 \times 30 - 32 \times 5$
    $= 1230 - 160 = 1070$.

29. Think like this:
    The average of the first 4 terms is 7, while the average of the first 8 terms must be 11.
    Now visualize this :

    1st 2nd 3rd 4th 5th 6th 7th 8th

    average = 7   average = 11

    Hence, $d = 4/2 = 2$ [Note: understand this as a property of an A.P.]
    Hence, the average of the 6th and 7th terms = 15 and the average of the 8th and 9th term = 19
    But this (19) also represents the average of the 16 term A.P.
    Hence, required answer = $16 \times 19 = 304$.

30. Go through the options. The correct option should give value as 1, when $n = 3$ and as 8 when $n = 8$. Only option (a) satisfies both conditions.

31. The series is: $1/81, -1/27, 1/9, -1/3, 1, -3, 9, -27, 81, -243, 729$. There are 11 terms in the series. Option (a) is correct.

32. $1/8 \times r^5 = 128 \rightarrow r^5 = 128 \times 8 = 1024 \rightarrow r = 4$. Thus, the series would be $1/8, 1/2, 2, 8, 32, 128$. The third geometric mean would be 8. Option (d) is correct.

33. AM = 25 means that their sum is 50 and GM = 7 means their product is 49. The numbers can only be 49 and 1. Option (c) is correct.

34. Trial and error gives us that for option (b):
    With the ratio 4:1, the numbers can be taken as $4x$ and $1x$. Their AM would be $2.5x$ and their GM would be $2x$. The GM can be seen to be 20% lower than the AM. Option (b) is thus the correct answer.

35. The total savings would be given by the sum of the series:
    $100 + 150 + 200 + 650 = 12 \times 375 = ₹ 4500$. Option (b) is correct.

36. In order to find how many times the alarm rings we need to find the number of numbers below 100 which are not divisible by 2,3, 5 or 7. This can be found by:
    100 – (numbers divisible by 2) – (numbers divisible by 3 but not by 2) – (numbers divisible by 5 but not by 2 or 3) – (numbers divisible by 7 but not by 2 or 3 or 5).
    Numbers divisible by 2 up to 100 would be represented by the series 2, 4, 6, 8, 10..100 → A total of 50 numbers.
    Numbers divisible by 3 but not by 2 up to 100 would be represented by the series 3, 9, 15, 21…99 → A total of 17 numbers. Note use short cut for finding the number of number in this series :
    [(last term – first term)/ common difference] + 1 = [(99 – 3)/6] + 1 = 16 + 1 = 17.
    Numbers divisible by 5 but not by 2 or 3: Numbers divisible by 5 but not by 2 up to 100 would be represented by the series 5, 15, 25, 35…95 → A total of 10 numbers. But from these numbers, the numbers 15, 45 and 75 are also divisible by 3. Thus, we are left with 10 – 3 = 7 new numbers which are divisible by 5 but not by 2 and 3.
    Numbers divisible by 7, but not by 2, 3 or 5:
    Numbers divisible by 7 but not by 2 upto 100 would be represented by the series 7, 21, 35, 49, 63, 77, 91 → A total of 7 numbers. But from these numbers we should not count 21, 35 and 63 as they are divisible by either 3 or 5. Thus a total of 7 – 3 = 4 numbers are divisible by 7 but not by 2, 3 or 5.

37. For looking at the zeroes in the expression we should be able to see that the number of zeroes in the third term onwards is going to be very high. Thus, the number of zeroes in the expression would be given by the number of zeroes in:

$4 + 24^{24}$. 24^{24} has a unit digit 6. Hence, the number of zeroes in the expression would be 1. Option (d) is correct.

38. Since the sum of 22 terms of the AP is 385, the average of the numbers in the AP would be 385/22 = 17.5. This means that the sum of the first and last terms of the AP would be 2 × 17.5 = 35. Trial and error gives us the terms of the required GP as 7, 14, 28. Thus, the common ratio of the GP can be 2.

39. The sum of the interior angles of a polygon are multiples of 180 and are given by $(n - 1) \times 180$ where n is the number of sides of the polygon. Thus, the sum of interior angles of a polygon would be a member of the series: 180, 360, 540, 720, 900, 1080, 1260

The sum of the series with first term 100 and common difference 10 would keep increasing when we take more and more terms of the series. In order to see the number of sides of the polygon, we should get a situation where the sum of the series represented by 100 + 110 + 120... should become a multiple of 180. The number of sides in the polygon would then be the number of terms in the series 100, 110, 120 at that point.

If we explore the sums of the series represented by

100 + 110 + 120...

We realize that the sum of the series becomes a multiple of 180 for 8 terms as well as for 9 terms.

It can be seen in: 100 + 110 + 120 + 130 + 140 + 150 + 160 + 170 = 1080

Or 100 + 110 + 120 + 130 + 140 + 150 + 160 + 170 + 180 = 1260.

40. The sum of the total distance it travels would be given by the infinite sum of the series:

420 × 8/1 + 367.5 × 8/1 = 3360 + 2940 = 6300. Option (b) is correct.

41. The two series till their hundredth terms are 13, 15, 17....211 and 14, 17, 20...311. The common terms of the series would be given by the series 17, 23, 29....209. The number of terms in this series of common terms would be 192/6 + 1 = 33. Option (d) is correct.

42. The area of the first square would be 64 sq cm. The second square would give 32, the third one 16 and so on. The infinite sum of the geometric progression 64 + 32 + 16 + 8... = 128. Option (a) is correct.

43. It can be seen that for the series the average of two terms is 2, for 3 terms the average is 3 and so on. Thus, the sum to 2 terms is 2^2, for 3 terms it is 3^2

and so on. For 11111 terms it would be 11111^2 = 123454321. Option (d) is correct.

44. The maximum score would be the sum of the series 9 + 13 + ... + 389 + 393 + 397 = 98 × 406/2 = 19894. Option (d) is correct.

45. The series would be 8, 8/3, 8/9 and so on. The sum of the infinite series would be 8/(1 – 1/3) = 8 × 3/2 = 12. Option (a) is correct.

46. The maximum sum would occur when we take the sum of all the positive terms of the series.

The series 25, 24.5, 24, 23.5, 23, ... 1, 0.5, 0 has 51 terms. The sum of the series would be given by:

$n \times$ average = 51 × 12.5 = 637.5

Option (a) is correct.

47. The side of the first equilateral triangle being 24 units, the first perimeter is 72 units. The second perimeter would be half of that and so on.

72, 36, 18 ...

The infinite sum of this series = 72(1 – 1/2) = 144. Option (d) is correct.

48. Solve using options. Option (a) fits the situation as 16 + 2 + 2/8 + 2/64 meets the conditions of the question. Option (a) is correct.

49. The 33rd term of the sequence would be the 17th term of the sequence 3, 9, 15, 21 ....

The 17th term of the sequence would be 3 + 6 × 16 = 99.

50. The sum to 33 terms of the sequence would be:

The sum to 17 terms of the sequence 3, 9, 15, 21, ...99 + The sum to 16 terms of the sequence 8, 13, 18, 83.

The required sum would be 17 × 51 + 16 × 45.5 = 867 + 728 = 1595.

Level of Difficulty (II)

1. Identify an A.P. which satisfies the given condition.

Suppose we are talking about the second and third terms of the A.P.

Then an A.P. with second term 3 and third term 2 satisfies the condition.

a times the ath term = b times the bth term.

In this case the value of $a = 2$ and $b = 3$.

Hence, for the $(a + b)$th term, we have to find the fifth term.

It is clear that the fifth term of this A.P. must be zero.

Check the other three options to see whether any option gives 0 when $a = 2$ and $b = 3$.

Since none of the options b, c or d gives zero for this particular value, option (a) is correct.

2. Since the four parts of the number are in *AP* and their sum is 20, the average of the four parts must be 5. Looking at the options for the largest part, only the value of 8 fits in, as it leads us to think of the *AP* 2, 4, 6, 8. In this case, the ratio of the product of the first and fourth (2×8) to the product of the first and second (4×6) are equal. The ratio becomes 2:3.

3. View: $1 - 4 + 5 - 8 + 9 - 12 \ldots\ldots 50$ terms as
   $(1 - 4) + (5 - 8) + (9 - 12) \ldots\ldots 25$ terms.
   Hence, $-3 + -3 + -3 \ldots. 25$ terms
   $= 25 \times - 3 = -75$.

4. In the course of 2 days the clock would strike 1 four times, 2 four times, 3 four times and so on. Thus, the total number of times the clock would strike would be:
   $4 + 8 + 12 + ..48 = 26 \times 12 = 312$. Option (b) is correct.

5. Since this is a decreasing A.P. with first term positive, the maximum sum will occur upto the point where the progression remains non – negative.
   44, 42, 40 ….. 0
   Hence, 23 terms $\times$ 22 = 506.

6. The sum of the required series of integers would be given by $7 + 14 + 21 + \ldots.196 = 28 \times 101.5 = 2842$. Option (b) is correct.

7. A little number juggling would give you 2nd term is 1/3 and 3rd term is ½ is a possible situation that satisfies the condition.
   The A.P. will become:
   1/6, 1/3, 1/2, 2/3, 5/6, 1
   or in decimal terms, 0.166, 0.333, 0.5, 0.666, 0.833, 1
   Sum to 6 terms = 3.5
   Check the option with $m = 2$ and $n = 3$. Only option (c) gives 3.5. Hence, must be the answer.

8. $101 + 103 + 105 + \ldots 199 = 150 \times 50 = 7500$

9. The required sum would be given by the sum of the series 105, 112, 119, …. 994. The number of terms in this series = $(994 - 105)/7 + 1 = 127 + 1 = 128$. The sum of the series = $128 \times$ (average of 105 and 994) = 70336. Option (c) is correct.

10. $5 \times$ average of 107 and 253 = $5 \times 180 = 900$. Option (c) is correct.

11. The first 100 terms of this series can be viewed as:
    $(1 - 2 -3) + (2 - 3 -4) + \ldots + (33 - 34 - 35) + 34$
    The first 33 terms of the above series (indicated inside the brackets) will give an A.P.: $-4, -5, -6 \ldots. -36$
    Sum of this A.P. = $33 \times -20 = -660$
    Answer = $-660 + 34 = -626$

12. Solve this one through trial and error. For $n = 2$ terms the sum upto 2 terms is equal to 96. Putting $n = 2$, in the options it can be seen that for option (b) the sum to two terms would be given by
    $8 \times (1000 - 10 - 18)/81 = 8 \times 972/81 = 8 \times 12 = 96$.

13. If we take the values of *a*, *b*, and *c* as 10,100 and 1000 respectively, we get log *a*, log *b* and log *c* as 1, 2 and 3 respectively. This clearly shows that the values of log *a*, log *b* and log *c* are in AP.

14. The path of the rubber ball is:

In the figure above, every bounce is 4/5th of the previous drop.
In the above movement, there are two infinite G.Ps (The GP representing the falling distances and the GP representing the Rising distances.)
The required answer: (Using $a/(1-r)$ formula)
$$\frac{120}{1/5} + \frac{96}{1/5} = 1080$$

15. Solve this for a sample GP. Let us say we take the GP as 2, 6, 18, 54. *x*, the first term is 2, let $n = 3$ then the 3rd term $y = 18$ and the product of 3 terms $p = 2 \times 6 \times 18 = 216 = 6^3$. The value of $p^2 = 216 \times 216 = 6^6$.
    Putting these values in the options we have:
    Option (a) gives us $(xy)^{n-1} = 36^2$ which is not equal to the value of p^2 we have from the options
    Option (b) gives us $(xy)^n = 36^3 = 6^6$ which is equal to the value of p^2 we have from the options.
    It can be experimentally verified that the other options yield values of p^2 which are different from 6^6 and hence we can conclude that option (b) is correct.

16. Trying to plug in values we can see that the infinite sum of the GP 16, 8, 4, 2… is 32 and hence the third term is 4.

17. The expression can be written as $x^{(1/2 + ¼ + 1/8 + 1/16 \ldots..)}$
    $= x^{\text{INFINTE SUM OF THE GP}} = x^1$. Option (b) is correct.

18. For $n = 1$, the sum should be 6. Option (b), (c) and (d) all give 6 as the answer.
    For $n = 2$, the sum should be 30.
    Only option *d* gives this value. Hence must be the answer.

19. From the facts given in the question it is self evident that the common ratio of the GP must be 2 (as the sum of the 2nd and 4th term is twice the sum of the

first and third term). After realizing this, the question is about trying to match the correct sums by taking values from the options.

The GP formed from option (c) with a common ratio of 2 is: 8,16,32,64 and this GP satisfies the conditions of the problem- sum of 1st and 3rd term is 40 and sum of 2nd and 4th term is 80.

20. Since the sum of the first five even terms is 15, we have that the 2nd, 4th, 6th, 8th and 10th term of the AP should add up to 15. We also need to understand that these 5 terms of the AP would also be in an AP by themselves and hence, the value of the 6th term (being the middle term of the AP) would be the average of 15 over 5 terms. Thus, the value of the 6th term is 3. Also, since the sum of the first three terms of the AP is –3, we get that the 2nd term would have a value of –1. Thus, the AP can be visualized as:

_, -1, _,_,_,3,....

Thus, it is obvious that the AP would be –2, –1, 0, 1, 2, 3. The second term is –1. Thus, option (c) is correct.

21. Second term $= a + d$, Fifth term $= a + 4d$; third term $= a + 2d$, seventh term $= a + 6d$.

Thus, $2a + 5d = 8$ and $2a + 8d = 14 \rightarrow d = 2$ and $a = -1$.

The eleventh term $= a + 10d = -1 + 20 = 19$. Thus, option (a) is correct.

22. If the difference between the seventh and the second term is 20, it means that the common difference is equal to 4. Since, the third term is 9, the *AP* would be 1, 5, 9, 13, 17, 21, 25, 29 and the sum to 8 terms for this *AP* would be 120. Thus, option (d) is correct.

23. $5d = 35 \rightarrow d = 7$. Thus, the numbers are 4, 11, 18, 25, 32, 39. The largest number is 32. Option (c) is correct.

24. Find sum of the series:

104, 109, 114 999

Average $\times n = 551.5 \times 180 = 99270$

25. Since the sum of the first three terms of the *AP* is 30, the average of the *AP* till 3 terms would be 30/3 = 10. The value of the second term would be equal to this average and hence the second term is 10. Using the information about the sum of squares of the first and second terms being 116, we have that the first term must be 4. Thus, the AP has a first term of 4 and a common difference of 6. The seventh term would be 40. Thus, option (b) is correct.

26. The combined travel would be 25 on the first day, 26 on the second day, 27 on the third day, 28 on the fourth day, 29 on the fifth day and 30 on the sixth day. They meet after 6 days. Option (c) is correct.

27. This is a calculation intensive problem and you are not supposed to know how to do the calculations in this question mentally. The problem has been put

here to test your concepts about whether you recognize how this is a question of GPs. If you feel like, you can use a calculator/ computer spreadsheet to get the answer to this question.

The logic of the question would hinge on the fact that the value of the investment of the fifteenth year would be 1000. At the end of the 15th year, the investment of the 14th year would be equal to 1000×1.05, the 13th year's investment would amount to 1000×1.05^2 and so on till the first year's investment which would amount to 1000×1.05^{14} after 15 years.

Thus, you need to calculate the sum of the GP: 1000, 1000×1.05, 1000×1.05^2, 1000×1.05^3 for 15 terms.

28. Since, sum to n terms is given by (n + 8),

Sum to 1 terms = 9

Sum to 2 terms = 10

Thus, the 2nd term must be 1.

29. Solve this question by looking at hypothetical values for n and $2n$ terms. Suppose, we take the sum to 1 ($n = 1$) term of the first series and the sum to 2 terms ($2n = 2$) of the second series we would get A/B as 1/1.5 = 2/3.

For $n = 2$ and $2n = 4$ we get $A = 1.25$ and $B = 1.875$ and $A/B = 1.25/1.875 = 2/3$.

Thus, we can conclude that the required ratio is always constant at 2/3 and hence the correct option is (c).

30. We need to find the infinite sum of the GP: 100, 90, 81…(first term = 100 and common ratio= 0.9)

We get: Infinite sum of the series as 1000. Thus, option (b) is correct.

31. Questions such as these have to be solved on the basis of a reading of the pattern of the question. The sum upto the first term is: 1/5. Upto the second term it is 2/9 and upto the third term it is 3/13. It can be easily seen that for the first term, second term and third term the numerators are 1, 2 and 3 respectively. Also, for 1/5 – the 5 is the second value in the denominator of $1/1 \times 5$ (the first term); for 2/9 also the same pattern is followed—as 9 comes out of the denominator of the second term of series and for 3/13 the 13 comes out of the denominator of the third term of the series and so on. The given series has 56 terms and hence the correct answer would be 56/225.

32. Solve this on the same pattern as Question 31 and you can easily see that for the first term sum of the series is $\sqrt{2} - 1$, for 2 terms we have the sum as $\sqrt{3} - 1$ and so on. For the given series of 120 terms the sum would be $\sqrt{121} - 1 = 10$.

Option (a) is correct.

33. If you look for a few more terms in the series, the series is:

1, 1/3, 1/6, 1/10, 1/15, 1/21, 1/28, 1/36, 1/45, 1/55, 1/66, 1/78, 1/91, 1/105, 1/120, 1/136, 1/153 and so on. If you estimate the values of the individual terms it can be seen that the sum would tend to 2 and would not be good enough to reach even 2.25. Thus, option (a) is correct.

34. Solve this using trial and error. For 1 term the sum should be 40 and we get 40 only from the first option when we put $n = 1$. Thus, option (a) is correct.

35. For this question too you would need to read the pattern of the values being followed. The given sum has 13 terms.
It can be seen that the sum to 1 term = ½
Sum to 2 terms = 2/3
Sum to 3 terms = ¾
Hence, the sum to 13 terms would be 13/14.

36. The sum to infinite terms would tend to 1 because we would get (infinity)/(infinity + 1).

37. All members of A are smaller than all members of B. In order to visualize the effect of the change in sign in A, assume that A is {1, 2, 3…124} and B is {126, 127…250}. It can be seen that for this assumption of values neither options (a), (b) or (c) is correct.

38. If elements of A are in ascending order a_{124} would be the largest value in A. Also a_{125} would be the largest value in B. On interchanging a_{124} and a_{125}, A continues to be in ascending order, but B would lose its descending order arrangement since a_{124} would be the least value in B. Hence, option a is correct.

39. Since the minimum is in A and the maximum is in B, the value of x cannot be *less than Max–Min*.

40. It is evident that the whole question is built around Arithmetic progressions. The 5th row has an average of 55, while the 15th row has an average of 65. Since even column wise each column is arranged in an *AP* we can conclude the following:
1st row – average 51 – total = 23 × 51
2nd row – average 52 – total 23 × 52…..
23rd row – average 73 – total 23 × 73
The overall total can be got by using averages as:
23 × 23 × 62 = 32798

41. The numbers forming an *AP* would be:
123, 135, 147, 159, 210, 234, 246, 258, 321, 345, 357, 369, 432, 420, 456, 468, 543, 531, 567, 579, 654, 642, 630, 678, 765, 753, 741, 789, 876, 864, 852, 840, 987, 975, 963 and 951. A total of 36 numbers.

If we count the GPs we get:
124, 139, 248, 421, 931, 842—a total of 6 numbers.
Hence, we have a total of 42 3 digit numbers where the digits are either APs or GPs.
Thus, option (d) is correct.

42. Total burgers made = 660
Burgers with chicken and mushroom patty = 165 (Number of terms in the series 1, 5, 9…657)
Burgers with vegetable patty = 95 (Number of terms in the series 2, 9, 16, …660)
Burgers with chicken, mushroom and vegetable patty = 24 (Number of terms in the series 9, 37, 65….653)
Required answer = 660 – 165 – 95 + 24 = 424

43. From the above question, we have 24 such burgers.

44. The key to this question is what you understand from the statement- 'for two progressions out of P_1, P_2 and P_3 the average is itself a term of the original progression P.' For option (a) which tells us that the Progression P has 20 terms, we can see that P_1 would have 7 terms, P_2 would have 7 terms and P_3 would have 6 terms. Since, both P_1 and P_2 have an odd number of terms we can see that for P_1 and P_2 their 4th terms (being the middle terms for an *AP* with 7 terms) would be equal to their average. Since, all the terms of P_1, P_2 and P_3 have been taken out of the original *AP* P, we can see that for P_1 and P_2 their average itself would be a term of the original progression P. This would not occur for P_3 as P_3 has an even number of terms. Thus, 20 is a correct value for n.
Similarly, if we go for $n = 26$ from the second option we get:
P_1, P_2 and P_3 would have 9, 9 and 8 terms respectively and the same condition would be met here too.
For $n = 36$ from the third option, the three progressions would have 12 terms each and none of them would have an odd number of terms.
Thus, option (d) is correct as both options (a) and (b) satisfy the conditions given in the problem.

45. Since, P_1 is formed out of every third term of P, the common difference of P_1 would be three times the common difference of P. Thus, the common difference of P would be 2.

TRAINING GROUND FOR BLOCK I

📶 HOW TO THINK IN PROBLEMS ON BLOCK I

1. A number x is such that it can be expressed as $a + b + c = x$ where a, b, and c are factors of x. How many numbers below 200 have this property?

    (a) 31   (b) 32
    (c) 33   (d) 5

Solution: In order to think about this question you need to think about whether the number can be divided by the initial numbers below the square root like 2, 3, 4, 5… and so on.

Let us say, if we think of a number that is not divisible by 2, in such a case if we take the number to be divisible by 3, 5 and 7, then the largest factors of x that we will get would be $\dfrac{x}{3}, \dfrac{x}{5}$ and $\dfrac{x}{7}$.

Even in this situation, the percentage value of these factors as a percentage of x would only be: for $\dfrac{x}{3} = 33.33\%$, $\dfrac{x}{5} = 20\%$ and $\dfrac{x}{7} = 14.28\%$

Hence, if we try to think of a situation where $a = \dfrac{x}{3}$, $b = \dfrac{x}{5}$, and $c = \dfrac{x}{7}$ the value of $a + b + c$ would give us only $(33.33\% + 20\% + 14.28\%) = 67.61\%$ of x, which is not equal to 100%

Since the problem states that $a + b + c = x$, the value of $a + b + c$ should have added up to 100% of x.

The only situation, for this to occur would be if

$$a = \dfrac{x}{2} = 50\% \text{ of } x \qquad b = \dfrac{x}{3} = 33.33\% \text{ of } x \text{ and}$$

$$c = \dfrac{x}{6} = 16.66\% \text{ of } x.$$

This means that 2, 3 and 6 should divide x necessarily. In other words x should be a multiple of 6. The multiples of 6 below 200 are 6, 12, 18 … 198, a total of 33 numbers.

Hence the correct answer is c.

2. Find the sum of all 3 digit numbers that leave a remainder of 3 when divided by 7.

    (a) 70821   (b) 60821
    (c) 50521   (d) 80821

Solution: In order to solve this question you need to visualise the series of numbers, which satisfy this condition of the remainder 3 when divided by 7.

The first number in 3 digits for this condition is 101 and the next will be 108, followed by 115, 122 …

This series would have its highest value in 3 digits as 997.

The number of terms in this series would be 129 (using the logic that for any AP, the number of terms is given by $\dfrac{D}{d} + 1$)

Also the average value of this series is the average of the first and the last term i.e., the average of 101 and 997. Hence the required sum $= 549 \times 129 = 70821$.

Hence the correct Option is (a).

3. How many times would the digit 6 be used in numbering a book of 639 pages?

    (a) 100   (b) 124
    (c) 150   (d) 164

Solution: In order to solve this question you should count the digit 6 appearing in units digit, separately from the instances of the digit 6 appearing in the tens place and appearing in the hundreds place.

When you want to find out the number of times 6 appears in the unit digit, you will have to make a series as follows: 6, 16, 26, 36 … 636.

It should be evident to you that the above series has 64 terms because it starts from 06, 16, 26 … and continues till 636. The digit 6 will appear once in the unit digit for each of these 64 numbers.

Next you need to look at how many times the digit 6 appears in the ten's place.

In order to do this we will need to look at instances when 6 appears in the tens place. These will be in 6 different ranges 60s, 160s, 260s, 360s, 460s, 560s and in each of these ranges there are 10 numbers each with exactly one instance of the digit 6 in the tens place, a total of 60 times.

Lastly, we need to look at the number of instances where 6 appears in the hundreds place. For this we need to form the series 600, 601, 602, 603 … 639. This series will have 40 numbers each with exactly one instance of the digit 6 appearing in the hundreds place.

Therefore the required answer would be $64 + 60 + 40 = 164$.

Hence, Option (d) is correct.

4. A number written in base 3 is 100100100100100100. What will be the value of this number in base 27?

    (a) 999999   (b) 900000
    (c) 989999   (d) 888888

The number can be visualised as:

1	0	0	1	0	0	1	0	0	1	0	0	1	0	0	1	0	0
3^{17}	3^{16}	3^{15}	3^{14}	3^{13}	3^{12}	3^{11}	3^{10}	3^9	3^8	3^7	3^6	3^5	3^4	3^3	3^2	3^1	3^0

Now in the base 27, we can visualise this number as:

—	—	—	—	—	—
27^5	27^4	27^3	27^2	27^1	27^0

When you want to write this number in Base 27 the unit digit of the number will have to account for the value of 3^2 in the above number. Since the unit digit of the number in Base 27 will correspond to 27^0 we would have to use 27^0, 9 times to make a value 3^2. The number would now become:

27^5	27^4	27^3	27^2	27^1	27^0
—	—	—	—	—	9

Similarly, the number of times that we will have to use 27^1 in order to make the value of 3^5 (or 243) will be $\frac{243}{27}$ = 9. Hence the second last digit of the number will also be 9.

Similarly, to make a value of 3^8 using 27^2 the number of times we will have to use 27^2 will be given by $\frac{3^8}{27^2} = \frac{3^8}{3^6}$ = 9. The number would now look as:

27^5	27^4	27^3	27^2	27^1	27^0
—	—	—	9	9	9

It can be further predicted that each of subsequent 1's in the original number will equal 9 in the number, which is being written in Base 27. Since the original number in Base 3 has 18 digits, the left most '1' in that number will be covered by a number corresponding to 27^5 in the new number (i.e. 3^{15}). Hence the required number will be a 6-digit number 999999. Hence, Option (a) is correct.

5. Let x = 1640, y = 1728 and z = 448. How many natural numbers are there that divide at least one amongst x, y, z.

    (a) 47   (b) 48
    (c) 49   (d) 50

Solution: 1640 can be prime factorised as $2^3 \times 5^1 \times 41^1$. This number would have a total of 16 factors.

Similarly, 1728 can be prime factorised as $2^6 \times 3^3$. Hence, it would have 28 factors. While $448 = 2^6 \times 7^1$ would have 14 factors. Thus there are a total of (16 + 28 + 14) = 58 factors amongst x, y and z.

However, some of these factors must be common between x, y, z. Hence, in order to find the number of natural numbers that would divide at least one amongst x, y, z, we will need to account for double and triple counted numbers amongst these 58 numbers (by reducing the count by 2 for each triple counted number and by reducing the count by 1 for each double counted number).

The number of cases of triple counting would be for all the common factors of (x, y, z). This number can be estimated by finding the HCF of x, y and z and counting the number of factors of the HCF. The HCF of 1640, 1728 and 448 is 8 and hence the factors of 8, i.e., 1, 2, 4 and 8 itself must have got counted in each of the 3 counts done above. Thus each of these 4 numbers should get subtracted twice to remove the triple count. This leaves us with 58 – 4 × 2 = 50 numbers.

We still need to eliminate numbers that have been counted twice, i.e., numbers, which belong to the factors of any two of these numbers (while counting this we need to ensure that we do not count the triple counted numbers again). This can be visualised in the following way:

Number of common factors that are common to only 1640 and 1728 and not to 448 (x and y but not z):

    $1640 = 2^3 \times 5^1 \times 41^1$
    $1728 = 2^6 \times 3^3$

It can be seen from these 2 standard forms of the numbers that the highest common factors of these 2 numbers is 8. Hence there is no new number to be subtracted for double counting in this case.

The case of 1640 and 448 is similar because $1640 = 2^3 \times 5^1 \times 41^1$ while $448 = 2^6 \times 7^1$ and HCF = 2^3 and hence they will not give any more numbers as common factors apart from 1, 2, 4 and 8.

Thus there is no need of adjustment for the pair 1640 and 448.

Finally when we look for 1728 and 448, we realise that the HCF = 2^6 = 64 and hence the common factors between 448 and 1728 are 1, 2, 4, 8, 16, 32, 64. But we are looking for factors which are common for 1728 and 448 but not common to 1640 to estimate the double counting error for this case.

Hence we can eliminate the number 1, 2, 4, 8 from this list and conclude that there are only 3 numbers 16, 32 and 64 that divide both 1728 and 448 but do not divide 1640.

If we subtract these numbers once each, from the 50 numbers we will end up with 50 – 3 × 1 = 47.

The complete answer can be visualised as 16 + 28 + 14 – 4 × 2 – 3 × 1 = 47.

Hence, Option (a) is correct.

6. How many times will the digit 6 be used when we write all the six digit numbers?

    (a) 5,50,000   (b) 5,00,000
    (c) 4,50,000   (d) 4,00,000

Solution: When we write all 6-digit numbers we will have to write all the numbers from 100000 to 999999, a total of 9 lac numbers in 6 digits without omitting a single number. There will be a complete symmetry and balance in the use of all the digits. However the digit 0 is not going to be used in the leftmost place.

Using this logic we can visualise that when we write 9 lakh, 6-digit numbers, the units place, tens place, hundreds place, thousands place, ten thousands place and lakh place – Each of these places will be written 9 lakh times. Thinking about the units place, we can think as follows: In writing the units place 9 lakh times (once for every number) we will be using the digit 0, 1, 2, 3 … 9 an equal number of times. Hence any particular digit like 6 would get used in the units digit a total number of 90000 times (9 lakh/10). The same logic will continue for tens, hundreds, thousands and ten thousands, i.e., the digit 6 will be used (9 lakh/10) = 90000 times in each of these places. (Note here that we are dividing by 10 because we have to equally distribute 9 lakh digits amongst the ten digits 0, 1, 2, 3,4, 5, 6, 7, 8, 9.)

Finally for the lakh place since "0" is not be used in the lakh place as it is the leftmost digit of the number, the number of times the digit 6 will be used would be 9 lakh/9 = 1 lakh. Hence the next time you are solving the problem of this type, you should solve directly using $\frac{9\,\text{lakh}}{9} + \frac{9\,\text{lakh}}{10} \times 5$ = 5,50,000.

Hence, Option (a) is the correct answer.

🎯 BLOCK REVIEW TESTS

REVIEW TEST 1

1. Lata has the same number of sisters as she has brothers, but her brother Shyam has twice as many sisters as he has brothers. How many children are there in the family?
   - (a) 7
   - (b) 6
   - (c) 5
   - (d) 3

2. How many times does the digit 6 appear when you count from 11 to 100?
   - (a) 9
   - (b) 10
   - (c) 19
   - (d) 20

3. If m < n, then
   - (a) $m.m < n.n$
   - (b) $m.m > n.n$
   - (c) $m.n.n < n.m.m$
   - (d) $m.m.m < n.n.n$

4. A square is drawn by joining the midpoints of the side of a given square. A third square is drawn in side the second square in the same way and this process is continued indefinitely. If a side of the first square is 8 cm, the sum of the areas of all the squares (in sq. cm) is
   - (a) 128
   - (b) 120
   - (c) 96
   - (d) None of these

5. Find the least number which when divided by 6, 15, 17 leaves a remainder 1, but when divided by 7 leaves no remainder.
   - (a) 211
   - (b) 511
   - (c) 1022
   - (d) 86

6. The number of positive integers not greater than 100, which are not divisible by 2, 3 or 5 is
   - (a) 26
   - (b) 18
   - (c) 31
   - (d) None of these

7. The smallest number which when divided by 4, 6 or 7 leaves a remainder of 2, is
   - (a) 44
   - (b) 62
   - (c) 80
   - (d) 86

8. An intelligence agency decides on a code of 2 digits selected from 0, 1, 2,....9. But the slip on which the code is hand-written allows confusion between top and bottom, because these are indistinguishable. Thus, for example, the code 91 could be confused with 16. How many codes are there such that there is no possibility of any confusion?
   - (a) 25
   - (b) 75
   - (c) 80
   - (d) None of these

9. Suppose one wishes to find distinct positive integers x, y such that $(x + y)/xy$ is also a positive integer. Identify the correct alternative.
   - (a) This is never possible
   - (b) This is possible and the pair (x, y) satisfying the stated condition is unique.
   - (c) This is possible and there exist more than one but a finite number of ways of choosing the pair (x, y).
   - (d) This is possible and the pair (x, y) can be chosen in infinite ways.

10. A young girl counted in the following way on the fingers of her left hand. She started calling the thumb 1, the index finger 2, middle finger 3, ring finger 4, little finger 5, then reversed direction, calling the ring finger 6, middle finger 7, index finger 8, thumb 9, then back to the index finger for 10, middle finger for 11, and so on. She counted up to 1994. She ended on her.
    - (a) thumb
    - (b) index finger
    - (c) middle finger
    - (d) ring finger

11. 139 persons have signed up for an elimination tournament. All players are to be paired up for the first round, but because 139 is an odd number one player gets a bye, which promotes him to the second round, without actually playing in the first round. The pairing continues on the next round, with a bye to any player left over. If the schedule is planned so that a minimum number of matches is required to determine the champion, the number of matches which must be played is
    - (a) 136
    - (b) 137
    - (c) 138
    - (d) 139

12. The product of all integers from 1 to 100 will have the following numbers of zeros at the end.
    - (a) 20
    - (b) 24
    - (c) 19
    - (d) 22

13. There are ten 50 paise coins placed on a table. Six of these show tails four show heads. A coin chosen at random and flipped over (not tossed). This operation is performed seven times. One of the coins is then covered. Of the remaining nine coins five show tails and four show heads. The covered coin shows
    - (a) a head
    - (b) a tail
    - (c) more likely a head
    - (d) more likely a tail

14. A five digit number is formed using digits 1, 3, 5, 7 and 9 without repeating any one of them. What is the sum of all such possible numbers?

(a) 6666600   (b) 6666660

(c) 6666666   (d) None

15. From each of two given numbers, half the smaller number is subtracted. Of the resulting numbers the larger one is three times as large as the smaller. What is the ratio of the two numbers?

(a) 2:1   (b) 3:1

(c) 3:2   (d) None

16. If the harmonic mean between two positive numbers is to the inverse of their geometric mean as 12:13; then the numbers could be in the ratio

(a) 12:13   (b) 1/12:1/13

(c) 4:9   (d) 2:3

17. Fourth term of an arithmetic progression is 8. What is sum of the first 7 terms of the arithmetic progression?

(a) 7   (b) 64

(c) 56   (d) Cannot be determined

18. It takes the pendulum of a clock 7 seconds to strike 4 o'clock. How much time will it take to strike 11 o'clock?

(a) 18 seconds   (b) 20 seconds

(c) 19.25 seconds   (d) 23.33 seconds

19. Along a road lie an odd number of stones placed at intervals of 10 m. These stones have to be assembled around the middle stone. A person can carry only one stone at a time. A man carried out the job starting with the stone in the middle, carrying stones in succession, thereby covering a distance of 4.8 km. Then the number of stones is

(a) 35   (b) 15

(c) 29   (d) 31

20. What is the smallest number which when increased by 5 is completely divisible by 8, 11 and 24?

(a) 264   (b) 259

(c) 269   (d) None of these

21. Which is the least number that must be subtracted from 1856, so that the remainder when divided by 7, 12 and 16 will leave the same remainder 4.

(a) 137   (b) 1361

(c) 140   (d) 172

22. Two positive integers differ by 4 and sum of their reciprocals is 10/21. Then one of the numbers is

(a) 3   (b) 1

(c) 5   (d) 21

23. $5^6 - 1$ is divisible by

(a) 13   (b) 31

(c) 5   (d) None of these

24. For the product $n(n + 1)(2n + 1)$. $n \in$ N, which one of the following is necessarily false?

(a) It is always even

(b) Divisible by 3

(c) Always divisible by the sum of the square of first n natural numbers

(d) Never divisible by 237

25. The remainder obtained when a prime number greater than 6 is divided by 6 is

(a) 1 or 3   (b) 1 or 5

(c) 3 or 5   (d) 4 or 5

Space for Rough Work

REVIEW TEST 2

Directions for Questions 1 to 4: Four sisters Suvarna, Tara, Uma and Vibha playing a game such that the loser doubles the money of each of the other player. They played four games and each sister lost one game in alphabetical order. At the end of fourth game each sister had ₹ 32.

1. Who started with the lowest amount?
   (a) Suvarna   (b) Tara
   (c) Uma   (d) Vibha

2. Who started with the highest amount?
   (a) Suvarna   (b) Tara
   (c) Uma   (d) Vibha

3. What was the amount with Uma at the end of the second round?
   (a) 36   (b) 72
   (c) 16   (d) None of these

4. How many rupees did Suvarna start with?
   (a) 60   (b) 34
   (c) 66   (d) 28

5. If n is an integer, how many values of n will give an integral value of $(16n^2+7n+6)/n$?
   (a) 2   (b) 3
   (c) 4   (d) None of these

6. A student instead of finding the value of $7/8^{th}$ of a number found the value of $7/18^{th}$ of the number. If his answer differed from the actual one by 770. Find the numbers.
   (a) 1584   (b) 2520
   (c) 1728   (d) 1656

7. P and Q are two integers such that $PQ = 8^2$. Which of the following cannot be the value of $P+Q$?
   (a) 20   (b) 65
   (c) 16   (d) 35

8. If m and n are integers divisible by 5, which of the following is not necessarily true?
   (a) $m - n$ is divisible by 5
   (b) $m^2 - n^2$ is divisible by 25
   (c) $m + n$ is divisible by 10
   (d) None of the above

9. Which of the following is true?
   (a) $7^{3^2} = (7^3)^2$ (b) $7^{3^2} > (7^3)^2$
   (c) $7^{3^2} < (7^3)^2$ (d) None of these

10. P, Q and R are three consecutive odd numbers in ascending order. If the value of three times P is three less than two times R. find the value of R.
    (a) 5   (b) 7
    (c) 9   (d) 11

11. ABC is a three-digit number in which $A > 0$. The value of ABC is equal to the sum of the factorials of its three digits. What is the value of B?

    (a) 9   (b) 7
    (c) 4   (d) 2

12. A, B and C are defined as follows:
    $A = (2.000004) \div [(2.000004)^2 + (4.000008)]$
    $B = (3.000003) \div [(3.000003)^2 + (9.000009)]$
    $C = (4.000002) \div [(4.000002)^2 + (8.000004)]$
    Which of the following is true about the value of the above three expressions?
    (a) All of them lie between 0.18 and 0.20
    (b) A is twice C
    (c) C is the smallest
    (d) B is the smallest

13. Let $x < 0.50$, $0 < y < 1$, $z > 1$. Given a set of numbers, the middle number, when they arranged in ascending order is called the median. So the median of the numbers x, y and z would be
    (a) less than one   (b) between 0 and 1
    (c) greater than one   (d) cannot say

14. let a, b, c d, and e be integers such that $a = 6b = 12c$, and $2b = 9d = 12e$. Then which of the following pairs contains a number that is not an integer?.
    (a) $\left(\dfrac{a}{27}, \dfrac{b}{e}\right)$ (b) $\left(\dfrac{a}{36}, \dfrac{c}{e}\right)$
    (c) $\left(\dfrac{a}{3}, \dfrac{bd}{9}\right)$ (d) $\left(\dfrac{a}{7}, \dfrac{c}{d}\right)$

15. If a, $a + 2$, and $a + 4$ are prime numbers, then the number of possible solutions for a is:
    (a) One   (b) Two
    (c) Three   (d) More than three

16. Let x and y be positive integers such that x is prime and y is composite. Then,
    (a) $y - x$ cannot be an even integer
    (b) xy cannot be an even integer
    (c) $(x + y)$ cannot be an even integer
    (d) None of the above statement is true

17. Let n (>1) be a composite natural number such that the square root of n is not an integer. Consider the following statements:
    A: n has a factor which is greater than 1 and less than square root n
    B: n has a factor which is greater than square root n but less than n
    Then
    (a) Both A and B are false
    (b) Both A and B are true
    (c) A is false but B is true
    (d) A is true and B is false

18. What is the remainder when 4^{96} is divided by 6?
    (a) 0   (b) 2
    (c) 3   (d) 4

19. What is the sum of all two-digit numbers that give a remainder of 3 when they are divided by 7?
    (a) 646
    (b) 676
    (c) 683
    (d) 797

20. The infinite sum $1 + \dfrac{4}{7} + \dfrac{9}{7^2} + \dfrac{16}{7^3} + \dfrac{25}{7^4} + - - - - -$
    (a) $\dfrac{27}{14}$
    (b) $\dfrac{29}{13}$
    (c) $\dfrac{49}{27}$
    (d) $\dfrac{256}{147}$

21. If the product of n positive real numbers is unity, then their sum is necessarily:
    (a) a multiple of n
    (b) equal to $n + \dfrac{1}{n}$
    (c) never less than n
    (d) None of these

22. How many three digit positive integer, with digits x, y and z in the hundred's, ten's and unit's place respectively, exist such that $x < y$, $z < y$ and $x \neq 0$?

    (a) 245
    (b) 285
    (c) 240
    (d) 320

23. How many even integers n, where $100 \leq n \leq 200$, are divisible neither by seven nor by nine?
    (a) 40
    (b) 37
    (c) 39
    (d) 38

24. A positive whole number M less than 100 is represented in base 2 notation, base 3 notation, and base 5 notation. It is found that in all three cases the last digit is 1, while in exactly two out of the three cases the leading digit in 1. Then M equals:
    (a) 31
    (b) 63
    (c) 75
    (d) 91

25. In a certain examinations paper, there are n questions. For $j = 1, 2 \ldots n$. there are 2^{n-1} students who answered j or more questions wrongly. If the total number of wrong answers is 4095, then the value of n is:
    (a) 12
    (b) 11
    (c) 10
    (d) 9

Space for Rough Work

REVIEW TEST 3

1. In 1936, I was as old as the number formed by the last two digits of my year of birth. Find the date of birth of my father who is 25 years older to me.
   (a) 1868   (b) 1893
   (c) 1902   (d) 1900
   (e) Can't be determined

2. Find the total number of integral solutions of the equation $(407)x - (ddd)y = 2589$, where 'ddd' is a three-digit number.
   (a) 0   (b) 1
   (c) 2   (d) 3
   (e) Can't be determined

3. Find the digit at the ten's place of the number $N = 7^{281} \times 3^{264}$.
   (a) 0   (b) 1
   (c) 6   (d) 5
   (e) None of these

4. Raju went to a shop to buy a certain number of pens and pencils. Raju calculated the amount payable to the shopkeeper and offered that amount to him. Raju was surprised when the shopkeeper returned him ₹ 24 as balance. When he came back home, he realized that the shopkeeper had actually transposed the number of pens with the number of pencils. Which of the following is certainly an invalid statement?
   (a) The number of pencils that Raju wanted to buy was 8 more than the number of pens.
   (b) The number of pens that Raju wanted to buy was 6 less than the number of pencils.
   (c) A pen cost ₹ 4 more than a pencil.
   (d) None of the above.

5. HCF of 384 and a^5b^2 is 16ab. What is the correct relation between a and b?
   (a) $a = 2b$ (b) $a + b = 3$
   (c) $a - b = 3$ (d) $a + b = 5$

6. In ancient India, 0 to 25 years of age was called Brahmawastha and 25 to 50 was called Grahastha. I am in Grahastha and my younger brother is also in Grahastha such as the difference in our ages is 6 years and both of our ages are prime numbers. Also twice my brother's age is 31 more than my age. Find the sum of our ages.
   (a) 80   (b) 68
   (c) 70   (d) 71

7. Volume of a cube with integral sides is the same as the area of a square with integral sides. Which of these can be the volume of the cube formed by using the square and its replicas as the 6 faces?
   (a) 19683   (b) 512
   (c) 256   (d) Both (a) and (b)

8. Let A be a two-digit number and B be another two-digit number formed by reversing the digits of A. If A + B + (Product of digits of the number A) = 145, then what is the sum of the digits of A?
   (a) 9   (b) 10
   (c) 11   (d) 12

9. When a two-digit number N is divided by the sum of its digits, the result is Q. Find the minimum possible value of Q.
   (a) 10   (b) 2
   (c) 5.5   (d) 1.9

10. A one-digit number, which is the ten's digit of a two digit number X, is subtracted from X to give Y which is the quotient of the division of 999 by the cube of a number. Find the sum of the digits of X.
   (a) 5   (b) 7
   (c) 6   (d) 8

11. After Yuvraj hit 6 sixes in an over, Geoffery Boycott commented that Yuvraj just made 210 runs in the over. Harsha Bhogle was shocked and he asked Geoffery which base system was he using? What must have been Geoffery's answer?
   (a) 9   (b) 2
   (c) 5   (d) 4

12. Find the ten's digit of the number 7^{2010}.
   (a) 0   (b) 1
   (c) 2   (d) 4

13. Find the HCF of 481 and the number 'aaa' where 'a' is a number between 1 and 9 (both included).
   (a) 73   (b) 1
   (c) 27   (d) 37

14. The number of positive integer valued pairs (x, y), satisfying $4x - 17y = 1$ and $x < 1000$ is:
   (a) 59   (b) 57
   (c) 55   (d) 58

15. Let a, b, c be distinct digits. Consider a two digit number 'ab' and a three digit number 'ccb' both defined under the usual decimal number system. If $(ab)^2 = ccb$ and $ccb > 300$ then the value of b is:
   (a) 1   (b) 0
   (c) 5   (d) 6

16. The remainder 7^{84} is divided by 342 is:
   (a) 0   (b) 1
   (c) 49   (d) 341

17. Let x, y and z be distinct integers, x and y are odd and positive, and z is even and positive. Which one of the following statements can't be true?
   (a) $(x - z)^2 y$ is even   (b) $(x - z)y^2$ is odd
   (c) $(x - y)y$ is odd   (d) $(x - y)^2 z$ is even

18. A boy starts adding consecutive natural numbers starting with 1. After some time he reaches a total

of 1000 when he realizes that he has made the mistake of double counting 1 number. Find the number double counted.

(a) 44   (b) 45

(c) 10   (d) 12

19. In a number system the product of 44 and 11 is 1034. The number 3111 of this system, when converted to decimal number system, becomes:

(a) 406   (b) 1086

(c) 213   (d) 691

20. Ashish is given ₹ 158 in one rupee denominations. He has been asked to allocate them into a number of bags such that any amount required between Re 1 and ₹ 158 can be given by handing out a certain number of bags without opening them. What is the minimum number of bags required?

(a) 11   (b) 12

(c) 13   (d) None of these

Space for Rough Work

REVIEW TEST 4

1. Find the number of 6-digit numbers that can be formed using the digits 1, 2, 3, 4, 5, 6 once such that the 6-digit number is divisible by its unit digit.
   (a) 648
   (b) 528
   (c) 728
   (d) 128

2. Which is the highest 3-digit number that divides the number 11111....1(27 times) perfectly without leaving any remainder?
   (a) 111
   (b) 333
   (c) 666
   (d) 999

3. W1, W2, ... , W7 are 7 positive integral values such that by attaching the coefficients of +1, 0 and -1 to each value available and adding the resultant values, any number from 1 to 1093 (both included) could be formed. If W1, W2, ... , W7 are in ascending order, then what is the value of W3?
   (a) 10
   (b) 9
   (c) 0
   (d) 1

4. What is the unit digit of the number $63^{25} + 25^{63}$?
   (a) 3
   (b) 5
   (c) 8
   (d) 2

5. Find the remainder when $(2222^{5555} + 5555^{2222})$ is divided by 7.
   (a) 1
   (b) 0
   (c) 2
   (d) 5

6. What is the number of nines used in numbering a 453 page book?
   (a) 86
   (b) 87
   (c) 84
   (d) 85

7. How many four digit numbers are divisible by 5 but not by 25?
   (a) 2000
   (b) 8000
   (c) 1440
   (d) 9999

8. The sum of two integers is 10 and the sum of their reciprocals is 5/12. What is the value of larger of these integers?
   (a) 7
   (b) 5
   (c) 6
   (d) 4

9. Saurabh was born in 1989. His elder brother Siddhartha was also born in the 1980's such that the last two digits of his year of birth form a prime number P. Find the remainder when $(P^2 + 11)$ is divided by 5.
   (a) 0
   (b) 1
   (c) 2
   (d) 3

10. The HCF of x and y is H. Find the HCF of $(x - y)$ and $(x^3 + y^3)/(x^2 - xy + y^2)$.
    (a) H – 1
    (b) H^2
    (c) H
    (d) H + 1

11. 4 bells toll together at 9:00 A.M. They toll after 7, 8, 11 and 12 seconds respectively. How many times will they toll together again in the next 3 hours?
    (a) 3
    (b) 5
    (c) 6
    (d) 9

12. What power of 210 will exactly divide 142!
    (a) 22
    (b) 11
    (c) 34
    (d) 33

13. Find the total numbers between 122 and 442 that are divisible by 3 but not by 9.
    (a) 70
    (b) 71
    (c) 72
    (d) 73

14. If 146! is divisible by 6^n, then find the maximum value of n.
    (a) 74
    (b) 75
    (c) 76
    (d) 70

15. If we add the square of the digit in the tens place of a positive two-digit number to the product of the digits of that number, we shall get 52, and if we add the square of the digit in the units place to the same product of the digits, we shall get 117. Find the two-digit number.
    (a) 18
    (b) 39
    (c) 49
    (d) 28

16. Find the smallest natural number n such that $(n + 1)$ $n[(n - 1)!]$ is divisible by 990.
    (a) 2
    (b) 4
    (c) 10
    (d) 11

17. If x, y and z are odd, even and odd respectively, then $(x^2 - yz^2 + y^3)$ and $(x^2 + y^2 + z^2)$ are respectively:
    (a) Odd & Odd
    (b) Even & Odd
    (c) Odd & Even
    (d) Odd & Odd

18. A two digit number N has its digits reversed to form another two digit number M. What could be the unit digit of M if product of M and N is 574?
    (a) 1
    (b) 3
    (c) 6
    (d) 9

19. For what relation between b and c is the number abcacb divisible by 7, if $b > c$?
    (a) $b + c = 7$
    (b) $b = c + 7$
    (c) $2bc = 7$
    (d) $c = 7b$

20. What is the remainder when a^6 is divided by $(a + 1)$?
    (a) $a + 1$
    (b) a
    (c) 0
    (d) 1

Space for Rough Work

REVIEW TEST 5

1. What is the last digit of 62^43^54^65^76^87?
   (a) 2   (b) 4
   (c) 6   (d) 8

2. $N = 99^3 - 36^3 - 63^3$, how many factors does N have?
   (a) 51   (b) 96
   (c) 128   (d) 192

3. Find the highest power of 2 in 1! + 2! + 3! + 4!.............600!
   (a) 1   (b) 494
   (c) 3.0   (d) 256

4. 100! is divisible by 160^n...what is the max. integral value of n?
   (a) 19   (b) 24
   (c) 26   (d) 28

5. What is the sum of the digits of the decimal form of the product $2^{999} * 5^{1001}$?
   (a) 2   (b) 4
   (c) 5   (d) 7

6. What is the remainder when 1*1 + 11*11 + 111*111 + 1111*1111 +......+ (2001 times 1)*(2001 times 1) is divided by 100 ?
   (a) 99   (b) 22
   (c) 01   (d) 21

7. What is the remainder when 789456123 is divided by 999?
   (a) 123   (b) 369
   (c) 963   (d) 189

8. What is the total number of the factors of 16!
   (a) 2016   (b) 1024
   (c) 3780   (d) 5376

9. Find the sum of the first 125 terms of the sequence 1, 2, 1, 3, 2, 1, 4, 3, 2, 1, 5, 4, 3, 2...
   (a) 616   (b) 460
   (c) 750   (d) 720

10. Umesh purchased a Tata Nano recently, but the faulty car odometer of Tata Nano proceeds from digit 4 to digit 6, always skipping the digit 5, regardless of position. If the odometer now reads 003008 (starting with 000000), how many km has Nano actually travelled?
    (a) 2100   (b) 1999
    (c) 2194   (d) 2195

11. What is the number of consecutive zeroes in the end of 1000!?
    (a) 248   (b) 249
    (c) 250   (d) 251

12. Mr. Ramlal lived his entire life during the 1800s. In the last year of his life, Ramlal stated: Once I was x years old in the year x^2. He was born in the year
    (a) 1822   (b) 1851
    (c) 1853   (d) 1806

13. Find the unit's digit of LCM of $13^{501} - 1$ and $13^{501} + 1$
    (a) 2   (b) 4
    (c) 5   (d) 8

14. If you were to add all odd numbers between 1 and 2007 (both inclusive), the result would be
    (a) A perfect square   (b) Divisible by 2008
    (c) Multiple of 251   (d) All of the above

15. Find the remainder when $971(30^{99} + 61^{100}) * (1148)^{56}$ is divided by 31
    (a) 25   (b) 0
    (c) 11   (d) 21

16. What is the remainder when 2^{100} is divided by 101?
    (a) 1   (b) 100
    (c) 0   (d) 99

17. Find the last two digits of 2^{134}
    (a) 04   (b) 84
    (c) 24   (d) 64

18. Find the remainder when $(10^3 + 9^3)^{1000}$ by 12^3
    (a) 01   (b) 11
    (c) 1001   (d) 1727

19. The number of factors of the number 3000 are:
    (a) 16   (b) 32
    (c) 24   (d) 28

20. If N! has 73 zeroes at the end then find the value of N?
    (a) 295   (b) 300
    (c) 290   (d) Not possible

Space for Rough Work

ANSWER KEY

Review Test 1

1. (a)	2. (c)	3. (d)	4. (a)
5. (b)	6. (a)	7. (d)	8. (c)
9. (a)	10. (b)	11. (c)	12. (b)
13. (a)	14. (a)	15. (a)	16. (c)
17. (c)	18. (d)	19. (d)	20. (b)
21. (d)	22. (a)	23. (b)	24. (d)
25. (b)			

Review Test 2

1. (d)	2. (a)	3. (b)	4. (c)
5. (c)	6. (a)	7. (d)	8. (c)
9. (b)	10. (c)	11. (c)	12. (d)
13. (b)	14. (d)	15. (a)	16. (d)
17. (b)	18. (d)	19. (b)	20. (c)
21. (c)	22. (c)	23. (c)	24. (d)
25. (a)			

Review Test 3

1. (b)	2. (a)	3. (c)	4. (d)
5. (d)	6. (a)	7. (d)	8. (c)
9. (d)	10. (a)	11. (d)	12. (d)
13. (d)	14. (a)	15. (a)	16. (b)
17. (a)	18. (c)	19. (a)	20. (d)

Review Test 4

1. (a)	2. (d)	3. (b)	4. (c)
5. (b)	6. (d)	7. (c)	8. (c)
9. (a)	10. (c)	11. (b)	12. (a)
13. (b)	14. (d)	15. (c)	16. (c)
17. (c)	18. (a)	19. (b)	20. (d)

Review Test 5

1. (a)	2. (b)	3. (c)	4. (a)
5. (d)	6. (c)	7. (b)	8. (d)
9. (c)	10. (c)	11. (b)	12. (d)
13. (b)	14. (d)	15. (b)	16. (a)
17. (b)	18. (a)	19. (b)	20. (d)

BLOCK II

AVERAGES AND MIXTURES

Chapter 3
Averages

Chapter 4
Alligations

...BACK TO SCHOOL

- **The Relevance of Average**

Average is one of the most important mathematical concepts that we use in our day-to-day life. In fact, even the most non-mathematical individuals regularly utilize the concept of averages on a day-to-day basis.

So, we use averages in all the following and many more instances.

- How a class of students fared in an exam is assessed by looking at the average score.
- What is the average price of items purchased by an individual.
- A person might be interested in knowing his average telephone expenditure, electricity expenditure, petrol expenditure, etc.
- A manager might be interested in finding out the average sales per territory or even the average growth rate month to month.
- Clearly there can be immense application of averages that you might be able to visualise on your own.

- **The Meaning of an Average**

An average is best seen as a representative value which can be used to represent the value of the general term in a group of values.

For instance, suppose that a cricket team had 10 partnerships as follows:

1st wicket 28   2nd wicket 42

3rd wicket 112   4th wicket 52

5th wicket 0   6th wicket 23

7th wicket 41   8th wicket 18

9th wicket 9   10th wicket 15

On adding the ten values above, we get a total of 340—which gives an average of 34 runs per wicket, i.e. the average partnership of the team was 34 runs.

In other words, if we were to replace the value of all the ten partnerships by 34 runs, we would get the same total score. Hence, 34 represents the average partnership value for the team.

Suppose, in a cricket series of 5 matches between 2 countries, you are given that Team A had an average partnership of 58 Runs per wicket while Team B had an average partnership of 34 runs per wicket. What conclusion can you draw about the performance of the two teams, given that both the teams played 5 complete test matches?

Obviously, Team B would have performed much worse than Team A: For that matter, if I tell you that the average daytime high temperature of Lucknow was 18° C for a particular month, you can easily draw some kind of conclusion in your mind about the month we could possibly be talking about.

Thus, you should realize that the beauty of averages lies in the fact that it is one single number that tells you a lot about the group of numbers—hence, it is one number that represents an entire group of numbers.

But one of the key concepts that you need to understand before you move into the chapters of this block is the concept of <u>WEIGHTED AVERAGES.</u>

As always, the concept is best explained through a concrete example.

Suppose I had to buy a shirt and a trousers and let us say that the average cost of a shirt was ₹ 1200 while that of a trousers was ₹ 900.

Contd

In such a case, the average cost of a shirt and a trousers would be given by (1200 + 900)/2 = 1050.

This can be visualised on the number line as:

(midpoint) = answer

As you can easily see in the figure, the average occurs at the midpoint of the two numbers.

Now, let us try to modify the situation:

Suppose, I were to buy 2 trousers and 1 shirt. In such a case I would end up spending (900 + 900 + 1200) = ₹ 3000 in buying a total of 3 items. What would be my average in this case?

Obviously, 3000/3 = ₹ 1000!!

Clearly, the average has shifted!!

On the number line we could visualise this as follows:

(Answer)   (midpoint)

It is clearly visible that the average has shifted towards 900 (which was the cost price of the trousers—the larger purchased item.)

In a way, this shift is similar to the way a two pan weighing balance shifts on weights being put on it. The balance shifts towards the pan containing the larger weight.

Similarly, in this case, the correct average (1000) is closer to 900 than it is to 1200. This has happened because the number of elements in the group of average 900 is greater than the number of elements in the group having average 1200. Since, this is very similar to the system of weights, we call this as a weighted average situation.

At this stage, you should realize that weighted averages are not solely restricted to two groups. We can also come up with a weighted average situation for three groups (although in such a case the representation of the weighted average on the number line might not be so easily possible.) In fact, it is the number line representation of a weighted average situation that is defined as alligation (when 2 groups are involved).

Pre-assessment Test

1. X's age is 1/10th of Y's present age. Y's age will be thrice of Z's age after 10 years. If Z's eighth birthday was celebrated two years ago, then the present age of X must be
   (a) 5 years
   (b) 10 years
   (c) 15 years
   (d) 20 years

2. Dravid was twice as old as Rahul 10 years back. How old is Rahul today if Dravid will be 45 years old 15 years hence?
   (a) 20 years
   (b) 10 years
   (c) 30 years
   (d) None of these

3. A demographic survey of 100 families in which two parents were present revealed that the average age A, of the oldest child, is 15 years less than ½ the sum of the ages of the two parents. If X represents the age of one parent and Y the age of the other parent, then which of the following is equivalent to A?
   (a) $\dfrac{X+Y}{2} - 15$
   (b) $\dfrac{X+Y}{2} + 15$
   (c) $\dfrac{X+Y}{2} - 15$
   (d) X + Y − 7.5

4. If 10 years are subtracted from the present age of Randy and the remainder divided by 12, then you would get the present age of his grandson Sandy. If Sandy is 19 years younger to Sundy whose age is 24, then what is the present age of Randy?
   (a) 80 years
   (b) 70 years
   (c) 60 years
   (d) None of these

5. Two groups of students, whose average ages are 15 years and 25 years, combine to form a third group whose average age is 23 years. What is the ratio of the number of students in the first group to the number of students in the second group?
   (a) 8 : 2
   (b) 2 : 8
   (c) 4 : 6
   (d) None of these

6. A year ago, Mohit was four times his son's age. In six years, his age will be 9 more than twice his son's age. What is the present age of the son?
   (a) 10 years
   (b) 9 years
   (c) 20 years
   (d) None of these

7. In 1952, I was as old as the number formed by the last two digits of my birth year. When I mentioned this interesting coincidence to my grandfather, he surprised me by saying that the same applied to him also.
   The difference in our ages is:
   (a) 40 years
   (b) 50 years
   (c) 60 years
   (d) None of these

8. The average age of three boys is 18 years. If their ages are in the ratio 4:5:9, then the age of the youngest boy is
   (a) 8 years
   (b) 9 years
   (c) 12 years
   (d) 16 years

9. "I am eight times as old as you were when I was as old as you are", said a man to his son. Find out their present ages if the sum of their ages is 75 years.
   (a) 40 years and 35 years
   (b) 56 years and 19 years
   (c) 48 years and 27 years
   (d) None of these

10. My brother was 3 years of age when my sister was born, while my mother was 26 years of age when I was born. If my sister was 4 years of age when I was born, then what was the age of my father and mother respectively when my brother was born?
    (a) 35 years, 33 years
    (b) 35 years, 29 years
    (c) 32 years, 23 years
    (d) None of these

11. Namrata's father is now four times her age. In five years, he will be three times her age. In how many years, will he be twice her age?
    (a) 5
    (b) 20
    (c) 25
    (d) 15

12. A father is twice as old as his daughter. 20 years back, he was seven times as old as the daughter. What are their present ages?
    (a) 24, 12
    (b) 44, 22
    (c) 48, 24
    (d) none of these

13. The present ages of three persons are in the proportion of 5:8:7. Eight years ago, the sum of their ages was 76. Find the present age of the youngest person.
    (a) 20
    (b) 25
    (c) 30
    (d) None of these

14. The average age of a class is 14.8 years. The average age of the boys in the class is 15.4 years and that of girls is 14.4 years. What is the ratio of boys to girls in the class?
    (a) 1 : 2
    (b) 3 : 2
    (c) 2 : 3
    (d) None of these

15. In an organisation, the daily average wages of 20 illiterate employees is decreased from ₹ 25 to ₹ 10, thus the average salary of all the literate (educated) and illiterate employees is decreased by ₹ 10 per day. The number of educated employees working in the organisation are:
    (a) 15
    (b) 20
    (c) 10
    (d) 25

16. Mr.Akhilesh Bajpai while going from Lucknow to Jamshedpur covered half the distance by train at the speed of 96 km/hr, half the rest of the distance by his scooter at the speed of 60 km/hr and the remaining distance at the speed of 40 km/hr by car. The average speed at which he completed his journey is:
    (a) 64 km/hr   (b) 56 km/hr
    (c) 60 km/hr   (d) 36 km/hr

17. There are four types of candidates in AMS Learning Systems preparing for the CAT. The number of students of Engineering, Science, Commerce and Humanities is 400, 600, 500 and 300 respectively and the respective percentage of students who qualified the CAT is 80%, 75%, 60% and 50% respectively the overall percentage of successful candidates in our institute is:
    (a) 67.77%   (b) 66.66%
    (c) 68.5%   (d) None of these

18. Mr. Jagmohan calculated the average of 10 'Three digit numbers'. But due to mistake he reversed the digits of a number and thus his average increased by 29.7. The difference between the unit digit and hundreds digit of that number is:
    (a) 4   (b) 3
    (c) 2   (d) can't be determined

Directions for Questions 19 and 20: Answer the questions based on the following Information.

Production pattern for number of units (in cubic feet) per day.

Days	1	2	3	4	5	6	7
Numbers of units	150	180	120	250	160	120	150

For a truck that can carry 2,000 cubic feet, hiring cost per day is ₹1,000. Storing cost per cubic feet is ₹5 per day. Any residual material left at the end of the seventh day has to be transferred.

19. If all the units should be sent to the market, then on which days should the trucks be hired to minimize the cost:
    (a) 2nd, 4th, 6th, 7th (b) 7th
    (c) 2nd, 4th, 5th, 7th (d) None of these

20. If the storage cost is reduced to ₹ 0.9 per cubic feet per day, then on which day/days, should the truck be hired?
    (a) 4th (b) 7th
    (c) 4th and 7th (d) None of these

ANSWER KEY

1. (a)	2. (a)	3. (a)	4. (b)
5. (b)	6. (b)	7. (b)	8. (c)
9. (c)	10. (d)	11. (b)	12. (c)
13. (b)	14. (c)	15. (c)	16. (a)
17. (a)	18. (b)	19. (a)	20. (b)

SCORE INTERPRETATION ALGORITHM FOR PRE-ASSESSMENT TEST OF BLOCK II

If You Scored: < 12: (In Unlimited Time)

Step One

Go through the first chapter of the block, viz., Averages. When you do so, concentrate on clearly understanding each of the concepts explained in the chapter theory.

Then move onto the LOD 1 exercises. These exercises will provide you with the first level of challenge. Try to solve each and every question provided under LOD 1. While doing so do not think about the time requirement .Once you finish solving LOD 1, revise the questions and their solution processes.

Also at this stage study the concept of averages from your school text books (Class 8, 9 & 10) and solve all the questions which are available to you in those books._

Step Two

After finishing LOD 1 of Averages, move into LOD 2 and then LOD 3 of this chapter.

Step Three

Go to the chapter of alligations and study the shortcuts provided carefully. Understand the use of the alligation process as clearly as possible.

Then move to the LOD 1 exercise of the same. (Note: The chapter of alligations does not have an LOD2 & LOD 3 exercise)

Step Four

Go to the practice test given at the end of the block and solve it. While doing so, first look at the score you get within the time limit mentioned. Then continue to solve the test further without a time limit and try to evaluate the improvement in your unlimited time score.

In case the growth in your score is not significant, go back to the theory of each chapter and review each of the questions you have solved for both the chapters.

If You Scored: > 12 (In Unlimited Time)

Follow the same process as above. The only difference is that the school book work is optional – do it only if you feel you need to. However, your concentration during the solving of the two chapters has to be on developing your speed at solving questions on this chapter.

3 Chapter Averages

THEORY

The average of a number is a measure of the central tendency of a set of numbers. In other words, it is an estimate of where the center point of a set of numbers lies.

The basic formula for the average of n numbers $x_1, x_2, x_3, \ldots x_n$ is

$A_n = (x_1 + x_2 + x_3 + \ldots + x_n)/n$ = (Total of set of n numbers)/n

This also means $A_n \times n$ = total of the set of numbers.

The average is always calculated for a set of numbers.

Concept of Weighted Average: When we have two or more groups whose individual averages are known, then to find the combined average of all the elements of all the groups we use weighted average. Thus, if we have k groups with averages $A_1, A_2 \ldots A_k$ and having $n_1, n_2 \ldots n_k$ elements then the weighted average is given by the formula:

$$A_w = \frac{n_1 A_1 + n_2 A_2 + n_3 A_3 + \ldots + n_k A_k}{n_1 + n_2 + n_3 + \ldots + n_k}$$

Another Meaning of Average The average [also known as *arithmetic mean* (AM)] of a set of numbers can also be defined as the number by which we can replace each and every number of the set without changing the total of the set of numbers.

Properties of Average (AM) The properties of averages [arithmetic mean] can be elucidated by the following examples:

Example 1: The average of 4 numbers 12, 13, 17 and 18 is:

Solution: Required average = (12 + 13 + 17 + 18)/4 = 60/4 = 15

This means that if each of the 4 numbers of the set were replaced by 15 each, there would be no change in the total.

This is an important way to look at averages. In fact, whenever you come across any situation where the average of a group of 'n' numbers is given, you should visualise that there are 'n' numbers, each of whose value is the average of the group. This view is a very important way to visualise averages.

This can be visualised as

$$
\begin{aligned}
12 &\rightarrow +3 \rightarrow 15 \\
13 &\rightarrow +2 \rightarrow 15 \\
17 &\rightarrow -2 \rightarrow 15 \\
18 &\rightarrow -3 \rightarrow 15 \\
\hline
60 &\rightarrow +0 \rightarrow 60
\end{aligned}
$$

Example 2: In Example 1, visualise addition of a fifth number, which increases the average by 1.

$$
\begin{aligned}
15 + 1 &= 16 \\
15 + 1 &= 16 \\
15 + 1 &= 16 \\
15 + 1 &= 16
\end{aligned}
$$

The +1 appearing 4 times is due to the fifth number, which is able to maintain the average of 16 first and then 'give one' to each of the first 4.

Hence, the fifth number in this case is 20

Example 3: The average always lies above the lowest number of the set and below the highest number of the set.

Example 4: The net deficit due to the numbers below the average always equals the net surplus due to the numbers above the average.

Example 5: *Ages and averages:* If the average age of a group of persons is x years today then after n years their average age will be $(x + n)$.

Also, n years ago their average age would have been $(x - n)$. This happens due to the fact that for a group of people, 1 year is added to each person's age every year.

Example 6: A man travels at 60 kmph on the journey from A to B and returns at 100 kmph. Find his average speed for the journey.

Solution:

> Average speed = (total distance)/(total time)

If we assume distance between 2 points to be d
Then

Average speed $= 2d/[(d/60) + (d/100)] = (2 \times 60 \times 100)/(60 + 100) = (2 \times 60 \times 100)/160 = 75$

> Average speed $= (2S_1 \cdot S_2)/(S_1 + S_2)$
> [S_1 and S_2 are speeds]

of going and coming back respectively.

Short Cut The average speed will always come out by the following process:

The ratio of speeds is $60:100 = 3:5$ (say $r_1 : r_2$)

Space for Notes

Then, divide the difference of speeds (40 in this case) by $r_1 + r_2$ (3 + 5 = 8, in this case) to get one part. (40/8 = 5, in this case)

The required answer will be three parts away (i.e. r_1 parts away) from the lower speed.

Check out how this works with the following speeds:

$$S_1 = 20 \quad \text{and} \quad S_2 = 40$$

Step 1: Ratio of speeds = $20:40 = 1:2$

Step 2: Divide difference of 20 into 3 parts $(r_1 + r_2) \rightarrow = 20/3 = 6.66$

Required average speed $= 20 + 1 \times 6.66$

Note: This process is essentially based on alligations and we shall see it again in the next chapter.

Exercise for Self-practice

Find the average speed for the above problem if

(1)	$S_1 = 20$	$S_2 = 200$
(2)	$S_1 = 60$	$S_2 = 120$
(3)	$S_1 = 100$	$S_2 = 50$
(4)	$S_1 = 60$	$S_2 = 180$

🎯 WORKED-OUT PROBLEMS

Problem 3.1 The average of a batsman after 25 innings was 56 runs per innings. If after the 26th inning his average increased by 2 runs, then what was his score in the 26th inning?

Solution *Normal process:*

Runs in 26th inning = Runs total after 26 innings – Runs total after 25 innings

$$= 26 \times 58 - 25 \times 56$$

For mental calculation use:

$$(56 + 2) \times 26 - 56 \times 25$$

$$= 2 \times 26 + (56 \times 26 - 56 \times 25)$$

$$= 52 + 56 = 108$$

Short Cut Since the average increases by 2 runs per innings it is equivalent to 2 runs being added to each score in the first 25 innings. Now, since these runs can only be added by the runs scored in the 26th inning, the score in the 26th inning must be $25 \times 2 = 50$ runs higher than the average after 26 innings (i.e. new average = 58).

Hence, runs scored in 26th inning = New Average + Old innings × Change in average

$$= 58 + 25 \times 2 = 108$$

Visualise this as

Average in first 25 innings	Average after 26 innings
56	58
56	58
56	58
…	…
…	…
25 times…	26 times…

Difference in total is two, 25 times and 58 once, that is, 58 + 25 × 2.

Problem 3.2 The average age of a class of 30 students and a teacher reduces by 0.5 years if we exclude the teacher. If the initial average is 14 years, find the age of the class teacher.

Solution *Normal process:*

Age of teacher = Total age of (students + teacher)

– Total age of students

$$= 31 \times 14 - 30 \times 13.5$$

$$= 434 - 405$$

$$= 29 \text{ years}$$

Short Cut The teacher after fulfilling the average of 14 (for the group to which he belonged) is also able to give 0.5 years to the age of each of the 30 students. Hence, he has $30 \times 0.5 \rightarrow 15$ years to give over and above maintaining his own average age of 14 years.

$$\text{Age of teacher} = 14 + 30 \times 0.5 = 29 \text{ years}$$

(*Note:* This problem should be viewed as change of average from 13.5 to 14 when teacher is included.)

Problem 3.3 The average marks of a group of 20 students on a test is reduced by 4 when the topper who scored 90 marks is replaced by a new student. How many marks did the new student have?

Solution *Normal process:*

Let initial average be x.

Then the initial total is $20x$

New average will be $(x - 4)$ and the new total will be $20(x - 4) = 20x - 80$.

The reduction of 80 is created by the replacement.

Hence, the new student has 80 marks less than the student he replaces. Hence, he must have scored 10 marks.

Short Cut The replacement has the effect of reducing the average marks for each of the 20 students by 4. Hence, the replacement must be $20 \times 4 = 80$ marks below the original.

Hence, answer = 10 marks.

Problem 3.4 The average age of 3 students A, B and C is 48 marks. Another student D joins the group and the new average becomes 44 marks. If another student E, who has 3 marks more than D, joins the group, the average of the 4 students B, C, D and E becomes 43 marks. Find how many marks A got in the exam.

Solution Solve while reading. The first sentence gives you a total of 144 for A, B and C's marks. *Second sentence:* When D joins the group, the total becomes $44 \times 4 = 176$. Hence D must get 32 marks.

Alternatively, you can reach this point by considering the first 2 statements together as:

D's joining the group reduces the average from 48 to 44 marks (i.e. 4 marks).

This means that to maintain the average of 44 marks, D has to take 4 marks from A, 4 from B and 4 from $C \rightarrow$ A total of 12 marks. Hence, he must have got 32 marks.

From here:

The first part of the third sentence gives us information about E getting 3 marks more than 32 → Hence, E gets 35 marks.

Now, it is further stated that when A is replaced by E, the average marks of the students reduces by 1 to 43.

Mathematically this can be shown as

$$A + B + C + D = 44 \times 4 = 176 \text{ while, } B + C + D + E$$
$$= 43 \times 4 = 172$$

Subtracting the two equations, we get $A - E = 4$ marks. Hence, A would have got 39 marks.

Alternatively, you can think of this as:

The replacement of A with E results in the reduction of 1 mark from each of the 4 people who belong to the group. Hence, the difference is 4 marks. Hence, A would get 4 marks more than E i.e. A gets 39 marks.

Problem 3.5 The mean temperature of Monday to Wednesday was 27 °C and of Tuesday to Thursday was 24 °C. If the temperature on Thursday was 2/3rd of the temperature on Monday, what was the temperature on Thursday?

Solution From the first sentence, we get that the total from Monday to Wednesday was 81 while from Tuesday to Thursday was 72. The difference is arising out of the replacement of Monday by Thursday.

This can be mathematically written as

$$\text{Mon} + \text{Tue} + \text{Wed} = 81 \qquad (1)$$

$$\text{Tue} + \text{Wed} + \text{Thu} = 72 \qquad (2)$$

Hence, $$\text{Mon} - \text{Thu} = 9$$

We have two unknown variables in the above equation. To solve for 2 unknowns, we need a new equation. Looking back at the problem we get the equation:

$$\text{Thu} = (2/3) \times \text{Mon}$$

Solving the two equations we get: Thursday = 18 °C.

However, in the exam, you should avoid using equation-solving as much as possible. You should, ideally, be able to reach half way through the solution during the first reading of the question, and then meet the gap through the use of options.

The answer to this problem should be got by the time you finish reading the question for the first time.

Thus suppose we have the equations:
$M - T = 9$ and $T = 2M/3$ or $T/M = 2/3$ and have the options for T as

    (a) 12   (b) 15

    (c) 18   (d) 27

To check which of these options is the appropriate value, we need to check one by one.

Option (a) gives $T = 12$, then we have $M = 21$. But $12/21 \neq 2/3$. Hence, this is not the correct option.

Option (b) gives $T = 15$, then $M = 24$. But again $15/24 \neq 2/3$. Hence, this is not the correct option.

Option (c) gives $T = 18$, then $M = 27$. Now $18/27 = 2/3$. Hence, this is the correct option.

So we no longer need to check for option (d).

However, if we had checked for option (d) then $T = 27$, so $M = 36$. But again $27/36 \neq 2/3$. Hence, this is not the correct option.

In the above, we used 'solving-while-reading' and 'option-based' approaches.

These two approaches are very important and by combining the two, you can reach amazing speeds in solving the question.

You are advised to practice both these approaches while solving questions, which will surely improve your efficiency and speed. You will see that, with practice, you will be able to arrive at the solution to most of the LOD I problems (given later in this chapter) even as you finish reading the questions. And since it is the LOD I level problems that appear in most examinations (like CMAT, Bank PO, MAT, Indo MAT, NMIMS, NIFT, NLS and most other aptitude exams) you will gain a significant advantage in solving these problems.

On LOD II, LOD III and CAT type problems, you will find that using solving-while-reading and option-based approaches together would take you through anywhere between 30–70% of the question by the time you finish reading the question for the first time.

This will give you a tremendous time advantage over the other students appearing in the examination.

Problem 3.6 A person covers half his journey by train at 60 kmph, the remainder half by bus at 30 kmph and the rest by cycle at 10 kmph. Find his average speed during the entire journey.

Solution Recognise that the journey by bus and that by cycle are of equal distance. Hence, we can use the short cut illustrated earlier to solve this part of the problem.

Using the process explained above, we get average speed of the second half of the journey as

$$10 + 1 \times 5 = 15 \text{ kmph}$$

Then we employ the same technique for the first part and get

$$15 + 1 \times 9 = 24 \text{ kmph (Answer)}$$

Problem 3.7 A school has only 3 classes that contain 10, 20 and 30 students respectively. The pass percentage of these classes are 20% , 30% and 40% respectively. Find the pass percentage of the entire school.

Solution

Using weighted average: $\dfrac{10 \times 0.2 + 20 \times 0.3 + 30 \times 0.4}{10 + 20 + 30}$

$= \dfrac{20}{60} = 33.33\%$

Alternatively, we can also use solving-while-reading as

Space for Rough Work

Recognize that the pass percentage would be given by

$$\dfrac{\text{Passed students}}{\text{Total students}}$$

As soon as you get into the second line of the question get back to the first sentence and get the total number of passed students = 2 + 6 + 12 and you are through with the problem.

LEVEL OF DIFFICULTY (I)

1. The average age of 24 students and the principal is 15 years. When the principal's age is excluded, the average age decreases by 1 year. What is the age of the principal?
   - (a) 38
   - (b) 40
   - (c) 39
   - (d) 37

2. The average weight of 3 men A, B and C is 84 kg. Another man D joins the group and the average now becomes 80 kg. If another man E, whose weight is 3 kg more than that of D, replaces A then the average weight of B, C, D and E becomes 78 kg. The weight of A is
   - (a) 70 kg
   - (b) 72 kg
   - (c) 79 kg
   - (d) 78 kg

3. The mean temperature of Monday to Wednesday was 37 °C and of Tuesday to Thursday was 34 °C. If the temperature on Thursday was 4/5 that of Monday, the temperature on Thursday was
   - (a) 38 °C
   - (b) 36 °C
   - (c) 40 °C
   - (d) 39 °C

4. Three years ago, the average age of A, B and C was 27 years and that of B and C 5 years ago was 20 years. A's present age is
   - (a) 30 years
   - (b) 35 years
   - (c) 40 years
   - (d) 48 years

5. Ajit Tendulkar has a certain average for 9 innings. In the tenth inning, he scores 100 runs thereby increasing his average by 8 runs. His new average is
   - (a) 20
   - (b) 24
   - (c) 28
   - (d) 32

6. The average of the first five multiples of 7 is
   - (a) 20
   - (b) 21
   - (c) 28
   - (d) 30

7. There are three fractions A, B and C. If $A = \dfrac{1}{4}$ and B = 1/6 and the average of A, B and C is 1/12. What is the value of C?
   - (a) −1/2
   - (b) − 1/6
   - (c) −1/3
   - (d) − 1/4

8. The marks obtained by Hare Rama in Mathematics, English and Biology are respectively 93 out of 100, 78 out of 150 and 177 out of 200. Find his average score in percent.
   - (a) 87.83
   - (b) 86.83
   - (c) 76.33
   - (d) 77.33

9. The average monthly expenditure of a family was ₹ 2750 for the first 3 months, ₹ 3150 for the next three months and ₹ 6750 for the next three months. Find the average income of the family for the 9 months, if they save ₹ 650 per month.
   - (a) 4866.66
   - (b) 5123.33
   - (c) 4666.66
   - (d) 4216.66

10. The average age of a family of 6 members is 22 years. If the age of the youngest member be 7 years, what was the average age of the family at the birth of the youngest member?
    - (a) 15
    - (b) 18
    - (c) 21
    - (d) 12

11. The average age of 8 persons in a committee is increased by 2 years when two men aged 35 years and 45 years are substituted by two women. Find the average age of the two women.
    - (a) 48
    - (b) 45
    - (c) 51
    - (d) 42

12. The average temperature for Wednesday, Thursday and Friday was 40 °C. The average for Thursday, Friday and Saturday was 41 °C. If the temperature on Saturday was 42 °C, what was the temperature on Wednesday?
    - (a) 39 °C
    - (b) 44 °C
    - (c) 38 °C
    - (d) 41 °C

13. The speed of the train in going from Nagpur to Allahabad is 100 km/hr while when coming back from Allahabad to Nagpur, its speed is 150 km/hr. Find the average speed during the whole journey.
    - (a) 125
    - (b) 75
    - (c) 135
    - (d) 120

14. The average weight of a class of 29 students is 40 kg. If the weight of the teacher be included, the average rises by 500 gm. What is the weight of the teacher?
    - (a) 40.5 kg
    - (b) 50.5 kg
    - (c) 45 kg
    - (d) 55 kg

15. The average of 3 numbers is 17 and that of the first two is 16. Find the third number.
    - (a) 15
    - (b) 16
    - (c) 17
    - (d) 19

16. The average weight of 19 men in a ship is increased by 3.5 kg when one of the men, who weighs 79 kg, is replaced by a new man. Find the weight of the new man upto 2 decimal places
    - (a) 105.75
    - (b) 107.55
    - (c) 145.50
    - (d) 140.50

17. The age of Shaurya and Kauravki is in the ratio 2 : 6. After 5 years, the ratio of their ages will become 6 : 8. Find the average of their ages after 10 years.

(a) 12   (b) 13

(c) 17   (d) 24

18. Find the average of the first 97 natural numbers.

    (a) 47   (b) 37

    (c) 48   (d) 49

19. Find the average of all prime numbers between 30 and 50.

    (a) 39.8   (b) 38.8

    (c) 37.8   (d) 41.8

20. If we take four numbers, the average of the first three is 16 and that of the last three is 15. If the last number is 18, the first number is

    (a) 20   (b) 21

    (c) 23   (d) 25

21. The average of 5 consecutive numbers is n. If the next two numbers are also included, the average will.

    (a) increase by 1   (b) remain the same

    (c) increase by 1.4   (d) increase by 2

22. The average of 50 numbers is 38. If two numbers, namely, 45 and 55 are discarded, the average of the remaining numbers is

    (a) 36.5   (b) 37

    (c) 37.6   (d) 37.5

23. The average of ten numbers is 7. If each number is multiplied by 12, then the average of the new set of numbers is

    (a) 7   (b) 19

    (c) 82   (d) 84

24. In a family of 8 males and a few ladies, the average monthly consumption of grain per head is 10.8 kg. If the average monthly consumption per head be 15 kg in the case of males and 6 kg in the case of females, find the number of females in the family.

    (a) 8   (b) 7

    (c) 9   (d) 15

25. Average marks obtained by a student in 3 papers is 52 and in the fourth paper he obtains 60 marks. Find his new average.

    (a) 54   (b) 52

    (c) 55   (d) 53.5

26. The average earning of Shambhu Nath Pandey for the initial three months of the calendar year 2002 is ₹ 1200. If his average earning for the second and third month is ₹ 1300 find his earning in the first month?

    (a) 900   (b) 1100

    (c) 1000   (d) 1200

27. In a hotel where rooms are numbered from 101 to 130, each room gives an earning of ₹ 3000 for the first fifteen days of a month and for the latter half, ₹ 2000 per room. Find the average earning per room per day over the month. (Assume 30 day month)

(a) 2250   (b) 2500

(c) 2750   (d) 2466.66

28. The average weight of 5 men is decreased by 3 kg when one of them weighing 150 kg is replaced by another person. Find the weight of the new person.

    (a) 165 kg   (b) 135 kg

    (c) 138 kg   (d) 162 kg

29. The average age of a group of men is increased by 5 years when a person aged 18 years is replaced by a new person of aged 38 years. How many men are there in the group?

    (a) 3   (b) 4

    (c) 5   (d) 6

30. The average score of a cricketer in three matches is 22 runs and in two other matches, it is 17 runs. Find the average in all the five matches.

    (a) 20   (b) 19.6

    (c) 21   (d) 19.5

31. The average of 13 papers is 40. The average of the first 7 papers is 42 and of the last seven papers is 35. Find the marks obtained in the 7th paper.

    (a) 23   (b) 38

    (c) 19   (d) 39

32. The average age of the Indian cricket team playing the Nagpur test is 30. The average age of 5 of the players is 27 and that of another set of 5 players, totally different from the first five, is 29. If it is the captain who was not included in either of these two groups, then find the age of the captain.

    (a) 75   (b) 55

    (c) 50   (d) 58

33. Siddhartha has earned an average of 4200 dollars for the first eleven months of the year. If he justifies his staying on in the US on the basis of his ability to earn at least 5000 dollars per month for the entire year, how much should he earn (in dollars) in the last month to achieve his required average for the whole year?

    (a) 14,600   (b) 5,800

    (c) 12,800   (d) 13,800

34. A bus goes to Ranchi from Patna at the rate of 60 km per hour. Another bus leaves Ranchi for Patna at the same time as the first bus at the rate of 70 km per hour. Find the average speed for the journeys of the two buses combined if it is known that the distance from Ranchi to Patna is 420 kilometers.

    (a) 64.615 kmph   (b) 64.5 kmph

    (c) 63.823 kmph   (d) 64.82 kmph

35. A train travels 8 km in the first quarter of an hour, 6 km in the second quarter and 40 km in the third quarter. Find the average speed of the train per hour over the entire journey.

(a) 72 km/h   (b) 18 km/h
(c) 77.33 km/h   (d) 78.5 km/h

36. The average weight of 6 men is 68.5 kg. If it is known that Ram and Tram weigh 60 kg each, find the average weight of the others.
    (a) 72.75 kg   (b) 75 kg
    (c) 78 kg   (d) 80 kg

37. The average score of a class of 40 students is 52. What will be the average score of the rest of the students if the average score of 10 of the students is 61.
    (a) 50   (b) 47
    (c) 48   (d) 49

38. The average age of 80 students of IIM, Bangalore of the 1995 batch is 22 years. What will be the new average if we include the 20 faculty members whose average age is 37 years?
    (a) 32 years   (b) 24 years
    (c) 25 years   (d) 26 years

39. Out of three numbers, the first is twice the second and three times the third. The average of the three numbers is 88. The smallest number is
    (a) 72   (b) 36
    (c) 42   (d) 48

40. The sum of three numbers is 98. If the ratio between the first and second is $2:3$ and that between the second and the third is $5:8$, then the second number is
    (a) 30   (b) 20
    (c) 58   (d) 48

41. The average height of 30 girls out of a class of 40 is 160 cm and that of the remaining girls is 156 cm. The average height of the whole class is
    (a) 158 cm   (b) 158.5 cm
    (c) 159 cm   (d) 157 cm

42. The average weight of 6 persons is increased by 2.5 kg when one of them whose weight is 50 kg is replaced by a new man. The weight of the new man is
    (a) 65 kg   (b) 75 kg
    (c) 76 kg   (d) 60 kg

43. The average age of three boys is 15 years. If their ages are in the ratio $3:5:7$, the age of the youngest boy is
    (a) 21 years   (b) 18 years
    (c) 15 years   (d) 9 years

44. The average age of A, B, C and D five years ago was 45 years. By including X, the present average age of all the five is 49 years. The present age of X is
    (a) 64 years   (b) 48 years
    (c) 45 years   (d) 40 years

45. The average salary of 20 workers in an office is ₹1900 per month. If the manager's salary is added,

the average salary becomes ₹ 2000 per month. What is the manager's annual salary?
    (a) ₹ 24,000   (b) ₹ 25,200
    (c) ₹ 45,600   (d) None of these

46. If a, b, c, d and e are five consecutive odd numbers, then their average is
    (a) $5(a + b)$ (b) $(a\,b\,c\,d\,e)/5$
    (c) $5(a + b + c + d + e)$ (d) None of these

47. The average of first five multiples of 3 is
    (a) 3   (b) 9
    (c) 12   (d) 15

48. The average weight of a class of 40 students is 40 kg. If the weight of the teacher be included, the average weight increases by 500 gm. The weight of the teacher is
    (a) 40.5 kg   (b) 60 kg
    (c) 62 kg   (d) 60.5 kg

49. In a management entrance test, a student scores 2 marks for every correct answer and loses 0.5 marks for every wrong answer. A student attempts all the 100 questions and scores 120 marks. The number of questions he answered correctly was
    (a) 50   (b) 45
    (c) 60   (d) 6 8

50. The average age of four children is 8 years, which is increased by 4 years when the age of the father is included. Find the age of the father.
    (a) 32   (b) 2 8
    (c) 16   (d) 24

51. The average of the first ten natural numbers is
    (a) 5   (b) 5.5
    (c) 6.5   (d) 6

52. The average of the first ten whole numbers is
    (a) 4.5   (b) 5
    (c) 5.5   (d) 4

53. The average of the first ten even numbers is
    (a) 18   (b) 22
    (c) 9   (d) 11

54. The average of the first ten odd numbers is
    (a) 11   (b) 10
    (c) 17   (d) 9

55. The average of the first ten prime numbers is
    (a) 15.5   (b) 12.5
    (c) 10   (d) 12.9

56. The average of the first ten composite numbers is
    (a) 12.9   (b) 11
    (c) 11.2   (d) 10

57. The average of the first ten prime numbers, which are odd, is
    (a) 12.9   (b) 13.8
    (c) 17   (d) 15.8

58. The average weight of a class of 30 students is 40 kg. If, however, the weight of the teacher is included, the average becomes 41 kg. The weight of the teacher is
    (a) 31 kg   (b) 62 kg
    (c) 71 kg   (d) 70 kg

59. Ram bought 2 toys for ₹ 5.50 each, 3 toys for ₹ 3.66 each and 6 toys for ₹ 1.833 each. The average price per toy is
    (a) ₹ 3   (b) ₹ 10
    (c) ₹ 5   (d) ₹ 9

60. 30 oranges and 75 apples were purchased for ₹ 510. If the price per apple was ₹ 2, then the average price of oranges was
    (a) ₹ 12   (b) ₹ 14
    (c) ₹ 10   (d) ₹ 15

61. The average income of Sambhu and Ganesh is ₹ 3,000 and that of Arun and Vinay is ₹ 500. What is the average income of Sambhu, Ganesh, Arun and Vinay?
    (a) ₹ 1750   (b) ₹ 1850
    (c) ₹ 1000   (d) ₹ 2500

62. A batsman made an average of 40 runs in 4 innings, but in the fifth inning, he was out on zero. What is the average after fifth inning?
    (a) 32   (b) 22
    (c) 38   (d) 49

63. The average weight of 40 teachers of a school is 80 kg. If, however, the weight of the principal be included, the average decreases by 1 kg. What is the weight of the principal?
    (a) 109 kg   (b) 29 kg
    (c) 39 kg   (d) None of these

64. The average temperature of 1st, 2nd and 3rd December was 24.4 °C. The average temperature of the first two days was 24 °C. The temperature on the 3rd of December was
    (a) 20 °C   (b) 25 °C
    (c) 25.2 °C   (d) None of these

65. The average age of Ram and Shyam is 20 years. Their average age 5 years hence will be
    (a) 25 years   (b) 22 years
    (c) 21 years   (d) 20 years

66. The average of 20 results is 30 and that of 30 more results is 20. For all the results taken together, the average is
    (a) 25   (b) 50
    (c) 12   (d) 24

67. The average of 5 consecutive numbers is 18. The highest of these numbers will be
    (a) 24   (b) 18
    (c) 20   (d) 22

68. The average of 6 students is 11 years. If 2 more students of age 14 and 16 years join, their average will become
    (a) 12 years   (b) 13 years
    (c) 21 years   (d) 19 years

69. The average of 8 numbers is 12. If each number is increased by 2, the new average will be
    (a) 12   (b) 14
    (c) 13   (d) 15

70. Three years ago, the average age of a family of 5 members was 17 years. A baby having been born, the average of the family is the same today. What is the age of the baby?
    (a) 1 year   (b) 2 years
    (c) 6 months   (d) 9 months

71. Sambhu's average daily expenditure is ₹ 10 during May, ₹ 14 during June and ₹ 15 during July. His approximate daily expenditure for the 3 months is
    (a) ₹ 13 approximately
    (b) ₹ 12
    (c) ₹ 12 approximately
    (d) ₹ 10

72. A ship sails out to a mark at the rate of 15 km per hour and sails back at the rate of 20 km/h. What is its average rate of sailing?
    (a) 16.85 km   (b) 17.14 km
    (c) 17.85 km   (d) 18 km

73. The average temperature on Monday, Tuesday and Wednesday was 41 °C and on Tuesday, Wednesday and Thursday it was 40 °C. If on Thursday it was exactly 39 °C, then on Monday, the temperature was
    (a) 42 °C   (b) 46 °C
    (c) 23 °C   (d) 26 °C

74. The average of 20 results is 30 out of which the first 10 results are having an average of 10. The average of the rest 10 results is
    (a) 50   (b) 40
    (c) 20   (d) 25

75. A man had seven children. When their average age was 12 years a child aged 6 years died. The average age of the remaining 6 children is
    (a) 6 years   (b) 13 years
    (c) 17 years   (d) 15 years

76. The average income of Ram and Shyam is ₹ 200. The average income of Rahul and Rohit is ₹ 250. The average income of Ram, Shyam, Rahul and Rohit is
    (a) ₹ 275   (b) ₹ 225
    (c) ₹ 450   (d) ₹ 250

77. The average weight of 35 students is 35 kg. If the teacher is also included, the average weight increases to 36 kg. The weight of the teacher is

(a) 36 kg   (b) 71 kg
(c) 70 kg   (d) 45 kg

78. The average of x, y and z is 45. x is as much more than the average as y is less than the average. Find the value of z.
(a) 45   (b) 25
(c) 35   (d) 15

79. Find the average of four numbers $2\frac{3}{4}, 5\frac{1}{3}, 4\frac{1}{6}, 8\frac{1}{2}$.
(a) $5\frac{3}{16}$ (b) $3\frac{3}{16}$
(c) $16\frac{5}{3}$ (d) $3\frac{16}{5}$

80. The average salary per head of all the workers in a company is ₹ 95. The average salary of 15 officers is ₹ 525 and the average salary per head of the rest is ₹ 85. Find the total number of workers in the workshop.
(a) 660   (b) 580
(c) 650   (d) 460

81. The average age of 8 men is increased by 2 years when one of them whose age is 24 years is replaced by a woman. What is the age of the woman?

(a) 35 years   (b) 28 years
(c) 32 years   (d) 40 years

82. The average monthly expenditure of Ravi was ₹ 1100 during the first 3 months, ₹ 2200 during the next 4 months and ₹ 4620 during the subsequent five months of the year. If the total saving during the year was ₹ 2100, find Ravi's average monthly income.
(a) ₹ 1858   (b) ₹ 3108.33
(c) ₹ 3100   (d) None of these

83. Shyam bought 2 articles for ₹ 5.50 each, and 3 articles for ₹ 3.50 each, and 3 articles for ₹ 5.50 each and 5 articles for ₹ 1.50 each. The average price for one article is
(a) ₹ 3   (b) ₹ 3.10
(c) ₹ 3.50   (d) ₹ 2

84. In a bag, there are 150 coins of Re. 1, 50 p and 25 p denominations. If the total value of coins is ₹ 150, then find how many rupees can be constituted by 50 p coins.
(a) 16   (b) 20
(c) 28   (d) None of these

Space for Rough Work

LEVEL OF DIFFICULTY (II)

1. With an average speed of 40 km/h, a train reaches its destination in time. If it goes with an average speed of 35 km/h, it is late by 15 minutes. The length of the total journey is:
   - (a) 40 km
   - (b) 70 km
   - (c) 30 km
   - (d) 80 km

2. In the month of July of a certain year, the average daily expenditure of an organisation was ₹ 68. For the first 15 days of the month, the average daily expenditure was ₹ 85 and for the last 17 days, ₹ 51. Find the amount spent by the organisation on the 15th of the month.
   - (a) ₹ 42
   - (b) ₹ 36
   - (c) ₹ 34
   - (d) ₹ 52

3. In 1919, W. Rhodes, the Yorkshire cricketer, scored 891 runs for his county at an average of 34.27; in 1920, he scored 949 runs at an average of 28.75; in 1921, 1329 runs at an average of 42.87 and in 1922, 1101 runs at an average of 36.70. What was his county batting average for the four years?
   - (a) 36.23
   - (b) 37.81
   - (c) 35.88
   - (d) 28.72

4. A train travels with a speed of 20 m/s in the first 10 minutes, goes 8.5 km in the next 10 minutes, 11 km in the next 10, 8.5 km in the next 10 and 6 km in the next 10 minutes. What is the average speed of the train in kilometer per hour for the journey described?
   - (a) 42 kmph
   - (b) 35.8 kmph
   - (c) 55.2 kmph
   - (d) 46 kmph

5. One-fourth of a certain journey is covered at the rate of 25 km/h, one-third at the rate of 30 km/h and the rest at 50 km/h. Find the average speed for the whole journey.
   - (a) 600/53 km/h
   - (b) 1200/53 km/h
   - (c) 1800/53 km/h
   - (d) 1600/53

6. Typist A can type a sheet in 6 minutes, typist B in 7 minutes and typist C in 9 minutes. The average number of sheets typed per hour per typist for all three typists is
   - (a) 265/33
   - (b) 530/63
   - (c) 655/93
   - (d) 530/33

7. Find the average increase rate if increase in the population in the first year is 30% and that in the second year is 40%.
   - (a) 41
   - (b) 56
   - (c) 40
   - (d) 38

8. The average income of a person for the first 6 days is ₹ 29, for the next 6 days it is ₹ 24, for the next 10 days it is ₹ 32 and for the remaining days of the month it is ₹ 30. Find the average income per day.
   - (a) ₹ 31.64
   - (b) ₹ 30.64
   - (c) ₹ 29.26
   - (d) Cannot be determined

9. In hotel Jaysarmin, the rooms are numbered from 101 to 130 on the first floor, 221 to 260 on the second floor and 306 to 345 on the third floor. In the month of June 2012, the room occupancy was 60% on the first floor, 40% on the second floor and 75% on the third floor. If it is also known that the room charges are ₹ 200, ₹ 100 and ₹ 150 on each of the floors, then find the average income per room for the month of June 2012.
   - (a) ₹ 151.5
   - (b) ₹ 88.18
   - (c) ₹ 78.3
   - (d) ₹ 65.7

10. A salesman gets a bonus according to the following structure: If he sells articles worth ₹ x then he gets a bonus of ₹ $(x/100 - 1)$. In the month of January, his sales value was ₹ 100, in February it was ₹ 200, from March to November it was ₹ 300 for every month and in December it was ₹ 1200. Apart from this, he also receives a basic salary of ₹ 30 per month from his employer. Find his average income per month during the year.
    - (a) ₹ 31.25
    - (b) ₹ 30.34
    - (c) ₹ 32.5
    - (d) ₹ 34.5

11. A man covers half of his journey by train at 60 km/h, half of the remainder by bus at 30 km/h and the rest by cycle at 10 km/h. Find his average speed during the entire journey.
    - (a) 36 kmph
    - (b) 30 kmph
    - (c) 24 kmph
    - (d) 18 kmph

12. The average weight of 5 men is decreased by 3 kg when one of them weighing 150 kg is replaced by another person. This new person is again replaced by another person whose weight is 30 kg lower than the person he replaced. What is the overall change in the average due to this dual change?
    - (a) 6 kg
    - (b) 9 kg
    - (c) 12 kg
    - (d) 15 kg

13. Find the average weight of four containers, if it is known that the weight of the first container is 100 kg and the total of the second, third and fourth containers' weight is defined by $f(x) = x^2 - 3/4 (x^2)$ where $x = 100$

(a) 650 kg   (b) 900 kg

(c) 750 kg   (d) 450 kg

14. There are five boxes in a cargo hold. The weight of the first box is 200 kg and the weight of the second box is 20% higher than the weight of the third box, whose weight is 25% higher than the first box's weight. The fourth box at 350 kg is 30% lighter than the fifth box. Find the difference in the average weight of the four heaviest boxes and the four lightest boxes.

(a) 51.5 kg   (b) 75 kg

(c) 37.5 kg   (d) 112.5 kg

15. For Question 14, find the difference in the average weight of the heaviest three and the lightest three.

(a) 116.66 kg   (b) 125 kg

(c) 150 kg   (d) 112.5 kg

16. A batsman makes a score of 270 runs in the 87th inning and thus increases his average by a certain number of runs that is a whole number. Find the possible values of the new average.

(a) 98   (b) 184

(c) 12   (d) All of these

17. 19 persons went to a hotel for a combined dinner party. 13 of them spent ₹ 79 each on their dinner and the rest spent ₹ 4 more than the average expenditure of all the 19. What was the total money spent by them?

(a) 1628.4   (b) 1534

(c) 1492   (d) None of these

18. There were 42 students in a hostel. Due to the admission of 13 new students, the expenses of the mess increase by ₹ 31 per day while the average expenditure per head diminished by ₹ 3. What was the original expenditure of the mess?

(a) ₹ 633.23   (b) ₹ 583.3

(c) ₹ 623.3   (d) ₹ 632

19. The average price of 3 precious diamond studded platinum thrones is ₹ 97610498312 if their prices are in the ratio 4:7:9. The price of the cheapest is:

(a) 5, 65, 66, 298.972   (b) 5, 85, 66, 29, 897.2

(c) 58, 56, 62, 889.72   (d) None of these

20. The average weight of 47 balls is 4 gm. If the weight of the bag (in which the balls are kept) be included, the calculated average weight per ball increases by 0.3 gm. What is the weight of the bag?

(a) 14.8 gm   (b) 15.0 gm

(c) 18.6 gm   (d) None of these

21. The average of 71 results is 48. If the average of the first 59 results is 46 and that of the last 11 is 52. Find the 60th result.

(a) 132   (b) 122

(c) 134   (d) 128

22. A man covers 1/3rd of his journey by cycle at 50 km/h, the next 1/3 by car at 30 km/h, and the rest by walking at 7 km/h. Find his average speed during the whole journey.

(a) 14.2 kmph   (b) 15.3 kmph

(c) 18.2 kmph   (d) 12.8 kmph

23. The average age of a group of 14 persons is 27 years and 9 months. Two persons, each 42 years old, left the group. What will be the average age of the remaining persons in the group?

(a) 26.875 years   (b) 26.25 years

(c) 25.375 years   (d) 25 years

24. In an exam, the average was found to be x marks. After deducting computational error, the average marks of 94 candidates got reduced from 84 to 64. The average thus came down by 18.8 marks. The numbers of candidates who took the exam were:

(a) 100   (b) 90

(c) 110   (d) 105

25. The average salary of the entire staff in an office is ₹ 3200 per month. The average salary of officers is ₹ 6800 and that of non-officers is ₹ 2000. If the number of officers is 5, then find the number of non-officers in the office?

(a) 8   (b) 12

(c) 15   (d) 5

26. A person travels three equal distances at a speed of x km/h, y km/h and z km/h respectively. What will be the average speed during the whole journey?

(a) $xyz/(xy + yz + zx)$ (b) $(xy + yz + zx)/xyz$

(c) $3xyz/(xy + yz + xz)$ (d) None of these

Directions for Questions 27 to 30: Read the following passage and answer the questions that follow.

In a family of five persons A, B, C, D and E, each and everyone loves one another very much. Their birthdays are in different months and on different dates. A remembers that his birthday is between 25th and 30th, of B it is between 20th and 25th, of C it is between 10th and 20th, of D it is between 5th and 10th and of E it is between 1st to 5th of the month. The sum of the date of birth is defined as the addition of the date and the month, for example 12th January will be written as 12/1 and will add to a sum of the date of 13. (Between 25th and 30th includes both 25 and 30).

27. What may be the maximum average of their sum of the dates of birth?

(a) 24.6   (b) 15.2

(c) 28   (d) 32

28. What may be the minimum average of their sum of the dates of births?

(a) 24.6   (b) 15.2

(c) 28   (d) 32

29. If it is known that the dates of birth of three of them are even numbers then find maximum average of their sum of the dates of birth.
    (a) 24.6   (b) 15.2
    (c) 27.6   (d) 28

30. If the date of birth of four of them are prime numbers, then find the maximum average of the sum of their dates of birth.
    (a) 27.2   (b) 26.4
    (c) 28   (d) None of these

31. The average age of a group of persons going for a picnic is 16.75 years. 20 new persons with an average age of 13.25 years join the group on the spot due to which the average of the group becomes 15 years. Find the number of persons initially going for the picnic.
    (a) 24   (b) 20
    (c) 15   (d) 18

32. A school has only four classes that contain 10, 20, 30 and 40 students respectively. The pass percentage of these classes are 20%, 30%, 60% and 100% respectively. Find the pass % of the entire school.
    (a) 56%   (b) 76%
    (c) 34%   (d) 66%

33. Find the average of $f(x)$, $g(x)$, $h(x)$, $d(x)$ at $x = 10$. $f(x)$ is equal to $x^2 + 2$, $g(x) = 5x^2 - 3$, $h(x) = \log x^2$ and $d(x) = (4/5)x^2$
    (a) 170   (b) 170.25
    (c) 70.25   (d) 70

34. Find the average of $f(x) - g(x)$, $g(x) - h(x)$, $h(x) - d(x)$, $d(x) - f(x)$
    (a) 0   (b) −2.25
    (c) 4.5   (d) 2.25

35. $\sum_{r=1}^{n} (n+1)\, r$ where $r = n$.
    (a) $\dfrac{(n-1)(n)(n+1)}{2}$ (b) $\dfrac{n(n+1)^2}{2}$
    (c) $\dfrac{n(n-1)^2}{2}$ (d) $\dfrac{n^2}{2}$

36. The average of 'n' numbers is z. If the number x is replaced by the number x^1, then the average becomes z^1. Find the relation between n, z, z^1, x and x^1.
    (a) $\left[\dfrac{z^1 - 2}{x^1 - x} = \dfrac{1}{n}\right]$ (b) $\left[\dfrac{x^1 - x}{z^1} = \dfrac{1}{n}\right]$
    (c) $\left[\dfrac{z - z^1}{x - x^1} = \dfrac{1}{n}\right]$ (d) $\left[\dfrac{x - x^1}{z - z^1} = \dfrac{1}{n}\right]$

37. The average salary of workers in Mindworkzz is ₹ 2,000, the average salary of faculty being ₹ 4,000 and the management trainees being ₹ 1,250. The total number of workers could be
    (a) 450   (b) 300
    (c) 110   (d) 500

Directions for Questions 38 to 41: Read the following and answer the questions that follows.

During a criket match, India playing against NZ scored in the following manner:

Partnership	Runs scored
1st wicket	112
2nd wicket	58
3rd wicket	72
4th wicket	92
5th wicket	46
6th wicket	23

38. Find the average runs scored by the first four batsmen.
    (a) 83.5   (b) 60.5
    (c) 66.8   (d) Cannot be determined

39. The maximum average runs scored by the first five batsmen could be
    (a) 80.6   (b) 66.8
    (c) 76   (d) Cannot be determined.

40. The minimum average runs scored by the last five batsmen to get out could be
    (a) 53.6   (b) 44.4
    (c) 66.8   (d) 0

41. If the fifth down batsman gets out for a duck, then find the average runs scored by the first six batsmen.
    (a) 67.1   (b) 63.3
    (c) 48.5   (d) Cannot be determined

42. The weight of a body as calculated by the average of 7 different experiments is 53.735 gm. The average of the first three experiments is 54.005 gm, of the fourth is 0.004 gm greater than the fifth, while the average of the sixth and seventh experiment was 0.010 gm less than the average of the first three. Find the weight of the body obtained by the fourth experiment.
    (a) 49.353 gm   (b) 51.712 gm
    (c) 53.072 gm   (d) 54.512 gm

43. A man's average expenditure for the first 4 months of the year was ₹ 251.25. For the next 5 months the average monthly expenditure was ₹ 26.27 more than what it was during the first 4 months. If the person spent ₹ 760 in all during the remaining 3 months of the year, find what percentage of his annual income of ₹ 3000 he saved in the year.
    (a) 14%   (b) −5.0866%
    (c) 12.5%   (d) None of these

44. A certain number of trucks were required to transport 60 tons of steel wire from the TISCO factory in Jamshedpur. However, it was found that since each truck could take 0.5 tons of cargo less, another 4 trucks were needed. How many trucks were initially planned to be used?

    (a) 10   (b) 15
    (c) 20   (d) 25

45. One collective farm got an average harvest of 21 tons of wheat and another collective farm that had 12 acres of land less given to wheat, got 25 tons from a hectare. As a result, the second farm harvested 300 tons of wheat more than the first. How many tons of wheat did each farm harvest?

    (a) 3150, 3450   (b) 3250, 3550
    (c) 2150, 2450   (d) None of these

Space for Rough Work

LEVEL OF DIFFICULTY (III)

Directions for Questions 1 to 8:   Read the following:

There are 3 classes having 20, 25 and 30 students respectively having average marks in an examination as 20, 25 and 30 respectively. If the three classes are represented by *A*, *B* and *C* and you have the following information about the three classes, answer the questions that follow:

$$A \rightarrow \text{Highest score 22, Lowest score 18}$$
$$B \rightarrow \text{Highest score 31, Lowest score 23}$$
$$C \rightarrow \text{Highest score 33, Lowest score 26}$$

If five students are transferred from *A* to *B*.

1. What will happen to the average score of *B*?
   (a) Definitely increase (b) Definitely decrease
   (c) Remain constant   (d) Cannot say
2. What will happen to the average score of *A*?
   (a) Definitely increase (b) Definitely decrease
   (c) Remain constant   (d) Cannot say

In a transfer of 5 students from *A* to *C*

3. What will happen to the average score of *C*?
   (a) Definitely increase (b) Definitely decrease
   (c) Remain constant   (d) Cannot say
4. What will happen to the average score of *A*?
   (a) Definitely increase (b) Definitely decrease
   (c) Remain constant   (d) Cannot say

In a transfer of 5 students from *B* to *C* (Questions 5–6)

5. What will happen to the average score of *C*?
   (a) Definitely increase (b) Definitely decrease
   (c) Remain constant   (d) Cannot say
6. Which of these can be said about the average score of *B*?
   (a) Increases if *C* decreases
   (b) Decreases if *C* increases
   (c) Increases if *C* decreases
   (d) Decreases if *C* decreases
7. In a transfer of 5 students from *A* to *B*, the maximum possible average achievable for group *B* is
   (a) 25   (b) 24.5
   (c) 25.5   (d) 24
8. For the above case, the maximum possible average achieved for group *A* will be
   (a) 20.66   (b) 21.5
   (c) 20.75   (d) 20.5
9. What will be the minimum possible average of Group *A* if 5 students are transferred from *A* to *B*?

10. (a) 19.55   (b) 21.5
    (c) 19.33   (d) 20.5
11. If 5 students are transferred from *B* to *A*, what will be the minimum possible average of *A*?
    (a) 20.69   (b) 21
    (c) 20.75   (d) 20.6
12. For question 10, what will be the maximum average of *A*?
    (a) 23.2   (b) 22.2
    (c) 18.75   (d) 19

Directions for Questions 12 to 17:   Read the following and answer the questions that follow.

If 5 people are transferred from *A* to *B* and another independent set of 5 people are transferred back from *B* to *A*, then after this operation (Assume that the set transferred from *B* to *A* contains none from the set of students that came to *B* from *A*)

12. What will happen to *B*'s average?
    (a) Increase if *A*'s average decreases
    (b) Decrease always
    (c) Cannot be said
    (d) Decrease if *A*'s average decreases
13. What can be said about *A*'s average?
    (a) Will decrease
    (b) Will always increase if *B*'s average changes
    (c) May increase or decrease
    (d) Will increase only if *B*'s average decreases
14. At the end of the 2 steps mentioned above (in the *direction*) what could be the maximum value of the average of class *B*?
    (a) 25.4   (b) 25
    (c) 24.8   (d) 24.6
15. For question 14, what could be the minimum value of the average of class *B*?
    (a) 22.4   (b) 24.2
    (c) 25   (d) 23
16. What could be the maximum possible average achieved by class *A* at the end of the operation?
    (a) 25.2   (b) 26
    (c) 23.25   (d) 23.75
17. What could be the minimum possible average of class *A* at the end of the operation?
    (a) 21.4   (b) 19.2
    (c) 28.5   (d) 20.25

Directions for Questions 18 to 23:   Read the following and answer the questions that follow.

If 5 people are transferred from *C* to *B*, further, 5 more people are transferred from *B* to *A*, then 5 are transferred from *A* to *B* and finally, 5 more are transferred from *B* to *C*.

18. What is the maximum possible average achieved by class *C*?
    (a) 30.833
    (b) 30
    (c) 29.66
    (d) 30.66

19. What is the maximum possible average of class *B*?
    (a) 26
    (b) 27
    (c) 25
    (d) 28

20. What is the maximum possible average value attained by class *A*?
    (a) 22.75
    (b) 23.75
    (c) 23.5
    (d) 24

21. The minimum possible value of the average of group *C* is:
    (a) 26.3
    (b) 27.5
    (c) 29.6
    (d) 28

22. The minimum possible average of group *B* after this set of operation is
    (a) 21.6
    (b) 21.4
    (c) 21.8
    (d) 21.2

23. The minimum possible average of group *A* after the set of 3 operation is
    (a) 20
    (b) 20.3
    (c) 20.4
    (d) 19.8

24. Which of these will definitely not constitute an operation for getting the minimum possible average value for group *A*:
    (a) Transfer of five 31s from *B* to *A*
    (b) Transfer of five 26s from *C* to *B*
    (c) Transfer of five 22s from *A* to *B*
    (d) Transfer of five 33s from *C* to *B*

25. For getting the lowest possible value of *C*'s average, the sequence of operations could be
    (a) Transfer five 33s from *C* to *B*, five 23s from *B* to *A*, five 18s from *A* to *B*, five 18s from *B* to *C*
    (b) Transfer five 33s from *C* to *B*, 31s from *B* to *A*,
    (c) Both a and b
    (d) None of the above

26. If we set the highest possible average of class *C* as the primary objective and want to achieve the highest possible value for class *B* as the secondary objective, what is the maximum value of class *B*'s average that is attainable?
    (a) 27
    (b) 26
    (c) 25
    (d) 24

27. For Question 26, if the secondary objective is changed to achieving the minimum possible average value of class *B*'s average, the lowest value of class *B*'s average that could be attained is

    (a) 22.2
    (b) 23
    (c) 22.6
    (d) 22

28. For question 27, what can be said about class *A*'s average?
    (a) Will be determined automatically at 22.25
    (b) Will have a maximum possible value of 22.25
    (c) Will have a minimum possible value of 22.25
    (d) Will be determined automatically at 22.5

29. A team of miners planned to mine 1800 tons of ore during a certain number of days. Due to technical difficulties in one-third of the planned number of days, the team was able to achieve an output of 20 tons of ore less than the planned output. To make up for this, the team overachieved for the rest of the days by 20 tons. The end result was that the team completed the task one day ahead of time. How many tons of ore did the team initially plan to ore per day?
    (a) 50 tons
    (b) 100 tons
    (c) 150 tons
    (d) 200 tons

30. According to a plan, a team of woodcutters decided to harvest 216 m³ of wheat in several days. In the first three days, the team fulfilled the daily assignment, and then it harvested 8 m³ of wheat over and above the plan everyday. Therefore, a day before the planned date, they had already harvested 232 m³ of wheat. How many cubic metres of wheat a day did the team have to cut according to the plan?
    (a) 12
    (b) 13
    (c) 24
    (d) 25

31. On an average, two liters of milk and one liter of water are needed to be mixed to make 1 kg of sudha shrikhand of type *A*, and 3 liters of milk and 2 liters of water are needed to be mixed to make 1 kg of sudha shrikhand of type *B*. How many kilograms of each type of shrikhand was manufactured if it is known that 130 liters of milk and 80 liters of water were used?
    (a) 20 of type *A* and 30 of type *B*
    (b) 30 of type *A* and 20 of type *B*
    (c) 15 of type *A* and 30 of type *B*
    (d) 30 of type *A* and 15 of type *B*

32. There are 500 seats in Minerva Cinema, Mumbai, placed in similar rows. After the reconstruction of the hall, the total number of seats became 10% less. The number of rows was reduced by 5 but each row contained 5 seats more than before. How many rows and how many seats in a row were there initially in the hall?
    (a) 20 rows and 25 seats
    (b) 20 rows and 20 seats
    (c) 10 rows and 50 seats
    (d) 50 rows and 10 seats

33. One fashion house has to make 810 dresses and another one 900 dresses during the same period of time. In the first house, the order was ready 3 days ahead of time and in the second house, 6 days ahead of time. How many dresses did each fashion house make a day if the second house made 21 dresses more a day than the first?

    (a) 54 and 75   (b) 24 and 48

    (c) 44 and 68   (d) 04 and 25

34. A shop sold 64 kettles of two different capacities. The smaller kettle cost a rupee less than the larger one. The shop made 100 rupees from the sale of large kettles and 36 rupees from the sale of small ones. How many kettles of either capacity did the shop sell and what was the price of each kettle?

    (a) 20 kettles for 2.5 rupees each and 14 kettles for 1.5 rupees each

    (b) 40 kettles for 4.5 rupees each and 24 kettles for 2.5 rupees each

    (c) 40 kettles for 2.5 rupees each and 24 kettles for 1.5 rupees each

    (d) either a or b

35. An enterprise got a bonus and decided to share it in equal parts between the exemplary workers. It turned out, however, that there were 3 more exemplary workers than it had been assumed. In that case, each of them would have got 4 rupees less. The administration had found the possibility to increase the total sum of the bonus by 90 rupees and as a result each exemplary worker got 25 rupees. How many people got the bonus?

    (a) 9   (b) 18

    (c) 8   (d) 16

Directions for Questions 36 to 39: Read the following and answer the questions that follows.

In the island of Hoola Boola Moola, the inhabitants have a strange process of calculating their average incomes and expenditures. According to an old legend prevalent on that island, the average monthly income had to be calculated on the basis of 14 months in a calendar year while the average monthly expenditure was to be calculated on the basis of 9 months per year. This would lead to people having an underestimation of their savings since there would be an underestimation of the income and an overestimation of the expenditure per month.

36. If the minister for economic affairs decided to reverse the process of calculation of average income and average expenditure, what will happen to the estimated savings of a person living on Hoola Boola Moola island?

    (a) It will increase

    (b) It will decrease

    (c) It will remain constant

    (d) Will depend on the value

37. If it is known that Mr. Magoo Hoola Boola estimates his savings at 10 Moolahs and if it is further known that his actual expenditure is 288 Moolahs in an year (Moolahs, for those who are not aware, is the official currency of Hoola Boola Moola), then what will happen to his estimated savings if he suddenly calculates on the basis of a 12 month calendar year?

    (a) Will increase by 5   (b) Will increase by 15

    (c) Will increase by 10   (d) Will triple

38. Mr. Boogie Woogie comes back from the USA to Hoola Boola Moola and convinces his community comprising 546 families to start calculating the average income and average expenditure on the basis of 12 months per calendar year. Now if it is known that the average estimated income on the island is (according to the old system) 87 Moolahs per month, then what will be the change in the average estimated savings for the island of Hoola Boola Moola. (Assume that there is no other change).

    (a) 251.60 Moolahs   (b) 565.5 Moolahs

    (c) 625.5 Moolahs   (d) Cannot be determined

39. Mr. Boogle Woogle comes back from the USSR and convinces his community comprising 273 families to start calculating the average income on the basis of 12 months per calendar year. Now if it is known that the average estimated income in his community is (according to the old system) 87 Moolahs per month, then what will be the change in the average estimated savings for the island of Hoola Boola Moola. (Assume that there is no other change).

    (a) 251.60 Moolahs   (b) 282.75 Moolahs

    (c) 312.75 Moolahs   (d) Cannot be determined

Directions for Questions 40 to 44: Read the following and answer the questions that follows.

The Indian cricket team has to score 360 runs on the last day of a test match in 90 overs, to win the test match. This is the target set by the opposing captain Brian Lara after he declared his innings closed at the overnight score of 411 for 7.

The Indian team coach has the following information about the batting rates (in terms of runs per over) of the different batsmen:

Assume that the run rate of a partnership is the weighted average of the individual batting rates of the batsmen involved in the partnership (on the basis of the ratio of the strike each batsman gets, i.e. the run rate of a partnership is defined as the weighted average of the run rates of the two batsmen involved weighted by the ratio of the number of balls faced by each batsman).

Since decimal fractions of runs are not possible for any batsman, assume that the estimated runs scored by a batsman in an inning (on the basis of his run rate and the number of overs faced by him) is rounded off to the next higher integer immediately above the estimated value of the runs scored during the innings.

For example, if a batsman scores at an average of 3 runs per over for 2.1666 overs, then he will be estimated to have scored $2.1666 \times 3 = 6.5$ runs in his innings, but since this is not possible, the actual number of runs scored by the batsman will be taken as 7 (the next higher integer above 6.5).

Runs scored per over in different batting styles

Name of Batsman	Defensive	Normal	Aggressive
Das	3	4	5
Dasgupta	2	3	4
Dravid	2	3	4
Tendulkar	4	6	8
Laxman	4	5	6
Sehwag	4	5	6
Ganguly	3	4	5
Kumble	2	3	4
Harbhajan	3	4	5
Srinath	3	4	5
Yohannan	2	3	4

Also, this rounding off can take place only once for one innings of a batsman.

Assume no extras unless otherwise stated.

Assume that the strike is equally shared unless otherwise stated.

40. If the first wicket pair of Das and Dasgupta bats for 22 overs and during this partnership Das has started batting normally and turned aggressive after 15 overs while Dasgupta started off defensively but shifted gears to bat normally after batting for 20 overs, find the expected score after 22 overs.
    (a) 65   (b) 71
    (c) 82   (d) 58

41. Of the first-wicket partnership between Das and Dasgupta as per the previous question, the ratio of the number of runs scored by Das to those scored by Dasgupta is:
    (a) 46:25   (b) 96:46
    (c) 41:32   (d) Cannot be determined

42. The latest time by which Tendulkar can come to bat and still win the game, assuming that the run rate at the time of his walking the wicket is into 2.5 runs per over, is (assuming he shares strike equally with his partner and that he gets the maximum possible support at the other end from his batting partner and both play till the last ball).

(a) After 50 overs   (b) After 55 overs
(c) After 60 overs   (d) Cannot be determined

43. For question 42, where Tendulkar batted aggressively and assuming that it is the Tendulkar-Laxman pair that wins the game for India (after Tendulkar walks into bat with the current run rate at 2.5 per over, and at the latest possible time for him to win the game with maximum possible support from the opposite end), what will be Tendulkar's score for the innings (assume equal strike)?
    (a) 105   (b) 120
    (c) 135   (d) None of these

44. For questions 42 and 43, if it was Laxman who batted with Tendulkar for his entire innings, then how many runs would Laxman score in the innings?
    (a) 105   (b) 75
    (c) 90   (d) Cannot be determined

Directions for Questions 45 to 49: Read the following and answer the questions that follow.

If Sachin Tendulkar walks into bat after the fall of the fifth wicket and has to share partnerships with Ganguly, Kumble, Harbhajan, Srinath and Yohannan, who have batted normally, defensively, defensively, defensively and defensively respectively while Tendulkar has batted normally, aggressively, aggressively, aggressively and aggressively respectively in each of the five partnerships that lasted for 12, 10, 8, 5 and 10 overs respectively, sharing strike equally with Ganguly and keeping two-thirds of the strike in his other four partnerships, then answer the following questions:

45. How many runs did Sachin score during his innings?
    (a) 128   (b) 212
    (c) 176   (d) None of these

46. The highest partnership that Tendulkar shared in was worth:
    (a) 60   (b) 61
    (c) 62   (d) 58

47. The above partnership was shared with:
    (a) Ganguly   (b) Yohannan
    (c) Kumble   (d) All three

48. If India proceeded to win the match based on the runs scored by these last five partnerships (assuming the last wicket pair remained unbeaten), what could be the maximum score at which Tendulkar could have come into bat:
    (a) 103 for 5   (b) 97 for 5
    (c) 100 for 5   (d) 104 for 5

49. For Question 48, what could be the minimum score at which Tendulkar could have come to bat:
    (a) 103 for 5   (b) 97 for 5
    (c) 104 for 5   (d) 98 for 5

ANSWER KEY

Level of Difficulty (I)

1. (c)	2. (c)	3. (b)	4. (c)
5. (c)	6. (b)	7. (b)	8. (d)
9. (a)	10. (b)	11. (a)	12. (a)
13. (d)	14. (d)	15. (d)	16. (c)
17. (a)	18. (d)	19. (a)	20. (b)
21. (a)	22. (d)	23. (d)	24. (b)
25. (a)	26. (c)	27. (b)	28. (b)
29. (b)	30. (a)	31. (c)	32. (c)
33. (d)	34. (a)	35. (a)	36. (a)
37. (d)	38. (c)	39. (d)	40. (a)
41. (c)	42. (a)	43. (d)	44. (c)
45. (d)	46. (d)	47. (b)	48. (d)
49. (d)	50. (b)	51. (b)	52. (a)
53. (d)	54. (b)	55. (d)	56. (c)
57. (d)	58. (c)	59. (a)	60. (a)
61. (a)	62. (a)	63. (c)	64. (c)
65. (a)	66. (d)	67. (c)	68. (a)
69. (b)	70. (b)	71. (a)	72. (b)
73. (a)	74. (a)	75. (b)	76. (b)
77. (b)	78. (a)	79. (a)	80. (a)
81. (d)	82. (b)	83. (c)	84. (d)

Level of Difficulty (II)

1. (b)	2. (c)	3. (c)	4. (c)
5. (c)	6. (b)	7. (a)	8. (d)
9. (a)	10. (c)	11. (c)	12. (a)
13. (a)	14. (b)	15. (a)	16. (d)
17. (d)	18. (a)	19. (d)	20. (d)
21. (b)	22. (b)	23. (c)	24. (a)
25. (c)	26. (c)	27. (c)	28. (b)
29. (d)	30. (a)	31. (b)	32. (d)
33. (b)	34. (a)	35. (b)	36. (c)
37. (c)	38. (d)	39. (a)	40. (d)
41. (d)	42. (c)	43. (b)	44. (c)
45. (a)			

Level of Difficulty (III)

1. (b)	2. (d)	3. (b)	4. (d)
5. (d)	6. (b)	7. (b)	8. (a)
9. (c)	10. (d)	11. (b)	12. (b)
13. (b)	14. (c)	15. (a)	16. (c)
17. (d)	18. (a)	19. (b)	20. (b)
21. (b)	22. (b)	23. (a)	24. (a)
25. (a)	26. (d)	27. (c)	28. (a)
29. (b)	30. (c)	31. (a)	32. (a)
33. (a)	34. (c)	35. (b)	36. (a)
37. (b)	38. (d)	39. (b)	40. (b)
41. (b)	42. (c)	43. (b)	44. (d)
45. (b)	46. (b)	47. (b)	48. (d)
49. (b)			

Level of Difficulty (I)

1. $P = 25 \times 15 - 24 \times 14 = 375 - 336 = 39$

2. D's weight = $4 \times 80 - 3 \times 84 = 320 - 252 = 68$.
   E's weight = $68 + 3 = 71$.
   Now, we know that $A + B + C + D = 4 \times 80 = 320$ and $B + C + D + E = 78 \times 4 = 312$. Hence, A's weight is 8 kg more than E's weight. $A = 71 + 8 = 79$.

3. Monday + Tuesday + Wednesday = $3 \times 37 = 111$;
   Tuesday + Wednesday + Thursday = $3 \times 34 = 102$.
   Thus, Monday – Thursday = 9 and
   Thursday = $4 \times$ Monday/5 → Thursday = 36 and Monday = 45.

4. Today's total age of A, B and C = $30 \times 3 = 90$.
   Today's total age for B and C = $25 \times 2 = 50$.
   C's age = $90 - 50 = 40$.

5. $9x + 100 = 10(x + 8) \rightarrow x = 20$ (average after 9 innings). Hence, new average = $20 + 8 = 28$.

6. $7 \times 3 = 21$.

7. $1/4 + 1/6 + C = 3 \times 1/12 \rightarrow C = -1/6$.

8. His total score is $93 + 78 + 177 = 348$ out of 450.
   % score = 77.33

9. Average income over 9 months = [$3 \times (2750 + 650) + 3 \times (3150 + 650) + 3 \times (6750+650)]/9$
   = [$3 \times 3400 + 3 \times 3800 + 3 \times 7400]/9 = 4866.66$

10. Today's total age = $6 \times 22 = 132$ years. Total age of the family excluding the youngest member (for the remaining 5 people) = $132 - 7 = 125$. Average age of the other 5 people in the family = 25 years.
    7 years ago their average age = $25 - 7 = 18$ years.

11. If the average age of 8 people has gone up by 2 years it means the total age has gone up by 16 years. Thus the total age of the two women would be: $35 + 45 + 16 = 96$. Hence, their average age = 48.

12. $W + T + F = 120$; $T + F + S = 123 \rightarrow S - W = 3$.
    Hence temperature on Wednesday = $42 - 3 = 39$.

13. The average speed can be calculated by assuming a distance of 300 km (LCM of 100 and 150). Then time taken @ 100 kmph = 3 hours and time taken @ 150kmph = 2 hours. Average speed = Total distance/total time = $600/5 = 120$ kmph.

14. Teacher's weight = $40.5 \times 30 - 40 \times 29 = 1215 - 1160 = 55$.

15. $3 \times 17 - 2 \times 16 = 51 - 32 = 19$.

16. The weight of the new man would be 19×3.5 kgs more than the weight of the man he replaces. New man's weight = $79 + 19 \times 3.5 = 145.5$ kgs.

17. Let their current ages be x and $3x$ (ratio of 2:6). Then their ages after 5 years would be $x + 5$ and $3x + 5$. Now it is given that $(x + 5)/(3x + 5) = ¾ \rightarrow x = 1$ and hence their current ages are 1 years and 3 years

respectively. After 10 years their average age would be 12 years.

18. The average would be given by the average of the first and last numbers (since the series 1, 2, 3, 4...97 is an Arithmetic Progression).
Hence, the average = $(1 + 97)/2 = 49$

19. We need the average of the numbers: 31, 37, 41, 43 and 47
Average = Total/number of numbers → $199/5 = 39.8$

20. Let the numbers be a, b, c and d respectively. $a + b + c = 16 \times 3 = 48$ and $b + c + d = 15 \times 3 = 45$. Also, since $d = 18$, we have $b + c = 45 - 18 = 27$. Hence, $a = 48 - (b + c) \to a = 21$.

21. If the numbers are $a + 1$, $a + 2$, $a + 3$, $a + 4$ and $a + 5$ the average would be $a + 3$. If we take 7 numbers as:
$a + 1$, $a + 2$, $a + 3$, $a + 4$, $a + 5$, $a + 6$ and $a + 7$ their average would be a+4. Hence, the average increases by 1.

22. Total of 48 numbers = $50 \times 38 - 45 - 55 = 1800$. Average of 48 numbers = $1800/48 = 37.5$.

23. When we multiply each number by 12, the average would also get multiplied by 12. Hence, the new average = $7 \times 12 = 84$.

24. Let the number of ladies be n. Then we have $8 \times 15 + n \times 6 = (8 + n) \times (10.8) \to 120 + 6n = 86.4 + 10.8n \to 4.8n = 33.6 \to n = 7$.

25. $(3 \times 52 + 60)/4 = 216/4 = 54$.

26. $1200 \times 3 - 1300 \times 2 = 1000$.

27. $(2000 \times 15 + 3000 \times 15)/30 = (2000 + 3000)/2 = 2500$.

28. The decrease in weight would be 15 kgs (5 people's average weight drops by 3 kgs). Hence, the new person's weight = $150 \times 15 = 135$.

29. When a person aged 18 years is replaced by a person aged 38 years, the total age of the group goes up by 20 years. Since this leads to an increase in the average by 5 years, it means that there are $20/5 = 4$ persons in the group.

30. $(22 \times 3 + 17 \times 2)/5 = 100/5 = 20$.

31. Let the number of marks in the 7th paper be M. Then the total of the first seven papers = 7×42 while the total of the last 7 (i.e. 7th to 13th papers) would be 7×35.
Total of 1st 7 + total of 7th to 13th = total of all 13 + marks in the 7th paper →
$7 \times 42 + 7 \times 35 = 13 \times 40 + M$
$539 = 520 + M \to M = 19$.
(**Note:** We write this equation since marks in the seventh paper is counted in both the first 7 and the last 7)

32. Let the captain's age by C. Then: $11 \times 30 = 27 \times 5 + 29 \times 5 + C \to 330 = 135 + 145 + C \to C = 50$.

33. His earning in the 12th month should be: $5000 \times 12 - 4200 \times 11 = 60000 - 46200 = 13800$.

34. Total distance by total time = $840/13 = 64.615$.

35. In three quarters of an hour the train has traveled 54 km. Thus, in a full hour the train would have traveled 1/3rd more (as it gets 1/3rd time more). Thus, the speed of the train = $54 + 1 \times 54/3 = 54 + 18 = 72$.

36. Total weight of all 6 = 68.5×6. Total weight of Ram and Tram = $60 \times 2 = 120$. Average weight of the 4 people excluding Ram and Tram = $(68.5 \times 6 - 120)/4 = 72.75$ kg.

37. $10 \times 61 + 30 \times A = 40 \times 52 \to A = (2080 - 610)/30 = 1470/30 = 49$.

38. $(80 \times 22 + 20 \times 37)/100 = 2500/100 = 25$

39. If we take the first number as 6n, the second number would be 3n and the third would be 2n. Sum of the three numbers = $6n + 3n + 2n = 11n = 88 \times 3 \to n = 24$. The smallest number would be $2n = 48$.

40. The ratio between the first, second and third would be: 10:15:24. Since their total is 98, the numbers would be 20, 30 and 48 respectively. The second number is 30.

41. $(30 \times 160 + 10 \times 156)/40 = 159$. (note this question can also be solved using the alligation method explained in the next chapter.

42. The total weight of the six people goes up by 15 kgs (when the average for 6 persons goes up by 2.5 kg). Thus, the new person must be 15 kgs more than the person who he replaces. Hence, the new person's weight = $50 + 15 = 65$ kg.

43. Total age = $3 \times 15 = 45$. Individual ages being in the ratio 3:5:7 their ages would be 9, 15 and 21 years respectively. The youngest boy would be 9 years.

44. $50 \times 4 + X = 49 \times 5 \to X = 45$.

45. $(20 \times 1900 + M) = 21 \times 2000 \to M = 4000$. Hence, the salary is ₹ 4000 per month which also means ₹ 48,000 per year.

46. 5 consecutive odd numbers would always be in an Arithmetic progression and their average would be the middle number. The average would be 'c' in this case.

47. The average of 3, 6, 9, 12 and 15 would be 9.

48. $40 \times 40 + T = 41 \times 40.5 \to T = 1660.5 - 1600 = 60.5$ kgs.

49. If the number of questions correct is N, then the number of wrong answers is $100 - N$. Using this we get:
$N \times 2 - (100 - N) \times 0.5 = 120 \to 2.5 N = 170 \to N = 68$.

50. Required age of the father will be given by the equation: $5 \times 12 = 4 \times 8 + F \to F = 28$.

51. Required average = $(1 + 2 + 3 + ... + 10)/10 = 55/10 = 5.5$. Alternately you could use the formula

for sum of the first n natural numbers as $n(n + 1)/2$ with n as 10. Then average = Sum/10 = $10 \times 11/2 \times 10$ = 5.5

52. Required average = $(0 + 1 + 2 + ... + 9)/10 = 45/10$ = 4.5

53. Required average = $(2 + 4 + 6 + 8 + 10 + 12 + 14 + 16 + 18 + 20)/10 = 110/10 = 11$. Alternately you could use the formula for sum of the first n even natural numbers as $n(n + 1)$ with n as 10. Then average = Sum/10 = $10 \times 11/10 = 11$.

54. The sum of the first n odd numbers = n^2. In this case $n = 10 \rightarrow$ Sum = $10^2 = 100$. Required average = $100/10 = 10$.

55. Required average = $(2 + 3 + 5 + 7 + 11 + 13 + 17 + 19 + 23 + 29)/10 = 129/10 = 12.9$

56. Required average = $(4 + 6 + 8 + 9 + 10 + 12 + 14 + 15 + 16 + 18)/10 = 112/10 = 11.2$

57. Required average = $(3 + 5 + 7 + 11 + 13 + 17 + 19 + 23 + 29 + 31)/10 = 158/10 = 15.8$

58. Teacher's weight = $31 \times 41 - 30 \times 40 = 1271 - 1200 = 71$.

59. Required average = $(2 \times 5.5 + 3 \times 3.666 + 6 \times 1.8333)/11 = (11 + 11 + 11)/11 = 3$

60. $30 \times P + 75 \times 2 = 510 \rightarrow P = (510 - 150)/30 = 12$

61. Required average = $(2 \times 3000 + 2 \times 500)/4 = 7000/4$ = 1750.

62. Required average = Total runs/ total innings = $(40 \times 4 + 0)/5 = 160/5 = 32$.

63. Principal's weight = $41 \times 79 - 40 \times 80 = 3239 - 3200 = 39$.

64. Temperature on 3rd December = $24.4 \times 3 - 24 \times 2 = 73.2 - 48 = 25.2$

65. Average age 5 years hence would be 5 years more than the current average age. Hence, $20 + 5 = 25$.

66. Required average = $(20 \times 30 + 30 \times 20)/50 = 1200/50$ = 24.

67. The numbers would form an AP with common difference 1 and the middle term (also the 3rd term) as 18. Thus, the numbers would be 16, 17, 18, 19 and 20. The highest of these numbers would be 20.

68. Required average = $(6 \times 11 + 14 + 16)/8 = 96/8 = 12$

69. The new average would also go up by 2. Hence, $12 + 2 = 14$.

70. Total age 3 years ago for 5 people = $17 \times 5 = 85$. Today, the family's total age = $17 \times 6 = 102$. The age of the 5 older people would be $85 + 3 \times 5 = 100$. Hence, the baby's age is 2 years.

71. Required average = $(10 \times 31 + 14 \times 30 + 15 \times 31)/92 = (310 + 420 + 465)/92 = 12.98$ (which is closest to 13.

72. Assume a distance of 60 km. In such a case, the Required average = Total distance/Total time = $(60 + 60)/(4 + 3) = 120/7 = 17.14$

73. (Mon + Tue + wed) = $41 \times 3 = 123$. (Tue + Wed + Thu) = $40 \times 3 = 120$.

Mon – Thu = $123 - 120 = 3$. Since Thursday's temperature is given as 39, Monday's temperature would be $39 + 3 = 42$.

74. Required average = $(30 \times 20 - 10 \times 10)/10 = 500/10$ = 50.

75. Total age of 7 children = $12 \times 7 = 84$ years. When the 6 year old child dies, the total age of the remaining 6 children would be $84 - 6 = 78$. Required average = $78/6 = 13$ years.

76. Required average = $(2 \times 200 + 2 \times 250)/4 = 900/4$ = 225.

77. Teacher's weight = $36 \times 36 - 35 \times 35 = 1296 - 1225$ = 71 kgs.

78. The statement 'x is as much more than the average as y is less than the average signifies that the numbers x, y, z form an Arithmetic Progression with z as the middle term. z's value would then be equal to the average of the three numbers. This average is given as 45. Hence, the correct answer is $z = 45$.

79. The sum of the given 4 numbers is 20.75. The required average = $20.75/4$. Option (a) is correct.

80. Let the number of non officer workers in the company be W. Then we will have the following equation: $(15 \times 525 + W \times 85) = (15 + W) \times 95 \rightarrow 10\ W = 15 \times 430 \rightarrow W = 645$. Thus, the total number of workers in the company would be $645 + 15 = 660$.

81. The woman's age would be $8 \times 2 = 16$ years more than the age of the man she replaces. Age of the woman = $24 + 2 \times 8 = 40$ years.

82. Required average income = (Total expenditure + total savings]/12
= [(1100 \times 3 + 2200 \times 4 + 4620 \times 5) + 2100]/12 = 37300/12 = 3108.333

83. Required average = $(2 \times 5.5 + 3 \times 3.5 + 3 \times 5.5 + 5 \times 1.5)/13 = 45.5/13 = 3.5$

84. For 150 coins to be of a value of ₹ 150, using only 25 paise, 50 paise and 1 Re coins, we cannot have any coins lower than ther value of 1 ₹. Thus, the number of 50 paise coins would be 0. Option (d) is correct.

Level of Difficulty (II)

1. The train needs to travel 15 minutes extra @35 kmph. Hence, it is behind by 8.75 kms. The rate of losing distance is 5 kmph. Hence, the train must have travelled for $8.75/5 = 1$ hour 45 minutes. @ 40 kmph $\rightarrow$ 70 km.

Alternatively, you can also see that 12.5% drop in speed results in 14.28% increase in time. Hence, total time required is 105 minutes @ 40 kmph $\rightarrow$ 70 kilometers.

Alternatively, solve through options.

2. Standard question requiring good calculation speed. Obviously, the 15th day is being double counted. Calculations can be reduced by thinking as:

   Surplus in first 15 days – Deficit in last 17 days = 255 – 289 → Net deficit of 34. This means that the average is reducing by 34 due to the double counting of the 15th day. This can only mean that the 15th day's expenditure is ₹ 68 – 34 = 34.

   (Lengthy calculations would have yielded the following calculations:

   85*15 + 51*17 – 68*31 = 34)

3. Find out the number of innings in each year. Then the answer will be given by:

   $$\frac{\text{Total runs in 4 years}}{\text{Total innings in 4 years}} \quad (4270/119 = 35.88)$$

4. Find the total distance covered in each segment of 10 minutes. You will get total distance = 46 kilometers in 50 mins.

5. Assume that the distance is 120 km. Hence, 30 km is covered @ 25 kmph, 40 @ 30 kmph and so on. Then average speed is 120/total time

6. In three hours the total number of sheets typed will be: 60/6 + 60/7 + 60/9 = 10 + 8.57 + 6.66.

   Hence the number of sheets/hour is 25.23/3 = 8.41 is equivalent to 530/63.

7. 100 → 130 → 182. Hence, 82/2 = 41.

8. You do not know the number of days in the month. Hence, the question cannot be answered.

9. The number of rooms is 18 + 16 + 30 on the three floors respectively.

   Total revenues are: 18*200 + 16*100 + 30*150 = 9700 required average = 9700/110 = 88.18.

   Note here that if you could visualize here that since the number of rooms is 110 the decimal values cannot be .3 or .7 which effectively means that options 3 and 4 are rejected.

10. Replace x with the sales value to calculate the bonus in a month.

11. Use the same process as Q. No. 5 above.

12. The weight of the second man is 135 and that of the third is 105. Hence, net result is a drop of 45 for 5 people. Hence, 9 kg is the drop.

13. Put $x = 100$ to get the weight of the containers. Use these weights to find average weight as 2600/4 = 650.

14. The weight of the boxes are 1st box → 200, 3rd box → 250 kg, 2nd box → 300 kg, 4th box → 350 and 5th box → 500 kg. Hence difference between the heavier 4 and the lighter 4 is 300. Hence, difference in the averages is 75.

15. Difference between heaviest three and lightest three totals is: (350 + 500) – (300 + 200) = 350

Difference in average weights is 350/3 = 116.66.

16. Part of the runs scored in the 87th innings will go towards increasing the average of the first 86 innings to the new average and the remaining part of the runs will go towards maintaining the new average for the 87th innings. The only constraint in this problem is that there is an increase in the average by a whole number of runs. This is possible for all three options.

17. Assume x is the average expenditure of 19 people. Then, $19x = 13*79 + 6(x + 4)$.

18. 42 A + 31 = 55 (A – 3) → 13 A = 196 → A = 196/13 = 15.07. Total expenditure original = 15.07 × 42 = 633.23

19. The total price of the three stones would be 97610498312 × 3 = 292831494936. Since, this price is divided into the three stones in the ratio of 4 : 7 : 9, the price of the cheapest one would be = (4 × 2928314936/20) = 58566298987.2

20. The average weight per ball is asked. Hence, the bag does not have to be counted as the 48th item.

21. 71*48 = 59*46 + x + 11*52 → x = 72.

   Alternately, this can be solved by using the concepts of surpluses and deficits as:

   2*59 (deficit) – 4 * 11(surplus) + 48 (average to be maintained by the 60th number) = 118-44 + 48 = 122.

22. Solve through the same process as the Q. No. 5 of this chapter.

23. (14 * 333 – 2 * 504)/12.

24. $\dfrac{(84 - 64) \times 94}{18.8}$.

25. Use alligation to solve. 20————32————68. Thus, 5 corresponds to 12, hence for 36 the answer will be 15.

26. Let the equal distances be 'd' each. Then 3d/(d/x + d/y + d/z) = 3xyz/(x + y + z).

27–30. You have to take between 25th and 30th to mean that both these dates are also included.

27. The maximum average will occur when the maximum possible values are used. Thus:

   A should have been born on 30th, B on 25th, C on 20th, D on 10th and E on 5th. Further, the months of births in random order will have to be between August to December to maximize the average.

   Hence the total will be 30 + 25 + 20 + 10 + 5 + 12 + 11 + 10 + 9 + 8 = 140. Hence average is 28.

28. The minimum average will be when we have 1 + 5 + 10 + 20 + 25 + 1 + 2 + 3 + 4 + 5 = 76. Hence, average is 15.2.

29. This does not change anything. Hence the answer is the same as Q. 27.

30. The prime dates must be 29th, 23rd, 19th and 5th. Hence, the maximum possible average will reduce by 4/5 = 0.8. Hence, answer will be 27.2.

31. Solve using alligation. Since 15 is the mid-point of 13.25 and 16.75, the ratio is 1:1 and hence there are 20 people who were going for the picnic initially.

32. The number of pass candidates are 2 + 6 + 18 + 40 = 66 out of a total of 100. Hence, 66%.

33&34. Put $x = 10$ in the given equations and find the average of the resultant values.

35. Solve through options.

36. $nz-x + x^1 = nz^1 \rightarrow$ Simplify to get Option (c) correct.

37. By alligation the ratio is 3:8. Hence, only 110 is possible.

Q38-41:

38. You don't know who got out when. Hence, cannot be determined.

39. Since possibilities are asked about, you will have to consider all possibilities. Assume, the sixth and seventh batsmen have scored zero. Only then will the possibility of the first 5 batsmen scoring the highest possible average arise. In this case the maximum possible average for the first 5 batsmen could be 403/5 = 80.6.

40. Again it is possible that only the first batsman has scored runs.

41. We cannot find out the number of runs scored by the 7th batsman. Hence answer is (d).

42. You can take 53 as the base to reduce your calculations. Otherwise the question will become highly calculation intensive.

43. 251.25*4 + 277.52 * 5 + 760 = 3152.6

44. Solve using options. 20 is the only possible value.

45. Check through options to solve.

Level of Difficulty (III)

1. Definitely decrease, since the highest marks in Class A is less than the lowest marks in Class B.

2. Cannot say since there is no indication of the values of the numbers which are transferred.

3. It will definitely decrease since the highest possible transfer is lower than the lowest value in C.

4. The effect on A will depend on the profile of the people who are transferred. Hence, anything can happen.

5. Cannot say since there is a possibility that the numbers transferred are such that the average can either increase, decrease or remain constant.

6. If C increases, then the average of C goes up from 30. For this to happen it is definite that the average of B should drop.

7. The maximum possible average for B will occur if all the 5 transferees from A have 22 marks.

8. The average of Group A after the transfer in Q. 7 above is:
(400 – 18*5)/15 = 310/15 = 20.66

9. (400 – 22*5)/15 = 19.33

10. 400 + 23*5 = 515. Average = 515/25 = 20.6

11. 400 + 31*5 = 555. Average = 555/25 = 22.2

12. Will always decrease since the net value transferred from B to A will be higher than the net value transferred from A to B.

13. Since the lowest score in Class B is 23 which is more than the highest score of any student in Class A. Hence, A's average will always increase.

14. The maximum possible value for B will happen when the A to B transfer has the maximum possible value and the reverse transfer has the minimum possible value.

15. For the minimum possible value of B we will need the A to B transfer to be the lowest possible value while the B to A transfer must have the highest possible value. Thus, A to B transfer → 18* 5 while B to A transfer will be 31*5. Hence answer is 22.4.

16. The maximum value for A will happen in the case of Q. 15. Then the increment for group A is:
31*5 – 18*5 = 5*(31 – 18) = 65.
Thus maximum possible value is 465/20 = 23.25.

17. Minimum possible average will happen for the transfer we saw in Q. 14. Thus the answer will be 405/20 = 20.25.

18. The maximum possible value for C will be achieved when the transfer from C is of five 26's and the transfer back from B is of five 31's. Hence, difference is totals will be +25. Hence, max. average = (900 + 25)/30 = 30.833.
[Note here that 900 has come by 30*30]

19. For the maximum possible value of Class B the following set of operations will have to hold:
Five 33's are transferred from C to B, whatever goes from B to A comes back from A to B, then five 23's are transferred from B to C. This leaves us with:
Increase of 50 marks → average increases by 2 to 27.

20. A will attain maximum value if five 33's come to A from C through B and five 18's leave A. In such a case the net result is going to be a change of +75. Thus the average will go up by 75/20 = 3.75 to 23.75.

21–23. Will be solved by the same pattern as the above questions.

24. Only option A will give us the required situation since the transfer of five 31's increases the value of the average of group A.

25–28. Will be solved by the same pattern as above questions.

29–35. These are standard questions using the concept of averages. Hence, analyse each and every sentence by itself and link the interpretations. If you are getting stuck, the only reason is that you have not used the information in the questions fully.

36. Monthly estimates of income is reduced as the denominator is increased from 12 to 14 at the same time the monthly estimate of expenditure is increased as the denominator is reduced from 12 to 9. Hence, the savings will be underestimated.

37–39. Use the averages formulae and common sense to answer.

40–49. The questions are commonsensical with a lot of calculations and assumptions involved. You have to solve these using all the information provided.

40. Das's score = $15*2 + 7*2.5 = 47.5 \rightarrow 48$.
    Dasgupta's score = $20*1 + 2*1.5 = 23$

41. From the above the answer is 48:23 = 96:46.

42–44. By maximum possible support from the other end, you have to assume that he has Laxman or Sehwag batting aggressively for the entire tenure at the crease. Strike has to be shared equally.

42. Through options, After 60 overs, score would be 150. Then Tendulkar can score @ 4 runs per over (sharing the strike and batting aggressively) and get maximum support @ 3 runs per over. Thus in 30 overs left the target will be achieved.

43. Tendulkar's score for the innings will be $30*4 = 120$.

44. We do not know when Laxman would have come into bat. Hence this cannot be determined.

45–49. Build in each of the conditions in the problem to form a table like:

	Partnership Partner	Overs faced	Tendulkar's score	Partner's score
6th wicket	Ganguly	12	6 overs × 6	6 overs × 4
7th wicket	and so on			
8th wicket				
9th wicket				
10th wicket				

4
Chapter

Alligations

INTRODUCTION

The chapter of alligation is nothing but a faster technique of solving problems based on the weighted average situation as applied to the case of two groups being mixed together. I have often seen students having a lot of difficulty in solving questions on alligation. Please remember that all problems on alligation can be solved through the weighted average method. Hence, the student is advised to revert to the weighted average formula in case of any confusion.

The use of the techniques of this chapter for solving weighted average problems will help you in saving valuable time wherever a direct question based on the mixing of two groups is asked. Besides, in the case of questions that use the concept of the weighted average as a part of the problem, you will gain a significant edge if you are able to use the techniques illustrated here.

THEORY

In the chapter on Averages, we had seen the use of the weighted average formula. To recollect, the weighted average is used when a number of smaller groups are mixed together to form one larger group.

If the average of the measured quantity was

A_1 for group	1	containing	n_1	elements
A_2 for group	2	containing	n_2	elements
A_3 for group	3	containing	n_3	elements
A_k for group	k	containing	n_k	elements

We say that the weighted average, Aw is given by:

$$Aw = (n_1 A_1 + n_2 A_2 + n_3 A_3 + \dots\dots + n_k A_k)/ (n_1 + n_2 + n_3 \dots + n_k)$$

That is, the weighted average

$$= \frac{\text{Sum total of all groups}}{\text{Total number of elements in all groups together}}$$

In the case of the situation where just two groups are being mixed, we can write this as:

$$Aw = (n_1 A_1 + n_2 A_2)/(n_1 + n_2)$$

Rewriting this equation we get: $(n_1 + n_2) Aw = n_1 A_1 + n_2 A_2$

$$n_1(Aw - A_1) = n_2 (A_2 - Aw)$$

or $n_1/n_2 = (A_2 - Aw)/(Aw - A_1) \rightarrow$ The alligation equation.

The Alligation Situation

Two groups of elements are mixed together to form a third group containing the elements of both the groups.

If the average of the first group is A_1 and the number of elements is n_1 and the average of the second group is A_2 and the number of elements is n_2, then to find the average of the new group formed, we can use either the weighted average equation or the alligation equation.

As a convenient convention, we take $A_1 < A_2$. Then, by the principal of averages, we get $A_1 < Aw < A_2$.

Illustration 1

Two varieties of rice at ₹ 10 per kg and ₹ 12 per kg are mixed together in the ratio 1 : 2. Find the average price of the resulting mixture.

Solution $1/2 = (12 - Aw)/(Aw - 10) \rightarrow Aw - 10 = 24 - 2Aw$

$$\Rightarrow 3Aw = 34 \qquad \Rightarrow Aw = 11.33 \text{ ₹/kg.}$$

Illustration 2

On combining two groups of students having 30 and 40 marks respectively in an exam, the resultant group has an average score of 34. Find the ratio of the number of students in the first group to the number of students in the second group.

Solution $n_1/n_2 = (40 - 34)/(34 - 30) = 6/4 = 3/2$

Graphical Representation of Alligation

The formula illustrated above can be represented by the following cross diagram:

[Note that the cross method yields nothing but the alligation equation. Hence, the cross method is nothing but a graphical representation of the alligation equation.]

As we have seen, there are five variables embedded inside the alligation equation. These being:

the three averages $\rightarrow A_1$, A_2 and Aw

and the two weights $\rightarrow n_1$ and n_2

Based on the problem situation, one of the following cases may occur with respect to the knowns and the unknown, in the problem.

Case	Known	Unknown
I	(a) A_1, A_2, Aw	(a) $n_1 : n_2$
	(b) A_1, A_2, Aw, n_1	(b) n_2 and $n_1 : n_2$
II	A_1, A_2, n_1, n_2	Aw
III	A_1, Aw, n_1, n_2	A_2

Now, let us try to evaluate the effectiveness of the cross method for each of the three cases illustrated above:

Case 1: A_1, A_2, Aw are known; may be one of n_1 or n_2 is known.

To find: $n_1 : n_2$ and n_2 if n_1 is known   OR n_1 if n_2 is known.

Let us illustrate through an example:

Illustration 3

On mixing two classes of students having average marks 25 and 40 respectively, the overall average obtained is 30 marks. Find

(a) The ratio of students in the classes

(b) The number of students in the first class if the second class had 30 students.

Solution

(a) Hence, solution is 2 : 1.

(b) If the ratio is 2 : 1 and the second class has 30 students, then the first class has 60 students.

Note: The cross method becomes pretty effective in this situation when all the three averages are known and the ratio is to be found out.

Case 2: A_1, A_2, n_1 and n_2 are known, Aw is unknown.

Illustration 4

4 kg of rice at ₹ 5 per kg is mixed with 8 kg of rice at ₹ 6 per kg. Find the average price of the mixture.

Solution

$$= (6 - Aw) : (Aw - 5)$$

$$\Rightarrow \quad (6 - Aw)/(Aw - 5) = 4/8 \rightarrow 12 - 2\,Aw = Aw - 5$$

$$3\,Aw = 17$$

$$\therefore \qquad Aw = 5.66 \text{ ₹/kg. (Answer)}$$

Task for student: Solve through the alligation formula approach and through the weighted average approach to get the solution. Notice, the amount of time required in doing the same.

Note: The cross method becomes quite cumbersome in this case, as this method results in the formula being written. Hence, there seems to be no logic in using the cross method in this case.

Case 3: A_1, Aw, n_1 and n_2 are known; A_2 is unknown.

Illustration 5

5 kg of rice at ₹ 6 per kg is mixed with 4 kg of rice to get a mixture costing ₹ 7 per kg. Find the price of the costlier rice.

Solution Using the cross method:

$$= (x - 7) : 1$$
$$\therefore \quad (x - 7)/1 = 5/4 \rightarrow 4x - 28 = 5$$
$$\therefore \quad x = ₹ 8.25.$$

Task for student: Solve through the alligation formula approach and through the weighted average approach to get the solution. Notice the amount of time required in doing the same.

Note: The cross method becomes quite cumbersome in this case since this method results in the formula being written. Hence, there seems to be no logic in using the cross method in this case.

The above problems can be dealt quite effectively by using the straight line approach, which is explained below.

The Straight Line Approach

As we have seen, the cross method becomes quite cumbersome in Case 2 and Case 3. We will now proceed to modify the cross method so that the question can be solved graphically in all the three cases.

Consider the following diagram, which results from closing the cross like a pair of scissors. Then the positions of A_1, A_2, Aw, n_1 and n_2 are as shown.

Visualise this as a fragment of the number line with points A_1, Aw and A_2 in that order from left to right. Then,

(a) n_2 is responsible for the distance between A_1 and Aw or n_2 corresponds to $Aw - A_1$
(b) n_1 is responsible for the distance between Aw and A_2. or n_1 corresponds to $A_2 - Aw$
(c) $(n_1 + n_2)$ is responsible for the distance between A_1 and A_2. or $(n_1 + n_2)$ corresponds to $A_2 - A_1$.

The processes for the 3 cases illustrated above can then be illustrated below:

Illustration 6

On mixing two classes of students having average marks 25 and 40 respectively, the overall average obtained is 30 marks. Find

(a) the ratio in which the classes were mixed.
(b) the number of students in the first class if the second class had 30 students.

Solution

Hence, ratio is 2 : 1, and the second class has 60 students.

Case 2 A_1, A_2, n_1 and n_2 are known; Aw is unknown.

Illustration 7

4 kg of rice at ₹ 5 per kg is mixed with 8 kg of rice at ₹ 6 per kg. Find the average price of the mixture.

Solution

is the same as

Then, by unitary method:

$$n_1 + n_2 \text{ corresponds to } A_2 - A_1$$
$$\rightarrow 1 + 2 \text{ corresponds to } 6 - 5$$

That is, 3 corresponds to 1

$\therefore$ n_2 will correspond to $\dfrac{(A_2 - A_1) \times n_2}{(n_1 + n_2)}$

In this case $(1/3) \times 2 = 0.66$.

Hence, the required answer is 5.66.

Note: In this case, the problem associated with the cross method is overcome and the solution becomes graphical.

Case 3: A_1, Aw, n_1 and n_2 are known; A_2 is unknown.

Illustration 8

5 kg of rice at ₹ 6 per kg is mixed with 4 kg of rice to get a mixture costing ₹ 7 per kg. Find the price of the costlier rice.

Using straight line method:

4 corresponds to $7 - 6$ and 5 corresponds to $x - 7$.

The thought process should go like:

$$4 \rightarrow 1$$

$\therefore$ $5 \rightarrow 1.25$

Hence, $x - 7 = 1.25$

and $x = 8.25$

SOME TYPICAL SITUATIONS WHERE ALLIGATIONS CAN BE USED

Given below are typical alligation situations, which students should be able to recognize. This will help them improve upon the time required in solving questions. Although in this chapter we have illustrated problems based on alligation at level 1 only, alligation is used in more complex problems where the weighted average is an intermediate step in the solution process.

The following situations should help the student identify alligation problems better as well as spot the way A_1, A_2, n_1 and n_2 and Aw are mentioned in a problem.

In each of the following problems the following magnitudes represent these variables:

$$A_1 = 20, \quad A_2 = 30, \quad n_1 = 40, \quad n_2 = 60$$

Each of these problems will yield an answer of 26 as the value of Aw.

1. A man buys 40 kg of rice at ₹ 20/kg and 60 kg of rice at ₹ 30/kg. Find his average price. (26/kg)
2. Pradeep mixes two mixtures of milk and water. He mixes 40 litres of the first containing 20% water and 60 litres of the second containing 30% water. Find the percentage of water in the final mixture. (26%)
3. Two classes are combined to form a larger class. The first class having 40 students scored an average of 20 marks on a test while the second having 60 students scored an average of 30 marks on the same test. What was the average score of the combined class on the test. (26 marks)
4. A trader earns a profit of 20% on 40% of his goods sold, while he earns a profit of 30% on 60% of his goods sold. Find his percentage profit on the whole. (26%)
5. A car travels at 20 km/h for 40 minutes and at 30 km/h for 60 minutes. Find the average speed of the car for the journey. (26 km/hr)
6. 40% of the revenues of a school came from the junior classes while 60% of the revenues of the school came from the senior classes. If the school raises its fees by 20% for the junior classes and by 30% for the senior classes, find the percentage increase in the revenues of the school. (26%)

Some Keys to spot A_1, A_2 and Aw and differentiate these from n_1 and n_2

1. Normally, there are 3 averages mentioned in the problem, while there are only 2 quantities. This isn't foolproof though, since at times the question might confuse the student by giving 3 values for quantities representing n_1, n_2 and $n_1 + n_2$ respectively.
2. A_1, A_2 and Aw are always rate units, while n_1 and n_2 are quantity units.
3. The denominator of the average unit corresponds to the quantity unit (i.e. unit for n_1 and n_2).
4. All percentage values represent the average values.

A Typical Problem

A typical problem related to the topic of alligation goes as follows:

4 litres of wine are drawn from a cask containing 40 litres of wine. It is replaced by water. The process is repeated 3 times

(a) What is the final quantity of wine left in the cask.
(b) What is the ratio of wine to water finally.

If we try to chart out the process, we get: Out of 40 litres of wine, 4 are drawn out.

This leaves 36 litres wine and 4 litres water. (Ratio of 9 : 1)

Now, when 4 litres are drawn out of this mixture, we will get 3.6 litres of wine and 0.4 litres of water (as the ratio is 9 : 1). Thus at the end of the second step we get: 32.4 litres of wine and 7.6 litres of water. Further, the process is repeated, drawing out 3.24 litres wine and 0.76 litres water leaving 29.16 litres of wine and 10.84 litres of water.

This gives the final values and the ratio required.

A closer look at the process will yield that we can get the amount of wine left by:

$$40 \times 36/40 \times 36/40 \times 36/40 = 40 \times (36/40)^3$$
$$\Rightarrow 40 \times (1 - 4/40)^3$$

Space for Notes

This yields the formula:

Wine left : Capacity $\times$ (1 – fraction of wine withdrawn)^n for n operations.

Thus, you could have multiplied:

$$40 \times (0.9)^3 \text{ to get the answer}$$

That is, reduce 40 by 10% successively thrice to get the required answer.

Thus, the thought process could be:

$$40 - 10\% \rightarrow 36 - 10\% \rightarrow 32.4 - 10\% \rightarrow 29.16$$

LEVEL OF DIFFICULTY (I)

1. If 5 kg of salt costing ₹ 5/kg and 3 kg of salt costing ₹ 4/kg are mixed, find the average cost of the mixture per kilogram.
   (a) ₹ 4.5
   (b) ₹ 4.625
   (c) ₹ 4.75
   (d) ₹ 4.125

2. Two types of oils having the rates of ₹ 4/kg and ₹ 5/kg respectively are mixed in order to produce a mixture having the rate of ₹ 4.60/kg. What should be the amount of the second type of oil if the amount of the first type of oil in the mixture is 40 kg?
   (a) 75 kg
   (b) 50 kg
   (c) 60 kg
   (d) 40 kg

3. How many kilograms of sugar worth ₹ 3.60 per kg should be mixed with 8 kg of sugar worth ₹ 4.20 per kg, such that by selling the mixture at ₹ 4.40 per kg, there may be a gain of 10%?
   (a) 6 kg
   (b) 3 kg
   (c) 2 kg
   (d) 4 kg

4. A mixture of 125 gallons of wine and water contains 20% water. How much water must be added to the mixture in order to increase the percentage of water to 25% of the new mixture?
   (a) 10 gals
   (b) 8.5 gals
   (c) 8 gals
   (d) 8.33 gals

5. Ravi lends ₹ 3600 on simple interest to Harsh for a period of 5 years. He lends a part of the amount at 4% interest and the rest at 6% and receives ₹ 960 as the amount of interest. How much money did he lend on 4% interest rate?
   (a) ₹ 2800
   (b) ₹ 2100
   (c) ₹ 2400
   (d) ₹ 1200

6. 400 students took a mock exam in Delhi. 60% of the boys and 80% of the girls cleared the cut off in the examination. If the total percentage of students qualifying is 65%, how many girls appeared in the examination?
   (a) 100
   (b) 120
   (c) 150
   (d) 300

7. A man purchased a cow and a calf for ₹ 1300. He sold the calf at a profit of 20% and the cow at a profit of 25%. In this way, his total profit was $23\frac{1}{13}$%. Find the cost price of the cow.
   (a) ₹ 1100
   (b) ₹ 600
   (c) ₹ 500
   (d) ₹ 800

8. The average salary per head of all employees of a company is ₹ 600. The average salary of 120 officers is ₹ 4000. If the average salary per head of the rest of the employees is ₹ 560, find the total number of workers in the company.
   (a) 10200
   (b) 10320
   (c) 10500
   (d) 10680

9. A dishonest milkman purchased milk at ₹ 10 per litre and mixed 5 litres of water in it. By selling the mixture at the rate of ₹ 10 per litre he earns a profit of 25%. The quantity of the amount of the mixture that he had was:
   (a) 15 litres
   (b) 20 litres
   (c) 25 litres
   (d) 30 litres

10. A cistern contains 50 litres of water. 5 litres of water is taken out of it and replaced by wine. The process is repeated again. Find the proportion of wine and water in the resulting mixture.
    (a) 1 : 4
    (b) 41 : 50
    (c) 19 : 81
    (d) 81 : 19

11. A container has a capacity of 20 gallons and is full of spirit. 4 gallons of spirit is drawn out and the container is again filled with water. This process is repeated 5 times. Find out how much spirit is left in the resulting mixture finally?
    (a) $6\frac{257}{525}$ gallons
    (b) $6\frac{346}{625}$ gallons
    (c) 6.5 gallons
    (d) 6.25 gallons

12. A vessel is full of refined oil. 1/4 of the refined oil is taken out and the vessel is filled with mustard oil. If the process is repeated 4 times and 10 litres of refined oil is finally left in the vessel, what is the capacity of the vessel?
    (a) 33 litres
    (b) $\frac{2460}{81}$ litres
    (c) $\frac{2560}{81}$ litres
    (d) 30 litres

13. In what ratio should two qualities of coffee powder having the rates of ₹ 47 per kg and ₹ 32 per kg be mixed in order to get a mixture that would have a rate of ₹ 37 per kg?
    (a) 1 : 2
    (b) 2 : 1
    (c) 1 : 3
    (d) 3 : 1

14. A thief steals four gallons of liquid soap kept in a train compartment's bathroom from a container that is full of liquid soap. He then fills it with water to avoid detection. Unable to resist the temptation he steals 4 gallons of the mixture again, and fills it with water. When the liquid soap is checked at a station it is

found that the ratio of the liquid soap now left in the container to that of the water in it is 36 : 13. What was the initial amount of the liquid soap in the container if it is known that the liquid soap is neither used nor augmented by anybody else during the entire period?

(a) 7 gallons   (b) 14 gallons
(c) 21 gallons   (d) 28 gallons

15. In what ratio should water be mixed with soda costing ₹ 12 per litre so as to make a profit of 25% by selling the diluted liquid at ₹ 13.75 per litre?

(a) 10 : 1   (b) 11 : 1
(c) 1 : 11   (d) 12 : 1

16. A sum of ₹ 36.90 is made up of 90 coins that are either 20 paise coins or 50 paise coins. Find out how many 20 paise coins are there in the total amount.

(a) 47   (b) 43
(c) 27   (d) 63

17. A dishonest grocer professes to sell pure butter at cost price, but he mixes it with adulterated fat and thereby gains 25%. Find the percentage of adulterated fat in the mixture assuming that adulterated fat is freely available.

(a) 20%   (b) 25%
(c) 33.33%   (d) 40%

18. A mixture of 70 litres of alcohol and water contains 10% of water. How much water must be added to the above mixture to make the water 12.5% of the resulting mixture?

(a) 1 litre   (b) 1.5 litre
(c) 2 litres   (d) 2.5 litres

19. A mixture of 20 litres of brandy and water contains 10% water. How much water should be added to it to increase the percentage of water to 25%?

(a) 2 litres   (b) 3 litres
(c) 2.5 litres   (d) 4 litres

20. A merchant purchased two qualities of pulses at the rate of ₹ 200 per quintal and ₹ 260 per quintal. In 52 quintals of the second quality, how much pulse of the first quality should be mixed so that by selling the resulting mixture at ₹ 300 per quintal, he gains a profit of 25%?

(a) 100 quintals   (b) 104 quintals
(c) 26 quintals   (d) None of these

21. A man buys milk at ₹ 8.5 per litre and dilutes it with water. He sells the mixture at the same rate and thus gains 11.11%. Find the quantity of water mixed by him in every litre of milk.

(a) 0.111 litres   (b) 0.909 litres
(c) 0.1 litre   (d) 0.125 litres

22. There are two mixtures of honey and water, the quantity of honey in them being 25% and 75% of

the mixture. If 2 gallons of the first are mixed with three gallons of the second, what will be the ratio of honey to water in the new mixture?

(a) 11 : 2   (b) 11 : 9
(c) 9 : 11   (d) 2 : 11

23. There are two kinds of alloys of tin and copper. The first alloy contains tin and copper such that 93.33% of it is tin. In the second alloy there is 86.66% tin. What weight of the first alloy should be mixed with some weight of the second alloy so as to make a 50 kg mass containing 90% of tin?

(a) 15 kg   (b) 30 kg
(c) 20 kg   (d) 25 kg

24. Two containers of equal capacity are full of a mixture of oil and water. In the first, the ratio of oil to water is 4 : 7 and in the second it is 7 : 11. Now both the mixtures are mixed in a bigger container. What is the resulting ratio of oil to water?

(a) 149 : 247   (b) 247 : 149
(c) 143 : 241   (d) 241 : 143

25. Two vessels contain spirit and water mixed respectively in the ratio of 1 : 3 and 3 : 5. Find the ratio in which these are to be mixed to get a new mixture in which the ratio of spirit to water is 1 : 2.

(a) 2 : 1   (b) 3 : 1
(c) 1 : 2   (d) 1 : 3

26. The price of a pen and a pencil is ₹ 35. The pen was sold at a 20% profit and the pencil at a 10% loss. If in the transaction a man gains ₹ 4, how much is cost price of the pen?

(a) ₹ 10   (b) ₹ 25
(c) ₹ 20   (d) None of these

27. A person purchased a cupboard and a cot for ₹ 18,000. He sold the cupboard at a profit of 20% and the cot at a profit of 30%. If his total profit was 25.833%, find the cost price of the cupboard.

(a) ₹ 10,500   (b) ₹ 12,000
(c) ₹ 7500   (d) ₹ 10,000

28. A vessel is full of a mixture of kerosene and petrol in which there is 18% kerosene. Eight litres are drawn off and then the vessel is filled with petrol. If the kerosene is now 15%, how much does the vessel hold?

(a) 40 litres   (b) 32 litres
(c) 36 litres   (d) 48 litres

29. Two solutions of 90% and 97% purity are mixed resulting in 21 litres of mixture of 94% purity. How much is the quantity of the first solution in the resulting mixture?

(a) 15 litres   (b) 12 litres
(c) 9 litres   (d) 6 litres

30. In the Singapore zoo, there are deers and there are ducks. If the heads are counted, there are 180, while the legs are 448. What will be the number of deers in the zoo?
    (a) 136   (b) 68
    (c) 44   (d) 22

31. A bonus of ₹ 9,85,000 was divided among 300 workers of a factory. Each male worker gets 5000 rupees and each female worker gets 2500 rupees. Find the number of male workers in the factory.
    (a) 253   (b) 47
    (c) 94   (d) 206

32. What will be the ratio of petrol and kerosene in the final solution formed by mixing petrol and kerosene that are present in three vessels of equal capacity in the ratios 4 : 1, 5 : 2 and 6 : 1 respectively?
    (a) 166 : 22   (b) 83 : 22
    (c) 83 : 44   (d) None of these

33. A mixture worth ₹ 3.25 a kg is formed by mixing two types of flour, one costing ₹ 3.10 per kg while the other ₹ 3.60 per kg. In what proportion must they have been mixed?
    (a) 3 : 7   (b) 7 : 10
    (c) 10 : 3   (d) 7 : 3

34. A 20 percent gain is made by selling the mixture of two types of ghee at ₹ 480 per kg. If the type costing 610 per kg was mixed with 126 kg of the other, how many kilograms of the former was mixed?
    (a) 138 kg   (b) 34.5 kg
    (c) 69 kg   (d) Cannot be determined

35. In what proportion must water be mixed with milk so as to gain 20% by selling the mixture at the cost price of the milk? (Assume that water is freely available)
    (a) 1 : 4   (b) 1 : 5
    (c) 1 : 6   (d) 1 : 12

36. A bartender stole champagne from a bottle that contained 50% of spirit and he replaced what he had stolen with champagne having 20% spirit. The bottle then contained only 25% spirit. How much of the bottle did he steal?
    (a) 80%   (b) 83.33%
    (c) 85.71%   (d) 88.88%

37. A bag contains a total of 105 coins of ₹ 1, 50 p and 25 p denominations. Find the total number of coins of Re 1 if there are a total of 50.5 rupees in the bag and it is known that the number of 25 paise coins are 133.33% more than the number of 1 rupee coins.
    (a) 56   (b) 25
    (c) 24   (d) None of these

38. A man possessing ₹ 6800, lent a part of it at 10% simple interest and the remaining at 7.5% simple interest. His total income after $3\frac{1}{2}$ years was ₹ 1904. Find the sum lent at 10% rates.
    (a) ₹ 1260   (b) ₹ 1700
    (c) ₹ 1360   (d) None of these

39. If a man decides to travel 80 kilometres in 8 hours partly by foot and partly on a bicycle, his speed on foot being 8 km/h and that on bicycle being 16 km/h, what distance would he travel on foot?
    (a) 20 km   (b) 30 km
    (c) 48 km   (d) 60 km

40. Two vessels contain a mixture of spirit and water. In the first vessel the ratio of spirit to water is 8 : 3 and in the second vessel the ratio is 5 : 1. A 35 litre cask is filled from these vessels so as to contain a mixture of spirit and water in the ratio of 4 : 1. How many litres are taken from the first vessel?
    (a) 11 litres   (b) 22 litres
    (c) 16.5 litres (d) 17.5 litres

Space for Rough Work

ANSWER KEY

Level of Difficulty (I)

1. (b)	2. (c)	3. (d)	4. (d)
5. (d)	6. (a)	7. (d)	8. (b)
9. (c)	10. (c)	11. (b)	12. (c)
13. (a)	14. (d)	15. (c)	16. (c)
17. (a)	18. (c)	19. (d)	20. (c)
21. (a)	22. (b)	23. (d)	24. (a)
25. (c)	26. (b)	27. (c)	28. (d)
29. (c)	30. (c)	31. (c)	32. (b)
33. (d)	34. (d)	35. (b)	36. (b)
37. (c)	38. (c)	39. (c)	40. (a)

Solutions and Shortcuts

Level of Difficulty (I)

1. Solving the following alligation figure:

The answer would be 4.625/kg.

2. Mixing ₹ 4/kg and ₹ 5/kg to get ₹ 4.6 per kg we get that the ratio of mixing is 2:3. If the first oil is 40 kg, the second would be 60 kg.

3. Since by selling at ₹ 4.40 we want a profit of 10%, it means that the average cost required is ₹ 4 per kg. Mixing sugar worth ₹ 3.6/kg and ₹4.2/kg to get ₹ 4/kg means a mixture ratio of 1:2. Thus, to 8 kg of the second variety we need to add 4 kg of the first variety to get the required cost price.

4. In 125 gallons we have 25 gallons water and 100 gallons wine. To increase the percentage of water to 25%, we need to reduce the percentage of wine to 75%. This means that 100 gallons of wine = 75% of the new mixture. Thus the total mixture = 133.33 gallons. Thus, we need to mx 133.33 − 125 = 8.33 gallons of water in order to make the water equivalent to 25% of the mixture.

5. Since, Ravi earns ₹ 960 in 5 years, it means that he earns an interest of 960/5 = ₹ 192 per year. On an investment of 3600, an annual interest of 192 represents an average interest rate of 5.33%. Then using the alligation figure below:

We get the ratio of investments as 1:2. Hence, he lent 1 × 3600/3 = 1200 at 4% per annum.

6. The ratio of boys and girls appearing for the exam can be seen to be 3:1 using the following alligation figure.

This means that out of 400 students, there must have been 100 girls who appeared in the exam.

7. The ratio of the cost of the cow and the calf would be 40:25 or 8:5 as can be seen from the following alligation figure:

Thus, the cost of the cow would be ₹800.

8.

From the figure it is clear that the ratio of the number of officers to the number of other employees would be 40:3400. Since there are 120 officers, there would be 3400 × 3 = 10200 workers in the company. Thus the total number of employees would be 10200 + 120 = 10320.

9. The cost price of the mixture would have been ₹ 8 per liter for him to get a profit of 25% by selling at ₹ 10 per liter. The ratio of mixing would have been 1:4 (water is to milk) as can be seen in the figure:

Ratio of mixing = 2:8 or 1:4

Since we are putting in 5 liters of water, the amount of milk must be 20 liters. The amount of mixture then would become 25 liters.

10. Amount of water left = 50 × 9/10 × 9/10 = 40.5 liters. Hence, wine = 9.5 liters. Ratio of wine and water = 19:81. Option (c) is correct.

11. The amount of spirit left = 20 × 4/5 × 4/5 × 4/5 × 4/5 × 4/5 = 4096/625 = 6 (346/625).

12. Let the quantity of refined oil initially be Q. Then we have $Q \times 3/4 \times 3/4 \times 3/4 \times 3/4 = 10 \to Q = 2560/81$ liters.

13. The ratio would be 1:2 as seen from the figure:

14. It can be seen from the ratio 36:13 that the proportion of liquid soap to water is 36/49 after two mixings. This means that 6/7th of the liquid soap must have been allowed to remain in the container and hence 1/7th of the conatiner's original liquid soap would

have been drawn out by the thief. Since he takes out 4 gallons every time, there must have been 28 gallons in the container. (as 4 should be 1/7th of 28).

15. In order to sell at a 25% profit by selling at 13.75 the cost price should be 13.75/1.25 = 11. Also since water is freely available, we can say that the ratio of water and soda must be 1:11.

16. The average value of a coin is 41 paise and there are only 20 paise and 50 paise coins in the sum. Hence, the ratio of the number of 20 paise coins to 50 paise coins would be 9:21 = 3:7. Since there are a total of 90 coins, the number of 20 paise coins would be 3 × 90/10 = 27 coins.

17.

The ratio of mixing required would be 1:4 which means that the percentage of adulterated fat would be 20%.

18. Solve using options. Initially there are 7 liters of water in 70 liters of the mixture. By mixing 2 liters of water we will have 9 liters of water in 72 liters of the mixture – which is exactly 12.5%.

19. Again solve this question using options. Initially there are 2 liters of water in 20 liters of the mixture. To take the water to 25% of the mixture we would need to add 4 liters of water as that would give us 6 liters of water in 24 liters of the mixture.

20. By selling at 300 if we need to get a profit of 25% it means that the cost price would be 300/1.25 = 240.

```
200              240              260
|----------------|----------------|
??                              52 quintals
```

Ratio of mixing required to get an average of Rs. 240 per quintal = 1:2

Thus, in 52 quintals of the second we need to mix 26 quintals of the first.

21. The requisite 11.11% profit can be got by mixing 0.111 liters of water in 1 liter of milk. In such a case the total milk quantity would be 1.111 liters and the price would be for 1 liter only. The profit would be 0.111/1 = 11.11%.

22. The percentage of honey in the new mixture would be:
(2 × 25 + 3 × 75)/5 = 275/5 =55%. The ratio of honey to water in the new mixture would be 55:45 = 11:9.

23. In order to mix two tin alloys containing 86.66% tin and 93.33% tin to get 90% tin, the ratio of mixing

should be 1:1. Thus, each variety should be 25 kgs each.

24. Assume the capacity of the two containers is 198 liters each. When we mix 198 liters of the first and 198 liters of the second the amount of oil would be:
198 × 4/11 + 198 × 7/18 = 72 + 77 = 149 liters.
Consequently the amount of water would be 396 – 149 = 247 liters. Option (a) is correct.

25. The first vessel contains 25% spirit while the second vessel contains 37.5 % spirit. To get a 1:2 ratio we need 33.33% spirit in the mixture. The ratio of mixing can be seen using the following alligation figure:

Ratio of mixing = 4.1666:8.333 = 1:2

26. Solve using options as that would be the best way to tackle this question. Option (b) fits the situation perfectly as if we take the price of the pen as ₹ 25, the cost of the pencil would be ₹ 10. The profit in selling the pen would be ₹5 while the loss in selling the pencil would be ₹ 1. The total profit would be ₹ 4 as stipulated by the problem.

27. The following alligation visualization would help us solve the problem:

Ratio of cost of cupboard to cost of COT
= 4.1666: 5.8333
= 25:35
= 5:7

Cost of cupboard = 5 × 18000/12 = 7500.

28. The following visualization would help:

From the figure we can see that the original mixture would be 40 liters and the petrol being mixed is 8 liters. Thus, the vessel capacity is 48 liters.

29. 90% and 97% mixed to form 94% means that the mixing ratio is 3:4. The first solution would be 3 × 21/7 = 9 liters.

30. If all the animals were ducks we would have 180 heads and 360 legs. If we reduce the number of ducks

by 1 to 179 and increase the number of deers by 1 to 1, we would get an incremental 2 legs.

Since, the number of legs we need to increment is 88 (448 – 360 = 88), we need to have 44 deers and 136 ducks.

31. Solve using options. Option (a) does not fit because $253 \times 5000 + 47 \times 2500$ is not equal to 985000.

Similarly option (b) does not fit because $253 \times 2500 + 47 \times 5000$ is not equal to 985000.

Option (c) fits as $94 \times 5000 + 206 \times 2500 = 985000$.

32. In order to solve this we need to assume a value for the amounts in the vessels. If we assume 35 liters as the quantities in all the three vessels we will get:

28 liters + 25 liters + 30 liters = 83 liters of petrol and 22 liters of kerosene in 105 liters of the mixture.

The required ratio is 83:22.

33. The required ratio would be 7:3 as seen in the following figure.

Ratio of mixing
= 35:15
= 7:3

34. We cannot determine the answer to this question as we do not know the price per kg of the other type of ghee. Hence, we cannot find the ratio of mixing which would be required in order to move further in this question.

Space for Rough Work

35. To gain 20% by selling at cost price, milk should comprise 83.33% of the total mixture. The ratio of mixing that achieves this is 1:5.

36. 20% spirit is mixed with 50% spirit to get 25% spirit. The ratio of mixing would be 5:1. This means he stole 5/6th of the bottle or 83.33% of the bottle.

37. $O + F + T = 95$

$O + 0.5F + 0.25T = 50.5$

$T = 1.333\ O$.

Solving we get: 24 coins of 25 paise each.

38. Annual interest income = 1904 /3.5 = 544. Interest of ₹ 544 on a lending of ₹ 6800 implies an 8% average rate of interest. This 8% is generated by mixing two loans @ 7.5% and 10% respectively. The ratio in which the two loans should be allocated would be 4:1. The amount lent at 10% would be 1 × 6800/5 = 1360.

39. Solve using options. If he travels 48 km on foot he would take 6 hours on foot. Also, in this case he would travel 32 km on bicycle @ 16kmph – which would take him 2 hours. Thus a total of 8 hours. Option (c) satisfies the conditions of the question.

40. Solving through options is the best way to tackle this question. Option (a) fits the conditions of the problem as if there are 11 liters in the first vessel, there would be 8 liters of spirit. Also it means that we would be taking 24 liters from the second vessel out of which there would be 20 liters of spirit. Thus, total spirit would be 28 out of 35 liters giving us 7 liters of water.

🎯 BLOCK REVIEW TEST

REVIEW TEST

1. Rakshit bought 19 erasers for ₹ 10. He paid 20 paise more for each white eraser than for each brown eraser. What could be the price of a white eraser and how many white erasers could he have bought?
   - (a) 60 paise, 8
   - (b) 60 paise, 12
   - (c) 50 paise, 8
   - (d) 50 paise, 10

2. After paying all your bills, you find that you have ₹ 7.20 in your pocket. You have equal number of 50 paise and 10 paise coins; but no other coins nor any other currency notes. How many coins do you have?
   - (a) 8
   - (b) 24
   - (c) 27
   - (d) 30

3. Suresh Kumar went to the market with ₹ 100. If he buys three pens and six pencils he uses up all his money. On the other hand if he buys three pencils and six pens he would fall short by 20%. If he wants to buy equal number of pens & pencils, how many pencils can he buy?
   - (a) 4
   - (b) 5
   - (c) 6
   - (d) 7

4. For the above question, what is the amount of money he would save if he were to buy 3 pens and 3 pencils?
   - (a) ₹ 50
   - (b) ₹25
   - (c) ₹75
   - (d) ₹40

5. Abdul goes to the market to buy bananas. If he can bargain and reduce the price per dozen by ₹ 2, he can buy 3 dozen bananas instead of 2 dozen with the money he has. How much money does he have?
   - (a) ₹ 6
   - (b) ₹ 12
   - (c) ₹ 18
   - (d) ₹ 24

6. Two oranges, three bananas and four apples cost ₹15. Three oranges, two bananas and one apple cost ₹10. I bought 3 oranges, 3 bananas and 3 apples. How much did I pay?
   - (a) ₹10
   - (b) ₹8
   - (c) ₹15
   - (d) cannot be determined

7. John bought five mangoes and ten oranges together for forty rupees. Subsequently, he returned one mango and got two oranges in exchange. The price of an orange would be
   - (a) ₹ 1
   - (b) ₹ 2
   - (c) ₹ 3
   - (d) ₹ 4

8. Two towns A and B are 100 km apart. A school is to be built for 100 students of Town B and 30 students of Town A. The Expenditure on transport is ₹1.20 per km per person. If the total expenditure on transport by all 130 students is to be as small as possible, then the school should be built at
   - (a) 33 km from Town A
   - (b) 33 km from Town B
   - (c) Town A
   - (d) Town B

9. A person who has a certain amount with him goes to the market. He can buy 50 oranges or 40 mangoes. He retains 10% of the amount for taxi fare and buys 20 mangoes and of the balance he purchases oranges. Number of oranges he can purchase is
   - (a) 36
   - (b) 40
   - (c) 15
   - (d) 20

10. 72 hens costs ₹ _96.7_. Then what does each hen cost, where numbers at "_" are not visible or are written in illegible hand?
    - (a) ₹3.43
    - (b) ₹5.31
    - (c) ₹5.51
    - (d) ₹6.22

Directions for Questions 10 to 12: There are 60 students in a class. These students are divided into three groups A, B and C of 15, 20 and 25 students each. The groups A and C are combined to form group D

11. What is the average weight of the students in group D?
    - (a) more than the average weight of A.
    - (b) more than the average weight of C.
    - (c) less than the average weight of C.
    - (d) Cannot be determined.

12. If one student from Group A is shifted to group B, which of the following will be true?
    - (a) The average weight of both groups increases
    - (b) The average weight of both groups decreases
    - (c) The average weight of the class remains the same.
    - (d) Cannot be determined.

13. If all the students of the class have the same weight then which of the following is false?
    - (a) The average weight of all the four groups is the same.
    - (b) The total weight of A and C is twice the total weight of B.
    - (c) The average weight of D is greater than the average weight of A.
    - (d) The average weight of all the groups remains the same even if a number of students are shifted from one group to another.

14. The average marks of a student in ten papers are 80. If the highest and the lowest score are not considered

the average is 81. If his highest score is 92 find the lowest.

(a) 55   (b) 60
(c) 62   (d) Cannot be determined

15. A shipping clerk has five boxes of different but unknown weights each weighing less than 100 kg. The clerk weighs the boxes in pairs. The weights obtained are 110, 112, 113, 114, 115, 116, 117,118, 120 and 121 kg. What is the weight of the heaviest box?

(a) 60 kg   (b) 62 kg
(c) 64 kg   (d) Cannot be determined

16. The total expenses of a boarding house are partly fixed and partly varying linearly with the number of boarders. The average expense per boarder is ₹ 700 when there are 25 boarders and ₹ 600 when there are 50 boarders. What is the average expense per boarder when there are 100 boarders?

(a) 550   (b) 580
(c) 540   (d) 570

17. A yearly payment to a servant is ₹ 90 plus one turban. The servant leaves the job after 9 months and receives ₹65 and a turban, then find the price of the turban.

(a) ₹10   (b) ₹15
(c) ₹7.50   (d) Cannot be determined

18. A leather factory produces two kinds of bags, standard and deluxe. The profit margin is ₹20 on a standard bag and ₹30 on a deluxe bag. Every bag must be processed on machine A and on Machine B. The processing times per bag on the two machines are as follows:

Time required (Hours/bag)

	Machine A	Machine B
Standard Bag	4	6
Deluxe Bag	5	10

The total time available on machine A is 700 hours and on machine B is 1250 hours. Among the following production plans, which one meets the machine availability constraints and maximizes the profit?

(a) Standard 75 bags, Deluxe 80 bags
(b) Standard 100 bags, Deluxe 60 bags
(c) Standard 50 bags, Deluxe 100 bags
(d) Standard 60 bags, Deluxe 90 bags

19. Three math classes: X, Y, and Z, take an algebra test.
The average score of class X is 83.
The average score of class Y is 76.
The average score of class Z is 85.
What is the average score of classes X, Y, Z ?

(a) 81.5   (b) 80.5
(c) 83   (d) Cannot be determined

20. Prabhat ordered 4 Arrow shirts and some additional Park Avenue shirts. The price of one Arrow shirt was twice that of one Park Avenue shirt. When the order was executed it was found that the number of the two brands had been interchanged. This increased the bill by 40%. The ratio of the number of Arrow shirts to the number of Park Avenue shirts in the original order was:

(a) 1:3   (b) 1:4
(c) 1:2   (d) 1:5

21. Three groups of companies: Tata, Birla and Reliance announced the average of the annual profit for all years since their establishment.
The average profit of Tata is ₹ 75,000 lakh
The average profit of Birla is ₹ 64000 lakh
The average profit of Reliance is ₹ 73000 lakh
The average profit of all results of Tata and Birla together is ₹ 70000 lakh.
The average profit of all results of Birla and Reliance together is ₹ 69000 lakh.
Approximately what is the average profit for all the three group of companies?

(a) ₹ 70800 lakh   (b) ₹ 71086 lakh
(c) ₹ 70666 lakh   (d) Cannot be determined

ANSWER KEY

Review Test

1. (b)	2. (b)	3. (a)	4. (b)
5. (b)	6. (c)	7. (b)	8. (d)
9. (d)	10. (c)	11. (d)	12. (c)
13. (c)	14. (b)	15. (b)	16. (a)
17. (a)	18. (a)	19. (d)	20. (a)
21. (b)			

ARITHMETIC AND WORD-BASED PROBLEMS

Chapter 5
Percentages

Chapter 6
Profit & Loss

Chapter 7
Interest

Chapter 8
Ratio, Proportion and Variation

Chapter 9
Time and Work

Chapter 10
Time, Speed and Distance

...BACK TO SCHOOL

As you are already aware, this block consists of the following chapters:
Percentages,
Profit & Loss,
Interest,
Ratio, Proportion and Variation,
Time and Work,
Time, Speed and Distance

To put it very simply, the reason for these seemingly diverse chapters to be under one block of chapters is: **Linear Equations**

Yes, the solving of linear equations is the common thread that binds all the chapters in this block.

But before we start going through what a linear equation is, let us first understand the concept of a variable and it's need in the context of solving mathematical expressions.

Let us start off with a small exercise first:

Think of a number.
Add 2 to it.
Double the number to get a new number.
Add half of this new number to itself.
Divide the no. by 3.
Take away the original number from it.
The number you now have is......... 2!!
How do I know this result?

The answer is pretty simple. Take a look. I am assuming that you had taken the initial number as 5 to show you what has happened in this entire process.

Instruction	You	Me
Think of a number.	5	X
Add 2 to it.	5 + 2 = 7	X + 2
Double the number to get a new number.	7 × 2 = 14	2X + 4
Add half of this new number to itself.	14 + 7 = 21	3X + 6
Divide the result by 3.	21/3 = 7	X + 2
Take away the original number from it.	7 – 5 = 2	X + 2 – X = 2
The number you now have is….. 2 and is independent of the value again.	The number you now have is….. 2!	The number you now have is….. 2!

The above is a perfect illustration of what a variable is and how it operates.

In this entire process, it does not matter to me as to what number you have assumed. All I set up is a kind of a parallel world wherein the number in your mind is represented by the variable X in my mind.

By ensuring that the final value does not have an X in it, I have ensured that the answer is independent of the value you would have assumed. Thus, even if someone had assumed 7 as the original value, his values would go as: 7, 9, 18, 27, 9, 2. *Contd*

What you need to understand is that in Mathematics, whenever we have to solve for the value of an unknown we represent that unknown by using some letter (like x, y, a etc.) These letters are then called as the variable representations of the unknown quantity.

Thus, for instance, if you come across a situation where a question says: The temperature of a city increases by 1°C on Tuesday from its value on Monday, you assume that if Monday's temperature was t, then Tuesday's temperature will be $t + 1$.

The opposite of a variable is a constant. Thus if it is said in the same problem that the temperature on Wednesday is 34° C, then 34 becomes a constant value in the context of the problem.

Thus although you do not have the actual value in your mind, you can still move ahead in the question by assuming a variable to represent the value of the unknowns. All problems in Mathematics ultimately take you to a point which will give the value of the unknown—which then becomes the answer to the question.

Hence, in case you are stuck in a problem in this block of chapters, it could be due to any one of the following three reasons:

Reason 1: You are stuck because you have either not used all the information given in the problem or have used them in the incorrect order.

In such a case go back to the problem and try to identify each statement and see whether you have utilized it or not. If you have already used all the information, you might be interested in knowing whether you have used the information given in the problem in the correct order. If you have tried both these options, you might want to explore the next reason for getting stuck.

Reason 2: You are stuck because even though you might have used all the information given in the problem, you have not utilized some of the information completely.

In such a case, you need to review each of the parts of the information given in the question and look at whether any additional details can be derived out of the same information. Very often, in Quants, you have situations wherein one sentence might have more than one connotation. If you have used that sentence only in one perspective, then using it in the other perspective will solve the question.

Reason 3: You are stuck because the problem does not have a solution.

In such a case, check the question once and if it is correct go back to Reasons 1 and 2. Your solution has to lie there.

My experience in training students tells me that the 1st case is the most common reason for not being able to solve questions correctly. (more than 90% of the times) Hence, if you consider yourself to be weak at Maths, concentrate on the following process in this block of chapters.

THE LOGIC OF THE STANDARD STATEMENT

What I have been trying to tell the students is that most of the times, you will get stuck in a problem only when you are not able to interpret a statement in the problem. Hence, my advise to students (especially those who are weak in these chapters)—concentrate on developing your ability to decode the mathematical meaning of a sentence in a problem.

To do this, even in problems that you are able to solve (easily or with difficulty) go back into the language of the question and work out the mathematical reaction that you should have with each statement.

It might not be a bad idea to make a list of standard statements along with their mathematical reactions for each chapter in this block of chapters. You will realise that in almost no time, you will come to a situation where you will only rarely encounter new language.

Coming back to the issue of **linear equations**:

Linear equations are expressions about variables that might help us get the value of the variable if we can solve the equation.

Depending upon the number of variables in a problem, a linear equation might have one variable, two variables or even three or more variables. The only thing you should know is that in order to get the value of a variable, the number of equations needed is always equal to the number of variables. In other words, if you have more variables in a system of equations than the number of equations, you cannot solve for the individual values of the variables.

The basic mathematical principle goes like this:

For a system of equations to be solvable, the number of equations should be equal to the number of variables in the equations.

Thus for instance, if you have two variables, you need two equations to get the values of the two variables, while if you have three variables you will need three equations.

This situation is best exemplified by the situation where you might have the following equation. $x + y = 7$. If it is known that both x and y are natural numbers, it yields a set of possibilities for the values of x & y as follows: (1, 6), (2, 5), (3, 4), (4, 3), (5, 2), (6, 1). One of these possibilities has to be the answer.

In fact, it might be a good idea to think of all linear equation situations in this fashion. Hence, before you go ahead to read about the next equation, you should set up this set of possibilities based on the first equation.

Consider the following situation where a question yields a set of possibilities:

Four enemies A, B, C and D gather together for a picnic in a park with their wives. A's wife consumes 5 times as many glasses of juice as A. B's wife consumes 4 times as many glasses of juice as B. C's wife consumes 3 times as many glasses of juice as C and D's wife consumes 2 times as many glasses of juice as D. In total, the wives of the four enemies consume a total of 44 glasses of juice. If A consumes at least 5 glasses of juice while each of the other men have at least one glass, find the least number of drinks that could have been consumed by the 4 enemies together.

(1) 9   (2) 12
(3) 11   (4) 10

In the question above, we have 8 variables—A, B, C & D and a, b, c, d – the number of glasses consumed by the four men and the number of glasses consumed by the four wives.

Also, the question gives us five informations which can be summarized into 5 equations as follows.

a = 5A
b = 4B
c = 3C
d = 2D
and a + b + c + d = 44
Also, A>5.

Under this condition, you do not have enough information to get all values and hence you will get a set of possibilities.

Since the minimal value of A is 5, a can take the values 25, 30, 35 and 40 when A takes the values 5, 6, 7 and 8 respectively. Based on these, and on the realization that b has to be a multiple of 4, c a multiple of 3 and d a multiple of 2, the following possibilities emerge:

At A = 5

a	(multiple of 5)	25	25	25	25	25
b	(multiple of 4)	12	8	8	4	4
c	(multiple of 3)	3	9	3	3	9
d	(multiple of 2)	4	2	8	12	6
	a + b + c + d	44	44	44	44	44

a		A=6, a=30	A=7, a=35	A=8, a=40
b	(multiple of 4)	4	4	No solution
c	(multiple of 3)	6	3	
d	(multiple of 2)	4	2	
	a + b + c + d	44	44	

In this case the answer will be 10, since in the case of a=35, b=4, c=3 & d=2, the values for A,B,C and D will be respectively 7,1,1 and 1. This solution is the least number of drinks consumed by the 4 enemies together as in all the other possibilities the number of glasses is greater than 10.

Such utilisations of linear equations are very common in CAT and top level aptitude examinations.

The relationship between the decimal value and the percentage value of a ratio:

Every ratio has a percentage value and a decimal value and the difference between the two is just in the positioning of the decimal point.

Thus 2/4 can be represented as 0.5 in terms of its decimal value and can be represented by 50% in terms of its percentage value.

Pre-assessment Test

1. Three runners A, B and C run a race, with runner A finishing 24 metres ahead of runner B and 36 metres ahead of runner C, while runner B finishes 16 metres ahead of runner C. Each runner travels the entire distance at a constant speed. .What was the length of the race?
   - (a) 72 metres
   - (b) 96 metres
   - (c) 120 metres
   - (d) 144 metres

2. A dealer buys dry fruits at ₹100, ₹ 80 and ₹ 60 per kilogram. He mixes them in the ratio 4:5:6 by weight, and sells at a profit of 50%. At what price per kilogram does he sell the dry fruit?
   - (a) ₹116
   - (b) ₹106
   - (c) ₹115
   - (d) None of these

3. There are two containers: the first contains 500 ml of alcohol, while the second contains 500 ml of water. Five cups of alcohol from the first container is taken out and is mixed well in the second container. Then, five cups of this mixture is taken out from the second container and put back into the first container. Let X and Y denote the proportion of alcohol in the first and the proportion of water in the second container. Then what is the relationship between X & Y? (Assume the size of the cups to be identical)
   - (a) X>Y
   - (b) X<Y
   - (c) X=Y
   - (d) Cannot be determined

4. Akhilesh took five papers in an examination, where each paper was of 200 marks. His marks in these' papers were in the proportion of 7: 8: 9 :10 : 11. In all papers together, the candidate obtained 60% of the total marks. Then, the number of papers in which he got more than 50% marks is:
   - (a) 1
   - (b) 3
   - (c) 4
   - (d) 5

5. A and B walk up an escalator (moving stairway). The escalator moves at a constant speed, A takes six steps for every four of B's steps. A gets to the top of the escalator after having taken 50 steps, while B (because his slower pace lets the escalator do a little more of the work) takes only 40 steps to reach the top. If the escalator were turned off, how many steps would they have to take to walk up?
   - (a) 80
   - (b) 100
   - (c) 120
   - (d) 160

6. Fifty per cent of the employees of a certain company are men, and 80% of the men earn more than ₹ 2.5 lacs per year. If 60% of the company's employees earn more than ₹ 2.5 lacs per year, then what fraction of the women employed by the company earn more than ₹ 2.5 lacs per year?
   - (a) 2/5
   - (b) 1/4
   - (c) 1/3
   - (d) 3/4

7. A piece of string is 80 centimeters long. It is cut into three pieces. The longest piece is 3 times as long as the middle-sized and the shortest piece is 46 centimeters shorter than the longest piece. Find the length of the shortest piece (in cm).
   - (a) 14
   - (b) 10
   - (c) 8
   - (d) 18

8. Three members of a family A, B, and C, work together to get all household chores done. The time it takes them to do the work together is six hours less than A would have taken working alone, one hour less than B would have taken alone, and half the time C would have taken working alone. How long did it take them to do these chores working together?
   - (a) 20 minutes
   - (b) 30 minutes
   - (c) 40 minutes
   - (d) 50 minutes

9. Fresh grapes contain 90% water by weight while dried grapes contain 20% water by weight. What is the weight of dry grapes available from 20 kg of fresh grapes?
   - (a) 2kg
   - (b) 2.4kg
   - (c) 2.5kg
   - (d) None of these

10. At the end of the year 2008, a shepherd bought twelve dozen goats. Henceforth, every year he added p% of the goats at the beginning of the year and sold q% of the goats at the end of the year where p> 0 and q >0. If the shepherd had twelve dozen goats at the end of the year 2012, (after making the sales for that year), which of the following is true?
    - (a) p = q
    - (b) p<q
    - (c) p>q
    - (d) p = q/2

Directions for Questions 11 and 12: Answer the questions based on the following information.

An Indian company purchases components X and Y from UK and Germany, respectively. X and Y form 40% and 30% of the total production cost. Current gain is 25%. Due to change in the international exchange rate scenario, the cost of the German mark increased by 50% and that of UK pound increased by 25%. Due to tough competitive market conditions, the selling price cannot be increased beyond 10%.

11. What is the maximum current gain possible?
    - (a) 10%
    - (b) 12.5%
    - (c) 0%
    - (d) 7.5%

12. If the UK pound becomes cheap by 15% over its original cost and the cost of German mark increased by 20%, what will be the gain if the selling price is not altered.
    (a) 10%   (b) 20%
    (c) 25%   (d) 7.5%

13. A college has raised 80% of the amount it needs for a new building by receiving an average donation of ₹ 800 from the people already solicited. The people already solicited represent 50% of the people, the college will ask for donations. If the college is to raise exactly the amount needed for the new building, what should be the average donation from the remaining people to be solicited?
    (a) 300   (b) 200
    (c) 400   (d) 500

14. A student gets an aggregate of 60% marks in five subjects in the ratio 10: 9: 8: 7: 6. If the passing marks are 45% of the maximum marks and each subject has the same maximum marks, in how many subjects did he pass the examination?
    (a) 2   (b) 3
    (c) 4   (d) 5

15. After allowing a discount of 12.5 % a trader still makes a gain of 40%. At what per cent above the cost price does he mark on his goods?
    (a) 45%   (b) 60%
    (c) 25%   (d) None of these

16. The owner of an art shop conducts his business in the following manner. Every once in a while he raises his prices by X%, then a while later he reduces all the new prices by X%. After one such up-down cycle, the price of a painting decreased by ₹ 441. After a second up-down cycle, the painting was sold for ₹ 1944.81. What was the original price of the painting (in ₹)?
    (a) 2756.25   (b) 2256.25
    (c) 2500   (d) 2000

17. Manas, Mirza, Shorty and Jaipal bought a motorbike for $60,000. Manas paid 50% of the amounts paid by the other three boys, Mirza paid one third of the sum of the amounts paid by the other boys; and Shorty paid one fourth of the sum of the amounts paid by the other boys. How much did Jaipal have to pay?
    (a) $15000   (b) $13000
    (c) $17000   (d) None of these

18. A train X departs from station A at 11.00 a.m. for station B, which is 180 km away. Another train Y departs from station B at 11.00 a.m. for station A. Train X travels at an average speed of 70 kms/hr and does not stop anywhere until it arrives at sta-

tion B. Train Y travels at an average speed of 50 km/hr, but has to stop for 10 minutes at station C, which is 60 kms away from station B enroute to station A. Ignoring the lengths of the trains, what is the distance, to the nearest km, from station A to the point where the trains cross each other?
    (a) 110   (b) 112
    (c) 116   (d) None of these

19. In a survey of political preferences, 81% of those asked were in favour of at least one of the three budgetary proposals A, B and C. 50% of those asked favoured proposal A, 30% favoured proposal B and 20% favoured proposal C. If 5% of those asked favoured all the three proposals, what percentage of those asked favoured more than one of the three proposals?
    (a) 10%   (b) 12%
    (c) 9%   (d) 14%

Directions for Questions 20 and 21: The petrol consumption rate of a new model car 'Palto' depends on its speed and may be described by the graph below:

20. Manasa makes the 240 km trip from Mumbai to Pune at a steady speed of 60 km per hour. What is the amount of petrol consumed for the journey?
    (a) 12.5 litres   (b) 16 litres
    (c) 15 litres   (d) 19.75 litres

21. Manasa would like to minimise the fuel consumption for the trip by driving at the appropriate speed. How should she change the speed?
    (a) Increase the speed
    (b) Decrease the speed
    (c) Maintain the speed at 60km/hour
    (d) Cannot be determined

Directions for Questions 22 and 23: Answer the questions based on the following information:

There are five machines—A, B, C, D, and E situated on a straight line at distances of 10m, 20 m, 30 m, 40 m and 50m respectively from the origin of the line. A robot is stationed at the origin of the line. The robot serves the machines with raw material whenever a machine becomes idle. All the raw materials are located at the origin. The robot is in an idle state at the origin at the beginning of a day. As soon as one or more machines become idle, they send messages to the robot-station and the robot starts and serves all the machines from which it received messages. If a message is received at the station while the robot is away from it, the robot takes notice of the message only when it returns to the station. While moving, it serves the machines in the sequence in which they are encountered, and then returns to the origin. If any messages are pending at the station when it returns, it repeats the process again. Otherwise, it remains idle at the origin till the next message(s) is (are) received.

22. Suppose on a certain day, machines A and D have sent the first two messages to the origin at the beginning of the first second, C has sent a message at the beginning of the 7th second, B at the beginning of the 8th second and E at the beginning of the 10th second. How much distance has the robot traveled since the beginning of the day, when it notices the message of E? Assume that the speed of movement of the robot is 10m/s.
    (a) 140 m   (b) 80 m
    (c) 340 m   (d) 360 m

23. Suppose there is a second station with raw material for the robot at the other extreme of the line which is 60 m from the origin, i.e., 10m from E. After finishing the services in a trip, the robot returns to the nearest station. If both stations are equidistant, it chooses the origin as the station to return to. Assuming that both stations receive the

messages sent by the machines and that all the other data remains the same, what would be the answer to the above question?
    (a) 120   (b) 160
    (c) 140   (d) 170

24. One bacteria splits into eight bacteria of the next generation. But due to environment, only 50% of a generation survive. If the eighth generation number is 8192 million, what is the number in the first generation?
    (a) I million   (b) 2 million
    (c) 4 million   (d) 8 million

25. I bought 10 pens, 14 pencils and 4 erasers. Ravi bought 12 pens, 8 erasers and 28 pencils for an amount which was half more what I had paid. What percent of the total amount paid by me was paid for the pens?
    (a) 37.5%   (b) 62.5%
    (c) 50%   (d) None of these

ANSWER KEY

1. (b)	2. (a)	3. (c)	4. (c)
5. (b)	6. (a)	7. (c)	8. (c)
9. (c)	10. (c)	11. (a)	12. (c)
13. (b)	14. (d)	15. (b)	16. (a)
17. (b)	18. (a)	19. (d)	20. (b)
21. (b)	22. (a)	23. (a)	24. (b)
25. (b)			

SCORE INTERPRETATION ALGORITHM FOR PRE-ASSESSMENT TEST OF BLOCK III

If You Scored: <7: (In Unlimited Time)

Step One

Go through the Block III **Back to School** Section carefully. Grasp each of the concepts explained in that part carefully. I would recommend that you go back to your Mathematics school books (ICSE/ CBSE) Class 8,9 & 10 if you feel you need it.

Step Two

Move into each of the chapters of Block III one by one.

When you do so, concentrate on clearly understanding each of the concepts explained in the chapter theory.

Step Three

Then move onto the LOD 1 exercises. These exercises will provide you with the first level of challenge. Try to solve each and every question provided under LOD 1. While doing so do not think about the time requirement. Once you finish solving LOD 1, revise the questions and their solution processes.

Step Four

Go to the first review test given at the end of the block and solve it. While doing so, first look at the score you get within the time limit mentioned. Then continue to solve the test further without a time limit and try to evaluate the improvement in your unlimited time score.

In case the growth in your score is not significant, go back to the theory of each chapter and review each of the LOD 1 questions for all the chapters.

Step Five

Move to LOD 2 and repeat the process that you followed in LOD 1 in each of the chapters. Concentrate on understanding each and every question and it's underlying concept.

Step Six

Go to the second review test given at the end of the block and solve it. Again, while doing so measure your score within the provided time limit first and then continue to solve the test further without a time limit and try to evaluate the improvement that you have had in your score.

Step Seven

Move to LOD 3 only after you have solved and understood each of the questions in LOD 1 & LOD 2. Repeat the process that you followed in LOD 1 – going into each chapter one by one.

Step Eight

Go to the remaining review tests given at the end of the block and solve them. Again, while doing so measure your score within the provided time limit first and then continue to solve the test further without a time limit and try to evaluate the improvement that you have had in your score.

In case the growth in your score is not significant, go back to the theory of each chapter and review each of the LOD 1,2 & 3 questions for all the chapters.

If You Scored:7–15 (In Unlimited Time)

Although you are better than the person following the instructions above, obviously there is a lot of scope for the development of your score. You will need to work both on your concepts as well as speed. Initially emphasize more on the concept development aspect of your preparations, then move your emphasis onto speed development. The following process is recommended for you:

Step One

Go through the **Block III Back to School Section** carefully. Revise each of the concepts explained in that part. Going through your 8th, 9th and 10th standard books will be an optional exercise for you. It will be recommended in case you scored in single digits, while if your score is in two digits, I leave the choice to you.

Step Two

Move into each of the chapters of Block III one by one.

When you do so, concentrate on clearly understanding each of the concepts explained in the chapter theory.

Step Three

Then move onto the LOD 1 & LOD 2 exercises. These exercises will provide you with the first level of challenge. Try to solve each and every question provided under LOD 1 & 2. While doing so do not think about the time requirement. Once you finish solving LOD 1, revise the questions and their solution processes. Repeat the same process for LOD 2.

Step Four

Go to the first review test given at the end of the block and solve it. While doing so, first look at the score you get within the time limit mentioned. Then continue to solve the test further without a time limit and try to evaluate the improvement in your unlimited time score.

Step Five

Go to the second review test given at the end of the block and solve it. Again, while doing so measure your score within the provided time limit first and then continue to solve the test further without a time limit and try to evaluate the improvement that you have had in your score.

In case the growth in your score is not significant, go back to the theory of each chapter and review each of the LOD 1& LOD 2 questions for all the chapters.

Step Six

Move to LOD 3 only after you have solved and understood each of the questions in LOD 1 & LOD 2. Repeat the process that you followed in LOD 1 – going into each chapter one by one.

Step Seven

Go to the remaining review tests given at the end of the block and solve them. Again, while doing so measure your score within the provided time limit first and then continue to solve the test further without a time limit and try to evaluate the improvement that you have had in your score.

In case the growth in your score is not significant, go back to the theory of both the chapters and re solve all LODs of all the chapters. While doing so concentrate more on the LOD 2 & LOD 3 questions.

If You Scored 15+ (In Unlimited Time)

Obviously you are much better than the first two category of students. Hence unlike them, your focus should be on developing your speed by picking up the shorter processes explained in this book. Besides, you might also need to pick up concepts that might be hazy in your mind. The following process of development is recommended for you:

Step One

Quickly review the concepts given in the Block III Back to School Section. Only go deeper into a concept in case you find it new. Going back to school level books is not required for you.

Step Two

Move into each of the chapters of Block III one by one.

When you do so, concentrate on clearly understanding each of the concepts explained in the chapter theory.

Then move onto the LOD 1 & LOD 2 exercises. These exercises will provide you with the first level of challenge. Try to solve each and every question provided under LOD 1 & 2. While doing so try to work on faster processes for solving the same questions. Concentrate on how you could have solved the same question faster. Also try to think of how much time you took over the calculations.

Step Three

Go to the first review test given at the end of the block and solve it. While doing so, first look at the score you get within the time limit mentioned. Then continue to solve the test further without a time limit and try to evaluate the improvement in your unlimited time score.

Step Four

Go to the second review test given at the end of the block and solve it. Again, while doing so measure your score within the provided time limit first and then continue to solve the test further without a time limit and try to evaluate the improvement that you have had in your score.

Step Five

In case the growth in your score is not significant (esp. under time limits), review each of the LOD 1 & LOD 2 questions for all the chapters.

Step Six

Move to LOD 3 only after you have solved and understood each of the questions in LOD 1 & LOD 2. Repeat the process that you followed in LOD 1 – going into each chapter one by one.

Step Seven

Go to the remaining review tests given at the end of the block and solve them. Again, while doing so measure your score within the provided time limit first and then continue to solve the test further without a time limit and try to evaluate the improvement that you have had in your score.

Percentages

INTRODUCTION

In my opinion, the chapter on Percentages forms the most important chapter (apart from Number Systems) in the syllabus of the CAT and the XLRI examination. The importance of 'percentages' is accentuated by the fact that there are a lot of questions related to the use of percentage in all chapters of commercial arithmetic (especially Profit and Loss, Ratio and Proportion, Time and Work, Time, Speed and Distance).

Besides, the calculation skills that you can develop while going through the chapter on percentages will help you in handling Data Interpretation (DI) calculations. A closer look at that topic will yield that at least 80% of the total calculations in any DI paper is constituted of calculations on additions and percentage.

BASIC DEFINITION AND UTILITY OF PERCENTAGE

Percent literally, means 'for every 100' and is derived from the French word 'cent', which is French for 100.

The basic utility of Percentage arises from the fact that it is one of the most powerful tools for comparison of numerical data and information. It is also one of the simplest tools for comparison of data.

In the context of business and economic performance, it is specifically useful for comparing data such as profits, growth rates, performance, magnitudes and so on.

Mathematical Definition of Percentage The concept of percentage mainly applies to ratios, and the percentage value of a ratio is arrived at by multiplying by 100 the decimal value of the ratio.

For example, a student scores 20 marks out of a maximum possible 30 marks. His marks can then be denoted as 20 out of 30 = (20/30) or (20/30) × 100% = 66.66%.

The process for getting this is perfectly illustrated through the unitary method:

$$\text{Marks scored} \qquad \text{Out of}$$

then,

$$20 \xrightarrow{\text{out of}} 30$$

$$x \xrightarrow{\text{out of}} 100$$

Then the value of $x \times 30 = 20 \times 100$

$x = (20/30) \times 100 \rightarrow$ the percentage equivalent of a ratio.

Now, let us consider a classic example of the application of percentage:

Example: Student *A* scores 20 marks in an examination out of 30 while another student *B* scores 40 marks out of 70. Who has performed better?

Solution: Just by considering the marks as 20 and 40, we do not a get clear picture of the actual performance of the two students. In order to get a clearer picture, we consider the percentage of marks.

$$\text{Thus, } A \text{ gets } (20/30) \times 100 = 66.66\%$$
$$\text{While } B \text{ gets } (40/70) \times 100 = 57.14\%$$

Now, it is clear that the performance of *A* is better. Consider another example:

Example: Company *A* increases its sales by 1 crore rupees while company *B* increases its sales by 10 crore rupees. Which company has grown more?

Solution: Apparently, the answer to the question seems to be company *B*. The question cannot be answered since we don't know the previous year's sales figure (although on the face of it Company *B* seems to have grown more).

If we had further information saying that company *A* had a sales turnover of ₹ 1 crore in the previous year and company *B* had a sales turnover of ₹ 100 crore in the previous year, we can compare growth rates and say that it is company *A* that has grown by 100%. Hence, company

A has a higher growth rate, even though in terms of absolute value increase of sales, company *B* has grown much more.

IMPORTANCE OF BASE/ DENOMINATOR FOR PERCENTAGE CALCULATIONS

Mathematically, the percentage value can only be calculated for ratios that, by definition, must have a denominator. Hence, one of the most critical aspects of the percentage is the denominator, which in other words is also called the base value of the percentage. No percentage calculation is possible without knowing the base to which the percentage is to be calculated.

Hence, whenever faced with the question 'What is the percentage ...?' always try first to find out the answer to the question 'Percentage to what base?'

CONCEPT OF PERCENTAGE CHANGE

Whenever the value of a measured quantity changes, the change can be captured through

(a) Absolute value change   or

(b) Percentage change.

Both these measurements have their own advantages and disadvantages.

Absolute value change: It is the actual change in the measured quantity. For instance, if sales in year 1 is ₹ 2500 crore and the sales in year 2 is ₹ 2600 crore, then the absolute value of the change is ₹ 100 crore.

Percentage change: It is the percentage change got by the formula

$$\text{Percentage change} = \frac{\text{Absolute value change}}{\text{Original quantity}} \times 100$$

$$= \frac{100}{2500} \times 100 = 4\%$$

As seen earlier, this often gives us a better picture of the effect of the change.

Note: The base used for the sake of percentage change calculations is always the original quantity unless otherwise stated.

Example: The population of a city grew from 20 lakh to 22 lakh. Find the

(a) percentage change

(b) percentage change based on the final value of population

Solution: (a) percentage change = (2/20) × 100 = 10%

(b) percentage change on the final value = (2/22) × 100 = 9.09%

Difference between the Percentage Point Change and the Percentage Change

The difference between the percentage point change and the percentage change is best illustrated through an example. Consider this:

The savings rate as a percentage of the GDP was 25% in the first year and 30% in the second year. Assume that there is no change in the GDP between the two years. Then:

Percentage point change in savings rate = 30%−25% = 5 percentage points.

Percentage change in savings rate = $\frac{30-25}{25} \times 100$ = 25%.

PERCENTAGE RULE FOR CALCULATING PERCENTAGE VALUES THROUGH ADDITIONS

Illustrated below is a powerful method of calculating percentages. In my opinion, the ability to calculate percentage through this method depends on your ability to handle 2 digit additions. Unless you develop the skill to add 2 digit additions in your mind, you are always likely to face problems in calculating percentage through the method illus- trated below. In fact, trying this method without being strong at 2-digit additions/subtractions (including 2 digits after decimal point) would prove to be a disadvantage in your attempt at calculating percentages fast.

This process, essentially being a commonsense process, is best illustrated through a few examples:

Example: What is the percentage value of the ratio: 53/81?

Solution: The process involves removing all the 100%, 50%, 10%, 1%, 0.1% and so forth of the denominator from the numerator.

Thus, 53/81 can be rewritten as: (40.5 + 12.5)/81 = 40.5/81 + 12.5/81 = 50% + 12.5/81

= 50% + (8.1 + 4.4)/81 = 50% + 10% + 4.4/81 = 60% + 4.4/81

At this stage you know that the answer to the question lies between 60 – 70% (Since 4.4 is less than 10% of 81)

At this stage, you know that the answer to the calculation will be in the form: 6*a.bcde* ....

All you need to do is find out the value of the missing digits.

In order to do this, calculate the percentage value of 4.4/81 through the normal process of multiplying the numerator by 100.

Thus the % value of $\frac{4.4}{81} = \frac{4.4 \times 100}{81} = \frac{440}{81}$

[*Note*: Use the multiplication by 100, once you have the 10% range. This step reduces the decimal calculations.]

Thus $\dfrac{440}{81}$ = 5% with a remainder of 35

Our answer is now refined to 65.*bcde*. (1% Range)

Next, in order to find the next digit (first one after the decimal add a zero to the remainder;

Hence, the value of '*b*' will be the quotient of

$b \rightarrow 350/81 = 4$ Remainder 26

Answer: 65.4*cde* (0.1% Range)

$c \rightarrow 260/81 = 3$ Remainder 17

Answer: 65.43 (0.01% Range)

and so forth.

The advantages of this process are two fold:

(1) You only calculate as long as you need to in order to eliminate the options. Thus, in case there was only a single option between 60 – 70% in the above question, you could have stopped your calculations right there.

(2) This process allows you to go through with the calculations as long as you need to.

However, remember what I had advised you right at the start: Strong Addition skills are a primary requirement for using this method properly.

To illustrate another example:

What is the percentage value of the ratio $\dfrac{223}{72}$?

223/72 $\rightarrow$ 300 – 310% Remainder 7

700/72 $\rightarrow$ 9. Hence 309 – 310%, Remainder 52

520/72 $\rightarrow$ 7. Hence, 309.7, Remainder 16

160/72 $\rightarrow$ 2. Hence, 309.72 Remainder 16

Hence, 309.7222 (2 recurs since we enter an infinite loop of 160/72 calculations).

In my view, percentage rule (as *I* call it) is one of the best ways to calculate percentages since it gives you the flexibility to calculate the percentage value up to as many digits after decimals as you are required to and at the same time allows you to stop the moment you attain the required accuracy range.

Effect of a Percent Change in the Numerator on a Ratio's Value

The numerator has a direct relationship with the ratio, that is, if the numerator increases the ratio increases. The percentage increase in the ratio is the same as the percentage increase in the numerator, if the denominator is constant.

Thus, $\dfrac{22}{40}$ is exactly 10% more than $\dfrac{20}{40}$. (in terms of percentage change)

Percentage Change Graphic and its Applications

In mathematics there are many situations where one is required to work with percentage changes. In such situations the following thought structure (Something I call Percentage Change Graphic) is a very useful tool:

What I call Percentage Change Graphic (PCG) is best illustrated through an example:

Suppose you have to increase the number 20 by 20%. Visualise this as follows:

$$20 \xrightarrow[= +4]{20\% \uparrow} 24$$

The PCG has 6 major applications listed and explained below: PCG applied to:

1. Successive changes
2. Product change application
3. Product constancy application
4. A $\rightarrow$ B$\rightarrow$A application
5. Denominator change to Ratio Change application
6. Use of PCG to calculate Ratio Changes

Application 1: PCG Applied to Successive Changes

This is a very common situation in most questions. Suppose you have to solve a question in which a number 30 has two successive percentage increases (20% and 10% respectively).

The situation is handled in the following way using PCG:

$$30 \xrightarrow[+6]{20\% \text{ increase}} 36 \xrightarrow[+3.6]{10\% \text{ increase}} 39.6$$

Illustration

A's salary increases by 20% and then decreases by 20%. What is the net percentage change in *A*'s salary?

Solution:

$$100 \xrightarrow[+20]{20\% \text{ inc.}} 120 \xrightarrow[-24]{20\% \text{ decrease}} 96$$

Hence, *A*'s salary has gone down by 4%

Illustration

A trader gives successive discounts of 10%, 20% and 10% respectively. The percentage of the original cost price he will recover is:

Solution:

$$100 \xrightarrow[-10]{10\% \text{ decrease}} 90 \xrightarrow[-18]{20\% \text{ decrease}} 72 \xrightarrow[-7.2]{10\% \text{ decrease}} 64.8$$

Hence the overall discount is 35.2% and the answer is 64.8%.

Illustration

A trader marks up the price of his goods by 20%, but to a particularly haggling customer he ends up giving a discount of 10% on the marked price. What is the percentage profit he makes?

Solution:

$$100 \xrightarrow[+20]{20\% \text{ increase}} 120 \xrightarrow[-12]{10\% \text{ decrease}} 108$$

Hence, the percentage profit is 8%.

Application 2: PCG applied to Product Change

Suppose you have a product of two variables say 10×10.

If the first variable changes to 11 and the second variable changes to 12, what will be the percentage change in the product? [Note there is a 10% increase in one part of the product and a 20% increase in the other part.]

The formula given for this situation goes as: $(a + b + ab/100)$

Hence, Required % change = $10 + 20 + \dfrac{10 \times 20}{100}$

(Where 10 and 20 are the respective percentage changes in the two parts of the product) (This is being taught as a shortcut at most institutes across the country currently.)

However, a much easier solution for this case can be visualized as:

$100 \xrightarrow[+20]{20\% \uparrow} 120 \xrightarrow[+12]{10\% \uparrow} 132$. Hence, the final product

shows a 32% increase.

Similarly suppose $10 \times 10 \times 10$ becomes $11 \times 12 \times 13$
In such a case the following PCG will be used:

$$100 \xrightarrow[+30]{30\% \uparrow} 130 \xrightarrow[+26]{20\% \uparrow} 156 \xrightarrow[+15.6]{10\% \uparrow} 171.6$$

Hence, the final product sees a 71.6 percent increase (Since, the product changes from 100 to 171.6)

Note: You will get the same result irrespective of the order in which you use the respective percentage changes.

Also note that this process is very similar to the one used for calculating successive percentage change.

Application for DI:

Suppose you have two pie charts as follows:

Scooters: 23.47%

Scooters: 26.55%

Total sales year 1: 17342.34 crores

Total sales Year 2: 19443.56 crores

If you are asked to calculate the percentage change in the sales revenue of scooters for the company from year one to year two, what would you do?

The formula for percentage change would give us:

$$\frac{(0.2655 \times 19443.56) - (0.2347 \times 17342.34) \times 100}{(0.2347 \times 17342.34)}$$

i.e. $\dfrac{\text{New Sales Revenue} - \text{Original Sales Revenue}}{\text{Original Sales Revenue}} \times 100$

Obviously this calculation is easier said than done.

However, the Product change application of PCG allows us to execute this calculation with a lot of ease comparatively. Consider the following solution:

Product for year one is: 0.2347×17342.34
Product for year two is: 0.2655×19443.56

These can be approximated into:

234×173 and 265×194 respectively (Note that by moving into three digits we do not end up losing any accuracy. We have elaborated this point in the chapter on Ratio and Proportions.)

The overall percentage change depends on two individual percentage changes:

234 increases to 265: A % change of $31/234 = 13.2$ % approx. This calculation has to be done using the percentage rule for calculating the percentage value of the ratio

173 increases to 194 – A percentage change of approximately 12%.

Thus PCG will give the answer as follows:

$$100 \xrightarrow[+13.2]{13.2\% \uparrow} 113.2 \xrightarrow[+13.56]{12\% \uparrow} 126.76$$

Hence, 26.76 % increase in the product's value. (Note that the value on the calculator for the full calculation sans any approximations is 26.82 %, and given the fact that we have come extremely close to the answer—the method is good enough to solve the question with a reasonable degree of accuracy.)

Application 3 of PCG: Product Constancy Application (Inverse proportionality)

Suppose you have a situation wherein the price of a commodity has gone up by 25%. In case you are required to keep the total expenditure on the commodity constant, you would obviously need to cut down on the consumption. By what percentage? Well, PCG gives you the answer as follows:

$$100 \xrightarrow[\substack{+25 \\ \text{Price effect}}]{25\% \uparrow} 125 \xrightarrow[\substack{-25 \\ \text{Consumption Effect}}]{} 100$$

Hence, the percentage drop in consumption to offset the price increase is 20%.

I leave it to the student to discover the percentage drop required in the second part of the product if one part increases by 50 percent.

Note: Product constancy is just another name for Inverse proportionality.

Table 5.1 gives you some standard values for this kind of a situation.

Application 4 of PCG: A→B→A.

Very often we are faced with a situation where we compare two numbers say A and B. In such cases, if we are given a relationship from A to B, then the reverse relationship can be determined by using PCG in much the same way as the product constancy use shown above.

Illustration

B's salary is 25% more than A's salary. By what percent is A's salary less than B's salary?

$$100(A) \xrightarrow[+25]{25\%\uparrow} 125(B) \xrightarrow{-25} 100(A)$$

A drop of 25 on 125 gives a 20% drop.
Hence A's salary is 20% less than B's.

Note: The values which applied for Product Constancy also apply here. Hence Table 4.1 is useful for this situation also.

Application 5 of PCG → Effect of change in Denominator on the Value of the Ratio

The denominator has an inverse relationship with the value of a ratio.

Hence the process used for product constancy (and explained above) can be used for calculating percentage change in the denominator.

For instance, suppose you have to evaluate the difference between two ratios:

Ratio 1   : 10/20
Ratio 2   : 10/25

As is evident the denominator is increasing from 20 to 25 by 25%.

If we calculate the value of the two ratios we will get:
Ratio 1 = 0.5,   Ratio 2 = 0.4.

% change between the two ratios = $\dfrac{0.1}{0.5} \times 100 = 20\%$ Drop

This value can be got through PCG as:
$100 \longrightarrow 125 \longrightarrow 100$ Hence, 20% drop.

Note: This is exactly the same as Product constancy and works here because the numerator is constant.

Hence, $R_1 = N/D_1$ and $R_2 = N/D_2$
i.e. $R_1 \times D_1 = N$ and $R_2 \times D_2 = N$, which is the product constancy situation.

Direct process for calculation

To find out the percentage change in the ratio due to a change in the denominator follow the following process:

In order to find the percentage change from 10/20 to 10/25, calculate the percentage change in the denominator in the reverse fashion.

i.e. The required percentage change from R_1 to R_2 will be given by calculating the percentage change in the

denominators from 25 to 20 (i.e. in a reverse fashion) & not from 20 to 25.

Table 5.1   **Product Constancy Table, Inverse Proportionality Table, A → B → A table, Ratio Change to Denominator table**

Product XY is Constant	X increases (%)	Y Decreases (%)
A→B→A	A → B % increase	B → A% decrease
X is inversely proportional to Y	X increases (%)	Y decreases (%)
Ratio change effect of Denominator change	Denominator increases (%)	(Ratio decreases (%)
Denominator change effect of Ratio change	Ratio increases (%)	As Denominator decreases (%)
Standard Value 1	9.09	8.33
Standard Value 2	10	9.09
Standard Value 3	11.11	10
Standard Value 4	12.5	11.11
Standard Value 5	14.28	12.5
Standard Value 6	16.66	14.28
Standard Value 7	20	16.66
Standard Value 8	25	20
Standard Value 9	33.33	25
Standard Value 10	50	33.33
Standard Value 11	60	37.5
Standard Value 12	66.66	40
Standard Value 13	75	42.85
Standard Value 14	100	50

Application 6: Use of PCG to Calculate Ratio Changes:

Under normal situations, you will be faced with ratios where both numerator and denominator change. The process to handle and calculate such changes is also quite convenient if you go through PCG.

Illustration

Calculate the percentage change between the Ratios.
Ratio 1 = 10/20   Ratio 2 = 15/25

The answer in this case is 0.5 → 0.6 (20% increase). However, in most cases calculating the values of the ratio will not be easy. The following PCG process can be used to get the answer:

When 10/20 changes to 15/25, the change occurs primarily due to two reasons:

(A) Change in the numerator (Numerator effect)
(B) Change in the denominator (Denominator effect)

By segregating the two effects and calculating the effect due to each separately, we can get the answer easily as follows:

Numerator Effect The numerator effect on the value of the ratio is the same as the change in the numerator.

Hence, to calculate the numerator effect, just calculate the percentage change in the numerator:

In this case the numerator is clearly changing from 10 to 15 (i.e. a 50% increase.) This signifies that the numerator effect is also 50%.

Denominator Effect As we have just seen above, the effect of a percentage change in the denominator on the value of the ratio is seen by calculating the denominator's percentage change in the reverse order.

In this case, the denominator is changing from 20 to 25. Hence the denominator effect will be seen by going reverse from 25 to 20 i.e. 20% drop.

With these two values, the overall percentage change in the Ratio is seen by:

$$100 \xrightarrow[\substack{+50 \\ \text{Numerator} \\ \text{Effect}}]{50\% \uparrow} 150 \xrightarrow[\substack{-30 \\ \text{Denominator} \\ \text{Effect}}]{20\% \downarrow} 120$$

This means that the ratio has increased by 20%.

I leave it to the student to practice such calculations with more complicated values for the ratios.

Implications for Data Interpretation

Percentage is perhaps one of the most critical links between QA and Data Interpretation.

In the chapter theory mentioned above, the Percentage Rule for Percentage Calculations and the PCG applied to product change and ratio change are the most critical.

As already shown, the use of PCG to calculate the percentage change in a product (as exhibited through the pie chart example above) as well as the use of PCG to calculate ratio changes are two extremely useful applications of the concepts of percentages into DI.

Applying Percentages for the special case of comparing two ratios to find the larger one.

Suppose you have two ratios to compare. Say $R_1 = N_1/D_1$ and $R_2 = N_2/D_2$

The first step is to find the ten percent ranges for each of these ratios. In case, they belong to different ranges of 10% (say R1 lies between 50-60 while R2 lies between 70 to 80), it becomes pretty simple to say which one will be higher.

In case, both of these values for percentage of the ratios belong to the same ten percent range, then we can use the following process

Step 1: Calculate the percentage change in the numerator

Step 2: Calculate the percentage change in the denominator.

There could be four cases in this situation, when we move from Ratio$_1$ to Ratio$_2$:

Case 1: **Numerator is increasing while denominator is decreasing** → obviously the net effect of the two changes will be an increase in the ratio. Hence, R_2 will be greater.

Case 2: **Numerator is decreasing while denominator is increasing** → obviously the net effect of the two changes will be a decrease in the ratio. Hence, R_1 will be greater.

It is only in the following cases that we need to look at the respective changes in the Numerator and denominator.

Case 3: Numerator and denominator are both increasing Calculate the percentage value of the respective increases. If the numerator is increasing more than the denominator the ratio will go up. On the other hand, if the denominator is increasing more than the numerator, Ratio$_2$ will be smaller than Ratio$_1$. (Note: Compare in percentage values)

Case 4: **Numerator and denominator are both decreasing** → Calculate the percentage value of the respective decreases. If the numerator is decreasing more than the denominator the ratio will go down. On the other hand, if the denominator is decreasing more than the numerator, Ratio$_2$ will be greater than Ratio$_1$.

FRACTION TO PERCENTAGE CONVERSION TABLE

The following percentage values appear repeatedly over the entire area where questions can be framed on the topic of percentage. Further, it would be of great help to you if you are able to recognize these values separately from values that do not appear in the Table 5.2.

Some Utilisations of the Table

- The values that appear in the table are all percentage values. These can be converted into decimals by just shifting the decimal point by two places to the left. Thus, 83.33% = 0.8333 in decimal value.

- A second learning from this table is in the process of division by any of the numbers such as 2, 3, 4, 5, 6, 7, 8, 9, 11, 12, 15, 16, 24 and so on, students normally face problems in calculating the decimal values of these divisions. However, if one gets used to the decimal values that appear in the Table 5.2, calculation of decimals in divisions will become very simple. For instance, when an integer is divided by 7, the decimal values can only be .14, .28, .42, .57, .71, .85 or .00. (There are approximate values)

- This also means that the difference between two ratios like $\dfrac{x}{6} - \dfrac{x}{7}$ can be integral if and only if x is divisible by both 6 and 7.

  This principle is very useful as an advanced short cut for option based solution of some questions. I leave it to the student to discover applications of this principle.

Calculation of Multiplication by Numbers like 1.21, 0.83 and so on

In my opinion, the calculation of multiplication of any number by a number of the form $0.xy$ or of the form $1.ab$

Table 5.2 Percentage Conversion Table

	1	2	3	4	5	6	7	8	9	10	11	12
1	100											
2	50	100										
3	33.33	66.66	100									
4	25	50	75	100								
5	20	40	60	80	100							
6	16.66	33.33	50	66.66	83.33	100						
7	14.28	28.57	42.85	57.14	71.42	85.71	100					
8	12.5	25	37.5	50	62.5	75	87.5	100				
9	11.11	22.22	33.33	44.44	55.55	66.66	77.77	88.88	100			
10	10	20	30	40	50	60	70	80	90	100		
11	9.09	18.18	27.27	36.36	45.45	54.54	63.63	72.72	81.81	90.09	100	
12	8.33	16.66	25	33.33	41.66	50	58.33	66.66	75	83.33	91.66	100
15	6.66	13.33	20	26.66	33.33	40						
16	6.25	12.5	18.75	25								
20	5	10	15	20	25							
24	4.166	8.33	12.5	16.66	20.83	25						
25	4	8	12	16	20	24	28	32	26	40		
30	3.33	6.66	10	13.33	16.66	20						
40	2.5	5	7.5	10	12.5	15	17.5	20				
60	1.66	3.33	5	6.66	8.33	10						

Formula for any cell = Column value × 100/Row value

should be viewed as a subtraction/addition situation and not as a multiplication situation. This can be explained as follows.

Example: Calculate 1.23 × 473.

Solution: If we try to calculate this by multiplying, we will end up going through a very time taking process, which will yield the final value at the end but nothing before that (i.e. you will have no clue about the answer's range till you reach the end of the calculation).

Instead, one should view this multiplication as an addition of 23% to the original number. This means, the answer can be got by adding 23% of the number to itself.

Space for Notes

Thus 473 × 1.23 = 473 + 23% of 473 = 473 + 94.6 + 3% of 473 = 567.6 + 14.19 = 581.79

(The percentage rule can be used to calculate the addition and get the answer.)

The similar process can be utilised for the calculation of multiplication by a number such as 0.87

(Answer can be got by subtracting 13% of the number from itself and this calculation can again be done by percentage rule.)

Hence, the student is advised to become thorough with the percentage rules. Percentage calculation & additions of 2 & 3 digit numbers.

WORKED-OUT PROBLEMS

Problem 5.1 *A* sells his goods 30% cheaper than *B* and 30% dearer than *C*. By what percentage is the cost of *C*'s goods cheaper than *B*'s goods.

Solution There are two alternative processes for solving this question:

1. Assume the price of *C*'s goods as *p*.: Then *A*'s goods are at 1.3 p and *B*'s goods are such that *A*'s goods are 30% cheaper than *B*'s goods. i.e. *A*'s goods are priced at 70% of *B*'s goods.

$$\text{Hence, } 1.3\ p \to 70$$
$$B\text{'s price} \to 100$$
$$B\text{'s price} = 130\ p/70 = 1.8571\ p$$

Then, the percentage by which *C*'s price is cheaper than *B*'s price =

$$(1.8571\ p - p) \times 100/(1.8571\ p) = 600/13 = \textbf{46.15\%}$$

Learning task for student Could you answer the question: Why did we assume *C*'s price as a variable *p* and then work out the problem on its basis. What would happen if we assumed *B*'s price as *p* or if we assumed *A*'s price as *p*?

2. Instead of assuming the price of one of the three as p, assume the price as 100.
Let *B* = 100. Then *A* = 70, which is 30% more than *C*. Hence *C* = 23.07% less than *A* (from Table 4.1) = approx. 53.84. Hence answer is 46.15% approximately.

(This calculation can be done mentally if you are able to work through the calculations by the use of percentage rule. The students are advised to try to assume the value of 100 for each of the variables *A*, *B* and *C* and see what happens to the calculations involved in the problem. Since the value of 100 is assumed for a variable to minimise the requirements of calculations to solve the problems, we should ensure that the variable assumed as 100 should have the maximum calculations associated with it.)

Note: In fact this question and the ones that follow contain some of the most basic operations in the chapter of percentages. The questions at the first level of difficulty would appear in examinations like CET Maharashtra, Bank P.O., MAT, NMAT, CLAT, NLS and most other aptitude exams. Hence, if you are able to do the operations illustrated here mentally, you would be able to solve LOD 1 questions easily and gain a significant time advantage over your competitors.

However, for the serious CAT aspirant, the logic used for LOD I questions would normally be used as a part of the entire logic. You would be able to see this in the questions of the second and the third level of difficulties in the exercises later in the chapter. Hence, developing the process for solving questions of the LOD 1 level mentally would help you gain an improved speed for the CAT level questions.

Also remember that since percentages are the basis for most of the commercial mathematics as well as for calculation and the Data Interpretation section, developing skills for calculation and problem solving illustrated here would go a long way towards helping you clear aptitude exams.

Problem 5.2 The length and the breadth of a rectangle are changed by +20% and by –10% respectively. What is the percentage change in the area of the rectangle.

Solution The area of a rectangle is given by: length × breadth. If we represent these by:

Area = $L \times B = LB \to$ then we will get the changed area as

$$\text{Area}_{(NEW)} = 1.2\ L \times 0.9\ B = 1.08\ LB$$

Hence, the change in area is 8% increase.

Note: You can solve (and in fact, finish the problem) during your first reading by using percentage change graphic as follows:

$$100 \xrightarrow{\ +20\%\ } 120 \xrightarrow{\ -10\%\ } 108.$$ Hence, the percentage change is **8%**.

Problem 5.3 Due to a 25% price hike in the price of rice, a person is able to purchase 20 kg less of rice for ₹ 400. Find the initial price.

Solution Since price is rising by 25%, consumption has to decrease by 20%. But there is an actual reduction in the consumption by 20 kg. Thus, 20% decrease in consumption is equal to a 20 kg drop in consumption.

Hence, original consumption is: 100 kg of rice.

Money spent being ₹ 400, the original price of rice is ₹ 4 per kg.

(There, you see the benefit of internalising the product constancy table! It is left to the student to analyze why and how the product constancy table applies here.)

Problem 5.4 *A*'s salary is 20% lower than *B*'s salary, which is 15% lower than *C*'s salary. By how much percent is *C*'s salary more than *A*'s salary?

Solution The equation approach here would be

$$A = 0.8\ B$$
$$B = 0.85\ C$$

Then $\qquad A = 0.8 \times 0.85\ C$

$A = 0.68\ C$ (Use percentage change graphic to calculate the value of 0.68)

Thus, A's salary is 68 % of C's salary.

If A's salary is 68, B's salary is 100.

Using percentage change graphic

$$68 \xrightarrow[+32]{(3200/68)\%} 100$$

Students are advised to refrain from using equations to solve questions of this nature. In fact, you can adopt the following process, which can be used while you are reading the problem, to get the result faster.

Assume one of the values as 100. (Remember, selection of the right variable that has to take the value of 100 may make a major difference to your solving time and effort required. The thumb rule for selecting the variable whose value is to be taken as 100 is based on three principal considerations:

Select as 100, the variable

1. With the maximum number of percentage calculations associated with it.
2. Select as 100 the variable with the most difficult calculation associated with it.
3. Select as 100 the variable at the start of the problem solving chain.

The student will have to develop his own judgment in applying these principles in specific cases.

Here I would take C as 100, getting B as 85 and A as 68. Hence, the answer is $(32 \times 100/68)$.

Problem 5.5 The cost of manufacture of an article is made up of four components A, B, C and D which have a ratio of 3 : 4 : 5 : 6 respectively. If there are respective changes in the cost of +10%, −20%, −30% and +40%, then what would be the percentage change in the cost?

Solution Assume the cost components to be valued at 30, 40, 50 and 60 as you read the question. Then we can get changed costs by effecting the appropriate changes in each of the four components.

Thus we get the new cost as 33, 32, 35 and 84 respectively.

The original total cost was 180 the new one is 184. The percent change is 4/180 = 2.22%.

Problem 5.6 Harsh receives an inheritance of a certain amount from his grandfather. Of this he loses 32.5% in his effort to produce a film. From the balance, a taxi driver stole the sum of ₹ 1,00,000 that he used to keep in his pocket. Of the rest, he donated 20% to a charity. Further he purchases a flat in Ganga Apartment for ₹ 7.5 lakh. He then realises that he is left with only ₹ 2.5 lakh cash of his inheritance. What was the value of his inheritance?

Solution These sort of problems should either be solved through the reverse process or through options.

Reverse process for this problem He is left with ₹ 2.5 lakh after spending ₹ 7.5 lakh on the apartment.

Therefore, before the apartment purchase he has ₹ 10 lakh. But this is after the 20% reduction in his net value due to his donation to charity. Hence, he must have given ₹ 2.5 lakh to charity (20% decrease corresponds to a 25% increase). As such, he had 12.5 lakh before the charity. Further, he must have had ₹ 13.5 lakh before the taxi driver stole the sum. From 13.5 lakh you can reach the answer by trial and error trying whole number values. You will get that if he had 20 lakh and lost 32.5% of it he would be left with the required 13.5 lakh.

Hence, the answer is ₹ 20 lakh.

This process can be done mentally by: 2.5 + 7.5 = 10 lakh → +25% → 12.5 lakh → + 1 lakh → 13.5 lakh.

From this point move by trial and error. You should try to find the value of the inheritance, which on reduction by 32.5%, would leave 13.5 lakh. A little experience with numbers leaves you with ₹ 20 lakh as the answer. This process should be started as soon as you finish reading the first time.

Through options Suppose the options were:

(a) 25 lakh (b) 22.5 lakh

(c) 20 lakh (d) 18 lakh

Start with any of the middle options. Then keep performing the mathematical operation in the order given in the problem. The final value that he is left with should be ₹ 2.5 lakh. The option that gives this, will be the answer. If the final value yielded is higher than ₹ 2.5 lakh in this case, start with a value lower than the option checked. In case it is the opposite, start with the option higher than the one used.

As a thumb rule, start with the most convenient option—the middle one. This would lead us to start with ₹ 20 lakh here.

However, if we had started with ₹ 25 lakh the following would have occurred.

25 lakh −32.5% → 16.875 lakh −1 lakh → 15.875 lakh −20% − 7.5 lakh, should equal 2.5 lakh → (Prior to doing this calculation, you should see that there is no way the answer will yield a nice whole number like 2.5 lakh. Hence, you can abandon the process here and move to the next option)

Trying with 20 lakh, 20 −32.5% → 13.5 lakh −1ac. → 12.5 lakh −20% → 10 lakh − 7.5 lakh = **2.5 lakh** → Required answer.

LEVEL OF DIFFICULTY (I)

1. Which of the following is the largest number?
   (a) 20% of 200   (b) 7% of 500
   (c) 1300% of 3   (d) 700% of 9

2. If 25% of a number is 75, then 45% of that number is:
   (a) 145   (b) 125
   (c) 150   (d) 135

3. What is 20% of 50% of 75% of 70?
   (a) 5.25   (b) 6.75
   (c) 7.25   (d) 5.5

4. If we express $41(3/17)\%$ as a fraction, then it is equal to
   (a) $\dfrac{17}{7}$ (b) $\dfrac{7}{17}$
   (c) $\dfrac{12}{17}$ (d) $\dfrac{3}{17}$

5. Mr. Abhimanyu Banerjee is worried about the balance of his monthly budget. The price of petrol has increased by 40%. By what percent should he reduce the consumption of petrol so that he is able to balance his budget?
   (a) 33.33   (b) 28.56
   (c) 25   (d) 14.28

6. In Question 5, if Mr. Banerjee wanted to limit the increase in his expenditure to 5% on his basic expenditure on petrol then what should be the corresponding decrease in consumption so that expenditure exceeds only by 5%?
   (a) 33.33   (b) 28.56
   (c) 25   (d) 20

7. Ram sells his goods 25% cheaper than Shyam and 25% dearer than Bram. How much percentage is Bram's goods cheaper than Shyam's?
   (a) 33.33%   (b) 50%
   (c) 66.66%   (d) 40%

8. In an election between 2 candidates, Bhiku gets 65% of the total valid votes. If the total votes were 6000, what is the number of valid votes that the other candidate Mhatre gets if 25% of the total votes were declared invalid?
   (a) 1625   (b) 1575
   (c) 1675   (d) 1525

9. In a medical certificate, by mistake a candidate gave his height as 25% more than normal. In the interview panel, he clarified that his height was 5 feet 5 inches.

Find the percentage correction made by the candidate from his stated height to his actual height.
   (a) 20   (b) 28.56
   (c) 25   (d) 16.66

10. Arjit Sharma generally wears his father's coat. Unfortunately, his cousin Shaurya poked him one day that he was wearing a coat of length more than his height by 15%. If the length of Arjit's father's coat is 120 cm then find the actual length of his coat.
    (a) 105   (b) 108
    (c) 104.34   (d) 102.72

11. A number is mistakenly divided by 5 instead of being multiplied by 5. Find the percentage change in the result due to this mistake.
    (a) 96%   (b) 95%
    (c) 2400%   (d) 200%

12. Harsh wanted to subtract 5 from a number. Unfortunately, he added 5 instead of subtracting. Find the percentage change in the result.
    (a) 300%   (b) 66.66%
    (c) 50%   (d) Cannot be determined

13. If 65% of x = 13% of y, then find the value of x if $y = 2000$.
    (a) 200   (b) 300
    (c) 400   (d) 500

14. In a mixture of 80 litres of milk and water, 25% of the mixture is milk. How much water should be added to the mixture so that milk becomes 20% of the mixture?
    (a) 20 litres   (b) 15 litres
    (c) 25 litres   (d) 24 litres

15. 50% of a% of b is 75% of b% of c. Which of the following is c?
    (a) $1.5a$ (b) $0.667a$
    (c) $0.5a$ (d) $1.25a$

16. A landowner increased the length and the breadth of a rectangular plot by 10% and 20% respectively. Find the percentage change in the cost of the plot assuming land prices are uniform throughout his plot.
    (a) 33%   (b) 35%
    (c) 22.22%   (d) None of these

17. The height of a triangle is increased by 40%. What can be the maximum percentage increase in length of the base so that the increase in area is restricted to a maximum of 60%?

(a) 50%   (b) 20%

(c) 14.28%   (d) 25%

18. The length, breadth and height of a room in the shape of a cuboid are increased by 10%, 20% and 50% respectively. Find the percentage change in the volume of the cuboid.

    (a) 77%   (b) 75%

    (c) 88%   (d) 98%

19. The salary of Amit is 30% more than that of Varun. Find by what percentage is the salary of Varun less than that of Amit?

    (a) 26.12%   (b) 23.07%

    (c) 21.23%   (d) 27.27%

20. The price of sugar is reduced by 25% but inspite of the decrease, Aayush ends up increasing his expenditure on sugar by 20%. What is the percentage change in his monthly consumption of sugar ?

    (a) +60%   (b) −10%

    (c) +33.33%   (d) 50%

21. The price of rice falls by 20%. How much rice can be bought now with the money that was sufficient to buy 20 kg of rice previously?

    (a) 5 kg   (b) 15 kg

    (c) 25 kg   (d) 30 kg

22. 30% of a number when subtracted from 91, gives the number itself. Find the number.

    (a) 60   (b) 65

    (c) 70   (d) 75

23. When 60% of a number A is added to another number B, B becomes 175% of its previous value. Then which of the following is true regarding the values of A and B?

    (a) $A > B$

    (b) $B > A$

    (c) $B \geq A$

    (d) Either (a) or (b) can be true depending upon the values of A and B

24. At an election, the candidate who got 56% of the votes cast won by 144 votes. Find the total number of voters on the voting list if 80% people cast their vote and there were no invalid votes.

    (a) 360   (b) 720

    (c) 1800   (d) 1500

25. The population of a village is 1,00,000. The rate of increase is 10% per annum. Find the population at the start of the third year.

    (a) 1,33,100   (b) 1,21,000

    (c) 1,18,800   (d) 1,20,000

26. The population of the village of Gavas is 10,000 at this moment. It increases by 10% in the first year. However, in the second year, due to immigration, the population

drops by 5%. Find the population at the end of the third year if in the third year the population increases by 20%.

    (a) 12,340   (b) 12,540

    (c) 1,27,540   (d) 12,340

27. A man invests ₹ 10,000 in some shares in the ratio 2 : 3 : 5 which pay dividends of 10%, 25% and 20% (on his investment) for that year respectively. Find his dividend income.

    (a) 1900   (b) 2000

    (c) 2050   (d) 1950

28. In an examination, Mohit obtained 20% more than Sushant but 10% less than Rajesh. If the marks obtained by Sushant is 1080, find the percentage marks obtained by Rajesh if the full marks is 2000.

    (a) 86.66%   (b) 72%

    (c) 78.33%   (d) 77.77%

29. In a class, 25% of the students were absent for an exam. 30% failed by 20 marks and 10% just passed because of grace marks of 5. Find the average score of the class if the remaining students scored an average of 60 marks and the pass marks are 33 (counting the final scores of the candidates).

    (a) 37.266   (b) 37.6

    (c) 37.8   (d) 36.93

30. Ram spends 20% of his monthly income on his household expenditure, 15% of the rest on books, 30% of the rest on clothes and saves the rest. On counting, he comes to know that he has finally saved ₹ 9520. Find his monthly income.

    (a) 10000   (b) 15000

    (c) 20000   (d) 12000

31. Hans and Bhaskar have salaries that jointly amount to ₹ 10,000 per month. They spend the same amount monthly and then it is found that the ratio of their savings is 6 : 1. Which of the following can be Hans's salary?

    (a) ₹ 6000   (b) ₹ 5000

    (c) ₹ 4000   (d) ₹ 3000

32. The population of a village is 5500. If the number of males increases by 11% and the number of females increases by 20%, then the population becomes 6330. Find the population of females in the town.

    (a) 2500   (b) 3000

    (c) 2000   (d) 3500

33. Vicky's salary is 75% more than Ashu's. Vicky got a raise of 40% on his salary while Ashu got a raise of 25% on his salary. By what percent is Vicky's salary more than Ashu's?

    (a) 96%   (b) 51.1%

    (c) 90%   (d) 52.1%

34. On a shelf, the first row contains 25% more books than the second row and the third row contains 25% less books than the second row. If the total number of books contained in all the rows is 600, then find the number of books in the first row.
    (a) 250
    (b) 225
    (c) 300
    (d) None of these.

35. An ore contains 25% of an alloy that has 90% iron. Other than this, in the remaining 75% of the ore, there is no iron. How many kilograms of the ore are needed to obtain 60 kg of pure iron?
    (a) 250 kg
    (b) 275 kg
    (c) 300 kg
    (d) 266.66 kg

36. Last year, the Indian cricket team played 40 one-day cricket matches out of which they managed to win only 40%. This year, so far it has played some matches, which has made it mandatory for it to win 80% of the remaining matches to maintain its existing winning percentage. Find the number of matches played by India so far this year.
    (a) 30
    (b) 25
    (c) 28
    (d) Insufficient Information

37. The population of a village is 1,00,000. Increase rate per annum is 10%. Find the population at the starting of the fourth year.
    (a) 1,33,100
    (b) 1,21,000
    (c) 1,33,000
    (d) None of these

38. In the recent, climate conference in New York, out of 700 men, 500 women, 800 children present inside the building premises, 20% of the men, 40% of the women and 10% of the children were Indians. Find the percentage of people who were not Indian.
    (a) 73%
    (b) 77%
    (c) 79%
    (d) 83%

39. A cow and a calf cost ₹ 2000 and ₹ 1400 respectively. If the price of the cow and that of the calf is increased by 20% and 30% respectively then the price of 1 dozen cows and 2 dozens calves is:
    (a) 72,480
    (b) 71,360
    (c) 74,340
    (d) None of these

40. Ram sells his goods 20% cheaper than Bobby and 20% dearer than Chandilya. How much percentage is Chandilya's goods cheaper/dearer than Bobby's?
    (a) 33.33%
    (b) 50%
    (c) 42.85%
    (d) None of these

41. During winters, an athlete can run 'x' metres on one bottle of Glucose. But in the summer, he can only run $0.5 x$ metres on one bottle of Glucose. How many bottles of Glucose are required to run 400 meters during summer?
    (a) $800/x$
    (b) $890/x$
    (c) 96
    (d) $454/x$

42. Out of the total production of iron from hematite, an ore of iron, 20% of the ore gets wasted, and out of the remaining ore, only 25% is pure iron. If the pure iron obtained in a year from a mine of hematite was 80,000 kg, then the quantity of hematite mined from that mine in the year is
    (a) 5,00,000 kg
    (b) 4,00,000 kg
    (c) 4,50,000 kg
    (d) None of these

43. A man buys a truck for ₹ 2,50,000. The annual repair cost comes to 2.0% of the price of purchase. Besides, he has to pay an annual tax of ₹ 2000. At what monthly rent must he rent out the truck to get a return of 15% on his net investment of the first year?
    (a) ₹ 3350
    (b) ₹ 2500
    (c) ₹ 4000
    (d) ₹ 3212.50

44. Recently, while shopping in Patna Market in Bihar, I came across two new shirts selling at a discount. I decided to buy one of them for my little boy Sherry. The shopkeeper offered me the first shirt for ₹ 42 and said that it usually sold for 8/7 of that price. He then offered me the other shirt for ₹ 36 and said that it usually sold for 7/6th of that price. Of the two shirts which one do you think is a better bargain and what is the percentage discount on it?
    (a) first shirt, 12.5%
    (b) second shirt, 14.28%
    (c) Both are same
    (d) None of these

45. 4/5th of the voters in Bellary promised to vote for Sonia and the rest promised to vote for Sushma. Of these voters, 10% of the voters who had promised to vote for Sonia, did not vote on the election day, while 20% of the voters who had promised to vote for Sushma did not vote on the election day. What is the total no. of votes polled if Sonia got 216 votes?
    (a) 200
    (b) 300
    (c) 264
    (d) 100

46. In an examination, 80% students passed in Physics, 70% in Chemistry while 15% failed in both the subjects. If 325 students passed in both the subjects. Find the total number of students who appeared in the examination.
    (a) 500
    (b) 400
    (c) 300
    (d) 600

47. Ravana spends 30% of his salary on house rent, 30% of the rest he spends on his children's education and 24% of the total salary he spends on clothes. After his expenditure, he is left with ₹ 2500. What is Ravana's salary?
    (a) ₹ 11,494.25
    (b) ₹ 20,000
    (c) ₹ 10,000
    (d) ₹ 15,000

48. The entrance ticket at the Minerva theatre in Mumbai is worth ₹ 250. When the price of the ticket was

lowered, the sale of tickets increased by 50% while the collections recorded a decrease of 17.5%. Find the deduction in the ticket price.

  (a) ₹ 150   (b) ₹ 112.5

  (c) ₹ 105   (d) ₹ 120

49. Ravi's monthly salary is A rupees. Of this, he spends X rupees. The next month he has an increase of C% in his salary and D% in his expenditure. The new amount saved is:

  (a) $A(1 + C/100) - X(1 + D/100)$

  (b) $(A/100)$ $(C - D)$ $X(1 + D/100)$

(c) $X(C - (D)/100$

(d) $X(C + D)/100$

50. In the year 2000, the luxury car industry had two car manufacturers—Maruti and Honda with market shares of 25% and 75% respectively. In 2001, the overall market for the product increased by 50% and a new player BMW also entered the market and captured 15% of the market share. If we know that the market share of Maruti increased to 50% in the second year, the share of Honda in that year was:

  (a) 50%   (b) 45%

  (c) 40%   (d) 35%

Space for Rough Work

LEVEL OF DIFFICULTY (II)

1. Bill Ambani, a very clever businessman, started off a business with very little capital. In the first year, he earned a profit of 50% and donated 50% of the total capital (initial capital + profit) to a charitable organisa-tion. The same course was followed in the 2nd and 3rd years also. If at the end of three years, he is left with ₹ 16,875, then find the amount donated by him at the end of the 2nd year.
   (a) ₹ 45,000   (b) ₹ 12,500
   (c) ₹ 22,500   (d) ₹ 20,000

2. In an examination, 48% students failed in Hindi and 32% students in History, 20% students failed in both the subjects. If the number of students who passed the examination was 880, how many students appeared in the examination if the examination consisted only of these two subjects?
   (a) 2000   (b) 2200
   (c) 2500   (d) 1800

3. At IIM Bangalore, 60% of the students are boys and the rest are girls. Further 15% of the boys and 7.5% of the girls are getting a fee waiver. If the number of those getting a fee waiver is 90, find the total number of students getting 50% concession if it is given that 50% of those not getting a fee waiver are eligible to get half fee concession?
   (a) 360   (b) 280
   (c) 320   (d) 330

4. A machine depreciates in value each year at the rate of 10% of its previous value. However, every second year there is some maintenance work so that in that particular year, depreciation is only 5% of its previous value. If at the end of the fourth year, the value of the machine stands at ₹ 1,46,205, then find the value of machine at the start of the first year.
   (a) ₹ 1,90,000   (b) ₹ 2,00,000
   (c) ₹ 1,95,000   (d) ₹ 2,10,000

5. Arushi's project report consists of 25 pages each of 60 lines with 75 characters on each line. In case the number of lines is reduced to 55 but the number of characters is increased to 90 per lines, what is the percentage change in the number of pages. (Assume the number of pages to be a whole number.)
   (a) +10%   (b) +5%
   (c) −8%   (d) −10%

6. The price of soap is collectively decided by five factors: research, raw materials, labour, advertise-ments and transportation. Assume that the functional relationship is

Price of soap = ($k \times$ Research costs × Raw material costs × Labour costs × Advertising cost × Transporta-tion cost).
   If there are respective changes of 10%, 20%, −20%, 25% and 50% in the five factors, then find the change in the price of soap.
   (a) 97%   (b) 95%
   (c) 98%   (d) 96%

7. After receiving two successive raises, Hursh's salary became equal to 15/8 times of his initial salary. By how much percent was the salary raised the first time if the second raise was twice as high (in percent) as the first?
   (a) 15%   (b) 20%
   (c) 25%   (d) 30%

8. The ratio of Jim's salary for October to his salary for November was 1.5 : 1.333 and the ratio of the salary for November to that for December was 2 : 2.6666. The worker got 40 rupees more for December than for October and received a bonus consti-tuting 40 per cent of the salary for three months. Find the bonus. (Assume that the number of workdays is the same in every month.)
   (a) 368.888 rupees (b) 152.5555 rupees
   (c) 222.22 rupees   (d) 265.6 rupees

9. After three successive equal percentage rise in the salary the sum of 100 rupees turned into 140 rupees and 49 paise. Find the percentage rise in the salary.
   (a) 12%   (b) 22%
   (c) 66%   (d) 82%

10. Prema goes to a shop to buy a sofa set costing ₹ 13,080. The rate of sales tax is 9%. She tells the shopkeeper to reduce the price of the sofa set to such an extent that she has to pay ₹13080 inclusive of sales tax. Find the percentage reduction needed in the price of the sofa set to just satisfy her require-ment.
   (a) 8.33%   (b) 8.26%
   (c) 9%   (d) 8.5%

11. The price of a certain article was raised by 10% in India. The consumption of the same article was increased from 200 tons to 225 tons. By how much percent will the expenditure on the article rise in the Indian economy?
   (a) 24.25%   (b) 22.5%
   (c) 23.75%   (d) 26.75%

12. In the university examination last year, Rajesh scored 65% in English and 82% in History. What is the min-imum percent he should score in Sociology, which

is out of 50 marks (if English and History were for 100 marks each), if he aims at getting 78% overall?

(a) 94%   (b) 92%

(c) 98%   (d) 96%

13. King Dashratha, at his eleventh hour, called his three queens and distributed his gold in the following way: He gave 50% of his wealth to his first wife, 50% of the rest to his second wife and again 50% of the rest to his third wife. If their combined share is worth 1,30,900 kilograms of gold, find the quantity of gold King Dashratha was having initially?

(a) 1,50,000 kg   (b) 1,49,600 kg

(c) 1,51,600 kg   (d) 1,52,600 kg

14. The population of New Foundland increases with a uniform rate of 8% per annum, but due to immigration, there is a further increase of population by 1% (however, this 1% increase in population is to be calculated on the population after the 8% increase and not on the previous years population). Find what will be the percentage increase in population after 2 years.

(a) 18.984   (b) 18.081

(c) 18.24   (d) 17.91

15. 10% of Mexico's population migrated to South Asia, 10% of the remaining migrated to America and 10% of the rest migrated to Australia. If the female population, which was left in Mexico, remained only 3,64,500, find the population of Mexico City before the migration and its effects if it is given that before the migration the female population was half the male population and this ratio did not change after the migration?

(a) 10,00,000   (b) 12,00,000

(c) 15,00,000   (d) 16,00,000

16. According to a recent survey report issued by the Commerce Ministry, Government of India, 30% of the total FDI goes to Gujarat and 20% of this goes to rural areas. If the FDI in Gujarat, which goes to urban areas, is $72 m, then find the size of FDI in rural Andhra Pradesh, which attracts 50% of the FDI that comes to Andhra Pradesh, which accounts for 20% of the total FDI?

(a) $30 m   (b) $9 m

(c) $60 m   (d) $40 m

17. If in question 16, the growth in the size of FDI for the next year with respect to the previous year is 20%, then find the share of urban Maharashtra next year if 12% of the total FDI going to Maharashtra went to urban areas (provided Maharashtra attracted only 10% of the total share for both years).

(a) $36 m   (b) $4.32 m

(c) $3 m   (d) $5 m

18. The cost of food accounted for 25% of the income of a particular family. If the income gets raised by 20%, then what should be the percentage point decrease in the food expenditure as a percentage of the total income to keep the food expenditure unchanged between the two years?

(a) 3.5   (b) 8.33

(c) 4.16   (d) 5

19. If the length, breadth and height of a cube are decreased, decreased and increased by 5%, 5% and 20% respectively, then what will be the impact on the surface area of the cube (in percentage terms)?

(a) 7.25%   (b) 5%

(c) 8.33%   (d) 20.75%

20. A's salary is first increased by 25% and then decreased by 20%. The result is the same as B's salary increased by 20% and then reduced by 25%. Find the ratio of B's salary to that of A's.

(a) 4 : 3   (b) 11 : 10

(c) 10 : 9   (d) 12 : 11

21. The minimum quantity of milk in litres (in whole number) that should be mixed in a mixture of 60 litres in which the initial ratio of milk to water is 1 : 4 so that the resulting mixture has 15% milk is

(a) 3   (b) 4

(c) 5   (d) This is not possible

22. A person saves 6% of his income. Two years later, his income shoots up by 15% but his savings remain the same. Find the hike in his expenditure.

(a) 15.95%   (b) 15%

(c) 14.8%   (d) 15.5%

23. A is 50% more than B, C is 2/3 of A and D is 60% more than C. Now, each of A, B, C and D is increased by 10%. Find what per cent of B is D (after the increase)?

(a) 150%   (b) 160%

(c) 175%   (d) 176%

24. A and B have, between them, ₹ 1200. A spends 12% of his money while B spends 20% of his money. They are then left with a sum that constitutes 85% of the whole sum. Find what amount is left with A.

(a) ₹ 750   (b) ₹ 800

(c) ₹ 700   (d) ₹ 660

25. Maya has ₹ M with her and her friend Chanda has ₹ C with her. Maya spends 12% of her money and Chanda also spends the same amount as Maya did. What percentage of her money did Chanda spend?

(a) $\dfrac{18M}{C}$ (b) $\dfrac{18C}{M}$

(c) $\dfrac{12M}{C}$ (d) $\dfrac{12C}{M}$

26. In a village consisting of p persons, x% can read and write. Of the males alone y%, and of the females alone z% can read and write. Find the number of males in the village in terms of p, x, y and z if $z < y$.

   (a) $\dfrac{p(x-z)}{(y+x-z)}$ (b) $\dfrac{p(x-z)}{(y+x-2z)}$

   (c) $\dfrac{p(y-x)}{(x-z)}$ (d) $\dfrac{p(x-z)}{(y-z)}$

27. In order to maximise his gain, a theatre owner decides to reduce the price of tickets by 20% and as a result of this, the sales of tickets increase by 40%. If, as a result of these changes, he is able to increase his weekly collection by ₹ 1,68,000, find by what value did the gross collection increase per day.

   (a) 14,000   (b) 18,000
   (c) 24,000   (d) 20,000

28. In a town consisting of three localities A, B and C, the population of the three localities A, B and C are in the ratio $9:8:3$. In locality A, 80% of the people are literate, in locality B, 30% of the people are illiterate. If 90% people in locality C are literate, find the percentage literacy in that town.

   (a) 61.5%   (b) 78%
   (c) 75%   (d) None of these

29. A fraction is such that if the double of the numerator and the triple of the denominator is changed by +10% and –30% respectively then we get 11% of 16/21. Find the fraction.

   (a) $\dfrac{4}{25}$ (b) $\dfrac{2}{25}$

   (c) $\dfrac{3}{25}$ (d) None of these

30. To pass an examination, 40% marks are essential. A obtains 10% marks less than the pass marks and B obtains 11.11% marks less than A. What percent less than the sum of A's and B's marks should C obtain to pass the exam?

   (a) 40%   (b) 41(3/17)%
   (c) 28%   (d) Any of these

31. The hourly wages of a female labour are increased by 12.5%, whereas the weekly working hours are reduced by 8%. Find the percentage change in the weekly wages if she was getting ₹ 1200 per week for 50 hours previously.

   (a) +3.5%   (b) 4%
   (c) 4.5%   (d) None of these

32. Two numbers X and Y are 20% and 28% less than a third number Z. Find by what percentage is the number Y less than the number X.

   (a) 8%   (b) 12%
   (c) 10%   (d) 9%

33. Price of a commodity is first increased by x% and then decreased by x%. If the new price is $K/100$, find the original price.

   (a) $(x-100)100/K$ (b) $(x^2-100^2)100/K$
   (c) $(100-x)100/K$ (d) $100K/(100^2-x^2)$

34. The salary of a person is increased by ₹ 4800 and the rate of tax is decreased by 2% from 12% to 10%. The effect is such that he is now paying the same tax as before. If in both the cases, the standard tax deduction is fixed at 20% of the total income, find the increased salary?

   (a) ₹ 32,800   (b) ₹ 36,800
   (c) ₹ 28,000   (d) None of these

35. Reena goes to a shop to buy a radio costing ₹ 2568. The rate of sales tax is 7% and the final value is rounded off to the next higher integer. She tells the shopkeeper to reduce the price of the radio so that she has to pay ₹ 2568 inclusive of sales tax. Find the reduction needed in the price of the radio.

   (a) ₹ 180   (b) ₹ 210
   (c) ₹ 168   (d) None of these

Directions for Questions 36 to 38: Read the following passage and answer the questions.

In a recent youth fete organised by Mindworkzz, the entry tickets were sold out according to the following scheme:

Tickets bought in one lot	6	12	18
Percentage discount	10%	20%	25%

Original price per ticket: ₹ 40

This offer could have been availed only when tickets were bought in a fixed lot according to the scheme and any additional ticket was available at its original price.

36. If a person has to buy 25 tickets, then what will be the minimum price per ticket?

   (a) Equal to ₹ 32   (b) 32.32
   (c) 31.84   (d) Cannot be determined.

37. In the above question, what will be the approximate possible maximum price per ticket (if discounts have been availed for 24 tickets)?

   (a) ₹ 30   (b) ₹ 32
   (c) ₹ 36   (d) ₹ 36.16

38. On the last day of the fete, with the objective of maximising participation, the number of tickets sold in a lot was halved with the same discount offer. Mr. X is in a fix regarding the number of tickets he can buy with ₹ 532. The maximum number of tickets he can purchase with this money is

   (a) 14   (b) 15
   (c) 16   (d) 17

39. 800 people were supposed to vote on a resolution, but 1/3rd of the people who had decided to vote for the motion were abducted. However, the opponents of the motion, through some means managed to increase their strength by 100%. The motion was then rejected by a majority, which was 50% of that by which it would have been passed if none of these changes would have occurred. How many people finally voted for the motion and against the motion?
    (a) 200 (for), 400 (against)
    (b) 100 (for) and 200 (against)
    (c) 150 (for), 300 (against)
    (d) 200 (for) and 300 (against)

40. Of the adult population in Nagpur, 45% of men and 25% of women are married. What percentage of the total population of adults is married (assume that no man marries more than one woman and vice versa)?
    (a) 33.33%   (b) 32.14%
    (c) 31.1%   (d) None of these

41. The weight of an iron bucket increases by 33.33% when filled with water to 50% of its capacity. Which of these may be 50% of the weight of the bucket when it is filled with water (assume the weight of bucket and its capacity in kg to be integers)?
    (a) 7 kg   (b) 6 kg
    (c) 5 kg   (d) 8 kg

42. Australia scored a total of x runs in 50 overs. India tied the scores in 20% less overs. If India's average run rate had been 33.33% higher the scores would have been tied 10 overs earlier. Find how many runs were scored by Australia.
    (a) 250   (b) 240
    (c) 200   (d) Cannot be determined

43. Due to a 25% hike in the price of rice per kilogram, a person is able to purchase 20 kg less for ₹ 400. Find the increased price of rice per kilogram.
    (a) ₹ 5   (b) ₹ 6
    (c) ₹ 10   (d) ₹ 4

44. A salesman is appointed on the basic salary of ₹ 1200 per month and the condition that for every sales of ₹ 10,000 above ₹ 10,000, he will get 50% of basic salary and 10% of the sales as a reward. This incentive scheme does not operate for the first ₹ 10000 of sales. What should be the value of sales if he wants to earn ₹ 7600 in a particular month?
    (a) ₹ 60,000   (b) ₹ 50,000
    (c) ₹ 40,000   (d) None of these

45. In Question 44, which of the following income cannot be achieved in a month?
    (a) ₹ 6000
    (b) ₹ 9000
    (c) Both a and b
    (d) Any income can be achieved

46. In Question 44, despite a 5 percentage point increment on the commission from 20%, the total commission remained unaltered. Find the change in the volume of the transaction.
    (a) −10%   (b) −16%
    (c) −25%   (d) −20%

47. In an assembly election at Surat, the total turnout was 80% out of which 16% of the total voters on the voting list were declared invalid. Find which of the following can be the percentage votes got by the winner of the election if the candidate who came second got 20% of the total voters on the voting list. (There were only three contestants, only one winner and the total number of voters on the voters' list was 20000.)
    (a) 44.8%   (b) 46.6%
    (c) 48%   (d) None of these

48. A watch gains by 2% per hour when the temperature is in the range of 40°C–50°C and it loses at the same rate when the temperature is in the range of 20°C–30°C. However, the watch owner is fortunate since it runs on time in all other temperature ranges. On a sunny day, the temperature started soaring up from 8 a.m. in the morning at the uniform rate of 2°C per hour and sometime during the afternoon it started coming down at the same rate. Find what time will it be by the watch at 7 p.m. if at 8 a.m. the temperature was 32°C and at 4 p.m., it was 40°C.
    (a) 6 : 55 p.m.   (b) 6 : 55 : 12 p.m.
    (c) 6 : 55 : 24 p.m.   (d) None of these

Questions 49 and 50: Study the following table and answer the questions that follow.

Beverages	% of Vitamin	% of Minerals	% of Micronutrients	Cost per 250 gram (In ₹)
Pepsi	12	18	30	8
Coke	15	20	10	10
Sprite	20	10	40	7

49. Which of the following beverages contains the maximum amount of vitamins?
    (a) Pepsi worth ₹ 16
    (b) Coke worth ₹ 15
    (c) Sprite worth ₹ 8
    (d) All the three worth ₹ 12.5 (125 grams of each)

50. Which of these is the cheapest?
    (a) 200 grams of Pepsi + 200 grams of Coke
    (b) 300 grams of Coke +100 grams of Pepsi
    (c) 100 grams of Coke + 100 grams of Pepsi + 100 grams of Sprite
    (d) 300 grams of Coke +100 grams of Sprite

LEVEL OF DIFFICULTY (III)

1. The price of raw materials has gone up by 15%, labour cost has also increased from 25% of the cost of raw material to 30% of the cost of raw material. By how much percentage should there be a reduction in the usage of raw materials so as to keep the cost same?

   (a) 17%   (b) 24%
   (c) 28%   (d) 25%

2. Mr. *A* is a computer programmer. He is assigned three jobs for which time allotted is in the ratio of 5 : 4 : 2 (jobs are needed to be done individually). But due to some technical snag, 10% of the time allotted for each job gets wasted. Thereafter, owing to the lack of interest, he invests only 40%, 30%, 20% of the hours of what was actually allotted to do the three jobs individually. Find how much percentage of the total time allotted is the time invested by *A*.

   (a) 38.33%   (b) 39.4545%
   (c) 32.72%   (d) 36.66%

3. In the Mock CAT paper at Mindworkzz, questions were asked in five sections. Out of the total students, 5% candidates cleared the cut-off in all the sections and 5% cleared none. Of the rest, 25% cleared only one section and 20% cleared four sections. If 24.5% of the entire candidates cleared two sections and 300 candidates cleared three sections, find out how many candidates appeared at the Mock CAT at Mindworkzz?

   (a) 1000   (b) 1200
   (c) 1500   (d) 2000

4. There are three galleries in a coal mine. On the first day, two galleries are operative and after some time, the third gallery is made operative. With this, the output of the mine became half as large again. What is the capacity of the second gallery as a percentage of the first, if it is given that a four-month output of the first and the third galleries was the same as the annual output of the second gallery?

   (a) 70%   (b) 64%
   (c) 60%   (d) 65%

5. 10% of salty sea water contained in a flask was poured out into a beaker. After this, a part of the water contained in the beaker was vapourised by heating and due to this, the percentage of salt in the beaker increased *M* times. If it is known that after the content of the beaker was poured into the flask, the percentage of salt in the flask increased by *x*%. Find the original quantity of sea water in the flask.

   (a) $\dfrac{9M + 1\%}{M - 1}$ (b) $\dfrac{(9M + 1)x\%}{M - 1}$

   (c) $\dfrac{9M - 1x\%}{M + 1}$ (d) $\dfrac{9M + x\%}{M + 1}$

6. In an election of 3 candidates *A*, *B* and *C*, *A* gets 50% more votes than *B*. *A* also beats *C* by 1,80,00 votes. If it is known that *B* gets 5 percentage point more votes than *C*, find the number of voters on the voting list (given 90% of the voters on the voting list voted and no votes were illegal)

   (a) 72,000   (b) 81,000
   (c) 90,000   (d) 1,00,000

7. A clock is set right at 12 noon on Monday. It loses 1/2% on the correct time in the first week but gains 1/4% on the true time during the second week. The time shown on Monday after two weeks will be

   (a) 12 : 25 : 12   (b) 11 : 34 : 48
   (c) 12 : 50 : 24   (d) 12 : 24 : 16

8. The petrol prices shot up by 7% as a result of the hike in the price of crudes. The price of petrol before the hike was ₹ 28 per litre. Vawal travels 2400 kilometres every month and his car gives a mileage of 18 kilometres to a litre. Find the increase in the expenditure that Vawal has to incur due to the increase in the price of petrol (to the nearest rupee)?

   (a) ₹ 270   (b) ₹ 262
   (c) ₹ 276   (d) ₹ 272

9. For Question 8, by how many kilometres should Vawal reduce his travel if he wants to maintain his expenditure at the previous level (prior to the price increase)?

   (a) 157 km   (b) 137 km
   (c) 168 km   (d) 180 km

10. In Question 8, if Vawal wants to limit the increase in expenditure to ₹ 200, what strategy should he adopt with respect to his travel?

    (a) Reduce travel to 2350 kilometres
    (b) Reduce travel to 2340 kilometres
    (c) Reduce travel to 2360 kilometres
    (d) None of these

11. A shopkeeper announces a discount scheme as follows: for every purchase of ₹ 3000 to ₹ 6000, the customer gets a 15% discount or a ticket that entitles him to get a 7% discount on a further purchase of goods costing more than ₹ 6000. The customer, how-

ever, would have the option of reselling his right to the shopkeeper at 4% of his initial purchase value (as per the right refers to the 7% discount ticket). In an enthusiastic response to the scheme, 10 people purchase goods worth ₹ 4000 each. Find the maximum. Possible revenue for the shopkeeper.

(a) ₹ 38,400   (b) ₹ 38,000
(c) ₹ 39,400   (d) ₹ 39,000

12. For question 11, find the maximum possible discount that the shopkeeper would have to offer to the customer.

(a) ₹ 1600   (b) ₹ 2000
(c) ₹ 6000   (d) ₹ 4000

Directions for Questions 13 to 16: Read the following and answer the questions that follow.

Two friends Shayam and Kailash own two versions of a car. Shayam owns the diesel version of the car, while Kailash owns the petrol version.

Kailash's car gives an average that is 20% higher than Shayam's (in terms of litres per kilometre). It is known that petrol costs 60% of its price higher than diesel.

13. The ratio of the cost per kilometre of Kailash's car to Shayam's car is

(a) 3 : 1   (b) 1 : 3
(c) 1.92 : 1   (d) 2 : 1

14. If Shayam's car gives an average of 20 km per litre, then the difference in the cost of travel per kilometre between the two cars is

(a) ₹ 4.3   (b) ₹ 3.5
(c) ₹ 2.5   (d) Cannot be determined

15. For Question 14, the ratio of the cost per kilometre of Shayam's travel to Kailash's travel is

(a) 3 : 1   (b) 1 : 3
(c) 1 : 1.92   (d) 2 : 1

16. If diesel costs ₹ 12.5 per litre, then the difference in the cost of travel per kilometre between Kailash's and Shayam's is (assume an average of 20 km per litre for Shayam's car and also assume that petrol is 50% of its own price higher than diesel)

(a) ₹ 1.75   (b) ₹ 0.875
(c) ₹ 1.25   (d) ₹ 1.125

Directions for Questions 17 to 23: Read the following and answer the questions that follow.

In the island of Hoola Boola Moola, the inhabitants have a strange process of calculating their average incomes and expenditures. According to an old legend prevalent on that island, the average monthly income had to be calculated on the basis of 14 months in a calendar year while the average monthly expenditure was to be calculated on the basis of 9 months per year. This would lead to people having an underestimation of their savings since there would be an underestimation of the income and an overestimation of the expenditure per month.

17. Mr. Boogle Woogle comes back from the USSR and convinces his community comprising 273 families to start calculating the average income and the average expenditure on the basis of 12 months per calendars year. Now if it is known that the average estimated income in his community is (according to the old system) 87 moolahs per month, then what will be the percentage change in the savings of the community of Mr. Boogle Woogle (assume that there is no other change)?

(a) 12.33%   (b) 22.22%
(c) 31.31%   (d) Cannot be determined

18. For Question 17, if it is known that the average estimated monthly expenditure is 19 moolahs per month for the island of Hoola Boola Moola, then what will be the percentage change in the estimated savings of the community?

(a) 32.42%   (b) 38.05%
(c) 25.23%   (d) Cannot be determined

19. For Question 18, if it is known that the average estimated monthly expenditure was 22 moolahs per month for the community of Boogle Woogle (having 273 families), then what will be the percentage change in the estimated savings of the community?

(a) 30.77%   (b) 28.18%
(c) 25.23%   (d) 25.73%

20. For Question 19, what will be the percentage change in the estimated average income of the community (calculated on the basis of the new estimated average)?

(a) 14.28% increase   (b) 14.28% decrease
(c) 16.66% increase   (d) 16.66% decrease

21. If the finance minister of the island Mr. Bhola Ram declares that henceforth the average monthly income has to be estimated on the basis of 12 months per year while the average monthly expenditure is to be estimated on the basis of 11 months to the year, what will happen to the savings in the economy of Hoola Boola Moola?

(a) Increase   (b) Decrease
(c) Remain constant   (d) Either (b) or (c)

22. For Question 21, what will be the percentage change in savings?

(a) 3.1%   (b) 1.52%
(c) 2.5%   (d) Cannot be determined

23. For Question 22, what will be the percentage change in the estimated monthly expenditure?

(a) 22.22% decrease   (b) 22.22% increase
(c) 18.18% decrease   (d) 18.18% increase

24. Abhimanyu Banerjee has 72% vision in his left eye and 68% vision in his right eye. On corrective therapy, he starts wearing contact lenses, which augment his vision by 15% in the left eye and 11% in the right eye. Find out the percentage of normal vision that he possesses after corrective therapy. (Assume that a person's eyesight is a multiplicative construct of the eyesight's of his left and right eyes)

    (a) 52.5%   (b) 62.5%
    (c) 72.5%   (d) 68.6%

25. A shopkeeper gives 3 consecutive discounts of 10%, 15% and 15% after which he sells his goods at a percentage profit of 30.05% on the C.P. Find the value of the percentage profit that the shopkeeper would have earned if he had given discounts of 10% and 15% only.

    (a) 53%   (b) 62.5%
    (c) 72.5%   (d) 68.6%

26. If the third discount in Question 25 was ₹ 2,29,50, then find the original marked price of the item.

    (a) ₹ 1,00,000   (b) ₹ 1,25,000
    (c) ₹ 2,00,000   (d) ₹ 2,50,000

27. Krishna Iyer, a motorist uses 24% of his fuel in covering the first 20% of his total journey (in city driving conditions). If he knows that he has to cover another 25% of his total journey in city driving conditions, what should be the minimum percentage increase in the fuel efficiency for non-city driving over the city driving fuel efficiency, so that he is just able to cover his entire journey without having to refuel? (Approximately)

    (a) 39.2%   (b) 43.5%
    (c) 45.6%   (d) 41.2%

Directions for Questions 28 to 30: Read the following and answer the questions that follow the BSNL announced a cut in the STD rates on 27 December 2011. The new rates and slabs are given in the table below and are to be implemented from 14 January 2012.

Slab Details

Distance	Rates (₹/min)			
	Peak Rates		Off Peak	
	Old	New	Old	New
50–200	4.8	2.4	1.2	1.2
200–500	11.6	4.8	3.0	2.4
500–1000	17.56	9.00	4.5	4.5
1000+	17.56	9.00	6.0	4.5

28. The maximum percentage reduction in costs will be experienced for calls over which of the following distances?

    (a) 50–200   (b) 500–1000
    (c) 1000+   (d) 200–500

29. The percentage difference in the cost of a set of telephone calls made on the 13th and 14th January having durations of 4 minutes over a distance of 350 km, 3 minutes for a distance of 700 km and 3 minutes for a distance of 1050 km is (if all the three calls are made in peak times)

    (a) 51.2%   (b) 51.76%
    (c) 59.8 %   (d) Cannot be determined

30. If one of the three calls in Question 29 were made in an off peak time on both days, then the percentage reduction in the total cost of the calls between 13th and 14th January will

    (a) Definitely reduce
    (b) Definitely increase
    (c) Will depend on which particular call was made in an off peak time
    (d) Cannot be determined

Directions for Questions 31 to 35: Read the following caselet and answer the questions that follow.

The circulation of the *Deccan Emerald* newspaper is 3,73,000 copies, while its closest competitors are *The Times of Hindustan* and *India's Times,* which sell 2,47,000 and 20% more than that respectively (rounded off to the higher thousand). All the newspapers cost ₹ 2 each. The hawker's commissions offered by the three papers are 20%, 25% and 30% respectively (these commissions are calculated on the sale price of the newspaper). Also, it is known that newspapers earn primarily through sales and advertising.

31. Taking the base as the net revenue of *Deccan Emerald*, the percentage difference of the net revenue (revenues – commission disbursed to hawkers) between *Deccan Emerald* and *India's Times* is

    (a) 24.62%   (b) 30.32%
    (c) 26.28%   (d) None of these

32. The ratio of the percentage difference in the total net revenue between *Deccan Emerald* and *India's Times* to the percentage difference in the total revenue between *Deccan Emerald* and *India's Times* is

    (a) 1.488   (b) 0.3727
    (c) 0.6720   (d) Cannot be determined

33. If the cost of printing the newspaper is ₹ 8, 7.5 and 7 respectively per day for *Deccan Emerald*, *Times of Hindustan* and *India's Times* respectively and on any day the available advertising space in the *Deccan Emerald* newspaper is 800 cc (column centimetres) and the advertising rate for *Deccan Emerald* is ₹ 3000 per cc then the percentage of the advertising space that must be utilised to ensure the full recovery of the day's cost for *Deccan Emerald* is

(a) 95.83%   (b) 99.46%

(c) 97.28%   (d) Cannot be determined

34. Based on the data in the previous question and the additional information that the space availability in *India's Times* is 1000 cc and that in the *Times of Hindustan* is 1100 cc, find the percentage point difference in the percentage of advertising space to be utilised in *India's Times* and that which must be utilised in *Times of Hindustan* so that both newspapers just break even.

(a) 4.5   (b) 5.2

(c) 10   (d) Cannot be determined

35. For the data in Questions 33 and 34 if it is known that the advertising rate in *Times of Hindustan* is ₹ 1800 per cc and that in the *India's Times* is ₹ 2100 per cc, then what is the percentage point difference in the percentage of advertising space to be utilised by *Times of Hindustan* and *India's Times* so that both of them are just able to break even?

(a) 4.18   (b) 5.6

(c) 4.09   (d) Cannot be determined

36. On a train journey, there are 5 kinds of tickets AC I, AC II, AC III, 3-tier, and general. The relationship between the rates of the tickets for the Eurail is:

AC II is 20% higher than AC III and AC I is 70% of AC III's value higher than the AC II ticket's value. The 3-tier ticket is 25% of the AC I's ticket cost and the general ticket is 1/3 the price of the AC II ticket. The AC II ticket costs 780 euros between London and Paris. The difference in the rates of 3 tier and general ticket is

(a) 41.25 euros   (b) 55.8 euros

(c) 48.75 euros   (d) 52.75 euros

37. For the above question, the total cost of one ticket of each class will be

(a) 3233.75   (b) 3533.75

(c) 4233.75   (d) 3733.75

Directions for Questions 38 to 40: Read the following and answer the questions that follow.

A Eurailexpress train has 2 AC I bogeys having 24 berths each, 3 AC II bogeys having 45 berths each, 2 AC III bogeys having 64 berths each and 12 3-tier bogeys having 64 berths each. There are no general bogeys in the train. If 200 euros is the cost of an AC 3-tier berth from London to Glasgow, answer the following questions:

38. The value of the maximum revenues possible from the Eurailexpress between Glasgow to London and back is

(a) 3,15,600   (b) 2,44,800

(c) 2,98,400   (d) 2,96,760

39. For a Eurailexpress journey from London to Glasgow, 80% of the train was uniformly booked across class-

es. What percentage of the total revenues came out of the sales of 3-tier tickets?

(a) 44.23%   (b) 52.18%

(c) 39.23%   (d) 48.9%

40. If bookings for the above question was 40% in AC I, 70% in AC II, 60% in AC III and 55% in 3-tier, then what will happen to the percentage contribution of 3-tier to the total revenues on the train journey?

(a) Decrease   (b) Increase

(c) Remain constant   (d) Cannot be determined

41. A 14.4 kg gas cylinder runs for 104 hours when the smaller burner on the gas stove is fully opened while it runs for 80 hours when the larger burner on the gas stove is fully opened. Which of these values are the closest to the percentage difference in the usage of gas per hour, between the smaller and the larger burner?

(a) 26.23%   (b) 30%

(c) 32.23%   (d) 23.07%

42. For Question 41, assume that the rate of gas dispersal is directly proportional to the degree of opening of the aperture of the gas. If we are given that the smaller burner is open to 60% of its maximum and the larger burner is open to 50% of its maximum, the percentage decrease in the percentage difference between the smaller burner and the larger burner (in terms of hours per kg) is

(a) 72.22%   (b) 73.33%

(c) 66.66%   (d) None of these

43. Hursh Sarma has a salary of ₹10,800 per month. In the first month of the year, he spends 40% of his income on food, 50% on clothing and saves 11.11% of what he has spent. In the next two months, he saves 9.09% of what he has spent (spending 38.33% of his income on food). In the fourth month, he gets an increment of 11.11% on his salary and spends every single paise on celebrating his raise. But from the fifth month onwards good sense prevails on him and he saves 12.5%, 15%, 20%, 10%, 8.33%, 12.5%, 15% and 20% on his new income per month. The ratio between the sum of the savings for the two months having the highest savings to the sum of the savings for the two months having the lowest savings is

(a) 2.6666   (b) 5.3333

(c) 8   (d) None of these

44. In an economy, the rate of savings has a relation to the investment in industry for that year and the following three years. The relation is such that a percentage point change in investment in industry for that year has a relation to the total production output in the next 4 years. A 2 percentage point increase in the savings rate in a year, increases the

investment in the industry of the economy by 1%. Further, the rate of investment also goes up by 0.5% in the next year, by 0.25% in the second year and again by 0.25% in the third year. Also assume that the investment in an economy is only dependent on the patterns of savings in the previous 3 years in the economy. Also, the percentage change in the investment in a particular year is got by adding the effect of the previous three years savings pattern.

In fiscal 2008–09, the rate of savings in the Indian economy is 25% while that in the Pakistani economy, is 20%. This has remained constant since 2003. In 2009–10 the savings rate in the Indian economy suddenly rises by 5 percentage points to 30% while that in the Pakistani economy rises by 2 percentage points to 22%. It is further known that the value of the investment in the industry in the 2 countries was 2 million dollars and 1.8 million dollars respectively (for the previous year). The percentage difference between the investment in the Pakistani economy to the investment in the Indian economy in 2010–11 will be (if it is known that there is no change in the savings rate in 2010–11):

(a) 13.6%   (b) 15.12%
(c) 11.18%   (d) 12.2%

Directions for Questions 45 to 48: In an economy the rate of savings has a relation to the investment in industry for that year and for the following three years and the investment in industry for that year has a relation to the total production output in the next 4 years.

45. For Question 44, if there is no additional change in the savings rate until 2011–12, then the percentage difference in the value of the investment in India to the investment in Pakistan in 2011–12 (as a percentage of the investment in India) is
   (a) 11.28%   (b) 14.18%
   (c) 14.02%   (d) None of these

46. If the change in production is directly related to the change in investment in the previous year, and if the data of the savings rate change for the previous 2 questions are to be assumed true, then for which year did the difference between the production in the Indian economy and the production in the Pakistani economy show the maximum percentage change?
   (a) 2010–11   (b) 2011–12
   (c) 2012–13   (d) Cannot be determined

47. For Question 44, it is known that the percentage change in investment in a year leads to a corresponding equal percentage increase in the manufacturing production in the next year. Further, if the growth

rate of manufacturing production is 27% of the GDP growth rate of the country, then what is the GDP growth rate of India in 2010–11?
   (a) 8.52%   (b) 7.28%
   (c) 9.26%   (d) None of these

48. The Euro was ushered in on the Ist January 2002 and the old currencies of the European economies were exchanged into Euros. In France, 4 Francs were exchanged for 1 Euro while in Germany 5 Deutsche Marks were exchanged for 1 Euro and in Italy 3 Liras were exchanged for 1 Euro. The exchange rate for Moolahs, the official currency of Hoola Boola Moola, was set at 185 Moolahs per Euro. Dr. Krishna Iyer, an NRI doctor based in Europe, had a practice across each of these three countries and he sends back money orders to his native island of Hoola Boola Moola. The existing exchange rate of Moolahs with the above-mentioned currencies was 51 moolahs per Franc, 36 Moolahs per Deutsche Mark and 70 moolahs per Lira. If Dr. Iyer has this information, then what should he do with his currency holdings in these three currencies on the 31st December 2001 so that he maximises his moolah value on the Ist of January 2002. (Assume no arbitrage possibilities between the three currencies)
   (a) Change to Francs
   (b) Change to Deutsche Marks
   (c) Change to Liras
   (d) Remain indifferent

49. For the above questions, the exchange rates for the three currencies with respect to a dollar was: 2$ per Lira, 1.5$ per Franc and 1.4 dollar per Deutshce Mark. If Dr. Iyer has 100 liras, 100 Deutsche Marks and 100 Francs on 31st December 2001, the maximum percentage change he can achieve in his net holding in terms of dollars due to the arbitrage created by the Euro conversion could be
   (a) 17.23%   (b) 7.33%
   (c) 11.2%   (d) Cannot be determined

50. For Question 48, which one of the following will allow the calculation of all possibilities of percentage change in terms of moolah value of Dr. Iyer's portfolio? (That is possible through currency conversions.)
   (a) Dr. Iyer's money holding in all three currencies
   (b) Dr. Iyer's monthly earnings in all three currencies
   (c) The inter-currency conversion rates between Liras, Deutsche Mark and Francs
   (d) Both (a) and (c)

ANSWER KEY

Level of Difficulty (I)

1. (d)	2. (d)	3. (a)	4. (b)
5. (b)	6. (c)	7. (d)	8. (b)
9. (a)	10. (c)	11. (a)	12. (d)
13. (c)	14. (a)	15. (b)	16. (d)
17. (c)	18. (d)	19. (b)	20. (a)
21. (c)	22. (c)	23. (d)	24. (d)
25. (b)	26. (b)	27. (d)	28. (b)
29. (b)	30. (c)	31. (a)	32. (a)
33. (a)	34. (a)	35. (d)	36. (d)
37. (a)	38. (c)	39. (a)	40. (a)
41. (a)	42. (b)	43. (d)	44. (b)
45. (c)	46. (a)	47. (c)	48. (b)
49. (a)	50. (d)		

Level of Difficulty (II)

1. (c)	2. (b)	3. (d)	4. (b)
5. (c)	6. (c)	7. (c)	8. (d)
9. (a)	10. (b)	11. (c)	12. (d)
13. (b)	14. (a)	15. (c)	16. (a)
17. (b)	18. (c)	19. (d)	20. (c)
21. (d)	22. (a)	23. (b)	24. (d)
25. (c)	26. (d)	27. (c)	28. (d)
29. (b)	30. (d)	31. (a)	32. (c)
33. (d)	34. (d)	35. (a)	36. (c)
37. (d)	38. (c)	39. (a)	40. (b)
41. (c)	42. (d)	43. (a)	44. (b)
45. (b)	46. (d)	47. (d)	48. (d)
49. (a)	50. (c)		

Level of Difficulty (III)

1. (a)	2. (c)	3. (b)	4. (c)
5. (b)	6. (d)	7. (a)	8. (b)
9. (a)	10. (d)	11. (a)	12. (c)
13. (a)	14. (d)	15. (a)	16. (b)
17. (d)	18. (d)	19. (a)	20. (c)
21. (a)	22. (d)	23. (c)	24. (b)
25. (a)	26. (c)	27. (b)	28. (d)
29. (b)	30. (a)	31. (b)	32. (a)
33. (b)	34. (c)	35. (b)	36. (c)
37. (a)	38. (c)	39. (a)	40. (a)
41. (b)	42. (a)	43. (b)	44. (a)
45. (c)	46. (d)	47. (c)	48. (b)
49. (d)	50. (d)		

Hints

Level of Difficulty (II)

1. Assume the initial value to be 100 and solve.

3. Total number of students = Full fee waver + 50% concession + No concession.

6. Assume initial value of price = 100.
Since, the price is a mutiplicative function, we have
$100 \times 1.1 \times 1.2 \times 0.8 \times 1.25 \times 1.5$
Solve using percentage change graphic.

8. Salary ratio is 2.25 : 2.2.6666.
Hence 0.41666 = ₹ 40.
Then, 6.9166 = ₹ 664

9. Solve using options

13. Assume initial amount of gold to be 100.
Then he gives away: 50 + 25 + 12.5 = 87.5
But 87.5 = 1309000 kg
Hence, 100 = 149600

18. If initial income = 100, initial food expenditure = 25.
New income = 120
Since, food expenditure is constant at 25, the percentage of the new income = 20.833.
Percentage point change = 25 − 20.833 = 4.166

24. Solve using options.

25. Use standard formulae of percentage.
Alternatively, this problem can also be solved by assuming values for p, x, y and z. Then compare the options to see which one fits.

29. Solve using options.

31. $100 \times 1.125 \times 0.92 = 103.5$

34. Solve using options.

35. Reduction required $= \dfrac{7}{107} \times 2568$

36-38. To maximise the discount, tickets, need to be bought in two groups of 18 and 6 respectively. The maximum possible price per ticket will occur when tickets are bought in sets of 6.

39. Solve through options.
Checking for option (a) → Final voting is 200 for and 400 against.
Hence, the motion is rejected by 200 votes. This means that if none of the things had occurred then the motion would have been passed by 400 votes. i.e. 600 (for) and 200 (against) 1/3 of 600 were abducted and the opponents doubled their voted from 200 to 400.
Since all the values fit; the answer is (a).

40. Take 45% men = 25% women.

42. Since, runs scored = overs × run rate. If overs reduce by 25%, run rate will go up by 33.33%. Hence, Australia could have scored any number of runs.

47. Valid votes = 64%
The second placed candidate gets 20% votes.
Then the winner can get between 20.01% to 44% votes.

Level of Difficulty (III)

1. Assume initial raw material price to be 100. This means that the initial labour cost is 25. Hence the

net cost is 125. Now, since there is a 15% increment in raw material cost and the labour cost has gone up to 30% of the raw material cost, it is clear that the new total expenditure is 115* 1.3 = 149.5. Reduce the cost to 125 by reducing the usage of raw materials used.

2. Assume that 50, 40 and 20 hours are available. There is no need to use 10% waste of time in this question.

4. Half as large again means 1.5 times (or an addition of 50%).

5. Assume values for M and x and solve through options.

6. $A = 1.5 B$, $A - C = 180000$ and $B = 1.05 C$. Solve to get A, B and C. Also, $A + B + C = 90\%$ of total voters on voting list. This will give you the answer. Ideally solve this question through options.

7. Clock loses 0.5% of 168 hours in the first week and gains 0.25% of 168 hours in the second week. Hence, net loss is 0.25% of 168 hours.

8. Vawal uses 133.33 litres of petrol every month, while the price of petrol has gone up by ₹ 1.96. Hence, the increase in expenditure = 133.33 * 1.96 = ₹ 261 approximately.

11. Maximum revenue for the shopkeeper will occur when the minimum discount offer is used by the customer. This level is 4%.

12. This is the case of maximum discounts.

Hints for Questions 13–16

	Diesel	Petrol
	Shyam	Kailash
Average (in litre per km)	x	$1.2x$
Cost of Fuel (in ₹/litre)	$0.4 p$	p

13. Average in liter per kilometre multiplied by the Cost of fuel in ₹/litre will give the required cost per kilometre.

14. Shyam's car gives 20 km/litre means 0.05 litres per kilometre then Kailash's car gives 0.06 litre/km. However, since we do not know the price of petrol or diesel we cannot find out the difference in the cost of travel.

15. This question is the opposite of question 13.

16. Cost of petrol is ₹ 25 per liter. Cost per kilometre for Shyam = 12.5 × 0.05

Also, cost per kilometre for Kailash = 25 × 0.06

Hints for Questions 17–23

Estimated average savings

$$= \frac{\text{Annual Income}}{14} - \frac{\text{Annual Expenditure}}{9}$$

17. The value will depend on the values of annual expenditure which is not available.

18. Average estimated monthly expenditure is given for the island of Hoola Boola Moola and not for Mr. Boogle Woogle's community.

19. Original estimated savings = 87 – 22 = 65 Moolahs. New estimated savings = 1218/12 – 198/12 = 85.

24. $0.72 \times 1.15 \times 0.68 \times 1.11$.

25. Solve through options: A 15% reduction on the correct answer will give a profit of 30.05%.
Option (a) is correct.

26. The last discount being 22,950, it means that the value prior to this 15% discount must have been 1,53,000 checking with options:

$$200{,}000 \xrightarrow{15\% \downarrow} 17{,}000 \xrightarrow{10\% \downarrow} 1{,}53{,}000.$$

Hence option (c) is correct.

27. For 45% of the journey in city driving conditions, 54% of the fuel is consumed.
Hence, for the remaining 55% journey, 46% fuel is left.

Required increase in fuel efficiency

$$= \frac{\dfrac{55}{46} - \dfrac{45}{54}}{\dfrac{45}{54}} \times 100.$$

28. The maximum percentage reduction in peak rates is for the 200 – 500 category.

29. $\dfrac{(4 \times 11.6 + 3 \times 17.56 + 3 \times 17.56) - (4 \times 4.8 + 3 \times 9 + 3 \times 9)}{4 \times 11.6 + 3 \times 17.56 + 3 \times 17.56}$

33. Loss to be made up everyday = 373000(8 – 1.60) = 6.4 × 373000.

No. of cc required to be sold = $\dfrac{373000 \times 6.4}{3000}$

34. Advertising rates have not been mentioned. Hence, we cannot solve the question.

36-40. The ticket cost are:
AC III → 100 (assume), AC – II → 120, AC I → 190, 3 Tier → 47.5, General → 40.
Also, AC – II = 780 Euros for a London – Paris journey

36. $(47.5 - 40) \times 6.5 = 48.75$

37. $(100 + 120 + 190 + 47.5 + 40) \times 6.5.$

38. Maximum revenues on a return journey means 100% bookings both ways.

39. $\dfrac{\text{Revenues from 3-Tier}}{\text{Total Revenues}} \times 100$

41. $\dfrac{\dfrac{14.4}{80} - \dfrac{14.4}{104}}{\dfrac{14.4}{104}} = \dfrac{104 - 80}{80} = 30\%$

42. Original percentage difference = 30%
At 60% aperture opening the smaller gas will last
$\dfrac{104}{0.6} = 173.33$ hours.

Similarly, the larger gas will last $\dfrac{80}{0.5} = 160$ hours.

Thus, the smaller gas lasts $\frac{173.33-160}{173.33} \times 100 =$ 8.33% more than the larger gas.

Then, required answer = $\frac{30-8.33}{30} \times 100 = 72.22\%$

44. The 5% point increase in savings rate will account for a 2.5% increase in investment in 2005–06 and a further 1.25% increase in investment in 2006–07.
Thus, Indian investment is 2006-07 = 2 million × 1.025 × 1.0125 similarly, calculate for Pakistan.

45. Use the same process as for the previous question.

46. Cannot be determined since we do not know the initial values of the production output.

47. Since there is a 2.5% increase in investment in 2005–06, there will be a 2.5% increase in manufacturing production is 2006–07.
Then, GDP growth rate = $\frac{2.5}{0.27} = 9.26\%$.

Solutions and Shortcuts

Level of Difficulty (I)

1. It can be clearly seen that 700% of 9 = 63 is the highest number.

2. $0.25 N = 75 \rightarrow = 300$. Thus, $0.45 \times 300 = 135$.

3. 20% of 50% of 75% of 70% = $20/100 \times 50/100 \times 75/100 \times 70 = 0.2 \times 0.5 \times 0.75 \times 70 = 5.25$.
A quicker way to think here would be: 20% of 70 = 14 → 50% of 14 = 7 → 75% of 7 = 5.25

4. 41 (3/17)% = 700/17. As a fraction, the value = $700/(17 \times 100) = 7/17$.

5. The following PCG will give the answer:

$$100 \xrightarrow[\text{Price effect}]{40\%\uparrow} 140 \xrightarrow[\substack{\text{Consumption}\\\text{effect}}]{} 100$$

Hence, the percentage reduction required is 28.56% (40/140)

6. 100 → 140 (after a 40% increase) → 105. The reduction from 140 to 105 is 25% and hence, it means that he needs to reduce his consumption by 25%.

7. Assume Ram as 100. Shyam will be 133.33 and Bram will be 80
Thus, Bram's goods are 40% cheaper than Shyam's (53.33/133.33)

8. Total votes = 6000. Valid votes = 75% of 6000 = 4500. Bhiku gets 65% of 4500 votes and Mhatre gets 35% of 4500. Hence, Mhatre gets: $0.35 \times 4500 = 1575$ votes.

9. If the candidate has inadvertently increased his height by 25% the correction he would need to make to go back to his original height would be to reduce the stated height by 20%.

10. Let Arjit's height be H. Then, $H \times 1.15 = 120 \rightarrow H = 120/1.15 = 104.34$.

11. Let the number be N. Then, 5N should be the correct outcome. But instead the value got is 0.2N. Change in value = 5N – 0.2N = 4.8N. The percentage change in the value = 4.8N × 100/5N = 96%.

12. The percentage difference would be given by thinking of the percentage change between two numbers: $(x - 5)$ to $(x + 5)$ ['What he wanted to get' to 'what he got by mistake'].
The value of the percentage difference in this case depends on the value of x. Hence, this cannot be answered. Option (d) is correct.

13. 65% of x = 13% of 2000 → $0.65 x = 260 \rightarrow x = 400$

14. From the first statement we get that out of 80 litres of the mixture, 20 litres must be milk. Since, we are adding water to this and keeping the milk constant, it is quite evident that 20 litres of milk should correspond to 20% of the total mixture. Thus, the amount in the total mixture must be 100, which means we need to add 20 litres of water to make 100 litres of the mixture.

15. $(50/100) \times (a/100) \times (b) = (75/100) \times (b/100) \times (c)$ → $50a = 75c \rightarrow c = 0.667a$

16. $100 \xrightarrow{10\%\uparrow} 110 \xrightarrow{20\%\uparrow} 132$
Hence, the required answer is 32%

17. The area of a triangle depends on the product base × height.
Since, the height increases by 40% and the area has to increase by 60% overall, the following PCG will give the answer.

$$100 \xrightarrow[\text{base}]{40\%\uparrow} 140 \xrightarrow[\text{height}]{?} 160$$

The required answer will be 20/140 = 14.28%

18. The volume goes up by:

$$100 \xrightarrow[\text{Height}]{50\%\uparrow} 150 \xrightarrow[\text{breadth}]{20\%\uparrow} 180 \xrightarrow[\text{length}]{10\%\uparrow} 198$$

Hence, 98%

19. $100 \longrightarrow 130 \longrightarrow 100$ (A→B→A use of PCG)
∴ Answer = 30/130 = 23.07%

20. $100 \xrightarrow{25\%\downarrow} 75 \xrightarrow{?} 120$
We have assumed initial expenditure to be 100, in the above figure. Then the final expenditure is 120. The percentage change in consumption can be seen to be $45/75 \times 100 = 60\%$

21. If the price of rice has fallen by 20% the quantity would be increased by 25% (if we keep the expenditure constant.)
This means that 20 kgs would increase by 25% to 25 kgs.

22. $91 - 0.3N = N \rightarrow 1.3 N = 91 \rightarrow N = 70$.

23. $B + 60\%$ of $A = 175\%$ of $B \rightarrow$

60% of A = 75% of B.

i.e. $\quad 0.6A = 0.75B$

$\quad\quad A/B = 5/4$

Apparently it seems that A is bigger, but if you consider A and B to be negative the opposite would be true.

Hence, option (d) is correct.

24. The winning candidate gets 56% of the votes cast and the losing candidate gets 44% of the votes cast. Thus, the gap between the two is 12% of the votes cast = 144 votes. Thus, the votes cast = 1200. Since, this is 80% of the number of voters on the voting list, the number of people on the voting list = 1200/0.8 = 1500.

25. $100000 \xrightarrow{10\%\uparrow} 110000 \xrightarrow{10\uparrow} 121000$

26. $10000 \rightarrow 11000$ (after a 10% increase) $\rightarrow 10450$ (after a 5% decrease) $\rightarrow 12540$ (after a 20% increase)

27. His investments are 2000, 3000 and 5000 respectively. His dividends are: 200, 750 and 1000, which means total dividend = 1950.

28. Sushant 1080, hence Mohit = $1080 \times 1.2 = 1296$. Rajesh = 1296/0.9 = 1440. 1440 out of 2000 means a percentage of 72%.

29. 30% students got a final score of 13. 10% students got a final score of 33 (inclusive of grace marks.) 35% students got a final score of 60

Hence, average score of the class

$$= \frac{0.35 \times 60 + 0.1 \times 33 + 0.3 \times 13}{0.75} = 37.6$$

30. Ram would spend 20%, 12% and 20.4% respectively on household expenditure, books and clothes. His savings would account for $100 - 20 - 12 - 20.4 = 47.6\%$ of his income. Since the savings = 9520, we get $0.476 \times$ Income = 9520 $\rightarrow$ Income = 9520/0.476 = 20000

31. The only logic for this question is that Hans' salary would be more than Bhaskar's salary. Thus, only option (a) is possible for Hans' salary.

32. By using options, you can easily see that option (a) satisfies.

2500 females means 3000 males.

Increase = $2500 \times 0.2 + 3000 \times 0.11 = 830$

33. If Ashu's salary =100, then Vicky's salary = 175. Ashu's new salary = 125, Vicky's new salary = $175 \times 1.4 = 245$. Percentage difference between Vicky's salary and Ashu' salary now = $120 \times 100/125 = 96\%$.

34. Let the second row contain 100 books. Then, the first row would contain 125 books and the third row would contain 75 books. The total number of books would be $100 + 125 + 75 = 300$. But this number is given as 600 which means that the total number of

books would be double the assumed value for each row. Thus, the first row would contain $125 \times 2 = 250$ books.

35. Since the only iron contained in the ore is 90% of 25%, the net iron percentage would be 22.5%. Thus, 60 kg should be 22.5% of the ore $\rightarrow$ 60/0.225 = 266.66

36. The data is insufficient since the number of matches to be played by India this year is not given. (You cannot assume that they will play 40 matches.)

37. $100000 \rightarrow 110000$ (after 1 year) $\rightarrow 121000$ (after 2 years) $\rightarrow 133100$ (after 3 years and at the start of the fourth year).

38. Total people present = $700 + 500 + 800 = 2000$. Indians = $0.2 \times 700 + 0.4 \times 500 + 0.1 \times 800 = 420 = 21\%$ of the population. Thus, 79% of the people were not Indians.

39. Price of a cow after increase = 2400. Price of a calf after 30% increase = 1820. Cost of 12 cows and 24 calves = $12 \times 2400 + 24 \times 1820 = 72480$

40. If we take Ram as 100, we will get Bobby as 125 and Chandilya as 83.33. This means Chandilya's goods are priced at $2/3^{rd}$ Bobby's and hence he sells his goods 33.33% cheaper than Bobby.

41. 1 Bottle $\rightarrow 0.5x$ metres

? Bottles $\rightarrow$ 400 meters

Using unitary method, we get no. of bottles = $400/0.5x$ = $800/x$ Bottles.

42. $(100 \times 0.8 \times 0.25)\% = 80000$ kg $\rightarrow 20\% = 80000$ kg. Thus, the total quantity of hematite mined = 400000.

43. The total cost for a year = $2,50,000 + 2\%$ of $2,50,000 + 2000$

$$= 2,55,000 + 2000 = 2,57,000$$

To get a return of 15% he must earn: $2,57,000 \times 0.15$ = 38,550 in twelve months.

Hence, the monthly rent should be 38550/12 = 3212.5.

44. The sales price of the first shirt is $8/7 \times 42 = ₹\ 48$.

Hence, I am being offered a discount of ₹ 6 on a price of ₹ 48 – a 12.5% discount.

The sales price of the second shirt is $7/6 \times 36$ = ₹ 42.

Hence, I am being offered a discount of ₹ 6 on ₹ 42 – a 14.28% discount. Hence, the second shirt is a better bargain.

45. 72% must have voted for Sonia Gandhi and 16% for Sushma Swaraj. Hence, $88 \times 3 = 264$.

46. The following Venn diagram would solve this problem:

Physics 80%   Chemistry 70%

15   Both 65   5

We can clearly see from the above figure that 65% of the people passed both subjects. Since this value is given as 325, we get that the total number of students who appeared for the exam is 500.

47. Ravana spends 30% on house rent, 21% on children's education and 24% on clothes. Thus, he spends 75% of his total salary. He thus saves 25% of his salary which is given as being equal to 2500. Thus, his salary is ₹ 10000.

48. $100 \xrightarrow[\text{Sales increase}]{50\%\uparrow} 150 \xrightarrow[\text{Price drop}]{?} 82.5$ (final sales figure)

    Hence, the required price drop is $67.5/150 = 45\%$ drop. Thus there is a drop of $250 \times .45 = 112.5$

49. A $C\%$ increase in income means the new income is $A(1 + C/100)$ while a $D\%$ increase in expenditure means that the new expenditure would be $X(1 + D/100)$. Thus, the new savings $= A(1 + C/100) - X(1 + D/100)$

50. In 2001, BMW = 15%, Maruti = 50% and hence Honda = 35%

Level of Difficulty (II)

1. $100 \longrightarrow 150 \underset{\text{(year 1)}}{\longrightarrow} 75 \longrightarrow 112.5 \underset{\text{(year 2)}}{\longrightarrow} 56.25$
   $\longrightarrow 84.375 \longrightarrow 42.1875$

   Now, $42.1875 = ₹ 16,875$

   Hence $1 \longrightarrow 400$

   Also, year 2 donation is $56.25 \times 400 = 22500$

2. The following figure shows the percentage of failures:

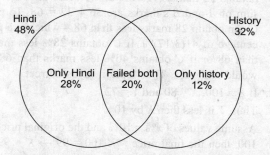

Hindi 48%   History 32%

Only Hindi 28%   Failed both 20%   Only history 12%

From the figure it is clear that 60% of the people have failed in at least one subject, which means that 40% of the students would have passed in both subjects. This value is given as 880 people. Hence, there would be $880/0.4 = 2200$ students who would appear in the examination.

3. The thought process would go like:
   If we assume 100 students

   Total   : 60 boys and 40 girls.
   Fee waiver   : 9 boys and 3 girls.

   This means that a total of 12 people are getting a fee waiver. (But this figure is given as 90.)
   Hence, 1 corresponds to 7.5.
   Now, number of students not getting a fee waiver
   = 51 boys and 37 girls
   50% concession → 25.5 boys and 18.5 girls (i.e. a total of 44.)
   Hence, the required answer = $44 \times 7.5 = 330$

4. Solve using options. Checking for option (b), gives us:
   $200000 \rightarrow 180000 \rightarrow 171000 \rightarrow 153900 \rightarrow 146205$
   (by consecutively decreasing 200000 by 10% and 5% alternately)

5. Total characters in her report = $25 \times 60 \times 75$.
   Let the new no. of pages be n.
   Then:
   $$n \times 55 \times 90 = 25 \times 60 \times 75$$
   $$n = 22.72$$
   This means that her report would require 23 pages. A drop of 8% in terms of the pages.

6. The following percentage change thinking would give us the value of the percentage increase as 98%

   $100 \xrightarrow[\text{increase}]{50\%} 150 \xrightarrow[\text{increase}]{20\%} 180 \xrightarrow[\text{20\% drop}]{} 144$

   $\xrightarrow[\text{25\% increase}]{} 180 \xrightarrow[\text{10\% increase}]{} 198$

7. The total raise of salary is 87.5% (That is what 15/8 means here).
   Using the options and PCG, you get option (c) as the correct answer.

8. October : November : December = 9 : 8 : 10.666
   since, he got ₹ 40 more in December than October, we can conclude that $1.666 = 40 \rightarrow 1 = 24$.
   Thus, total Bonus for the three months is:
   $$0.4 \times 27.666 \times 24 = 265.6$$

9. Solve through trial and error using the options. 12% (option a) is the only value that fits the situation.

10. 9% increase is offset by 8.26% decrease. Hence, option (b) is correct.

11. The expenditure increase can be calculated using PCG as:
    $$100 \rightarrow 112.5 \rightarrow 123.75.$$
    A 23.75% increase.

12. Rajesh's scores in each area is 65 and 82 respectively out of 100 each. Since, the exam is of a total of 250 marks (100+100+50) he needs a total of 195 marks in order to get his target of 78% overall. Thus, he

should score 195-65-82 = 195-147=48 marks in Sociology which would mean 96%.

13. The total wealth given would be 50% + 25% (which is got by 50% of the remaining 50%) + 12.5% (which is got by 50% of the remaining 25%). Thus, the total wealth given by him would be equivalent to 87.5% of the total. Since, this is equal to 130900 kilograms of gold, the total gold would be:
130900 × 8/7 = 149600.

14. Population at the start = 100.
Population after 2 years = 100 × 1.08 × 1.01 × 1.08 × 1.01 = 108.984
Thus, the required percentage increase = 18.984%

15. After the migrations, 72.9% of the people would remain in the country. This would comprise females and males in the ratio of 1:2 (as given) and hence, the women's population left would be 1/3rd of 72.9% = 24.3% which is given as being equal to 364500. Thus, the total population would be
364500 × 100/24.3 = 1500000

16. 24% of the total goes to urban Gujarat $72 m
∴ 1% = $ 3 mn.
The required value for Rural AP
= 50% of 20% = 10%
Hence, required answer = $ 30 mn

17. In the previous question, the total FDI was $ 300 mn. A growth of 20% this year means a total FDI of $360 mn.
The required answer is 12% of 10% of 360 mn
= 1.2% of 360 = $4.32 mn.

18. The income goes to 120. Food expenditure has to be maintained at 25. (i.e. 20.833%)
Hence, percentage point drop from 25 to 20.833 is 4.16%

19. Assume the initial surface area as 100 on each side. A total of 6 such surfaces would give a total surface area of 600. Two surface areas would be impacted by the combined effect of length and breadth, two would be affected by length and height and two would be affected by breadth and height. Thus, the respective surface areas would be (110.25 twice, 126 twice and 126 twice) Thus, new surface area = 220.5 + 504 = 724.5. A percentage increase of 20.75%. Option (d) is correct.

20. Option (c) fits the situation as if the ratio is 10:9, the value of B's salary would first go up from 10 to 12 and then come down from 12 to 9 (after a 25% decrease). On the other hand, the value of A's salary would go up from 9 to 11.25 and then come back to 9 (Note that a 25% increase followed by a 20% decrease gets one back to the starting value.)

21. Initial quantity of milk and water = 12 and 48 liters respectively. Since, this is already containing 20% milk, adding more milk to the mixture cannot make the mixture reach 15% milk. Hence, it is not possible.

22. On ₹100 he saves ₹6. On 115 he still saves ₹6. Thus, his expenditure goes up from 94 to 109- a percentage increase of 15 on 94 = 15.95%.

23. B = 100, A = 150, C = 100, D = 160. D is 160% of B. Note that this does not change if all the values are incremented by the same percentage value.

24. Think about this problem through alligation. Since, A spends 12% of his money and B spends 20% of his money and together they spend 15% of their money- we can conclude that the ratio of the money A had to the money B had would be 5:3. Hence, Total money with A = 5 × 1200/8 =750.
Money spent by A = 12% of 750 = 90.
Money left with A = 750 × 90 = 660.

25. Chanda would have spent 12% of Maya
Thus, her percentage of expenditure would be 0.12 M × 100/C = 12 M/C

26. Option (d) is correct and can be verified experimentally by using values for x, y, z and p.

27. The weekly change is equal to ₹ 1,68,000.
Hence, the daily collection will go up by 1,68,000/7 = 24,000.

28. The total population of the town can be taken as 9 + 8 + 3 = 20.
The number of literates would be:
80% of 9 + 70% of 8 + 90% of 3 = 7.2 + 5.6 + 2.7 = 15.5
15.5 out of 20 represents a 77.5% literacy rate.

29. Solve using options. 2/25 fits the requirement.

30. Let the exam be of 100 marks. A obtains 36 marks (10% or 1/10th less than the pass marks) while B obtains 32 marks (11.11% or 1/9th less than A). The sum of A and B's marks are 36 + 32 = 68. To pass C can obtain 28 marks less than 68 – which is a percentage of 41(3/17)%. If C obtains 28% less marks than 68 or if C obtains 40% less marks than 68 he would still pass. Thus, option (d) is correct.

32. If Z = 100, X = 80 and Y = 72.
Thus, Y is less then X by 10%

33. Assume values of x% = 10% and the original price as 100, then the final price = K/100 = 99 → K = 9900.
(Note: After an increase of 10% followed by a decrease of 10% a price of 100 would become 99).
Put these values of x, and K in the options. The option that gives a value of 100 for the original price should be the correct answer.
Option (d) is correct.

34. The correct answer should satisfy the following condition: If 'x' is the increased salary

$$x \times 0.8 \times 0.1 = (x - 4800) \times 0.8 \times 0.12.$$

None of the first 3 options satisfies this.

In fact, solving for x we get $x = 25800$.

Option (d) is correct.

35. A sales tax of 7% on a price of 2568 would amount to a tax amount of 179.76. Since, the price is rounded off to the next higher integer, the tax would be rounded off to ₹180. This would also be the amount of discount (or reduction in price) that Reena is asking for.

36. The minimum price occurs at:

$$18 \times 30 + 6 \times 36 + 1 \times 40$$

Hence, 796/25 = 31.84

37. $36 \times 24 + 40 \times 1 = 904$

Required answer = 904/25 = 36.16.

38. If the ticket lots are halved, the maximum discount will be available for 9 tickets (25%). A maximum number of 16 tickets can be bought in ₹ 532 as: 9 tickets for ₹ 30 each. 6 tickets for ₹ 32 each and 1 ticket for ₹ 40

39. Solve using options.

Checking for option (a) will go as: According to this option 400 people have voted against the motion. Hence, originally 200 people must have favoured the motion. (Since, there is a 100% increase in the opponents)

This means that 200 people who were for the motion initially went against it.

This leaves us with 400 people who were for the motion initially (after the abduction.)

1/3rd of the original having been abducted, they should amount to half what is left.

This means that 600 (for) and 200 (against) were the original distribution of 800.

This option fits perfectly (given all the constraints) and hence is the correct answer.

40. 1 man is married to 1 woman.

Hence, 45% of men = 25% of women.

i.e. 0.45 M = 0.25 W

Hence $\dfrac{0.45}{0.25} = \dfrac{M}{W}$

Women to men ratio of 9:5

Using alligation, the required answer is 32.14

41. The required weight of the bucket to the water when full is 3:2.

If both the weights (bucket and water) are integers, then the total weight must be a multiple of 5.

Only option (c) shows this characteristic.

42. We do not have sufficient information to solve the question.

43. A 25% hike in the price would result in a 20% drop in consumption (if we are keeping expenditure constant). Thus, the drop in what he can buy of 20kg is equivalent to 20% of the original consumption. Hence, the original consumption should be 100 kg and the new consumption should be 80 kg. The increased price of rice would be 400/80 = ₹5

44. Income of the salesman = 1200 + (1600 × x)

Where x is the number of ₹ 10000 sales he achieves over the initial ₹ 10000.

For $\quad$ 1200 + 1600 × x = 7600

We get $\quad\quad\quad\quad\quad$ $x = 4$.

This means that the sales value must be ₹ 50000.

45. A sales value of ₹ 9000 cannot be achieved.

46. This question is based on a product constancy situation. A 25% increment in the commission (How?? Note: When the commission goes up by 5 percentage points from 20 to 25, there is a 25% increment in the commission) would get offset by a 20% drop in the volume of the transaction. Option (d) is correct.

47. Out of a total of 100% votes; 80% voted. 16% were invalid and 20% went to the second placed candidate. This means that the maximum the winner can get is 44%. Options a, b and c are greater them 44% and hence cannot be correct. Hence, none of these.

48. At 12 noon, the watch would show the correct time (since till then the temperature range was below 40°C). The watch would gain 2% every hour between 12 and 4. An hour having 3600 seconds, it would gain 72 seconds in each of these hours. Thus, at 7 pm it would be 72 × 4 = 288 seconds ahead. The time exhibited would be 7: 04: 48.

49. Pepsi worth ₹ 16 would be containing 60 grams of vitamins.

50. Option (a) would cost: 6 + 7.5 = 13.5

Option (b) would cost: 12 + 3.2 = 15.2

Option (c) would cost: 4 + 3.2 + 2.8 = 10

Option (d) would cost: 12 + 2.8 = 14.8

Option (c) is the cheapest.

Level of Difficulty (III)

1. Let the initial price of raw materials be 100. The new cost of the same raw material would be 115.

The initial cost of labour would be 25 and the new cost would be 30% of 115 = 34.5

The total cost initially would be ₹125.

The total cost for the same usage of raw material would now be: 115+34.5= 149.5

This cost has to be reduced to 125. The percentage reduction will be given by 24.5/149.5 = 17 % approx.

2. Let the initial times allotted be: 50,40 and 20 hours. Then, the time used in each activity is:
   20,12 and 4 hours. Thus, 36 hours out of 110 are used in all.
   Hence, the answer is 36/110 = 32.72 %

3. The following structure would follow:
   Passed all: 5%
   Passed 4: 20% of 90% =18%
   Passed 1: 25% of 90% = 22.5%
   Passed 2: 24.5%
   Passed None: 5%
   Passed 3: Rest (100 – 5-18-22.5-24.5-5 = 25%)
   But it is given that 300 people passed 3. Hence, 25% = 300.
   Hence, 1200 students must have appeared in the test.

4. The third gallery making the capacity 'half as large again' means: an increase of 50%.
   Further, it is given that : 4(first + third) = 12 (second)
   In order to get to the correct answer, try to fit in the options into this situation.
   (Note here that the question is asking you to find the capacity of the second gallery as a percentage of the first.)
   If we assume option (a) as correct – 70% the following solution follows:
   If second is 70, then first is 100 and first + second is 170. Then third will be 85 (50% of first + second).
   Then the equation:
   $4 \times (100 + 85)$ should be equal to 12×70
   But this is not true.
   Through trial and error, you can see that the third option fits correctly.
   $4 \times (100 + 80) = 12 \times 60$.
   Hence, it is the correct answer.

5. Let the initial percentage of salt be 10% in 100 liters of sea water in the flask.
   10% of this is poured out (i.e. 10 liters are poured out) and the water heated so as to increase the percentage of salt in the beaker 5 times (we have assumed M as 5 here.)
   This means that there will be 30% salt in the beaker. Since, the salt concentration is increased by only evaporating water, the amount of salt remains the same.
   Initially the salt was 10% of 10 liters (= worth 1 liter). Hence, the water must have been worth 9 liters.
   Now, since this amount of salt becomes worth 50% of the total solution, the amount of water left after evaporation would have been 1 liter and the total would be 2 liters.
   When the 2 liters are mixed back again: The new concentration of salt in sea water would go up. In this specific case by alligation we would get the following alligation situation:
   Mix 90 liters of 10% salted sea water with 2 liters of 50% salted sea water.
   The result using alligation will be: [10 + 40/46] % concentration of salted sea water. The value of the increase percentage will be 400/46. (this will be the value of x)
   Now, try to use the given options in order to match the fact that originally the flask contained 100 liters of sea water.
   Use $M = 5, x = 400/46,$
   Only option (b) matches the situation.
   $$\frac{(9 \times 5 + 1)\,400/46}{(5 - 1)} = 100$$

6. The only values that fit this situation are C 25%, B 30%, and A 45%. These are the percentage of votes polled. (Note: these values can be got either through trial and error or through solving $c + c + 5 + 1.5$ $(c + 5) = 100\%$
   Then, 20% is 18000 (the difference between A & C.)
   Hence, 90000 people must have voted and 100000 people must have been on the voter's list.

7. The net time lost over two weeks would be 0.25% of a week's time (since in the first week the clock loses ½% and in the second week the clock gains ¼% on the true time.)
   A week contains 168 hours. Hence, the clock loses 0.42 hours.i.e. 25.2 minutes or 25 minutes 12 seconds. Hence, the correct time would be 12:25:12.

8. Traveling for 2400 kms at 18 kmph, Vawal will use 133.33 liters of petrol every month. The increase in expenditure for Vawal will be 133.33 × 0.7 × 28 = ₹ 262 (approx).

9. The required answer will be given by: (7/107) × 2400 = 157 km

10. The original expenditure is 28* 133.333 = ₹ 3733.333
    The new expenditure will be given by 28 × 1.07 × n/18 where n = the no. of kilometers to travel.
    Since the new expenditure should increase by ₹ 200, its value has to be equal to ₹ 3933.333
    This gives us $n = 2363.15$
    Hence, the answer is e.

11. The shopkeeper would get the maximum revenue when everybody opts for a 4% resale of the right. In such a case, the revenue for the shopkeeper from each customer would be: 96% of 4000 = 4000 – 160 = 3840. hence, total revenue is 38400.

12. Similarly, the highest discount would be if everybody opts for the 15% discount. In such a case, the total discount would be: 600 × 10 = 6000.

13-16. Detailed solutions for 13–16 are given in the hints of LOD III.

17–23. The average income estimated would be: Annual Income/14 (Underestimated savings).

The average monthly expenditure would be: Annual expenditure/9 (Overestimated expenditure)

17–19 are explained in the hints of LOD III.

20. $x/14 = 87$. Hence, annual income = 1218.

New income = 1218/12 = 101.5

Change in estimated income due to the change in process of average calculation = $14.5/87 \rightarrow 16.66\%$ increase.

21. Estimated monthly income would go up, while the estimated monthly expenditure would go down. Hence, Savings (estimated) would increase.

22. Cannot be determined since the percentage change would depend on the actual values which are not available for this question.

23. The estimated monthly expenditure would change from: $x/9$ to $x/11$. Hence, percentage drop in the ratio will be $2/11 \rightarrow 18.18\%$

24 to 29 are explained in the hints to LOD III.

31-34. The following table will give a clearer picture of the situation:

Newspaper	Circulation (in 000)	Revenues	Commission	Net Revenues
Deccan Emerald	373	746	20%	596.8
Times of Hindustan	247	494	25%	395.2
India's Times	297	594	30%	415.8

31. Reduction of $\dfrac{181*100}{596.8} = 30.32\%$

32. The percentage difference between the revenues is: $(746–594) \times 100/746 = 20.37$

Hence, the required value is 30.32/20.37 = 1.488

33. The day's cost of printing 373000 copies of Deccan Emerald is: $373000 \times 8 = 2984000$

Out of this, the paper recovers 596800. The remaining cost to be recovered would be: 2387200.

At ₹ 3000 per cc, 795.733 cc will have to be booked on any given day in order to obtain the cost. This represents 99.46% of the total value.

35. Times of Hindustan:

Total cost = $2,47,000 \times 7.5 = 18,52,500$

Net revenues from newspaper sales is 3,95,200

Cost to be covered through advertising = 18,52,500 – 3,95,200 = 14,57,300.

At an ad rate of ₹1800 per cc, they would have to sell 809.61 cc i.e.73.6%

Similar calculations for India's Times will give 79.2%.

Hence, the percentage point difference = 5.6

36. If Ac 3rd costs 100, Ac 2nd would cost 120 and AC 1st would cost 190. 3 Tier ticket would cost : 47.5 and general ticket would cost 40.

$$AC\ 2^{nd} \rightarrow 780 = 120$$

Then the difference between 3 Tier and general ticket would be: $7.5 \times 780 = 48.75$

37. Total cost $\rightarrow 100 + 120 + 190 + 47.5 + 40 = 497.5$

This gives $(497.5/120) \times 780 = 3233.75$.

43. Hursh Sarma's savings:

Month	Salary	Savings
1	10800	1080
2	10800	900
3	10800	900
4	10800	0
5	12000	1500
6	12000	1800
7	12000	2400
8	12000	1200
9	12000	1000
10	12000	1500
11	12000	1800
12	12000	2400

Required Ratio = 4800/900 = 5.333

48. Assume he has 1200 francs, 1200 DM and 1200 Liras. If he converts everything to francs, the result will be: 1200 DM will convert to 240 Euros which will convert to 960 francs. But 51 Moolas = 1 franc. Thus the value of 1200 DM in terms of Moolas goes up from $1200 \times 36 = 43200$ to $960 \times 51 = 48960$. This increase in value has occurred only because of the change of currency. Hence, he should convert all his DM into Francs. However, before concluding on this you also will need to consider the effect of Liras.

It is evident that 1200 DM will yield 240 Euros, which would yield 720 Liras (since 1 euro is 3 lira), which in turn would yield $720 \times 70 = 5040$ Moolas. Thus, it is evident that by converting DM into Liras the increase in value is higher than that achieved by converting DM into Francs.

Similarly, converting Francs to Liras also increases the value of the Francs.

1200×51 becomes equivalent to 900×70.

Note: The thought process goes like this: 1200 Francs = 300 Euros (since 1 euro = 4 francs). Further 300 Euros equals 900 liras which equal 900×70 Moolas.

49. Cannot be determined since the conversion from dollar to Euro is not given, neither is the inter currency exchange rate between Lira, Francs and DMs.

50. Obviously, both a and c are required in order to answer this question.

6 Chapter

Profit & Loss

INTRODUCTION

Traditionally, Profit & Loss has always been an important chapter for CAT. Besides, all other Management entrance exams like SNAP, CMAT, MAT, ATMA as well as Bank P.O. exams extensively use questions from this chapter. From the point of view of CAT, the relevance of this chapter has been gradually reducing. However, CAT being a highly unpredictable exam, my advice to students and readers would be to go through this chapter and solve it at least up to LOD II, so that they are ready for any changes in patterns.

Further, the Level of Difficulties at which questions are set in the various exams can be set as under:

LOD I: CAT, XLRI, IRMA, IIFT, CMAT, Bank PO aspirants, MAT, NIFT, NMAT, and SNAP and all other management exams.

LOD II: CAT, XLRI, IRMA (partially), etc.

LOD III: CAT, XLRI (students aiming for 60% plus in Maths in CAT).

THEORY

Profit & Loss are part and parcel of every commercial transaction. In fact, the entire economy and the concept of capitalism is based on the so called "Profit Motive".

Profit & Loss in Case of Individual Transactions

We will first investigate the concept of Profit & Loss in the case of individual transactions. Certain concepts are important in such transactions. They are:

The price at which a person buys a product is the cost price of the product for that person. In other words, the amount paid or expended in either purchasing or producing an object is known as its Cost Price (also written as CP).

The price at which a person sells a product is the sales price of the product for that person. In other words, the amount got when an object is sold is called as the *Selling Price* (*SP*) of the object from the seller's point of view.

When a person is able to sell a product at a price higher than its cost price, we say that he has earned a profit. That is,

If SP > CP, the difference, SP – CP is known as the profit or gain.

Similarly, if a person sells an item for a price lower than its cost price, we say that a loss has been incurred.

The basic concept of profit and loss is as simple as this.

If, however, SP < CP, then the difference, CP – SP is called the loss.

It must be noted here that the Selling Price of the seller is the Cost Price of the buyer.

Thus we can say that in the case of profit the following formulae hold true:

1. Profit = SP – CP
2. SP = Profit + CP
3. CP = SP – Profit
4. Percentage Profit = $\dfrac{\text{Profit} \times 100}{\text{CP}}$

Percentage Profit is always calculated on CP unless otherwise stated.

Notice that SP = CP + Gain
$$= CP + (\text{Gain on Re } 1) \times CP$$
$$= CP + (\text{Gain\%}/100) \times CP$$

Example: A man purchases an item for ₹ 120. If he sells it at a 20 per cent profit find his selling price.

Solution: The selling price is given by $120 + 120 \times 0.2 = 144$

$$= CP + (Gain\%/100) \times CP = CP\left[1 + \frac{\%Gain}{100}\right]$$

For the above problem, the selling price is given by this method as: Selling Price = $1.2 \times 120 = 144$.

Hence, we also have the following:

1. $SP = \left[1 + \dfrac{\%Gain}{100}\right] \times C.P = \dfrac{(100 + Gain\%) \times CP}{100}$

2. $CP = \dfrac{100 \times SP}{(100 \times Gain\%)}$

In case of loss
1. $Loss = CP - SP$
2. $SP = CP - Loss$
3. $CP = SP + Loss$
4. $Loss\% = Loss \text{ on } ₹ 100 = \dfrac{Loss \times 100}{CP}$

Precentage Loss is always calculated on CP unless otherwise stated.

The above situation (although it is the basic building block of Profit and Loss) is not the normal situation where we face Profit and Loss problems. In fact, there is a wide application of profit and loss in day-to-day business and economic transactions. It is in these situations that we normally have to work out profit and loss problems.

Having investigated the basic concept of profit and loss for an individual transaction of selling and buying one unit of a product, let us now look at the concept of profit and loss applied to day-to-day business and commercial transactions.

Profit & Loss as Applied to Business and Commercial Transactions

Profit & Loss when Multiple Units of a Product are Being Bought and Sold The basic concept of profit and loss remains unchanged for this situation. However, a common mistake in this type of problem can be avoided if the following basic principle is adopted:

Profit or Loss in terms of money can only be calculated when the number of items bought and sold are equal.

That is, Profit or Loss in money terms cannot be calculated unless we equate the number of products bought and sold.

This is normally achieved by equating the number of items bought and sold at 1 or 100 or some other convenient figure as per the problem asked.

Overlooking of this basic fact is one of the most common mistakes that students are prone to making in the solving of profit and loss problems.

Types of Costs In any business dealing, there is a situation of selling and buying of products and services. From the sellers point of view, his principle interest, apart from maximising the sales price of a product/service, is to minimise the costs associated with the selling of that product/service. The costs that a businessman/trader faces in the process of day-to-day business transaction can be subdivided into three basic categories:

1. **Direct Costs or Variable Costs** This is the cost associated with direct selling of product/service. In other words, this is the cost that varies with every unit of the product sold. Hence, if the variable cost in selling a pen for ₹ 20 is ₹ 5, then the variable cost for selling 10 units of the same pen is $10 \times 5 = ₹ 50$.

   As is clear from the above example, that part of the cost that varies directly for every additional unit of the product sold is called as direct or variable cost. *Typical examples of direct costs are:* Raw material used in producing one unit of the product, wages to labour in producing one unit of the product when the wages are given on a piece rate basis, and so on. In the case of traders, the cost price per unit bought is also a direct cost (i.e. every such expense that can be tied down to every additional unit of the product sold is a direct cost).

2. **Indirect Costs (Overhead Costs) or Fixed Costs** There are some types of costs that have to be incurred irrespective of the number of items sold and are called as fixed or indirect costs. For example, irrespective of the number of units of a product sold, the rent of the corporate office is fixed. Now, whether the company sells 10 units or 100 units, this rent is fixed and is hence a fixed cost.

   Other examples of indirect or fixed costs: Salary to executives and managers, rent for office, office telephone charges, office electricity charges.

   Apportionment of indirect (or fixed) costs: Fixed Costs are apportioned equally among each unit of the product sold. Thus, if *n* units of a product is sold, then the fixed cost to be apportioned to each unit sold is given by

   $$\frac{Fixed\ costs}{n}$$

3. **Semi-Variable Costs** Some costs are such that they behave as fixed costs under normal circumstances but have to be increased when a certain level of sales figure is reached. For instance, if the sales increase to such an extent that the company needs to take up additional office space to accommodate the increase in work due to the increase in sales then the rent for the of-

fice space becomes a part of the semi-variable cost.

The Concept of Margin or Contribution Per Unit The difference between the value of the selling price and the variable cost for a product is known as the margin or the contribution of the product. This margin goes towards the recovery of the fixed costs incurred in selling the product/service.

The Concept of the Break-even Point The break-even point is defined as the volume of sale at which there is no profit or no loss. In other words, the sales value in terms of the number of units sold at which the company breaks even is called the break-even point. This point is also called the break-even sales.

Since for every unit of the product the contribution goes towards recovering the fixed costs, as soon as a company sells more than the break-even sales, the company starts earning a profit. Conversely, when the sales value in terms of the number of units is below the break-even sales, the company makes losses.

The entire scenario is best described through the following example.

Let us suppose that a *paan* shop has to pay a rent of ₹ 1000 per month and salaries of ₹ 4000 to the assistants.

Also suppose that this *paan* shop sells only one variety of *paan* for ₹ 5 each. Further, the direct cost (variable cost) in making one *paan* is ₹ 2.50 per *paan*, then the margin is ₹ (5 – 2.50) = ₹ 2.50 per *paan*.

Now, break-even sales will be given by:

Break-even-sales = Fixed costs/Margin per unit = 5000/2.5 = 2000 *paans*.

Hence, the *paan* shop breaks-even on a monthly basis by selling 2000 *paans*.

Selling every additional *paan* after the 2000th *paan* goes towards increasing the profit of the shop. Also, in the case of the shop incurring a loss, the number of *paans* that are left to be sold to break-even will determine the quantum of the loss.

Note the following formulae:

Profit = (Actual sales – Break-even sales) × Contribution per unit

Also in the case of a loss:

Loss = (Break-even sales – Actual sales) × Contribution per unit

Also, if the break-even sales equals the actual sales, then we reach the point of no profit no loss, which is also the technical definition of the break-even point.

Note that the break-even point can be calculated on the basis of any time period (but is normally done annually or monthly).

Profit Calculation on the Basis of Equating the Amount Spent and the Amount Earned

We have already seen that profit can only be calculated in the case of the number of items being bought and sold being equal. In such a case, we take the difference of the money got and the money given to get the calculation of the profit or the loss in the transaction.

There is another possibility, however, of calculating the profit. This is done by equating the money got and the money spent. In such a case, the profit can be represented by the amount of goods left. This is so because in terms of money the person going through the transaction has got back all the money that he has spent, but has ended up with some amount of goods left over after the transaction. These left over items can then be viewed as the profit or gain for the individual in consideration.

Hence, profit when money is equated is given by Goods left. Also, cost in this case is represented by Goods sold and hence percentage profit = $\frac{\text{Goods left}}{\text{Goods sold}} \times 100$.

Example: A fruit vendor recovers the cost of 25 mangoes by selling 20 mangoes. Find his percentage profit.

Solution: Since the money spent is equal to the money earned the percentage profit is given by:

$$\% \text{ Profit} = \frac{\text{Goods left}}{\text{Goods sold}} \times 100 = 5 \times 100/20 = 25\%$$

Concept of Mark Up

Traders/businessmen, while selling goods, add a certain percentage on the cost price. This addition is called percentage mark up (if it is in money terms), and the price thus obtained is called as the marked price (this is also the price printed on the product in the shop).

The operative relationship is

	CP + Mark up = Marked price
or	CP + % Mark up on CP = Marked Price

The product is normally sold at the marked price in which case the marked price = the selling price

If the trader/shopkeeper gives a discount, he does so on the marked price and after the discount the product is sold at its discounted price.

Hence, the following relationship operates:

CP + % Mark up (Calculated on CP) = Marked Price
Marked price – % Discount = Selling price

Use of PCG in Profit and Loss

1. The relationship between CP and SP is typically defined through a percentage relationship. As we have seen earlier, this percentage value is called as

the percentage mark up. (And is also equal to the percentage profit if there is no discount).

Consider the following situation —

Suppose the SP is 25% greater than the CP. This relationship can be seen in the following diagram.

$$CP \xrightarrow{\;25\%\uparrow\;} SP$$

In such a case the reverse relationship will be got by the A→B→A application of PCG and will be seen as follows:

If the profit is 25% :

Space for Notes

Example: $CP \xrightarrow{\;25\%\uparrow\;} SP \xrightarrow{\;20\%\downarrow\;} CP$

Suppose you know that by selling an item at 25%, profit the Sales price of a bottle of wine is ₹ 1600. With this information, you can easily calculate the cost price by reducing the sales price by 20%. Thus, the CP is

$$1600 \xrightarrow[-320]{\;20\%\downarrow\;} 1280$$

WORKED-OUT PROBLEMS

Before we go into problems based on profit and loss, the reader should realize that there are essentially four phases of a profit and loss problem. These are connected together to get higher degrees of difficulty.

These are clues for (a) Cost calculations (b) Marked price calculations (c) Selling price calculations (d) Overheads/fixed costs calculations.

It is left to the reader to understand the interrelationships between *a*, *b*, *c* and *d* above. (These have already been stated in the earlier part of this chapter.)

Problem 6.1   A shopkeeper sold goods for ₹ 2000 at a profit of 50%. Find the cost price for the shopkeeper.

Solution   The shopkeeper sells his items at a profit of 50%. This means that the selling price is 150% of cost price (Since CP + % Profit = SP)

For short you should view this as SP = 1.5 CP.

The problem with this calculation is that we know what 150% of the cost price is but we do not know what the cost price itself is. Hence, we have difficulty in directly working out this problem. The calculation will become easier if we know the percentage calculation to be done on the basis of the selling price of the goods.

Hence look at the equation from the angle → CP = SP/1.5.

Considering the SP as SP/1, we have to find CP as SP/1.5. This means that the denominator is increasing by 50%. But from the table of denominator change to ratio change of the chapter of percentages, we can see that when the denominator increases by 50% the ratio decreases by 33.33%.

Interpret this as the CP can be got from the SP by reducing the SP by 33.33%. Hence, the answer is 2000 − (1/3) × 2000 = ₹ 1333.33

Also, this question can also be solved through options by going from CP (assumed from the value of the option) to the SP by increasing the assumed CP by 50% to check whether the SP comes out to 2000. If a 50% increase in the assumed CP does not make the SP equal 2000 it means that the assumed CP is incorrect. Hence, you should move to the next option. Use logic to understand whether you go for the higher options or the lower options based on your rejection of the assumed option.

Note: The above question will never appear as a full question in the examination but might appear as a part of a more complex question. If you are able to interpret this statement through the denominator change to ratio change table, the time requirement will reduce significantly and you will gain a significant time advantage over this statement.

Problem 6.2   A man buys a shirt and a trousers for ₹ 371. If the trouser costs 12% more than the shirt, find the cost of the shirt.

Solution   Here, we can write the equation: $s + 1.12s = 371 \to s = 371/2.12$ (however, this calculation is not very easily done)

An alternate approach will be to go through options. Suppose the options are

(a)	₹ 125	(b)	₹ 150
(c)	₹ 175	(d)	₹ 200

Checking for, say, ₹ 150, the thought process should go like:

Let s = cost of a shirt

If $s = 150$, $1.12s$ will be got by increasing s by 12% i.e. 12% of 150 = 18. Hence the value of $1.12s = 150 + 18 = 168$ and $s + 1.12s = 318$ is not equal to 371. Hence check the next higher option.

If $s = 175$, $1.12s = s + 12\%$ of $s = 175 + 21 = 196$. i.e. $2.12 s = 371$.

Hence, Option (c) is correct.

Problem 6.3   A shopkeeper sells two items at the same price. If he sells one of them at a profit of 10% and the other at a loss of 10%, find the percentage profit/loss.

Generic question: A shopkeeper sells two items at the same price. If he sells one of them at a profit of x% and the other at a loss of x%, find the percentage profit/loss.

Solution   The result will always be a loss of $[x/10]^2$%. Hence, the answer here is $[10/10]^2$% = 1% loss.

Problem 6.4   For Problem 6.3, find the value of the loss incurred by the shopkeeper if the price of selling each item is ₹ 160.

Solution   When there is a loss of 10% → 160 = 90% of CP_1. ∴ $CP_1 = 177.77$

When there is a profit of 10% → 160 = 110% of CP_2 ∴ $CP_2 = 145.45$

Hence total cost price = 177.77 + 145.45 = 323.23 while the net realisation is ₹ 320.

Hence loss is ₹ 3.23.

Short cut for calculation: Since by selling the two items for ₹ 320 the shopkeeper gets a loss of 1% (from the previous problem), we can say that ₹ 320 is 99% of the value of the cost price of the two items. Hence, the total cost is given by 320/0.99 (solution of this calculation can be approximately done on the percentage change graphic).

Problem 6.5   If by selling 2 items for ₹ 180 each the shopkeeper gains 20% on one and loses 20% on the other, find the value of the loss.

Solution The percentage loss in this case will always be $(20/10)^2 = 4\%$ loss.

We can see this directly as $360 \rightarrow 96\%$ of the CP $\rightarrow$ CP = 360/0.96. Hence, by percentage change graphic 360 has to be increased by 4.166 per cent = 360 + 4.166% of 360 = 360 + 14.4 + 0.6 = ₹ 375.

Hence, the loss is ₹ 15.

Problem 6.6 By selling 15 mangoes, a fruit vendor recovers the cost price of 20 mangoes. Find the profit percentage.

Solution Here since the expenditure and the revenue are equated, we can use percentage profit = (goods left × 100)/ goods sold = 5 × 100/15 = 33.33%.

Problem 6.7 A dishonest shopkeeper uses a 900 gram weight instead of 1 kilogram weight. Find his profit percent if he sells per kilogram at the same price as he buys a kilogram.

Solution Here again the money spent and the money got are equal. Hence, the percentage profit is got by goods left × 100/goods sold.

This gives us 11.11%.

Problem 6.8 A manufacturer makes a profit of 15% by selling a colour TV for ₹ 6900. If the cost of manufacturing increases by 30% and the price paid by the retailer is increased by 20%, find the profit percent made by the manufacturer.

Solution For this problem, the first line gives us that the cost price of the TV for the manufacturer is ₹ 6000.

(By question stem analysis you should be able to solve this part of the problem in the first reading and reach at the figure of 6000 as cost, before you read further. This can be achieved advantageously if your percentage rule calculations are strong. Hence, work on it. The better you can get at it the more it will benefit you. In fact, one of the principal reasons I get through the CAT every year is the strength in percentage calculation. Besides, percentage calculation will also go a long way in improving your scores in data Interpretation.)

Further, if you have got to the 6000 figure by the end of the first line, reading further you can increase this advantage by calculating while reading as follows:

Manufacturing cost increase by 30% → New manufacturing cost = 7800 and new selling price is 6900 + 20% of 6900 = 6900 + 1380 = 8280.

Hence, profit = 8280 – 7800 = 480 and profit percent = 480 × 100/7800 = 6.15%.

Problem 6.9 Find a single discount to equal three consecutive discounts of 10%, 12% and 5%.

Solution Using percentage change graphic starting from 100: we get 100 → 88 → 83.6 → 75.24 (Note we can change percentages in any order).

Hence, the single discount is 24.76%.

Problem 6.10 A reduction in the price of petrol by 10% enables a motorist to buy 5 gallons more for $180. Find the original price of petrol.

Solution 10% reduction in price → 11.11% increase in consumption.

But 11.11% increase in consumption is equal to 5 gallons. Hence, original consumption is equal to 45 gallons for $180. Hence, original price = 4$ per gallon.

Problem 6.11 Ashok bought an article and spent ₹ 110 on its repairs. He then sold it to Bhushan at a profit of 20%. Bhushan sold it to Charan at a loss of 10%. Charan finally sold it for ₹ 1188 at a profit of 10%. How much did Ashok pay for the article.

(a) ₹ 890   (b) ₹ 1000

(c) ₹ 780   (d) ₹ 840

Solution Solve through options using percentage rule and keep checking options as you read. Try to finish the first option-check before you finish reading the question for the first time. Also, as a thumb rule always start with the middle most convenient option. This way you are likely to be required lesser number of options, on an average.

Also note that LOD II and LOD III questions will always essentially use the same sentences as used in LOD I questions. The only requirement that you need to have to handle LOD II and III questions is the ability to string together a set of statements and interconnect them.

Problem 6.12 A dishonest businessman professes to sell his articles at cost price but he uses false weights with which he cheats by 10% while buying and by 10% while selling. Find his percentage profit.

Solution Assume that the businessman buys and sells 1 kg of items. While buying he cheats by 10%, which means that when he buys 1 kg he actually takes 1100 grams. Similarly, he cheats by 10% while selling, that is, he gives only 900 grams when he sells a kilogram. Also, it must be understood that since he purportedly buys and sells the same amount of goods and he is trading at the same price while buying and selling, money is already equated in this case. Hence, we can directly use: % Profit = (Goods left × 100/Goods sold) = 200 × 100/900 = 22.22% (Note that you should not need to do this calculation since this value comes from the fraction to percentage conversion table).

If you are looking at 70% plus net score in quantitative ability you should be able to come to the solution in about 25 seconds inclusive of problem reading time. And the calculation should go like this:

Money is equated → % profit = 2/9 = 22.22%

The longer process of calculation in this case would be involving the use of equating the amount of goods bought and sold and the money value of the profit. However, if you try to do this you will easily see that it requires a much higher degree of calculations and the process will tend to get messy.

The options for doing this problem by equating goods would point to comparing the price per gram bought or sold. Alternatively, we could use the price per kilogram bought and sold (which would be preferable to equating on a per gram basis for this problem).

Here the thought process would be:

Assume price per kilogram = ₹ 1000. Therefore, he buys 1100 grams while purchasing and sells 900 grams while selling.

To equate the two, use the following process:

	Money paid		Amount of goods
Buying	₹ 1000	1100	grams (Reduce this by 10%)
After reduction	₹ 900	990	grams
Selling	₹ 1000	900	grams (Increase this by 10%)
After increase	₹ 1100	990	

Problem 6.13 RFO Tripathi bought some oranges in Nagpur for ₹ 32. He has to sell it off in Yeotmal. He is able to sell off all the oranges in Yeotmal and on reflection finds that he has made a profit equal to the cost price of 40 oranges. How many oranges did RFO Tripathi buy?

Solution Suppose we take the number of oranges bought as x. Then, the cost price per orange would be ₹ $32/x$, and his profit would by $40 \times 32/x = 1280/x$.

To solve for x, we need to equate this value with some value on the other side of the equation. But, we have no information provided here to find out the value of the variable x. Hence, we cannot solve this equation.

Problem 6.14 By selling 5 articles for ₹ 15, a man makes a profit of 20%. Find his gain or loss percentage if he sells 8 articles for ₹ 18.4?

Questions of this type normally appear as part of a more complex problem in an exam like the CAT.

Remember, such a question should be solved by you as soon as you finish reading the question by solving-while-reading process, as follows.

By selling 5 articles for ₹ 15, a man makes a profit of 20% → SP = 3. Hence, CP = 2.5, if he sells 8 articles for ₹ 18.4 → SP = 2.3. Hence percentage loss = 8%. For solving this question through this method with speed you need to develop the skill and ability to calculate percentage changes through the percentage change graphic. For this purpose, you should not be required to use a pencil and a paper.

Problem 6.15 Oranges are bought at 12 for a rupee and are sold at 10 for a rupee. Find the percentage profit or loss.

Solution Since money spent and got are equated, use the formula for profit calculation in terms of goods left/goods sold.

This will give you percentage profit = 2/10 = 20%.

Alternatively, you can also equate the goods and calculate the percentage profit on the basis of money as

CP of 1 orange = 8.33 paise

SP of 1 orange = 10 paise

8.33 paise → 10 paise (corresponds to a percentage increase of 20% on CP)

Problem 6.16 In order to maximise its profits, AMS Corporate defines a function. Its unit sales price is ₹ 700 and the function representing the cost of production = 300 + $2p^2$, where p is the total units produced or sold. Find the most profitable production level. Assume that everything produced is necessarily sold.

Solution The function for profit is a combination of revenue and costs. It is given by Profit = Revenue − Costs = $700\,p - (300 + 2p^2) = -2p^2 + 700p - 300$.

In order to find the maxima or minima of any quadratic function, we differentiate it and equate the differentiated equation to zero.

Thus, the differentiated profit function is $-4p + 700 = 0 \rightarrow p = 175$. This value of production will yield the maximum profits in this case.

Note: Whether a quadratic function is maximum or minimum is decided by redifferentiating the differentiated equation. We then look at the sign of the constant term to determine whether the value got by equating the differentiated equation to zero corresponds to the maximum or the minimum. In the case of the constant term, left being negative, we say that the function is a maxima function and hence the solution point got would be a maximum point. In the event that the final constant term is positive, it is a minimum function.

Short cut Just look at the coefficient of x^2 in the function. If it is positive, equating the first differentiation to zero would yield the minimum point, and if the coefficient of x^2 is negative, the function is a maximum function.

Problem 6.17 For Problem 6.16, what is the value of the maximum profits for AMS Corporate?

Solution For this, continuing from the previous question's solution, we just put the value of $p = 175$ in the equation for profit. Thus, substitute $p = 175$ in the equation. Profit = $-2p^2 + 700p - 300$ and get the answer.

Problem 6.18 A shopkeeper allows a rebate of 25% to the buyer. He sells only smuggled goods and as a bribe, he pays 10% of the cost of the article. If his cost price is ₹ 2500, then find what should be the marked price if he desires to make a profit of 9.09%.

Solution Use solving-while-reading as follows: Cost price (= 2500) + Bribe (= 10% of cost of article = 250) = Total cost to the shopkeeper (2500 + 250 = 2750).

He wants a profit of 9.09 percent on this value → Using fraction to percentage change table we get 2750 + 9.09% of 2750 = 2750 + 250 = ₹ 3000.

But this ₹ 3000 is got after a rebate of 25%. Since we do not have the value of the marked price on which 25% rebate is to be calculated, it would be a good idea to work reverse through the percentage change graphic:

Going from the marked price to ₹ 3000 requires a 25% rebate. Hence the reverse process will be got by increasing ₹ 3000 by 33.33% and getting ₹ 4000.

[Notice the use of percentage change graphic in general and the product constancy table in particular in the solving of this question]

Problem 6.19 A man sells three articles, one at a loss of 10%, another at a profit of 20% and the third one at a loss of 25%. If the selling price of all the three is the same, find by how much percent is their average CP lower than or higher than their SP.

Solution

Note: It is always convenient to solve questions involving percentages by using the number 100. The reason for this is that it reduces the amount of effort required in calculating the solution. Hence, it goes without saying that the variable to be fixed at 100 should be the one with the highest

number of calculations associated with it. Another thumb rule for this is that the variable to be fixed at 100 should be the one with which the most difficult calculation set is associated.

We have to calculate: (average CP – average SP)/average SP.

Here, the selling price is equal in all three cases. Since the maximum number of calculations are associated with the SP, we assume it to be 100. This gives us an average SP of 100 for the three articles. Then, the first article will be sold at 111.11, the second at 83.33 and the third at 133.33. (The student is advised to be fluent at these calculations) Further, the CP of the three articles is 111.11 + 83.33 + 133.33 = 327.77.

The average CP of the three articles is 327.77/3 = 109.2566.

Hence, (average CP – average SP)/average SP = 9.2566%. higher

Any other process adopted for this problem is likely to require much more effort and time.

Note: This process will be feasible if you have worked well with the percentage calculation techniques of the previous chapter.

Space for Rough Work

LEVEL OF DIFFICULTY (I)

1. By selling a watch for ₹ 495, a shopkeeper incurs a loss of 10%. Find the cost price of the watch for the shopkeeper.
   - (a) ₹ 545
   - (b) ₹ 550
   - (c) ₹ 555
   - (d) ₹ 565

2. By selling a cap for ₹ 34.40, a man gains 7.5%. What will be the CP of the cap?
   - (a) ₹ 32.80
   - (b) ₹ 32
   - (c) ₹ 32.40
   - (d) ₹ 28.80

3. A cellular phone when sold for ₹ 4600 fetches a profit of 15%. Find the cost price of the cellular phone.
   - (a) ₹ 4300
   - (b) ₹ 4150
   - (c) ₹ 4000
   - (d) ₹ 4500

4. A machine costs ₹ 375. If it is sold at a loss of 20%, what will be its cost price as a percentage of its selling price?
   - (a) 80%
   - (b) 120%
   - (c) 110%
   - (d) 125%

5. A shopkeeper sold goods for ₹ 2400 and made a profit of 25% in the process. Find his profit per cent if he had sold his goods for ₹ 2040.
   - (a) 6.25%
   - (b) 7%
   - (c) 6.20%
   - (d) 6.5%

6. A digital diary is sold for ₹ 935 at a profit of 10%. What would have been the actual profit or loss on it, if it had been sold for ₹ 810?
   - (a) ₹ 45
   - (b) ₹ 40
   - (c) ₹ 48
   - (d) ₹ 50

7. A music system when sold for ₹ 4500 gives a loss of 16.66% to the merchant who sells it. Calculate his loss or gain per cent, if he sells it for ₹ 5703.75.
   - (a) Loss of 5.625%
   - (b) Profit of 8.33%
   - (c) Loss of 7%
   - (d) Profit of 5.625%

8. By selling bouquets for ₹ 63, a florist gains 5%. At what price should he sell the bouquets to gain 10% on the cost price?
   - (a) ₹ 66
   - (b) ₹ 69
   - (c) ₹ 72
   - (d) ₹ 72.50

9. A shopkeeper bought 240 chocolates at ₹ 9 per dozen. If he sold all of them at Re. 1 each, what was his profit per cent?
   - (a) 66(1/6)%
   - (b) 33(1/3)%
   - (c) 24%
   - (d) 27%

10. A feeding bottle is sold for ₹ 120. Sales tax accounts for one-fifth of this and profit one-third of the remainder. Find the cost price of the feeding bottle.
    - (a) ₹ 64
    - (b) ₹ 72
    - (c) ₹ 68
    - (d) ₹ 76

11. A coal merchant makes a profit of 20% by selling coal at ₹ 25 per quintal. If he sells the coal at ₹ 22.50 per quintal, what is his profit per cent on the whole investment?
    - (a) 6%
    - (b) 6.66%
    - (c) 7.5%
    - (d) 8%

12. The cost price of a shirt and a pair of trousers is ₹ 371. If the shirt costs 12% more than the trousers, find the cost price of the trouser.
    - (a) ₹ 125
    - (b) ₹ 150
    - (c) ₹ 175
    - (d) ₹ 200

13. A pet shop owner sells two puppies at the same price. On one he makes a profit of 20% and on the other he suffers a loss of 20%. Find his loss or gain per cent on the whole transaction.
    - (a) Gain of 4%
    - (b) No profit no loss
    - (c) Loss of 10%
    - (d) Loss of 4%

14. The marked price of a table is ₹ 1200, which is 20% above the cost price. It is sold at a discount of 10% on the marked price. Find the profit per cent.
    - (a) 10%
    - (b) 8%
    - (c) 7.5%
    - (d) 6%

15. 125 toffees cost ₹ 75. Find the cost of one million toffees if there is a discount of 40% on the selling price for this quantity.
    - (a) ₹ 3,00,000
    - (b) ₹ 3,20,000
    - (c) ₹ 3,60,000
    - (d) ₹ 4,00,000

16. A shopkeeper marks the price of an article at ₹ 80. Find the cost price if after allowing a discount of 10% he still gains 20% on the cost price.
    - (a) ₹ 53.33
    - (b) ₹ 70
    - (c) ₹ 75
    - (d) ₹ 60

17. In Question 16, what will be the selling price of the article if he allows two successive discounts of 5% each?
    - (a) ₹ 72
    - (b) ₹ 72.20
    - (c) ₹ 75
    - (d) ₹ 71.66

18. A dozen pairs of gloves quoted at ₹ 80 are available at a discount of 10%. Find how many pairs of gloves can be bought for ₹ 24.
    - (a) 4
    - (b) 5
    - (c) 6
    - (d) 8

19. Find a single discount equivalent to the discount series of 20%, 10%, 5%.
    (a) 30%   (b) 31.6%
    (c) 68.4%   (d) 35%

20. The printed price of a calculator is ₹ 180. A retailer pays ₹ 137.7 for it by getting successive discounts of 10% and another rate which is illegible. What is the second discount rate?
    (a) 12%   (b) 12.5%
    (c) 15%   (d) 20%

21. How much percent more than the cost price should a shopkeeper mark his goods, so that after allowing a discount of 12.5% he should have a gain of 5% on his outlay?
    (a) 9.375   (b) 16.66%
    (c) 20%   (d) 25%

22. In order to maintain the price line, a trader allows a discount of 10% on the marked price of goods in his shop. However, he still makes a gross profit of 17% on the cost price. Find the profit per cent he would have made on the selling price had he sold at the marked price.
    (a) 23.07%   (b) 30%
    (c) 21.21%   (d) 25%

23. A whole-seller allows a discount of 20% on the list price to a retailer. The retailer sells at 5% discount on the list price. If the customer paid ₹ 38 for an article, what profit is made by the retailer?
    (a) ₹ 10   (b) ₹ 8
    (c) ₹ 6   (d) ₹ 12

24. In Question 23, also find the retailer's percentage profit on his cost giving your answer correct to two decimal places.
    (a) 12.5%   (b) 16.66%
    (c) 18.75%   (d) 20%

25. The cost of production of a cordless phone set in 2011 is ₹ 900, divided between material, labour and overheads in the ratio 3 : 4 : 2. If the cordless phone set is marked at a price that gives a 20% profit on the component of price accounted for by labour, what is the marked price of the set?
    (a) ₹ 980   (b) ₹ 1080
    (c) ₹ 960   (d) ₹ 1020

26. For Question 25, if subsequently in 2012, the cost of material, labour and overheads increased by 20%, 30% and 10% respectively, calculate the cost of manufacturing in 2012.
    (a) ₹ 1150   (b) ₹ 1050
    (c) ₹ 1080   (d) ₹ 1100

27. What should be the new marked price if the criteria for profit is to remain the same as for Question 25 above?
    (a) ₹ 1320   (b) ₹ 1204
    (c) ₹ 1244   (d) None of these

28. By selling a casserole for ₹ 960, a man incurs a loss of 4%. At what price should he sell the casserole to gain 16%?
    (a) ₹ 1160   (b) ₹ 1080
    (c) ₹ 1120   (d) None of these

29. A man sells 5 articles for ₹ 15 and makes a profit of 20%. Find his gain or loss percent if he sells 8 such articles for ₹ 18.40.
    (a) 2.22% profit (b) 2.22% loss
    (c) 8% loss   (d) 8% profit

30. The cost price of 50 mangoes is equal to the selling price of 40 mangoes. Find the percentage profit.
    (a) 20%   (b) 25%
    (c) 30%   (d) None of these

31. A owns a house worth ₹ 10,000. He sells it to B at a profit of 15%. After some time, B sells it back to A at 15% loss. Find A's loss or gain percent.
    (a) 2.25% gain   (b) 6.25% gain
    (c) 17.64% gain (d) 17.25% gain

32. A shopkeeper bought locks at the rate of 8 locks for ₹ 34 and sold them at the rate of 12 locks for ₹ 57. Calculate his gain percent.
    (a) 9.33%   (b) 12.5%
    (c) 11.11%   (d) 11.76%

33. Anil bought an article at ₹ 200 and sold it at a profit of 10%. What would have been the increase in the profit percent if it was sold for ₹ 230?
    (a) 5%   (b) 10%
    (c) 15%   (d) None of these

34. A makes an article for ₹ 120 and sells it to B at a profit of 25%. B sells it to C who sells it for ₹ 198, making a profit of 10%. What profit percent did B make?
    (a) 25%   (b) 20%
    (c) 16.66%   (d) 15%

35. A reduction of 10% in the price of sugar enables a housewife to buy 6.2 kg. more for ₹ 279. Find the reduced price per kilogram
    (a) ₹ 5   (b) ₹ 4.5
    (c) ₹ 4.05   (d) None of these

36. A man buys 50 kg of oil at ₹ 10 per kilogram and another 40 kg of oil at ₹ 12 kilogram and mixes them. He sells the mixture at the rate of ₹ 11 per kilogram. What will be his gain percent if he is able to sell the whole lot?
    (a) $\dfrac{100}{98}$%   (b) 100(10/49)%
    (c) 10(1/49)%   (d) None of these

37. If the cost price of 30 articles is equal to the selling price of 20 articles, find the profit percent.
    (a) 33.33%   (b) 40%
    (c) 50%   (d) 60%

38. A shopkeeper sells sugar in such a way that the selling price of 950 gm is the same as the cost price of one kilogram. Find his gain percent.
    (a) 100/17%   (b) 150/17%
    (c) 5(5/19)%   (d) 1/19%

39. A dealer buys eggs at ₹ 36 per gross. He sells the eggs at a profit of 12(1/2) % on the cost price. What is the selling price per egg (approximately)?
    (a) 33 paise   (b) 30 paise
    (c) 29 paise   (d) 28 paise

40. *A* sold a table to *B* at a profit of 20%. *B* sold the same table to *C* for ₹ 75 thereby making a profit of 25%. Find the price at which *A* bought the table from *X* if it is known that *X* gained 25% in the transaction.
    (a) ₹ 30   (b) ₹ 40
    (c) ₹ 50   (d) ₹ 60

41. *A* sold a table to *B* at a profit of 15%. Later on, *B* sold it back to *A* at a profit of 20%, thereby gaining ₹ 69. How much did *A* pay for the table originally?
    (a) ₹ 300   (b) ₹ 320
    (c) ₹ 345   (d) ₹ 350

42. A dealer sold two TV sets for ₹ 2400 each, gaining 20% on one and losing 20% on the other set. Find his net gain or net loss.
    (a) ₹ 300 loss   (b) ₹ 200 loss
    (c) ₹ 200 gain   (d) ₹ 300 gain

43. On selling tea at ₹ 40 per kg a loss of 10% is incurred. Calculate the amount of tea (in kg) sold if the total loss incurred is ₹ 80.
    (a) 12 kg   (b) 15 kg
    (c) 18 kg   (d) 20 kg

44. A colour TV and a VCP were sold for ₹ 12,000 each. The TV was sold at a loss of 20% whereas the VCP was sold at a gain of 20%. Find gain or loss in the whole transaction.
    (a) ₹ 1200 loss   (b) ₹ 1000 loss
    (c) ₹ 960 loss   (d) ₹ 1040 loss
    (*Note:*   In this case there will always be a loss)

45. A man sells a TV set for ₹ 3450 and makes a profit of 15%. He sells another TV at a loss of 10%. If on the whole, he neither gains nor loses, find the selling price of the second TV set.
    (a) ₹ 4000   (b) ₹ 4400
    (c) ₹ 4050   (d) ₹ 4500

46. A man sells an article at 5% above its cost price. If he had bought it at 5% less than what he paid for it and sold it for ₹ 2 less, he would have gained 10%.

Find the cost price of the article.
    (a) ₹ 500   (b) ₹ 360
    (c) ₹ 425   (d) ₹ 400

47. A briefcase was sold at a profit of 10%. If its cost price was 5% less and it was sold for ₹ 7 more, the gain would have been 20%. Find the cost price of the briefcase.
    (a) ₹ 175   (b) ₹ 200
    (c) ₹ 225   (d) ₹ 160

48. A man sells a plot of land at 6% profit. If he had sold it at 10% profit, he would have received ₹ 200 more. What is the selling price of the land?
    (a) ₹ 5000   (b) ₹ 5300
    (c) ₹ 4800   (d) ₹ 5500

49. Ashok bought an article and spent ₹ 110 on its repairs. He then sold it to Bhushan at a profit of 20%. Bhushan sold it to Charan at a loss of 10%. Charan finally sold it for ₹ 1188 at a profit of 10%. How much did Ashok pay for the article?
    (a) ₹ 890   (b) ₹ 1000
    (c) ₹ 780   (d) ₹ 840

50. A man buys two cycles for a total cost of ₹ 900. By selling one for 4/5 of its cost and other for 5/4 of its cost, he makes a profit of ₹ 90 on the whole transaction. Find the cost price of lower priced cycle.
    (a) ₹ 360   (b) ₹ 250
    (c) ₹ 300   (d) ₹ 420

51. A merchant bought two transistors, which together cost him ₹ 480. He sold one of them at a loss of 15% and other at a gain of 19%. If the selling price of both the transistors are equal, find the cost of the lower priced transistor.
    (a) ₹ 300   (b) ₹ 180
    (c) ₹ 200   (d) ₹ 280

52. A manufacturer makes a profit of 15% by selling a colour TV for ₹ 5750. If the cost of manufacturing increases by 30% and the price paid by the retailer is increased by 20%, find the profit percent made by the manufacturer.
    (a) 6(2/13)%   (b) 4 (8/13)%
    (c) 6(1/13)%   (d) 7(4/13)%

53. The cost of manufacturing an article is made up of materials, labour and overheads in the ratio 4 : 3 : 2. If the cost of labour is ₹ 45, find the profit percent if the article is sold for ₹ 180.
    (a) 50%   (b) 33.33%
    (c) 25%   (d) 20%

54. Two dealers *X* and *Y* selling the same model of refrigerator mark them under the same selling prices. *X* gives successive discounts of 25% and 5% and *Y* gives successive discounts of 16% and 12%. From

whom is it more profitable to purchase the refrigerator?

(a) From *Y*

(b) From *X*

(c) Indifferent between the two

(d) Cannot be determined

55. A sells a car priced at ₹ 36,000. He gives a discount of 8% on the first ₹ 20,000 and 5% on the remaining ₹ 16,000. His competitor *B* sells a car of the same make, priced at ₹ 36,000. If he wants to be competitive what percent discount should *B* offer on the marked price.

(a) 5%

(b) 5.5%

(c) 6.66%

(d) 8.33%

56. An article costs ₹ 700 to a manufacturer who lists its price at ₹ 800. He sells it to a trader at a discount of 5%. The trader gets a further discount of 5% on his net payment for paying in cash. Calculate the amount that the trader pays to the manufacturer.

(a) ₹ 722

(b) ₹ 720

(c) ₹ 725

(d) None of these

57. In Question 56, find the profit percent that the manufacturer makes on the sale.

(a) 1500/7%

(b) 22/7%

(c) 2000/7%

(d) None of these

58. A firm dealing in furniture allows 4% discount on the marked price of each item. What price must be marked on a dining table that cost ₹ 400 to assemble, so as to make a profit of 20%?

(a) ₹ 475

(b) ₹ 480

(c) ₹ 500

(d) ₹ 520

59. A shopkeeper allows a discount of 12.5% on the marked price of a certain article and makes a profit of 20%. If the article cost the shopkeeper ₹ 210, what price must be marked on the article?

(a) ₹ 280

(b) ₹ 288

(c) ₹ 300

(d) None of these

60. A Camera shop allows a discount of 10% on the advertised price of a camera. What price must be marked on the camera, that costs him ₹ 600, so that he makes a profit of 20%?

(a) ₹ 800

(b) ₹ 720

(c) ₹ 750

(d) ₹ 850

61. A watch dealer pays 10% custom duty on a watch that costs ₹ 250 abroad. For how much should he mark it, if he desires to make a profit of 20% after giving a discount of 25% to the buyer?

(a) ₹ 400

(b) ₹ 440

(c) ₹ 275

(d) ₹ 330

62. A shopkeeper buys an article for ₹ 400 and marks it for sale at a price that gives him 80% profit on his cost. He, however, gives a 15% discount on the marked price to his customer. Calculate the actual percentage profit made by the shopkeeper.

(a) 62%

(b) 64%

(c) 53%

(d) 54%

63. In the land of the famous milkman Merghese Durian, a milkman sells his buffalo for ₹ 720 at some profit. Had he sold his buffalo at ₹ 510, the quantum of the loss incurred would have been double that of the profit earned. What is the cost price?

(a) ₹ 600

(b) ₹ 625

(c) ₹ 675

(d) None of these

64. A trader purchases apples at ₹ 60 per hundred. He spends 15% on the transportation. What should be the selling price per 100 to earn a profit of 20%?

(a) ₹ 72

(b) ₹ 81.8

(c) ₹ 82.8

(d) ₹ 83.8

65. A dishonest dealer professes to sell at cost price but uses a 900 gram weight instead of a 1 kilogram weight. Find the percent profit to the dealer.

(a) 10%

(b) 11.11%

(c) 12.5%

(d) None of these

Space for Rough Work

LEVEL OF DIFFICULTY (II)

1. Mithilesh makes 750 articles at a cost of 60 paise per article. He fixes the selling price such that if only 600 articles are sold, he would have made a profit of 40% on the outlay. However, 120 articles got spoilt and he was able to sell 630 articles at this price. Find his actual profit percent as the percentage of total outlay assuming that the unsold articles are useless.
   - (a) 42%
   - (b) 53%
   - (c) 47%
   - (d) 46%

2. A manufacturer estimates that on inspection 12% of the articles he produces will be rejected. He accepts an order to supply 22,000 articles at ₹ 7.50 each. He estimates the profit on his outlay including the manufacturing of rejected articles, to be 20%. Find the cost of manufacturing each article.
   - (a) ₹ 6
   - (b) ₹ 5.50
   - (c) ₹ 5
   - (d) ₹ 4.50

3. The cost of setting up the type of a magazine is ₹ 1000. The cost of running the printing machine is ₹ 120 per 100 copies. The cost of paper, ink and so on is 60 paise per copy. The magazines are sold at ₹ 2.75 each. 900 copies are printed, but only 784 copies are sold. What is the sum to be obtained from advertisements to give a profit of 10% on the cost?
   - (a) ₹ 730
   - (b) ₹ 720
   - (c) ₹ 726
   - (d) ₹ 736

4. A tradesman fixed his selling price of goods at 30% above the cost price. He sells half the stock at this price, one-quarter of his stock at a discount of 15% on the original selling price and rest at a discount of 30% on the original selling price. Find the gain percent altogether.
   - (a) 14.875%
   - (b) 15.375%
   - (c) 15.575%
   - (d) 16.375%

5. A tradesman marks an article at ₹ 205 more than the cost price. He allows a discount of 10% on the marked price. Find the profit percent if the cost price is ₹ x.
   - (a) $\dfrac{\left[\dfrac{x}{(18450)} - 10\right]}{x}$
   - (b) $\dfrac{[(18450)] - 10x}{x}$
   - (c) $\dfrac{\left[\dfrac{x}{(18450)} - 100\right]}{x}$
   - (d) $\dfrac{\left[\dfrac{18450}{x} - 100\right]}{x}$

6. Dolly goes to a shop to purchase a doll priced at ₹ 400. She is offered 4 discount options by the shop-keeper. Which of these options should she opt for to gain maximum advantage of the discount offered?
   - (a) Single discount of 30%
   - (b) 2 successive discounts of 15% each
   - (c) 2 successive discounts of 20% and 10%
   - (d) 2 successive discounts of 20% and 12%

7. A dishonest dealer marks up the price of his goods by 20% and gives a discount of 10% to the customer. He also uses a 900 gram weight instead of a 1 kilogram weight. Find his percentage profit due to these maneuvers.
   - (a) 8%
   - (b) 12%
   - (c) 20%
   - (d) 16%

8. A dishonest dealer marks up the price of his goods by 20% and gives a discount of 10% to the customer. Besides, he also cheats both his supplier and his buyer by 100 grams while buying or selling 1 kilogram. Find the percentage profit earned by the shopkeeper.
   - (a) 20%
   - (b) 25%
   - (c) 32%
   - (d) 27.5%

9. For Question 8, if it is known that the shopkeeper takes a discount of 10% from his supplier and he disregards this discount while marking up (i.e. he marks up at the undiscounted price), find the percentage profit for the shopkeeper if there is no other change from the previous problem.
   - (a) 32%
   - (b) 36.66%
   - (c) 40.33%
   - (d) 46.66%

10. Cheap and Best, a *kirana* shop bought some apples at 4 per rupee and an equal number at 5 per rupee. He then sold the entire quantity at 9 for 2 rupees. What is his percentage profit or loss?
    - (a) 1.23% loss
    - (b) 6.66%
    - (c) 8.888%
    - (d) No profit no loss

11. A watch dealer sells watches at ₹ 600 per watch. However, he is forced to give two successive discounts of 10% and 5% respectively. However, he recovers the sales tax on the net sale price from the customer at 5% of the net price. What price does a customer have to pay him to buy the watch?
    - (a) ₹ 539.75
    - (b) ₹ 539.65
    - (c) ₹ 538.75
    - (d) ₹ 538.65

12. Deb bought 100 kg of rice for ₹ 1100 and sold it at a loss of as much money as he received for 20 kg rice. At what price did he sell the rice?
    - (a) ₹ 9 per kg
    - (b) ₹ 9.1666 per kg
    - (c) ₹ 9.5 per kg
    - (d) ₹ 10.33 per kg

13. A carpenter wants to sell 40 chairs. If he sells them at ₹ 156 per chair, he would be able to sell all the chairs. But for every ₹ 6 increase in price, he will be left with one additional unsold chair. At what selling price would he be able to maximise his profits (assuming unsold chairs remain with him)?
    (a) 198   (b) 192
    (c) 204   (d) 210

Directions for Questions 14 and 15: Read the following and answer the questions that follow.

Doctors have advised Renu, a chocolate freak, not to take more than 20 chocolates in one day. When she went to the market to buy her daily quota, she found that if she buys chocolates from the market complex she would have to pay ₹ 3 more for the same number of chocolates than she would have spent had she bought them from her uncle Scrooge's shop, getting two sweets less per rupee. She finally decided to get them from Uncle Scrooge's shop paying only in one rupee coins.

14. How many chocolates did she buy?
    (a) 12   (b) 9
    (c) 18   (d) 15

15. How much would she have spent at the market complex?
    (a) ₹ 6   (b) ₹ 12
    (c) ₹ 9   (d) ₹ 5

16. A shopkeeper makes a profit of Q% by selling an object for ₹ 24. Had the cost price and selling price been interchanged, it would have led to a loss of $62.5Q$%. With the latter cost price, what should be the new selling price to get a profit of Q%?
    (a) ₹ 34.40   (b) ₹ 32.50
    (c) ₹ 25.60   (d) ₹ 38.4

17. Find the change in the percentage profit for a fruit vendor who, after finding 20% of the fruits rotten, increased his selling price by 10% over and above 15% that he was already charging?
    (a) −15   (b) +11.5
    (c) −13.8   (d) −11.5

Directions for Questions 18 and 19: Read the following and answer the questions that follow.

Ramu and Shyamu decided to sell their cars each at ₹ 36,000. While Ramu decided to give a discount of 8% on the first ₹ 8000, 5% on next ₹ 12,000 and 3% on the rest to buyer Sashi, Shyamu decided to give a discount of 7% on the first 12,000, 6% on the next 8,000 and 5% on the rest to buyer Rajesh. These discounts were, however, subject to the buyers making the payment on time failing which the discount gets reduced by 1% for every delay of a week. In each case, the selling price of 36,000 was arrived at by increasing the cost price by 25%.

18. If each of them got the payments on time, what is the approximate percentage profit of the person getting the higher profit?
    (a) 19%   (b) 21%
    (c) 25%   (d) 17%

19. If Sashi defaults by 1 and 2 weeks in the second and third payments respectively, what would be the profit of Ramu in the sale of the car?
    (a) ₹ 5920   (b) ₹ 6240
    (c) ₹ 5860   (d) ₹ 5980

20. What would be the difference in the profits if both the buyers default in each payment by a week?
    (a) ₹ 200   (b) ₹ 300
    (c) ₹ 400   (d) ₹ 500

21. Find the selling price of goods if two salesmen claim to make 25% profit each, one calculating it on cost price while another on the selling price, the difference in the profits earned being ₹ 100 and selling price being the same in both the cases.
    (a) ₹ 2000   (b) ₹ 1600
    (c) ₹ 2400   (d) ₹ 2500

22. A shopkeeper calculates percentage profit on the buying price and another on the selling price. What will be their difference in profits if both claim a profit of 20% on goods sold for ₹ 3000?
    (a) ₹ 200   (b) ₹ 100
    (c) ₹ 400   (d) ₹ 150

23. A pharmaceutical company made 3000 strips of tablets at a cost of ₹ 4800. The company gave away 1000 strips of tablets to doctors as free samples. A discount of 25% was allowed on the printed price. Find the ratio of profit if the price is raised from ₹ 3.25 to ₹ 4.25 per strip and if at the latter price, samples to doctors were done away with. (New profit/old profit)
    (a) 55.5   (b) 63.5
    (c) 75   (d) 99.25

24. A merchant makes a profit of 20% by selling an article. What would be the percentage change in the profit percent had he paid 10% less for it and the customer paid 10% more for it?
    (a) 120%   (b) 125%
    (c) 133.33%   (d) 150%

25. An article costing ₹ 20 was marked 25% above the cost price. After two successive discounts of the same percentage, the customer now pays ₹ 20.25. What would be the percentage change in profit had the price been increased by the same percentage twice successively instead of reducing it?
    (a) 3600%   (b) 3200%
    (c) 2800%   (d) 4000%

26. Divya goes to buy fruits and after a lot of bargaining is able to get the price of a dozen apples reduced

by Re. 1 from the initial price, thereby enabling her to get 1 apple extra for every rupee saved. (Getting no discount on the extra apple). What is the initial price of a dozen apples?

(a) ₹ 10 (b) ₹ 13
(c) ₹ 12 (d) ₹ 15

27. The accounts of a company show sales of ₹ 12,600. The primary cost is 35% of sales and trading cost accounts for 25% of the gross profit. Gross profit is arrived at by excluding the primary cost plus the cost of advertising expenses of ₹ 1400, director's salary of ₹ 650 per annum plus 2% of annual sales as miscellaneous costs. Find the percentage profit (approx) on a capital investment of ₹ 14,000?

(a) 35% (b) 31%
(c) 28% (d) Cannot be determined

28. Jonny has two cycles and one rickshaw. The rickshaw is worth ₹ 96. If he sells the rickshaw along with the first cycle, he has an amount double that of the value of the second cycle. But if he decides to sell the rickshaw along with the second cycle, the amount received would be less than the value of first cycle by ₹ 306. What is the value of first cycle?

(a) ₹ 900 (b) ₹ 600
(c) ₹ 498 (d) None of these

29. David sells his Laptop to Goliath at a loss of 20% who subsequently sells it to Hercules at a profit of 25%. Hercules, after finding some defect in the laptop, returns it to Goliath but could recover only ₹ 4.50 for every ₹ 5 he had paid. Find the amount of Hercules' loss if David had paid ₹ 1.75 lakh for the laptop.

(a) ₹ 3500 (b) ₹ 2500
(c) ₹ 17,500 (d) None of these

30. A dishonest shopkeeper, at the time of selling and purchasing, weighs 10% less and 20% more per kilogram respectively. Find the percentage profit earned by treachery. (Assuming he sells at Cost Price)

(a) 30% (b) 20%
(c) 25% (d) 33.33%

31. A dealer marks articles at a price that gives him a profit of 30%. 6% of the consignment of goods was lost in a fire in his premises, 24% was soiled and had to be sold at half the cost price. If the remainder was sold at the marked price, what percentage profit or loss did the dealer make on that consignment?

(a) 2% (b) 2.5%
(c) 3% (d) 6.2%

32. A book was sold for a certain sum and there was a loss of 20%. Had it been sold for ₹ 12 more, there would have been a gain of 30%. What would be the profit if the book were sold for ₹ 4.8 more than what it was sold for?

(a) No profit, no loss (b) 20%
(c) 10% (d) 25%

For Questions 33 to 36 use the following data:

33. Two thousand people lived in Business Village of which 55% were male and the rest were female. The male population earned a profit of 5% and the female population earned 8% on an investment of ₹ 50 each. Find the change in the percentage profit of the village if the ratio of male to female gets reversed the next year, population remaining the same.

(a) Drop of 0.3 (b) Increase of 0.3
(c) Increase of 0.45 (d) Drop of 0.45

34. In Question 33, find the change in the percentage profit of the village, if the population increases by 10%. (Assume the ratio remains the same)

(a) Increase of 10% (b) Increase of 11.11%
(c) No change (d) Cannot be determined

35. For Question 34, find the percentage change in the profit.

(a) Increase of 10% (b) Increase of 11.11%
(c) No change (d) Cannot be determined

36. For Question 33, what would be the change in the percentage profit, if alongwith the reversal of the ratio of males to females, the profit also increases by 1% for both males and females?

(a) Drop of 1.3 (b) Increase of 1.3
(c) Increase of 0.8 (d) None of these

37. A rickshaw dealer buys 30 rickshaws for ₹ 4725. Of these, 8 are four-seaters and the rest are two-seaters. At what price must he sell the four-seaters so that if he sells the two-seaters at 3/4th of this price, he makes a profit of 40% on his outlay?

(a) ₹ 180 (b) ₹ 270
(c) ₹ 360 (d) ₹ 450

38. A flat and a piece of land were bought by two friends Raghav and Sita respectively at prices of ₹ 2 lakh and ₹ 2.2 lakh. The price of the flat rises by 20 percent every year and that of land by 10% every year. After two years, they decide to exchange their possessions. What is percentage gain of the gainer?

(a) 7.56% (b) 6.36%
(c) 4.39% (d) None of these

39. A, B and C form a company. A invests half of C expecting a return of 10%. B invests three-fourths of C, expecting a return of 15% on it. C invests ₹ 3000 and the profit of the firm is 25%. How much would B's share of profit be more than that of A's share if B gets an additional 8% for managing the business? (Assume that their expectations with respect to returns on capital invested are met before profit is divided in the ratio of capitals invested).

(a) 20% (b) 18%
(c) 15% (d) Cannot be determined

40. A driver of a autorickshaw makes a profit of 20% on every trip when he carries 3 passengers and the price of petrol is ₹ 30 a litre. Find the percentage profit for the same journey if he goes for four passengers per trip and the price of petrol reduces to ₹ 24 litre. (Assume that revenue per passenger is the same in both the cases.)
    (a) 33.33%
    (b) 65.66
    (c) 100%
    (d) Data inadequate

41. Raghav bought 25 washing machines and microwave ovens for ₹ 2,05,000. He sold 80% of the washing machines and 12 microwave ovens for a profit of ₹ 40,000. Each washing machine was marked up by 20% over cost and each microwave oven was sold at a profit of ₹ 2,000. The remaining washing machines and 3 microwave ovens could not be sold. What is Raghav's overall profit/loss?
    (a) ₹ 1000 profit
    (b) ₹ 2500 loss
    (c) ₹ 1000 loss
    (d) Cannot be determined

42. After selling a watch, Shyam found that he had made a loss of 10%. He also found that had he sold it for ₹ 27 more, he would have made a profit of 5%. The actual initial loss was what percentage of the profit earned, had he sold the watch for a 5% profit?
    (a) 23%
    (b) 150%
    (c) 200%
    (b) 180%

43. Sambhu buys rice at ₹ 10/kg and puts a price tag on it so as to earn a profit of 20%. However, his faulty balance shows 1000 gm when it is actually 800 gm. What is his actual gain percentage?
    (a) 50%
    (b) 40%
    (c) 18%
    (d) 10%

44. The profit earned when an article is sold for ₹ 800 is 20 times the loss incurred when it is sold for ₹ 275. At what price should the article be sold if it is desired to make a profit of 25%.
    (a) ₹ 300
    (b) ₹ 350
    (c) ₹ 375
    (d) ₹ 400

45. A sells to B goods at five-thirds the rate of profit at which B has decided to sell it to C. C, on other hand, sells it to D at one-third the rate of profit at which B sold it to C. If D gives ₹ 2145 to C at 10% profit, how much did A buy it for?
    (a) ₹ 1000
    (b) ₹ 2000
    (c) ₹ 1500
    (d) ₹ 1800

46. In the town of Andher Nagari Chaupat Raja, shopkeepers have to buy and sell goods in the range of ₹ 500 to ₹ 999. A shopkeeper in such a town decides not to buy or sell goods for amounts that contain the digit 9 or for amounts that add up to 13 or are a multiple of 13. What is the maximum possible profit he can earn?
    (a) ₹ 388
    (b) ₹ 389
    (c) ₹ 488
    (d) None of these

47. Manish bought a combined total of 25 monitors and printers. He marked up the monitors by 20% on the cost price, while each printer was marked up by ₹ 2000. He was able to sell 75% of the monitors and 2 printers and make a profit of ₹ 49,000. The remaining monitors and 3 printers could not be sold by him. Find his overall profit or loss if he gets no return on unsold items and it is known that a printer costs 50% of a monitor.
    (a) Loss of ₹ 48,500
    (b) Loss of 21,000
    (c) Loss of ₹ 41,000
    (d) Inadequate data

48. For Question 47, Manish's approximate percentage profit or loss is
    (a) 14.37% loss
    (b) 16.5% loss
    (c) 12.14% loss
    (d) Insufficient information

49. An orange vendor makes a profit of 20% by selling oranges at a certain price. If he charges ₹ 1.2 higher per orange he would gain 40%. Find the original price at which he sold an orange.
    (a) ₹ 5
    (b) ₹ 4.8
    (c) ₹ 6
    (d) None of these

50. The Mindworkzz prints 5000 copies of a magazine for ₹ 5,00,000 every month. In the July issue of the magazine, Mindworkzz distributed 500 copies free. Besides, it was able to sell 2/3 of the remaining magazines at 20% discount. Besides, the remaining magazines were sold at the printed price of the magazine (which was ₹ 200). Find the percentage profit of Mindworkzz in the magazine venture in the month of July (assume a uniform 20% of the sale price as the vendor's discount and also assume that Mindworkzz earns no income from advertising for the issue).
    (a) 56%
    (b) 24.8%
    (c) 28.5%
    (d) 22.6%

Space for Rough Work

LEVEL OF DIFFICULTY (III)

The charges of a taxi journey are decided on the basis of the distance covered and the amount of the waiting time during a journey. Distance wise, for the first 2 kilometers (or any part thereof) of a journey, the metre reading is fixed at ₹ 10 (if there is no waiting). Also, if a taxi is boarded and it does not move, then the meter reading is again fixed at ₹ 10 for the first ten minutes of waiting. For every additional kilometre the meter reading changes by ₹ 5 (with changes in the meter reading being in multiples of Re. 1 for every 200 meters travelled). For every additional minute of waiting, the meter reading changes by ₹ 1. (no account is taken of a fraction of a minute waited for or of a distance less than 200 meters travelled). The net meter reading is a function of the amount of time waited for and the distance travelled.

The cost of running a taxi depends on the fuel efficiency (in terms of mileage/liter), depreciation (straight line over 10 years) and the driver's salary (not taken into account if the taxi is self owned).

Depreciation is ₹ 100 per day everyday of the first 10 years. This depreciation has to be added equally to the cost for every customer while calculating the profit for a particular trip. Similarly, the driver's daily salary is also apportioned equally across the customers of the particular day. Assume, for simplicity, that there are 50 customers every day (unless otherwise mentioned). The cost of fuel is ₹ 15 per liter (unless otherwise stated).

The customer has to pay 20% over the meter reading while settling his bill. Also assume that there is no fuel cost for waiting time (unless otherwise stated).

Based on the above facts, answer the following:

1. If Sardar Preetpal Singh's taxi is 14 years old and has a fuel efficiency of 12 km/litre of fuel, find his profit in a run from Howrah Station to Park Street (a distance of 7 km) if the stoppage time is 8 minutes. (Assume he owns the taxi)
   (a) ₹ 32.25   (b) ₹ 40.85
   (c) ₹ 34.25   (d) ₹ 42.85

2. For question 2, Sardar Preetpal Singh's percentage profit is
   (a) 391.42%   (b) 380%
   (c) 489.71%   (d) 438.23%

3. For the same journey as in question 1 if on another day, with heavier traffic, the waiting time increases to 13 minutes, find the percentage change in the profit.
   (a) 12%   (b) 14%
   (c) 13%   (d) 16%

4. For Question 3, if Sardar Preetpal Singh idled his taxi for 7 minutes and if the fuel consumption dur-

ing idling is 50 ml per minute, find the percentage decrease in the profits.
   (a) 10.74%   (b) 11.21%
   (c) 10.87%   (d) 9.94%

Directions for Questions 5 to 10: Answer questions based on this additional information:

Mr. Vikas Verma owns a fleet of 3 taxis, where he pays his driver ₹ 3000 per month. He also insists on keeping an attendant for ₹ 1500 per month in each of his taxis. Idling requires 50 ml of fuel for every minute of idling. For a moving taxi, the fuel consumption is given by 12 km/per litre. On a particular day, he received the following reports about the three taxis.

Taxi code	Total kilometres	Waiting time	Waiting time with idling	Waiting time without idling
A	260		190 min	30 min
B	264		170 min	80 min
C	275		180 min	60 min

5. The maximum revenue has been generated by which taxi?
   (a) A   (b) B
   (c) C   (d) Cannot be determined

   If it is to be assumed that every customer travelled at least 2 kilometres:

6. Which of the three taxis generated the maximum revenue?
   (a) A   (b) B
   (c) C   (d) Both A & B
   (e) Cannot be determined

7. What percentage of the total revenue was generated by taxi B?
   (a) 32.30   (b) 33.36
   (c) 34.32   (d) 34.36

8. The highest profit was yielded by which taxi?
   (a) A   (b) B
   (c) C   (d) Both A & B

9. The taxi which had the highest percentage profit for the day was
   (a) A   (b) B
   (c) C   (d) B & C

10. The profit as a percentage of costs for the day was:
    (a) 179.46%   (b) 150.76%
    (c) 163.28%   (d) 173.48%

Directions for Questions 11 to 15: Read the following and answer the questions that follow.

The Coca-Cola Company is setting up a plant for manufacture and sale of the soft drink.

The investment for the plant is ₹ 10 crore (to be invested in plant, machinery, advertising, infrastructure, etc.).

The following information is available about the different bottle sizes planned:

Bottle size	Bottling cost	Cost of liquid	Transportation cost	Sale price	Dealer margin
300 ml	₹ 2	₹ 0.6	10 paise per bottle	₹ 10	₹ 3
500 ml	₹ 5	₹ 1	15 paise per bottle	₹ 18	₹ 6
1.5 litre	₹ 10	₹ 3	20 paise per bottle	₹ 40	₹ 12

Based on this information answer the questions given below:

11. For which bottle should Coca-Cola try to maximise sales to maximise its profits? (Assume that the total number of litres of Coca-Cola sold is constant irrespective of the break up of the sales in terms of the bottle sizes)
    (a) 300 ml
    (b) 500 ml
    (c) 1.5 litres
    (d) Indifferent between the three sizes

12. If the company sells only 300 ml bottles in the first year, how many bottles should it sell to recover the investment made in the first year only?
    (a) 23,255,814
    (b) 232,558,140
    (c) 32,255,814
    (d) 322,558,140

13. If sales of 300 ml bottles to 500 ml bottles is 4 : 1, and there is no sale of 1500 ml bottles how many 300 ml bottles will be required to recover the investment?
    (a) 1,73,53,580
    (b) 2,93,25,512
    (c) 16,25,848
    (d) 16,25,774

14. For Question 13, the total number of both the types to be sold in India in order to recover the whole investment is
    (a) 3665890
    (b) 2032310
    (c) 21691975
    (d) 21723165

15. If we add administrative costs @ Re. 1 per litre, which bottle size will have the maximum profitability?
    (a) 300 ml
    (b) 500 ml
    (c) 1.5 litres
    (d) Indifferent between the three sizes

16. Hotel Chanakya in Chankyapuri has a fixed monthly cost of ₹ 1,000,00. The advertising cost is ₹ 10,000 per month. It has 5 A/C rooms, which cost ₹ 600 per day and 10 non-A/C rooms, which cost ₹ 350 per day. Direct costs are ₹ 100 per day for an A/C room, and ₹ 50 for a non-A/C room. In the month of April 2020, the occupancy rate of A/C rooms is 50% while that of non-A/C rooms is 45%. Find the profit of the hotel in rupee terms for the month of April 2020.
    (a) 33,600
    (b) 28,800
    (c) (32,000) Loss
    (d) (17,750) Loss

17. For the above question, keeping the A/C occupancy constant at 50%, what should be the minimum occupancy rate for non-A/C rooms for incurring no loss for the month?
    (a) 75.66%
    (b) 80.66%
    (c) 83.33%
    (d) 86.66%

18. For Questions 15 and 16: ₹ 25,000 worth of advertising a sales promotion of 20% off on the bill doubles the occupancy rate. If this is done, what is the change in the profit or loss?
    (a) Reduction of loss by ₹ 5,900
    (b) Reduction of loss to ₹ 5,900
    (c) Reduction of loss by ₹ 26,100
    (d) Both b and c

19. Advertising worth ₹ 50,000 is done for the sales promotion of A/C rooms (advertising a 20% reduction in the bill for A/C rooms). This leads to a doubling of the occupancy rate of A/C rooms. Besides, it also has an effect of increasing non-A/C room occupancy by 20%. Is this advised?
    (a) Yes
    (b) No
    (c) Indifferent
    (d) Cannot be determined

A restaurant has a pricing policy that allows for the following mark-ups:

Soups	Mark-up of	40%
Starters	Mark-up of	50%
Meals	Mark-up of	25%
Breads	Mark-up of	75%
Sweets	Mark-up of	75%

20. Mr. Amarnath and his family of 4 went to the restaurant and got a bill for: Soups (₹ 126), Starters (₹ 180), Meals (₹ 300), Breads (₹ 245) and Sweets (₹ 210). Find the profit for the restaurant.
    (a) ₹ 341
    (b) ₹ 351
    (c) ₹ 361
    (d) ₹ 371

21. The approximate percentage profit for the restaurant on the bill is
    (a) 40%
    (b) 45%
    (c) 50%
    (d) 55%

22. Which of these are true:
   (i) Profit increases if a part of the money spent on starters was spent on breads and another part of the starters was spent on snacks.
   (ii) Profit increases if a part of the money spent on meal items was spent on starters and another part spent on soups was spent on breads.
   (iii) Profit decreases if a certain amount (say x) of the spending on soups was spent on starters and the same amount (₹ x) of the spending on soups is spent on meal items.
   (a) (ii) only
   (b) (iii) only
   (c) (ii) and (iii)
   (d) All the three

Directions for Questions 23 to 28: Read the following and answer the questions that follow.

Prabhat Ranjan inaugurates his internet cafe on the 1st of January 2003. He invests in 10 computers @ ₹ 30,000 per computer. Besides, he also invests in the other infrastructure of the centre, a sum of ₹ 1 lakh only. He charges his customers on the time spent on the internet a flat rate of ₹ 50 per hour. His initial investment on computers has to be written off equally in 3 years (1 lakh per year) and the infrastructure has to be written off in 5 years (@ ₹ 20,000 per year).

He has to pay a fixed rental of ₹ 8000 per month for the space and also hires an assistant at ₹ 2000 per month.

For every hour that he is connected to the internet, he has to bear a telephone charge of ₹ 20 irrespective of the number of machines operational on the internet at that time. On top of this, he also has to pay an electricity charge of ₹ 5 per computer per hour. Assume that there are no other costs involved unless otherwise mentioned. The internet cafe is open 12 hours a day and is open on all 7 days of the week. (Assume that if a machine is not occupied, it is put off and hence consumes no electricity).

23. Assuming a uniform 80% occupancy rate for the month of April 2003, find his profit or loss for the month.
   (a) ₹ 1,02,400
   (b) ₹ 1,22,400
   (c) ₹ 1,23,600
   (d) ₹ 1,20,733.33

24. If the occupancy rate drops to 60% in the month of June, what is the value of the profit for the month?
   (a) ₹ 90,000
   (b) ₹ 70,000
   (c) ₹ 1,23,600
   (d) ₹ 90,633.33

25. If Prabhat estimates a fixed occupancy rate of 80% during the peak hours of 2 to 8 pm and 40% in the off peak hours of 8 am to 2 pm find the expected profit for him in the month of July 2006.
   (a) ₹ 73,000
   (b) ₹ 93,000
   (c) ₹ 96,000
   (d) ₹ 1,27,500

26. The percentage margin is defined as the margin as a percentage of the variable cost for an hour of opera-

tion. Find the percentage margin of the cyber cafe Prabhat runs.
   (a) 600 %
   (b) 533.33%
   (c) 525%
   (d) Cannot be determined

27. For Question 25 above, how many 30-day months will be required for Prabhat to recover back the investment?
   (a) 3.58 months
   (b) 3.72 months
   (c) 5.71 months
   (d) Cannot be determined

28. If the internet rates per hour have to be dropped drastically to ₹ 20 per hour in the fourth year of operation, what is Prabhat's expected profit for the calendar year 2010 assuming an average of 60% occupancy rate for the year?
   (a) ₹ 2,66,600
   (b) ₹ 1,66,600
   (c) ₹ 88,500
   (d) ₹ 91,500

Directions for Questions 29 to 33: Read the following and answer the questions that follow.

A train journey from Patna to Delhi by the Magadh Express has 4 classes:
The fares of the 4 classes are as follows:

3 tier: ₹ 330	No. of berths per bogey: 72	No. of bogeys: 8
AC 3 tier: ₹ 898	No. of berths per bogey: 64	No. of bogeys: 2
AC 2 tier: ₹ 1388	No. of berths per bogey: 45	No. of bogeys: 2
AC first: ₹ 2691	No. of berths per bogey: 26	No. of bogeys: 1

Patna to Delhi distance: 1100 kilometres. Assume the train does not stop at any station unless otherwise indicated. Running cost per kilometre: AC bogey → ₹ 25, non AC bogey → ₹ 10.

29. Assuming full occupancy, a bogey of which class exhibits the highest profit margin?
   (a) AC 3 tier
   (b) AC 2 tier
   (c) AC first class
   (d) 3 tier

30. Assuming full occupancy in all the classes, for a journey between Patna to Delhi, the profit margin (as a percentage of the running costs) of the class showing the lowest profit is approximately.
   (a) 116%
   (b) 127%
   (c) 109%
   (d) None of these

31. What is the approximate profit for the railways in rupees if the Magadh Express runs at full occupancy on a particular day?
   (a) ₹ 250,000
   (b) ₹ 275,000
   (c) ₹ 300,000
   (d) Cannot be determined

32. For Question 31, the percentage of the total profit that comes out of AC bogeys is (approximately)

(a) 50%   (b) 60%

(c) 70%   (d) 80%

33. The highest revenue for a journey from Patna to Delhi will always be generated by

    (a) 3 tier   (b) AC 3 tier

    (c) AC 2 tier   (d) Cannot be determined

34. A newspaper vendor sells three kinds of periodicals-dailies, weeklies and monthlies.

    The weeklies sell for ₹ 12 at a profit of 20%, the monthlies sell for ₹ 50 at a profit of 25%, while the dailies sell at ₹ 3 at a profit of 50%. If there is a government restriction on the total number of periodicals that one particular news vendor, can sell, and Kalu a newspaper vendor, has sufficient demand for all the three types of periodicals, what should he do to maximise profits?

    (a) Sell maximum weeklies

    (b) Sell maximum monthlies

    (c) Sell maximum dailies

    (d) Cannot be determined

35. Without the restriction mentioned in the problem above, what should the newspaper vendor do to maximise his profits if his capital is limited?

    (a) Sell maximum weeklies

    (b) Sell maximum monthlies

    (c) Sell maximum dailies

    (d) Cannot be determined

36. A fruit vendor buys fruits from the fruit market at wholesale prices and sells them at his shop at retail prices. He operates his shop 30 days a month, as a rule. He buys in multiples of 100 fruits and sells them in multiples of a dozen fruits. He purchases mangoes for ₹ 425 per hundred and sells at ₹ 65 per dozen, he buys apples at ₹ 150 per hundred and sells at ₹ 30 per dozen, he buys watermelons (always of equal size) at ₹ 1800 per hundred and sells at ₹ 360 per dozen. Which of the three fruits yields him the maximum percentage profit?

(a) Mangoes   (b) Apples

(c) Watermelons   (d) Both (b) and (c)

37. For Question 36, if he adds oranges, which he buys at ₹ 180 per hundred and sells at ₹ 33 per dozen, what can be his maximum profit on a particular day if he invests ₹ 1800 in purchasing fruits everyday and he sells everything that he buys?

    (a) ₹ 1200   (b) ₹ 1180

    (c) ₹ 1260   (d) ₹ 1320

38. For Questions 36 and 37, if the fruit vendor hires you as a consultant and pays you 20% of his profit in the month of July 2006 as a service charge, what can be the maximum fees that you will get for your consultancy charges?

    (a) ₹ 7200   (b) ₹ 14,400

    (c) ₹ 7440   (d) Cannot be determined

39. A newspaper costs ₹ 11 to print on a daily basis. Its sale price (printed) is ₹ 3. The newspaper gives a sales incentive of 40% on the printed price, to the newspaper vendors. The newspaper makes up for the loss through advertisements, which are charged on the basis of per column centimetre rates. The advertisement rates of the newspaper are ₹ 300 per cc (column centimetre). It has to give an incentive of 15% on the advertising bill to the advertising agency. If the newspaper has a circulation of 12,000 copies, what is the approximate minimum advertising booking required if the newspaper has to break-even on a particular day. (Assume there is no wastage)

    (a) 300 cc   (b) 350 cc

    (c) 435 cc   (d) 450 cc

40. For Question 39, if it is known that the newspaper house is unable to recover 20% of its dues, what would be the approximate advertising booking target on a particular day in order to ensure the break-even point?

    (a) 375 cc   (b) 438 cc

    (c) 544 cc   (d) 562.5 cc

Space for Rough Work

ANSWER KEY

Level of Difficulty (I)

1. (b)	2. (b)	3. (c)	4. (d)
5. (a)	6. (b)	7. (d)	8. (a)
9. (b)	10. (a)	11. (d)	12. (c)
13. (d)	14. (b)	15. (c)	16. (d)
17. (b)	18. (a)	19. (b)	20. (c)
21. (c)	22. (b)	23. (c)	24. (c)
25. (a)	26. (d)	27. (b)	28. (a)
29. (c)	30. (b)	31. (d)	32. (d)
33. (a)	34. (b)	35. (b)	36. (a)
37. (c)	38. (c)	39. (d)	40. (c)
41. (a)	42. (b)	43. (c)	44. (b)
45. (c)	46. (d)	47. (a)	48. (b)
49. (a)	50. (c)	51. (c)	52. (a)
53. (b)	54. (b)	55. (c)	56. (a)
57. (b)	58. (c)	59. (b)	60. (a)
61. (b)	62. (c)	63. (d)	64. (c)
65. (b)			

Level of Difficulty (II)

1. (c)	2. (b)	3. (c)	4. (b)
5. (b)	6. (a)	7. (c)	8. (c)
9. (d)	10. (a)	11. (d)	12. (b)
13. (a)	14. (a)	15. (a)	16. (d)
17. (c)	18. (a)	19. (a)	20. (c)
21. (a)	22. (b)	23. (b)	24. (c)
25. (d)	26. (c)	27. (b)	28. (a)
29. (c)	30. (d)	31. (c)	32. (a)
33. (b)	34. (c)	35. (a)	36. (b)
37. (b)	38. (d)	39. (d)	40. (c)
41. (c)	42. (c)	43. (a)	44. (c)
45. (a)	46. (a)	47. (a)	48. (a)
49. (d)	50. (b)		

Level of Difficulty (III)

1. (d)	2. (c)	3. (b)	4. (a)
5. (d)	6. (c)	7. (b)	8. (c)
9. (a)	10. (b)	11. (a)	12. (a)
13. (a)	14. (c)	15. (a)	16. (c)
17. (b)	18. (d)	19. (b)	20. (b)
21. (c)	22. (c)	23. (a)	24. (b)
25. (a)	26. (d)	27. (d)	28. (b)
29. (c)	30. (c)	31. (b)	32. (b)
33. (d)	34. (b)	35. (c)	36. (d)
37. (a)	38. (a)	39. (c)	40. (c)

Hints

Level of Difficulty (II)

1. Cost of 750 articles = ₹ 450 → outlay.

   Hence, SP of 600 articles = ₹ 630. (@40% profit on his outlay)

   ∴ SP of each article = ₹ 1.05.

2. When the manufacturer makes 100 articles, he sells only 88.

   Revenues = $88 \times 7.5 = $ ₹ 660

   But profit being 20% of outlay, total outlay is ₹ 550.

3. Total cost = Type + Running cost of printing machine + paper, ink

   $= 1000 + 120 \times 9 + 540 = 2620$

   ∴ Net sum to be recovered = ₹ 2882.

4. Assume CP of goods = 100.

   Then marked price = 130.

   Revenues = $\dfrac{1}{2} \times 130 + \dfrac{1}{4} \times 0.85 \times 130 + \dfrac{1}{4} \times 0.7 \times 130$

5. If CP = x, then marked price = $x + 205$ and

   Selling price = $0.9x + 184.5$.

   Profit = $184.5 - 0.1x$

7. Assume CP as 1 Re/gram.

   Then, he sells 900 grams for ₹ 1080,

   While the CP of 900 grams is ₹ 900.

8. He buys 1100 grams for ₹1000 and sells 900 grams for ₹ 1080.

   To calculate profit percentage, either equate the money or the goods.

9. He buys 1100 grams for ₹ 900 and sells 900 grams for ₹ 1080.

   To calculate percentage profit, either equate the money or equate the goods.

10. Take the LCM of 4 and 5 and assume 20 apples bought at each price.

   Ensure that you equate either the goods or the money.

12. The loss is covered by the sale of 20 extra kgs of rice.

   i.e.   CP of 100 kg = SP of 120 kg

13. Profit maximisation is totally dependent on revenue maximisation, since the cost is constant.

14-15. Solve using options.

16. Difference between original CP and SP is Q%, while the reverse difference is 62.5% of Q.

   The only values satisfying these are 60% and 37.5%. Hence $Q = 60$%.

17. If CP = 100, original marked price = 115 and new marked price = 126.5. But he now sells on 80% of his marked price.

21. Assume the SP to be 125 for both the salesmen.

24. If initial cost price is 100, then initial selling price will be 120. Then, the new cost price is 90, while the new selling price is 132.

25. The successive percentage drops in marked price to get the selling price are 10% each.

27. Primary cost = 0.35×12600

Gross profit = 12600 – (1400 + 650 + 252) – 0.35 × 12600.

∴ Trading cost = 25% of Gross profit.

∴ Net profit = Gross profit – 25% of Gross profit = 75% of Gross profit.

and percent profit = $\dfrac{\text{Net Profit}}{\text{Outlay}} \times 100$.

28. Solve using options.

29. Assume David's cost price as 100. Then, Goliath buys at 80, sells at 100 and buys back from Hercules at 90.

30. Buys 1200 when he pays for 1000 and sells 900 when he receives money for 1000.

33-36. Investments are ₹ 55000 for men and ₹ 45000 for women.

The rate of return being given, we can find out the percentage profit overall.

37. Solve through options.

39. A's share is only dependent on the ratio of capital investment.

40. Assume cost = 100 and SP = 120.

Then, when price of petrol is reduced →

Cost = 80 and SP = 160.

41. The number of washing machines plus the number of microwaves = 25.

Unsold items = 2 washing machines + 3 microwaves.

Goods sold = 8 washing machines + 12 microwaves = 80% of total value.

44. If L represents the loss, then 20 L represents the profit. Hence, $L = \dfrac{525}{21} = 25$.

Hence, CP = 300.

45. A sells at 50% profit, while B sells at 30% profit.

46. The required profit will be given by:

Maximum possible selling price – Minimum possible purchase price.

50. Sales of 3000 copies for ₹160 and 1500 copies for ₹ 200 each.

Level of Difficulty (III)

1-10. Concentrate on creation of the revenue equation and the cost equations separately. Revenue from a journey will depend on
(a) length of journey (over 2 kilometres)
(b) time of waiting.

Besides, the fixed metre reading of ₹ 10 at the start is used up at the rate of 1 Re per 200 metres and/or 1 Re/minute of waiting.

11. Coca-Cola earns (10 – 3) – (2 + 0.6 + 0.1) = ₹ 4.3 per 300 ml bottle.

Similarly, for 500 ml bottle, the profit is

12 – 6.15 = ₹ 5.85.

and for 1500 ml bottle, 28 – 13.2 = 14.8 for 1500 ml bottle.

The profit per ml sold has to be maximised.

12. $\dfrac{\text{Rs.10 crore}}{4.3} = 2,32,55,814$.

13-14. The earning for one set of 5 bottles = 4.3 × 4 + 5.85 = ₹ 23.05.

15. Maximum profitability = $\dfrac{\text{Margin per bottle}}{\text{Cost per bottle}}$.

16-19. Profit = Revenue – Expenses.

20-22. Observe the profitability rates for each type of item.

23. Revenues = 8 computers × ₹ 50/hr × 12 hours × 30 days

Costs = monthly cost + $\dfrac{\text{Depreciation}}{12}$ + Hourly cost

× 12 hours × 30 days.

24-28. Will be solved on the same principle as question 23.

29-33. Revenues = occupancy × cost/ticket.

$\dfrac{\text{Cost}}{\text{Kilometer}} \times$ no. of kilometres.

Solutions and Shortcuts

Level of Difficulty (I)

1. 0.9 × Price = 495 → Price 550.

2. The SP = 107.5% of the CP. Thus, CP = 34.4/1.075 = ₹ 32.

3. 1.15 × Price = 4600 → Price = 4000.

4. A loss of 20% means a cost price of 100 corresponding to a selling price of 80. CP as a percentage of the SP would then be 125%

5. 2400 = 1.25 × cost price → Cost price = 1920
Profit at 2040 = ₹ 120
Percentage profit = (120/2040) × 100 = 6.25%

6. CP = 935/1.1 = 850. Selling this at 810 would mean a loss of ₹40 on a CP of ₹ 850.

7. The CP will be ₹ 5400. Hence at an S.P. of 5703.75 the percentage profit will be 5.625%

8. CP = 63/1.05 = 60. Thus, the required SP for 10% profit = 1.1 × 60 = 66.

9. The buying price is ₹ 9 per dozen, while the sales price is ₹ 12 per dozen – a profit of 33.33%

10. Sales tax = 120/5 =24. Thus, the SP contains ₹ 24 component of sales tax. Of the remainder (120 – 24 = 96) 1/3rd is the profit. Thus, the profit = 96/3 = 32. Cost price = 96 – 32 = 64.

11. C.P × 1.2 = 25 → CP = 20.833
At a selling price of ₹ 22.5, the profit percent 1.666/20.833 = 8%

12. Solve using options. Option (c) gives you ₹ 175 as the cost of the trouser. Hence, the shirt will cost 12% more i.e. 175 + 17.5 + 3.5 = 196.
This satisfies the total cost requirement of ₹ 371.

13. The formula that satisfies this condition is:
    Loss of $a^2/100\%$ (Where a is the common profit and loss percentage). Hence, in this case $400/100 = 4\%$ loss.

14. Use PCG as follows:

    $$100 \xrightarrow{\;20\%\uparrow\;} 120 \xrightarrow{\;10\%\downarrow\;} 108$$

    Hence, 8% is the correct answer.

15. The cost per toffee = $75/125 = ₹ 0.6 = 60$ paise. Cost of 1 million toffees = 600000. But there is a discount of 40% offered on this quantity. Thus, the total cost for 1 million toffees is 60% of 600000 = 360000.

16. On a marked price of ₹ 80, a discount of 10% would mean a selling price of ₹ 72. Since this represents a 20% profit we get:

    $$1.2 \times CP = 72 \rightarrow CP = 60.$$

17. The thought process in this question would go as follows:
    $80 – 5\%$ of $80 = 76$ (after the first discount). $76 – 5\%$ of $76 = 76 – 3.8 = 72.2$ (after the second discount)

18. For ₹ 72, we can buy a dozen pair of gloves. Hence, for ₹ 24 we can buy 4 pairs of gloves.

19. $100 \rightarrow 80$ (after 20% discount) $\rightarrow 72$ (after 10% discount) $\rightarrow 68.4$ (after 5% discount).
    Thus, the single discount which would be equivalent would be 31.6%.

20. $180 \times 0.9 \times x = 137.7 \rightarrow x = 0.85$
    Which means a 15% discount.

21. If you assume the cost price to be 100 and we check from the options, we will see that for Option (c) the marked price will be 120 and giving a discount of 12.5% would leave the shopkeeper with a 5% profit.

22. Solve by trial and error using the options. If he marks his goods 30% above the cost price he would be able to generate a 17% profit inspite of giving a 10% discount.

23. The customer pays ₹ 38 after a discount of 5%. Hence, the list price must be ₹ 40.
    This also means that at a 20% discount, the retailer buys the item at ₹ 32.
    Hence, the profit for the retailer will be ₹ 6 (38 – 32).

24. The profit would be given by the percentage value of the ratio $6/32 = 18.75\%$.

25. The labour price accounts for ₹ 400. Since the profit percentage gives a 20% profit on this component i.e. ₹ 80.
    Hence, the marked price is ₹ 980.

26. The costs in 2006 were 300,400 and 200 respectively. An increase of 20% in material → increase of 60. An increase of 30% in labor → increase of 120. Increase of 10% in overheads → increase of 20.
    Total increase = 60 + 120 + 20 = 200. New cost = 900 + 200 = 1100

27. For a 20% profit on labout cost, he should mark his goods at 1100 + 20% of 520 = 1204. Note, 520 is the new cost of labout after a 30% increase as described in Question 26.

28. SP = $960 = 0.96 \times CP \rightarrow CP = 1000$. To gain a profit of 16%, the marked price should be 116% of 1000 = 1160.

29. The SP per article = ₹ 3. This represents a profit of 20%. Thus, CP = $3/1.2 = 2.5$. 8 articles would cost ₹ 20 and hence selling at 18.40 would represent a loss of ₹ 1.6 which would mean an 8% loss on ₹ 20.

30. The percentage profit $= \dfrac{\text{Goods left}}{\text{Goods sold}} \times 100$
    $= 10/40 \times 100 = 25\%$

31. In the question, A's investment has to be considered as ₹ 10,000 (the house he puts up for sale).
    He sells at 11,500 and buys back at ₹ 9775. Hence his profit is ₹ 1725.

    Required answer $= \dfrac{1725}{10000} \times 100 = 17.25$

32. For 12 locks, he would have paid ₹ 51, and sold them at ₹ 57. This would mean a profit percentage of 11.76%

33. $230/200 = 1.15 \rightarrow$ the profit percentage would be 15% if sold at 230. Thus, the increase in profit percent = $15 – 10 = 5\%$.

34. A's selling price = $1.25 \times 120 = 150$. C's Cost price = B's selling price = $198/1.1 = 180$. Thus, B's profit = ₹ 30 and his profit percent = $30 \times 100/150 = 20\%$.

35. A 10% reduction in price increases the consumption by 11.11% (Refer Table 4.1). But the increase in consumption is 6.2 kg.
    Hence, the consumption (original) will be $6.2 \times 9 = 55.8$ kg.
    Hence, original price = $279/55.8 = ₹5$.
    Hence, reduced price = ₹ 4.5

36. Total cost = $50 \times 10 + 40 \times 12 = 980$. Total revenue = $90 \times 11 = 990$. Gain percent = $(10 \times 100)/980 = 100/98$ %.

37. Percentage profit $= \dfrac{\text{Goods left}}{\text{Goods sold}} \times 100$
    $= 10/20 \times 100 = 50\%$

38. The profit percent would be equal to $50 \times 100 /950 = 5000/950 = 100/19\% = 5\,(5/19)\%$

39. A gross means 144 eggs. Thus, the cost price per egg = 25 paise and the selling price after a 12.5% profit = 28 paise approx.

40. B sold the table at 25% profit at ₹ 75. Thus cost price would be given by: $CP_B \times 1.25 = 75$
    $$B\text{'s Cost price} = ₹ 60.$$
    We also know that A sold it to B at 20% profit.
    Thus,

A's Cost price $\times$ 1.2 = 60
$\rightarrow$ A's cost price = 50.

41. 300 (A buys at this value) $\rightarrow$ 345 (sells it to B at a profit of 15%) $\rightarrow$ 404 (B sells it back to A at a profit of 20% gaining ₹ 69 in the process). Thus, A's original cost = ₹300.

42. Net loss = $(20/100)^2$ = 4% of cost price. Thus, 4800 (total money realized) represents 96% of the value. Thus, the cost price would be ₹ 5000 and the loss would be ₹ 200.

43. CP $\times$ 0.9 = 40 $\rightarrow$ CP = ₹ 44.444. Loss per kg = ₹ 4.44. To incur a loss of ₹80, we need to sell 80/4.44 = 18 kgs of tea.

44. The CP of the TV $\rightarrow$ CP_{TV} $\times$ 0.8 =12000 $\rightarrow$ CP_{TV} = 15000
The CP of the VCP $\rightarrow$ CP_{VCP} $\times$ 1.2 = 12000 $\rightarrow$ CP_{VCP} = 10000.
Total sales value = 12000 $\times$ 2 = 24000.
Total cost price = 15000 + 10000 = 25000. Loss = 25000 – 24000= 1000.

45. The profit of 15% amounts to ₹ 450. This should also be the actual loss on the second TV.
Thus, the actual loss = ₹ 450 (10% of C.P.)
Hence, the CP of the second set = ₹ 4500.

46. Let the cost price be P. Then, P $\times$ 0.95 $\times$ 1.1 = P $\times$ 1.05 – 2 $\rightarrow$ P = 400. Alternately, you could have solved this using options.

47. Let the cost price be P. Then, P $\times$ 0.95 $\times$ 1.2 = P $\times$ 1.1 + 7 $\rightarrow$ P = 175. Alternately, you could have solved this using options.

48. 4% of the cost price = ₹ 200.
Thus, cost price = ₹ 5000
and selling price @ 6% profit = ₹ 5300.

49. From the last statement we have: Charan's cost price = 1188/1.1 = 1080 = Bhushan's selling price. Then, Bhushan's CP would be given by the equation: CP $\times$ 0.9 = 1080 $\rightarrow$ CP for Bhushan = 1200 = SP for Ashok.
Also, Ashok gains 20%. Hence, CP for Ashok $\rightarrow$ CP $\times$ 1.2 = 1200 $\rightarrow$ CP for Ashok = 1000.
This includes a ₹ 110 component of repairs. Thus, the purchase price for Ashok would be 1000 – 110 = 890.

50. Solve through the values given in the options. Option (c) is correct because at 4/5 $\times$ 300 + 5/4 $\times$ 600 we see that the profit earned = ₹ 90.

51. Solve this question using the options. The first thing you should realize is that the cost of the lower priced item should be less than 240. Thus, we can reject options a and d. Checking option (c) we can see that if the lower priced item is priced at 200, the higher priced item would be priced at ₹ 280. Then:

1.19 $\times$ 200 = 238 and 0.85 $\times$ 280 = 238. It can be seen that in this condition the values of the selling price of both the items would be equal (as required by the conditions given in the problem). Thus, option (c) is the correct answer.

52. Original Cost Price = ₹ 5000
New Cost Price = 1.3 $\times$ 5000 = ₹ 6500
Price paid by retailer = 1.2 $\times$ 5750 = ₹ 6900
Profit percentage = (400/6500) $\times$ 100 = 6 (2/13)%

53. The total manufacturing cost of the article = 60 + 45 + 30 = 135. SP = 180. Thus, profit = ₹ 45.
Profit Percent = 45 $\times$ 100/135 = 33.33%

54. Assume marked price for both to be 100.
X's selling price = 100 $\times$ 0.75 $\times$ 0.95 = 71.25
Y's selling price = 100 $\times$ 0.84 $\times$ 0.88 = 73.92.
Buying from 'X' is more profitable.

55. The total discount offered by A = 8% on 20000 + 5% on 16000 = 1600 + 800 = 2400.
If B wants to be as competitive, he should also offer a discount of ₹ 2400 on 3600. Discount percentage = 2400 $\times$ 100/36000 = 6.66% discount.

56. The trader pays 800 $\times$ 0.95 $\times$ 0.95 = ₹ 722

57. Manufacturer's profit percentage
= (22/700) $\times$ 100 = (22/7)%

58. For a cost price of ₹ 400, he needs a selling price of 480 for a 20% profit. This selling price is arrived at after a discount of 4% on the marked price. Hence, the marked price MP = 480/0.96 = 500.

59. Solve using options. Option (b) fits the situation as a 12.5% discount on 288 would mean a discount of ₹ 36. This would leave us with a selling price of 252 which represents a profit percent of 20% on ₹ 210.

60. If he marks the camera at 800, a 10% discount would still allow him to sell at 720 – a profit of 20%.

61. Cost price to the watch dealer
= 250 + 10% of 250 = ₹275
Desired selling price for 20% profit
= 1.2 $\times$ 275 = 330
But 330 is the price after 25% discount on the marked price.
Thus,
Marked price $\times$ 0.75 = 330 $\rightarrow$ MP = 440
Hence, he should mark the item at ₹ 440.

62. If the cost price is 100, a mark up of 80% means a marked price of 180. Further a 15% discount on the marked price would be given by:
180 – 15% of 180 = 180 – 27 =153. Thus, the percentage profit is 53%.

63. A cost price of ₹ 650 would meet the conditions in the problem as it would give us a loss of 140 (if sold at 510) and a profit of 70 (when sold at 720)

64. Cost per 100 apples = 60 + 15% of 60 = ₹ 69.
    Selling price @ 20% profit = 1.2 × 69 = ₹ 82.8

65. Profit percent = (100/900) × 100 = 11.11%

Level of Difficulty (II)

1. Total outlay (initial investment) = 750 × 0.6 = ₹ 450.

   By selling 600, he should make a 40% profit on the outlay. This means that the selling price for 600 should be 1.4 × 450 → ₹ 630

   Thus, selling price per article = 630/600 = 1.05. Since, he sells only 630 articles at this price, his total recovery = 1.05 × 630 = 661.5

   Profit percent (actual) = (211.5/450) × 100 = 47%

2. In order to solve this problem, first assume that the cost of manufacturing 1 article is ₹1. Then 100 articles would get manufactured for ₹100. For a 20% profit on this cost, he should be able to sell the entire stock for ₹120. However since he would be able to sell only 88 articles (given that 12% of his manufactured articles would be rejected) he needs to recover ₹120 from selling 88 articles only. Thus, the profit he would need would be given by the ratio 32/88.

   Now it is given to us that his selling price is ₹7.5. The same ratio of profitability i.e.32/88 is achieved if his cost per article is ₹ 5.5.

3. The total cost to print 900 copies would be given by:

   Cost for setting up the type + cost of running the printing machine + cost of paper/ink etc

   = 1000 + 120 × 9 + 900 × 0.6 = 1000 + 1080 + 540 = 2620.

   A 10% profit on this cost amounts to ₹ 262. Hence, the total amount to be recovered is ₹ 2882.

   Out of this, 784 copies are sold for ₹ 2.75 each to recover ₹ 2156.

   The remaining money has to be recovered through advertising.

   Hence, The money to be recovered through advertising = 2882 – 2156 = ₹ 726. Option (c) is correct.

4. Total cost (assume) = 100.

   Recovered amount = 65 + 0.85 × 32.5 + 0.7 × 32.5
   $$= 65 + 27.625 + 22.75 = 115.375$$

   Hence, profit percent = 15.375%

5. Cost price = x

   Marked Price = $x + 205$

   Selling Price = $0.9x + 184.5$

   Percentage Profit = $[(-0.1x + 184.5)/x] \times 100$.

   $$= \frac{18450 - 10x}{x}$$

6. She should opt for a straight discount of 30% as that gives her the maximum benefit.

7. If you assume that his cost price is 1 Re per gram, his cost for 1000 grams would be ₹ 1000. For supposed 1 kg sale he would charge a price of 1080 (after an increase of 20% followed by a decrease of 10%).

   But, since he gives away only 900 grams the cost for him would be ₹ 900.

   Thus he is buying at 900 and selling at 1080 – a profit percentage of 20%

8. While buying

   He buys 1100 gram instead of 1000 grams (due to his cheating).

   Suppose he bought 1100 grams for ₹ 1000

   While selling:

   He sells only 900 grams when he takes the money for 1 kg.

   Now according to the problems he sells at a 8% profit (20% mark up and 10% discount).

   Hence his selling price is ₹ 1080 for 900 grams.

   To calculate profit percentage, we either equate the goods or the money.

   In this case, let us equate the money as follows:
   Buying;

   1100 grams for ₹ 1000

   Hence   1188 grams for ₹ 1080

   Selling: 900 grams for ₹ 1080

   Hence, profit% = 288/900 = 32%

   (using goods left by goods sold formula)

9. The new situation is
   Buying:

   1100 grams for ₹ 900

   Hence, 1320 grams for ₹ 1080

   Selling: 900 grams for ₹ 1080

   Profit % = $\dfrac{420}{900} \times 100 = 46.66\%$

10. Assume he bought 20 apples each. Net investment ⇒ ₹ 5 + ₹ 4 = ₹ 9 for 40 apples. He would sell 40 apples @ (40 × 2)/9 = ₹ 8.888 → Loss of ₹ 0.111 on ₹ 9 investment

    Loss percentage = 1.23%

11. 600 – 10% of 600 = 540. 540 – 5% of 540 = 513. 513 + 5% of 513 = 538.65

12. The problem is structured in such a way that you should be able to interpret that if he had sold 120 kg of rice he would recover the investment on 100 kg of rice.

    % Loss/Profit = $\dfrac{\text{Goods left}}{\text{Goods sold}} \times 100$

    (–20/120) × 100 = 16.66% loss.

    Since, cost price for Deb is ₹ 11; selling price per kg would be ₹ 9.166.

13. Comparisons have to be made between:
    192×34, 198×33, 204×32 and 210×31 for the highest product amongst them.
    The highest value of revenue is seen at a price of ₹ 198.

14 & 15: Using options from question 15. Suppose she had spent ₹ 6 at the market complex, she would spend ₹ 3 at her uncle's shop. The other condition (that she gets 2 sweets less per rupee at the market complex) gets satisfied in this scenario if she had bought 12 chocolates overall. In such a case, her buying would have been 2 per Rupee at the market and 4 per rupee at Uncle Scrooge's shop.
    Trial and error will show that this condition is not satisfied for any other option combination.

16. The given situation fits if we take Q as 60% profit and then the loss would be 37.5% (which is 62.5%) of Q). Thus, if ₹ 24 is the cost price, the selling price should be 24×1.6 = ₹ 38.4

17. Assume the price of 1 kg as 100. He initially sells the kg at 115. His original profit is 15%. When he is able to sell only 80% of his items: his new revenue would be given by $80 \times 1.265 = 101.2$ on a cost of 100. Profit percentage = 1.2%
    Change in profit percent = –13.8 (It drops from 15 to 1.2)

18. Ramu's total discount:

8% on 8000	= ₹ 640
5% on 12000	= ₹ 600
3% on 16000	= Rs. 480
Total	= ₹ 1720 on ₹ 36000.

    Hence, Realised value = 34280.
    Shyamu's Discounts:

7% on 12000	= 840
6% on 8000	= 480
5% on 16000	= 800
	₹ 2120 on ₹ 36000

    Hence, Realised value = 33880.
    The higher profit is for Ramu.
    Also, the CP has a mark up of 25% for the Marked price. Thus the CP must have been 28800 (This is got by 36000 – 20% of 36000 – PCG thinking)
    Thus, the profit % for Ramu would be: $(5480*100)/28800 \rightarrow 19\%$ approx.

19. In the case of the given defaults, the discount for Ramu would have gone down to:
    4% on 12000 (the second payment) and the second discount would thus have been ₹480 meaning that the sale price would have risen by ₹120 (since there is a ₹120 drop in the discount)
    1% on 16000 → A reduction of 2% of 16000 in the discount → a reduction of ₹ 320.

Hence, Ramu's profit would have gone up by ₹440 in all & would yield his new profit as:
5480 + 440 = ₹ 5920

20. The following working would show the answer:
    Ramu's Discounts

7% on 8000	= ₹ 560
4% on 12000	= ₹ 480
2% on 16000	= Rs. 320
Total	= ₹ 1360 on ₹ 36,000.

    Shyamu's discounts:

6% on 12000	= 720
5% on 8000	= 400
4% on 16000	= 640
	₹ 1760 on ₹ 36000

    Thus, their profits would vary by ₹ 400 (since their cost price is the same)

21. Solve using options. Option (a) fits as if we take SP as 2000, we get CP_1 as 1500 and CP_2 as 1600 which gives us the required difference of ₹ 100.

22. The first one would get a profit of ₹ 500 (because his cost would be 2500 for him to get a 20% profit on cost price by selling at 3000).
    The second one would earn a profit of 600 (20% of 3000).
    Difference in profits = ₹100

23. Find out the total revenue realization for both the cases:
    Case 1: (Old) Total sales revenue = $2000 \times 3.25 \times 0.75$.
    Profit_{old} = Total sales revenue – 4800
    Case 2: (New) Total sales revenue = $3000 \times 4.25 \times 0.75$
    Profit_{new} = Total sales revenue – 4800
    The ratio of profit will be given by $\text{Profit}_{new}/\text{Profit}_{old}$

24. Profit in original situation = 20%.
    In new situation, the purchase price of 90 (buys at 10% less) would give a selling price of 132 (sells at 10% above 120).
    The new profit percent = $[(132 – 90) \times 100]/90 = 46.66$
    Change in profit percent = $[(46.66 – 20) \times 100]/20 = 133.33\%$

25. The successive discounts must have been of 10% each. The required price will be got by reducing 25 by 10% twice consecutively. (use PCG application for successive change)

26. From the options you can work out that if the original price was ₹ 12 per dozen, the cost per apple would be ₹1.
    If she is able to get a dozen apples at a reduced price (reduction of ₹ 1 per dozen), she would be able to

purchase 1 extra apple for the 1 Rupee she saved. Thus, option (c) is correct.

27. The following calculations will show the respective costs:

    Primary Cost: 35% of 12600 = 4410

    Miscellaneous costs = 2% of 12600 = 252

    Gross Profit = 12600 – 4410 – 1400 – 650 – 252 = 5888

    Trading cost = 0.25 × 5888 = 1472

    Hence, Net profit = 4416.

    Percentage profit = 4416/14000 = 31.54%

28. If we assume the value of the first cycle as ₹ 900. Then 900 + 96 = 996 should be equal to twice the value of the second cycle. Hence, the value of the second cycle works out to be: 498.

    Also 498 + 96 = 594 which is ₹306 less than 900.

    Hence, Option (a) fits the situation perfectly and will be the correct answer.

    Note here that if you had tried to solve this through equations, you would have got stuck for a very long time.

29. David (100) → Goliath (80) → Hercules (100) → Goliath (90)

    Hercules loss corresponds to 10 when David buys the laptop for 100.

    Hence, Hercules's loss would be ₹17500 when David buys the laptop for 1,75,000.

30. While purchasing he would take 1200 grams for the price of 1000 grams.

    While selling he would sell 900 grams for the price of 1000 grams. Since CP = SP, the profit earned is through the weight manipulations. It will be given by:

    Goods left/goods sold = 300 × 100/900 = 33.33%

31. Assume that for 100 items the cost price is ₹ 100, then the selling price is ₹ 130. Since 24 is sold at half the price, he would recover 24 × 1/2 = ₹12 (since it is sold at half the cost price)

    The remaining 70 would be sold at 70 × 1.3 = ₹91.

    Total revenue = 91 + 12 = 103 → a profit of 3% (on a cost of 100).

32. An increase in the price by ₹12 will correspond to 50% of the CP.

    Hence, The CP is ₹24 and initially the book was being sold at ₹19.2. Hence, if there is an increment of ₹ 4.8 in the selling price, there would be no profit or loss.

33. In the first year, the profit percentage would be:

    Old Profit Percentage = $\dfrac{0.55 \times 5 + 0.45 \times 8}{1}$ = 6.35%

    New Profit Percentage = $\dfrac{0.55 \times 8 + 0.45 \times 5}{1}$ = 6.65

34. Since the ratio remains unchanged the percentage profit of the village will remain unchanged too.

35. The profit would increase by 10% as there is no change in the percentage profit.

36. Since the answer to question 33 is 0.3, if we increase the percentage profit for both men and women by 1 % the overall percentage profit would also go up by 1% - thus 0.3 + 1 = 1.3%

37. $x \times 8 + 0.75x \times 22 = 1.4 \times 4725 \rightarrow x = 270$.

    On an investment of ₹ 4725, a profit of 40% means a profit of 1890.

    Hence, the targeted sales realization is ₹ 6615.

    The required equation would be:

    $8p + 22 (3p)/4 = 6615$

    $\rightarrow 8p + 33p/2 = 6615$

    In this expression for LHS to be equal to RHS, we need $33p/2$ to be an odd number. This can only happen when p is not a multiple of 4 (why?? Apply your mind). Hence, options a & c get eliminated automatically.

38. After 2 years, the flat would be worth ₹ 288000, while the land would be worth ₹ 266200. The profit percentage of the gainer would be given by:

    $$(21800/266200) \times 100 = 8.189\%$$

    Hence (d).

39. The total investment will be $A + B + C$.

    C being 3000, B will be 2250 and A will be 1500.

    The total investment is: 6750.

    Returns to be given on their expectations:

    $A = 150$, $B = 337.5$ and $C = 0$.

    From this point calculate the total profit, subtract A's and B's expected returns and B's share of the profits for managing the business before dividing the profits in the ratio of capital invested. However, most of this information is unknown. Hence option (d) is correct.

40. The cost of the trip would be proportional to the price of petrol. So, if initially the cost is 100, the new cost would be 80. Also, initially since his profit is 20%, his revenue would be 120. When he takes 4 passengers instead of 3 his revenue would go up to 160 – and his profit would become 100% (cost 80 and revenue 160).

41. Total number of microwave ovens = 15

    Hence, washing machines = 10

    Thus, He sells 80% of both at a profit of ₹ 40,000.

    Cost of 80% of the goods = 0.8 × 2,05,000 = 1,64,000.

    Total amount recovered = 1,64,000 + 40,000 = 2,04,000

    Hence, loss = ₹ 1000

42. Since the actual initial loss was 10% and it is to be compared to a profit of 5%, it is 200% of the profit. Option (c) is correct.

43. He would be selling 800 grams for ₹12. Since a kg costs ₹10 800 grams would cost ₹ 8.
    Hence, his profit percentage is 50%.

44. The interpretation of the first statement is that if the loss at 275 is L, the profit at 800 is 20L.
    Thus, 21L = 800 – 275 = 525 → L = 25.
    Thus, the cost price of the item is ₹300.
    To get a profit of 25%, the selling price should be 1.25 × 300 = 375.

45. C's purchase price = 2145 × 10/11 =1950
    B's rate of profit is 3 times C's rate of profit. Hence, B sells to C at 30% profit.
    B's price + 30% profit = 1950 (C's price).
    Hence, B's Price = 1500.
    Further, since A's profit rate is 5/3rd the rate of profit of B, A's profit percent would be 30 × 5/3 = 50%.
    Thus, A's Price + 50% profit = 1500 (B's price)
    Thus, A's price = 1000

46. He would buy at 500 and sell at 888 to get a profit of 388

47. There were 5 printers (2 + 3) and 20 monitors. He sells 2 printers for a profit of ₹ 2000 each. Hence, profit from printer sales = ₹ 4000.

Then, profit from monitor sales = ₹ 45000

Thus, profit per monitor $= \dfrac{45000}{15} = ₹\,3000$

(Since, 15 monitors were sold in all.)
Hence, C.P. of monitor   = ₹ 15000
And C.P. of Printer   = ₹ 7500
Total cost = 15000 × 20 + 7500 × 5 = 3,37,500
Total Revenues = 18000 × 15 + 9500 × 2 = 28,900
Hence, loss of ₹ 48,500

48. Loss% $= \dfrac{48,500}{3,37,500} \times 100 = 14.37\%$

49. By charging ₹ 1.2 more his profit should double to 40%. This means that his profit of 40% should be equal to ₹ 2.4. Thus, his cost price must be ₹6 and his original selling price should be 7.2. Hence, option (d) is correct.

50. Total cost = 5 lacs
    Total revenue = 3000 × 160 + 1500 × 200 – vendors discount of 20% of revenues
    = 7.8 lacs – 1.56 lacs = 6.24 lacs.
    Profit percent = (1.24 × 100)/5 = 24.8%

Space for Notes

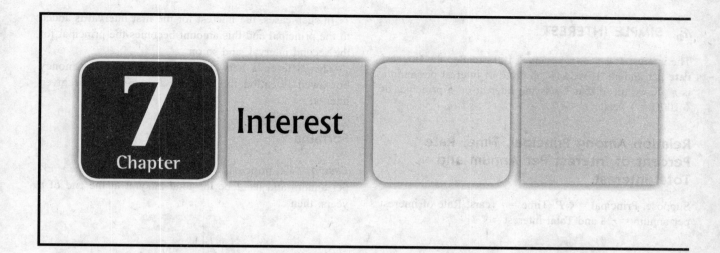

7 Chapter — Interest

INTRODUCTION

The chapter on Interest forms another important topic from the CAT's point of view. However, this relevance/importance is only restricted to the use of interest and its concepts in Data Interpretation.

However, it's relevance to Data Interpretation remains as high as always.

Prior to studying this chapter however, you are required to ensure that a clear understanding of percentages and percentage calculation is a must. The faster you are at percentage calculation, the faster you will be in solving questions of interests.

However, questions on interest are still important for exams like MAT, SNAP, ATMA, CMAT, IRMA and Bank P.O. exams. Hence, if you are planning to go for the entire spectrum of management exams—this chapter retains its importance in terms of mathematics too.

Questions from LOD I and LOD II of the chapter regularly appear in exams like the Bank PO or others management exams.

CONCEPT OF TIME VALUE OF MONEY

The value of money is not constant. This is one of the principal facts on which the entire economic world is based. A rupee today will not be equal to a rupee tomorrow. Hence, a rupee borrowed today cannot be repaid by a rupee tomorrow. This is the basic need for the concept of interest. The rate of interest is used to determine the difference between what is borrowed and what is repaid.

There are two basis on which interests are calculated:

Simple Interest It is calculated on the basis of a basic amount borrowed for the entire period at a particular rate of interest. The amount borrowed is the principal for the entire period of borrowing.

Compound Interest The interest of the previous year/s is/are added to the principal for the calculation of the compound interest.

This difference will be clear from the following illustration:

A sum of ₹ 1000 at 10% per annum will have

Simple interest		Compound interest
₹ 100	First year	₹ 100
₹ 100	Second year	₹ 110
₹ 100	Third year	₹ 121
₹ 100	Fourth year	₹ 133.1

Note that the previous years' interests are added to the original sum of ₹ 1000 to calculate the interest to be paid in the case of compound interest.

Terminology Pertaining to Interest

The man who lends money is the **Creditor** and the man who borrows money is the **Debtor**.

The amount of money that is initially borrowed is called the **Capital** or **Principal** money.

The period for which money is deposited or borrowed is called **Time**.

The extra money, that will be paid or received for the use of the principal after a certain period is called the **Total interest** on the capital.

The sum of the principal and the interest at the end of any time is called the **Amount**.

So, **Amount = Principal + Total Interest**.

Rate of Interest is the rate at which the interest is calculated and is always specified in percentage terms.

SIMPLE INTEREST

The interest of 1 year for every ₹ 100 is called the **Interest rate** per annum. If we say "the rate of interest per annum is r%", we mean that ₹ r is the interest on a principal of ₹ 100 for 1 year.

Relation Among Principal, Time, Rate Percent of Interest Per Annum and Total Interest

Suppose, Principal = ₹ P, Time = t years, Rate of interest per annum = r% and Total interest = ₹ I

Then

$$I = \frac{P \times t \times r}{100}$$

i.e. Total interest

$$= \frac{\text{Principal} \times \text{Time} \times \text{Rate of interest per annum}}{100}$$

Since the Amount = Principal + Total interest, we can write

$$\therefore \quad \text{Amount } (A) = P + \frac{P \times t \times r}{100}$$

$$\text{Time} = \left(\frac{\text{Total interest}}{\text{Interest on the Principal for one year}} \right) \text{years}$$

Thus, if we have the total interest as ₹ 300 and the interest per year is ₹ 50, then we can say that the number of years is 300/50 = 6 years.

Note: The rate of interest is normally specified in terms of annual rate of interest. In such a case we take the time t in years.

However, if the rate of interest is specified in terms of 6-monthly rate, we take time in terms of 6 months.

Also, the half-yearly rate of interest is half the annual rate of interest. That is if the interest is 10% per annum to be charged six-monthly, we have to add interest every six months @ 5%.

COMPOUND INTEREST

In monetary transactions, often, the borrower and the lender, in order to settle an account, agree on a certain amount of interest to be paid to the lender on the basis of specified unit of time. This may be yearly or half-yearly or quarterly, with the condition that the interest accrued to the principal at a certain interval of time be added to the principal so that the total amount at the end of an interval becomes the principal for the next interval. Thus, it is different from simple interest.

In such cases, the interest for the first interval is added to the principal and this amount becomes the principal for the second interval, and so on.

The difference between the amount and the money borrowed is called the *compound interest* for the given interval.

Formula

Case 1: Let principal = P, time = n years and rate = r% per annum and let A be the total amount at the end of n years, then

$$A = P \left[1 + \frac{r}{100} \right]^n$$

Case 2: When compound interest is reckoned half-yearly.

If the annual rate is r% per annum and is to be calculated for n years.

Then in this case, rate = $(r/2)$% half-yearly and time = $(2n)$ half-years.

∴ From the above we get

$$A = P \left[1 + \frac{r/2}{100} \right]^{2n}$$

Case 3: When compound interest is reckoned quarterly.

In this case, rate = $(r/4)$% quarterly and time = $(4n)$ quarter years.

∴ As before,

$$A = P \left[1 + \frac{r/4}{100} \right]^{4n}$$

Note: The difference between the compound interest and the simple interest over two years is given by

$$Pr^2/100^2 \quad \text{or} \quad P \left(\frac{r}{100} \right)^2$$

DEPRECIATION OF VALUE

The value of a machine or any other article subject to wear and tear, decreases with time.

This decrease is called its *depreciation*.

Thus if V_0 is the value at a certain time and r% per annum is the rate of depreciation per year, then the value V_1 at the end of t years is

$$V_1 = V_0 \left[1 - \frac{r}{100} \right]^t$$

POPULATION

The problems on Population change are similar to the problems on Compound Interest. The formulae applicable to the problems on compound interest also apply to those on population. The only difference is that in the application of formulae, the annual rate of change of population replaces the rate of compound interest.

However, unlike in compound interest where the rate is always positive, the population can decrease. In such a case, we have to treat population change as we treated depreciation of value illustrated above.

The students should see the chapter on interests essentially as an extension of the concept of percentages. All the rules of percentage calculation, which were elucidated in the chapter of percentages, will apply to the chapter on interests. Specifically, in the case of compound interests, the percentage rule for calculation of percentage values will be highly beneficial for the student.

Besides, while solving the questions on interests the student should be aware of the possibility of using the given options to arrive at the solution. In fact, I feel that the formulae on Compound Interest (CI) unnecessarily make a very simple topic overly mathematical. Besides, the CI formulae are the most unusable formulae available in this level of mathematics since it is virtually impossible for the student to calculate a number like 1.08 raised to the power 3, 4, 5 or more.

Instead, in my opinion, you should view CI problems simply as an extension of the concept of successive percentage increases and tackle the calculations required through approximations and through the use of the percentage rule of calculations.

Thus, a calculation: 4 years increase at 6% pa CI on ₹ 120 would yield an expression: 120×1.06^4. It would be impossible for an average student to attempt such a question and even if one uses advanced techniques of calculations, one will end up using more time than one has. Instead, if you have to solve this problem, you should look at it from the following percentage change graphic perspective:

$$120 \xrightarrow[= 7.2]{+6\%} 127.2 \xrightarrow[6 + 1.62]{+6\%}$$

$$134.82 \xrightarrow[6 + 2.1]{+6\%} 142.92 \xrightarrow[6 + 2.58]{+6\%} 15.15 \text{ (approx.)}$$

If you try to check the answer on a calculator, you will discover that you have a very close approximation. Besides, given the fact that you would be working with options and given sufficiently comfortable options, you need not calculate so closely; instead, save time through the use of approximations.

APPLICATIONS OF INTEREST IN D.I.

The difference between Simple Annual Growth Rate and Compound Annual Growth Rate:

The Measurement of Growth Rates is a prime concern in business and Economics. While a manager might be interested in calculating the growth rates in the sales of his product, an economist might be interested in finding out the rate of growth of the GDP of an economy.

In mathematical terms, there are basically two ways in which growth rates are calculated. To familiarize yourself with this, consider the following example.

The sales of a brand of scooters increase from 100 to 120 units in a particular city. What does this mean to you? Simply that there is a percentage increase of 20% in the sales of the scooters. Now read further:

What if the sales moves from 120 to 140 in the next year and 140 to 160 in the third year? Obviously, there is a constant and uniform growth from 100 to 120 to 160 — i.e. a growth of exactly 20 units per year. In terms of the overall growth in the value of the sales over there years, it can be easily seen that the sale has grown by 60 on 100 i.e. 60% growth.

In this case, what does 20% represent? If you look at this situation as a plain problem of interests 20% represents the simple interest that will make 100 grow to 160.

In the context of D.I., this value of 20% interest is also called the Simple Annual Growth Rate. (SAGR)

The process for calculating SAGR is simply the same as that for calculating Simple Interest.

Suppose a value grows from 100 to 200 in 10 years — the SAGR is got by the simple calculation 100%/10 = 10%

What is Compound Annual Growth Rate (CAGR)?

Let us consider a simple situation. Let us go back to the scooter company.

Suppose, the company increases it's sales by 20% in the first year and then again increases its' sales by 20% in the second year and also the third year. In such a situation, the sales (taking 100 as a starting value) trend can be easily tracked as below:

$$100 \xrightarrow[+ 20]{20\% \uparrow} 120 \xrightarrow[+ 24]{20\% \uparrow} 144 \xrightarrow[+ 28.8]{20\% \uparrow} 172.8$$

As you must have realised, this calculation is pretty similar to the calculation of Compound interests. In the above case, 20% is the rate of compound interest which will change 100 to 172.8 in three years.

This 20% is also called as the Compound Annual Growth Rate (CAGR) in the context of Data interpretation.

Obviously, the calculation of the CAGR is much more difficult than the calculation of the SAGR and the Compound Interest formula is essentially a waste of time for anything more than 3 years.

(upto three years, if you know your squares and the methods for the cubes you can still feasibly work things out

– but beyond three years it becomes pretty much infeasible to calculate the compound interest).

So is there an alternative? Yes there is and the alternative largely depends on your ability to add well. Hence, before trying out what I am about to tell you, I would recommend you should strengthen yourself at addition.

Suppose you have to calculate the C.I. on ₹ 100 at the rate of 10% per annum for a period of 10 years.

You can combine a mixture of PCG used for successive changes with guesstimation to get a pretty accurate value.

In this case, since the percentage increase is exactly 10% (Which is perhaps the easiest percentage to calculate), we can use PCG all the way as follows:

$$100 \xrightarrow[+10]{10\%\uparrow} 110 \xrightarrow[+4]{10\%\uparrow} 121 \xrightarrow[+12.1]{10\%\uparrow} 133.1$$

$$\xrightarrow[+13.31]{10\%\uparrow} 146.4$$

$$\xrightarrow[14.64]{10\%\uparrow} 161.04 \xrightarrow[16.10]{10\%\uparrow} 177.14 \xrightarrow[17.71]{10\%\uparrow} 194.8$$

$$\xrightarrow[19.48]{10\%\uparrow} \dots$$

$$214.3 \xrightarrow[21.43]{10\%\uparrow} 235.7 \xrightarrow[23.57]{10\%\uparrow} 259.2$$

Thus, the percentage increase after 10 years @ 10% will be 159.2 (approx).

However, this was the easy part. What would you do if you had to calculate 12% CI for 10 years. The percentage calculations would obviously become much more difficult and infeasible. How can we tackle this situation?

$$100 \xrightarrow[+12]{12\%\uparrow} 112 \xrightarrow[?]{12\%\uparrow} ?$$

In order to understand how to tackle the second percentage increase in the above PCG, let's try to evaluate where we are in the question.

We have to calculate 12% of 112, which is the same as 12% of 100 + 12% of 12.

But we have already calculated 12% of 100 as 12 for the first arrow of the PCG. Hence, we now have to calculate 12% of 12 and add it to 12% of 100.

Hence the addition has to be:

$$12 + 1.44 = 13.44$$

Take note of the addition of 1.44 in this step. It will be significant later. The PCG will now look like:

$$100 \longrightarrow 112 \longrightarrow 125.44 \xrightarrow[?]{12\%\uparrow} ?$$

We are now faced with a situation of calculating 12% of 125.44. Obviously, if you try to do this directly, you will have great difficulty in calculations. We can sidestep this as follows:

12% of 125.44 = 12% of 112 + 12% of 13.44.

But we have already calculated 12% of 112 as 13.44 in the previous step.

Hence, our calculation changes to:

12% of 112 + 12% of 13.44 = 13.44 + 12% of 13.44

But 12% of 13.44 = 12% of 12 + 12% of 1.44. We have already calculated 12% of 12 as 1.44 in the previous step.

Hence 12% of 13.44 = 1.44 + 12% of 1.44

$$= 1.44 + 0.17 = 1.61 \text{ (approx)}$$

Hence, the overall addition is

$$13.44 + 1.61 = 15.05$$

Now, your PCG looks like:

$$100 \xrightarrow{+12} 112 \xrightarrow{+13.44} 125.44 \xrightarrow{+15.05} 140.49$$

$$\xrightarrow{+?} ?$$

You are again at the same point—faced with calculating the rather intimidating looking 12% of 140.49

$$12\% \text{ of } 140.49 = \underbrace{12\% \text{ of } 125.44 + 12\% \text{ of } 15.05}$$

already calculated

Compare this to the previous calculation:

$$12\% \text{ of } 125.44 = \underbrace{12\% \text{ of } 112 + 12\% \text{ of } 13.44}$$

already calculated

The only calculation that has changed is that you have to calculate 12% of 15.05 instead of 12% of 13.44. (which was approx 1.61). In this case it will be approximately 1.8. Hence you shall now add 16.85 and the PCG will look as:

$$100 \xrightarrow{+12} 112 \xrightarrow{+13.44} 125.44 \xrightarrow{+15.05} 140.49$$

$$\xrightarrow{+16.85} 166.34$$

If you evaluate the change in the value added at every arrow in the PCG above, you will see a trend—

The additions were:

+12, +13.44 (change in addition = 1.44), +15.05(change in addition = 1.61), +16.85 (change in addition = 1.8)

If you now evaluate the change in the change in addition, you will realize that the values are 0.17, 0.19. This will be a slightly increasing series (And can be easily approximated).

Thus, the following table shows the approximate calculation of 12% CI for 10 years with an initial value of 100.

Thus, 100 becomes 309.78

(a percentage increase of 209.78%)

Similarly, in the case of every other compound interest calculation, you can simply find the trend that the first 2 – 3 years interest is going to follow and continue that trend to get a close approximate value of the overall percentage increase.

Thus for instance 7% growth for 7 years at C.I. would mean:

$$100 \xrightarrow{+7} 107 \xrightarrow{+7.49} 114.49 \xrightarrow{+8.01} 122.5$$

$$\xrightarrow{+8.55} 131.05$$

$$\xrightarrow{+9.11} 140.16 \xrightarrow{+9.75} 149.91 \xrightarrow{+10.35} 160.24$$

At the end of	Principal (approx.)	Interest for the year	Change in Addition	Change in change in Addition
year 0	100	+12		
			1.44	0.17
year 1	112	+13.44		
			1.61	0.19
year 2	125.44	+15.05		
			1.8	0.21
year 3	140.49	+16.85		
			2.01	0.24
year 4	157.36	+18.86		
			2.25	0.24
year 5	176.2	21.11		
			2.51	0.28
year 6	197.3	23.62		
			2.79	0.31
year 7	220.92	26.41		
			3.1	0.35
year 8	247.33	29.5		
			3.45	
year 9	276.83	32.95		
year 10	309.78			

This series is approximated giving all values in this table.

An approximate growth of 60.24%

The actual value (on a calculation) is around 60.57% – Hence as you can see we have a pretty decent approximation for the answer.

Note: The increase in the addition will need to be increased at a greater rate than as an A.P. Thus, in this case if we had considered the increase to be an A.P. the respective addition would have been:

+7, +7.49, +8.01, +8.55, +9.11, +9.69, +10.29.

However +7, +7.49, +8.01, +8.55, +9.11, +9.75, +10.35 are the actual addition used. Notice that using 9.75 instead of 9.69 is a deliberate adjustment, since while using C.I. the impact on the addition due to the interest on the interest shows an ever increasing behaviour.

Space for Notes

🎯 WORKED-OUT PROBLEMS

Problem 7.1 The SI on a sum of money is 25% of the principal, and the rate per annum is equal to the number of years. Find the rate percent.

    (a) 4.5%   (b) 6%
    (c) 5%   (d) 8%

Solution

Let principal = x, time = t years
Then interest = $x/4$, rate = $t\%$
Now, using the SI formula, we get
      Interest = (Principal × Rate × Time)/100
$\Rightarrow$ $x/4 = (x \times t \times t)/100$
$\Rightarrow$ $t^2 = 25$
$\Rightarrow$ $t = 5\%$

Alternatively, you can also solve this by using the options, wherein you should check that when you divide 25 by the value of the option, you get the option's value as the answer.

    Thus, 25/4.5 ≠ 4.5. Hence, option (a) is incorrect.

    Also, 25/6 ≠ 6. Hence option (b) is incorrect.

    Checking for option (c) we get, 25/5 = 5. Hence, (c) is the answer.

Problem 7.2 The rate of interest for first 3 years is 6% per annum, for the next 4 years, 7 per cent per annum and for the period beyond 7 years, 7.5 percentages per annum. If a man lent out ₹ 1200 for 11 years, find the total interest earned by him?

    (a) ₹ 1002   (b) ₹ 912
    (c) ₹ 864   (d) ₹ 948

Solution

Whenever it is not mentioned whether we have to assume SI or CI we should assume SI.

    For any amount, interest for the 1st three years @ 6% SI will be equal to 6 × 3 = 18%

    Again, interest for next 4 years will be equal to 7 × 4 = 28%.

    And interest for next 4 years (till 11 years) – 7.5 × 4 = 30%

    So, total interest = 18 + 28 + 30 = 76%

    So, total interest earned by him = 76% of the amount

$$= \frac{(76 \times 1200)}{100} = ₹\,912$$

This calculation can be done very conveniently using the percentage rule as 75% + 1% = 900 + 12 = 912.

Problem 7.3 A sum of money doubles itself in 12 years. Find the rate percentage per annum.

    (a) 12.5%   (b) 8.33%
    (c) 10%   (d) 7.51%

Solution Let principal = x, then interest = x, time = 12 years.

Using the formula, Rate = (Interest × 100)/Principal × Time

$$= (x \times 100)/(x \times 12) = 8.33\%$$

Alternatively: It is obvious that in 12 years, 100% of the amount is added as interest.

    So, in 1 year = (100/12)% of the amount is added.

    Hence, every year there is an addition of 8.33% (which is the rate of simple interest required).

    Alternatively, you can also use the formula.

    If a sum of money gets doubled in x years, then rate of interest = $(100/x)\%$.

Problem 7.4 A certain sum of money amounts to ₹ 704 in 2 years and ₹ 800 in 5 years. Find the principal.

    (a) ₹ 580   (b) ₹ 600
    (c) ₹ 660   (d) ₹ 640

Solution Let the principal be ₹ x and rate = $r\%$.

    Then, difference in between the interest of 5 years and of 2 years equals to

₹ 800 – ₹ 704 = ₹ 96
So, interest for 3 years = ₹ 96
Hence, interest/year = ₹ 96/3 = ₹ 32
So, interest for 2 years → 2 × ₹ 32 = ₹ 64
So, the principal = ₹ 704 – ₹ 64 = ₹ 640

Thought process here should be
₹ 96 interest in 3 years → ₹ 32 interest every year.
Hence, principal = 704 – 64 = 640

Problems 7.5 A sum of money was invested at SI at a certain rate for 3 years. Had it been invested at a 4% higher rate, it would have fetched ₹ 480 more. Find the principal.

    (a) ₹ 4000   (b) ₹ 4400
    (c) ₹ 5000   (d) ₹ 3500

Solution Let the rate be $y\%$ and principal be ₹ x and the time be 3 years.

    Then according to the question = $(x(y + 4) \times 3)/100 - (xy \times 3)/100 = 480$

$\Rightarrow$ $xy + 4x - xy = 160 \times 100$
$\Rightarrow$ $x = (160 \times 100)/4 = ₹\,4000$

Alternatively: Excess money obtained = 3 years @ 4% per annum

$$= 12\% \text{ of whole money}$$

So, according to the question, 12% = ₹ 480

So, 100% = ₹ 4000 (answer arrived at by using unitary method.)

Problem 7.6 A certain sum of money trebles itself in 8 years. In how many years it will be five times?

(a) 22 years   (b) 16 years
(c) 20 years   (d) 24 years

Solution It trebles itself in 8 years, which makes interest equal to 200% of principal.

So, 200% is added in 8 years.

Hence, 400%, which makes the whole amount equal to five times of the principal, which will be added in 16 years.

Problem 7.7 If CI is charged on a certain sum for 2 years at 10% the amount becomes 605. Find the principal?

(a) ₹ 550   (b) ₹ 450
(c) ₹ 480   (d) ₹ 500

Solution Using the formula, amount = Principal (1 + rate/100)^{time}

$$605 = p(1 + 10/100)^2 = p(11/10)^2$$
$$p = 605(100/121) = ₹ 500$$

Alternatively: Checking the options,

Option (a) ₹ 550

First year interest = ₹ 55, which gives the total amount ₹ 605 at the end of first year. So not a valid option.

Option (b) ₹ 450

First year interest = ₹ 45
Second year interest = ₹ 45 + 10% of ₹ 45 = 49.5
So, amount at the end of 2 years = 450 + 94.5 = 544.5
So, not valid.

Hence answer has to lie between 450 and 550 (since 450 yields a shortfall on ₹ 605 while 550 yields an excess.)

Option (c) ₹ 480

First year interest = ₹ 48
Second year interest = ₹ 48 + 10% of ₹ 48 = 52.8
So, amount at the end of 2 years = 580.8 ≠ 605

Option (d) ₹ 500

First year's interest = ₹ 50
Second year's interest = ₹ 50 + 10% of ₹ 50
                       = ₹ 55.
∴   Amount = 605.

Note: In general, while solving through options, the student should use the principal of starting with the middle (in terms of value), more convenient option. This will often reduce the number of options to be checked by the student, thus reducing the time required for problem solving drastically. In fact, this thumb rule should be used not only for the chapter of interests but for all other chapters in maths.

Furthermore, a look at the past question papers of exams like Lower level MBA exams and bank PO exams will yield that by solving through options and starting with the middle more convenient option, there will be significant time savings for these exams where the questions are essentially asked from the LOD I level.

Problem 7.8 If the difference between the CI and SI on a certain sum of money is ₹ 72 at 12 per cent per annum for 2 years, then find the amount.

(a) ₹ 6000   (b) ₹ 5000
(c) ₹ 5500   (d) ₹ 6500

Solution Let the principal = x

Simple interest = $(x \times 12 \times 2)/100$
Compound interest = $x[1 + 12/100]^2 - x$
So, $x[112/100]^2 - x - 24x/100 = 72$
$x[112^2/100^2 - 1 - 24/100] = 72 \Rightarrow x[12544/10000 - 1 - 24/100] = 72$
$\Rightarrow x = 72 \times 10000/144 = ₹ 5000$

Alternatively: Simple interest and compound interest for the first year on any amount is the same.

Difference in the second year's interest is due to the fact that compound interest is calculated over the first year's interest also.

Hence, we can say that ₹ 72 = Interest on first year's interest → 12% on first year's interest = ₹ 72.

Hence, first year's interest = ₹ 600 which should be 12% of the original capital. Hence, original capital = ₹ 5000 (this whole process can be done mentally).

You can also try to solve the question through the use of options as follows.

Option (a) ₹ 6000

First year's CI/SI = ₹ 720

Difference between second year's CI and SI = 12% of ₹ 720 ≠ ₹ 72

Hence, not correct.

Option (b) ₹ 5000

First year's CI/SI = 12% of ₹ 5000 = ₹ 600

Difference between second year's CI and SI = 12% of 600 = 72 year's CI and SI = 12% of 600 = ₹ 72

Hence option (b) is the correct answer.

Therefore we need not check any other options.

Problem 7.9 The population of Jhumri Tilaiya increases by 10% in the first year, it increases by 20% in the second year and due to mass exodus, it decreases by 5% in the third year. What will be its population after 3 years, if today it is 10,000?

(a) 11,540   (b) 13,860
(c) 12,860   (d) 12,540

Solution Population at the end of 1 year will be → 10,000 + 10% of 10,000 = 11,000

At the end of second year it will be 11,000 + 20% of 11,000 = 13,200

At the end of third year it will be 13,200-5% of 13,200 = 12,540.

Problem 7.10 Seth Ankoosh Gawdekar borrows a sum of ₹ 1200 at the beginning of a year. After 4 months, ₹ 1800 more is borrowed at a rate of interest double the previous one. At the end of the year, the sum of interest on both the loans is ₹ 216. What is the first rate of interest per annum?

    (a) 9%   (b) 6%

    (c) 8%   (d) 12%

Solution Let the rate of interest be = r%

Then, interest earned from ₹ 1200 at the end of year = $(1200r)/100 = ₹ 12r$

Again, interest earned from ₹ 1800 at the end of year = $(1800/100) \times (8/12) \times 2r = ₹ 24r$

So, total interest earned = $36r$, which equals 216

$\Rightarrow r = 216/36 = 6\%$

Alternatively: Checking the options.

Option (a) 9%

Interest from ₹ 1200 = 9% of 1200 = 108

Interest from ₹ 1800 = two-thirds of 18% on ₹ 1800 = 12% on ₹ 1800 = ₹ 216

Total interest = ₹ 324

Option (b) 6%

Interest earned from ₹ 1200 = 6% on 1200 = ₹ 72

Interest earned from ₹ 1800 = two-thirds of 12% on ₹ 1800 = ₹ 144

(We were able to calculate the interest over second part very easily after observing in option (a) that interest earned over second part is double the interest earned over first part).

Total interest = ₹ 216

We need not check any other option now.

Problem 7.11 Rajiv lend out ₹ 9 to Anni on condition that the amount is payable in 10 months by 10 equal instalments of Re. 1 each payable at the start of every month. What is the rate of interest per annum if the first instalment has to be paid one month from the date the loan is availed.

Solution Money coming in : ₹ 9 today

Money going out:

Re. 1 one month later + Re. 1, 2 months later ... + Re. 1, 10 months later.

The value of the money coming in should equal the value of the money going out for the loan to be completely paid off.

In the present case, for this to happen, the following equation has to hold:

₹ 9 + Interest on ₹ 9 for 10 months = (Re. 1 + Interest on Re. 1 for 9 months) + (Re. 1 + interest on Re. 1 for 8 months)

+ (Re. 1 + interest on Re. 1 for 7 months) + (Re. 1 + interest on Re. 1 for 6 months)

+ (Re. 1 + interest on Re. 1 for 5 months) + (Re. 1 + interest on Re. 1 for 4 months)

+ (Re. 1 + interest on Re. 1 for 3 months) + (Re. 1 + interest on Re. 1 for 2 months)

+ (Re. 1 + interest on Re. 1 for 1 months) + (Re. 1)

₹ 9 + Interest on ₹ 1 for 90 months = ₹ 10 + Interest on ₹ 10 for 45 months.

→ Interest on Re. 1 for 90 months – Interest on Re. 1 for 45 months = ₹ 10 – ₹ 9

→ Interest on Re. 1 for 45 months = Re. 1 (i.e. money would double in 45 months.)

Hence the rate of interest = $\dfrac{100\%}{45} = 2.222\%$

Note: The starting equation used to solve this problem comes from crediting the borrower with the interest due to early payment for each of his first nine instalments.

Space for Rough Work

LEVEL OF DIFFICULTY (I)

1. ₹ 1200 is lent out at 5% per annum simple interest for 3 years. Find the amount after 3 years.
   - (a) ₹ 1380
   - (b) ₹ 1290
   - (c) ₹ 1470
   - (d) ₹ 1200

2. Interest obtained on a sum of ₹ 5000 for 3 years is ₹ 1500. Find the rate percent.
   - (a) 8%
   - (b) 9%
   - (c) 10%
   - (d) 11%

3. ₹ 2100 is lent at compound interest of 5% per annum for 2 years. Find the amount after two years.
   - (a) ₹ 2300
   - (b) ₹ 2315.25
   - (c) ₹ 2310
   - (d) ₹ 2320

4. ₹ 1694 is repaid after two years at compound interest. Which of the following is the value of the principal and the rate?
   - (a) ₹ 1200, 20%
   - (b) ₹ 1300, 15%
   - (c) ₹ 1400, 10%
   - (d) ₹ 1500, 12%

5. Find the difference between the simple and the compound interest at 5% per annum for 2 years on a principal of ₹ 2000.
   - (a) 5
   - (b) 105
   - (c) 4.5
   - (d) 5.5

6. Find the rate of interest if the amount after 2 years of simple interest on a capital of ₹ 1200 is ₹ 1440.
   - (a) 8%
   - (b) 9%
   - (c) 10%
   - (d) 11%

7. After how many years will a sum of ₹ 12,500 become ₹ 17,500 at the rate of 10% per annum?
   - (a) 2 years
   - (b) 3 years
   - (c) 4 years
   - (d) 5 years

8. What is the difference between the simple interest on a principal of ₹ 500 being calculated at 5% per annum for 3 years and 4% per annum for 4 years?
   - (a) ₹ 5
   - (b) ₹ 10
   - (c) ₹ 20
   - (d) ₹ 40

9. What is the simple interest on a sum of ₹700 if the rate of interest for the first 3 years is 8% per annum and for the last 2 years is 7.5% per annum?
   - (a) ₹ 269.5
   - (b) ₹ 283
   - (c) ₹ 273
   - (d) ₹ 280

10. What is the simple interest for 9 years on a sum of ₹ 800 if the rate of interest for the first 4 years is 8% per annum and for the last 4 years is 6% per annum?

    - (a) 400
    - (b) 392
    - (c) 352
    - (d) Cannot be determined

11. What is the difference between compound interest and simple interest for the sum of ₹ 20,000 over a 2 year period if the compound interest is calculated at 20% and simple interest is calculated at 23%?
    - (a) ₹ 400
    - (b) ₹ 460
    - (c) ₹ 440
    - (d) ₹ 450

12. Find the compound interest on ₹ 1000 at the rate of 20% per annum for 18 months when interest is compounded half-yearly.
    - (a) ₹ 331
    - (b) ₹ 1331
    - (c) ₹ 320
    - (d) ₹ 325

13. Find the principal if the interest compounded at the rate of 10% per annum for two years is ₹ 420.
    - (a) ₹ 2000
    - (b) ₹ 2200
    - (c) ₹ 1000
    - (d) ₹ 1100

14. Find the principal if compound interest is charged on the principal at the rate of $16\frac{2}{3}$% per annum for two years and the sum becomes ₹ 196.
    - (a) ₹ 140
    - (b) ₹ 154
    - (c) ₹ 150
    - (d) ₹ 144

15. The SBI lent ₹ 1331 to the Tata group at a compound interest and got ₹ 1728 after three years. What is the rate of interest charged if the interest is compounded annually?
    - (a) 11%
    - (b) 9.09%
    - (c) 12%
    - (d) 8.33%

16. In what time will ₹ 3300 become ₹ 3399 at 6% per annum interest compounded half-yearly?
    - (a) 6 months
    - (b) 1 year
    - (c) $1\frac{1}{2}$ year
    - (d) 3 months

17. Ranjan purchased a Maruti van for ₹ 1,96,000 and the rate of depreciation is $14\frac{2}{7}$% per annum. Find the value of the van after two years.
    - (a) ₹ 1,40,000
    - (b) ₹ 1,44,000
    - (c) ₹ 1,50,000
    - (d) ₹ 1,60,000

18. At what percentage per annum, will ₹ 10,000 amount to 17,280 in three years? (Compound Interest being reckoned)
    - (a) 20%
    - (b) 14%
    - (c) 24%
    - (d) 11%

19. Vinay deposited ₹ 8000 in ICICI Bank, which pays him 12% interest per annum compounded quar-

terly. What is the amount that he receives after 15 months?

(a) ₹ 9274.2   (b) ₹ 9228.8

(c) ₹ 9314.3   (d) ₹ 9338.8

20. What is the rate of simple interest for the first 4 years if the sum of ₹ 360 becomes ₹ 540 in 9 years and the rate of interest for the last 5 years is 6%?

(a) 4%   (b) 5%

(c) 3%   (d) 6%

21. Harsh makes a fixed deposit of ₹ 20,000 with the Bank of India for a period of 3 years. If the rate of interest be 13% SI per annum charged half-yearly, what amount will he get after 42 months?

(a) 27,800   (b) 28,100

(c) 29,100   (d) 28,500

22. Ranjeet makes a deposit of ₹ 50,000 in the Punjab National Bank for a period of $2\frac{1}{2}$ years. If the rate of interest is 12% per annum compounded half-yearly, find the maturity value of the money deposited by him.

(a) 66,911.27   (b) 66,123.34

(c) 67,925.95   (d) 65,550.8

23. Vinod makes a deposit of ₹ 100,000 in Syndicate Bank for a period of 2 years. If the rate of interest be 12% per annum compounded half-yearly, what amount will he get after 2 years?

(a) 122,247.89   (b) 125,436.79

(c) 126,247.69   (d) 122436.89

24. What will be the simple interest on ₹ 700 at 9% per annum for the period from February 5, 1994 to April 18, 1994?

(a) ₹ 12.60   (b) ₹ 11.30

(c) ₹ 15   (d) ₹ 13

25. Ajay borrows ₹ 1500 from two moneylenders. He pays interest at the rate of 12% per annum for one loan and at the rate of 14% per annum for the other. The total interest he pays for the entire year is ₹ 186. How much does he borrow at the rate of 12%?

(a) ₹ 1200   (b) ₹ 1300

(c) ₹ 1400   (d) ₹ 300

26. A sum was invested at simple interest at a certain interest for 2 years. It would have fetched ₹ 60 more had it been invested at 2% higher rate. What was the sum?

(a) ₹ 1500   (b) ₹ 1300

(c) ₹ 2500   (d) ₹ 1000

27. The difference between simple and compound interest on a sum of money at 5% per annum is ₹ 25. What is the sum?

(a) ₹ 5000   (b) ₹ 10,000

(c) ₹ 4000   (d) Data insufficient

28. A sum of money is borrowed and paid back in two equal annual instalments of ₹ 882, allowing 5% compound interest. The sum borrowed was

(a) ₹ 1640   (b) ₹ 1680

(c) ₹ 1620   (d) ₹ 1700

29. Two equal sums were borrowed at 8% simple interest per annum for 2 years and 3 years respectively. The difference in the interest was ₹ 56. The sum borrowed were

(a) ₹ 690   (b) ₹ 700

(c) ₹ 740   (d) ₹ 780

30. In what time will the simple interest on ₹ 1750 at 9% per annum be the same as that on ₹ 2500 at 10.5% per annum in 4 years?

(a) 6 years and 8 months

(b) 7 years and 3 months

(c) 6 years

(d) 7 years and 6 months

31. In what time will ₹ 500 give ₹ 50 as interest at the rate of 5% per annum simple interest?

(a) 2 years   (b) 5 years

(c) 3 years   (d) 4 years

32. Shashikant derives an annual income of ₹ 688.25 from ₹ 10,000 invested partly at 8% p.a. and partly at 5% p.a. simple interest. How much of his money is invested at 5%?

(a) ₹ 5000   (b) ₹ 4225

(c) ₹ 4800   (d) ₹ 3725

33. If the difference between the simple interest and compound interest on some principal amount at 20% per annum for 3 years is ₹ 48, then the principle amount must be

(a) ₹ 550   (b) ₹ 500

(c) ₹ 375   (d) ₹ 400

34. Raju lent ₹ 400 to Ajay for 2 years, and ₹ 100 to Manoj for 4 years and received together from both ₹ 60 as interest. Find the rate of interest, simple interest being calculated.

(a) 5%   (b) 6%

(c) 8%   (d) 9%

35. In what time will ₹ 8000 amount to 40,000 at 4% per annum? (simple interest being reckoned)

(a) 100 years   (b) 50 years

(c) 110 years   (d) 160 years

36. What annual payment will discharge a debt of ₹ 808 due in 2 years at 2% per annum?

(a) ₹ 200   (b) ₹ 300

(c) ₹ 400   (d) ₹ 350

37. A sum of money becomes 4 times at simple interest in 10 years. What is the rate of interest?

(a) 10%   (b) 20%

(c) 30%   (d) 40%

38. A sum of money doubles itself in 5 years. In how many years will it become four fold (if interest is compounded)?

(a) 15   (b) 10

(c) 20   (d) 12

39. A difference between the interest received from two different banks on ₹ 400 for 2 years is ₹ 4. What is the difference between their rates?

(a) 0.5%   (b) 0.2%

(c) 0.23%   (d) 0.52%

40. A sum of money placed at compound interest doubles itself in 3 years. In how many years will it amount to 8 times itself?

(a) 9 years   (b) 8 years

(c) 27 years (d) 7 years

41. If the compound interest on a certain sum for 2 years is ₹ 21. What could be the simple interest?

(a) ₹ 20   (b) ₹ 16

(c) ₹ 18   (d) ₹ 20.5

42. Divide ₹ 6000 into two parts so that simple interest on the first part for 2 years at 6% p.a. may be equal to the simple interest on the second part for 3 years at 8% p.a.

(a) ₹ 4000, ₹ 2000   (b) ₹ 5000, ₹ 1000

(c) ₹ 3000, ₹ 3000   (d) None of these

43. Divide ₹ 3903 between Amar and Akbar such that Amar's share at the end of 7 years is equal to Akbar's share at the end of 9 years at 4% p.a. rate of compound interest.

(a) Amar = ₹ 2028, Akbar = ₹ 1875

(b) Amar = ₹ 2008, Akbar = ₹ 1000

(c) Amar = ₹ 2902, Akbar = ₹ 1001

(d) Amar = ₹ 2600, Akbar = ₹ 1303

44. A sum of money becomes 7/4 of itself in 6 years at a certain rate of simple interest. Find the rate of interest.

Space for Rough Work

(a) 12%   (b) 12.5%

(c) 8%   (d) 14%

45. Sanjay borrowed ₹ 900 at 4% p.a. and ₹ 1100 at 5% p.a. for the same duration. He had to pay ₹ 364 in all as interest. What is the time period in years?

(a) 5 years   (b) 3 years

(c) 2 years   (d) 4 years

46. If the difference between compound and simple interest on a certain sum of money for 3 years at 2% p.a. is ₹ 604, what is the sum?

(a) 5,00,000 (b) 4,50,000

(c) 5,10,000 (d) None of these

47. If a certain sum of money becomes double at simple interest in 12 years, what would be the rate of interest per annum?

(a) 8.33   (b) 10

(c) 12   (d) 14

48. Three persons Amar, Akbar and Anthony invested different amounts in a fixed deposit scheme for one year at the rate of 12% per annum and earned a total interest of ₹ 3,240 at the end of the year. If the amount invested by Akbar is ₹ 5000 more than the amount invested by Amar and the amount invested by Anthony is ₹ 2000 more than the amount invested by Akbar, what is the amount invested by Akbar?

(a) ₹ 12,000 (b) ₹ 10,000

(c) ₹ 7000   (d) ₹ 5000

49. A sum of ₹ 600 amounts to ₹ 720 in 4 years at Simple Interest. What will it amount to if the rate of interest is increased by 2%?

(a) ₹ 648   (b) ₹ 768

(c) ₹ 726   (d) ₹ 792

50. What is the amount of equal instalment, if a sum of ₹1428 due 2 years hence has to be completely repaid in 2 equal annual instalments starting next year.

(a) 700   (b) 800

(c) 650   (d) Cannot be determined

LEVEL OF DIFFICULTY (II)

1. A sum of money invested at simple interest triples itself in 8 years at simple interest. Find in how many years will it become 8 times itself at the same rate?
   - (a) 24 years
   - (b) 28 years
   - (c) 30 years
   - (d) 21 years

2. A sum of money invested at simple interest triples itself in 8 years. How many times will it become in 20 years time?
   - (a) 8 times
   - (b) 7 times
   - (c) 6 times
   - (d) 9 times

3. If ₹ 1100 is obtained after lending out ₹ x at 5% per annum for 2 years and ₹ 1800 is obtained after lending out ₹ y at 10% per annum for 2 years, find $x + y$.
   - (a) ₹ 2500
   - (b) ₹ 3000
   - (c) ₹ 2000
   - (d) ₹ 2200

Directions for Questions 4 to 6: Read the following and answer the questions that follow.

4. A certain sum of money was lent under the following repayment scheme based on Simple Interest:
   8% per annum for the initial 2 years
   9.5% per annum for the next 4 years
   11% per annum for the next 2 years
   12% per annum after the first 8 years
   Find the amount which a sum of ₹ 9000 taken for 12 years becomes at the end of 12 years.
   - (a) 20,200
   - (b) 19,800
   - (c) 20,000
   - (d) 20,160

5. If a person repaid ₹ 22,500 after 10 years of borrowing a loan, at 10% per annum simple interest find out what amount did he take as a loan?
   - (a) 11,225
   - (b) 11,250
   - (c) 10,000
   - (d) 7500

6. Mr. X, a very industrious person, wants to establish his own unit. For this he needs an instant loan of ₹ 5,00,000 and, every five years he requires an additional loan of ₹100,000. If he had to clear all his outstandings in 20 years, and he repays the principal of the first loan equally over the 20 years, find what amount he would have to pay as interest on his initial borrowing if the rate of interest is 10% p.a. Simple Interest.
   - (a) ₹ 560,000
   - (b) ₹ 540,000
   - (c) ₹ 525,000
   - (d) ₹ 500,000

7. The population of a city is 200,000. If the annual birth rate and the annual death rate are 6% and 3% respectively, then calculate the population of the city after 2 years.
   - (a) 212,090
   - (b) 206,090
   - (c) 212,000
   - (d) 212,180

8. A part of ₹ 38,800 is lent out at 6% per six months. The rest of the amount is lent out at 5% per annum after one year. The ratio of interest after 3 years from the time when first amount was lent out is 5 : 4. Find the second part that was lent out at 5%.
   - (a) ₹ 26,600
   - (b) ₹ 28,800
   - (c) ₹ 27,500
   - (d) ₹ 28,000

9. If the simple interest is 10.5% annual and compound interest is 10% annual, find the difference between the interests after 3 years on a sum of ₹ 1000.
   - (a) ₹ 15
   - (b) ₹ 12
   - (c) ₹ 16
   - (d) ₹ 11

10. A sum of ₹ 1000 after 3 years at compound interest becomes a certain amount that is equal to the amount that is the result of a 3 year depreciation from ₹ 1728. Find the difference between the rates of CI and depreciation. (Given CI is 10% p.a.). (Approximately)
    - (a) 3.33%
    - (b) 0.66%
    - (c) 3%
    - (d) 2%

11. The RBI lends a certain amount to the SBI on simple interest for two years at 20%. The SBI gives this entire amount to Bharti Telecom on compound interest for two years at the same rate annually. Find the percentage earning of the SBI at the end of two years on the entire amount.
    - (a) 4%
    - (b) 3(1/7)%
    - (c) 3(2/7)%
    - (d) 3(6/7)%

12. Find the compound interest on ₹ 64,000 for 1 year at the rate of 10% per annum compounded quarterly (to the nearest integer).
    - (a) ₹ 8215
    - (b) ₹ 8205
    - (c) ₹ 8185
    - (d) None of these

13. If a principal P becomes Q in 2 years when interest R% is compounded half-yearly. And if the same principal P becomes Q in 2 years when interest S% is compound annually, then which of the following is true?
    - (a) $R > S$
    - (b) $R = S$
    - (c) $R < S$
    - (d) $R \le S$

14. Find the compound interest at the rate of 10% for 3 years on that principal which in 3 years at the rate of 10% per annum gives ₹ 300 as simple interest.

(a) ₹ 331   (b) ₹ 310
(c) ₹ 330   (d) ₹ 333

15. The difference between CI and SI on a certain sum of money at 10% per annum for 3 years is ₹ 620. Find the principal if it is known that the interest is compounded annually.
    (a) ₹ 200,000   (b) ₹ 20,000
    (c) ₹ 10,000   (d) ₹ 100,000

16. The population of Mangalore was 1283575 on 1 January 2011 and the growth rate of population was 10% in the last year and 5% in the years prior to it, the only exception being 2009 when because of a huge exodus there was a decline of 20% in population. What was the population on January 1, 2005?
    (a) 1,000,000   (b) 1,200,000
    (c) 1,250,000   (d) 1,500,000

17. According to the 2011 census, the population growth rate of Lucknow is going to be an increasing AP with first year's rate as 5% and common difference as 5%, but simultaneously the migration, rate is an increasing GP with first term as 1% and common ratio of 2. If the population on 31 December 2010 is 1 million, then find in which year will Lucknow witness its first fall in population?
    (a) 2015   (b) 2016
    (c) 2017   (d) 2018

18. Mohit Anand borrows a certain sum of money from the Mindworkzz Bank at 10% per annum at compound interest. The entire debt is discharged in full by Mohit Anand on payment of two equal amounts of ₹ 1000 each, one at the end of the first year and the other at the end of the second year. What is the approximate value of the amount borrowed by him?
    (a) ₹ 1852   (b) ₹ 1736
    (c) ₹ 1694   (d) ₹ 1792

19. In order to buy a car, a man borrowed ₹ 180,000 on the condition that he had to pay 7.5% interest every year. He also agreed to repay the principal in equal annual instalments over 21 years. After a certain number of years, however, the rate of interest has been reduced to 7%. It is also known that at the end of the agreed period, he will have paid in all ₹ 270,900 in interest. For how many years does he pay at the reduced interest rate?
    (a) 7 years   (b) 12 years
    (c) 14 years   (d) 16 years

20. A sum of ₹ 8000 is borrowed at 5% p.a. compound interest and paid back in 3 equal annual instalments. What is the amount of each instalment?
    (a) ₹ 2937.67   (b) ₹ 3000
    (c) ₹ 2037.67   (d) ₹ 2739.76

21. Three amounts x, y and z are such that y is the simple interest on x and z is the simple interest on y. If in all the three cases, rate of interest per annum and the time for which interest is calculated is the same, then find the relation between x, y and z.
    (a) $xyz = 1$ (b) $x^2 = yz$
    (c) $z = x^2y$ (d) $y^2 = xz$

22. A person lent out some money for 1 year at 6% per annum simple interest and after 18 months, he again lent out the same money at a simple interest of 24% per annum. In both the cases, he got ₹ 4704. Which of these could be the amount that was lent out in each case if interest is paid half-yearly?
    (a) ₹ 4000   (b) ₹ 4400
    (c) ₹ 4200   (d) ₹ 3600

23. A person bought a motorbike under the following scheme: Down payment of ₹ 15,000 and the rest amount at 8% per annum for 2 years. In this way, he paid ₹ 28,920 in total. Find the actual price of the motorbike. (Assume simple interest).
    (a) ₹ 26,000   (b) ₹ 27,000
    (c) ₹ 27,200   (d) ₹ 26,500

24. Hans Kumar borrows ₹ 7000 at simple interest from the village moneylender. At the end of 3 years, he again borrows ₹ 3000 and closes his account after paying ₹ 4615 as interest after 8 years from the time he made the first borrowing. Find the rate of interest.
    (a) 3.5%   (b) 4.5%
    (c) 5.5%   (d) 6.5%

25. Some amount was lent at 6% per annum simple interest. After one year, ₹ 6800 is repaid and the rest of the amount is repaid at 5% per annum. If the second year's interest is 11/20 of the first year's interest, find what amount of money was lent out.
    (a) ₹ 17,000   (b) ₹ 16,800
    (c) ₹ 16,500   (d) ₹ 17,500

26. An amount of ₹ 12820 due 3 years hence, is fully repaid in three annual instalments starting after 1 year. The first instalment is 1/2 the second instalment and the second instalment is 2/3 of the third instalment. If the rate of interest is 10% per annum, find the first instalment.
    (a) ₹ 2400   (b) ₹ 1800
    (c) ₹ 2000   (d) ₹ 2500

Directions for Questions 27 and 28: Read the following and answer the questions that follow.

The leading Indian bank ISBI, in the aftermath of the Kargil episode, announced a loan scheme for the Indian Army. Under this scheme; the following options were available.

	Loans upto	Soft loan	Interest (Normal)
Scheme 1	₹ 50,000	50% of total	8%
Scheme 2	₹ 75,000	40% of total	10%
Scheme 3	₹ 100,000	30% of total	12%
Scheme 4	₹ 200,000	20% of total	14%

Soft loan is a part of the total loan and the interest on this loan is half the normal rate of interest charged.

27. Soldier *A* took some loan under scheme 1, soldier *B* under scheme 2, soldier *C* under scheme 3 and soldier *D* under scheme 4. If they get the maximum loan under their respective schemes for one year, find which loan is MUL (MUL—Maximum Utility Loan, is defined as the ratio of the total loan to interest paid over the time. Lower this ratio the better the MUL).
   (a) *A* (b) *B*
   (c) *C* (d) *D*

28. Extending this plan, ISBI further announced that widows of all the martyrs can get the loans in which the proportion of soft loan will be double. This increase in the proportion of the soft loan component is only applicable for the first year. For all subsequent years, the soft loan component applicable on the loan, follows the values provided in the table. The widow

of a soldier takes ₹ 40,000 under scheme 1 in one account for 1 year and ₹ 60,000 under scheme 2 for 2 years. Find the total interest paid by her over the 2 year period.
   (a) ₹ 11,600 (b) ₹ 10,000
   (c) ₹ 8800 (d) None of these

29. A sum is divided between *A* and *B* in the ratio of 1 : 2. *A* purchased a car from his part, which depreciates $14\frac{2}{7}$% per annum and *B* deposited his amount in a bank, which pays him 20% interest per annum compounded annually. By what percentage will the total sum of money increase after two years due to this investment pattern (approximately)?
   (a) 20% (b) 26.66%
   (c) 30% (d) 25%

30. Michael Bolton has $90,000 with him. He purchases a car, a laptop and a flat for $15,000, $13,000 and $35,000 respectively and puts the remaining money in a bank deposit that pays compound interest @15% per annum. After 2 years, he sells off the three items at 80% of their original price and also withdraws his entire money from the bank by closing the account. What is the total change in his asset?
   (a) −4.5% (b) +3.5%
   (c) −4.32% (d) +5.5%

Space for Rough Work

ANSWER KEY

Level of Difficulty (I)

1. (a)	2. (c)	3. (b)	4. (c)
5. (a)	6. (c)	7. (c)	8. (a)
9. (c)	10. (d)	11. (a)	12. (a)
13. (a)	14. (d)	15. (b)	16. (a)
17. (b)	18. (a)	19. (a)	20. (b)
21. (c)	22. (a)	23. (c)	24. (a)
25. (a)	26. (a)	27. (d)	28. (a)
29. (b)	30. (a)	31. (a)	32. (d)
33. (c)	34. (a)	35. (a)	36. (c)
37. (c)	38. (b)	39. (a)	40. (a)
41. (a)	42. (a)	43. (a)	44. (b)
45. (d)	46. (a)	47. (a)	48. (b)
49. (b)	50. (d)		

Level of Difficulty (II)

1. (b)	2. (c)	3. (a)	4. (d)
5. (b)	6. (c)	7. (d)	8. (b)
9. (c)	10. (d)	11. (a)	12. (d)
13. (c)	14. (a)	15. (b)	16. (b)
17. (b)	18. (b)	19. (c)	20. (a)
21. (d)	22. (c)	23. (b)	24. (d)
25. (a)	26. (c)	27. (a)	28. (b)
29. (a)	30. (c)		

Hints

Level of Difficulty (II)

3. $x + 0.1x = 1100$
   $y + 0.2y = 1800$
6. Interest will be charged on the initial amount borrowed, on the amount of principal still to be paid.
7. Required value = $200000 \times (1.03)^2$
   (Solve using percentage change graphic)
9. $(1.105)^3 \times 1000 - 1.3 \times 1000$
12. $64000 \times (1.025)^4$
13. Half-yearly compounding always increases the value of the amount more than annual compounding. Since, increase over 2 years is equal, the annual compounding rate has to be more than the half-yearly compounding rate. Hence $S > R$.
15. Solve through options and use percentage change graphic.
16. If P is the population on 1 January 1995 then
    $P \times 1.05 \times 1.05 \times 1.05 \times 1.05 \times 0.8 \times 1.1 = 1283575$.
    Use options and percentage change graphic to calculate.
20. $8000 \times (1.05)^3 = x \times (1.05)^2 + x \times (1.05) + x$.
24. Solve through options.
27-28. The meaning of the table is

Under Scheme 1 the maximum borrowing allowed is ₹ 50000. The normal interest to be charged is 8% per annum and for the soft loan component 4% per annum has to be charged. It is also given that 50% of the loan taken is the soft loan component.

29. Difference between the total values at the start and at the end is
$$\left(200 \times 1.2 \times 1.2 + 100 \times \frac{6}{7} \times \frac{6}{7}\right) - (200 + 100)$$
30. Final assets = $63000 \times 0.8 + 27000 \times (1.15)^2$
    Calculate using percentage change graphic.

Solutions and Shortcuts

Level of Difficulty (I)

1. The annual interest would be ₹ 60. After 3 years the total value would be $1200 + 60 \times 3 = 1380$
2. The interest earned per year would be $1500/3=500$. This represents a 10% rate of interest.
3. $2100 + 5\%$ of $2100 = 2100 + 105 = 2205$ (after 1 year). Next year it would become:
   $2205 + 5\%$ of $2205 = 2205 + 110.25 = 2315.25$
4. $1400 \xrightarrow{10\%\uparrow} 1540 \xrightarrow{10\%\uparrow} 1694$.
5. Simple Interest for 2 years = $100 + 100 = 200$.
   Compound interest for 2 years: Year 1 = 5% of 2000 = 100.
   Year 2: 5% of 2100 = 105 → Total compound interest = ₹ 205.
   Difference between the Simple and Compound interest = $205 - 200 = ₹ 5$
6. Interest in 2 years = ₹ 240.
   Interest per year = ₹ 120
   Rate of interest = 10%
7. 12500 @ 10% simple interest would give an interest of ₹ 1250 per annum. For a total interest of ₹ 5000, it would take 4 years.
8. 5% for 3 years (SI) = 15% of the amount; At the same time 4% SI for 4 years means 16% of the amount. The difference between the two is 1% of the amount. 1% of 500 = ₹ 5
9. 8% @ 700 = ₹ 56 per year for 3 years
   7.5% @ 700 = ₹ 52.5 per year for 2 years
   Total interest = $56 \times 3 + 52.5 \times 2 = 273$.
10. 8% of 800 for 4 years + 6% of 800 for 4 years = $64 \times 4 + 48 \times 4 = 256 + 192 = 448$. However, we do not know the rate of interest applicable in the 5th year and hence cannot determine the exact simple interest for 9 years.
11. Simple interest @ 23% = $4600 \times 2 = 9200$
    Compound interest @ 20%
    $20000 \xrightarrow{20\%\uparrow} 24000 \xrightarrow{20\%\uparrow} 28800$

→ ₹ 8800 compound interest.

Difference = 9200 – 8800 = ₹ 400.

12. $1000 \xrightarrow{10\%\uparrow} 1100 \xrightarrow{10\%\uparrow} 1210 \xrightarrow{10\%\uparrow} 1331$.

Compound interest = 1331 – 1000 = ₹ 331

13. Solve using options. Thinking about option (a):

2000 → 2200 (after 1 year) → 2420 (after 2 years) which gives us an interest of ₹420 as required in the problem. Hence, this is the correct answer.

14. $P \times 7/6 \times 7/6 = 196 \to P = (196 \times 6 \times 6)/7 \times 7 = 144$.

15. $1331 \times 1.090909 \times 1.090909 \times 1.090909 = 1331 \times 12/11 \times 12/11 \times 12/11 = 1728$. Hence, the rate of compound interest is 9.09%.

16. Since compounding is half yearly, it is clear that the rate of interest charged for 6 months would be 3%

$3300 \xrightarrow{3\%\uparrow} 3399$.

17. The value of the van would be $196000 \times 6/7 \times 6/7 = 144000$

18. Solve through options:

$10000 \xrightarrow{20\%\uparrow} 12000 \xrightarrow{20\%\uparrow} 14400 \xrightarrow{20\%\uparrow} 17280$.

19. 12% per annum compounded quarterly means that the amount would grow by 3% every 3 months.

Thus, 8000 → 8000 + 3% of 8000 = 8240 after 3 months → 8240 + 3% of 8240 = 8487.2 after 6 months and so on till five3 month time periods get over. It can be seen that the value would turn out to be 9274.2.

20. For the last 5 years, the interest earned would be: 30% of 360 = 108. Thus, interest earned in the first 4 years would be ₹ 72 → ₹ 18 every year on an amount of ₹ 360- which means that the rate of interest is 5%

21. He will get 20000 + 45.5% of 20000 = 29100.

[Note: In this case we can take 13% simple interest compounded half yearly to mean 6.5% interest getting added every 6 months. Thus, in 42 months it would amount to 6.5 × 7 = 45.5%]

22. $50000 \xrightarrow{6\%\uparrow} 53000 \xrightarrow{6\%\uparrow} 56180 \xrightarrow{6\%\uparrow} 59550.8 \xrightarrow{6\%\uparrow} 63123.84 \xrightarrow{6\%\uparrow} 66911.27$

23. 100000 + 6% of 100000 (after the first 6 months) = 106000.

After 1 year: 106000 + 6% of 106000 = 112360

After 1 ½ years: 112360 + 6% of 112360 = 119101.6

After 2 years: 119101.6 + 6% of 119101.6 = 126247.69

24. $(73/365) \times 0.09 \times 700 = ₹ 12.6$.

(Since the time period is 73 days)

25. The average rate of interest he pays is $186 \times 100/1500 = 12.4\%$.

The average rate of interest being 12.4%, it means that the ratio in which the two amounts would be distributed would be 4:1 (using alligation). Thus, the borrowing at 12% would be ₹ 1200.

26. Based on the information we have, we can say that there would have been ₹ 30 extra interest per year. For 2% of the principal to be equal to ₹ 30, the principal amount should be ₹ 1500

27. The data is insufficient as we do not know the time period involved.

28. $882 \times (1.05) + 882 = P \times (1.05)^2$

Solve for P to get $P = 1640$

29. The difference would amount to 8% of the value borrowed. Thus 56 = 0.08 × sum borrowed in each case → Sum borrowed = ₹ 700.

30. 42% on 2500 = ₹ 1050. The required answer would be: 1050/157.5 = 6 years and 8 months.

31. Interest per year = ₹ 25. Thus, an interest of ₹ 50 would be earned in 2 years.

32. The average Rate of interest is 6.8825%. The ratio of investments would be 1.1175: 1.8825 (@5% is to 8%). The required answer = 10000 × 1.1175/3 = 3725.

33. Solve using options. If we try 500 (option b) for convenience, we can see that the difference between the two is ₹ 64 (as the SI would amount to 300 and CI would amount to 100 + 120 + 144 = 364).

Since, we need a difference of only ₹ 48 we can realize that the value should be 3/4th of 500. Hence, 375 is correct.

34. Total effective amount lent for 1 year

$= ₹ 400 \times 2 + ₹ 100 \times 4 = ₹ 1200$

Interest being ₹ 60, Rate of interest 5%

35. The value would increase by 4% per year. To go to 5 times it's original value, it would require an increment of 400%. At 4% SI it would take 100 years.

36. $A \times (1.02) + A = 808 \times (1.02)^2 \to A = ₹ 400$

37. The sum becomes 4 times → the interest earned is 300% of the original amount. In 10 years the interest is 300% means that the yearly interest must be 30%.

38. It would take another 5 years to double again. Thus, a total of 10 years to become four fold.

39. The difference in Simple interest represents 1% of the amount invested. Since this difference has occurred in 2 years, annually the difference would be 0.5%.

40. If it doubles in 3 years, it would become 4 times in 6 year and 8 times in 9 years.

41. If we take the principal as 100, the CI @ 10% Rate of interest would be ₹ 21. In such a case, the SI would be ₹ 20.

42. 12% of x = 24% of $(600 - x) \to x = 4000$

Thus, the two parts should be ₹ 4000 and ₹ 2000.

43. Akbars' share should be such that at 4% p.a. compound interest it should become equal to Amar's share in 2 years. Checking thorugh the options it is clear that option (a) fits perfectly as 1875 would become 2028 in 2 years @4% p.a. compound interest.

44. The total interest in 6 years = 75%
Thus per year = SI = 12.5%

45. The interest he pays per year would be 36 + 55 = 91. Thus, in 4 years the interest would amount to ₹ 364.

46. Solve through trial and error using the values of the options. Option (a) 500000 fits the situation perfectly as the SI = ₹ 30000 while the CI = 30604.

47. 100/12 = 8.33%

48. 12% Rate of interest on the amount invested gives an interest of ₹ 3240. This means that 0.12 A = 3240 → A = ₹ 27000. The sum of the investments should be ₹ 27000. If Akbar invests x, Amar invests $x - 5000$ and Anthony invests $x + 2000$. Thus:
$x + x - 5000 + x + 2000 = 27000 \rightarrow x = 10000.$

49. 600 becomes 720 in 4 years SI → SI per year = ₹ 30 and hence the SI rate is 5%.
At 7% rate of interest the value of 600 would become 768 in 4 years. (600 + 28% of 600)

50. The rate of interest is not defined.
Hence, option (d) is correct.

Level of Difficulty (II)

1. In 8 years, the interest earned = 200%
Thus, per year interest rate = 200/8 = 25%
To become 8 times we need a 700% increase
700/25 = 28 years.

2. Tripling in 8 years means that the interest earned in 8 years is equal to 200% of the capital value. Thus, interest per year (simple interest) is 25% of the capital. In 20 years, total interest earned = 500% of the capital and hence the capital would become 6 times it's original value.

3. x = ₹ 1000 (As 1000 @ 5% for 2 years = 1100).
Similarly y = ₹ 1500.
$x + y = 2500.$

4. 9000 + 720 + 720 + 855 + 855 + 855 + 855 + 990 + 990 + 1080 + 1080 + 1080 + 1080
= 9000 + 720 × 2 + 855 × 4 + 990 × 2 + 1080 × 4
= 20160

5. At 10% simple interest per year, the amount would double in 10 years. Thus, the original borrowin would be 22500/2 = 11250.

6. The simple interest would be defined on the basis of the sum of the AP.
50000 + 47500 + 45000 + ... + 2500 = 525000.

7. The yearly increase in the population is 3%. Thus, the population would increase by 3% each year. 200000 would become 206000 while 206000 would become 212180.

8. $$\frac{F \times (0.06) \times 6}{(38800 - F) \times 0.05 \times 2} = 5/4$$
where F is the first part.
$$1.44F = 19400 - 0.5F$$
$$F = 19400/1.94 = 10000.$$
Thus, the second part = 38800 − 10000 = 28800

9. At 10% compound interest the interest in 3 years would be 33.1% = ₹331
At 10.5% simple interest the interest in 3 years would be 31.5% = ₹315
Difference = ₹16

10. The amount @ 10% CI could become ₹ 1331. Also, ₹ 1728 depreciated at R% has to become ₹1331.
Thus,
$$1728 \times [(100-R)/100]^3 = 1331 \text{ (approximately)}.$$
The closest value of R = 8%
Thus, the difference is 2%.

11. SBI would be paying 40% on the capital as interest over two years and it would be getting 44% of the capital as interest from Bharti Telecom. Hence, it earns 4%.

12. $64000 \times (1.025)^4 = 70644.025.$
Interest 6644.025
Option (d). None of these is correct.

13. Since the interest is compounded half yearly at R% per annum, the value of R would be lesser than the value of S. (Remember, half yearly compounding is always profitable for the depositor).

14. At 10% per annum simple interest, the interest earned over 3 years would be 30% of the capital. Thus, 300 is 30% of the capital which means that the capital is 1000. In 3 years, the compound interest on the same amount would be 331.

15. Go through trial and error of the options. You will get:
$20000 \times (1.3) = 26000$ (@ simple interest)
$20000 \times 1.1 \times 1.1 \times 1.1 = 26620$ @ compound interest.
Thus 20000 is the correct answer.

16. Solve through options to see that the value of 1200000 fits the given situation.

17. Population growth rate according to the problem:
Year 1 = 5% , year 2 = 10% , year 3 = 15%
Year 4 = 20%, year 5 = 25%, year 6 = 30%.
Population decrease due to migration:
Year 1 = 1% , year 2 = 2% , year 3 = 4%
Year 4 = 8%, year 5 = 16%, year 6 = 32%.
Thus, the first fall would happen in 2006.

18. P + 2 years interest on P = 1000 + 1 years interest on 1000 + 1000

    → 1.21P = 2100 → P = 1736 (approx).

19. Solve this one through options. Option (c) reduced rate for 14 years fits the conditions.

20. Let the repayment annually be X. Then:

    8000 + 3 years interest on 8000 (on compound interest of 5%) = X + 2 years interest on X + X + 1 years interest on X + X → X = 2937.67

21. You can think about this situation by taking some values. Let $x = 100$, $y = 10$ and $z = 1$ (at an interest rate of 10%). We can see that $10^2 = 100 → y^2 = xz$

22. 4200 + (4 % of 4200) 3 times = 4200 + 0.04 × 3 × 4200 = 4704.

23. Solve using options. If the price is 27000, the interest on 12000 (after subtracting the down payment) would be 16% of 12000 = 1920. Hence, the total amount paid would be 28920.

24. The interest would be paid on

    7000 for 3 years + 10000 for 5 years.

    @ 6.5% the total interest for 8 years

    $$= 1365 + 3250$$
    $$= ₹ 4615$$

25. It can be seen that for 17000, the first year interest would be 1020, while the second year interest after a repayment of 6800 would be on 10200 @ 5% per annum. The interest in the second year would thus be ₹510 which is exactly half the interest of the first year. Thus, option (a) is correct.

26. Solve using options. Option (c) fits the situation as:

    12820 = 2000 + 2 years interest on 2000 + 4000 + 1 years interest on 4000 + 6000 (use 10% compound interest for calculation of interest) →

    12820 = 2000 + 420 + 4000 + 400 + 6000.

    Thus, option (c) fits the situation perfectly.

27. Interest for A = 6% of 50000.

    Interest for B, C and D the interest is more than 6%. Thus A's loan is MUL.

28. Interest she would pay under scheme 1:

    Year 1 the entire loan would be @ 4% – hence interest on 40000 = ₹1600.

    Total interest = 1600

    Interest on loan 2:

    In year 1: 80% of the loan (I.e 48000) would be on 5%, 12000 would be @10% – hence total interest = 3600

    Year 2: 40% of the loan (24000) would be on 5%, while the remaining loan would be on 10% – hence total interest = 4800

    Thus, total interest on the two loans would be 1600 + 3600 + 4800 = 10000.

29. Let the amounts be ₹100 and ₹200 respectively. The value of the 100 would become 100 × 6/7 × 6/7 = 3600/49 = 73.46

    The other person's investment of 200 would become 200 × 1.2 × 1.2 = 288

    The total value would become 288 + 73.46 = 361.46

    This represents approximately a 20% increase in the value of the amount after 2 year. Hence, option (a) is correct.

30. The final value would be:

    0.8 × 63000 + 27000 × 1.15 × 1.15 = 86107.5.

    → Drop in value = 4.32%

8 Chapter — Ratio, Proportion and Variation

INTRODUCTION

The concept of ratio, proportion and variation is an important one for the aptitude examinations. Questions based on this chapter have been regularly asked in the CAT exam (direct or application based). In fact, questions based on this concept regularly appear in all aptitude tests (XLRI, CMAT, NMIMS, SNAP, NIFT, IRMA, Bank PO, etc.).

Besides, this concept is very important in the area of Data Interpretation, where ratio change and ratio comparisons are very popular question types.

RATIO

When comparing any two numbers, sometimes, it is necessary to find out how many times one number is greater (or less) than the other. In other words, we often need to express one number as a fraction of the other.

In general, the ratio of a number x to a number y is defined as the quotient of the numbers x and y.

The numbers that form the ratio are called the terms of the ratio. The numerator of the ratio is called the *antecedent* and the denominator is called the *consequent* of the ratio.

The ratio may be taken for homogenous quantities or for heterogeneous quantities. In the first case, the ratio has no unit (or is unitless), while in the second case, the unit of the ratio is based on the units of the numerator and that of the denominator.

Ratios can be expressed as percentages. To express the value of a ratio as a percentage, we multiply the ratio by 100.

Thus, $4/5 = 0.8 = 80\%$

The Calculation of a ratio:
Percentage and decimal values

The calculation of ratio is principally on the same lines as the calculation of a percentage value.

Hence, you should see it as:

The ratio 2/4 has a percentage value of 50% and it has a decimal value of 0.5.

It should be pretty obvious to you that in order to find out the decimal value of any ratio, calculate the percentage value using the percentage rule method illustrated in the chapter of percentage and then shift the decimal point 2 places to the left.

Thus a ratio which has a percentage value of 62.47% will have a decimal value of 0.6247.

Some Important Properties of Ratios

1. If we multiply the numerator and the denominator of a ratio by the same number, the ratio remains unchanged.

   That is, $\dfrac{a}{b} = \dfrac{ma}{mb}$

2. If we divide the numerator and the denominator of a ratio by the same number, the ratio remains unchanged. Thus

   $$a/b = \dfrac{(a/d)}{(b/d)}$$

3. Denominator equation method:
   The magnitudes of two ratios can be compared by equating the denominators of the two ratios and then checking for the value of the numerator.

Contd

Some Important Properties of Ratios
(*Contd*)

Thus, if we have to check for

$$8/3 \quad \text{vs} \quad 11/4$$

We can compare $\dfrac{(8 \times 1.33)}{(3 \times 1.33)}$ vs $\dfrac{11}{4}$

That is, $\dfrac{10.66}{4} < \dfrac{11}{4}$

In fact, the value of a ratio has a direct relationship with the value of the numerator of the ratio. At the same time, it has an inverse relationship with the denominator of the ratio. Since the denominator has an inverse relationship with the ratio's value, it involves an unnecessary inversion in the minds of the reader. Hence, in my opinion, we should look at maintaining constancy in the denominator and work all the requisite calculations on the numerator's basis.

The reader should recall here the Product Constancy Table (or the denominator change to ratio change table) explained in the chapter of percentages to understand the mechanics of how a change in the denominator affects the value of the ratio. A clear understanding of these dynamics will help the student become much faster in solving the problems based on ratios.

4. The ratio of two fractions can be expressed as a ratio of two integers. Thus the ratio:

$$a/b : c/d = \dfrac{(a/b)}{(c/d)} = \dfrac{ad}{bc}$$

5. If either or both the terms of a ratio are a surd quantity, then the ratio will never evolve into integral numbers unless the surd quantities are equal. Use this principle to spot options in questions having surds.

Example: $\dfrac{\sqrt{3}}{\sqrt{2}}$ can never be represented by integers.

This principle can also be understood in other words as follows:

Suppose while solving a question, you come across a situation where $\sqrt{3}$ appears as a part of the process. In such a case, it would be safe to assume that $\sqrt{3}$ will also be part of the answer. Since the only way the $\sqrt{3}$ can be removed from the answer is by multiplying or dividing the expression by $\sqrt{3}$. Thus for instance, the formula for the area of an equilateral triangle is $(\sqrt{3}/4)a^2$.

Some Important Properties of Ratios
(*Contd*)

Hence, you can safely assume that the area of any equilateral triangle will have $\sqrt{3}$ in its answer. The only case when this gets negated would be when the value of the side has a component which has the fourth root of three.

6. The multiplication of the ratios $\dfrac{a}{b}$ and $\dfrac{c}{d}$ yields:

$$a/b \times c/d = \dfrac{ac}{bd}$$

7. When the ratio a/b is compounded with itself, the resulting ratio is a^2/b^2 and is called the duplicate ratio. Similarly, a^3/b^3 is the triplicate ratio and $a^{0.5}/b^{0.5}$ is the sub-duplicate ratio of a/b.

8. If $a/b = c/d = e/f = g/h = k$ then

$$k = \dfrac{(a + c + e + g)}{(b + d + f + h)}$$

9. If $a_1/b_1, a_2/b_2, a_3/b_3 \ldots a_n/b_n$ are unequal fractions Then the ratio:

$$\dfrac{(a_1 + a_2 + a_3 + \ldots + a_n)}{(b_1 + b_2 + b_3 + \ldots b_n)}$$

lies between the lowest and the highest of these fractions.

10. If we have two equations containing three unknowns as

$$a_1 x + b_1 y + c_1 z = 0 \qquad (1)$$

and $\qquad a_2 x + b_2 y + c_2 z = 0 \qquad (2)$

Then, the value of x, y and z cannot be resolved without having a third equation.

However, in the absence of a third equation, we can find the proportion $x : y : z$. This will be given by $b_1 c_2 - b_2 c_1 : c_1 a_2 - c_2 a_1 : a_1 b_2 - a_2 b_1$. This can be remembered by writing as follows:

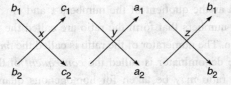

Fig. 8.1

Multiply the coefficients across the arrow indicated always taking a multiplication as positive if the arrow points downwards and taking it as negative if the arrow points upwards.

Thus x corresponds to $b_1 c_2 - b_2 c_1$ and so on.

Some Important Properties of Ratios
(*Contd*)

11. If the ratio $a/b > 1$ (called a ratio of greater inequality) and if k is a positive number:

    $(a + k)/(b + k) < a/b$ and $(a - k)/(b - k) > a/b$

    Similarly if $a/b < 1$ then

    $(a + k)/(b + k) > a/b$ and $(a - k)/(b - k) < a/b$

    [The student should try assuming certain values and check the results]

12. Maintenance of equality when numbers are added in both the numerator and the denominators.

    This if best illustrated through an example:

    $$20/30 = (20 + 2)/(30 + 3)$$

    i.e. $a/b = (a + c)/(b + d)$ if and only if $c/d = a/b$. In other words, the ratio of the additions should be equal to the original ratio to maintain equality of ratios when two different numbers are added in the numerator and denominator.

    Consequently,   if $c/d > a/b$ then $(a + c)/(b + d) > a/b$
    and   if $c/d < a/b$ then $(a + c)/(b + d) < a/b$

    The practical applications of (11) and (12) is of immense importance for all aptitude exams.

MATHEMATICAL USES OF RATIOS

Use 1

As a bridge between 3 or more quantities:

Suppose you have a ratio relationship given between the salaries of two individuals A and B. Further, if there is another ratio relationship between B and C. Then, by combining the two ratios, you can come up with a single consolidated ratio between A, B and C. This ratio will give you the relationship between A and C.

Illustration

The Ratio of A's salary to B's salary is 2:3. The ratio of B's salary to C's salary is 4:5. What is the ratio of A's salary to C's salary?

Using the conventional process in this case:

Take the LCM of 3 and 4 (the two values representing B's amount). The LCM is 12.

Then, convert B's value in each ratio to 12.

Thus, Ratio 1 = 8/12 and Ratio 2 = 12/15

Thus, $A:B:C$ = 8:12:15

Hence, $A:C$ = 8:15

Further, if it were given that A's salary was 800, you could derive the values of C's salary (as 1500).

SHORTCUT for this process:

The LCM process gets very cumbersome especially if you are trying to create a bridge between more than 3 quantities.

Suppose, you have the ratio train as follows:

$A:B$ = 2:3
$B:C$ = 4:5
$C:D$ = 6:11
$D:E$ = 12:17

In order to create one consolidated ratio for this situation using the LCM process becomes too long.

The short cut goes as follows:

$A:B:C:D:E$ can be written directly as:

$2 \times 4 \times 6 \times 12 : 3 \times 4 \times 6 \times 12 : 3 \times 5 \times 6 \times 12 : 3 \times 5 \times 11 \times 17$

The thought algorithm for this case goes as:

To get the consolidated ratio $A:B:C:D:E$, A will correspond to the product of all numerators ($2 \times 4 \times 6 \times 12$) while B will take the first denominator and the last 3 numerators ($3 \times 4 \times 6 \times 12$). C on the other hand takes the first two denominators and the last 2 numerators ($3 \times 5 \times 6 \times 12$), D takes the first 3 denominators and the last numerator ($3 \times 5 \times 11 \times 12$) and E takes all the four denominators ($3 \times 5 \times 11 \times 17$).

In mathematical terms this can be written as:

If $a/b = N_1/D_1$, $b/c = N_2/D_2$, $c/d = N_3/D_3$ and $d/e = N_4/D_4$ then $a : b : c : d : e = N_1N_2N_3N_4 : D_1N_2N_3N_4 : D_1D_2N_3N_4 : D_1D_2D_3N_4 : D_1D_2D_3D_4$

Use 2

Ratio as a Multiplier

This is the most common use of Ratios:

If $A:B$ is 3:1, then the value of B has to be multiplied by 3 to get the value of A.

CALCULATION METHODS related to RATIOS

(A) Calculation methods for Ratio comparisons:

There could be four broad cases when you might be required to do ratio comparisons:

The table below clearly illustrates these:

	Numerator	Denominator	Ratio	Calculations
Case 1	Increases	Decreases	Increase	Not required
Case 2	Increases	Increases	May Increase or Decrease	Required
Case 3	Decreases	Increases	Decreases	Not required
Case 4	Decreases	Decreases	May Increase or Decrease	Required

In case 2 and 4 in the table, calculations will be necessitated. In such a situation, the following process can be used for ratio comparisons.

1. The Cross Multiplication Method

Two ratios can be compared using the cross multiplication method as follows. Suppose you have to compare

12/17 with 15/19

Then, to test which ratio is higher cross multiply and compare 12×19 and 15×17.

If 12×19 is bigger the Ratio 12/17 will be bigger. If 15×17 is higher, the ratio 15/19 will be higher.

In this case, 15×17 being higher, the Ratio 15/19 is higher.

Note: In real time usage (esp. in D.I.) this method is highly impractical and calculating the product might be more cumbersome than calculating the percentage values.

Thus, this method will not be able to tell you the answer if you have to compare $\dfrac{3743}{5624}$ with $\dfrac{3821}{5783}$

2. Percentage value comparison method:

Suppose you have to compare: $\dfrac{173}{212}$ with $\dfrac{181}{241}$

In such a case just by estimating the 10% ranges for each ratio you can clearly see that —
the first ratio is > 80% while the second ratio is < 80%

Hence, the first ratio is obviously greater.

This method is extremely convenient if the two ratios have their values in different 10% ranges.

However, this problem will become slightly more difficult, if the two ratios fall in the same 10% range. Thus, if you had to compare $^{173}/_{212}$ with $^{181}/_{225}$, both the values would give values between 80 – 90%. The next step would be to calculate the 1% range.

The first ratio here is 81 – 82% while the second ratio lies between 80 – 81%

Hence the first ratio is the larger of the two.

Note: For this method to be effective for you, you'll first need to master the percentage rule method for calculating the percentage value of a ratio. Hence if you cannot see that 169.6 is 80% of 212 or for that matter that 81% of 212 is 171.72 and 82% is 172.84 you will not be able to use this method effectively. (This is also true for the next method.) However, once you can calculate percentage values of 3 digit ratios to 1% range, there is not much that can stop you in comparing ratios. The CAT and all other aptitude exams normally do not challenge you to calculate further than the 1% range when you are looking at ratio comparisons.

---

3. Numerator denominator percentage change method:
There is another way in which you can compare close ratios like 173/212 and 181/225. For this method, you need to calculate the percentage changes in the numerator and the denominator.
Thus:

$173 \rightarrow 181$ is a % increase of 4 – 5%
While $212 \rightarrow 225$ is a % increase of 6 – 7%.

In this case, since the denominator is increasing more than the numerator, the second ratio is smaller.

This method is the most powerful method for comparing close ratios—provided you are good with your percentage rule calculations.

(B) Method for calculating the value of a percentage change in the ratio:
PCG (Percentage Change Graphic) gives us a convenient method to calculate the value of the percentage change in a ratio.

Suppose, you have to calculate the percentage change between 2 ratios. This has to be done in two stages as:

Original Ratio $\xrightarrow[\text{numerator}]{\text{Effect of}}$ Intermediate Ratio

$\xrightarrow[\text{Denominator}]{\text{Effect of}}$ Final Ratio

Thus if 20/40 becomes 22/50
Effect of numerator = 20 → 22(10% increase)
Effect of denominator = 50 → 40(25% decrease) (reverse fashion)
Overall effect on the ratio:

$$100 \xrightarrow[\substack{\text{Numerator}\\\text{Effect}}]{10\%\uparrow} 110 \xrightarrow[\substack{\text{Denominator}\\\text{Effect}}]{25\%\downarrow} 82.5$$

Hence, overall effect = 17.5% decrease.

PROPORTION

When two ratios are equal, the four quantities composing them are said to be proportionals. Thus if $a/b = c/d$, then a, b, c, d are proportionals. This is expressed by saying that a is to b as c is to d, and the proportion is written as

$$a:b::c:d$$
or
$$a:b = c:d$$

• The terms a and d are called the extremes while the terms b and c are called the means.
• **If four quantities are in proportion, the product of the extremes is equal to the product of the means.**
Let a, b, c, d be the proportionals.
Then by definition $a/b = c/d$

$\therefore \qquad\qquad ad = bc$

Hence if any three terms of proportion are given, the fourth may be found. Thus if a, c, d are given, then $b = ad/c$.
• **If three quantities a, b and c are in continued proportion, then $a:b = b:c$**

$\therefore \qquad\qquad ac = b^2$

In this case, b is said to be a *mean proportional* between a and c; and c is said to be a *third proportional* to a and b.
• **If three quantities are proportionals the first is to the third is the duplicate ratio of the first to the second.**
That is: for $a:b::b:c$

$$a:c = a^2:b^2$$

• If four quantities a, b, c and d form a proportion, many other proportions may be deduced by the properties of fractions. The results of these operations are very useful. These operations are

1. **Invertendo:** If $a/b = c/d$ then $b/a = d/c$
2. **Alternando:** If $a/b = c/d$, then $a/c = b/d$
3. **Componendo:** If $a/b = c/d$, then $\left(\dfrac{a+b}{b}\right) = \left(\dfrac{c+d}{d}\right)$
4. **Dividendo:** If $a/b = c/d$, then $\left(\dfrac{a-b}{b}\right) = \left(\dfrac{c-d}{d}\right)$
5. **Componendo and Dividendo:** If $a/b = c/d$, then $(a + b)/(a - b) = (c + d)/(c - d)$

🎧 VARIATION

Essentially there are two kinds of proportions that two variables can be related by:

(1) Direct Proportion
When it is said that A varies directly as B, you should understand the following implications:

(a) **Logical implication:** When A increases B increases
(b) **Calculation implication:** If A increases by 10%, B will also increase by 10%
(c) **Graphical implications:** The following graph is representative of this situation.

(d) **Equation implication:** The ratio A/B is constant.

(2) Inverse Proportion:
When A varies inversely as B, the following implication arise.

Space for Notes

(a) **Logical implication:** When A increases B decreases
(b) **Calculation implication:** If A decreases by 9.09%, B will increase by 10%.
(c) **Graphical implications:** The following graph is representative of this situation.

(d) **Equation implication:** The product $A \times B$ is constant.

A quantity 'A' is said to vary directly as another 'B' when the two quantities depend upon each other in such a manner that if B is changed, A is changed in the same ratio.

Note: The word directly is often omitted, and A is said to vary as B.

The symbol $\propto$ *is used to denote variation. Thus, $A \propto B$ is read "A varies as B".*

If $A \propto B$ then, $A = KB$ where K is any constant.

Thus to find $K = A/B$, we need one value of A and a corresponding value of B.

where $K = 3/12 = 1/4 \Rightarrow A = B \times (1/4)$.

A quantity A is said to vary inversely as another B when A varies directly as the reciprocal of B. Thus if A varies inversely as B, $A = m/B$, where m is constant.

A quantity is said to vary jointly as a number of others when it varies directly as their product. Thus A varies jointly as B and C, when $A = mBC$.

If A varies as B when C is constant, and A varies as C when B is constant, then A will vary as BC when both B and C vary.

The variation of A depends partly on that of B and partly on that of C. Assume that each letter variation takes place separately, each in its turn producing its own effect on A.

🎯 WORKED-OUT PROBLEMS

Problem 8.1 ₹ 5783 is divided among Sherry, Berry, and Cherry in such a way that if ₹ 28, ₹ 37 and ₹ 18 be deducted from their respective shares, they have money in the ratio 4 : 6 : 9. Find Sherry's share.

(a) ₹ 1256   (b) ₹ 1228
(c) ₹ 1456   (d) ₹ 1084

Solution The problem clearly states that when we reduce 28, 37 and 18 rupees respectively from Sherry's, Berry's and Cherry's shares, the resultant ratio is: 4 : 6 : 9.

Thus, if we assume the reduced values as

$$4x, 6x \text{ and } 9x, \text{ we will have} \rightarrow$$

Sherry's share → $4x + 28$, Berry's share → $6x + 37$ and Cherry's share → $9x + 18$ and thus we have

$(4x + 28) + (6x + 37) + (9x + 18) = 5783$
$\rightarrow 19x = 5783 - 83 = 5700$
Hence, $x = 300$.
Hence, Sherry's share is ₹ 1228.

Note: For problems based on this chapter we are always confronted with ratios and proportions between different number of variables. For the above problem we had three variables which were in the ratio of 4 : 6 : 9. When we have such a situation we normally assume the values in the same proportion, using one unknown 'x' only (in this example we could take the three values as $4x$, $6x$ and $9x$ respectively).

Then, the total value is represented by the addition of the three giving rise to a linear equation, which on solution, will result in the answer to the value of the unknown 'x'.

However, the student should realise that most of the time this unknown 'x' is not needed to solve the problem. This is illustrated through the following alternate approach to solving the above problem:

Assume the three values as 4, 6 and 9
Then we have

$(4 + 28) + (6 + 37) + (9 + 18) = 5783$
$\rightarrow 19 = 5783 - 83 = 5700 \rightarrow 1 = 300$

Hence, $4 + 28 = 1228$.
While adopting this approach the student should be careful in being able to distinguish the numbers in bold as pointing out the unknown variable.

Problem 8.2 Two numbers are in the ratio $P : Q$. When 1 is added to both the numerator and the denominator, the ratio gets changed to R/S. Again, when 1 is added to both the numerator and the denominator, it becomes 1/2. Find the sum of P and Q.

(a) 3   (b) 4
(c) 5   (d) 6

Solution The normal process of solving this problem would be through the writing of equations.

Approach 1: We have: Final ratio is $x/2x$.

Then, $\dfrac{x-2}{2x-2} = P/Q$

Then, $Qx - 2Q = 2Px - 2P$
$2(P - Q) = x(2P - Q)$ (At this stage we see that the solution is a complex one)

Approach 2: $\dfrac{R+1}{S+1} = \dfrac{1}{2}$

$$2R + 2 = S + 1 \rightarrow R = \dfrac{S-1}{2}$$

Now, $\dfrac{P+1}{Q+1} = \dfrac{R}{S} = \dfrac{S-1}{2S}$ (At this time we realise that we are getting stuck)

Start from front:
$\dfrac{P+2}{Q+2} = 1/2 \rightarrow 2P + 4 = Q + 2$ (Again the solution is not visible and we are likely to get stuck)

Note: Such problems should never be attempted by writing the equations since this process takes more time than is necessary to solve the problem and is impractical in the exam situation due to the amount of time required in writing.

Besides, in complex problems where the final solution is not visible to the student while starting off, many a times the student has to finally abort the problem midway. This results in an unnecessary wastage of time if the student has attempted to write equations.

In fact, the student should realise that selecting the correct questions to solve in aptitude exams like the CAT is more important than being aware of how all the problems are solved.

The following process will illustrate the option based solution process.

Option A: It has $P + Q = 3$. The possible values of P/Q are 1/2 or 2/1.

Using 1/2, we see that on adding 2 to both the numerator and the denominator we get
3/4 (Not the required value.)

Similarly, we see that 2/1 will also not give the answer. We should also realise that the numerator has to be lower than the denominator to have the final value of 1/2.

Next we try **Option B,** where we have 1/3 as the only possible ratio.

Then we get the final value as 3/5 (Not equal to 1/2) Hence, we reject option B.

Next we try **Option C,** where we have 1/4 or 2/3

Checking for 1/4 we get 3/6 = 1/2. Hence, the option is correct.

Problem 8.3 If 10 persons can clean 10 floors by 10 mops in 10 days, in how many days can 8 persons clean 8 floors by 8 mops?

    (a) 12 ½ days   (b) 8 days

    (c) 10 days   (d) 8 ⅓ days

Solution Do not get confused by the distractions given in the problem. 10 men and 10 days means 100 man-days are required to clean 10 floors.

That is, 1 floor requires 10 man-days to get cleaned. Hence, 8 floors will require 80 man-days to clean.

Therefore, 10 days are required to clean 8 floors.

Problem 8.4 Three quantities A, B, C are such that $AB = KC$, where K is a constant. When A is kept constant, B varies directly as C; when B is kept constant, A varies directly C and when C is kept constant, A varies inversely as B.

Initially, A was at 5 and $A:B:C$ was $1:3:5$. Find the value of A when B equals 9 at constant C.

    (a) 8   (b) 8.33

    (c) 9   (d) 9.5

Solution Initial values are 5, 15 and 25.

Thus we have $5 \times 15 = K \times 25$.

Hence, $K = 3$.

Thus, the equation is $AB = 3C$.

For the problem, keep C constant at 25. Then, $A \times 9 = 3 \times 25$.

i.e. $A = 75/9 = 8.33$

Problem 8.5 If $x/y = 3/4$, then find the value of the expression, $(5x - 3y)/(7x + 2y)$.

    (a) 3/21   (b) 5/29

    (c) 3/29   (d) 5/33

Solution Assume the values as $x = 3$ and $y = 4$.

Then we have

$$\frac{(15 - 12)}{(21 + 8)} = 3/29$$

Problem 8.6 ₹ 3650 is divided among 4 engineers, 3 MBAs and 5 CAs such that 3 CAs get as much as 2 MBAs and 3 Engineers as much as 2 CAs. Find the share of an MBA.

    (a) 300   (b) 450

    (c) 475   (d) None of these

Solution

$$4E + 3M + 5C = 3650$$

Also, $3C = 2M$, that is, $M = 1.5\,C$

and $3E = 2C$ that is, $E = 0.66C$

Thus, $4 \times 0.66C + 3 \times 1.5\,C + 5C = 3650$

                        $C = 3650/12.166$

That is, $C = 300$

Hence, $M = 1.5\,C = 450$

Problem 8.7 The ratio of water and milk in a 30 litre mixture is 7 : 3. Find the quantity of water to be added to the mixture in order to make this ratio 6 : 1.

    (a) 30   (b) 32

    (c) 33   (d) 35

Solution Solve while reading → As you read the first sentence, you should have 21 litres of water and 9 litres of milk in your mind.

In order to get the final result, we keep the milk constant at 9 litres.

Then, we have 9 litres, which corresponds to 1

Hence, '?' corresponds to 6.

Solving by using unitary method we have

54 litres of water to 9 litres of milk.

Hence, we need to add 33 litres of water to the original mixture.

Alternatively, we can solve this by using options. The student should try to do the same.

Problem 8.8 Three containers A, B and C are having mixtures of milk and water in the ratio of $1:5$, $3:5$ and $5 : 7$ respectively. If the capacities of the containers are in the ratio $5:4:5$, find the ratio of milk to water, if the mixtures of all the three containers are mixed together.

Solution Assume that there are 500, 400 and 500 litres respectively in the 3 containers.

Then we have, 83.33,150 and 208.33 litres of milk in each of the three containers.

Thus, the total milk is 441.66 litres. Hence, the amount of water in the mixture is

$$1400\text{--}441.66 = 958.33 \text{ litres.}$$

Hence, the ratio of milk to water is

441.66 : 958.33 → 53 : 115 (Using division by 0.33333)

The calculation thought process should be:

$(441 \times 3 + 2) : (958 \times 3 + 1) = 1325 : 2875$.

Dividing by 25 → 53 : 115.

LEVEL OF DIFFICULTY (I)

1. Divide ₹ 1870 into three parts in such a way that half of the first part, one-third of the second part and one-sixth of the third part are equal.
   (a) 241, 343, 245   (b) 400, 800, 670
   (c) 470, 640, 1160   (d) None of these

2. Divide ₹ 500 among A, B, C and D so that A and B together get thrice as much as C and D together, B gets four times of what C gets and C gets 1.5 times as much as D. Now the value of what B gets is
   (a) 300   (b) 75
   (c) 125   (d) 150

3. If $\dfrac{a}{b+c} = \dfrac{b}{c+a} = \dfrac{c}{a+b}$, then each fraction is equal to
   (a) $(a+b+c)^2$ (b) 1/2
   (c) 1/4   (d) 0

4. If $6x^2 + 6y^2 = 13xy$, what is the ratio of x to y?
   (a) 1:4   (b) 3:2
   (c) 4:5   (d) 1:2
   (Hint: Use options to solve fast)

5. If $a:b = c:d$ then the value of $\dfrac{a^2 + b^2}{c^2 + d^2}$ is
   (a) 1/2   (b) $\dfrac{a+b}{c+d}$
   (c) $\dfrac{a-b}{c-d}$ (d) $\dfrac{ab}{cd}$

6. A crew can row a certain course up the stream in 84 minutes; they can row the same course down stream in 9 minutes less than they can row it in still water. How long would they take to row down with the stream.
   (a) 45 or 23 minutes   (b) 63 or 12 minutes
   (c) 60 minutes   (d) 19 minutes

7. If a, b, c, d are in continued proportion then $\dfrac{a-d}{b-c} \geq x$. What is the value of x.
   (a) 2   (b) 3
   (c) 1   (d) 0

8. If 4 examiners can examine a certain number of answer books in 8 days by working 5 hours a day, for how many hours a day would 2 examiners have to work in order to examine twice the number of answer books in 20 days.
   (a) 6   (b) 7 ½
   (c) 8   (d) 9

9. If a, b, c, d are proportional, then $(a-b)(a-c)/a =$
   (a) $a+c+d$ (b) $a+d-b-c$
   (c) $a+b+c+d$ (d) $a+c-b-d$

10. In a mixture of 40 litres, the ratio of milk and water is 4 : 1. How much water must be added to this mixture so that the ratio of milk and water becomes 2 : 3.
    (a) 20 litres   (b) 32 litres
    (c) 40 litres   (d) 30 litres

11. If A varies as C, and B varies as C, then which of the following is false:
    (a) $(A+B) \propto C$ (b) $(A-B) \propto 1/C$
    (c) $\sqrt{AB} \propto C$ (d) $AB \propto C^2$

12. If three numbers are in the ratio of 1 : 2 : 3 and half the sum is 18, then the ratio of squares of the numbers is:
    (a) 6 : 12 : 13   (b) 1 : 2 : 4
    (c) 36 : 144 : 324   (d) 3 : 5 : 7

13. The ratio between two numbers is 3 : 4 and their LCM is 180. The first number is:
    (a) 60   (b) 45
    (c) 15   (d) 20

14. A and B are two alloys of argentum and brass prepared by mixing metals in proportions 7 : 2 and 7 : 11 respectively. If equal quantities of the two alloys are melted to form a third alloy C, the proportion of argentum and brass in C will be:
    (a) 5 : 9   (b) 5 : 7
    (c) 7 : 5   (d) 9 : 5

15. If 30 men working 7 hours a day can do a piece of work in 18 days, in how many days will 21 men working 8 hours a day do the same work?
    (a) 24 days   (b) 22.5 days
    (c) 30 days   (d) 45 days

16. The incomes of A and B are in the ratio 3 : 2 and their expenditures are in the ratio 5 : 3. If each saves ₹ 1000, then, A's income can be:
    (a) ₹ 3000   (b) ₹ 4000
    (c) ₹ 6000   (d) ₹ 9000

17. If the ratio of sines of angles of a triangle is $1 : 1 : \sqrt{2}$, then the ratio of square of the greatest side to sum of the squares of other two sides is
    (a) 3 : 4   (b) 2 : 1
    (c) 1 : 1   (d) 1 : 2

18. Divide ₹ 680 among A, B and C such that A gets 2/3 of what B gets and B gets 1/4th of what C gets. Now the share of C is:

(a) ₹ 480   (b) ₹ 300

(c) ₹ 420   (d) ₹ 360

19. A, B, C enter into a partnership. A contributes one-third of the whole capital while B contributes as much as A and C together contribute. If the profit at the end of the year is ₹ 84,000, how much would each receive?

  (a) 24,000, 20,000, 40,000

  (b) 28,000, 42,000, 14,000

  (c) 28,000, 42,000, 10,000

  (d) 28,000, 14,000, 42,000

20. The students in three batches at Mindworkzz are in the ratio $2:3:5$. If 20 students are increased in each batch, the ratio changes to $4:5:7$. The total number of students in the three batches before the increases were

  (a) 10   (b) 90

  (c) 100   (d) 150

21. The speeds of three cars are in the ratio $2:3:4$. The ratio between the times taken by these cars to travel the same distance is

  (a) $2:3:4$ (b) $4:3:2$

  (c) $4:3:6$ (d) $6:4:3$

22. If a, b, c and d are proportional then the mean proportion between $a^2 + c^2$ and $b^2 + d^2$ is

  (a) ac/bd (b) $ab + cd$

  (c) $a/b + d/c$ (d) $a^2/b^2 + c^2/d^2$

23. A number z lies between 0 and 1. Which of the following is true?

  (a) $z > \sqrt{z}$ (b) $z > 1/z$

  (c) $z^3 > z^2$ (d) $1/z > \sqrt{z}$

24. ₹ 2250 is divided among three friends Amar, Bijoy and Chandra in such a way that 1/6th of Amar's share, 1/4th of Bijoy's share and 2/5th of Chandra's share are equal. Find Amar's share.

  (a) ₹ 720   (b) ₹ 1080

  (c) ₹ 450   (d) ₹ 1240

25. After an increment of 7 in both the numerator and denominator, a fraction changes to 3/4. Find the original fraction.

  (a) 5/12   (b) 7/9

  (c) 2/5   (d) 3/8

26. The difference between two positive numbers is 10 and the ratio between them is $5:3$. Find the product of the two numbers.

  (a) 375   (b) 175

  (c) 275   (d) 125

27. If 30 oxen can plough 1/7th of a field in 2 days, how many days 18 oxen will take to do the remaining work?

(a) 30 days   (b) 20 days

(c) 15 days   (d) 18 days

28. A cat takes 5 leaps for every 4 leaps of a dog, but 3 leaps of the dog are equal to 4 leaps of the cat. What is the ratio of the speed of the cat to that of the dog?

  (a) $11:15$ (b) $15:11$

  (c) $16:15$ (d) $15:16$

29. The present ratio of ages of A and B is $4:5$. 18 years ago, this ratio was $11:16$. Find the sum total of their present ages.

  (a) 90 years   (b) 105 years

  (c) 110 years   (d) 80 years

30. Four numbers in the ratio $1:3:4:7$ add up to give a sum of 105. Find the value of the biggest number.

  (a) 42   (b) 35

  (c) 49   (d) 63

31. Three men rent a farm for ₹ 7000 per annum. A puts 110 cows in the farm for 3 months, B puts 110 cows for 6 months and C puts 440 cows for 3 months. What percentage of the total expenditure should A pay?

  (a) 20%   (b) 14.28%

  (c) 16.66%   (d) 11.01%

32. 10 students can do a job in 8 days, but on the starting day, two of them informed that they are not coming. By what fraction will the number of days required for doing the whole work get increased?

  (a) 4/5   (b) 3/8

  (c) 3/4   (d) 1/4

33. A dishonest milkman mixed 1 litre of water for every 3 litres of milk and thus made up 36 litres of milk . If he now adds 15 litres of milk to the mixture, find the ratio of milk and water in the new mixture.

  (a) $12:5$ (b) $14:3$

  (c) $7:2$ (d) $9:4$

34. ₹ 3000 is distributed among A, B and C such that A gets 2/3rd of what B and C together get and C gets 1/2 of what A and B together get. Find C's share.

  (a) ₹ 750   (b) ₹ 1000

  (c) ₹ 800   (d) ₹ 1200

35. If the ratio of the ages of Maya and Chhaya is $6:5$ at present, and fifteen years from now, the ratio will get changed to $9:8$, then find Maya's present age.

  (a) 24 years   (b) 30 years

  (c) 18 years   (d) 33 years

36. At constant temperature, pressure of a definite mass of gas is inversely proportional to the volume. If the pressure is reduced by 20%, find the respective change in volume.

(a) −16.66%   (b) +25%

(c) −25%   (d) +16.66%

37. If ₹ 58 is divided among 150 children such that each girl and each boy gets 25 p and 50 p respectively. Then how many girls are there?

(a) 52   (b) 54

(c) 68   (d) 62

38. If 391 bananas were distributed among three monkeys in the ratio 1/2 : 2/3 : 3/4, how many bananas did the first monkey get?

(a) 102   (b) 108

(c) 112   (d) 104

39. A mixture contains milk and water in the ratio 5 : 1. On adding 5 litres of water, the ratio of milk to water becomes 5 : 2. The quantity of milk in the mixture is:

(a) 16 litres   (b) 25 litres

(c) 32.5 litres   (d) 22.75 litres

40. A beggar had ten paise, twenty paise and one rupee coins in the ratio 10 : 17 : 7 respectively at the end of day. If that day he earned a total of ₹ 57, how many twenty paise coins did he have?

(a) 114   (b) 171

(c) 95   (d) 85

41. Vijay has coins of the denomination of Re. 1, 50 p and 25 p in the ratio of 12 : 10 : 7. The total worth of the coins he has is ₹ 75. Find the number of 25 p coins that Vijay has

(a) 48   (b) 72

(c) 60   (d) None of these

42. If two numbers are in the ratio of 5 : 8 and if 9 be added to each, the ratio becomes 8 : 11. Now find the lower number.

(a) 5   (b) 10

(c) 15   (d) None of these

43. What number must be taken from each term of the fraction 27/35 that it may become 2 : 3?

(a) 9   (b) 10

(c) 11   (d) None of these

44. If x varies inversely as $y^2 - 1$ and is equal to 24 when $y = 10$, find x when $y = 5$.

(a) 99   (b) 101

(c) 91   (d) 93

45. If x varies as y, and $y = 7$ when $x = 18$, find x when $y = 21$

(a) 36   (b) 54

(c) 72   (d) 18

46. A varies jointly as B and C; and $A = 6$ when $B = 3$, $C = 2$; find A when $B = 5$, $C = 7$.

(a) 17.5   (b) 35

(c) 70   (d) 105

47. If x varies as y directly, and as z inversely, and $x = 14$ when $y = 10$; find z when $x = 49$, $y = 45$.

(a) 14/10   (b) 10

(c) 10/14   (d) Cannot be determined

48. A cask contains a mixture of 49 litres of wine and water in the proportion 5 : 2. How much water must be added to it so that the ratio of wine to water may be 7 : 4?

(a) 3.5   (b) 6

(c) 7   (d) None of these

49. A cask contains 12 gallons of mixture of wine and water in the ratio 3 : 1. How much of the mixture must be drawn off and water substituted, so that wine and water in the cask may become half and half.

(a) 3 litres   (b) 5 litres

(c) 6 litres   (d) None of these

50. The total number of pupils in three classes of a school is 333. The number of pupils in classes I and II are in the ratio 3 : 5 and those in classes II and III are in the ratio 7 : 11. Find the number of pupils in the class that had the highest number of pupils.

(a) 63   (b) 105

(c) 165   (d) 180

Space for Rough Work

LEVEL OF DIFFICULTY (II)

1. If the work done by $(x - 1)$ men in $(x + 1)$ days is to the work done by $(x + 2)$ men in $(x - 1)$ days is in the ratio $9 : 10$, then the value of x is
   (a) 10
   (b) 12
   (c) 8
   (d) 15

2. The duration of a railway journey varies as the distance and inversely as the velocity; the velocity varies directly as the square root of the quantity of coal used, and inversely as the number carriages in the train. In a journey of 50 km in half an hour with 18 carriages, 100 kg of coal is required. How much coal will be consumed in a journey of 42 km in 28 minutes with 16 carriages.
   (a) 64 kg
   (b) 49 kg
   (c) 25 kg
   (d) 36 kg

3. The weight of a circular disc varies as the square of the radius when the thickness remains the same; it also varies as the thickness when the radius remains the same. Two discs have their thicknesses in the ratio of 9:8; the ratio of the radii if the weight of the first is twice that of the second is
   (a) 4 : 3
   (b) 5 : 2
   (c) 2 : 1
   (d) 1 : 2

4. If a and b are positive integers then $\sqrt{2}$ always lies between:
   (a) $(a + b)/(a - b)$ and ab
   (b) a/b and $(a + 2b)/(a + b)$
   (c) a and b
   (d) $ab/(a + b)$ and $(a - b)/ab$

5. The cost of digging a pit was ₹ 1,347. How much will it cost (approximately) if the wages of workmen per day had been increased by 1/8 of the former wages and length of the working day increased by 1/20 of the former period?
   (a) ₹ 1443
   (b) ₹ 1234
   (c) ₹ 1439
   (d) ₹ 1000

6. A vessel contains a litres of wine, and another vessel contains b litres of water. c litres are taken out of each vessel and transferred to the other if $c \times (a + b) = ab$. If A and B are the respective values of the amount of wine contained in the respective containers after this operation, then what can be said about the relationship between A and B.
   (a) $A = B$
   (b) $\dfrac{A - C}{B - C} > 2$
   (c) $A - B = 4c$
   (d) None of these

7. If sum of the roots and the product of the roots of a quadratic equation S are in the ratio of $2 : 1$, then which of the following is true?
   (a) $f(S) < 0$
   (b) $(b^2 - 4ac) < 0$
   (c) S is a perfect square
   (d) None of these

8. A factory employs skilled workers, unskilled workers and clerks in the proportion $8 : 5 : 1$, and the wages of a skilled worker, an unskilled worker and a clerk are in the ratio $5 : 2 : 3$. When 20 unskilled workers are employed, the total daily wages of all amount to ₹ 318. The wages paid to each category of workers are
   (a) ₹ 240, ₹ 60, ₹ 18
   (b) ₹ 200, ₹ 90, ₹ 28
   (c) ₹ 150, ₹ 108, ₹ 60
   (d) ₹ 250, ₹ 50, ₹ 18

9. If $a : b = c : d$, and $e : f = g : h$, then $(ae + bf) : (ae - bf) = ?$
   (a) $\dfrac{(e + f)}{(e - f)}$
   (b) $\dfrac{(cg + dh)}{(cg - dh)}$
   (c) $\dfrac{(cg + dh)}{(cg - dh)}$
   (d) $\dfrac{e - f}{e + f}$

10. Brass is an alloy of copper and zinc. Bronze is an alloy containing 80% of copper, 4 % of zinc and 16% of tin. A fused mass of brass and bronze is found to contain 74% of copper, 16% of zinc, and 10% of tin. The ratio of copper to zinc in Brass is:
    (a) 64% and 36%
    (b) 33% and 67%
    (c) 50% and 75%
    (d) 35% and 65%

11. The Lucknow Indore Express without its rake can go 24 km an hour, and the speed is diminished by a quantity that varies as the square root of the number of wagons attached. If it is known that with four wagons its speed is 20 km/h, the greatest number of wagons with which the engine can just move is
    (a) 144
    (b) 140
    (c) 143
    (d) 124

12. If x varies as y then $x^2 + y^2$ varies as
    (a) $x + y$
    (b) $x - y$
    (c) $x^2 - y^2$
    (d) None of these

13. If $f(x) = \dfrac{(x + 1)}{(x - 1)}$, then the ratio of x to $f(y)$ where $y = f(x)$ is
    (a) $x : y$
    (b) $x^2 : y^2$
    (c) $1 : 1$
    (d) $y : x$

14. A contractor employs 200 men to build a bund. They finish 5/6 of the work in 10 weeks. Then rain sets in and not only does the work remain suspended for 4 weeks but also half of the work already done is washed away. After the rain, when the work is resumed, only 140 men turn up. The total time in which the contractor is able to complete the work assuming that there are no further disruptions in the schedule is
    (a) 25 weeks   (b) 26 weeks
    (c) 24 weeks   (d) 20 weeks

15. In a journey of 48 km performed by tonga, rickshaw and cycle in that order, the distance covered by the three ways in that order are in the ratio of $8:1:3$ and charges per kilometre in that order are in the ratio $8:1:4$. If the tonga charges being 24 paise per kilometre, the total cost of the journey is
    (a) ₹ 9.24   (b) ₹ 10
    (c) ₹ 12   (d) None of these

16. A bag contains 25 paise, 50 paise and 1 Re. coins. There are 220 coins in all and the total amount in the bag is ₹ 160. If there are thrice as many 1 Re. coins as there are 25 paise coins, then what is the number of 50 paise coins?
    (a) 60   (b) 40
    (c) 120   (d) 80

Directions for Questions 17 to 19: Read the following and answer the questions that follow.

Tuliram runs in a triathlon consisting of three phases in the following manner. Running 12 km, cycling 24 km and swimming 5 km. His speeds in the three phases are in the ratio $2:6:1$. He completes the race in n minutes. Later, he changes his strategy so that the distances he covers in each phase are constant but his speeds are now in the ratio $3:8:1$. The end result is that he completes the race taking 20 minutes more than the earlier speed. It is also known that he has not changed his running speed when he changes his strategy.

17. What is his initial speed while swimming?
    (a) 1/2 km/min   (b) 0.05 km/min
    (c) 0.15 km/min   (d) None of these

18. If his speeds are in the ratio 1:3:1, with the running time remaining unchanged, what is his finishing time?
    (a) 500/3 min   (b) 250/3 min
    (c) 200/3 min   (d) 350/3 min

19. What is Tuliram's original speed of running?
    (a) 9 kmph   (b) 18 kmph
    (c) 54 kmph   (d) 12 kmph

20. Concentrations of three wines A, B and C are 10%, 20% and 30% respectively. They are mixed in the ratio $2:3:x$ resulting in a 23% concentration solution. Find x.

    (a) 7   (b) 6
    (c) 5   (d) 4

21. The cost of an article (which is composed of raw materials and wages) was 3 times the value of the raw materials used. The cost of raw materials increased in the ratio $3:7$ and wages increased in the ratio $4:9$. Find the present cost of the article if its original cost was ₹ 18.
    (a) ₹ 41   (b) ₹ 30
    (c) ₹ 40   (d) ₹ 46

22. In a co-educational school there are 15 more girls than boys. If the number of girls is increased by 10% and the number of boys is also increased by 16%, there would be 9 more girls than boys. What is the number of students in the school?
    (a) 140   (b) 125
    (c) 265   (d) 255

23. At IIM Bangalore class of 1995, Sonali, a first year student has taken 10 courses, earning grades A (worth 4 points each), B (worth 3 points each) and C (worth 2 points each). Her grade point average is 3.2, and if the course in which she get C's were deleted, her GPA in the remaining courses would be 3.333. How many A's, B's and C's did she get?
    (a) 3, 1 and 6   (b) 1, 3 and 6
    (c) 3, 6 and 1   (d) 1, 6 and 3

24. Total expenses of running the hostel at Harvard Business School are partly fixed and partly varying linearly with the number of boarders. The average expense per boarder is $70 when there are 25 boarders and $60 when there are 50 boarders. What is the average expense per boarder when there are 100 boarders?
    (a) 55   (b) 56
    (c) 54   (d) 50

25. The speed of the engine of Gondwana Express is 42 km/h when no compartment is attached, and the reduction in speed is directly proportional to the square root of the number of compartments attached. If the speed of the train carried by this engine is 24 km/h when 9 compartments are attached, the maximum number of compartments that can be carried by the engine is
    (a) 49   (b) 48
    (c) 46   (d) 47

Three drunkards agree to pool their vodka and decided to share it with a fourth drunkard (who had no vodka) at a price equal to 5 roubles a litre. The first drunkard contributed 1 litre more than the second and the second contributed a litre more than the third. Then all four of them divided the vodka equally and drank it. The fourth drunkard paid money, which was divided in the ratio of each drunkard's contribution towards his portion. It was found that the first drunkard should get twice as much money as the second. Based on this information answer the questions 26–28. (Assume that all shares are integral).

26. How much money did the second drunkard get (in roubles)?

    (a) 8   (b) 10
    (c) 5   (d) Data insufficient

27. How many litres of vodka was consumed in all by the four of them?

    (a) 12   (b) 16
    (c) 10   (d) None of these

28. What proportion of the fourth drunkard's drink did the second drunkard contribute?

    (a) 1/3   (b) 2/3
    (c) 1/2   (d) None of these

29. In Ramnagar Colony, the ratio of school going children to non-school going children is 5 : 4. If in the next year, the number of non-school going children is increased by 20%, making it 35,400, what is the new ratio of school going children to non-school going children?

    (a) 4 : 5   (b) 3 : 2
    (c) 25 : 24   (d) None of these

30. A precious stone weighing 35 grams worth ₹ 12,250 is accidentally dropped and gets broken into two pieces having weights in the ratio of 2 : 5. If the price varies as the square of the weight then find the loss incurred.

    (a) ₹ 5750   (b) ₹ 6000
    (c) ₹ 5500   (d) ₹ 5000

31. On his deathbed, Mr. Kalu called upon his three sons and told them to distribute all his assets worth ₹ 525,000 in the ratio of 1/15 : 1/21 : 1/35 amongst themselves. Find the biggest share amongst the three portions.

    (a) 17,500   (b) 245,000
    (c) 10,500   (d) 13,250

32. Three jackals—Paar, Maar and Taar together have 675 loaves of bread. Paar has got three times as much as Maar but 25 loaves more than Taar. How many does Taar have?

    (a) 175   (b) 275
    (c) 375   (d) None of these

33. King Sheru had ordered the distribution of apples according to the following plan : for every 20 apples the elephant gets, the zebra should get 13 apples and the deer should get 8 apples. Now his servant Shambha jackal is in a fix. Can you help him by telling how much should he give to the elephant if there were 820 apples in total?

34. In the famous Bhojpur island, there are four men for every three women and five children for every three men. How many children are there in the island if it has 531 women?

    (a) 454   (b) 1180
    (c) 1070   (d) 389

35. Which of the following will have the maximum change in their values if 5 is added to both the numerator and denominator of all the fractions?

    (a) 3/4   (b) 2/3
    (c) 4/7   (d) 5/7

36. 40 men could have finished the whole project in 28 days but due to the inclusion of a few more men, work got done in 3/4 of the time. Find out how many more men were included (in whole numbers).

    (a) 12   (b) 13
    (c) 14   (d) None of these

37. Mr *AM*, the magnanimous cashier at *XYZ* Ltd., while distributing salary, adds whatever money is needed to make the sum a multiple of 50. He adds ₹ 10 and ₹ 40 to *A*'s and *B*'s salary respectively and then he realises that the salaries of *A*, *B* and *C* are now in the ratio 4 : 5 : 7. The salary of *C* could be

    (a) ₹ 2300   (b) ₹ 2150
    (c) ₹ 1800   (d) ₹ 2100

38. A mother divided an amount of ₹ 61,000 between her two daughters aged 18 years and 16 years respectively and deposited their shares in a bond. If the interest rate is 20% compounded annually and if each received the same amount as the other when she attained the age of 20 years, their shares are

    (a) ₹ 35,600 and ₹ 25,400
    (b) ₹ 30500 each
    (c) ₹ 24,000 and ₹ 37000
    (d) None of these

Directions for Questions 39 to 41: Read the passage below and answer the questions that follow:

Anshu gave Bobby and Chandana as many pens as each one of them already had. Then Chandana gave Anshu and Bobby as many pens as each already had. Now each had an equal number of pens. The total number of pens is 72.

39. How many pens did Bobby have initially?

    (a) 24   (b) 18
    (c) 12   (d) 6

40. How many pens did Chandana have initially?

    (a) 24   (b) 18
    (c) 12   (d) 6

41. How many pens did Anshu have initially?

    (a) 30   (b) 36
    (c) 42   (d) 48

42. The volume of a pyramid varies jointly as its height and the area of its base; and when the area of the base is 60 square dm and the height 14 dm, the volume is 280 cubic dm. What is the area of the base of a pyramid whose volume is 390 cubic dm and whose height is 26 dm?
    (a) 40
    (b) 45
    (c) 50
    (d) None of these

43. The expenses of an all boys' institute are partly constant and partly vary as the number of boys. The expenses were ₹ 10,000 for 150 boys and ₹ 8400 for 120 boys. What will the expenses be when there are 330 boys?
    (a) 18,000
    (b) 19,600
    (c) 22,400
    (d) None of these

44. The distance of the horizon at sea varies as the square root of the height of the eye above sea-level. When the distance is 14.4 km, the height of the eye is 18 metres. Find, in kilometres, the distance when the height of the eye is 8 metres.
    (a) 4.8 km
    (b) 7.2 km
    (c) 9.6 km
    (d) 12 km

45. A mixture of cement, sand and gravel in the ratio of 1 : 2 : 4 by volume is required. A person wishes to measure out quantities by weight. He finds that the weight of one cubic foot of cement is 94 kg, of sand 100 kg and gravel 110 kg. What should be the ratio of cement, sand and gravel by weight in order to give a proper mixture?
    (a) 47 : 100 : 220
    (b) 94 : 100 : 220
    (c) 47 : 200 : 440
    (d) None of these

Space for Rough Work

LEVEL OF DIFFICULTY (III)

1. An alloy of gold and silver is taken in the ratio of 1:2, and another alloy of the same metals is taken in the ratio of 2:3. How many parts of the two alloys must be taken to obtain a new alloy consisting of gold and silver that are in the ratio 3:5?
   (a) 3 and 5
   (b) 2 and 9
   (c) 2 and 5
   (d) 1 and 5

2. There are two quantities of oil, with the masses differing by 2 kg. The same quantity of heat, equal to 96 kcal, was imparted to each mass, and the larger mass of oil was found to be 4 degrees cooler than the smaller mass. Find the mass of oil in each of the two quantities.
   (a) 6 and 8
   (b) 4 and 6
   (c) 2 and 9
   (d) 4 and 9

3. There are two alloys of gold and silver. In the first alloy, there is twice as much gold as silver, and in the second alloy there is 5 times less gold than silver. How many times more must we take of the second alloy than the first in order to obtain a new alloy in which there would be twice as much silver as gold?
   (a) Two times
   (b) Three times
   (c) Four times
   (d) Ten times

4. Calculate the weight and the percentage of zinc in the zinc-copper alloy being given that the latter's alloy with 3 kg of pure zinc contains 90 per cent of zinc and with 2 kg of 90% zinc alloy contains 84% of zinc.
   (a) 2.4 kg or 80%
   (b) 1.4 kg or 88%
   (c) 3.4 kg or 60%
   (d) 7.4 kg or 18%

5. Two solutions, the first of which contains 0.8 kg and the second 0.6 kg of salt, were poured together and 10 kg of a new salt solution were obtained. Find the weight of the first and of the second solution in the mixture if the first solution is known to contain 10 per cent more of salt than the second.
   (a) 4 kg, 6 kg
   (b) 3 kg, 7 kg
   (c) 4 kg, 9 kg
   (d) 5 kg, 9 kg

6. From a full barrel containing 729 litres of honey we pour off 'a' litre and add water to fill up the barrel. After stirring the solution thoroughly, we pour off 'a' litre of the solution and again add water to fill up the barrel. After the procedure is repeated 6 times, the solution in the barrel contains 64 litres of honey. Find a.
   (a) 243 litres
   (b) 81 litres
   (c) 2.7 litres
   (d) 3 litres

7. In two alloys, the ratios of nickel to tin are 5:2 and 3:4 (by weight). How many kilogram of the first alloy and of the second alloy should be alloyed together to obtain 28 kg of a new alloy with equal contents of nickel and tin?
   (a) 9 kg of the first alloy and 22 kg of the second
   (b) 17 kg of the first alloy and 11 kg of the second
   (c) 7 kg of the first alloy and 21 kg of the second
   (d) 8 kg and 20 kg respectively

8. In two alloys, aluminium and iron are in the ratios of 4:1 and 1:3. After alloying together 10 kg of the first alloy, 16 kg of the second and several kilograms of pure aluminium, an alloy was obtained in which the ratio of aluminium to iron was 3:2. Find the weight of the new alloy.
   (a) 15
   (b) 35
   (c) 65
   (d) 95

9. There are two alloys of gold, silver and platinum. The first alloy is known to contain 40 per cent of platinum and the second alloy 26 per cent of silver. The percentage of gold is the same in both alloys. Having alloyed 150 kg of the first alloy and 250 kg of the second, we get a new alloy that contains 30 per cent of gold. How many kilogram of platinum is there in the new alloy?
   (a) 170 kg
   (b) 175 kg
   (c) 160 kg
   (d) 165 kg

10. Two alloys of iron have different percentage of iron in them. The first one weighs 6 kg and second one weighs 12 kg. One piece each of equal weight was cut off from both the alloys and the first piece was alloyed with the second alloy and the second piece alloyed with the first one. As a result, the percentage of iron became the same in the resulting two new alloys. What was the weight of each cut-off piece?
    (a) 4 kg
    (b) 2 kg
    (c) 3 kg
    (d) 5 kg

11. Two litres of a mixture of wine and water contain 12% water. They are added to 3 litres of another mixture containing 7% water, and half a litre of water is then added to whole. What is the percentage of water in resulting concoction?
    (a) 17(2/7)%
    (b) 15 (7/11)%
    (c) 17(3/11)%
    (d) 16 (2/3)%

12. Three vessels having volumes in the ratio of 1:2:3 are full of a mixture of coke and soda. In the first vessel, ratio of coke and soda is 2:3, in second, 3:7

and in third, 1:4. If the liquid in all the three vessels were mixed in a bigger container, what is the resulting ratio of coke and soda?

(a) 4:11   (b) 5:7

(c) 7:11   (d) 7:5

13. Two types of tea are mixed in the ratio of 3:5 to produce the first quality and if they are mixed in the ratio of 2:3, the second quality is obtained. How many kilograms of the first quality has to be mixed with 10 kg of the second quality so that a third quality having the two varieties in the ratio of 7:11 may be produced?

(a) 5 kg   (b) 10 kg

(c) 8 kg   (d) 9 kg

14. A toy weighing 24 grams of an alloy of two metals is worth ₹ 174, but if the weights of metals in alloy be interchanged, the toy would be worth ₹ 162. If the price of one metal be ₹ 8 per gram, find the price of the other metal in the alloy used to make the toy.

(a) ₹ 10 per gram   (b) ₹ 6 per gram

(c) ₹ 4 per gram   (d) ₹ 5 per gram

15. The weight of three heaps of gold are in the ratio 5:6:7. By what fractions of themselves must the first two be increased so that the ratio of the weights may be changed to 7:6:5?

(a) $\dfrac{24}{25}, \dfrac{2}{5}$ (b) $\dfrac{48}{50}, \dfrac{4}{5}$

(c) $\dfrac{48}{50}, \dfrac{3}{5}$ (d) $\dfrac{24}{25}, \dfrac{3}{7}$

16. An alloy of gold, silver and bronze contains 90% bronze, 7% gold and 3% silver. A second alloy of bronze and silver only is melted with the first and the mixture contains 85% of bronze, 5% of gold and 10% of silver. Find the percentage of bronze in the second alloy.

(a) 75%   (b) 72.5%

(c) 70%   (d) 67.5%

17. Gunpowder can be prepared by saltpetre and nitrous oxide. Price of saltpetre is thrice the price of nitrous oxide. Notorious gangster Kallu Bhai sells the gunpowder at ₹ 2160 per 10 g, thereby making a profit of 20%. If the ratio of saltpetre and nitrous oxide in the mixture be 2:3, find the cost price of saltpetre.

(a) ₹ 210/gm   (b) ₹ 300/gm

(c) ₹ 120/gm   (d) None of these

18. Two boxes A and B were filled with a mixture of rice and dal—in A in the ratio of 5:3, and in B in the ratio of 7:3. What quantity must be taken from the first to form a mixture that shall contain 8 kg of rice and 3 kg of dal?

(a) 4 kg

(b) 5 kg

(c) 6 kg

(d) This cannot be achieved

19. A person buys 18 local tickets for ₹ 110. Each first class ticket costs ₹ 10 and each second class ticket costs ₹ 3. What will another lot of 18 tickets in which the number of first class and second class tickets are interchanged cost?

(a) 112   (b) 118

(c) 121   (d) 124

20. Two jars having a capacity of 3 and 5 litres respectively are filled with mixtures of milk and water. In the smaller jar 25% of the mixture is milk and in the larger 25% of the mixture is water. The jars are emptied into a 10 litre cask whose remaining capacity is filled up with water. Find the percentage of milk in the cask.

(a) 55%   (b) 50%

(c) 45%   (d) None of these

21. Two cubes of bronze have their total weight equivalent to 60 kg. The first piece contains 10 kg of pure zinc and the second piece contains 8 kg of pure zinc. What is the percentage of zinc in the first piece of bronze if the second piece contains 15 per cent more zinc than the first?

(a) 15%   (b) 25%

(c) 55%   (d) 24%

22. Sonu gets a jewellery made of an alloy of copper and silver. The alloy with a weight of 8 kg contains p per cent of copper. What piece of a copper-silver alloy containing 40 per cent of silver must be alloyed with the first piece in order to obtain a new alloy with the minimum percentage of copper if the weight of the second piece is 2 kg?

(a) 2 kg for $p > 60$, a kg, where $a \in [0, 2]$, for $p = 60$, 0 kg for $0 < p < 60$

(b) 0 kg for $p > 60$, a kg, where $a \in [0, 2]$, for $p = 60$, 2 kg for $0 < p < 60$

(c) 0 kg for $p > 60$, a kg, where $a \in [0, 3]$, for $p = 70$, 0 kg for $0 < p < 70$

(d) None of these

23. From a vessel filled up with pure spirit to the brim, two litres of spirit was removed and 2 litres of water were added. After the solution was mixed, 2 litres of the mixture was poured off and again 2 litres of water was added. The solution was stirred again and 2 litres of the mixture was removed and 2 litres of water was added. As a result of the above operations, the volume of water in the vessel increased by 3 litres than the volume of spirit remaining in it. How many litres of spirit and water were there in the vessel after the above procedure was carried out?

(a) 0.7 litre of spirit and 3.7 litres of water

(b) 1.5 litres of spirit and 4.5 litres of water

(c) 8.5 litre of spirit and 11.5 litres of water

(d) 0.5 litre of spirit and 3.5 litres of water

24. There are two qualities of milk—Amul and Sudha having different prices per litre, their volumes being 130 litres and 180 litres respectively. After equal amounts of milk was removed from both, the milk removed from Amul was added to Sudha and vice-versa. The resulting two types of milk now have the same price. Find the amount of milk drawn out from each type of milk.

(a) 58.66

(b) 75.48

(c) 81.23

(d) None of these

25. Assume that the rate of consumption of coal by a locomotive varies as the square of the speed and is 1000 kg per hour when the speed is 60 km per hour. If the coal costs the railway company ₹ 15 per 100 kg and if the other expenses of the train be ₹ 12 per hour, find a formula for the cost in paise per kilometre when the speed is S km per hour.

(a) $1200 + \dfrac{5S^2}{18}$

(b) $1200 + \dfrac{75S^2}{18}$

(c) $\dfrac{1200}{S} + \dfrac{75S}{18}$

(d) None of these

Space for Rough Work

ANSWER KEY

Level of Difficulty (I)

1. (d)	2. (a)	3. (b)	4. (b)
5. (d)	6. (b)	7. (b)	8. (c)
9. (b)	10. (c)	11. (b)	12. (c)
13. (b)	14. (c)	15. (b)	16. (c)
17. (c)	18. (a)	19. (b)	20. (c)
21. (d)	22. (b)	23. (d)	24. (b)
25. (c)	26. (a)	27. (b)	28. (d)
29. (a)	30. (c)	31. (b)	32. (d)
33. (b)	34. (b)	35. (b)	36. (b)
37. (c)	38. (a)	39. (b)	40. (d)
41. (d)	42. (c)	43. (c)	44. (a)
45. (b)	46. (b)	47. (d)	48. (b)
49. (d)	50. (c)		

Level of Difficulty (II)

1. (c)	2. (a)	3. (a)	4. (b)
5. (a)	6. (d)	7. (d)	8. (a)
9. (b)	10. (a)	11. (c)	12. (d)
13. (c)	14. (c)	15. (a)	16. (a)
17. (d)	18. (b)	19. (b)	20. (c)
21. (a)	22. (c)	23. (c)	24. (a)
25. (b)	26. (c)	27. (a)	28. (a)
29. (c)	30. (d)	31. (b)	32. (b)
33. (d)	34. (b)	35. (b)	36. (c)
37. (d)	38. (d)	39. (d)	40. (a)
41. (c)	42. (b)	43. (b)	44. (c)
45. (a)			

Level of Difficulty (III)

1. (a)	2. (a)	3. (a)	4. (a)
5. (a)	6. (a)	7. (c)	8. (b)
9. (a)	10. (a)	11. (c)	12. (a)
13. (c)	14. (b)	15. (a)	16. (b)
17. (b)	18. (d)	19. (d)	20. (c)
21. (b)	22. (a)	23. (d)	24. (b)
25. (c)			

Hints

Level of Difficulty (II)

1. Check the equation: $\dfrac{(x-1)(x+1)}{(x+2)(x-1)} = \dfrac{9}{10}$

Through options

2. $S = k\dfrac{\sqrt{Q}}{N}$ where Q is the quantity of coal used per km and N is the number of carriages.

$$100 = k\frac{\sqrt{2}}{18}$$

$$\therefore \qquad k = \frac{1800}{\sqrt{2}}\ 900\sqrt{2} \text{ and}$$

$$S = 900\sqrt{2} \times \frac{\sqrt{Q}}{N}$$

Then $150 = 900\sqrt{2} \times \dfrac{\sqrt{Q}}{16}$

3. $\dfrac{w_1}{w_2} = \dfrac{r_1^2 t_1}{r_2^2 t_2} = \dfrac{2w_2}{w_2}$

5. $1347 \times 1.125 \times 0.9523$

6. Assume values of a, b and c such that they satisfy $c(a+b) = ab$.

Then $A = a - c$ and $B = c$

8. Number of workers—32 skilled, 20 unskilled and 4 clerks.

Then, wages are divided in the ratio 160 : 40 : 12.

11. $S = 24 - k\sqrt{N}$

13. $y = \dfrac{(x+1)}{(x-1)}, f(y) = \dfrac{\dfrac{x+1}{x-1}+1}{\dfrac{x+1}{x-1}-1} = x$

14. 2000 man weeks = $\dfrac{5}{6}$ of the total work.

$\therefore$ Total work = 2400 man weeks

Work left after disruption = 1400 men weeks.

17–19. Let the running speed be $2x$, then $6x$ and x are the cycling and swimming speeds respectively

Then, $\dfrac{n}{60} = \dfrac{12}{2x} + \dfrac{24}{6x} + \dfrac{5}{x}$ (1)

Also, $\dfrac{n+20}{60} = \dfrac{12}{3y} + \dfrac{24}{8y} + \dfrac{5}{y}$ (2)

And $3y = 2x$ (3)

23. Solve using options

24. Variable cost per boarder = $\dfrac{60 \times 50 - 70 \times 25}{25} = 50$

26–28. Let the contributions be C, $C+1$ and $C+2$. Total Vodka = $3C + 3 = 3(C+1)$

The total Vodka should be divisible into 4 parts. Hence, C can take values like 3, 7, 11 etc.

Proceed with trial and error and check the value for which all conditions are met.

31. The ratio is 7 : 5 : 3

34. Ratios are 3 : 4 and 3 : 5 i.e. 9 : 12 : 20

37. The question asks for a possible answer and not for a definite answer.

44. $D = k\sqrt{h}$

$$k = \frac{14.4}{3\sqrt{2}}$$

Level of Difficulty (III)

1. One alloy contains 33.33% gold, the other contains 40% gold. The mixture must contain 37.5% gold. Solve using alligation.

2. $\dfrac{96}{x} - \dfrac{96}{(x+2)} = 4$ (Required difference). Check using options.

3.
```
33.33            66.66              83.33
|-----------------|-------------------|      gives 1 : 2
1st                                  2nd
Alloy                                Alloy
```

4. Check using options whether the given conditions of mixing are met.
   Option (a) gives : 2.4 kg of zinc @ 80% concentration. i.e. 3 kg alloy of 80% zinc concentration is mixed with 3 kg of pure zinc. Satisfies the given condition.

5. Solve using options the following equation $\dfrac{0.8}{x} - \dfrac{0.6}{10-x} = 0.1$

7. Check the options.

8. 80% aluminium (4: 1) and 25% aluminium (1 : 3) have to be mixed with pure aluminium to obtain an alloy with 60% aluminium.
$$\therefore \quad \frac{10 \times 0.8 + 16 \times 0.25 + x}{10 + 16 + x} = 0.6$$

9. Since the percentage of gold in both alloys is the same, any mixture of the two will contain the same percentage concentration of gold.
   Hence, we get

First alloy :	Gold :	Silver :	Platinum
	30 :	30 :	40

AND Second alloy:	Gold :	Silver :	Platinum
	30 :	26 :	44

10. Let 'w' be the weight of the cut off piece.
    Then, $\dfrac{6-w}{w} = \dfrac{w}{12-w}$

13. First alloy has 37.5% of the first tea type. Similarly, the second alloy has 40% of the first tea type. The mixture should contain 42.85% of the first tea type. This is not possible.

16. When one alloy having 7% gold is mixed with another alloy having no gold, the result is a new alloy with 5% gold. Hence, ratio of mixing is 2 : 5.

19. $10x + (18-x) \times 3 = 110$

20. Out of 8 liters milk and water mixture poured into the 10 liter cask, the milk is $0.25 \times 3 + 0.75 \times 5 = 4.5$.

21. $\dfrac{8}{x} - \dfrac{10}{60-x} = 0.15$.

22. Since the second alloy contains 60% copper, the requirement for the minimisation of copper will be fulfilled by option 2. Note, that the values of the number of kgs required of the second alloy will depend on the value of p.

24. Solve through options.

25. Total cost = Other expenses (paise/km) + Coal cost (paise/km).
    Coal Consumption = $k \times s^2$
    $\therefore \quad 1000 = k \times 60^2$
    $k = \dfrac{5}{18}$ and Coal consumption = $\dfrac{5}{18} \times s^2$
    $\therefore$ Required expression is
    Total cost = $\dfrac{1200}{s} + \dfrac{5}{18} s \times 15$.

Solutions and Shortcuts

Level of Difficulty (I)

1. Solve this question using options. 1/2 of the first part should equal 1/3rd of the second part and $\dfrac{1}{6}$ of the third part. This means that the first part should be divisible by 2, the second one by 3, and the third one by 6. Looking at the options, none of the first 3 options has its third number divisible by 6. Thus, option (d) is correct.

2. $(A + B) = 3 (C + D) \rightarrow A + B$
   $= 375$ and $C + D = 125$.
   Also, since C gets 1.5 times D we have
   $C = 75$ and $D = 50$, and $B = 4 C = 300$.

3. The given condition has a, b and c symmetrically placed. Thus, if we use $a = b = c = 2$ (say) we get each fraction as 1/2.

4. Solve using options. Since $x > y > 0$ it is clear that a ratio of $x{:}y$ as 3:2 fits the equation.

5. $1 : 2 = 3 : 6$ So, $(a^2 + b^2)/(c^2 + d^2) = 5/45 = 1/9$
   From the given options, only ab/cd gives us this value.

6. If you try to solve this question through equations, the process becomes too long and almost inconclusive. The best way to approach this question is by trying to use options.
   The question asks us to find the time in which the boat can move downstream.
   The basic situation in this question is:
   Percentage increase over still water speed while going downstream = Percentage decrease over still water speed while going upstream.
   (Since: $S_{downstream} = S_{boat} + S_{stream}$ and $S_{upstream} = S_{boat} - S_{stream}$)
   Hence, the percentage increase in time while going upstream should match the percentage decrease in time while going downstream in such a way that the percentage change in the speed is same in both the cases).

Testing for option (a):

Time$_{upstream}$ = 84 minutes (given)

Time$_{downstream}$ = 45 minutes (first value from the option)

Time$_{Stillwater}$ = 54 minutes (45 + 9)

% increase in time when going upstream = 30/54

[**Note:** The percentage increase should be written as 30*100/54. However, as I have repeatedly pointed out right from the chapter of percentages, you need to be able to look at % values of ratios directly by using the Percentage rule for calculations)

% decrease in time when going downstream = 9/54 =16.66%

Since, the % decrease is 16.66%, this should correspond to a % increase in speed by 20% (Since, product speed × time is constant).

This means that the speed should drop by 20% while going upstream and hence the time should increase by 25% while going upstream. But, 30/54 does not give us a value of 25% increase. Hence this option is incorrect.

Testing for option (b):

Time$_{upstream}$ = 84 minutes (given)

Time$_{downstream}$ = 63 minutes (first value from the option)

Time$_{Stillwater}$ = 72 minutes (63 + 9)

% increase in time when going upstream = 12/72 = 16.66%

% decrease in time when going downstream = 9/72 =12.5%

Since, the % decrease is 12.5%, this should correspond to a % increase in speed by 14.28% (Since, product speed × time is constant).

This means that the speed should drop by 14.28% while going upstream and hence the time should increase by 16.66% while going upstream. This is actually occurring. Hence, this option is correct.

Options (c) & (d) can be seen to be incorrect in this context.

7. Experimentally if you were to take the value of a, b, c, and d as 1 : 2 : 4 : 8, you get the value of the expression as 3.5. If you try other values for a, b, c and d experimentally you can see that while you can approach 3, you cannot get below that.

For instance,

$$1 : 1.1 :: 1.21 : 1.331$$

Gives us: – 0.331/–0.11 which is slightly greater than 3.

8. 4 × 8 × 5 = 160 man-hours are required for 'x' no. of answer sheets. So, for '2x' answer sheets we would require 320 man-hours = 2 × 20 × n → n = 8 Hours a day.

9. Assume a set of values for a, b, c, d such that they are proportional i.e. a/b = c/d. Suppose we take a:b

as 1:4 and c:d as 3:12 we get the given expression: $(a - b)(a - c)/a = -3 \times -2/1 = 6$. This value is also given by $a + d - b - c$ and hence option (b) is correct.

10. In 40 litres, milk = 32 and water = 8. We want to create 2 : 3 milk to water mixture, for this we would need: 32 milk and 48 water. (Since milk is not increasing). Thus, we need to add 40 litres of water.

11. Option (b) is not true.

12. 1 : 2 : 3 → x, 2x and 3x add up to 36.

So the numbers are: 6, 12 and 18.

Ratio of squares = 36 : 144 : 324.

13. The numbers would be 3x and 4x and their LCM would be 12x. This gives us the values as 45 and 60. The first number is 45.

14. Since equal quantities are being mixed, assume that both alloys have 18 kgs (18 being a number which is the LCM of 9 and 18).

The third alloy will get, 14 kg of argentum from the first alloy and 7 kg of argentum from the second alloy. Hence, the required ratio: 21:15 = 7:5

15. The total number of manhours required = 30 × 7 × 18 = 3780

21 × 8 × no. of days → 3780/168 = 22.5 days

Note, you could have done this directly by: (30 × 7 × 18)/(21 × 8).

16. Solve using options. Option (c) fits the situation as if you take A's income as ₹ 6,000, B's income will become ₹ 4,000 and if they each save ₹ 1,000, their expenditures would be ₹ 5,000 , ₹ 3,000 respectively. This gives the required 5: 3 ratio.

17. The given ratio for sines would only be true for a 45-45-90 triangle. The sides of such a triangle are in the ratio $1:1:\sqrt{2}$. The square of the longest side is 2 while the sum of the squares of the other two sides is also 2. Hence, the required ratio is 1:1.

18. Solve by options. Option (a) C = 480 fits perfectly because if C = 480, B = 120 and A = 80.

19. A's contribution = 33.33%

B's contribution = 50%

C's contribution = 16.66%

Ratio of profit sharing = Ratio of contribution

= 2 : 3 : 1

Thus, profit would be shared as : 28000 : 42000 : 14000.

20. 2x + 20 : 3x + 20 : 5x + 20 = 4 : 5 : 7 → x = 10 and initially the number of students would be 20, 30 and 50 → a total of 100.

21. The ratio of time would be such that speed × time would be constant for all three. Thus if you take the speeds as 2x, 3x and 4x respectively, the times would be 6y, 4y and 3y respectively.

22. Again in order to solve this question, try to assume values for a, b, c and d such that $a:b = c:d$ (i.e. a, b, c and d are proportional). Let us say we assume $a = 1$, $b = 4$, $c = 3$ and $d = 12$ we get:

$a^2 + c^2 = 10$ and $b^2 + d^2 = 160$. The mean proportional between 10 and 160 is 40. $ab + cd$ gives us this value and can be checked by taking another set of values to see that it still works.

23. Option (d) is true since $1/z$ will be greater than 1 and $\sqrt{z}$ would be less then 1.

24. Amar's share should be divisible by 6. Option d gets rejected by this logic.

Further: $A + B + C = 2250$. If Amar's share is 720 (acc. To option a) Bijoy's share should be 480 & Chandra's share should be 300. (Gives us a total of $720 + 480 + 300 = 1500$).

But the required total is 2250 (50% more than 1500). Since all relationships are linear, 1500 will increase to 2250 if we increase all values by 50%. Hence, Amar's share should be 1080.

25. Trial and error would give us 2/5 as the original fraction.

26. Their ratio being 5:3, the difference according to the ratio is 2. But this difference is 10. To get the values, expand the ratio 5 times. This gives 25 and 15 as the required values. Hence, the product is 375.

27. 60 oxen days = 1/7 of the field → 420 oxen days are required to plough the field. Thus, the remaining work would be 360 oxen days. With 18 oxen, it would take 20 days.

28. Assume that 1 cat leap is equal to 3 metres and 1 dog leap is equal to 4 metres.

Then the speed of the cat in one unit time $= 3 \times 5 = 15$ meters.

Also, the speed of the dog in one unit time $= 4 \times 4 = 16$ meters.

The required ratio is 15:16

29. $4x$, and $5x$ are their current ages. According to the problem, $4x - 18 : 5x - 18 = 11:16 \rightarrow x = 10$ and hence the sum total of their present ages is 90 years $(40 + 50)$.

30. $x + 3x + 4x + 7x = 105 \rightarrow x = 7$

Thus, $7x = 49$.

31. The share of the rent is on the basis of the ratio of the number of cow months. A uses 330 cow months (110×3), B uses $660 (110 \times 6)$ and C uses 1320 cow months (440×3)

Hence, the required ratio is: $330:660:1320 = 1:2:4$

32. $10 \times 8 = 80$ man days is required for the job. If only 8 students turn up, they would require 10 days to complete the task. The number of days is increasing by 1/4.

33. The initial amount of water is 9 liters and milk is 27 liters. By adding 15 liters of milk the mixture becomes 42 milk and 9 water → 14:3 the required ratio.

34. From the first statement $A = 1200$ and $B + C = 1800$. From the second statement $C = 1000$ and $A + B = 2000$.

35. $6x + 15 : 5x + 15 = 9 : 8$

$\rightarrow 45x + 135 = 48x + 120$

$3x = 15 \rightarrow x = 5$

Maya's present age $= 6x = 30$

36. Since pressure and volume are inversely proportional, we get that if one is reduced by 20% the other would grow by 25%. Option (b) is correct.

37. Solve using options.

For option (c), 68 girls. Hence, 82 boys

Amount with Girls $= 68 \times 0.25 = 17$

Amount with Boys $= 82 \times 0.5 = 41$.

Total of ₹ 58.

Thus, option (c) fits the conditions.

38. The ratio : 1/2 : 2/3 : 3/4

Converts to 6 : 8 : 9 (on multiplying by 12)

Thus, the first monkey would get $(391/23) \times 6 = 102$ bananas.

39. Let the values of milk and water be $5x$ and x respectively. Then when we add 5 liters of water to this mixture, water would become $x + 5$.

Now: $5x/(x + 5) = 5:2 \rightarrow x = 5$. Thus, $5x$ is 25.

40. The ratio of the values of the three coins are:

$10 \times 10 : 17 \times 20 : 7 \times 100 = 100:340:700$

$= 5:17:35$ is the ratio of division of value of coins.

Thus, 20 paise coins correspond to ₹ 17. Hence, there will be 85 coins.

41. Ratio of no. of coins $= 12 : 10 : 7$

Ratio of individual values of coins $= 1 : 0.5 : 0.25$

Ratio of gross value of coins $= 12 : 5 : 1.75$

$= 48 : 20 : 7 \rightarrow 75$ ₹

Thus, he has ₹ 7 in 25 paisa coins. Which means that he would have 28 such coins.

42. Solve using options. 15/24 becomes 24/33 → 8/11

43. $\dfrac{27 - 11}{35 - 11} = 16/24 = 2/3$.

Thus option (c) is correct.

44. $x = k/(y^2 - 1)$. This gives $k = 24 \times 99 = 2376$.

The equation becomes $x = 2376/(24) = 99$.

45. $x = ky \rightarrow 18 = 7k \rightarrow k = 18/7$

Hence, $x = 18/7 \times y$

When $y = 21, x = 54$.

46. $A = K \times B \times C \rightarrow$ It is known that when $A = 6$, $B = 3$ and $C = 2$. Thus we get $6 = 6K \rightarrow K = 1$.

Thus, our relationship between A, B and C becomes $A = B \times C$. Thus, when $B = 5$ and $C = 7$ we get $A = 35$.

47. $x = ky/z$

We cannot determine the value of k from the given information and hence cannot answer the question.

48. Initial wine = 35 litres

Initial water = 14 litres

Since, we want to create 7 : 4 mixture of wine and water by adding only water, it mean that the amount of wine is constant at 35 litres. Thus 7 : 4 = 35 : 20. So, we need 6 litres of water.

49. If we were to draw out 4 litres of wine and substitute it with plain water, the ratio of wine to water would become 1:1. Hence, option (d) is correct.

50. The overall ratio is: 21:35:55. Dividing 333 in 111 parts (21 + 35 + 55) each part will be 3 and Class III will have the highest number of pupils → 55 × 3 = 165

Level of Difficulty (II)

1. By taking the value of $x = 8$ from Option (c), the required ratio of 9:10 is achieved.

2. $T = KD/V$. $V = (K_1Q^{1/2})/N$ where K and K_1 are constants, T is the time duration of the journey, Q is the quantity of coal used and N is the number of carriages.

    Thus, $T = (KDN)/(K_1Q^{1/2})$ or $T = (K_2DN)/(Q^{1/2})$ → if we take K/K_1 as K_2.

    From the information provided in the question: 30 = $(K_2 \times 50 \times 18)/10$ 24 K_2 = 1/3

    Thus, the equation becomes: $T = (DN)/(3Q^{1/2})$. Then, when $D = 42$, $T = 28$, and $N = 16$ we get:

    $28 = 42 \times 16/(3Q^{1/2})$ → $Q = 64$

3. $\dfrac{2w_2}{w_2} = \dfrac{9r_1^2}{8r_2^2}$

    Thus, $r_1/r_2 = 4:3$

4. Suppose you take $a = 3$ and $b = 2$. It can be clearly seen that the square root of 2 does not lie between 2 and 3. Hence, option c is incorrect.

    Further with these values for a and b option a also can be ruled out since it means that the value should lie between 5 and 6 which it obviously does not.

    Also, Option d gives 6/5 and 1/6. This means that the value should lie between 0.1666 and 1.2 (which it obviously does not). Hence, option (b) is correct.

5. $(1347 \times 1.125)/1.05 = 1443$.

6. The constraint given to us for the values of a, b, and c is

    $$c(a + b) = a \times b$$

    So, if we take $a = 6$, $b = 3$ and $c = 2$, we have 18 = 18 and a feasible set of values for a, b and c respectively. With this set of values, we can complete the operation as defined and see what happens.

A. Wine left in the first vessel = 4 = (6 – 2)

B. Wine in the second vessel = 2

With these values none of the first 3 options matches. Thus, option (d) is correct.

7. The only information available here is that $-b/c$ should be equal to 2/1. This is not sufficient to make any of the first three options as conclusions. Hence, option (d) is correct.

8. The ratio of total salaries will be:

    40:10:3. This gives 53 corresponds to 318. Hence, 1 corresponds to 6.

    Thus the wages are: 240, 60 and 18 respectively.

9. Solve by taking values of a, b, c, d and e, f, g, and h independently of each other

    $$a = 1, b = 2, c = 3, d = 6$$

    and $\qquad e = 3, f = 9, g = 4$

    and $\qquad h = 12$

    gives $\quad (ae + bf) : (ae – bf) = 21: -15 = -7/5$

    Option (b) $(cg + dh)/(cg – dh) = 84/-60 = -7/5$.

10. Since Brass has 0% tin and bronze has 16% tin, the ratio of mixing in the fused mass must be 3:5. Using alligation as follows:

Hence, 6:10 or 3:5

Then, percentage of copper in brass can be got as follows:

x = 64%

11. Speed = $24 - k\sqrt{N}$.

    Putting value of $N = 4$ we get:

    $20 = 24 - 2k$. Hence, $k = 2$

    Thus the equation is: $S = 24 - 2\sqrt{N}$

    This means that when $N = 144$, the speed will become zero. Hence, the train can just move when 143 wagons are attached.

12. x varies as y, means $x = ky$. This does not have any relation to the variance of $x^2 + y^2$.

13. Let $x = 5$

    Then $\qquad f(x) = 6/4 = 1.5 = y$

    And $\qquad f(y) = 2.5/0.5 = 5$.

    Thus, the ratio of $x : f(y) = 1 : 1$

Note: Even if you take some other value of *y*, you would still get the same answer.

14. 2000 man weeks before the rain, 5/6th of the work is completed. Hence, 2400 men weeks will be the total amount of work. However, due to the rain half the work gets washed off → This means that 1000 man weeks worth of work must have got washed off. This leaves 1400 men weeks of work to be completed by the 140 men. They will take 10 more weeks and hence the total time required is 24 weeks.

15. Total distances covered under each mode = 32, 4 and 12 km respectively.

   Total charges = $32 \times 24 + 4 \times 3 + 12 \times 12 = 924$ paise = ₹ 9.24.

16. The no. of coins of 1 Re = $3x$ and 25p = x.

   Conventionally, we can solve this using equations as follows.

$$A + B + C = 220 \quad (1)$$
$$A = 3C \quad (2)$$
$$A + 0.5B + 0.25C = 160 \quad (3)$$

   We have a situation with 3 equations and 3 unknowns. and we can solve for

   A (no. of 1 Re coins),
   B (no. of 50 paise coins)
   and *C* (no. of 25 paise coins)

   However, a much smarter approach would be to go through the options. If we check option (a) – no. of 50 paise coins = 60 we would get the number of 1 Re coins as 120 and the number of 25 paise coins as 40.

$$120 \times 1 + 60 \times 0.5 + 40 \times 0.25 = 160$$

   This fits the conditions perfectly and is hence the correct answer.

17–19. In order to solve this question, if you try going through equation and expressions, it would lead you in to a very long drawn solution.

   Thus: $12/2x + 24/6x + 5/x = n/60$
   and $12/3y + 24/8y + 5/y = n + 20/60$
   We also know that $3y = 2x$.

   In order to handle this expression, you can try be substituting the values of the speeds. Also, we know that his running speed (initially) is twice his swimming speed.

   Question 17 is asking us his swimming speed, while 19 is asking us his running speed. So the answer of the two questions should be in the ratio 1 : 2.

   However, a scrutiny of the options shows us that none of the 4 options (values) in question 17 have a value which is half the values provided for in 19. (you would need to check for this after converting the values into kmph).

   So, we can start by checking individual options from question 19.

   Amongst the 4 values (9, 18, 54, and 12) 12 kmph is the easiest to check.

   Checking for it we have:
   Scenario 1: $12/12 + 24/36 + 5/6 = 1 + 1$ hr + 40 mins + 50 mins = 2 hr 30 minutes.
   Scenario 2: $12/12 + 24/32 + 5/4 = 1$hr + 45 minutes + 1 hr 15 minutes = 3 hrs.

   This doesn't match the condition of 20 minutes extra.

   If you check for 18 kmph, you will get all values fitting in perfectly.

   Scenario 1 would give you 1 hr 40 minutes and Scenario 2 would give you 2 hours.

   Answers are: 17. d
   18. b
   19. b

20. $(20 + 60 + 30x)/(2 + 3 + x) = 23 \rightarrow 80 + 30x = 115 + 23x \rightarrow x = 5$.

21. Assume raw materials cost as 150 and total cost as 450. (Thus, wages cost is 300)

   Since, the cost of raw materials goes up in the ratio of 3:7 the new raw material cost would become 350 and the new wages cost would become in the ratio 4:9 as 675.

   The new cost would become, 1025.

   Since 450 become 1025 (change in total cost), unitary method calculation would give us that 18 would become ₹ 41.

22. Solve using options. For option (c), we will get that initially there are 125 boys and 140 girls. After the given increases, the number of boys would be 145 and the number of girls would become 154 which gives a difference of 9 as required.

23. From the question, it is evident that after leaving out the *C* courses, Sonali's GPA goes to 3.33. This means that the number of subjects she must have had after leaving out the *C*'s must be a multiple of 3. This only occurs in Option c. Hence, that is the answer.

24. When there are 25 boarders, the total expenses are $1750. When there are 50 boarders, the total expenses are $ 3000. The change in expense due to the coming in of 25 boarders is $ 1250. Hence, expense per boarder is equal to $50. This also means that when there are 25 boarders, the variable cost would be $25 \times 50 = \$1250$. Hence, $500 must be the fixed expenses.

   So for 100 boarders, the total cost would be: $ 500 (fixed) + $ 5000 = $5500

25. $S = 42 - k\sqrt{n}$

$$24 = 42 - k \times 3 \rightarrow k = 6$$

So, $\quad S = 42 - 6\sqrt{n}$

For 49 compartments the train would not move. Hence it would move for 48 compartments.

26-28:

Let the third drunkard get in x litres. Then the second will contribute $x + 1$ and the first will contribute $x + 2$ litres. Thus in all they have $3x + 3$ litres of the drink. Using option a in question 27, this value is 12, giving x as 3.

Also, each drunkard will drink 3 litres.

Thus, the first drunkard brings 5 litres and the second 4 litres. Their contribution to the fourth drunkard will be in the ratio 2:1 and hence their share of money would be also in the ratio 2:1. Hence, this option is correct for question 27.

Hence, for question 26, the second drunkard will get 5 roubles (for his contribution of 1 litre to the fourth) and for question 28, the answer would be 1:3

29. $5 : 4 \rightarrow 5 : 4.8 \rightarrow 25 : 24$.

Option (c) is correct.

30. $P = K \times W^2 \rightarrow 12250 = K \times 35^2 \rightarrow K = 10$.

Thus our price and weight relationship is: $P = 10W^2$.

When the two pieces are in the ratio 2:5 (weight wise) then we know that their weights must be 10 grams and 25 grams respectively. Their values would be:

10 gram piece: $10 \times 10^2 = $ ₹ 1000;

25 gram piece: $10 \times 25^2 = $ ₹6250.

Total Price = 1000 + 62450 = 7250. From an initial value of 12250, this represents a loss of ₹ 5000.

31. The ratio of distribution should be:

$21 \times 35 : 15 \times 35 : 15 \times 21 \rightarrow 147 : 105:63 \rightarrow 7:5:3$

The biggest share will be worth: $7 \times 525000/15 = 245000$.

32. $P + M + T = 675 \rightarrow 3M + M + 3M - 25 = 675 \rightarrow 7M = 700$. Hence, $M = 100$. $P = 300$ and $T = 275$.

33. Ratio of distribution = 20 : 13 : 8

So the elephant should get $(20/41) \times 820 = 400$.

34. Women : Men = 3 : 4

Men : Children = 3 : 5

$\rightarrow$ Women : Men : children = 9 : 12 : 20

In the ratio, $9 \rightarrow 531$ Women

Thus, $\quad 20 \rightarrow 1180$ children.

35. 2/3 becomes 7/8 a change from 0.666 to 0.875 while the other changes are smaller than this. For instance 4/7 becomes 9/12 a change from 0.5714 to 0.75 which is smaller than the change in 2/3. Similarly the other options can be checked and rejected.

36. Since, the work gets done in 25% less time there must have been an addition of 33.33% men.

This would mean 13.33 men extra $\rightarrow$ which would mean 14 extra men (in whole nos.)

37. From the given options, we just need to look for a multiple of 7. 2100 is the only option which is a multiple of 7 and is hence the correct answer.

38. This is a simple question if you can catch hold of the logic of the question. i.e. the younger daughter's share must be such after adding a CI of 20% for two years, she should get the same value as her elder sister.

None of the options meets this requirement. Hence, None of these is correct.

39-41. You should realise that when Anshu gives her pens to Bobby & Chandana, the number of pens for both Bobby & Chandana should double. Also, the number of pens for Anshu & Bobby should also double when Chandana gives off her pens. Further the final condition is that each of them has 24 pens. The following table will emerge on the basis of this logic.

	Anshu	Bobby	Chandana
Final	24	24	24
Second round	12	12	48
Initial	42	6	24

42. $V = k\,AH \rightarrow 280 = k \times 60 \times 14 \rightarrow 280 = 840k$. Thus, $k = 1/3$ and the equation becomes:

$V = AH/3$ and $390 = 26A/3 \rightarrow A = 45$.

43. Expenses for 120 boys = 8400

Expenses for 150 boys = 10000.

Thus, variable expenses are ₹ 1600 for 30 boys.

If we add 180 more boys to make it 330 boys, we will get an additional expense of $1600 \times 6 = $ ₹ 9600.

Total expenses are ₹ 19600.

44. Let the distance be d. Then, $d/14.4 = \sqrt{8}/\sqrt{18} \rightarrow d = 9.6$

45. 47 : 100: 220 would give: 0.5 cubic feet of Cement, 1cubic feet of sand and 2 cubic feet of gravel. Required ratio. 1 : 2 : 4 is satisfied.

Level of Difficulty (III)

1. You can use alligation between 33.33% and 40% to get 37.5%. Hence the ratio of mixing must be 2.5:4.16 $\rightarrow$ 3:5

6. Check each of the options as follows:

Suppose you are checking option b which gives the value of a as 81 litres.

Then, it is clear that when you are pouring out 81 litres, you are leaving 8/9 of the honey in the barrel. Thus the amount of honey contained after 6 such operations will be given by:

$729 \times (8/9)^6$. If this answer has to be correct this value must be equal to 64 (which it clearly is not since the value will be in the form of a fraction.)

Hence, this is not the correct option. You can similarly rule out the other options.

7. It is clear that if 7 kg of the first is mixed with 21 kg of the second you will get $5 + 9 = 14$ kg of nickel and 14 kg of tin. You do not need to check the other options since they will go into fractions.

10. The piece that is cut off should be such that the fraction of the first to the second alloy in each of the two new alloys formed should be equal.

    If you cut off 4 kg, the respective ratios will be:

    First alloy: 2 kg of first alloy and 4 kg of second alloy

    Second alloy: 4 kg of first alloy and 8 kg of the second alloy. It can easily be seen that the ratios are equal to 1:2 in each case.

13. This is again the typical alligation situation.

    The required ratio will be given by $(7/18 - 3/8)$: $(2/5 - 7/18)$

Alternately, you can also look at it through options. It can be easily seen that if you take 8 kg of the first with 10 kg of the second you will get the required 7:11 ratio.

17. The cost of making one gram of gun powder would be ₹ 180. This will contain 0.4 gm of saltpetre and 0.6 gm of nitrous oxide. Check through options.

    At the rate of saltpetre of 300/gm, the nitrous oxide will cost ₹100/gm. The total cost of 0.4 grams of saltpetre will be 120 and 0.6 grams of nitrous oxide will be ₹ 60 giving the total cost as 180.

20. There will be a total of 4.5 litres of milk (25% of 3 + 75% of 5) giving a total of 4.5. Hence, 45%.

23. Go through the options as follows:

    According to option d, if the initial quantity of spirit is 4 litres, half the spirit is taken out when 2 litres are drawn out. Thus the spirit after three times of the operation would be:

    $4 \times (1/2)^2 = 0.5$ litres. This matches the option. You can check for yourself that the first three options will not work.

9 Chapter
Time and Work

INTRODUCTION

The concept of time and work is another important topic for the aptitude exams. Questions on this chapter have been appearing regularly over the past decade in all aptitude exams. Questions on Time and Work have regularly appeared in the CAT especially in its online format.

Theory

In the context of the CAT, you have to understand the following basic concepts of this chapter:

If A does a work in a days, then in one day A does $\rightarrow \dfrac{1}{a}$ of the work.

If B does a work in b days, then in one day B does $\rightarrow \dfrac{1}{b}$ of the work.

Then, in one day, if A and B work together, then their combined work is $\dfrac{1}{a} + \dfrac{1}{b}$.

or $\dfrac{a+b}{ab}$

In the above case, we take the total work to be done as "1 unit of work". Hence, the work will be completed when 1 unit of work is completed.

For example, if A can do a work in 10 days and B can do the same work in 12 days, then the work will be completed in how many days.

One day's work = 1/10 + 1/12 = (12 + 10)/120

[Taking LCM of the denominators]

= 22/120

Then the number of days required to complete the work is 120/22.

Note that this is a reciprocal of the fraction of work done in one day. This is a benefit associated with solving time and work through fractions. It can be stated as—the number of time periods required to complete the full work will be the reciprocal of the fraction of the work done in one time period.

ALTERNATIVE APPROACH

Instead of taking the value of the total work as 1 unit of work, we can also look at the total work as 100 per cent work. In such a case, the following rule applies:

If A does a work in a days, then in one day A does $\rightarrow \dfrac{100}{a}$% of the work.

If B does a work in b days, then in one day B does $\rightarrow \dfrac{100}{b}$% of the work.

Then, in one day, if A and B work together, then their combined work is

$$\dfrac{100}{a} + \dfrac{100}{b}$$

This is often a very useful approach to look at the concept of time and work because thinking in terms of percentages gives a direct and clear picture of the actual quantum of work done.

What I mean to say is that even though we can think in either a percentage or a fractional value to solve the problem, there will be a thought process difference between the two.

Thinking about work done as a percentage value gives us a linear picture of the quantum of the work that has been done and the quantum of the work that is to be done. On the other hand, if we think of the work done as a fractional value, the thought process will have to be slightly longer to get a full understanding of the work done.

For instance, we can think of work done as 7/9 or 77.77%. The percentage value makes it clear as to how much quantum is left. The percentage value can be visualised on the number line, while the fractional value requires a mental inversion to fully understand the quantum.

An additional advantage of the percentage method of solving time and work problems would be the elimination of the need to perform cumbersome fraction additions involving LCMs of denominators.

However, you should realise that this would work only if you are able to handle basic percentage calculations involving standard decimal values. If you have really internalised the techniques of percentage calculations given in the chapter of percentages, then you can reap the benefits for this chapter.

The benefit of using this concept will become abundantly clear by solving through percentages the same example that was solved above using fractions.

Example: If A can do a work in 10 days and B can do the same work in 12 days, then the work will be completed in how many days.

One day's work = 10% + 8.33% = 18.33% (Note, no LCMs required here)

Hence, to do 100% work, it will require: 100/18.33.

This can be solved by adding 18.33 mentally to get between 5–6 days. Then on you can go through options and mark the closest answer.

The process of solving through percentages will yield rich dividends if and only if you have adequate practice on adding standard percentage values. Thus, $18.33 \times 5 = 91.66$ should not give you any headaches and should be done while reading for the first time.

Thus a thought process chart for this question should look like this.

If A can do a work in 10 days ($\rightarrow$ means 10% work) and B can do the same work in 12 days ($\rightarrow$ 8.33% work $\rightarrow$ 18.33% work in a day in 5 days 91.66% work $\rightarrow$ leaves 8.33% work to be done $\rightarrow$ which can be done in 8.33/18.33 of a day = 5/11 of a day (since both the numerator and the denominator are divisible by 1.66), then the work will be completed in $5\frac{5}{11}$ days.

The entire process can be done mentally.

The Concept of Negative Work

Suppose, that A and B are working to build a wall while C is working to break the wall. In such a case, the wall is being built by A and B while it is being broken by C. Here, if we consider the work as the building of the wall, we can say that C is doing negative work.

Example: A can build a wall in 10 days and B can build it in 5 days, while C can completely destroy the wall in 20 days. If they start working at the same time, in how many days will the work be completed.

Solution: The net combined work per day here is:

A's work + B's work – C's work = 10% + 20% – 5% = 25% work in one day.

Hence, the work will get completed (100% work) in 4 days.

The concept of negative work commonly appears as a problem based on pipes and cisterns, where there are inlet pipes and outlet pipes/leaks which are working against each other.

If we consider the work to be filling a tank, the inlet pipe does positive work while the outlet pipe/leak does negative work.

Application of Product Constancy Table to Time and Work

The equation that applies to Time and Work problems is

$$\text{Work Rate} \times \text{Time} = \text{Work done}$$

This equation means that if the work done is constant, then $\rightarrow$

Work rate is inversely proportional to time. Hence, the Product Constancy Table will be directly applicable to time and work questions.

[Notice the parallelism between this formula and the formula of time speed and distance, where again there is product constancy between speed and time if the distance is constant.]

Time is usually in days or hours although any standard unit of time can be used. The unit of time that has to be used in a question is usually decided by the denominator of the unit of work rate.

Here, there are two ways of defining the Work rate.

(a) In the context of situations where individual working efficiencies or individual time requirements are given in the problem, the work rate is defined by the unit: Work done per unit time.

In this case, the total work to be done is normally considered to be 1 (if we solve through fractions) or 100% (if we solve through percentages).

Thus, in the solved problem above, when we calculated that A and B together do 18.33% work in a day, this was essentially a statement of the rate of work of A and B together.

Then the solution proceeded as:

18.33% work per day × No. of days required = 100% work

Giving us: the no. of days required = $100/18.33 = 5\frac{5}{11}$

(b) In certain types of problems (typically those involving projects that are to be completed), where a certain category of worker has the same rate of working, the Work rate will be defined as the number of workers of a particular category working on the project.

For instance, questions where all men work at a certain rate, the work rate when 2 men are working together will be double the work rate when 1 man is working alone. Similarly, the work rate when 10 men are working together will be 10 times the work rate when 1 man is working alone.

In such cases, the work to be done is taken as the number of man-days required to finish the work.

Note, for future reference, that the *work to be done can also be measured in terms of the volume of work defined in the context of day-to-day life.*

For example, the volume of a wall to be built, the number of people to be interviewed, the number of *chapattis* to be made and so on.

WORK EQUIVALENCE METHOD (To Solve Time and Work Problems)

The work equivalence method is nothing but an application of the formula:

Work rate × Time = Work done (or work to be done)

Thus, if the work to be done is doubled, the product of *work rate × time* also has to be doubled. Similarly, if the work to be done increases by 20%, the product of *work rate × time* also has to be increased by 20% and so on.

This method is best explained by an example:

A contractor estimates that he will finish the road construction project in 100 days by employing 50 men.

However, at the end of the 50th day, when as per his estimation half the work should have been completed, he finds that only 40% of his work is done.

(a) How many more days will be required to complete the work?
(b) How many more men should he employ in order to complete the work in time?

Solution:

(a) The contactor has completed 40% of the work in 50 days.

If the number of men working on the project remains constant, the rate of work also remains constant. Hence, to complete 100% work, he will have to complete the remaining 60% of the work.

For this he would require **75** more days. (This calculation is done using the unitary method.)

(b) In order to complete the work on time, it is obvious that he will have to increase the number of men working on the project.

This can be solved as:

50 men working for 50 days → 50 × 50 = 2500 man-days.

2500 man-days has resulted in 40% work completion. Hence, the total work to be done in terms of the number of man-days is got by using unitary method:

Work left = 60% = 2500 × 1.5 = 3750 man-days

This has to be completed in 50 days. Hence, the number of men required per day is 3750/50 = 75 men.

Since, 50 men are already working on the project, the contractor needs to hire 25 more men.

[Note, this can be done using the percentage change graphic for product change. Since, the number of days is constant at 50, the 50% increase in work from 40% to 60% is solely to be met by increasing the number of men. Hence, the number of men to be increased is 50% of the original number of men = 25 men.]

The Specific Case of Building a Wall (Work as Volume of Work)

As already mentioned, in certain cases, the unit of work can also be considered to be in terms of the volume of work. For example, building of a wall of a certain length, breadth and height.

In such cases, the following formula applies:

$$\frac{L_1 B_1 H_1}{L_2 B_2 H_2} = \frac{m_1 t_1 d_1}{m_2 t_2 d_2}$$

where L, B and H are respectively the length, breadth and height of the wall to be built, while m, t and d are respectively the number of men, the amount of time per day and the number of days. Further, the suffix 1 is for the first work situation, while the suffix 2 is for the second work situation.

Consider the following problem:

Example: 20 men working 8 hours a day can completely build a wall of length 200 meters, breadth 10 metres and height 20 metres in 10 days. How many days will 25 men working 12 hours a day require to build a wall of length 400 meters, breadth 10 metres and height of 15 metres.

This question can be solved directly by using the formula above

$$\frac{L_1 B_1 H_1}{L_2 B_2 H_2} = \frac{m_1 t_1 d_1}{m_2 t_2 d_2}$$

Here,	L_1 is 200 metres	L_2 is 400 metres
	B_1 is 10 metres	B_2 is 10 metres
	H_1 is 20 metres	H_2 is 15 metres
while	m_1 is 20 men	m_2 is 25 men
	d_1 is 10 days	d_2 is unknown
and	t_1 is 8 hours a day	t_2 is 12 hours a day

Then we get $(200 × 10 × 20)/(400 × 10 × 15) = (20 × 8 × 10)/(25 × 12 × d_2)$

$\therefore$ $\qquad$ $d_2 = 5.333/0.6666 = 8$ days

Alternatively, you can also directly write the equation as follows:

$d_2 = 10 \times (400/200) \times (10/10) \times (20/15) \times (20/25) \times (8/12)$

This can be done by thinking of the problem as follows:

The number of days have to be found out in the second case. Hence, on the LHS of the equation write down the unknown and on the RHS of the equation write down the corresponding knowns.

$d_2 = 10 \times \ldots$

Then, the length of the wall has to be factored in. There are only two options for doing so. viz:

Multiplying by 200/400 (< 1, which will reduce the number of days) or multiplying by 400/200 (>1, which will increase the number of days).

The decision of which one of these is to be done is made on the basis of the fact that when the length of the wall is increasing, the number of days required will also increase.

Hence, we take the value of the fraction greater than 1 to get

$d_2 = 10 \times (400/200)$

We continue in the same way to get

No change in the breadth of the wall → hence, multiply by 10/10 (no change in d_2)

Height of the wall is decreasing → hence, multiply by 15/20 (< 1 to reduce d_2)

Number of men working is increasing → hence, multiply by 20/25 (< 1 to reduce d_2)

Number of hours per day is increasing → hence, multiply by 8/12 (< 1 to reduce the number of days)

Space for Notes

The Concept of Efficiency

The concept of efficiency is closely related to the concept of work rate.

When we make a statement saying A is twice as efficient as B, we mean to say that A does twice the work as B in the same time. In other words, we can also understand this as A will require half the time required by B to do the same work.

In the context of efficiency, another statement that you might come across is A is two times more efficient than B. This is the same as A is thrice as efficient as B or A does the same work as B in 1/3rd of the time.

Equating Men, Women and Children This is directly derived from the concept of efficiencies.

Example: 8 men can do a work in 12 days while 20 women can do it in 10 days. In how many days can 12 men and 15 women complete the same work.

Solution: Total work to be done = $8 \times 12 = 96$ man-days.
or total work to be done = $20 \times 10 = 200$ woman-days.

Since, the work is the same, we can equate 96 man-days = 200 woman-days.

Hence, 1 man-day = 2.08333 woman-days.

Now, if 12 men and 15 women are working on the work we get

12 men are equal to $12 \times 2.08333 = 25$ women

Hence, the work done per day is equivalent to $25 + 15$ women working per day.

That is, 40 women working per day.

Hence, $40 \times$ no. of days = 200 woman days
Number of days = 5 days.

🎯 WORKED-OUT PROBLEMS

Problem 9.1 *A* can do a piece of work in 10 days and *B* in 12 days. Find how much time they will take to complete the work under the following conditions:

(a) Working together

(b) Working alternately starting with *A*.

(c) Working alternately starting with *B*.

(d) If *B* leaves 2 days before the actual completion of the work.

(e) If *B* leaves 2 days before the scheduled completion of the work.

(f) If another person *C* who does negative work (i.e. works against *A* and *B* and can completely destroy the work in 20 days) joins them and they work together all the time.

Solution

(a) 1 day's work for *A* is 1/10 and 1 day's work for *B* is 1/12.

Then, working together, the work in one day is equal to:

$\frac{1}{10} + \frac{1}{12} = \frac{11}{60}$ of the work. Thus working together they

need 60/11 days to complete the work → 5.45 days.

Alternately, you can use percentage values to solve the above question:

A's work =10%, *B*'s work = 8.33%. Hence, *A* + *B* = 18.33% of the work in one day.

Hence, to complete 100% work, we get the number of days required = 100/18.33 → 5.55 days.

This can be calculated as

@ 18.33% per day in 5 days, they will cover 18.33 × 5 = 91.66%. (The decimal value 0.33 is not difficult to handle if you have internalised the fraction to percentage conversion table of the chapter of percentages).

Work left on the sixth day is: 8.33%, which will require: 8.33/18.33 of the sixth day.

Since, both these numbers are divisible by 1.66 we get 5/11 of the sixth day will be used → 0.45 of the sixth day is used.

Hence, 5.45 days are required to finish the work.

Note: Although the explanation to the question through percentages seems longer, the student should realise that if the values in the fraction-to-percentage table is internalised by the student, the process of solution through percentage will take much lesser time because we are able to eliminate the need for the calculation of LCMs, which are often cumbersome. (if the numbers in the problem are those that are covered in the fraction to percentage conversion table). In fact, the percentage method allows for solving while reading.

(b) Working alternately: When two people are working alternately the question has to be solved by taking 2 days as a unit of time instead of 1 day.

So in (a) above, the work done in 1 day will be covered in 2 days here.

Thus, in 2 days the work done will be 18.33%. In 10 days it will be 91.66%. On the 11th day *A* works by himself.

But *A*'s work in 1 day is 10%. Therefore, he will require 4/5 of the 11th day to finish the work.

(c) Working alternately starting with *B*: Here, there will be no difference in work completed by the 10th day. On the 11th day, *B* works alone and does 8.33% of the work (which was required to complete the work). Hence, the whole of the 11th day will get used.

(d) If *B* leaves 2 days before the actual completion of the work: In this case, the actual completion of the work is after 2 days of *B*'s leaving. This means, that *A* has worked alone for the last 2 days to complete the work. But *A* does, 10% work in a day. Hence, *A* and *B* must have done 80% of the work together (@18.33% per day). Then, the answer can be found by

80/18.33 + 20/10 days.

Note: For calculation of 80/18.33, we can use the fact that the decimal value is a convenient one. If they worked together they would complete 73.33% of the work in 4 days and the work that they would have done on the 5th day would be 6.66%.

At the rate of 18.33% work per day while working together, they would work together for 6.66/18.33 of the 5th day. Since both the numerator and denominator are divisible by 1.66 the above ratio is converted into 4/11 = 0.3636.

Hence, they work together for 4.3636 days after which *B* leaves and then *A* completes the work in 2 more days. Hence, the time required to finish the work would be = 6.3636 days.

(e) If *B* leaves 2 days before the scheduled completion of the work: Completion of the work would have been scheduled assuming that *A* and *B* both worked together for completing the work (say, this is *x* days). Then, the problem has to be viewed as *x* – 2 days was the time for which *A* and *B* worked together. The residual amount of work left (which will be got by 2 days work of *A* and *B* together) would be done by *A* alone at his own pace of work.

Thus we can get the solution by:

Number of days required to complete the work =

$$[(100/18.33) - 2] + \frac{36.66}{10}$$

(f) If C joins the group and does negative work, we can see that one day's work of the three together would be

A's work + B's work − C's work = 10% + 8.33% − 5% = 13.33%

Hence, the work will be completed in (100/13.33) days.

[*Note:* This can be calculated by $13.33 \times 7 = 13 \times 7 + 0.33 \times 7 = 93.33$.

Then, work left = 6.66, which will require half a day more at the rate of 13.33% per day.

Advantage of Solving Problems on Time and Work through Percentages

Students should understand here, that most of the times the values given for the number of days in which the work is completed by a worker will be convenient values like: 60 days, 40 days, 30 days, 25 days, 24 days, 20 days, 16 days, 15 days, 12 days, 11 days, 10 days, 9 days, 8 days, 7 days, 6 days, 5 days, 4 days, 3 days and 2 days. All these values for the number of days will yield convenient decimal values. If your fraction to percentage table is internalised, you can use the process of solving while reading by taking the percentage of work done per day process rather than getting delayed by the need to find LCM's while solving through the process of the fraction of work done per day.]

Problem 9.2 A contractor undertakes to build a wall in 50 days. He employs 50 people for the same. However, after 25 days he finds that the work is only 40% complete. How many more men need to be employed to:

(a) complete the work in time?

Solution In order to complete the work in time, the contractor has to finish the remaining 60% of the work in 25 days.

Now, in the first 25 days the work done = 50×25 =1250 man-days → 40% of the work.

Hence, work left = 60% of the work = 1875 man-days.

Since, 25 days are left to complete the task, the number of people required is 1875/25 = 75 men.

Since, 50 men are already working, 25 more men are needed to complete the work.

Thought process should go like: 1250 → 40% of work. Hence, 1875 man-days required to complete the work.

Since there are only 25 days left, we need 1875/25 = 75 men to complete the work.

(b) Complete the work 10 days before time?

For this purpose, we have to do 1875 man-days of work in 15 days. Hence, men = 1875/15 = 125 men.

Problem 9.3 For the previous problem, if the contractor continues with the same workforce:

(a) how many days behind schedule will the work be finished?

Solution He has completed 40% work in 25 days. Hence, to complete the remaining 60% of the work, he would require 50% more days (i.e. 37.5 days) (Since, 60% is 1.5 times of 40%)

Hence, the work would be done 12.5 days behind schedule.

(b) how much increase in efficiency is required from the work force to complete the work in time?

Solution If the number of men working is kept constant, the only way to finish the work in time is by increasing the efficiency so that more work is done every man-day. This should be mathematically looked at as follows: Suppose, that 1 man-day takes care of 1 unit of work. Then, in the first 25 days, work done = 25 (days) × 50 (men) × 1 (work unit per man-day) = 1250 units of work. Now, this 1250 units of work is just 40% of the work. Hence, work left = 1875 units of work.

Then, 25 (days) × 50 (men) × z (work units per man-day) = 1875 → $z = 1.5$

Thus, the work done per man-day has to rise from 1 to 1.5, that is, by 50%. Hence, the efficiency of work has to rise by **50%.**

Problem 9.4 A is twice as efficient as B. If they complete a work in 30 days find the times required by each to complete the work individually.

Solution When we say that A is twice as efficient as B, it means that A takes half the time that B takes to complete the same work.

Thus, if we denote A's 1 day's work as A and B's one day's work as B, we have

$$A = 2B$$

Then, using the information in the problem, we have: 30 A + 30 B = 100% work

That is, 90 B = 100% work → $B = 1.11$ % (is the work done by B in 1 day) → B requires **90 days** to complete the work alone.

Since, $A = 2B$ → we have $A = 2.22$ % → A requires 45 days to do the work alone.

You should be able to solve this mentally with the following thought process while reading for the first time:

$\frac{100}{30} = 3.33\%$. $\frac{3.33}{3} = 1.11\%$. Hence, work done is 1.11% per day and 2.22% per day → 90 and 45 days.

Problem 9.5 A is two times more efficient than B. If they complete a work in 30 days, then find the times required by each to complete the work individually.

Solution Interpret the first sentence as $A = 3B$ and solve according to the process of the previous problem to get the answers. (You should get A takes 40 days and B takes 120 days.)

LEVEL OF DIFFICULTY (I)

1. Raju can do 25% of a piece of work in 5 days. How many days will he take to complete the work ten times?
   - (a) 150 days
   - (b) 250 days
   - (c) 200 days
   - (d) 180 days

2. 6 men can do a piece of work in 12 days. How many men are needed to do the work in 18 days.
   - (a) 3 men
   - (b) 6 men
   - (c) 4 men
   - (d) 2 men

3. *A* can do a piece of work in 20 days and *B* can do it in 15 days. How long will they take if both work together?
   - (a) $8\left(\dfrac{6}{7}\right)$ days
   - (b) $8\left(\dfrac{4}{7}\right)$ days
   - (c) $9\left(\dfrac{3}{7}\right)$ days
   - (d) $9\left(\dfrac{4}{7}\right)$ days

4. In question 3 if *C*, who can finish the same work in 25 days, joins them, then how long will they take to complete the work?
   - (a) $6\left(\dfrac{18}{47}\right)$ days
   - (b) 12 days
   - (c) $2\left(\dfrac{8}{11}\right)$ days
   - (d) $47\left(\dfrac{6}{18}\right)$ days

5. Nishu and Archana can do a piece of work in 10 days and Nishu alone can do it in 12 days. In how many days can Archana do it alone?
   - (a) 60 days
   - (b) 30 days
   - (c) 50 days
   - (d) 45 days

6. Baba alone can do a piece of work in 10 days. Anshu alone can do it in 15 days. If the total wages for the work is ₹ 50. How much should Baba be paid if they work together for the entire duration of the work?
   - (a) ₹ 30
   - (b) ₹ 20
   - (c) ₹ 50
   - (d) ₹ 40

7. 4 men and 3 women finish a job in 6 days, and 5 men and 7 women can do the same job in 4 days. How long will 1 man and 1 woman take to do the work?
   - (a) $22\left(\dfrac{2}{7}\right)$ days
   - (b) $25\left(\dfrac{1}{2}\right)$ days
   - (c) $5\left(\dfrac{1}{7}\right)$ days
   - (d) $12\left(\dfrac{7}{22}\right)$ days

8. If 8 boys and 12 women can do a piece of work in 25 days, in how many days can the work be done by 6 boys and 11 women working together?
   - (a) 15 days
   - (b) 10 days
   - (c) 12 days
   - (d) Cannot be determined

9. *A* can do a piece of work in 10 days and *B* can do the same work in 20 days. With the help of *C*, they finish the work in 5 days. How long will it take for *C* alone to finish the work?
   - (a) 20 days
   - (b) 10 days
   - (c) 35 days
   - (d) 15 days

10. *A* can do a piece of work in 20 days. He works at it for 5 days and then *B* finishes it in 10 more days. In how many days will *A* and *B* together finish the work?
    - (a) 8 days
    - (b) 10 days
    - (c) 12 days
    - (d) 6 days

11. *A* and *B* undertake to do a piece of work for ₹ 100. *A* can do it in 5 days and *B* can do it in 10 days. With the help of *C*, they finish it in 2 days. How much should *C* be paid for his contribution?
    - (a) ₹ 40
    - (b) ₹ 20
    - (c) ₹ 60
    - (d) ₹ 30

12. Twenty workers can finish a piece of work in 30 days. After how many days should 5 workers leave the job so that the work is completed in 35 days?
    - (a) 5 days
    - (b) 10 days
    - (c) 15 days
    - (d) 20 days

13. Arun and Vinay together can do a piece of work in 7 days. If Arun does twice as much work as Vinay in a given time, how long will Arun alone take to do the work.
    - (a) 6.33 days
    - (b) 10.5 days
    - (c) 11 days
    - (d) 72 days

14. Subhash can copy 50 pages in 10 hours; Subhash and Prakash together can copy 300 pages in 40 hours. In how much time can Prakash copy 30 pages?
    - (a) 13 h
    - (b) 12 h
    - (c) 11 h
    - (d) 9 h

15. *X* number of men can finish a piece of work in 30 days. If there were 6 men more, the work could be finished in 10 days less. What is the original number of men?
    - (a) 10
    - (b) 11
    - (c) 12
    - (d) 15

16. Sashi can do a piece of work in 25 days and Rishi can do it in 20 days. They work for 5 days and then

Sashi goes away. In how many more days will Rishi finish the work?
   (a) 10 days   (b) 12 days
   (c) 14 days   (d) None of these

17. Raju can do a piece of work in 10 days, Vicky in 12 days and Tinku in 15 days. They all start the work together, but Raju leaves after 2 days and Vicky leaves 3 days before the work is completed. In how many days is the work completed?
   (a) 5 days   (b) 6 days
   (c) 7 days   (d) 8 days

18. Sambhu can do 1/2 of the work in 8 days while Kalu can do 1/3 of the work in 6 days. How long will it take for both of them to finish the work?
   (a) $\frac{88}{17}$ days   (b) $\frac{144}{17}$ days
   (c) $\frac{72}{17}$ days   (d) 8 days

19. Manoj takes twice as much time as Anjay and thrice as much as Vijay to finish a piece of work. Together they finish the work in 1 day. What is the time taken by Manoj to finish the work?
   (a) 6 days   (b) 3 days
   (c) 2 days   (d) 4 days

20. An engineer undertakes a project to build a road 15 km long in 300 days and employs 45 men for the purpose. After 100 days, he finds only 2.5 km of the road has been completed. Find the (approx.) number of extra men he must employ to finish the work in time.
   (a) 43   (b) 45
   (c) 55   (d) 68

21. Apurva can do a piece of work in 12 days. Apurva and Amit complete the work together and were paid ₹ 54 and ₹ 81 respectively. How many days must they have taken to complete the work together?
   (a) 4 days   (b) 4.5 days
   (c) 4.8 days   (d) 5 days

22. Raju is twice as good as Vijay. Together, they finish the work in 14 days. In how many days can Vijay alone do the same work?
   (a) 16 days   (b) 21 days
   (c) 32 days   (d) 42 days

23. In a company XYZ Ltd. a certain number of engineers can develop a design in 40 days. If there were 5 more engineers, it could be finished in 10 days less. How many engineers were there in the beginning?
   (a) 18   (b) 20
   (c) 25   (d) 15

24. If 12 men and 16 boys can do a piece of work in 5 days and 13 men and 24 boys can do it in 4 days,

compare the daily work done by a man with that done by a boy?
   (a) 1:2   (b) 1:3
   (c) 2:1   (d) 3:1

25. A can do a work in 10 days and B can do the same work in 20 days. They work together for 5 days and then A goes away. In how many more days will B finish the work?
   (a) 5 days   (b) 6.5 days
   (c) 10 days   (d) $8\frac{1}{3}$ days

26. 30 men working 5 h a day can do a work in 16 days. In how many days will 20 men working 6 h a day do the same work?
   (a) $22\frac{1}{2}$ days   (b) 20 days
   (c) 21 days   (d) None of these

27. Ajay and Vijay undertake to do a piece of work for ₹ 200. Ajay alone can do it in 24 days while Vijay alone can do it in 30 days. With the help of Pradeep, they finish the work in 12 days. How much should Pradeep get for his work?
   (a) ₹ 20   (b) ₹ 100
   (c) ₹ 180   (d) ₹ 50

28. 15 men could finish a piece of work in 210 days. But at the end of 100 days, 15 additional men are employed. In how many more days will the work be complete?
   (a) 80 days   (b) 60 days
   (c) 55 days   (d) 50 days

29. Ajay, Vijay and Sanjay are employed to do a piece of work for ₹ 529. Ajay and Vijay together are supposed to do 19/23 of the work and Vijay and Sanjay together 8/23 of the work. How much should Ajay be paid?
   (a) ₹ 245   (b) ₹ 295
   (c) ₹ 300   (d) ₹ 345

30. Anmol is thrice as good a workman as Vinay and therefore is able to finish the job in 60 days less than Vinay. In how many days will they finish the job working together?
   (a) $22\left(\frac{1}{2}\right)$ days   (b) $11\left(\frac{3}{2}\right)$ days
   (c) 15 days   (d) 20 days

31. In a fort there was sufficient food for 200 soldiers for 31 days. After 27 days 120 soldiers left the fort. For how many extra days will the rest of the food last for the remaining soldiers?
   (a) 12 days   (b) 10 days
   (c) 8 days   (d) 6 days

32. Anju, Manju and Sanju together can reap a field in 6 days. If Anju can do it alone in 10 days and Manju

in 24 days. In how many days will Sanju alone be able to reap the field?

(a) 40 days   (b) 36 days

(c) 35 days   (d) 32 days

33. Ajay and Vijay can do a piece of work in 28 days. With the help of Manoj, they can finish it in 21 days. How long will Manoj take to finish the work all alone?

(a) 84 days   (b) 80 days

(c) 75 days   (d) 70 days

34. Ashok and Mohan can do a piece of work in 12 days. Mohan and Binod together do it in 15 days. If Ashok is twice as good a workman as Binod. In how much time will Mohan alone can do the work?

(a) 15 days   (b) 20 days

(c) 25 days   (d) 35 days

35. Ajay and Vijay together can do a piece of work in 6 days. Ajay alone does it in 10 days. What time does Vijay require to do it alone?

(a) 20 days   (b) 15 days

(c) 25 days   (d) 30 days

36. A cistern is normally filled in 5 hours. However, it takes 6 hours when there is leak in its bottom. If the cistern is full, in what time shall the leak empty it?

(a) 6 h   (b) 5 h

(c) 30 h   (d) 15 h

37. Pipe A and B running together can fill a cistern in 6 minutes. If B takes 5 minutes more than A to fill the cistern, then the time in which A and B will fill the cistern separately will be respectively?

(a) 15 min, 20 min   (b) 15 min, 10 min

(c) 10 min, 15 min   (d) 25 min, 20 min

38. A can do a work in 18 days, B in 9 days and C in 6 days. A and B start working together and after 2 days C joins them. In how many days will the job be completed?

(a) 4.33 days   (b) 4 days

(c) 4.66 days   (d) 5 days

39. 24 men working 8 h a day can finish a work in 10 days. Working at a rate of 10 h a day, the number of men required to finish the work in 6 days is

(a) 30   (b) 32

(c) 34   (d) 36

40. A certain job was assigned to a group of men to do it in 20 days. But 12 men did not turn up for the job and the remaining men did the job in 32 days. The original number of men in group was

(a) 32   (b) 34

(c) 36   (d) 40

41. 12 men complete a work in 18 days. 6 days after they had started working, 4 men join them. How many more days will all of them take to complete the remaining work?

(a) 10 days   (b) 12 days

(c) 15 days   (d) 9 days

42. A takes 5 days more than B to do a certain job and 9 days more than C; A and B together can do the job in the same time as C. How many days A would take to do it?

(a) 16 days   (b) 10 days

(c) 15 days   (d) 20 days

43. A cistern is normally filled in 6 h but takes 4 h longer to fill because of a leak in its bottom. If the cistern is full, the leak will empty it in how much time?

(a) 15 h   (b) 16 h

(c) 20 h   (d) None of these

44. If three taps are open together, a tank is filled in 10 h. One of the taps can fill in 5 h and another in 10 h. At what rate does the 3rd pipe work?

(a) Waste pipe emptying the tank is 10 h

(b) Waste pipe emptying the tank is 20 h

(c) Waste pipe emptying the tank is 5 h

(d) Fills the tank in 10 h

45. There are two pipes in a tank. Pipe A is for filling the tank and Pipe B is for emptying the tank. If A can fill the tank in 10 hours and B can empty the tank in 15 hours then find how many hours will it take to completely fill a half empty tank?

(a) 30 hours   (b) 15 hours

(c) 20 hours   (d) 33.33 hours

46. Abbot can do some work in 10 days, Bill can do it in 20 days and Clinton can do it in 40 days. They start working in turns with Abbot starting to work on the first day followed by Bill on the second day and by Clinton on the third day and again by Abbot on the fourth day and so on till the work is completed fully. Find the time taken to complete the work fully?

(a) 16 days   (b) 15 days

(c) 17 days   (d) 16.5 days

47. A, B and C can do some work in 36 days. A and B together do twice as much work as C alone and A and C together can do thrice as much work as B alone. Find the time taken by C to do the whole work.

(a) 72 days   (b) 96 days

(c) 108 days   (d) 120 days

48. There are three Taps A, B and C in a tank. They can fill the tank in 10 hrs, 20 hrs and 25 hrs respectively. At first, all of them are opened simultaneously. Then after 2 hours, tap C is closed and A and B are kept running. After the 4th hour, tap B is also closed. The remaining work is done by Tap A alone. Find the percentage of the work done by Tap A by itself.

(a) 32%   (b) 52%

(c) 75%   (d) None of these

49. Two taps are running continuously to fill a tank. The 1st tap could have filled it in 5 hours by itself and the second one by itself could have filled it in 20 hours. But the operator failed to realise that there was a leak in the tank from the beginning which caused a delay of one hour in the filling of the tank. Find the time in which the leak would empty a filled tank.

(a) 15 hours   (b) 20 hours

(c) 25 hours   (d) 40 hours

50. *A* can do some work in 24 days, *B* can do it in 32 days and *C* can do it in 60 days. They start working together. *A* left after 6 days and *B* left after working for 8 days. How many more days are required to complete the whole work?

(a) 30   (b) 25

(c) 22   (d) 20

Space for Rough Work

LEVEL OF DIFFICULTY (II)

1. Two forest officials in their respective divisions were involved in the harvesting of *tendu* leaves. One division had an average output of 21 tons from a hectare and the other division, which had 12 hectares of land less, dedicated to *tendu* leaves, got 25 tons of *tendu* from a hectare. As a result, the second division harvested 300 tons of *tendu* leaves more than the first. How many tons of *tendu* leaves did the first division harvest?
   (a) 3150   (b) 3450
   (c) 3500   (d) 3600

2. According to a plan, a drilling team had to drill to a depth of 270 metres below the ground level. For the first three days the team drilled as per the plan. However, subsequently finding that their resources were getting underutilised according to the plan, it started to drill 8 metres more than the plan every day. Therefore, a day before the planned date they had drilled to a depth of 280 metres. How many metres of drilling was the plan for each day.
   (a) 38 metres   (b) 30 metres
   (c) 27 metres   (d) 28 metres

3. A pipe can fill a tank in x hours and another can empty it in y hours. If the tank is 1/3rd full then the number of hours in which they will together fill it in is
   (a) $\dfrac{(3xy)}{2(y-x)}$ (b) $\dfrac{(3xy)}{(y-x)}$

   (c) $\dfrac{xy}{3(y-x)}$ (d) $\dfrac{2xy}{3(y-x)}$

4. Dev and Tukku can do a piece of work in 45 and 40 days respectively. They began the work together, but Dev leaves after some days and Tukku finished the remaining work in 23 days. After how many days did Dev leave
   (a) 7 days   (b) 8 days
   (c) 9 days   (d) 11 days

5. A finishes 6/7th of the work in $2z$ hours, B works twice as fast and finishes the remaining work. For how long did B work?
   (a) $\left(\dfrac{2}{3}\right)z$ (b) $\left(\dfrac{6}{7}\right)z$

   (c) $\left(\dfrac{6}{49}\right)z$ (d) $\left(\dfrac{3}{18}\right)z$

Directions for Questions 6 to 10: Read the following and answer the questions that follow.

A set of 10 pipes (set X) can fill 70% of a tank in 7 minutes. Another set of 5 pipes (set Y) fills 3/8 of the tank in 3 minutes. A third set of 8 pipes (set Z) can empty 5/10 of the tank in 10 minutes.

6. How many minutes will it take to fill the tank if all the 23 pipes are opened at the same time?
   (a) 5 minutes   (b) $5\dfrac{5}{7}$ minutes

   (c) 6 minutes   (d) $6\dfrac{5}{7}$ minutes

7. If only half the pipes of set X are closed and only half the pipes of set Y are open and all other pipes are open, how long will it take to fill 49% of the tank?
   (a) 16 minutes   (b) 13 minutes
   (c) 7 minutes   (d) None of these

8. If 4 pipes are closed in set Z, and all others remain open, how long will it take to fill the tank?
   (a) 5 minutes   (b) 6 minutes
   (c) 7 minutes   (d) 7.5 minutes

9. If the tank is half full and set X and set Y are closed, how many minutes will it take for set Z to empty the tank if alternate taps of set Z are closed.
   (a) 12 minutes   (b) 20 minutes
   (c) 40 minutes   (d) 16 minutes

10. If one pipe is added for set X and set Y and set Z's capacity is increased by 20% on its original value and all the taps are opened at 2.58 p.m., then at what time does the tank get filled? (If it is initially empty.)
    (a) 3.05 p.m.   (b) 3.04 p.m.
    (c) 3.10 p.m.   (d) 3.03 p.m.

11. Ajit can do as much work in 2 days as Baljit can do in 3 days and Baljit can do as much in 4 days as Diljit in 5 days. A piece of work takes 20 days if all work together. How long would Baljit take to do all the work by himself?
    (a) 82 days   (b) 44 days
    (c) 66 days   (d) 50 days

12. Two pipes can fill a cistern in 14 and 16 hours respectively. The pipes are opened simultaneously and it is found that due to leakage in the bottom of the cistern, it takes 32 minutes extra for the cistern to be filled

up. When the cistern is full, in what time will the leak empty it?

(a) 114 h   (b) 112 h
(c) 100 h   (d) 80 h

13. A tank holds 100 gallons of water. Its inlet is 7 inches in diameter and fills the tank at 5 gallons/min. The outlet of the tank is twice the diameter of the inlet. How many minutes will it take to empty the tank if the inlet is shut off, when the tank is full and the outlet is opened? (*Hint:* Rate of filling or emptying is directly proportional to the diameter)

(a) 7.14 min   (b) 10.0 min
(c) 0.7 min   (d) 5.0 min

14. A tank of capacity 25 litres has an inlet and an outlet tap. If both are opened simultaneously, the tank is filled in 5 minutes. But if the outlet flow rate is doubled and taps opened the tank never gets filled up. Which of the following can be outlet flow rate in liters/min?

(a) 2   (b) 6
(c) 4   (d) 3

15. X takes 4 days to complete one-third of a job, Y takes 3 days to complete one-sixth of the same work and Z takes 5 days to complete half the job. If all of them work together for 3 days and X and Z quit, how long will it take for Y to complete the remaining work done.

(a) 6 days   (b) 8.1 days
(c) 5.1 days   (d) 7 days

16. A completes 2/3 of a certain job in 6 days. B can complete 1/3 of the same job in 8 days and C can complete 3/4 of the work in 12 days. All of them work together for 4 days and then A and C quit. How long will it take for B to complete the remaining work alone?

(a) 3.8 days   (b) 3.33 days
(c) 2.22 days   (d) 4.3 days

17. Three diggers dug a ditch of 324 m deep in six days working simultaneously. During one shift, the third digger digs as many metres more than the second as the second digs more than the first. The third digger's work in 10 days is equal to the first digger's work in 14 days. How many metres does the first digger dig per shift?

(a) 15 m   (b) 18 m
(c) 21 m   (d) 27 m

18. A, B and C working together completed a job in 10 days. However, C only worked for the first three days when 37/100 of the job was done. Also, the work done by A in 5 days is equal to the work done by B in 4 days. How many days would be required by the fastest worker to complete the entire work?

(a) 20 days   (b) 25 days
(c) 30 days   (d) 40 days

19. A and B completed a work together in 5 days. Had A worked at twice the speed and B at half the speed, it would have taken them four days to complete the job. How much time would it take for A alone to do the work?

(a) 10 days   (b) 20 days
(c) 25 days   (d) 15 days

20. Two typists of varying skills can do a job in 6 minutes if they work together. If the first typist typed alone for 4 minutes and then the second typist typed alone for 6 minutes, they would be left with 1/5 of the whole work. How many minutes would it take the slower typist to complete the typing job working alone?

(a) 10 minutes   (b) 15 minutes
(c) 12 minutes   (d) 20 minutes

21. Three cooks have to make 80 idlis. They are known to make 20 pieces every minute working together. The first cook began working alone and made 20 pieces having worked for sometime more than three minutes. The remaining part of the work was done by the second and the third cook working together. It took a total of 8 minutes to complete the 80 idlis. How many minutes would it take the first cook alone to cook 160 idlis for a marriage party the next day?

(a) 16 minutes   (b) 24 minutes
(c) 32 minutes   (d) 40 minutes

22. It takes six days for three women and two men working together to complete a work. Three men would do the same work five days sooner than nine women. How many times does the output of a man exceed that of a woman?

(a) 3 times   (b) 4 times
(c) 5 times   (d) 6 times

23. Each of A, B and C need a certain unique time to do a certain work. C needs 1 hour less than A to complete the work. Working together, they require 30 minutes to complete 50% of the job. The work also gets completed if A and B start working together and A leaves after 1 hour and B works for a further 3 hours. How much work does C do per hour?

(a) 16.66%   (b) 33.33%
(c) 50%   (d) 66.66%

24. Two women Renu and Ushi are working on an embroidery design. If Ushi worked alone, she would need eight hours more to complete the design than if they both worked together. Now if Renu worked alone, it would need 4.5 hours more to complete the design than they both working together. What time would it take Renu alone to complete the design?

(a) 10.5 hours   (b) 12.5 hours

(c) 14.5 hours   (d) 18.5 hours

25. Mini and Vinay are quiz masters preparing for a quiz. In x minutes, Mini makes y questions more than Vinay. If it were possible to reduce the time needed by each to make a question by two minutes, then in x minutes Mini would make $2y$ questions more than Vinay. How many questions does Mini make in x minutes?

(a) $1/4[2(x+y) - \sqrt{(2x^2 + 4y^2)}\,]$

(b) $1/4[2(x-y) - \sqrt{(2x^2 + 4y^2)}\,]$

(c) Either a or b

(d) $1/4\,[2(x-y) - \sqrt{(2x^2 - 4y^2)}\,]$

26. A tank of 3600 cu m capacity is being filled with water. The delivery of the pump discharging the tank is 20% more than the delivery of the pump filling the same tank. As a result, twelve minutes more time is needed to fill the tank than to discharge it. Determine the delivery of the pump discharging the tank.

(a) 40 m³/min   (b) 50 m³/min

(c) 60 m³/min   (d) 80 m³/min

27. Two pipes A and B can fill up a half full tank in 1.2 hours. The tank was initially empty. Pipe B was kept open for half the time required by pipe A to fill the tank by itself. Then, pipe A was kept open for as much time as was required by pipe B to fill up 1/3 of the tank by itself. It was then found that the tank was 5/6 full. The least time in which any of the pipes can fill the tank fully is

(a) 4.8 hours   (b) 4 hours

(c) 3.6 hours   (d) 6 hours

28. A tank of 425 litres capacity has been filled with water through two pipes, the first pipe having been opened five hours longer than the second. If the first pipe were open as long as the second, and the second pipe was open as long as the first pipe was open, then the first pipe would deliver half the amount of water delivered by the second pipe; if the two pipes were open simultaneously, the tank would be filled up in 17 hours. How long was the second pipe open?

(a) 10 hours   (b) 12 hours

(c) 15 hours   (d) 18 hours

29. Two men and a woman are entrusted with a task. The second man needs three hours more to cope with the job than the first man and the woman would need working together. The first man, working alone, would need as much time as the second man and the woman working together. The first man, working alone, would spend eight hours less than the double period of time the second man would spend working alone. How much time would the two men and the woman need to complete the task if they all worked together?

(a) 2 hours   (b) 3 hours

(c) 4 hours   (d) 5 hours

30. The Bubna dam has four inlets. Through the first three inlets, the dam can be filled in 12 minutes; through the second, the third and the fourth inlet, it can be filled in 15 minutes; and through the first and the fourth inlet, in 20 minutes. How much time will it take all the four inets to fill up the dam?

(a) 8 min   (b) 10 min

(c) 12 min   (d) None of these

Space for Rough Work

LEVEL OF DIFFICULTY (III)

Directions for Questions 1 to 10: Study the following tables and answers the questions that follow.

Darbar Toy Company has to go through the following stages for the launch of a new toy:

		Expert man-days required	Non-expert man-days required
1.	Design and development	30	60
2.	Prototype creation	15	20
3.	Market survey	30	40
4.	Manufacturing setup	15	30
5.	Marketing and launch	15	20

The profile of the company's manpower is

Worker name	Expert at	Non-Expert at	Refusal to work on
A	Design and development	All others	Market survey
B	Prototype creation	All others	Market survey
C	Market survey and marketing and launch	All others	Design and development
D	Manufacturing	All others	Market survey
E	Market survey	All others	Manufacturing

1. Given this situation, the minimum number of days in which the company can launch a new toy going through all the stages is
   (a) 40 days
   (b) 40.5 days
   (c) 45 days
   (d) 44 days

2. If A and C refuse to have anything to do with the manufacturing set up. The number of days by which the project will get delayed will be
   (a) 5 days
   (b) 4 days
   (c) 3 days
   (d) 6 days

3. If each of the five works is equally valued at ₹10,000, the maximum amount will be received by
   (a) A
   (b) C
   (c) D
   (d) E

4. For question 3, the second highest amount will be received by
   (a) A
   (b) C
   (c) D
   (d) E

5. If C works at 90.909% of his efficiency during marketing and launch, who will be highest paid amongst the five of them?
   (a) A
   (b) C
   (c) D
   (d) E

6. If the company decides that the first 4 works can be started simultaneously and the experts will be allocated to their respective work areas only and a work will be done by a non-expert only if the work in his area of expertise is completed, then the expert who will first be assisted in his work will be (assume that marketing and launch can only be done after the first four are fully completed)
   (a) A
   (b) B
   (c) C
   (d) D

7. For the question above, the minimum number of days in which the whole project will get completed (assume everything is utilised efficiently all the time, and nobody is utilised in a work that he refuses to work upon)
   (a) 22.5 days
   (b) 15 days
   (c) 24.75 days
   (d) 25.25 days

8. For the situation in question 6, the highest earning will be for
   (a) A
   (b) Both B and D
   (c) C
   (d) Cannot be determined

9. If each work has an equal payment of ₹10,000, the lowest earning for the above situation will be for
   (a) A
   (b) E
   (c) C
   (d) B

10. The value of the earning for the highest earning person, (if the data for questions 6–9 are accurate) will be
    (a) 19,312.5
    (b) 13,250
    (c) 12,875
    (d) B

Directions for Questions 11 to 20: Read the following and answer the questions that follow.

A fort contains a granary, that has 1000 tons of grain. The fort is under a siege from an enemy army that has blocked off all the supply routes.

The army in the fort has three kinds of soldiers:
Sepoys → 2,00,000.
Mantris → 1,00,000
Footies → 1,00,000
100 Sepoys can hold 5% of the enemy for one month.
100 Mantris can hold 10% of the enemy for 15 days.
50 Footies can hold 5% of the enemy for one month.

A sepoy eats 1 kg of food per month, a Mantri eats 0.5 kg of food per month and a footie eats 3 kg of food. (Assume 1 ton = 1000 kg).

The king has to make some decisions based on the longest possible resistance that can be offered to the enemy.

If a king selects a soldier, he will have to feed him for the entire period of the resistance. The king is not obliged to feed a soldier not selected for the resistance.

(Assume that the entire food allocated to a particular soldier for the estimated length of the resistance is redistributed into the king's palace in case a soldier dies and is not available for the other soldiers.)

11. If the king wants to maximise the time for which his resistance holds up, he should
    (a) Select all mantris   (b) Select all footies
    (c) Select all sepoys   (d) None of these

12. Based on existing resources, the maximum number of months for which the fort's resistance can last is
    (a) 5 months   (b) 20 months
    (c) 7.5 months   (d) Cannot be determined

13. If the king makes a decision error, the maximum reduction in the time of resistance could be
    (a) 15 months   (b) 12.5 months
    (c) 16.66 months   (d) Cannot be determined

14. If the king estimates that the attackers can last for only 50 months, what should the king do to ensure victory?
    (a) Select all mantris
    (b) Select the mantris and the sepoys
    (c) Select the footies
    (d) The king cannot achieve this

15. If a reduction in the ration allocation by 10% reduces the capacity of any soldier to hold off the enemy by 10%, the number of whole months by which the king can increase the life of the resistance by reducing the ration allocation by 10% is
    (a) 4 months   (b) 2 months
    (c) No change   (d) This will reduce the time

16. The minimum amount of grain that should be available in the granary to ensure that the fort is not lost (assuming the estimate of the king of 50 months being the duration for which the enemy can last is correct) is
    (a) 2000 tons   (b) 2500 tons
    (c) 5000 tons   (d) Cannot be determined

17. If the king made the worst possible selection of his soldiers to offer the resistance, the percentage increase in the minimum amount of grain that should be available in the granary to ensure that the fort is not lost is
    (a) 100%   (b) 500%
    (c) 600%   (d) Cannot be determined

18. The difference in the minimum grain required for the second worst choice and the worst choice to ensure that the resistance lasts for 50 months is
    (a) 5000 tons   (b) 7500 tons
    (c) 10000 tons   (d) Cannot be determined

19. If the king strategically attacks the feeder line on the first day of the resistance so that the grain is no longer a constraint, the maximum time for which the resistance can last is
    (a) 100 months   (b) 150 months
    (c) 250 months   (d) Cannot be determined

20. If the feeder line is opened after 6 months and prior to that the king had made decisions based on food availability being a constraint then the number of months (maximum) for which the resistance could last is
    (a) 100 months   (b) 150 months
    (c) 5 months   (d) Cannot be determined

Directions for Questions 21 to 25: Study the following and answer the questions that follow.

A gas cylinder can discharge gas at the rate of 1 cc/minute from burner A and at the rate of 2 cc/minute from burner B (maximum rates of discharge). The capacity of the gas cylinder is 1000 cc of gas.

The amount of heat generated is equal to 1 kcal per cc of gas.

However, there is wastage of the heat as per follows:

Gas discharge@	Loss of heat
0–0.5 cc/minute	10%
0.5–1 cc/minute	20%
1–1.5 cc/minute	25%
1.5 + cc/minute	30%

@(Include higher extremes)

21. If both burners are opened simultaneously such that the first is opened to 90% of its capacity and the second is opened to 80% of its capacity, the amount of time in which the gas cylinder will be empty (if it was half full at the start) will be:
    (a) 250 minutes   (b) 400 minutes
    (c) 200 minutes   (d) None of these

22. The maximum amount of heat with the fastest speed of cooking that can be utilised for cooking will be when:
    (a) The first burner is opened upto 50% of it's aperture
    (b) The second burner is opened upto 25% of it's aperture
    (c) Either (a) or (b)
    (d) None of these

23. The amount of heat utilised for cooking if a full gas cylinder is burnt by opening the aperture of burner *A* 100% and that of burner *B* 50% is
    - (a) 900 kcal
    - (b) 800 kcal
    - (c) 750 kcal
    - (d) Cannot be determined

24. For Question 23, if burner *A* had been opened only 25% and burner *B* had been opened 50%, the amount of heat available for cooking would be

    - (a) 820 kcal
    - (b) 800 kcal
    - (c) 750 kcal
    - (d) Cannot be determined

25. For Question 24, the amount of time required to finish a full gas cylinder will be
    - (a) 900 minutes
    - (b) 833.33 minutes
    - (c) 800 minutes
    - (d) None of these

Space for Rough Work

ANSWER KEY

Level of Difficulty (I)

1. (c)	2. (c)	3. (b)	4. (a)
5. (a)	6. (a)	7. (a)	8. (d)
9. (a)	10. (a)	11. (a)	12. (c)
13. (b)	14. (b)	15. (c)	16. (d)
17. (c)	18. (b)	19. (a)	20. (d)
21. (c)	22. (d)	23. (d)	24. (c)
25. (a)	26. (b)	27. (a)	28. (c)
29. (d)	30. (a)	31. (d)	32. (a)
33. (a)	34. (b)	35. (b)	36. (c)
37. (c)	38. (b)	39. (b)	40. (a)
41. (d)	42. (c)	43. (a)	44. (c)
45. (b)	46. (d)	47. (c)	48. (d)
49. (b)	50. (c)		

Level of Difficulty (II)

1. (a)	2. (b)	3. (d)	4. (c)
5. (d)	6. (b)	7. (d)	8. (a)
9. (b)	10. (d)	11. (c)	12. (b)
13. (b)	14. (b)	15. (c)	16. (b)
17. (a)	18. (a)	19. (a)	20. (b)
21. (c)	22. (d)	23. (c)	24. (a)
25. (a)	26. (c)	27. (b)	28. (c)
29. (a)	30. (b)		

Level of Difficulty (III)

1. (b)	2. (b)	3. (b)	4. (d)
5. (b)	6. (a)	7. (c)	8. (d)
9. (c)	10. (c)	11. (a)	12. (b)
13. (c)	14. (d)	15. (c)	16. (b)
17. (b)	18. (a)	19. (c)	20. (c)
21. (c)	22. (c)	23. (b)	24. (a)
25. (c)			

Hints

Level of Difficulty (II)

2. They drill at planned rate for 3 days (say x)
$$3x + 5(x + 8) = 280$$

5. Work left = 1/7th of original work. A would have done it in $z/3$ hours.

6–10. First set of ten pipes operate at 10%/min (filling) i.e.
Filling done by 1 pipe = 1%/minute
Second set of five pipes operate at 12.5%/minute (filling)
i.e. Filling done by 1 pipe = 2.5%/minute
Set Z (Emptying) = 5%/minute.
Emptying per pipe = 0.625%/minute.

11. $8A = 12B = 15D$.

13. Since (rate of filling or emptying) α diameter, the emptying rate is 10 gallons/minute.

14. The net flow in the original situation is 5 litres/minutes. The required answer will be such that when it is doubled, the increase in emptying rate (in litres/minute) should be more than 5 litres/minute.

15. Required answer = $\dfrac{\text{work left after 3 days}}{Y\text{'s work rate}}$.

17. Ditch dug per day = $\dfrac{324}{6}$ = 54 metres
$\therefore \qquad x + (x + y) + (x + 2y) = 54$
$$10(x + 2y) = 14x$$
Use options to solve.

18. Work done on the first three days is 37%. Hence, work done on the next 7 days is 63%.
Since, this is $A + B$'s work we get
One day's work of $(A + B)$ = 9%
Also, $5A = 4B$.
Hence A = 4% and B = 5%
B, turns out to be the fastest worker.

19. Solve through options.

20. Work done by the first typist in 2 minutes = 20%.
Hence, the first typist's work rate = 10% per minute.

22. Solve through options.

23. Solve through options.

24. Let x hours be required to complete the work together.
Then, $\dfrac{1}{(x + 4.5)} + \dfrac{1}{(x + 8)} = \dfrac{1}{x}$. Check the options to see which one fits the equation.

27. $A + B = \dfrac{50\%}{1.2}$ = 41.66%
(where A and B represent the work per hour of pipes A and B respectively).
Solve using options to see which one fits the remaining conditions of the problem.
For example, if we check option b (4 hrs), then we get that the work of the faster pipe (say A) = 25%. Then B = 16.66%.
Then B was open for 4/2 = 2 hours and A was open for 6/3 = 2 hours.
Work done = 25% × 2 + 16.66% × 2 = 83.33%
$= \dfrac{5}{6}$ of work.
Hence, this option is correct.

28. Let the discharges per pipe be A and B litres/hr.
Then $\qquad 17(A + B) = 425$
i.e. $\qquad A + B = 25$
From this point of the solution, proceed to check the conditions of the question through options.

29. Difference in times required by the first man (A) and the second man (B) = 3 hours. Also, if t_A and t_B are the respective times, then

$$2t_B - t_A = 8 \quad \text{and} \quad t_B - t_A = 3$$

30. Let the work/minute of the four pipes be A, B, C and D respectively.

Then, $D - A = 1.66\%$ and $D + A = 5\%$

Level of Difficulty (III)

1–10. Interpretation of the first row of the first table in the question:

Design and Development requires 30 expert man-days or 60 non-expert man-days.

Hence, work done in 1 expert man-day = 3.33% and work done in 1 non-expert man-day = 1.66%. Further, from the second table, it can be interpreted that: A is an expert at design and development. Hence, his work rate is 3.33% per day and B, D and E are ready to work as non-experts on design and development, hence their work rate is 1.66% per day each.

Thus, in 1 day the total work will be

$A + B + D + E = 3.33 + 1.66 + 1.66 + 1.66 = 8.33\%$ work.

Thus, 12 days will be required to finish the design and development phase.

1. $\dfrac{100}{8.33} + \dfrac{100}{26.66} + \dfrac{100}{6.66} + \dfrac{100}{16.66} + \dfrac{100}{26.66} = 40.5$

2. Increase of number of days → $\dfrac{100}{10} - \dfrac{100}{16.66} = 4$ days.

[This happens since the work rate will drop from 16.66% to 10% due to A and C's refusal to work.]

3–4. Find out the work done by each of the 5 workers.

11–20. The resistance offered is equal for 100 numbers of all types of soldiers.

11–13. If all sepoys are chosen, the food requirement will be 200 tons/month. The resistance will last for 5 months.

If footies are chosen, the food will last for $\dfrac{1000}{100 \times 3}$ = 3.33 months.

If mantris are chosen, the food will last for $\dfrac{1000}{100 \times 0.5}$ = 20 months.

Hence, all mantris must be chosen.

19–20. For these questions, since food is no longer a constraint, the constraint then becomes the number of lives. Then, the assumption will be that the resistance lasts for one month with a loss of either 2000 sepoys, 2000 mantris or 1000 footies.

19. Length of resistance = $\dfrac{200000}{2000} + \dfrac{100000}{2000} + \dfrac{100000}{1000}$
= 250 months.

20. In 6 months, the resistance will have lost 12000 mantris. He would also have lost all other soldiers since he has not fed them.

21. $\dfrac{500}{0.9 + 1.6} = 200.$

23. At 1 cc/minute, the loss of heat is 20%. Hence, when 1000 cc of the gas is used, out of the 1000 kcal of heat generated 200 kcal will be lost.

Solutions and Shortcuts

Level of Difficulty (I)

1. He will complete the work in 20 days. Hence, he will complete ten times the work in 200 days.

2. 6 men for 12 days means 72 mandays. This would be equal to 4 men for 18 days.

3. A's one day work will be 5%, while B will do 6.66% of the work in one day. Hence, their total work will be 11.66% in a day.

In 8 days they will complete → $11.66 \times 8 = 93.33\%$

This will leave 6.66% of the work. This will correspond to 4/7 of the ninth day since in 6.66/11.66 both the numerator and the denominator are divisible by 1.66.

4. A's work = 5% per day

B's work = 6.66% per day

C's work = 4% per day.

Total no. of days = 100/15.66 = 300/47 = 6(18/47)

5. $N + A = 10\%$

$N = 8.33\%$

Hence $A = 1.66\% \rightarrow 60$ days.

6. The ratio of the wages will be the inverse of the ratio of the number of days required by each to do the work. Hence, the correct answer will be 3:2 → ₹ 30

7. 24 man days + 18 women days = 20 man days + 28 woman days

→ 4 man days = 10 woman days.

→ 1 man day = 2.5 woman days

Total work = 24 man days + 18 woman days = 60 woman days + 18 woman days = 78 woman days.

Hence, 1 man + 1 woman = 3.5 women can do it in 78/3.5 = 156/7 = 22(2/7) days.

8. The data is insufficient, since we only know that the work gets completed in 200 boy days and 300 women days.

9. A = 10%, B = 5% and Combined work is 20%. Hence, C's work is 5% and will require 20 days.

10. In 5 days, A would do 25% of the work. Since, B finishes the remaining 75% work in 10 days, we can conclude that B's work in a day = 7.5%

Thus, $(A + B) = 12.5\%$ per day.

Together they would take $100/12.5 = 8$ days.

11. $A = 20\%$, $B = 10\%$ and $A + B + C = 50\%$. Hence, $C = 20\%$. Thus, in two days, C contributes 40% of the total work and should be paid 40% of the total amount.

12. Total man days required = 600 man days. If 5 workers leave the job after 'n' days, the total work would be done in 35 days. We have to find the value of 'n' to satisfy:

$$20 \times n + (35 - n) \times 15 = 600.$$

Solving for n, we get

$$20n - 15n + 35 \times 15 = 600$$
$$5n = 75$$
$$n = 15.$$

13. Let the time taken by Arun be 't' days. Then, time taken by Vinay = $2t$ days.

$1/t + 1/2t = 1/7 \rightarrow t = 10.5$

14. Subhash can copy 200 pages in 40 hours (reaction to the first sentence). Hence, Prakash can copy 100 pages in 40 hours. Thus, he can copy 30 pages in 30% of the time: i.e. 12 hours.

15. $30X = 20 (X + 6) \rightarrow 10X = 120 \rightarrow X = 12$.

16. Sashi = 4%, Rishi = 5%. In five days, they do a total of 45% work. Rishi will finish the remaining 55% work in 11 more days.

17. Raju = 10%, Vicky = 8.33% and Tinku = 6.66%. Hence, total work for a day if all three work = 25%.

In 2 days they will complete, 50% work. On the third day onwards Raju doesn't work. The rate of work will become 15%. Also, since Vicky leaves 3 days before the actual completion of the work, Tinku works alone for the last 3 days (and must have done the last $6.66 \times 3 = 20\%$ work alone). This would mean that Vicky leaves after 80% work is done. Thus, Vicky and Tinku must be doing 30% work together over two days.

Hence, total time required = 2 days (all three) + 2 days (Vicky and Tinku) + 3 days (Tinku alone)

18. Sambhu requires 16 days to do the work while Kalu requires 18 days to do the work.

$$(1/16 + 1/18) \times n = 1$$
$$\rightarrow n = 288/34 = 144/17$$

19. Let Anjay take $3t$ days, Vijay take $2t$ days and Manoj take $6t$ days in order to complete the work. Then we get:

$1/3t + 1/2t + 1/6t = 1 \rightarrow t = 1$. Thus, Manoj would take $6t = 6$ days to complete the work.

20. After 100 days and 4500 mandays, only 1/6th of the work has been completed. You can use the product change algorithm of PCG to solve this question.

$100 \times 45 = 16.66\%$ of the work. After this you have 200 days (i.e. 100% increase in the time available) while the product $200 \times$ no. of men should correspond to five times times the original product.

$$100 \xrightarrow[\substack{+100}]{\substack{\text{TIME} \\ \text{100\% increase}}} 200 \xrightarrow[\substack{+300 \text{ required}}]{\substack{?}} 500$$

This will be got by increasing the no. of men by 150% (300/200).

21. Since the ratio of money given to Apurva and Amit is 2:3, their work done would also be in the same ratio. Thus, their time ratio would be 3:2 (inverse of 2:3). So, if Apurva takes 12 days, Amit would take 8 days and the total number of days required (t) would be given by the equation:

$(1/12 + 1/8)t = 1 \rightarrow t = 24/5 = 4.8$ days

22. Raju being twice as good a workman as Vijay, you can solve the following equation to get the required answer:

$1/R + 1/2R = 1/14$.

Solving will give you that Vijay takes 42 days.

23. $40n = 30 (n + 5) \rightarrow n = 15$

24. 12×5 man days + 16×5 Boy days
$$= 13 \times 4 \text{ man days} + 24 \times 4 \text{ Boy days}$$
$$\rightarrow 8 \text{ man days} = 16 \text{ Boy days}$$
$$1 \text{ man day} = 2 \text{ Boy days}.$$

Required ratio of man's work to boy's work = 2 : 1.

25. A's rate of working is 10 per cent per day while B's rate of working is 5 per cent per day. In 5 days they will complete 75 per cent work. Thus the last 25 per cent would be done by B alone. Working at the rate of 5 per cent per day, B would do the work in 5 days.

26. Work equivalence method:

$30 \times 5 \times 16 = 20 \times 6 \times n$

Gives the value of n as 20 days

27. Ajay's daily work = 4.1666%, Vijay's daily work = 3.33% and the daily work of all the three together is 8.33%. Hence, Pradeep's daily work will be 0.8333%. Hence, he will end up doing 10% of the total work in 12 days. This will mean that he will be paid ₹ 20.

28. Total work = $15 \times 210 = 3150$ mandays.

After 100 days, work done = $15 \times 100 = 1500$ mandays.

Work left = $3150 - 1500 = 1650$ mandays.

This work has to be done with 30 men working each day.

The number of days (more) required = 1650/30 = 55 days.

29. $$A + V + S = 1 \qquad (1)$$
$$A + V = 19/23$$
$$V + S = 8/23$$

$\rightarrow A + 2V + S = 27/23$ (2)

(2)–(1) gives us: $V = 4/23$.

30. Interpret the starting statement as: Anmol takes 30 days and Vinay takes 90 days. Hence, the answer will be got by:

    $(1/30 + 1/90) * n = 1$

    Alternatively, you can also solve using percentages as: $3.33 + 1.11 = 4.44\%$ is the daily work. Hence, the no. of days required is $100/4.44 = 22.5$ days.

31. After 27 days, food left $= 4 \times 200 = 800$ soldier days worth of food. Since, now there are only 80 soldiers, this food would last for $800/80 = 10$ days. Number of extra days for which the food lasts $= 10 - 4 = 6$ days.

32. Total work of Anju, Manju and Sanju $= 16.66\%$

            Anju's work $= 10\%$

            Manju's work $= 4.166\%$

            Sanju's work $= 2.5\%$

    So Sanju can reap the field in 40 days.

33. Ajay + Vijay $= 1/28$ and Ajay + Vijay + Manoj $= 1/21$.

    Hence, Manoj $= 1/21 - 1/28 = 1/84$.

    Hence, Manoj will take 84 days to do the work.

34. $A + M = 8.33$, $M + B = 6.66$ and $A = 2B \rightarrow$ A's 1 days work $= 3.33\%$, M's $= 5\%$ and B's $= 1.66\%$. Thus, Mohan would require $100/5 = 20$ days to complete the work if he works alone.

35. $A + V = 16.66\%$ and $A = 10\% \rightarrow V = 6.66\%$. Consequently Vijay would require $100/6.66 = 15$ days to do it alone.

36. The rate of filling will be 20% and the net rate of filling (including the leak) is 16.66%. Hence, the leak accounts for 3.33% per. i.e. it will take 30 hours to empty the tank.

37. $A + B = 16.66\%$. From here solve this one using the options. Option (c) fits the situation as it gives us A's work $= 10\%$, B's work $= 6.66\%$ as also that B takes 5 minutes more than A (as stipulated in the problem).

38. $A + B = 5.55 + 11.11 = 16.66$. In two days, 33.33% of the work will be done. C adds 16.66% of work to that of A and B. Hence, the rate of working will go to 33.33%. At this rate it would take 2 more days to complete the work.

    Hence, in total it will take 4 days to complete the entire work.

39. $24 \times 8 \times 10 = N \times 10 \times 6 \rightarrow N = 32$

40. $n \times 20 = (n - 12) \times 32 \rightarrow n = 32$.

41. $12 \times 18 = 12 \times 6 + 16 \times t \rightarrow t = 9$

42. $(A + B)$'s work $= C$'s work.

    Also if A takes 'a' days

    B would take '$a - 5$' days

and C would take '$a - 9$' days.

Solving through options, option 'c' fits.

     A (15 days) $\rightarrow$ A's work $= 6.66\%$

     B (10 days) $\rightarrow$ B's work $= 10\%$

     C (6 days) $\rightarrow$ C's work $= 16.66\%$

43. The cistern fills in 6 hours normally, means that the rate of filling is 16.66% per hour. With the leak in the bottom, the rate of filling becomes 10% per hour (as it takes 10 hours to fill with the leak).

    This means that the leak drains out water at the rate of 6.66% per hour. This in turn means that the leak would take $100/6.66 = 15$ hours to drain out the entire cistern.

44. Since the net work of the three taps is 10% and the first and second do $20\% + 10\% = 30\%$. Hence, the third pipe must be a waste pipe emptying at the rate of 20% per hour. Hence, the waste pipe will take a total of 5 hours to empty the tank.

45. A's work $= 10\%$

         B's negative work $= 6.66\%$

         $(A + B)$'s work $= 3.33\%$

    To fill a half empty tank, they would take $50/3.33 = 15$ hours.

46. The work rate would be 10% on the first day, 5% on the second day and 2.5% on the third day. For every block of 3 days there would be 17.5% work done. In 15 days, the work completed would be $17.5 \times 5 = 87.5\%$. On the sixteenth day, work done $= 10\% \rightarrow 2.5\%$ work would be left after 16 days. On the 17th day the rate of work would be 5% and hence it would take half of the 17th day to complete the work. Thus, it would take 16.5 days to finish the work in this fashion.

47. $(A + B) = 2C$.

    Also, $(A + C) = 3B$

       $36(A + B + C) = 1$

    Solving for C, we get:

    $36 (2C + C) = 1 \rightarrow 108C = 1$

                    $C = 1/108$

    Hence, C takes 108 days.

48. $A + B + C = 19\%$. In the first two hours they will do 38 % of the work. Further, for the next two hours work will be done at the rate of 15% per hour. Hence, after 4 hours 68% of the work will be completed, when tap B is also closed. The last 32% of the work will be done by A alone. Hence, A does 40% (first 4 days) $+ 32\% = 72\%$ of the work.

49. Without the leak:

    Rate of work $= 20\% + 5\% = 25\%$. Thus, it would have taken 4 hours to complete the work.

    Due to the leak the filling gets delayed by 1 hour. Thus, the tank gets filled in 5 hours. This means that the effective rate of filling would be 20% per hour. This means that the rate at which the leak empties the tank is 5% per hour and hence it would have taken 20 hours to empty a filled tank.

50. In 6 days A would do 25% of the work and in 8 days B would do 25% of the work himself. So, C has to complete 50% of the work by himself.

In all C would require 30 days to do 50% of the work. So, he would require 22 more days.

Level of Difficulty (II)

1. $25(n-12) = 21n + 300$. Solving this equation, $n = 150$. Hence, the first division harvest 3150 tons.

2. Let n be the number of meters planned per day. Start from the options to find the number of planned days. In the options the 2 feasible values are 30 meters and 27 meters (as these divide 270). Suppose we check for 30 meters per day, the work would have got completed in 9 days as per the original plan. In the new scenario:

$3n + 5(n+8) = 280 \rightarrow n = 30$ too. Hence, this option is correct.

Note that if we tried with 27 meters per day the final equation would not match as we would get:

$3n + 6(n+8) = 280 \rightarrow$ which does not give us the value of n as 27 and hence this option is rejected.

3. To solve this question first assume the values of x and y (such that $x < y$). If you take x as 10 hours and y as 15 hours, you will get a net work of 3.33% per hour. At this rate it will take 20 hours to fill the tank from one third full. Using this condition try to put these values of x and y into the options to check the values.

For instance option (a) gives the value as $3 \times 10 \times 15/10 = 45$ which is not equal to 20.

4. $n(1/45 + 1/40) + 23/40 = 1 \rightarrow n = 9.$

5. Since A finishes $6/7^{th}$ of the work in $2z$ hours.

B would finish 12/7 of the work in $2z$ hours.

Thus, to do $1/7^{th}$ of the work (which represents the remaining work), B would require $2z/12 = z/6$ hours. Option (d) is correct.

6–10.

Set X can fill 10% in a minute. Hence, every Pipe of set X can do 1% work per minute. Set Y has a filling capacity of 12.5% per minute (or 2.5% per minute for each tap in set Y). Set Z has a capacity of emptying the tank at the rate of 5% per minute and each tap of set Z can empty at the rate of 0.625% per minute.

6. If all the 23 pipes are opened the per minute rate will be:

$10 + 12.5 - 5 = 17.5\% \rightarrow$ Option b is correct.

7. Set X will do 5% per minute and Set Y will do 6.25% per minute, while set Z will do 5% per minute (negative work). Hence, Net work will be 6.25% per minute. To fill 49% it will take slightly less than eight minutes and the value will be a fraction. None of the first three options matches this requirement. Hence, the answer will be (d).

8. If 4 of the taps of set Z are closed, the net work done by Set Z would be –2.5% while the work done by Sets X and Y would remain 10% and 12.5% respectively. Thus, the total work per minute would be 20% and hence the tank would take 5 minutes to fill up.

9. Again if we close 4 taps of set Z, the rate of emptying by set Z would be 2.5% per minute. A half filled tank would contain 50% of the capacity and hence would take 50/2.5 = 20 minutes to empty.

10. The rate per minute with the given changes (in percentage terms) would be:

Set X =11%, Set Y = 15% and Set Z = –6%.

Hence, the net rate = 11 + 15 – 6 = 20% per minute and it would take 5 minutes for the tank to fill. If all pipes are opened at 7:58, the tank would get filled at 3:03.

11. Let Ajit's rate of work be 100/2 = 50 work units per day. Baljit would do 100/3 = 33.33 work units per day and Diljit does 133.33/5 = 26.66 units of work per day. Their 1 days work = 50 + 33.33 + 26.66 = 110 units of work per day. In 20 days, the total work done would be 2200 units of work and hence for Baljit to do it alone it would take: 2200/33.33 = 66 days to complete the same work.

12. The 32 minutes extra represents the extra time taken by the pipes due to the leak.

Normal time for the pipes $\rightarrow n \times (1/14 + 1/16) = 1$ $\rightarrow n = 112/15 = 7$ hrs 28 minutes.

Thus, with 32 minutes extra, the pipes would take 8 hours to fill the tank.

Thus, $8(1/14 + 1/16) - 8 \times (1/L) = 1 \rightarrow 8/L$
$= 8(15/112) - 1$
$1/L = 15/112 - 1/8$
$= 1/112.$

Thus, L = 112 hours.

13. The outlet pipe will empty the tank at a rate which is double the rate of filling (Hence, 10 gallons per minute). If the inlet is shut off, the tank will get emptied of 100 gallons of water in ten minutes.

14. The net inflow when both pipes are opened is 5 litres a minute.

The outlet flow should be such that if its rate is doubled the net inflow rate should be negative or 0. Only an option greater than or equal to '5' would satisfy this condition.

Option (b) is the only possible value.

15. X→12 days → 8.33% of the work per day.

Y → 18 days → 5.55% of the work per day

Z → 10 days → 10% of the work per day.

In three days, the work done will be 25 + 16.66 + 30 = 71.66%. The remaining work will get done by Y in 28.33/5.55 = 5.1 days.

[*Note:* You need to be fluent with your fraction to percentage conversions in order to do well at these kinds of calculations.]

16. A takes 9 days to complete the work

B takes 24 days to complete the work

C takes 16 days to complete the work

In 4e days, work done by all three would be:

$4 \times (1/9 + 1/24 + 1/16)$

$$= 4 \times \frac{(16 + 6 + 9)}{144} = 124/144$$

$$= 31/36 \text{ of the work.}$$

Work left for B would be 5/36 of the work.

B would require: $(5/36) \times 24 = 3.33$ days.

17. The per day digging of all three combined is 54 meters. Hence, their average should be 18. This means that the first should be $18 - x$, the second, 18 & the third $18 + x$.

The required conditions are met if we take the values as 15,18,21 meters for the first, second and third diggers respectively. Hence, (a) is the correct answer.

18. The equations are:

$3(A + B + C) = 37/100 = 37\%$ of the work.

$7(A + B) = 63/10 \rightarrow A + B = 9/100 = 9\%$

(Where A, B and C are 1 day's work of the three respectively).

Further, $5A = 4B$ gives us

$A = 4\%$ and $B = 5\%$ work per day.

In 3 days $(A + B + C)$ do 37% of the work.

Out of this A and B would do 27% (= 3 × 9%) of the work. So, C would do 3.33% of the work per day.

$$\frac{37 - 27}{3}$$

Thus, B is the fastest and he would require 20 days to complete the work.

19. $A + B = 20\%$ of the work. Use trial and error with the options to get the answer.

Checking for option (a), $A = 10\%$ and $B = 10\%$. If A doubles his work and B halves his work rate, the total work in a day would become $A = 20, B = 5$. This would mean that the total work would get completed in 4 days which is the required condition that needs to be matched if the option is to be correct. Hence, this option is correct.

20. Since the first typist types for 4 minutes and the second typist types for exactly 6 minutes, the work left (which is given as 1/5 of the total work) would be the work the first typist can do in 2 minutes. Thus, the time taken by the first typist to do the work would be 10 minutes and his rate of work would be 10% per minute. Also, since both the typists can do the work together in 6 minutes, their combined rate of work would be 100/6 = 16.66% per minute.

Thus, the second typist's rate of work would be 16.66 – 10 = 6.66% per minute.

He would take 100/6.66 = 15 minutes to complete the task alone.

21. From the condition of the problem and a little bit of trial and error we can see that the first cook worked for 4 minutes and the 2nd and 3rd cooks also worked for 4 minutes. As $4(A) + 4(B + C) = 4(A + B + C)$ and we know that $A + B + C = 20$ idlis per minute.

Thus, the first cook make 20 idlis in 4 minutes. To make 160 idlis he would take 32 minutes.

22. Solve this using options. If we check for option (c) i.e. the work of a man exceeds the work of a woman by 5 times, we would get the following thought process:

Total work = 6 days × (3 women + 2 men) = 18 woman days + 12 man days = 18 woman days + 60 woman days = 78 woman days.

Thus, 9 women would take 78/9 days = 8.66 days and hence 3 men should do the same work in 3.66 days. This translates to 3 × 3.66 = 10 man days or 50 woman days which is incorrect as the number of woman days should have been 78.

Thus, we can reject this option.

If we check for option (d) i.e. the work of a man exceeds the work of a woman by 6 times, we would get the following thought process:

Total work = 6 days × (3 women + 2 men) = 18 woman days + 12 man days = 18 woman days + 72 woman days = 90 woman days.

Thus, 9 women would take 90/9 days = 10 days and hence 3 men should do the same work in 5 days. This translates to 3 × 5 = 15 man days or 90 woman days which is correct as the number of woman days should be 90.

Thus, we select this option.

23. $0.5(A + B + C) = 50\%$ of the work.

Means → A, B and C can do the full work in 1 hour.

Thus, $(A + B + C) = 100\%$

From this point it is better to solve through options. Option (c) gives the correct answer based on the following thought process.

If c = 50% work per hour, it means C takes 2 hours to complete the work.

Consequently, A would take 3 hours and hence do 33.33% work per hour.

Since, $A + B + C$ = 100%, this gives us B's hourly work rate = 16.66%.

For this option to be correct these nos. should match the second instance and the information given there.

According to the second condition:

$A + 4B$ should be equal to 100%. Putting A = 33.33% and B = 16.66% we see that the condition is satisfied. Hence, this option is correct.

24. Option (a) is correct because: $1/10.5 + 1/14 = 1/6$ which matches all the conditions of the problem.

25. Solve by trial and error by putting values for x and y in the options.

26. Use options for this question as follows:

If discharging delivery is 40, filling delivery will be 16.66% less (this will give a decimal value right at the start and is unlikely to be the answer. Hence, put this option aside for the time being.)

Option (c) gives good values. If discharging delivery is 60, filling delivery will be 50. Also, time taken for discharge of 3600 cu m will be 60 minutes and the time taken for delivery will be 72 minutes (12 minutes more – which is the basic condition of the problem).

27. The interpretation of the first statement is that (a) & (b) do 41.66 percent of the work per hour. From this point if we go through the options, option (b) fits the situation as 4 hours per one person means 25 percent work per hour per person. Consequently this means 16.66 percent per work per hour per other person.

28. From the last statement we know that since both the pipes would require 17 hours to fill the tank together, they would discharge $425/17$ = 25 liters per hour together.

From this point try to fit the values from the options in order to see which one satisfies all the conditions.

In the case of option (a): Second pipe open for 10 hours, first pipe open for 15 hours.

When the interchange occurs: Second pipe open for 15 hours, first pipe open for 10 hours → gives us that the respective rates of the two pipes would be 3:4 (as the first pipe delivers half the amount of the second pipe- if it delivers 3 liters per minute the second pipe would need to deliver 4 liters per minute).

Thus, if the delivery of the first pipe is $3n$ liters per minute, the delivery of the second pipe would be $4n$ liters per minute. Then, in 10 hours of the second

pipe and 15 hours of the first pipe, the total water would be $85n$, which should be equal to the total water of the two pipes in 17 hours each. But in 17 hours each, the two pipes would discharge $17 \times 7n$ = $119n$. Thus, we reject this option.

In the case of option (c): Second pipe open for 15 hours, first pipe open for 20 hours.

When the interchange occurs: Second pipe open for 20 hours, first pipe open for 15 hours → gives us that the respective rates of the two pipes would be 2:3 (as the first pipe delivers half the amount of the second pipe- if it delivers 2 liter per minute the second pipe would need to deliver 3 liters per minute).

Thus, if the delivery of the first pipe is $2n$ liters per minute, the delivery of the second pipe would be $3n$ liters per minute. Then, in 15 hours of the second pipe and 20 hours of the first pipe, the total water would be $85n$, which should be equal to the total water of the two pipes in 17 hours each. In 17 hours each, the two pipes would discharge $17 \times 5n$ = $85n$. Thus, we realize that this is the correct option.

29. In order to solve this question, if we look at the first statement, we could think of the following scenarios:

If the time taken by the first man and the woman is 1 hour (100% work per hour) , the time taken by the second man would be 4 hours (25% work per hour). In such a case, the total time taken by all three to complete the task would be $100/125$ = 0.8 hours. But this value is not there in the options. Hence, we reject this set of values.

If the time taken by the first man and the woman is 2 hours (50% work per hour) , the time taken by the second man would be 5 hours (20% work per hour). In such a case, the total time taken by all three to complete the task would be $100/70$ = $10/7$ hours. But this value is not there in the options. Hence, we reject this set of values.

If the time taken by the first man and the woman is 3 hours (33.33% work per hour) , the time taken by the second man would be 6 hours (16.66% work per hour). In such a case, the total time taken by all three to complete the task would be $100/50$ = 2 hours. Since this value is there in the options we should try to see whether this set of values meets the other conditions in the question.

In this case, it is given that the first man working alone takes as much time as the second man and the woman. Since, the work of all three is 50%, this means that the work of the first man is 25%. Consequently the work of the woman is 8.33%.

Looking at the third condition given in the problem – the time taken by the first man to do the work alone (@ 25% per hour he would take 4 hours) should be

8 hours less than double the time taken by the second man. This condition can be seen to be fulfilled here because the second man would take 6 hours to complete his work (@ 16.66% per hour) and hence, double his time would be 12 hours- which satisfies the difference of 8 hours.

Thus, the total time taken is 2 hours.

30. Let the inlets be A, B, C and D.

$$A + B + C = 8.33\%$$

$$B + C + D = 6.66\%$$

$$A + D = 5\%$$

Thus, $$2A + 2B + 2C + 2D = 20\%$$

and $$A + B + C + D = 10\%$$

→ 10 minutes would be required to fill the tank completely.

10 Chapter

Time, Speed and Distance

INTRODUCTION

The concepts underlying the chapter of Time, Speed and Distance (TSD) are amongst the most important for the purpose of the Maths section in aptitude exams. The basic concepts of TSD are used in solving questions based on motion in a straight line, relative motion, circular motion, problems based on trains, problem based on boats, clocks, races, etc. Besides, these concepts can also be used for the creation of new types of problems. Your ability to solve these problems will depend only on the depth of your understanding.

Due to this diversity in the possibilities for question setting, this chapter is very important for CAT aspirants. Besides, all other exams based on Aptitude (CMAT, XLRI, FMS, IIFT, Bank PO) also require the use of TSD.

This chapter is one of the most important chapters in the entire portion of quantitative aptitude. The students are therefore advised to closely understand the concepts contained in this chapter to be comfortable with the problems related to this topic in the examination.

THEORY OF TSD

Concept of Motion and Mathematical Representation of Motion

Motion/movement occurs when a body of any shape or size changes its position with respect to any external stationary point. Thus, when a person travels from city A to city B, we say that he has moved from city A to city B. In general, whenever a body moves with respect to a stationary point, we say that the body has undergone a displacement/

motion with respect to the starting point. Thus, for motion to have occurred, there must have been some displacement with respect to a stationary point on the ground.

The mathematical model that describes motion has three variables, namely: Speed, Time and Distance. The interrelationship between these three is also the most important formula for this chapter, namely:

Speed × Time = Distance (Equation for the description of one motion of one body)

The above equation is the mathematical description of the movement of a body. In complex problems, students tend to get confused regarding the usage of this equation and often end up mixing up the speed, time and distance of different motions of different bodies.

It must be mentioned here that this formula is the cornerstone of the chapter Time, Speed and Distance.

Besides, this formula is also the source of the various formulae applied to the problems on the applications of time, speed and distance—to trains, boats and streams, clocks and races, circular motion and straight line motion.

In the equation above, *speed* can be defined as the rate at which distance is covered during the motion. It is measured in terms of *distance* per unit time and may have any combination of units of distance and time in the numerator and the denominator respectively. (m/s, km/hour, m/min, km/min, km/day, etc.)

When we say that the speed of a body is S kmph, we mean to say that the body moves with S kmph towards or away from a stationary point (as the case may be).

Time (t) is the time duration over which the movement/ motion occurs/has occurred. The unit used for measuring time is synchronous with the denominator of the unit used for measuring speed. Thus, if the speed is measured in terms of km/h then time is measured in hours.

Distance (d) is the displacement of the body during the motion.

The above equation, as is self-evident, is such that the interrelationship between the three parameters defines the value of the third parameter if two of the three are known. Hence we can safely say that if we know two of the three variables describing the motion, then the motion is fully described and every aspect of it is known.

The Proportionalities Implicit in the Equation $S \times T = D$

The above equation has three implicit proportionality dimensions each of which has its own critical bearing on the solving of time, speed and distance problems.

1. **Direct proportionality between time and distance (when the speed is constant) time $\propto$ distance**

Illustration

A car moves for 2 hours at a speed of 25 kmph and another car moves for 3 hours at the same speed. Find the ratio of distances covered by the two cars.

Solution: Since, the speed is constant, we can directly conclude that time $\propto$ distance.

Hence $\qquad \dfrac{t_A}{t_B} = \dfrac{d_A}{d_B}$

Since, the times of travel are 2 and 3 hours respectively, the ratio of distances covered is also 2/3.

Note: This can be verified by looking at the actual distances travelled—being 50 km and 75 km in this case.

2. **Direct Proportionality between speed and distance (when the time is constant) speed $\propto$ distance**

(a) *A body travels at S_1 kmph for the first 2 hours and then travels at S_2 kmph for the next two hours.* Here two motions of one body are being described and between these two motions the time is constant hence speed will be proportional to the distance travelled.

(b) *Two cars start simultaneously from A and B respectively towards each other with speeds of S_1 kmph and S_2 kmph. They meet at a point C....* Here again, the speed is directly proportional to the distance since two motions are described where the time of both the motions is the same, that is, it is evident here that the first and the second car travel for the same time.

In such a case the following ratios will be valid:

$$S_1/S_2 = d_1/d_2$$

Illustrations

(i) A car travels at 30 km/h for the first 2 hours of a journey and then travels at 40 km/h for the next 2 hours of the journey. Find the ratio of the distances travelled at the two speeds.

Solution: Since time is constant between the two motions described, we can use the proportionality between speed and distance.

Hence, $\qquad d_1/d_2 = s_1/s_2 = 3/4$

Alternatively, you can also think in terms of percentage as d_2 will be 33.33% higher than d_1 since S_2 is 33.33% higher than S_1 and time is constant.

(ii) Two cars leave simultaneously from points A and B on a straight line towards each other. The distance between A and B is 100 km. They meet at a point 40 km from A. Find the ratio of their speeds.

Solution: Since time is the same for both the motions described, we have ratio of speed = ratio of distance.

$$S_A/S_B = 40/60 = 2/3$$

(iii) Two cars move simultaneously from points A and B towards each other. The speeds of the two cars are 20 m/s and 25 m/s respectively. Find the meeting point if $d(AB) = 900$ km.

Solution: For the bodies to meet, the time of travel is constant (since the two cars have moved simultaneously).

Hence, speed ratio = distance ratio
$\rightarrow$ 4/5 = distance ratio

Hence, the meeting point will be 400 km from A and 500 km from B.

3. **Inverse proportionality between speed and time (when the distance is constant) Speed $\propto$ 1/time**

(a) *A body travels at S_1 kmph for the first half of the journey and then travels at S_2 kmph for the second half of the journey.* Here two motions of one body are being described and between these two motions the distance travelled is constant. Hence the speed will be inversely proportional to the time travelled for.

(b) *Two cars start simultaneously from A and B respectively towards each other. They meet at a point C and reach their respective destinations B and A in t_1 and t_2 hours respectively...* Here again, the speed is inversely proportional to the time since two motions are described where the distance of both the motions is the same, that is, it is evident here that the first and the second car travel for the distance, viz., AB. In such a case, the following ratio will be valid:

$$S_1/S_2 = t_2/t_1 \quad \text{i.e.} \quad S_1 t_1 = S_2 t_2 = S_3 t_3 = K$$

Illustrations

(i) A train meets with an accident and moves at 3/4 its original speed. Due to this, it is 20 minutes late. Find the original time for the journey beyond the point of accident.

Solution: Speed becomes 3/4 (Time becomes 4/3)
Extra time = 1/3 of normal time = 20 minutes
Normal time = 60 minutes

Alternatively, from the table on product constancy in the chapter of percentages, we get that a 25% reduction in speed leads to a 33.33% increase in time.

But, 33.33% increase in time is equal to 20 minutes increase in time.

Hence, total time (original) = 60 minutes.

(ii) A body travels half the journey at 20 kmph and the other half at 30 kmph. Find the average speed.

Solution: The short-cut process is elucidated in the chapter on 'averages'. Answer = 24 kmph.

(iii) A man travels from his house to his office at 5 km/h and reaches his office 20 minutes late. If his speed had been 7.5 km/h, he would have reached his office 12 minutes early. Find the distance from his house to his office.

Solution: Notice that here the distance is constant. Hence, speed is inversely proportional to time.
Solving mathematically

$$S_1/S_2 = t_2/(t_2 + 32)$$
$$5/7.5 = t_2/(t_2 + 32)$$
$$5t_2 + 160 = 7.5\ t_2$$
$$t_2 = 160/2.5 = 64 \text{ minutes}$$

Hence, the distance is given by 7.5 × 64/60 = 8 km.

Alternatively, using the Product Constancy Table from the chapter of percentages. If speed increases by 50%, then time will decrease by 33.33%.

But the decrease is equal to 32 minutes.

Hence, original time = 96 minutes and new time is 64 minutes.

Hence, the required distance = 5 × 96/60 km = 8 km.
or distance = 7.5 × 64/60 km = 8 km

[*Note:* The entire process can be worked out mentally while reading the problem.]

CONVERSION BETWEEN kmph to m/s

1 km/h = 1000 m/h = 1000/3600 m/s = 5/18 m/s.

Hence, to convert y km/h into m/s multiply by 5/18.

Thus, y km/h = $\dfrac{5y}{18}$ m/s.

And vice versa : y m/s = 18 y/5 km/h. To convert from m/s to kmph, multiply by 18/5.

Relative Speed : Same Direction and Opposite Direction

Normally, when we talk about the movement of a body, we mean the movement of the body with respect to a stationary point. However, there are times when we need to determine the movement and its relationships with respect to a moving point/body. In such instances, we have to take into account the movement of the body/point with respect to which we are trying to determine relative motion.

Relative movement, therefore, can be viewed as the movement of one body relative to another moving body.

The following formulae apply for the relative speed of two **independent** bodies with respect to each other:

Case I: Two bodies are moving in *opposite* directions at speeds S_1 and S_2 respectively.
The relative speed is defined as $S_1 + S_2$

Case II: Two bodies are moving in the *same direction*.

The relative speed is defined as

(a) $S_1 - S_2$ when S_1 is greater than S_2.
(b) $S_2 - S_1$ when S_1 is lesser than S_2.

In other words, the relative speed can also be defined as the positive value of the difference between the two speeds, that is, $|S_1 - S_2|$.

Motion in a Straight Line

Problems on situations of motion in a straight line are one of the most commonly asked questions in the CAT and other aptitude exams. Hence a proper understanding of the following concepts and their application to problem solving will be extremely important for the student.

Motion in a straight line is governed by the rules of relative speed enumerated above.

A. Two or more bodies starting from the same point and moving in the same direction: Their relative speed is $S_1 - S_2$.

(a) *In the case of the bodies moving to and fro between two points A and B:* The faster body will reach the end first and will meet the second body on its way back. The relative speed $S_1 - S_2$ will apply till the point of reversal of the faster body and after that the two bodies will start to move in the opposite directions at a relative speed of $S_1 + S_2$. The relative speed governing the movement of the two bodies will alternate between $S_1 - S_2$ and $S_1 + S_2$ everytime any one of the bodies reverses directions. However, if both the bodies reverse their direction at the same instant, there will be no change in the relative speed equation.

In this case, the description of the motion of the two bodies between two consecutive meetings will also be governed by the proportionality between speed and distance (since the time of movement between any two meetings will be constant).

Distances covered in this case: For every meeting, the total distance covered by the two bodies will be 2D (where D is the distance between the extreme points). However, notice that the value of $2D$ would be applicable only if both the bodies reverse the direction between two meetings. In case only one body has reversed direction, the total distance would need to be calculated on a case-by-case basis. The respective coverage of the distance is in the ratio of the individual speeds.

Thus, for the 9th meeting (if both bodies have reversed direction between every 2 meetings) the total distance covered will be $9 \times 2D = 18D$.

This will be useful for solving problems that require the calculation of a meeting point.

(b) *In the case of the bodies continuing to move in the same direction without coming to an end point and reversing directions*: The faster body will take a lead and will keep increasing the lead and the movement of the two bodies will be governed by the relative speed equation: $S_1 - S_2$.

Here again, if the two bodies start simultaneously, their movement will be governed by the direct proportionality between speed and distance.

B. Moving in the opposite direction: Their relative speed will be initially given by $S_1 + S_2$.

(a) *In the case of the bodies moving to and fro between two points A and B starting from opposite ends of the path*: The two bodies will move towards each other, meet at a point in between A and B, then move apart away from each other. The faster body will reach its extreme point first followed by the slower body reaching its extreme point next. Relative speed will change every time; one of the bodies reverses direction.

The position of the meeting point will be determined by the ratio of the speeds of the bodies (since the 2 movements can be described as having the time constant between them).

Distances covered in the above case: For the first meeting, the total distance covered by the two bodies will be D (the distance between the extreme points). The coverage of the distance is in the ratio of the individual speeds.

Thereafter, as the bodies separate and start coming together, the combined distance to be covered is $2D$. Note that if only one body is reversing direction between two meetings, this would not be the case and you will have to work it out.

Thus, for the 10th meeting (if both bodies have reverse direction between every 2 meetings) the total distance covered will be $D + 9 \times 2D = 19D$.

This will be useful for solving of problems that require the calculation of a meeting point.

Illustrations

(i) Two bodies A and B start from opposite ends P and Q of a straight road. They meet at a point $0.6D$ from P. Find the point of their fourth meeting.

Solution: Since time is constant, we have ratio of speeds as 3 : 2.

Also, total distance to be covered by the two together for the fourth meeting is $7D$. This distance is divided in a ratio of 3 : 2 and thus we have that A will cover $4.2D$ and B will cover $2.8D$.

The fourth meeting point can then be found out by tracking either A or B's movement. A, having moved a distance of $4.2D$, will be at a point $0.2D$ from P. This is the required answer.

(ii) A starts walking from a place at a uniform speed of 2 km/h in a particular direction. After half an hour, B starts from the same place and walks in the same direction as A at a uniform speed and overtakes A after 1 hour 48 minutes. Calculate the speed of B.

Solution: Start solving as you read the question. From the first two sentences you see that A is 1 km ahead of B when B starts moving.

This distance of 1 km is covered by B in 9/5 hours [1 hour 48 minutes = 1(4/5) = 9/5 hours].
The equation operational here $(S_B - S_A) \times T =$ initial distance
$$(S_B - 2) \times 9/5 = 1$$
Solving, we get $S_B = 23/9$ km/h.

(b) *In the case of the bodies continuing to move in the same direction without coming to an end point and reversing directions*: The bodies will meet and following their meeting they will start separating and going away from each other. The relative speed will be given by $S_1 + S_2$ initially while approaching each other and, thereafter, it will be $S_1 + S_2$ while moving away from each other.

Important: The student is advised to take a closer look and get a closer understanding of these concepts by taking a few examples with absolute values of speed, time and distance. Try to visualise how two bodies separate and then come together. Also, clearly understand the three proportionalities in the equation $s \times t = d$, since these are very important tools for problem solving.

Concept of Acceleration

Acceleration is defined as the rate of change of speed.

Acceleration can be positive (speed increases) or negative (speed decreases → also known as deceleration)

The unit of acceleration is speed per unit time (e.g. m/s^2)

For instance, if a body has an initial speed of 5 m/s and a deceleration of 0.1 m/s^2 it will take 50 seconds to come to rest.

Final speed = Initial speed + Acceleration × Time

Some more examples:

(i) Water flows into a cylindrical beaker at a constant rate. The base area of the beaker is 24 cm^2. The water level rises by 10 cm every second. How quickly will the water level rise in a beaker with a base area of 30 cm^2.

Solution: The flow of water in the beaker is 24 cm^2 × 10 cm/s = 240 cm^3/s.

If the base area is 30 cm^2 then the rate of water level rise will be 240/30 = 8 cm/s.

Note: In case of confusion in such questions the student is advised to use dimensional analysis to understand what to multiply and what to divide.

(ii) A 2 kilowatt heater can boil a given amount of water in 10 minutes. How long will it take for
   (a) a less powerful heater of 1.2 kilowatts to boil the same amount of water?
   (b) a less powerful heater of 1.2 kilowatts to boil double the amount of water?

Solution:

(a) The heating required to boil the amount of water is $2 \times 10 = 20$ kilowatt minutes. At the rate of 1.2 kilowatt, this heat will be generated in 20/1.2 minutes = 16.66 minutes.

(b) When the water is doubled, the heating required is also doubled. Hence, heating required = 40 kilowatt minutes. At the rate of 1.2 kilowatt, this heat will be generated in 40/1.2 = 33.33 minutes.

AN APPLICATION OF ALLIGATION IN TIME, SPEED AND DISTANCE

Consider the following situation:

Suppose a car goes from A to B at an average speed of S_1 and then comes back from B to A at an average speed of S_2. If you had to find out the average speed of the whole journey, what would you do?

The normal short cut given for this situation gives the average speed as:

$$\frac{2S_1 S_2}{S_1 + S_2}$$

However, this situation can be solved very conveniently using the process of alligation as explained below:

Since, the two speeds are known to us, we will also know their ratio. The ratio of times for the two parts of the journey will then be the inverse ratio of the ratio of speeds. (Since the distance for the two journeys are equal). The answer will be the weighted average of the two speeds (weighted on the basis of the time travelled at each speed)

The process will become clear through an example:

A car travels at 60 km/h from Mumbai to Poona and at 120 km/h from Poona to Mumbai. What is the average speed of the car for the entire journey.

Solution

The process of alligation, will be used here to give the answer as 80. (*Note:* For the process of alligation, refer to the chapter of Alligations.)

Note here, that since the speed ratio is 1:2, the value of the time ratio used for calculating the weighted average will be 2:1.

What will happen in case the distances are not constant?

For instance, if the car goes 100 km at a speed of 66kmph and 200 km at a speed of 110 kmph, what will be the average speed?

In this case the speed ratio being 6:10 i.e. 3:5 the inverse of the speed ratio will be 5:3. This would have been the ratio to be used for the time ratio in case the distances were the same (for both the speeds). But since the distances are different, we cannot use this ratio in this form. The problem is overcome by multiplying this ratio (5:3) by the distance ratio (in this case it is 1:2) to get a value of 5:6. This is the ratio which has to be applied for the respective weights. Hence, the alligation will look like:

Solution

Thus the required answer is 90 kmph. (The student is advised to check this value through normal mathematical processes.)

APPLICATIONS OF TIME, SPEED AND DISTANCE

Trains

Trains are a special case in questions related to time, speed and distance because they have their own theory and distinct situations.

The basic relation for trains problems is the same: Speed × Time = Distance.

The following things need to be kept in mind before solving questions on trains:

(a) When the train is crossing a moving object, the speed has to be taken as the **relative speed** of the train with respect to the object. All the rules for relative speed will apply for calculating the relative speed.

(b) The distance to be covered when crossing an object whenever a train crosses an object will be equal to: **Length of train + Length of object**

Thus, the following cases will yield separate equations, which will govern the crossing of the object by the train:

For each of the following situations the following notations have been used:

S_T = Speed of train S_O = Speed of object t = time
L_T = Length of train L_O = Length of object

Case I: Train crossing a stationary object without length:
$$S_T \times t = L_T$$
Case II: Train crossing a stationary object with length:
$$S_T \times t = (L_T + L_O)$$

Case III: Train crossing a moving object without length:

- In opposite direction: $(S_T + S_O) \times t = L_T$
- In same direction: $(S_T - S_O) \times t = L_T$

Case IV: Train crossing a moving object with length:

- In opposite direction: $(S_T + S_O) \times t = (L_T + L_O)$
- In same direction: $(S_T - S_O) \times t = (L_T + L_O)$

[*Note:* In order for a train to completely cross a stationary point on the ground, the train has to traverse a distance that is equal to its entire length.

This can be visualised by remembering yourself stationary on a railway platform and being crossed by a train. You would say that the train starts crossing you when the engine of the train comes in line with you. Also, you would say that you have been crossed by the train when the end of the guard's compartment comes in line with you. Thus, the train would have travelled its own length in crossing you].

Illustrations

(i) A train crosses a pole in 8 seconds. If the length of the train is 200 metres, find the speed of the train.

Solution: In this case, it is evident that the situation is one of the train crossing a stationary object without length. Hence, Case I is applicable here.

Thus, $S_T = 200/8 = 25$ m/s $\rightarrow 25 \times \dfrac{18}{5} = 90$ kmph.

(ii) A train crosses a man travelling in another train in the opposite direction in 8 seconds. However, the train requires 25 seconds to cross the same man if the trains are travelling in the same direction. If the length of the first train is 200 metres and that of the train in which the man is sitting is 160 metres, find the speed of the first train.

Solution: Here, the student should understand that the situation is one of the train crossing a moving object without length. Thus the length of the man's train is useless or redundant data.

Then applying the relevant formulae after considering the directions of the movements we get the equations:

$$S_T + S_M = 25$$
$$S_T - S_M = 8$$

$$S_T = \frac{33}{2} = \frac{33 \times 18}{2 \times 5} = 59.4 \text{ kmph}$$

Boats and Streams

The problems of boats and streams are also dependent on the basic equation of time, speed and distance : Speed × Time = Distance.

However, as in the case of trains the adjustments to be made for solving questions on boats and streams are:

The boat has a speed of its own, which is also called the *speed of the boat in still water* (S_B).

Another variable that is used in boats and streams problems is the *speed of the stream* (S_S).

The speed of the movement of the boat is dependent on whether the boat is moving:

(a) In still water the speed of movement is given by $\rightarrow S_B$.

(b) While *moving upstream* (or against the flow of the water), the speed of movement is given by $\rightarrow S_U = S_B - S_S$

(c) While *moving downstream* (or with the flow of the water), the speed of movement is given by $\rightarrow S_D = S_B + S_S$

The time of movement and the distance to be covered are to be judged by the content of the problem.

Circular motion: A special case of movement is when two or more bodies are moving around a circular track.

The relative speed of two bodies moving around a circle in the same direction is taken as $S_1 - S_2$.

Also, *when two bodies are moving around a circle in the opposite direction, the speed of the two bodies is taken to be $S_1 + S_2$.*

The peculiarity inherent in moving around a circle in the same direction is that when the faster body overtakes the slower body it goes ahead of it. And for every unit time that elapses, the faster body keeps increasing the distance by which the slower body is behind the faster body. However, when the distance by which the faster body is in front of the slower body becomes equal to the circumference of the circle around which the two bodies are moving, the faster body again comes in line with the slower body. This event is called as overlapping or lapping of the slower body by the faster body. We say that the slower body has been lapped or overlapped by the faster body.

First meeting: Three or more bodies start moving simultaneously from the same point on the circumference of the circle, in the same direction around the circle. They will first meet again in the LCM of the times that the fastest runner takes in totally overlapping each of the slower runners.

For instance, if A, B, C and D start clockwise from a point X on the circle such that A is the fastest runner then we can define T_{AB} as the time in which A completely overlaps B, T_{AC} as the time in which A completely overlaps C and T_{AD} as the time in which A completely overlaps D. Then the LCM of T_{AB}, T_{AC} and T_{AD} will be the time in which A, B, C and D will be together again for the first time.

First meeting at starting point: Three or more bodies start moving simultaneously from the same point on the circumference of a circle, in the same direction around the circle. Their first meeting at the starting point will occur after a time that is got by the LCM of the times that each of the bodies takes to complete one full round.

For instance, if A, B and C start from a point X on the circle such that T_A, T_B and T_C are the times in which A, B and C respectively cover one complete round around the circle, then they will all meet together at the starting point in the LCM of T_A, T_B and T_C.

Clocks

Problems on clocks are based on the movement of the minute hand and that of the hour hand as well as on the relative movement between the two. In my opinion, it is best to solve problems on clocks by considering a clock to be a circular track having a circumference of 60 km and each kilometre being represented by one minute on the dial of the clock. Then, we can look at the minute hand as a runner running at the speed of 60 kmph while we can also look at the hour hand as a runner running at an average speed of 5 kmph.

Since, the minute hand and the hour hand are both moving in the same direction, the relative speed of the minute hand with respect to the hour hand is 55 kmph, that is, for every hour elapsed, the minute hand goes 55 km (minute) more than the hour hand.

(Beyond this slight adjustment, the problems of clocks require a good understanding of unitary method. This will be well illustrated through the solved example below.)

Important Information

Number of right angles formed by a clock: A clock makes 2 right angles between any 2 hours. Thus, for instance, there are 2 right angles formed between 12 to 1 or between 1 and 2 or between 2 and 3 or between 3 and 4 and so on.

However, contrary to expectations, the clock does not make 48 right angles in a day. This happens because whenever the clock passes between the time period 2–4 or between the time period 8–10 there are not 4 but only 3 right angles.

This happens because the second right angle between 2–3 (or 8–9) and the first right angle between 3–4 (or 9–10) are one and the same, occurring at 3 or 9.

Contd

Space for Notes

Important Information (*Contd*)

Right angles are formed when the distance between the minute hand and the hour hand is equal to 15 minutes.

Exactly the same situation holds true for the formation of straight lines. There are 2 straight lines in every hour. However, the second straight line between 5–6 (or 11–12) and the first straight line between 6–7 (or 12–1) coincide with each other and are represented by the straight line formed at 6 (or 12).

Straight lines are formed when the distance between the minute hand and the hour hand is equal to either 0 minutes or 30 minutes.

Illustration

At what time between 2–3 p.m. is the first right angle in that time formed by the hands of the clock?

Solution: At 2 p.m. the minute hand can be visualised as being 10 kilometres behind the hour hand. (considering the clock dial to be a race track of circumference 60 km such that each minute represents a kilometre).

Also, the first right angle between 2–3 is formed when the minute hand is 15 kilometres ahead of the hour hand.

Thus, the minute hand has to cover 25 kilometres over the hour hand.

This can be written using the unitary method:

Distance covered by the minute hand over the hour hand.

55 kilometres ——————— in 1 hour
25 kilometres ——————— in what time?
→ 5/11 of an hour.

Thus, the first right angle between 2–3 is formed at 5/11 hours past 2 o'clock.

This can be converted into minutes and seconds using unitary method again as:

1 hour ——————— 60 minutes
5/11 hours ——————— ? minutes
→ 300/11 minutes = 27 (3/11) minutes
1 minute ——————— 60 seconds
3/11 minutes ——————— ? seconds → 180/11 seconds = 16.3636 seconds.

Hence, the required answer is: **2 : 27 : 16.36 seconds**.

LEVEL OF DIFFICULTY (I)

1. The Sinhagad Express left Pune at noon sharp. Two hours later, the Deccan Queen started from Pune in the same direction. The Deccan Queen overtook the Sinhagad Express at 8 p.m. Find the average speed of the two trains over this journey if the sum of their average speeds is 70 km/h.
   - (a) 34.28 km/h
   - (b) 35 km/h
   - (c) 50 km/h
   - (d) 12 km/h

2. Walking at 3/4 of his normal speed, Abhishek is 16 minutes late in reaching his office. The usual time taken by him to cover the distance between his home and his office is
   - (a) 48 minutes
   - (b) 60 minutes
   - (c) 42 minutes
   - (d) 62 minutes

3. Ram and Bharat travel the same distance at the rate of 6 km per hour and 10 km per hour respectively. If Ram takes 30 minutes longer than Bharat, the distance travelled by each is
   - (a) 6 km
   - (b) 10 km
   - (c) 7.5 km
   - (d) 20 km

4. Two trains for Mumbai leave Delhi at 6:00 a.m. and 6:45 am and travel at 100 kmph and 136 kmph respectively. How many kilometres from Delhi will the two trains be together?
   - (a) 262.4 km
   - (b) 260 km
   - (c) 283.33 km
   - (d) 275 km

5. Two trains, Calcutta Mail and Bombay Mail, start at the same time from stations Kolkata and Mumbai respectively towards each other. After passing each other, they take 12 hours and 3 hours to reach Mumbai and Kolkata respectively. If the Calcutta Mail is moving at the speed of 48 km/h, the speed of the Bombay Mail is
   - (a) 24 km/h
   - (b) 22 km/h
   - (c) 21 km/h
   - (d) 96 km/h

6. Shyam's house, his office and his gym are all equidistant from each other. The distance between any 2 of them is 4 km. Shyam starts walking from his gym in a direction parallel to the road connecting his office and his house and stops when he reaches a point directly east of his office. He then reverses direction and walks till he reaches a point directly south of his office. The total distance walked by Shyam is
   - (a) 6 km
   - (b) 9 km
   - (c) 16 km
   - (d) 12 km

7. Lonavala and Khandala are two stations 600 km apart. A train starts from Lonavala and moves towards Khandala at the rate of 25 km/h. After two hours, another train starts from Khandala at the rate of 35 km/h. How far from Lonavala will they will cross each other?
   - (a) 250 km
   - (b) 300 km
   - (c) 279.166 km
   - (d) 475 km

8. Walking at 3/4 of his normal speed, a man takes 2(1/2) hours more than the normal time. Find the normal time.
   - (a) 7.5 h
   - (b) 6 h
   - (c) 8 h
   - (d) 12 h

9. Alok walks to a viewpoint and returns to the starting point by his car and thus takes a total time of 6 hours 45 minutes. He would have gained 2 hours by driving both ways. How long would it have taken for him to walk both ways?
   - (a) 8 h 45 min
   - (b) 7 h 45 min
   - (c) 5 h 30 min
   - (d) 6 h 45 min

10. Sambhu beats Kalu by 30 metres or 10 seconds. How much time was taken by Sambhu to complete a race 1200 meters.
    - (a) 6 min 30 s
    - (b) 3 min 15 s
    - (c) 12 min 10 s
    - (d) 2 min 5 s

11. What is the time taken by Chandu to cover a distance of 360 km by a motorcycle moving at a speed of 10 m/s?
    - (a) 10 h
    - (b) 5 h
    - (c) 8 h
    - (d) 6 h

12. Without stoppage, a train travels a certain distance with an average speed of 60 km/h, and with stoppage, it covers the same distance with an average speed of 40 km/h. On an average, how many minutes per hour does the train stop during the journey?
    - (a) 20 min/h
    - (b) 15 min/h
    - (c) 10 min/h
    - (d) 10 min/h

13. Rajdhani Express travels 650 km in 5 h and another 940 km in 10 h. What is the average speed of train?
    - (a) 1590 km/h
    - (b) 168 km/h
    - (c) 106 km/h
    - (d) 126 km/h

14. Rishikant, during his journey, travels for 20 minutes at a speed of 30 km/h, another 30 minutes at a speed of 50 km/h, and 1 hour at a speed of 50 km/h and 1 hour at a speed of 60 km/h. What is the average velocity?
    - (a) 51.18 km/h
    - (b) 63 km/h
    - (c) 39 km/h
    - (d) 48 km/h

15. A car travels from A to B at V_1 km/h, travels back from B to A at V_2 km/h and again goes back from A to B at V_2 km/h. The average speed of the car is:

    (a) $\dfrac{2V_1 V_2}{V_1 + 2V_2}$

    (b) $\dfrac{2V_1 V_2}{V_2 + 2V_1}$

    (c) $\dfrac{3V_1 V_2}{V_2 + 2V_1}$

    (d) $\dfrac{3V_1 V_2}{V_1 + 2V_2}$

16. Narayan Murthy walking at a speed of 20 km/h reaches his college 10 minutes late. Next time he increases his speed by 5 km/h, but finds that he is still late by 4 minutes. What is the distance of his college from his house?

    (a) 20 km   (b) 6 km

    (c) 12 km   (d) None of these

17. Jayshree goes to office at a speed of 6 km/h and returns to her home at a speed of 4 km/h. If she takes 10 hours in all, what is the distance between her office and her home?

    (a) 24 km   (b) 12 km

    (c) 10 km   (d) 30 km

18. A motor car does a journey in 17.5 hours, covering the first half at 30 km/h and the second half at 40 km/h. Find the distance of the journey.

    (a) 684 km   (b) 600 km

    (c) 120 km   (d) 540 km

19. Sujit covers a distance in 40 minutes if he drives at a speed of 60 kilometer per hour on an average. Find the speed at which he must drive at to reduce the time of the journey by 25%?

    (a) 60 km/h   (b) 70 km/h

    (c) 75 km/h   (d) 80 km/h

20. Manish travels a certain distance by car at the rate of 12 km/h and walks back at the rate of 3 km/h. The whole journey took 5 hours. What is the distance he covered on the car?

    (a) 12 km   (b) 30 km

    (c) 15 km   (d) 6 km

21. A railway passenger counts the telegraph poles on the rail road as he passes them. The telegraph poles are at a distance of 50 metres. What will be his count in 4 hours, if the speed of the train is 45 km per hour?

    (a) 600   (b) 2500

    (c) 3600   (d) 5000

22. Two trains A and B start simultaneously in the opposite direction from two points A and B and arrive at their destinations 9 and 4 hours respectively after their meeting each other. At what rate does the second train B travel if the first train travels at 80 km per hour.

    (a) 60 km/h   (b) 100 km/h

    (c) 120 km/h   (d) 80 km/h

23. Vinay fires two bullets from the same place at an interval of 12 minutes but Raju sitting in a train approaching the place hears the second report 11 minutes 30 seconds after the first. What is the approximate speed of train (if sound travels at the speed of 330 metre per second)?

    (a) 660/23 m/s   (b) 220/7 m/s

    (c) 330/23 m/s   (d) 110/23 m/s

24. A car driver, driving in a fog, passes a pedestrian who was walking at the rate of 2 km/h in the same direction. The pedestrian could see the car for 6 minutes and it was visible to him up to a distance of 0.6 km. What was the speed of the car?

    (a) 30 km/h   (b) 15 km/h

    (c) 20 km/h   (d) 8 km/h

25. Harsh and Vijay move towards Hosur starting from IIM, Bangalore, at a speed of 40 km/h and 60 km/h respectively. If Vijay reaches Hosur 200 minutes earlier then Harsh, what is the distance between IIM, Bangalore, and Hosur?

    (a) 600 km   (b) 400 km

    (c) 900 km   (d) 200 km

26. A journey of 192 km takes 2 hours less by a fast train than by a slow train. If the average speed of the slow train be 16 kmph less than that of fast train, what is the average speed of the faster train?

    (a) 32 kmph   (b) 16 kmph

    (c) 12 kmph   (d) 48 kmph

27. A passenger train takes 2 h less for a journey of 300 kilometres if its speed is increased by 5 kmph over its usual speed. Find the usual speed.

    (a) 10 kmph   (b) 12 kmph

    (c) 20 kmph   (d) 25 kmph

28. If Arun had walked 1 km/h faster, he would have taken 10 minutes less to walk 2 kilometre. What is Arun's speed of walking?

    (a) 1 kmph   (b) 2 kmph

    (c) 3 kmph   (d) 6 kmph

29. A plane left half an hour later than the scheduled time and in order to reach its destination 1500 kilometre away in time, it had to increase its speed by 33.33 per cent over its usual speed. Find its increased speed.

    (a) 250 kmph   (b) 500 kmph

    (c) 750 kmph   (d) 1000 kmph

30. A train moves at a constant speed of 120 km/h for one kilometre and at 40 kmph for the next one kilometre. What is the average speed of the train?

    (a) 48 kmph   (b) 50 kmph

    (c) 80 kmph   (d) 60 kmph

31. A cyclist moving on a circular track of radius 100 metres completes one revolution in 2 minutes. What is the average speed of cyclist (approximately)?

(a) 314 m/minute   (b) 200 m/minute
(c) 300 m/minute   (d) 900 m/minute

32. A person travelled a distance of 200 kilometre between two cities by a car covering the first quarter of the journey at a constant speed of 40 km/h and the remaining three quarters at a constant speed of x km/h. If the average speed of the person for the entire journey was 53.33 km/h what is the value of x?

(a) 55 km/h   (b) 60 km/h
(c) 70 km/h   (d) 80 km/h

33. A car travels 1/3 of the distance on a straight road with a velocity of 10 km/h, the next 1/3 with a velocity of 20 km/h and the last 1/3 with a velocity of 60 km/h. What is the average velocity of the car for the whole journey?

(a) 18 km/h   (b) 10 km/h
(c) 20 km/h   (d) 15 km/h

34. Two cars started simultaneously toward each other from town A and B, that are 480 km apart. It took the first car travelling from A to B 8 hours to cover the distance and the second car travelling from B to A 12 hours. Determine at what distance from A the two cars meet.

(a) 288 km   (b) 200 km
(c) 300 km   (d) 196 km

35. Walking at 3/4 of his usual speed, a man is 16 minutes late for his office. The usual time taken by him to cover that distance is

(a) 48 minutes   (b) 60 minutes
(c) 42 minutes   (d) 62 minutes

36. A and B travel the same distance at the rate of 8 kilometre and 10 kilometre an hour respectively. If A takes 30 minutes longer than B, the distance travelled by B is

(a) 6 km   (b) 10 km
(c) 16 km   (d) 20 km

37. Two trains for Patna leave Delhi at 6 a.m. and 6:45 a.m. and travel at 98 kmph and 136 kmph respectively. How many kilometres from Delhi will the two trains meet?

(a) 262.4 km   (b) 260 km
(c) 200 km   (d) None of these

38. Two trains A and B start from station X to Y, Y to X respectively. After passing each other, they take 12 hours and 3 hours to reach Y and X respectively. If train A is moving at the speed of 48 km/h, the speed of train B is

(a) 24 km/h   (b) 96 km/h
(c) 21 km/h   (d) 20 km/h

39. X and Y are two stations 600 km apart. A train starts from X and moves towards Y at the rate of 25 km/h.

Another train starts from Y at the rate of 35 km/h. How far from X they will cross each other?

(a) 250 km   (b) 300 km
(c) 450 km   (d) 475 km

40. A starts from a point that is on the circumference of a circle, moves 600 metre in the North direction and then again moves 800 metre East and reaches a point diametrically opposite the starting point. Find the diameter of the circle?

(a) 1000 m   (b) 500 m
(c) 800 m   (d) 900 m

41. Ram and Shyam run a race of 2000 m. First, Ram gives Shyam a start of 200 m and beats him by 30 s. Next, Ram gives Shyam a start of 3 min and is beaten by 1000 metres. Find the time in minutes in which Ram and Shyam can run the race separately.

(a) 8, 10   (b) 4, 5
(c) 5, 9   (d) 6, 9

42. A motorboat went downstream for 28 km and immediately returned. It took the boat twice as long to make the return trip. If the speed of the river flow were twice as high, the trip downstream and back would take 672 minutes. Find the speed of the boat in still water and the speed of the river flow.

(a) 9 km/h, 3 km/h   (b) 9 km/h, 6 km/h
(c) 8 km/h, 2 km/h   (d) 12 km/h, 3 km/h

43. A train requires 7 seconds to pass a pole while it requires 25 seconds to cross a stationary train which is 378 metres long. Find the speed of the train.

(a) 75.6 km/h   (b) 75.4 km/h
(c) 76.2 km/h   (d) 21 km/h

44. A boat sails downstream from point A to point B, which is 10 km away from A, and then returns to A. If the actual speed of the boat (in still water) is 3 km/h, the trip from A to B takes 8 hours less than that from B to A. What must the actual speed of the boat for the trip from A to B to take exactly 100 minutes?

(a) 1 km/h   (b) 2 km/h
(c) 3 km/h   (d) 4 km/h

45. A boat sails down the river for 10 km and then up the river for 6 km. The speed of the river flow is 1 km/h. What should be the minimum speed of the boat for the trip to take a maximum of 4 hours?

(a) 2 kmph   (b) 3 kmph
(c) 4 kmph   (d) 5 kmph

46. A man rows 6 km/h in still water. If the river is running at 3 km per hour, it takes him 45 minutes to row to a place and back. How far is the place?

(a) 1.12 km   (b) 1.25 km
(c) 1.6875 km   (d) 2.5 km

47. A boat goes 40 km upstream in 8 h and a distance of 49 km downstream in 7 h. The speed of the boat in still water is
    (a) 5 km/h   (b) 5.5 km/h
    (c) 6 km/h   (d) 6.5 km/h

48. Two trains are running on parallel lines in the same direction at speeds of 40 kmph and 20 kmph respectively. The faster train crosses a man in the second train in 36 seconds. The length of the faster train is
    (a) 200 metres   (b) 185 metres
    (c) 225 metres   (d) 210 metres

49. The speed of the boat in still water is 12 km/h and the speed of the stream is 2 km/h. A distance of 8 km, going upstream, is covered in
    (a) 1 h   (b) 1 h 15 min
    (c) 1 h 12 min   (d) None of these

50. A boat goes 15 km upstream in 80 minutes. The speed of the stream is 5 km/h. The speed of the boat in still water is
    (a) 16.25 km/h   (b) 16 km/h
    (c) 15 km/h   (d) 17 km/h

51. In a stream, B lies in between A and C such that it is equidistant from both A and C. A boat can go from A to B and back in 6 h 30 minutes while it goes from A to C in 9 h. How long would it take to go from C to A?
    (a) 3.75 h   (b) 4 h
    (c) 4.25 h   (d) 4.5 h

52. Two trains pass each other on parallel lines. Each train is 100 metres long. When they are going in the same direction, the faster one takes 60 seconds to pass the other completely. If they are going in opposite directions they pass each other completely in 10 seconds. Find the speed of the slower train in km/h.
    (a) 30 km/h   (b) 42 km/h
    (c) 48 km/h   (d) 60 km/h

53. Vinay runs 100 metres in 20 seconds and Ajay runs the same distance in 25 seconds. By what distance will Vinay beat Ajay in a hundred metre race?
    (a) 10 m   (b) 20 m
    (c) 25 m   (d) 12 m

54. In a 100 m race, Shyam runs at 1.66 m/s. If Shyam gives Sujit a start of 4 m and still beats him by 12 seconds, what is Sujit's speed?
    (a) 1.11 m/s   (b) 0.75 m/s
    (c) 1.33 m/s   (d) 1 km/h

55. At a game of billiards, A can give B 15 points in 60 and A can give C 20 in 60. How many points can B give C in a game of 90?
    (a) 11   (b) 13
    (c) 10   (d) 14

56. In a 500 m race, the ratio of speed of two runners Vinay and Shyam is 3 : 4. If Vinay has a start of 140 m then Vinay wins by
    (a) 15 m   (b) 20 m
    (c) 25 m   (d) 30 m

57. How many seconds will a caravan 120 metres long running at the rate 10 m/s take to pass a standing boy.
    (a) 10 s   (b) 12 s
    (c) 11 s   (d) 14 s

58. Two trains are travelling in the same direction at 50 km/h and 30 km/h respectively. The faster train crosses a man in the slower train in 18 seconds. Find the length of the faster train.
    (a) 0.1 km   (b) 1 km
    (c) 1.5 km   (d) 1.4 km

59. Two trains for Howrah leave Muzaffarpur at 8:30 a.m. and 9:00 a.m. respectively and travel at 60 km/h and 70 km/h respectively. How many kilometres from Muzaffarpur will the two trains meet?
    (a) 210 km   (b) 180 km
    (c) 150 km   (d) 120 km

60. Without stoppage, a train travels at an average speed of 75 km/h and with stoppages it covers the same distance at an average speed of 60 km/h. How many minutes per hour does the train stop?
    (a) 10 minutes   (b) 12 minutes
    (c) 14 minutes   (d) 18 minutes

61. A boat rows 16 km up the stream and 30 km downstream taking 5 h each time. The velocity of the current
    (a) 1.1 km/h   (b) 1.2 km/h
    (c) 1.4 km/h   (d) 1.5 km/h

62. Vijay can row a certain distance downstream in 6 h and return the same distance in 9 h. If the stream flows at the rate of 3 km/h, find the speed of Vijay in still water.
    (a) 12 km/h   (b) 13 km/h
    (c) 14 km/h   (d) 15 km/h

63. Subbu can row 6 km/h in still water. When the river is running at 1.2 km/h, it takes him 1 hour to row to a place and back. How far in the place?
    (a) 2.88 km   (b) 2.00 km
    (c) 3.12 km   (d) 2.76 km

64. A dog is passed by a train in 8 seconds. Find the length of the train if its speed is 36 kmph.
    (a) 70 m   (b) 80 m
    (c) 85 m   (d) 90 m

65. A lazy man can row upstream at 16 km/h and downstream at 22 km/h. Find the man's rate in still water (in kmph).

(a) 19   (b) 14
(c) 17   (d) 18

66. A man can row 30 km upstream and 44 km downstream in 10 hours. It is also known that he can row 40 km upstream and 55 km downstream in 13 hours. Find the speed of the man in still water.
    (a) 4 km/h   (b) 6 km/h
    (c) 8 km/h   (d) 12 km/h

67. In a stream that is running at 2 km/h, a man goes 10 km upstream and comes back to the starting point in 55 minutes. Find the speed of the man in still water.
    (a) 20 km/h   (b) 22 km/h
    (c) 24 km/h   (d) 28 km/h

68. A man goes down stream at x km/h and upstream at y km/h. The speed of the boat in still water is
    (a) 0.5 $(x + y)$ (b) 0.5 $(x - y)$
    (c) $x + y$ (d) $x - y$

69. The length of the minutes hand of a clock is 8 cm. Find the distance travelled by its outer end in 15 minutes.
    (a) 4π cm   (b) 8π cm
    (c) 12π cm   (d) 16π cm

70. Between 5 a.m. and 5 p.m. of a particular day for how many times are the minute and the hour hands together?
    (a) 11   (b) 22
    (c) 33   (d) 44

71. At what time are the hands of clock together between 2 and 3 p.m.?

(a) 2/11 hours past 2 p.m.
(b) 2/9 hours past 2 p.m.
(c) 2:10 p.m.
(d) None of these

72. A motorboat went down the river for 14 km and then up the river for 9 km. It took a total of 5 hours for the entire journey. Find the speed of the river flow if the speed of the boat in still water is 5 km/h.
    (a) 1 kmph   (b) 1.5 kmph
    (c) 2 kmph   (d) 3 kmph

73. A motorboat whose speed in still water is 10 km/h went 91 km downstream and then returned to its starting point. Calculate the speed of the river flow if the round trip took a total of 20 hours.
    (a) 3 km/h   (b) 4 km/h
    (c) 6 km/h   (d) 8 km/h

74. In a race of 600 meters, Ajay beats Vijay by 60 metres and in a race of 500 meters Vijay beats Anjay by 25 meters. By how many meters will Ajay beat Anjay in a 400 meter race?
    (a) 48 m   (b) 52 m
    (c) 56 m   (d) 58 m

75. A motorboat whose speed in still water is 15 kmph goes 30 km downstream and comes back in a total 4 hours 30 min. Determine the speed of the stream.
    (a) 2 kmph   (b) 3 kmph
    (c) 4 kmph   (d) 5 kmph

Space for Rough Work

LEVEL OF DIFFICULTY (II)

1. The J&K Express from Delhi to Srinagar was delayed by snowfall for 16 minutes and made up for the delay on a section of 80 km travelling with a speed 10 km per hour higher than its normal speed. Find the original speed of the J&K Express (according to the schedule)
   - (a) 60 km/h
   - (b) 66.66 km/h
   - (c) 50 km/h
   - (d) 40 km/h

2. Ayrton Senna had to cover a distance of 60 km. However, he started 6 minutes later than his scheduled time and raced at a speed 1 km/h higher than his originally planned speed and reached the finish at the time he would reach it if he began to race strictly at the appointed time and raced with the assumed speed. Find the speed at which he travelled during the journey described.
   - (a) 25 km/h
   - (b) 15 km/h
   - (c) 10 km/h
   - (d) 6 km/h

3. Amitabh covered a distance of 96 km two hours faster than he had planned to. This he achieved by travelling 1 km more every hour than he intended to cover every 1 hour 15 minutes. What was the speed at which Amitabh travelled during the journey?
   - (a) 16 km/h
   - (b) 26 km/h
   - (c) 36 km/h
   - (d) 30 km/h

4. An urgent message had to be delivered from the house of the Peshwas in Pune to Shivaji who was camping in Bangalore. A horse rider travels on horse back from Pune to Bangalore at a constant speed. If the horse increased its speed by 6 km/h, it would take the rider 4 hours less to cover that distance. And travelling with a speed 6 km/h lower than the initial speed, it would take him 10 hours more than the time he would have taken had he travelled at a speed 6 kmph higher than the initial speed. Find the distance between Pune and Bangalore.
   - (a) 120 km
   - (b) 600 km
   - (c) 720 km
   - (d) 750 km

5. A pedestrian and a cyclist start simultaneously towards each other from Aurangabad and Paithan which are 40 km apart and meet 2 hours after the start. Then they resumed their trips and the cyclist arrives at Aurangabad 7 hours 30 minutes earlier than the pedestrian arrives at Paithan. Which of these could be the speed of the pedestrian?
   - (a) 4 km/h
   - (b) 5 km/h
   - (c) 3 km/h
   - (d) 6 km/h

6. Two motorists met at 10 a.m. at the Dadar railway station. After their meeting, one of them proceeded in the East direction while the other proceeded in the North direction. Exactly at noon, they were 60 km apart. Find the speed of the slower motorist if the difference of their speeds is 6 km/h.
   - (a) 28 km/h
   - (b) 18 km/h
   - (c) 9 km/h
   - (d) 19 km/h

7. Two cyclists start simultaneously towards each other from Aurangabad and Ellora, which are 28 km apart. An hour later they meet and keep pedalling with the same speed without stopping. The second cyclist arrives at Ellora 35 minutes later than the first arrives at Aurangabad. Find the speed of the cyclist who started from Ellora.
   - (a) 12 km/h
   - (b) 16 km/h
   - (c) 15 km/h
   - (d) 10 km/h

8. Two ants start simultaneously from two ant holes towards each other. The first ant coveres 8% of the distance between the two ant holes in 3 hours, the second ant covered $\frac{7}{120}$ of the distance in 2 hours 30 minutes. Find the speed (feet/h) of the second ant if the first ant travelled 800 feet to the meeting point.
   - (a) 15 feet/h
   - (b) 25 feet/h
   - (c) 45 feet/h
   - (d) 35 feet/h

9. A bus left point X for point Y. Two hours later a car left point X for Y and arrived at Y at the same time as the bus. If the car and the bus left simultaneously from the opposite ends X and Y towards each other, they would meet 1.33 hours after the start. How much time did it take the bus to travel from X to Y?
   - (a) 2 h
   - (b) 4 h
   - (c) 6 h
   - (d) 8 h

10. A racetrack is in the form of a right triangle. The longer of the legs of the track is 2 km more than the shorter of the legs (both these legs being on a highway). The start and end points are also connected to each other through a side road. The escort vehicle for the race took the side road and rode with a speed of 30 km/h and then covered the two intervals along the highway during the same time with a speed of 42 km/h. Find the length of the racetrack.
    - (a) 14 km
    - (b) 10 km
    - (c) 24 km
    - (d) 36 km

11. Two planes move along a circle of circumference 1.2 km with constant speeds. When they move in

different directions, they meet every 15 seconds and when they move in the same direction, one plane overtakes the other every 60 seconds. Find the speed of the slower plane.

(a) 0.04 km/s   (b) 0.03 km/s
(c) 0.05 km/s   (d) 0.02 km/s

12. Karim, a tourist leaves Ellora on a bicycle. Having travelled for 1.5 h at 16 km/h, he makes a stop for 1.5 h and then pedals on with the same speed. Four hours after Karim started, his friend and local guide Rahim leaves Ellora on a motorcycle and rides with a speed of 28 km/h in the same direction as Karim had gone. What distance will they cover before Rahim overtakes Karim?

(a) 88 km   (b) 90.33 km
(c) 93.33 km   (d) 96.66 km

13. A tourist covered a journey partly by foot and partly by tonga. He walked for 90 km and rode the tonga for 10 km. He spent 4 h less on the tonga than on walking. If the tourist had reversed the times he travelled by foot and on tonga, the distances travelled on each part of the journey would be equal. How long did he ride the tonga?

(a) He rode for 6 hours (b) He rode for 4 hours
(c) He rode for 2 hours (d) He rode for 5 hours

14. Two Indian tourists in the US cycled towards each other, one from point A and the other from point B. The first tourist left point A 6 hrs later than the second left point B, and it turned out on their meeting that he had travelled 12 km less than the second tourist. After their meeting, they kept cycling with the same speed, and the first tourist arrived at B 8 hours later and the second arrived at A 9 hours later. Find the speed of the faster tourist.

(a) 4 km/h   (b) 6 km/h
(c) 9 km/h   (d) 2 km/h

15. Two joggers left Delhi for Noida simultaneously. The first jogger stopped 42 min later when he was 1 km short of Noida and the other one stopped 52 min later when he was 2 km short of Noida. If the first jogger jogged as many kilometres as the second and the second as many kilometres as the first, the first one would need 17 min less than the second. Find the distance between Delhi and Noida.

(a) 5 km   (b) 15 km
(c) 25 km   (d) 35 km

16. A tank of 4800 m³ capacity is full of water. The discharging capacity of the pump is 10 m³/min higher than its filling capacity. As a result the pump needs 16 min less to discharge the fuel than to fill up the tank. Find the filling capacity of the pump.

(a) 50 m³/min   (b) 25 m³/min
(c) 55 m³/min   (d) 24 m³/min

17. An ant climbing up a vertical pole ascends 12 meters and slips down 5 meters in every alternate hour. If the pole is 63 meters high how long will it take it to reach the top?

(a) 18 hours
(b) 17 hours
(c) 16 hours 35 minutes
(d) 16 hours 40 minutes

18. Two ports A and B are 300 km apart. Two ships leave A for B such that the second leaves 8 hours after the first. The ships arrive at B simultaneously. Find the time the slower ship spent on the trip if the speed of one of them is 10 km/h higher than that of the other.

(a) 25 hours   (b) 15 hours
(c) 10 hours   (d) 20 hours

19. An ant moved for several seconds and covered 3 mm in the first second and 4 mm more in each successive second than in its predecessor. If the ant had covered 1 mm in the first second and 8 mm more in each successive second, then the difference between the path it would cover during the same time and the actual path would be more than 6 mm but less than 30 mm. Find the time for which the ant moved (in seconds).

(a) 5 s   (b) 4 s
(c) 6 s   (d) 2 s

20. The Sabarmati Express left Ahmedabad for Mumbai. Having travelled 300 km, which constitutes 66.666 per cent of the distance between Ahmedabad and Mumbai, the train was stopped by a red signal. Half an hour later, the track was cleared and the engine-driver, having increased the speed by 15 km per hour, arrived at Mumbai on time. Find the initial speed of the Sabarmati Express.

(a) 50 kmph   (b) 60 kmph
(c) 75 kmph   (d) 40 kmph

21. Two swimmers started simultaneously from the beach, one to the south and the other to the east. Two hours later, the distance between them turned out to be 100 km. Find the speed of the faster swimmer, knowing that the speed of one of them was 75% of the speed of the other.

(a) 30 kmph   (b) 40 kmph
(c) 45 kmph   (d) 60 kmph

22. A motorcyclist left point A for point B. Two hours later, another motorcyclist left A for B and arrived at B at the same time as the first motorcyclist. Had both the motorcyclists started simultaneously from A and B travelling towards each other, they would have met in 80 minutes. How much time did it take the faster motorcyclist to travel from A to B?

(a) 6 hours   (b) 3 hours
(c) 2 hours   (d) 4 hours

23. Two horses started simultaneously towards each other and meet each other 3 h 20 min later. How much time will it take the slower horse to cover the whole distance if the first arrived at the place of departure of the second 5 hours later than the second arrived at the point of departure of the first?
    - (a) 10 hours
    - (b) 5 hours
    - (c) 15 hours
    - (d) 6 hours

24. The difference between the times taken by two buses to travel a distance of 350 km is 2 hours 20 minutes. If the difference between their speeds is 5 kmph, find the slower speed.
    - (a) 35 kmph
    - (b) 30 kmph
    - (c) 25 kmph
    - (d) 20 kmph

25. One bad day, at 7 a.m. I started on my bike at the speed of 36 kmph to meet one of my relatives. After I had travelled some distance, my bike went out of order and I had to stop. After resting for 35 minutes, I returned home on foot at a speed of 14 kmph and reached home at 1 p.m. Find the distance from my house at which my bike broke down.
    - (a) 54 km
    - (b) 63 km
    - (c) 72 km
    - (d) None of these

Direction for Questions 26 to 30:   Read the following data and answer the questions that follow.

Three brothers, Ram, Shyam and Mohan, travelled by road. They all left the college at the same time—12 noon. The description of the motions of the three are detailed below:

Name	Ram	Shyam	Mohan
Phase I	Bus for 2 hours @ 10 mph	Bike for @ 1 hours 30 mph	Foot for 3 hours @ 3.33 mph
Phase II	Bike for 1.5 hours @ 40 mph	Foot for 3 hours @ 3.33 mph	Bus for 3 hours @ 10 mph
Phase III	Foot for 3 hours @ 3.33 mph	Bus for 4 hours @ 10 mph	Bike for 2 hours @ 30 mph

26. When did Ram overtake Shyam?
    - (a) 3:15 p.m.
    - (b) 2:22 p.m.
    - (c) 2:30 p.m.
    - (d) 2:20 p.m.

27. At what distance from the start does Mohan overtake Shyam?
    - (a) 40 miles
    - (b) 57 miles
    - (c) 70 miles
    - (d) 80 miles

28. If Ram travelled by bike instead of foot in the last leg of his journey (for the same distance as he had covered by foot), what is the difference in the times of Ram and Mohan to cover 90 miles?
    - (a) 6 h 50 minutes
    - (b) 10 h 40 minutes
    - (c) 3 hrs 55 minutes
    - (d) 4 hrs 10 minutes

29. If all of them travelled a distance of 100 miles, who reached first and at what time (assume the last leg time increases to cover 100 miles)?
    - (a) Mohan at 6 p.m.
    - (b) Ram at 8 p.m.
    - (c) Shyam at 6 p.m.
    - (d) Mohan at 8 p.m.

30. In the above question, who reached last and at what time?
    - (a) Ram at 9:30 p.m.
    - (b) Ram at 10 p.m.
    - (c) Shyam at 9:30 p.m.
    - (d) Shyam at 10 p.m.

31. A motorcyclist rode the first half of his way at a constant speed. Then he was delayed for 5 minutes and, therefore, to make up for the lost time he increased his speed by 10 km/h. Find the initial speed of the motorcyclist if the total path covered by him is equal to 50 km.
    - (a) 36 km/h
    - (b) 48 km/h
    - (c) 50 km/h
    - (d) 62 km/h

32. Ram Singh and Priyadarshan start together from the same point on a circular path and walk around, each at his own pace, until both arrive together at the starting point. If Ram Singh performs the circuit in 3 minutes 44 seconds and Priyadarshan in 6 minutes 4 seconds, how many times does Ram Singh go around the path?
    - (a) 8
    - (b) 13
    - (c) 15
    - (d) Cannot be determined

33. Ravi, who lives in the countryside, caught a train for home earlier than usual yesterday. His wife normally drives to the station to meet him. But yesterday he set out on foot from the station to meet his wife on the way. He reached home 12 minutes earlier than he would have done had he waited at the station for his wife. The car travels at a uniform speed, which is 5 times Ravi's speed on foot. Ravi reached home at exactly 6 O'clock. At what time would he have reached home if his wife, forewarned of his plan, had met him at the station?
    - (a) 5 : 48
    - (b) 5 : 24
    - (c) 5 : 00
    - (d) 5 : 36

34. Hemant and Ajay start a two-length swimming race at the same moment but from opposite ends of the pool. They swim in lane and at uniform speeds, but Hemant is faster than Ajay. They first pass at a point 18.5 m from the deep end and having completed one length, each one is allowed to rest on the edge for exactly 45 seconds. After setting off on the return length, the swimmers pass for the second time just 10.5 m from the shallow end. How long is the pool?
    - (a) 55.5 m
    - (b) 45 m
    - (c) 66 m
    - (d) 49 m

35. Rahim sets out to cross a forest. On the first day, he completes 1/10th of the journey. On the second day, he covers 2/3rd of the distance travelled the first day.

He continues in this manner, alternating the days in which he travels 1/10th of the distance still to be covered, with days on which he travels 2/3 of the total distance already covered. At the end of seventh day, he finds that $22\frac{1}{2}$ km more will see the end of his journey. How wide is the forest?

(a) $66\frac{2}{3}$ km   (b) 100 km

(c) 120 km   (d) 150 km

36. The metro service has a train going from Mumbai to Pune and Pune to Mumbai every hour, the first one at 6 a.m. The trip from one city to other takes $4\frac{1}{2}$ hours, and all trains travel at the same speed. How many trains will you pass while going from Mumbai to Pune if you start at 12 noon?

(a) 8   (b) 10

(c) 9   (d) 13

37. The distance between two towns is x km. A car travelling between the towns covers the first k km at an average speed of y km/h and the remaining distance at z km/h. The time taken for the journey is

(a) $\dfrac{k}{y} + \dfrac{(x-k)}{z}$ (b) $ky + \dfrac{(k-x)}{z}$

(c) $\dfrac{k}{y} + \dfrac{(k-x)}{z}$ (d) $ky + z(x-k)$

38. Two rifles are fired from the same place at a difference of 11 minutes 45 seconds. But a man who is coming towards the place in a train hears the second sound after 11 minutes. Find the speed of train.

(a) 72 km/h·   (b) 36 km/h

(c) 81 km/h   (d) 108 km/h

Directions for Questions 39 and 40: Read the following and answer the questions that follow.

The Kalinga Express started from Patna to Tata at 7 p.m. at a speed of 60 km/h. Another train, Rajdhani Express, started from Tata to Patna at 4 a.m. next morning at a speed of 90 km/h. The distance between Patna to Tata is 800 km.

39. How far from Tata will the two trains meet?

(a) 164 km   (b) 156 km

(c) 132 km   (d) 128 km

40. At what time will the two trains meet?

(a) 5 : 32 a.m.   (b) 5 : 28 a.m.

(c) 5 : 36 a.m.   (d) 5 : 44 a.m.

Directions for Questions 41 to 43: Read the following and answer the question that follow.

A naughty bird is sitting on top of a car. It sees another car approaching it at a distance of 12 km. The speed of the two cars is 60 kmph each. The bird starts flying from the first car and moves towards the second car, reaches the second car and comes back to the first car and so on. If the speed at which the bird flies is 120 kmph then answer the following questions. Assume that the two cars have a crash.

41. The total distance travelled by the bird before the crash is

(a) 6 km   (b) 12 km

(c) 18 km   (d) None of these

42. The total distance travelled by the bird before it reaches the second car for the second time is

(a) 10.55 km   (b) 11.55 km

(c) 12.33 km   (d) None of these

43. The total number of times that the bird reaches the bonnet of the second car is (theoretically):

(a) 12 times   (b) 18 times

(c) Infinite times   (d) Cannot be determined

44. A dog sees a cat. It estimates that the cat is 25 leaps away. The cat sees the dog and starts running with the dog in hot pursuit. If in every minute, the dog makes 5 leaps and the cat makes 6 leaps and one leap of the dog is equal to 2 leaps of the cat. Find the time in which the cat is caught by the dog (assume an open field with no trees)

(a) 12 minutes   (b) 15 minutes

(c) 12.5 minutes   (d) None of these

45. Two people A and B start from P and Q (distance = D) at the same time towards each other. They meet at a point R, which is at a distance $0.4D$ from P. They continue to move to and fro between the two points. Find the distance from point P at which the fourth meeting takes place.

(a) $0.8D$ (b) $0.6D$

(c) $0.3D$ (d) $0.4D$

46. A wall clock gains 2 minutes in 12 hours, while a table clock loses 2 minutes in 36 hours; both are set right at noon on Tuesday. The correct time when they both show the same time next would be

(a) 12:30 night   (b) 12 noon

(c) 1:30 night   (d) 12 night

47. Two points A and B are located 48 km apart on the riverfront. A motorboat must go from A to B and return to A as soon as possible. The river flows at 6 km/h. What must be the least speed of the motorboat in still water for the trip from A to B and back again to be completed in not more than six hours (assume that the motorboat does not stop at B)?

(a) 18 km/h   (b) 16 km/h

(c) 25 km/h   (d) 46 km/h

48. Two *ghats* are located on a riverbank and are 21 km apart. Leaving one of the ghats for the other, a motorboat returns to the first *ghat* in 270 minutes, spending 40 min of that time in taking the passengers at the second *ghat*. Find the speed of the boat in still water if the speed of the river flow is 2.5 km/h?

(a) 10.4 km/h   (b) 12.5 km/h

(c) 22.5 km/h   (d) 11.5 km/h

49. A train leaves Muzaffarpur for Hazipur at 2:15 p.m. and travels at the rate of 50 kmph. Another train leaves Hazipur for Muzaffarpur at 1:35 p.m. and travels at the rate of 60 kmph. If the distance between Hazipur and Muzaffarpur is 590 km at what distance from Muzaffarpur will the two trains meet?
    - (a) 200 km
    - (b) 300 km
    - (c) 250 km
    - (d) 225 km

50. A dog after travelling 50 km meets a *swami* who counsels him to go slower. He then proceeds at 3/4 of his former speed and arrives at his destination 35 minutes late. Had the meeting occurred 24 km further the dog would have reached its destination 25 minutes late. The speed of the dog is
    - (a) 48 km/h
    - (b) 36 km/h
    - (c) 54 km/h
    - (d) 58 km/h

Space for Rough Work

LEVEL OF DIFFICULTY (III)

1. Two people started simultaneously towards each other from Siliguri and Darjeeling, which are 60 km apart. They met 5 hours later. After their meeting, the first person, who travelled from Siliguri to Darjeeling, decreased his speed by 1.5 km/h and the other person, who travelled from Darjeeling to Siliguri, increased his speed by 1.5 km/h. The first person is known to arrive at Darjeeling 2.5 hours earlier than the second person arrived at Siliguri. Find the initial speed of the first person.
   (a) 4.5 km/h (b) 6 km/h
   (c) 7.5 km/h (d) 9 km/h

2. Two friends Arun and Nishit, on their last day in college, decided to meet after 20 years on a river. Arun had to sail 42 km to the meeting place and Nishit had to sail $35\frac{5}{7}$ per cent less. To arrive at the meeting place at the same time as his friend Nishit, Arun started at the same time as Nishit and sailed with the speed exceeding by 5 km/h the speed of Nishit. Find the speed of Arun.
   (a) 10 kmph (b) 14 km/h
   (c) 9 kmph (d) Both b and c

3. Three cars leave Patna for Ranchi after equal time intervals. They reach Ranchi simultaneously and then leave for Vizag, which is 120 km from Ranchi. The first car arrives there an hour after the second car, and the third car, having reached Vizag, immediately reverses the direction and 40 km from Vizag meets the first car. Find the speed of the first car.
   (a) 30 km/h (b) 19 km/h
   (c) 32 km/h (d) 22 km/h

4. Two sea trawlers left a sea port simultaneously in two mutually perpendicular directions. Half an hour later, the shortest distance between them was 17 km, and another 15 min later, one sea trawler was 10.5 km farther from the origin than the other. Find the speed of each sea trawler.
   (a) 16 km/h, 30 km/h (b) 18 km/h, 24 km/h
   (c) 20 km/h, 22 km/h (d) 18 km/h, 36 km/h

5. Shaurya and Arjit take a straight route to the same terminal point and travel with constant speeds. At the initial moment, the positions of the two and the terminal point form an equilateral triangle. When Arjit covered a distance of 80 km, the triangle becomes right-angled. When Arjit was at a distance of 120 km from the terminal point, the Shaurya arrived at the point. Find the distance between them at the initial moment assuming that there are integral distances throughout the movements described.

6. Mrinalini and Neha travel to Connaught Place along two straight roads with constant speeds. At the initial moment, the positions of Mrinalini, Neha, and Connaught Place form a right triangle. After Mrinalini travelled 30 km, the triangle between the points became equilateral. Find the distance between Mrinalini and Neha at the initial moment if at the time Mrinalini arrived at Connaught Place, Neha had to cover 6.66 km to reach Connaught Place.
   (a) $10\sqrt{3}$ km (b) $12\sqrt{3}$ km
   (c) $30\sqrt{5}$ km (d) None of these

7. Three cars started simultaneously from Ajmer to Benaras along the same highway. The second car travelled with a speed that was 10 km/h higher than the first car's speed and arrived at Benaras 1 hour earlier than the first car. The third car arrived at Benaras 33.33 minutes earlier than the first car, travelling half the time at the speed of the first car and the other half at the speed of the second car. Find the total distance covered by these three cars during their journey between Ajmer and Benaras.
   (a) 360 km (b) 600 km
   (c) 540 km (d) 840 km

8. Three sprinters A, B, and C had to sprint from points P to Q and back again (starting in that order). The time interval between the starting times of the three sprinters A, B and C was 5 seconds each. Thus C started 10 seconds after A, while B started 5 seconds after A. The three sprinters passed a certain point R, which is somewhere between P and Q, simultaneously (none of them having reached point Q yet). Having reached Q and reversed the direction, the third sprinter met the second one 9 m short of Q and met the first sprinter 15 m short of Q. Find the speed of the first sprinter if the distance between PQ is equal to 55 m.
   (a) 4 m/s (b) 3 m/s
   (c) 2 m/s (d) 1 m/s

9. Two trains start from the same point simultaneously and in the same direction. The first train travels at 40 km/h, and the speed of the second train is 25 per cent more than the speed of the first train. Thirty minutes later, a third train starts from the same point and in the same direction. It overtakes the second train 90 minutes later than it overtook the first train. What is the speed of the third train?

(a) 20 km/h   (b) 40 km/h

(c) 60 km/h   (d) 80 km/h

10. A passenger train left town Alpha for town Beta. At the same time, a goods train left Beta for Alpha. The speed of each train is constant throughout the whole trip. Two hours after the trains met, they were 450 km apart. The passenger train arrived at the place of destination 16 hours after their meeting and the goods train, 25 hours after the meeting. How long did it take the passenger train to make the whole trip?

(a) 21 hours   (b) 28 hours

(c) 14 hours   (d) None of these

11. Two ducks move along the circumference of a circular pond in the same direction and come alongside each other every 54 minutes. If they moved with the same speeds in the opposite directions, they would meet every 9 minutes. It is known that when the ducks moved along the cicumference in opposite directions, the distance between them decreased from 54 to 14 feet every 48 seconds. What is the speed of the slower duck?

(a) 20 feet/min   (b) 15 feet/min

(c) 30 feet/min   (d) 20.83 feet/min

12. Dev and Nishit started simultaneously from opposite points X and Y on a straight road, at constant speeds. When Dev had covered 40% of the distance from X to Y, Nishit was 4 km away from Dev after having crossed Dev. When Nishit had covered half the way, Dev was 10 km short of the mid point. Find a possible of the time it took Dev to cover the distance from X to Y to the time it took Nishit to cover the same distance.

(a) $\left[\dfrac{1+\sqrt{3}}{2}\right]$ (b) $\dfrac{3\sqrt{2}+4}{2\sqrt{2}+1}$

(c) Either a or b   (d) None of these

13. For Question 12 which of these is a possible value of the distance between the points X and Y:

(a) $20(2+\sqrt{3})$ (b) $20(1+\sqrt{2})$

(c) 60 km   (d) Both (a) and (b)

14. Two ships sail in a fog towards each other with the same speed. When they are 4 km apart, the captains decelerate the engines for 4 minutes with a deceleration rate of 0.1 m/s², and then the ships continue sailing with the speeds attained. For what range of values of the initial speed V_0 will the ships avoid collision?

(a) $0 < V_0 < 10$ m/s   (b) $0 < V_0 < 20$ m/s

(c) $0 < V_0 < 30$ m/s   (d) None of these

15. Three points A, B and C are located at the vertices of an equilateral triangle with sides equal to 168 metres. A donkey called Dinky starts from A to B

at 60 metres/hour and at the same time a cow called Moo starts from B to C at 30 metres/hour. In what time after their departure will the distance between the donkey and the cow be the least?

(a) 2 h   (b) 3 h

(c) 0.5 h   (d) 8 h

16. A train has to travel the distance between Aurangabad and Daulatabad, equal to 20 km, at a constant speed. It travelled half the way with the specified speed and stopped for three minutes, to arrive at Daulatabad on time, it had to increase its speed by 10 km/h for the rest of the way. Next time the train stopped half-way for five minutes. By what speed must it increase its speed for the remaining half of the distance to arrive at Daulatabad as per the schedule?

(a) 10 kmph   (b) 20 kmph

(c) 15 kmph   (d) 16 kmph

17. Nishit travels from Patna to Kolkata, a distance of 200 km at the speed of 40 km/h. At the same time, Ravi starts from Kolkata at a speed of 20 kmph along a road, which is perpendicular to the road on which Nishit is travelling. When will Nishit and Ravi be closest to each other?

(a) In 1.5 hours   (b) In 4 hours

(c) In 3.33 hours   (d) In 5 hours

18. Two towns are at a distance of 240 km from each other. A motorist takes 8 hours to cover the distance if he travels at a speed of V_0 km/h from town A to an intermediate town C, and then continues on his way with an acceleration of x km/hr². He needs the same time to cover the whole distance if he travels from A to C at V_0 km/h and from C to B at V_1 km/h or from A to C at V_1 km/h and from C to B at V_0 km/h. Find V_0 if the acceleration 'x' is double V_0 in magnitude and $V_0 \neq V_1$.

(a) 15 km/h   (b) 10 km/h

(c) 20 km/h   (d) 8 km/h

19. Jaideep travels from Alaska, which is on a highway, to Burgen, which is 16 km from the highway. The distance between Alaska and Burgen along a straight line is 34 km. At what point should Jaideep turn from the highway to reach Burgen in the shortest possible time, if his speed along the highway is 10 km/h and 6 km/h otherwise.

(a) 30 km away from A

(b) 20 km away from A

(c) 18 km away from A

(d) 15 km away from A

20. An object begins moving at time moment $t = 0$ and 4 s after the beginning of the motion, attains the acceleration of 3 m/s². Find the speed of the object 6 s after the beginning of motion if it is known that the speed of the body varies accordingly to the law $v(t) =$

$(t^2 + 2b.t + 4)$ m/s and the object moves along a straight line.

(a) 22 m/s   (b) 10 m/s

(c) 30 m/s   (d) 15 m/s

21. For problem 20, find the distance covered by the object in the first 7 seconds if we assume that the speed of the object in a particular second is the speed it attains at the start of the second.

(a) 15 metres   (b) 14 metres

(c) 10 metres   (d) 5 metres

22. Three *ghats* X, Y and Z on the Yamuna in Delhi are located on the river bank. The speed of the river flow is 8 km/h in the direction of its flow, *Ghat Y* being located midway between X and Z. A raft and a launch leave Y at the same time, the raft travelling down the river to Z and the launch travelling to X. The speed of the launch in still water is 5 km/h. Having reached X, the launch reverses its direction and starts to Z. Find the range of values of V for which the launch arrives at Z later than the raft.

(a) $8 < V < 24$ km/h   (b) $8 < V < 16$ km/h

(c) $8 < V < 20$ km/h   (d) $12 < V < 24$ km/h

23. A pedestrian left point A for a walk, going with the speed of 5 km/h. When the pedestrian was at a distance of 6 km from A, a cyclist followed him, starting from A and cycling at a speed 9 km/h higher than that of the pedestrian. When the cyclist overtook the pedestrian, they turned back and returned to A together, at the speed of 4 km/h. At what v will the time spent by the pedestrian on his total journey from A to A be the least?

(a) 5 km/h   (b) 6 km/h

(c) 6.1 kmph   (d) 5.5 km/h

24. A cyclist left point A for point B and travelled at the constant speed of 25 km/h. When he covered the distance of 8.33 km, he was overtaken by a car that left point A twelve minutes after the cyclist and travelled at a constant speed too. When the cyclist travelled another 30 km, he encountered the car returning from B. Assume that the car did not stop at point B. Find the distance between A and B.

(a) 39.5833 km   (b) 41.0833 km

(c) 60.833 km   (d) 43.33 km

25. A robot began moving from point A in a straight line at 6 p.m. with an initial speed of 3 m/s. One second later, the speed of the robot became equal to 4 m/s. Find the acceleration of the robot at the end of the 2nd second if its speed changes by the law $s(t) = (at^2 + 2t + (b))$

(a) 1 m/s²   (b) −2 m/s²

(c) 0 m/s²   (d) 2 m/s²

26. For Question 25, the distance of the robot from point A after 6 seconds will be (assuming that for every

second the robot travels at a constant speed equal to its starting speed for that second and any acceleration occurs at the start of the next second)

(a) 45 m   (b) 36 m

(c) 10 m   (d) 17 m

27. Two friends Amit and Akshay began moving simultaneously from point A along a straight line in the same direction: Amit started moving at the speed of 5 m/s and moved with an uniform acceleration of 4 m/s², while his friend Akshay moved at a uniform speed. The limits for Akshay's speed (S) so that he should first leave Amit behind and then get overtaken by Amit at a distance of 18 m from A are

(a) $5 < S < 9$ (b) $3 < S < 5$

(c) $4 < S < 8$ (d) None of these

28. On the banks of the river Ganges there are two bathing points in Varanasi and Patna. A *diya* left in the river at Varanasi reaches Patna in 24 hours. However, a motorboat covers the whole way to and fro in exactly 10 hours. If the speed of the motorboat in still water is increased by 40%, then it takes the motorboat 7 hours to cover the same way (from Varanasi to Patna and back again). Find the time necessary for the motorboat to sail from Varanasi to Patna when its speed in still water is not increased.

(a) 3 hours   (b) 4 hours

(c) 4.8 hours   (d) None of these

29. Two friends started walking simultaneously from points A and B towards each other. 144 minutes later the distance between them was 20% of the original distance. How many hours does it take the faster walker to cover the distance AB if he needs eight hours less to travel the distance than his friend (assume all times to be in whole numbers and in hours)?

(a) 3 hours   (b) 6 hours

(c) 12 hours   (d) 4 hours

30. Two cars left points A and B simultaneously, travelling towards each other. 9 hours after their meeting, the car travelling from A arrived at B, and 16 hours after their meeting, the car travelling from B arrived at A. How many hours did it take the slower car to cover the whole distance?

(a) 36 hours   (b) 21 hours

(c) 25 hours   (d) 28 hours

31. A pedestrian and a cyclist left Nagpur for Buti Bori at the same time. Having reached Buti Bori, the cyclist turned back and met the pedestrian an hour after the start. After their meeting, the pedestrian continued his trip to Buti Bori and the cyclist turned back and also headed for Buti Bori. Having reached Buti Bori, the cyclist turned back again and met the pedestrian 30 mins after their first meeting. Determine what time it takes the pedestrian to cover the distance between Nagpur and Buti Bori.

(a) 1 hour   (b) 2 hours

(c) 2.5 hours   (d) 3 hours

32. Points A, B and C are at the distances of 120, 104.66 and 112 km from point M respectively. Three people left these points for point M simultaneously: the first person started from point A, the second from B and the third from C. The first person covered the whole way at a constant speed and arrived at M an hour before the second and the third persons (who arrived simultaneously). The third person covered the whole way at a constant speed. The second person, having travelled 72 km at the same speed as the first, stopped for 2 hours. The rest of the way he travelled at a speed that is less than the speed of the third person by the same amount as the speed of the third is less than that of the first. Determine the speed of the first person.

(a) 6 kmph   (b) 5 kmph

(c) 4 kmph   (d) 3 kmph

33. Two people started simultaneously from points A and B towards each other. At the moment the person who started from A had covered two-thirds of the way, the other person had covered 2 km less than half the total distance. If it is known that when the person who started from B had covered 1/4 of the way, the other person was 3 km short of the mid point. Find the distance between A and B. The speeds of the two people were constant.

(a) $(15 - 3\sqrt{17})$ km   (b) $(15 + 3\sqrt{17})$ km

(c) Both a and b   (d) $3\sqrt{17} - 5$ km

34. Sohan and Lallan left their house simultaneously. Thirty six minutes later, Sohan met his uncle travelling to their house, while Lallan met the uncle twelve minutes after Sohan. Twenty four minutes after his meeting with Lallan, the uncle rang the door bell at Sohan and Lallan's house. Assume each person travels at a constant speed. Find the ratio of the speeds of Sohan to Lallan to the uncle.

(a) 1 : 2 : 2   (b) 1 : 3 : 2

(c) 3 : 1 : 3   (d) 2 : 1 : 2

35. The distance between two towns—Aurangabad and Jalna is 80 km. A bus left Aurangabad and travelled at a constant speed towards Jalna. Thirty minutes later, Deepak Jhunjhunwala left Aurangabad in his car towards Jalna. He overtook the bus in thirty minutes and continued on his way to Jalna. Without stopping at Jalna, he turned back and again encountered the bus 80 minutes after he had left Aurangabad. Determine the speed of the bus.

(a) 40 kmph   (b) 45 kmph

(c) 50 kmph   (d) None of these

36. Rohit left Mahabaleshwar for Nashik at 6 a.m. An hour and a half later Vimal, whose speed was 5 km/h

higher than that of Rohit left Mahabaleshwar. At 10 : 30 p.m. of the same day the distance between the two friends was 21 km. Find the speed of Vimal.

(a) 40 kmph   (b) 41 kmph

(c) 69 kmph   (d) Either b or c

37. Aurangzeb and Babar with their troops left from Delhi and Daulatabad towards each other simultaneously. Each of them marched at a constant speed and, having arrived at their respective points of destination, went back at once. Their first meeting was 14 km from Daulatabad, and the second meeting, eight hours after the first meeting was at a distance of 2 km from Delhi. Find the distance between the Delhi and Daulatabad.

(a) 30 km   (b) 25 km

(c) 35 km   (d) None of these

38. Two tourists left simultaneously point A for point B, the first tourist covers each kilometre 2 minutes faster than the second. After travelling 30 per cent of the way, the first tourist returned to A, stopped there for 102 minutes and again started for B. The two tourists arrived at B simultaneously. What is the distance between A and B if the second tourist covered it in 2.5 hours?

(a) 60 km   (b) 70 km

(c) 45 km   (d) None of these

39. Amar and Akbar left Bhubaneshwar simultaneously and travelled towards Cuttack. Amar's speed was 15 km/h and that of Akbar was 12 km/h. Half an hour later, Anthony left Bhubaneshwar and travelled in the same direction. Some time later, he overtook Akbar and 90 minutes further on he overtook Amar. Find Anthony's speed.

(a) 18 kmph   (b) 24 kmph

(c) 20 kmph   (d) 16 kmph

40. Two bodies, moving along a circle in the same direction, meet every 49 minutes. Had they moved at the same speeds in the opposite directions, they would meet every 7 minutes. If, moving in the opposite directions, the bodies are at the distance of 40 m from each other along the arc at time $t = 0$, then at $t = 24$ seconds, their distance will be 26 metres (the bodies do not meet during those 24 seconds). Find the speed of the faster body in metres per minute.

(a) 15   (b) 20

(c) 25   (d) None of these

41. The distance between Varanasi and Lucknow is 220 km. Two buses start from these towns towards each other. They can meet halfway if the first bus leaves 2 hours earlier than the second. If they start simultaneously, they will meet in 4 hours. Find the speeds of the buses.

(a) $17.5(3 + \sqrt{5})$ km/h, $17.5(1 + \sqrt{5})$ km/h

(b) $27.5(3 + \sqrt{5})$ km/h, $27.5(1 + \sqrt{5})$ km/h

(c) $27.5(3 - \sqrt{5})$ km/h, $27.5(\sqrt{5} - 1)$ km/h

(d) None of these

42. A road passes through the towns Sangamner and Yeotmal. A cyclist started from Sangamner in the direction of Yeotmal. At the same time, two pedestrians started from Yeotmal travelling at the same speed, the first of them towards Sangamner and the other in the opposite direction. The cyclist covered the distance between the towns in half an hour and, continued ahead in the same direction. He overtook the second pedestrian, 1.2 hours after he met the first pedestrian. Determine the time the cyclist spent travelling from Sangamner to the point of the meeting with the first pedestrian (assuming the speeds of the cyclist and the pedestrians to be constant).

(a) 24 min   (b) 18 min

(c) 30 min   (d) Cannot be determined

43. Two people A and B start moving from P and Q that are 200 km apart, towards each other A is on a moped and B on foot. They meet at a point R when A gives B a lift to P and returns to his original path to reach Q. On reaching Q he finds that he has taken 2.6 times his normal time. B on the other hand realises that he has saved 40 minutes over his normal travel time. Find the ratio of their speeds.

(a) 3 : 2   (b) 4 : 3

(c) 3 : 1   (d) None of these

44. For Question 43, find the speed of the moped.

(a) 160 kmph   (b) 180 kmph

(c) 200 kmph   (d) None of these

45. Three friends A, B and C start from P to Q that are 100 km apart. A is on a moped while B is riding pillion and C walks on. A takes B to a point R and returns to pick up C on the way and takes him to point Q. B, on the other hand, walks to Q from point R (R is the mid-point between P and Q).

If the ratio of speeds of the three people is 5 : 2 : 2, find where will the last person be when the first person reaches Q.

(a) 12.85 km from Q (b) 12.75 km from Q

(c) 16.66 km from Q (d) 83.33 km from P

Space for Rough Work

46. A motorboat moves from point A to point B and back again, both points being located on the riverbank. If the speed of the boat in still water is doubled, then the trip from A to B and back again would take 20% of the time that the motorboat usually spends in the journey. How many times is the actual speed of the launch higher than the speed of the river flow?

(a) $\sqrt{\dfrac{3}{2}}$ (b) $\dfrac{\sqrt{3}}{3}$

(c) $\dfrac{2}{3}$ (d) $\dfrac{3}{2}$

47. A watch loses 2/3% time during the 1st week and gains 1/3% time during the next week. If on a Sunday noon, it showed the right time, what time will it show at noon on the Sunday after the next.

(a) 11 : 26 : 24 a.m.   (b) 10 : 52 : 18 a.m.

(c) 10 : 52 : 48 a.m.   (d) 11 : 36 : 24 a.m.

48. Clocks A, B and C strikes every hour. B slows down and takes 2 min longer than A per hour while C become faster and takes 2 min less than A per hour. If they strike together at 12 midnight, when will they strike together again

(a) 10 a.m.   (b) 11 a.m.

(c) 9 p.m.   (d) 8 p.m.

49. A boat went down the river for a distance of 20 km. It then turned back and returned to its starting point, having travelled a total of 7 hours. On its return trip, at a distance of 12 km from the starting point, it encountered a log, which had passed the starting point at the moment at which the boat had started downstream. The downstream speed of the boat is

(a) 7 kmph   (b) 13 kmph

(c) 16 kmph   (d) 10 kmph

50. Two boats go downstream from point X to point Y. The faster boat covers the distance from X to Y 1.5 times as fast as the slower boat. It is known that for every hour the slower boat lags behind the faster boat by 8 km. However, if they go upstream, then the faster boat covers the distance from Y to X in half the time as the slower boat. Find the speed of the faster boat in still water.

(a) 12 kmph   (b) 20 kmph

(c) 24 kmph   (d) 25 kmph

ANSWER KEY

Level of Difficulty (I)

1. (a)	2. (a)	3. (c)	4. (c)
5. (d)	6. (d)	7. (c)	8. (a)
9. (a)	10. (a)	11. (a)	12. (a)
13. (c)	14. (a)	15. (c)	16. (d)
17. (a)	18. (b)	19. (d)	20. (a)
21. (c)	22. (c)	23. (c)	24. (d)
25. (b)	26. (d)	27. (d)	28. (c)
29. (d)	30. (d)	31. (a)	32. (b)
33. (a)	34. (a)	35. (a)	36. (d)
37. (d)	38. (b)	39. (a)	40. (a)
41. (b)	42. (a)	43. (a)	44. (d)
45. (c)	46. (c)	47. (c)	48. (a)
49. (d)	50. (a)	51. (b)	52. (a)
53. (b)	54. (c)	55. (c)	56. (b)
57. (b)	58. (a)	59. (a)	60. (b)
61. (c)	62. (d)	63. (a)	64. (b)
65. (a)	66. (c)	67. (b)	68. (a)
69. (a)	70. (a)	71. (a)	72. (c)
73. (a)	74. (d)	75. (d)	

Level of Difficulty (II)

1. (c)	2. (a)	3. (a)	4. (c)
5. (a)	6. (b)	7. (b)	8. (d)
9. (b)	10. (a)	11. (b)	12. (c)
13. (c)	14. (b)	15. (c)	16. (a)
17. (c)	18. (d)	19. (b)	20. (b)
21. (b)	22. (c)	23. (a)	24. (c)
25. (d)	26. (b)	27. (c)	28. (c)
29. (d)	30. (d)	31. (c)	32. (b)
33. (d)	34. (b)	35. (c)	36. (c)
37. (a)	38. (c)	39. (b)	40. (d)
41. (b)	42. (b)	43. (c)	44. (c)
45. (a)	46. (b)	47. (a)	48. (b)
49. (c)	50. (a)		

Level of Difficulty (III)

1. (c)	2. (b)	3. (a)	4. (a)
5. (b)	6. (d)	7. (b)	8. (d)
9. (c)	10. (d)	11. (d)	12. (b)
13. (b)	14. (b)	15. (a)	16. (d)
17. (b)	18. (c)	19. (c)	20. (b)
21. (b)	22. (a)	23. (b)	24. (c)
25. (b)	26. (d)	27. (a)	28. (b)
29. (d)	30. (d)	31. (b)	32. (a)
33. (c)	34. (d)	35. (a)	36. (d)
37. (d)	38. (a)	39. (a)	40. (b)
41. (d)	42. (b)	43. (d)	44. (d)
45. (a)	46. (a)	47. (c)	48. (b)
49. (d)	50. (b)		

Hints

Level of Difficulty (II)

1. The train saves 16 minutes by travelling faster over a section of 80 km.

   Thus, $\dfrac{80}{S} - \dfrac{80}{S+10} = \dfrac{16}{60} = 0.2666$

   Check the options.

2. $\dfrac{60}{S} - \dfrac{60}{S+1} = \dfrac{6}{60}$. Check the options to solve.

3. Solve through options.

4. Solve through options.

5. Relative speed (in opposite direction) = 20 km/hr. Use the options after this.

6. The question is based on Pythagoras' triplets.

8. Assume the distance between the two ant holes is 600 feet. Then, the first ant's speed is 16 feet/hr while the second ant's speed is 14 feet/hr.

   If the first ant covers 800 feet, the second will cover 700 feet (since, distance is proportional to speed). Hence total distance is 1500 feet and required speed is $14 \times 2.5 = 35$ feet/hr.

9. Solve through options.

13. Solve using options as follows.

    Check for option (a). (He rode for 6 hours)

    Then, walking time = 10 hrs

    Thus, speed of the tonga = 1.66 km/hr

    And speed of walking = 9 km/hr.

    As per the question, if the times are reversed, the distances travelled by each mode will be equal.

    Thus, 10×1.66 should be equal to 6×9.

    But, this is not so. Hence, move to the next option.

14. Solve using options.

15. Solve using options, the following equations.

    Speed of first = $\left(\dfrac{x-1}{42} \times 60 \right)$ km/hr = S_A

    Speed of second = $\dfrac{x-2}{52} \times 60$ km/hr = S_B.

    Then, $\dfrac{x-2}{S_B} - \dfrac{x-1}{S_A} = \dfrac{17}{60}$

19. The first pattern of movement is

    $3 + 7 + 11 + 15 + 19 + 23$

    The second pattern of movement is

    $1 + 9 + 17 + 25 + 33 + 41$

    It is evident that the difference in the net movements between the second pattern and the first pattern is more than 6 mm and less than 30 mm for a movement of 4 seconds.

20. By increasing speed by 15 kmph, the time reduces by 30 minutes.

22. Given that they meet in 80 minutes, when moving towards each other, the sum of their speeds should be such that they cover 1.25% of the distance per minute (i.e. 75% of the distance per hour).

25. Ratio of time taken in going and coming back is 7 : 18.

    Also, total time of travel is 325 minutes.

26-30. Chart out the distances covered by the three of them in each leg of their journeys.

32. The answer would have been 13, if the question had stated the initial directions of their walking. Hence, we cannot determine the answer.

33. Solve on the basis of the would be wife's movement.

36. The train will meet all trains that start from Pune between 8 a.m. and 4 p.m.

38. Assume speed of sound = 330 m/s.

    Then, distance covered by sound in 45 seconds = distance covered by the trains in 11 minutes.

39-40. Use the concept of relative speed to solve.

41. The bird will fly for the time which the two cars take in approaching one another.

42. Chart the relative movements of the two cars and the bird.

46. The wall clock gains 6 minutes in 36 hours, while the table clock loses 2 minutes in 36 hours. Hence, time differential in 36 hours = 8 minutes. For them to show the same time again, we need a total time differential of 12 hours.

48. Solve through options.

Level of Difficulty (III)

1. The first person who travels from Siliguri to Darjeeling is obviously faster than the second. Hence, reject Options (a) and (b). Then, check all the conditions with Options (c) and (d) and select the one which satisfies the conditions.

2. Since distance to be travelled by Nishit is $35\frac{5}{7}\%$ less, his speed will also be $35\frac{5}{7}\%$ less than Arun's speed. Check the options with the conditions that Arun's speed is 5 kmph higher than that of Nishit.

3. Let S_1, S_2 and S_3 be the speeds of the three cars.

   Then: $\dfrac{120}{S_1} - \dfrac{120}{S_2} = 1$ hour \hfill (1)

   It is also known that the speed of the third car is double the speed of the first car.

   With these realisations, check for factors of 120 which can satisfy the equation above.

   [Note that in equations like (1) above, normally the respective values of S_1 and S_2 will be factors of 120.]

5. If the side of the initial equilateral triangle is S, then when Arjit covers $(S - 120)$ kms, Shaurya covers S

kilometres. Also, when Arjit covers a distance of 80 kilometres, Shaurya covers a distance such that the resultant triangle is right angled.

Check these conditions through options.

6. Solve through a process similar to the previous question.

7. If S_1 is the speed of the first car, then $(S_1 + 10)$ will be the second car's speed. If t_1 hours is the time required for the first car, then $(t_1 - 1)$ hours is the time required for the second car in covering the same distance, while that of the third car is $\left(t_1 - \dfrac{33.33}{60}\right)$ hours.

   Check these conditions through options.

10. The relative speed is 225 km/hr.

11. The sum of the speeds of the ducks is 50 feet/min Hence, circumference = $9 \times 50 = 450$ feet and difference of speeds = $\dfrac{450}{54} = 8.33$.

15. Use options to solve.

16. Through trial and error try to find the initial speed of the train, so that the first condition is met.

17. Use options to solve.

18. Let the distance $AC = d$

    Then, $\dfrac{d}{V_0} + \dfrac{240 - d}{V_1} = \dfrac{d}{V_1} + \dfrac{240 - d}{V_0}$

    If $V_0 \neq V_1$, then the above condition will be satisfied only if $d = 120$ km.

19. The time required will be represented by

    $$\frac{\text{Distance travelled on highway}}{10}$$

    $$+ \frac{\text{Distance travelled on side roads}}{10}$$

    This has to be minimised, check the options.

20-21. Acceleration is $\dfrac{dv}{dt} = 2t + 2b$

    At $t = 4$, the acceleration is given to be 3.

    Hence, $b = \dfrac{-5}{2}$

    Hence, the velocity equation becomes
    $V_{(t)} = t_2 - 5t + 4$

29. Total time taken to cover the entire distance together
    $= 144 \times \dfrac{5}{4} = 180$ minutes $= 3$ hours.

    Hence, distance covered per hour = 33.33% of the total by both of them combined.

    Check this condition for all the options.

31. Suppose A and B are the points where the first and the second meetings took place.

The total distance covered by the pedestrian and the cyclist before the first meeting = Twice the distance between Nagpur and Buti Bori.

Total time taken is 1 hour.

Total distance covered by the pedestrian and the cyclist between the two meetings = Twice the distance between A and Buti Bori.

and time taken is half an hour.

Hence, A is the mid-point. This will result in a GP.

32. Solve through options by checking all the conditions given in the question.

33. If $2d$ is the distance between A and B, then

$$\frac{\frac{2}{3} \times 2d}{d-2} = \frac{d-3}{2d \times \frac{1}{4}}$$

34. In 24 minutes, the uncle covers the distance for which Lallan requires 48 minutes.

35. Check the options for all the conditions.

36. Vimal could either be 21 km behind Rohit or 21 km ahead of Rohit.

37. If d is the distance between Delhi and Daulatabad, then you will get the following equation.

$$\frac{d-14}{14} = \frac{28+(d-16)}{(d-14)+2}$$

38. Check the conditions through the options.

47. The net time loss is 1/3% of 168 hours.

49. In the time taken by the boat in traveling $d + (d - 12)$ kms, the log travels 12 km. Let, S_B be the speed of the boat is still water and, S_S be the speed of the stream.

Then

$$\frac{12}{S_S} = \frac{20}{(S_S + S_B)} + \frac{8}{(S_B - S_S)} \qquad (1)$$

It is also known that,

$$\frac{20}{(S_S + S_B)} + \frac{20}{(S_B - S_S)} = 7 \text{ hours} \qquad (2)$$

Solve through options.

Solutions and Shortcuts

Level of Difficulty (I)

1. The ratio of time for the travel is 4:3 (Sinhagad to Deccan Queen). Hence, the ratio of speeds would be 3:4. Since, the sum of their average speeds is 70 kmph, their respective speeds would be 30 and 40 kmph respectively. Use alligation to get the answer as 34.28 kmph.

2. When speed goes down to three fourth (i.e. 75%) time will go up to 4/3rd (or 133.33%) of the original time. Since, the extra time required is 16 minutes, it

should be equated to 1/3rd of the normal time. Hence, the usual time required will be 48 minutes.

3. Since, the ratio of speeds is 3:5, the ratio of times would be 5:3. The difference in the times would be 2 (if looked at in the 5:3 ratio context.) Further, since Ram takes 30 minutes longer, 2 corresponds to 30. Hence, using unitary method, 5 will correspond to 75 and 3 will correspond to 45 minutes. Hence at 10 kmph, Bharat would travel 7.5 km.

4. The train that leaves at 6 am would be 75 km ahead of the other train when it starts. Also, the relative speed being 36 kmph, the distance from Mumbai would be:

$$(75/36) \times 136 = 283.33 \text{ km}$$

5. If you assume that the initial stretch of track is covered by the two trains in time t each, the following figure will give you a clearer picture.

From the above figure, we can deduce that,
$t/3 = 12/t$.

Hence, $t^2 = 36$, gives us $t = 6$.

Hence, the distance between Kolkata to the starting point is covered by the Calcutta Mail in 6 hours, while the same distance is covered by the Bombay Mail in 3 hours.

Hence, the ratio of their speeds would be 1:2. Hence, the Bombay Mail would travel at 96 kmph.

6.

From the figure above we see that Shyam would have walked a distance of $4 + 4 + 4 = 12$ km. (G to P_1, P_1 to G and G to P_2).

7. When the train from Khandala starts off, the train from Lonavala will already have covered 50 kms. Hence, 550 km at a relative speed of 60 kmph will take 550/60 hrs. From this, you can get the answer as:

$$50 + (550/60) * 25 = 279.166 \text{ km}.$$

8. When his speed becomes 3/4th, his time would increase by 1/3rd. Thus, the normal time = 7.5 hrs. (since increased time = 2.5 hrs).

9. Since he gains 2 hours by driving both ways (instead of walking one way) the time taken for driving would

be 2 hours less than the time taken for walking. Hence, he stands to lose another two hours by walking both ways. Hence his total time should be 8 hrs 45 minutes.

10. Kalu's speed = 3 m/s.
    For 1200 m, Kalu would take 400 seconds and Sambhu would take 10 seconds less. Hence, 390 seconds.

11. Since Chandu is moving at a speed of 10 m/s and he has to cover 360 km or 360000 meters, the time taken would be given by 360000/10 seconds = 36000 seconds = 36000/60 minutes = 600 minutes = 10 hours.

12. Since the train travels at 60 kmph, it's speed per minute is 1 km per minute. Hence, if it's speed with stoppages is 40 kmph, it will travel 40 minutes per hour.

13. Total distance/Total time = 1590/15 = 106 kmph.

14. The distance covered in the various phases of his travel would be:
    10 km + 25 km + 50 km + 60 km. Thus the total distance covered = 145 km in 2 hours 50 minutes → 145 km in 2.8333 hours → 51.18 kmph

15. The average speed would be given by:
$$\frac{3d}{\dfrac{d}{v_1}+\dfrac{d}{v_2}+\dfrac{d}{v_2}} = \frac{3v_1v_2}{2v_1+v_2}$$

16. By increasing his speed by 25%, he will reduce his time by 20%. (This corresponds to a 6 minute drop in his time for travel—since he goes from being 10 minutes late to only 4 minutes late.) Hence, his time originally must have been 30 minutes. Hence, the required distance is 20 kmph × 0.5 hours = 10 km.

17. $d/6 + d/4 = 10 \rightarrow d = 24$ km.

18. If the car does half the journey @ 30 kmph and the other half at 40 kmph it's average speed can be estimated using weighted averages.
    Since, the distance traveled in each part of the journey is equal, the ratio of time for which the car would travel would be inverse to the ratio of speeds. Since, the speed ratio is 3:4, the time ratio for the two halves of the journey would be 4:3. The average speed of the car would be:
    (30 × 4 + 40 × 3)/7 = 240/7 kmph.
    It is further known that the car traveled for 17.5 hours (which is also equal to 35/2 hours).
    Thus, total distance = average speed × total time = (240 × 35)/(2 × 7) = 120 × 5 = 600 km

19. To reduce the time of the journey by 25%, he should increase his speed by 33.33% or 1/3rd. Thus, required speed = 80 kmph.

20. You can solve this question using the options. Option (a) fits the given situation best as if we take

the distance as 12 km he would have taken 1 hour to go by car and 4 hours to come back walking—a total of 5 hours as given in the problem.

21. In four hours, the train will travel 180 km (180,000 metres). The number of poles would be 180,000/50 = 3600.

22. Is the same question as Question No. 5.

23.

    In the above figure, the train travels from A to B in 11:30 minutes.
    Suppose, you denote the time at which the first gunshot is heard as t = 0. Also, if you consider the travel of the sound of the second the gunshot is heard at point B at t = 11:30 minutes. Also, the second gunshot should reach point B at t = 12 minutes. Hence, the sound of the 2nd gunshot would take 30 seconds to travel from B to A.

    Thus, $\dfrac{S_{train}}{S_{sound}} = \dfrac{t_{sound}}{t_{train}}$

    $S_{train} = 330 \times \dfrac{30}{690} = \dfrac{330}{23}$ m/s.

24. In 6 minutes, the car goes ahead by 0.6 km. Hence, the relative speed of the car with respect to the pedestrian is equal to 6 kmph, since, the pedestrian is walking at 2 kmph, hence, the net speed is 8 kmph.

25. At 40 kmph, Harsh would cover (200/60) × 40 km.
    = 400/3 km. = 133.33 km.
    This represents the distance by which Vijay would be ahead of Harsh, when Vijay reaches the endpoint means in essence that Vijay must have travelled for 133.33/20 hours → 6.66 hours
    Hence, the distance is 60 × 6.66 = 400 km.

26. Solve this question using the values given in the options. Option (d) can be seen to fit the situation given by the problem as it gives us the following chain of thought:
    If the average speed of the faster train is 48 kmph, the average speed of the slower train would be 32 kmph. In this case, the time taken by the faster train (192/48 = 4 hours) is 2 hours lesser than the time taken by the slower train (192/32 = 6 hours). This satisfies the condition given in the problem and hence option (d) is correct.

27. The required speed s would be satisfying the equation:
    $$300/s - 300/(s + 2) = 5$$
    Solving for s from the options it is clear that s = 25.

28. Solve through options using trial and error. For usual speed 3 kmph we have:
    Normal time → 2/3 hours = 40 minutes.

At 4 kmph the time would be 2/4 hrs, this gives us a distance of 10 minutes. Hence option (c) is correct.

29. By increasing the speed by 33.33%, it would be able to reduce the time taken for travel by 25%. But since this is just able to overcome a time delay of 30 minutes, 30 minutes must be equivalent to 25% of the time originally taken. Hence, the original time must have been 2 hours and the original speed would be 750 kmph. Hence, the new speed would be 1000 kmph.

30. The average speed would be given by:

$$\frac{(120 \times 1 \times 40 \times 3)}{4} = 60 \text{ kmph.}$$

31. The length of the circular track would be equal to the circumference of the circle. In 2 minutes thus, the cyclist covers 3.14 × 200 = 628 meters (using the formula for the circumference of a circle).

Thus, the cyclist's speed would be 628/2 = 314 meters/minute.

32. The total time taken by the motorist would be 200/53.333 = 200 × 3/160 = 3.75 hours = 3 hours 45 minutes. In the first half of the journey the motorist covers 1/4th the distance @ 40kmph. This means that he takes 50/40 = 1.25 hours = 1 hour 15 minutes in covering the first 50 kms. This also means that he covers the remaining distance of 150 km in 2 hours 30 minutes → a speed of 60 kmph. Hence, option (b) is correct.

33. Assume a distance of 60 km in each stretch. Get the average speed by the formula. Total distance/ Total time = 180/10 = 18 kmph.

34. The speed of the first car would be 60 kmph while the speed of the second car would be 40 kmph. The relative speed of the two cars would be 100 kmph. To cover 480 km they would take 480/100 = 4.8 hours → In 4.8 hours, the car traveling from *A* to *B* would have traveled 4.8 × 60 = 288 kms.

35. At 3/4th speed, extra time = 1/3rd of time = 16 minutes. Normal time = 48 minutes.

36. Solve using options. The value in option (d) fits the situation as 20/8 – 20/10 = 2.5 – 2 = 0.5 hours = 30 minutes.

37. [73.5 × 136]/38. Same logic as for Question 4.

38. The time taken before their meeting would be given by $t^2 = 12 \times 3 = 36 \rightarrow t = 6$ hours. This means that their ratio of speeds is 1:2. Since train *A* is traveling slower, the speed of train *B* would be double the speed of train *A*. Required answer = 48 × 2 = 96. (Please take a look at the solution of question number 5).

39. The distance would get divided in the ratio of speeds (since time is constant). Thus, the distance ratio would be 5 : 7 and required distance = 5/12 × 600 = 250 km.

40. The diameter of the circle would be given by the hypotenuse of the right triangle with legs 600 and 800 respectively. Hence, the required diameter = 1000 meters.

41. When Ram runs 2000 m, Shyam runs (1800 – 30s) When Ram runs 1000 m, Shyam runs (2000 – 180s). Then:

$$2000/1000 = \frac{1800 - 30s}{2000 - 180s}$$

Solving , we get *s* = 6.66 m/s

Thus, Shyam's speed = 400 m/minute and he would take 5 minutes to cover the distance. Option (b) fits.

42. From the situation described in the first condition itself we can see that the speed of coming back has to be double the speed of going downstream. Checking the options, only option (a) fits this condition i.e. Downstream speed = 2 × Upstream speed. Hence, option (a) is correct.

43. $7 \times S_t = L_t$ (1)
$25 \times S_t = L_t + 378$ (2)
Solving, $S_t = 21$ m/sec.
    = 21 × 18/5 = 75.6 kmph.

44. In order to solve this, you first need to think of the speed of the river flow (if the speed of the boat in still water is 3 kmph). If we take the speed of the river flow as *s*, we get downstream speed as 3 + *s* and upstream speed as 3 – *s*.
$10/(3 - s) - 10/(3 + s) = 8$ hours → *s* = 2kmph.
Note: It is obvious that since the difference between the downstream time and the upstream time is 8 hours, the upstream and downstream speeds would both be factors of 10. The only value of *s* such that both 3 + *s* and 3 – *s* are factors of 10 is *s* = 2.
If the boat needs to reach 10 km downstream in 100 minutes (1.66 hours) it means: 10/1.66 = 6 kmph is the downstream speed.
Since, the speed of the stream is 2 kmph, the required speed of the boat = 4 kmph

45. Solve through options. For option (c) at 4 kmph, the boat would take exactly 4 hours to cover the distance.

46. $x/9 + x/3 = 3/4 \rightarrow 4x/9 = 3/4 \rightarrow x = 27/16$ kms = 1.6875 kms.

47. Upstream speed = 40/8 = 5 kmph.
Downstream speed = 49/7 = 7 kmph.
Speed in still water = average of upstream and downstream speed = 6 kmph.

48. $(20 \times 5/18) \times 36 = L_t \rightarrow L_t = 200$ m.

49. 8/(12 – 2) = 8/10 = 0.8 hours

50. 15 km upstream in 80 minutes → 15/1.33 = 11.25 kmph. (upstream speed of the boat).
Thus, still water speed of the boat
    = 11.25 + 5 = 16.25 kmph

51. Since A to C is double the distance of A to B, it is evident that the time taken for A to C and back would be double the time taken from A to B and back (i.e. double of 6.5 hours = 13 hours). Since going from A to C takes 9 hours, coming back from C to A would take 4 hours (Since 9 + 4 = 13).

52. $(S_f - S_s) \times 60 = 200$
    Where S_f and S_s are speeds of the faster and slower train respectively
    $\rightarrow S_f - S_s = 3.33$
    Also, $(S_f + S_s) \times 10 = 200$.
    $\rightarrow S_f + S_s = 20$.
    Solving we get $S_s = 8.33$ m/s
    $= 8.33 \times 18/5 = 30$ kmph.

53. Speed of Vinay = 5 m/s, Speed of Ajay = 4m/s. In a hundred meter race, Vinay would take 20 seconds to complete and in this time Ajay would only cover 80 meters. Thus, Vinay beats Ajay by 20 meters in a hundred meter race.

54. Solve using options 1.33 m/s fits perfectly.

55. Solve using options 1.33 m/s fits perfectly. When A scores 60 points B scores 45, and C scores 40.
    Thus, when B scores 90, C would score 80. So, B can give C 10 points in 90.

56. When Shyam does 500, Vinay does 375. Since Vinay has a start of 140 m, it means that Vinay only needs to cover 360 m to reach the destination.
    When Vinay does 360, Shyam would cover 480 m and lose by 20 m. (Since the ratio of their speeds is 3:4)

57. Distance to be covered = 120 meters. Speed = 10m/s $\rightarrow$ Time required = 120/10 =12 seconds.

58. $20 \times (5/18) \times 18 = 100$ m = 0.1 km.

59. When the second train leaves Muzaffarpur, the first train would have already traveled 30 km. Now, after 9 AM, the relative speed of the two trains would be 10 kmph (i.e. the rate at which the faster train would catch the slower train).
    Since the faster train has to catch up a relative distance of 30 km in order for the trains to meet, it would take 30/10 = 3 hours to catch up.
    Distance from Muzaffarpur = 70 × 3 = 210 km

60. Speed of running of the train = 1.25 km/hr.
    With stoppage, an effective speed of 60 kmph means that the time of travel per hour would be 60/1.25 = 48 minutes.
    Thus, the train stops for 12 minutes per hour.

61. Upstream speed = 3.2 kmph
    Downstream speed = 6 kmph.
    Thus, speed of stream = 1.4 kmph.

62. Vijay takes 9 hours to return upstream after going for 6 hours downstream. Solve using options. Option (d) fits as we get Downstream speed = 18 kmph $\rightarrow$ distance = 18 × 6 =108 km

Also, upstream speed = 12 kmph $\rightarrow$ distance = 12 × 9 = 108 km

63. Upstream speed = 4.8 kmph
    Downstream speed = 7.2 kmph.
    $d/4.8 + d/7.2 = 1$
    Solving we get $d = 2.88$ km.

64. The length of the train would be given by: $36 \times 5/18 \times 8 = 80$ meters.

65. Rate in still water = (16 + 22)/2 = 19 kmph

66. The given situations are satisfied with the speed of the boat as 8 kmph and the speed of the stream as 3 kmph. Option (c) is correct.

67. $10/(x-2) + 10/(x+2) = 55/60 = 11/12$ hours.
    $x = 22$ fits the expression.

68. The speed of the boat in still water is the average of the upstream and downstream speeds. $(x + y)/2$.

69. $(1/4) \times 2\pi r = 4\pi$ (Since $r = 8$ cm).

70. The hands would be together once in each hour. However, the 12 noon time would be counted in both 11 to 12 and 12 to 1. Hence, the no. of times = 12 – 1 = 11.

71. If we consider the clock to be a circle with circumference 60 km, the speed of the Minute hand = 60 kmph, while the speed of the hour hand = 5 kmph. The relative speed = 55 kmph. At 2 PM, the distance between the two would be seen as 10 km. This would get covered in 10/55 = 2/11 hours. Option (a) is correct.

72. $14/(5+x) + 9/(5-x) = 5$
    $x = 2$, fits this equation.

73. Look for the solution by thinking of the factors of 91. It can be seen that 91/13 + 91/7 = 7 + 13 = 20 hours. This means that the speed of the boat in still water is 10 kmph and the speed of the water flow would be 3 kmph. Option (a) is correct.

74. When Ajay does 600 metres, Vijay does 540 m.
    When Vijay does 500 metres, Anjay does 475 m
    Thus, Ajay : Vijay : Anjay = 600 : 540 : 513.
    Thus, Ajay would beat Anjay by (87 × 2/3) = 58 m in a 400 m race.

75. $30/(15+x) + 30/(15-x) = 4$ hrs 30 minutes.
    At $x = 5$, the equation is satisfied.

Level of Difficulty (II)

1. By travelling at 10 kmph higher than the original speed, the train is able to make up 16 minutes while traveling 80 km.
   This condition is only satisfied at an initial speed of 50 (and a new speed of 60 kmph).

2. Solve this question through options. For instance, if he traveled at 25 kmph, his original speed would have been 24 kmph.

The time difference can be seen to be 6 minutes in this case:

60/24 – 60/25 = 0.1 hrs = 6 mins. Thus, this is the correct answer.

3. In 1 hours 15 minutes an individual will be able to cover 25% more than his speed per hour. The relationship between the original speed and the new speed is best represented as below:

Original speed $\xrightarrow{\text{25\% increase}}$ speed per 75 minutes $\xrightarrow{+1 \text{ increase}}$ New speed.

Thus, to go from the new speed to the original speed the process would be:

New speed $\xrightarrow{-1}$ Speed per 75 minutes $\xrightarrow{20\% \downarrow}$ Original speed.

We need to use this process to check the option. Only the first option satisfies this condition. (at 16 kmph it would take 6 hours while at 12 kmph it would take 8 hours).

4. The question's structure (and solving) have to be done on the basis of integers. The following equations emerge:

$$\frac{d}{s} - \frac{d}{(s+6)} = 4 \text{ and } \frac{d}{(S-6)} - \frac{d}{(S+6)} = 10$$

Solving these expressions through normal solving methods is close to impossible (at the very least it would take a huge amount of time.) Instead this question has to be solved using the logic that integral difference in ratios in such a situation can only occur in all the three ratios (d/s), $d/(s+6)$ and $d/(s-6)$) are integers.

Hence, d should have three divisors which are 6 units apart from each other.

5. The relative speed is 20 kmph. Also, the pedestrian should take 7:30 hours more than the cyclist. Using option (a) the speeds of the two people are 4km/hr and 16 km/hr respectively. At this speed, the respective times would be 10 hrs and 2:30 hours, giving the required answer.

6.

The distance between the motorists will be shown on the hypotenuse. Using the 3,4,5 Pythagoras triplet and the condition that the two speeds are 6 kmph different from each other, you will get the triplet as: 18,24,30. Hence, the slower motorist travelled at 18 kmph.

7. Since the two motorists meet after an hour, their relative speed is 28 kmph. Use options to check out the values. Since the speed of the faster cyclist is asked for it has to be greater than 14 kmph. Hence only check options > 14 kmph.

8. Since the second ant covers 7/120 of the distance in 2 hours 30 minutes, we can infer that is covers 8.4/120 = 7% of the distance in 3 hours. Thus, in 3 hours both ants together cover 15% of the distance → 5% per hour → they will meet in 20 hours.

Also, ratio of speeds = 8 : 7.

So, the second ant would cover 700 ft to the meeting profit in 20 hours and its speed would be 35 feet/hr.

9. In this question consider the total distance as 100%. Hence the sum of their speeds will be 75% per hour. Checking option (c)

If the bus took 6 hours, it would cover 16.66% distance per hour and the car would cover 25% distance per hour. (as it takes 2 hours less than the bus.) This gives an addition of only 41.66%. Hence, the answer is not correct.

Option (b) is the correct answer.

10. The requisite conditions are met on a Pythagoras triplet 6,8,10. Since the racetrack only consists of the legs of the right triangle the length must be 6 + 8 = 14 km.

11. The sum of speeds would be 0.08 m/s (relative speed in opposite direction). Also if we go by option (b), the speeds will be 0.03 and 0.05 m/s respectively.

At this speed the overlapping would occur every 60 seconds.

12. When Rahim starts, Karim would have covered 40 km. Also, their relative speed is 12 kmph and the distance between the two would get to 0 in 40/12 = 3.33 hours.

Distance covered = 28 × 3.33 = 93.33 km.

13. Solve this question through options.

For option (c), the conditions match since: If he rode for 2 hours (speed = 5 kmph), he would have walked for 6 hours (4 hours more) and his walking speed would be 15 kmph.

If we interchange the times, we get 15 × 2 = 5 × 6.

14. This is a complex trial and error based question and the way you would have to think in this is:

From the figure above, it is clear that A is faster as he takes only $t + 2$ hours while B has taken $t + 9$ hours to complete the journey.

Then, we get: $(t - 6)/9 = 8/t$

Solving for t, we get $t = -6$ (not possible)

Or $t = 12$. Putting this value of t in the figure it changes to:

We also get ratio of speeds = 3 : 2 (inverse of ratio of times)

The next part of the puzzle is to think of the 12 km less traveled by the first person till the meeting point. If the speed of the faster person is 3s, that of the slower person = 2s.

Further

$$12 \times 2s - 6 \times 3s = 12 \text{ km}$$
$$s = 2 \text{ kmph.}$$

The speed of the faster tourist is $3 \times 2 = 6$ kmph

15. Solve using options. The first option you would check for (given the values in the questions) would be option (b). This would give that the first jogger would run at 3 min per km, while the second jogger would run at 4 min per km. In the new condition, the first jogger would jog for 13 km while the second jogger would jog fo 14 km and their respective times would be 39 mins and 56 minutes. This is consistent with the condition in the question which talks about a difference of 17 minutes in their respective times.

16. Solve this through options as: For option (a)
$$4800/60 - 4800/50 = 16 \text{ minutes}$$

17. The ant would cover $7 \times 8 = 56$ meters in 16 hours. Further, it would require 7/12 of the 17th hour to reach the top. Thus time required = 16 hours 35 minutes

18. If the slower ship took 20 hours (option d) the faster ship would take 12 hours and their respective speeds would be 15 and 25 kmph. This satisfies the basic condition in the question.

19. The movement of the ant in the two cases would be 3, 7, 11, 15, 19, 23 and 1, 9, 17, 25, 33, 41. It can be seen that after 3 seconds the difference is 6mm, after 4 seconds, the difference is 16mm and after 5 seconds the difference is 30 mm. Thus, it is clearly seen that the ant moved for 4 seconds.

20. When the signal happened distance left was 150 km.
$$150/(s) - 150/(s + 15) = 1/2 \text{ hours} \rightarrow s = 60.$$

21. The following figure gives us the movement of the two swimmers:

The faster swimmer must have traveled 80 km in 2 hours and hence his speed is 40 kmph.

22. Since they cover the distance in 80 minutes traveling in opposite directions we infer 100% distance is covered in 80 minutes → 1.25% per minute → 75% per hour.
i.e. their combined distance coverage is 75% per hour. Since we are asked for the time the faster motorcyclist takes, we can pick up this time from the options.

Options	Time for faster motorcyclist	Faster's % coverage per hour	Slower's % coverage per hour
a	6 hours	16.66	58.33
b	3 hours	33.33	41.66
c	2 hours	50	25
d	4 hours	25	50
e	5 hours	20	55

It is clear that options a, b, d and e are not feasible as it is making the faster motorcyclist slower.

Thus option (c) has to be correct.

Note: You can use the values in option (c) to check the other condition in problem and see that it works.

23. Since the two horses meet after 200 minutes, they cover 0.5% of the distance per minute (combined) or 30% per hour. This condition is satisfied only if you the slower rider takes 10 hours (thereby covering 10% per hour) and the faster rider takes 5 hours (thereby covering 20% per hour).

24. Solve through options the equation: $350/s - 350/(3 + 5) = 2.33$ hours.
$$\rightarrow s = 25.$$

25. Solve this question through options. The total travel time should be 5 hours 25 minutes.
or $5(5/12)$ hours = 65/12 hours
$$d/36 + d/14 = 65/12 \rightarrow d = 54.6 \text{ km.}$$

Thus, option (d) none of these is correct.

26–28. You can make the following table to chart out the motions of the three.

Hour	Ram	Shyam	Mohan
1	10	30	3.33
2	20	33.33	6.66
3	60	36.66	10
4	81.66	40	20
5	85	50	30
6	88.33	60	40
	90(6.5)	70(7)	70(7)
		80(8)	100(8)

26. It is evident that Ram would overtake Shyam between 2 and 3. At x, Shyam is ahead by 13.33 km.
Relative speed between 2 – 3 = 36.66 kmph.
Time required = 13.33/36.66 of the hour
= 4/11 of the hour
= 2 : 22. (approx)

27. Mohan would overtake Shyam after 70 miles.

28. Ram would cover 90 miles in 3 hours 45 minutes.
Mohan would cover 90 miles in 7 hours 40 minutes.
Time difference = 3 hours 55 minutes.

29. Mohan at 8 pm (each of the others would reach later).

30. Ram would reach at 9:30 p.m., while Shyam would reach at 10:00 p.m.

31. $25/s - 25/(s + 10) = 1/2$
$S = 50$ km/hr.

32. The respective times are 224 seconds and 364 seconds. They will meet at the starting point in the LCM of these times i.e. 224×13. Hence, Ram Singh will cover the circle 13 times.

33. The wife drives for 12 minutes less than her driving on normal days.
Thus, she would have saved 6 minutes each way. Hence, Ravi would have walked for 30 minutes (since his speed is 1/5th of the car's speed).
In effect, Ravi spends 24 minutes extra on the walking (rather than if he had traveled the same distance by car).
Thus, if Ravi had got the car at the station only, he would have saved 24 minutes more and reached at 5:36.

34. The following figure represents the travel of the two:

Once, you can visualize this figure, try to extract the value of x by taking the length as given in the options. For option (a) length of pool is 55.5 meters, the ratio of speeds of Ajay to Hemant on the basis

of the first meeting = 18.5/37. The ratio of speeds on the basis of the second meeting = Ajay's travel to Hemant's travel = 47.5/ 63.5. The two ratios are not the same- which they should have been as both these ratios represent the speed ratio between Ajay and Hemant.
For option (b), length of pool is 45 meters, the ratio of speeds of Ajay to Hemant on the basis of the first meeting = 18.5/26.5. The ratio of speeds on the basis of the second meeting = Ajay's travel to Hemant's travel = 37/ 53. The two ratios are the same- which they should have been as both these ratios represent the speed ratio between Ajay and Hemant. Hence, this is the correct answer.

35. The distances covered in percentage would be, 10% + 6.66% + 8.33% + 16.66% + 5.833% + 31.666 + 2.0833 = 81.25%
$(22.5/18.75) \times 100 = 120$ km

36. If you start at 12 noon, you would reach at 4:30 PM. You would be able to meet the train which left Mumbai at 8 AM, 9 AM, 10 AM, 11 AM, 12 Noon, 1 PM, 2 PM, 3 PM and 4 PM – a total of 9 trains.

37. The total time = time in the first part of the journey + time for the second part of the journey= $k/y + (x - k)/z$. Option (a) is correct.

38. If we assume the speed of the sound as 330 m/s, we can see that the distance traveled by the sound in 45 seconds is the distance traveled by the train in 11 minutes.
$330 \times 45 = 660 \times s \rightarrow s = 22.5$ m/s = 81 kmph

39–40. In 9 hours, (7 pm to 4 pm) the Kalinga Express would cover 540 kms.
Remaining distance = 260 kms
Relative speed = 150 kmph.
Time required = 260/150 =1.733 hours
= 104 minutes.

39. $1.733 \times 90 = 156$ km.

40. 4 A.M. + 1 hr 44 minutes = 5 : 44 A.M.

41. The total distance the bird would travel would be dependent on the time that the cars crash with each other. Also, the speed of the bird is the same as the relative speed of the cars. Hence, the answer to question 41 will be 12 km.

42. The bird would travel at 120 kmph for 4 + 4/3 + 4/9 minutes. i.e 5.77 minutes. Hence, the answer is $(5.77/60) \times 120 = 11.55$ km.

43. The bird would be able to theoretically reach the bonnet of the second car an infinite number of times.

44. Initial distance = 25 dog leaps.
Per minute → dog makes 5 dog leaps
Per minute → Cat makes 6 cat leaps = 3 dog leaps.

Relative speed = 2 dog leaps/minutes.

An initial distance of 25 dog leaps would get covered in 12.5 minutes.

45. Refer to the following figure which helps us understand that the ratio of speeds of A to B would be 2:3.

P ―――――――――――――――――――――――――――― Q

0.4 D means ratio of speeds = 2:3

The 4th meeting would occur after a combined movement of $D + 6D = 7D$. 2/5th of this distance would be covered by A and 3/5th of this distance would be the distance covered by B. Thus, distance covered by A would be 2/5th of $7D$ --: distance covered by $A = 2.8D$ – which means that the 4th meeting occurs at a distance of $0.8D$ from P.

46. In 36 hours, there would be a gap of 8 minutes. The two watches would show the same time when the gap would be exactly 12 hours or 720 minutes.

The no. of 36 hour time frames required to create this gap = 720/8 = 90.

Total time = 90 × 36 = 3240 hours. Since this is divisible by 24, the watches would show 12 noon.

47. Solve through options. At 18 kmph the motorboat would take exactly 6 hours.

48. Check through options. Option (d) will give us 14 kmph and 9 kmph as the down stream and up stream speeds. This would mean that the total travel time would be 1.5 hours and 2.33 hours down stream and up stream respectively.

49. At 2:15 PM the distance between the two trains would be 550 km as the train from Hazipur to Muzaffarpur would already have traveled for 40 minutes. After that they would take 550/110 = 5 hours to meet. Thus, the train from Muzaffarpur would have traveled 250 kms before meeting. Option (c) is correct.

50. The dog loses 1/3rd of his normal time from the meeting point. (Thus normal time = 35 × 3 = 105 minutes)

If the meeting occurred 24 km further, the dog loses 25 minutes.

This means that the normal time for the new distance would be 75 minutes. Thus, normally the dog would cover this distance of 24 km in 30 minutes. Thus, normal speed = 48 km/hr.

Space for Notes

EXERCISE ON APPLICATIONS OF TIME, SPEED AND DISTANCE

1. At the ancient Athens Olympic games, in a duel between two runners, Portheus and Morpheus, they were made to start running in opposite direction from diametrically opposite ends of a circular race track of length (circumference) 2 kms. The first time they met was after 24 minutes. If the distance between them exactly 'n' minutes after they start is equal to a quarter of the length of the track, which of the following is a possible value of 'n'?
   (a) 124
   (b) 184
   (c) 160
   (d) 204

2. Aman and Biman started a walkathon around a circular track starting from the same point on the track in opposite directions. They met for the first after time 't'. Had they walked in the same direction with their speeds intact, they would have met after a time '$7t$'. It was also observed that Aman was slower than Biman, and Aman's speed was measured at 12 kmph. Find the speed of Biman.
   (a) 4 m/s
   (b) 5 m/s
   (c) 6 m/s
   (d) None of these

3. Abhishek and Aiswarya start from two opposite ends of a tunnel AB, which is 182 meters in length. Abhishek starts from A and Aiswarya starts from B. After they meet, they continue moving in their respective directions, till one of them reaches his end point and immediately reverses direction and starts walking back towards the other end. The ratio of their speeds is 7:6. At what distance (in metres) from A will they meet when Abhishek is in his 8th round?
   (a) 105
   (b) 130
   (c) 125
   (d) They would not meet.

4. For the above question, at what distance (in metres) from A will they meet when Abhishek is in his 12th round?
   (a) 126
   (b) 118
   (c) 91
   (d) They would not meet.

5. Two runners Portheus and Zeus, are running around a circular track at different speeds such that they meet after regular time intervals. The length of the track (circumference) is 1600 meters. If they run in opposite directions, they meet at eight different points while if they run in the same direction it is observed that they meet at 2 distinct points on the circular track. If they meet at intervals of 1.33 minutes when they run in the same direction, how much time does the faster runner (Portheus) take to complete one round?

   (a) 80 secs
   (b) 128 secs
   (c) 120 secs
   (d) None of these

6. At the Vijayantkhand Mini Stadium there are two circular race tracks— A with radii 40m and B 80 m respectively such that they touch each other at a point X. The coach Vijay Sir has a particular ritual with his best athletes Mridul and Odeon. Mridul runs at a speed of 80π m/min on Race Track A and Odeon runs at a speed of 40π m/min along the Race Track B. Both of them start from the point X and run multiple rounds. If Mridul gives Odeon a start of 4 mins exactly before he starts running himself, after how much time (in minutes) will the straight line distance between the two be exactly 240 m?
   (a) 6
   (b) 10
   (c) 12.5
   (d) Never

7. Bolt and Milkha, start running around a race track simultaneously. Bolt runs at a speed of 's' kmph, while Milkha runs at a speed of 'm' kmph. They meet for the first time when Bolt is in his third round. Which of the following can be the value of $x:y$?
   (a) 11 : 6
   (b) 11 : 5
   (c) 17 : 8
   (d) 9 : 4

8. Amar, Abhijit and Arun start running on a circular race track (from the same point). Amar and Abhijit run in a clockwise fashion while Arun runs anticlockwise. When Amar and Arun meet for the first time, Arun is at a distance which is equal to a quarter of the circumference of the circular race track. It is also known that Amar runs faster than Arun. The ratio of speeds of Amar, Arun and Abhijit cannot be...?
   (a) 5 : 1 : 2
   (b) 3 : 1 : 1
   (c) 4 : 2 : 1
   (d) 3 : 2 : 1

9. At what time between 6 and 7 o'clock is the miniute hand of a clock 4 minutes ahead of the hour hand?
   (a) $34\frac{1}{11}$ minutes past 6
   (b) $36\frac{5}{11}$ minutes past 6
   (c) $37\frac{1}{11}$ minutes past 6
   (d) None of these

10. The minute hand of a clock overtakes the hour hand at intervals of 66 minutes of the correct time. How much time does the clock gain or lose in 4 hours?
    (a) $1\frac{119}{121}$ minutes
    (b) $1\frac{114}{121}$ minutes
    (c) 2 minutes
    (d) None of these

11. Robin Varkey's watch always runs faster than the actual time – and gains time unifromly. He sets the watch to be 10 minutes behind time at 12 noon on a Sunday. He observes that the watch is 5 minutes 48 seconds faster the following Sunday at 12 noon. At what exact time would the watch be correct?

    (a) $\frac{26}{79}$ hours past 10 PM on Thursday

    (b) $\frac{13}{79}$ hours past 8 PM on Thursday

    (c) $\frac{26}{79}$ hours past 6 PM on Thursday

    (d) None of these

12. Prawin Tiwari sets his clock right at 10 AM on Monday morning. However, being a defective piece (the clock), it loses 32 minutes every day. He has to get up on Friday at exactly 2 AM to catch his flight to Lebuana. At what time on Friday morning should he set the alarm on his watch in order for the watch to ring at exactly 2 AM?

    (a) 3 AM   (b) 4 AM
    (c) 5 AM   (d) None of these

13. At what time, in minutes , between 4 o'clock and 5 o'clock, would both the hands of a clock coincide with each other?

    (a) $22\frac{1}{11}$ (b) $21\frac{9}{11}$

    (c) $22\frac{4}{11}$ (d) $21\frac{7}{11}$

14. At what time between 8 PM to 9 PM will the hands of a clock be in the same straight line pointing away from each other?

    (a) $10\frac{8}{11}$ minutes past 8

    (b) $10\frac{10}{11}$ minutes past 8

    (c) $10\frac{3}{11}$ minutes past 8

    (d) $9\frac{10}{11}$ minutes past 8

15. A watch which gains 5 seconds in 3 minutes was set right at 7 am. In the afternoon of the same day, when it indicated quarter past 4 o'clock, the true time is:

    (a) $59\frac{7}{12}$ min. past 3   (b) 4 p.m

    (c) $58\frac{7}{11}$ min. past 3   (d) $2\frac{3}{11}$ min. past 4

16. In a 2000 m race between Portheus and Cassius, Portheus gives Cassius a head start of a minute but still beats him by 200 m. When, he increases the head start to 80 seconds, the race ends in a dead heat. Find the speed of Portheus.

    (a) 25 m/s   (b) 18 m/s
    (c) 13.33 m/s   (d) 16.66 m/s

17. How many right angles would be formed between the minute and the hour hand of a watch in a day?

    (a) 48   (b) 46
    (c) 45   (d) 44

18. How many times between 2 PM and 4 PM does the minutes hand coincide with the seconds hand?

    (a) 118   (b) 119
    (c) 120   (d) 121

19. A man enters his house at some time between 6 to 7 PM. When he leaves his house sometime between 7 to 8, he observes that the minute hand and the hour hand have interchanged positions. At what exact time did the man enter the house?

    (A) $38\frac{82}{121}$ minutes past 6

    (b) $37\frac{42}{121}$ minutes past 6

    (c) $37\frac{82}{121}$ minutes past 6

    (d) $37\frac{62}{121}$ minutes past 6

20. How many straight lines would be formed between the minute and the hour hand of a watch in a day?

    (a) 48   (b) 46
    (c) 45   (d) 44

21. Two friends started simultaneously from Lucknow towards Kanpur in the same direction along a straight road. The faster friend Raveesh was on a bike while Prakash was in an auto. The ratio of their speeds was 1 : 5 respectively. Two hours later, Raveesh parked his bike and started running back towards Prakash's auto. His speed dropped by 80% as a result of this. They meet at a point which is 15 km from Kanpur. What was the speed of the auto?

    (a) 2 km/hr   (b) 2.5 km/hr
    (c) 3 km/hr   (d) None of these.

22. Two brothers came to know about their sister's wedding at the last minute. The wedding was to be held at a location which was 800 kms away from Mumbai where both of them lived. The elder brother Kanhaiya came to know about the wedding at 6 PM and left immediately in his car. His younger brother Ramaiyya came to know about the wedding at 9:30 PM and left in his car immediately at a speed which was 15 kmph higher than the speed of his elder brother. At 4:30 AM it was found that the two cars were 70 km apart. If the cars had travelled continuously without taking any rest, find the speed (in km/hr) of car A.

    (a) 40   (b) 50
    (c) 60   (d) Cannot be determined

23. Ranatunga once challenged Bolt to a race. The distance of the race was set at 2 km. They start at the same time and the ratio of their speeds is seen to be 4:1 (obviously Bolt would be faster). After some time passes, Bolt realises that he is far ahead and calculates that even if he stops for a snack and a nap for 'n' minutes, he would still reach his destination and beat Ranatunga by 13 minutes. Hence, he plans to take a break of 'n' minutes. Ranatunga keeps walking during this whole time. However, when Bolt wakes up, he realises that he has stopped for a total of (n+15) minutes. He redoubles his efforts by increasing his speed to double his original speed. The race eventually ended in a dead heat. If it is known that Bolt overstayed his stop by 6n/5 mins, how long did Ranatunga take to complete the race?

  (a) 32 mins   (b) 34 mins
  (c) 25 mins   (d) None of these

24. A and B run a 300 m race where the initial speed of B is double the speed of A. After some time, going on these speeds, A realising that he would be losing the race redoubled his effort and increased his speed to four times his initial speed. As a result, they reached the end point at the same time and the race resulted in a dead heat. What was the distance traveled by B, when A quadrupled his speed?

  (a) 100 m   (b) 200 m
  (c) 150 m   (d) None of these

25. Amit and Bimal start running around a circular track of circumference 4200 metres. Their respective speeds are 15m/s and 3 m/s. Their 14th meeting occurs at point P and their 22nd meeting occurs at the point Q. Find the longer distance (along the circumference) between Points P and Q.

  (a) 2800   (b) 1400
  (c) 3500   (d) 3150

26. In a 2 km race, Ravi beats Sandeep by 45 seconds and Sandeep beats Tarun by a further 75 seconds. In the same race, Ravi beats Tarun by 400 m. Find the time in which Ravi can run the race (in seconds).

  (a) 240   (b) 300
  (c) 360   (d) 480

ANSWER KEY

1. (d)	2. (d)	3. (d)	4. (a)
5. (b)	6. (d)	7. (a)	8. (d)
9. (c)	10. (a)	11. (a)	12. (b)
13. (b)	14. (b)	15. (b)	16. (d)
17. (d)	18. (d)	19. (a)	20. (c)
21. (b)	22. (b)	23. (b)	24. (b)
25. (a)	26. (d)		

Solutions

1. They would first meet after 24 minutes (after covering 50% of the distance represented by the circumference of the circle). The next time they would meet would be at 72 minutes, then 120 minutes, then 168 minutes, 216 minutes and so on.

Every time they meet they would be together and after the meeting point they continue running in opposite directions till they meet again. Between two meeting points, the distance between them would be 25% of the length of the circle's circumference in two cases: first when they are going away from each other after meeeting (this would occur at a time of 12 minutes after the meeting point) and second when they are approaching each other before their next meeting (this would occur at a time of 12 minutes before the next meeting point.

The meeting times 24, 72, 120, 168, 216, 264 etc, the table would represent the times at which the distance would be 25% of the circumference:

(24 –12 = 12); (24 + 12 = 36); (72 – 12 = 60);
(72 + 12 = 84); (120 – 12 = 108); (120 + 12 = 132);
(168 – 12 = 156); (168 + 12 = 180);
(216 – 12 = 204).

Only Option (d) is possible and hence is the correct answer.

2. Let the speed of Biman be b kmph. The value of b should be such that. be x.
$b = 16$ kmph $= 16 \times 5 \div 18 = 80 \div 18$ m/s $= 4.44$ m/s.
Option (d) is the correct answer.

3. When Abhishek would complete 7 rounds, Aiswarya would have completed: $7 \times 6 \div 7 = 6$ rounds.

This means that both of them would be at the point B at this time. Since Abhishek is faster than Aiswarya, during his eighth round there would be no meeting with Aiswarya. Hence, Option (d) is correct.

4. When Abhishek would complete 11 rounds, Aiswarya would have completed: $11 \times 6 \div 7$ rounds $= 9\frac{3}{7}$ rounds.

This means that Aiswarya would be at a distance of 3/7 from A, while Abhishek would be at B at this point of time. The distance between them would be 4/7 of the total distance between A and B. Aiswarya would further cover a distance of $4/7 \times 6/13$ in order to meet Abhishek. Thus the total distance from A is $(3/7 + 24/91) \times 182 = 63 \times 182 \div 91 = 126$ meters from A and 56 meters from B. Option (a) is correct.

5. Let the ratio of speeds be P:Z (where P>Z).
Since they meet at 8 distinct points on the circle when they move in opposite directions, it automatically means that the sum of P+Z = 8. (I would like to encourage you to discover this piece of logic through trial and error.)

Similar logic gives us that P-Z = 2 (since they meet at two distinct points when travelling in the same direction.

Using these two equations, we can determine that if P = 5, Z=3. Let the speeds of P be 5x and Z be 3x (in m/s). Then we have: 1600/8x = 80 secs → x = 2.5 and hence the speeds are P= 12.5 m/s and Z=7.5 m/s.

P would take 1600 ÷ 12.5 = 128 seconds to complete one round.

Option (b) would be the correct answer.

6. Since the radii of the circles are 40m and 80m respectively, the circumference would be 80π and 160π meters respectively. Since Odeon's speed is 40πm/min, he would take 4 minutes to cover a round. This also means that when Mridul starts running, they would both be at point X, since Odeon would have covered 1 round exactly in 4 minutes. Also, for the straight line distance to be 240 m they should be at the diametrically opposite ends from the point X (of their respective circles). Mridul reaches the diametrically opposite end (from X) of his circle for the first time in 30 seconds and after that he would reach the same point every 1 minute at 1:30, 2:30 and so on. Odeon on the other hand would reach the diametrically opposite end at 2 minutes, 6 minutes, 10 minutes and so on. They would never be exactly 240 m apart. Option (d) is correct.

7. Check using the options. You can see that only in the case of Option (a) do they meet when Bolt is in his third round. For all other options, Bolt would cross Milkha when Bolt is in his second round.

8. Checking the options, it can be seen that the condition of diametrically opposite is satisfied in each of the first three options. It is only in Option (d) that it is not satisfied. Hence, Option (d) is correct.

9. At 6 o'clock, the minute hand is 30 minutes behind the hour hand.

From this position, we need to reach a position, where the minute hand is 4 minutes ahead of the hour hand. For this to occur, the minute hand has to gain (30 + 4) = 34 minute spaces on the hour hand. In one hour, the minute hand moves 60 mintues while the hour hand moves 5 minute spaces on the clock. Hence, the minute hand gains 55 minutes on the hour hand in an hour.

Hence, to gain, 34 minutes, the minute hand would take $\left(\frac{60}{55} \times 34\right) = 37\frac{1}{11}$ min.

The required answer would be $37\frac{1}{11}$ minutes past 6. Option (c) is correct.

10. Assume the clock to be a circular race track of 60 kms with each minute denoting 1 km. Also imagine two runners Mr. Minute and Mr. Hour running on this track. Normally, in a correct clock, Mr. Minute would cover 55 kms more than Mr. Hour every hour. This means that they would be together (meaning Mr. Minute would overtake Mr. Hour) every $\left(\frac{60}{55} \times 60\right)$ min. = $65\frac{5}{11}$ minutes. If they meet at longer time intervals than this, it means that the clock is slow. If the time intervals are shorter it would mean that the clock is fast.

In this problem they are together after 66 minutes. Thus, the clock loses time.

Loss in 66 minutes = $\left(66 - 65\frac{5}{11}\right) = \frac{6}{11}$ minutes.

Using unitary method we get loss in 4 hours = $\left(\frac{6}{11} \times \frac{60 \times 4}{66}\right)$ min. = $1\frac{119}{121}$ minutes.

11. In one week the time elapsed is exaclty 168 hours. Robin's watch gains 15 minutes 48 seconds in 168 hours. In other words it gains $\left(10 + 5\frac{4}{5}\right)$ min. or $\frac{79}{5}$ minutes in 168 hrs.

To be showing the exact time, the watch should have gained exactly 10 minutes.

Using Unitary method it can be seen that 10 minutes would be gained by the watch in: $\left(168 \times \frac{5}{79} \times 10\right)$ hrs. = $106\frac{26}{79}$ hours.

∴ Watch is correct at $\frac{26}{79}$ hours past 10 PM on Thursday. Option (a) is the correct answer.

12. Time from 10 AM on Monday to 2 AM on Friday = 88 hours.

Now 23 hrs 28 minutes of this clock = 24 hours of correct clock.

∴ $\frac{352}{15}$ hrs of this clock = 24 hours of correct clock

88 hrs of this clock = $\left(24 \times \frac{15}{352} \times 88\right)$ hrs of correct clock.

= 90 hrs of correct clock. This means that at 2 AM on Friday his clock would show 4 AM. Hence, if he needs to wake up at 2 AM, he should set his clock's alarm at 4 AM.

Hence, Option (b) is the correct answer.

13. Assume the clock to be a circular race track of 60 kms with each minute denoting 1 km. Also imagine two runners Mr. Minute and Mr. Hour running on this track. Normally, in a correct clock, Mr. Minute would cover 55 kms more than Mr. Hour every hour. At 4 o'clock, the minute hand is 20 kms behind the hour hand.

It would hence, need to gain 20 kms to coincide with the hour hand.

In 60 minutes, it gains 55 kms.

In t minutes, it gains 20 kms.

$$t = \left(\frac{60}{55} \times 20\right) \text{min.} = 21\frac{9}{11} \text{ minutes.}$$

14. Thinking as in the previous question, we can think that at 8 PM the minute hand is 40 kms behind the hour hand. For it to become 30 kms behind the hour hand, we would need it to cover 10 kms over the hour hand.

In 60 minutes, it gains 55 kms.

In t minutes, it gains 10 kms.

$$t = \left(\frac{60}{55} \times 10\right) \text{min.} = 10\frac{10}{11} \text{ minutes.}$$

Option (b) is correct.

15. Time from 7 am to 4:15 pm = 9 hrs 15min = $\frac{37}{4}$ hrs

3 min 5 sec of this clock = 3 min of the correct clock.

$\Rightarrow \frac{37}{720}$ hrs of this clock = $\frac{1}{20}$ hrs of the clock.

$\Rightarrow \frac{37}{4}$ hrs of this clock = $\left(\frac{1}{20} \times \frac{720}{37} \times \frac{37}{4}\right)$ hrs of the correct clock

= 9 hrs of the correct clock

The correct time is 9 hrs after 7 AM i.e. 4 PM.

16. Since Cassius is able to get a dead heat when he gets a head start of 80 seconds, it means that he would cover 200 meters in 20 seconds. Hence, his speed is 10m/s.

Let the time taken by Portheus to finish the race be *t* seconds. Then tracking the movement of Cassius we get:

$t \times 10 + 60 \times 10 = 2000 - 200$.

So $t = 120$ seconds.

Hence, the speed of Portheus would be = 2000/120 = 250/15 = 50/3 = 16.666 m/s. Option (d) is correct.

17. There are 2 right angles that are formed every hour between the hands of a watch. Hence, in 24 hours, we would expect 48 right angles. However, between 2 to 4 AM and 2 to 4 PM the number of right angles formed is only 3, because the right angle formed at 3 O'Clock (both AM and PM) is the second right angle for the hour between 2 O'Clock and 3 O'Clock. It is also the first right angle between 3 O'Clock and 4 O'Clock. This makes the clock lose two of its 48 expected right angles. Similarly, two right angles are lost when the clock passes through 8 O'Clock to 10 O'Clock. Hence, ther would be a total of 44 right angles formed. Option (d) is correct.

18. In two hours, the minute hand completes 2 rounds around the circumference of the clock's dial. In the same time, the seconds hand covers 120 rounds. If we count 2 PM coincidence as the first one, the 4 pm coincidence would be the last one. There would be a total of 121 coincidences in 2 hours. Option (d) is correct.

19. Assume the clock to be a circular race track of 60 kms with each minute denoting 1 km. Also imagine two runners Mr. Minute and Mr. Hour running on this track. Normally, in a correct clock, Mr. Minute would cover 55 kms more than Mr. Hour every hour. For the conditions given in the problem, when the man enters the house, the time would be somewhere between 6:35 to 6:40 while when he leaves the time would be somewhere between 7:30 to 7:35.

Let, the distance between the two be equal to *x* kms. When the hands interchange positions, the hour hand would have traveled *x* kms and the minute hand would have traveled $(60 - x)$ kms.

Using unitary method we get:

When the minute hand travels 60 kms, the hour hand travels 5 kms.

When the minute hand travels '$60 - x$' kms, the hour hand travels '*x*' kms.

$60x = 300 - 5x \rightarrow x = \frac{300}{55} = 5\frac{5}{11}$ minutes.

This means that when he comes home, the minute hand is $5\frac{5}{11}$ minutes ahead of the hour hand.

In order to find the exact time at which this happens between 6 to 7, we know that at 6, the minute hand is 30 kms behind the hour hand. For the minute hand to move $5\frac{5}{11}$ minutes ahead of the hour hand we would need the minute hand to cover $35\frac{5}{11}$ kms.

In 60 minutes, the minute hand covers 55 kms.

In *t* minutes, the minute hand covers $35\frac{5}{11}$ minutes.

$t = 60 \times 35\frac{5}{11} \div 55 = \frac{12}{11} \times \frac{390}{11}$ minutes = 4680 ÷ 121 = $38\frac{82}{121}$ minutes.

He comes home at $38\frac{82}{121}$ minutes past 6.

20. There are 2 times that the hands of a watch form straight lines every hour. Hence, in 24 hours, we would expect 48 straight lines. However, between 11 to 1 and between 5 to 7 we would 'lose' one straight line as the 12 o'clock straight line and the 6 o'clock straight lines are double counted. Hence, the number of straight lines = 48 – 1 (for 5 AM to 7AM) – 1 (for 11 AM to 1 PM) – 1 (for 5 PM to 7 PM). Hence, there would be a total of 45 straight lines formed in a day. Option (c) is correct.

21. Solve this through options. Option (b) matches the conditions of the problem and is hence the correct answer.

The thought process for this goes as follows:
If the auto's speed is 2.5, the bike's speed would be 12.5. Naturally 2 hours later, Raveesh would be at 25 kms. while Prakash would be at 5 kms. A distance of 20 kms. When Raveesh starts back his speed would be 2.5 kmph and hence the total speed at which they would approach each other would be 5 kmph. They would meet 6 hours after starting – and in this time Prakash would have covered 15 km and hence they would meet at 15 km from Kanpur. (This last bit would not match for the other options.)
For example if we check Option (a):
The thought process for this goes as follows:
If the auto's speed is 2, the bike's speed would be 10. Naturally 2 hours later, Raveesh would be at 20 kms while Prakash would be at 4 kms. A distance of 16 kms. When Raveesh starts back his speed would be 2 kmph and hence the total speed at which they would approach each other would be 4 kmph. They would meet 6 hours after starting – and in this time Prakash would have covered 12 km and hence they would meet at 12 km from Kanpur which does not match the information in the problem.

22. Solve using options. For option (b), at 4:30 AM the elder brother has travelled for 10:30 hours and hence must have covered 525 kms. The younger brother has traveled only for 7 hours and at a speed of 65 kmph, the distance traveled would be 455 km. This would mean that the distance between them would be 70 km (as given). Hence, this option works correctly. The other options do not work and can be tested in a similar way. For instance for option (a), 40 kmph does not work because $10.5 \times 40 - 7 \times 55 \neq 70$.
Similarly, Option (c) can be rejected because $10.5 \times 60 - 7 \times 75 \neq 70$

23. Since Bolt outstretched his time by $6n/5$ mins and this is also equal to 15 mins. Solving we get: $n = 12.5$ mins.

Space for Rough Work

Let their original speeds be '$4s$' and 's' kmph respectively.
Had Bolt not overstretched his nap, he would have beaten Ranatunga by 13 min.

$$\therefore \frac{2000}{4s} + 12.5 + 13 = \frac{2000}{s} \Rightarrow s = 1000/17$$

Hence, the time taken by Ranatunga to complete the race = $2000 \times 17 \div 1000 = 34$ minutes.
Hence, Option (b) is correct.

24. The distance traveled by B in the initial phase of the race would be double the distance traveled by A during the same time. Likewise, in the second phase of the race, the distance traveled by A would be double the distance traveled by B. Also the total distance traveled by A and B would be 300 m. The only value which creates this symmetircal situation is if the initial phase is such that B travels 200 m and A travels 100 m. Hence, Option (b) is correct.

25. Imagine the circle to be a clock with 12 divisions on the circumference- each division equal to a distance of $4200 \div 12 = 350$ metres. (Imagine these are representing 1 o'Clock to 12 o'Clock for ease of understanding). Since they travel at a ratio of speed as 5:1, imagine Amit travels clockwise and Bimal travels anti clockwise. Their first meeting would occur at the point representing 10 o'Clock, the next at 8 o'clock, then 6 o'clock and so on. It can be seen that the 14th meeting would occur at 8 o'Clock and the 22nd meeting at 4 o'Clock. The longer distance between them would be equal to 8 markings on the clock. This distance would be $8 \times 350 = 2800$ metres. Option (a) is correct.

26. Ravi beats Tarun by 120 seconds or 400 meters. Hence, Tarun's speed is $400 \div 2 = 200$ m/minute. Also, when Ravi does 2000 meters, Tarun does 1600 meters – which he would do in 8 minutes. Thus Ravi takes 8 minutes = 480 seconds to complete the race. Option (d) is correct

BLOCK REVIEW TESTS

REVIEW TEST 1

1. A man earns x% on the first ₹ 5,000 of his investment and y% on the rest of his investment. If he earns ₹ 1250 from ₹7,000 and ₹1750 from ₹ 9,000 invested, find the value of x.
   - (a) 20%
   - (b) 15%
   - (c) 25%
   - (d) None of these

2. The price of a telelvision set drops by 30% while the sales of the set goes up by 50% What is the percentage change in the total revenue from the sales of the set?
   - (a) –4%
   - (b) –2%
   - (c) +5%
   - (d) +2%

3. A person who has a certain amount with him goes to the market. He can buy 100 oranges or 80 mangoes. He retains 20% of the amount for petrol expenses and buys 40 mangoes and of the balance, he purchases oranges. The number of oranges he can purchase is:
   - (a) 30
   - (b) 40
   - (c) 15
   - (d) 20

4. A cloth merchant cheats his supplier and his customer to the tune of 20% while buying and selling cloth respectively. He professes to sell at the cost price but also offers a discount of 20% on cash payment, what is his overall profit percentage?
   - (a) 20%
   - (b) 25%
   - (c) 40%
   - (d) 15%

5. I sold two horses for ₹ 50000 each, one at the loss of 20% and the other at the profit of 20%. What is the percentage of loss (–) or profit (+) that resulted from the transaction?
   - (a) (+) 20
   - (b) (–) 4
   - (c) (+) 4
   - (d) (–) 20

6. The cost of a diamond varies directly as the square of its weight. A diamond fell and broke into four pieces whose weights were in the ratio 1:2:3:4. As a result the merchant had a loss of ₹700000. Find the original price of the diamond.
   - (a) ₹ 14 lacs
   - (b) ₹ 20 lacs
   - (c) ₹ 10 lacs
   - (d) ₹ 25 lacs

7. Two oranges, three bananas and four apples cost ₹ 25. Three oranges, two bananas and one apple cost ₹ 20. I brought 3 oranges, 3 bananas and 3 apples. How much did I pay ?
   - (a) ₹22.5
   - (b) ₹27
   - (c) ₹30
   - (d) Cannot be determined

8. From each of two given numbers, half the smaller number is subtracted. Of the resulting numbers the larger one is five times as large as the smaller one. What is the ratio of the two numbers?
   - (a) 2: 1
   - (b) 3: 1
   - (c) 3: 2
   - (d) None of these

Directions for Questions 9 and 10: Answer these questions based on the following information.

A watch dealer incurs an expense of ₹150 for producing every watch. He also incurs an additional expenditure of ₹ 30,000, which is independent of the number of watches produced. If he is able to sell a watch during the season, he sells it for ₹ 250. If he fails to do so, he has to sell each watch for ₹ 100.

9. If he is able to sell only 1,000 out of 1,500 watches he has made in the season, then he has made a profit of:
   - (a) ₹90,000
   - (b) ₹75,000
   - (c) ₹45,000
   - (d) ₹60, 000

10. If he produces 2000 watches, what is the number of watches that he must sell during the season (to the nearest 100) in order to break-even, given that he is able to sell all the watches produced?
   - (a) 700
   - (b) 800
   - (c) 900
   - (d) 1,000

11. A stockist wants to make some profit by selling oil. He contemplates about various methods. Which of the following would maximise his profit?
   - I. Sell oil at 20% profit.
   - II. Use 800 g of weight instead of 1 kg
   - III. Mix 20% impurities in oil and selling it at cost price.
   - IV. Increase the price by 10% and reduce weights by 10%.
   - (a) I or III
   - (b) II
   - (c) II and IV
   - (d) Profits are same

12. A dealer offers a cash discount of 20% and still makes a profit of 20%, when he further allows 160 articles when the customer buys 120. How much percent above the cost price were his wares listed?
   - (a) 100%
   - (b) 80%
   - (c) 75%
   - (d) 66(2/3)%

13. A man buys spirit at ₹ 600 per litre, adds water to it and then sells it at ₹ 750 per litre. What is the ratio of the spirit's weight to the weight of the water if his profit in the deal is 37.5%?

(a) 9:1   (b) 10:1

(c) 11:1   (d) None of these

Directions for Questions 14 to 16: Answer these questions based on the following information.

Aamir, on his death bed, keeps half his property for his wife and divides the rest equally among his three sons: Bimar, Cumar and Danger. Some years later, Bimar dies, leaving half his property to his widow and half to his brothers, Cumar and Danger together, sharing equally. When Cumar makes his will, he keeps half his property for his widow and the rest he bequeaths to his younger brother Danger. When Danger dies some years later, he keeps half his property for his widow and the remaining for his mother. The mother now has ₹15,75,0000

14. What was the worth of the total property?
    (a) ₹3 crore   (b) ₹0.8 crore
    (c) ₹1.8 crore   (d) ₹2.4 crore

15. What was Cumar's original share ?
    (a) ₹40 lakh   (b) ₹120 lakh
    (c) ₹60 lakh   (d) ₹50 lakh

16. What was the ratio of the property owned by the widows of the three sons, in the end?
    (a) 7:9:13   (b) 8:10:17
    (c) 5:7:9   (d) 9:12:13

17. At a bookstore, "MODERN BOOK STORE" is flashed using neon lights. The words are individually flashed at long intervals of $2\frac{1}{2}$, $4\frac{1}{4}$, $5\frac{1}{8}$ seconds respectively, and each word is put off after a second. The least time after which the full name of the bookstore can be read again, is:
    (a) 49.5 seconds   (b) 73.5 seconds
    (c) 1744.5 seconds (d) 855 seconds

18. A train approaches a tunnel AB. Inside the tunnel a cat is located at a point that is $2/5$th the distance AB measured from the entrance A. When the train whistles, the cat runs. If the cat moves to the entrance of the tunnel, A, the train catches the cat exactly at the entrance. If the cat moves to the exit B, the train catches the cat at exactly the exit. The speed of the train is greater than the speed of the cat by what order?
    (a) 3 : 1   (b) 4 : 1
    (c) 5 : 1   (d) None of these

19. Six technicians working at the same rate complete the work of one server in 2.5 hrs. If one of them starts at 11:00 a.m. and one additional technician per hour is added beginning at 5:00 p.m., at what time the server will be complete?
    (a) 6:40 p.m,   (b) 7 p.m.
    (c) 7:20 p.m.   (d) 8:00 p.m.

Directions for Questions 20 and 21: Answer the questions based on the following information.

A thief, after committing the burglary, started fleeing at 12 noon, at a speed of 60 km/hr. He was then chased by a policeman X. X started the chase, 15 min after the thief had started, at a speed of 65 km/hr.

20. At what time did X catch the thief?
    (a) 3.30p.m.   (b) 3 p.m.
    (c) 3.15 p.m.   (d) None of these

21. If another policeman had started the same chase along with X, but at a speed of 60 km/hr, then how far behind was he when X caught the thief?
    (a) 18.75 km   (b) 15 km
    (c) 21 km   (d) 37.5km

22. Two typists undertake to do a job. The second typist begins working one hour after the first. Three hours after the first typist has begun working, there is still 9/20 of the work to be done. When the assignment is completed, it turns out that each typist has done half the work. How many hours would it take each one to do the whole job individually?
    (a) 12 hr and 8 hr (b) 8 hr and 5.6 hr
    (c) 10 hr and 8hr   (d) 5 hr and 4 hr

23. A man can walk up a moving 'up' escalator in 30 s. The same man can walk down this moving 'up' escalator in 90s. Assume that his walking speed is same upwards and downwards. How much time will he take to walk up the escalator, when it is not moving?
    (a) 30s   (b) 45s
    (c) 60s   (d) 90s

Directions for Questions 24 and 26: Answer the questions based on the following information.

Boston is 4 hr ahead of Frankfurt and 2 hrs behind India. X leaves Frankfurt at 6 p.m. on Friday and reaches Boston the next day. After waiting there for 2 hrs, he leaves exactly at noon and reaches India at 1 a.m. On his return journey, he takes the same route as before, but halts at Boston for 1 hr less than his previous halt there. He then proceeds to Frankfurt.

24. If his journey, including stoppage, is covered at an average speed of 180 mph, what is the distance between Frankfurt and India?
    (a) 3,600 miles   (b) 4,500 miles
    (c) 5580 miles   (d) Data insufficient

25. If X had started the return journey from India at 2.55 a.m. on the same day that he reached there, after how much time would he reach Frankfurt?
    (a) 24 hrs   (b) 25 hrs
    (c) 26 hrs   (d) Data insufficient

26. What is X's average speed for the entire journey (to and fro)?
    (a) 176 mph   (b) 180 mph
    (c) 165 mph   (d) Data insufficient

REVIEW TEST 2

1. A car after traveling 18 km from a point A developed some problem in the engine and the speed became $4/5^{th}$ of its original speed. As a result, the car reached point B 45 minutes late. If the engine had developed the same problem after travelling 30 km from A, then it would have reached B only 36 minutes late. The original speed of the car (in km per hour) and the distance between the points A and B (in km) are
   - (a) 25,130
   - (b) 30,150
   - (c) 20,190
   - (d) None of these

2. A, B and C individually can finish a work in 6,8 and 15 hours respectively. They started the work together and after completing the work got ₹94.60. when they divide the money among themselves. A, B and C will get respectively (in ₹)
   - (a) 44,33,17.60
   - (b) 43,27,24.60
   - (c) 45,30,19.60
   - (d) 42,28,24.60

3. Two trains are traveling in opposite direction at uniform speed 60 and 50 km per hour respectively. They take 5 seconds to cross each other. If the two trains had traveled in the same direction, then a passenger sitting in the faster moving train would have overtaken the other train in 18 seconds. The length of the trains in metres are
   - (a) 112, 78.40
   - (b) 97.78, 55
   - (c) 102.78, 50
   - (d) 102.78, 55

4. Assume that an equal number of people are born on each day. Find approximately the percentage of the people whose birthday will fall on 29th February.
   - (a) 0.374
   - (b) 0.5732
   - (c) 0.0684
   - (d) None of these.

5. A sum of money compounded annually becomes ₹625 in two years and ₹675 in three years. The rate of interest per annum is
   - (a) 7%
   - (b) 8%
   - (c) 6%
   - (d) 5%

6. Every day Asha's husband meets her at the city railway station at 6:00 p.m. and drives her to their residence. One day she left early from the office and reached the railway station at 5:00 p.m. She started walking towards her home, met her husband coming from their residence on the way and they reached home 10 minutes earlier than the usual time. For how long did she walk?
   - (a) 1 hour
   - (b) 50 minutes
   - (c) ½ hour
   - (d) 55 minutes

7. Three machines, A, B and C can be used to produce a product. Machine A will take 60 hours to produce a million units. Machine B is twice as fast as Machine A. Machine C will take the same amount of time to produce a million units as A and B running together. How much time will be required to produce a million units if all the three machines are used simultaneously?
   - (a) 12 hours
   - (b) 10 hours
   - (c) 8 hours
   - (d) 6 hours

8. Mr. and Mrs. Shah travel from City A to City B and break journey at City C in between. Somewhere between City A and City C, Mrs. Shah asks "How far have we travelled?" Mr. Shah replies, "Half as far as the distance from here to city C". Somewhere between City C and City B, exactly 200 km from the point where she asked the first question, Mrs. Shah asks "How far do we have to go?" Mr. Shah replies "Half as far as the distance from City C to here." The distance between Cities A and B in km. is
   - (a) 200
   - (b) 100
   - (c) 400
   - (d) 300

9. A shop sells ball point pens and refills. It used to sell refills for 50 paise each, but there were hardly any takers. When he reduced the price, the remaining refills were sold out enabling the shopkeeper to realize ₹ 35.89. How many refills were sold at the reduced price?
   - (a) 37
   - (b) 71
   - (c) 89
   - (d) 97

10. Anand and Bharat can cut 5 kg of wood in 20 min, Bharat and Chandra can cut 5 kg of wood in 40 min. Chandra and Anand can cut 5 kg. of wood in 30 min. How much time Chandra will take to cut 5 kg of wood alone?
    - (a) 120 minutes
    - (b) 48 minutes
    - (c) 240 minutes
    - (d) (240/7) minutes

11. If 200 soldiers eat 10 tons of food in 200 days, how much will 20 soldiers eat in 20 days?(1ton = 1000 kgs)
    - (a) 1 ton
    - (b) 10 kg
    - (c) 100 kg
    - (d) 50 kg

12. A servant is paid ₹ 100 plus one shirt for a full year of work. He works for 6 months and gets ₹ 30 plus the shirt. What is the cost of the shirt? (in Rupees)?
    - (a) 20
    - (b) 30
    - (c) 40
    - (d) 50

13. A train without stopping travels at 60 km per hour and with stoppages at 40 km per hour. What is the time taken for stoppages on a route of 300 km?
    - (a) 11 hours
    - (b) 22 hours
    - (c) 5 hours
    - (d) 2.5 hours

14. A contractor receives a certain sum every week for paying wages. His own capital together with the weekly sum enables him to pay 45 men for 52 weeks. If he had 60 men and the same wages his capital and weekly sum would suffice for 13 weeks, how many

men can be maintained for 26 weeks?
(a) 60   (b) 52
(c) 50   (d) 65

15. A supply of water lasts for 150 days if 12 gallons leak off every day, but only for 100 days if 15 gallons leak off daily. What is the total quantity of water in the supply?
(a) 900   (b) 1125
(c) 3350   (d) 1250

16. If a dealer were to diminish the selling price of his wares by 10% he would double his sale making the same profit as before. In what ratio would his profit diminish if he were to increase his selling price by 10% and thereby halve his sale?
(a) 2:1.5   (b) 5:4
(c) 1:1.5   (d) 9:7

17. A can is full of paint. Out of this 5 litres are removed and a thinning liquid substituted. The process is repeated. Now the ratio of paint to thinner is 49:15. What is the full capacity of the can?
(a) 20 litres   (b) 60 litres
(c) 40 litres   (d) 50 litres

Directions for Questions 18 to 20: Use the following information.

Kachua Bhaiya started to move from point B towards point A exactly an hour after Jiggly Pup started from A in the opposite direction. Kachua Bhaiyas's speed was twice that of Jiggly Pup. When Jiggly Pup had covered one-sixth of the distance between the points A and B, Kachua Bhaiya had also covered the same distance.

18. The point where the two would meet is
(a) Closer to A
(b) Exactly between A and B
(c) Closer to B
(d) P and Q will not meet at all

19. How many hours would Jiggly Pup take to reach B?
(a) 2   (b) 5
(c) 6   (d) 12

20. How many more hours would Jiggly Pup (compared

Space for Rough Work

to Kachua Bhaiya) take to complete his journey?
(a) 4   (b) 5
(c) 6   (d) 7

21. A group of workers was put on a publishing job. From the second day onwards one worker was withdrawn each day. The job was finished when the last worker was withdrawn. Had no worker been withdrawn at any stage, the group would have finished the job in two-thirds the time. How many workers were there in the group?
(a) 2   (b) 3
(c) 5   (d) 10

22. A ship leaves on a long voyage. When it is 18 miles from the shore, a seaplane, whose speed is ten times that of the ship, is sent to deliver mail. How far from the shore does the seaplane catch up with the ship?
(a) 24 miles   (b) 25 miles
(c) 22 miles   (d) 20 miles

23. One man can do as a woman can do in 2 days. A child does one-third the work in a day as a woman. If an estate-owner hires 39 pairs of hands, men, women and children in the ratio 6:5:2 and pays them in all ₹1113 at the end of days work, what must the daily wages of a child be, if the wages are proportional to the amount of work done?
(a) ₹14   (b) ₹5
(c) ₹20   (d) ₹7

24. A water tank has three taps A, B and C. A fills four buckets in 24 mins, B fills 8 buckets in 1 hour and C fills 2 buckets in 20 minutes. If all the taps are opened together a full tank is emptied in 2 hours. If a bucket can hold 5 litres of water, what is the capacity of the tank?
(a) 120 litres   (b) 240 litres
(c) 180 litres   (d) 60 litres

25. A man buys spirit at ₹60 per litre, adds water to it and then sells it at ₹75 per litre. What is the ratio of spirit to water if his profit in the deal is 37.5%?
(a) 9:1   (b) 10:1
(c) 11:1   (d) None of these

REVIEW TEST 3

1. There is a leak in the bottom of a tank. This leak can empty a full tank in 8 hours. When the tank is full, a tap is opened into the tank which admits 6 litres per hour and the tank is now emptied in 12 hours. What is the capacity of the tank?
   - (a) 28.8 litres
   - (b) 36 litres
   - (c) 144 litres
   - (d) cannot be determined

2. The winning relay team in a high school sports competition clocked 48 minutes for a distance of 13.2 km. Its runners A, B, C and D maintained speeds of 15 kmph, 16, 17 kmph and 18 kmph respectively. What is the ratio of the time taken by B to that taken by D?
   - (a) 5:16
   - (b) 5:17
   - (c) 9:8
   - (d) 8:9

3. Three bells chime at intervals of 18,24 and 32 minutes respectively. At a certain time they begin to chime together. What length of time will elapse before they chime together again?
   - (a) 2 hours 24 minutes
   - (b) 4 hours 48 minutes
   - (c) 1 hours 36 minutes
   - (d) 5 hours

4. In a race of 200 meters run, Ashish beats Sunil by 20 metres and Nalin by 40 metres. If Sunil and Nalin are running a race of 100 metres with exactly the same speeds as before, then by how many metres will Sunil beat Nalin?
   - (a) 11.11 metres
   - (b) 10 metres
   - (c) 12 metres
   - (d) 25 metres

5. A man invests ₹3000 at a rate of 5% per annum. How much more should he invest at a rate of 8%, so that he can earn a total of 6% per annum?
   - (a) ₹1200
   - (b) ₹1300
   - (c) ₹1500
   - (d) ₹2000

Use the following data for Questions 6 to 9: Helitabh and Ruk Ruk are running along a circular course of radius 14 km in opposite directions such that when they meet they reverse their directions as well as they interchange their speeds i.e. after they meet Helitabh will run at the speed of Ruk Ruk and vice-versa. However, this interchange occurs only when they meet outside the starting point. They do not interchange directions or speeds when they meet at the starting point. Initially, the speed of Helitabh is thrice the speed of Ruk Ruk. Assume that they start from M_0 and they first meet at M_1, then at M_2, next M_3, and finally at M_4.

6. What is the shortest distance between M_1 and M_2?
   - (a) 22 km.
   - (b) $14\sqrt{2}$ km
   - (c) 14 km
   - (d) 28 km

7. What is the shortest distance between M_1 and M_3 along the course?

8. (a) 44 km
   (b) $28\sqrt{2}$ km
   (c) $44\sqrt{2}$ km
   (d) 28 km

8. Which is the point that coincides with M_0?
   - (a) M_1
   - (b) M_2
   - (c) M_3
   - (d) M_4

9. What is the distance travelled by Helitabh when they meet at M_3?
   - (a) 154 km.
   - (b) 132 km
   - (c) 198 km
   - (d) 176 km

Directions for Questions 10 to 12: A certain race is made up of three stretches A, B and C, each 4 km long, and to be covered by a certain mode of transport. The following table gives these modes of transport for the stretches, and the minimum and maximum possible speeds (in kmph) over these stretches. The speed over a particular stretch is assumed to be constant. The previous record for the race is ten minutes.

Stretch	Mode of transport	Min. Speed	Max Speed
A	Car	80	120
B	Motor-cycle	60	100
C	Bicycle	20	40

10. Anshuman travels at minimum speed by car over A and completes stretch B at the fastest possible speed. At what speed should he cover stretch C in order to break the previous record?
    - (a) Max. speed for C
    - (b) Min. speed for C
    - (c) This is not possible
    - (d) None of these

11. Mr. Hare completes the first stretch at the minimum speed and takes the same time for stretch B. He takes 50% more time than the previous record to complete the race. What is Mr. Hare's speed for the stretch C?
    - (a) 21.8 kmph
    - (b) 26.66 kmph
    - (c) 34.2 kmph
    - (d) None of these

12. Mr. Tortoise completes the race at an average speed of 40 kmph. His average speed for the first two stretches is 4 times that for the last stretch. Find his speed over stretch C.
    - (a) 30 kmph
    - (b) 24 kmph
    - (c) 20 kmph
    - (d) This is not possible

13. After allowing a discount of 11.11% a trader still makes a gain of 20%. At what percent above the cost price does he mark his goods?
    - (a) 28.56%
    - (b) 35%
    - (c) 22.22%
    - (d) None of these

14. A dealer buys oil at ₹100, ₹80 and ₹60 per liter. He mixes them in the ratio 5:6:7 by weight and sells them at a profit of 50%. At what price does he sell oil?

(a) ₹80/liter   (b) ₹116.666/ liter
(c) ₹95/liter   (d) None of these

15. An express train travelling at 80 kmph overtakes a goods train twice as long and going at 40 kmph on a parallel track, in 54 seconds. How long will the express train take to cross a station 400 m long?

(a) 36 sec   (b) 45 sec
(c) 27 sec   (d) none of these

16. A man earns x% on the first 2000 rupees and y% on the rest of his income. If he earns ₹700 from ₹4000 and ₹900 from ₹5000 of income. Find x.

(a) 20   (b) 15
(c) 25   (d) None of these

17. In the famous Harrods museum, the value of each of a set of gold coins varies as the square of its diameter, if its thickness remains constant and it varies as the thickness, if the diameter remains constant. If the diameters of the two coins are in the ratio 4:3, what should the ratio of their thickness be if the value of the first is 4 times that of the second?

(a) 16:9   (b) 9:4
(c) 9:16   (d) 4:9

A thief after committing a burglary, started fleeing at 12:00 noon at the speed of 60 kmph. He was then chased by a policeman X. X started the chase 15 minutes after the thief had started at a speed of 65 kmph.

18. At what time did X catch the thief?

(a) 3:30 p.m.   (b) 3:00p.m.
(c) 3:15 p.m.   (d) None of these

19. If another policeman has started the same chase along with X, but at a speed of 60 kmph, then how far behind was he when X caught the thief?

(a) 18.75 km   (b) 15 km
(c) 21 km   (d) 47.5 km

20. A and B walk from X to Y, a distance of 27 km at 5 kmph and 7 kmph respectively. B reaches Y and immediately turns back meeting A at Z. What is the distance from Y to Z?

(a) 2 km   (b) 4.5 km
(c) 3 km   (d) 7 km

21. A motorist leaves the post office to go to the airport to collect mail. The plane arrives early, and the mail is sent on a horse-cart. After half an hour, the motorist meets the horse-cart, collects the mail and returns to the post office, thus saving 20 minutes. How many minutes early did the plane arrive?

(a) 20   (b) 25
(c) 30   (c) 40

22. In his book on Leonardo da Vinci, Sigmund Freud, after a detailed psychoanalysis concluded that Goethe could complete the masterpiece in nine days as he could channelize overly but was more possessed as a result of which he could generate 50% more efficiency than Goethe. The number of days it takes Leonardo da Vinci to do the same piece of work that Goethe completes in nine days is:

(a) 4 (1/2) days   (b) 6 days
(c) 13 (1/2) days   (d) None of these

23. The North South Express is a pair of trains between the cities Jammu & Chennai. A train leaves Jammu for Chennai exactly at 12 noon every day of the week. Similarly, there is a train that leaves from Chennai to Jammu on every day of the week at exactly 12 noon. The time required by a train to cover the distance between Chennai & Jammu is exactly 7 days and 1 minute. Find the number of trains from Chennai to Jammu which a train from Jammu to Chennai will encounter in completing its journey. (Assume all trains run exactly on time).

(a) 7   (b) 8
(c) 14   (d) 15

24. For the question above, the minimum number of rakes that the Indian Railways will have to devote for running this daily service will be:

(a) 16   (b) 32
(c) 30   (d) None of these

25. There are two candles each of the same initial length. The first candle can burn for 24 hours, while the second candle can burn for 16 hours. Both of them are lit at the same time. After sometime, it was found that one of the candles was twice as long as the second. For how long had the candle been burning?

(a) 6 hours   (b) 8 hours
(c) 10 hours   (d) 12 hours

Space for Rough Work

REVIEW TEST 4

1. The menu at a local café at Mumbai reads as under:

Item	Price (₹)
Samosa and Coffee	– ac
Parathe	– bc
Sweet Dish, Samosa and Coffee	– bd
Samosa, Coffee and Parathe	– ca
Parathe, Sweet Dish, Samosa and Coffee	– db

In the price list, each of the entry in the right hand column stands for a two digit number and each of the different letter stands for a different digit. What is the price of the sweet dish?

(a) ₹ 6   (b) ₹ 11
(c) ₹ 41   (d) ₹ 22

2. Two trains, a passenger train and a freight train, are running in the same direction on parallel railway tracks. The passenger train takes three times as long to pass the freight train as when they are going in opposite directions.

If the trains run at uniform speeds with goods train running at a maximum speed of 25 km/h, what is the speed of passenger train (p) in km/h?

(a) $p = 50$ (b) $p \le 50$ $(p > 0)$
(c) $0 \le p \le 50$ (d) $20 \le p \le 50$

3. Rambilas, a rice merchant does not think much of ethical practice and neither does he think too much about his reputation; his only aim is to earn as much profit as possible. Which of the following would serve his purpose best?

I. Fixing selling price one-eighth above the cost price.

II. Mix stones (available for free) 12.5% by weight and fixing selling price at cost price

III. Use an 8.75 kg weight for 10 kg weight and selling at cost price

IV. Selling 15/16th only, by cheating, of the weight kept on balance and fixing the selling price 6.25% above cost price.

(a) I   (b) I and II
(c) IV   (d) II and III

Directions for Questions 4 to 6: A motorboat race is held in the Suvarnarekha river in Jharkhand. The race is held over 3 stretches namely M, N and O. The maximum speed allowed in the stretch M is 80 km/hr and the maximum speeds allowed in stretches N and O are 65 km/hr and 30 km/hr respectively. The minimum speeds allowed over the 3 stretches are 50 km/hr, 40 km/hr and 15 km/hr respectively. Each of the stretches is 4 km in length and speed over a stretch is assumed constant. Current record for the race is 12 min. 30 sec.

4. Shoaib completes the first stretch at minimum speed but is able to maintain the same speed in the second stretch also. If he takes 60% more time than the current record, then speed of Shoalb over stretch O is approximately:

(a) 23 km/hr   (b) 17 km/hr
(c) 28.8 km/hr   (d) 32 km/hr

5. Amitabh covers stretch M at minimum speed but completes the next stretch at maximum permissible speed. What should be Amithabh's speed in the stretch O if he now aims at breaking the current record?

(a) 30 km/hr   (b) Indeterminate
(c) Breaking Record is not possible
(d) 40 km/hr

6. Steven Miles completes the race at an average speed 30 km/hr. If his average speed over stretches M and N is 300% more than his speed over stretch O, what is his speed over stretch O?

(a) 24 km/hr   (b) 27 km/hr
(c) 18 km/hr   (d) 15 km/hr

7. Ali along with his friend embarked on a boat journey. While making all his preparations for the journey, he checked with the boat manufacturer's data and was glad to learn that the boat was really dependable as it could float even if it was upto 75% full of water (with more water it could sink). Unfortunately, the boat developed a hole during his journey—the hole filling up water @ 2 liter per minute. The boat was also equipped with a drainage pump which could empty a boatful of water in 32 hrs. If Ali figures that they have a maximum of 12 hrs to reach a safe place (before they sink), what is the capacity of the boat?

(a) 1280 liter   (b) 1480 liter
(c) 1600 liter   (d) 1056 liter

8. The number of votes not cast for Pappu's party increased by $33\frac{1}{3}$% over those not cast for it in the previous polls in the Farrukhabad city constituency where the only other candidate belongs/belonged to the Jhussu Party. If a total of 4,50,000 people voted each time and Pappu's Party loses by a majority one-third times as large as that by which it had won in the last polls, How many people voted for Pappu's Party in the current polls?

(a) 150000   (b) 210000
(c) 240000   (d) 180000

Directions for Questions 9 and 10: On the planet of Krypton (yes the same one from where Superman originated) A small scale businessman owns an ancillary unit that manufactures 6 types of tools namely A, B, C, D, E and F. These tools for their manufacturing require work on machine X and machine Y in that order. The time taken on these machines to manufacture one unit of a tool is as follows:

Tool →	A	B	C	D	E	F
Time (hrs) Machine X	6	24	10	4	18	22
Machine Y	16	20	18	12	6	2

Presently, the businessman has received orders to manufacture one unit of each of the tools. There is no constraint to work on the machines and these machines can be run non-stop.

9. For a particular order from Earth, the tools are to be manufactured in the sequence FEBCAD, what is the minimum time taken to execute the order?
   (a) 158 hrs
   (b) 110 hrs
   (c) 130 hrs
   (d) 120 hrs

10. If a revolutionary technology is imported from the earth, the time required for working on each tool is reduced to half it's current time on both machines. With this technology in place, what is the shortest possible time in which the above order can be executed?
   (a) 65 hrs
   (b) 51 hrs
   (c) 55 hrs
   (d) None of these

11. A man can climb up a greased pole 30 ft high in 15 seconds (where 10 seconds is used for climbing up and 5 seconds when he is slipping down). If grease causes a downward slip of 2 ft a second, the time taken by the man to climb a non greased pole would be:
   (a) 8 seconds
   (b) 10 seconds
   (c) 7.5 seconds
   (d) 9 seconds

12. A state's GDP during 2011-12 grew by a healthy 6.3%. During the same period service sector growth was 7.0%: average growth for agricultural, manufacturing, and service sector (excluding ITES and IT) was 5.8%. If weightage given to agricultural sector is 25%, to manufacturing sector 42%, and to service sector as a whole 33% (IT sector 13% and ITES 9%), then what is the approximate growth rate for service sector (excluding ITES and IT)?
   (a) 6.4%
   (b) 5.9%
   (c) 5.0%
   (d) 5.8% to 7.0% (depending on weightage)

13. The village of Hara Kiri has two-thirds of its male population married to 90% of its women population. Each of such man is married to exactly two of such women. What is the minimum possible 4 digit population of the village (Children are not counted as part of the population unless they are married)?
   (a) 1005
   (b) 1026
   (c) 1080
   (d) Cannot be determined/None of these

14.

The figure contains three squares with areas of 100 m², 49 m², and 16 m² lying side by side. Rahim wishes to reduce the length AB to 19 m by reducing area of only one of the squares without altering its shape, what is the maximum reduction (in %) in the area of that square?
   (a) (Approx) 33%
   (b) 50%
   (c) (Approx) 66%
   (d) 75%

15. Tingal and Sagar practice in the local Gomati Nagar stadium daily. One day, they started running around the circular track simultaneously from the same point in opposite directions. Thereafter they met a total of ten times when the practice session was terminated. If they meet at a point diametrically opposite to the starting point when they meet for the second time, what could be ratio of their speed?
   (a) 1 : 1
   (b) 2 : 1
   (c) 1 : 3
   (d) Data insufficient

16. The Sinhagad Express and the Gomati Express consisting of 41 and 42 carriages respectively are traveling @ 36 kmph in opposite directions. The carriage length (including inter-carriage lengths averaged over number of carriages) averages 10 m and is half the engine length. If the trains cross each other on parallel tracks, in how much time will they complete the crossing?
   (a) 1 min 20 sec
   (b) 42 seconds
   (c) 38 seconds
   (d) 40 seconds

17. The selling price and the cost price of an article which is being sold at a profit have increased by r% YOY for a period of 3 years. Which of the following statements summarizes the effect of the inflationary pressure?
   (a) The profitability of the article has increased at the same rate r% every year for the 3-year period.
   (b) The profit has increased YOY at the same rate of r% while the profitability has remained constant.
   (c) The profit has increased YOY at the same rate r% but profitability has increased at a rate which is less than the rate of increase of profits.
   (d) The profit has increased YOY at the same rate of r%, while the profitability has decreased over the 3 year period.

18. The Hosur Computer Company gets a large supply order for assembled computers of two different configurations A and B from the Karnataka government. The supply order for A-type computers being double that of the B-type. A team of hardware experts was

assigned the task which worked on *A*-type computers. For the second day, the team was split into two equal groups: the first continued work on *A*-type computers and completed the work order by day end. The second group, however could not complete work order for *B*-type computers on the second day and this work order could only be completed by employing two experts for the whole of the third day. What was the strength of the team if it is known that a *B*-type computer takes 20% less time to assemble than *A*-type?

(a) 5   (b) 20

(c) 16   (d) 24

19. In a learning experiment at Stanford University it was found that the square of the inverse of learning time varies directly as the age of a rat in weeks, while the inverse of learning time and complexity index of the maze are directly related. If the age of

the rat in the second trial of the experiment is 40% more than in the first trial and the learning time is 16.67% less, then find change in complexity index of the maze

(a) Increase of 10%   (b) Increase of 5%

(c) Increase of 1%   (d) Decrease of 5%

20. Ramu is standing at an intersection where two roads intersect at right angles. He observes through his binoculars that two cars start moving towards the intersection at the same time along these two roads, one of them is moving at a speed of 13.333 m/sec and starts at a point 40 km from the intersection. The second car is moving at 10 m/sec and starts at a point 50 km from the intersection. In how many minutes from the start will the distance between the two be minimum?

(a) 83 min   (b) 62 min

(c) 50 min   (d) (1) or (3)

Space for Rough Work

REVIEW TEST 5

Directions for Questions 1 and 2: Refer to data below: In a motorcycle race, three motorcycles started out. The first motorcycle was 15 km/h faster than the second, while the third was 3 km/h slower than the second. The second motorcycle driven by Ayrton Senna arrived at the finish 12 min after the first motorcycle and 3 minutes before the third one. There were no stops on route.

1. What is the length of the race?
   - (a) 150 km
   - (b) 72 km
   - (c) 75 km
   - (d) 90 km

2. What is the speed of the slowest motor cycle?
   - (a) 75 km/h
   - (b) 90 km/h
   - (c) 72 km/h
   - (d) 64 km/h

3. Naman Sweets, a sweet shop in down town Allahabad, manufactures Rossagullas for export. They are currently experimenting with an ideal sugar syrup concentration for their new product. Originally, the sugar in the syrup is $33\frac{1}{3}$% by weight. The syrup is heated till 25% of the water in it evaporates. The resultant solution is mixed with a 40% sugar syrup in the ratio 5 : 3. The sugar syrup so obtained is again heated to evaporate $33\frac{1}{3}$% of water in it. Find the strength of this solution assuming the solution never saturates.
   - (a) 50%
   - (b) slightly more than 90%
   - (c) slightly more than 75%
   - (d) 35%

4. Two sets of boys are playing a match of catching. It is decided that once the ball falls on the ground from the hands of a side it would get the other side as many points as the number of meters the ball travels before coming to rest and the play won't resume until that happens. It is also known that height of a fall is exactly 150% of that of the bounce for the kind of balls to be used for the match. In the first instance Raghav's team dropped the ball a height of 45 m. How many points does Shaurya's team gain?
   - (a) 90
   - (b) 135
   - (c) 225
   - (d) None of these

5. Akhilesh was experimenting with time measurement using a pair of sandglasses. The following pairs of sand glasses are available (sand glass of one pair cannot be combined with sand glass of another pair)

A	–	9 min and 12 min
B	–	4 min and 7 min
C	–	6 min and 7 min

   In how many ways can he choose his pair of sand glasses in order to be able to measure exactly 15 minutes?
   - (a) 3
   - (b) 2
   - (c) 1
   - (d) None

6. In a 4000 meter race around a circular track (in the stadium at IIM Bangalore) having a circumference of 1000 meters, the fastest runner and the slowest runner reach the same point at the end of the 5th minute, for the first time after the start of the race. All the runners have the same starting point and each runner maintains a uniform speed throughout the race. If the slowest runner runs at half the speed of the fastest runner, what is the time taken by the slowest runner to finish the race?
   - (a) 40 min.
   - (b) 30 min.
   - (c) 20 min.
   - (d) 15 min.

Directions for Questions 7 and 8: Answer these questions based on the following information:

Prabhjeet made a trip from Hyderabad to Bengaluru to attend an interview. He had been traveling at a speed which would have ensured that he reaches the interview on time. He had a flat tyre on the way and it took 100 min. to mend it. He arrived 15 min. late for the interview. The distance between Bengaluru and Hyderabad is 260 km.

7. If the speed after the flat tyre was 20% more than the original speed, find the normal time taken by Prabhjeet to reach the destination from the site of the accident.
   - (a) 8 hr. 30 min.
   - (b) 1 hr. 45 min.
   - (c) 6 hr.
   - (d) 8 hr. 30 min.

8. If the normal time taken to reach Bengaluru after the start was 10 hr. at what distance from Bengaluru did the flat tyre occur? (Use data of Question 7)
   - (a) 39 km.
   - (b) 221 km.
   - (c) 169 km.
   - (d) Can't be determined

9. Steven fell in love with Ankita who lived 630 miles away. He decided to propose his beloved and invited her to travel to his place and offered to meet her en route and bring her home. Steven is able to cover 4 miles per hour to Ankita's 3 miles per hour. How far will each have travelled upon meeting?
   - (a) Steven = 270 miles; Ankita = 360 miles
   - (b) Steven = 360 miles; Ankita = 270 miles
   - (c) Steven = 400 miles; Ankita = 230 miles
   - (d) Steven = 450 miles; Ankita = 180 miles

10. The evergreen shrubs at Ramesh's nursery are planted in rows on a square plot of land measuring 2,401 sq. ft. The shrubs are planted in such a manner that the centers of the shrubs are 7 ft. apart and the outer shrubs are planted along the edges of the plot, with a shrub at each corner. Ramesh spent $1792 to cover

all the costs necessary for raising this crop of the evergreen shrubs. If Ramesh succeeds in selling each shrub for $63, his profit will be what percentage of his total cost?

(a) 100%   (b) 50%

(c) 125%   (d) 150%

11. Chashmish is repaid a loan that he had given to Mucchad such that each year the amount he gets is 1/20 lesser than what he got in the previous year. Mucchad being a sly person, decides to give Chashmish ₹ 2500 as a lump sum and not pay anything later. Who gains from this agreement and what is the breakeven value, if the initial installment is ₹ 100? (Consider no time value of money.)

(a) Chashmish, ₹ 2000

(b) Mucchad, ₹ 3000

(c) Chashmish, ₹ 100

(d) Mucchad, ₹ 10000

12. NTPC Gas power plant in Dibyapur can produce upto 120 MW of power every month. The cost of the power is partly fixed and partly varying. The cost is ₹ 250 million, when 80 MW are produced and it is ₹ 300 million, when 100 MW is produced. On the other hand, the part of selling price per unit goes on decreasing linearly as more power is consumed. The selling rate per unit is ₹ 3.30 at 80 MW sell and it is ₹ 3.20, when 100 MW power is sold. What will be the profit or loss when it produces 110 MW of power and sells it all?

(a) Profit, ₹ 26.5 million

(b) Profit, ₹ 21.5 million

(c) Loss, ₹ 26.5 million

(d) Loss, ₹ 21.5 million

13. Divyansh Awasthi buys some apples and Chikoos from the market at a rate such that a Chikoo is two times costlier than an apple and he sells them such that a Chikoo is sold at thrice the cost price of an apple. By selling the apple at twice its cost price, he makes 150% profit. Find the proportion of Chikoos to the apples.

(a) 1 : 6   (b) 3 : 4

(c) 1 : 2   (d) Cannot be determined

14. Arundhati bets a certain portion of her total money on betting. On a particular day, when she won, the betting rate was 12 : 1 (i.e. if you bet 1 rupee you stand to gain 12 rupees if you win the bet) and her total money became 8 times the initial total money. What is the proportion of her initial total money to the money she put on bet?

(a) 3 : 2   (b) 7 : 5

(c) 8 : 5   (d) None of these

15. On 26th July, Mumbai was flooded. Rainshield enterprises is in the business of manufacturing umbresl-

las and raincoats. An umbrella can shield 2 people while a raincoat can shield 1 person. People under an umbrella can walk at 1/3rd the speed of a person wearing a raincoat. The cost of an umbrella and cost of the raincoat are in the ratio 2 : 5. Points A and B are 100 m apart and it takes 20 minutes for a person wearing a raincoat to travel the distance. At the maximum how many people will be transported today from A to B, if only ₹ 1000 is available for transporting 20 people? Cost of traveling time is ₹ 2 per min. per head (Assume cost of a raincoat to be ₹ 100.)

(a) 6   (b) 7

(c) 4   (d) None of these

16. A manufacturing job was wrongly estimated to be completed in 10 days by x machines. By deploying 3 extra machines, the job was completed in 12 days. If only one additional machine was used, how many days more than that estimated would it have taken to complete the job?

(a) $\dfrac{2x - 18}{x + 3}$ (b) $\dfrac{2x + 13}{x + 1}$

(c) $\dfrac{2x + 26}{x + 1}$ (d) Cannot be determined

17. A tank in Gauri Apartments is full of water and is fitted with pumps of equal capacity. Besides it is also fitted with a certain number of inlet pipes which are always kept open. When the tank is full, 10 pumps of equal capacity empty the tank in 12 hrs., while 15 pumps of the same capacity empty the tank in 6 hrs. In how much time would 25 pumps of the same capacity empty the tank, if the tank is initially full? (All the pipes pouring water into the tank are always open)

(a) 3 hrs.   (b) $2\dfrac{1}{2}$ hrs.

(c) 4 hrs.   (d) $3\dfrac{1}{2}$ hrs.

18. A group of 4 people—Raghav, Golu, Shaurya and Arjit, arrive in a car to a friend's house. The group was forced to park around the corner due to lack of parking space. It was raining heavily and the group had only one umbrella. They decided to share it. Two persons would go at a time to the friends house and one of them would come back with the umbrella. The process would be repeated unless all four people reach the friends house. If Raghav, Golu, Shaurya and Arjit take 1, 2, 5 and 10 minutes respectively at their fastest speed to go to the friend's house, what is the minimum time required for all of them to reach

the friend's house? (A faster person slows down to accompany a slower one)

(a) 15 mins   (b) 17 mins

(c) 22 mins   (d) 19 mins.

19. At a shooting competition, Rathore and Bindra had x bullets between them. Bindra fired 'a' bullets per min. while Rathore fired 'b' bullets per min. After time 't', both of them had the same number of bullets. What is the initial number of bullets with Rathore?

(a) $x - \dfrac{a+b}{2}$ (b) $x + \dfrac{t(a-b)}{2}$

(c) $\dfrac{x - t(a-b)}{2}$ (d) None of these

Space for Rough Work

ANSWER KEY

Review Test 1

1. (b)	2. (c)	3. (a)	4. (a)
5. (b)	6. (c)	7. (b)	8. (b)
9. (c)	10. (c)	11. (b)	12. (a)
13. (b)	14. (d)	15. (a)	16. (b)
17. (b)	18. (c)	19. (d)	20. (c)
21. (b)	22. (c)	23. (b)	24. (b)
25. (a)	26. (a)		

Review Test 2

1. (d)	2. (a)	3. (c)	4. (c)
5. (b)	6. (d)	7. (b)	8. (d)
9. (d)	10. (c)	11. (c)	12. (c)
13. (d)	14. (c)	15. (a)	16. (a)
17. (c)	18. (a)	19. (d)	20. (c)
21. (b)	22. (d)	23. (d)	24. (b)
25. (b)			

Review Test 3

1. (c)	2. (c)	3. (b)	4. (a)
5. (c)	6. (b)	7. (a)	8. (d)
9. (a)	10. (c)	11. (b)	12. (c)
13. (b)	14. (b)	15. (c)	16. (b)
17. (b)	18. (c)	19. (b)	20. (b)
21. (d)	22. (b)	23. (d)	24. (a)
25. (d)			

Review Test 4

1. (b)	2. (b)	3. (d)	4. (a)
5. (c)	6. (d)	7. (a)	8. (b)
9. (c)	10. (a)	11. (c)	12. (c)
13. (a)	14. (d)	15. (c)	16. (c)
17. (b)	18. (b)	19. (b)	20. (b)

Review Test 5

1. (d)	2. (c)	3. (a)	4. (c)
5. (a)	6. (c)	7. (a)	8. (b)
9. (b)	10. (c)	11. (a)	12. (b)
13. (c)	14. (a)	15. (b)	16. (a)
17. (a)	18. (d)	19. (d)	

Geometry

Chapter 11
Geometry and
Mensuration

Chapter 12
Coordinate
Geometry

...BACK TO SCHOOL

The word GEOMETRY is derived from two words—GEO meaning earth and METRY meaning measurement. Hence, it is quite evident that geometry as a mathematical science developed mainly due to the human need of measuring land masses and distances. The major developments in the fields of Geometry and Mensuration are mainly credited to the ancient Egyptian and Greek civilisations. (In fact, this is one of the reasons why all formulae and theorems primarily carry Greek names.)

Key Geometrical Concepts

Point: The point should be visualised as a singular dot. In physical terms, a point can be defined as a single dot that can be created on a plain paper by a very sharp pencil. It could also be visualised as a singular prick on a piece of paper by a very sharp nail or pin.

Line: Mathematically, lines are defined as a group of points which are straight one after another. All lines are supposed to extend infinitely in two directions.

Segment of a Line

If a part of a line is cut out, we get a segment of a line.

Physically, the closest representations of a segment of a line would be a tight thread or the straight crease of a piece of paper.

Plane: The surface of a smooth wall or a table top is the closest representation of a portion of a plane.

Some Geometrical Properties

1. Lines Between Points: Let us take two distinct points in a plane. You can easily verify that an infinite number of lines can be drawn in the plane passing through any one of these two points. However, if you wanted to draw a line which passes through both the points, you will be able to draw only one line. This is an important result in Geometry.

Property: Given any two distinct points in a plane, there exists one and only one line containing both the points. Alternately, we can state that two distinct points in a plane determine a unique line.

2. Collinearity of Points: Collinear or non-collinear points are only defined in the context of 3 or more points.

Consider the situation of three points. There can only be two cases with respect to three points:

1. All the points lie on the same line. (Here, the points are said to be collinear).
2. All the three points do not lie on the same line (In this case the points are said to be non-collinear).

Note: It is quite evident that we would discuss collinear or non-collinear points only if the number of points is more than two. Obviously, if there are only two points they would always lie on one line.

Contd

3. Points in Common between Distinct Lines: In the case of distinct lines, there can only be two cases:

(a) There is one point in common: In such a case, the common point is called as the point of intersection, and the two lines are called as intersecting lines.

(b) There is no point in common: In such a case, the two lines are non-intersecting and are also called as parallel lines.

The property can thus be stated as:

Property: Two distinct lines in a plane cannot have more than one point in common.

4. Lines and Points:

Property: Given a line and a point in the same plane, such that the point is not on the line, there is one and only one line which passes through the point and is parallel to the given line.

5. Lines:

Property: Two intersecting lines cannot be parallel to the same line.

6. Multiple Lines: There can be four distinct possibilities in such a case.

1. No two lines intersect each other
2. Some lines intersect
3. Every line intersects all other lines, but their respective points of intersection are different from each other.
4. Every pair of lines is intersecting and all the points of intersection coincide.

The reader is required to visualise the figures for each of these situations.

The remaining formulae and results for geometry have been given within the chapter. You are required to move to the respective formulae. However, an important note while you are doing this.

Important Note

One of the least understood issues with respect to this block is:

How does a person move from:

"Cannot Solve Geometry and Mensuration!" to "Can Solve Geometry and Mensuration!"

In fact, this transition should be your sole aim while studying and solving this block of chapters.

As you are already aware, mere knowledge of formulae does not guarantee this movement. Then in that case what should a person do if he/she has to engineer this transition of abilities?

Well, the answer is really quite simple and for understanding the same you need to move out of conventional mathematical study processes. In your mind you need to create an awareness of how to think while solving a geometry/mensuration question. Here are a few tips that will help you through this transition:

1. Some Formulae are More Important than Others: For the CAT (and indeed all other MBA and aptitude examinations) your concentration should not be on memorizing complex formulae. A close study of the past trends for questions from this block will show you that the formulae themselves can be graded into the important and the not so important formulae. In fact, if you study over 200 questions from this block that have been asked in the CAT in the past decade or more, you will realise that over 98% of the questions are simply based on a small subset of geometrical formulae and results. This important set of formulae are listed below for your convenience:

Lines: Properties related to intersecting lines and angles formed.

Polygons: Basic properties of regular polygons.

Triangles: Pythagoras theorem, 30-60-90 triangle, 45-45-90 triangle, Sine rule, Properties of Exterior angles of a triangle, equilateral triangle, isosceles triangle.

Quadrilaterals: Areas, perimeters, diagonals and angles between diagonals for all standard quadrilaterals.

Hexagon: A Hexagon can be divided into six equal triangles.

2. Length/Area/Volume Measuring Formulae versus Angle Measuring Formulae: In your mind, divide the formulae into length/area/volume measuring formulae on the one hand and Angle measuring formulae on the other hand. This will be very helpful, since most questions in this block can be clearly segregated as length or angle measuring questions. In such a scenario, in case you have a question requiring angle measurements, you will only require to think of angle measuring formulae.

Note: There are very few formulae that connect lengths with angles. (e.g. Sine rule and Cosine rule in the context of triangles).

---

3. The Use of Reverse Flowcharting for Solving Questions: All questions in geometry and mensuration ask you to find a particular value. Very often, it makes the question much more convenient to solve if instead of trying to find what is asked, you try to find a value which is related to the required value.

Thus, for example, if in a triangle *ABC* angle *A* is given to be 40° & angle *B* is asked for and you are not getting a clear strategy for getting the value of angle

B, then it might be wise to try to derive the value of angle C. If you can get C, then B will be got by 140-C..

This process is called as reverse flowcharting and is an extremely crucial process for solving questions in geometry.

In other words, it can also be seen to be a deflection of the original question into a more convenient question.

Note: You are advised to concentrate on the special note for solving CAT questions provided prior to the LOD I Questions while studying this block.

Pre-assessment Test

1. In the figure below, $AB=BC=CD=DE=EF=FG=GA$. Then, $\angle DAE$ is approximately:

   (a) 15°   (b) 20°
   (c) 30°   (d) 25°

2. The figure below shows three circles, each of radius 25 and centres at P, Q and R respectively. Further $AB = 6, CD = 12$ and $EF = 15$. What is the perimeter of the triangle PQR?

   (a) 117   (b) 116
   (c) 113   (d) 121

3. The figure shows a circle which has a diameter AB and a radius 13. If chord CA is 10 cm long, then find the area of $\triangle ABC$.

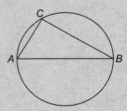

   (a) 240 sq.cm   (b) 120 sq.cm
   (c) 160 sq.cm   (d) None of these

4. The line AB is 12 metres in length and is tangent to the inner one of the two concentric circles at point C. It is known that the radii of the two circles are integers. The radius of the inner circle is:

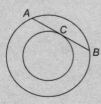

   (a) 5 metres   (b) 8 metres
   (c) 6 metres   (d) 3 metres

5. Four cities are connected by a road network as shown in the figure. In how many ways can you start from any city and come back to it without travelling on the same road more than once?

   (a) 14   (b) 12
   (c) 10   (d) 15

6. In the figure (not drawn to scale) given below, if $AL = LC = CT$, and $\angle TCD = 96°$. What is the value of the $\angle LTC$?

   (a) 32°   (b) 84°
   (c) 64°   (d) Cannot be determined

Directions for Questions 7 to 9: Answer the questions on the basis of the information given below.

Consider a cylinder of height h cm and radius $r = 2/\pi$ cm as shown in the figure (not drawn to scale). A string of a certain length, when wound on its cylindrical surface, starting at point A and ending at point B, gives a maximum of n turns (in other words, the string's length is the minimum length required to wind n turns).

7. What is the vertical spacing in cm between two consecutive turns?
   (a) h/n
   (b) $h/\sqrt{n}$
   (c) h/n^2
   (d) Cannot be determined with given information.

8. The same string, when wound on the four exterior four walls of a cube of side n cm, starting at point C and ending at point D, can give exactly one turn (as shown in the figure). The length of the string, in cm, is:

(a) $\sqrt{2}\ n$ (b) $\sqrt{17}\ n$

(c) n (d) $\sqrt{13}\ n$

9. In the setup of the previous two questions, how is h related to n?

(a) $h = \sqrt{2}\ n$ (b) $h = \sqrt{17}\ n$

(c) $h = n$ (d) $h = \sqrt{13}\ n$

10. Let $LMNOPQ$ be a regular hexagon. What is the ratio of the area of the triangle LNP to that of the hexagon $LMNOPQ$?

(a) 1/3   (b) 1/2

(c) 2/3   (d) 5/6

11. In the figure below, a circle is inscribed inside a square. In the gap between the circle and the square (at the corner) a rectangle measuring 20 cm × 10 cm is drawn such that the corner A of the rectangle is also a point on the circumference of the circle. What is the radius of the circle in cm?

(a) 30 cm   (b) 40 cm

(c) 50 cm   (d) None of these

12. In the figure below $ABCDEF$ is a regular hexagon. The $\angle AOF = 90°$ and FO is parallel to ED. What is the ratio of the area of the triangle AOF to that of the hexagon $ABCDEF$?

(a) 1/12   (b) 1/8

(c) 1/24   (d) 1/18

13. Sherry a naughty boy after a lot of convincing by his mother has agreed to mow the farm lawn, which is a 30 m by 40 m rectangle. The mower mows a 1 m wide strip. If Sherry starts at one corner and mows around the lawn towards the centre, about how many times would he go round before he has mowed half the lawn?

(a) 4.3   (b) 4.5

(c) 4.9   (d) 5.0

14. Two sides of a plot measure 32 metres and 24 metres and the angle between them is a perfect right angle. The other two sides measure 25 metres each and the other three angles are not right angles.

What is the area of the plot (in m²)?

(a) 768   (b) 534

(c) 696.5   (d) 684

15. Euclid has a triangle in mind. Its longest side has length 20 and another of its sides has length 10. Its area is 80 sq. cm. What is the exact length of its third side?

(a) $\sqrt{260}$ (b) $\sqrt{250}$

(c) $\sqrt{240}$ (d) $\sqrt{270}$

16. Consider a circle with unit radius. There are seven adjacent sectors, $S_1, S_2, S_3, \ldots\ldots, S_7$, in the circle such that their total area is 1/16 of the area of the circle. Further, the area of jth sector is twice that of the $(j-1)$th sector, for $j = 2\ldots\ldots, 7$. What is the angle, in radians, subtended by the arc of S_1 at the centre of the circle?

(a) $\pi/508$ (b) $\pi/2040$

(c) $\pi/1016$ (d) $\pi/2032$

17. The figure below shows a set of concentric squares. If the diagonal of the innermost square is 2 units, and if the distance between the corresponding corners of any two successive squares is 1 unit find the difference between the areas of the sixth and the seventh squares, counting from the innermost square.

(a) $\sqrt{2}$ sq. units   (b) 26 sq. units

(c) 30 sq. units   (d) None of these

18. In the figure (not drawn to scale), rectangle $ABCD$ is inscribed in the circle with center at O. The length of side AB is greater than that of side BC. The ratio of the area of the circle to the area of the rectangle $ABCD$ in $\pi : \sqrt{3}$. The line segment

DE intersects *AB* at *E* such that ∠*ODC* = ∠*ADE*. What is the ratio *AE* : *AD*?

(a) $1 : \sqrt{13}$ (b) $1 : \sqrt{2}$
(c) $\sqrt{13} : 1$ (d) $1 : 2$

19. In Δ*ABC*, ∠*B* is a right angle, *AC* = 16 cm, and *D* is the mid-point of *AC*. The length of *BD* is:

(a) 10 cm   (b) $\sqrt{15}$ cm
(c) 8 cm   (d) 7.5 cm

20. In triangle *DEF* shown below, points *A*, *B*, and *C* are taken on *DE*, *DF* and *EF* respectively such that *EC* = *AC* and *CF* : *BC*. If angle *D* = 50 degrees then what is angle *ACB* in degrees?

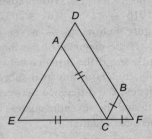

(a) 120   (b) 80
(c) 90   (d) None of these

21. *PQRS* is a square. *SR* is a tangent (at point *S*) to the circle with centre *O* and *TR* = *OS*. Then, the ratio of area of the square to the area of the circle is :

(a) π/3   (b) 11/7
(c) 3/π   (d) 7/11

22. In the adjoining figure, *AC* + *AB* = 5 *AD* and *AC* − *AD* = 8. Then, the area of the rectangle *ABCD* is:

(a) 45
(b) 50
(c) 60
(d) Cannot be answered

23. The figure shows the rectangle *ABCD* with a semicircle and a circle inscribed inside it as shown. What is the ratio of the area of the circle to that of the semicircle?

(a) $(\sqrt{2}-1)^2 : 1$ (b) $2(\sqrt{2}-1)^2 : 1$
(c) $(\sqrt{2}-1)^2 : 2$ (d) None of these

24. A right circular cone of height *h* is cut by a plane parallel to the base and at a distance *h*/3 from the base then the volumes of the frustum of the cone and the resulting frustum of the cone are in the ratio:

(a) 1 : 3   (b) 8 : 19
(c) 19 : 8   (d) 7 : 1

25. Three identical cones with base radius *m* are placed on their bases so that each is touching the other two. There will be one and only one circle that would pass through each of the three vertices. What can be said about the radius of this circle?

(a) It would be smaller than *m*
(b) It would be equal to *m*
(c) It would be larger than *m*
(d) depends on the height of the cones

ANSWER KEY

1. (d)	2. (a)	3. (b)	4. (a)
5. (b)	6. (c)	7. (a)	8. (b)
9. (c)	10. (b)	11. (c)	12. (a)
13. (c)	14. (d)	15. (a)	16. (d)
17. (b)	18. (a)	19. (c)	20. (b)
21. (c)	22. (c)	23. (d)	24. (c)
25. (c)			

Chapter 11

Geometry and Mensuration

The chapters of geometry and mensuration have their share of questions in the CAT and other MBA entrance exams. For doing well in questions based on this chapter, the student should familiarise himself/herself with the basic formulae and visualisations of the various shapes of solids and two-dimensional figures based on this chapter.

The following is a comprehensive collection of formulae based on two-dimensional and three-dimensional figures.

For the purpose of this chapter we have divided the theory in two parts:

- Part I consists of geometry and mensuration of two-dimensional figures
- Part II consists of mensuration of three-dimensional figures.

PART I: GEOMETRY

🕮 INTRODUCTION

Geometry and Mensuration are important areas in the CAT examination. In the Online CAT, the Quantitative Aptitude and Data Interpretation section has consisted by an average between 3–5 questions out of 30 from these chapters. Besides, questions from these chapters appear prominently in all major aptitude based exams like MBAs, Bank POs, etc.

Hence, the student is advised to ensure that he/she studies this chapter completely and thoroughly. Skills to be developed while studying and practising this chapter will be application of formula and visualisation of figures and solids.

The principal skill required for doing well in this chapter is the ability to apply the formulae and theorems.

The following is a comprehensive collection of formulae based on two-dimensional figures. The student is advised to remember the formulae in this chapter so that he is able to solve all the questions based on this chapter.

🕮 THEORY

Basic Conversions	
A. 1 m = 100 cm = 1000 mm 1 km = 1000 m = 5/8 miles 1 inch = 2.54 cm	B. 1 m = 39.37 inches 1 mile = 1760 yd = 5280 ft 1 nautical mile (knot) = 6080 ft
C. 100 kg = 1 quintal 10 quintal = 1 tonne = 1000 kg 1 kg = 2.2 pounds (approx.)	D. 1 litre = 1000 cc 1 acre = 100 sq m 1 hectare = 10000 sq m

🕮 STRAIGHT LINES

Parallel Lines: Two straight lines are parallel if they lie on the same plane and do not intersect however far produced.

Transversal: It is a straight line that intersects two parallel lines. When a transversal intersects two parallel lines then

1. Corresponding angles are equal, (that is: For the following figure)

   1 = 5; 2 = 6; 4 = 8; 3 = 7

2. Alternate interior angles are equal, that is (Refer following figure)

   4 = 6; 5 = 3

3. Alternate exterior angles are equal, that is
2 = 8; 1 = 7

4. Interior angles on the same side of transversal add
up to 180°, that is
4 + 5 = 3 + 6 = 180°

5. Perimeter = $n \times s$.

POLYGONS

Polygons are plane figures formed by a closed series of
rectilinear (straight) segments. *Example:* Triangle, Rectangle...

Polygons can broadly be divided into two types:

(a) *Regular polygons:* Polygons with all the sides and
angles equal.

(b) *Irregular polygons:* Polygons in which all the sides
or angles are not of the same measure.

Polygon can also be divided as *concave* or *convex* polygons.

Convex polygons are the polygons in which all the
diagonals lie inside the figure otherwise it's a concave
polygon

Polygons can also be divided on the basis of the number
of sides they have.

No. of sides	Name of the polygon	Sum of all the angles
3	Triangle	180°
4	Quadrilateral	360°
5	Pentagon	540°
6	Hexagon	720°
7	Heptagon	500°
8	Octagon	1080°
9	Nonagon	1260°
10	Decagon	1440°

Properties

1. Sum of all the angles of a polygon with n sides
= $(2n - 4)\pi/2$ or $(n - 2)\pi$ Radians = $(n - 2)$ 180°
degrees

2. Sum of all exterior angles = 360°.
i.e. In the figure below:
$\theta_1 + \theta_2 + ... + \theta_6 = 360°$
In general, $\theta_1 + \theta_2 + ... + \theta_n = 360°$

3. No. of sides = 360°/exterior angle.

4. Area = $(ns^2/4) \times \cot (180/n)$; where s = length of
side, n = no. of sides.

TRIANGLES (Δ)

A triangle is a polygon having three sides. Sum of all the
angles of a triangle = 180°.

Types 1. *Acute angle triangle:* Triangles with all three
angles acute (less than 90°).

2. *Obtuse angle triangle:* Triangles with one of the
angles obtuse (more than 90°).
Note: we cannot have more than one obtuse angle
in a triangle.

3. *Right angle triangle:* Triangle with one of the angles
equal to 90°.

4. *Equilateral triangle:* Triangle with all sides equal.
All the angles in such a triangle measure 60°.

5. *Isosceles triangle:* Triangle with two of its sides
equal and consequently the angles opposite the equal
sides are also equal.

6. *Scalene Triangle:* Triangle with none of the sides
equal to any other side.

Properties (General)

• Sum of the length of any two sides of a triangle has
to be always greater than the third side.

• Difference between the lengths of any two sides of
a triangle has to be always lesser than the third side.

• Side opposite to the greatest angle will be the
greatest and the side opposite to the smallest angle
the smallest.

• The sine rule: $a/\sin A = b/\sin B = c/\sin C = 2R$
(where R = circum radius.)

• The cosine rule: $a^2 = b^2 + c^2 - 2bc \cos A$
This is true for all sides and respective angles.

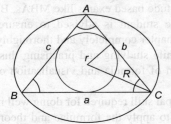

In case of a right $\angle$, the formula reduces to $a^2 = b^2 + c^2$

Since cos 90 = 0

- The exterior angle is equal to the sum of two interior angles not adjacent to it.

$$\angle ACD = \angle BCE = \angle A + \angle B$$

Area

1. Area = 1/2 base × height or 1/2 bh.

   Height = Perpendicular distance between the base and vertex opposite to it

2. Area = $\sqrt{s(s-a)(s-b)(s-c)}$ (Hero's formula)

   where $S = \dfrac{a+b+c}{2}$ (a, b and c being the length of the sides)

3. Area = rs (where r is in radius)

4. Area = 1/2 × product of two sides × sine of the included angle

   $$= 1/2\ ac \sin B$$
   $$= 1/2\ ab \sin C$$
   $$= 1/2\ bc \sin A$$

4. Area = $abc/4R$

   where R = circum radius

Congruency of Triangles Two triangles are congruent if all the sides of one are equal to the corresponding sides of another. It follows that all the angles of one are equal to the corresponding angles of another. The notation for congruency is $(\cong)$.

Conditions for Congruency

1. *SAS congruency*: If two sides and an included angle of one triangle are equal to two sides and an included angle of another, the two triangles are congruent. (See figure below.)

   Here, $AB = PQ$

   $$BC = QR$$

   and $\angle B = \angle Q$

   So $\Delta ABC \cong \Delta PQR$

2. *ASA congruency*: If two angles and the included side of one triangle is equal to two angles and the included side of another, the triangles are congruent. (See figure below.)

   Here, $\angle A = \angle P$

   $$\angle B = \angle Q$$

   and $AB = PQ$

   So $\Delta ABC \cong \Delta PQR$

3. *AAS congruency*: If two angles and side opposite to one of the angles is equal to the corresponding angles and the side of another triangle, the triangles are congruent. In the figure below:

   $$\angle A = \angle P$$
   $$\angle B = \angle Q$$

   and $AC = PR$

   So $\Delta ABC \cong \Delta PQR$

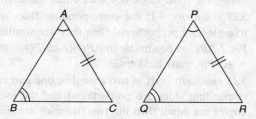

4. *SSS congruency*: If three sides of one triangle are equal to three sides of another triangle, the two triangles are congruent. In the figure below:

$$AB = PQ$$
$$BC = QR$$
$$AC = PR$$

$$\therefore \quad \triangle ABC \cong \triangle PQR$$

5. *SSA congruency*: If two sides and the angle opposite the greater side of one triangle are equal to the two sides and the angle opposite to the greater side of another triangle, then the triangles are congruent. The congruency doesn't hold if the equal angles lie opposite the shorter side. In the figure below, if

$$AB = PQ$$
$$AC = PR$$
$$\angle B = \angle Q$$

Then the triangles are congruent.

i.e. $\triangle ABC \cong \triangle PQR$.

Similarity of triangles Similarity of triangles is a special case where if either of the conditions of similarity of polygons holds, the other will hold automatically.

Types of Similarity

1. *AAA similarity:* If in two triangles, corresponding angles are equal, that is, the two triangles are equiangular then the triangles are similar.
   Corollary (AA similarity): If two angles of one triangle are respectively equal to two angles of another triangle then the two triangles are similar. The reason being, the third angle becomes equal automatically.

2. *SSS similarity:* If the corresponding sides of two triangles are proportional then they are similar.
   For $\triangle ABC$ to be similar to $\triangle PQR$, $AB/PQ = BC/QR = AC/PR$, must hold true.

3. *SAS similarity:* If in two triangles, one pair of corresponding sides are proportional and the included angles are equal then the two triangles are similar.

$$\triangle ABC \sim \triangle PQR$$

If $\quad AB/BC = PQ/QR \quad$ and $\quad \angle B = \angle Q$

Note: In similar triangles; the following identity holds:

Ratio of medians = Ratio of heights = Ratio of circumradii = Ratio of inradii = Ratio of angle bisectors

While there are a lot of methods through which we see similarity of triangles, the one thing that all our Maths teachers forgot to tell us about similarity is the basic real life concept of similarity. i.e. **Two things are similar if they look similar!!**

If you have been to a toy shop lately, you would have come across models of cars or bikes which are made so that they look like the original—but are made in a different size from the original. Thus you might have seen a toy Maruti car which is built in a ratio of 1:25 of the original car. The result of this is that the toy car would look very much like the original car (of course if it is built well!!). Thus if you have ever seen a father and son looking exactly like each other, you have experienced similarity!!

You should use this principle to identify similar triangles. In a figure two triangles would be similar simply if they look like one another.

Thus, in the figure below if you were to draw the radii OB and O'A the two triangles MOB and MO'A will be similar to each other. Simply because they look similar. Of course, the option of using the different rules of similarity of triangles still remains with you.

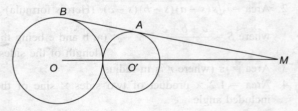

Equilateral Triangles (of side *a*):

1. $\qquad\qquad (\therefore \sin 60 = \sqrt{3}/2 = h/\text{side})$
   $$h = \frac{a\sqrt{3}}{2}$$

2. Area = 1/2 (base) × (height) = $\frac{1}{2} \times a \times \frac{a\sqrt{3}}{2} = \frac{\sqrt{3}}{4}a^2$

3. R (circum radius) $= \frac{2h}{3} = \frac{a}{\sqrt{3}}$.

4. r (in radius) = $\dfrac{h}{3} = \dfrac{a}{2\sqrt{3}}$.

Properties

1. The incentre and circumcentre lies at a point that divides the height in the ratio $2:1$.
2. The circum radius is always twice the in radius. [$R = 2r$.]
3. Among all the triangles that can be formed with a given perimeter, the equilateral triangle will have the maximum area.
4. An equilateral triangle in a circle will have the maximum area compared to other triangles inside the same circle.

Isosceles Triangle

Area = $\dfrac{b}{4}\sqrt{4a^2 - b^2}$

In an isosceles triangle, the angles opposite to the equal sides are equal.

Right-Angled Triangle

Pythagoras Theorem In the case of a right angled triangle, the square of the hypotenuse is equal to the sum of the squares of the other two sides. In the figure below, for triangle ABC, $a^2 = b^2 + c^2$

Area = 1/2 (product of perpendicular sides)

R(circumradius) = $\dfrac{\text{hypotenuse}}{2}$

Area = rs

(where r = in radius and $s = (a + b + c)/2$ where a, b and c are sides of the triangle)

$\Rightarrow \qquad 1/2\ bc = r(a + b + c)/2$

$\Rightarrow \qquad\quad r = (bc)/(a + b + c)$

In the triangle ABC,

$$\Delta ABC \sim \Delta DBA \sim \Delta DAC$$

(*Note:* A lot of questions are based on this figure.)
Further, we find the following identities:

1. $\Delta ABC \sim \Delta DBA$
   $\therefore \qquad AB/BC = DB/BA$
   $\Rightarrow \qquad AB^2 = DB \times BC$
   $\Rightarrow \qquad\quad c^2 = pa$
2. $\Delta ABC \sim \Delta DAC$
   $\qquad\quad AC/BC = DC/AC$
   $\Rightarrow \qquad AC^2 = DC \times BC$
   $\Rightarrow \qquad\quad b^2 = qa$
3. $\quad \Delta DBA \sim \Delta DAC$
   $\qquad\quad DA/DB = DC/DA$
   $\qquad\quad DA^2 = DB \times DC$
   $\Rightarrow \qquad AD^2 = pq$

Basic Pythagorean Triplets

$\rightarrow$ 3, 4, 5 $\rightarrow$ 5, 12, 13 $\rightarrow$ 7, 24, 25 $\rightarrow$ 8, 15, 17 $\rightarrow$ 9, 40, 41 $\rightarrow$ 11, 60, 61 $\rightarrow$ 12, 35, 37 $\rightarrow$ 16, 63, 65 $\rightarrow$ 20, 21, 29 $\rightarrow$ 28, 45, 53. These triplets are very important since a lot of questions are based on them.

Any triplet formed by either multiplying or dividing one of the basic triplets by any positive real number will be another Pythagorean triplet.

Thus, since 3, 4, 5 form a triplet so also will 6, 8 and 10 as also 3.3, 4.4 and 5.5.

Similarity of Right Triangles Two right triangles are similar if the hypotenuse and side of one is proportional to hypotenuse and side of another. (RHS–similarity–Right angle hypotenuse side).

Important Terms with Respect to a Triangle

1. Median A line joining the mid-point of a side of a triangle to the opposite vertex is called a median. In the figure the three medians are PG, QF and RE where G, E and F are mid-points of their respective sides.

- A median divides a triangle into two parts of equal area.
- The point where the three medians of a triangle meet is called the *centroid* of the triangle.
- The centroid of a triangle divides each median in the ratio $2:1$.
  i.e. $PC:CG = 2:1 = QC:CF = RC:CE$

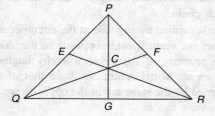

Important formula with respect to a median

→ 2 × (median)² + 2 × (1/2 the third side)²

= Sum of the squares of other two sides

$$\Rightarrow \quad 2(PG)^2 + 2 \times \left(\frac{QR}{2}\right)^2$$

$$= (PQ)^2 + (PR)^2$$

2. Altitude/Height A perpendicular drawn from any vertex to the opposite side is called the *altitude*. (In the figure, *AD, BF* and *CE* are the altitudes of the triangles).

- All the altitudes of a triangle meet at a point called the *orthocentre* of the triangle.
- The angle made by any side at the orthocentre and the vertical angle make a supplementary pair (i.e. they both add up to 180°). In the figure below:

$$\angle A + \angle BOC = 180° = \angle C + \angle AOB$$

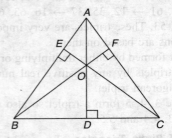

3. Perpendicular Bisectors A line that is a perpendicular to a side and bisects it is the perpendicular bisector of the side.

- The point at which the perpendicular bisectors of the sides meet is called the *circumcentre* of the triangle
- The circumcentre is the centre of the circle that circumscribes the triangle. There can be only one such circle.
- Angle formed by any side at the circumcentre is two times the vertical angle opposite to the side. This is the property of the circle whereby angles formed by an arc at the centre are twice that of the angle formed by the same arc in the opposite arc. Here we can view this as:

∠QCR = 2 ∠QPR (when we consider arc QR and it's opposite arc QPR)

4. Incenter
- The lines bisecting the interior angles of a triangle are the angle bisectors of that triangle.
- The angle bisectors meet at a point called the *incentre* of the triangle.
- The incentre is equidistant from all the sides of the triangle.

- From the incentre with a perpendicular drawn to any of the sides as the radius, a circle can be drawn touching all the three sides. This is called the *incircle* of the triangle. The radius of the incircle is known as *inradius*.
- The angle formed by any side at the incentre is always a right angle more than half the angle opposite to the side.

This can be illustrated as ∠QIR = 90 + 1/2 ∠P
- If QI and RI be the angle bisectors of exterior angles at Q and R then,

QIR = 90 − 1/2 ∠P.

QUADRILATERALS

Area

(A) Area = 1/2 (product of diagonals) × (sine of the angle between, them)

If θ_1 and θ_2 are the two angles made between themselves by the two diagonals, we have by the property of intersecting lines → $\theta_1 + \theta_2 = 180°$

Then, the area of the quadrilateral = $\frac{1}{2} d_1 d_2 \sin \theta_1$

$= \frac{1}{2} d_1 d_2 \sin \theta_2$.

(B) Area = 1/2 × diagonal × sum of the perpendiculars to it from opposite vertices = $\frac{d(h_1 + h_2)}{2}$.

(C) Area of a circumscribed quadrilateral

$$A = \sqrt{(S-a)(S-b)(S-c)(S-d)}$$

Where $S = \dfrac{a+b+c+d}{2}$

(where a, b, c and d are the lengths of the sides.)

Properties

1. In a convex quadrilateral inscribed in a circle, the product of the diagonals is equal to the sum of the products of the opposite sides. For example, in the figure below:

$$(a \times c) + (b \times d) = AC \times BD$$

2. Sum of all the angles of a quadrilateral = 360°.

TYPES OF QUADRILATERALS

1. Parallelogram (|| gm)

A parallelogram is a quadrilateral with opposite sides parallel (as shown in the figure below.)

(A) Area = Base (b) × Height (h)
   = bh

Base

(B) Area = product of any two adjacent sides × sine of the included angle.
   = $ab \sin Q$

(C) Perimeter = $2(a+b)$
   where a and b are any two adjacent sides.

Properties

(a) Diagonals of a parallelogram bisect each other.
(b) Bisectors of the angles of a parallelogram form a rectangle.

(c) A parallelogram inscribed in a circle is a rectangle.
(d) A parallelogram circumscribed about a circle is a rhombus.
(e) The opposite angles in a parallelogram are equal.
(f) The sum of the squares of the diagonals is equal to the sum of the squares of the four sides in the figure:

$$AC^2 + BD^2 = AB^2 + BC^2 + CD^2 + AD^2$$
$$= 2(AB^2 + BC^2)$$

2. Rectangles

A rectangle is a parallelogram with all angles 90°
   (a) Area = Base × Height = $b \times h$

Note: Base and height are also referred to as the length and the breadth in a rectangle.

(b) Diagonal (d) = $\sqrt{b^2 + h^2}$ → by Pythagoras theorem

Properties of a Rectangle

(a) Diagonals are equal and bisect each other.
(b) Bisectors of the angles of a rectangle (a parallelogram) form another rectangle.
(c) All rectangles are parallelograms but the reverse is not true.

3. Rhombus

A parallelogram having all the sides equal is a rhombus.
   (a) Area = 1/2 × product of diagonals × sine of the angle between them.
   = 1/2 × d_1 × d_2 sin 90° (Diagonals in a rhombus intersect at right angles)
   = 1/2 × $d_1 d_2$ (since sin 90° = 1)
   (b) Area = product of adjacent sides × sine of the angle between them.

Properties

(a) Diagonals bisect each other at right angles.
(b) All rhombuses are parallelograms but the reverse is not true.
(c) A rhombus may or may not be a square but all squares are rhombuses.

4. Square

A square is a rectangle with adjacent sides equal or a rhombus with each angle 90°

  (a) Area = base × height = a^2
  (b) Area = 1/2 (diagonal)^2 = 1/2 d^2 (square is a rhombus too).
  (c) Perimeter = $4a$ (a = side of the square)
  (d) Diagonal = $a\sqrt{2}$
  (e) In radius = $\dfrac{a}{2}$

Properties

  (a) Diagonals are equal and bisect each other at right angles.
  (b) Side is the diameter of the inscribed circle.
  (c) Diagonal is the diameter of the circumscribing circle.
    ⇒   Diameter = $a\sqrt{2}$.
        Circumradius = $a/\sqrt{2}$

5. Trapezium

A trapezium is a quadrilateral with only two sides parallel to each other.

  (a) Area = 1/2 × sum of parallel sides × height = 1/2 $(AB + DC) \times h$—For the figure below.
  (b) Median = 1/2 × sum of the parallel sides (median is the line equidistant from the parallel sides)
    For any line EF parallel to AB

$$EF = \frac{\{[P \times (AB)] + [Q \times (DC)]\}}{AD}$$

Properties

  (a) If the non-parallel sides are equal then diagonals will be equal too.

🔊 REGULAR HEXAGON

  (a) Area = $[(3\sqrt{3})/2]$ (side)^2

$$= \frac{3\sqrt{3} \times a^2}{2}$$

  (b) A regular hexagon is actually a combination of 6 equilateral triangles all of side 'a'.
    Hence, the area is also given by: 6 × side of equilateral triangles = $6 \times \dfrac{\sqrt{3}}{4} a^2$

  (c) If you look at the figure closely it will not be difficult to realise that circumradius (R) = a; i.e the side of the hexagon is equal to the circumradius of the same.

🔊 CIRCLES

  (a) Area = πr^2
  (b) Circumference = $2\pi r$ (r = radius)
  (c) Area = 1/2 × circumference × r
    Arc: It is a part of the circumference of the circle. The bigger one is called the *major arc* and the smaller one the *minor arc*.

  (d) Length (Arc XY) = $\dfrac{\theta}{360} \times 2\pi r$

  (e) **Sector of a circle** is a part of the area of a circle between two radii.

  (f) Area of a sector = $\dfrac{\theta}{360} \times \pi r^2$

    (where θ is the angle between two radii)
    = $(1/2)r \times$ length (arc xy)
    ($\therefore$ $\pi r\theta / 180$ = length arc xy)

$$= \frac{1}{2} \times r \times \frac{\pi r \theta}{360}$$

(g) **Segment:** A sector minus the triangle formed by the two radii is called the segment of the circle.

(h) Area = Area of the sector − Area $\triangle OAB$ =
$$\frac{\theta}{360} \times \pi r^2 - \frac{1}{2} \times r^2 \sin\theta$$

(i) Perimeter of segment = length of the arc + length of segment AB

$$= \frac{\theta}{360} \times 2\pi r + 2r \sin\left(\frac{\theta}{2}\right)$$

$$= \frac{\pi r \theta}{180} + 2r \sin\left(\frac{\theta}{2}\right)$$

(j) **Congruency:** Two circles can be congruent if and only if they have equal radii.

Properties

(a) The perpendicular from the centre of a circle to a chord bisects the chord. The converse is also true.

(b) The perpendicular bisectors of two chords of a circle intersect at its centre.

(c) There can be one and only one circle passing through three or more non-collinear points.

(d) If two circles intersect in two points then the line through the centres is the perpendicular bisector of the common chord.

(e) If two chords of a circle are equal, then the centre of the circle lies on the angle bisector of the two chords.

(f) Equal chords of a circle or congruent circles are equidistant from the centre.

(g) Equidistant chords from the centre of a circle are equal to each other in terms of their length.

(h) The degree measure of an arc of a circle is twice the angle subtended by it at any point on the alternate

segment of the circle. This can be clearly seen in the following figure:

With respect to the arc AB, $\angle AOB = 2\ \angle ACB$.

(i) Any two angles in the same segment are equal. Thus, $\angle ACB = \angle ADB$.

(j) The angle subtended by a semi-circle is a right angle. Conversely, the arc of a circle subtending a right angle at any point of the circle in its alternate segment is a semi-circle.

(k) Any angle subtended by a minor arc in the alternate segment is acute, and any angle subtended by a major arc in the alternate segment is obtuse.

In the figure below

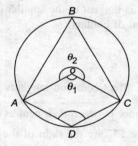

$\angle ABC$ is acute and

$\qquad \angle ADC$ = obtuse

Also $\qquad \theta_1 = 2\ \angle B$

And $\qquad \theta_2 = 2\ \angle D$

$\therefore \qquad \theta_1 + \theta_2 = 2(\angle B + \angle D)$

$\qquad\qquad = 360° = 2(\angle B + \angle D)$

or $\angle B + \angle D = 180°$

or sum of opposite angles of a cyclic quadrilateral is 180°.

(l) If a line segment joining two points subtends equal angles at two other points lying on the same side of the line, the four points are concyclic. Thus, in the following figure:

If, $\qquad \theta_1 = \theta_2$

Then $ABCD$ are concyclic, that is, they lie on the same circle.

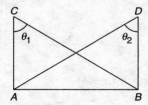

(m) Equal chords of a circle (or of congruent circles) subtend equal angles at the centre (at the corresponding centres.) The converse is also true.

(n) If the sum of the opposite angles of a quadrilateral is 180°, then the quadrilateral is cyclic.

Secant: A line that intersects a circle at two points.

Tangent: A line that touches a circle at exactly one point.

(o) If a circle touches all the four sides of a quadrilateral then the sum of the two opposite sides is equal to the sum of other two

$$AB + DC = AD + BC$$

(p) In two concentric circles, the chord of the larger circle that is tangent to the smaller circle is bisected at the point of contact.

Tangents

- Length of direct common tangents is

$$= \sqrt{(\text{Distance between their centres})^2 - (r_1 - r_2)^2}$$

where r_1 and r_2 are the radii of the circles

$$= \sqrt{(OO')^2 - (r_1 - r_2)^2}$$

- Length of transverse common tangents is

$$= \sqrt{(\text{distance between their centres})^2 - (r_1 + r_2)^2}$$

$$= \sqrt{(OO')^2 - (r_1 + r_2)^2}$$

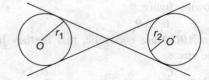

ELLIPSE

- Perimeter = $\pi (a + b)$
- Area = πab

STAR

Sum of angles of a star = $(2n - 8) \times \pi/2 = (n - 4)\pi$

PART II: MENSURATION

The following formulae hold true in the area of mensuration:

1. Cuboid

A cuboid is a three dimensional box. It is defined by the virtue of it's length *l*, breadth *b* and height *h*. It can be visualised as a room which has its length, breadth and height different from each other.

1. Total surface area of a cuboid = 2 (*lb* + *bh* + *lh*)
2. Volume of the cuboid = *lbh*

2. Cube of side s

A cube is a cuboid which has all its edges equal i.e. length = breadth = height = *s*.

1. Total surface area of a cube = $6s^2$.
2. Volume of the cube = s^3.

3. Prism

A prism is a solid which can have any polygon at both its ends. It's dimensions are defined by the dimensions of the polygon at it's ends and its height.

1. Lateral surface area of a right prism = Perimeter of base * height
2. Volume of a right prism = area of base* height
3. Whole surface of a right prism = Lateral surface of the prism + the area of the two plane ends.

4. Cylinder

A cylinder is a solid which has both its ends in the form of a circle. Its dimensions are defined in the form of the radius of the base (*r*) and the height *h*. A gas cylinder is a close approximation of a cylinder.

1. Curved surface of a right cylinder = $2\pi rh$ where *r* is the radius of the base and *h* the height.
2. Whole surface of a right circular cylinder = $2\pi rh + 2\pi r^2$
3. Volume of a right circular cylinder = $\pi r^2 h$

5. Pyramid

A pyramid is a solid which can have any polygon as its base and its edges converge to a single apex. Its dimensions are defined by the dimensions of the polygon at its base and the length of its lateral edges which lead to the apex. The Egyptian pyramids are examples of pyramids.

1. Slant surface of a pyramid = 1/2 * Perimeter of the base* slant height

2. Whole surface of a pyramid = Slant surface + area of the base

3. Volume of a pyramid = $\dfrac{\text{area of the base*}}{3}$ height

6. Cone

A cone is a solid which has a circle at its base and a slanting lateral surface that converges at the apex. Its dimensions are defined by the radius of the base (r), the height (h) and the slant height (l). A structure similar to a cone is used in ice cream cones.

1. Curved surface of a cone = $\pi r l$ where l is the slant height

2. Whole surface of a cone = $\pi r l + \pi r^2$

3. Volume of a cone = $\dfrac{\pi r^2 h}{3}$

7. Sphere

A sphere is a solid in the form of a ball with radius r.

Space for Notes

1. Surface Area of a sphere = $4\pi r^2$

2. Volume of a sphere = $\dfrac{4}{3}\pi r^3$

8. Frustum of a pyramid

When a pyramid is cut the left over part is called the frustum of the pyramid.

1. Slant surface of the frustum of a pyramid = 1/2 * sum of perimeters of end * slant height.

2. Volume of the frustum of a pyramid = $\dfrac{k}{3}[E_1 + (E_1 \cdot E_2)^{1/2} + E_2]$ where k is the thickness and E_1, E_2 the areas of the ends.

9. Frustum of a cone

When a cone is cut the left over part is called the frustum of the cone.

1. Slant surface of the frustum of a cone = $\pi(r_1 + r_2)l$ where l is the slant height.

2. Volume of the frustum of a cone = $\dfrac{\pi}{3}k(r_1^2 + r_1 r_2 + r_2^2)$

🎯 WORKED-OUT PROBLEMS

Problem 11.1 A right triangle with hypotenuse 10 inches and other two sides of variable length is rotated about its longest side thus giving rise to a solid. Find the maximum possible area of such a solid.

(a) $(250/3)\pi\,in^2$ (b) $(160/3)\pi\,in^2$
(c) $325/3\pi\,in^2$ (d) None of these

Solution Most of the questions like this that are asked in the CAT will not have figures accompanying them. Drawing a figure takes time, so it is always better to strengthen our imagination. The beginners can start off by trying to imagine the figure first and trying to solve the problem. They can draw the figure only when they don't arrive at the right answer and then find out where exactly they went wrong. The key is to spend as much time with the problem as possible trying to understand it fully and analysing the different aspects of the same without investing too much time on it.

Let's now look into this problem. The key here lies in how quickly you are able to visualise the figure and are able to see that

(i) the triangle has to be an isosceles triangle,
(ii) the solid thus formed is actually a combination of two cones,
(iii) the radius of the base has to be the altitude of the triangle to the hypotenuse.

After you have visualised this comes the calculation aspect of the problem. This is one aspect where you can score over others.

In this question the figure would be somewhat like this (as shown alongside) with triangles ABC and ADC representing the cones and AC being the hypotenuse around which the triangle ABC revolves. Now that the area has to be maximum with AC as the hypotenuse, we must realise that ADB has to be an isosceles triangle, which automatically makes BCD an isosceles triangle too. The next step is to calculate the radius of the base, which is essentially the height of the triangle ABC. To find that, we have to first find AB. We know

$$AC^2 = AB^2 + BC^2$$

For triangle to be one with the greatest possible area AB must be equal to BC that is, $AB = BC = \sqrt{50}$, since $AO = 1/2 AC = 5$ inches.

Now take the right angle triangle ABO, BO being the altitude of triangle AOC. By Pythagoras theorem, $AB^2 = AO^2 + BO^2$, so $BO^2 = 25$ inches

The next step is to find the area of the cone ABD and multiply it with two to get the area of the whole solid

Area of the cone $ADB = \pi/3\ (BO)^2 \times AO$
$$= (1/3)\ (25) \times 5\pi = (125/3)\pi$$
Therefore, area solid $ABCD = 2 \times (125/3)\pi = (250/3)\pi$

Problem 11.2 A right circular cylinder is to be made out of a metal sheet such that the sum of its height and radius does not exceed 9 cm can have an area of maximum.

(a) 54 p cm²   (b) 108 p cm²
(c) 81 p cm²   (d) None of these

Solution Solving this question requires the knowledge of ratio and proportion also. To solve this question, one must know that for $a^2b^3c^4$ to have the maximum value when $(a + b + c)$ is constant, a, b and c must be in the ratio $1:2:3$.

Now lets look at this problem. Volume of a cylinder $= \pi r^2 h$.

If you analyse this formula closely, you will find that r and h are the only variable term. So for volume of the cylinder to be maximum, r^2h has to be maximum under the condition that $r + h = 9$. By the information given above, this is possible only when $r:h = 2:1$, that is, $r = 6$, $h = 3$. So,

Volume of the cone $= \pi r^2 h$
$$= \pi \times 6^2 \times 3$$
$$= 108\pi$$

Problem 11.3 There are five concentric squares. If the area of the circle inside the smallest square is 77 square units and the distance between the corresponding corners of consecutive squares is 1.5 units, find the difference in the areas of the outermost and innermost squares.

Solution Here again the ability to visualise the diagram would be the key. Once you gain expertise in this aspect, you will be able to see that you will be able to see that the diameter of the circle is equal to the side of the innermost square that is

$$\pi r^2 = 77$$
or $$r = 3.5\sqrt{2}$$
or $$2r = 7\sqrt{2}$$

Then the diagonal of the square is 14 sq units.
Which means the diagonal of the fifth square would be 14 + 12 units = 26.

Which means the side of the fifth square would be $13\sqrt{2}$.

Therefore, the area of the fifth square = 338 sq units
Area of the first square = 98 sq units
Hence, the difference would be 240 sq. units.

Problem 11.4   A spherical pear of radius 4 cm is to be divided into eight equal parts by cutting it in halves along the same axis. Find the surface area of each of the final piece.

Fig. (a)

(a) 20 π (b) 25 π
(c) 24 π (d) 19 π

Solution   The pear after being cut will have eight parts each of same volume and surface area. The figure will be somewhat like the above Figure (a) if seen from the top before cutting. After cutting it look something like the Figure (b).

Now the surface area of each piece = Area *ACBD* + 2 (Area *CODB*).

The darkened surface is nothing but the arc *AB* from side glance which means its surface area is one eighth the area of the sphere, that is, $1/8 \times 4\pi r^2 = (1/2)\pi r^2$.

Now *CODB* can be seen as a semicircle with radius 4 cm.

1/8 surface area

4 cm

Fig. (b)

Therefore, 2 (Area *CODB*) = $2[(1/2)] \pi r^2 = \pi r^2$
$\Rightarrow$ surface area of each piece = $(1/2) \pi r^2 + \pi r^2$
$$= (3/2) \pi r^2$$
$$= 24\pi$$

Problem 11.5   A solid metal sphere is melted and smaller spheres of equal radii are formed. 10% of the volume of the sphere is lost in the process. The smaller spheres have a radius, that is 1/9th the larger sphere. If 10 litres of paint were needed to paint the larger sphere, how many litres are needed to paint all the smaller spheres?

(a) 90   (b) 81
(c) 900   (d) 810

Solution   Questions like this require, along with your knowledge of formulae, your ability to form equations. Stepwise, it will be something like this

Step 1: Assume values.

Step 2: Find out volume left.

Step 3: Find out the number of small spheres possible.

Step 4: Find out the total surface area of each small spheres as a ratio of the original sphere.

Step 5: Multiply it by 10.

Step 1:   Let radius of the larger sphere be *R* and that of smaller ones be *r*.

Then,   volume $= \frac{4}{3} \pi R^3$ and $\frac{4}{3} \pi r^3 = \frac{4}{3} \pi (R/9)^3$ respectively for the larger and smaller spheres.

Step 2:   Volume lost due to melting $= \frac{4}{3} \pi R^3 \times \frac{10}{100}$
$$= \frac{4\pi R^3}{30}$$

Volume left $= \frac{4}{3} \pi R^3 \times \frac{90}{100} = \frac{4\pi R^3 \times 0.9}{3}$

Step 3:   Number of small spheres possible = Volume left/Volume of the smaller sphere

$$= \frac{\frac{4}{3} \pi R^3 \times 0.9}{\frac{4}{3} \pi \times (R/9)^3} = 9^3 \times 0.9$$

Step 4:   Surface area of larger sphere $= 4\pi R^2$
Surface area of smaller sphere $= 4\pi r^2 = 4\pi (R/9)^2$
$$= \frac{4\pi R^2}{81}$$

Surface area of all smaller spheres = Number of small spheres $\times$ Surface area of smaller sphere
$$= (9^3 \times .9) \times (4\pi R^2)/81$$
$$= 8.1 \times (4\pi R^2)$$

Therefore, ratio of the surface area is $\dfrac{[8.1 \times (4\pi R^2)]}{4\pi R^2} = 8.1$

Step 5:
$$8.1 \times \text{number of litres} = 8.1 \times 10 = 81$$

Problem 11.6   A solid wooden toy in the shape of a right circular cone is mounted on a hemisphere. If the radius of the hemisphere is 4.2 cm and the total height of the toy is 10.2 cm, find the volume of the wooden toy.

(a) 104 cm³   (b) 162 cm³
(c) 427 cm³   (d) 266 cm²

Solution   Volume of the cone is given by $-1/3 \times \pi r^2 h$
Here, $r = 4.2$ cm; $h = 10.2 - r = 6$ cm
Therefore the volume of the cone $= 1/3 \pi \times (4.2)^2 \times 6$ cm
$$= 110.88 \text{ cm}^3$$

Volume of the hemisphere $= \frac{1}{2} \times \frac{4}{3} \pi r^3 = 155.23$

Total volume = $110.88 + 155.232 = 266.112$

Problem 11.7 A vessel is in the form of an inverted cone. Its depth is 8 cm and the diameter of its top, which is open, is 10 cm. It is filled with water up to the brim. When bullets, each of which is a sphere of radius 0.5 cm, are dropped into the vessel 1/4 of the water flows out. Find the number of bullets dropped in the vessel.

(a) 50   (b) 100   (c) 150   (d) 200

Solution In these type of questions it is just your calculation skills that is being tested. You just need to take care that while trying to be fast you don't end up making mistakes like taking the diameter to be the radius and so forth. The best way to avoid such mistakes is to proceed systematically. For example, in this problem we can proceed thus:

Volume of the cone = $\dfrac{1}{3}\pi r^2 h = \dfrac{200}{3}\pi$ cm^3

volme of all the lead shots = Volume of water that spilled out = $\dfrac{50}{3}\pi$ cm^3

Volume of each lead shot = $\dfrac{4}{3}\pi r^3 = \dfrac{\pi}{6}$ cm^3

Number of lead shots = (Volume of water that spilled out)/(Volume of each lead shot)

$$= \dfrac{\dfrac{50}{3}\pi}{\dfrac{\pi}{6}} = \dfrac{50}{3}\times 6 = 100$$

Problem 11.8 *AB* is a chord of a circle of radius 14 cm. The chord subtends a right angle at the centre of the circle. Find the area of the minor segment.

(a) 98 sq cm   (b) 56 sq cm
(c) 112 sq cm   (d) None of these

Solution Area of the sector *ACBO* = $\dfrac{90\pi \times 14^2}{360}$

= 154 sq cm

Area of the triangle *AOB* = $\dfrac{14\times 14}{2}$

= 98 sq cm

Area of the segment *ACB* = Area sector *ACBO* – Area of the triangle *AOB* = **56 sq cm**

Problem 11.9 A sphere of diameter 12.6 cm is melted and cast into a right circular cone of height 25.2 cm. Find the diameter of the base of the cone.

(a) 158.76 cm   (b) 79.38 cm
(c) 39.64 cm   (d) None of these

Solution In questions like this, do not go for complete calculations. As far as possible, try to cancel out values in the resulting equations.

Volume of the sphere = $\dfrac{4}{3}\pi r^3 = \dfrac{4}{3}\pi(6.3)^3$

Volume of the cone = $\dfrac{1}{3}\pi r^2 h = \dfrac{\pi}{3}r^2(25.2)$

Now, volume of the cone = volume of the sphere

Therefore, *r* (radius of the cone) = 39.69 cm

Hence the diameter = **79.38 cm**

Problem 11.10 A chord *AB* of a circle of radius 5.25 cm makes an angle of 60° at the centre of the circle. Find the area of the major and minor segments.   (Take π = 3.14)

(a) 168 cm^2 (b) 42 cm^2
(c) 84 cm^2 (d) None of these

Solution The moment you finish reading this question, it should occur to you that this has to be an equilateral triangle. Once you realise this, the question is reduced to just calculations.

Area of the minor sector = $\dfrac{60}{360}\times \pi \times 5.25^2$

= 14.4375 cm^2

Area of the triangle = $\dfrac{\sqrt{3}}{4}\times 5.25^2$ = 11.93 cm^2

Area of the minor segment = Area of the minor sector – Area of the triangle = 2.5 cm^2

Area of the major segment = Area of the circle – Area of the minor segment.

= 86.54 cm^2 – 2.5 cm^2 = **84 cm^2**

Problem 11.11 A cone and a hemisphere have equal bases and equal volumes. Find the ratio of their heights.

(a) 1:2   (b) 2:1
(c) 3:1   (d) None of these

Solution Questions of this type should be solved without the use of pen and paper. A good authority over formulae will make things easier.

Volume of the cone = $\dfrac{\pi r^2 h}{3}$ = Volume of a hemisphere

$= \dfrac{2}{3}\pi r^3$.

Height of a hemisphere = Radius of its base
So the question is effectively asking us to find out *h/r*
By the formula above we can easily see that *h/r* = **2/1**

GEOMETRY

LEVEL OF DIFFICULTY (I)

1. A vertical stick 20 m long casts a shadow 10 m long on the ground. At the same time, a tower casts the shadow 50 m long on the ground. Find the height of the tower.
   - (a) 100 m
   - (b) 120 m
   - (c) 25 m
   - (d) 200 m

2. In the figure, ΔABC is similar to ΔEDC.

   If we have $AB = 4$ cm,
   $ED = 3$ cm, $CE = 4.2$ and
   $CD = 4.8$ cm, find the value of CA and CB
   - (a) 6 cm, 6.4 cm
   - (b) 4.8 cm, 6.4 cm
   - (c) 5.4 cm, 6.4 cm
   - (d) 5.6 cm, 6.4 cm

3. The area of similar triangles, ABC and DEF are 144 cm² and 81 cm² respectively. If the longest side of larger ΔABC be 36 cm, then the longest side of smaller ΔDEF is
   - (a) 20 cm
   - (b) 26 cm
   - (c) 27 cm
   - (d) 30 cm

4. Two isosceles Δs have equal angles and their areas are in the ratio 16:25. Find the ratio of their corresponding heights.
   - (a) 4/5
   - (b) 5/4
   - (c) 3/2
   - (d) 5/7

5. The areas of two similar Δs are respectively 9 cm² and 16 cm². Find the ratio of their corresponding sides.
   - (a) 3:4
   - (b) 4:3
   - (c) 2:3
   - (d) 4:5

6. Two poles of height 6 m and 11 m stand vertically upright on a plane ground. If the distance between their foot is 12 m, find the distance between their tops.
   - (a) 12 cm
   - (b) 14 cm
   - (c) 13 cm
   - (d) 11 cm

7. The radius of a circle is 9 cm and length of one of its chords is 14 cm. Find the distance of the chord from the centre.
   - (a) 5.66 cm
   - (b) 6.3 cm
   - (c) 4 cm
   - (d) 7 cm

8. Find the length of a chord that is at a distance of 12 cm from the centre of a circle of radius 13 cm.
   - (a) 9 cm
   - (b) 8 cm
   - (c) 12 cm
   - (d) cm

9. If O is the centre of circle, find $\angle x$

   - (a) 35°
   - (b) 30°
   - (c) 39°
   - (d) 40°

10. Find the value of $\angle x$ in the given figure.

    - (a) 120°
    - (b) 130°
    - (c) 110°
    - (d) 100°

11. Find the value of x in the figure, if it is given that AC and BD are diameters of the circle.

    - (a) 60°
    - (b) 45°
    - (c) 15°
    - (d) 30°

12. Find the value of x in the given figure.

    - (a) 2.2 cm
    - (b) 1.6 cm
    - (c) 3 cm
    - (d) 2.6 cm

13. Find the value of x in the given figure.

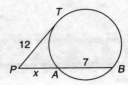

    (a) 16 cm   (b) 9 cm
    (c) 12 cm   (d) 7 cm

14. Find the value of x in the given figure.

    (a) 13 cm   (b) 12 cm
    (c) 16 cm   (d) 15 cm

15. ABC is a right angled triangle with $BC = 6$ cm and $AB = 8$ cm. A circle with centre O and radius x has been inscribed in $\triangle ABC$. What is the value of x.

    (a) 2.4 cm   (b) 2 cm
    (c) 3.6 cm   (d) 4 cm

16. In the given figure AB is the diameter of the circle and $\angle PAB = 25°$. Find $\angle TPA$.

    (a) 50°   (b) 65°
    (c) 70°   (d) 45°

17. In the given figure find $\angle ADB$.

    (a) 132°   (b) 144°
    (c) 48°   (d) 96°

18. In the given two straight line, PQ and RS intersect each other at O. If $\angle SOT = 75°$, find the value of a, b and c.

    (a) $a = 84°$, $b = 21°$, $c = 48°$
    (b) $a = 48°$, $b = 20°$, $c = 50°$
    (c) $a = 72°$, $b = 24°$, $c = 54°$
    (d) $a = 64°$, $b = 28°$, $c = 45°$

19. In the following figure A, B, C and D are the concyclic points. Find the value of x.

    (a) 130°   (b) 50°
    (c) 60°   (d) 30°

20. In the following figure, it is given that O is the centre of the circle and $\angle AOC = 140°$. Find $\angle ABC$.

    (a) 110°   (b) 120°
    (c) 115°   (d) 130°

21. In the following figure, O is the centre of the circle and $\angle ABO = 30°$, find $\angle ACB$.

    (a) 60°   (b) 120°
    (c) 75°   (d) 90°

22. In the following figure, find the value of x

    (a) 40°   (b) 25°
    (c) 30°   (d) 45°

23. If $L_1 \parallel L_2$ in the figure below, what is the value of x.

(a) 80°   (b) 100°

(c) 40°   (d) Cannot be determined

24. Find the perimeter of the given figure.

- 10 cm
- 6 cm

(a) $(32 + 3\pi)$ cm   (b) $(36 + 6\pi)$ cm

(c) $(46 + 3\pi)$ cm   (d) $(26 + 6\pi)$ cm

25. In the figure, AB is parallel to CD and $RD \parallel SL \parallel TM \parallel AN$, and $BR:RS:ST:TA = 3:5:2:7$. If it is known that $CN = 1.333\ BR$. find the ratio of $BF:FG:GH:HI:IC$

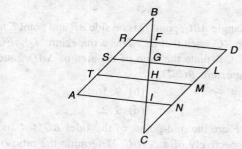

(a) 3:7:2:5:4   (b) 3:5:2:7:4

(c) 4:7:2:5:3   (d) 4:5:2:7:3

Space for Rough Work

LEVEL OF DIFFICULTY (II)

1. In a triangle *ABC*, point *D* is on side *AB* and point *E* is on side *AC*, such that *BCED* is a trapezium. *DE* : *BC* = 3 : 5. Calculate the ratio of the area of Δ*ADE* and the trapezium *BCED*.

   (a) 3 : 4
   (b) 9 : 16
   (c) 3 : 5
   (d) 9 : 25

2. *D*, *E*, *F* are the mid-points of the sides *BC*, *CA* and *AB* respectively of a Δ*ABC*. Determine the ratio of the area of triangles *DEF* and *ABC*.

   (a) 1 : 4
   (b) 1 : 2
   (c) 2 : 3
   (d) 4 : 5

3. In the adjoining figure, *ABCD* is a trapezium in which *AB* || *DC* and *AB* = 3 *DC*. Determine the ratio of the areas of (Δ*AOB* and Δ*COD*).

   (a) 9 : 1
   (b) 1 : 9
   (c) 3 : 1
   (d) 1 : 3

4. A ladder reaches a window that is 8 m above the ground on one side of the street. Keeping its foot on the same point, the ladder is twined to the other side of the street to reach a window 12 m high. Find the width of the street if the ladder is 13 m.

   (a) 15.2 m
   (b) 14 m
   (c) 14.6 m
   (d) 12 m

5. In the adjoining figure ∠*A* = 60° and ∠*ABC* = 80°, ∠*BQC*

   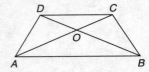

   (a) 40°
   (b) 80°
   (c) 20°
   (d) 30°

6. The diagram below represents three circular garbage cans, each of diameter 2 m. The three cans are touching as shown. Find, in metres, the perimeter of the rope encompassing the three cans.

   (a) 2π + 6
   (b) 3π + 4
   (c) 4π + 6
   (d) 6π + 6

7. In the figure below, *PQ* = *QS*, *QR* = *RS* and angle *SRQ* = 100°. How many degrees is angle *QPS*?

   (a) 20°
   (b) 40°
   (c) 15°
   (d) 30°

8. In the figure, *ABDC* is a cyclic quadrilateral with *O* as centre of the circle. If ∠*BOC* = 136°, find ∠*BDC*.

   (a) 110°
   (b) 112°
   (c) 109°
   (d) 115°

9. In the given figure, *AD* || *BC*. Find the value of *x*.

   (a) *x* = 8, 9
   (b) *x* = 7, 8
   (c) *x* = 8, 10
   (d) *x* = 7, 10

10. In the given figure $\dfrac{AO}{OC} = \dfrac{DO}{OB} = 1/2$ and *AB* = 4 cm.

    Find the value of *BC* in the above figure, $\dfrac{AO}{OC} = \dfrac{BO}{OD} = \dfrac{1}{2}$ and *AD* = 4 cm. Find the value of *BC*.

(a) 7 cm   (b) 8 cm

(c) 9 cm   (d) 10 cm

11. In the above figure, AD is the bisector of $\angle BAC$, AB = 6 cm, AC = 5 cm and BD = 3 cm. Find DC.

(a) 11.3 cm   (b) 2.5 cm

(c) 3.5 cm   (d) 4 cm

12. In a ΔABC, AD is the bisector of $\angle BAC$, AB = 8 cm, BD = 6 cm and DC = 3 cm. Find AC.

(a) 4 cm   (b) 6 cm

(c) 3 cm   (d) 5 cm

13. If ABC is a quarter circle and a circle is inscribed in it and if AB = 1 cm, find radius of smaller circle.

(a) $\sqrt{2} - 1$ (b) $(\sqrt{2} + 1)/2$

(c) $\sqrt{2} - 1/2$ (d) $1 - 2\sqrt{2}$

14. ABC is an equilateral triangle. Point D is on AC and point E is on BC, such that $AD = 2CD$ and $CE = EB$. If we draw perpendiculars from D and E to other two sides and find the sum of the length of two perpendiculars for each set, that is, for D and E individually and denote them as per (D) and per (E) respectively, then which of the following option will be correct.

(a) Per (D) > per (E) (b) Per (D) < per (E)

(c) Per (D) = per (E) (d) None of these

15. $ABCD$ is a trapezium in which AB is parallel to DC, $AD = BC$, $AB = 6$ cm, $AB = EF$ and $DF = EC$. If two lines AF and BE are drawn so that area of $ABEF$ is half of $ABCD$. Find DF/CD.

(a) 1/4   (b) 1/3

(c) 2/5   (d) 1/6

16. In the given figure, ΔABC and ΔACD are right angle triangles and $AB = x$ cm, $BC = y$ cm, $CD = z$ cm and $x \cdot y = z$ and x, y and z has minimum integral value. Find the area of $ABCD$

(a) 36 cm^2 (b) 64 cm^2

(c) 24 cm^2 (d) 25 cm^2

17. OD, OE and OF are perpendicular bisectors to the three sides of the triangle. What is the relationship between $m \angle BAC$ and $m \angle BOC$?

(a) $m\angle BAC = 180 - m\angle BOC$

(b) $m\angle BOC = 90 + 1/2\ m\angle BAC$

(c) $m\angle BAC = 90 + 1/2\ m\angle BOC$

(d) $m\angle BOC = 2m\angle BAC$

18. If two equal circles of radius 5 cm have two common tangent AB and CD which touch the circle on A, C and B, D respectively and if $CD = 24$ cm, find the length of AB.

(a) 27 cm   (b) 25 cm

(c) 26 cm   (d) 30 cm

19. If a circle is provided with a measure of 19° on centre, is it possible to divide the circle into 360 equal parts?
    (a) Never
    (b) Possible when one more measure of 20° is given
    (c) Always
    (d) Possible if one more measure of 21° is given

20. O is the centre of a circle of radius 5 cm. The chord AB subtends an angle of 60° at the centre. Find the area of the shaded portion (approximate value).

    (a) 50 cm²   (b) 62.78 cm²
    (c) 49.88 cm²   (d) 67.67 cm²

21. Two circles $C\ (O, r)$ and $C\ (O', r')$ intersect at two points A and B and O lies on $C\ (O', r')$. A tangent CD is drawn to the circle $C\ (O', r')$ at A. Then

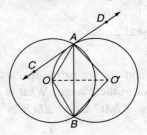

    (a) $\angle OAC = \angle OAB$ (b) $\angle OAB = \angle AO'O$
    (c) $\angle AO'B = \angle AOB$ (d) $\angle OAC = \angle AOB$

22. PP' and QQ' are two direct common tangents to two circles intersecting at points A and B. The common chord on produced intersects PP' in R and QQ' in S. Which of the following is true?

    (a) $RA^2 + BS^2 = AB^2$ (b) $RS^2 = PP'^2 + AB^2$
    (c) $RS^2 = PP'^2 + QQ'^2$ (d) $RS^2 = BS^2 + PP'^2$

23. Two circles touch internally at point P and a chord AB of the circle of larger radius intersects the other circle in C and D. Which of the following holds good?

    (a) $\angle CPA = \angle DPB$
    (b) $2\ \angle CPA = \angle CPD$
    (c) $\angle APX = \angle ADP$
    (d) $\angle BPY = \angle CPD + \angle CPA$

24. In a trapezium $ABCD$, $AB \parallel CD$ and $AD = BC$. If P is point of intersection of diagonals AC and BD, then all of the following is wrong except
    (a) $PA \cdot PB = PC \cdot PD$ (b) $PA \cdot PC = PB \cdot PD$
    (c) $PA \cdot AB = PD \cdot DC$ (d) $PA \cdot PD = AB \cdot DC$

25. All of the following is true except:
    (a) The points of intersection of direct common tangents and indirect common tangents of two circles divide the line segment joining the two centres respectively externally and internally in the ratio of their radii.
    (b) In a cyclic quadrilateral $ABCD$, if the diagonal CA bisects the angle C, then diagonal BD is parallel to the tangent at A to the circle through A, B, C, D.
    (c) If TA, TB are tangent segments to a circle $C(O, r)$ from an external point T and OT intersects the circle in P, then AP bisects the angle TAB.
    (d) If in a right triangle ABC, BD is the perpendicular on the hypotenuse AC, then
        (i) $AC \cdot AD = AB^2$ and
        (ii) $AC \cdot AD = BC^2$

Space for Rough Work

MENSURATION

LEVEL OF DIFFICULTY (I)

1. In a right angled triangle, find the hypotenuse if base and perpendicular are respectively 36015 cm and 48020 cm.
   - (a) 69125 cm
   - (b) 60025 cm
   - (c) 391025 cm
   - (d) 60125 cm

2. The perimeter of an equilateral triangle is $72\sqrt{3}$ cm. Find its height.
   - (a) 63 metres
   - (b) 24 metres
   - (c) 18 metres
   - (d) 36 metres

3. The inner circumference of a circular track is 440 cm. The track is 14 cm wide. Find the diameter of the outer circle of the track.
   - (a) 84 cm
   - (b) 168 cm
   - (c) 336 cm
   - (d) 77 cm

4. A race track is in the form of a ring whose inner and outer circumference are 352 metre and 396 metre respectively. Find the width of the track.
   - (a) 7 metres
   - (b) 14 metres
   - (c) 14π metres
   - (d) 7π metres

5. The outer circumference of a circular track is 220 metre. The track is 7 metre wide everywhere. Calculate the cost of levelling the track at the rate of 50 paise per square metre.
   - (a) ₹ 1556.5
   - (b) ₹ 3113
   - (c) ₹ 593
   - (d) ₹ 693

6. Find the area of a quadrant of a circle whose circumference is 44 cm
   - (a) 77 cm^2
   - (b) 38.5 cm^2
   - (c) 19.25 cm^2
   - (d) 19.25π cm^2

7. A pit 7.5 metre long, 6 metre wide and 1.5 metre deep is dug in a field. Find the volume of soil removed in cubic metres.
   - (a) 135 m^3
   - (b) 101.25 m^3
   - (c) 50.625 m^3
   - (d) 67.5 m^3

8. Find the length of the longest pole that can be placed in an indoor stadium 24 metre long, 18 metre wide and 16 metre high.
   - (a) 30 metres
   - (b) 25 metres
   - (c) 34 metres
   - (d) $\sqrt{580}$ metres

9. The length, breadth and height of a room are in the ratio of $3:2:1$. If its volume be 1296 m^3, find its breadth

10. The volume of a cube is 216 cm^3. Part of this cube is then melted to form a cylinder of length 8 cm. Find the volume of the cylinder.
    - (a) 342 cm^3
    - (b) 216 cm^3
    - (c) 36 cm^3
    - (e) Data inadequate

11. The whole surface of a rectangular block is 8788 square cm. If length, breadth and height are in the ratio of $4:3:2$, find length.
    - (a) 26 cm
    - (b) 52 cm
    - (c) 104 cm
    - (d) 13 cm

12. Three metal cubes with edges 6 cm, 8 cm and 10 cm respectively are melted together and formed into a single cube. Find the side of the resulting cube.
    - (a) 11 cm
    - (b) 12 cm
    - (c) 13 cm
    - (d) 24 cm

13. Find curved and total surface area of a conical flask of radius 6 cm and height 8 cm.
    - (a) $60\pi, 96\pi$
    - (b) $20\pi, 96\pi$
    - (c) $60\pi, 48\pi$
    - (d) $30\pi, 48\pi$

14. The volume of a right circular cone is 100π cm^3 and its height is 12 cm. Find its curved surface area.
    - (a) 130π cm^2
    - (b) 65π cm^2
    - (c) 204π cm^2
    - (d) 65 cm^2

15. The diameters of two cones are equal. If their slant height be in the ratio $5:7$, find the ratio of their curved surface areas.
    - (a) $25:7$
    - (b) $25:49$
    - (c) $5:49$
    - (d) $5:7$

16. The curved surface area of a cone is 2376 square cm and its slant height is 18 cm. Find the diameter.
    - (a) 6 cm
    - (b) 18 cm
    - (c) 84 cm
    - (d) 12 cm

17. The ratio of radii of a cylinder to a that of a cone is $1:2$. If their heights are equal, find the ratio of their volumes?
    - (a) $1:3$
    - (b) $2:3$
    - (c) $3:4$
    - (d) $3:1$

18. A silver wire when bent in the form of a square, encloses an area of 484 cm^2. Now if the same wire is bent to form a circle, the area of enclosed by it would be

(a) 308 cm²   (b) 196 cm²
(c) 616 cm²   (d) 88 cm²

19. The circumference of a circle exceeds its diameter by 16.8 cm. Find the circumference of the circle.
    (a) 12.32 cm   (b) 49.28 cm
    (c) 58.64 cm   (d) 24.64 cm

20. A bicycle wheel makes 5000 revolutions in moving 11 km. What is the radius of the wheel?
    (a) 70 cm   (b) 135 cm
    (c) 17.5 cm   (d) 35 cm

21. The volume of a right circular cone is 100π cm³ and its height is 12 cm. Find its slant height.
    (a) 13 cm   (b) 16 cm
    (c) 9 cm   (d) 26 cm

22. The short and the long hands of a clock are 4 cm and 6 cm long respectively. What will be sum of distances travelled by their tips in 4 days? (Take $\pi = 3.14$)
    (a) 954.56 cm   (b) 3818.24 cm
    (c) 2909.12 cm   (d) 2703.56 cm

23. The surface areas of two spheres are in the ratio of 1 : 4. Find the ratio of their volumes.
    (a) 1 : 2   (b) 1 : 8
    (c) 1 : 4   (d) 2 : 1

24. The outer and inner diameters of a spherical shell are 10 cm and 9 cm respectively. Find the volume of the metal contained in the shell. (Use $\pi = 22/7$)
    (a) 6956 cm³   (b) 141.95 cm³
    (c) 283.9 cm³   (d) 478.3 cm³

25. The radii of two spheres are in the ratio of 1 : 2. Find the ratio of their surface areas.
    (a) 1 : 3   (b) 2 : 3
    (c) 1 : 4   (d) 3 : 4

26. A sphere of radius r has the same volume as that of a cone with a circular base of radius r. Find the height of cone.
    (a) $2r$ (b) $r/3$
    (c) $4r$ (d) $(2/3)r$

27. Find the number of bricks, each measuring 25 cm × 12.5 cm × 7.5 cm, required to construct a wall 12 m long, 5 m high and 0.25 m thick, while the sand and cement mixture occupies 5% of the total volume of wall.
    (a) 6080   (b) 3040
    (c) 1520   (d) 12160

28. A road that is 7 m wide surrounds a circular path whose circumference is 352 m. What will be the area of the road?
    (a) 2618 cm²   (b) 654.5 cm²
    (c) 1309 cm²   (d) 5236 cm²

29. In a shower, 10 cm of rain falls. What will be the volume of water that falls on 1 hectare area of ground?
    (a) 500 m³   (b) 650 m³
    (c) 1000 m³   (d) 750 m³

30. Seven equal cubes each of side 5 cm are joined end to end. Find the surface area of the resulting cuboid.
    (a) 750 cm²   (b) 1500 cm²
    (c) 2250 cm²   (d) 700 cm²

31. In a swimming pool measuring 90 m by 40 m, 150 men take a dip. If the average displacement of water by a man is 8 cubic metres, what will be rise in water level?
    (a) 30 cm   (b) 50 cm
    (c) 20 cm   (d) 33.33 cm

32. How many metres of cloth 5 m wide will be required to make a conical tent, the radius of whose base is 7 m and height is 24 m?
    (a) 55 m   (b) 330 m
    (c) 220 m   (d) 110 m

33. Two cones have their heights in the ratio 1 : 2 and the diameters of their bases are in the ratio 2 : 1. What will be the ratio of their volumes?
    (a) 4 : 1   (b) 2 : 1
    (c) 3 : 2   (d) 1 : 1

34. A conical tent is to accommodate 10 persons. Each person must have 6 m² space to sit and 30 m³ of air to breath. What will be the height of the cone?
    (a) 37.5 m   (b) 150 m
    (c) 75 m   (d) None of these

35. A closed wooden box measures externally 10 cm long, 8 cm broad and 6 cm high. Thickness of wood is 0.5 cm. Find the volume of wood used.
    (a) 230 cubic cm   (b) 165 cubic cm
    (c) 330 cubic cm   (d) 300 cubic cm.

36. A cuboid of dimension 24 cm × 9 cm × 8 cm is melted and smaller cubes are of side 3 cm is formed. Find how many such cubes can be formed.
    (a) 27   (b) 64
    (c) 54   (d) 32

37. Three cubes each of volume of 216 m³ are joined end to end. Find the surface area of the resulting figure.
    (a) 504 m²   (b) 216 m²
    (c) 432 m²   (d) 480 m²

38. A hollow spherical shell is made of a metal of density 4.9 g/cm³. If its internal and external radii are 10 cm and 12 cm respectively, find the weight of the shell. (Take $\pi = 3.1416$)
    (a) 5016 gm   (b) 1416.8 gm
    (c) 14942.28 gm   (d) 5667.1 gm

39. The largest cone is formed at the base of a cube of side measuring 7 cm. Find the ratio of volume of cone to cube.
    (a) 20:21   (b) 22:21
    (c) 21:22   (d) 42:11

40. A spherical cannon ball, 28 cm in diameter, is melted and cast into a right circular conical mould the base of which is 35 cm in diameter. Find the height of the cone correct up to two places of decimals.
    (a) 8.96 cm   (b) 35.84 cm
    (c) 5.97 cm   (d) 17.92 cm

41. Find the area of the circle circumscribed about a square each side of which is 10 cm.
    (a) 314.28 cm³   (b) 157.14 cm³
    (c) 150.38 cm³   (d) 78.57 cm³

42. Find the radius of the circle inscribed in a triangle whose sides are 8 cm, 15 cm and 17 cm.
    (a) 4 cm   (b) 5 cm
    (c) 3 cm   (d) $2\sqrt{2}$ cm

43. In the given diagram a rope is wound round the outside of a circular drum whose diameter is 70 cm and a bucket is tied to the other end of the rope. Find the number of revolutions made by the drum if the bucket is raised by 11 m.

    (a) 10   (b) 2.5
    (c) 5   (d) 5.5

44. A cube whose edge is 20 cm long has circle on each of its faces painted black. What is the total area of the unpainted surface of the cube if the circles are of the largest area possible?
    (a) 85.71 cm²   (b) 257.14 cm²
    (c) 514.28 cm²   (d) 331.33 cm²

45. The areas of three adjacent faces of a cuboid are x, y, z. If the volume is V, then V^2 will be equal to
    (a) xy/z (b) yz/x^2
    (c) x^2y^2/z^2 (d) xyz

46. In the adjacent figure, find the area of the shaded region. (Use = 22/7)

    (a) 15.28 cm²   (b) 61.14 cm²
    (c) 30.57 cm²   (d) 40.76 cm²

47. The diagram represents the area swept by the wiper of a car. With the dimensions given in the figure, calculate the shaded area swept by the wiper.

    (a) 102.67 cm   (b) 205.34 cm
    (c) 51.33 cm   (d) 208.16 cm

48. Find the area of the quadrilateral ABCD. (Given, $\sqrt{3}$ = 1.73)

    (a) 452 sq units   (b) 269 sq units
    (c) 134.5 sq units (d) 1445 g cm

49. The base of a pyramid is a rectangle of sides 18 m × 26 m and its slant height to the shorter side of the base is 24 m. Find its volume.

    (a) $156\sqrt{407}$ (b) $78\sqrt{407}$
    (c) $312\sqrt{407}$ (d) $234\sqrt{407}$

50. A wire is looped in the form of a circle of radius 28 cm. It is bent again into a square form. What will be the length of the diagonal of the largest square possible thus?
    (a) 44 cm   (b) $44\sqrt{2}$
    (c) $176/2\sqrt{2}$ (d) $88\sqrt{2}$

Space for Rough Work

LEVEL OF DIFFICULTY (II)

1. The perimeter of a sector of a circle of radius 5.7 m is 27.2 m. Find the area of the sector.
   - (a) 90.06 cm²
   - (b) 135.09 cm²
   - (c) 45 cm²
   - (d) None of these

2. The dimensions of a field are 20 m by 9 m. A pit 10 m long, 4.5 m wide and 3 m deep is dug in one corner of the field and the earth removed has been evenly spread over the remaining area of the field. What will be the rise in the height of field as a result of this operation?
   - (a) 1 m
   - (b) 2 m
   - (c) 3 m
   - (d) 4 m

3. A vessel is in the form of a hollow cylinder mounted on a hemispherical bowl. The diameter of the sphere is 14 cm and the total height of the vessel is 13 cm. Find the capacity of the vessel. (Take $\pi = 22/7$).

   - (a) 321.33 cm
   - (b) 1642.67 cm³
   - (c) 1232 cm³
   - (d) 1632.33 cm³

4. The sides of a triangle are 21, 20 and 13 cm. Find the area of the larger triangle into which the given triangle is divided by the perpendicular upon the longest side from the opposite vertex.
   - (a) 72 cm²
   - (b) 96 cm²
   - (c) 168 cm²
   - (d) 144 cm²

5. A circular tent is cylindrical to a height of 3 metres and conical above it. If its diameter is 105 m and the slant height of the conical portion is 53 m, calculate the length of the canvas 5 m wide to make the required tent.
   - (a) 3894
   - (b) 973.5
   - (c) 1947 m
   - (d) 1800 m

6. A steel sphere of radius 4 cm is drawn into a wire of diameter 4 mm. Find the length of wire.
   - (a) 10,665 mm
   - (b) 42,660 mm
   - (c) 21,333 mm
   - (d) 14,220 mm

7. A cylinder and a cone having equal diameter of their bases are placed in the Qutab Minar one on the other, with the cylinder placed in the bottom. If their curved surface area are in the ratio of 8 : 5, find the ratio of their heights. Assume the height of the cylinder to be equal to the radius of Qutab Minar. (Assume Qutab Minar to be having same radius throughout).
   - (a) 1:4
   - (b) 3:4
   - (c) 4:3
   - (d) 2:3

8. If the curved surface area of a cone is thrice that of another cone and slant height of the second cone is thrice that of the first, find the ratio of the area of their base.
   - (a) 81:1
   - (b) 9:1
   - (c) 3:1
   - (d) 27:1

9. A solid sphere of radius 6 cm is melted into a hollow cylinder of uniform thickness. If the external radius of the base of the cylinder is 5 cm and its height is 32 cm, find the uniform thickness of the cylinder.
   - (a) 2 cm
   - (b) 3 cm
   - (c) 1 cm
   - (d) 3.5 cm

10. A hollow sphere of external and internal diameters 6 cm and 4 cm respectively is melted into a cone of base diameter 8 cm. Find the height of the cone
    - (a) 4.75 cm
    - (b) 9.5 cm
    - (c) 19 cm
    - (d) 38 cm

11. Three equal cubes are placed adjacently in a row. Find the ratio of total surface area of the new cuboid to that of the sum of the surface areas of the three cubes.
    - (a) 7:9
    - (b) 49:81
    - (c) 9:7
    - (d) 27:23

12. If V be the volume of a cuboid of dimension x, y, z and A is its surface, then A/V will be equal to
    - (a) $x^2y^2z^2$
    - (b) $1/2 (1/xy + 1/xz + 1/yz)$
    - (c) $\dfrac{1}{2}\left(\dfrac{1}{x} + \dfrac{1}{y} + \dfrac{1}{z}\right)$
    - (d) $1/xyz$

13. The minute hand of a clock is 10 cm long. Find the area of the face of the clock described by the minute hand between 9 a.m. and 9 : 35 a.m.
    - (a) 183.3 cm²
    - (b) 366.6 cm²
    - (c) 244.4 cm²
    - (d) 188.39 cm²

14. Two circles touch internally. The sum of their areas is 116π cm² and distance between their centres is 6 cm. Find the radii of the circles.
    - (a) 10 cm, 4 cm
    - (b) 11 cm, 4 cm
    - (c) 9 cm, 5 cm
    - (d) 10 cm, 5 cm

15. A toy is in the shape of a right circular cylinder with a hemisphere on one end and a cone on the other. The height and radius of the cylindrical part

are 13 cm and 5 cm respectively. The radii of the hemispherical and conical parts are the same as that of the cylindrical part. Calculate the surface area of the toy if the height of conical part is 12 cm.

(a) 1440 cm²   (b) 385 cm²

(c) 1580 cm²   (d) 770 cm²

16. A solid wooden toy is in the form of a cone mounted on a hemisphere. If the radii of the hemisphere is 4.2 cm and the total height of the toy is 10.2 cm, find the volume of wood used in the toy.

(a) 343.72 cm³   (b) 266.11 cm³

(c) 532.22 cm³   (d) 133.55 cm³

17. A cylindrical container whose diameter is 12 cm and height is 15 cm, is filled with ice cream. The whole ice-cream is distributed to 10 children in equal cones having hemispherical tops. If the height of the conical portion is twice the diameter of its base, find the diameter of the ice-cream cone.

(a) 6 cm   (b) 12 cm

(c) 3 cm   (d) 18 cm

18. A solid is in the form of a cylinder with hemispherical ends. The total height of the solid is 19 cm and the diameter of the cylinder is 7 cm. Find the total surface area of the solid.   (Use = 22/7).

(a) 398.75 cm²   (b) 418 cm²

(c) 444 cm²   (d) 412 cm²

19. A cone, a hemisphere and a cylinder stand on equal bases and have the same height. What is the ratio of their volumes?

(a) 2 : 1 : 3   (b) 2.5 : 1 : 3

(c) 1 : 2 : 3   (d) 1.5 : 2 : 3

20. The internal and external diameters of a hollow hemispherical vessel are 24 cm and 25 cm respectively. The cost of painting 1 cm² of the surface is ₹ 0.05. Find the total cost of painting the vessel all over.   (Take π = 22/7)

(a) ₹ 97.65   (b) ₹ 86.4

(c) ₹ 184   (d) ₹ 96.28

21. A solid is in the form of a right circular cylinder with a hemisphere at one end and a cone at the other end. Their common diameter is 3.5 cm and the heights of conical and cylindrical portion are respectively 6 cm and 10 cm. Find the volume of the solid.

(Use π = 3.14)

(a) 117 cm²   (b) 234 cm²

(c) 58.5 cm²   (d) None of these

22. In the adjoining figure, *AOBCA* represents a quadrant of a circle of radius 3.5 cm with centre *O*. Calculate the area of the shaded portion.   (Use π = 22/7)

(a) 35 cm²   (b) 7.875 cm²

(c) 9.625 cm²   (d) 6.125 cm²

23. Find the area of the shaded region if the radius of each of the circles is 1 cm.

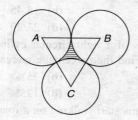

(a) $2 - \dfrac{\pi}{3}$ (b) $\sqrt{3} - \pi$

(c) $\sqrt{3} - \dfrac{\pi}{2}$ (d) $\sqrt{3} - \pi/4$

24. A right elliptical cylinder full of petrol has its widest elliptical side 2.4 m and the shortest 1.6 m. Its height is 7 m. Find the time required to empty half the tank through a hose of diameter 4 cm if the rate of flow of petrol is 120 m/min

(a) 60 min   (b) 90 min

(c) 75 min   (d) 70 min

25. Find the area of the trapezium *ABCD*.

(a) 5/2(13 + 2√3)   (b) $\dfrac{5\sqrt{3}(13 + 5\sqrt{3})}{2}$

(c) 13(13 + 2√3)   (d) None of these

26. *PQRS* is the diameter of a circle of radius 6 cm. The lengths *PQ*, *QR* and *RS* are equal. Semi-circles are drawn with *PQ* and *QS* as diameters as shown in the figure alongside. Find the ratio of the area of the shaded region to that of the unshaded region.

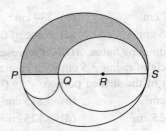

(a) 1:2   (b) 25:121

(c) 5:18   (d) 5:13

27. In the right angle triangle *PQR*, find *Rr*.

(a) 13/60   (b) 13/45

(c) 60/13   (d) 23/29

28. The radius of a right circular cylinder is increased by 50%. Find the percentage increase in volume

(a) 120%   (b) 75%

(c) 150%   (d) 125%

29. Two persons start walking on a road that diverge at an angle of 120°. If they walk at the rate of 3 km/h and 2 km/h repectively. Find the distance between them after 4 hours.

(a) $4\sqrt{19}$ km   (b) 5 km

(c) 7 km   (d) $8\sqrt{19}$ km

30. Water flows out at the rate of 10 m/min from a cylindrical pipe of diameter 5 mm. Find the time taken to fill a conical tank whose diameter at the surface is 40 cm and depth 24 cm.

(a) 50 min   (b) 102.4 min

(c) 51.2 min   (d) 25.6 min

31. The section of a solid right circular cone by a plane containing vertex and perpendicular to base is an equilateral triangle of side 12 cm. Find the volume of the cone.

(a) 72 cc   (b) 144 cc

(c) $72\sqrt{2}\,\pi$ cc   (d) $72\sqrt{3}\,\pi$ cc

32. Iron weighs 8 times the weight of oak. Find the diameter of an iron ball whose weight is equal to that of a ball of oak 18 cm in diameter.

(a) 4.5 cm   (b) 9 cm

(c) 12 cm   (d) 15 cm

33. In the figure, *ABC* is a right angled triangle with $\angle B = 90°$, *BC* = 21 cm and *AB* = 28 cm. With *AC* as diameter of a semicircle and with *BC* as radius, a quarter circle is drawn. Find the area of the shaded portion correct to two decimal places

(a) 428.75 cm²   (b) 857.50 cm²

(c) 214.37 cm²   (d) 371.56

34. Find the perimeter and area of the shaded portion of the adjoining diagram:

(a) 90.8 cm, 414 cm²   (b) 181.6 cm, 423.7 cm²

(c) 90.8 cm, 827.4 cm²   (d) 181.6 cm, 827.4 cm²

35. In the adjoining figure, a circle is inscribed in the quadrilateral *ABCD*. Given that *BC* = 38 cm, *AB* = 27 cm and *DC* = 25 cm, and that *AD* is perpendicular to *DC*. Find the maximum limit of the radius and the area of the circle.

(a) 10 cm; 226 cm²   (b) 14 cm; 616 cm²

(c) 14 cm; 216 cm²   (d) 28 cm; 616 cm²

36. From a piece of cardboard, in the shape of a trapezium *ABCD* and *AB* ∥ *DC* and $\angle BCD = 90°$, a quarter circle (*BFEC*) with *C* as its centre is removed. Given *AB* = *BC* = 3.5 cm and *DE* = 2 cm, calculate the area of the remaining piece of the cardboard.

(Take $\pi = 22/7$)

(a) 3.325 cm²   (b) 3.125 cm²
(c) 6.125 cm²   (d) 12.25 cm²

37. The inside perimeter of a practice running track with semi-circular ends and straight parallel sides is 312 m. The length of the straight portion of the track is 90 m. If the track has a uniform width of 2 m throughout, find its area.

90 cm

(a) 5166 m²   (b) 5802.57 m²
(c) 636.57 m²   (d) 1273.14 m²

38. Find the area of the triangle inscribed in a circle circumscribed by a square made by joining the mid-points of the adjacent sides of a square of side a.

(a) $3a^2/16$ (b) $\dfrac{3\sqrt{3}\,a^2}{16}$

(c) $3/4\,a^2(\pi - 1/2)$ (d) $\dfrac{3\sqrt{3}\,a^2}{32}$

39. Two goats are tethered to diagonally opposite vertices of a field formed by joining the mid-points of the adjacent sides of another square field of side $20\sqrt{2}$. What is the total grazing area of the two goats?

(a) $100\pi\,m^2$ (b) $50\,(\sqrt{2} - 1)\pi\,m^2$

(c) $100\pi\,(3 - 2\sqrt{2})\,m^2$ (d) $200\pi\,(2 - \sqrt{2})\,m^2$

40. The area of the circle circumscribing three circles of unit radius touching each other is

(a) $(\pi/3)\,(2 + \sqrt{3})^2$ (b) $6\pi\,(2 + \sqrt{3})^2$

(c) $3\pi\,(2 + \sqrt{3})^2$ (d) $\left(\dfrac{\pi}{6}\right)(2 + \sqrt{3})^2$

41. Find the ratio of the diameter of the circles inscribed in and circumscribing an equilateral triangle to its height.
(a) 1:2:1   (b) 1:2:3
(c) 1:3:4   (d) 3:2:1

42. Find the sum of the areas of the shaded sectors given that ABCDFE is any hexagon and all the circles are of same radius r with different vertices of the hexagon as their centres as shown in the figure.

(a) πr^2 (b) $2\pi r^2$
(c) $5\pi r^2/4$ (d) $3\pi r^2/2$

43. Circles are drawn with four vertices as the centre and radius equal to the side of a square. If the square is formed by joining the mid-points of another square of side $2\sqrt{6}$, find the area common to all the four circles.

(a) $[(\sqrt{3} - 1)/2)]\,6\pi$ (b) $4\pi - 3\sqrt{3}$

(c) $1/2\,(\pi - 3\sqrt{3})$ (d) $4\pi - 12(\sqrt{3} - 1)$

44. ABDC is a circle and circles are drawn with AO, CO, DO and OB as diameters. Areas E and F are shaded. E/F is equal to

(a) 1   (b) 1/2
(c) 1/2   (d) $\pi/4$

45. The diagram shows six equal circles inscribed in equilateral triangle ABC. The circles touch externally among themselves and also touch the sides of the triangle. If the radius of each circle is R, area of the triangle is

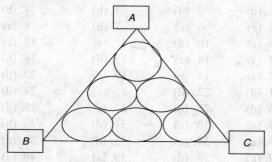

(a) $(6 + \pi\sqrt{3})\,R^1$ (b) $9\,R^2$

(c) $R^2\,(12 + 7\sqrt{3})$ (d) $R^2\,(9 + 6\sqrt{3})$

ANSWER KEY

GEOMETRY

Level of Difficulty (I)

1. (a)	2. (d)	3. (c)	4. (a)
5. (a)	6. (c)	7. (a)	8. (d)
9. (a)	10. (d)	11. (d)	12. (a)
13. (b)	14. (a)	15. (b)	16. (b)
17. (a)	18. (a)	19. (b)	20. (a)
21. (b)	22. (a)	23. (d)	24. (d)
25. (b)			

Level of Difficulty (II)

1. (b)	2. (a)	3. (a)	4. (a)
5. (c)	6. (a)	7. (a)	8. (b)
9. (a)	10. (b)	11. (b)	12. (a)
13. (a)	14. (c)	15. (b)	16. (a)
17. (d)	18. (c)	19. (c)	20. (d)
21. (a)	22. (a)	23. (a)	24. (b)
25. (d)			

MENSURATION

Level of Difficulty (I)

1. (b)	2. (d)	3. (b)	4. (a)
5. (d)	6. (b)	7. (d)	8. (c)
9. (d)	10. (d)	11. (b)	12. (b)
13. (a)	14. (b)	15. (d)	16. (c)
17. (c)	18. (c)	19. (d)	20. (d)
21. (a)	22. (b)	23. (b)	24. (b)
25. (c)	26. (c)	27. (a)	28. (a)
29. (c)	30. (a)	31. (d)	32. (d)
33. (b)	34. (d)	35. (b)	36. (b)
37. (a)	38. (c)	39. (d)	40. (b)
41. (b)	42. (c)	43. (c)	44. (c)
45. (d)	46. (c)	47. (a)	48. (b)
49. (a)	50. (b)		

Level of Difficulty (II)

1. (d)	2. (d)	3. (b)	4. (b)
5. (c)	6. (c)	7. (b)	8. (a)
9. (c)	10. (d)	11. (a)	12. (c)
13. (a)	14. (a)	15. (d)	16. (b)
17. (a)	18. (b)	19. (c)	20. (d)
21. (d)	22. (d)	23. (c)	24. (d)
25. (d)	26. (d)	27. (c)	28. (d)
29. (a)	30. (c)	31. (d)	32. (b)
33. (a)	34. (a)	35. (d)	36. (c)
37. (c)	38. (d)	39. (a)	40. (a)
41. (b)	42. (b)	43. (d)	44. (a)
45. (c)			

Solutions and Shortcuts

GEOMETRY

Level of Difficulty (I)

1. (a)
   When the length of stick = 20 m, then length of shadow = 10 m i.e. in this case length = 2 × shadow with the same angle of inclination of the sun, the length of tower that casts a shadow of 50 m ⇒ 2 × 50 m = 100 m
   i.e. height of tower = 100 m

2. (d)
   $\triangle ABC \sim \triangle EDC$

   Then $\dfrac{AC}{EC} = \dfrac{BC}{DC} = \dfrac{AB}{ED}$

   Then $\dfrac{AC}{4.2} = \dfrac{4}{3} = AC = 5.6$ cm and

   $\dfrac{BC}{4.8} = \dfrac{4}{3} = BC = 6.4$ cm

3. (c)
   For similar triangles ⇒ (Ratio of sides)² = Ratio of areas

   Then as per question $= \left(\dfrac{36}{x}\right)^2 = \dfrac{144}{81}$

   {Let the longest side of $\triangle DEF = x$}

   $\Rightarrow \dfrac{36}{x} = \dfrac{12}{9} = x = 27$ cm

4. (a)
   (Ratio of corresponding sides)² = Ratio of area of similar triangle
   ∴ Ratio of corresponding sides in this question

   $= \sqrt{\dfrac{16}{25}} = \dfrac{4}{5}$

5. (a)
   Ratio of corresponding sides $= \sqrt{\dfrac{9}{16}} = \dfrac{3}{4}$

6. (c)

   $BC = ED = 6$ m
   So $AB = AC - BC = 11 - 6 = 5$ m
   $CD = BE = 12$ m

Then by Pythagoras theorem:

$$AE^2 = AB^2 + BE^2 \Rightarrow AE = 13 \text{ m}$$

7. (a)

In the ΔOBC; $BC = 7$ cm and $OC = 9$ cm, then using Pythagoras theorem.

$$OB^2 = OC^2 - BC^2$$

$$OB = \sqrt{32} = 5.66 \text{ cm (approx)}$$

8. (d)

In the ΔOBC, $OB = 12$ cm, $OC = $ radius $= 13$ cm. Then using Pythagoras theorem;

$$BC^2 = OC^2 - OB^2 = 25; BC = 5 \text{ cm}$$

Length of the chord $= 2 \times BC = 2 \times 5 = 10$ cm

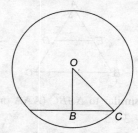

9. (a)

$\angle x = 35°$; because angles subtended by an arc, anywhere on the circumference are equal.

10. (d)

$\angle AOM = 2\angle ABM$ and

$\angle AON = 2\angle ACN$

because angle subtended by an arc at the centre of the circle is twice the angle subtended by it on the circumference on the same segment.

$\angle AON = 60°$ and $\angle AOM = 40°$

$\angle X = \angle AON + \angle AOM$

(∵ vertically opposite angles).

$\angle X = 100°$

11. (d)

ΔBCO and ΔAOD are similar (∵ AC and BD one diameters). Thus

$\angle ADO = \angle CBD$ (alternate opposite angles)

∴ $\angle X = 30°$

12. (a)

By the rule of tangents, we know:

$6^2 = (5 + n)5 \Rightarrow 36 = 25 + 5x \Rightarrow 11 = 5x \Rightarrow x = 2.2$ cm

13. (b)

By the rule of tangents, we get

$$12^2 = (x + 7)x \Rightarrow 144 = x^2 + 7x$$

$\Rightarrow x^2 + 7x - 144 = 0 \Rightarrow x^2 + 16x - 9x - 144 = 0$

$\Rightarrow x(x + 16) - 9(x + 16) \Rightarrow x = 9$ or -16

-16 can't be the length, hence this value is discarded, thus, $x = 9$

14. (a)

By the rule of chords, cutting externally, we get

$\Rightarrow (9 + 6)6 = (5 + x)5 \Rightarrow 90 = 25 + 5x \Rightarrow 5x = 65$

$\Rightarrow x = 13$ cm

15. (b)

Inradius = area/semi perimeter

$= 24/12 = 2$ cm

16. (b)

$\angle APB$ = 90° (angle in a semicircle = 90°)

$\angle PBA$ = $180 - (90 + 25) = 65°$

$\angle TPA$ = $\angle PBA$(the angle that a chord makes with the tangent, is subtended by the chord on the circumference in the alternate segment).

$= 65°$

17. (a)

$ADBC$ is a cyclic quadrilateral as all its four vertices are on the circumference of the circle. Also, the opposite angles of the cyclic quadrilateral are supplementary.

Therefore, $\angle ADB = 180 - 48° = 132°$

18. (a)

$\angle POS = \angle QOR$ (vertically opposite angles)

So $a = 4b$

$\angle SOT + \angle TOQ + \angle QOR = 180°$

(sum of angles on a line = 180°)

$4b + 2c = 180°$

$84 + 2c = 180°$

$\Rightarrow$ $2c = 96° \Rightarrow c = 48°$

So $a = 84°, b = 21°, c = 48°$

19. (b)
$\angle ABC = 180° - 130° = 50°$
   (∴ sum of angles on a line = 180°)
$\angle ADC = 180° - \angle ABC = 130°$
   (∵ opposite angles of a cyclic quadrilateral are supplementary).
$\angle x = 180° - 130° = 50°$
   (∴ sum of angles on a line = 180°)

20. (a)

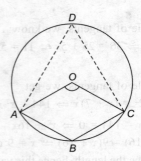

$\angle ADC = \dfrac{140}{2} = 70°$ (because the angle subtended by an arc on the circumference is half of what it subtends at the centre). $ABCD$ one cyclic quadrilateral So $\angle ABC = 180° - 70° = 110°$ (because opposite angles of a cyclic quadrilateral are supplementary).

21. (b)

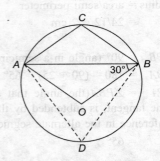

$OB = OA$ = radius of the circle
$\angle AOB = 180 - (30 + 30)$
   {Sum of angles of a triangle = 180°}
$\Rightarrow 120°$

Then $\angle ADB = \dfrac{120}{2} = 60°$; because the angle subtended by a chord at the centre is twice of what it can subtend at the circumference. Again, $ABCD$ is a cyclic quadrilateral;
So $\angle ACB = 180° - 60° = 120°$ (because opposite angles of cyclic quadrilateral are supplementary).

22. (a)
$\angle BAC = 30°$ (∵ angles subtended by an arc anywhere on the circumference in the same segment are equal).

In $\triangle BAC$; $\angle x = 180° - (110° + 30°) = 40°$
   (∵ sum of angles of a triangle = 180°)

23. (d)
As L_4 and L_3 are not parallel lines, so there can't be any relation between 80° and $x°$.
Hence the answer cannot be determined.

24. (d)
Perimeter of the figure $= 10 + 10 + 6 + 3\pi$
$= 26 + 3\pi$

25. (b) $CN : BR = 4 : 3$
So the required answer is $3 : 5 : 2 : 7 : 4$
Option (b) is correct.

Level of Difficulty (II)

1. (b)

$\triangle ADE$ is similar to $\triangle ABC$ (AAA property)
$ED : BC = 3 : 5$
Area of $\triangle ADE$: Area of $\triangle ABC = 9 : 25$
Area of trapezium = area of ABC − Area of ADE
$= 25 - 9 = 16$
Thus,
Area of $\triangle ADE$: Area of trapezium $EDBC = 9 : 16$

2. (a)

The area of a triangle formed by joining the mid-points of the sides of another triangle is always 1/4th of the area of the bigger triangle.
   So, the ratio is $= 1 : 4$

3. (a)
$\triangle DOC$ and $\triangle AOB$ are similar (by AAA property)
$AB : DC = 3 : 1$
So area of AOB : Area of $DOC = (3 : 1)^2 \Rightarrow 9 : 1$

4. (a)

In ΔABC; $BC = \sqrt{13^2 - 12^2} = 5$

In ΔCDE; $CE = \sqrt{13^2 - 8^2} = \sqrt{105} = 10.2$

Width of street $= BC + CE = 5 + 10.2 = 15.2$ m

5. (c)

$ABCD$ is a cyclic quadrilateral. Therefore

$\angle DCB = 180 - \angle A = 180 - 60 = 120°$

$\angle ABC = 80°$; therefore $\angle BCQ = 180° - 120° = 60°$

And $\angle CBQ = 180° - 80° = 100°$

         (because, sum of angles on a line=180°)

Then in ΔBCQ; $\angle Q = 180 - (100 + 60) = 20$

         ($\because$ sum of angles of triangle = 180°)

6. (a)

$\angle AOB = \angle CO'D = \angle FO''E = 120°$

Distance between 2 centres = 2 m

$\therefore$ $BC = DE = FA = 2$ m

Perimeter of the figure $= BC + DE + FA +$ circumference of sectors AOB, $CO'B$ and $FO''E$.

    But three equal sectors of 120° = 1 full circle of same radius.

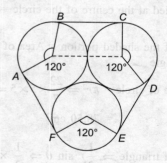

Therefore, perimeter of surface
$$= 2\pi r + BC + DE + FA = (2\pi + 6)\,m$$

7. (a)

In ΔQRS; $QR = RS$, therefore $\angle RQS = \angle RSQ$ (because angles opposite to equal sides are equal).

Thus $\angle RQS + \angle RSQ = 180° - 100° = 80°$

$\therefore$ $\angle RQS = \angle RSQ = 40°$

        $\angle PQS = 180° - 40° = 140°$

        (sum of angles on a line = 180°)

Then again $\angle QRS = \angle QSP$

        ($\because$ angles opposite to equal sides are equal)

Thus $\angle QPS + \angle QSP = 180° - 140° = 40°$

And $\angle QPS = \angle QSP = 20°$

8. (b)

        $\angle BOC = 136°$

$\angle BAC = \dfrac{136}{2} = 68°$ (because angle subtended by an arc anywhere on the circumference is half of the angle it subtends at the centre).

$\angle BDC = 180° - 68° = 112°$ ($\therefore$ $ABCD$ is a cyclic quadrilateral and its opposite angles are supplementary)

9. (a)

ΔADO and ΔBOC are similar (AAA property)

Then $\dfrac{3}{3x - 19} = \dfrac{x - 5}{x - 3}$

$\Rightarrow$ $3x - 9 = 3x^2 - 15x - 19x + 95$

$\Rightarrow$ $3x^2 - 37x + 104 = 0$

On solving this quadratic equation, we get $x = 8$ or 9.

10. (b)

ΔAOD and ΔBOC are similar (AAA property)

$\dfrac{AO}{OC} = \dfrac{1}{2}$; therefore $\dfrac{AD}{BC} = \dfrac{1}{2} \Rightarrow \dfrac{4}{BC} = \dfrac{1}{2}$

$\Rightarrow$ $BC = 8$ cm

11. (b)

In the given figure, ΔABD is similar to ΔADC

Then $\dfrac{AB}{BD} = \dfrac{AC}{DC} \Rightarrow \dfrac{6}{3} = \dfrac{5}{DC} \Rightarrow DE = 2.5$ cm

12. (a)

As AD bisects $\angle CAB$, so ΔABD is similar to ΔADC

Then $\dfrac{AB}{DB} = \dfrac{AC}{DC} \Rightarrow \dfrac{8}{6} = \dfrac{AC}{3} \Rightarrow AC = 4$ cm

13. (a)

Area of the quarter circle = $\dfrac{\pi r^2}{4} \Rightarrow 0.25\pi$. Going by

options, we have to see that the area of the inserted circle is less than the area of the quarter circle.

Option (b) $\dfrac{(\sqrt{2}+1)}{2} \Rightarrow$ Area $= (1.5 + \sqrt{2})\pi$

$2.9\pi > 0.25\pi$. Hence discarded.

Option (c) $\sqrt{2} - \dfrac{1}{2} \Rightarrow$ Area $= \pi\left(2 + \dfrac{1}{4} - \sqrt{2}\right) \Rightarrow 0.75\pi$

$> 0.25\pi$. Hence discarded.

Option (d) $1 - \sqrt[2]{2} \Rightarrow$ Area $= \pi(1 + 8 - \sqrt[4]{2} \Rightarrow 0.85\pi$

$> 0.25\pi$. Hence discarded.

Option (a) $\sqrt{2} - 1 =$ Area $\pi(2 + 1 - \sqrt[2]{2}) \Rightarrow 0.20\pi$

$< 0.25\pi$.

Hence this option is correct.

14. (c)

Sum of length of all perpendiculars drawn on the sides of any equilateral triangle is constant. Perpendicular (D) = Perpendicular (E)

15. (b)

In the above question:

$FE = AB = 6$ cm

$\Delta ADF \cong \Delta BEC$; so $DF = EC$

Let $DF = EC = x$

Solving through options; e.g. option (b) 1/3; $x = 6$

Then by Pythagoras triplet $AF = 8$

Area of $ABEF = 8 \times 6 = 48$ cm^2

Area of $\Delta AFD + \Delta BEC = 2 \times \dfrac{1}{2} \times 6 \times 8 \Rightarrow 48$ cm^2

$\therefore$ Area of $ABCD = 48 + 48 = 96$ cm^2. Hence the condition is proved.

16. (a)

Find the indivisible area of ΔABC and ΔACD

Add them then;

$\dfrac{1}{2} AB \times BC + \dfrac{1}{2} AC \times CD \Rightarrow \dfrac{1}{2}xy + \dfrac{1}{2}z\sqrt{x^2 + y^2}$

$\Rightarrow$ replace x, y, z by the lowest integral values.

Here as we are talking about right angles, so we have to take the smallest Pythagorean triplet, which in this case would be = 3, 4, 5

Answer $\Rightarrow 36$ cm^2

17. (d)

As the point 'O' is formed by the $\perp$ bisects to the three sides of the Δ, so point 'O' is the circumcenter. This means that virtually, points A, B and C are on the circumference of the circle.

Thus $m\angle BOC = 2\, m\angle BAC$ ($\because$ angle subtended by an arc at the centre of the circle is twice the angle subtended at the circumference).

18. (c)

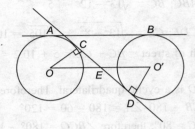

$OC = O'D = 5$ cm (radius)

$CD = 24$ cm

ΔCOE and $\Delta EO'D$ are similar therefore $OE = O'E$ and $CE = ED = 12$ cm

In ΔCOD; $OE^2 = CE^2 + OC^2$

$= 12^2 + 5^2 = 169$

$OE = 13$

$\therefore \qquad OO' = OE + EO' = 13 + 13 = 26$ cm

19. (c)

It will always be possible to divide a circle into 360 equal parts, because the sum of angles that can be subtended at the centre of the circle = 360°

20. (d)

Area of the shaded portion = Area of circle – Area of triangle

$\Rightarrow$ Area of circle $= \pi r^2 \Rightarrow \dfrac{22}{7} \times 5 \times 5 \Rightarrow \dfrac{22 \times 25}{7}$ cm^2

$= 78.50$ cm^2

Area of triangle $\Rightarrow \dfrac{1}{2} r^2 \sin\theta \Rightarrow \dfrac{1}{2} \times 25 \times \sin\theta$

$\Rightarrow \dfrac{25\sqrt{3}}{4} \Rightarrow 6.25 \times 1.732 \Rightarrow 10.8$

$\therefore$ Area of shaded portion $= 78.50 - 10.8 = 67.7$ cm^2

21. (a)

$OB = OA$ – radius of circle

$\Rightarrow \quad \angle CAO = \angle OBA$

(angles in alternate segments are equal).

Now, if $\angle CAO = \angle OBA$

∴   ∠CAO = ∠OAB
∴ option (a) is correct.

22. (b)

23. (a)

Angle *XPA* = angle *ABP* = *x*

Angle *CPX* = angle *CDP* = *x* + *y*

Anlge *CDP* is exterior angle of triangle *PDB*

So angle *CDP* = *DBP* + *DPB*

    X + *y* = *x* + *DPB*

    DPB = *y*

So angle   *CPA* = *DPB*

24. (b)

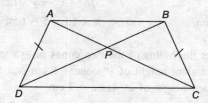

ΔAPD ~ ΔCPB

∴ $\frac{PA}{PB} = \frac{PD}{PC}$

i.e.   *PA* · *PC* = *PB* · *PD*.

∴ option (b)

25. (d)

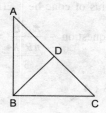

    AC · *AD* = *AB*²
    AC · *AD* = *BC*²
ΔABC N ΔADB
∴ $\frac{AC}{AB} = \frac{AB}{AD}$

    (Corresponding sides of similar triangle
    are proportional)
    AC · *AD* = *AB*²   (i)

Also, ΔABC N ΔBDC ⇒ $\frac{AC}{BC} = \frac{BC}{CD}$

    AC · *CD* = *BC*²   (ii)

Both conditions of option (d) are found, therefore
(d) is the answer.

MENSURATION
Level of Difficulty (I)

1. (b)

Let hypotenuse = *x* cm
Then, by Pythagoras theorem:
    *x*² = (48020)² + (36015)²
    x ⇒ 60025 cm

2. (d)

Let one side of the Δ be = *a*
Perimeter of equilateral triangle = 3*a*
∴   3*a* = 72√3 = *a* = 24√3 cm

Height = *AC*; by Pythagoras theorem
    $AC^2 = a^2 - \left(\frac{a}{2}\right)^2$
    AC = 36 cm

3. (b)
Let inner radius = *A*; then 2π*r* = 440   ∴ π = 70
Radius of outer circle = 70 + 14 = 84 cm
∴   Outer diameter = 2 × Radius = 2 × 84 = 168

4. (a)
Let inner radius = *r* and outer radius = *R*
Width = $R - r = \frac{396}{2\pi} - \frac{352}{2\pi}$
⇒ $(R - r) = \frac{44}{2\pi} = 7$ meters

5. (d)
Let outer radius = *R*; then inner radius = *r* = *R* − 7
    2π*R* = 220 ⇒ 35m;
    r = 35 − 7 = 28 m
Area of torch = π*R*² − π*r*² ⇒ π(*R*² − *r*²) = 1386 m²
Cost of traveling it = 1386 × $\frac{1}{2}$ = ₹ 693

6. (b)

Circumference of circle = $2\pi r = 44$

$= r = 7$ cm

Area of a quadrant = $\dfrac{\pi r^2}{4} = 38.5$ cm^2

7. (d)

Volume of soil removed = $l \times b \times h$

$= 7.5 \times 6 \times 1.5 = 67.5$ m^3

8. (c)

The longest pole can be placed diagonally (3-dimensional)

$BC = \sqrt{18^2 + 24^2} = 30$

$AC = \sqrt{30^2 + 16^2} = 34$ m

9. (d)

Let the common ratio be = x

Then; length = $3x$, breadth = $2x$ and height = x

Then; as per question $3x \cdot 2x \cdot x = 1296 \Rightarrow 6x^3 = 1296$

$\Rightarrow x = 6$ m

Breadth = $2x = 12$ m

10. (d)

Data is inadequate as it's not mentioned that what part of the cube is melted to form cylinder.

11. (b)

Let the common ratio be = x

Then, length = $4x$, breadth = $3x$ and height = $2x$

As per question;

$2(4x \cdot 3x + 3x \cdot 2x + 2x \cdot 4x) = 8788$

$2(12x^2 + 6x^2 + 8x^2) = 8788 \Rightarrow 52x^2 = 8788$

$\Rightarrow \qquad\qquad x = 13$

Length = $4x = 52$ cm

12. (b)

The total volume will remain the same, let the side of the resulting cube be = a. Then,

$6^3 + 8^3 + 10^3 = a^3 \Rightarrow a = \sqrt[3]{1728} = 12$ cm

13. (a)

Slant length = $l = \sqrt{6^2 + 8^2} = 10$ cm

Then curved surface area = $\pi r l = \pi \times 6 \times 10 \Rightarrow 60\pi$

And total surface area = $\pi r l + \pi r^2 \Rightarrow \pi((6 \times 10) + 6^2)$

$= 96\pi$

14. (b)

Volume of a cone = $\dfrac{\pi r^2 h}{3}$

Then; $\qquad 100\pi = \dfrac{\pi r^2 \cdot 12}{3} \Rightarrow r = 5$ cm

Curved surface area = $\pi r l$

$l = \sqrt{h^2 + r^2} \Rightarrow \sqrt{12^2 + 5^2} = 13$

then, $\qquad \pi r l = \pi \times 13 \times 5 = 65\pi$ cm^2

15. (d)

Let the radius of the two cones be = x cm

Let slant height of 1st cone = 5 cm and

Slant height of 2nd cone = 7 cm

Then ratio of covered surface area = $\dfrac{\pi \times 5}{\pi \times 7} = 5 : 7$

16. (c)

Radius = $\dfrac{\pi r l}{\pi l} = \dfrac{2376}{3.14 \times 18} = 42$ cm

Diameter = $2 \times$ Radius = $2 \times 42 = 84$ cm

17. (c)

Let the radius of cylinder = $1(r)$

Then the radius of cone be = $2(R)$

Then as per question = $\dfrac{\pi r^2 h}{\dfrac{\pi R^2 h}{3}} \Rightarrow \dfrac{3\pi r^2 h}{\pi R^2 h}$

$\Rightarrow \dfrac{3r^2}{R^2} \Rightarrow 3 : 4$

18. (c)

The perimeter would remain the same in any case.

Let one side of a square be = a cm

Then $a^2 = 484 \Rightarrow a = 22$ cm $\therefore$ perimeter $= 4a = 88$ cm

Let the radius of the circle be = r cm

Then $2\pi r = 88 \Rightarrow r = 14$ cm

Then area = $\pi r^2 = 616$ cm^2

19. (d)

Let the radius of the circle be = π

Then $\quad 2\pi r - 2r = 16.8 \Rightarrow r = 3.92$ cm

Then $\qquad\quad 2\pi r = 24.6$ cm

20. (d)

Let the radius of the wheel be = π

Then $5000 \times 2\pi r = 1100000$ cm $\Rightarrow r = 35$ cm

21. (a)

Let the slant height be = l

Let radius = r

Then $v = \dfrac{\pi r^2 h}{3} \Rightarrow r = \sqrt{\dfrac{3v}{\pi h}} \Rightarrow \sqrt{\dfrac{3 \times 100\pi}{\pi \times 12}} = 5$ cm

$l = \sqrt{h^2 + r^2} = \sqrt{12^2 + 5^2} = 13$ cm

22. (b)

In 4 days, the short hand covers its circumference
$4 \times 2 = 8$ times long hand covers its circumference
$4 \times 24 = 96$ times
Then they will cover a total distance of:-
$(2 \times \pi \times 4)8 + (2 \times \pi \times 6)96 \Rightarrow 3818.24$ cm

23. (b)

Let the radius of the smaller sphere = r
Then, the radius of the bigger sphere = R
Let the surface area of the smaller sphere = 1
Then, the surface area of the bigger sphere = 4
Then, as per question

$\Rightarrow \dfrac{4\pi r^2}{4\pi R^2} = \dfrac{1}{4} \Rightarrow \dfrac{r}{R} = \dfrac{1}{2} \Rightarrow R = 2r$

Ratio of their volumes

$= \dfrac{4\pi r^3}{3} \times \dfrac{3}{4\pi (2r)^3} \Rightarrow 1:8$

24. (b)

Inner radius(r) = $\dfrac{9}{2}$ = 4.5 cm

Outer radius (R) = $\dfrac{10}{2}$ = 5 cm

Volume of metal contained in the shell = $\dfrac{4\pi R^3 - 4\pi r^3}{3}$

$\Rightarrow \dfrac{4\pi}{3} (R^3 - r^3)$

$\Rightarrow 141.9$ cm³

25. (c)

Let smaller radius (r) = 1
Then bigger radius (R) = 2
Then, as per question

$\Rightarrow \dfrac{4\pi r^2}{4\pi R^2} = \left(\dfrac{r}{R}\right)^2 \Rightarrow \left(\dfrac{1}{2}\right)^2 = 1:4$

26. (c)

As per question $\Rightarrow \dfrac{4\pi r^3}{3} = \dfrac{\pi r^2 h}{3} \Rightarrow h = 4r$

27. (a)

Volume of wall = $1200 \times 500 \times 25 = 15000000$ cm³
Volume of cement = 5% of $15000000 = 750000$ cm³
Remaining volume = $15000000 - 750000$
$= 14250000$ cm³

Volume of a brick = $25 \times 12.5 \times 7.5 = 2343.75$ cm³

Number of bricks used = $\dfrac{14250000}{2343.75} = 6080$

28. (a)

Let the inner radius = r
Then $2\pi r = 352$ m. Then $r = 56$
Then outer radius = $r + 7 = 63 = R$
Now, $\pi R^2 - \pi r^2$ = Area of road
$\Rightarrow \pi(R^2 - r^2) = 2618$ m²

29. (c)

1 hectare = 10000 m²

Height = 10 cm = $\dfrac{1}{10}$ m

Volume = $10000 \times \dfrac{1}{10} = 1000$ m³

30. (a)

Total surface area of 7 cubes $\Rightarrow 7 \times 6a^2 = 1050$
But on joining end to end, 12 sides will be covered.
So there area = $12 \times a^2 \Rightarrow 12 \times 25 = 300$
So the surface area of the resulting figure = $1050 - 300 = 750$

31. (d)

Let the rise in height be = h
Then, as per the question, the volume of water should be equal in both the cases.
Now, $90 \times 40 \times h = 150 \times 8$

$h = \dfrac{150 \times 8}{90 \times 40} = \dfrac{1}{3}$ m = $\dfrac{100}{3}$ cm
$= 33.33$ cm

32. (d)

Slant height (l) = $\sqrt{7^2 + 24^2} = 25$ m
Area of cloth required = covered surface area of cone
$= \pi r l = \dfrac{22}{7} \times 7 \times 25 = 550$ m²

Amount of cloth required = $\dfrac{550}{5} = 110$ m

33. (b)

If the ratio of their diameters = 2 : 1, then the ratio of their radii will also be = 2 : 1
Let the radii of the broader cone = 2 and height be = 1
Then the radii of the smaller cone = 1 and height be = 2

Ratio of volumes = $\dfrac{\pi 2^2 \cdot 1}{3} \div \dfrac{\pi 1^2 \cdot 2}{3}$

$\dfrac{4\pi}{3} \times \dfrac{3}{2\pi} \Rightarrow 2:1$

34. (d)

Area of base = $6 \times 10 = 60$ m²
Volume of tent = $30 \times 10 = 300$ m³

Let the radius be $= r$, height $= h$, slant height $= l$

$$\pi r^2 = 60 \Rightarrow r = \sqrt{\frac{60}{\pi}}$$

$$300 = \frac{\pi r^2 h}{3} \Rightarrow 900 = \pi \cdot \frac{60}{\pi} \cdot h \Rightarrow h = 15 \text{ m}$$

35. (b)
Volume of wood used = External volume – Outer Volume
$\Rightarrow (10 \times 8 \times 6) - (10 - 1) \times (8 - 1) \times (6 - 1)$
$\Rightarrow 480 - (9 \times 7 \times 5) = 165 \text{ cm}^2$

36. (b)
Total volume in both the cones will be equal. Let the number of smaller cubes $= x$

$$x \cdot 3^3 = 24 \times 9 \times 8 \Rightarrow x = \frac{24 \times 72}{27} = 64$$

37. (a)
Let one side of the cube $= a$
Then $\qquad a^3 = 216 \Rightarrow a = 6 \text{ m}$
Area of the resultant figure
= Area of all 3 cubes – Area of covered figure
$\Rightarrow 216 \times 3 - (4 \times a^2) \Rightarrow 648 - 144 \Rightarrow 504 \text{ m}^2$

38. (c)

Volume of metal used $= \dfrac{4\pi R^3}{3} - \dfrac{4\pi r^3}{3}$

$$= \frac{4\pi}{3}(12^3 - 10^3)$$
$$= 3047.89 \text{ cm}^3$$

Weight = volume × density $\Rightarrow 4.9 \times 3047.89$
$$\Rightarrow 14942.28 \text{ gm}$$

39. (d)
Volume of cube $= 7^3 = 343 \text{ cm}^3$

Radius of cone $= \dfrac{7}{2} = 3.5 \text{ cm}$

Height of cone $= 7$

Ratio of volumes $= \dfrac{\frac{\pi r^2 h}{3}}{343} = \dfrac{22 \times 3.5 \times 3.5 \times 7}{7 \times 3 \times 343}$

$\Rightarrow 11:42$

40. (b)
The volume in both the cases will be equal. Let the height of cone be $= h$

$$4 \times \frac{22}{7} \times (14)^3 \times \frac{1}{3} = \frac{22}{7} \times \left(\frac{35}{2}\right)^2 \times \frac{h}{3}$$

$$\Rightarrow \qquad 4(14)^3 = h\left(\frac{35}{2}\right)^2 = h$$

$$= \frac{4 \times 14 \times 14 \times 14 \times 2 \times 2}{35 \times 35}$$

$$= h = 35.84 \text{ cm}$$

41. (b)
Diameter of circle = diagonal of square
$$= \sqrt{10^2 + 10^2} = \sqrt{200} = 10\sqrt{2}$$

$\therefore$ Radius $= \dfrac{10\sqrt{2}}{2} = 5\sqrt{2}$

Area of circle $= \pi r^2 \Rightarrow 50\pi = 50 \times 3.14 = 157.14 \text{ cm}^3$

42. (c)
Area of triangle $= rS$; where r = inradius

$$S = \frac{15 + 8 + 17}{2} = 20 \text{ cm}$$

$$\Delta = \sqrt{S(S-a)(S-b)(S-c)}$$

$$\Rightarrow \Delta\sqrt{20(20-15)(20-8)(20-17)}$$

$$\Delta = \sqrt{20 \times 5 \times 12 \times 3} = 60 \text{ cm}^2$$

$$r = \frac{\Delta}{S} = \frac{60}{20} = 3 \text{ cm}$$

43. (c)
Circumference of the circular face of the cylinder
$= 2\pi r$

$$\Rightarrow 2 \times \frac{22}{7} \times \frac{35}{100} = 2.2 \text{ m}$$

Number of revolutions required to lift the bucket by

$11 \text{ m} = \dfrac{11}{2.2} = 5$

44. (c) Surface area of the cube $= 6a^2 = 6 \times (20)^2$
$$= 2400$$
Area of 6 circles of radius 10 cm $= 6\pi r^2$
$$= 6 \times \pi \times 100$$
$$= 1885.71$$
Remaining area $= 2400 - 1884 = 514.28$

45. (d)
$$x \cdot y \cdot z = lb \times bh \times lh = (lbh)^2$$
(V) Volume of a cuboid $= lbh$
So $\qquad V^2 = (lbh)^2 = xyz$

46. (c)
Diameter of the circle = diagonal of rectangle
$$= \sqrt{8^2 + 6^2} = 10 \text{ cm}$$

Radius $= \dfrac{10}{2} = 5 \text{ cm}$

Area of shaded portion $= \pi r^2 - lb$
$$= 3.14 \times 5^2 - 8 \times 6$$
$$= 30.57 \text{ cm}^2$$

47. (a)
Larger Radius $(R) = 14 + 7 = 21 \text{ cm}$
Smaller Radius $(r) = 7 \text{ cm}$

Area of shaded portion $\pi R^2 \dfrac{\theta}{360} - \dfrac{\pi r^2 \theta}{360}$

$\Rightarrow \dfrac{\pi\theta}{360}(21^2 - 7^2) \Rightarrow 102.67$ cm

48. (b)

Area of quadrilateral = Area of right angled triangle + Area of equilateral triangle $x = \sqrt{20^2 - 12^2} = 16$

Area of quadrilateral = $\left(\dfrac{1}{2} \times 16 \times 12\right) + \dfrac{\sqrt{3}}{4} \times 20 \times 20$

$= 269$ units^2

49. (a)

Height $= \sqrt{24^2 - 13^2} = \sqrt{407}$

Volume $= \dfrac{\text{Area of base} \times \text{height}}{3} \Rightarrow \dfrac{18 \times 26 \times \sqrt{407}}{3}$

$\Rightarrow 156\sqrt{407}$

50. (b)

The perimeter would remain the same in both cases.

Circumference of circle $= 2\pi r = 2 \times \dfrac{22}{7} \times 28 = 176$ cm

Perimeter of square = 176

Greatest side possible $= \dfrac{176}{4} = 44$ cm

Length of diagonal $= \sqrt{44^2 + 44^2} = 62.216$

$= \dfrac{88}{2} \cdot \sqrt{2} = 44\sqrt{2}$

Level of Difficulty (II)

1. (d)

Let the angle subtended by the sector at the centre be $= \theta$

Then,

$5.7 + 5.7 + (2\pi) \times 5.7 \times \dfrac{\theta}{360} = 27.2$

$11.4 + \dfrac{11.4 \times 3.14 \times \theta}{360} = 27.2$

$\Rightarrow \qquad \dfrac{\theta}{360} = 0.44$

Area of the sector $= \pi r^2 \dfrac{\theta}{360} \Rightarrow (22/7) \times (5.7)^2 \times 0.44$

$= 44.92$ approx.

2. (a)

Volume of mud dug out $= 10 \times 4.5 \times 3 = 135$ m^3

Let the remaining ground rise by $= h$ m

Then $\{(20 \times 9) - (10 \times 4.5)\}h = 135$

$135h = 135 \Rightarrow h = 1$ m

3. (b)

Height of the cylinder $= 13 - 7 = 6$ cm

Radius of the cylinder and the hemisphere = 7 cm

Volume of the vessel = volume of cylinder + volume of hemisphere

$\Rightarrow \pi r^2 h + \dfrac{4\pi r^3}{3 \times 2} \Rightarrow 3.14 \times (7)^2 \times 6 + \dfrac{4 \times 3.14 \times (7)^3}{3 \times 2}$

$\Rightarrow 1642.6$ cm^2

4. (b)

Let the original triangle be $= ACD$

Longest side $= AC = 21$cm

In the right angled $\triangle ABD$, by Pythagorean triplets, we get $AB = 5$ and $BD = 12$

Then, $BC = 21 - 5 = 16$

By Pythagoras theorem,

$BD^2 = CD^2 - BC^2 \Rightarrow BD = 12$ cm

Thus, on assumption is correct.

Area of the larger $\triangle BDC = \dfrac{1}{2} \times 16 \times 12 \Rightarrow 96$ cm^2

5. (c)

Radius $= \dfrac{105}{2} = 52.5$ cm

Area of the entire canvas, used for the tent

= Area of cylinder + centre of cone

= $2\pi rh + \pi rl$

= $\pi r(2h + l) = 3.14 \times 52.5 \ (2\sqrt{53^2 - 52.5^2} + 53)$

= $5 \times l$ (because area of canvas $= l \times b$ also)

= $l \Rightarrow 1947$ m

6. (c)

The volume in both the cases would be the same.

Therefore $= \dfrac{4\pi r^3}{3} = \pi r^2 h$

$\dfrac{4 \times 3.14 \times (4 \times 10)^3}{3} = 3.14 \times 2^2 \times h$

$\Rightarrow \qquad h = \dfrac{64000}{3} = 21333.33$ mm

7. (b)

As the cylinder and cone have equal diameters. So they have equal area. Let cone's height be h_2 and as per question, cylinder's height be h_1.

$$\frac{2\pi r h_1}{\pi r \sqrt{h_2^2 + r^2}} = \frac{8}{5}.$$

On solving we get the desired ratio as 3 : 4

8. (a)

Let the slant height of 1st cone = L

Then the slant height of 2nd cone = $3L$

Let the radius of 1st cone = r_1

And let the radius of 2nd cone = r_2

Then, $\qquad \pi r_1 L = 3 \times \pi r_2 \times 3L$

$\Rightarrow \qquad \pi r_1 L = 9\pi r_2 L \Rightarrow r_1 = 9r_2$

Ratio of area of the base

$$\frac{\pi r_1^2}{\pi r_2^2} \Rightarrow \left(\frac{r_1}{r_2}\right)^2 = \left(\frac{9}{1}\right)^2 \Rightarrow 81 : 1$$

9. (c)

Let the internal radius of the cylinder = r

Then, the volume of sphere = Volume of sphere cylinder

$\Rightarrow \qquad \dfrac{4\pi \cdot 6^3}{3} = \pi h(5^2 - r^2)$

$\Rightarrow \qquad \dfrac{864\pi}{3} = 32\pi(25 - r^2)$

$\Rightarrow \qquad r^2 = 16 = r = 4$ cm

So thickness of the cylinder = $5 - 4 = 1$ cm

10. (d)

The volume in both the cases would be the same.

Let the height of the cone = h

Then, external radius = 6 cm

Internal radius = 4 cm

$\Rightarrow \qquad \dfrac{4\pi(6^3 - 4^3)}{3} = \dfrac{\pi \cdot 4^2 \cdot h}{3}$

$\Rightarrow \qquad h = \dfrac{6^3 - 4^3}{4} \Rightarrow h = \dfrac{216 - 64}{4} = 38$ cm

11. (a)

Let arc side of the cube be = a units

Total surface area of 3 cubes = $3 \times 6a^2$
$$= 18a^2$$

Total surface area of cuboid = $18a^2 - 4a^2 = 14a^2$

Ratio = $\dfrac{14a^2}{18a^2} = 7 : 9$

12. (c)

$A = 2(xy + yz + zx)$

$V = xyz$

$A/V = \dfrac{2(xy + yz + zx)}{xyz} = \dfrac{2}{z} + \dfrac{2}{x} + \dfrac{2}{y}$

$\Rightarrow 2\left(\dfrac{1}{x} + \dfrac{1}{y} + \dfrac{1}{z}\right)$

13. (a)

The entire dial of the clock = 360°

Every 5 minutes = $\dfrac{360}{12} = 30°$

So 35 minutes = $30 \times 17 = 210$

Area = $\pi r^2 \times \dfrac{8}{360} = 3.14 \times 100 \times \dfrac{210}{360}$

$\Rightarrow 183.3$ cm^2

14. (a)

Let the radius of the bigger circle = R

Let the radius of the smaller circle = r

Then as per question; $R - r = 6$

Solving through options; only option (a) satisfies this condition.

15. (d)

Radius of cylinder, hemisphere and cone = 5 cm

Height of cylinder = 13 cm

Height of cone = 12 cm

Surface area of toy = $2\pi r h + \dfrac{4\pi r^2}{2} + \pi r L$

$$L = \sqrt{h^2 + r^2} = \sqrt{12^2 + 5^2} = 13$$

Then $\Rightarrow (2 \times 3.14 \times 5 \times 13) + (2 \times 3.14 \times 25) + (3.14 \times 5 \times 13) \Rightarrow 770$ cm^2

16. (b)

Height of cone = $10.2 - 4.2 = 6$ cm

Volume of wood = $\dfrac{\pi r^2 h}{3} + \dfrac{4\pi r^5}{3 \times 2}$

$\Rightarrow \dfrac{3.14 \times (4.2)^2 \times 6}{3} + \dfrac{4 \times 3.14 \times (4.2)^3}{3 \times 2}$

$\Rightarrow 266$ cm^3

17. (a)

Volume of ice cream = $\pi r^2 h$
$$= 3.14 \times (6)^2 \times 15$$
$$= 1695.6 \text{ cm}^2$$

Volume of 1 cone = $\dfrac{\pi r^2 \times 24}{3}$

Then $\Rightarrow 10 \times 3.14 \times r^2 \times 8 = 1695.6$

$\Rightarrow \qquad r = 3$ cm (approx.)

So $\qquad$ diameter = $2 \times r = 6$ cm

18. (b)

Radius of cylinder and hemispheres = $\dfrac{7}{2} = 3.5$ cm

Height of cylinder = $19 - (3.5 \times 2) = 12$ cm

Total surface area of solid = $2\pi r h + 4\pi r^2$

$\Rightarrow 2 \times 3.14 \times 3.5 \times 12 + 4 \times 3.14 \times (3.5)^2$

$\Rightarrow 418$ cm^2

19. (c)
As they stand on the same base so their radius is also same.

Then; volume of cone = $\dfrac{\pi r^2 h}{3}$

Volume of hemisphere = $\dfrac{2\pi r^2}{3}$

Volume of cylinder = $\pi r^2 h$

Ratio = $\dfrac{\pi r^2 h}{3} : \dfrac{2\pi r^3}{3} : \pi r^2 h$

$\Rightarrow \qquad \dfrac{h}{3} : \dfrac{2r}{3} : h$

$\Rightarrow \qquad h : 2r : 3h$

Radius of a hemisphere = Its height
So $\qquad h : 2h : 3h \Rightarrow 1 : 2 : 3$

20. (d)
Total surface to be painted
= external surface area + internal surface + surface area of ring area
$\Rightarrow 2\pi R^2 + 2\pi r^2 = 2\pi(R^2 + r^2) + 2\pi(R^2 - r^2)$

Cost of painting

$\Rightarrow 2 \times 3.14 \times \left\{ \left(\dfrac{25}{2}\right)^2 + \left(\dfrac{24}{2}\right)^2 + \left(\dfrac{25}{2}\right)^2 - \left(\dfrac{24}{2}\right)^2 \right\}$
$\hspace{9cm} \times 0.05$

$\Rightarrow 2 \times 6.28 \times (12.5)^2 \times 0.05 = ₹\ 96.28$

21. (e)
Radius = $\dfrac{3.5}{2} = 1.75$ cm

Volume of solid = $\pi r^2 h + \dfrac{\pi r^2 h}{3} + \dfrac{2\pi r^3}{3}$

$\Rightarrow \pi r^2 \left(h + \dfrac{h}{3} + \dfrac{r}{3} \right)$

$\Rightarrow 3.14 \times (1.75)^2 \times \left(10 + \dfrac{6}{3} + \dfrac{1.75}{3} \right)$

$\Rightarrow 121$ cm^3

22. (d)
Area of shaded portion = Area of quadrant – Area of triangle

$\Rightarrow \dfrac{\pi r^2}{4} - \dfrac{1}{2} \times 3.5 \times 2 = \dfrac{3.14 \times (3.5)^2}{4} - 3.5$

$\Rightarrow 6.1$ cm^2

23. (c)
ABC is an equilateral triangle with sides = 2 cm
Area of shaded portion = Area of equilateral triangle
–Area of 3 quadrant

$\Rightarrow$ i.e. $\dfrac{\sqrt{3}}{4} a^2 - 3 \left(\pi r^2 \dfrac{\theta}{360} \right)$; $\theta = 60°$ ($\because$ *A*, *B*, *C* is an equilateral triangle)

$\Rightarrow \dfrac{\sqrt{3}}{4} \times 2^2 - 3 \left(3.14 \times 1 \times \dfrac{60}{360} \right)$

$\Rightarrow \sqrt{3} - \dfrac{3.14}{2} = \sqrt{3} - \dfrac{\pi}{2}$

24. (d)
Volume of the elliptical cylinder

$= \pi \times \dfrac{2.4}{2} \times \dfrac{1.6}{2} \times 7$

$= 3.14 \times 1.2 \times 0.8 \times 7 \Rightarrow 9$ m^3

Amount of water emptied per minute

$= 120 \times 3.14 \times \left(\dfrac{2}{100} \right)^2$

Time required to empty half the tank

$= \dfrac{4.5}{120 \times 3.14 \times (0.02)^2} = 70$ min

25. (e)

Triangles

AB and *DC* are the parallel sides
Height = *AM* = *BN*
$\qquad AB = MN = 4$

ΔBNC and ΔAMD are right angled triangles

In $\Delta BNC \Rightarrow \sin 30 = \dfrac{BN}{10} \Rightarrow BN = 5$

Using Pythagoras theorem $NC = \sqrt{10^2 - 5^2} = 5\sqrt{3}$

In ΔADM; $AM = 5$; $\tan 45 = \dfrac{AM}{DM} = 1 = \dfrac{5}{DM}$

$\Rightarrow \qquad DM = 5$

Area of trapezium $\Rightarrow \dfrac{1}{2}$ (Sum of 11 sides) $\times$ height

$\Rightarrow \dfrac{1}{2} (4 + 4 + 5\sqrt{3} + 5) \times 5 = \dfrac{5(13 + 5\sqrt{3})}{2}$ (Answer)

26. (d)

$PQ = QR = RS = \dfrac{12}{3} = 4$ cm

Area of unshaded region $\Rightarrow \dfrac{\pi 6^2}{2} + \dfrac{\pi 4^2}{2}$

$\Rightarrow 18\pi + 8\pi \Rightarrow 26\pi$

Area of shaded region $\Rightarrow \dfrac{\pi 6^2}{2} - \dfrac{\pi 4^2}{2}$

$\Rightarrow 18\pi - 8\pi = 10\pi$

Ratio $= \dfrac{10\pi}{26\pi} \Rightarrow \dfrac{5}{13} \Rightarrow 5:13$

27. (c)

$QP = \sqrt{5^2 + 12^2} = 13$

Area of the triangle $= \dfrac{1}{2} \times b \times h = 30$

$\Rightarrow$ As Rx is $a \perp$ drawn to the hypotenuse

So $Rx = \dfrac{2 \times \text{Area}}{\text{Hypotenuse}} = \dfrac{60}{13}$

28. (d)

Let initial area $= \pi$

Then volume $= \pi r^2 h$

New radius $= \pi + \dfrac{\pi}{2} \Rightarrow \dfrac{3\pi}{2}$

New volume $= \pi - \dfrac{9}{4} r^2 h$

Increased volume $= \dfrac{5}{4} \pi r^2 h$

Percent increase $= \dfrac{5\pi r^2 h}{4\pi r^2 h} \times 100 = 125\%$

29. Distance after 4 hours $= AB = C$

$a = 3 \times 4 = 12$; $b = 2 \times 4 = 8$

and $\dfrac{a+b+c}{2} \Rightarrow \dfrac{12+8+C}{2} \Rightarrow \left(\dfrac{10+C}{2}\right)$

Area $= \sqrt{S(S-a)(S-b)(S-c)}$

Area $= \dfrac{1}{2} ab \sin 120°$

Area $\Rightarrow 48 \times \dfrac{\sqrt{3}}{2} = 24\sqrt{3}$

As per question:

$24\sqrt{3} = \sqrt{\left(10 + \dfrac{c}{2}\right)\left(\dfrac{c}{2} - 2\right)\left(2 + \dfrac{c}{2}\right)\left(10 - \dfrac{c}{2}\right)}$

On solving, we get $c = 4\sqrt{19}$ km

30. (c)

Volume of the cone $= \dfrac{\pi r^2 h}{3} \Rightarrow \dfrac{3.14 \times 20 \times 20 \times 24}{3}$

$\Rightarrow 10048$ cm^3

Diameter of pipe $= 5$ m

Volume of water flowing out of the pipe per minute

$\Rightarrow 10 \times (2.5)^2 \times 3.14 \Rightarrow 196.25$ cm^3

Time taken to fill the tank $= \dfrac{10048}{196.25} = 51.2$ mins

31. (d)

One side of the equilateral triangle = diameter of cone.

Therefore radius of cone $= \dfrac{12}{2} = 6$

Height of cone = Height of equilateral triangle be

$\because$ Height of cone $= \dfrac{\sqrt{3}a}{2} = 6\sqrt{3}$

Volume of cone $= \dfrac{\pi r^2 h}{3}$

$\Rightarrow$ $\dfrac{\pi \times 6^2 \times 6\sqrt{3}}{3} = 72\sqrt{3}\pi$ cm^3

32. (b)

Let the radius of iron ball $= r_1$

Let the radius of oak ball $= r_0$

Then, as iron weights 8 times more than Oak

$\therefore$ $\dfrac{4\pi r_0^3}{3} = \dfrac{8 \times 4\pi r_1^3}{3} = \dfrac{r_0}{r_1} = 2 \Rightarrow r_0 = 2r_1$

So diameter of iron $= \dfrac{1}{2}$ diameter of oak

$\Rightarrow$ $\dfrac{1}{2} \times 18 = 9$ cm

33. (a)

Area of shaded portion = Area of ADC – Area of sector DC + Area of $\triangle ADB$ – sector BED

$\Rightarrow$ Area of $ADC = \pi \times (17.5)^2 \times \dfrac{1}{2} = 481$ cm^2

$\dfrac{\angle DBC}{\angle ABC} = \dfrac{21}{28} \Rightarrow \angle DBC = 67.5$ and $\angle DBA = 22.5$

$\Rightarrow$ Area of sector $DC = \left(\pi \times 21^2 \times \dfrac{67.5}{360}\right)$

$-\left(\dfrac{1}{2} \times 21^2 \times Sin 67.5\right) = 56$ cm^2

$\Rightarrow$ Area of $ADE = \left(\frac{1}{2} \times 28 \times 21\right)$

$- \left(204 + \frac{1}{2} \times 21^2 \times \sin 22.5\right) = 5.6$ cm^2

Thus area of shaded portion = 480 – 56 + 5.6 = 429 cm^2

34. (a)

KJ = radius of semicircles = 10 cm

4 Quadrants of equal radius = 1 circle of that radius

Area of shaded portion $\Rightarrow$ Area of rectangle – Area of circle

$\Rightarrow (28 \times 26) - (3.14 \times 10^2) \Rightarrow 414$ cm^2

$BC = 28 - (10 + 10) = 8$ and $EF = 26 - (10 + 10) = 6$

Perimeter of shaded portion = 28 cm + $2\pi r$

Answer $\Rightarrow$ 414 cm^2 = Area and

Perimeter = 90.8

35. (d)

Go through the option

Only option (d) is correct.

36. (c)

Area of remaining cardboard = Area of trapezium

– Area of quadrant

$\Rightarrow$ Area of trapezium = $\frac{1}{2}$(sum of parallel sides)

$\times$ height

$= \frac{1}{2} \times (AB + DC) \times BC$

$\Rightarrow \frac{1}{2} \times (3.5 + 5.5) \times 3.5$

$= 4.5 \times 3.5 = 15.75$ cm^2

Area of quadrant $= \frac{\pi r^2}{4} \Rightarrow \frac{3.14 \times 3.5 \times 3.5}{4} = 9.6$

$\Rightarrow$ Area of remaining cardboard = 15.7 – 9.6 = 6.1 cm^2

37. (c)

Circumference of the 2 semicircles = 21 – (90 + 90)

= 132

2 semicircles = 1 circle with equal radius

So $2\pi r = 132 \Rightarrow 2r = \frac{132}{3.14} \Rightarrow 42$ m diameter

Area of track = Area within external border – Area within internal border

$\Rightarrow \pi(23^2 - 21^2) + 90 \times 46 - 90 \times 4^2$

$\Rightarrow 88\pi + 360 \Rightarrow 636.3$ m^2

38. (d)

AB = side of the outermost triangle = a

$AC = CB = a/2$

$HC = \sqrt{\frac{a^2}{4} + \frac{a^2}{4}} = \frac{a}{\sqrt{2}}$

Diameter of circle $= \frac{a}{\sqrt{2}}$; radius $= \frac{a}{2\sqrt{2}}$

O is the centre of the circle. Then $\angle EOF = 120°$

Then Area of $\Delta EOF = \frac{1}{2} EO \cdot OF \cdot \sin 120°$

$\Rightarrow \quad \frac{1}{2} \times \frac{a^2}{8} \times \frac{\sqrt{3}}{2} = \frac{\sqrt{3}a^2}{32}$

Then area of $\Delta EFG = \frac{3\sqrt{3}a^2}{32}$

39. (a)

The length of rope of goat = $10\sqrt{2}$ m

Then the two goats will graze an area = Area of a semicircle with area $10\sqrt{2}$ m.

So total area grazed $= \frac{\pi r^2}{2} \Rightarrow 100\pi$ m^2

40. (a)

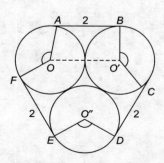

In this figure, the sides $AB = CD = FE$ = distance between 2 radii = 2 cm

$\angle AOP = \angle BO'C = \angle EO''D = 120°$

So perimeter of the bigger triangle = (2 + 2 + 2 + 2 × 3.14 × 1) (because 3 sectors of circles of 120° = 1 full circle of same radius)

Let the radius of longer circle be = R

Then $2 \times \pi \times R = 12.28 \Rightarrow R = \dfrac{12.28}{2 \times 3.14} = 2$

Area = $AR^2 \Rightarrow 3.14 \times 4 \Rightarrow 13$ cm² (approximately)

Option (a) is closest to the answer.

41. (b)

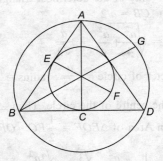

Let arc side of equilateral triangle = a

Then height = $\dfrac{a\sqrt{3}}{2}$

Area = $\dfrac{\sqrt{3}}{2}a^2$; $S = \dfrac{a+a+a}{2} = \dfrac{3a}{2}$

Diameter of inner circle = $\dfrac{2 \times \text{Area}}{5}$

$= \dfrac{\sqrt{3}}{2}a^2 \times \dfrac{2}{3a} = \dfrac{a}{\sqrt{3}}$

Diameter of outer circle = $\dfrac{a^3}{2 \times \text{Area}} = a^3 \times \dfrac{a}{\sqrt{3}a^2}$

$\Rightarrow \dfrac{2a}{\sqrt{3}}$

Ratio = $\dfrac{a}{\sqrt{3}} : \dfrac{2a}{\sqrt{3}} : \dfrac{a\sqrt{3}}{2} \Rightarrow$ Ratio = 1 : 2 : 3

42. (b)

Sum of interior angles of a hexagon = 120°

6 sectors with same radius o = 2 full circles of same radius

So area of shaded region $\Rightarrow 2\pi r^2$

43. (d)

44. (a)

$AO = CO = DO = OB$ = radius of bigger circle = r(let)

Then area of $(G + F) = \dfrac{\pi r^2}{2}$

Area of $2(G + F) = \pi r^2$. Also area of $2G + F + E = \pi r^2$

i.e. $2G + F + F = 2G + F + E \Rightarrow F = E$

So the ratio of areas E and F = 1 : 1

45. (c)

Space for Rough Work

Extra Practice Exercise
on Geometry and Mensuration

1. In the figure given what is the measure of $\angle ACD$

   (a) 75° (b) 80°
   (c) 90° (d) 105°

2. Two circles C_1 and C_2 of radius 2 and 3 respectively touch each other as shown in the figure. If AD and BD are tangents then the length of BD is

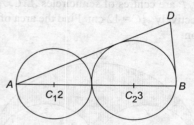

   (a) $3\sqrt{6}$ (b) $5\sqrt{6}$
   (c) $(7\sqrt{6})/3$ (d) 6

3. If the sides of a triangle measure 13, 14, 15 cm respectively, what is the height of the triangle for the base side 14.
   (a) 10 (b) 12
   (c) 14 (d) 13

4. A right angled triangle is drawn on a plane such that sides adjacent to right angle are 3 cm and 4 cm. Now three semi-circles are drawn taking all three sides of the triangle as diameters respectively (as shown in the figure). What is the area of the shaded regions $A_1 + A_2$

   (a) 3π (b) 4π
   (c) 5π (d) None of these

5. A lateral side of an isosceles triangle is 15 cm and the altitude is 8 cm. What is the radius of the circumscribed circle

   (a) 9.625 (b) 9.375
   (c) 9.5 (d) 9.125

6. Let a, b, c be the length of the sides of triangle ABC. Given $(a + b + c)(b + c - a) = \alpha bc$. Then the value of α will lie in between
   (a) −1 and 1 (b) 0 and 4
   (c) 0 and 1 (d) 0 and

7. In the figure given below (not drawn to scale). A, B and C are three points on a circle with centre O. The chord BC is extended to point T such that AT becomes a tangent to the circle at point A. If $\angle CTA = 35°$ and $\angle CAT = 45°$ calculate $x°$ ($\angle BOC$)

   (a) 100° (b) 90°
   (c) 110° (d) 65°

8. In the given figure

   $AB = 20$
   $BC = 15$
   $CA = 19$
   Calculate a, b, c.
   (a) $a = 12, b = 8, c = 7$
   (b) $a = 8, b = 12, c = 7$
   (c) $a = 9, b = 10, c = 15$
   (d) $a = 10, b = 15, c = 9$

9. In the figure given below, AB is perpendicular to ED. $\angle CED = 75°$ and $\angle ECF = 30°$. What is the measure of $\angle ABC$?

(a) 60°   (b) 45°
(c) 55°   (d) 30°

10. The angle between lines *L* and *M* measures 35° degrees. If line *M* is rotated 45° degrees counter clockwise about point *P* to line *M*¹ what is the angle in degrees between lines *L* and *M*¹

(a) 90°   (b) 80°
(c) 75°   (d) 60°

11. In the figure given below, *XYZ* is a right angled triangle in which ∠*Y* = 45° and ∠*X* = 90°. *ABCD* is a square inscribed in it whose area is 64 cm². What is the area of triangle *XYZ*?

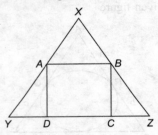

(a) 100   (b) 64
(c) 144   (d) 81

12. The area of circle circumscribed about a regular hexagon is 144π. What is the area of hexagon?

(a) $300\sqrt{3}$ (b) $216\sqrt{3}$
(c) 256   (d) 225

13. Find the area of the shaded portion

(a) 4 − π   (b) 6 − π
(c) 5 − π   (d) π

14. The numerical value of the product of the three sides (which are integers when measured in cm) of a right angled triangle having a perimeter of 56 cm is 4200. Find the length of the hypotenuse.

(a) 24   (b) 25
(c) 15   (d) 30

15. In the figure *ABDC* is a cyclic quadrilateral with *O* as centre of the circle. Find ∠*BDC*.

(a) 105°   (b) 120°
(c) 130°   (d) 95°

16. *B, O, P* are centres of semicircles *AXC, AYB* & *BZC* respectively. *AC* = 12 cm. Find the area of the shaded region.

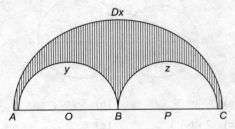

(a) 9π   (b) 18π
(c) 20π   (d) 25π

17. *O* is the centre of the circle. *OP* = 5 and *OT* = 4, and *AB* = 8. The line *PT* is a tangent to the circle. Find *PB*

(a) 9 cm   (b) 10 cm
(c) 7 cm   (d) 8 cm

18. In the figure given below, *AB* = 16, *CD* = 12 and *OM* = 6. Calculate *ON*.

(a) 8   (b) 10
(c) 12   (d) 14

19. In the figure, M is the centre of the circle. $l(QS) = 10\sqrt{2}$, $l(PR) = l(RS)$ and PR is parallel to QS. Find the area of the shaded region.

   (a) $90\pi - 90$ (b) $50\pi - 100$

   (c) $150\pi - 150$ (d) $125\pi - 125$

20. In the given figure PBC and PKH are straight lines. If $AH = AK$, $b = 70°$, $c = 40°$, the value of d is

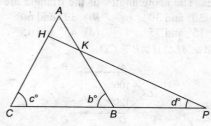

   (a) $20°$ (b) $25°$

   (c) $15°$ (d) $35°$

21. In the given figure, circle AXB passes through 'O' the centre of circle AYB. AX and BX and AY and BY are tangents to the circles AYB and AXB respectively. The value of $y°$ is

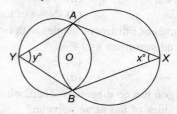

   (a) $180° - x°$,   (b) $180° - 2x°$

   (c) $½ (90° - x°)$ (d) $90° - (x°/2)$

22. In the figure, $AB = x$
Calculate the area of triangle ADC ($\angle B = 90°$)

   (a) $½ x^2 \sin 30°$ (b) $½ x^2 \cos 30°$

   (c) $½ x^2 \tan 30°$ (d) $½ x^2(\tan 45° - \tan 30°)$

23. In the given figure $SQ = TR = a$, $QT = b$, $QM \perp PR$, ST is parallel to PR.

$m \angle STQ = 30°$
$m \angle SQT = 90°$

Find QM.

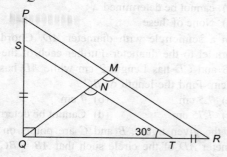

   (a) $(a + b)/2$ (b) $2(a + b)$

   (c) $(2a + b)/2$ (d) $(a + 2b)/2$

24. In the figure given, AB is a diameter of the circle and C and D are on the circumference such that $\angle CAD = 40°$. Find the measure of the $\angle ACD$

   (a) $40°$ (b) $50°$

   (c) $60°$ (d) None of these

25. Six solid hemispherical balls have to be arranged one upon the other vertically. Find the minimum total surface area of the cylinder in which the hemispherical balls can be arranged, if the radii of each hemispherical ball is 7 cm.

   (a) 2056   (b) 2156

   (c) 1232   (d) None of these

Questions 26 and 27: In the following figure, there is a cone which is being cut and extracted in three segments having heights h_1, h_2 and h_3 and the radius of their bases 1 cm, 2 cm and 3 cm respectively, then

26. The ratio of the volumes of the smallest segment to that of the largest segment is

   (a) $1 : 27$ (b) $27 : 1$

   (c) $1 : 19$ (d) None of these

27. The ratio of the curved surface area of the second largest segment to that of the full cone is:
    (a) 2 : 9   (b) 4 : 9
    (c) cannot be determined
    (d) None of these

28. On a semicircle with diameter *AD*, Chord *BC* is parallel to the diameter. Further each of the chords *AB* and *CD* has Length 2 cm while *AD* has length 8 cm. Find the length of *BC*.
    (a) 7.5 cm   (b) 7 cm
    (c) 7.75 cm   (d) Cannot be determined

29. In the given figure, *B* and *C* are points on the diameter *AD* of the circle such that *AB* = *BC* = *CD*. Then find the ratio of area of the shaded portion to that of the whole circle.

    (a) 1 : 3   (b) 2 : 3
    (c) 1 : 2   (d) None of these

30. In the given figure, *ABC* is a triangle in which *AD* and *DE* are medians to *BC* and *AB* respectively, the ratio of the area of Δ*BED* to that of Δ*ABC* is

    (a) 1 : 4   (b) 1 : 16
    (c) Data inadequate   (d) None of these

31. Two identical circles intersect so that their centres, and the points at which they intersect, from a square of side 1 cm. The area in square cm of the portion that is common to the two circles is
    (a) π/4   (b) $\pi/2 - 1$
    (c) π/5   (d) $\sqrt{2} - 1$

32. If the height of a cone is trebled and its base diameter is doubled, then the ratio of the volume of the resultant cone to that of the original cone is
    (a) 9 : 1   (b) 9 : 2
    (c) 12 : 1   (d) 6 : 1

33. If two cylinders of equal volume have their heights in the ratio 2 : 3, then the ratio of their radii is
    (a) $\sqrt{3} : \sqrt{2}$ (b) 2 : 3
    (c) $\sqrt{5} : \sqrt{3}$ (d) $\sqrt{6} : \sqrt{3}$

34. Through three given non-collinear points, how many circles can pass.
    (a) 2   (b) 3
    (c) Both 1 and 2   (d) None of these

35. The area of the rectangle *ABCD* is 2 and *BD* = *DE*. Find the area of the shaded region

    (a) $\sqrt{5}$ (b) $2\sqrt{5}$
    (c) $\sqrt{(5/2)}$ (d) 1

36. In a right-angled triangle, the square of the hypotenuse is equal to twice the product of the other two sides. The acute angles of the triangle are
    (a) 30° and 30°   (b) 30° and 60°
    (c) 15° and 75°   (d) 45° and 45°

37. Find ∠*ALC* if *AB* ∥ *CD*

    (a) 75   (b) 135
    (c) 110   (d) 145

38. If the sides of a triangle are in the ratio of ½ : $^1/_3$: ¼ , the perimeter is 52 cm, then the length of the smallest side is
    (a) 12 cm   (b) 11 cm
    (c) 8 cm   (d) None of these

39. The number of distinct triangles with integral valued sides and perimeter as 14 is
    (a) 2   (b) 3
    (c) 4   (d) 5

40. A polygon has 65 diagonals. Then, what is the number of sides of the same polygon?
    (a) 11   (b) 12
    (c) 14   (d) None of these

41. *PQRS* is a square drawn inside square *ABCD* of side 2*x* units by joining the midpoints of the sides *AB*, *BC*, *CD*, *DA*. The square *TUVW* is drawn inside *PQRS*, where *T*, *U*, *V*, *W* are the midpoints of *SP*, *PQ*, *QR* and ₹ If the process is repeated an infinite number of times the sum of the areas of all the squares will be equal to:

(a) $8x^2$ (b) $6x^2$

(c) $16x^2$ (d) $6x^2/2$

42. Suppose the same thing is done with an equilateral triangle of side x, wherein the mid points of the sides are connected to each other to form a second triangle and the mid points of the sides of the second triangle are connected to form a third triangle and so on an infinite number of times—then the sum of the areas of all such equilateral triangles would be:

(a) $3x^2$ (b) $6x^2$

(c) $12x^2$ (d) None of these

43. If in the figure given below $OP = PQ = 28$ cm and OQ, PQ and OP are all joined by semicircles, then the perimeter of the figure (shaded area) is equal to

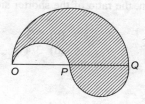

(a) 352 cm   (b) 264 cm

(c) 176 cm   (d) 88 cm

44. For the question above, what is the shaded area?

(a) 1352 sq. cm   (b) 1264 sq. cm

(c) 1232 sq. cm   (d) 1188 sq. cm

45. What is the area of the shaded portion? It is given that $ZV\|XY$, $WZ = ZX$, $ZV = 2a$ and $ZX = 2b$.

(a) $\dfrac{4ab}{2}$ (b) $\dfrac{8ab}{3}$

(c) $6ab$ (d) $3ab$

46. In the given figure there is an isosceles triangle ABC with angle A = angle C = 50° $ABDE$ and $BCFG$ are two rectangles drawn on the sides AB and BC respectively, such that $BD = BG = AE = CF$.

Find the value of the angle DBG.

(a) 80°   (b) 120°

(c) 100°   (d) 140°

47. In the figure, ABE, DCE, BCF and ADF are straight lines. $E = 50°$, $F = 56°$, find $\angle A$.

(a) 47°   (b) 37°

(c) 40°   (d) 42°

48. ABC is an equilateral triangle. $PQRS$ is a square inscribed in it. Therefore

(a) $AR^2 = RC^2$ (b) $2AR^2 = RC^2$

(c) $3AR^2 = 4RC^2$ (d) $4AR^2 = 3RC^2$

49. Consider the five points comprising the vertices of a square and the intersection point of its diagonals. How many triangles can be formed using these points?

(a) 4   (b) 6

(c) 8   (d) 10

50. In a triangle ABC, the internal bisector of the angle A meets BC at D. If $AB = 4$, $AC = 3$ and $\angle A = 60°$. Then, the length of AD is:

(a) $2\sqrt{3}$ (b) $(12\sqrt{3})/7$

(c) $(15\sqrt{3})/8$ (d) $(6\sqrt{3})/7$

Directions for Questions 51 and 52: Answer the questions based on the following information.

A rectangle $PRSU$, is divided into two smaller rectangles $PQTU$ and $QRST$ by the line QT. $PQ = 40$ cm. $QR = 20$ cm, and $RS = 40$cm. Points A, B, F are within rectangle $PQTU$, and points C, D, E are within the rectangle $QRST$. The closest pair of points among the pairs (A, C), (A, D), (A, E), (F, C), (F, D), (F, E), (B, C), (B, D), (B, E) are 40 $\sqrt{3}$ cm apart.

51. Which of the following statements is necessarily true?

(a) The closest pair of points among the six given points cannot be (F, C).

(b) Distance between A and B is greater than that between F and C.

(c) The closest pair of points among the six given points is (C, D), (D, E) or (C, E).

(d) None of the above.

52. $AB > AF > BF$; $CD > DE > CE$; and $BF = 24\sqrt{5}$ cm. Which is the closest pair of points among all the six given points?

(a) B, F (b) C, D

(c) A, B (d) None of these

53. If $ABCD$ is a square and CDE is an equilateral triangle, what is the measure of $\angle DEB$?

(a) $15°$ (b) $30°$

(c) $20°$ (d) $45°$

54. $AB \perp BC$, $BD \perp AC$ and CE bisects $\angle C$, $\angle A = 30°$. Then, what is $\angle CED$?

(a) $30°$ (b) $60°$

(c) $45°$ (d) $65°$

55. Instead of walking along two adjacent sides of a rectangular field, a boy took a short cut along the diagonal and saved a distance equal to half the longer side. Then, the ratio of the shorter side to the longer side is:

(a) $1/2$ (b) $2/3$

(c) $1/4$ (d) $3/4$

Space for Rough Work

ANSWER KEY

1. (b)	2. (c)	3. (b)	4. (d)
5. (b)	6. (b)	7. (c)	8. (a)
9. (b)	10. (b)	11. (c)	12. (b)
13. (a)	14. (b)	15. (c)	16. (a)
17. (a)	18. (a)	19. (b)	20. (c)
21. d	22. (d)	23. (a)	24. (d)

25. (b)	26. (c)	27. (a)	28. (b)
29. (a)	30. (a)	31. (b)	32. (c)
33. (a)	34. (d)	35. (d)	36. (d)
37. (b)	38. (a)	39. (c)	40. (d)
41. (a)	42. (d)	43. (c)	44. (c)
45. (c)	46. (a)	47. (b)	48. (d)
49. (c)	50. (b)	51. (d)	52. (d)
53. (a)	54. (b)	55. (d)	

12 Chapter

Coordinate Geometry

From the CAT point of view, Coordinate Geometry by itself is not a very significant chapter. Basically, applied questions are asked in the form of tabular representation or regarding the shape of the structure formed. However, it is advised to go through the basics and important formulae to have a feel-good effect as also to be prepared for surprises, if any, in the examination. Logical questions might be asked based on the formulae and concepts contained in this chapter. Besides, the student will have an improved understanding of the graphical representation of functions if he/she has gone through coordinate geometry.

The students who face any problems in this chapter can stop after solving LOD II instead of getting frustrated.

CARTESIAN COORDINATE SYSTEM

Rectangular Coordinate Axes

Let $X'OX$ and $Y'OY$ be two mutually perpendicular lines through any point O in the plane of the paper. Point O is known as the origin. The line $X'OX$ is called the x-axis or axis of x; the line $Y'OY$ is known as the y-axis or axis of y; and the two lines taken together are called the coordinate axes or the axes of coordinates.

Fig. 12.1

Any point can be represented on the plane described by the coordinate axes by specifying its x and y coordinates.

The x coordinate of the point is also known as the abscissa while the y coordinate is also known as the ordinate.

1. Distance Formula If two points P and Q are such that they are represented by the points (x_1, y_1) and (x_2, y_2) on the x-y plane (cartesian plane), then the distance between the points P and $Q = \sqrt{(x_1 - x_2)^2 + (y_1 - y_2)^2}$.

Illustration

Question 1: Find the distance between the points $(5, 2)$ and $(3, 4)$.

Answer: Distance $= \sqrt{(5 - 3)^2 + (2 - 4)^2}$

$$\left[\text{Using the formula } \sqrt{(x_1 - x_2)^2 + (y_1 - y_2)^2} \right]$$

$$= 2\sqrt{2} \text{ units}$$

2. Section Formula If any point (x, y) divides the line segment joining the points (x_1, y_1) and (x_2, y_2) in the ratio $m:n$ internally,

then

$$x = (mx_2 + nx_1)/(m + n)$$
$$y = (my_2 + ny_1)/(m + n) \qquad \text{(See figure)}$$

A (x_1, y_1) *m*   *P*   *n*   *B* (x_2, y_2)

Fig. 12.2

If any point (x, y) divides the line segment joining the points (x_1, y_1) and (x_2, y_2) in the ratio $m:n$ externally,

then

$$x = (mx_2 - nx_1)/(m - n)$$
$$y = (my_2 - ny_1)/(m - n)$$

Illustration

Question 2: Find the point which divides the line segment joining (2, 5) and (1, 2) in the ratio 2:1 internally.

Answers: $X = (2.1 + 1.2)/(1 + 2) = 4/3$

$Y = (2.2 + 1.5)/(2 + 1) = 9/3 = 3$

3. Area of a Triangle The area of a triangle whose vertices are $A(x_1, y_1)$, $B(x_2, y_2)$ and $C(x_3, y_3)$ is given by

$$\left[\frac{\{x_1(y_2 - y_3) + x_2(y_3 - y_1) + x_3(y_1 - y_2)\}}{2} \right]$$

Fig. 12.3

[**Note:** Since the area cannot be negative, we have to take the modulus value given by the above equation.]

Corollary: If one of the vertices of the triangle is at the origin and the other two vertices are $A(x_1, y_1)$, $B(x_2, y_2)$, then the area of triangle is $\left| \dfrac{(x_1 y_2 - x_2 y_1)}{2} \right|$.

Illustration

Question 3: Find the area of the triangle (0, 4), (3, 6) and (–8, –2).

Answer: Area of triangle $= |1/2 \{0 (6 - (-2)) + 3 ((-2) -4) + (-8)(4-6)\}|$

$= |1/2 \{(0) + 3 (-6) + (-8)(-2)\}|$

$= |1/2 (-2)| = |-1| = 1$ square unit.

4. Centre of Gravity or Centroid of a Triangle The centroid of a triangle is the point of intersection of its medians (the line joining the vertex to the middle point of the opposite side). Centroid divides the medians in the ratio 2:1. In other words, the CG or the centroid can be viewed as a point at which the whole weight of the triangle is concentrated.

Formula: If $A(x_1, y_1)$, $B(x_2, y_2)$ and $C(x_3, y_3)$ are the coordinates of the vertices of a triangle, then the coordinates of the centroid G of that triangle are

$$x = (x_1 + x_2 + x_3)/3 \text{ and } y = (y_1 + y_2 + y_3)/3$$

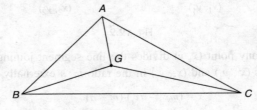

Fig. 12.4

Illustration

Question 4: Find the centroid of the triangle whose vertices are (5, 3), (4, 6) and (8, 2).

Answer: X coordinate $= (5 + 4 + 8)/3 = 17/3$

Y coordinate $= (3 + 6 + 2)/3 = 11/3$

5. In-centre of a Triangle The centre of the circle that touches the sides of a triangle is called its In-centre. In other words, if the three sides of the triangle are tangential to the circle then the centre of that circle represents the in-centre of the triangle.

The in-centre is also the point of intersection of the internal bisectors of the angles of the triangle. The distance of the in-centre from the sides of the triangle is the same and this distance is called the in-radius of the triangle.

If $A(x_1, y_1)$, $B(x_2, y_2)$ and $C(x_3, y_3)$ are the coordinates of the vertices of a triangle, then the coordinates of its in-centre are

$$x = \frac{(ax_1 + bx_2 + cx_3)}{(a+b+c)} \quad \text{and} \quad y = \frac{(ay_1 + by_2 + cy_3)}{(a+b+c)}$$

where $BC = a$, $AB = c$ and $AC = b$.

Fig. 12.5

Illustration

Question 5: Find the in-centre of the right angled isosceles triangle having one vertex at the origin and having the other two vertices at (6, 0) and (0, 6).

Answer: Obviously, the length of the two sides AB and BC of the triangle is 6 units and the length of the third side is $(6^2 + 6^2)^{1/2}$.

Hence $a = c = 6$, $b = 6\sqrt{2}$

Fig. 12.6

In-centre will be at

$$\frac{(6.0 + 6\sqrt{2}.0 + 6.6)}{(6 + 6 + \sqrt{2})}, \frac{(6.6 + 6\sqrt{2}.0 + 6.0)}{(6 + 6 + \sqrt{2})}$$

$$= \frac{36}{12 + 6\sqrt{2}}, \frac{36}{12 + 6\sqrt{2}}$$

6. Circumcentre of a Triangle The point of intersection of the perpendicular bisectors of the sides of a triangle is called its circumcentre. It is equidistant from the vertices of the triangle. It is also known as the centre of the circle which passes through the three vertices of a triangle (or the centre of the circle that circumscribes the triangle.)

Let ABC be a triangle. If O is the circumcentre of the triangle ABC, then $OA = OB = OC$ and each of these three represent the circum radius.

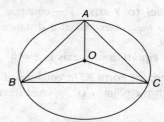

Fig. 12.7

Illustration

Question 6: What will be the circumcentre of a triangle whose sides are $3x - y + 3 = 0$, $3x + 4y + 3 = 0$ and $x + 3y + 11 = 0$?

Answer: Let ABC be the triangle whose sides AB, BC and CA have the equations $3x - y + 3 = 0$, $3x + 4y + 3 = 0$ and $x + 3y + 11 = 0$ respectively.

Solving the equations, we get the points A, B and C as $(-2, -3)$, $(-1, 0)$ and $(7, -6)$ respectively.

The equation of a line perpendicular to BC is $4x - 3y + k = 0$.

[For students unaware of this formula, read the section on straight lines later in the chapter.]

This will pass through $(3, -3)$, the mid-point of BC, if $12 + 9 + k = 0 \Rightarrow k = -21$

Putting $k_1 = -21$ in $4x - 3y + k = 0$, we get $4x - 3y - 21 = 0$ (i)

as the equation of the perpendicular bisector of BC.

Again, the equation of a line perpendicular to CA is $3x - y + k_1 = 0$.

This will pass through $(5/2, -9/2)$, the mid-point of AC if

$$15/2 + 9/2 + k_1 = 0 \Rightarrow k_1 = -12$$

Putting $k_1 = -12$ in $3x - y + k_1 = 0$, we get $3x - y - 12 = 0$ (ii)

as the perpendicular bisector of AC.

Solving (i) and (ii), we get $x = 3$, $y = -3$.

Hence, the coordinates of the circumcentre of $\triangle ABC$ are $(3, -3)$.

7. Orthocentre of a Triangle The orthocentre of a triangle is the point of intersection of the perpendiculars drawn from the vertices to the opposite sides of the triangle.

Fig. 12.8

Illustration

Question 7: Find the orthocentre of the triangle whose sides have the equations $y = 15$, $3x = 4y$, and $5x + 12y = 0$.

Answer: Let ABC be the triangle whose sides BC, CA and AB have the equations $y = 15$, $3x = 4y$, and $5x + 12y = 0$ respectively.

Solving these equations pairwise, we get coordinates of A, B and C as $(0, 0)$, $(-36, 15)$ and $(20, 15)$ respectively.

AD is a line passing through A $(0, 0)$ and perpendicular to $y = 15$.

So, equation of AD is $x = 0$.

The equation of any line perpendicular to $3x - 4y = 0$ is represented by $4x + 3y + k = 0$.

This line will pass through $(-36, 15)$ if $-144 + 45 + k = 0 \Rightarrow k = 99$.

So the equation of BE is $4x + 3y + 99 = 0$.

Solving the equations of AD and BE we get $x = 0$, $y = -33$.

Hence the coordinates of the orthocentre are $(0, -33)$.

8. Collinearity of Three Points: Three given points A, B and C are said to be collinear, that is, lie on the same straight line, if any of the following conditions occur:

(i) Area of triangle formed by these three points is zero.

(ii) Slope of AB = Slope of AC.

(iii) Any one of the three points (say C) lies on the straight line joining the other two points (here A and B).

Fig. 12.9

Illustration

Question 8: Select the right option the points $(-a, -b)$, $(0, 0)$ and (a, b) are

(a) Collinear   (b) Vertices of square

(c) Vertices of a rectangle   (d) None of these

Answer: We can use either of the three methods to check whether the points are collinear.

But the most convenient one is (ii) in this case.

Let A, B, C are the points whose coordinates are $(-a, -b)$, $(0, 0)$ and (a, b)

Slope of $BC = b/a$

Slope of $AB = b/a$

So, the straight line made by points A, B and C is collinear.

Hence, (a) is the answer.

[If you have not understood this here, you are requested to read the following section on straight lines and their slopes and then re-read this solution]

Alternative: Draw the points on paper assuming the paper to be a graph paper. This will give you an indication regarding the nature of points. In the above question, point (a, b) is in first quadrant for $a > 0$, $b > 0$ and point $(-a, -b)$ is directly opposite to the point (a, b) in the third quadrant with the third point $(0, 0)$ in the middle of the straight line joining the points A and B.

You can check this by assuming any value for 'a' and 'b'.

Also, you can use this method for solving any problem involving points and diagrams made by those points. However you should be fast enough to trace the points on paper. A little practice of tracing points might help you.

9. Slope of a Line The slope of a line joining two points A (x_1, y_1) and B (x_2, y_2) is denoted by m and is given by $m = (y_2 - y_1)/(x_2 - x_1) = \tan \theta$, where θ is the angle that the line makes with the positive direction of x-axis. This angle θ is taken positive when it is measured in the anti-clockwise direction from the positive direction of the axis of x.

Fig. 12.10

Illustration

Question 9: Find the equation of a straight line passing through $(2, -3)$ and having a slope of 1 unit.

Answer: Here slope = 1

And point given is $(2, -3)$.

So, we will use point-slope formula for finding the equation of straight line. This formula is given by:

$$(y - y_1) = m (x - x_1)$$

So, equation of the line will be $y - (-3) = 1 (x - 2)$

$\Rightarrow \qquad\qquad y + 3 = x - 2$

$\Rightarrow \qquad\qquad y - x + 5 = 0$

10. Different Forms of the Equations of a Straight Line

(a) General Form The general form of the equation of a straight line is $ax + by + c = 0$.

(First degree equation in x and y). Where a, b and c are real constants and a, b are not simultaneously equal to zero.

In this equation, slope of the line is given by $\dfrac{-a}{b}$.

The general form is also given by $y = mx + c$; where m is the slope and c is the intercept on y-axis.

In this equation, slope of the line is given by m.

(b) Line Parallel to the X-axis The equation of a straight line *parallel to the x-axis* and at a distance b from it, is given by $y = b$.

Obviously, the **equation of the x-axis is $y = 0$**

(c) Line Parallel to Y-axis The equation of a straight line *parallel to the y-axis* and at a distance a from it, is given by $x = a$.

Obviously, the **equation of y-axis is $x = 0$**

(d) Slope Intercept Form The equation of a straight line passing through the point A (x_1, y_1) and having a slope m is given by

$$(y - y_1) = m (x - x_1)$$

(e) Two Points Form The equation of a straight line passing through two points A (x_1, y_1) and B (x_2, y_2) is given by

$$(y - y_1) = \frac{(y_2 - y_1) (x - x_1)}{(x_2 - x_1)}$$

Its slope $= \left(\dfrac{y_2 - y_1}{x_2 - x_1} \right)$

(f) Intercept Form The equation of a straight line making intercepts a and b on the axes of x and y respectively is given by

$$x/a + y/b = 1$$

Fig. 12.11

If a straight line cuts x-axis at A and the y-axis at B then OA and OB are known as the intercepts of the line on x-axis and y-axis respectively.

11. Perpendicularity and Parallelism

Condition for two lines to be parallel: Two lines are said to be parallel if their slopes are equal.

For this to happen, ratio of coefficient of x and y in both the lines should be equal.

In a general form, this can be stated as: line parallel to $ax + by + c = 0$ is $ax + by + k = 0$
or $dx + ey + k = 0$ if $a/d = b/e$ where k is a constant.

Illustration

Question 10: Which of the lines represented by the following equations are parallel to each other?

1. $x + 2y = 5$ 2. $2x - 4y = 6$
3. $x - 2y = 4$ 4. $2x + 6y = 8$

(a) 1 and 2   (b) 2 and 4   (c) 2 and 3   (d) 1 and 4

Answer: Go through the options and check which of the two lines given will satisfy the criteria for two lines to be parallel. It will be obvious that option c is correct, that is, the line $2x - 4y = 6$ is parallel to the line $x - 2y = 4$.

Question 11: Find the equation of a straight line parallel to the straight line $3x + 4y = 7$ and passing through the point $(3, -3)$.

Answer: Equation of the line parallel to $3x + 4y = 7$ will be of the form $3x + 4y = k$.

This line passes through $(3, -3)$, so this point will satisfy the equation of straight line $3x + 4y = k$. So, $3.3 + 4. (-3) = k \Rightarrow k = -3$.

Hence, equation of the required straight line will be $3x + 4y + 3 = 0$.

Condition for two lines to be perpendicular: Two lines are said to be perpendicular if product of the slopes of the lines is equal to -1.

For this to happen, the product of the coefficients of x + the product of the coefficients of y should be equal to zero.

Illustration

Question 12: Which of the following two lines are perpendicular?

1. $x + 2y = 5$ 2. $2x - 4y = 6$
3. $2x + 3y = 4$ 4. $2x - y = 4$

(a) 1 and 2   (b) 2 and 4   (c) 2 and 3   (d) 1 and 4

Check the equations to get option 4 as the correct answer.

Question 13: Find the equation of a straight line perpendicular to the straight line $3x + 4y = 7$ and passing through the point $(3, -3)$.

Answer: Equation of the line perpendicular to $3x + 4y = 7$ will be of the form $4x - 3y = K$.

This line passes through $(3, -3)$, so this point will satisfy the equation of straight line $4x - 3y = K$. So, $4.3 - 3.-3 \Rightarrow K = 21$.

Hence, equation of required straight line will be $4x - 3y = 21$.

12. Length of Perpendicular or Distance of a Point from a Line The length of perpendicular from a given point (x_1, y_1) to a line $ax + by + c = 0$ is

$$\frac{|ax_1 + by_1 + c|}{\sqrt{a^2 + b^2}}$$

Corollary:

(a) Distance between two parallel lines.

If two lines are parallel, the distance between them will always be the same.

When two straight lines are parallel whose equations are $ax + by + c = 0$ and $ax + by + c_1 = 0$, then the distance between them is given by $\dfrac{|c - c_1|}{\sqrt{a^2 + b^2}}$.

(b) The length of the perpendicular from the origin to the line $ax + by + c = 0$ is given by $\dfrac{|c|}{\sqrt{a^2 + b^2}}$

Illustration

Question 14: Two sides of a square lie on the lines $x + y = 2$ and $x + y = -2$. Find the area of the square formed in this way.

Answer: Obviously, the difference between the parallel lines will be the side of the square.

To convert it into the form of finding the distance of a point from a line, we will have to find out a point at which any one of these two lines cut the axes and then we will draw a perpendicular from that point to the other line, and this distance will be the side of the square.

To find the point at which the equation of the line $x + y = 2$ cut the axes, we will put once $x = 0$ and then again $y = 0$.

When $x = 0$, $y = 2$, so the coordinates of the point where it cuts y-axis is $(0, 2)$.

Now the point is $(0, 2)$, and the equation of line on which perpendicular is to be drawn is $x + y = -2$.

So, distance $= \dfrac{|1.0 + 1.2 + 2|}{\sqrt{1^2 + 1^2}} = \dfrac{4}{\sqrt{2}}$.

$\therefore$ Area $= \dfrac{16}{2} = 8$

Alternatively: Draw the points on the paper and you will get the length of diagonal as 4 units; so, length of side will be $2\sqrt{2}$ and, therefore, the area will be 8 sq units.

Alternatively: You can also use the formula for the distance between two parallel lines as

$$\frac{|2 + 2|}{\sqrt{1^2 + 1^2}} = \frac{4}{\sqrt{2}}$$

13. Change of Axes If origin (0, 0) is shifted to (h, k) then the coordinates of the point (x, y) referred to the old axes and (X, Y) referred to the new axes can be related with the relation $x = X + h$ and $y = Y + k$.

Fig. 12.12

Illustration

Question 15: If origin (0, 0) is shifted to (5, 2), what will be the coordinates of the point in the new axis which was represented by (1, 2) in the old axis?

Space for Rough Work

Answer: Let (X, Y) be the coordinates of the point in the new axis.

Then,
$$1 = X + 5 \qquad \therefore \quad X = -4$$
$$2 = Y + 2 \qquad \therefore \quad Y = 0$$

So, the new coordinates of the point will be (−4, 2).

14. Point of Intersection of Two Lines Point of intersection of two lines can be obtained by solving the equations as simultaneous equations.

An Important Result

If all the three vertices of a triangle have integral coordinates, then that triangle cannot be an Equilateral triangle.

LEVEL OF DIFFICULTY (I)

1. Find the distance between the points (3, 4) and (8, –6).
   (a) $\sqrt{5}$ (b) $5\sqrt{5}$
   (c) $2\sqrt{5}$ (d) $4\sqrt{5}$

2. Find the distance between the points (5, 2) and (0, 0).
   (a) $\sqrt{27}$ (b) $\sqrt{21}$
   (c) $\sqrt{29}$ (d) $\sqrt{31}$

3. Find the value of p if the distance between the points (8, p) and (4, 3) is 5.
   (a) 6   (b) 0
   (c) Both (a) and (b)   (d) None of these

4. Find the value of c if the distance between the point (c, 4) and the origin is 5 units.
   (a) 3   (b) –3
   (c) Both a and b   (d) None of these

5. Find the mid-point of the line segment made by joining the points (3, 2) and (6, 4).
   (a) $\left(\dfrac{9}{2}, 3\right)$ (b) $\left(\dfrac{-3}{2}, -1\right)$
   (c) $\left(\dfrac{9}{2}, -\dfrac{3}{2}\right)$ (d) $\left(\dfrac{3}{-1}\right)$

6. If the origin is the mid-point of the line segment joined by the points (2, 3) and (x, y), find the value of (x, y).
   (a) (2, 3)   (b) (–2, 3)
   (c) (–2, –3)   (d) (2, –3)

7. Find the points that divide the line segment joining (2, 5) and (–1, 2) in the ratio 2 : 1 internally.
   (a) (1, 2)   (b) (–3, 2)
   (c) (3, 1)   (d) (0, 3)

8. In what ratio does the x-axis divide the line segment joining the points (2, –3) and (5, 6)?
   (a) 2 : 1   (b) 1 : 2
   (c) 3 : 4   (d) 2 : 3

9. How many squares are possible if two of the vertices of a quadrilateral are (1, 0) and (2, 0)?
   (a) 1   (b) 2
   (c) 3   (d) 4

10. If the point R (1, –2) divides externally the line segment joining P (2, 5) and Q in the ratio 3 : 4, what will be the coordinates of Q?
    (a) (–3, 6)   (b) (2, –4)
    (c) (3, 6)   (d) (1, 2)

11. Find the coordinates of the points that trisect the line segment joining (1, –2) and (–3, 4).
    (a) $\left(\dfrac{-1}{3}, 0\right)$ (b) $\left(\dfrac{-5}{3}, 2\right)$
    (c) Both (a) and (b)   (d) None of these

12. Find the coordinates of the point that divides the line segment joining the points (6, 3) and (–4, 5) in the ratio 3 : 2 internally.
    (a) $\left(0, \dfrac{-21}{5}\right)$ (b) $\left(0, \dfrac{21}{5}\right)$
    (c) $\left(\dfrac{11}{2}, \dfrac{14}{3}\right)$ (d) $\left(\dfrac{-11}{2}, \dfrac{-14}{3}\right)$

13. In Question 12 question, find the coordinates of the point if it divides the points externally.
    (a) (24, –9)   (b) (3, –5)
    (c) (–24, 9)   (d) (5, –3)

14. In what ratio is the line segment joining (–1, 3) and (4, –7) divided at the point (2, –3)?
    (a) 3 : 2   (b) 2 : 3
    (c) 3 : 5   (d) 5 : 3

15. In question 14, find the nature of division?
    (a) Internal   (b) External
    (c) Cannot be said

16. In what ratio is the line segment made by the points (7, 3) and (–4, 5) divided by the y-axis?
    (a) 2 : 3   (b) 4 : 7
    (c) 3 : 5   (d) 7 : 4

17. What is the nature of the division in the above question?
    (a) External   (b) Internal
    (c) Cannot be said

18. If the coordinates of the mid-point of the line segment joining the points (2, 1) and (1, –3) is (x, y) then the relation between x and y can be best described by
    (a) $3x + 2y = 5$ (b) $6x + y = 8$
    (c) $5x - 2y = 4$ (d) $2x - 5y = 4$

19. Points (6, 8), (3, 7), (–2, –2) and (1, –1) are joined to form a quadrilateral. What will be this structure?
    (a) Rhombus   (b) Parallelogram
    (c) Square   (d) Rectangle

20. Points (4, –1), (6, 0), (7, 2) and (5, 1) are joined to be a vertex of a quadrilateral. What will be the structure?
    (a) Rhombus   (b) Parallelogram
    (c) Square   (d) Rectangle

21. What will be the centroid of a triangle whose vertices are (2, 4), (6, 4) and (2, 0)?

    (a) $\left(\dfrac{7}{2}, \dfrac{5}{2}\right)$
    (b) (3, 5)

    (c) $\left(\dfrac{10}{3}, \dfrac{8}{3}\right)$
    (d) (1, 4)

22. The distance between the lines $4x + 3y = 11$ and $8x + 6y = 15$ is

    (a) 4
    (b) $\dfrac{7}{10}$

    (c) $\dfrac{5}{7}$
    (d) 26

23. If the mid-point of the line joining (3, 4) and (p, 7) is (x, y) and $2x + 2y + 1 = 0$, then what will be the value of p?

    (a) 15
    (b) $\dfrac{-17}{2}$

    (c) −15
    (d) $\dfrac{17}{2}$

24. Find the third vertex of the triangle whose two vertices are (−3, 1) and (0, −2) and the centroid is the origin.

    (a) (2, 3)
    (b) $\left(\dfrac{-4}{3}, \dfrac{14}{3}\right)$

    (c) (3, 1)
    (d) (6, 4)

25. Find the area of the triangle whose vertices are (1, 3), (−7, 6) and (5, −1).

    (a) 20
    (b) 10
    (c) 18
    (d) 24

26. Find the area of the triangle whose vertices are $(a, b + c)$, $(a, b − c)$ and $(− a, c)$.

    (a) $2ac$
    (b) $2bc$
    (c) $b(a + c)$
    (d) $c(a − b)$

27. The number of lines that are parallel to $2x + 6y + 7 = 0$ and have an intercept of length 10 between the coordinate axes is

    (a) 0
    (b) 1
    (c) 2
    (d) Infinite

28. Which of the following three points represent a straight line?

    (a) $\left(\dfrac{-1}{2}, 3\right)$, (−5, 6) and (− 8, 8)

    (b) $\left(\dfrac{-1}{2}, 3\right)$, (5, 6) and (− 8, 8)

    (c) $\left(\dfrac{1}{2}, 3\right)$, (−5, 6) and (− 8, 8)

    (d) $\left(\dfrac{-1}{2}, 3\right)$, $\left(\dfrac{5}{6}\right)$ and (8, 8)

29. Which of the following will be the equation of a straight line that is parallel to the y-axis at a distance 11 units from it?

    (a) $x = + 11, x = −11$
    (b) $y = 11, y = −11$
    (c) $y = 0$
    (d) None of these

30. Which of the following will be the equation of a straight line parallel to the y-axis at a distance of 9 units to the left?

    (a) $x = − 9$
    (b) $x = 9$
    (c) $y = 9$
    (d) $y = − 9$

31. What can be said about the equation of the straight line $x = 7$?

    (a) It is the equation of a straight line at a distance of 7 units towards the right of the y-axis.

    (b) It is the equation of a straight line at a distance of 7 units towards the left of the y-axis.

    (c) It is the equation of a straight line at a distance of 7 units below the x-axis.

    (d) It is the equation of a straight line at a distance of 7 units above the x-axis.

32. What can be said about the equation of the straight line $y = −8$?

    (a) It is the equation of a straight line at a distance of 8 units below the x-axis.

    (b) It is the equation of a straight line at a distance of 8 units above the x-axis.

    (c) It is the equation of a straight line at a distance of 8 units towards the right of the y-axis.

    (d) It is the equation of a straight line at a distance of 8 units towards the left of the y-axis.

33. Which of the following straight lines passes through the origin?

    (a) $x + y = 4$
    (b) $x^2 + y^2 = − 6$
    (c) $x + y = 5$
    (d) $x = 4y$

34. What will be the point of intersection of the equation of lines $2x + 5y = 6$ and $3x + 4y = 7$?

    (a) $\left(\dfrac{11}{7}, \dfrac{4}{7}\right)$
    (b) $\left(\dfrac{-11}{7}, 4\right)$

    (c) $\left(3, \dfrac{-2}{7}\right)$
    (d) $\left(4, \dfrac{-2}{5}\right)$

35. If P (6, 7), Q (2, 3) and R (4, −2) be the vertices of a triangle, then which of the following is not a point contained in this triangle?

    (a) (4, 3)
    (b) (3, 3)
    (c) (4, 2)
    (d) (6, 1)

36. What will be the reflection of the point (4, 5) in the second quadrant?

    (a) (− 4, − 5)
    (b) (− 4, 5)
    (c) (4, − 5)
    (d) None of these

37. What will be the reflection of the point (4, 5) in the third quadrant?

(a) $(-4, -5)$ (b) $(-4, 5)$

(c) $(4, -5)$ (d) None of these

38. What will be the reflection of the point $(4, 5)$ in the second quadrant?

(a) $(-4, -5)$ (b) $(-4, 5)$

(c) $(4, -5)$ (d) None of these

39. If the origin gets shifted to $(2, 2)$, then what will be the new coordinates of the point $(4, -2)$?

(a) $(-2, 4)$ (b) $(2, 4)$

(c) $(4, 2)$ (d) $(2, -4)$

40. What will be the length of the perpendicular drawn from the point $(4, 5)$ upon the straight line $3x + 4y = 10$?

(a) $\dfrac{12}{5}$ (b) $\dfrac{32}{5}$

(c) $\dfrac{22}{5}$ (d) $\dfrac{42}{5}$

Space for Rough Work

1. Find the area of the quadrilateral the coordinates of whose angular points taken in order are (1, 1), (3, 4), (5, −2) and (4, −7).
   - (a) 20.5
   - (b) 41
   - (c) 82
   - (d) 61.5

2. Find the area of the quadrilateral the coordinates of whose angular points taken in order are (−1, 6), (−3, −9), (5, −8) and (3, 9).
   - (a) 48
   - (b) 96
   - (c) 192
   - (d) 72

3. Two vertices of a triangle are (5, −1) and (−2, 3). If the orthocenter of the triangle is the origin, what will be the coordinates of the third point?
   - (a) (4, 7)
   - (b) (−4, 7)
   - (c) (−4, −7)
   - (d) (4, −7)

4. Find the equation of the straight line passing through the origin and the point of intersection of the lines $x/a + y/b = 1$ and $x/b + y/a = 1$.
   - (a) $y = x$
   - (b) $y = -x$
   - (c) $y = 2x$
   - (d) $y = -2x$

5. One side of a rectangle lies along the line $4x + 7y + 5 = 0$. Two of its vertices are (−3, 1) and (1, 1). Which of the following may be an equation which represents any of the other three straight lines?
   - (a) $7x - 4y = 3$
   - (b) $7x - 4y + 3 = 0$
   - (c) $y + 1 = 0$
   - (d) $4x + 7y = 3$

6. The points $(p-1, p + 2)$, $(p, p + 1)$, $(p + 1, p)$ are collinear for
   - (a) $p = 0$
   - (b) $p = 1$
   - (c) $p = -1/2$
   - (d) Any value of p

7. The straight line joining (1, 2) and (2, −2) is perpendicular to the line joining (8, 2) and (4, p). What will be the value of p?
   - (a) −1
   - (b) 1
   - (c) 3
   - (d) None of these

8. What will be the length of the perpendicular drawn from the point (−3, −4) to the straight line $12 (x + 6) = 5 (y - 2)$?
   - (a) $5\left(\dfrac{4}{13}\right)$
   - (b) $5\left(\dfrac{1}{13}\right)$
   - (c) $3\left(\dfrac{2}{13}\right)$
   - (d) $3\left(\dfrac{1}{13}\right)$

9. The area of the triangle with vertices at $(a, b + c)$, $(b, c + a)$ and $(c, a + b)$ is
   - (a) 0
   - (b) $a + b + c$
   - (c) $a^2 + b^2 + c^2$
   - (d) 1

10. Find the distance between the two parallel straight lines $y = mx + c$ and $y = mx + d$? [Assume $c > d$]
    - (a) $\left(\dfrac{(c - d)}{(1 + m^2)^{\frac{1}{2}}}\right)$
    - (b) $\left(\dfrac{(d - c)}{(1 + m^2)^{\frac{1}{2}}}\right)$
    - (c) $\left(\dfrac{d}{(1 + m^2)^{\frac{1}{2}}}\right)$
    - (d) $\left(\dfrac{-d}{(1 + m)^{\frac{1}{2}}}\right)$

11. What will be the equation of the straight line that passes through the intersection of the straight lines $2x - 3y + 4 = 0$ and $3x + 4y - 5 = 0$ and is perpendicular to the straight line $3x - 4y = 5$?
    - (a) $8x + 6y = \dfrac{32}{7}$
    - (b) $4x + 3y = \dfrac{84}{17}$
    - (c) $4x + 3y = \dfrac{62}{17}$
    - (d) $8x + 6y = \dfrac{58}{17}$

12. In question 11, find the equation of the straight line if it is parallel to the straight line $3x + 4y = 5$?
    - (a) $12x + 16y = \dfrac{58}{17}$
    - (b) $3x + 4y = \dfrac{58}{17}$
    - (c) $6x + 8y = \dfrac{58}{17}$
    - (d) None of these

13. The orthocenter of the triangle formed by the points (0, 0), (8, 0) and (4, 6) is
    - (a) $\left(4, \dfrac{8}{3}\right)$
    - (b) (3, 4)
    - (c) (4, 3)
    - (d) $\left(3, \dfrac{5}{2}\right)$

14. The area of a triangle is 5 square units, two of its vertices are (2, 1) and (3, −2). The third vertex lies on $y = x + 3$. What will be the third vertex?
    - (a) $\left(\dfrac{5}{3}, \dfrac{13}{3}\right)$
    - (b) $\left(\dfrac{7}{2}, \dfrac{13}{2}\right)$
    - (c) (3, 4)
    - (d) (1, 2)

15. The equations of two equal sides AB and AC of an isosceles triangle ABC are $x + y = 5$ and $7x - y = 3$ respectively. What will be the equation of the side BC if area of triangle ABC is 5 square units.
    - (a) $x + 3y - 1 = 0$
    - (b) $x - 3y + 1 = 0$
    - (c) $2x - y = 5$
    - (d) $x + 2y = 5$

16. Three vertices of a rhombus, taken in order are (2, −1), (3, 4) and (−2, 3). Find the fourth vertex.
    - (a) (3, 2)
    - (b) (−3, −2)
    - (c) (−3, 2)
    - (d) (3, −2)

17. Four vertices of a parallelogram taken in order are $(-3, -1)$, (a, b), $(3, 3)$ and $(4, 3)$. What will be the ratio of a to b?

   (a) 4:1
   (b) 1:2
   (c) 1:3
   (d) 3:1

18. What will be the new equation of straight line $3x + 4y = 6$ if the origin gets shifted to $(3, -4)$?

   (a) $3x + 4y = 5$
   (b) $4x - 3y = 4$
   (c) $3x + 4y + 1 = 0$
   (d) $3x + 4y - 13 = 0$

19. What will be the value of p if the equation of straight line $2x + 5y = 4$ gets changed to $2x + 5y = p$ after shifting the origin at $(3, 3)$?

   (a) 16
   (b) −17
   (c) 12
   (d) 10

20. A line passing through the points $(a, 2a)$ and $(-2, 3)$ is perpendicular to the line $4x + 3y + 5 = 0$. Find the value of a?

   (a) −14/3
   (b) 18/5
   (c) 14/3
   (d) −18/5

Space for Rough Work

LEVEL OF DIFFICULTY (III)

1. The area of a triangle is 5 square units. Two of its vertices are (2, 1) and (3, –2). The third vertex lies on $y = x + 3$. What will be the third vertex?
   (a) (4, –7) (b) (4, 7)
   (c) (– 4, –7) (d) (– 4, 7)

2. One side of a rectangle lies along the line $4x + 7y + 5 = 0$. Two of its vertices are (–3, 1) and (1, 1). Which of the following is not an equation of the other three straight lines?
   (a) $14x – 8y = 6$ (b) $7x – 4y = –25$
   (c) $4x + 7y = 11$ (d) $14x – 8y = 20$

3. The area of triangle formed by the points $(p, 2–2p)$, $(1–p, 2p)$ and $(–4–p, 6–2p)$ is 70 units. How many integral values of p are possible?
   (a) 2 (b) 3
   (c) 4 (d) None of these

4. What are the points on the axis of x whose perpendicular distance from the straight line $x/p + y/q = 1$ is p?
   (a) $\dfrac{p}{q}\left[q + \sqrt{(p^2 + q^2)}\right], 0$
   (b) $\dfrac{p}{q}\left[q - \sqrt{(p^2 + q^2)}\right], 0$
   (c) Both (a) and (b)
   (d) None of these

5. If the medians PT and RS of a triangle with vertices $P(0, b)$, $Q(0, 0)$ and $R(a, 0)$ are perpendicular to each other, which of the following satisfies the relationship between a and b?
   (a) $4b^2 = a^2$ (b) $2b^2 = a^2$
   (c) $a = –2b$ (d) $a^2 + b^2 = 0$

6. The point of intersection of the lines $x/a + y/b = 1$ and $x/b + y/b = 1$ lies on the line
   (a) $x + y = 1$ (b) $x + y = 0$
   (c) $x – y = 1$ (d) $x – y = 0$

7. PQR is an isosceles triangle. If the coordinates of the base are $Q(1, 3)$ and $R(–2, 7)$, then the coordinates of the vertex P can be
   (a) $\left(4, \dfrac{7}{2}\right)$ (b) $(2, 5)$
   (c) $\left(\dfrac{5}{6}, 6\right)$ (d) $\left(\dfrac{1}{3}, 2\right)$

8. The extremities of a diagonal of a parallelogram are the points (3, – 4) and (– 6, 5). If the third vertex is the point (–2, 1), the coordinate of the fourth vertex is
   (a) (1, 0) (b) (–1, 0)
   (c) (–1, 1) (d) (1, –1)

9. If the points $(a, 0)$, $(0, b)$ and $(1, 1)$ are collinear then which of the following is true?
   (a) $\dfrac{1}{a} + \dfrac{1}{b} = 2$ (b) $\dfrac{1}{a} - \dfrac{1}{b} = 1$
   (c) $\dfrac{1}{a} - \dfrac{1}{b} = 2$ (d) $\dfrac{1}{a} + \dfrac{1}{b} = 1$

10. If P and Q are two points on the line $3x + 4y = –15$, such that $OP = OQ = 9$ units, the area of the triangle POQ will be
    (a) $18\sqrt{2}$ sq units (b) $3\sqrt{2}$ sq units
    (c) $6\sqrt{2}$ sq units (d) $15\sqrt{2}$ sq units

11. If the coordinates of the points A, B, C and D are (6, 3), (–3, –5), (4, –2) and $(a, 3a)$ respectively and if the ratio of the area of triangles ABC and DBC is 2 : 1, then the value of a is
    (a) $\dfrac{-9}{2}$ (b) $\dfrac{9}{2}$
    (c) $\dfrac{-23}{36}$ (d) $\dfrac{23}{18}$

12. The equations of two equal sides AB and AC of an isosceles triangle ABC are $x + y = 5$ and $7x – y = 3$ respectively. What will be the length of the intercept cut by the side BC on the y-axis?
    (a) $\dfrac{9}{5}$ (b) 8
    (c) 1.5 (d) No unique solution

13. A line is represented by the equation $4x + 5y = 6$ in the coordinate system with the origin (0, 0). You are required to find the equation of the straight line perpendicular to this line that passes through the point (1, –2) [which is in the coordinate system where origin is at (–2, –2)].
    (a) $5x – 4y = 11$ (b) $5x – 4y = 13$
    (c) $5x – 4y = –3$ (d) $5x – 4y = 7$

14. $P(3, 1)$, $Q(6, 5)$ and $R(x, y)$ are three points such that the angle PRQ is a right angle and the area of $\triangle PRQ$ is 7. The number of such points R that are possible is
    (a) 1 (b) 2
    (c) 3 (d) 4

15. Two sides of a square lie on the lines $x + y = 1$ and $x + y + 2 = 0$. What is its area?
    (a) $\dfrac{11}{2}$ (b) $\dfrac{9}{2}$
    (c) 5 (d) 4

16. Find the value of k if the straight line $2x + 3y + 4 + k$ $(6x - y + 12) = 0$ is perpendicular to the line $7x + 5y = 4$.

(a) $\dfrac{-33}{37}$

(b) $\dfrac{-29}{37}$

(c) $\dfrac{19}{37}$

(d) None of these

17. If p is the length of the perpendicular from the origin to the line $\dfrac{x}{a} + \dfrac{y}{b} = 1$, then which of the following is true?

(a) $\dfrac{1}{p^2} = \dfrac{1}{b^2} - \dfrac{1}{a^2}$

(b) $\dfrac{1}{p^2} = \dfrac{1}{a^2} - \dfrac{1}{b^2}$

(c) $\dfrac{1}{p^2} = \dfrac{1}{a^2} + \dfrac{1}{b^2}$

(d) None of these

18. How many points on $x + y = 4$ are there that lie at a unit distance from the line $4x + 3y = 10$?

(a) 1

(b) 2

(c) 3

(d) None of these

19. What will be the area of the rhombus $ax \pm by \pm c = 0$?

(a) $\dfrac{3c^2}{ab}$

(b) $\dfrac{4c^2}{ab}$

(c) $\dfrac{2c^2}{ab}$

(d) $\dfrac{c^2}{ab}$

20. The coordinates of the mid-points of the sides of a triangle are (4, 2), (3, 3) and (2, 2). What will be the coordinates of the centroid of the triangle?

(a) $\left(3, \dfrac{7}{3}\right)$

(b) $\left(-3, \dfrac{-7}{3}\right)$

(c) $\left(3, \dfrac{-7}{3}\right)$

(d) $\left(-3, \dfrac{7}{3}\right)$

Space for Rough Work

ANSWER KEY

Level of Difficulty (I)

1. (b)	2. (c)	3. (c)	4. (c)
5. (a)	6. (c)	7. (d)	8. (b)
9. (c)	10. (c)	11. (c)	12. (b)
13. (c)	14. (a)	15. (a)	16. (d)
17. (b)	18. (b)	19. (b)	20. (a)
21. (c)	22. (b)	23. (c)	24. (c)
25. (b)	26. (a)	27. (c)	28. (a)
29. (a)	30. (a)	31. (a)	32. (a)
33. (d)	34. (a)	35. (d)	36. (b)
37. (a)	38. (b)	39. (d)	40. (c)

Level of Difficulty (II)

1. (a)	2. (b)	3. (c)	4. (a)
5. (a)	6. (d)	7. (b)	8. (b)
9. (a)	10. (a)	11. (c)	12. (d)
13. (a)	14. (b)	15. (d)	16. (b)
17. (a)	18. (c)	19. (b)	20. (b)

Level of Difficulty (III)

1. (c)	2. (d)	3. (d)	4. (c)
5. (b)	6. (d)	7. (c)	8. (b)
9. (d)	10. (a)	11. (c)	12. (b)
13. (a)	14. (b)	15. (b)	16. (b)
17. (c)	18. (b)	19. (c)	20. (a)

Hints

Level of Difficulty (II)

1. Use the area of a triangle formula for the two parts of the quadrilateral separately and then add them.

4. Find the point of intersection of the lines by solving the simultaneous equations and then use the two-point formula of a straight line.
   Alternative: After finding out the point of intersection, use options to check.

6. For 3 points to be collinear,
   (i) Either the slope of any two of the 3 points should be equal to the slope of any other two points. OR
   (ii) The area of the triangle formed by the three points should be equal to zero.
   Solve using options.

7. Form the equation of the straight lines and then use the options.

10. Point of intersection of $y = mx + c$ with x-axis is $(-c/m, 0)$.
    Now use the formula for the distance of a point to a straight line.

11. Find the point of intersection of the lines and then put the coordinate of this point into the equation $4x + 3y = K$, which is perpendicular to the equation of straight line $3x - 4y = 5$, to find out K.

13. Orthocenter is the point of intersection of altitudes of a triangle and centroid divides the straight line

formed by joining circumcenter and the orthocenter in the ratio 2 : 1.
Let the vertices of the triangle be $O(0, 0)$, $A(8, 0)$ and $B(4, 6)$.
The equation of an altitude through O and perpendicular to AB is $y = 2/3x$ and similarly the equation of an altitude through A and perpendicular to OB is $2x + 3y = 16$. Now find the point of intersection of these two straight lines.

14. Use the options.
    Alternative: Draw the points in the cartesian co-ordinate system and then use the simple geometry formula to calculate the point using the options.

15. Draw the points and then check with the options.
    Alternative: Find out the point of intersection with the help of options and then use the formula for area of ?.

17. Sum of x and y co-ordinates of opposite vertices in a parallelogram are same.

19. If the origin gets changed to (h, k) from $(0, 0)$ then
    Old x co-ordinate = New x co-ordinate + h
    Old y co-ordinate = New y co-ordinate + k

20. Equation of any straight line perpendicular to the line $4x + 3y + 5 = 0$ will be of the form of $3x - 4y = k$, where k is any constant.
    Now form the equation of the straight line with the given two points and then equate.

Level of Difficulty (III)

1. First check the options to see that which of the points lie on the equation of straight line $y = x + 3$.
   And then again check the options, if needed, to confirm the second constraint regarding area of triangle.

2. Use the options.

3. Use the formula of area of a quadrilateral which will lead to a quadratic equation. Now solve the quadratic equation to see the number of integral solutions it can have.

4. Use the formula of distance of a point from the straight line using the options.

7. Use the options to find the length using the distance formula.

9. Make the slope of any two points equal to the slope of any other two points.
   Slope = Difference of Y coordinates/Difference of X coordinates.

14. Draw the points on cartesian coordinate system.

15. Length of the square can be find out using the method of finding out the distance between two parallel lines.

17. Use the formula (perpendicular distance of a point from a straight line.)

TRAINING GROUND FOR BLOCK IV

HOW TO THINK IN PROBLEMS ON BLOCK IV

In the back to school section of this block, I have already mentioned that there is very little use of complex and obscure formulae and results while solving questions on this block.

The following is a list of questions (with solutions) of what has been asked in previous years' CAT questions from this chapter. Hopefully you will realise through this exercise, what I am talking about when I say this. For each of the questions given below, try to solve on your own first, before looking at the solution provided.

1. A circle with radius 2 is placed against a right angle. As shown in the figure below, another smaller circle is placed in the gap between the circle and the right angle. What is the radius of the smaller circle?

    (a) $3 - 2\sqrt{2}$ (b) $4 - 2\sqrt{2}$

    (c) $7 - 4\sqrt{2}$ (d) $6 - 4\sqrt{2}$

Solution: The solution of the above question is based on the following construction.

In the right triangle $OO'P$,

$$OP = (2 - r), \quad O'P = (2 - r) \text{ and } OO' = 2 + r$$

where r is the radius of the smaller circle.
Using Pythagoras theorem:

$$(2 + r)^2 = (2 - r)^2 + (2 - r)^2$$

Solving, we get $r = 6 \pm 4\sqrt{2}$

$6 + 4\sqrt{2}$ cannot be correct since the value of r should be less than 2.

Note: The key to solving this question is in the visualisation of the construction. If you try to use complex formulae while solving, your mind unnecessarily gets cluttered. The key to your thinking in this question is:

(1) Realise that you only have to use length measuring formulae. Hence, put all angle measurement formulae into the back seat.

(2) A quick mental search of the length measuring formulae available for this situation will narrow down your mind to the Pythagoras theorem.

(3) The key then becomes the construction of a triangle (right angled of course) where the only unknown is r.

---

2. ABCDEFGH is a cube. If the length of the diagonals DF, AG & CE are equal to the sides of a triangle, then the circumradius of that triangle would be

    (a) Equal to the side of the cube

    (b) $\sqrt{3}$ times the side of the cube

    (c) $1/\sqrt{3}$ times the side of the cube

    (d) Indeterminate

Solution: If we assume the side of the cube to be a the triangle will be an equilateral triangle with side $a\sqrt{3}$. (we get this using Pythagoras theorem). Also, we know that the circumradius of an equilateral triangle is $1/\sqrt{3}$ times the side of the triangle.

Hence, in this case the circumradius would be a—equal to the side of the cube.

(Again the only formula used in this question would be the Pythagoras theorem.)

3. On a semicircle (diameter AD), chord BC is parallel to the diameter AD. Also, $AB = CD = 2$, while $AD = 8$, what is the length of BC?

    (a) 7.5   (b) 7

    (c) 7.75   (d) None of these

Solution: Think only of length measuring formulae (Pythagoras theorem is obvious in this case).

If we can find the value of x, we will get the answer for BC as $AD - 2x$. Hence, we need to focus our energies in finding the value of x.

The construction above gives us two right angled triangles (OEC and DEC).

In Δ OCE, $OC = 4$ (radius) and $OE = (4 - x)$, Then: $(CE)^2 = 8x - x^2$. (Using Pythagoras Theorem)

Then in triangle CED:

$$(8x - x^2) + x^2 = 2^2$$

Hence, $x = 0.5$

Thus, $BC = 8 - 2 \times 0.5 = 7$

4. In the given circle, AC is the diameter of the circle. ED is parallel to AC. $\angle CBE = 65°$, find $\angle DEC$.
   (a) 35°   (b) 55°
   (c) 45°   (d) 25°

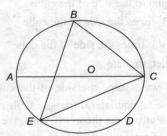

Solution: Obviously this question has to be solved using only angle measuring tools. Further from the figure, it is obvious that we have to use angle measurement tools related to arcs of circles.

Reacting to the 65° information in the question above, you will get $\angle EOC = 130°$ (Since, the angle at the centre of the circle is twice the angle at any point of the circle).

Hence, $\angle AOE = 180 - 130 = 50°$

This, will be the same as $\angle COD$ since the minor arc AE = minor arc CD.

Also, $\angle DEC = \frac{1}{2} \times \angle COD$

Hence, $\angle DEC = 25°$

Directions for Questions 5 to 7: In the figure below, X and Y are circles with centres O and O' respectively. MAB is a common tangent. The radii of X and Y are in the ratio 4 : 3 and $OM = 28$ cm.

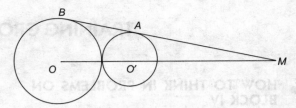

5. What is the ratio of the length of OO' to that of $O'M$?
   (a) 1 : 4   (b) 1 : 3
   (c) 3 : 8   (d) 3 : 4
6. What is the radius of circle X?
   (a) 2 cm   (b) 3 cm
   (c) 4 cm   (d) 5 cm
7. The length of AM is
   (a) $8\sqrt{3}$ cm   (b) $10\sqrt{3}$ cm
   (c) $12\sqrt{3}$ cm   (d) $14\sqrt{3}$ cm

Solution: Construct OB and $O'A$ as shown below.

In this construction it is evident that the two right angled triangles formed are similar to each other. i.e. ΔOBM is similar to $\Delta O'AM$.

Hence, $OM : O'M = 4 : 3$ (since $OB : O'A = 4 : 3$)

Also, $OM = 28$ cm, $\therefore$ $O'M = 21$ cm. $\rightarrow OO' = 7$ cm.

Hence, the radius of circle X is 4 cm (Answer to Q. 6).

5. Also: $OO' = 7$ and $O'M = 21$. Hence, required ratio = 1 : 3
7. AM can be found easily using Pythagoras theorem.

$$AM^2 = 21^2 - 3^2 = 432$$

$$\therefore \quad AM = \sqrt{432} = 12\sqrt{3}.$$

(Note: Only similarity of triangles and Pythagoras theorem was used here.)

8. In the figure, $ABCD$ is a rectangle inscribed inside a circle with center O. Side AB > Side BC. The ratio of the area of the circle to the area of the rectangle is π : $\sqrt{3}$. Also, $\angle ODC = \angle ADE$. Find the ratio $AE : AD$.

(a) $1 : \sqrt{3}$

(b) $1 : \sqrt{2}$

(c) $2\sqrt{3} : 1$

(d) $1 : 2$

Solution: In my experience, questions involving ratios of length typically involves the use of similar triangles. This question is no different.

Make the following construction:

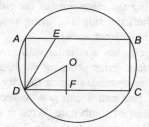

ΔOFD is similar to ΔAED. Hence, the required ratio $AE : AD = OF/FD$

But $OF = \frac{1}{2}$ side BC while $FD = \frac{1}{2}$ side CD.

Hence, we need the ratio of the side of the rectangle $BC : DC$ (This will give the required answer.)

From this point, you can get to the answer through a little bit of unconventional thinking.

The ratio of the area of the circle to that of the rectangle is given as $\pi : \sqrt{3}$. Hence, it is obvious that one of the sides has to have a $\sqrt{3}$ component in it. Hence, options 2 and 4 can be rejected. Also the required ratio has to be less than 1, hence, option (1) is correct.

9. Find $\angle BOA$.

(a) $100°$

(b) $150°$

(c) $80°$

(d) Indeterminate

Solution: Obviously this question has to be solved using angle measurement tools.

In order to measure $\angle BOA$, you could either try to use theorems related to the angle subtended by arcs of a circle or solve using the isosceles ΔBOA.

With this thought in mind start reacting to the information in the question.

$\angle CAF = 100°$. Hence $\angle BAC = 80°$

Also, $\angle OCA = (90 - ACF) = 90 - 50 = 40° = \angle OAC$ (Since the triangle OCA is isosceles)

Hence $\angle OAB = 40°$

In isosceles ΔOAB, $\angle OBA$ will also be $40°$

Hence $\angle BOA = 180 - 40 - 40 = 100°$

10. In the figure $AD = CD = BC$ and $\angle BCE = 96°$. How much is $\angle DBC$?

(a) $32°$

(b) $84°$

(c) $64°$

(d) Indeterminate

Solution: Get out your angle measuring formulae and start reacting to the information.

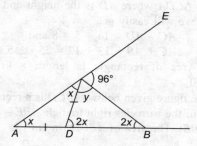

From the figure above, it is clear that

$$x + y = 180 - 96 = 84°$$

Also $\qquad 4x + y = 180°$

Solving we get $x = 32°$

Hence, $\qquad \angle DBC = 2x = 64°$.

11. $PQRS$ is a square. SR is a tangent (at point S) to the circle with centre O and $TR = OS$. Then the ratio of area of the circle to the area of the square is

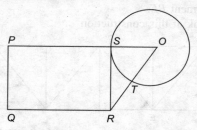

(a) $\pi/3$

(b) $11/7$

(c) $3/\pi$

(d) $7/11$

Solution: Looking at the options we can easily eliminate option (b) and (d), because in the ratio of the area of the circle to the area of the triangle we cannot eliminate π and hence the answer should contain π.

Further the question is asking for the ratio $\dfrac{\text{Area of the circle}}{\text{Area of the square}}$ so, π should be in the numerator.

Hence (a).

12. In the adjoining figure, $AC + AB = 5AD$ and $AC - AD = 8$. Then the area of the rectangle $ABCD$ is

(a) 36   (b) 50

(c) 60   (d) Cannot be answered

Solution: Think only of length measuring formulae (Pythagoras Theorem is obvious in this case).

There is no need of forming equations if you have the knowledge of some basic triplets like 3, 4, 5; 5, 12, 13 etc.

Now looking at the equations given in the question and considering ΔCDA where AD is the height and AC is the hypotenuse we will easily get,

$$AC - AD = 13 - 5 = 8 \text{ and}$$
$$AC + AB = 13 + 12 = 25 \text{ i.e. } 5AD$$

Hence, Area of rectangle is length × breadth i.e. $5 \times 12 = 60$

13. In the figure given below. $ABCD$ is a rectangle. The area of the isosceles right triangle $ABE = 7$ cm², $EC = 3(BE)$. The area of $ABCD$ (in cm²) is

Solution: The key to solve this question is in the visualisation of the construction and the equations.

It is given that $EC = 3 (BE)$ from this we can conclude that the whole side BC can be divided in four equal parts of measurement BE.

Now look at this construction

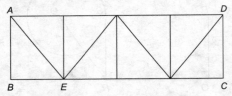

Each part is of equal area as 7 cm². Hence $7 \times 8 = 56$ cm²

14. In the given figure. $EADF$ is a rectangle and ABC is a triangle whose vertices lie on the sides of $EADF$. $AE = 22$, $BE = 6$ $CF = 16$ and $BF = 2$. Find the length of the line joining the mid–points of the side AB and BC

(a) $4\sqrt{2}$ (b) 5

(c) 3.5   (d) None of these

Solution: Think only of length measuring formulae and triplets.

$EA = 22$ and $FC = 16$, So, $CD = 6$

$EF = 8$ So, AD is also 8. Now using the triplet 6, 8, 10 based on basic triplet 3, 4, 5 we will get that $AC = 10$.

The line joining the midpoints of the sides AB and BC will be exactly half the side AC (using similar triangles).

Hence, 5 is the correct answer.

15. A certain city has a circular wall around it and this wall has four gates pointing north, south, east and west. A house stands outside the city, 3 km north of the north gate and it can just be seen from a point nine km east of south gate. What is the diameter of the wall that surrounds the city?

Solution: Make this construction

Given $AN = 3$, $BC = 9$ and $\angle B$ is 90°. Now according to conventional method, we have to use tangent theorem to get to the answer, which will be very long.

Instead if we were to use the Pythagorean triplets again we would easily see the (9, 12, 15) triplet which is based on the basic triplet 3, 4, 5. Here $BC = 9$, Hence, $AC = 15$ and $AB = 12$. Hence, the diameter will be $12 - 3 = 9$ km.

16. Let $ABCDEF$ be a regular hexagon: What is the ratio of the area of the triangle ACE to that of the hexagon $ABCDEF$?

Solution: Make the following construction:

Now we have to find the ratio $\dfrac{\text{Area of } ACE}{\text{Area of } ABCDEF}$.

In order to do so we use the property of a regular hexagon (that it is a combination of 6 equilateral triangles).

We can easily see that we have divided all 6 equilateral triangles into two equal parts of the same area.

If we number all the equal areas as 1, 2, 3 ⋯ 12 as shown in the above construction we will get the answer as

$$\frac{\text{Sum of area of triangles } 1+2+3+4+5+6}{\text{Sum of area of triangle } 1+2+3\ldots+12}$$

Hence ½.

17. Euclid has a triangle in mind. Its longest side has length 20 and another of its side has length 10. Its area is 80. What is the exact length of its third side?

  (a) $\sqrt{260}$ (b) $\sqrt{250}$

  (c) $\sqrt{240}$ (d) $\sqrt{270}$

Solution: The solution of the above question is based on the following construction, where $AB = 20$ and $BD = 10$

Space for Rough Work

The question is asking for the exact length AD, of triangle ABD.

Think only of length measuring formulae (Pythagoras theorem is obvious in this case).

If we extend the side BD upto a point C, the length AC will give the Altitude or height of the ΔABD. Then we will get:

½ $b \times h \Rightarrow 80 \Rightarrow$ ½ $\times 10 \times h = 80 \Rightarrow h = 16$. i.e. $AC = 16$.

And now as ΔABC is a right angled triangle, we can easily get the length of DC as 2, based on the triplet 12, 16, 20.

Now, if $AC = 16$, $DC = 2$, we can easily get the exact length of AD using Pythagoras theorem i.e. $AC = \sqrt{2^2 + 16^2}$ = $\sqrt{260}$

Hence (1).

(*Note:* In this solution we have only used Pythagorean triplet 12, 16, 20 to solve the question. The alternate method for solving this question is through the use of the semi perimeter of the triangle. This will lead to a very cumbersome and long solution to this question. For experimentation purposes you can try this solution for yourself.)

🎯 BLOCK REVIEW TESTS

REVIEW TEST 1

1. A piece of paper is in the shape of a right angled triangle. This paper is cut along a line that is parallel to the hypotenuse, leaving a smaller triangle. The cut was done in such a manner that there was a 35% reduction in the length of the hypotenuse of the triangle. If the area of the original triangle was 54 square inches before the cut, what is the area (in square inches) of the smaller triangle?
    (a) 26.685   (b) 22.815
    (c) 23.465   (d) 24.365

2. Consider two different cloth-cutting processes. In the first one, n square cloth pieces of the same size are cut from a square cloth piece of the size a; then a circle of maximum possible area is cut from each of the smaller squares. In the second process, only one circle of maximum possible area is cut from a square of the same size and the process ends there. The cloth pieces remaining after cutting the circles are scrapped in both the processes. The ratio of the total area of .scrap cloth generated in the former to that in the latter is:
    (a) $1 : 1$ (b) $\sqrt{2} : 1$
    (c) $2 : 1$ (d) $\dfrac{4n - \pi}{n(4 - \pi)}$

3. The length of the circumference of a circle equals the perimeter of a triangle of equal sides. This is also equal to the the perimeter of a square and also the perimeter of a regular pentagon. The areas covered by the circle, triangle, pentagon and square are c. t, p and s respectively. Then:
    (a) $s > t > c > p$ (b) $c > p > t > s$
    (c) $c > p > s > t$ (d) $s > p > c > t$

4. Three horses are grazing within a semi-circular field. In the diagram given below, AB is the diameter of the semi-circular field with centre at O. Horses are tied up at P, R and S such that PO and RO are the radii of the two semi circles drawn with centers at P and R respectively. S is the centre of the circle touching the two semi-circles with diameters AO and OB. The horses tied at P and R can graze within the respective semi-circles and the horse tied at S can graze within the circle centred at S. The percentage of the area of the semi-circle with diameter AB that cannot be grazed by the horses is nearest to:

    (a) 16   (b) 24
    (c) 36   (d) 32

5. A certain city has a circular wall around it with four gates pointing north, south, east and west. A house stands outside the city, three km north of the north gate, and it can just be seen from a point nine km east of the south gate. What is the diameter of the wall that surrounds the city?
    (a) 6 km   (b) 9 km
    (c) 12 km   (d) None of these

6. Based on the figure below, what is the value of x, if $y = 10$.

    (a) 10   (b) 11
    (c) 12   (d) None of these

7. What is the number of distinct triangles with integral valued sides and perimeter as 12?
    (a) 6   (b) 5
    (c) 4   (d) 3

Directions for Questions 8 and 9: Answer the question based on the following information.

A cow is tethered at point A by a rope. Neither the rope nor the cow is allowed to enter the triangle ABC.
$$\angle BAC = 30°.$$
$$AB = AC = 10 \text{ m}.$$

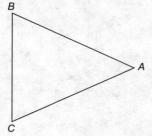

8. What is the area that can be grazed by the cow if the length of the rope is 8 m ?
    (a) $134\pi\dfrac{1}{3}$ sq. m   (b) 121π sq. m

(c) 132π sq. m   (d) $\dfrac{176\pi}{3}$ sq. m

9. What is the area that can be grazed by the cow if the length of the rope is 12 m?

     (a) $134\pi\dfrac{1}{3}$ sq. m   (b) 121π sq. m

     (c) 132π sq. m   (d) $\dfrac{176\pi}{3}$ sq. m

10. *AB* is the diameter of the given circle, while points *C* and *D* lie on the circumference as shown. If *AB* is 25 cm, *AC* is 20 cm and *BD* is 7 cm, find the area of the quadrilateral *ACBD*.

     (a) 160 sq. cm   (b) 240 sq. cm

     (c) 320 sq. cm   (d) None of these

11. The value of each of a set of coins varies as the square of its diameter, if its thickness remains constant, varies as the thickness, if the diameter remains constant. If the diameter of two coins are in the ratio 3 : 4, what should be the ratio of their thicknesses be if the value of the second is four times that of the first?

     (a) 9 : 16   (b) 4 : 9

     (c) 16 : 9   (d) 9 : 4

12. If *a*, *b* and *c* are the sides of a triangle, and $a^2 + b^2 + c^2 = bc + ca + ab$, then the triangle is:

     (a) equilateral   (b) isosceles

     (c) right-angled   (d) obtuse-angled

Directions for Questions 13 and 14: Use the following information: *XYZ* is an equilateral triangle in which *Y* is 2 km from *X*. Safdar starts walking from *Y* in a direction parallel to *XZ* and stops when he reaches a point *M* directly east of *Z*. He, then, reverses direction and walks till he reaches a point *N* directly south of *Z*.

13. Then *M* is
     (a) 3 km east and 1 km north of *X*
     (b) 3 km east and $\sqrt{3}$ km north of *X*
     (c) $\sqrt{3}$ km east and 1 km south of *X*
     (d) $\sqrt{3}$ km west and 3 km north of *X*

14. The total distance walked by Safdar is:
     (a) 3 km   (b) 4 km
     (c) $2\sqrt{3}$ km   (d) 6 km

15. The sides of a triangle are 5, 12 and 13 units. A rectangle is constructed, which has an area twice the area of the triangle, and has a width of 10 units. Then, the perimeter of the rectangle is:
     (a) 30 units   (b) 36 units
     (c) 32 units   (d) None of these

16. The diameter of a hollow cone is equal to the diameter of a spherical ball. If the ball is placed at the base of the cone, what portion of the ball will be inside the cone?
     (a) 50%   (b) less than 50%
     (c) more than 50%   (d) 100%

17. The length of a ladder is exactly equal to the height of the wall it is leaning against. If lower end of the ladder is kept on a platform of height 3 feet and the platform is kept 9 feet away from the wall, the upper end of the ladder coincides with the top of the wall. Then, the height of the wall is:
     (a) 12 feet   (b) 15 feet
     (c) 18 feet   (d) 16 feet

18. A cube of side 12 cm is painted red on all the faces and then cut into smaller cubes, each of side 3 cm. What is the total number of smaller cubes having none of their faces painted?
     (a) 16   (b) 8
     (c) 12   (d) None of these

19. From a circular sheet of paper with a radius 20 cm, four circles of radius 5 cm each are cut out. What is the ratio of the cut to the uncut portion?
     (a) 1 : 3   (b) 4 : 1
     (c) 3 : 1   (d) 4 : 3

20. Four friends Mani, Sunny, Honey & Funny start from four towns Mindain, Sindain, Hindain and Findain respectively. The four towns are at the four corners of an imaginary rectangle. They meet at a point which falls inside this imaginary rectangle. At that point three of them (Mani, Sunny and Honey had travelled distances of 40 m, 50 m and 60 m respectively). The maximum distance that Funny could have travelled is near about:
     (a) 67 m   (b) 53 m
     (c) 24 m   (d) Cannot be determined

21. Each side of a given polygon is parallel to either the *X* or the *Y* axis. A corner of such a polygon is said to be convex if the internal angle is 90° or concave if the internal angle is 270°. If the number of convex corners in such a polygon is 29, the number of concave corners must be
     (a) 20   (b) 0
     (c) 25   (d) 26

22. In the figure (not drawn to scale) given below, *L* is a point on *AB* such that *AL* : *LB* = 4 : 3. *LQ* is parallel to *AC* and *QD* is parallel to *CL*. In $\triangle ARC$, $\angle ARC = 90°$, and in $\triangle LQS$, $\angle LSQ = 90°$. What is ratio *AL* : *LD*?

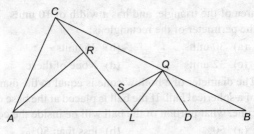

(a) 3 : 7   (b) 4 : 3
(c) 7 : 3   (d) 8 : 3

23. In the diagram given below, $\angle ABC = \angle CDB = \angle PQD$ = 90°. If $AB : CD = 3 : 1$, the ratio of $CD : PQ$ is:

Space for Rough Work

(a) 1 : 0.666   (b) 1 : 0.75
(c) 1 : 0.54   (d) None of the above

24. In the figure given below, $ABCD$ is a rectangle. The area of the isosceles right triangle ABE = 9 cm². $EC = 3(BE)$. The area of $ABCD$ (in cm²) is:

(a) 27   (b) 36
(c) 54   (d) 72

25. The length of the common chord of two circles of radii 15 cm and 20 cm whose centres are 25 cm apart, is (in cm):

(a) 24   (b) 10
(c) 12   (d) 20

REVIEW TEST 2

1. A square tin sheet of side 24 inches is converted into a box with open top in the following steps: The sheet is placed horizontally. Then, equal sized squares, each of side x inches, are cut from the four corners of the sheet. Finally, the four resulting sides are bent vertically upwards in the shape of a box. If x is an Integer, then what value of x maximizes the volume of the box?

   (a) 6   (b) 8
   (c) 2   (d) 4

2. Let S_1 be a square of side a. Another square S_2 is formed by joining the mid-points of the sides of S_1. The same process is applied to S_2 to form yet another square S_3, and so on. If $A_1, A_2, A_3, \ldots\ldots$ be the areas and $P_1, P_2, P_3, \ldots\ldots$ be the perimeters of $S_1, S_2, S_3, \ldots\ldots$, respectively, then the ratio $\dfrac{A_1 + A_2 + A_3 + \ldots}{P_1 + P_2 + P_3 + \ldots}$ equals:

   (a) $1/2(1 + \sqrt{2})$ (b) $a/2(2 - \sqrt{2})$
   (c) $a/2(2 + \sqrt{2})$ (d) $a/2(1 + 2\sqrt{2})$

3. There are two concentric circles such that the area of the outer circle is four times the area of the inner circle. Let A, B and C be three distinct points on the perimeter of the outer circle such that AB and AC are tangents to the inner circle. If the area of the triangle ABC is $\dfrac{9\sqrt{3}}{\pi}$ then what would be the area of the outer circle?

   (a) 9/4   (b) 9/π
   (c) 12   (d) None of these

4. Four horses are tethered at four corners of a square plot of side 42 meters so that the adjacent horses can just reach one another. There is a small circular pond of area 20 m² at the center. Find the ungrazed area.

   (a) 378 m²   (b) 388 m²
   (c) 358 m²   (d) 368 m²

5. A square, whose side is 2 meters, has its corners cut away so as to form an octagon with all sides equal. Then length of each side of the octagon, in metres is:

   (a) $\dfrac{\sqrt{2}}{\sqrt{2}+1}$ (b) $\dfrac{2}{\sqrt{2}+1}$

   (c) $\dfrac{2}{\sqrt{2}-1}$ (d) $\dfrac{\sqrt{2}}{\sqrt{2}-1}$

6. A rectangular pool 30 metres wide and 50 metres long is surrounded by a walkway of uniform width. If the area of the walkway is 516 square meters, how wide, in metres, is the walkway?

   (a) 1   (b) 2
   (c) 3   (d) None of these

7. A farmer has decided to build a wire fence along one straight side of his property. For this purpose he has planned to place several fence-posts at 12 m intervals, with posts fixed at both ends of the side. After he bought the posts and wire, he found that the number of posts he had bought was 5 less than required. However, he discovered that the number of posts he had bought would be just sufficient if he spaced them 16 m apart. What is the length of the side of his property and how many posts did he buy?

   (a) 200 m, 15   (b) 200 m, 16
   (c) 240 m, 15   (d) 240 m, 16

8. The figure below shows two concentric circles with centre O. PQRS is a square inscribed in the outer circle. It also circumscribes the inner circle, touching it at points B, C, D and A. What is the ratio of the perimeter of the polygon ABCD to that of the outer circle?

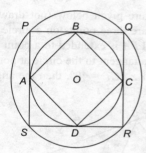

   (a) 4/π (b) 2/3π
   (c) 2/π (d) 1/π

9. Four identical coins are placed in a square. For each coin, the ratio of area to circumference is same as the ratio of circumference to area. Then, find the area of the square that is covered by the coins.

   (a) 16π (b) 32π
   (c) 8π (d) Insufficient data

10. The sum of the areas of two circles, which touch each other externally, is 153π. If the sum of their radii is 15, the ratio of the smaller to the larger radius is:

    (a) 1 : 4   (b) 1 : 2
    (c) 1 : 3   (d) None of these

11. In ΔABC, points P, Q and R are the mid-points of sides AB, BC and CA respectively. If area of ΔABC, is 40 sq units, find the area of ΔPQR.
    (a) 10 sq. units
    (b) $10\sqrt{3}$ sq. units
    (c) 5 sq. units
    (d) None of these

12. A wooden box (open at the top) of thickness 0.5 cm, length 21 cm, width 11 cm and height 6 cm is painted on the inside. The expenses of painting are ₹ 140. What is the rate of painting per square centimeter?
    (a) ₹ 1.4
    (b) ₹ 0.5
    (c) ₹ 1
    (d) ₹ 2

13. Which one of the following cannot be the ratio of angles in a right-angled triangle?
    (a) $1:2:3$
    (b) $1:1:2$
    (c) $1:3:5$
    (d) None of these

14. A slab of ice 10 inches in length, 15 inches in breadth, and 3 inches thick was melted and re-solidified in the form of a rod of 10 inches diameter. The length of such a rod, in inches, is nearest to:
    (a) 5
    (b) 5.7
    (c) 4.5
    (d) 5.5

15. In the figure given below (not drawn to scale), A, B and C are three points on a circle with centre O. The chord BA is extended to a point T such that CT becomes a tangent to the circle at point C. If $\angle ATC = 20°$ and $\angle ACT = 40°$, then the angle $\angle BOA$ is:

    (a) 160°
    (b) 150°
    (c) 140°
    (d) Not possible to determine

16. A vertical tower OP stands at the center O of a square $ABCD$. Let x and y denote the height of the tower OP and the side of the square AB respectively. Suppose $\angle APB = 60°$ then the relationship between x and y can be expressed as:
    (a) $2y^2 = x^2$
    (b) $2x^2 = y^2$
    (c) $3y^2 = 2x^2$
    (d) $3x^2 = 2y^2$

17. In a triangle XYZ, $XY = 6$, $YZ = 8$ and $XZ = 10$. A perpendicular dropped from Y, meets the side XZ at M. A circle of radius YM (with center Y) is drawn. If the circle cuts XY and YZ at P and Q respectively, then $QZ : XP$ is equal to:

(a) $1:1$
(b) $2:3$
(c) $1:4$
(d) $8:3$

18. In the figure below, AB is the chord of a circle with center O. AB is extended to C such that $BC = OB$. The straight line CO is produced to meet the circle at D. If $\angle ACD = 20°$ and $\angle AOD = x$ degrees then the value of x is:

    (a) 20
    (b) 40
    (c) 60
    (d) None of these

19. The area of the triangle whose vertices are (a, a), $(a + 1, a + 1)$, $(a + 2, a)$ is:
    (a) a^3
    (b) 1
    (c) $2a$
    (d) $2^{1/2}$

20. In the given figure, AB is the diameter of the circle and points C and D are on the circumference such that $\angle CAD = 40°$ and $\angle CBA = 60°$. What is the measure of $\angle ACD$?

    (a) 20°
    (b) 30°
    (c) 40°
    (d) 50°

21. A ladder leans against a vertical wall. The top of the ladder is 12 m above the ground. When the bottom of the ladder is moved 4 m farther away from the wall, the top of the ladder rests against the foot of the wall. What is the length of the ladder?
    (a) 16 m
    (b) 15 m
    (c) 20 m
    (d) 17 m

22. In the below diagram, $ABCD$ is a rectangle with $AE = 2EF = 3FB$. What is the ratio of the area of the rectangle to that of the triangle CEF?

    (a) $11:3$
    (b) $22:3$
    (c) $11:6$
    (4) None of these

23. In the given figure, *EADF* is a rectangle and *ABC* is a triangle whose vertices lie on the sides of *EADF*. *AE* = 30, *BE* = 12, *CF* = 18 and *BF* = 4. Find the length of the line joining the mid-points of the sides *AB* and *BC*.

(a) 5

(b) 10

(c) 15

(d) None of these

24. In the figure, points *A*, *B*, *C* and *D* lie on the circle. *AD* = 44 and *BC* = 11. What is the ratio of the area of Δ *CBE* to that of the triangle Δ *ADE*?

(a) 1 : 4

(b) 1 : 16

(c) 1 : 16

(d) Data insufficient

25. In a rectangle, the difference between the sum of the adjacent sides and the diagonal is two-thirds the length of the shorter side. What is the ratio of the shorter to the longer side?

(a) $\sqrt{3}$: 2

(b) 1 : $\sqrt{3}$

(c) 2 : 5

(d) 3 : 4

Space for Rough Work

REVIEW TEST 3

1. In the figure given below, if angle $ABC = 90$, and BD is perpendicular to AC, & $BD = 4$ cm and $AD = 3$ cm , what will be the length of BC

   (a) 13   (b) 15
   (c) 10   (d) 9

2. In the figure below, the measure of an angle formed by the bisectors of two angles in a triangle ABC is 130 find the measure of an angle B.
   (a) 40   (b) 45
   (c) 50   (d) 80

3. The perimeter of right triangle is 36 and the sum of the square of its sides is 450. The area of the right triangle is
   (a) 42   (b) 54
   (c) 62   (d) 100

4. The circles are tangent to one another and each circle is tangent to the sides of the right triangle ABC with right angle ABC. If the larger circle has radius 12 and the smaller circle has radius 3, what is the area of the triangle?

   (a) 420   (b) 620
   (c) 540   (d) 486

5. All the circles are tangent to one another / or the sides of the rectangle. All circles have radius 1. What is the area of the shaded region to the nearest whole unit, i.e. the region outside all the circles but inside the rectangle?

   (a) 27   (b) 28
   (c) 29   (d) 30

6. Given below are six congruent circles drawn internally tangent to a circle of a radius 21; each smaller circle is also tangent to each of its adjacent circles. Find the shaded area between the circle and the six smaller circles.

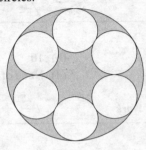

   (a) 136π (b) 196π
   (c) 180π (d) 147π

7. In the figure below, O_1 and O_2 are centers of the circles O_1A is the circle centers at O_2.

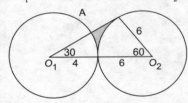

   Find the area of the shaded region.
   (a) $22 - 7\pi$ (b) $24\sqrt{2} - 7\pi$
   (c) $18 - 9\pi$ (d) $24 - \pi22/3$

8. In the figure, which of the following is correct?

   (a) $x = 60$ (b) $x = 70$
   (c) $x = 10$ (d) $x = 90$

9. Triangle PAB is formed by three tangents to circle O and angle $APB = 40$; then the angle BOA equals

(a) 70   (b) 55

(c) 60   (d) 50

10. *PQRS* is a cyclic quadrilateral. The angle bisector of angle *P*, *Q*, *R* and *S* intersect at *A*, *B*, *C* and *D* as shown in the figure below. Then these four points form a quadrilateral *ABCD* is a:

(a) Rectangle   (b) square

(c) rhombus   (d) cyclic quadrilateral

11. In the given figure, *O* is the center of the circle; angle $BOC = m°$, angle $BAC = n°$.then which of the following is correct?

(a) $m + n = 90$ (b) $m + n = 180$

(c) $2m + n = 180$ (d) $m + 2n = 180$

12. Find the area of shaded portion given that the circles with centers *O* and *O′* are 6 cm and 18 cm in diameter respectively and *ACB* is a semi circle.

(a) $54 \pi \, cm^2$ (b) $27 \pi \, cm^2$

(c) $36 \pi \, cm^2$ (d) $18 \pi \, cm^2$

13. There are two spheres and one cube. The cube is inside the bigger sphere and the smaller sphere is inside the cube. Find the ratio of surface areas of the bigger sphere to the smaller sphere?

(a) 3 : 1   (b) 2 : 1

(c) 4 : 1   (d) 2 : 1

14. In the adjoining figure, a star is shown. What is the sum of the angles *P*, *Q*, *R*, *S* and *T*?

(a) 240   (b) 180

(c) 120   (d) Can't be determined

15. In the figure given below *PS* & *RT* are the medians each measuring 4 cm. triangle *PQR* is right angled at *Q*. what is the area of the triangle *PQR*?

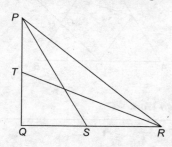

(a) 5.2   (b) 6.4

(d) 6.2   (d) 7.2

16. The area of the largest triangle that can be inscribed in a semi circle whose radius is

(a) $2R^2$ (b) $3R^2$

(c) R^2 (d) $3R^2/2$

17. *R* is *O* is the center of the circle having radius (*OP*) = *r*. *PQRSTU* is a regular hexagon and *PAQBRCS-DTEUFP* is a regular six pointed star.

Find the perimeter of hexagon *PQRSTU*.

(a) 12*r*   (b) 9*r*

(c) 6*r*   (d) 8*r*

18. In the given figure *ABC* is a triangle in which *AD* = 3*CD* and *E* lies on *BD*, *DE* = 2*BE*. What is the ratio of area of triangle *ABE* and area of triangle *ABC*?

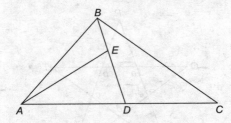

(a) 1/12   (b) 1/8

(c) 1/6   (d) 1/10

19. In the given figure, P and Q are the mid points of AC and AB. Also, $PG = GR$ and $HQ = HR$. what is the ratio of area of triangle PQR: area of triangle ABC?

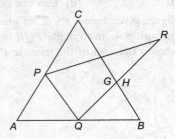

(a) 1/2   (b) 2/3

(c) 3/5   (d) 1/3

20. In the given figure, it is given that angle $C = 90$, $AD = DB$, DE is perpendicular to $AB = 20$, and $AC = 12$. The area of quadrilateral $ADEC$ is:

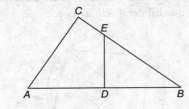

(a) 37(1/2)   (b) 75

(c) 48   (d) 58(1/2)

Space for Rough Work

REVIEW TEST 4

1. Rectangle *PQRS* contains 4 congruent rectangles. If the smaller dimension of one of the small rectangles is 4 units, what is the area of rectangle *PQRS* in square units?
   - (a) 144
   - (b) 172
   - (c) 156
   - (d) 192

2. If the radii of the circles with centers *O* and *P*, as shown below are 4 and 2 units respectively. Find the area of triangle *ABC*.
   Given: angle *DOA* = angle *EPC* = 90

   - (a) 36
   - (b) 62
   - (c) 18
   - (d) 48

3. A cube of side 16 cm is painted red on all the faces and then cut into smaller cubes, each of side 4 cm. What is the total number of smaller cubes having none of their faces painted?
   - (a) 16
   - (b) 8
   - (c) 12
   - (d) 24

4. Identical regular pentagons are placed together side by side to form a ring in the manner shown. The diagram shows the first two pentagons. How many are needed to make a full ring?

   - (a) 9
   - (b) 10
   - (c) 11
   - (d) 12

5. Find angle *EBC* + angle *ECB* from the given figure, given *ADE* is an equilateral triangle and angle *DCE* = 20°
   - (a) 160
   - (b) 140
   - (c) 100
   - (d) 120

6. *PQRS* is a square and *POQ* is an equilateral triangle. What is the value of angle *SOR*?

   - (a) 150
   - (b) 120
   - (c) 125
   - (d) 100

7. In the following figure *ABCD* is a square, angle *DAO* = 40 then find angle *BNO*.

   - (a) 50
   - (b) 60
   - (c) 30
   - (d) 40

8. From an external point *P*, tangents *PA* and *PB* are drawn to a circle with center *O*. If *CO* is the tangent to the circle at a point *E* and *PA* = 14 cm, find the perimeter of Δ*CPD*.

   - (a) 21
   - (b) 28
   - (c) 24
   - (d) 25

9. A circle is inscribed in an equilateral triangle; the radius of the circle is 2 cm. Find the area of triangle.
   - (a) $12\sqrt{3}$
   - (b) $15\sqrt{3}$
   - (c) $12\sqrt{2}$
   - (d) $18\sqrt{3}$

10. If interior angle of a regular polygon is 168°, then find no. of sides in that polygon.

    (a) 10   (b) 20
    (c) 30   (d) 25

11. In the given figure, *PQ* and *PR* are two tangents to the circle, whose center is *O*. If angle *QPR* = 40°, find angle *QSR*.

    (a) 60   (b) 70
    (c) 80   (d) 50

12. In the figure *AB* \\ *DE*, angle *BAD* = 20° and angle *DAE* = 30°, and *DE* = *EC*. Then *x* equals:

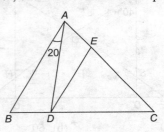

    (a) 60   (b) 65
    (c) 75   (d) 70

13. There is an equilateral triangle of side 32 cm. The mid-points of the sides are joined to form another triangle, whose mid-points are again joined to form still another triangle. This process is continued for '*n*' number of times. The sum of the perimeters of all the triangles is 180 cm. Find the value of *n*.

    (a) 4   (b) 5
    (c) 8   (d) 3

14. There is a circle of diameter *AB* and radius 26 cm. If chord *CA* is 10 cm long, find the ratio of area of triangle *ABC* to the remaining area of circle.

15. Ram Singh has a rectangular plot of land of dimensions 30 m * 40 m. He wants to construct a unique swimming pool which is in the shape of an equilateral triangle. Find the area of the largest swimming pool which he can have?

    (a) 300 $\sqrt{3}$ sq cm   (b) 225 $\sqrt{3}$ sq cm
    (c) 300 sq cm   (d) 225$\sqrt{}$ sq cm

16. The perimeter of a triangle is 105 cm. The ratio of its altitudes is 3 : 5 : 6. Find the sides of the triangle.

    (a) 72, 46, 36   (b) 62, 28, 41
    (c) 30, 60, 25   (d) 50, 30, 25

17. Rizwan gave his younger sister a rectangular sheet of paper. He halved it by folding it at the mid point of its longer side. The piece of paper again became a rectangle whose longer and shorter sides were in the same proportion as the longer and shorter sides of the original rectangle. If the shorter side of the original rectangle was 4 cm, find the diagonal of the smaller rectangle?

    (a) $3(3)^{1/2}$ (b) $5(3)^{1/2}$
    (c) $4(3)^{1/2}$ (d) $2(3)^{1/2}$

18. A rectangular hall, 50 m in length and 75 m in width has to be paved with square tiles of equal size. What is the minimum number of tiles required?

    (a) 4   (b) 5
    (c) 6   (d) 8

19. In triangle *ABC* we have angle *A* = 100 degree and *B* = *C* = 40. The side *AB* is produced to a point *D* so that *B* lies between *A* and *D* and *AD* = *BC*. Then angle *BCD* =?

    (a) 20°   (b) 10°
    (c) 30°   (4) 40°

20. The sides of a cyclic quadrilateral are 9,10,12 and 16. If one of its diagonals is 14, then find the other diagonal?

    (a) 16   (b) 17
    (c) 18   (d) 19

21. Segments starting with points *M* and *N* and ending with vertices of the rectangle *ABCD* divide the given figure into eight parts (see the figure). The areas of three parts of the rectangle are indicated in the picture. What is the area of the shaded region?

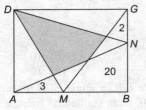

    (a) 25   (b) 40
    (c) 29   (d) 20

(a) 0.60   (b) 0.30
(c) 0.29   (d) 0.52

ANSWER KEY

Review Test 1

1. (b)	2. (a)	3. (c)	4. (c)
5. (b)	6. (b)	7. (d)	8. (d)
9. (c)	10. (d)	11. (b)	12. (a)
13. (b)	14. (d)	15. (c)	16. (b)
17. (b)	18. (b)	19. (a)	20. (a)
21. (c)	22. (c)	23. (b)	24. (d)
25. (a)			

Review Test 2

1. (d)	2. (c)	3. (c)	4. (c)
5. (a)	6. (c)	7. (d)	8. (c)
9. (a)	10. (a)	11. (a)	12. (c)
13. (c)	14. (b)	15. (a)	16. (b)
17. (d)	18. (c)	19. (b)	20. (a)

21. (c)	22. (b)	23. (b)	24. (b)
25. (b)			

Review Test 3

1. (b)	2. (d)	3. (b)	4. (d)
5. (d)	6. (d)	7. (d)	8. (d)
9. (a)	10. (d)	11. (a)	12. (b)
13. (a)	14. (b)	15. (b)	16. (c)
17. (c)	18. (a)	19. (a)	20. (d)

Review Test 4

1. (d)	2. (a)	3. (b)	4. (b)
5. (c)	6. (a)	7. (d)	8. (b)
9. (a)	10. (c)	11. (b)	12. (b)
13. (a)	14. (c)	15. (a)	16. (d)
17. (c)	18. (c)	19. (b)	20. (c)
21. (a)			

BLOCK V

ALGEBRA

Chapter 13
Functions

Chapter 14
Inequalities

Chapter 15
Quadratic
and other
Equations

Chapter 16
Logarithms

...BACK TO SCHOOL

This block of chapters (consisting of Functions, Inequalities, Quadratic and other Equations and Logarithms) has always been a source of discomfort for students who have had negative experiences with Mathematics. At the same time students who have had a positive experience with mathematics throughout their school, junior college and college years find these chapters extremely easy.

Throughout my experience in training students preparing for the CAT exam and other aptitude exams like CMAT, SNAP, IIFT, MAT, XAT, etc. I have always critically tried to understand the key mental representations that differentiate the two categories of students I have mentioned above—how is it that two students who are basically similarly talented with similar IQs be so different when it comes to Higher Maths?

The reason I am talking about this issue is that Block V consists of some of the most critical areas of the entire QA Section for the CAT exam. Besides the XLRI entrance test, XAT also has a very high focus on this block of chapters. Hence, this is one area where you simply cannot allow yourselves to remain in the *'I cannot solve Block V questions'* category if you want to seriously take a crack at the CAT Exam. However to enable students who are weak at Maths to move from the 'I cannot' to the 'I can' category in this block of chapters you will first have to believe that this can happen.

And the good news is that in my experience of having trained over 50000 students for aptitude examinations, I have seen a lot of mediocre students in Maths transit from being initially poor at the chapters of this block to becoming strong in the same.

If you belong to such a category of students what you first need to understand is that the reason for your inability in Higher Maths lies in the way you have approached it up to now. There is simply no reason that a better approach will not help you.

WHAT APPROACH CHANGE DO YOU NEED?

To put it simply—rather than trying to study these Higher Maths chapters in so called Mathematical language, you need to study the same in plain logical language (with as little Maths as possible). The following write up is an attempt at the same. My attempt in the following part of this section is to give you in as simple language as possible some of the missing technology that makes you consider yourself weak at Maths (esp. this block of chapters).

The following is a list of startup issues you need to resolve in your mind in order to make yourself comfortable with this block of chapters.

ISSUE 1: The $X - Y$ Plot:

ISSUE 2: Locus of points

ISSUE 3: What is an equation?

ISSUE 4: Equations and Functions:

ISSUE 5: How inequalities relate to Graphs of functions?

Let us Now Start to Look at these Issues One by One

ISSUE 1: The X – Y Plot: The need for an $X - Y$ plot essentially arises out of the need to measure anything which cannot be measured in a single dimension.

Contd

For instance, any object that can be represented on a straight line (like a rope, a tape etc.) could be easily represented on the number line itself. However, when you are required to represent any two dimensional figures (like table top, a book etc.) simply unidimensional representations (which can be done on the number line only) are not sufficient.

You are required to be able to represent things in two dimensions.

For this purpose, a vertical line is drawn from point '0' of the number line. This line is perpendicular to the number line and is called the Y-axis (which in plain language terms can be understood as the axis which provides the vital second dimension of measurement which helps us describe plain figures better.)

In this situation, the horizontal line (which we know as the number line) is called the X-axis and the diagram which emerges represents what is known as the $X - Y$ plane and is also called as the $X - Y$ plot.

The number line (The X-axis) has a positive measurement direction on the right side of zero (and keeps going to a mathematically defined, in reality non-existent point called infinity.) On the left side of zero the X axis shows negative measurements and keeps going to negative infinity.

In a similar manner, the Y-axis starts from 0 and moves upwards to positive infinity and moves downwards to negative infinity.

The following figures illustrate this point.

Fig. 1   The number line (Also the X axis)

As can be seen the $X - Y$ plot divides the plane into 4 parts (Quadrants). The origin is the point where both X and Y are zero.

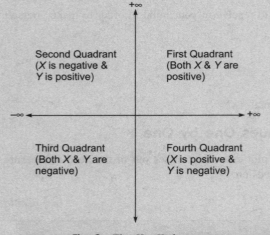

Fig. 2   The $X - Y$ plot

Plotting a Point on the *X – Y* Plot

Suppose we have to plot the point (2, 3) on the $X - Y$ plot. In order to do so, we first need to understand what $x = 2$ means on the $X - Y$ chart. On the $X - Y$ plot if you start from the $x = 2$ point on the X-axis and draw a line parallel to the Y-axis you will get a set of points which represent a constant value of x (=2). Similarly for $y = 3$, draw a line parallel to the X-axis from the $y = 3$ point on the Y-axis.

In this situation, the point of intersection between these two lines will be the point (2, 3).

I would encourage the reader to try to draw the figure as described above.

ISSUE 2: Locus of Points   In the above situation we have come across a set of points which represents $x = 2$. In mathematics lingo, a set of points is also referred to as a locus of points.

ISSUE 3: What is an Equation?   Consider the following:

   (a) $2x + 3 = 0$
   (b) $x^2 - 5x + 6 = 0$
   (c) $4x^3 - 3x^2 - 11x - 18 = 0$

In each of the above cases, we have a situation where there is an equality between what is written on the left side of the equality sign and the right side of the equality sign. i.e. LHS = RHS (Left Hand Side = Right Hand Side)

This is the basic definition of an equation.

All Equations have solutions

Consider the first equation above:

Here you have: $2x + 3 = 0 \rightarrow 2x = -3 \rightarrow x = -3/2$ i.e. $x = -1.5$

This means that at the value $x = -1.5$, the condition of the equation (i.e. LHS = RHS) is satisfied. This value of x is called the 'solution' or the 'root' of the equation.

Note: The equation we have just seen had a highest power of 'x' as 1. Such equations are called as linear equations. [We shall come to this issue of why they are called as linear equations shortly]. What you need to remember at this stage is that linear equations have only one solution. (or Root as mathematicians prefer to call it.)

ISSUE 4: Equations and Functions: Before we move ahead into the second and third equations given above, let us first try to connect equations and functions.

If you remember we studied in school a chapter called as the equation of a straight line. For instance, parallel to the equation $2x + 3 = 0$ we have $y = 2x + 3$ (which was defined as the equation of a straight line – hence $2x + 3 = 0$ is called a linear equation).

In $y = 2x + 3$ we have a consistent relationship between the values of x and the corresponding values of y that we could get.

Thus for $y = 2x + 3$, we can create the following table giving us the specific points which satisfy the equation as below:

x	–3	–2	–1	0	1	2
y	–3	–1	+1	3	5	7

If you plot these points on the $X - Y$ plane, you will get the following figure.

'All the points in the table above will lie on this line. The locus of points which are commonly represented by $y = 2x + 3$ is represented by the line above.

In higher mathematics instead of calling expressions like $y = 2x + 3$ as linear equations, they are called as linear functions. (Perhaps the reason for this is that in higher maths, we are interested in identifying relationships and behaviors of interdependent variables especially how a change in one variable changes the other variables. Hence, while equations which are of the form $f(x) = 0$ deal with only one variable x, functions represent relationships between two or more variables. They are denoted in Maths as $y = f(x)$ [Reads as: y is a function of x] or $y = f(a, b)$ [Read as: y is function of a and b].

In general whenever we have any expression in x (denoted by $f(x)$) we can use it either as

$$y = f(x) \text{ [which is what a function is !!]}$$

$$f(x) = 0 \text{ [An equation]}$$

Other Principles Related to Functions and Equations

(a) Every function of the form $y = f(x)$ can be plotted on the $X - Y$ plane.

For instance, consider what we did with the function $y = 2x + 3$. [This form of writing a function is called as its analytical representation, while the graph plotted is called as the graphical representation of the function.]

We first created a table where we started putting values of x and getting the respective value for y. Thus, we got a locus of points (as shown in the table above) which represented the function $y = 2x + 3$. This representation of the function is called as the analytical representation of the function.

Further, the line representing $y = 2x + 3$ was plotted on the $X - Y$ plane. This is called as the graphical representation of the function.

(b) The point/points where the graph of the function $y = f(x)$ cuts the x-axis, represents the solution of the equation $f(x) = 0$.

Thus, if you noticed $y = 2x + 3$ cuts the x axis at $x = -1.5$. At the same time the root or solution of the equation $2x + 3 = 0$ is $x = -1.5$.

This is not accidental but will happen in each and every case. Thus, in general you can state that the point where the graph of a function $y = f(x)$ cuts the x-axis is the solution of the equation $f(x) = 0$. [**Note:** This will be true for every expression in x-irrespective of the highest power of 'x' in the expression.]

It is a consequence of this logic, that linear functions will cut the x-axis only once (since linear equations have only one solution.)

(c) **Quadratic Equations and Quadratic Functions:** Let us now pick up the equation: $x^2 - 5x + 6 = 0$.

If you solve this equation you will get the solution of this equation at two values of x. viz. at $x = 2$ as well as at $x = 3$.

[Remember, the root/solution of an equation is that value of the variable which makes the LHS = RHS in the equation. You can easily see that at both $x = 2$ and $x = 3$ the expression $x^2 - 5x + 6$ yields a value of 0.

At $x = 2$, $x^2 - 5x + 6 \rightarrow 2^2 - 5 \times 2 + 6 = 0$
At $x = 3$, $x^2 - 5x + 6 \rightarrow 3^2 - 5 \times 3 + 6 = 0$

At this point you can predict that the graph of the expression $y = x^2 - 5x + 6$ will cut the x axis at both these points viz. $x = 2$ and $x = 3$.

If you now try to plot $y = x^2 - 5x + 6$, your tabular representation will be:

x	–5	–4	–3	–2	–1	0	1	2	3	4	5
y	56	42	30	20	12	6	2	0	0	2	6

This locus of points will look like the figure below:

Naturally, the graph cuts the *x* axis at $x = 2$ and $x = 3$.

Special Note on Quadratic Equations

Since all quadratic equations have two solutions, graph of the function for the same expression should cut the *x*-axis at two points.

However, this might not always be true.

For instance, look at the following graphs.

Case 1:

In this case the roots are said to be real and equal.

Case 2:

In this case the roots of the quadratic equation are imaginary with respect to the *x*-axis.

Note: You also need to know that quadratic functions can also look inverted as shown below. This occurs when the coefficient of x^2 is negative.

Plot of $-x^2 + x + 6$

In general, quadratic equations then can take any of six shapes (with respect to the *x*-axis):

(d)   How cubic functions look: Cubic functions have x^3 as their highest power of *x*. Cubic equations have three solutions and hence cubic functions will cut the *x*-axis thrice.

They can look like:

CASE 1: When the Coefficient of x^3 is Positive

(A)   Cubic functions with 3 distinct real roots (e.g.: $y = x^3 - 6x^2 + 11x - 6$)

(B)   Cubic function with three real and equal roots. e.g.: $y = (x - 1)^3$

(C)   Cubic function with one real and two imaginary roots

CASE 2: When the Coefficient of x^3 is Negative

(A) Cubic function with 3 distinct real roots.

(B) Cubic function with three real and equal roots.

(C) Cubic function with one real and two imaginary roots.

You can similarly visualize functions with highest power 4, 5 and so on to have shapes such that they can cut the x – axis 4 times, 5 times and so on. The following are standard figures for expressions with

(a) Degree 4 (i.e. x^4) [4 roots]

(b) Degree 5 [5 roots]

A Key Note

Graphical representations and ability to understand how an expression in x will look on the $X - Y$ plot is a very key factor in your moving towards proficiency and self dependence in this crucial block of chapters. Hence, I would encourage you to try to plot the graphs of as many $y = f(x)$ functions as you can imagine. To give you a target, I would recommend a minimum of 100 graphs to be plotted by you. Only then would you be able to move to a level of comfort in visualizing graphs.

ISSUE 5: How Inequalities Relate to Graphs of Functions?

We have just seen the relationship between a function and an equation. While a function is written in the $y = f(x)$ form, an equation is written in the $f(x) = 0$ form.

An inequality (or an inequation) can be written in the form $f(x) > 0$ or $f(x) \geq 0$.

Thus, if we say $x^2 - 5x + 6 > 0$, we are looking for those values of x where the above expression yields values above 0.

Going back to the graph for $x^2 - 5x + 6$, it is obvious that the function is greater than 0 when $x > 3$ or $x < 2$.

In such a case, the solution of the inequality $x^2 - 5x + 6 > 0$ becomes $x > 3$ or $x < 2$.

Understand here that when we are solving an inequality all we are bothered about is to see at what values of x does the inequality hold true.

Pre-assessment Test

Directions for Questions 1 to 3: Answer the questions on the basis of the tables given below.

Two binary operations (+) and * are defined over the set $\{i, j, k, l, m\}$ as per the following tables:

(+)	i	j	k	l	m
i	i	j	k	l	m
j	j	k	l	m	i
k	k	l	m	i	J
l	l	m	i	j	k
m	m	i	j	k	l

*	i	j	k	l	m
i	i	i	i	i	I
j	i	j	k	l	m
k	i	k	m	j	L
l	i	l	j	l	k
m	i	m	l	k	j

Thus according to the first table k (+) $l = i$ while according to the second table $l* m = k$, and so on. Also, let $k^2 = k * k$, $l^3 = l * l * l$, and so on.

1. What is the smallest positive integer n such that $k^n = l$?
   (a) 4
   (b) 5
   (c) 2
   (d) 3

2. Upon simplification m (+) $[k * \{k$ (+) $(k * k)\}]$ equals
   (a) j
   (b) k
   (c) l
   (d) m

3. Upon simplification, $\{i^{10} * (k^{10}$ (+) $l^9)\}$ (+) j^8 equals
   (a) j
   (b) k
   (c) l
   (d) m

4. What is the sum of n terms in the series: $\log m + \log (m^2/n) + \log (m^4/n^3) + \ldots\ldots$
   (a) $\log [n^{(n-1)}/m^{(n+1)}]^{n/2}$
   (b) $\log [m^m/n^n]^{n/2}$
   (c) $\log [m^{(1-n)}/n^{(1-m)}]^{n/2}$
   (d) $\log [m^{(n+1)}/n^{(n-1)}]^{n/2}$

5. If n is such that $36 \le n \le 72$, then $x = (n^2 + 2\sqrt{n(n+4)} + 16)/(n + 4\sqrt{n+4})$ satisfies:
   (a) $20 < x < 54$
   (b) $23 < x < 58$
   (c) $25 < x < 64$
   (d) $28 < x < 60$

6. A real number x is such that it satisfies the condition: $2-1/m < x \le 4 + 1/m$, for every positive integer m. Which of the following best describes the range of values that x can take:
   (a) $1 < x < 5$
   (b) $1 < x \le 4$
   (c) $1 < x \le 5$
   (d) $1 \le x \le 4$

7. If $1/3 \log_3 M + 3 \log_3 N = 1 + \log_{0.008} 5$, then:
   (a) $M^9 = 9/N$
   (b) $N^9 = 9/M$
   (c) $M^3 = 3/N$
   (d) $N^9 = 3/M$

8. If $f(x) = \log \{(1 + x)/(1 - x)\}$, then $f(x) + f(y)$ is:
   (a) $f(x + y)$
   (b) $f\{(x + y)/(1 + xy)\}$
   (c) $(x + y) f \{1/(1 + xy)\}$
   (d) $f(x) + f(y)/(1 + xy)$

9. The nth element of a series is represented as:
   $X_n = (-2)^n X_{n-1}$
   If $X_0 = x$ and $x > 0$ then the following is always true.
   (a) X_n is positive if n is even
   (b) X_n is positive if n is odd
   (c) X_n is negative if n is even
   (d) None of these

10. The number of roots common between the two equations $x^3 + 3x^2 + 4x + 7 = 0$ and $x^3 + 2x^2 + 7x + 5 = 0$ is:
    (a) 0
    (b) 1
    (c) 2
    (d) 3

11. If $|y| \ge 1$ and $x = -|a|\, y$, then which one of the following is necessarily true?
    (a) $a - xy < 0$
    (b) $a - xy \ge 0$
    (c) $a - xy > 0$
    (d) $a - xy \le 0$

12. Consider the sets $T_n = \{n, n + 1, n + 2, n + 3, n + 4\}$, where $n = 1, 2, 3, \ldots., 96$. How many of these sets do not contain 6 or any integral multiple thereof (i.e., any one of the numbers 6, 12, 18, ….)?
    (a) 16
    (b) 15
    (c) 14
    (d) 13

13. If $13m + 1 < 2n$, and $n + 3 = 5y^2$, then:
    (a) m is necessarily less than n
    (b) m is necessarily greater than n
    (c) m is necessarily equal to n
    (d) None of the above is necessarily true

14. If both a and b belong to the set $\{1, 2, 3, 4\}$, then the number of equations of the form $ax^2 + bx + 1 = 0$ having real roots is:
    (a) 10
    (b) 7
    (c) 6
    (d) 12

15. If three positive real numbers x, y and z satisfy $y - x = z - y$ and $xyz = 4$, then what is the minimum possible value of y?
    (a) $2^{1/3}$
    (b) $2^{2/3}$
    (c) $2^{1/4}$
    (d) $2^{3/4}$

16. There are 12 towns grouped into four zones with three towns per zone. It is intended to connect the

towns with telephone lines such that every two towns are connect with three direct lines if they belong to the same zone, and with only one direct line otherwise. How many direct telephone lines are required?

(a) 72   (b) 90
(c) 96   (d) 144

17. If $\log_{10} x + \log_{10} x = 2 \log_x 10$, then a possible value of x is given by:

(a) 10   (b) 1/10
(c) 1/100   (d) None of these

18. Find the area enclosed by the region in sq. units described by $0 = x = 5$ and $0 \leq |y| \leq 8$.

(a) 40   (b) 80
(c) 160   (d) 120

19. The value of the expression $[(1/2) + (1/100)] + [(1/2) + (2/100)] + [(1/2) + (3/100)] + \ldots [(1/2) + (103/100)]$ is equal to

(a) 53   (b) 54
(c) 52   (d) None of these

20. The number of non-negative real roots of $2^x - x - 1 =$ equals:

(a) 0   (b) 1
(c) 2   (d) 3

21. Let a, b, c and d be four integers such that $a + b + c + d = 4m + 1$ where m is a positive integer. Given m, which one of the following is necessarily true?

(a) The minimum possible value of $a^2 + b^2 + c^2 + d^2$ is $4m^2 - 2m + 1$
(b) The minimum possible value of $a^2 + b^2 + c^2 + d^2$ is $4m^2 + 2m + 1$
(c) The maximum possible value of $a^2 + b^2 + c^2 + d^2$ is $4m^2 - 2m + 1$

(d) The maximum possible value of $a^2 + b^2 + c^2 + d^2$ is $4m^2 + 2m + 1$

22. The 288th term of the series $a, b, b, c, c, c, d, d, d, d, e, e, e, e, e, f, f, f, f, f, f \ldots$ is

(a) u (b) v
(c) w (d) x

23. Find the area enclosed by the curve $|x| + |y| = 4$.

(a) 24   (b) 28
(c) 32   (d) 36

24. Let $y = \min \{(x + 8), (6 - x)\}$. If $x \, \varepsilon \, R$, what is the maximum value of y?

(a) 8   (b) 7
(c) 6   (d) 10

25. Let S be the set of integers $\{3, 11, 19, 27, \ldots 451, 459, 467\}$ and M be a subset of S such that no two elements of M add up to 470. The maximum possible number of elements in M is:

(a) 32   (b) 28
(c) 29   (d) 30

ANSWER KEY

1. (a)	2. (a)	3. (d)	4. (d)
5. (d)	6. (c)	7. (b)	8. (b)
9. (d)	10. (a)	11. (b)	12. (a)
13. (d)	14. (b)	15. (b)	16. (b)
17. (b)	18. (b)	19. (b)	20. (c)
21. (b)	22. (d)	23. (c)	24. (b)
25. (d)			

13 Chapter — Functions

Quantities of various characters such as length, area, mass, temperature and volume either have constant values or they vary based on the values of other quantities. Such quantities are called constant and variable respectively.

Function is a concept of mathematics that studies the dependence between variable quantities in the process of their change. For instance, with a change in the side of a square, the area of the square also varies. The question of how the change in the side of the square affects the area is answered by a mathematical relationship between the area of the square and the side of the square.

Let the variable x take on numerical values from the set D.

A function is a rule that attributes to every number x from D one definite number y where y belongs to the set of real numbers.

Here, x is called the independent variable and y is called the dependent variable.

The set D is referred to as the *domain of definition* of the function and the set of all values attained by the variable y is called the *range of the function*.

In other words, a variable y is said to be the value of function of a variable x in the domain of definition D if to each value of x belonging to this domain there corresponds a definite value of the variable y.

This is symbolised as $y = f(x)$ where f denotes the rule by which y varies with x.

🎧 BASIC METHODS OF REPRESENTING FUNCTIONS

Analytical Representation

This is essentially representation through a formula.

This representation could be a uniform formula in the entire domain, for example, $y = 3x^2$

or

by several formulae which are different for different parts of the domain.

Example: $y = 3x^2$ if $x < 0$
and $y = x^2$ if $x > 0$

In analytical representations, the domain of the function is generally understood as the set of values for which the equation makes sense.

For instance, if $y = x^2$ represents the area of a square then we get that the domain of the function is $x > 0$.

Problems based on the analytical representation of functions have been a favourite for the XLRI exam and have also become very common in the CAT over the past few years. Other exams are also moving towards asking questions based on this representation of functions.

Tabular Representation of Functions

For representing functions through a table, we simply write down a sequence of values of the independent variable x and then write down the corresponding values of the dependent variable y. Thus, we have tables of logarithms, trigonometric values and so forth, which are essentially tabular representations of functions.

The types of problems that appear based on tabular representation have been restricted to questions that give a table and then ask the student to trace the appropriate analytical representation or graph of the function based on the table.

Graphical Representation of Functions

This is a very important way to represent functions. The process is: on the coordinate xy plane for every value of x from the domain D of the function, a point $P(x, y)$ is constructed whose abscissa is x and whose ordinate y is got by putting the particular value of x in the formula representing the function.

For example, for plotting the function $y = x^2$, we first decide on the values of x for which we need to plot the graph.

Thus we can take $x = 0$ and get $y = 0$ (means the point $(0, 0)$ is on the graph).

Then for $x = 1$, $y = 1$; for $x = 2$, $y = 4$; for $x = 3$, $y = 9$ and for $x = -1$ $y = 1$; for $x = -2$, $y = 4$, and so on.

EVEN AND ODD FUNCTIONS

Even Functions

Let a function $y = f(x)$ be given in a certain interval. The function is said to be even if for any value of x

$$\rightarrow \qquad f(x) = f(-x)$$

Properties of even functions:

(a) The sum, difference, product and quotient of an even function is also an even function.

(b) The graph of an even function is symmetrical about the y-axis.

However, when y is the independent variable, it is symmetrical about the x-axis. In other words, if $x = f(y)$ is an even function, then the graph of this function will be symmetrical about the x-axis. Example: $x = y^2$.

Examples of even functions: $y = x^2$, $y = x^4$, $y = -3x^8$, $y = x^2 + 3$, $y = x^4/5$, $y = |x|$ are all even functions.

The symmetry about the y-axis of an even function is illustrated below.

Odd Functions

Let a function $y = f(x)$ be given in a certain interval. The function is said to be odd if for any value of x

$$f(x) = -f(-x)$$

Properties of odd functions.

(a) The sum and difference of an odd function is an odd function.

(b) The product and quotient of an odd function is an even function.

(c) The graph of an odd function is symmetrical about the origin.

The symmetry about the origin of an odd function is illustrated below.

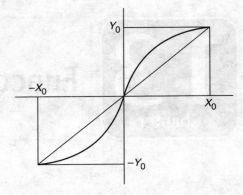

Examples of odd functions $y = x^3$, $y = x^5$, $y = x^3 + x$, $y = x/(x^2 + 1)$.

Not all functions need be even or odd. However, every function can be represented as the sum of an even function and an odd function.

Inverse of a Function

Let there be a function $y = f(x)$, which is defined for the domain D and has a range R.

Then, by definition, for every value of the independent variable x in the domain D, there exists a certain value of the dependent variable y. In certain cases the same value of the dependent variable y can be got for different values of x. For example, if $y = x^2$, then for $x = 2$ and $x = -2$ give the value of y as 4.

In such a case, the inverse function of the function $y = f(x)$ *does not exist.*

However, if a function $y = f(x)$ is such that for every value of y (from the range of the function R) there corresponds one and only one value of x from the domain D, then the inverse function of $y = f(x)$ exists and is given by $x = g(y)$. Here it can be noticed that x becomes the dependent variable and y becomes the independent variable. Hence, this function has a domain R and a range D.

Under the above situation, the graph of $y = f(x)$ and $x = g(y)$ are one and the same.

However, when denoting the inverse of the function, we normally denote the independent variable by y and, hence, the inverse function of $y = f(x)$ is denoted by $y = g(x)$ and not by $x = g(y)$.

The graphs of two inverse functions when this change is used are symmetrical about the line $y = x$ (which is the bisector of the first and the third quadrants).

Graphs of Some Simple Functions The student is advised to familiarise himself/herself with the following figures.

Graphs of $y = b$, $y = kx$, $y = kx + b$, $y = kx - b$.

Note the shifting of the line when a positive number b is added and subtracted to the function's equation.

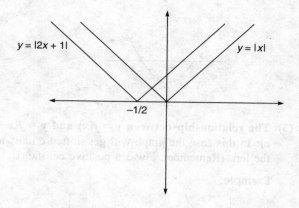

SHIFTING OF GRAPHS

The ability to visualize how graphs shift when the basic analytical expression is changed is a very important skill. For instance if you knew how to visualize the graph of $(x + 2)^2 - 5$, it will definitely add a lot of value to your ability to solve questions of functions and all related chapters of block 5 graphically.

In order to be able to do so, you first need to understand the following points clearly:

(1) **The relationship between the graph of $y = f(x)$ and $y = f(x) + c$ (where c represents a positive constant.):** The shape of the graph of $y = f(x) + c$ will be the same as that of the $y = f(x)$ graph. The only difference would be in terms of the fact that $f(x) + c$ is shifted c units up on the $x - y$ plot.

The following figure will make it clear for you:

Example: Relationship between $y = x^2$ and $y = x^2 + 2$.

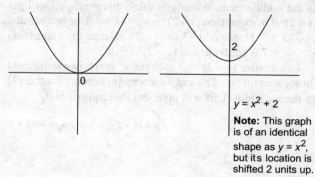

Note: This graph is of an identical shape as $y = x^2$, but its location is shifted 2 units up.

(2) **The relationship between $y = f(x)$ and $y = f(x) - c$:** In this case while the shape remains the same, the position of the graph gets shifted c units down.

$y = x^2 - 2$

(3) The relationship between $y = f(x)$ and $y = f(x + c)$: In this case the graph will get shifted c units to the left. (Remember, c was a positive constant)

Example:

$y = x^2$ $y = (x + 2)^2$

(4) The relationship between $y = f(x)$ and $y = f(x - c)$: In this case the graph will get shifted c units to the right on the $x - y$ plane.

$y = (x - 2)^2$

COMBINING MOVEMENTS

It is best understood through an example:

Visualizing a graph for a function like $x^2 - 4x + 7$.

First convert $x^2 - 4x + 7$ into $(x - 2)^2 + 3$.

[Note: In order to do this conversion, the key point of your thinking should be on the $-4x$. Your first focus has to be to put down a bracket $(x - a)^2$ which on expansion gives $-4x$ as the middle term. When you think this way, you will get $(x - 2)^2$. On expansion $(x - 2)^2 = x^2 - 4x + 4$. But you wanted $x^2 - 4x + 7$. Hence add $+3$ to $(x - 2)^2$. Hence the expression $x^2 - 4x + 7$ is equivalent to $(x - 2)^2 + 3$.]

To visualize $(x - 2)^2 + 3$ shift the x^2 graph two units right [to account for $(x - 2)^2$] and 3 units up [to account for the $+3$] on the $x - y$ plot. This will give you the required plot.

$y = (x - 2)^2 + 3$ or $y = x^2 - 4x + 7$

$y = x^2$ 7 Up   +2 Right

Task for the student: I would now like to challenge and encourage you to think of how to add and multiply functions graphically.

INEQUALITIES

The Logical Graphical Process for Solving Inequalities

Your knowledge of the standard graphs of functions and how these shift can help you immensely while solving inequalities.

Thus, for instance if you are given an inequality question based on a quadratic function like $ax^2 + bx + c < 0$ (and a is positive) you should realize that the curve will be U shaped. And the inequality would be satisfied between the roots of the quadratic equation $ax^2 + bx + c = 0$. [Remember, we have already seen and understood that the solution of an equation $f(x) = 0$ is seen at the points where the graph of $y = f(x)$ cuts the x axis.]

Similarly, for a cubic curve like the one shown below, you should realize that it is greater than 0 to the left of the point 1 shown in the figure. This is also true between points 2 and 3. At the same time the function is less than zero between points 1 and 2 and to the right of point 3. (on the x-axis.)

1   2   3

Another important point to note is that in the case of strict inequalities (i.e. inequalities with the '<' or '>' sign) the answer will also consist of strict inequalities only. On the other hand in the case of slack inequalities (inequalities having ≤ or ≥ sign) the solution of the inequality will also have a slack inequality sign.

LOGARITHMS

Graphical View of the Logarithmic Function

The typical logarithmic function is shown in the graph below:

Note the following points about the logarithmic function $y = \log x$.

(1) It is only defined for positive values of x.

(2) For values of x below 1, the logarithmic function is negative. At the same time for $x = 1$, the logarithmic function has a value of 0. (Irrespective of the base)

(3) The value of $\log x$ becomes 2, when the value of x becomes equal to the square of the base.

(4) As we go further right on the x axis, the graph keeps increasing. However, this increase becomes more and more gradual and hence the shape of the graph becomes increasingly flatter as we move further on the x axis.

Space for Notes

🎯 WORKED-OUT PROBLEMS

Problem 13.1 Find the domain of the definition of the function $y = 1/(x^2 - 2x)^{1/2}$

    (a) $(-\infty, -2)$ (b) $(-\infty, +\infty)$ except $[0, 2]$

    (c) $(2, +\infty)$ (d) $(-\infty, 0)$

Solution For the function to be defined, the expression under the square root should be non-negative and the denominator should not be equal to zero.

So, $x^2 - 2x > 0$ and $(x^2 - 2x) \neq 0$

or, $x(x - 2) > 0$ or $(x^2 - 2x) \neq 0$

So, x won't lie in between 0 and 2 and $x \neq 0$, $x \neq 2$.

So, x will be $x(-\infty, +\infty)$ excluding the range $0 \leq x$ is ≤ 2.

In exam situations, to solve the above problem, you should check the options as below.

In fact, for solving all questions on functions, the student should explore the option-based approach.

Often you will find that going through the option-based approach will help you save a significant amount of time. The student should try to improve his/her selection of values through practice so that he/she is able to eliminate the maximum number of options on the basis of every check. The student should develop a knack for disproving three options so that the fourth automatically becomes the answer. It should also be noted that if an option cannot be disproved, it means that it is the correct option.

What I am trying to say will be clear from the following solution process.

For this question, if we check at $x = 3$, the function is defined. However, $x = 3$ is outside the ambit of option a and d. Hence, a and d are rejected on the basis of just one value check, and b or c has to be the answer.

Alternately, you can try to disprove each and every option one by one.

Problem 13.2 Which of the following is an even function?

    (a) $|x^2| - 5x$ (b) $x^4 + x^5$

    (c) $e^{2x} + e^{-2x}$ (d) $|x|^2/x$

Solution Use options for solving.

If a function is even it should satisfy the equation $f(x) = f(-x)$.

We now check the four options to see which of them represents an even function.

Checking option (a) $f(x) = |x^2| - 5x$

Putting $-x$ in the place of x.

$$f(x) = |(-x)^2| - 5(-x)$$
$$= |x^2| + 5(x) \neq f(x)$$

Checking option (b) $f(x) = x^4 + x^5$.

Putting $(-x)$ at the place of x,

$$f(-x) = (-x)^4 + (-x)^5 = x^4 - x^5 \neq f(x)$$

Checking option (c), $f(x) = e^{2x} + e^{-2x}$

Putting $(-x)$ at the place of x.

$$f(-x) = e^{-2x} + e^{-(-2x)} = e^{-2x} + e^{2x} = f(x)$$

So (c) is the answer.

You do not need to go further to check for d. However, if you had checked, you would have been able to disprove it as follows:

Checking option (d), $f(x) = |x|^2/x$

Putting $f(x)$ at the place of x,

$$f(-x) = |-x|^2/-x = |x^2|/-x \angle \neq f(-x)$$

Directions for Questions 13.3–13.6:

Mark (a) if $f(-x) = f(x)$

Mark (b) if $f(-x) = -f(x)$

Mark (c) if neither (a) nor (b)

Problem 13.3

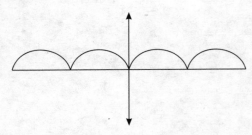

Solution The graph is symmetrical about the y-axis. This is the definition of an even function. So (a).

Problem 13.4

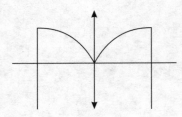

Solution The graph is symmetrical about the y-axis. This is the definition of an even function. So (a).

Problem 13.5

Solution The graph is symmetrical about origin. This is the definition of an odd function. So (b).

Problem 13.6

Solution The graph is neither symmetrical about the y-axis nor about origin. So (c).

Problem 13.7 Which of the following two functions are identical?

(a) $f(x) = x^2/x$ (b) $g(x) = (\sqrt{x})^2$
(c) $h(x) = x$

(i) (a) and (b)   (ii) (b) and (c)
(iii) (a) and (c)   (iv) None of these

Solution For two functions to be identical, their domains should be equal.

Checking the domains of $f(x)$, $g(x)$ and $h(x)$,

$f(x) = x^2/x$, x should not be equal to zero.

So, domain will be all real numbers except at $x = 0$.

$g(x) = (\sqrt{x})^2$, x should be non-negative.

So, domain will be all positive real numbers.

$h(x) = x$, x is defined every where.

So, we can see that none of them have the same domain. Hence, (d) is the correct option.

Problem 13.8 If $f(x) = 1/x$, $g(x) = 1/(1 - x)$ and $h(x) = x^2$, then find *fogoh* (2).

(a) −1   (b) 1
(c) 1/2   (d) None of these

Solution *fogoh* (2) is the same as $f(g(h(2)))$

To solve this, open the innermost bracket first. This means that we first resolve the function $h(2)$. Since $h(2) = 4$ we will get

$f(g(h(2))) = f(g(4)) = f(-1/3) = -3$. Hence, the option (d) is the correct answer.

Read the instructions below and solve Problems 11.9 and 11.10.

$$A * B = A^3 - B^3$$
$$A + B = A - B$$
$$A - B = A/B$$

Problem 13.9 Find the value of (3 * 4) − (8 + 12).

(a) 9   (b) 9.25
(c) −9.25   (d) None of these

Solution Such problems should be solved by the BOD-MAS rule for sequencing of operations.

Solving, thus, we get: (3 * 4) − (8 + 12)

= −37 − (−4). [Note here that the '−' sign between −37 and −4 is the operation defined above.]

= 37/4 = 9.25

Problem 13.10 Which of the following operation will give the sum of the reciprocals of x and y and unity?

(a) $(x + y) * (x - y)$
(b) $[(x * y) - x] - y$
(c) $[\{(x * y) - (x + y)\} - x] - y$
(d) $(x + y) - (x - y)$

For solving questions containing a function in the question as well as a function in the options (where values are absent), the safest process for students weak at math is to assume certain convenient values of the variables in the expression and checking for the correct option that gives us equality with the expression in the question. The advantages of this process of solution is that there is very little scope for making mistakes. Besides, if the expression is not simple and directly visible, this process takes far less time as compared to simplifying the expression from one form to another.

This process will be clear after perusing the following solution to the above problem.

Solution The problem statement above defines the expression: $(1/x) + (1/y) + 1$ and asks us to find out which of the four options is equal to this expression. If we try to simplify, we can start from the problem expression and re-write it to get the correct option. However, in the above case this will become extremely complicated since the symbols are indirect. Hence, if we have to solve through simplifying, we should start from the options one by one and try to get the problem expression. However, this is easier said than done and for this particular problem, going through this approach will take you at least two minutes plus.

Hence, consider the following approach:

Take the values of x and y as 1 each. Then,

$$(1/x) + (1/y) + 1 = 3$$

Put the value of x and y as 1 each in each of the four options that we have to consider.

Option (a) will give a value of −1 ≠ 3. Hence, option (a) is incorrect.

Opton (b) will give a value of 0. 0 ≠ 3. Hence, option (b) is incorrect.

Option (c) gives an answer of 3. Hence, option (c) could be the answer.

Option (d) gives an answer of 0. 0 ≠ 3. Hence, option (d) is incorrect.

Now since options (a), (b) and (d) are incorrect and option (c) is the only possibility left, it has to be the answer.

[Note that in case there is a fourth option of 'none of these' then we have to be careful before marking the answer.]

LEVEL OF DIFFICULTY (I)

1. Find the domain of the definition of the function $y = |x|$.
   - (a) $0 \leq x$
   - (b) $-\infty < x < +\infty$
   - (c) $x < +\infty$
   - (d) $0 \leq x < +\infty$

2. Find the domain of the definition of the function $y = \sqrt{x}$.
   - (a) $-\infty < x < +\infty$
   - (b) $x \leq 0$
   - (c) $x > 0$
   - (d) $x \geq 0$

3. Find the domain of the definition of the function $y = \left|\sqrt{x}\right|$.
   - (a) $x \geq 0$
   - (b) $-\infty < x < +\infty$
   - (c) $x > 0$
   - (d) $x < +\infty$

4. Find the domain of the definition of the function $y = (x - 2)^{1/2} + (8 - x)^{1/2}$.
   - (a) All the real values except $2 \leq x \leq 8$
   - (b) $2 \leq x$
   - (c) $2 \leq x \leq 8$
   - (d) $x \leq 8$

5. Find the domain of the definition of the function $y = (9 - x^2)^{1/2}$.
   - (a) $-3 \leq x \leq 3$
   - (b) $(-\infty, -3] \cup [3, \infty)$
   - (c) $-3 \leq x$
   - (d) $x \leq 3$

6. Find the domain of the definition of the function $y = 1/(x^2 - 4x + 3)$.
   - (a) $1 \leq x \leq 3$
   - (b) $(-\infty, -3) \cup (3, \infty)$
   - (c) $x = (1, 3)$
   - (d) $-\infty < x < \infty$, excluding 1, 3

7. The values of x for which the functions $f(x) = x$ and $g(x) = (\sqrt{x})^2$ are identical is
   - (a) $-\infty < x < +\infty$
   - (b) $x \geq 0$
   - (c) $x > 0$
   - (d) $x \leq 0$

8. The values of x for which the functions $f(x) = x$ and $g(x) = x^2/x$ are identical is
   - (a) Set of real numbers excluding 0
   - (b) Set of real numbers
   - (c) $x \geq 0$
   - (d) $x > 0$

9. If $f(x) = \sqrt{x^3}$, then $f(3x)$ will be equal to
   - (a) $\sqrt{3x^3}$
   - (b) $3\sqrt{x^3}$
   - (c) $3\sqrt{(3x^3)}$
   - (d) $3\sqrt{x^5}$

10. If $f(x) = e^x$, then the value of $7 f(x)$ will be equal to
    - (a) e^{7x}
    - (b) $7e^x$
    - (c) $7 e^{7x}$
    - (d) e^x

11. If $f(x) = \log x^2$ and $g(x) = 2 \log x$, then $f(x)$ and $g(x)$ are identical for
    - (a) $-\infty < x < +\infty$
    - (b) $0 \leq x < \infty$
    - (c) $-\infty x \leq 0$
    - (d) $0 < x < \infty$

12. If $f(x)$ is an even function, then the graph $y = f(x)$ will be symmetrical about
    - (a) x-axis
    - (b) y-axis
    - (c) Both the axes
    - (d) None of these

13. If $f(x)$ is an odd function, then the graph $y = f(x)$ will be symmetrical about
    - (a) x-axis
    - (b) y-axis
    - (c) Both the axes
    - (d) origin

14. Which of the following is an even function?
    - (a) x^{-8}
    - (b) x^3
    - (c) x^{-33}
    - (d) x^{73}

15. Which of the following is not an odd function?
    - (a) $(x + 1)^3$
    - (b) x^{23}
    - (c) x^{53}
    - (d) x^{77}

16. For what value of x, $x^2 + 10x + 11$ will give the minimum value?
    - (a) 5
    - (b) $+10$
    - (c) -5
    - (d) -10

17. In the above question, what will be the minimum value of the function?
    - (a) -14
    - (b) 11
    - (c) 86
    - (d) 0

18. Find the maximum value of the function $1/(x^2 - 3x + 2)$.
    - (a) $11/4$
    - (b) $1/4$
    - (c) 0
    - (d) None of these

19. Find the minimum value of the function $f(x) = \log_2 (x^2 - 2x + 5)$.
    - (a) -4
    - (b) 2
    - (c) 4
    - (d) -2

20. $f(x)$ is any function and $f^{-1}(x)$ is known as inverse of $f(x)$, then $f^{-1}(x)$ of $f(x) = \dfrac{1}{x} + 1$ is
    - (a) $\dfrac{1}{x} - 1$
    - (b) $x - 1$
    - (c) $\dfrac{1}{(x-1)}$
    - (d) $\dfrac{1}{x+1}$

Directions for Questions 21 to 23: Read the instructions below and solve.

$f(x) = f(x - 2) - f(x - 1)$, x is a natural number
$f(1) = 0$, $f(2) = 1$

21. The value of $f(8)$ is
    (a) 0   (b) 13
    (c) −5   (d) −9

22. The value of $f(7) + f(4)$ is
    (a) 11   (b) −6
    (c) −12   (d) 12

23. What will be the value of $\sum_{n=1}^{9} f(n)$?

    (a) −12   (b) −15
    (c) −14   (d) −13

24. What will be the domain of the definition of the function $f(x) = {}^{8-x}C_{5-x}$ for positive values of x?
    (a) {1, 2, 3}   (b) {1, 2, 3, 4}
    (c) {1, 2, 3, 4, 5}   (d) {1, 2, 3, 4, 5, 6, 7, 8}

Directions for Questions 25 to 38:
Mark a if $f(-x) = f(x)$
Mark b if $f(-x) = -f(x)$
Mark c if neither a nor b is true
Mark d if $f(x)$ does not exist at at least one point of the domain.

25.

26.

27.

28.

29.

30.

31.

32.

33.

34.

(−1, 0)

35.

Assume
$f(x) = 0$, at $x = 0$

36.

37.

38.

Directions for Questions 39 to 43: Define the following functions:

(i) $a @ b = \dfrac{a+b}{2}$

(ii) $a \# b = a^2 - b^2$

(iii) $(a\,!\,b) = \dfrac{a-b}{2}$

39. Find the value of $\{[(3@4)!(3\#2)] @ [(4!3)@(2\#3)]\}$.
   (a) −0.75
   (b) −1
   (c) −1.5
   (d) −2.25

40. Find the value of $(4\#3)@(2!3)$.
   (a) 3.25
   (b) 3.5
   (c) 6.5
   (d) 7

41. Which of the following has a value of 0.25 for $a = 0$ and $b = 0.5$?
   (a) $a @ b$
   (b) $a \# b$
   (c) Either a or b
   (d) Cannot be determined

42. Which of the following expressions has a value of 4 for $a = 5$ and $b = 3$?
   (a) $\dfrac{(a!b)}{(a\#b)}$
   (b) $(a!b)(a@b)$
   (c) $\dfrac{(a\#b)}{(a!b)(a@b)}$
   (d) Both (b) and (c)

43. If we define $a\$b$ as $a^3 - b^3$, then for integers a, $b > 2$ and $a > b$ which of the following will always be true?

(a) $(a@b) > (a!b)$
(b) $(a@b) \geq (a!b)$
(c) $(a\#b) < (a\$b)$
(d) Both a and c

Directions for Questions 44 to 48: Define the following functions:

(a) $(a\,M\,b) = a - b$
(b) $(a\,D\,b) = a + b$
(c) $(a\,H\,b) = (ab)$
(d) $(a\,P\,b) = a/b$

44. Which of the following functions will represent $a^2 - b^2$?
   (a) $(a\,M\,b)\,H\,(a\,D\,b)$
   (b) $(a\,H\,b)\,M\,(a\,P\,b)$
   (c) $(a\,D\,b)/(a\,M\,b)$
   (d) None of these

45. Which of the following represents a^2?
   (a) $(a\,M\,b)\,H\,(a\,D\,b) + b^2$
   (b) $(a\,H\,b)\,M\,(a\,P\,b) + b^2$
   (c) $\dfrac{(a\,M\,b)}{(a\,P\,b)}$
   (d) Both (a) and (c)

46. What is the value of $(3M4H2D4P8M2)$?
   (a) 6.5
   (b) 6
   (c) −6.5
   (d) None of these

47. Which of the four functions defined has the maximum value?
   (a) $(a\,M\,b)$
   (b) $(a\,D\,b)$
   (c) $(a\,P\,b)$
   (d) Cannot be determined

48. Which of the four functions defined has the minimum value?
   (a) $(a\,M\,b)$
   (b) $(a\,D\,b)$
   (c) $(a\,H\,b)$
   (d) Cannot be determined

49. If $0 < a < 1$ and $0 < b < 1$ and $a > b$, which of the 4 expressions will take the highest value?
   (a) $(a\,M\,b)$
   (b) $(a\,D\,b)$
   (c) $(a\,P\,b)$
   (d) Cannot be determined

50. If $0 < a < 1$ and $0 < b < 1$ and if $a < b$, which of the following expressions will have the highest value?
   (a) $(a\,M\,b)$
   (b) $(a\,D\,b)$
   (c) $(a\,P\,b)$
   (d) Cannot be determined

51. A function $F(n)$ is defined as $F(n-1) = \dfrac{1}{(2 - F(n))}$ for all natural numbers 'n'. If $F(1) = 3$, then what is the value of $[F(1)] + [F(2)] + \ldots + [F(1000)]$? (Here, $[x]$ is equal to the greatest integer less than or equal to 'x')
   (a) 1001
   (b) 1002
   (c) 3003
   (d) None of these

52. For the above question find the value of the expression: $F(1) \times F(2) \times F(3) \times F(4) \times \ldots F(1000)$
   (a) 2001
   (b) 1999
   (c) 2004
   (d) 1997

53. A function $f(x)$ is defined for all real values of x as $f(x) = ax^2 + bx + c$. If $f(3) = f(-3) = 18$, $f(0) = 15$, then what is the value of $f(12)$?

(a) 63   (b) 159

(c) 102   (d) None of these

54. Two operations, for real numbers x and y, are defined as given below.

  (i) $M(x \, \theta \, y) = (x + y)^2$

  (ii) $f(x \, \psi \, y) = (x - y)^2$

  If $M(x^2 \theta y^2) = 361$ and $M(x^2 \psi y^2) = 49$, then what is the value of the square root of $((x^2 y^2) + 3)$?

(a) ± 81 (b) ± 9

(c) ± 7 (d) ± 11

55. The function $\Psi(m) = [m]$, where $[m]$ represents the greatest integer less than or equal to m. Two real numbers x and y are such that $\Psi(4x + 5) = 5y + 3$ and $\Psi(3y + 7) = x + 4$, then find the value of $x^2 \times y^2$.

(a) 1   (b) 2

(c) 4   (d) None of these

56. A certain function always obeys the rule: If $f(x.y) = f(x).f(y)$ where x and y are positive real numbers. A certain Mr. Mogambo found that the value of $f(128) = 4$, then find the value of the variable $M = f(0.5)$.

$f(1).f(2).f(4).f(8).f(16).f(32).f(64).f(128).f(256)$

(a) 128   (b) 256

(c) 512   (d) 1024

57. x and y are non negative integers such that $4x + 6y = 20$, and $x^2 \le M/y^{2/3}$ for all values of x, y. What is the minimum value of M?

(a) $2^{2/3}$ (b) $2^{1/3}$

(c) $2^{4/3}$ (d) $4^{2/3}$

58. Let $\Psi(x) = \dfrac{x+3}{2}$ and $\theta(x) = 3x^2 + 2$. Find the value of $\theta(\Psi(-7))$.

(a) 12   (b) 14

(c) 50   (d) 42

59. If $F(a + b) = F(a).F(b) \div 2$, where $F(b) \ne 0$ and $F(a) \ne 0$, then what is the value of $F(12b)$?

(a) $(F(b))^{12}$ (b) $F(b)^{12} \div 2$

(c) $(F(b))^{12} \div 2^{12}$ (d) $(F(b))^{12} \div 2^{11}$

60. A function $a = \theta(b)$ is said to be reflexive if $b = \theta(a)$. Which of the following is/are reflexive functions?

  (i) $\dfrac{3b+5}{4b-3}$ (ii) $\dfrac{3b+5}{5b-2}$

  (iii) $\dfrac{2b+12}{12b-2}$

(a) All of these are reflexive

(b) Only (i) and (ii) are reflexive

(c) Only (i) and (iii) are reflexive

(d) None of these are reflexive.

Space for Rough Work

LEVEL OF DIFFICULTY (II)

1. Find the domain of the definition of the function $y = 1/(4 - x^2)^{1/2}$.
   (a) $(-2, 2)$
   (b) $[-2, 2]$
   (c) $(-\infty, -2) \cup (2, \infty)$ excluding -2 and 2
   (d) $(2, \infty)$

2. The domain of definition of the function
   $$y = \frac{1}{\log_{10}(1-x)} + (x+2)^{1/2} \text{ is}$$
   (a) $(-3, -2)$
   (b) $[0, 1)$
   (c) $[-2, 1]$
   (d) $[-2, 1)$ excluding 0

3. The domain of definition of $y = [\log_{10}\left(\dfrac{5x - x^2}{4}\right)]^{1/2}$ is
   (a) $[1, 4]$
   (b) $[-4, -1]$
   (c) $[0, 5]$
   (d) $[-1, 5]$

4. Which of the following functions is an odd function?
   (a) $2^{-x.x}$
   (b) $2^{x - x.x.x}$
   (c) Both (a) and (b)
   (d) Neither (a) nor (b)

5. The domain of definition of $y = [1 - |x|]^{1/2}$ is
   (a) $[-1, 0]$
   (b) $[0, 1]$
   (c) $(-1, 1)$
   (d) $[-1, 1]$

6. The domain of definition of $y = [3/(4 - x^2)] + \log_{10}$ $(x^3 - x)$ is
   (a) $(-1, 0) \cup (1, \infty)$
   (b) Not 2 or -2
   (c) (a) and (b) together
   (d) None of these

7. If $f(t) = 2^t$, then $f(0), f(1), f(2)$ are in
   (a) AP
   (b) HP
   (c) GP
   (d) Cannot be said

8. Centre of a circle $x^2 + y^2 = 16$ is at $(0, 0)$. What will be the new centre of the circle if it gets shifted 3 units down and 2 units left?
   (a) $(2, 3)$
   (b) $(-2, -3)$
   (c) $(-2, 3)$
   (d) $(2, -3)$

9. If $u(t) = 4t - 5$, $v(t) = t^2$ and $f(t) = 1/t$, then the formula for $u(f(v(t)))$ is
   (a) $\dfrac{1}{(4t - 5)^2}$
   (b) $\dfrac{4}{(t - 5)}$
   (c) $\dfrac{4}{t^2} - 5$
   (d) None of these

10. If $f(t) = \sqrt{t}$, $g(t) = t/4$ and $h(t) = 4t - 8$, then the formula for $g(f(h(t)))$ will be
    (a) $\dfrac{\sqrt{t - 2}}{4}$
    (b) $2\sqrt{t} - 8$
    (c) $\dfrac{\sqrt{(4t - 8)}}{4}$
    (d) $\dfrac{\sqrt{(t - 8)}}{4}$

11. In the above question, find the value of $h(g(f(t)))$.
    (a) $\sqrt{t} - 8$
    (b) $2\sqrt{t - 8}$
    (c) $\dfrac{\sqrt{t} + 8}{4}$
    (d) None of these

12. In question number 10, find the formula of $f(h(g(t)))$.
    (a) $\sqrt{t} - 8$
    (b) $\sqrt{(t - 8)}$
    (c) $2\sqrt{t} - 8$
    (d) None of these

13. The values of x, for which the functions $f(x) = x$, $g(x) = (\sqrt{x})^2$ and $h(x) = x^2/x$ are identical, is
    (a) $0 \le x$
    (b) $0 < x$
    (c) All real values
    (d) All real values except 0

14. Which of the following is an even function?
    (a) e^x
    (b) e^{-x}
    (c) $e^x + e^{-x}$
    (d) $\dfrac{e^x + e^{-x}}{e^x - e^{-x}}$

15. The graph of $y = (x + 3)^3 + 1$ is the graph of $y = x^3$ shifted
    (a) 3 units to the right and 1 unit down
    (b) 3 units to the left and 1 unit down
    (c) 3 units to the left and 1 unit up
    (d) 3 units to the right and 1 unit up

16. If $f(x) = 5x^3$ and $g(x) = 3x^5$, then $f(x).g(x)$ will be
    (a) Even function
    (b) Odd function
    (c) Both
    (d) None of these

17. If $f(x) = x^2$ and $g(x) = \log_e x$, then $f(x) + g(x)$ will be
    (a) Even function
    (b) Odd function
    (c) Both
    (d) Neither (a) nor (b)

18. If $f(x) = x^3$ and $g(x) = x^2/5$, then $f(x) - g(x)$ will be
    (a) Odd function
    (b) Even function
    (c) Neither (a) nor (b)
    (d) Both

19. $f(x)$ is any function and $f^{-1}(x)$ is known as inverse of $f(x)$, then $f^{-1}(x)$ of $f(x) = 1/(x - 2)$ is
    (a) $\dfrac{1}{x} + 2$
    (b) $\dfrac{1}{(x + 2)}$
    (c) $\dfrac{1}{x} + 0.5$
    (d) None of these

20. $f(x)$ is any function and $f^{-1}(x)$ is known as inverse of $f(x)$, then $f^{-1}(x)$ of $f(x) = e^x$ is
    (a) $-e^x$
    (b) e^{-x}
    (c) $\log_e x$
    (d) None of these

21. $f(x)$ is any function and $f^{-1}(x)$ is known as inverse of $f(x)$, then $f^{-1}(x)$ of $f(x) = x/(x - 1)$, $x \ne 1$ is

(a) $x/(1 + x)$ (b) $\dfrac{x}{x^2 - 1}$

(c) $x/(x - 1)$ (d) $-x/(x + 1)$

22. Which of the following functions will have a minimum value at $x = -3$?

  (a) $f(x) = 2x^3 - 4x + 3$ (b) $f(x) = 4x^4 - 3x + 5$

  (c) $f(x) = x^6 - 2x - 6$ (d) None of these

Directions for Questions 23 to 32:

Mark (a) if $f(-x) = f(x)$

Mark (b) if $f(-x) = -f(x)$

Mark (c) if neither (a) nor (b) is true

Mark (d) if $f(x)$ does not exist at at least one point of the domain.

23.

24.

25.

26.

27.

28.

29.

30.

31.

$(x^3 - x)$

32.

Directions for Questions 33 to 36:   If $f(x)$ is represented by the graph below.

33. Which of the following will represent the function $-f(x)$?

34. Which of the following will represent the function $-f(x) + 1$?

35. Which of the following will represent the function $f(x) - 1$?

36. Which of the following will represent the function $f(x) + 1$?

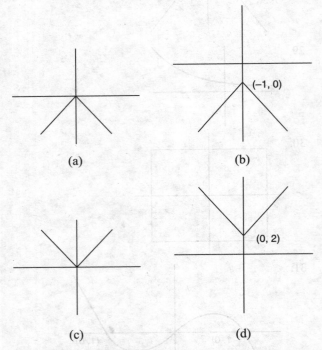

(a)

(b) (−1, 0)

(c)

(d) (0, 2)

Directions for Questions 37 to 40: Define the following functions:

$$f(x, y, z) = xy + yz + zx$$
$$g(x, y, z) = x^2y + y^2z + z^2x \text{ and}$$
$$h(x, y, z) = 3\ xyz$$

Find the value of the following expressions:

37. $h[f(2, 3, 1), g(3, 4, 2), h(1/3, 1/3, 3)]$
   (a) 0   (b) 23760
   (c) 2640   (d) None of these

38. $g[f(1, 0, 0), g(0, 1, 0), h(1, 1, 1)]$
   (a) 0   (b) 9
   (c) 12   (d) None of these

39. $f[f(1, 1, 1), g(1, 1, 1), h(1, 1, 1)]$
   (a) 9   (b) 18
   (c) 27   (d) None of these

40. $f(1, 2, 3) - g(1, 2, 3) + h(1, 2, 3)$
   (a) −6   (b) 6
   (c) 12   (d) 8

41. If $f(x) = 1/\ g(x)$, then which of the following is correct?
   (a) $f(f(g(f(x)))) = f(g(f(f(x))))$
   (b) $f(g(g(f(f(x))))) = f(f(g(g(g(x)))))$
   (c) $g(g(f(f(g(f(x)))))) = f(f(g(g(f(g(x))))))$
   (d) $f(g(g(g(f(x))))) = g(g(f(f(f(x)))))$

42. If $f(x) = 1/g(x)$, then the minimum value of $f(x) + g(x)$, $f(x) > 0$ and $g(x) > 0$, will be
   (a) 0
   (b) 2
   (c) Depends upon the value of $f(x)$ and $g(x)$
   (d) None of these

Directions for Questions 43 to 45:

If $R(a/b)$ = Remainder when a is divided by b;
   $Q(a/b)$ = Quotient obtained when a is divided by b;
   $SQ(a)$ = Smallest integer just bigger than square root of a.

43. If $a = 12$, $b = 5$, then find the value of $SQ[R \{(a + b)/b\}]$.
   (a) 0   (b) 1
   (c) 2   (d) 3

44. If $a = 9$, $b = 7$, then the value of $Q [[SQ(ab)+b]/a]$ will be
   (a) 0   (b) 1
   (c) 2   (d) None of these

45. If $a = 18$, $b = 2$ and $c = 7$, then find the value of $Q [\{SQ(ab) + R(a/c)\}/b]$.
   (a) 3   (b) 4
   (c) 5   (d) 6

Directions for Questions 46 to 48: Read the following passage and try to answer questions based on them.

   $[x]$ = Greatest integer less than or equal to x.
   $\{x\}$ = Smallest integer greater than or equal to x.

46. If x is not an integer, what is the value of $([x] - \{x\})$?
   (a) 0   (b) 1
   (c) −1   (d) 2

47. If x is not an integer, then $(\{x\} + [x])$ is
   (a) An even number
   (b) An odd integer
   (c) $> 3x$
   (d) $< x$

48. What is the value of x if $5 < x < 6$ and $\{x\} + [x] = 2x$?
   (a) 5.2   (b) 5.8
   (c) 5.5   (d) 5.76

49. If $f(t) = t^2 + 2$ and $g(t) = (1/t) + 2$, then for $t = 2$, $f[g(t)] - g[f(t)] = ?$
   (a) 1.2   (b) 2.6
   (c) 4.34   (d) None of these

50. Given $f(t) = kt + 1$ and $g(t) = 3t + 2$. If $fog = gof$, find k.
   (a) 2   (b) 3
   (c) 5   (d) 4

51. Let $F(x)$ be a function such that $F(x)\ F(x + 1) =$ $- F(x - 1)F(x-2)F(x-3)F(x-4)$ for all $x \geq 0$. Given the values of If $F(83) = 81$ and $F(77) = 9$, then the value of $F(102)$ equals to
    (a) 27   (b) 54
    (c) 729   (d) Data Insufficient

52. Let $f(x) = 121 - x^2$, $g(x) = |x - 8| + |x + 8|$ and $h(x)$ $= \min (f(x), g(x))$. What is the number of integer values of x for which $h(x)$ is equal to a positive integral value?
    (a) 17   (b) 19
    (c) 21   (d) 23

53. If the function $R(x) = \max (x^2 - 8, 3x, 8)$, then what is the max value of $R(x)$?
    (a) 4   (b) $\dfrac{1+\sqrt{5}}{2}$
    (c) ∞ (d) 0

54. If the function $R(x) = \min (x^2 - 8, 3x, 8)$, what is the max value of $R(x)$?
    (a) 4   (b) 8
    (c) ∞ (d) None of these

55. The minimum value of $ax^2 + bx + c$ is 7/8 at $x = 5/4$. Find the value of the expression at $x = 5$, if the value of the expression at $x = 1$ is 1.
    (a) 75   (b) 79
    (c) 121   (d) 129

56. Find the range of the function $f(x) = (x + 4)(5 - x)$ $(x + 1)$.

57. The function $f(x)$ is defined for positive integers and is defined as:

    $f(x) = 6^x - 3$, if x is a number in the form $2n$.
    $= 6^x + 4$, if x is a number in the form $2n + 1$.

    What is the remainder when $f(1) + f(2) + f(3) + ... + f(1001)$ is divided by 2?
    (a) 1   (b) 0
    (c) -1 (d) None of the above

58. p, q and r are three non-negative integers such that $p + q + r = 10$. The maximum value of $pq + qr + pr + pqr$ is
    (a) ≥ 40 and < 50 (b) ≥ 50 and < 60
    (c) ≥ 60 and < 70 (d) ≥ 70 and < 80

59. A function $\alpha(x)$ is defined for x as $3\alpha(x) + 2\alpha (2 - x) = (x + 3)^2$. What is the value of $[G (-5)]$ where $[x]$ represents the greatest integer less than or equal to x?
    (a) 37   (b) -38
    (c) -37 (d) Cannot be determined

60. For a positive integer x, $f(x + 2) = 3 + f(x)$, when x is even and $f(x + 2) = x + f(x)$, when x is odd. If $f(1) = 6$ and $f(2) = 4$, then find $f(f(f(f(1)))) + f(f(f(f(2))))$.
    (a) 1375   (b) 1425
    (c) 1275   (d) None of these

Options (from top right):
(a) $[-2, 3]$ (b) $(-\infty, 20]$
(c) $(-\infty, +\infty)$ (d) $[-20, \infty)$

Space for Rough Work

LEVEL OF DIFFICULTY (III)

1. Find the domain of the definition of the function $y = 1/(x - |x|)^{1/2}$.
   - (a) $-\infty < x < \infty$
   - (b) $-\infty < x < 0$
   - (c) $0 < x < \infty$
   - (d) No where

2. Find the domain of the definition of the function $y = (x - 1)^{1/2} + 2(1 - x)^{1/2} + (x^2 + 3)^{1/2}$.
   - (a) $x = 0$
   - (b) $[1, \infty)$
   - (c) $[-1, 1]$
   - (d) 1

3. Find the domain of the definition of the function $y = \log_{10}[(x - 5)/(x^2 - 10x + 24)] - (x + 4)^{1/2}$.
   - (a) $x > 6$
   - (b) $4 < x < 5$
   - (c) Both a and b
   - (d) None of these

4. Find the domain of the definition of the function $y = [(x - 3)/(x + 3)]^{1/2} + [(1 - x)/(1 + x)]^{1/2}$.
   - (a) $x > 3$
   - (b) $x < -3$
   - (c) $-3 \le x \le 3$
   - (d) Nowhere

5. Find the domain of the definition of the function $y = (2x^2 + x + 1)^{-3/4}$.
   - (a) $x \ge 0$
   - (b) All x except $x = 0$
   - (c) $-3 \le x \le 3$
   - (d) Everywhere

6. Find the domain of the definition of the function $y = (x^2 - 2x - 3)^{1/2} - 1/(-2 + 3x - x^2)^{1/2}$.
   - (a) $x > 0$
   - (b) $-1 < x < 0$
   - (c) x^2
   - (d) None of these

7. Find the domain of the definition of the function $y = \log_{10}[1 - \log_{10}(x^2 - 5x + 16)]$.
   - (a) $(2, 3]$
   - (b) $[2, 3)$
   - (c) $[2, 3]$
   - (d) None of these

8. If $f(t) = (t - 1)/(t + 1)$, then $f(f(t))$ will be equal to
   - (a) $1/t$
   - (b) $-1/t$
   - (c) t
   - (d) $-t$

9. If $f(x) = e^x$ and $g(x) = \log_e x$ then value of fog will be
   - (a) x
   - (b) 0
   - (c) 1
   - (d) e

10. In the above question, find the value of gof.
    - (a) x
    - (b) 0
    - (c) 1
    - (d) e

11. The function $y = 1/x$ shifted 1 unit down and 1 unit right is given by
    - (a) $y - 1 = 1/(x + 1)$
    - (b) $y - 1 = 1/(x - 1)$
    - (c) $y + 1 = 1/(x - 1)$
    - (d) $y + 1 = 1/(x + 1)$

12. Which of the following functions is an even function?

    - (a) $f(t) = (a^t + a^{-t})/(a^t - a^{-t})$
    - (b) $f(t) = (a^t + 1)/(a^t - 1)$
    - (c) $f(t) = t \cdot (a^t - 1)/(a^t + 1)$
    - (d) None of these

13. Which of the following functions is not an odd function?
    - (a) $f(t) = \log_2(t + \sqrt{t^2 + 1})$
    - (b) $f(t) = (a^t + a^{-t})/(a^t - a^{-t})$
    - (c) $f(t) = (a^t + 1)/(a^t - 1)$
    - (d) All of these

14. Find fof if $f(t) = t/(1 + t^2)^{1/2}$.
    - (a) $1/(1 + 2t^2)^{1/2}$
    - (b) $t/(1 + 2t^2)^{1/2}$
    - (c) $(1 + 2t^2)$
    - (d) None of these

15. At what integral value of x will the function $\dfrac{(x^2 + 3x + 1)}{(x^2 - 3x + 1)}$ attain its maximum value?
    - (a) 3
    - (b) 4
    - (c) -3
    - (d) None of these

16. Inverse of $f(t) = (10^t - 10^{-t})/(10^t + 10^{-t})$ is
    - (a) $1/2 \log\{(1 - t)/(1 + t)\}$
    - (b) $0.5 \log\{(t - 1)/(t + 1)\}$
    - (c) $1/2 \log_{10}(2^t - 1)$
    - (d) None of these

17. If $f(x) = |x - 2|$, then which of the following is always true?
    - (a) $f(x) = (f(x))^2$
    - (b) $f(x) = f(-x)$
    - (c) $f(x) = x - 2$
    - (d) None of these

Directions for Questions 18 to 20: Read the instructions below and solve:

$f(x) = f(x - 2) - f(x - 1)$, x is a natural number
$f(1) = 0, f(2) = 1$

18. The value of $f(x)$ is negative for
    - (a) All $x > 2$
    - (b) All odd $x(x > 2)$
    - (c) For all even $x(x > 0)$
    - (d) $f(x)$ is always positive

19. The value of $f[f(6)]$ is
    - (a) 5
    - (b) -1
    - (c) -3
    - (d) -2

20. The value of $f(6) - f(8)$ is
    - (a) $f(4) + f(5)$
    - (b) $f(7)$
    - (c) $-\{f(7) + f(5)\}$
    - (d) $-f(5)$

21. Which of the following is not an even function ?
    (a) $f(x) = e^x + e^{-x}$ (b) $f(x) = e^x - e^{-x}$
    (c) $f(x) = e^{2x} + e^{-2x}$ (d) None of these

22. If $f(x)$ is a function satisfying $f(x). f(1/x) = f(x) + f(1/x)$ and $f(4) = 65$, what will be the value of $f(6)$?
    (a) 37   (b) 217
    (c) 64   (d) None of these

Directions for Questions 23 to 34:

Mark (a) if $f(-x) = f(x)$,
Mark (b) if $f(-x) = -f(x)$
Mark (c) if neither (a) nor (b) is true
Mark (d) if $f(x)$ does not exist at at least one point of the domain.

23.

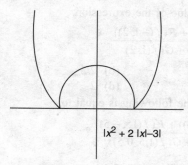

$|x^2 + 2 |x| - 3|$

24.

$x = 1/4$

25.

26.

27.

28.

29.

30.

31.

32.

33.

34.

Directions for Questions 35 to 40: Define the functions:

$A(x, y, z) = $ Max (max (x, y), min (y, z) min (x, z))
$B(x, y, z) = $ Max (max (x, y), min (y, z) max (x, z))
$C(x, y, z) = $ Max (min (x, y), min (y, z) min (x, z))
$D(x, y, z) = $ Min (max (x, y), max (y, z) max (x, z))
Max $(x, y, z) = $ Maximum of x, y and z.
Min $(x, y, z) = $ Minimum of x, y and z.
Assume that x, y and z are distinct integers.

35. For what condition will $A(x, y, z)$ be equal to Max (x, y, z)?
    (a) When x is maximum (b) When y is maximum
    (c) When z is maximum (d) Either (a) or (b)

36. For what condition will $B(x, y, z)$ be equal to Min (x, y, z)?
    (a) When y is minimum (b) When z is minimum
    (c) Either (a) or (b)   (d) Never

37. For what condition will $A(x, y, z)$ not be equal to $B(x, y, z)$?
    (a) $x > y > z$ (b) $y > z > x$
    (c) $z > y > x$ (d) None of these

38. Under what condition will $C(x, y, z)$ be equal to $B(x, y, z)$?
    (a) $x > y > z$ (b) $z > y > x$
    (c) Both a and b (d) Never

39. Which of the following will always be true?
    (I) $A(x, y, z)$ will always be greater than Min (x, y, z)
    (II) $B(x, y, z)$ will always be lower than Max (x, y, z)
    (III) $A(x, y, z)$ will never be greater than $B(x, y, z)$
    (a) I only   (b) III only
    (c) Both a and b (d) All the three

40. The highest value amongst the following will be
    (a) Max/Min   (b) A/B
    (c) C/D (d) Cannot be determined

Directions for Questions 41 to 49: Suppose x and y are real numbers. Let $f(x, y) = |x + y|$ $F(f(x, y)) = -f(x, y)$ and $G(f(x, y)) = -F(f(x, y))$

41. Which one of the following is true?
    (a) $F(f(x, y)).G(f(x, y)) = -F(f(x, y)). G.(f(x, y))$
    (b) $F(f(x, y)).G(f(x, y)) < -F(f(x, y)). G.(f(x, y))$
    (c) $G(f(x, y)).f(x, y) = F(f(x, y)). (f(x, y)$
    (d) $G(f(x, y)).F(f(x, y)) = f(x, y). f(x, y)$

42. Which of the following has a^2 as the result?
    (a) $F(f(a, -a)).G(f(a, -a))$
    (b) $-F(f(a, a).G(f(a, a))/4$
    (c) $F(f(a, a)).G(f(a, a))/2^2$
    (d) $f(a, a).f(a, a)$

43. Find the value of the expression.
$$\frac{G(f(3, 2)) + F(f(-1, 2))}{f(2, -3) + G(f(1, 2)}\ ...$$
    (a) 3/2   (b) 2/3
    (c) 1   (d) 2

44. Which of the following is equal to
$$\frac{G(f(32, 13)) + F(f(15, -5))}{f(2, 3) + G(f(1.5, 0.5))}?$$
    (a) $\dfrac{2G(f(1, 2)) + (f(-3, 1))}{G(f(2, 6) + F(f(-8, 2))}$

    (b) $\dfrac{3.G(f(3, 4)) + F(f(1, 0))}{f(1, 1) + G(f(2, 0))}$

    (c) $\dfrac{(f(3, 4)) + F(f(1, 2))}{G(f(1, 1))}$

    (d) None of these

Now if $A(f(x, y) = f(x, y)$
$\qquad B(f(x, y) = -f(x, y)$
$\qquad C(f(x, y) = f(x, y)$
$\qquad D(f(x, y) = -f(x, y)$ and similarly
$\qquad Z (f(x, y) = -f(x, y)$

Now, solve the following:

45. Find the value of $A(f(0, 1)) + B(f(1, 2)) + C(f(2, 3)) + ... + Z(f(25, 26))$.
    (a) −50   (b) −52
    (c) −26   (d) None of these

46. Which of the following is true?
    (i) $A(f(0, 1)) < B(f(1, 2)) < C(f(2, 3)...$
    (ii) $A(f(0, 1)). B(f(1, 2)) > B(f(1, 2)).C(f(2, 3)) > C(f(2, 3)). D(f(3, 4))$
    (iii) $A(f(0, 0)) = B(f(0, 0)) = C(f(0, 0)) = ... = Z(f(0, 0))$
    (a) only (i) and (ii)   (b) only (ii) and (iii)
    (c) only (ii)   (d) only (i)

47. If max (x, y, z) = maximum of x, y and z
    Min (x, y, z) = minimum of x, y and z
    $f(x, y) = |x + y|$
    $F(f(x, y)) = -f(x, y)$
    $G(f(x, y)) = -F(f(x, y))$
    Then find the value of the following expression:
    Min (max [$f(2, 3)$, $F(f(3, 4))$, $G(f(4, 5))$], min [$f(1, 2)$, $F(f(-1, 2))$, $G(f(1, -2))$], max [$f(-3, -4)$, $f(-5, -1)$, $G(f(-4, -6))$])
    (a) −1   (b) −7
    (c) −6   (d) −10

48. Which of the following is the value of
    Max. [$f(a, b)$, $F(f(b, c))$, $G(f(c, d))$]
    For all $a > b > c > d$?
    (a) Anything but positive
    (b) Anything but negative
    (c) Negative or positive
    (d) Any real value

49. If another function is defined as $P(x, y) = \dfrac{F(f(x, y))}{(x, y)}$
    which of the following is second lowest in value?
    (a) Value of $P(x, y)$ for $x = 2$ and $y = 1$
    (b) Value of $P(x, y)$ for $x = 3$ and $y = 4$
    (c) Value of $P(x, y)$ for $x = 3$ and $y = 5$
    (d) Value of $P(x, y)$ for $x = 3$ and $y = 2$

50. If $f(s) = (b^s + b^{-s})/2$, where $b > 0$. Find $f(s + t) + f(s - t)$.
    (a) $f(s) - f(t)$ (b) $2 f(s).f(t)$
    (c) $4 f(s).f(t)$ (d) $f(s) + f(t)$

Questions 51 to 60 are all actual questions from the XAT exam.

51. A0, A1, A2,...... is a sequence of numbers with
    A0 = 1, A1 = 3, and At = $(t +1)$ At−1 − t At−2 = 2, 3, 4,....
    Conclusion I. A8 = 77
    Conclusion II. A10 = 121
    Conclusion III. A12 = 145
    (a) Using the given statement, only Conclusion I can be derived.
    (b) Using the given statement, only Conclusion II can be derived.
    (c) Using the given statement, only Conclusion III can be derived.
    (d) Using the given statement, Conclusion I, II and III can be derived.
    (e) Using the given statement, none of the three Conclusions I, II and III can be derived.

52. A, B, C be real numbers satisfying A < B < C, A + B + C = 6 and AB + BC + CA = 9
    Conclusion I. 1 < B < 3
    Conclusion II. 2 < A < 3
    Conclusion III. 0 < C < 1

(a) Using the given statement, only Conclusion I can be derived.
(b) Using the given statement, only Conclusion II can be derived.
(c) Using the given statement, only Conclusion III can be derived.
(d) Using the given statement, Conclusion I, II and III can be derived.
(e) Using the given statement, none of the three Conclusions I, II and III can be derived.

53. If $F(x, n)$ be the number of ways of distributing "x" toys to "n" children so that each child receives at the most 2 toys, then $F(4, 3) = $ ___?
    (a) 2   (b) 6
    (c) 3   (d) 4
    (e) 5

54. The figure below shows the graph of a function $f(x)$. How many solutions does the equation $f(f(x)) = 15$ have?
    (a) 5   (b) 6
    (c) 7   (d) 8
    (e) Cannot be determined from the given graph

55. A sequence of positive integers is defined as $A_{n+1} = A^2_{n+1}$ for each $n \geq 0$. What is the value of Greatest Common Divisor of A_{900} and A_{1000}?
    I. A0 = 1   II. $A_1 = 2$

56. A manufacturer produces two types of products—A and B, which are subjected to two types of operations, viz., grinding and polishing. Each unit of product A takes 2 hours of grinding and 3 hours of polishing whereas product B takes 3 hours of grinding and 2 hours of polishing. The manufacturer has 10 grinders and 15 polishers. Each grinder operates for 12 hours/day and each polisher 10 hours/day. The profit margin per unit of A and B are ₹ 5/- and ₹ 7/- respectively. If the manufacturer utilises all his resources for producing these two types of items, what is the maximum profit that the manufacturer can earn?

(a) ₹ 280/-   (b) ₹ 294/-

(c) ₹ 515/-   (d) ₹ 550/-

(e) None of the above

57. Consider a function $f(x) = x^4 + x^3 + x^2 + x + 1$, where x is a positive integer greater than 1. What will be the remainder if $f(x^5)$ is divided by $f(x)$?

(a) 1   (b) 4

(c) 5   (d) A monomial in x

(e) A polynomial in x

58. For all real numbers x, except $x = 0$ and $x = 1$, the function F is defined by $F\left(\dfrac{x}{x-1}\right) = \dfrac{1}{x}$

If $0 < \alpha < 90°$ then $F((\text{cosec } \alpha)^2) =$

(a) $(\sin \alpha)^2$ (b) $(\cos \alpha)^2$

(c) $(\tan \alpha)^2$ (d) $(\cot \alpha)^2$

(e) $(\sec \alpha)^2$

59. $F(x)$ is a fourth order polynomial with integer coefficients and with no common factor. The roots of $F(x)$ are –2, –1, 1, 2. If p is a prime number greater than 97, then the largest integer that divides $F(p)$ for all values of p is:

(a) 72   (b) 120

(c) 240   (d) 360

(e) None of the above.

60. If $x = (9 + 4\sqrt{5})^{48} = [x] + f$, where $[x]$ is defined as integral part of x and f is a fraction, then $x(1 - f)$ equals–

(a) 1

(b) Less than 1

(c) More than 1

(d) Between 1 and 2

(e) None of the above

Space for Rough Work

ANSWER KEY

Level of Difficulty (I)

1. (b)	2. (d)	3. (a)	4. (c)
5. (a)	6. (d)	7. (b)	8. (a)
9. (c)	10. (b)	11. (d)	12. (b)
13. (d)	14. (a)	15. (a)	16. (c)
17. (a)	18. (d)	19. (b)	20. (c)
21. (b)	22. (b)	23. (a)	24. (c)
25. (a)	26. (d)	27. (c)	28. (c)
29. (c)	30. (d)	31. (a)	32. (a)
33. (a)	34. (a)	35. (b)	36. (c)
37. (d)	38. (d)	39. (c)	40. (a)
41. (a)	42. (d)	43. (d)	44. (a)
45. (a)	46. (c)	47. (d)	48. (d)
49. (d)	50. (d)	51. (b)	52. (a)
53. (a)	54. (b)	55. (d)	56. (d)
57. (c)	58. (b)	59. (d)	60. (c)

Level of Difficulty (II)

1. (a)	2. (d)	3. (a)	4. (d)
5. (d)	6. (c)	7. (c)	8. (b)
9. (c)	10. (c)	11. (a)	12. (b)
13. (b)	14. (c)	15. (c)	16. (a)
17. (d)	18. (c)	19. (a)	20. (c)
21. (c)	22. (d)	23. (b)	24. (a)
25. (d)	26. (d)	27. (c)	28. (a)
29. (c)	30. (d)	31. (b)	32. (d)
33. (b)	34. (a)	35. (c)	36. (d)
37. (c)	38. (a)	39. (c)	40. (b)
41. (c)	42. (b)	43. (c)	44. (b)
45. (c)	46. (c)	47. (b)	48. (c)
49. (d)	50. (a)	51. (a)	52. (c)
53. (c)	54. (b)	55. (b)	56. (c)
57. (a)	58. (c)	59. (c)	60. (a)

Level of Difficulty (III)

1. (d)	2. (d)	3. (c)	4. (d)
5. (d)	6. (d)	7. (d)	8. (b)
9. (a)	10. (a)	11. (c)	12. (c)
13. (a)	14. (b)	15. (a)	16. (b)
17. (d)	18. (b)	19. (c)	20. (b)
21. (b)	22. (b)	23. (a)	24. (b)
25. (b)	26. (d)	27. (b)	28. (a)
29. (c)	30. (a)	31. (d)	32. (a)
33. (d)	34. (a)	35. (d)	36. (d)
37. (c)	38. (d)	39. (c)	40. (d)
41. (b)	42. (b)	43. (c)	44. (b)
45. (c)	46. (b)	47. (a)	48. (b)
49. (b)	50. (b)	51. (e)	52. (a)
53. (b)	54. (e)	55. (d)	56. (b)
57. (c)	58. (b)	59. (d)	60. (a)

Solutions and Shortcuts

Level of Difficulty (I)

1. $y = |x|$ will be defined for all values of x. From $= -\infty$ to $+\infty$

   Hence, option (b).

2. For $y = \sqrt{x}$ to be defined, x should be non-negative. i.e. $x \geq 0$.

3. Since the function contains $a \sqrt{x}$ in it, $x \geq 0$ would be the domain.

4. For $(x - 2)^{1/2}$ to be defined $x \geq 2$.

   For $(8 - x)^{1/2}$ to be defined $x \leq 8$.

   Thus, $2 \leq x \leq 8$ would be the required domain.

5. $(9 - x^2) \geq 0 \Rightarrow -3 \leq x \leq 3$.

6. The function would be defined for all values of x except where the denominator viz: $x^2 - 4x + 3$ becomes equal to zero.

   The roots of $x^2 - 4x + 3x = 0$ being 1, 3, it follows that the domain of definition of the function would be all values of x except $x = 1$ and $x = 3$.

7. $f(x) = x$ and $g(x) = (\sqrt{x})^2$ would be identical if $\sqrt{x}$ is defined.

   Hence, $x \geq 0$ would be the answer.

8. $f(x) = x$ is defined for all values of x.

   $g(x) = x^2/x$ also returns the same values as $f(x)$ except at $x = 0$ where it is not defined.

   Hence. option (a).

9. $f(x) = \sqrt{x^3} \Rightarrow f(3x) = \sqrt{(3x)^3} = 3\sqrt{3x^3}$.

   Option (c) is correct.

10. $7 f(x) = 7 e^x$.

11. While $\log x^2$ is defined for $-\infty < x < \infty$, $2 \log x$ is only defined for $0 < x < \infty$. Thus, the two functions are identical for $0 < x < \infty$.

12. y – axis by definition.

13. Origin by definition.

14. x^{-8} is even since $f(x) = f(-x)$ in this case.

15. $(x + 1)^3$ is not odd as $f(x) \neq -f(-x)$.

16. $dy/dx = 2x + 10 = 0 \Rightarrow x = -5$.

17. Required value $= (-5)^2 + 10(-5) + 11$

    $= 25 - 50 + 11 = -14$.

18. Since the denominator $x^2 - 3x + 2$ has real roots, the maximum value would be infinity.

19. The minimum value of the function would occur at the minimum value of $(x^2 - 2x + 5)$ as this quadratic function has imaginary roots.

    For $\qquad y = x^2 - 2x + 5$

    $\qquad\qquad dy/dx = 2x - 2 = 0 \Rightarrow x = 1$

    $\Rightarrow \quad x^2 - 2x + 5 = 4$.

    Thus, minimum value of the argument of the log is 4.

    So minimum value of the function is $\log_2 4 = 2$.

20. $y = 1/x + 1$

    Hence, $y - 1 = 1/x$

$\Rightarrow \qquad x = 1/(y-1)$

Thus $\quad f^{-1}(x) = 1/(x-1).$

21–23.

$$f(1) = 0, \; f(2) = 1,$$
$$f(3) = f(1) - f(2) = -1$$
$$f(4) = f(2) - f(3) = 2$$
$$f(5) = f(3) - f(4) = -3$$
$$f(6) = f(4) - f(5) = 5$$
$$f(7) = f(5) - f(6) = -8$$
$$f(8) = f(6) - f(7) = 13$$
$$f(9) = f(7) - f(8) = -21$$

21. 13
22. $-8 + 2 = -6$
23. $0 + 1 - 1 + 2 - 3 + 5 - 8 + 13 - 21 = -12.$
24. For any ${}^nC_r$, n should be positive and $r \geq 0.$

Thus, for positive x, $5 - x \geq 0$

$\Rightarrow x = 1, 2, 3, 4, 5.$

Directions for Questions 25 to 38: You essentially have to mark (a) if it is an even function, mark (b) if it is an odd function, mark (c) if the function is neither even nor odd.

Also, option (d) would occur if the function does not exist atleast one point of the domain. This means one of two things.

Either the function is returning two values for one value of x. (as in questions 26, 30, 37 and 38) or the function has a break in between (not seen in any of these questions).

We see even functions in: 25, 31, 32, 33 and 34, [Symmetry about the y axis].

We see odd functions in question 35.

While the figures in Questions 27, 28, 29 and 36 are neither odd nor even.

39. $\{[(3@4)! \; (3 \; \#2)] \; @ \; [(4!3) \; @ \; (2 \; \# \; 3)]\}$
$\{[(3.5) \; ! \; (5)] \; @ \; [\; (0.5) \; @ \; (-5)]\}$
$\{[-0.75] \; @ \; [-2.25]\} = -1.5.$

40. $(7) \; @ \; (-0.5) = 3.25.$
41. $0 \; @ \; 0.5 = 0.25.$ Thus, a
42. $b = (1) \; (4) = 4.$

$$C = \frac{(16)}{(1) \; (4)}$$
$$16/4 = 4$$

Hence, both (b) and (c).

43. (a) will always be true because $(a + b)/2$ would always be greater then $(a - b)/2$ for the given value range.

Further, $a^2 - b^2$ would always be less than $a^3 - b^3$. Thus, option (d) is correct.

44–48.

44. Option $a = (a - b) \; (a + b) = a^2 - b^2$
45. Option $a = (a^2 - b^2) + b^2 = a^2.$

46. $3 - 4 \times 2 + 4/8 - 2 = 3 - 8 + 0.5 - 2 = -6.5$

(using BODMAS rule)

47. The maximum would depend on the values of a and b. Thus, cannot be determined.

48. The minimum would depend on the values of a and b. Thus, cannot be determined.

49. Any of $(a + b)$ or a/b could be greater and thus we cannot determine this.

50. Again $(a + b)$ or a/b can both be greater than each other depending on the values we take for a and b. E.g. for $a = 0.9$ and $b = 0.91$, $a + b > a/b$. For $a = 0.1$ and $b = 0.11$, $a + b < a/b$

51. Given that $F(n - 1) = \dfrac{1}{(2 - F(n))}$, we can rewrite the expression as $F(n) = (2F(n-1) -1)/((F(n-1)).$

For $n = 2$: $F(2) = \dfrac{6-1}{3} \Rightarrow F(2) = \dfrac{5}{3}.$

The value of $F(3)$ would come out as $7/5$ and $F(4)$ comes out as $9/7$ and so on. What we realise is that for each value of n, after and including $n = 2$, the value of $F(n) = \dfrac{2n+1}{2n-1}.$

This means that the greatest integral value of $F(n)$ would always be 1 for $n = 2$ to $n = 1000$.

Thus, the value of the given expression would turn out to be:

$3 + 1 \times 999 = 1002$. Option (b) is the correct answer.

52. From the solution to the previous question, we already know how the value of the given functions at $n = 1, 2, 3$ and so on would behave.

Thus, we can try to see what happens when we write down the first few terms of the expression:

$F(1) \times F(2) \times F(3) \times F(4) \times \; \ldots . \; F(1000)$

$= 3 \times \dfrac{5}{3} \times \dfrac{7}{5} \times \dfrac{9}{7} \times \cdots \times 2001 .$

53. Since $f(0) = 15$, we get $c = 15.$

Next, we have $f(3) = f(-3) = 18$. Using this information, we get:

$9a + 3b + c = 9a - 3b + c \to 3b = -3b$

$\therefore \quad 6b = 0 \to b = 0.$

Also, since

$f(3) = 9a + 2b + c = 18 \to$ we get: $9a + 15 = 18$

$\to a = 1/3$

The quadratic function becomes $f(x) = x^2/3 + 15.$

$f(12) = 144/3 + 15 = 63.$

54. What you need to understand about $M(x^2 \theta y^2)$ is that it is the square of the sum of two squares. Since $M(x^2 \theta y^2) = 361$, we get $(x^2 + y^2)^2 = 361$, which means that the sum of the sqaures of x and y viz. $x^2 + y^2 = 19$. (Note it cannot be -19 as we are talking about the sum of two squares, which cannot be negative under any circumstance).

Also, from $M(x^2 \psi y^2) = 49$, we get $(x^2 - y^2)^2 = 49$, $\rightarrow (x^2 - y^2) = \pm 7$

Based on these two values, we can solve for two distinct situations:

(a) When $x^2 + y^2 = 19$ and $x^2 - y^2 = 7$, we get $x^2 = 13$ and $y^2 = 6$

(b) When $x^2 + y^2 = 19$ and $x^2 - y^2 = -7$, we get $x^2 = 6$ and $y^2 = 13$

In both cases, we can see that the value of: $((x^2 y^2) + 3)$ would come out as $13 \times 6 + 3 = 81$ and the square root of its value would turn out to ±9. Option (b) is correct.

55. The first thing you need to understand while solving this question is that, since $[m]$ will always be integral, hence $\Psi(4x + 5)$ will also be integral. Since $\Psi(4x + 5) = 5y + 3$, naturally, the value of $5y + 3$ will also be integral. This means that y is an integer. By a similar logic, the value of x will also be an integer considering the second equation: $\Psi(3y + 7) = x + 4$. Using, this logic we know that $\Psi(4x+5) = 4x+5$ (because, whenever m is an integer the value of $[m] = m$).

This leads us to two linear equations as follows:
$4x + 5 = 5y + 3$ ...(i)
$3y + 7 = x + 4$ ...(ii)
Solving simultaneously, we will get: $x = -2$ and $y = -3$. Thus, $x^2 \times y^2 = 4 \times 9 = 36$.

56. Since $f(128) = 4$, we can see that the product of $f(256).f(0.5) = f(256 \times 0.5) = f(128) = 4$.

Similarly, the products $f(1).f(128) = f(2).f(64) = f(4).f(32) = f(8).f(16) = 4$.

Thus, M = $4 \times 4 \times 4 \times 4 \times 4 = 1024$.

Option (d) is the correct answer.

57. The only values of x and y that satisfy the equation $4x + 6y = 20$ are $x = 2$ and $y = 2$ (since, x, y are non negative integers). This gives us: $4 \le M/2^{2/3}$. M has to be greater than $2^{4/3}$ for this expression to be satisfied. Option (c) is correct.

58. $\theta(\Psi(-7)) = \theta(-2) = 14$. Option (b) is correct.

59. $F(2b) = F(b + b) = F(b).F(b) \div 2 = (F(b))^2 \div 2$

Similarly, $F(3b) = F(b + b + b) = F(b + b).F(b) \div 2 = \{F(b)^2 \div 2\}.\{F(b)\} \div 2 = (F(b))^3 \div 2^2$

Similarly, $F(4b) = (F(b))^4 \div 2^3$.

Hence, $F(12b) = (F(b))^{12} \div 2^{11}$. Option (d) is correct.

60. To test for a reflexive function as defined in the problem use the following steps:

Step 1: To start with, assume a value of 'b' and derive a value for 'a' using the given function.

Step 2: Then, insert the value you got for 'a' in the first step into the value of 'b' and get a new value of 'a'. This value of 'a' should be equal to the first value of 'b' that you used in the first step. If this

occurs the function would be reflexive. Else it is not reflexive.

Checking for the expression in (i) if we take $b = 1$, we get:

$a = 8/1 = 8$. Inserting, $b = 8$ in the function gives us $a = 29/29 = 1$. Hence, the function given in (i) is reflexive.

Similarly checking the other two functions, we get that the function in (ii) is not reflexive while the function in (iii) is reflexive.

Thus, Option (c) is the correct answer.

Level of Difficulty (II)

1. For the function to be defined $4 - x^2 > 0$
This happens when $-2 < x < 2$.
Option (a) is correct.

2. For the function to be defined two things should happen
(a) $(1 - x) > 0 \Rightarrow x < 1$ and
(b) $(x + 2) \ge 0 \Rightarrow x \ge -2$. Also $x \ne 0$
Thus, option (d) is correct.

3. $\dfrac{5x - x^2}{4} \ge 1 \Rightarrow 1 \le x \le 4$.

4. Neither $2^{-x \cdot x}$ nor $2^{x - x \cdot x \cdot x}$ is an odd function as for neither of them is $f(x) = -f(-x)$.

5. $1 - |x|$ should be non negative.
$[-1, 1]$ would satisfy this.

6. $4 - x^2 \ne 0$ and $(x^3 - x) > 0 \Rightarrow (-1, 0) \cup (1, \infty)$ but not 2 or -2.

7. $f(0) = 1$, $f(1) = 2$ and $f(2) = 4$
Hence, they are in G.P.

8. x would become -2 and $y = -3$.

9. $u(f(v(t))) = u(f(t^2)) = u(1/t^2) = \left(\dfrac{4}{t^2}\right) - 5$.

10. $g(f(h(t))) = g(f(4t - 8)) = g\left(\sqrt{4t - 8}\right)$
$= \dfrac{\sqrt{4t - 8}}{4}$

11. $h(g(f(t)) = h(g(\sqrt{t})) = h(\sqrt{t}/4)$
$= \sqrt{t} - 8$

12. $f(h(g(t))) = f(h(t/4)) = f(t - 8) = \sqrt{t - 8}$.

13. All three functions would give the same values for $x > 0$. As $g(x)$ is not defined for negative x, and $h(x)$ is not defined for $x = 0$.

14. $e^x + e^{-x} = e^{-x} + e^x$
Hence, this is an even function.

15. $(x + 3)^3$ would be shifted 3 units to the left and hence $(x + 3)^3 + 1$ would shift 3 units to the left and 1 unit up. Option (c) is correct.

16. $f(x) \cdot g(x) = 15x^8$ which is an even function. Thus, option (a) is correct.

17. $(x^2 + \log_e x)$ would be neither odd nor even since it obeys neither of the rules for even function ($f(x) = f(-x)$) nor for odd functions ($f(x) = -f(-x)$).

18. $(x^3 - x^2/5) = f(x) - g(x)$ is neither even nor odd.

19. $y = 1/(x - 2) \Rightarrow (x - 2) = 1/y \Rightarrow x = 1/y + 2$.
    Hence, $f^{-1}(x) = 1/x + 2$.

20. $y = e^x$
    $\Rightarrow \log_e y = x$.
    $\Rightarrow f^{-1}(x) = \log_e x$.

21. $y = x/(x - 1)$
    $\Rightarrow \qquad (x - 1)/x = 1/y$
    $\Rightarrow \qquad 1 - (1/x) = 1/y$
    $\Rightarrow \qquad 1/x = 1 - 1/y \Rightarrow 1/x = (y - 1)/y$
    $\Rightarrow \qquad x = y/(y - 1)$
    Hence, $f^{-1}(x) = x/(x - 1)$.

22. If you differentiate each function with respect to x, and equate it to 0 you would see that for none of the three options will get you a value of $x = -3$ as its solution. Thus, option (d) viz. None of these is correct.

Directions for Questions 23 to 32: You essentially have to mark (a) if it is an even function, mark (b) if it is an odd function, mark (c) if the function is neither even nor odd.

Also, option (d) would occur if the function does not exist atleast one point of the domain. This means one of two things.

Either the function is returning two values for one value of x or the function has a break in between. This is seen in Questions 25, 26, 30 and 32.

We see even functions in Questions 24 and 28. [Symmetry about the y axis]. We see odd functions in Questions 23 and 31.

While the figures in Questions 27 and 29 are neither odd nor even.

Even $\Rightarrow$ 24, 28,
Odd 23, 31.
Neither 27, 29,
doesn't exist: 25, 26, 30 and 32.

33. $-f(x)$ would be the mirror image of the function, about the 'x' axis which is seen in option (b).

34. $-f(x) + 1$ would be mirror image about the x axis and then shifted up by 1. Option (a) satisfies this.

35. $f(x) - 1$ would shift down by 1 unit. Thus option (c) is correct.

36. $f(x) + 1$ would shift by 1 unit. Thus, option (d) is correct.

37. The given function would become $h[11, 80, 1] = 2640$.

38. The given function would become $g[0, 0, 3] = 0$.

39. The given function would become $f[3, 3, 3] = 27$.

40. $f(1, 2, 3) - g(1, 2, 3) + h(1, 2, 3) = 11 - 23 + 18 = 6$.

41. The number of g's and f's should be equal on the LHS and RHS since both these functions are essentially inverse of each other.
    Option (c) is correct.

42. The required minimum value would occur at $f(x) = g(x) = 1$.

43. $SQ[R[(a + b)/b]] = SQ[R[17/5]] \Rightarrow SQ[2] = 2$.

44. $Q[[SQ(63) + 7]/9] = Q[[8 + 7]/9] = Q[15/9] = 1$.

45. $Q[[SA(36) + R(18/7)]/2] = Q[(7 + 4)/2] = Q[11/2] = 5$.

46. $[x] - \{x\} = -1$

47. $[x] + \{x\}$ will always be odd as the values are consecutive integers.

48. At $x = 5.5$, the given equation can be seen to be satisfied as: $6 + 5 = 2 \times 5.5 = 11$.

49. $f(g(t)) - g(f(t)) = f(2.5) - g(6) = 8.25 - 2.166 = 6.0833$.

50. fog $= f(3t + 2) = K(3t + 2) + 1$
    gof $= g(kt + 1) = 3(kt + 1) + 2$
    $\qquad K(3t + 2) + 1 = 3(kt + 1) + 2$
    $\Rightarrow \qquad 2k + 1 = 5$
    $\Rightarrow \qquad k = 2$.

51. When the value of $x = 81$ and 82 is substituted in the given expression, we get,
    $F(81) \, F(82) = -F(80) \, F(79) \, F(78) \, F(77)$ ...(i)
    $F(82) \, F(83) = -F(81) \, F(80) \, F(79) \, F(78)$ ...(ii)
    On dividing (i) by (a), we get
    $$\frac{F(81)}{F(83)} = \frac{F(77)}{F(81)} \Rightarrow F(81) \times F(81) = 81 \times 9$$
    $\Rightarrow F(81) = 27$
    Option (a) is the correct answer.

52. In order to understand this question, you first need to develop your thought process about what the value of $h(x)$ is in various cases. A little bit of trial and error would show you that the value of $h(x)$ since it depends on the minimum of $f(x)$ and $g(x)$, would definitely be dependant on the value of $f(x)$ once x becomes greater than 11 or less than -11. Also, the value of $g(x)$ is fixed as an integer at 16. It can be observed that when $f(x) > g(x)$ i.e. $f(x) > 16$, the values of $h(x)$ would also be 16 and hence would be a positive integer.

With this thought when you look at the expression of $f(x) = 121 - x^2$, you realise that the value of x can be $-10, -9, -8, -7, \ldots 0, 1, 2, 3, \ldots 8, 9, 10$, i.e., 21 values of x when $h(x) = g(x) = 16$. When we use $x = 11$ or $x = -11$, the vlaue of $f(x) = \min(0, 16) = 0$ and is not a positive integral value.

Hence, the correct answer is Option (c).

53. Since, $R(x)$ is the maximum amongst the three given functions, its value would always be equal to the highest amongst the three. It is easy to imagine that $x^2 - 8$ and $3x$ are increasing functions, therefore the value of the function is continuously increasing as you increase the value of x. Similarly $x^2 - 8$ would be increasing continuously as you go farther and farther down on the negative side of the x-axis. Hence, the

maximum value of $R(x)$ would be infinity. Option (c) is the correct answer.

54. In this case, the value of the function, is the minimum of the three values. If you visualise the graphs of the three functions (viz: $y = x^2 - 8$, $y = 3x$ and $y = 8$) you realise that the function $y = 3x$ (being a straight line) will keep going to negative infinity as you move to the left of zero on the negative side of the x-axis.

Hence, the minimum value of the function $R(x)$ after a certain point (when x is negative) would get dictated by the value of $3x$. This point will be the intersection of the line $y = 3x$ and the function $y = x^2 - 8$ when x is negative.

The two intersection points of the line $(3x)$ and the quadratic curve $(x^2 - 8)$ would be got by equating $3x = x^2 - 8$. Solving this equation tells us that the intersection points are:

$$\frac{3 - \sqrt{41}}{2} \text{ and } \frac{3 + \sqrt{41}}{2}.$$

$R(x)$ would depend on the following structures based on the value of x:

(i) When x is smaller than $\dfrac{3 - \sqrt{41}}{2}$, the value of the function $R(x)$ would be given by the value of $3x$.

(ii) When x is between $\dfrac{3 - \sqrt{41}}{2}$ and 4 the value of the function $R(x)$ would be given by the value of $x^2 - 8$, since that would be the least amongst the three functions.

(iii) After $x = 4$, on the positive side of the x-axis, the value of the function would be defined by the third function viz: $y = 8$.

A close look at these three ranges would give you that amongst these three ranges, the third range would yield the highest value of $R(x)$. Hence, the maximum possible value of $R(x) = 8$. Option (b) is correct.

55. The expression is $2x^2 - 5x + 4$, and its value at $x = 5$ would be equal to $100 - 25 + 4 = 79$. Option (b) is correct.

56. At $x = 0$, the value of the function is 20 and this value rejects the first option. Taking some higher values of x, we realise that on the positive side, the value of the function will become negative when we take x greater than 5 since the value of $(5 - x)$ would be negative. Also, the value of $f(x)$ would start tending to $-\infty$, as we take bigger values of x.

Similarly, on the negative side, when we take the value of x lower than -4, $f(x)$ becomes positive and when we take it farther away from 0 on the negative side, the value of $f(x)$ would continue tending to $+\infty$. Hence, Option (c) is the correct answer.

57. The remainder when $6^x + 4$ is divided by 2 would be 0 in every case (when x is odd)

Also, when x is even, we would get $6^x - 3$ as an odd number. In every case the remainder would be 1 (when it is divided by 2.)

Between $f(2)$, $f(4)$, $f(6)$,....$f(1000)$ there are 500 instances when x is even. In each of these instances the remainder would be 0 and hence the remainder would be 0 (in total). Option (b) is correct.

58. The product of p, q and r will be maximum if p, q and r are as symmetrical as possible. Therefore, the possible combination is (4, 3, 3).

Hence, maximum value of $pq + qr + pr + pqr = 4 \times 3 + 4 \times 3 + 3 \times 3 + 4 \times 3 \times 3 = 69$.

Hence, Option (c) is correct.

59. The equation given in the question is: $3\alpha(x) + 2\alpha (2-x) = (x + 3)^2$ ....(i)

Replacing x by $(2-x)$ in the above equation, we get

$3\alpha(2-x) + 2\alpha(x) = (5-x)^2$

Solving the above pairs of equation, we get

$\alpha(x) = (x^2 + 38 - 23)/5$

Thus, $G(-5) = -188/5 = -37.6$. The value of $[-37.6] = -37$. Hence, Option (c) is the correct answer.

60. The first thing you do in this question is to create the chain of values of $f(x)$ for $x = 1, 2, 3$ and so on. The chain of values would look something like this:

When x is odd			When x is even		
$f(1)$	Value is given	6	$f(2)$	Value is given	4
$f(3)$	$= 1 + f(1)$	7	$f(4)$	$= 3 + f(2)$	7
$f(5)$	$= 3 + f(3)$	10	$f(6)$	$= 3 + f(4)$	10
$f(7)$	$= 5 + f(5)$	15	$f(8)$	$= 3 + f(6)$	13
$f(9)$	$= 7 + f(7)$	22	$f(10)$	$= 3 + f(8)$	16
$f(11)$	$= 9 + f(9)$	31			

In order to evaluate the value of the embedded function represented by $f(f(f(f(f(f(1))))))$, we can use the above values and think as follows:

$f(f(f(f(1)))) = f(f(f(6))) = f(f(10)) = f(16) = 25$

Also, $f(f(f(f(2)) = f(f(f(4))) = f(f(7)) = f(15) = 55$

Hence, the product of the two values is $25 \times 55 = 1375$.

Option (a) is correct.

Level of Difficulty (III)

1. $x - |x|$ is either negative for $x < 0$ or 0 for $x \geq 0$. Thus, option (d) is correct.

2. The domain should simultaneously satisfy:

$$x - 1 \geq 0, (1 - x) \geq 0 \text{ and } (x^2 + 3) \geq 0.$$

Gives us: $x \geq 1$ and $x \leq 1$

The only value that satisfies these two simultaneously is $x = 1$.

3. For the function to exist, the argument of the logarithmic function should be positive. Also, $(x + 4) \geq 0$ should be obeyed simultaneously.

For $\dfrac{(x-5)}{(x^2-10x+24)}$ to be positive both numerator and denominator should have the same sign. Considering all this, we get:

$$4 < x < 5 \text{ and } x > 6.$$

Option (c) is correct.

4. Both the brackets should be non-negative and neither $(x + 3)$ nor $(1+ x)$ should be 0.

For $(x - 3)/(x + 3)$ to be non negative we have $x > 3$ or $x < -3$.

Also for $(1- x)/(1+ x)$ to be non-negative $-1 < x < 1$. Since there is no interference in the two ranges, Option (d) would be correct.

8. $f(f(t)) = f((t-1)/(t+1))$

$$= \left[\left(\frac{t-1}{t+1}\right)-1\right]\Big/\left[\left(\frac{t-1}{t+1}\right)+1\right] = \frac{t-1-t-1}{t-1+t+1}$$

$$= -2/2t = -1/t.$$

9. fog $= f(\log_e x) = e^{\log e x} = x$.

10. gof $= g(e^x) = \log_e e^x = x$.

11. Looking at the options, one unit right means x is replaced by $(x - 1)$. Also, 1 unit down means -1 on the RHS.

Thus, $(y + 1) = 1/(x - 1)$

12. For none of these is $f(t) = f(-t)$

Thus, Option (d) is correct.

13. Option (b) is odd because:

$$\frac{a^{-t}+a^t}{a^t-a^{-t}} = -1 \times \left(\frac{a^{-t}+a^t}{a^{-t}-a^t}\right)$$

Similarly option (c) is also representing an odd function. The function in option (a) is not odd.

14. $f(f(t)) = f[t/(1+t^2)^{1/2}] = t/(1 + 2t^2)^{1/2}$.

15. By trial and error it is clear that at $x = 3$, the value of the function is 19. At other values of 'x' the value of the function is less than 19.

17. Take different values of n to check each option. Each of Options (a), (b) and (c) can be ruled out. Hence, Option (d) is correct.

Solutions to 18 to 20:

$$f(1) = 0, f(2) = 1,$$
$$f(3) = f(1) - f(2) = -1$$
$$f(4) = f(2) - f(3) = 2$$
$$f(5) = f(3) - f(4) = -3$$
$$f(6) = f(4) - f(5) = 5$$
$$f(7) = f(5) - f(6) = -8$$
$$f(8) = f(6) - f(7) = 13$$

18. It can be seen that $f(x)$ is positive wherever x is even and negative whenever x is odd.

19. $f(f(6)) = f(5) = -3$.

20. $f(6) - f(8) = 5 - 13 = -8 = f(7)$.

21. Option (b) is not even since $e^x - e^{-x} \neq e^{-x} - e^x$.

22. We have $f(x) \cdot f(1/x) = f(x) + f(1/x)$

$\Rightarrow \quad f(1/x)[f(x) - 1] = f(x)$

For $x = 4$, we have $f(1/4)[f(4) - 1] = f(4)$

$\Rightarrow \quad f(1/4)[64] = 65$

$\Rightarrow \qquad f(1/4) = 65/64 = 1/64 + 1$

This means $f(x) = x^3 + 1$

For $f(6)$ we have $f(6) = 216 + 1 = 217$.

Directions for Questions 23 to 34: You essentially have to mark (a) if it is an even function, mark (b) if it is an odd function, mark (c) if the function is neither even nor odd.

Also, Option (d) would occur if the function does not exist at, atleast one point of the domain. This means one of two things.

Either the function is returning two values for one value of x or the function has a break in between (as in questions 26, 31 and 33).

We see even functions in Questions 23, 28, 30, 32 and 34 [Symmetry about the y axis]. We see odd functions in Questions 24, 25 and 27.

While the figure in Question 29 is neither odd nor even.

Solutions to 35–40:
In order to solve this set of questions first analyse each of the functions:

$A(x, y, z) = $ will always return the value of the highest between x and y.

$B(x, y, z)$ will return the value of the maximum amongst x, y and z.

$C(x, y, z)$ and $D(x, y, z)$ would return the second highest values in all cases while max (x, y, z) and min(x, y, z) would return the maximum and minimum values amongst x, y, and z respectively.

35. When either x or y is maximum.
36. This would never happen.
37. When z is maximum, A and B would give different values. Thus, option (c) is correct.
38. Never.
39. I and III are always true.
40. We cannot determine this because it would depend on whether the integers x, y, and z are positive or negative.

Solutions to 41 to 49:

$F(x, y)$ is always positive
$F(f(x, y))$ is always negative
$G(f(x, y))$ is always positive

41. $F \times G$ would always be negative while $-F \times G$ would always be positive.

Hence, Option (b) $F \times G < -F \times G$ is correct.

42. Option (b) can be seen to give us $4a^2/4 = a^2$.

43. $(5 - 1)/(1 + 3) = 4/4 = 1.$

44. The given expression $= (45 - 10)/(5 + 2) = 35/7 = 5.$
    Option (b) $= 20/4 = 5.$

Directions for Questions 45 to 49: Do the following analysis:

$A(f(x, y))$ is positive
$B(f(x, y))$ is negative
$C(f(x, y))$ is positive
$D(f(x, y))$ is positive
$E(f(x, y))$ is positive and so on.

45. $1 - 3 + 5 - 7 + 9 - 11 + \ldots - 51$
    $= (1 + 5 + 9 + 13 + \ldots 49) - (3 + 7 + 11 \ldots + 51)$
    $= -26$

46. Verify each statement to see that (ii) and (iii) are true.

47. The given expression becomes:
    Min (max [5, -7, 9], min [3, -1, 1], max [7, 6, 10])
    $=$ Min [9, -1, 10]
    $= -1.$

48. The given expression becomes:
    $$\text{Max } [|a + b|, -|b + c|, |c + d|]$$
    This would never be negative.

49. The respective values are:
    $$-3/2, -7/12, -8/15, \text{ and } -5/6.$$
    Option (b) is second lowest.

50. Let $s = 1$, $t = 2$ and $b = 3$
    Then, $f(s + t) + f(s - t)$
    $= f(3) + f(-1) = (3^3 + 3^{-3})/2 + (3^{-1} + 3^1)/2$
    $= [(27 + (1/27)]/2 + [3 + (1/3)]/2$
    $= 730/54 + 10/6$
    $= 820/54 = 410/27$
    Option (b) $2 f(s) \times f(t)$ gives the same value.

51. This question is based on the logic of a chain function. Given the relationship
    $At = (t + 1) At - 1 - t At - 2$
    We can clearly see that the value of A2 would depend on the values of A_0 and A_1. Putting $t = 2$ in the expression, we get:
    $A_2 = 3A1 - 2A0 = 7$; $A_3 = 19$; $A_4 = 67$ and $A_5 = 307$.
    Clearly, A6 onwards will be larger than 307 and hence none of the three conclusions are true. Option (e) is the correct answer.

52. In order to solve this question, we would need to check each of the value ranges given in the conclusions: Checking whether Conclusion I is possible
    For B = 2, we get A + C = 4 (since A + B + C = 6). This transforms the second equation AB + BC + CA = 9 to:
    $2(A + C) + CA = 9 \rightarrow CA = 1.$
    Solving CA = 1 and A + C = 4 we get: $(4 - A)A = 1 \rightarrow A^2 - 4A + 1 = 0 \rightarrow A = 2 + 3^{1/2}$ and C = $2 - 3^{1/2}$. Both these numbers are real and it satisfies A < B < C and hence, Conclusion I is true.

Checking Conclusion II: If we chose A = 2.5, the condition is not satisfied since we get the other two variables as $(3.5 + 11.25^{1/2}) \div 2 \approx 3.4$ and $(3.5 - 11.25^{1/2}) \div 2 \approx 0.1$. In this case, A is no longer the least value and hence Conclusion II is rejected.

Checking Conclusion III we can see that $0 < C < 1$ cannot be possible since C being the largest of the three values has to be greater than 3 (the largest amongst A, B, and C would be greater than the average of A, B, C).

Option (a) is correct.

53. The number of ways of distributing n identical things to r people such that any person can get any number of things including 0 is always given by $^{n+r-1}C_{r-1}$. In the case of $F(4,3)$, the value of $n = 4$ and $r = 3$ and hence the total number of ways without any constraints would be given by $^{4+3-1}C_{3-1} = {}^6C_2 = 15$. However, out of these 15 ways of distributing the toys, we cannot count any way in which more than 2 toys are given to any one child. Hence, we need to reduce as follows:

The distribution of 4 toys as (3, 1, 0) amongst three children A, B and C can be done in 3! = 6 ways.

Also, the distribution of 4 toys as (4, 0, 0) amongst three children A, B and C can be done in 3 ways.

Hence, the value of $F(4, 3) = 15 - 6 - 3 = 6.$

Option (b) is correct.

54. $f(f(x)) = 15$ when $f(x) = 4$ or $f(x) = 12$ in the given function. The graph given in the figure becomes equal to 4 at 4 points and it becomes equal to 12 at 2 points in the figure. This gives us 6 points in the given figure when $f(f(x)) = 15$. However, the given function is continuous beyond the part of it which is shown between -10 and $+13$ in the figure. Hence, we do not know how many more solutions to $f(f(x)) = 15$ would be there. Hence, Option (e) is the correct answer.

55. The given function is a chain function where the value of A_{n+1} depends on the value A_n.

Thus for $n = 0$, A1 = $A_0^2 + 1$.

For n = 1, $A_2 = A_1^2 + 1$ and so on.

In such functions, if you know the value of the function at any one point, the value of the function can be calculated for any value till infinity.

Hence, Statement I is sufficient by itself to find the value of the GCD of A_{900} and A_{1000}.

So also, the Statement II is sufficient by itself to find the value of the GCD of A_{900} and A_{1000}.

Hence, Option (d) is correct.

56. This question can be solved by first putting up the information in the form of a table as follows:

	Product A	Product B	No of machines available	No of Hours/day per Machine.	Total Hrs. per day available for each activity
Grinding	2 hr	3 hr	10	12	120
Polishing	3 hr	2 hr	15	10	150
Profit	₹ 5	₹ 7			

On the surface, the profit of Product B being higher, we can think about maximising the number of units of Product B. Grinding would be the constraint when we maximise Product B production and we can produce a maximum of $120 \div 3 = 40$ units of Product B to get a profit of ₹ 280. The clue that this is not the correct answer comes from the fact that there is a lot of 'polishing' time left in this situation. In order to try to increase the profit we can check that if we reduce production of Product B and try to increase the production of Product A, does the profit go up? When we reduce the production of Product B by 2 units, the production of Product A goes up by 3 units and the profit goes up by +1 ($-2 \times 7 + 3 \times 5$ gives a net effect of +1). In this case, the grinding time remains the same (as there is a reduction of 2 units $\times$ 3 hours/unit = 6 hours in grinding time due to the reduction in Product B's production, but there is also a simultaneous increase of 6 hours in the use of the grinders in producing 3 units of Product A). Given that a reduction in the production of Product B, with a simultaneous maximum possible increase in the production of Product A, results in an increase in the profit, we would like to do this as much as possible. To think about it from this point this situation can be tabulated as under for better understanding:

	Product A Production (A)	Product B Production (B)	Grinding Machine Usage = 3A + 2B	Polishing Machine Usage = 2A + 3B	Time Left on Grinding Machine	Time Left on Polishing Machine	Profit = 7A+5B
Case 1	40	0	120	80	0	70	280
Case 2	38	3	120	85	0	65	281
Case 3	36	6	120	90	0	60	281

The limiting case would occur when we reduce the time left on the polishing machine to 0. That would happen in the following case:

Optimal case	12	42	120	150	0	0	294

Hence, the answer would be 294.

57. The value of $f(x)$ as given is: $f(x) = x^4 + x^3 + x^2 + x + 1 = 1 + x + x^2 + x^3 + x^4 + x^5$. This can be visualised as a geometric progression with 5 terms with the first term 1 and common ratio x. The sum of the GP = $f(x) = \dfrac{x^5 - 1}{x - 1}$

The value of $f(x^5) = x^{20} + x^{15} + x^{10} + x^5 + 1$ and this can be rewritten as:
$F(x^5) = (x^{20} - 1) + (x^{15} - 1) + (x^{10} - 1) + (x^5 - 1) + 5$. When this expression is divided by $f(x) = \dfrac{x^5 - 1}{x - 1}$ we get each of the first four terms of the expression would be divisible by it, i.e. $(x^{20} - 1)$ would be divisible by $f(x) = \dfrac{x^5 - 1}{x - 1}$ and would leave no remainder (because $x^{20} - 1$ can be rewritten in the form $(x^5 - 1) \times (x^{15} + x^{10} + x^5 + 1)$ and when you divide this expression by $\left(\dfrac{x^5 - 1}{x - 1}\right)$ we get the remainder as 0.)

A similar logic would also hold for the terms $(x^{15} - 1)$, $(x^{10} - 1)$ and $(x^5 - 1)$. The only term that would leave a

remainder would be 5 when it is divided by $\left(\dfrac{x^5 - 1}{x - 1}\right)$

Also, for $x \geq 2$ we can see the value of $\left(\dfrac{x^5 - 1}{x - 1}\right)$ would be more than 5. Hence, the remainder would always be 5 and Option (c) is the correct answer.

58. Start by putting $\dfrac{x}{x - 1} = (\operatorname{cosec} \alpha)^2$ in the given expression

$F\left(\dfrac{x}{x - 1}\right) = \dfrac{1}{x}$

Now for $0 < \alpha < 90°$

$\dfrac{x}{x - 1} = (\operatorname{cosec} \alpha)^2 \Rightarrow x = \dfrac{1}{1 - \sin^2 \alpha} \Rightarrow \dfrac{1}{x} = \cos^2 \alpha$

Hence, Option (b) is correct.

59. Given that the roots of the equation $F(x) = 0$ are -2, -1, 1 and 2 respectively and the $F(x)$ is a polynomial with the highest power of x as x^4, we can create the value of
$F(x) = (x + 2)(x + 1)(x - 1)(x - 2)$

Hence, $F(p) = (P + 2)(P + 1)(P - 1)(P - 2)$

It is given to us that P is a prime number greater than 97. Hence, p would always be of the form $6n \pm 1$ where n is a natural number greater than or equal to 17.

Thus, we get two cases for $F(p)$.

Case 1: If $p = 6n + 1$.

$F(6n + 1) = (6n + 3)(6n + 2)(6n)(6n - 1)$
$= 3(2n + 1) \cdot 2(3n + 1)(6n)(6n - 1)$
$= (36)(2n + 1)(3n + 1)(n)(6n - 1)$ ...(i)

If you try to look for divisibility of this expression by numbers given in the options for various values of $n \geq 17$, we see that the for $n = 17$ and 18 both 360 divides the value of $F(p)$. However at $n = 19$, none of the values in the four options divides $36 \times 39 \times 58 \times 19 \times 113$. In this case however, at $n = 19$, $6n + 1$ is not a prime number hence, this case is not to be considered. Whenever we put a value of n as a value greater than 17, such that $6n+1$ becomes a prime number, we also see that the value of $F(p)$ is divisible by 360. This divisibility by 360 happens since the expression $(2n + 1)(3n + 1)(n)(6n - 1)$ ... is always divisible by 10 in all such cases. A similar logic can be worked out when we take $p = gn-1$. Hence, the Option (d) is the correct answer.

60. In order to solve this question, we start from the value of $x = (9 + 4\sqrt{5})^{48}$.

Let the value of $x(1-f) = xy$. (We are assuming $(1-f) = y$, which means that y is between 0 to 1).

The value of $x = (9 + 4\sqrt{5})^{48}$ can be rewritten as $[^{48}C_0 \, 9^{48} + {}^{48}C_1 \, 9^{47}(4\sqrt{5}) + {}^{48}C_2 \, 9^{46}(4\sqrt{5})^2 + \ldots + {}^{48}C_{47}(9)(4\sqrt{5})^{47} + {}^{48}C_{48}(4\sqrt{5})^{48}]$ using the binary theorem.

In this value, it is going to be all the odd powers of the $(4\sqrt{5})$ which would account for the value of 'f' in the value of x. Thus, for instance it can be seen that the terms $^{48}C_0 \, 9^{48}, {}^{48}C_2 \, 9^{46}(4\sqrt{5})^2, \ldots {}^{48}C_{48}(4\sqrt{5})^{48}$ would all be integers. It is only the terms: $^{48}C_1 9^{47}(4\sqrt{5}), {}^{48}C_3 \, 9^{45}(4\sqrt{5})^3, \ldots {}^{48}C_{47}(9)(4\sqrt{5})^{47}$ which would give us the value of 'f' in the value of x.

Hence, $x(1-f) = x [1 - {}^{48}C_1 \, 9^{47}(4\sqrt{5}) - {}^{48}C_3 \, 9^{45}(4\sqrt{5})^3 - \ldots - {}^{48}C_{47}(9)(4\sqrt{5})^{47}]$

In order to think further from this point, you would need the following thought. Let $y = (9 - 4\sqrt{5})^{48}$.

Also, $x + y = \{{}^{48}C_0 9^{48} + {}^{48}C_1 9^{47}(4\sqrt{5}) + {}^{48}C_2 9^{46}(4\sqrt{5})^2 + \ldots + {}^{48}C_{47}(9)(4\sqrt{5})^{47} + {}^{48}C_{48}(4\sqrt{5})^{48}\} + \{{}^{48}C_0 9^{48} - {}^{48}C_1 9^{47}(4\sqrt{5}) + {}^{48}C_2 9^{46}(4\sqrt{5})^2 + \ldots - {}^{48}C_{47}(9)(4\sqrt{5})^{47} + {}^{48}C_{48}(4\sqrt{5})^{48}\} = 2\{{}^{48}C_0 9^{48} + {}^{48}C_2 9^{46}(4\sqrt{5})^2 + \ldots {}^{48}C_{48}(4\sqrt{5})^{48}\}$ – the bracket in this expression has only retained the even terms which are integral. Hence, the value of $x+y$ is an integer.

Further, $x+y = [x] + f$ and hence, if $x+y$ is an integer, $[x] + f + y$ would also be an integer. This automatically means that $f+y$ must be an integer (as $[x]$ is an integer).

Now, the value of y is between 0 to 1 and hence when we add the fractional part of x i.e. 'f' to y, and we need to make it an integer, the only possible integer that $f + y$ can be equal to is 1.

Thus, if $f + y = 1 \rightarrow y = (1 - f)$.

In order to find the value of $x(1 - f)$ we can find the value of $x \times y$.

Then, $x(1 - f) = x \times y = (9 + 4\sqrt{5})^{48} \times (9 - 4\sqrt{5})^{48}$
$= (81 - 80)^{48} = 1$
$x(1 - f) = 1$

Space for Rough Work

14 Chapter

Inequalities

This chapter will seem to be highly mathematical to you when you read the theory contained in the chapter and look at the solved examples. For students weak in Math, there is no need to be disheartened about the seemingly high mathematical content. I would advise you to go through this chapter and internalise the concepts. However, keep in mind the fact that in an aptitude test, the questions will have options, and with options all you will need to do will be check the validity of the inequality for the different options.

In fact, the questions in this chapter have options on all three levels and with option-based solutions, all these questions will seem easy to you.

However, I would advise students aiming to score high marks in Quantitative Ability to try to mathematically solve all the questions on all three levels in this chapter (even though option-based solution will be much easier.)

Two real numbers or two algebraic expressions related by the symbol > ("Greater Than") or < ("Less Than") (and also by the signs ≥ or ≤) form an inequality.

$A < B$, $A > B$ (are plain inequalities)

$A ≥ B$, $A ≤ B$ (are called as inequations)

The inequality consists of two sides—the left hand side, A and the right hand side, B. A and B can be algebraic expressions or they can be numbers.

An inequality with the < or > sign is called a *strict inequality* while an inequality having ≥ or ≤ sign is called a *slack inequality*. The expressions A and B have to be considered on the set where A and B have sense simultaneously. This set is called the set of permissible values of the inequality. If the terms on the LHS and the RHS are algebraic equations/identities, then the inequality may or may not hold true for a particular value of the variable/set of variables assumed.

The direction in which the inequality sign points is called *the sense of the inequality*. If two or several inequalities contain the same sign (< or >) then they are called *inequalities of the same sense*. Otherwise they are called *inequalities of the opposite sense*.

Now let us consider some basic *definitions* about inequalities.

For 2 real numbers a and b

The inequality $a > b$ means that the difference $a − b$ is positive.

The inequality $a < b$ means that the difference $a − b$ is negative.

PROPERTIES OF INEQUALITIES

For any two real numbers a and b, only one of the following restrictions can hold true:

$$a = b, a > b \text{ or } a < b$$

Definitions of Slack Inequalities

The inequality $a ≥ b$ means that $a > b$ or $a = b$, that is, a is not less than b.

The inequality $a ≤ b$ means that $a < b$ or $a = b$, that is, a is not greater than b.

We can also have the following double inequalities for simultaneous situations:

$$a < b < c, a < b ≤ c, a ≤ b < c, a ≤ b ≤ c$$

Properties of Inequalities

1. If $a > b$ then $b < a$ and vice versa.
2. If $a > b$ and $b > c$ then $a > c$.
3. If $a > b$ then for any c, $a + c > b + c$. In other words, an inequality remains true if the same number is added on both sides of the inequality.

Contd

Properties of Inequalities (*Contd*)

4. Any number can be transposed from one side of an inequality to the other side of the inequality with the sign of the number reversed. This does not change the sense of the inequality.

5. If $a > b$ and $c > 0$ then $ac > bc$. Both sides of an inequality may be multiplied (or divided) by the same positive number without changing the sense of the inequality.

6. If $a > b$ and $c < 0$ then $ac < bc$. That is, both sides of an inequality may be multiplied (or divided) by the same negative number but then the sense of the inequality is reversed.

7. If $a > b$ and $c > d$ then $a + c > b + d$. (Two inequalities having the same sense may be added termwise.)

8. If $a > b$ and $c < d$ then $a - c > b - d$
   From one inequality it is possible to subtract termwise another inequality of the opposite sense, retaining the sense of the inequality from which the other was subtracted.

9. If a, b, c, d are positive numbers such that $a > b$ and $c > d$ then $ac > bd$, that is, two inequalities of the same sense in which both sides are positive can be multiplied termwise, the resulting inequality having the same sense as the multiplied inequalities.

10. If a and b are positive numbers where $a > b$, then $a^n > b^n$ for any natural n.

11. If a and b are positive numbers where $a > b$ then $a^{1/n} > b^{1/n}$ for any natural $n \geq 2$.

12. Two inequalities are said to be equivalent if the correctness of one of them implies the correctness of the other, and vice versa.

    Students are advised to check these properties with values and form their own understanding and language of these rules.

Certain Important Inequalities

1. $a^2 + b^2 \geq 2ab$ (Equality for $a = b$)
2. $|a + b| \leq |a| + |b|$ (Equality reached if both a and b are of the same sign or if one of them is zero.)
   This can be generalised as $|a_1 + a_2 + a_3 + \ldots + a_n| \leq |a_1| + |a_2| + |a_3| + \ldots |a_n|$
3. $|a - b| \geq |a| - |b|$
4. $ax^2 + bx + c \geq 0$ if $a > 0$ and $D = b^2 - 4ac \leq 0$. The equality is achieved only if $D = 0$ and $x = -b/2a$.
5. Arithmetic mean $\geq$ Geometric mean. That is, $\dfrac{(a + b)}{2} \geq ab$
6. $a/b + b/a \geq 2$ if $a > 0$ and $b > 0$ or if $a < 0$ and $b < 0$, that is, both a and b have the same sign.

Certain Important Inequalities (*Contd*)

7. $a^3 + b^3 \geq ab(a + b)$ if $a > 0$ and $b > 0$, the equality being obtained only when $a = b$.
8. $a^2 + b^2 + c^2 \geq ab + ac + bc$
9. $(a + b)(b + c)(a + c) \geq 8\,abc$ if $a \geq 0$, $b \geq 0$ and $c \geq 0$, the equation being obtained when $a = b = c$
10. For any 4 numbers x_1, x_2, y_1, y_2 satisfying the conditions
$$x_1^2 + x_2^2 = 1$$
$$y_1^2 + y_2^2 = 1$$
    the inequality $|x_1 y_1 + x_2 y_2| \leq 1$ is true.

11. $\dfrac{a}{b^{1/2}} + \dfrac{b}{a^{1/2}} \geq a^{1/2} + b^{1/2}$ where $a \geq 0$ and $b \geq 0$

12. If $a + b = 2$, then $a^4 + b^4 \geq 2$
13. The inequality $|x| \leq a$, means that
$$-a \leq x \leq a \text{ for } a > 0$$
14. $2^n > n^2$ for $n \geq 5$

Some Important Results

- If $a > b$, then it is evident that
$$a + c > b + c$$
$$a - c > b - c$$
$$ac > bc$$
$$a/c > b/c; \text{ that is,}$$
  an inequality will still hold after each side has been increased, diminished, multiplied, or divided by the same positive quantity.

  If $a - c > b$,
  By adding c to each side,
  $a > b + c$; which shows that
  in an inequality any term may be transposed from one side to the other if its sign is changed.

- If $a > b$, then evidently $b < a$; that is,

  if the sides of an inequality be transposed, the sign of inequality must be reversed.

- If $a > b$, then $a - b$ is positive, and $b - a$ is negative; that is, $-a - (-b)$ is negative, and therefore $-a < -b$; hence,

  if the signs of all the terms of an inequality be changed, the sign of inequality must be reversed.

  Again, if $a > b$, then $-a < -b$ and, therefore, $-ac < -bc$; that is,

  if the sides of an inequality be multiplied by the same negative quantity, the sign of inequality must be reversed.

Contd

Contd

Some Important Results (Contd)

If $a_1 > b_1, a_2 > b_2, a_3 > b_3, \ldots a_m > b_m$, it is clear that $a_1 + a_2 + a_3 + \ldots + a_m > b_1 + b_2 + b_3 + \ldots + b_m$; and $a_1 a_2 a_3 \ldots a_m > b_1 b_2 b_3 \ldots b_m$.

- If $a > b$, and if p, q are positive integers, then or $a^{1/q} > b^{1/q}$ and, therefore, $a^{p/q} > b^{p/q}$; that is, $a^n > b^n$, where n is any positive quantity. Further,

$$1/a^n < 1/b^n; \text{ that is } a^{-n} < b^{-n}$$

The square of every real quantity is positive, and therefore greater than zero. Thus $(a-b)^2$ is positive.

Let a and b be two positive quantities, S their sum and P their product. Then from the identity

$$4ab = (a+b)^2 - (a-b)^2$$

we have $\quad 4P = S^2 - (a-b)^2$, and $S^2 = 4P + (a-b)^2$

Hence, if S is given, P is greatest when $a = b$; and if P is given, S is least when $a = b$;

That is, *if the sum of two positive quantities is given, their product is greatest when they are equal; and if the product of two positive quantities is given, their sum is least when they are equal.*

To Find the Greatest Value of a Product, the Sum of Whose Factors is Constant

Let there be n factors $a, b, c, \ldots n$, of a composite number and suppose that their sum is constant and equal to S.

Consider the product $abc \ldots n$, and suppose that a and b are any two unequal factors. If we replace the two unequal factors a and b by the two equal factors $(a+b)/2$, and $(a+b)/2$, the product is increased while the sum remains unaltered. Hence, so *long as the product contains two unequal factors it can be increased altering the sum of the factors; therefore, the product is greatest when all the factors are equal.* In this case the value of each of the n factors is S/n, and the greatest value of the product is $(S/n)^n$, or $\{(a + b + c + \ldots + n/n\}^n$

This will be clearer through an example.

Let us define a number as $a \times b = c$ such that we restrict $a + b = 100$ (maximum).

Then, the maximum value of the product will be achieved if we take the value of a and b as 50 each.

Thus $50 \times 50 = 2500$ will be the highest number achieved for the restriction $a + b \leq 100$.

Further, you can also say that $50 \times 50 > 51 \times 49 > 52 \times 48 > 53 \times 47 > 54 \times 46 > \ldots > 98 \times 2 > 99 \times 1$

Thus if we have a larger multiplication as $4 \times 6 \times 7 \times 8$ this will always be less than $5 \times 5 \times 7 \times 8$. [Holds true only for positive numbers.]

Corollary If $a, b, c \ldots k$, are unequal, $\{(a + b + c + \ldots + k)/n\}^n > abc \ldots k$;

that is , $(a + b + c + \ldots + k)/n > (abc \ldots k)^{1/n}$.

By an extension of the meaning of the arithmetic and geometric means this result is usually quoted as follows: *The arithmetic mean of any number of positive quantities is greater than the geometric mean.*

Definition of Solution of an Inequality

The solution of an inequality is the value of an unknown for which this inequality reduces to a true numerical identity. That is, to solve an inequality means to find all the values of the variable for which the given inequality is true.

An inequality has no solution if there is no such value for which the given inequality is true.

Equivalent Inequalities: Two inequalities are said to be equivalent if any solution of one is also a solution of the other and vice versa.

If both inequalities have no solution, then they are also regarded to be equivalent.

To solve an inequality we use the basic properties of an inequality which have been illustrated above.

Notation of Ranges

1. Ranges Where the Ends are Excluded If the value of x is denoted as $(1, 2)$ it means $1 < x < 2$ i.e. x is greater than 1 but smaller than 2.

Similarly, if we denote the range of values of x as $-(7, -2)U(3, 21)$, this means that the value of x can be denoted as $-7 < x < -2$ and $3 < x < 21$. This would mean that the inequality is satisfied between the two ranges and is not satisfied outside these two ranges.

Based on this notation write the ranges of x for the following representations:

$$(1, +\infty) \, U \, (-\infty, -7)$$
$$(-\infty, 0) \, U \, (4, +\infty), \, (-\infty, 50) \, U \, (-50, +\infty)$$

2. Ranges where the Ends are Included

$$[2, 5] \text{ means } 2 \leq x \leq 5$$

3. Mixed Ranges

$$(3, 21] \text{ means } 3 < x \leq 21$$

Solving Linear Inequalities in one Unknown

A linear inequality is defined as an inequality of the form

$$ax + b \, I \, 0$$

where the symbol 'I' represents any of the inequalities $<, >, \geq, \leq$.

For instance if $ax + b \leq 0$, then $ax \leq -b$

$\rightarrow x \leq -b/a$ if $a > 0$ and $x \geq -b/a$ if $a < 0$

Example: Solve the inequality $2(x - 3) - 1 > 3(x - 2) - 4(x + 1)$

$\rightarrow 2x - 7 > 3x - 6 - 4x - 4 \rightarrow 3x > -3$. Hence, $x > -1$

This can be represented in mathematical terms as $(-1, +\infty)$

Example: Solve the inequality $2(x - 1) + 1 > 3 - (1 - 2x)$
$\rightarrow 2x - 1 > 2 + 2x \rightarrow 0.x > 3 \rightarrow$ This can never happen. Hence, no solution.

Example: Solve the inequality $2(x - 1) + 1 < 3 - (1 - 2x)$

Gives: $\qquad 0.x < 3.$

This is true for all values of x

Example: Solve the inequality $ax > a$.

This inequality has the parametre a that needs to be investigated further.

$$\text{If } a > 0, \text{ then } x > 1$$
$$\text{If } a < 0, \text{ then } x < 1$$

Solving Quadratic Inequalities

A quadratic inequality is defined as an inequality of the form:

$$ax^2 + bx + c \, I \, 0 \, (a \neq 0)$$

where the symbol I represents any of the inequalities $<, >, \geq, \leq$.

For a quadratic expression of the form $ax^2 + bx + c$, $(b^2 - 4ac)$ is defined as the discriminant of the expression and is often denoted as D. i.e. $D = b^2 - 4ac$.

The following cases are possible for the value of the quadratic expression:

Case 1: If $D < 0$

1. If $a < 0$ then $ax^2 + bx + c < 0$ for all x
2. If $a > 0$ then $ax^2 + bx + c > 0$ for all x.

In other words, we can say that if D is negative then the values of the quadratic expression takes the same sign as the coefficient of x^2.

This can also be said as

If $D < 0$ then all real values of x are solutions of the inequalities $ax^2 + bx + c > 0$ and $ax^2 + bx + c \geq 0$ for $a > 0$ and have no solution in case $a < 0$.

Also, for $D < 0$, all real values of x are solutions of the inequalities $ax^2 + bx + c < 0$ and $ax^2 + bx + c \leq 0$ if $a < 0$ and these inequalities will not give any solution for $a > 0$.

Case 2: $D = 0$

If the discriminant of a quadratic expression is equal to zero, then the value of the quadratic expression takes the same sign as that of the coefficient of x^2 (except when

$x = -b/2a$ at which point the value of the quadratic expression becomes 0).

We can also say the following for $D = 0$:

1. The inequality $ax^2 + bx + c > 0$ has as a solution any $x \neq -(b/2a)$ if $a > 0$ and has no solution if $a < 0$.

2. The inequality $ax^2 + bx + c < 0$ has as a solution any $x \neq -(b/2a)$ if $a < 0$ and has no solution if $a > 0$.

3. The inequality $ax^2 + bx + c \geq 0$ has as a solution any x if $a > 0$ and has a unique solution $x = -b/2a$ if $a < 0$.

4. The inequality $ax^2 + bx + c \leq 0$ has as a solution any x if $a < 0$ and has a unique solution $x = -b/2a$ for $a > 0$.

Case 3: $D > 0$

If x_1 and x_2 are the roots of the quadratic expression then it can be said that:

1. For $a > 0$, $ax^2 + bx + c$ is positive for all values of x outside the interval $[x_1, x_2]$ and is negative for all values of x within the interval (x_1, x_2). Besides for values of $x = x_1$ or $x = x_2$, the value of the quadratic expression becomes zero (By definition of the root).

2. For $a < 0$, $ax^2 + bx + c$ is negative for all values of x outside the interval $[x_1, x_2]$ and is positive for all values of x within the interval (x_1, x_2). Besides for values of $x = x_1$ or $x = x_2$, the value of the quadratic expression becomes zero (By definition of the root).

Here are a few examples illustrating how quadratic inequalities are solved.

Solve the following inequalities.

Example 1: $x^2 - 5x + 6 > 0$

Solution: (a) The discriminant $D = 25 - 4 \times 6 > 0$ and a is positive $(+1)$; the roots of the quadratic expression are real and distinct: $x_1 = 2$ and $x_2 = 3$.

By the property of quadratic inequalities, we get that the expression is positive outside the interval $[2, 3]$. Hence, the solution is $x < 2$ and $x > 3$.

We can also see it as $x^2 - 5x + 6 = (x - 2)(x - 3)$ and the given inequality takes the form $(x - 2)(x - 3) > 0$.

The solutions of the inequality are the numbers $x < 2$ (when both factors are negative and their product is positive) and also the numbers $x > 3$ (when both factors are positive and, hence, their product is also positive).

Answer: $x < 2$ and $x > 3$.

Example 2: $2x^2 + x + 1 \geq 0$

Solution: The discriminant $D = 1 - 4 \cdot (-2) = 9 > 0$; the roots of the quadratic expression are real and distinct:

$$x_{1,2} = \frac{-1 \pm \sqrt{9}}{2 \cdot (-2)} = \frac{-1 \pm 3}{-4}$$

hence, $x_1 = -1/2$ and $x_2 = 1$, and consequently, $-2x^2 + x + 1 = -2(x + 1/2) \times (x - 1)$. We have

$$-2(x + 1/2)(x - 1) \geq 0 \text{ or } (x + 1/2)(x - 1) \leq 0$$

(When dividing both sides of an inequality by a negative number, the sense of the inequality is reversed). The inequality is satisfied by all numbers from the interval

$$[-1/2, 1]$$

Please note that this can also be concluded from the property of quadratic expressions when $D > 0$ and a is negative.

Answer: $-1/2 \leq x \leq 1$.

Example 3: $2x^2 + x - 1 < 0$

Solution: $D = 1 - 4 \cdot (-2) \cdot (-1) < 0$, the coefficient of x^2 is negative. By the property of the quadratic expression when $D < 0$ and a is negative $-2x^2 + x - 1$ attains only negative values.

Answer: x can take any value.

Example 4: $3x^2 - 4x + 5 < 0$

Solution: $D = 16 - 4 \times 3 \times 5 < 0$, the coefficient of x^2 is positive. The quadratic expression $3x^2 - 4x + 5$ takes on only positive values.

Answer: There is no solution.

Example 5: $4x^2 + 4x + 1 > 0$.

Solution: $D = 16 - 4 \times 4 = 0$. The quadratic expression $4x^2 + 4x + 1$ is the square $(2x + 1)^2$, and the given inequality takes the form $(2x + 1)^2 > 0$. It follows that all real numbers x, except for $x = -1/2$, are solutions of the inequality.

Answer: $x \neq -1/2$.

Example 6: Solve the inequality $(a - 2)x^2 - x - 1 \geq 0$

Here, the value of the determinant $D = 1 - 4(-1)(a - 2) = 1 + 4(a - 2) = 4a - 7$

There can then be three cases:

Case 1: $D < 0 \rightarrow a < 7/4$

Then the coefficient of $x^2 \rightarrow a - 2$ is negative. Hence, the inequality has no solution.

Case 2: $D = 0$

$a = 7/4$. Put $a = 7/4$ in the expression and then the inequality becomes

$-(x - 2)^2 \geq 0$. This can only happen when $x = 2$.

Case 3: $D > 0$

Then $a > 7/4$ and $a \neq 2$, then we find the roots x_1 and x_2 of the quadratic expression:

$$x_1 = \frac{1 + \sqrt{4a - 7}}{2(a - 2)} \text{ and } x_2 = \frac{1 - \sqrt{4a - 7}}{2(a - 2)}$$

Using the property of quadratic expression's values for $D > 0$ we get

If $a - 2 < 0$, the quadratic expression takes negative values outside the interval $[x_1, x_2]$. Hence, it will take positive values inside the interval (x_1, x_2).

If $a - 2 > 0$, the quadratic expression takes positive values outside the interval $[x_1, x_2]$ and becomes zero for x_1 and x_2.

If $a - 2 = 0$, then we get a straight linear equation. $-x - 1 \geq 0 \rightarrow x \leq -1$.

System of Inequalities in One Unknown

Let there be given several inequalities in one unknown. If it is required to find the number that will be the solution of all the given equalities, then the set of these inequalities is called a *system of inequalities*.

The solution of a system of inequalities in one unknown is defined as the value of the unknown for which all the inequalities of the system reduce to true numerical inequalities.

To solve a system of inequalities means to find all the solutions of the system or to establish that there is none.

Two systems of inequalities are said to be *equivalent* if any solution of one of them is a solution of the other, and vice versa. If both the systems of inequalities have no solution, then they are also regarded to be equivalent.

Example 1: Solve the system of inequalities:

$$3x - 4 < 8x + 6$$
$$2x - 1 > 5x - 4$$
$$11x - 9 \leq 15x + 3$$

Solution: We solve the first inequality:

$$3x - 4 < 8x + 6$$
$$-5x < 10$$
$$x > -2$$

It is fulfilled for $x > -2$.

Then we solve the second inequality

$$2x - 1 > 5x - 4$$
$$-3x > -3$$
$$x < 1$$

It is fulfilled for $x < 1$.

And, finally, we solve the third inequality:

$$11x - 9 \leq 15x + 3$$
$$-4x \leq 12$$
$$x \geq -3$$

It is fulfilled for $x \geq -3$. All the given inequalities are true for $-2 < x < 1$.

Answer: $-2 < x < 1$.

Example 2: Solve the inequality $\frac{2x - 1}{x + 1} < 1$

We have $\frac{2x - 1}{x + 1} - 1 < 0 \rightarrow \frac{x - 2}{x + 1} < 0$

This means that the fraction above has to be negative. A fraction is negative only when the numerator and the denominator have opposite signs.

Hence, the above inequality is equivalent to the following set of 2 inequalities:

$$x - 2 > 0 \quad \text{and} \quad x - 2 < 0$$
$$\text{and} \quad x + 1 < 0 \quad \quad x + 1 > 0$$

From the first system of inequalities, we get $x > 2$ or $x < -1$. This cannot happen simultaneously since these are inconsistent.

From the second system of inequalities we get

$$x < 2 \text{ or } x > -1 \text{ i.e } -1 < x < 2$$

Inequalities Containing a Modulus

Result:

$|x| \leq a$, where $a > 0$ means the same as the double inequality

$$-a \leq x \leq a$$

This result is used in solving inequalities containing a modulus.

Space for Notes

Example 1: $|2x - 3| \leq 5$

This is equivalent to $-5 \leq 2x - 3 \leq 5$

i.e. $\quad\quad 2x - 3 \geq -5 \quad \text{and} \quad 2x - 3 \leq 5$
$$2x \geq -2 \quad\quad\quad x \leq 4$$
$$x \geq -1$$

The solution is

$$-1 \leq x \leq 4$$

Example 2: $|1 - x| > 3$

$$|1 - x| = |x - 1|$$

Hence, $\quad\quad |x - 1| > 3 \rightarrow x - 1 > 3 \text{ i.e } x > 4$

or $\quad\quad\quad x - 1 < -3 \text{ or } x < -2$

Answer: $x > 4$ or $x < -2$.

🎯 WORKED-OUT PROBLEMS

Problem 14.1 Solve the inequality $\dfrac{1}{x} < 1$.

Solution $\dfrac{1}{x} < 1 \Leftrightarrow \dfrac{1}{x} - 1 < 0 \Leftrightarrow \dfrac{1-x}{x} < 0 \Leftrightarrow \dfrac{x-1}{x} > 0$.

This can happen only when both the numerator and denominator take the same sign (Why?)

Case 1: Both are positive: $x - 1 > 0$ and $x > 0$ i.e. $x > 1$.

Case 2: Both are negative: $x - 1 < 0$ and $x < 0$ i.e. $x < 0$.

Answer: $(-\infty, 0)\ U\ (1 + \infty)$

Problem 14.2 Solve the inequality $\dfrac{x}{x+2} \le \dfrac{1}{x}$.

Solution $\dfrac{x}{x+2} \le \dfrac{1}{x} \Leftrightarrow \dfrac{x}{x+2} - \dfrac{1}{x} \le 0 \Leftrightarrow \dfrac{x^2 - x - 2}{x(x+2)}$

$\le 0 \Leftrightarrow \dfrac{(x-2)(x+1)}{x(x+2)} \le 0.$

The function $f(x) = \dfrac{(x-2)(x+1)}{x(x+2)}$ becomes negative

when numerator and denominator are of opposite sign.

Case 1: Numerator positive and denominator negative: This occurs only between $-2 < x < -1$.

Case 2: Numerator negative and Denominator Positive: Numerator is negative when $(x - 2)$ and $(x + 1)$ take opposite signs. This can be got for:

Case A: $x - 2 < 0$ and $x + 1 > 0$ i.e. $x < 2$ and $x > -1$

Case B: $x - 2 > 0$ and $x + 1 < 0$ i.e. $x > 2$ and $x < -1$. Cannot happen.

Hence, the answer is $-2 < x \le 2$.

Problem 14.3 Solve the inequality $\dfrac{x}{x-3} \le \dfrac{1}{x}$.

Solution $\dfrac{x}{x-3} \le \dfrac{1}{x} \Leftrightarrow \dfrac{x}{x-3} - \dfrac{1}{x} \ge 0 \Leftrightarrow \dfrac{x^2 - x + 3}{x(x-3)}$

$\le 0.$ The function $f(x) = \dfrac{x^2 - x + 3}{x(x-3)}$

The numerator being a quadratic equation with $D < 0$ and $a > 0$, we can see that it will always be positive for all values of x. (From the property of quadratic inequalities).

Further, for the expression to be negative, the denominator should be negative.

That is, $x^2 - 3x < 0$. This will occur when $x < 3$ and x is positive.

Answer: **(0, 3)**

Suppose $F(x) = (x - x_1)^{k_1} (x - x_2)^{k_2} ... (x_1 - x_n)^{k_n}$, where k_1, $k_2 ..., k_n$ are integers. If k_j is an even number, then the function $(x - x_j)^{k_j}$ does not change sign when x passes through the point x_j and, consequently, the function $F(x)$ does not change sign. If k_p is an odd number, then the function $(x - x_p)^{k_p}$ changes sign when x passes through the point x_p and, consequently, the function $F(x)$ also changes sign.

Problem 14.4 Solve the inequality $(x - 1)^2 (x + 1)^3 (x - 4) < 0$.

Solution The above inequality is valid for

Case 1: $x + 1 < 0$ and $x - 4 > 0$

That is, $x < -1$ and $x > 4$ simultaneously. This cannot happen together.

Case 2: $x + 1 > 0$ and $x - 4 < 0$

That is $x > -1$ or $x < 4$, i.e. $-1 < x < 4$ is the answer

Problem 14.5 Solve the inequality $\dfrac{(x-1)^2(x+1)^3}{x^4(x-2)} \le 0$

Solution The above expression becomes negative when the numerator and the denominator take opposite signs.

That means that the numerator is positive and the denominator is negative or vice versa.

Case 1: Numerator positive and denominator negative: The sign of the numerator is determined by the value of $x + 1$ and that of the denominator is determined by $x - 2$.

This condition happens when $x < 2$ and $x > -1$ simultaneously.

Case 2: Numerator negative and denominator positive: This happens when $x < -1$ and $x > 2$ simultaneously. This will never happen.

Hence, the answer is $-1 \le x < 2$.

Space for Rough Work

LEVEL OF DIFFICULTY (I)

Solve the following inequalities:

1. $3x^2 - 7x + 4 \leq 0$
   - (a) $x > 0$
   - (b) $x < 0$
   - (c) All x
   - (d) None of these

2. $3x^2 - 7x - 6 < 0$
   - (a) $-0.66 < x < 3$
   - (b) $x < -0.66$ or $x > 3$
   - (c) $3 < x < 7$
   - (d) $-2 < x < 2$

3. $3x^2 - 7x + 6 < 0$
   - (a) $0.66 < x < 3$
   - (b) $-0.66 < x < 3$
   - (c) $-1 < x < 3$
   - (d) None of these

4. $x^2 - 3x + 5 > 0$
   - (a) $x > 0$
   - (b) $x < 0$
   - (c) Both (a) and (b)
   - (d) $-\infty < x < \infty$

5. $x^2 - 14x - 15 > 0$
   - (a) $x < -1$
   - (b) $15 < x$
   - (c) Both (a) and (b)
   - (d) $-1 < x < 15$

6. $2 - x - x^2 \geq 0$
   - (a) $-2 \leq x \leq 1$
   - (b) $-2 < x < 1$
   - (c) $x < -2$
   - (d) $x > 1$

7. $|x^2 - 4x| < 5$
   - (a) $-1 \leq x \leq 5$
   - (b) $1 \leq x \leq 5$
   - (c) $-1 \leq x \leq 1$
   - (d) $-1 < x < 5$

8. $|x^2 + x| - 5 < 0$
   - (a) $x < 0$
   - (b) $x > 0$
   - (c) All values of x
   - (d) None of these

9. $|x^2 - 5x| < 6$
   - (a) $-1 < x < 2$
   - (b) $3 < x < 6$
   - (c) Both (a) and (b)
   - (d) $-1 < x < 6$

10. $|x^2 - 2x| < x$
    - (a) $1 < x < 3$
    - (b) $-1 < x < 3$
    - (c) $0 < x < 4$
    - (d) $x > 3$

11. $|x^2 - 2x - 3| < 3x - 3$
    - (a) $1 < x < 3$
    - (b) $-2 < x < 5$
    - (c) $x > 5$
    - (d) $2 < x < 5$

12. $|x^2 - 3x| + x - 2 < 0$
    - (a) $(1 - \sqrt{3}) < x < (2 + \sqrt{2})$
    - (b) $0 < x < 5$
    - (c) $(1 - \sqrt{3}, 2 - \sqrt{2})$
    - (d) $1 < x < 4$

13. $x^2 - 7x + 12 < |x - 4|$
    - (a) $x < 2$
    - (b) $x > 4$
    - (c) $2 < x < 4$
    - (d) $2 \leq x \leq 4$

14. $x^2 - |5x - 3| - x < 2$
    - (a) $x > 3 + 2\sqrt{2}$
    - (b) $x < 3 + 2\sqrt{2}$
    - (c) $x > -5$
    - (d) $-5 < x < 3 + 2\sqrt{2}$

15. $|x - 6| > x^2 - 5x + 9$
    - (a) $1 \leq x < 3$
    - (b) $1 < x < 3$
    - (c) $2 < x < 5$
    - (d) $-3 < x < 1$

16. $|x - 6| < x^2 - 5x + 9$
    - (a) $x < 1$
    - (b) $x > 3$
    - (c) $1 < x < 3$
    - (d) Both (a) and (b)

17. $|x - 2| \leq 2x^2 - 9x + 9$
    - (a) $x > (4 - \sqrt{2})/2$
    - (b) $x < (5 + \sqrt{3})/2$
    - (c) Both (a) and (b)
    - (d) None of these

18. $3x^2 - |x - 3| > 9x - 2$
    - (a) $x < (4 - \sqrt{19})/3$
    - (b) $x > (4 + \sqrt{19})/3$
    - (c) Both (a) and (b)
    - (d) $-2 < x < 2$

19. $x^2 - |5x + 8| > 0$
    - (a) $x < (5 - \sqrt{57})/2$
    - (b) $x < (5 + \sqrt{57})/2$
    - (c) $x > (5 + \sqrt{57})/2$
    - (d) Both (a) and (b)

20. $3|x - 1| + x^2 - 7 > 0$
    - (a) $x > -1$
    - (b) $x < -1$
    - (c) $x > 2$
    - (d) Both (b) and (c)

21. $|x - 6| > |x^2 - 5x + 9|$
    - (a) $x < 1$
    - (b) $x > 3$
    - (c) $(1 < x < 3)$
    - (d) both (a) and (b)

22. $(|x - 1| - 3)$ $(|x + 2| - 5)$ < 0
    - (a) $-7 < x < -2$ and $3 < x < 4$
    - (b) $x < -7$ and $x > 4$
    - (c) $x < -2$ and $x > 3$
    - (d) Any of these

23. $|x^2 - 2x - 8| > 2x$
    - (a) $x < 2\sqrt{2}$
    - (b) $x < 3 + 3\sqrt{5}$
    - (c) $x > 2 + 2\sqrt{3}$
    - (d) Both (a) and (c)

24. $(x - 1)\sqrt{x^2 - x - 2} \geq 0$
    - (a) $x \leq 2$
    - (b) $x \geq 2$
    - (c) $x \leq -2$
    - (d) $x \geq 0$

25. $(x^2 - 1)\sqrt{x^2 - x - 2} \geq 0$
    - (a) $x \leq -1$
    - (b) $x \geq -1$
    - (c) $x \geq 2$
    - (d) (a) and (c)

26. $\sqrt{\dfrac{x - 2}{1 - 2x}} > -1$
    - (a) $0.5 > x$
    - (b) $x > 2$
    - (c) Both (a) and (b)
    - (d) $0.5 < x \leq 2$

27. $\sqrt{\dfrac{3x-1}{2-x}} > 1$

    (a) $0 < x < 2$ (b) $0.75 < x < 4$
    (c) $0.75 < x < 2$ (d) $0 < x < 4$

28. $\sqrt{3x-10} > \sqrt{6-x}$

    (a) $4 < x \le 6$ (b) $x < 4$ or $x > 6$
    (c) $x < 4$ (d) $x > 8$

29. $\sqrt{x^2 - 2x - 3} < 1$

    (a) $(-1-\sqrt{5} < x < -3)$ (b) $1 \le x < (\sqrt{5}-1)$
    (c) $x > 1$ (d) None of these

30. $\sqrt{1 - \dfrac{x+2}{x^2}} < \dfrac{2}{3}$

    (a) $(-6/5) < x \le -1$ or $2 \le x < 3$
    (b) $(-6/5) \le x < -1$
    (c) $2 \le x < 3$
    (d) $(-6/5) \le x < 3$

31. $2\sqrt{x-1} < x$

    (a) $x > 1$ (b) $x \ge 1, x \ne 2$
    (c) $x < 1$ (d) $1 < x < 5$

32. $\sqrt{x+18} < 2 - x$

    (a) $x \le -18$ (b) $x < -2$
    (c) $x > -2$ (d) $-18 \le x < -2$

33. $x > \sqrt{24 + 5x}$

    (a) $x < 3$ (b) $3 < x \le 4.8$
    (c) $x \ge 24/5$ (d) $x > 8$

34. $\sqrt{9x-20} < x$

    (a) $4 < x < 5$ (b) $20/9 \le x < 4$
    (c) $x > 5$ (d) Both (b) and (c)

35. $\sqrt{x+7} < x$

    (a) $x > 2$ (b) $x > \sqrt{30}/2$
    (c) $x > (1 + \sqrt{29})/2$ (d) $x > 1 + \sqrt{29}/2$

36. $\sqrt{2x-1} < x - 2$

    (a) $x < 5$ (b) $x > 5$
    (c) $x > 5$ or $x < -5$ (d) $5 < x < 15$

37. $\sqrt{x+78} < x + 6$

    (a) $x < 3$ (b) $x > 3$ or $x < 2$
    (c) $x > 3$ (d) $3 < x < 10$

38. $\sqrt{5-2x} < 6x - 1$

    (a) $0.5 < x$ (b) $x < 2.5$
    (c) $0.5 < x < 2.5$ (d) $x > 2.5$

39. $\sqrt{x+61} < x + 5$

    (a) $x < 3$ (b) $x > 3$ or $x < 1$
    (c) $x > 3$ (d) $3 < x < 15$

40. $x < \sqrt{2-x}$

    (a) $x > 1$ (b) $x < 1$
    (c) $-2 < x < 1$ (d) $-1 < x$

41. $x + 3 < \sqrt{x+33}$

    (a) $x > 3$ (b) $x < 3$
    (c) $-3 < x < 3$ (d) $-33 < x < 3$

42. $\sqrt{2x+14} > x + 3$

    (a) $x < -7$ (b) $-7 \le x < 1$
    (c) $x > 1$ (d) $-7 < x < 1$

43. $x - 3 < \sqrt{x-2}$

    (a) $2 \le x < (7 + \sqrt{5})/2$ (b) $2 \le x$
    (c) $x < (7 + \sqrt{5})/2$ (d) $x \le 2$

44. $x + 2 < \sqrt{x+14}$

    (a) $-14 \le x < 2$ (b) $x > -14$
    (c) $x < 2$ (d) $-11 < x < 2$

45. $x - 1 < \sqrt{7-x}$

    (a) $x > 3$ (b) $x < 3$
    (c) $-53 < x < 3$ (d) $-103 < x < 3$

46. $\sqrt{9x-20} > x$

    (a) $x < 4$ (b) $x > 5$
    (c) $x \le 4$ or $x \ge 5$ (d) $4 < x < 5$

47. $\sqrt{11-5x} > x - 1$

    (a) $x > 2, x < 5$ (b) $-3 < x < 2$
    (c) $-25 < x < 2$ (d) $x < 2$

48. $\sqrt{x+2} > x$

    (a) $-2 \le x < 2$ (b) $-2 \le x$
    (c) $x < 2$ (d) $x = -2$ or $x > 2$

Directions for Questions 49 to 53: Find the largest integral x that satisfies the following inequalities.

49. $\dfrac{x-2}{x^2-9} < 0$

    (a) $x = -4$ (b) $x = -2$
    (c) $x = 3$ (d) None of these

50. $\dfrac{1}{x+1} - \dfrac{2}{x^2 - x + 1} < \dfrac{1-2x}{x^3+1}$

    (a) $x = 1$ (b) $x = 2$
    (c) $x = -1$ (d) None of these

51. $\dfrac{x+4}{x^2-9} - \dfrac{2}{x+3} < \dfrac{4x}{3x-x^2}$

    (a) $x = 1$ (b) $x = 2$
    (c) $x = -1$ (d) None of these

52. $\dfrac{4x+19}{x+5} < \dfrac{4x-17}{x-3}$

    (a) $x = 1$ (b) $x = 2$
    (c) $x = -1$ (d) None of these

53. $(x + 1)(x - 3)^2(x - 5)(x - 4)^2(x - 2) < 0$

    (a) $x = 1$ (b) $x = -2$
    (c) $x = -1$ (d) None of these

Directions for Questions 54 to 69: Solve the following inequalities:

54. $(x - 1)(3 - x)(x - 2)^2 > 0$
    (a) $1 < x < 3$ (b) $1 < x < 3$ but $x \neq 2$
    (c) $0 < x < 2$ (d) $-1 < x < 3$

55. $\dfrac{6x - 5}{4x + 1} < 0$
    (a) $-1/4 < x < 1$ (b) $-1/2 < x < 1$
    (c) $-1 < x < 1$ (d) $-1/4 < x < 5/6$

56. $\dfrac{2x - 3}{3x - 7} > 0$
    (a) $x < 3/2$ or $x > 7/3$ (b) $3/2 < x < 7/3$
    (c) $x > 7/3$ (d) None of these

57. $\dfrac{3}{x - 2} < 1$
    (a) $2 < x < 5$ (b) $x < 2$
    (c) $x > 5$ (d) $x < 2$ or $x > 5$

58. $\dfrac{1}{x - 1} \leq 2$
    (a) $x < 1$ (b) $x \geq 1.5$
    (c) $-5 < x < 1$ (d) Both (a) and (b)
    or $x \geq 1.5$

59. $\dfrac{4x + 3}{2x - 5} < 6$
    (a) $x < 2.5$ (b) $x < 33/8$
    (c) $x \geq 2.5$ (d) $x < 2.5$ or $x > 33/8$

60. $\dfrac{5x - 6}{x + 6} < 1$
    (a) $-6 < x < 6$ (b) $-6 < x < 0$
    (c) $-6 < x < 3$ (d) None of these

61. $\dfrac{5x + 8}{4 - x} < 2$
    (a) $x < 0$ or $x > 4$ (b) $0 < x < 4$
    (c) $0 \leq x < 4$ (d) $x > 4$

62. $\dfrac{x - 1}{x + 3} > 2$
    (a) $x < -7$ (b) $x < -3$
    (c) $-7 < x < -3$ (d) None of these

63. $\dfrac{7x - 5}{8x + 3} > 4$

    (a) $-17/25 < x < -3/8$ (b) $x > -17/25$
    (c) $0 < x < 3/8$ (d) $-17/25 < x < 0$

64. $\dfrac{x}{x - 5} > \dfrac{1}{2}$
    (a) $-5 < x < 5$ (b) $-5 < x < 0$
    (c) $-5 \leq x \leq 5$ (d) $x < -5$ or $x > 5$

65. $x \leq \dfrac{6}{x - 5}$
    (a) $x < -1$ (b) $x > 5$
    (c) $x < 6$ (d) $x \leq -1$ or $5 < x \leq 6$

66. $\dfrac{30x - 9}{x - 2} \geq 25(x + 2)$

    (a) $x < -1.4$ or $x > 2$
    (b) $x < -1.4$ or $2 < x \leq 2.6$
    (c) $x \leq -1.4$ or $2 < x \leq 2.6$
    (d) None of these

67. $\dfrac{4}{x + 2} > 3 - x$
    (a) $-2 < x < -1$ or $x > 2$
    (b) $-2 < x < 2$
    (c) $-2 < x < -1$
    (d) $0 < x < 3$

68. $x - 17 \geq \dfrac{60}{x}$
    (a) $x < -3$
    (b) $x < 20$
    (c) $-3 \leq x < 0$ or $x \geq 20$
    (d) $-3 < x \leq 0$ or $x \geq 20$

69. $\sqrt{x^2} < x + 1$
    (a) $x > 0.5$ (b) $x > 0$
    (c) All x (d) $x > -0.5$

70. Find the smallest integral x satisfying the inequality
    $$\dfrac{x - 5}{x^2 + 5x - 14} > 0$$
    (a) $x = -6$ (b) $x = -3$
    (c) $x = -7$ (d) None of these

Space for Rough Work

LEVEL OF DIFFICULTY (II)

1. $x^2 - 5|x| + 6 < 0$
   (a) $-3 < x < -2$
   (b) $2 < x < 3$
   (c) Both (a) and (b)
   (d) $-3 < x < 3$

2. $x^2 - |x| - 2 \geq 0$
   (a) $-2 < x < 2$
   (b) $x \leq -2$ or $x \geq 2$
   (c) $x < -2$ or $x > 1$
   (d) $-2 < x < 1$

Directions for Questions 3 to 16: Solve the following polynomial inequalities

3. $(x-1)(3-x)(x-2)^2 > 0$
   (a) $1 < x < 2$
   (b) $-1 < x < 3$
   (c) $-3 < x < -1$
   (d) $1 < x < 3, x \neq 2$

4. $\dfrac{0.5}{x - x^2 - 1} < 0$
   (a) $x > 0$
   (b) $x \leq 0$
   (c) $x \geq 0$
   (d) For all real x

5. $\dfrac{x^2 - 5x + 6}{x^2 + x + 1} < 0$
   (a) $x < 2$
   (b) $x > 3$
   (c) $2 < x < 3$
   (d) $x < 2$ or $x > 3$

6. $\dfrac{x^2 + 2x - 3}{x^2 + 1} < 0$
   (a) $x < -3$
   (b) $-7 < x < -3$
   (c) $-3 < x < 1$
   (d) $-7 < x < 1$

7. $\dfrac{(x-1)(x+2)^2}{-1-x} < 0$
   (a) $x < -1$
   (b) $x < -1$ or $x > 1$
   (c) $x < -1$ and $x \neq 2$
   (d) $x < -1$ or $x > 1$ and $x \neq -2$

8. $\dfrac{x^2 + 4x + 4}{2x^2 - x - 1} > 0$
   (a) $x < -2$
   (b) $x > 1$
   (c) $x \neq 2$
   (d) None of these

9. $x^4 - 5x^2 + 4 < 0$
   (a) $-2 < x < 1$
   (b) $-2 < x < 2$
   (c) $-2 < x < -1$ or $1 < x < 2$
   (d) $1 < x < 2$

10. $x^4 - 2x^2 - 63 \leq 0$
    (a) $x \leq -3$ or $x \geq 3$
    (b) $-3 \leq x \leq 0$
    (c) $0 \leq x \leq 3$
    (d) $-3 \leq x \leq 3$

Directions for Questions 11 to 67: Solve the following polynomial and quadratic inequalities

11. $\dfrac{5x - 1}{x^2 + 3} < 1$
    (a) $x < 4$
    (b) $1 < x < 4$
    (c) $x < 1$ or $x > 4$
    (d) $1 < x < 3$

12. $\dfrac{x - 2}{x^2 + 1} < -\dfrac{1}{2}$
    (a) $-3 < x < 3$
    (b) $x < -3$
    (c) $-3 < x < 6$
    (d) $-3 < x < 1$

13. $\dfrac{x + 1}{(x-1)^2} < 1$
    (a) $x > 3$ or x is negative
    (b) $x > 3$
    (c) $x > 3$ or $-23 < x < 0$
    (d) x is negative and $x > 2$

14. $\dfrac{x^2 - 7x + 12}{2x^2 + 4x + 5} > 0$
    (a) $x < 3$ or $x > 4$
    (b) $3 < x < 4$
    (c) $4 < x < 24$
    (d) $0 < x < 3$

15. $\dfrac{x^2 + 6x - 7}{x^2 + 1} \leq 2$
    (a) x is negative
    (b) $x \geq 0$
    (c) $x > 0$ or $x < 0$
    (d) Always

16. $\dfrac{x^4 + x^2 + 1}{x^2 - 4x - 5} < 0$
    (a) $x < -1$ or $x > 5$
    (b) $-1 < x < 5$
    (c) $x > 5$
    (d) $-5 < x < -1$

17. $\dfrac{1 + 3x^2}{2x^2 - 21x + 40} < 0$
    (a) $0 < x < 8$
    (b) $2.5 < x < 8$
    (c) $-8 < x < 8$
    (d) $3 < x < 8$

18. $\dfrac{1 + x^2}{x^2 - 5x + 6} < 0$
    (a) $x < 2$
    (b) $x > 3$
    (c) Both a and b
    (d) $2 < x < 3$

19. $\dfrac{x^4 + x^2 + 1}{x^2 - 4x - 5} > 0$
    (a) $-1 < x < 5$
    (b) $x < -1$ or $x > 5$
    (c) $x \leq -1$ or $x > 5$
    (d) $-1 < x < 1$

20. $\dfrac{1 - 2x - 3x^2}{3x - x^2 - 5} > 0$

(a) $x < -1$ or $x > 1/3$ (b) $x < -1$ or $x = 1/3$

(c) $-1 < x < 1/3$ (d) $x < 1/3$

21. $\dfrac{x^2 - 5x + 7}{-2x^2 + 3x + 2} > 0$

(a) $x > 0.5$ (b) $x > -0.5$

(c) $-0.5 < x < 5$ (d) $-0.5 < x < 2$

22. $\dfrac{2x^2 - 3x - 459}{x^2 + 1} > 1$

(a) $x > -20$ (b) $x < 0$

(c) $x < -20$ (d) $-20 < x < 20$

23. $\dfrac{x^2 - 1}{x^2 + x + 1} < 1$

(a) $x > -2$ (b) $x > 2$

(c) $-2 < x < 2$ (d) $x < 2$

24. $\dfrac{1 - 2x - 3x^2}{3x - x^2 - 5} > 0$

(a) $1 < x < 3$ (b) $1 < x < 7$

(c) $-3 < x < 3$ (d) None of these

25. $\dfrac{x}{x^2 - 3x - 4} > 0$

(a) $-1 < x < 0$ (b) $4 < x$

(c) both (a) and (b)   (d) $-1 < x < 4$

26. $\dfrac{x^2 + 7x + 10}{x + 2/3} > 0$

(a) $-5 < x < -2$ or $\dfrac{-2}{3} < x < \infty$

(b) $-5 < x < 8$

(c) $x < -2$

(d) $x > -2$

27. $\dfrac{3x^2 - 4x - 6}{2x - 5} < 0$

(a) $x < (2 - \sqrt{22})/3$

(b) $x > (2 + \sqrt{22})/3$

(c) $(2 - \sqrt{22})/3 < x < (2 + \sqrt{22})/3$

(d) None of these

28. $\dfrac{17 - 15x - 2x^2}{x + 3} < 0$

(a) $-8.5 < x \le -3$

(b) $-17 < x < -3$

(c) $-8.5 < x < -3$ or $x > 1$

(d) $-8.5 < x < 1$

29. $\dfrac{x^2 - 9}{3x - x^2 - 24} < 0$

(a) $-3 < x < 3$ (b) $x < -3$ or $x > 3$

(c) $x < -5$ or $x > 5$ (d) $x < -7$ or $x > 7$

30. $\dfrac{x + 7}{x - 5} + \dfrac{3x + 1}{2} \ge 0$

(a) $1 < x < 5$ (b) $-1 < x < 5$

(c) $1 \le x \le 3$ or $x > 5$ (d) $-1 < x < 3$

31. $2x^2 + \dfrac{1}{x} > 0$

(a) $x > 0$ (b) $x < -1/2$

(c) Both (a) and (b)   (d) None of these

32. $\dfrac{x^2 - x - 6}{x^2 + 6x} \ge 0$

(a) $x < -6$ (b) $-2 \le x < 0$

(c) $x > 3$ (d) All of these

33. $\dfrac{x^2 - 5x + 6}{x^2 - 11x + 30} < 0$

(a) $x < 3$ or $x > 5$

(b) $2 < x < 4$ or $5 < x < 7$

(c) $2 < x < 3$ or $5 < x < 6$

(d) $2 < x < 3$ or $5 < x < 7$

34. $\dfrac{x^2 - 8x + 7}{4x^2 - 4x + 1} < 0$

(a) $x < 1$ or $x > 7$ (b) $1 < x < 7$

(c) $-7 < x < 1$ (d) $-7 < x < 7$

35. $\dfrac{x^2 - 36}{x^2 - 9x + 18} < 0$

(a) $-6 < x < 3$ (b) $-6 < x < 6$

(c) $x < -6$ or $x > 3$ (d) $-3 < x < 3$

36. $\dfrac{x^2 - 6x + 9}{5 - 4x - x^2} \ge 0$

(a) $-5 < x < 1$ or $x = 3$ (b) $-5 \le x < 1$ or $x = 3$

(c) $-5 < x \le 1$ or $x = 3$ (d) $-5 \le x \le -1$

37. $\dfrac{x - 1}{x + 1} < x$

(a) $x < -1$ (b) $x > -1$

(c) $-1 < x < 1$ (d) For all real values of x

38. $\dfrac{1}{x + 2} < \dfrac{3}{x - 3}$

(a) $-4.5 < x < -2$ (b) $-4.5 < x < -2$ or $3 < x$

(c) $-4.5 < x < -2, x > 3$ (d) (b) or (c)

39. $\dfrac{14x}{x + 1} - \dfrac{9x - 30}{x - 4} < 0$

(a) $-1 < x < 1$ or $4 < x < 6$

(b) $-1 < x < 4, 5 < x < 7$

(c) $1 < x < 4$ or $5 < x < 7$

(d) $-1 < x < 1$ or $5 < x < 7$

40. $\dfrac{5x^2 - 2}{4x^2 - x + 3} < 1$

(a) $x < 1$

(b) $-2 < x < 2$

(c) $-2.7 < x < 1.75$

(d) $(-(1 + \sqrt{21})/2 < x < (\sqrt{21} - 1)/2$

41. $\dfrac{x^2 - 5x + 12}{x^2 - 4x + 5} > 3$

(a) $x > 0.5$ (b) $1/2 < x < 3$

(c) $x < 0.5, x > 3$ (d) $1 < x < 3$

42. $\dfrac{x^2 - 3x + 24}{x^2 - 3x + 3} < 4$

(a) $x < -1$ (b) $4 < x < 8$

(c) $x < 4$ or $x > 8$ (d) Both (a) and (b)

43. $\dfrac{x^2 - 1}{2x + 5} < 3$

(a) $x < -2.5$ or $-2 < x < 8$

(b) $-2.5 < x < -2$

(c) $-2.5 < x < 8$

(d) Both (a) and (b)

44. $\dfrac{x^2 + 1}{4x - 3} > 2$

(a) $x > 7$ (b) $x > 7, x < 87$

(c) $0.75 < x < 1, x > 7$ (d) $0.25 < x < 1, x > 7$

45. $\dfrac{x^2 + 2}{x^2 - 1} < -2$

(a) $-1 < x < 2$

(b) $-1 < x < 1,$

(c) $-1 < x < 0, 0 < x < 1$

(d) $-2 < x < 2$

46. $\dfrac{3x - 5}{x^2 + 4x - 5} > \dfrac{1}{2}$

(a) $x < -5$ (b) $x > 1$

(c) $-5 < x < 1$ (d) $-5 < x < 5$

47. $\dfrac{2x + 3}{x^2 + x - 12} \leq \dfrac{1}{2}$

(a) $-4 < x < -3, 3 < x < 6$

(b) $-4 < x < -3, 0 < x < 6$

(c) $x < -4, -3 < x < 3, x > 6$

(d) $x < -4, x > 6$

48. $\dfrac{5 - 2x}{3x^2 - 2x - 16} < 1$

(a) $x < -\sqrt{7}$ (b) $-2 < x < \sqrt{7}$

(c) $8/3 \leq x$ (d) All of these

49. $\dfrac{15 - 4x}{x^2 - x - 12} < 4$

(a) $x < -\sqrt{63}/2, -3 < x < \sqrt{63}/2$

(b) $x > 4$

(c) Both (a) and (b)

(d) $x > 4, x < -63/2$

(e) None of these

50. $\dfrac{1}{x^2 - 5x + 6} \geq 2$

(a) $1 < x < 2, 3 < x < 4$ (b) $1 < x < 4$

(c) $x < 1, x > 3$ (d) $x < 1, x > 4$

(e) $2 < x < 4$

51. $\dfrac{5 - 4x}{3x^2 - x - 4} < 4$

(a) $x < -\dfrac{\sqrt{7}}{2}$ (b) $-1 < x < \dfrac{\sqrt{7}}{2}$

(c) $x > 4/3$ (d) All of these

52. $\dfrac{(x + 2)(x^2 - 2x + 1)}{4 + 3x - x^2} \geq 0$

(a) $x < -2$ or $-1 < x < 4$

(b) $-2 < x < 4$ or $x > 6$

(c) $-2 < x < -1$ or $x > 4$

(d) None of these

53. $\dfrac{4}{1 + x} + \dfrac{2}{1 - x} < 1$

(a) $-1 < x < 1$ (b) $x < -1$

(c) $x > 1$ (d) both (b) and (c)

54. $2 + 3/(x + 1) > 2/x$

(a) $x < -2$ (b) $-1 < x < 0$

(c) $1/2 < x$ (d) All of these

55. $1 + \dfrac{2}{x - 1} > \dfrac{6}{x}$

(a) $0 \leq x \leq 1$ (b) $2 \leq x \leq 3$

(c) $-\infty < x < 1$ (d) Always except (a) and (b)

56. $\dfrac{x^4 - 3x^3 + 2x^2}{x^2 - x - 30} > 0$

(a) $x < -5$ (b) $1 < x < 2$

(c) $x > 6$ (d) All of these

57. $\dfrac{x - 1}{x} - \dfrac{x + 1}{x - 1} < 2$

(a) $-1 \leq x \leq 0$ (b) $1/2 \leq x \leq 1$

(c) $0 < x < 1/2$ (d) Always except (a) and (b)

58. $\dfrac{2(x - 3)}{x(x - 6)} \leq \dfrac{1}{x - 1}$

(a) $x < 0$ (b) $1 < x < 6$

(c) Both (a) and (b)   (d) Always except (a) and (b)

59. $\dfrac{2(x - 4)}{(x - 1)(x - 7)} \geq \dfrac{1}{x - 2}$

(a) $1 < x < 2$ or $7 < x$ (b) $2 < x$

(c) $2 < x < 7$ (d) Both (a) and (c)

60. $\dfrac{2x}{x^2-9} \le \dfrac{1}{x+2}$

    (a) $x<-3$ (b) $-2<x<3$

    (c) All except (a) and (b)(d) Both (a) and (b)

61. $\dfrac{1}{x-2} + \dfrac{1}{x-1} > \dfrac{1}{x}$

    (a) $-\sqrt{2}<x<0$ or $2<x$

    (b) $\sqrt{2}<x$

    (c) $1<x<\sqrt{2}$

    (d) Both (a) and (c)

62. $\dfrac{7}{(x-2)(x-3)} + \dfrac{9}{x-3} + 1 < 0$

    (a) $-5<x<4$

    (b) $-5<x<1$ and $1<x<3$

    (c) $-5<x<1$ and $2<x<3$

    (d) $x<1$

63. $\dfrac{20}{(x-3)(x-4)} + \dfrac{10}{x-4} + 1 > 0$

    (a) $x<-2$ (b) $-1<x<3$ and $4<x$

    (c) All except (a) and (b)(d) Both (a) and (b)

64. $\dfrac{(x-2)(x-4)(x-7)}{(x+2)(x+4)(x+7)} > 1$

    (a) $x<-7$ (b) $x<-7$ and $-4<x<-2$

    (c) $-4<x<2$ (d) None of these

65. $\dfrac{(x-1)(x-2)(x-3)}{(x+1)(x+2)(x+3)} > 1$

    (a) $-3 \le x \le -2$ (b) $x<-3$

    (c) $-2<x<-1$ (d) None of these

66. $(x^2 + 3x + 1)(x^2 + 3x - 3) \ge 5$

    (a) $x<-4$ or $-2<x$

    (b) $-2<x<-1$ or $1<x$

    (c) $x \le -4$; $-2 \le x \le -1$; $1 \le x$

    (d) $x<-4$ or $1<x$

67. $(x^2 - x - 1)(x^2 - x - 7) < -5$

    (a) $-2<x$

    (b) $-2<x<-1$ and $1<x<4$

    (c) $-2<x<-1$ and $2<x<3$

    (d) $-2<x<0$ and $2<x<3$

Directions for Questions 68 to 92: Solve inequalities based on modulus

68. $|x^3 - 1| \ge 1 - x$

    (a) $-1<x<0$ (b) $x<-1$

    (c) $0<x$ (d) Always except (a)

69. $\dfrac{x^2 - 5x + 6}{|x| + 7} < 0$

    (a) $2 \le x \le 3$ (b) $2<x$

    (c) $1<x<3$ (d) $2<x<3$

70. $\dfrac{x^2 + 6x - 7}{|x+4|} < 0$

    (a) $-7<x<-5$ and $-4<x<1$

    (b) $-7<x<-5$ and $-4<x<0$

    (c) $-7<x<-4$ and $-4<x<1$

    (d) None of these

71. $\dfrac{|x-2|}{x-2} > 0$

    (a) $2<x<10$ (b) $3 \le x$

    (c) $2 \le x$ (d) $2<x$

72. $\left|\dfrac{2}{x-4}\right| > 1$

    (a) $2<x<4$; $4 \le x \le 5$

    (b) $2<x \le 4$; $4 \le x \le 5$

    (c) $2<x<4$; $4<x<6$

    (d) $2<x<4$; $4 \le x \le 6$

73. $\left|\dfrac{2x-1}{x-1}\right| > 2$

    (a) $2<x$ (b) $1<x$

    (c) $3/4<x<1$ (d) Both (b) and (c)

74. $\left|\dfrac{x^2 - 3x - 1}{x^2 + x + 1}\right| < 3$

    (a) $x<-2$ (b) $-1<x$

    (c) Always except (b)   (d) Both (a) and (b)

75. $\dfrac{x^2 - 7|x| + 10}{x^2 - 6x + 9} < 0$

    (a) $-5 \le x \le -2$; $2<x<5$

    (b) $-5<x<-2$; $2<x<5$

    (c) $-5<x<-2$; $2<x<3$; $3<x<5$

    (d) $-5<x<-2$; $3<x<5$

76. $\dfrac{|x+3| + x}{x+2} > 1$

    (a) $-5<x \le -2$ (b) $-2 \le x \le -1$

    (c) $-1<x$ (d) Always except (b)

77. $\dfrac{|x-1|}{x+2} < 1$

    (a) $-8<x \le -3$ (b) $-3<x \le -2$

    (c) Always except (b)   (d) Both (a) and (b)

78. $\dfrac{|x+2| - x}{x} < 2$

    (a) $-5 \le x < 0$ (b) $0 \le x \le 1$

    (c) Both (a) and (b)   (d) Always except (b)

79. $\dfrac{1}{|x| - 3} < \dfrac{1}{2}$

    (a) $x<-5$ and $-3<x<3$

    (b) $3 \le x \le 5$

(c) $-5 \le x \le -3$

(d) Always except (b) and (c)

80. $\left| \dfrac{3x}{x^2 - 4} \right| \le 1$

(a) $x \le -4$ and $-1 \le x \le 1$

(b) $4 \le x$

(c) Both of these

(d) None of these

81. $\left| \dfrac{x^2 - 5x + 4}{x^2 - 4} \right| \le 1$

(a) $[0 < x < 8/5]\ U\ [5/2 < x < +\infty]$

(b) $[0, 5/2]\ U\ [16/5, +\infty]$

(c) $[0, 8/5]\ U\ [5/2, +\infty]$

(d) $[0, 8/5]\ U\ [5/2, +\infty]$

82. $\dfrac{|x - 3|}{x^2 - 5x + 6} \ge 2$

(a) $[3/2, 1]$ (b) $[1, 2]$

(c) $[1.5, 2]$ (d) None of these

83. $\dfrac{x^2 - |x| - 12}{x - 3} \ge 2x$

(a) $-101 < x < 25$ (b) $[-\infty, 3]$

(c) $x \le 3$ (d) $x < 3$

84. $|x| < \dfrac{9}{x}$

(a) $x < -1$ (b) $0 < x < 3$

(c) $1 < x < 3; x < -1$ (d) $-\infty < x < 3$

85. $1 + \dfrac{12}{x^2} < \dfrac{7}{x}$

(a) $x < -2; 2 < x < 3$ (b) $3 \le x < 4$

(c) Both (a) and (b)   (d) None of these

86. $\dfrac{(x^2 - 4x + 5)}{(x^2 + 5x + 6)} \ge 0$

(a) $-\infty < x < \infty$ (b) $x < -3$

(c) $x > -2$ (d) Both (b) and (c)

Space for Rough Work

87. $\dfrac{x + 1}{x - 1} \ge \dfrac{x + 5}{x + 1}$

(a) $x < -1$ (b) $0 < x < 3$

(c) $1 < x \le 3, x < -1$ (d) $-\infty < x < 3$

88. $\dfrac{x - 1}{x^2 - x - 12} \le 0$

(a) $x < -3; 2 < x < 3$ (b) $3 \le x < 4$

(c) Both (a) and (b)   (d) None of these

89. $1 < (3x^2 - 7x + 8)/(x^2 + 1) \le 2$

(a) $1 < x < 6$ (b) $1 \le x < 6$

(c) $1 < x \le 6$ (d) $1 \le x \le 6$

90. If $f'(x) \ge g(x)$, where $f(x) = 5 - 3x + \dfrac{5}{2}x^2 - \dfrac{x^3}{3}$, $g(x) = 3x - 7$

(a) $[2, 3]$ (b) $[2, 3]$

(c) $x = 2.5$ (d) None of these

91. $f'(x) \ge g'(x)$, if $f(x) = 10x^3 - 13x^2 + 7x$, $g(x) = 11x^3 - 15x^2 - 3$

(a) $[-1, 7/3]$ (b) $[-1, 3.5]$

(c) $[-1, 7/3]$ (d) $[1, 7/3]$

92. $\dfrac{1}{x - 2} - \dfrac{1}{x} \le \dfrac{2}{x + 2}$

(a) $(-2, -1)\ U\ (2, +\infty)$ (b) $-2 < x < 1$

(c) Both (a) and (b)   (d) None of these

Directions for Questions 93 to 95: Solve the following irrational inequalities.

93. $(x - 1)\sqrt{x^2 - x - 2} \ge 0$

(a) $x < 2$ (b) $3 \le x < \infty$

(c) Always except (a) (d) Both (a) and (b)

94. $(x^2 - 1)\sqrt{x^2 - x - 2} \ge 0$

(a) $x < -1$ (b) $2 \le x$

(c) Both (a) and (b)   (d) None of these

95. $\dfrac{\sqrt{x - 3}}{x - 2} > 0$

(a) $0 \le x < 2$ (b) $x > 3$

(c) $0 < x < 1$ (d) Both (b) and (c)

ANSWER KEY

Level of Difficulty (I)

1. (d)	2. (a)	3. (d)	4. (d)
5. (c)	6. (a)	7. (d)	8. (d)
9. (c)	10. (a)	11. (d)	12. (c)
13. (c)	14. (d)	15. (b)	16. (d)
17. (d)	18. (c)	19. (d)	20. (d)
21. (c)	22. (a)	23. (d)	24. (b)
25. (d)	26. (d)	27. (c)	28. (a)
29. (d)	30. (a)	31. (b)	32. (d)
33. (d)	34. (d)	35. (c)	36. (b)
37. (c)	38. (c)	39. (c)	40. (b)
41. (d)	42. (b)	43. (a)	44. (a)
45. (b)	46. (d)	47. (d)	48. (a)
49. (a)	50. (a)	51. (b)	52. (b)
53. (b)	54. (b)	55. (d)	56. (a)
57. (d)	58. (d)	59. (d)	60. (d)
61. (a)	62. (c)	63. (a)	64. (d)
65. (d)	66. (c)	67. (a)	68. (c)
69. (b)	70. (a)		

Level of Difficulty (II)

1. (c)	2. (b)	3. (d)	4. (d)
5. (c)	6. (c)	7. (d)	8. (d)
9. (c)	10. (d)	11. (c)	12. (d)
13. (a)	14. (a)	15. (d)	16. (b)
17. (b)	18. (d)	19. (b)	20. (a)
21. (d)	22. (c)	23. (a)	24. (d)
25. (c)	26. (a)	27. (e)	28. (c)
29. (b)	30. (c)	31. (d)	32. (d)
33. (c)	34. (b)	35. (a)	36. (a)
37. (b)	38. (b)	39. (a)	40. (d)
41. (b)	42. (d)	43. (d)	44. (c)
45. (c)	46. (c)	47. (c)	48. (d)
49. (c)	50. (a)	51. (d)	52. (a)
53. (d)	54. (d)	55. (d)	56. (d)
57. (d)	58. (c)	59. (a)	60. (d)
61. (d)	62. (c)	63. (d)	64. (b)
65. (d)	66. (c)	67. (c)	68. (d)
69. (d)	70. (c)	71. (d)	72. (c)
73. (d)	74. (d)	75. (c)	76. (d)
77. (c)	78. (d)	79. (d)	80. (c)
81. (a)	82. (d)	83. (d)	84. (b)
85. (d)	86. (d)	87. (c)	88. (d)
89. (d)	90. (d)	91. (a)	92. (d)
93. (c)	94. (c)	95. (b)	

Solutions and Shortcuts

While practically solving inequalities remember the following:

1. The answer to an inequality question is always in the form of a range and represents the range of values where the inequality is satisfied.

2. In the cases of all continuous functions, the point at which the range of the correct answer will start, will always be a solution of the same function if written as an equation.

   This rule is only broken for non-continuous functions.

   Hence, if you judge that a function is continuous always check the options for LHS = RHS at the starting point of the option.

3. The correct range has to have two essential properties if it has to be the correct answer:
   (a) The inequality should be satisfied for each and every value of the range.
   (b) There should be no value satisfying the inequality outside the range of the correct option.

   Questions on inequalities are always solved using options and based on (3) (a) and (3) (b) above we would reject an option as the correct answer if:
   (i) we find even a single value not satisfying the inequality within the range of a single option.
   (ii) we can reject given option, even if we find a single value satisfying the inequality but not lying within the range of the option under check.

   I will now show you certain solved questions on this pattern of thinking.

Level of Difficulty (I)

1. At $x = 0$, inequality is not satisfied. Thus, option (c) is rejected. Also $x = 0$ is not a solution of the equation. Since, this is a continuous function, the solution cannot start from 0. Thus options (a) and (b) are not right. Further, we see that the given function is quadratic with real roots. Hence, option (d) is also rejected.

2. At $x = 0$, inequality is satisfied. Hence, options (b) and (c) are rejected. $x = 3$ gives LHS = RHS. and $x = -0.66$ also does the same. Hence. roots of the equation are 3 and -0.66.

   Thus, option (a) is correct.

3. At $x = 0$, inequality is not satisfied.

   Hence, options (b), (c) and (d) are rejected. At $x = 2$, inequality is not satisfied. Hence, option (a) is rejected.

   Thus, option (d) is correct.

4. The given quadratic equation has imaginary roots and is hence always positive.

   Thus, option (d) is correct

5. At $x = 0$ inequality is not satisfied. Thus option (d) is rejected.

   $x = -1$ and $x = 15$ are the roots of the quadratic equation. Thus, option (c) is correct.

6. At $x = 0$, inequality is satisfied.

   Thus, options, (c) and (d) are rejected.

   At $x = 1$, inequality is satisfied

Hence, we choose option (a).

7. At $x = 0$ inequality is satisfied, option (b) is rejected.
   At $x = 2$, inequality is satisfied, option (c) is rejected.
   At $x = 5$, LHS = RHS.
   At $x = -1$, LHS = RHS.
   Thus, option (d) is correct.

8. At $x = 0$ inequality is satisfied.
   Thus, options (a), (b), and (d) are rejected.
   Option (c) is correct.

10. At $x = 1$ and $x = 3$ LHS = RHS.
    At $x = 2$ inequality is satisfied.
    At $x = 0.1$ inequality is not satisfied.
    At $x = 2.9$ inequality is satisfied.
    At $x = 3.1$ inequality is not satisfied.
    Thus, option (a) is correct.

12. The options need to be converted to approximate values before you judge the answer. At $x = 0$, inequality is satisfied.
    Thus, option (a) is rejected.
    Option (c) is correct.

13. At $x = 0$, inequality is not satisfied, option (a) is rejected.

At $x = 5$, inequality is not satisfied, option (b) is rejected.

At $x = 2$ inequality is not satisfied.

Options (d) are rejected.

Option (c) is correct.

14. At $x = 0$, inequality is satisfied, option (a) rejected.
    At $x = 10$, inequality is not satisfied, option (c) rejected.
    At $x = -5$, LHS = RHS.

    Also at $x = 5$, inequality is satisfied and at $x = 6$, inequality is not satisfied.

    Thus, option (d) is correct.

15. At $x = 2$, inequality is satisfied.

    At $x = 0$, inequality is not satisfied.

    At $x = 1$, inequality is not satisfied but LHS = RHS.

    At $x = 3$, inequality is not satisfied but LHS = RHS.

    Thus, option (b) is correct.

    Solve other questions of LOD I and LOD II in the same fashion.

We have already seen in the *Back to School* part of this block the key interrelationship between functions, equations and inequalities. In this chapter we are specifically looking at questions based on equations—with an emphasis on quadratic equations. Questions based on equations are an important component of the CAT exam and hence your ability to formulate and solve equations is a key skill in the development of your thought process for QA.

As you go through with this chapter, focus on understanding the core concepts and also look to create a framework in your mind which would account for the typical processes that are used for solving questions based on equations.

THEORY OF EQUATIONS

Equations in one variable

An equation is any expression in the form $f(x) = 0$; the type of equation we are talking about depends on the expression that is represented by $f(x)$. The expression $f(x)$ can be linear, quadratic, cubic or might have a higher power and accordingly the equation can be referred to as linear equations, quadratic equations, cubic equations, etc. Let us look at each of these cases one by one.

Linear Equations

$2x + 4 = 0$; **we have the expression for $f(x)$ as a linear expression in x.** Consequently, the equation $2x + 4 = 0$ would be charaterised as a linear equation. This equation has exactly 1 root (solution) and can be seen by solving $2x + 4 = 0 \rightarrow x = -2$ which is the root of the equation. Note that the root or solution of the equation is the value of 'x' which would make the LHS of the equation equal the RHS of the equation. In other words, the equation is

satisfied when the value of x becomes equal to the root of the equation.

The linear function $f(x)$ when drawn would give us a straight line and this line would be intersecting with the x-axis at the point where the value of x equals the root (solution) of the equation.

Quadratic Equations

An equation of the form: $2x^2 - 5x + 4 = 0$; we have the expression for $f(x)$ as a quadratic expression in x. Consequently, the equation $2x^2 - 5x + 4 = 0$ would be charaterised as a quadratic equation. This equation has exactly 2 roots (solutions) and leads to the following cases with respect to whether these roots are real/imaginary or equal/unequal.

Case 1: Both the roots are real and equal;
Case 2: Both the roots are real and unequal;
Case 3: Both the roots are imaginary.

A detailed discussion of quadratic equations and the analytical formula based approach to identify which of the above three cases prevails follows later in this chapter.

The graph of a quadratic function is always U shaped and would just touch the X-Axis in the first case above, would cut the X-Axis twice in the second case above and would not touch the X-Axis at all in the third case above.

Note that the roots or solutions of the equation are the values of 'x' which would make the LHS of the equation equal the RHS of the equation. In other words, the equation is satisfied when the value of x becomes equal to the root of the equation.

Cubic Equations

An equation of the form: $x^3 + 2x^2 - 5x + 4 = 0$ where the expression $f(x)$ is a cubic expression in x. Consequently, the expression would have three roots or solutions.

Depending on whether the roots are real or imaginary we can have the following two cases in this situation:

Case 1: All three roots are real; (Graph might touch/cut the x-axis once, twice or thrice.)

In this case depending on the equality or inequality of the roots we might have the following cases:

Case (i) All three roots are equal; (The graph of the function would intersect the X-axis only once as all the three roots of the equation coincide.)

Case (ii) Two roots are equal and one root is distinct; (In this case the graph cuts the X-axis at one point and touches the X-Axis at another point where the other two roots coincide.)

Case (iii) All three roots are distinct from each other. (In this case the graph of the function cuts the x-axis at three distinct points.)

Case 2: One root is real and two roots are imaginary. (Graph would cut the X-axis only once.)

The shapes of the graph that a cubic function can take has already been discussed as a part of the discussion on the *Back to School* write up of this block.

Note: For a cubic equation $ax^3 + bx^2 + cx + d = 0$ with roots as l, m and n:

The product of its three roots viz: $l \times m \times n = -d/a$;

The sum of its three roots viz: $l + m + n = -b/a$

The pairwise sum of its roots taken two at a time viz: $lm + ln + mn = c/a$.

THEORY OF QUADRATIC EQUATIONS

An equation of the form

$$ax^2 + bx + c = 0 \qquad (1)$$

where a, b and c are all real and a is not equal to 0, is a quadratic equation. Then,

$D = (b^2 - 4ac)$ is the discriminant of the quadratic equation.

If $D < 0$ (i.e. the discriminant is negative) then the equation has no real roots.

If $D > 0$, (i.e. the discriminant is positive) then the equation has two distinct roots, namely,

$x_1 = (-b + \sqrt{D})/2a$, and $x_2 = (-b - \sqrt{D})/2a$

and then $ax^2 + bx + c = a(x - x_1)(x - x_2) \qquad (2)$

If $D = 0$, then the quadratic equation has equal roots given by

$$x_1 = x_2 = -b/2a$$

and then $ax^2 + bx + c = a(x - x_1)^2 \qquad (3)$

To represent the quadratic $ax^2 + bx + c$ in form (2) or (3) is to expand it into linear factors.

Properties of Quadratic Equations and Their Roots

(i) If D is a *perfect square* then the roots are *rational* and in case it is not a perfect square then the roots are *irrational*.

(ii) In the case of imaginary roots ($D < 0$) and if $p + iq$ is one root of the quadratic equation, then the other must be the conjugate $p - iq$ and vice versa (where p and q are real and $i = \sqrt{-1}$)

(iii) If $p + \sqrt{q}$ is one root of a quadratic equation, then the other must be the conjugate $p - \sqrt{q}$ and vice versa. (where p is rational and $\sqrt{q}$ is a surd).

(iv) If $a = 1$, b, $c \in I$ and the roots are rational numbers, then the root must be an integer.

(v) If a quadratic equation in x has more than two roots, then it is an identity in x.

The Sign of a Quadratic Expression

Let $f(x) = y = ax^2 + bx + c$ where a, b, c are real and $a \neq 0$, then $y = f(x)$ represents a parabola whose axis is parallel to y-axis. For some values of x, $f(x)$ may be positive, negative or zero. Also, if $a > 0$, the parabola opens upwards and for $a < 0$, the parabola opens downwards. This gives the following cases:

(i) $a > 0$ and $D < 0$ (The roots are imaginary)

The function $f(x)$ will always be positive for all real values of x. So $f(x) > 0 \ \forall \ x \in R$. Naturally the graph as shown in the figure does not cut the X-Axis.

(ii) When $a > 0$ and $D = 0$ (The roots are real and identical.)

$f(x)$ will be positive for all values of x except at the vertex where $f(x) = 0$.

So $f(x) \geq 0 \ \forall \ x \in R$. Naturally, the graph touches the X-Axis once.

(iii) When $a > 0$ and $D > 0$ (The roots are real and distinct)

Let $f(x) = 0$ have two real roots α and β ($\alpha < \beta$) then $f(x)$ will be positive for all real values of x which are lower than α or higher than β; $f(x)$ will be equal to zero when x is equal to either of α or β.

When x lies between α and β then $f(x)$ will be negative. Mathematically, this can be represented as

$f(x) > 0 \ \forall \ x \in (-\infty, \alpha) \cup (\beta, \infty)$

and $f(x) < 0 \ \forall \ x \in (\alpha, \beta)$ (Naturally the graph cuts the X axis twice)

(iv) When $a < 0$ and $D < 0$ (Roots are imaginary)

$f(x)$ is negative for all values of x. Mathematically, we can write $f(x) < 0 \ \forall \ x \in R$. (The graph will not cut or touch the X axis.)

(v) When $a < 0$ and $D = 0$ (Roots are real and equal)

$f(x)$ is negative for all values of x except at the vertex where $f(x) = 0$. i.e. $f(x) \leq 0 \ \forall \ x \in R$ (The graph touches the X axis once.)

(vi) When $a < 0$ and $D > 0$

Let $f(x) = 0$ have two roots α and β ($\alpha < \beta$) then $f(x)$ will be negative for all real values of x that are lower than α or higher than β. $f(x)$ will be equal to zero when x is equal to either of α or β. The graph cuts the X axis twice.

When x lies between α and β then $f(x)$ will be positive.

Mathematically, this can be written as

$f(x) < 0 \ \forall \ x \in (-\infty, \alpha) \cup (\beta, \infty)$ and $f(x) > 0 \ \forall \ x \in (\alpha, \beta)$.

Sum of the roots of a quadratic

Equation $= -b/a$.

Product of the roots of a quadratic equation $= c/a$

Equations in more than one Variable

Sometimes, an equation might contain not just one variable but more than one variable. In the context of an aptitude examination like the CAT, multiple variable equations may be limited to two or three variables. Consider this question from an old CAT examination which required the student to understand the interrelationship between the values of x and y.

The question went as follows:

$4x - 17y = 1$ where x and y are integers with $x, y > 0$ and $x, y < 1000$. How many pairs of values of (x, y) exist such that the equation is satisfied?

In order to solve this equation, you need to consider the fact that $4x$ in this equation should be looked upon as a multiple of 4 while $17y$ should be looked upon as a multiple of 17. A scan of values which exist such that a multiple of 4 is 1 more than a multiple of 17 starts from $52 - 51 = 1$, in which case the value of $x = 13$ and $y = 3$. This represents the first set of values for (x, y) that satisfies the equation.

The next pair of values in this case would happen if you increase x from 13 to 30 (increase by 17 which is the coefficient of y); at the same time increase y from 3 to 7 (increase by 4 which is the coefficient of x). The effect this has on $4x$ is to increase it by 68 while $17y$ would also increase by 68 keeping the value of $4x$ exactly 1 more than $17y$. In other words, at $x = 30$ and $y = 7$ the equation would give us $120 - 119 = 1$. Going further, you should realise that the same increases need to be repeated to again identify the pair of x, y values. ($x = 47$ and $y = 11$ gives us $188 - 187 = 1$)

Once, you realise this, the next part of the visualisation in solving this question has to be on creating the series of values which would give us our desired outcomes everytime.

This series can be viewed as

(13,3); (30,7); (47,11); (64,15)....and the series would basically be two arithmetic progressions running parallel to each other (viz: 13, 30, 47, 64, 81,....) and (3, 7, 11, 15, 19,...) and obviously the number of such pairs would depend on the number of terms in the first of these arithmetic progressions (since that AP would cross the upper limit of 1000 first).

You would need to identify the last term of the series below 1000. The series can be visualised as 13, 30, 47, 64,... 999 and the number of terms in this series is $986/17 + 1 = 59$ terms. [Refer to the chapter on arithmetic Progressions for developing the thinking that helps us do these last two steps.]

🎯 WORKED-OUT PROBLEMS

Problem 15.1 Find the value of $\sqrt{6+\sqrt{6+\sqrt{6+...}}}$

    (a) 4   (b) 3

    (c) 3.5   (d) 2.5

Solution Let $y = \sqrt{6+\sqrt{6+\sqrt{6+...}}}$

Then, $y = \sqrt{6+y}$ $\Rightarrow$ or $y^2 - y - 6 = 0$

or, $(y+2)(y-3) = 0$ $\Rightarrow$ $y = -2, 3$

          $y = -2$ is not admissible

Hence $y = 3$

Alternative: Going through options:

Option (a): For 4 to be the solution, value of the whole expression should be equal to 16. Looking into the expression, it cannot be equal to 16. So, option (a) cannot be the answer. Option (b): For 3 to be the solution, the value of the expression should be 9.

So, the expression is $= \sqrt{6+\sqrt{6+\sqrt{6+...}}}$

But $\sqrt{6} \approx 2.9$, hence $= \sqrt{6+2.9+\sqrt{\cdots}} \cong \sqrt{8.9+\cdots} \cong 3$

(Since, the remaining part is negligible in value)

Problem 15.2 One of the two students, while solving a quadratic equation in x, copied the constant term incorrectly and got the roots 3 and 2. The other copied the constant term and coefficient of x^2 correctly as –6 and 1 respectively. The correct roots are

    (a) 3, –2   (b) –3, 2

    (c) –6, –1   (d) 6, –1

Solution Let α, β be the roots of the equation. Then $\alpha + \beta = 5$ and $\alpha\beta = -6$. So, the equation is $x^2 - 5x - 6 = 0$. The roots of the equation are 6 and –1.

Problem 15.3 If p and q are the roots of the equation $x^2 + px + q = 0$

    (a) $p = 1$ (b) $p = 1$ or 0 or $-\dfrac{1}{2}$

    (c) $p = -2$ (d) $p = -2$ or 0

Solution Since p and q are roots of the equation $x^2 + px + q = 0$,

        $p^2 + p^2 + q = 0$ and $q^2 + pq + q = 0$

$\Rightarrow$ $2p^2 + q = 0$ and $q(q + p + 1) = 0$

$\Rightarrow$ $2p^2 + q = 0$ and $q = 0$ or $q = -p - 1$

When we use, $q = 0$ and $2p^2 + q = 0$

we get $p = 0$.

or when we use $q = -p - 1$ and $2p^2 + q = 0$

we get $2p^2 - p - 1 = 0 \rightarrow$ which gives us

          $p = 1$ or $p = -1/2$

Hence, there can be three values for p

i.e. $p = 1$, $p = 0$, or $p = -\dfrac{1}{2}$

Problem 15.4 If the roots of the equation $a(b - c)x^2 + b(c - a)x + c(a - b) = 0$ are equal, then a, b, c are in

    (a) AP   (b) GP

    (c) HP   (d) Cannot be determined

Solution Since roots of the equation $a(b - c)x^2 + b(c - a)x + c(a - b) = 0$ are equal

$\Rightarrow$ $b^2(c - a)^2 - 4ac(b - c)(a - b) = 0$

$\Rightarrow$ $b^2(c + a)^2 - 4abc(a + c) + 4a^2c^2 = 0$

$\Rightarrow$ $[b(c + a) - 2ac]^2 = 0$ $\Rightarrow$ $b(c + a) - 2ac = 0$

$\Rightarrow$ $b = (2ac)/(a + c)$ $\Rightarrow$ a, b, c, are in HP

Problem 15.5 The number of roots of the equation

$x - \dfrac{2}{(x-1)} = 1 - \dfrac{2}{(x-1)}$ is

    (a) 0   (b) 1

    (c) 2   (d) infinite

Solution The equation gives $x = 1$.

But $x = 1$ is not admissible because it gives $x - 1 = 0$ which, in turn, makes the whole expression like this: $x - 2/0 = 1 - 2/0$. But $2/0$ gives the value as infinity so, no solution is possible.

Problem 15.6 If the roots of the equation $x^2 - bx + c = 0$ differ by 2, then which of the following is true?

    (a) $c^2 = 4(c + 1)$ (b) $b^2 = 4c + 4$

    (c) $c^2 = b + 4$ (d) $b^2 = 4(c + 2)$

Solution Let the roots be α and $\alpha + 2$.

Then $\alpha + \alpha + 2 = b$ $\Rightarrow$ $\alpha = (b - 2)/2$ (1)

and $\alpha(\alpha + 2) = c$ $\Rightarrow$ $\alpha^2 + 2\alpha = c$ (2)

Putting the value of α from (1) in (2).

    $((b-2)/2)^2 + 2(b-2)/2) = c$

$\Rightarrow$ $(b^2 + 4 - 4b)/4 + b - 2 = c$

$\Rightarrow$ $b^2 + 4 - 8 = 4c$

$\Rightarrow$ $b^2 = 4c + 4$

$\therefore$ Option (b) is the correct answer.

Problem 15.7 What is the condition for one root of the quadratic equation $ax^2 + bx + c = 0$ to be twice the other?

    (a) $b^2 = 4ac$ (b) $2b^2 = 9ac$

    (c) $c^2 = 4a + b^2$ (d) $c^2 = 9a - b^2$

Solution

$\therefore$ $\alpha + 2\alpha = -(b/a)$ and $\alpha \times 2\alpha = c/a$

$\Rightarrow$ $3\alpha = -(b/a)$ $\Rightarrow$ $\alpha = -b/3a$

and $\quad 2\alpha^2 = c/a \quad \Rightarrow \quad 2(-b/3a)^2 = c/a$

$\Rightarrow \quad 2b^2/9a^2 = c/a \quad \Rightarrow \quad 2b^2 = 9ac$

Hence the required condition is $2b^2 = 9ac$.

Alternative: Assume any equation having two roots as 2 and 4 or any equation having two roots one of which is twice the other.

When roots are 2 and 4, then equation will be $(x - 2)(x - 4) = x^2 - 6x + 8 = 0$.

Now, check the options one by one and you will find only **(b)** as a suitable option.

Problem 15.8 Solve the system of equations

$$\begin{cases} 1/x + 1/y = 3/2, \\ 1/x^2 + 1/y^2 = 5/4 \end{cases}$$

Solution Let $1/x = u$ and $1/y = v$. We then obtain

$$\begin{cases} u + v = 3/2, \\ u^2 + v^2 = 5/4 \end{cases}$$

From the first equation, we find $v = (3/2) - u$ and substitute this expression into the second equation

$$u^2 + ((3/2) - u)^2 = 5/4 \text{ or } 2u^2 - 3u + 1 = 0$$

when $u_1 = 1$ and $u_2 = 1/2$; consequently, $v_1 = 1/2$ and $v_2 = 1$. Therefore, $x_1 = 1$,

$$y_1 = 2 \quad \text{and} \quad x_2 = 2, y_2 = 1$$

Answer: (1, 2) and (2, 1).

Problem 15.9 The product of the roots of the equation $mx^2 + 6x + (2m - 1) = 0$ is -1. Then m is

(a) 1   (b) 1/3

(c) -1 (d) $-1/3$

Solution We have $(2m - 1)/m = -1 \Rightarrow m = 1/3$

Problem 15.10 If $13x + 17y = 643$, where x and y are natural numbers, what is the value of two times the product of x and y?

(a) 744   (b) 844

(c) 924   (d) 884

Solution The solution of this question depends on your visualisation of the multiples of 13 and 17 which would satisfy this equation. (Note: your reaction to $13x$ should be to look at it as a multiple of 13 while $17y$ should be looked at as a multiple of 17). A scan of multiples of 13 and 17 gives us the solution at $286 + 357$ which would mean 13×22 and 17×21 giving us x as 22 and y as 21. The value of $2xy$ would be $2 \times 22 \times 21 = 2 \times 462 = 924$.

Problem 15.11 If $[x]$ denotes the greatest integer $\leq x$, then

$$\left[\frac{1}{3}\right] + \left[\frac{1}{3} + \frac{1}{99}\right] + \left[\frac{1}{3} + \frac{2}{99}\right] + \cdots \left[\frac{1}{3} + \frac{198}{99}\right] =$$

(a) 99   (b) 66

(c) 132   (d) 167

Solution When the value of the sum of the terms inside the function is less than 1, the value of its greatest integer function would be 0. In the above sequence of values, the value inside the bracket would become equal to 1 or more from the value $\left[\frac{1}{3} + \frac{66}{99}\right]$.

Further, this value would remain between 1 to 2 till the term $\left[\frac{1}{3} + \frac{164}{99}\right]$.

There would be 99 terms each with a value of 1 between 66/99 to 164/99. Hence, this part of the expression would each yield a value of 1 giving us:

$$\left[\frac{1}{3} + \frac{66}{99}\right] + \left[\frac{1}{3} + \frac{67}{99}\right] + \cdots \left[\frac{1}{3} + \frac{164}{99}\right] = 99$$

Further, from $\left[\frac{1}{3} + \frac{165}{99}\right] + \left[\frac{1}{3} + \frac{167}{99}\right] + \cdots \left[\frac{1}{3} + \frac{198}{99}\right]$

$= 2 \times 34 = 68$

This gives us a total value of $99 + 68 = 167$ which means that Option (d) is the correct answer.

Space for Rough Work

LEVEL OF DIFFICULTY (I)

1. Find the maximum value of the expression

$$\frac{1}{x^2 + 5x + 10}$$

(a) $\frac{15}{2}$ (b) 1

(c) $\frac{4}{15}$ (d) $\frac{1}{3}$

2. Find the maximum value of the expression $(x^2 + 8x + 20)$.

(a) 4   (b) 2

(c) 29   (d) None of these

3. Find the minimum value of the expression $(p + 1/p)$; $p > 0$.

(a) 1   (b) 0

(c) 2

(d) Depends upon the value of p

4. If the product of roots of the equation $x^2 - 3(2a + 4)x + a^2 + 18a + 81 = 0$ is unity, then a can take the values as

(a) 3, – 6   (b) 10, – 8

(c) –10, –8   (d) –10, – 6

5. For the equation $2^{a+3} = 4^{a+2} - 48$, the value of a will be

(a) $\frac{-3}{2}$ (b) –3

(c) –2   (d) 1

6. The expression $a^2 + ab + b^2$ is _____ for $a < 0$, $b < 0$.

(a) $\neq 0$ (b) < 0

(c) > 0 (d) $= 0$

7. If the roots of equation $x^2 + bx + c = 0$ differ by 2, then which of the following is true?

(a) $a^2c^2 = 4(1 + c)$ (b) $4b + c = 1$

(c) $c^2 = 4 + b$ (d) $b^2 = 4(c + 1)$

8. If $f(x) = (x + 2)$ and $g(x) = (4x + 5)$, and $h(x)$ is defined as $h(x) = f(x) \cdot g(x)$, then sum of roots of $h(x)$ will be

(a) $\frac{3}{4}$ (b) $\frac{13}{4}$

(c) $\frac{-13}{4}$ (d) $\frac{-3}{4}$

9. If equation $x^2 + bx + 12 = 0$ gives 2 as its one of the roots and $x^2 + bx + q = 0$ gives equal roots then

the value of b is

(a) $\frac{49}{4}$ (b) – 8

(c) 4   (d) $\frac{25}{2}$

10. If the roots of the equation $(a^2 + b^2)x^2 - 2(ac + bd)x + (c^2 + d^2) = 0$ are equal then which of the following is true?

(a) $ab = cd$ (b) $ad = bc$

(c) $ad = \sqrt{bc}$ (d) $ab = \sqrt{cd}$

11. For what value of c the quadratic equation $x^2 - (c + 6)x + 2(2c - 1) = 0$ has sum of the roots as half of their product?

(a) 5   (b) – 4

(c) 7   (d) 3

12. Two numbers a and b are such that the quadratic equation $ax^2 + 3x + 2b = 0$ has – 6 as the sum and the product of the roots. Find $a + b$.

(a) 2   (b) –1

(c) 1   (d) –2

13. If α and β are the roots of the Quadratic equation $5y^2 - 7y + 1 = 0$ then find the value of $\frac{1}{\alpha} + \frac{1}{\beta}$.

(a) $\frac{7}{25}$ (b) –7

(c) $\frac{-7}{25}$ (d) 7

14. Find the value of the expression

$$\left(\sqrt{x + \left(\sqrt{x + \left(\sqrt{x \cdots +} \right)} \right)} \right)$$

(a) $\frac{1}{2}\left[2\sqrt{(2x-1)} + 1 \right]$ (b) $\frac{1}{2}\left[\sqrt{(4x+1)} + 1 \right]$

(c) $\frac{1}{2}\left[2\sqrt{(2x-1)} - 1 \right]$ (d) $\frac{1}{2}\left[\sqrt{(4x-1)} - 1 \right]$

15. If $a = \sqrt{(7 + 4\sqrt{3})}$, what will be the value of $\left(a + \frac{1}{a} \right)$?

(a) 7   (b) 4

(c) 3   (d) 2

16. If the roots of the equation $(a^2 + b^2)x^2 - 2b(a + c)x + (b^2 + c^2) = 0$ are equal then a, b, c, are in

(a) AP   (b) GP

(c) HP   (d) Cannot be said

17. If α and β are the roots of the equation $ax^2 + bx + c = 0$ then the equation whose roots are $\alpha + \frac{1}{\beta}$ and $\beta + \frac{1}{\alpha}$ is

(a) $abx^2 + b(c + a)x + (c + a)^2 = 0$

(b) $(c + a)x^2 + b(c + a)x + ac = 0$

(c) $cax^2 + b(c + a)x + (c + a)^2 = 0$

(d) $cax^2 + b(c + a)x + c(c + a)^2 = 0$

18. If $x^2 + ax + b$ leaves the same remainder 5 when divided by $x - 1$ or $x + 1$ then the values of a and b are respectively

    (a) 0 and 4   (b) 3 and 0

    (c) 0 and 3   (d) 4 and 0

19. Find all the values of b for which the equation $x^2 - bx + 1 = 0$ does not possess real roots.

    (a) $-1 < b < 1$ (b) $0 < b < 2$

    (c) $-2 < b < 2$ (d) $-1.9 < b < 1.9$

Directions for Questions 20 to 24:   Read the data given below and it solve the questions based on.

     If α and β are roots of the equation $x^2 + x - 7 = 0$ then.

20. Find $\alpha^2 + \beta^2$

    (a) 10   (b) 15

    (c) 5   (d) 18

21. Find $\alpha^3 + \beta^3$

    (a) 22   (b) -22

    (c) 44   (d) 36

22. For what values of c in the equation $2x^2 - (c^3 + 8c - 1)x + c^2 - 4c = 0$ the roots of the equation would be opposite in signs?

    (a) $c \in (0, 4)$ (b) $c \in (-4, 0)$

    (c) $c \in (0, 3)$ (d) $c \in (-4, 4)$

23. The set of real values of x for which the expression $x^2 - 9x + 20$ is negative is represented by

    (a) $4 < x < 5$ (b) $4 < x < 5$

    (c) $x < 4$ or $x > 5$ (d) $-4 < x < 5$

24. The expression $x^2 + kx + 9$ becomes positive for what values of k (given that x is real)?

    (a) $k < 6$ (b) $k > 6$

    (c) $|k| < 6$ (d) $|k| \le 6$

25. If $9^{a-2} \div 3^{a+4} = 81^{a-11}$, then find the value of $3^{a-8} + 3^{a-6}$.

    (a) 972   (b) 2916

    (c) 810   (d) 2268

26. Find the number of solutions of $a^3 + 2^{a+1} = a^4$, given that n is a natural number less than 100.

    (a) 0   (b) 1

    (c) 2   (d) 3

27. The number of positive integral values of x that satisfy $x^3 - 32x - 5x^2 + 64 \le 0$ is/are

    (a) 4   (b) 5

    (c) 6   (d) More than 6

28. Find the positive integral value of x that satisfies the equation $x^3 - 32x - 5x^2 + 64 = 0$.

    (a) 5   (b) 6

    (c) 7   (d) 8

29. If a, b, c are positive integers, such that $\dfrac{1}{a} + \dfrac{1}{b} + \dfrac{1}{c} = \dfrac{29}{72}$ and $c < b < a < 60$, how many sets of (a, b, c) exist?

    (a) 3   (b) 4

    (c) 5   (d) 6

30. The variables p, q, r and s are correlated with each other with the following relationship: $s^{0.5}/p = q/r^2$. The ranges of values for p, q and r are respectively: $-0.04 \le p \le -0.03$, $-0.25 \le q \le -0.09$, $1 \le r \le 7$ Determine the difference between the maximum and minimum value of s?

    (a) -0.2 (b) 0.02

    (c) 0.1   (d) None of these

Space for Rough Work

LEVEL OF DIFFICULTY (II)

1. In the Maths Olympiad of 2020 at Animal Planet, two representatives from the donkey's side, while solving a quadratic equation, committed the following mistakes:
   (i) One of them made a mistake in the constant term and got the roots as 5 and 9.
   (ii) Another one committed an error in the coefficient of x and he got the roots as 12 and 4.
   But in the meantime, they realised that they are wrong and they managed to get it right jointly. Find the quadratic equation.
   (a) $x^2 + 4x + 14 = 0$ (b) $2x^2 + 7x - 24 = 0$
   (c) $x^2 - 14x + 48 = 0$ (d) $3x^2 - 17x + 52 = 0$

2. If the roots of the equation $a_1x^2 + a_2x + a_3 = 0$ are in the ratio $r_1 : r_2$ then
   (a) $r_1 \cdot r_2 \cdot a_1^2 = (r_1 + r_2) a_3^2$
   (b) $r_1 \cdot r_2 \cdot a_2^2 = (r_1 + r_2)^2 a_1 \cdot a_3$
   (c) $r_1 \cdot r_2 \cdot a_2 = (r_1 + a_2)^2 a_1 \cdot a_2$
   (d) $r_1 \cdot r_2 \cdot a_1^2 = (r_1 + r_2)^2 a_3 \cdot a_2$

3. For what value of a do the roots of the equation $2x^2 + 6x + a = 0$, satisfy the conditions $\left(\dfrac{\alpha}{\beta}\right) + \left(\dfrac{\beta}{\alpha}\right) < 2$.
   (a) $a < 0$ or $a > \dfrac{9}{2}$ (b) $a > 0$
   (c) $-1 < a < 0$ (d) $-1 < a < 1$

4. For what value of b and c would the equation $x^2 + bx + c = 0$ have roots equal to b and c.
   (a) $(0, 0)$ (b) $(1, -2)$
   (c) $(1, 2)$ (d) Both (a) and (b)

5. The sum of a fraction and its reciprocal equals 85/18. Find the fraction.
   (a) $\dfrac{2}{6}$ (b) $\dfrac{2}{3}$
   (c) $\dfrac{2}{9}$ (d) $\dfrac{4}{9}$

6. A journey between Mumbai and Pune (192 km apart) takes two hours less by a car than by a truck. Determine the average speed of the car if the average speed of the truck is 16 km/h less than the car.
   (a) 48 km/h   (b) 64 km/h
   (c) 16 km/h   (d) 24 km/h

7. If both the roots of the quadratic equation $ax^2 + bx + c = 0$ lie in the interval $(0, 3)$ then a lies in

(a) $(1, 3)$ (b) $(-1, -3)$
(c) $(-\sqrt{121}/91, -\sqrt{8})$ (d) None of these

8. If the common factor of $(ax^2 + bx + c)$ and $(bx^2 + ax + c)$ is $(x + 2)$ then
   (a) $a = b$, or $a + b + c = 0$
   (b) $a = c$, or $a + b + c = 0$
   (c) $a = b = c$
   (d) $b = c$, $a + b + c = 0$

9. If $P = 2^{2/3} + 2^{1/3}$ then which of the following is true?
   (a) $p^3 - 6p - 6 = 0$ (b) $p^3 - 6p + 6 = 0$
   (c) $p^3 + 6p - 6 = 0$ (d) $p^3 + 6p + 6 = 0$

10. If $f(x) = x^2 + 2x - 5$ and $g(x) = 5x + 30$, then the roots of the quadratic equation $g[f(x)]$ will be
    (a) $-1, -1$ (b) $2, -1$
    (c) $-1 + \sqrt{2}, -1 - \sqrt{2}$ (d) $1, 2$

11. If one root of the quadratic equation $ax^2 + bx + c = 0$ is three times the other, find the relationship between a, b and c.
    (a) $3b^2 = 16\, ac$ (b) $b^2 = 4ac$
    (c) $(a + c)^2 = 4b$ (d) $(a^2 + c^2)/ac = \dfrac{b}{2}$

12. If $x^2 - 3x + 2$ is a factor of $x^4 - ax^2 + b = 0$ then the values of a and b are
    (a) $-5, -4$ (b) $5, 4$
    (c) $-5, 4$ (d) $5, -4$

13. Value of the expression $(x^2 - x + 1)/(x - 1)$ cannot lie between
    (a) $1, 3$ (b) $-1, -3$
    (c) $1, -3$ (d) $-1, 2$

14. The value of p satisfying $\log_3 (p^2 + 4p + 12) = 2$ are
    (a) $1, -3$ (b) $-1, -3$
    (c) $-4, 2$ (d) $-4, -2$

15. If $q, r > 0$ then roots of the equation $x^2 + qx - r = 0$ are
    (a) Both negative   (b) Both positive
    (c) Of opposite sign but equal magnitude
    (d) Of opposite sign

16. If two quadratic equations $ax^2 + ax + 3 = 0$ and $x^2 + x + b = 0$ have a common root $x = 1$ then which of the following statements hold true?
    (a) $a + b = -3.5$ (b) $ab = 3$
    (c) $\dfrac{a}{b} = \dfrac{3}{4}$ (d) $a - b = -0.5$

    (a) A, B, C (b) B, C, D
    (c) A, C, D (d) A, B, D

17. If the expression $ax^2 + bx + c$ is equal to 4 when $x = 0$ leaves a remainder 4 when divided by $x + 1$ and a remainder 6 when divided by $x + 2$, then the values of a, b and c are respectively
    (a) 1, 1, 4   (b) 2, 2, 4
    (c) 3, 3, 4   (d) 4, 4, 4

18. If p and q are the roots of the equation $x^2 - px + q = 0$, then
    (a) $p = 1, q = -2$ (b) $p = 0, q = 1$
    (c) $p = -2, q = 0$ (d) $p = -2, q = 1$

19. Sum of the real roots of the equation $x^2 + 5|x| + 6 = 0$
    (a) Equals to 5   (b) Equals to 10
    (c) Equals to –5   (d) None of these

20. The value of p for which the sum of the square of the roots of $2x^2 - 2(p - 2)x - p - 1 = 0$ is least is
    (a) 1   (b) $\dfrac{3}{2}$
    (c) 2   (d) –1

21. For what values of p would the equation $x^2 + 2(p - 1)x + p + 5 = 0$ possess at least one positive root?
    (a) $P \in (-\infty, -5)$ (b) $P \in (-\infty, -1]$
    (c) $P \in (1, \infty)$ (d) $P \in (-5, 1)$

22. If $a, b \in \{1, 2, 3, 4\}$, then the number of the equations of the form $ax^2 + bx + 1 = 0$ having real roots is
    (a) 10   (b) 7
    (c) 6   (d) 12

23. If $a^2 + b^2 + c^2 = 1$, then which of the following cannot be a value of $(ab + bc + ca)$?
    (a) 0   (b) 1/2
    (c) $\dfrac{-1}{4}$ (d) –1

24. If one root of the equation $(I - m)x^2 + Ix + 1 = 0$ is double of the other and is real, find the greatest value of m.
    (a) $\dfrac{9}{8}$ (b) $\dfrac{8}{7}$
    (c) $\dfrac{8}{6}$ (d) $\dfrac{7}{5}$

25. The set of values of p for which the roots of the equation $3x^2 + 2x + p(p - 1) = 0$ are of opposite sign is
    (a) $(-\infty, 0)$ (b) $(0, 1)$
    (c) $(1, \infty)$ (d) $(0, \infty)$

26. One day each of Neha's friends consumed some cold drink and some orange squash. Though the quantities of cold drink and orange squash varied for the friends, the total consumption of the two liquids was exactly 9 litres for each friend. If Neha had one-ninth of the total cold drink consumed and one-eleventh of the total orange squash consumed. Find the ratio of the quantity of cold drink to that of orange squash consumed by Neha on that day?
    (a) 3 : 2   (b) 5:4
    (c) 2 : 1   (d) 1:1

27. $Q_1(x)$ and $Q_2(x)$ are quadratic functions such that $Q_1(10) = Q_2(8) = 0$. If the corresponding equations $Q_1(x) = 0$ and $Q_2(x) = 0$ have a common root and $Q_1(4) \times Q_2(5) = 36$, what is the value of the common root?
    (a) 10   (b) 6
    (c) Either 9 or 6   (d) Cannot be determined

28. For the above question if it is known that the coefficient of x^2 for $Q_1(x) = 0$ is 1/15 and that of $Q_2(x) = 0$ is 1, then which of the following options is a possible value of the sum of the roots of $Q_2(x) = 0$?
    (a) 18   (b) 36
    (c) 25   (d) 11

29. Which of the following could be a possible value of 'x' for which, each of the fractions is in its simplest form, where $[x]$ stands for the greatest integer less than or equal to 'x'?

    $$\frac{[x]+7}{10}, \frac{[x]+18}{11}, \frac{[x]+31}{12}, \frac{[x]+46}{13}, \ldots, \frac{[x]+1489}{39} \text{ and }$$
    $$\frac{[x]+1567}{40}$$

    (a) 95.71   (b) 93.71
    (c) 94.71   (d) 92.71

30. $x - y = 8$ and $P = 7x^2 - 12y^2$, where $x, y > 0$. What is the maximum possible value of P?
    (a) Infinite   (b) 352.8
    (c) 957.6   (d) 604.8

31. If the equations $5x + 9y + 17z = a$, $4x + 8y + 12z = b$ and $2x + 3y + 8z = c$ have at least one solution for x, y and z and a, b, and $c \neq 0$, then which of the following is true?
    (a) $4a - 3b - 3c = 0$ (b) $3a - 4b - 3c = 0$
    (c) $4a - 3b - 4c = 0$ (d) Nothing can be said

32. If the roots of the equation $x^3 - ax^2 + bx - 1080 = 0$ are in the ratio 2 : 4 : 5, find the value of the coefficient of x^2.
    (a) 33   (b) 66
    (c) –33   (d) 99

33. If the roots of the equation $px^3 - 20x^2 + 4x - 5 = 0$, where $m \neq 0$, are l, m and n, then what is the value of $\dfrac{1}{lm} + \dfrac{1}{mn} + \dfrac{1}{ln}$?
    (a) 5   (b) –4
    (c) 4   (d) 8

34. The cost of 10 pears, 8 grapes and 6 mangoes is ₹ 44. The cost of 5 pears, 4 grapes and 3 mangoes is ₹ 22. Find the cost of 4 mangoes and 3 grapes, if the cost of each of the items, in rupees, is a natural number and the cost of no two items is the same.

(a) ₹ 17   (b) ₹18

(c) ₹ 14   (d) Cannot be determined

35. The number of positive integral solutions to the system of equations $a_1 + a_2 + a_3 + a_4 + a_5 = 47$ and $a_1 + a_2 = 37$ is

(a) 2044   (b) 2246

(c) 2024   (d) 2376

36. If $f(x)$ is a quadratic polynomial, such that $f(5) = 75$ and $f(-5) = 55$, and $f(p) = f(q) = 0$, then find $p \times q$, given that the value of the constant term in the polynomial is 10.

(a) 2   (b) −3

(c) 5   (d) Cannot be determined

37. If $|a| + a + b = 75$ and $a + |b| - b = 150$, then what is the value of $|a| + |b|$?

(a) 105   (b) 60

(c) 90   (d) Cannot be determined

38. If $[x]$ represents the greatest integer less than or equal to x, then the value of $\left[315^{\frac{1}{3}}\right] + \left[316^{\frac{1}{3}}\right] + \left[317^{\frac{1}{3}}\right] + ... + \left[515^{\frac{1}{3}}\right]$ is

(a) 1383   (b) 1379

(c) 1183   (d) 1351

39. a, b, c, d and e are five consecutive integers $a < b < c < d < e$ and $a^2 + b^2 + c^2 = d^2 + e^2$. What is/are the possible value(s) of d?

(a) −2 and 10   (b) −1 and 11

(c) 0 and 12   (d) None of these

40. The 9 to 9 supermarket purchases x liters of fruit juice from the Fruit Garden Inc for a total price of $\$ 4x^2$ and sells the entire x liters at a total price of $\$ 10 \times (15 + 16x)$. Find the minimum amount of profit that the 9 to 9 supermarket makes in the process.

(a) 1700   (b) 1,000

(c) 1,750   (d) 1,300

Space for Rough Work

ANSWER KEY

Level of Difficulty (I)

1. (c)	2. (d)	3. (c)	4. (c)
5. (d)	6. (c)	7. (d)	8. (c)
9. (b)	10. (b)	11. (c)	12. (b)
13. (d)	14. (b)	15. (b)	16. (b)
17. (c)	18. (a)	19. (c)	20. (b)
21. (b)	22. (a)	23. (b)	24. (c)
25. (c)	26. (b)	27. (d)	28. (d)
29. (d)	30. (b)		

Level of Difficulty (II)

1. (c)	2. (b)	3. (d)	4. (d)
5. (c)	6. (a)	7. (d)	8. (a)
9. (a)	10. (a)	11. (a)	12. (b)
13. (d)	14. (b)	15. (d)	16. (a)
17. (a)	18. (c)	19. (d)	20. (b)
21. (b)	22. (b)	23. (d)	24. (a)
25. (b)	26. (a)	27. (d)	28. (a)
29. (c)	30. (d)	31. (c)	32. (c)
33. (c)	34. (b)	35. (d)	36. (c)
37. (a)	38. (a)	39. (d)	40. (c)

Solutions and Shortcuts

Level of Difficulty (I)

1. For the given expression to be a maximum, the denominator should be minimized. (Since, the function in the denominator has imaginary roots and is always positive). $x^2 + 5x + 10$ will be minimized at $x = -2.5$ and its minimum values at $x = -2.5$ is 3.75.

   Hence, required answer = 1/3.75 = 4/15.

2. Has no maximum.

3. The minimum value of $(p + 1/p)$ is at $p = 1$. The value is 2.

4. The product of the roots is given by: $(a^2 + 18a + 81)/1$.

   Since product is unity we get: $a^2 + 18a + 81 = 1$

   Thus, $a^2 + 18a + 80 = 0$

   Solving, we get: $a = -10$ and $a = -8$.

5. Solve through options. LHS = RHS for $a = 1$.

6. For a, b negative the given expression will always be positive since, a^2, b^2 and ab are all positive.

7. To solve this take any expression whose roots differ by 2.

   Thus, $(x - 3)(x - 5) = 0$
   $\Rightarrow$ $x^2 - 8x + 15 = 0$

   In this case, $a = 1$, $b = -8$ and $c = 15$.

   We can see that $b^2 = 4(c + 1)$.

8. $h(x) = 4x^2 + 13x + 10$.

   Sum of roots $- 13/4$.

9. $x^2 + bx + 12 = 0$ has 2 as a root.

   Thus, $b = -8$.

10. Solve this by assuming each option to be true and then check whether the given expression has equal roots for the option under check.

    Thus, if we check for option (b).

    $ad = bc$.

    We assume $a = 6$, $d = 4$ $b = 12$ $c = 2$ (any set of values that satisfies $ad = bc$).

    Then $(a^2 + b^2)x^2 - 2(ac + bc)x + (c^2 + d^2) = 0$
    $$180x^2 - 120x + 20 = 0.$$

    We can see that this has equal roots. Thus, option (b) is a possible answer. The same way if we check for a, c and d we see that none of them gives us equal roots and can be rejected.

11. $(c + 6) = 1/2 \times 2(2c - 1) \Rightarrow c + 6 = 2c - 1 \Rightarrow c = 7$

12. $-3/a = -6 \Rightarrow a = \frac{1}{2}$,

    $2b/a = -6$ and $a = \frac{1}{2}$

    Gives us $b = -1.5$.
    $\qquad a + b = -1$.

13. $1/\alpha + 1/\beta = (\alpha + \beta)/\alpha\beta$
    $= (7/5)/(1/5) = 7$.

14. $y = \sqrt{x + \sqrt{x + \sqrt{x + \cdots}}}$
    $\Rightarrow \qquad y = \sqrt{x + y}$
    $\Rightarrow \qquad y^2 = x + y$
    $y^2 - y - x = 0$

    Solving quadratically, we have option (b) as the root of this equation.

15. The approximate value of $a = \sqrt{13.92} = 3.6$ (approx).

    $a + 1/a = 3.6 + 1/3.6$ is closest to 4.

16. Solve by assuming values of a, b, and c in AP, GP and HP to check which satisfies the condition.

17. Assume any equation:

    Say $x^2 - 5x + 6 = 0$

    The roots are 2, 3.

    We are now looking for the equation, whose roots are:

    $(2 + 1/3) = 2.33$ and $(3 + 1/2) = 3.5$.

    Also $a = 1$, $b = -5$ and $c = 6$.

    Put these values in each option to see which gives 2.33 and 3.5 as its roots.

18. Remainder when $x^2 + ax + b$ is divided by $x - 1$ is got by putting $x = 1$ in the expression. Thus, we get.
    $$a + b + 1 = 5 \text{ and}$$
    $$b - a + 1 = 5$$
    $\Rightarrow \qquad b = 4$ and $a = 0$

19. $b^2 - 4 < 0 \Rightarrow -2 < b < 2$

20. $(\alpha^2 + \beta^2) = (\alpha + \beta)^2 - 2\alpha\beta$
    $$= (-1)^2 - 2 \times (-7) = 15.$$

21. $(\alpha^3 + \beta^3) = (\alpha + \beta)^3 - 3\alpha\beta(\alpha + \beta)$

$$= (-1)^3 - 3 \times (-7)(-1)$$
$$= -1 - 21 = -22$$

22. For the roots to be opposite in sign, the product should be negative.
$(c^2 - 4c)/2 < 0 \Rightarrow 0 < c < 4.$

23. The roots of the equation $x^2 - 9x + 20 = 0$ are 4 and 5. The expression would be negative for $4 < x < 5$.

24. The roots should be imaginary for the expression to be positive
i.e. $k^2 - 36 < 0$
thus $-6 < k < 6$ or $|k| < 6$.

25. Simplifying the equation $9^{a-2} 3^{a+4} = 81^{a-11}$ we will get: $3^{2a-4} \div 3^{a+4} = 3^{4a-44}$. This gives us:
$2a-4 - a - 4 = 4a-44 \rightarrow a-8 = 4a-44 \rightarrow 3a = 36$
$\rightarrow a = 12.$
Hence, we have to evaluate the value of $3^4 + 3^6 = 81 + 729 = 810$. Option (c) is correct.

26. In order to think of this situation, you need to think of the fact that "the cube of a number + a power of two" (LHS of the equation) should add up to the fourth power of the same number.
The only in which situation this happens is for $8 + 8 = 16$ where $a = 2$ giving us $2^3 + 2^3 = 2^4$.
Hence, Option (b) is the correct answer.

27. The values of x, where the above expression turns out to be negative or 0 are $x = 2, 3, 4, 5, 6, 7$ or 8. Hence, Option (d) is correct.

28. The value of the LHS would become $512 - 256 - 320 + 64 = 0$ when $x = 8$.

29. The above equation gets satisfied at $a = 9$, $b = 8$ and $c = 6$. (In order to visualise this, look for sets of 3 numbers with an LCM of 72). All different arrangements of $(9, 8, 6)$ will be possible values of (a, b, c). Possible arrangements of (a, b, c) are $(9, 8, 6)$, $(8, 9, 6)$, $(6, 8, 9)$, $(8, 6, 9)$, $(6, 9, 8)$, $(9, 6, 8)$. Thus, there are a total of 6 such sets possible. So option (d) is correct.

30. The equation can be rewritten as $s^{0.5} = \dfrac{pq}{r^2}$ or $s = \dfrac{(pq)^2}{r^4}$
The maximum value of s will happen when pq is maximum and r is minimum. pq is maximum when $p = -0.04$ and $q = -0.25$ and $r = 1$ similarly s will be minimum when $p = -0.03$ and $q = -0.09$ and $r = 7$.
$$s_{max} = \frac{(-0.04 \times -0.25)^2}{1} \quad s_{min} = \frac{(-0.03 \times -0.09)^2}{7^4}$$
$$s_{max} - s_{min} = \frac{(-0.04 \times -0.25)^2}{1} - \frac{(-0.03 \times -0.09)^2}{7^4}$$
$$\approx 0.0001$$

Level of Difficulty (II)

1. From (i) we have sum of roots = 14 and from (ii) we have product of roots = 48.
Option (c) is correct.

2. Assume the equation to be $(x - 1)(x - 2) = 0$ which gives $a_1 = 1$, $a_2 = -3$ and $a_3 = 2$ and $r_1 = 1$, $r_2 = 2$. With this information check the options.

3. $\dfrac{\alpha}{b} + \dfrac{\beta}{\alpha} < 2 \rightarrow \dfrac{\alpha^2 + \beta^2}{\alpha\beta} < 2$
$\rightarrow \dfrac{(\alpha + \beta)^2 - 2\alpha^2\beta^2}{\alpha\beta} < 2$
Use the formulae for sum of the roots and product of the roots.

4. Solve using options. It can be seen that at $b = 0$ and $c = 0$ the condition is satisfied. It is also satisfied at $b = 1$ and $c = -2$.

5. $2/9 + 9/2 = 85/18$.

6. Solve using options, If the car's speed is 48 kmph, the truck's speed would be 32 kmph. The car would take 4 hours and the bus 6 hours.

7. For each of the given options it can be seen that the roots do not lie in the given interval. Thus, option (d) is correct.

8. Using $x = -2$, we get $4a - 2b + c = 4b - 2a + c = 0$. Thus, $a = b$ and $a + b + c = 0$.

9. Use an approximation of the value of p to get the correct option. Such questions are generally not worth solving through mathematical approaches under the constraint of time in the examination.

10. $g(f(x)) = 5x^2 + 10x + 5$
Roots are -1 and -1.

11. Solve using options.
For option a, $3b^2 = 16ac$
We can assume $b = 4$, $a = 1$ and $c = 3$.
Then the equation $ax^2 + bx + c = 0$ becomes:
$x^2 + 4x + 3 = 0 \Rightarrow x = -3$ or $x = -1$
which satisfies the given conditions.

12. $x^2 - 3x + 2 = 0$ gives its roots as $x = 1, 2$.
Put these values in the equation and then use the options.

13. Trial and error gives us value as -1 at $x = 0$. If you try more values, you will see that you cannot get a value between -1 and 2 for this expression.

14. $p^2 + 4p + 12 = 9$
$\Rightarrow p^2 + 4p + 3 = 0$
$p = -3$ and -1.

15. The roots would be of opposite sign as the product of roots is negative.

16. Use the value of $x = 1$ in each of the two quadratic equations to get the value of a and b respectively. With these values check the options for their validity.

17. We get $c = 4$ (by putting $x = 0$)
Then, at $x = -1$, $a - b + 4 = 4$. So $a - b = 0$.
At $x = -2$, $4a - 2b + 4 = 6 \Rightarrow 4a - 2b = 2 \Rightarrow 2a = 2 \Rightarrow a = 1$, Thus, option (a) is correct.

18. Solve by checking each option for the condition given. Option c gives: $x^2 + 2x = 0$ whose roots are -2 and 0.

19. The following cases will arise

    Case 1: $x > 0$

    $x^2 + 5x + 6 = 0$

    On solving we get $x = -2, -3$ which is not possible as $x > 0$.

    Case 2: $x < 0$

    $x^2 - 5x + 6 = 0$

    On solving we get $x = 2, 3$ which is not possible as $x < 0$.

    So no real root is possible. Option (d) is correct.

20. We have to minimize : $R_1^2 + R_2^2$ or $(R_1 + R_2)^2 - 2 R_1 R_2$

    $\Rightarrow (p - 2)^2 - 2 \times (-(p + 1)/2) = p^2 - 4p + 4 + p + 1$

    $= p^2 - 3p + 5$.

    This is minimized at $p = 1.5$. or $3/2$.

21. Go through trial and error. At $p = 2$, both roots are negative. So, option (c) is rejected.

    At $p = 0$, roots are imaginary. So option (d) is rejected.

    At $p = -1$, we have both roots positive and equal.

    At $p > -1$, roots are imaginary Thus, option (b) is correct.

22. $b^2 - 4a \geq 0$ for real roots.

    If $b = 1$, no value possible for a.

    If $b = 2$, $a = 1$ is possible.

    If $b = 3$, a can be either 1 or 2 and if $b = 4$, a can be 1, 2, 3 or 4.

    Thus, we have 7 possibilities overall.

23. $(a + b + c)^2 = a^2 + b^2 + c^2 + 2 (ab + bc + ca)$

    $\Rightarrow 1 + 2(ab + bc + ca)$.

    Since, $(a + b + c)^2 = \geq 0 \Rightarrow ab + bc + ca \geq -1/2$

    Option (d) is not in this range and is hence not possible.

25. $p(p - 1)/3 < 0$ (Product of roots should be negative).

    $\Rightarrow p (p - 1) < 0$

    $p^2 - p < 0$.

    This happens for $0 < p < 1$.

    Option (b) is correct.

26. Let there be 'n' friends of Neha which would mean that the amount of total liquids consumed by the group would be $9n$. Further let the total amount (in litres) of cold drink consumed by Neha and her friends be 'x' liters. Then, the amount of orange squash consumed by the friends will be $9n-x$. As per the given information, we know that Neha has consumed one-ninth of the total cold drink (i.e. $x/9$) and also that she has consumed one-eleventh of the total orange squash $(9n-x)/11$. Also, since Neha has consumed a total of 9 liters of the liquids we will get:

    $\dfrac{x}{9} + \dfrac{(9n - x)}{11} = 9$

$\Rightarrow 11x + 81n - 9x = 891$

$\rightarrow 2x + 81n = 891 \rightarrow x = (891 - 81n) \div 2$.

In this equation, n is an integer and x should be less than $9n$. This gives rise to the inequality:

$0 < x < 9n \rightarrow 0 < (891-81n)/2 < 9n \rightarrow 0 < 891 - 81n < 18n$.

The only value of n that satisfies this inequality is at $n = 10$.

This means that there were 10 friends in the group and the amount of liquids consumed in total would have been 90 liters (9 liters each). Putting this value in the equation, we get: $2x + 810 = 891 \rightarrow x = 40.5$. This would mean that Neha consumes $40.5/9 = 4.5$ liters of cold drink and hence she would consume 4.5 liters of orange squash. The required ratio would be 1:1.

27. Let the common root be 'm'. Since we know that $Q_1(10) = 0$, it means that 10 would be one of the roots of Q_1. By the same logic it is given to us that 8 is one of the roots of Q_2. Using this information we have:

    $Q_1 = c_1 \times (x - 10) \times (x - m)$

    and $Q_2 = c_2 \times (x - 8) \times (x - m)$. Note: c_1 and c_2 are constants (each not equal to 0).

    The only information we have beyond this is that the product $Q_1 (4) \times Q_2 (5) = 36$. However, it is evident that by replacing $x = 4$ and $x = 5$ in the expressions for Q_1 and Q_2 respectively, we would not get any conclusive value for m since the value of m would depend on the values of c_1 and c_2. You can see this happening here:

    $c_1 \times -6 \times (4 - m) \times c_2 \times -3 \times (5 - m) = 36$

    $c_1 \times c_2 \times (20 - 9m + m^2) = 2$

    In this equation it can be clearly seen that the value of the common root 'm' would be dependent on the values of c_1 and c_2 and hence we cannot determine the answer to the question. Option (d) becomes the correct answer.

28. Since we got: $c_1 \times c_2 \times (20 - 9m + m^2) = 2$ as the equation in the previous solution, we can see that if we insert $c_1 = 1/15$ and $c_2 = 1$ in this equation we will get:

    $m^2 - 9m + 20 = 30 \rightarrow m^2 - 9m - 10 = 0 \rightarrow (m-10)(m+1) = 0 \rightarrow m = 10$ or $m = -1$. i.e., the common roots for the two equations could either be 10 or -1 giving rise to two cases for the quadratic equation $Q_2 = 0$:

    Case 1: When the common root is 10; Q_2 would become $\rightarrow (x - 8) (x - 10) = x_2 - 18x + 80$. The sum of roots for $Q_2(x) = 0$ in this case would be 18.

    Case 2: When the common root is -1; Q_2 would become $\rightarrow (x - 8) (x + 1) = x_2 - 7x - 8$. The sum of roots for $Q_1(x) = 0$ in this case would be 7.

Option (a) gives us a possible sum of roots as 18 and hence is the correct answer.

29. In order to solve this question, the first thing we need to do is to identify the pattern of the numbers in the expression. The series 7, 18, 31, 46 etc can be identified as 7, $7 + 11 \times 1$; $7 + 12 \times 2$; $7 + 13 \times 3$ and so on. Thus, the logic of the term when 39 is in the denominator is $7 + 39 \times 38 = 1489$ and the last term is $7 + 40 \times 39 = 1567$.

The series can be rewritten as:

$$\frac{[x]+7}{10}, 1+\frac{[x]+8}{11}, 2+\frac{[x]+7}{12}, 3+\frac{[x]+7}{13} \cdots 29+\frac{[x]+7}{39}$$

and $30 + \dfrac{[x]+7}{40}$

For each of these to be in their simplest forms, the value of $[x]$ should be such that $[x] + 7$ is co-prime to each of the 31 denominators (from 10 to 40). From amongst the options, Option (c) gives us a value such that $[x] + 7 = 101$ which is a prime number and would automatically be co-prime with the other values.

30. $x - y = 6$ $x = 6 + y$. Substituting this value of x in the expression for the value of P we get:

$P = 7(6 + y)^2 - 12y^2$

$P = 252 + 7y^2 + 84y - 12y^2 = 84y - 5y^2 + 252$

Differentiating P with respect to y and equating to zero we get:

$84 - 10y = 0 \rightarrow y = 8.4$

The maximum value of P would be got by inserting $y = 8.4$ in the expression. It gives us:

$84 \times 8.4 - 5 \times 8.4^2 + 252 = 705.6 - 5 \times 70.56 + 252 = 957.6 - 352.8 = 604.8$.

31. Only in the case of Option (c) do we get the LHS of the equation $4a - 3b - 4c = 0$ such that all the x, y and z cancel each other out. Hence, Option (c) is the sole correct answer.

32. The equation can be thought of as $(x - 2m)(x - 4m)(x - 5m) = 0$. The value of the constant term would be given by $(-2m) \times (-4m) \times (-5m)$ which would give us an outcome of $-40m^3$ which is equal to -320. Solving $-40m^3 = -1080 \rightarrow m = 3$. Hence, the roots of the equation being $2m$, $4m$ and $5m$ would be 6,12 and 15 respectively. Hence, the equation would become $(x - 6)(x - 12)(x - 15) = 0$. The coefficient of x^2 would be $(-15x^2 - 6x^2 - 12x^2) = -33x^2$. Hence, the value of '$a$' would be -33. Option (c) would be the correct answer.

33. The value of the expression $\dfrac{1}{lm} + \dfrac{1}{mn} + \dfrac{1}{ln} = lmn$

$(l + m + n)/l^2 m^2 n^2 = (l + m + n)/lmn$. For any cubic equation of the form $ax^3 + bx^2 + cx + d = 0$, the sum of the roots is given by $-b/a$; while the product of the roots is given by $-d/a$. The ratio $(l + m + n)/lmn = b/d = -20/-5 = 4$.

Option (c) is correct.

34. When you look at this question it seems that there are two equations with three unknowns. However a closer look of the second equation shows us that the second equation is the same as the first equation- i.e. $10p + 8g + 6m = 44$ and $5p + 4g + 3m = 22$ are nothing but one and the same equation. Hence you have only one equation with three unknowns. However, before you jump to the 'cannot be determined' answer consider this thought process.

The cost of 10 pears would be a multiple of 10 (since all costs are natural numbers). Similarly, the cost of 8 grapes would be a multiple of 8 while the cost of 6 mangoes would be a multiple of 6.

Thus, the first equation can be numerically thought of as follows :

By fixing the cost of 10 pears as a multiple of 10 and the cost of 8 grapes as a multiple of 8, we can see whether the cost of mangoes turns out to be a multiple of 6.

Total cost	Total cost of 10 pears	Total cost of 8 grapes	Total cost of 6 mangoes	
44	10	16	18	Possible
44	10	24	10	Not possible
44	10	32	2	Not possible
44	20	8	16	Not possible
44	20	24	0	Not possible
44	30	8	6	Not possible since both the cost of mangoes and grapes turns out to be Re 1 per unit. (They have to be distinct.)

Thus, there is only one possibility that fits into the situation. The cost per pear = Re 1. The cost per grape = ₹ 2 per unit and the cost per mango = ₹ 3 per unit. Hence, the total cost of 4 mangoes + 3 grapes = 12 + 6 = ₹ 18.

Option (b) is correct.

35. There are 36 ways of distributing the sum of 37 between a_1 and a_2 such that both a_1 and a_2 are positive and integral. (From 1,36; 2,35; 3,34; 4,33...; 36,1) Similarly, there are $^{12}C_2$ (= 66) ways of distributing the residual value of 10 amongst a_3, a_4 and a_5. Thus, there are a total of $36 \times 66 = 2376$ ways of distributing the values amongst the five variables such that each of them is positive and integral. Option (d) is the correct answer.

36. Let the polynomial be $f(x) = ax^2 + bx + 10$.

    The value of $f(5)$ in this case would be:

    $f(5) = 25a + 5b + 10 = 75$

    $f(-5) = 25a - 5b + 10 = 45$

    $f(5) - f(-5) = 10b = 30 \rightarrow b = 3$. The polynomial expression is: $ax^2 + 3x + 10$.

    Further, if we put the value of $b = 3$ in the equation for $f(5)$ we would get: $25a + 15 + 10 = 75 \rightarrow 25a = 50 \rightarrow a = 2$.

    Since $f(p)$ and $f(q)$ are both equal to zero it means that p and q are the roots of the equation $2x^2 + 3x + 10 = 0$. Finding $p \times q$ would mean that we have to find the sum of the roots of the equation. The sum of the roots would be equal to $10/2 = 5$. Option (c) is the correct answer.

37. The various possibilities for the values of a and b (in terms of their being positive or negative) would be as follows:

    Possibility 1: a positive and b positive;

    Possibility 2: a positive and b negative;

    Possibility 3: a negative and b positive;

    Possibility 4: a negative and b negative.

    Let us look at each of these possibilities one by one and check out which one of them is possible.

    Possibility 1: If a and b are both positive the second equation becomes $a = 150$ (since the value of $|b| - b$ would be equal to zero if b is positive). However, this value of 'a' does not fit the first equation since the value of the LHS would easily exceed 75 if we use $a = 150$ in the first equation. Hence, the possibility of both a and b being positive is not feasible and can be rejected.

    Through similar thinking the possibilities 3 and 4 are also rejected. Consider this:

    For possibility 3: a negative and b positive the second equation would give us $a = 150$ which contradicts the presupposition that a is negative. Hence, this possibility can be eliminated.

    For possibility 4: a negative and b negative- the first equation would give us $b = 75$ (since the value of $|a| - a$ would be equal to zero if a is negative) which contradicts the presupposition that b is negative. Hence, this possibility can be eliminated.

    The only possibility that remains is Possibility 2: a positive and b negative. In this case, the equations would transform as follows:

    $|a| + a + b = 75$ would become $2a + b = 75$;

    $a + |b| - b = 150$ would become $a - 2b = 150$.

    Solving the two equations simultaneously we will get the value of $a = 60$ and $b = -45$.

    The sum of $|a| + |b| = 60 + 45 = 105$

    Option (a) is the correct answer.

38. The value of the expression would be dependent on the individual values of each of the terms in the expression. $[315^{1/3}]$ would give us a value of 6 and so would all the terms upto $[342^{1/3}]$. (as $6^3 = 216$ and $7^3 = 343$) Hence, the value of the expression from $[315^{1/3}] + [316^{1/3}] + ... + [342^{1/3}] = 28 \times 6 = 168$

    Similarly, the value of the expression from $[343^{1/3}] + [344^{1/3}] + ... + [511^{1/3}] = 169 \times 7 = 1183$.

    Also, the value of the expression from $[512^{1/3}] + [513^{1/3}] + ... + [515^{1/3}] = 4 \times 8 = 32$.

    Thus, the answer $= 168 + 1183 + 32 = 1383$. Option (a) is correct.

39. The five consecutive integers can be represented by: $(c - 2)$; $(c - 1)$; c; $(c + 1)$ and $(c + 2)$.

    Then we have $a^2 + b^2 + c^2 = d^2 + e^2$ giving us:

    $(c - 2)^2 + (c - 1)^2 + c^2 = (c + 1)^2 + (c + 2)^2 \rightarrow$

    $3c^2 - 6c + 5 = 2c^2 + 6c + 5 \rightarrow$

    $c^2 - 12c = 0 \rightarrow$

    $c = 0$ or $c = 12$.

    Hence, the possible values of $d = c + 1$ would be 1 or 13.

    Option (d) is correct.

40. The profit of the 9 to 9 supermarket would be:

    Total Sales Price – Total cost price

    $= 10 \times (15 + 16x) - 4x^2$

    $= -4x^2 + 160x + 150$

    The minimum value of this function can be traced by differentiating it with respect to x and equating to 0. We get:

    $-8x + 160 = 0 \rightarrow x = 20$. The minimum value of Profit would occur at $x = 20$.

    The minimum profit would be $= -4 \times 20^2 + 160 \times 20 + 150 = -1600 + 3200 + 150 = 1750$.

    Option (c) is the correct answer.

16 Chapter

Logarithms

INTRODUCTION

Questions based on this chapter are not so frequent in management entrance exams. In exams, most problems that have used the concept of logs have been of an applied nature. However, the aspirants should know the basic concepts of logarithms to ensure there are no surprises in the paper.

While studying this chapter the student should pay particular attention to the basic rules of logarithms as well as develop an understanding of the range of the values of logs.

THEORY

Let a be a positive real number, $a \neq 1$ and $a^x = m$. Then x is called the logarithm of m to the base a and is written as $\log_a m$, and conversely, if $\log_a m = x$, then $a^x = m$.

Note: Logarithm to a negative base is not defined.

Also, logarithm of a negative number is not defined. Hence, in the above logarithmic equation, $\log_a m = x$, and we can say that $m > 0$ and $a > 0$.

Thus $a^x = m \Rightarrow x = \log_a m$ and $\log_a m = x \Rightarrow a^x = m$

In short, $a^x = m \Rightarrow x = \log_a m$.

$x = \log_a m$ is called the logarithmic form and $a^x = m$ is called the exponential form of the equation connecting a, x and m.

Two Properties of Logarithms

1. $\log_a 1 = 0$ for all $a > 0$, $a \neq 1$
   That is, log 1 to any base is zero
   Let $\log_a 1 = x$. Then by definition, $a^x = 1$.
   But $a^0 = 1$ ∴ $a^x = a^0 \Leftrightarrow x = 0$.
   Hence $\log_a 1 = 0$ for all $a > 0$, $a \neq 1$

2. $\log_a a = 1$ for all $a > 0$, $a \neq 1$
   That is, log of a number to the same base is 1
   Let $\log_a a = x$. Then by definition, $a^x = a$.
   But $a^1 = a$ ∴ $a^x = a^1 \Rightarrow x = 1$.
   Hence $\log_a a = 1$ for all $a > 0$, $a \neq 1$.

Laws of Logarithms

First Law: $\log_a (mn) = \log_a m + \log_a n$
           That is, log of product = sum of logs

Second Law: $\log_a (m/n) = \log_a m - \log_a n$
           That is, log of quotient
           = difference of logs

Note: The first theorem converts a problem of multiplication into a problem of addition and the second theorem converts a problem of division into a problem of subtraction, which are far easier to perform than multiplication or division. That is why logarithms are so useful in all numerical calculations.

Third Law: $\log_a m^n = n \log_a m$

Generalisation

1. $\log (mnp) = \log m + \log n + \log p$
2. $\log (a_1 a_2 a_3 \dots a_k) = \log a_1 + \log a_2 + \dots + \log a_k$

Note: *Common logarithms*: We shall assume that the base $a = 10$ whenever it is not indicated. Therefore, we shall denote $\log_{10} m$ by $\log m$ only. The logarithm calculated to base 10 are called common logarithms.

The Characteristic and Mantissa of a Logarithm

The logarithm of a number consists of two parts: the

integral part and the *decimal* part. The integral part is known as the *characteristic* and the decimal part is called the *mantissa*.

For example,

In log 3257 = 3.5128, the integral part is 3 and the decimal part is .5128; therefore, characteristic = 3 and mantissa = .5128.

It should be remembered that the mantissa is always written as positive.

Rule: To make the mantissa positive (in case the value of the logarithm of a number is negative), subtract 1 from the integral part and add 1 to the decimal part.

Thus, $\quad -3.4328 = -(3 + .4328) = -3 - 0.4328$
$$= (-3 - 1) + (1 - 0.4328)$$
$$= -4 + .5672.$$

so the mantissa is = .5672.

Note: The characteristic may be positive or negative. When the characteristic is negative, it is represented by putting a bar on the number.

Thus instead of −4, we write $\overline{4}$.

Hence we may write −4 + .5672 as $\overline{4}$.5672.

Base Change Rule

Till now all rules and theorems you have studied in Logarithms have been related to operations on logs with the same basis. However, there are a lot of situations in Logarithm problems where you have to operate on logs having different basis. The base change rule is used in such situations.

This rule states that

(i) $\log_a (b) = \log_c (b)/\log_c (a)$

It is one of the most important rules for solving logarithms.

Space for Notes

(ii) $\log_b (a) = \log_c (a)/\log_b (c)$

A corollary of this rule is

(iii) $\log_a (b) = 1/\log_b (a)$

(iv) log c to the base a^b is equal to $\dfrac{\log a^c}{b}$.

Results on Logarithmic Inequalities

(a) If $a > 1$ and $\log_a x_1 > \log_a x_2$ then $x_1 > x_2$

(b) If $a < 1$ and $\log_a x_1 > \log_a x_2$ then $x_1 < x_2$

Applied conclusions for logarithms

1. The characteristic of common logarithms of any positive number less than 1 is negative.

2. The characteristic of common logarithm of any number greater than 1 is positive.

3. If the logarithm to any base a gives the characteristic n, then we can say that the number of integers possible is given by $a^{n+1} - a^n$.

Example: $\log_{10} x = 2.bcde...$, then the number of integral values that x can take is given by: $10^{2+1} - 10^2 = 900$. This can be physically verified as follows. Log to the base 10 gives a characteristic of 2 for all 3 digit numbers with the lowest being 100 and the highest being 999. Hence, there are 900 integral values possible for x.

4. If $-n$ is the characteristic of $\log_{10} y$, then the number of zeros between the decimal and the first significant number after the decimal is $n - 1$.

Thus if the log of a number has a characteristic of −3 then the first two decimal places after the decimal point will be zeros.

Thus, the value will be $-3.00ab...$

◎ WORKED-OUT PROBLEMS

Problem 16.1 Find the value of x in $3^{|3x-4|} = 9^{2x-2}$

    (a) 8/7   (b) 7/8

    (c) 7/4   (d) 16/7

Solution Take the log of both sides, then we get,

$$|3x-4|\log 3 = (2x-2)\log 9$$
$$= (2x-2)\log 3^2$$
$$= (4x-4)\log 3$$

Dividing both sides by log 3, we get

$$|3x-4| = (4x-4) \tag{1}$$

Now, $|3x-4| = 3x-4$ if $x > 4/3$

so if $x > 4/3$

$$3x-4 = 4x-4$$

or $3x = 4x$

or $3 = 4$

But this is not possible.

Let's take the case of $x < 4/3$

Then $|3x-4| = 4-3x$

Therefore, $4-3x = 4x-4$ from   (1)

or $7x = 8$

or $x = 8/7$

Problem 16.2 Solve for x.

$$\log_{10}x - \log_{10}\sqrt{x} = 2\log_x 10$$

Solution Now, $\log_{10}\sqrt{x} = \dfrac{1}{2} \times \log_{10}x$

Therefore, the equation becomes

$$\log_{10}x - \frac{1}{2}\log_{10}x = 2\log_x 10$$

or $\dfrac{1}{2}\log_{10}x = 2\log_x 10 \tag{2}$

Using base change rule $(\log_b a = 1/\log_a b)$

Therefore, equation (2) becomes

$$\frac{1}{2}\log_{10}x = 2/\log_{10}x$$

$\Rightarrow$ $(\log_{10}x)^2 = 4$

or $\log_{10}x = 2$

Therefore, $x = 100$

Space for Rough Work

Problem 16.3 If $7^{x+1} - 7^{x-1} = 48$, find x.

Solution Take 7^{x-1} as the common term. The equation then reduces to

$$7^{x-1}(7^2 - 1) = 48$$

or $7^{x-1} = 1$

or $x-1 = 0$ or $x = 1$

Problem 16.4 Calculate: $\log_2(2/3) + \log_4(9/4)$

$$= \log_2(2/3) + (\log_2(9/4)/\log_2 4)$$
$$= \log_2(2/3) + 1/2\log_2(9/4)$$
$$= \log_2(2/3) + 1/2(2\log_2 3/2)$$
$$= \log_2 2/3 + \log_2 3/2 = \log_2 1 = 0$$

Problem 16.5 Find the value of the expression

$$1/\log_3 2 + 2/\log_9 4 - 3/\log_{27} 8$$

Passing to base 2

we get

$$\log_2 3 + 2\log_2 9 - 3\log_2 27$$

$$= \log_2 3 + \frac{4\log_2 3}{2} - \frac{9\log_2 3}{3}$$

$$= 3\log_2 3 - 3\log_2 3$$

$$= 0$$

Problem 16.6 Solve the inequality.

(a) $\log_2(x+3) < 2$

$\Rightarrow$ $2^2 > x+3$

$\Rightarrow$ $4 > x+3$

             $1 > x$

or $x < 1$

But log of negative number is not possible.

Therefore, $x+3 \geq 0$

That is, $x \geq -3$

Therefore, $-3 \leq x < 1$

(b) $\log_2(x^2 - 5x + 5) > 0$

$$= x^2 - 5x + 5 > 1$$
$$\rightarrow x^2 - 5x + 4 > 0$$
$$\rightarrow (x-4)(x-1) > 0$$

Therefore, the value of x will lie outside 1 and 4.

That is, $x > 4$ or $x < 1$.

Space for Rough Work

LEVEL OF DIFFICULTY (I)

1. log 32700 = ?
   (a) log 3.27 + 4
   (b) log 3.27 + 2
   (c) 2 log 327
   (d) 100 × log 327

2. log . 0867 = ?
   (a) log 8.67 + 2
   (b) log 8.67 − 2
   (c) $\dfrac{\log 867}{1000}$
   (d) −2 log 8.67

3. If $\log_{10} 2 = .301$ find $\log_{10} 125$.
   (a) 2.097
   (b) 2.301
   (c) 2.10
   (d) 2.087

4. $\log_{32} 8 = ?$
   (a) 2/5
   (b) 5/3
   (c) 3/5
   (d) 4/5

Find the value of x in equations 5–6.

5. $\log_{0.5} x = 25$
   (a) 2^{-25}
   (b) 2^{25}
   (c) 2^{-24}
   (d) 2^{24}

6. $\log_3 x = \dfrac{1}{2}$
   (a) 3
   (b) $\sqrt{3}$
   (c) $\dfrac{3}{2}$
   (d) $\dfrac{2}{3}$

7. $\log_{15} 3375 \times \log_4 1024 = ?$
   (a) 16
   (b) 18
   (c) 12
   (d) 15

8. $\log_a 4 + \log_a 16 + \log_a 64 + \log_a 256 = 10$. Then $a = $?
   (a) 4
   (b) 2
   (c) 8
   (d) 5

9. $\log_{625} \sqrt{5} = ?$
   (a) 4
   (b) 8
   (c) 1/8
   (d) 1/4

10. If log x + log (x + 3) = 1 then the value(s) of x will be, the solution of the equation
    (a) x + x + 3 = 1
    (b) x + x + 3 = 10
    (c) x (x + 3) = 10
    (d) x (x + 3) = 1

11. If $\log_{10} a = b$, find the value of 10^{3b} in terms of a.
    (a) a^3
    (b) 3a
    (c) a × 1000
    (d) a × 100

12. 3 log 5 + 2 log 4 − log 2 = ?
    (a) 4
    (b) 3
    (c) 200
    (d) 1000

Solve equations 13–25 for the value of x.

13. log (3x − 2) = 1
    (a) 3
    (b) 2
    (c) 4
    (d) 6

14. log (2x − 3) = 2
    (a) 103
    (b) 51.5
    (c) 25.75
    (d) 26

15. log (12 − x) = −1
    (a) 11.6
    (b) 12.1
    (c) 11
    (d) 11.9

16. $\log (x^2 − 6x + 6) = 0$
    (a) 5
    (b) 1
    (c) Both (a) and (b)
    (d) 3 and 2

17. $\log 2^x = 3$
    (a) 9.87
    (b) 3 log 2
    (c) 3/log 2
    (d) 9.31

18. $3^x = 7$
    (a) $1/\log_7 3$
    (b) $\log_7 3$
    (c) $1/\log_3 7$
    (d) $\log_3 7$

19. $5^x = 10$
    (a) log 5
    (b) log 10/log 2
    (c) log 2
    (d) 1/log 5

20. Find x, if $0.01^x = 2$
    (a) log 2/2
    (b) 2/log 2
    (c) −2/log 2
    (d) − log 2/2

21. Find x if log x = log 7.2 − log 2.4
    (a) 1
    (b) 2
    (c) 3
    (d) 4

22. Find x if log x = log 1.5 + log 12
    (a) 12
    (b) 8
    (c) 18
    (d) 15

23. Find x if log x = 2 log 5 + 3 log 2
    (a) 50
    (b) 100
    (c) 150
    (d) 200

24. log (x − 13) + 3 log 2 = log (3x + 1)
    (a) 20
    (b) 21
    (c) 22
    (d) 24

25. log (2x − 2) − log (11.66 − x) = 1 + log 3
    (a) 452/32
    (b) 350/32
    (c) 11
    (d) 11.33

Space for Rough Work

LEVEL OF DIFFICULTY (II)

1. Express $\log \dfrac{\sqrt[3]{a^2}}{b^5\sqrt{c}}$ or $\dfrac{a^{2/3}}{b^5\sqrt{c}}$ in terms of $\log a$, $\log b$ and $\log c$.

   (a) $\dfrac{3}{2}\log a + 5\log b - 2\log c$

   (b) $\dfrac{2}{3}\log a - 5\log b - \dfrac{1}{2}\log c$

   (c) $\dfrac{2}{3}\log a - 5\log b + \dfrac{1}{2}\log c$

   (d) $\dfrac{3}{2}\log a + 5\log b - \dfrac{1}{2}\log c$

2. If $\log 3 = .4771$, find $\log(.81)^2 \times \log\left(\dfrac{27}{10}\right)^{\frac{2}{3}} \div \log 9$.

   (a) 2.689   (b) -0.0552
   (c) 2.2402   (d) 2.702

3. If $\log 2 = .301$, $\log 3 = .477$, find the number of digits in $(108)^{10}$.

   (a) 21   (b) 27
   (c) 20   (d) 18

4. If $\log 2 = .301$, find the number of digits in $(125)^{25}$.

   (a) 53   (b) 50
   (c) 25   (d) 63

5. Which of the following options represents the value of $\log \sqrt{128}$ to the base .625?

   (a) $\dfrac{2+\log_8 2}{\log_8 5 - 1}$ (b) $\dfrac{\log_8 128}{2\log_8 0.625}$

   (c) $\dfrac{2+\log_8 2}{2(\log_8 5 - 1)}$ (d) Both (b) and (c)

6-8. Solve for x:

   $\log \dfrac{75}{35} + 2\log \dfrac{7}{5} - \log \dfrac{105}{x} - \log \dfrac{13}{25} = 0$.

   (a) 90   (b) 65
   (c) 13   (d) 45

7. $2\log \dfrac{4}{3} - \log \dfrac{x}{10} + \log \dfrac{63}{160} = 0$

   (a) 7   (b) 14
   (c) 9   (d) 3

8. $\log \dfrac{12}{13} - \log \dfrac{7}{25} + \log \dfrac{91}{3} = x$

   (a) 0   (b) 1
   (c) 2   (d) 3

Questions 9 to 11: Which one of the following is true

9. (a) $\log_{17}275 = \log_{19}375$ (b) $\log_{17}275 < \log_{19}375$
   (c) $\log_{17}275 > \log_{19}375$ (d) Cannot be determined

10. (a) $\log_{11}1650 > \log_{13}1950$
    (b) $\log_{11}1650 < \log_{13}1950$
    (c) $\log_{11}1650 = \log_{13}1950$
    (d) None of these

11. (a) $\dfrac{\log_2 4096}{3} = \log_8 4096$

    (b) $\dfrac{\log_2 4096}{3} < \log_8 4096$

    (c) $\dfrac{\log_2 4096}{3} > \log_8 4096$

    (d) Cannot be determined

12. $\log \dfrac{16}{15} + 5\log \dfrac{25}{24} + 3\log \dfrac{81}{80} = \log x$, $x = ?$

    (a) 2   (b) 3
    (c) 0   (d) None of these

If $\log 2 = .3030$ and $\log 3 = .4771$ then find the number of digits in the following.

13. 60^{12}

    (a) 25   (b) 22
    (c) 23   (d) 24

14. 72^9

    (a) 17   (b) 20
    (c) 18   (d) 15

15. 27^{25}

    (a) 38   (b) 37
    (c) 36   (d) 35

Questions 16 to 18: Find the value of the logarithmic expression in the questions below.

16. $\dfrac{\log\sqrt{27} + \log 8 - \log\sqrt{1000}}{\log 1.2}$

    where, $\log_{10}2 = 0.30103$, $\log_{10}3 = 0.4771213$

    (a) 1.77   (b) 1.37
    (c) 2.33   (d) 1.49

17. $\dfrac{1}{\log_{xy}(xyz)} + \dfrac{1}{\log_{yz}(xyz)} + \dfrac{1}{\log_{zx}(xyz)} =$

    (a) 1   (b) 2
    (c) 3   (d) 4

18. $\log a^n/b^n + \log b^n/c^n + \log c^n/a^n$

    (a) 1   (b) n
    (c) 0   (d) 2

19. $\log_{10} x - \log_{10} \sqrt{x} = 2 \log_x 10$ then $x = ?$
    (a) 50
    (b) 100
    (c) 150
    (d) 200

20. $\left(\dfrac{21}{10}\right)^x = 2.$ Then $x = ?$

    (a) $\dfrac{\log 2}{\log 3 + \log 7 - 1}$
    (b) $\dfrac{\log 2}{\log 3 + \log 7 + 1}$

    (c) $\dfrac{\log 3}{\log 2 + \log 7 - 1}$
    (d) $\dfrac{\log 2}{\log 3 - \log 7 + 1}$

21. $\log(x^3 + 5) = 3 \log(x + 2)$ then $x = ?$

    (a) $\dfrac{-2 + \sqrt{2}}{2}$
    (b) $\dfrac{-2 - \sqrt{2}}{2}$

    (c) Both (a) and (b)
    (d) None of these

22. $(a^4 - 2a^2 b^2 + b^4)^{x-1} = (a - b)^{-2} (a + b)^{-2}$ then $x = ?$
    (a) 1
    (b) 0
    (c) None of these
    (d) 2

23. If $\log_{10} 242 = a$, $\log_{10} 80 = b$ and $\log_{10} 45 = c$, express $\log_{10} 36$ in terms of a, b and c.

    (a) $\dfrac{(c-1)(3c+b-4)}{2}$
    (b) $\dfrac{(c-1)(3c+b-4)}{3}$

    (c) $\dfrac{(c-1)(3c-b-4)}{2}$
    (d) None of these

24. For the above problem, express $\log_{10} 66$ in terms of a, b and c.

    (a) $\dfrac{(c-1)(3c+b-4)}{8}$
    (b) $\dfrac{3(a+c)+(2b+-5)}{6}$

    (c) $\dfrac{3(a+c)+(2b-5)}{6}$
    (d) $\dfrac{3(c-1)(3c+b-4)}{6}$

25. $\log_2 (9 - 2^x) = 10^{\log (3-x)}.$ Solve for x.
    (a) 0
    (b) 3
    (c) Both (a) and (b)
    (d) 0 and 6

Space for Rough Work

ANSWER KEY

Level of Difficulty (I)

1. (a)	2. (b)	3. (a)	4. (c)
5. (a)	6. (b)	7. (d)	8. (a)
9. (c)	10. (c)	11. (a)	12. (b)
13. (c)	14. (b)	15. (d)	16. (c)
17. (c)	18. (a)	19. (d)	20. (d)
21. (c)	22. (c)	23. (d)	24. (b)
25. (c)			

Level of Difficulty (II)

1. (b)	2. (b)	3. (a)	4. (a)
5. (d)	6. (c)	7. (a)	8. (c)
9. (b)	10. (a)	11. (a)	12. (d)
13. (b)	14. (a)	15. (c)	16. (d)
17. (b)	18. (c)	19. (b)	20. (a)
21. (d)	22. (b)	23. (d)	24. (c)
25. (a)			

Solutions and Shortcuts

Level of Difficulty (I)

1. Log 32700 = log 3.27 + log 10000 = log 3.27 + 4
2. Log 0.0867 = log (8.67/100) = log 8.67 – log 100
   Log 8.67 – 2
3. $\log_{10} 125 = \log_{10}(1000/8) = \log.1000 - 3\log2$
   $= 3 - 3 \times 0.301 = 2.097$
4. $\log_{32} 8 = \log 8/\log 32$ (By base change rule)
   $= 3 \log2/5\log2 = 3/5$.
5. $\log_{0.5} x = 25 \Rightarrow x = 0.5^{25} = (\frac{1}{2})^{25} = 2^{-25}$
6. $x = 3^{1/2} = \sqrt{3}$.
7. $\log_{15}3375 \times \log_4 1024$
   $= 3 \log_{15} 15 \times 5 \log_4 4 = 3 \times 5 = 15$.
8. The given expression is:
   $\log_a (4 \times 16 \times 64 \times 256) = 10$
   i.e. $\log_a 4^{10} = 10$
   Thus, $a = 4$.
9. $1/2 \log_{625} 5 = [1/(2 \times 4)] \log_5 5 = 1/8$.
10. $\log x (x + 3) = 1 \Rightarrow 10^1 = x^2 + 3x$.
    or $x(x + 3) = 10$.
11. $\log_{10} a = b \Rightarrow 10^b = a \Rightarrow$ By definition of logs.
    Thus $10^{3b} = (10^b)^3 = a^3$.
12. $3 \log 5 + 2 \log 4 - \log 2$
    $= \log 125 + \log 16 - \log 2$
    $= \log (125 \times 16)/2 = \log 1000 = 3$.
13. $10^1 = 3x - 2 \Rightarrow x = 4$.
14. $10^2 = 2x - 3 \Rightarrow x = 51.5$
15. $1/10 = 12 - x \Rightarrow x = 11.9$
16. $x^2 - 6x + 6 = 10^\circ \Rightarrow x^2 - 6x + 6 = 1$
    $\Rightarrow x^2 - 6x + 5 = 0$
    Solving gives us $x = 5$ and 1.

17. $x \log 2 = 3$
    $\log 2 = 3/x$.
    Therefore, $x = 3/\log 2$
18. $3^x = 7 \Rightarrow \log_3 7 = x$
    Hence $x = 1/\log_7 3$
19. $x = \log_5 10 = 1/\log_{10} 5 = 1/\log 5$.
20. $x = \log_{0.01} 2 = -\log 2/2$.
21. $\log x = \log (7.2/2.4) = \log 3 \Rightarrow x = 3$
22. $\log x = \log 18 \Rightarrow x = 18$
23. $\log x = \log 25 + \log 8 = \log (25 \times 8) = \log 200$.
24. $\log (x - 13) + \log 8 = \log [3x + 1]$
    $\Rightarrow \log (8x - 104) = \log (3x + 1)$
    $\Rightarrow 8x - 104 = 3x + 1$
    $5x = 105 \Rightarrow x = 21$
25. $\log (2x - 2)/(11.66 - x) = \log 30$
    $\Rightarrow (2x - 2)/(11.66 - x) = 30$
    $2x - 2 = 350 - 30x$
    Hence, $32x = 352 \Rightarrow x = 11$.

Level of Difficulty (II)

1. $2/3 \log a - 5 \log b - 1/2 \log c$.
2. $2 \text{Log} (81/100) \times 2/3 \log (27/10) \div \log 9$
   $= 2 [\log3^4 - \log 100] \times 2/3 [(\log 3^3 - \log10)] \div 2 \log 3$
   $= 2 [\log3^4 - \log 100] \times 2/3 [(3\log 3 - 1)] \div 2 \log 3$
   Substitute $\log 3 = 0.4771 \Rightarrow - 0.0552$.
3. Let the number be y.
   $$y = 108^{10}$$
   $\Rightarrow \log y = 10 \log 108$
   $\text{Log } y = 10 \log (27 \times 4)$
   $\text{Log } y = 10 [3\log3 + 2 \log 2]$
   $\text{Log } y = 10 [1.43 + 0.602]$
   Hence $\log y = 10[2.03] = 20.3$
   Thus, y has 21 digits.
4. $\log y = 25 \log 125$
   $= 25 [\log 1000 - 3 \log 2] = 25 \times (2.097)$
   $= 52 +$
   Hence 53 digits.
5. $0.5 \log_{0.625} 128$
   $= 0.5 [\log_8 128/\log_8 0.625]$
   $= 1/2 [\log_8 128/\log_8 0.625]$
   $\dfrac{\text{Log}_8 128}{2(\log_8 5 - \log_8 8)} = \dfrac{\text{Log}_8 128}{2[\log_8 5 - 1]} = \dfrac{2 + \log_8 2}{2(\log_8 5 - 1)}$
6. $(75/35) \times (49/25) \times (x/105) \times (25/13) = 1$
   $\Rightarrow x = 13$
7. $(16/9) \times (10/x) \times (63/160) = 1$
   $\Rightarrow x = 7$
8. Solve in similar fashion.

9. $\text{Log}_{17}275 < \log_{19}375$

Because the value of $\text{Log}_{17}275$ is less than 2 while $\log_{19}375$ is greater then 2.

10. $\log_{11}1650 > 3$

$\text{Log}_{13}1950 < 3$

Hence, $\log_{11}1650 > \log_{13}1950$

11. $\dfrac{\log_2 4096}{3} = \log_8 4096$

12. $x = (16/15) \times (25^5/24^5) \times (81^3/80^3)$

None of these is correct.

13 – 15.

Solve similarly as 3 and 4.

18. $\log (a^n b^n c^n / a^n b^n c^n) = \log 1 = 0$

19. $(1/2) \log x = 2\log_x 10$

$\Rightarrow \quad \log x = 4 \log_x 10$

$\Rightarrow \quad \log x = 4/\log_{10} x \ (\log x)^2 = 4$

So $\log x = 2$ and $x = 100$.

20. $\log x = \log_{(21/10)} 2$

$= \dfrac{\text{Log} 2}{\text{Log} 21 - \log 10} = \dfrac{\text{Log} 2}{[\text{Log} 3 + \log 7 - 1]}$

21. $6x^2 + 12x + 3 = 0 \quad \text{or} \quad 2x^2 + 4x + 1 = 0$

Solving we get none of these.

25. For $x = 0$, we have LHS

$\text{Log}_2 8 = 3$.

RHS: $10^{\log 3} = 3$.

We do not get LHS = RHS for either $x = 3$ or $x = 6$.

Thus, option (a) is correct.

Space for Rough Work

TRAINING GROUND FOR BLOCK V

🎧 HOW TO THINK IN PROBLEMS ON BLOCK V

1. Let $x_1, x_2, \ldots, x_{100}$ be positive integers such that $x_1 + x_{1-1} + 1 = k$ for all !, where k is a constant. If $x_{10} = 1$, then the value of x_1 is

    (a) k (b) $k-2$

    (c) $k+1$ (d) 1

Solution: Using the information in the expression which defines the function, we realise that if we use x_{10} as $x_!$, the expression gives us:

$x_{10} + x_9 + 1 = k \rightarrow x_9 = k-2$; Further, using the value of x_9 to get the value of x_8 as follows:

$x_9 + x_8 + 1 = k \rightarrow k - 2 + x_8 + 1 = k \rightarrow x_8 = 1$;

Next: $x_8 + x_7 + 1 = k \rightarrow x_7 = k - 2$.

In this fashion, we can clearly see that x_6 would again be 1 and x_5 be $k-2$; $x_4 = 1$ and $x_3 = k-2$; $x_2 = 1$ and $x_1 = k-2$. Option (b) is correct.

2. If $a_0 = 1$, $a_1 = 1$ and $a_n = a_{n-2} a_{n-1} + 3$ for $n > 1$, which of the following options would be true?

    (a) a_{450} is odd and a_{451} is even

    (b) a_{450} is odd and a_{451} is odd

    (c) a_{450} is even and a_{451} is even

    (d) a_{450} is even and a_{451} is odd

Solution: In order to solve this question, you need to think about how the initial values of a_x would behave in terms of being even and odd.

The value of $a_2 = 1 \times 1 + 3 = 4$ (This is necessarily even since we have the construct as follows: Odd × Odd + Odd = Odd + Odd = Even.)

The value of $a_3 = 1 \times 4 + 3 = 7$ (This is necessarily odd since we have the construct as follows: Odd × Even + Odd = Even + Odd = Odd.)

The value of $a_4 = 4 \times 7 + 3 = 31$ (This is necessarily odd since we have the construct as follows: Odd × Even + Odd = Even + Odd = Odd.)

The value of $a_5 = 7 \times 31 + 3 = 220$ (This is necessarily even since we have the construct as follows: Odd × Odd + Odd = Odd + Odd = Even.)

The next two in the series values viz: a_6 and a_7 would be odd again since they would take the construct of Odd × Even + Odd = Even + Odd = Odd. Also, once, a_6 and a_7 turn out to be odd, it is clear that a_8 would be even and a_9 a_{10} would be odd again. Thus, we can understand that the terms a_2, a_5, a_8, a_{11}, a_{14} are even while all other terms in the series are odd. Thus, the even terms occur when we take a term whose number answers the description of a_{3n+2}. If you look at the options, all the four options in this question are asking about the value of a_{450} and a_{451}. Since, neither of these terms is in the series of a_{3n+2}, we can say that both of these are necessarily odd and hence, Option (b) would be the correct answer.

3. If $\dfrac{a+b}{b+c} = \dfrac{c+d}{d+a}$, then

    (a) $a = c$

    (b) either $a = c$ or $a + b + c + d = 0$

    (c) $a + b + c + d = 0$

    (d) $a = c$ and $b = d$

Solution: Such problems should be solved using values and also by doing a brief logical analysis of the algebraic equation. In this case, it is clear that if $a = c = k$ (say), the LHS of the expression would become equal to the RHS of the expression (and both would be equal to 1). Once we realise that the expression is satisfied for LHS = RHS, we have to choose between Options a, b and d. However, a closer look at Option (d) shows us that since it says $a = c$ and $b = d$ it is telling us that both of these (i.e., $a = c$ as well as $b = d$) get satisfied and we have already seen that even if only $a = c$ is true, the expression gets satisfied. Thus, there is no need to have $b = d$ as simultaneously true with $a = c$ as true. Based on this logic we can reject Option (d). To check for Option (b) we need to see whether $a + b + c + d = 0$ would necessarily be satisfied if the expression is true. In order to check this, we can take a set of values for a, b, c and d such that their sum is equal to 0 and check whether the equation is satisfied. Taking, a, b, c and d as 1, 2, 3 and –6 respectively we get the LHS of the expression as $3/(-1) = -3$; the RHS of the expression would be $(-3)/(-5) = 3/5$ which is not equal to the LHS. Thus, we can understand that $a + b + c + d = 0$ would not necessarily satisfy the equation. Hence, Option (a) is the correct answer.

4. If a, b, c and d satisfy the equations

$a + 7b + 3c + 5d = 0$

$8a + 4b + 6c + 2d = -32$

$2a + 6b + 4c + 8d = 32$

$5a + 3b + 7c + d = -32$

Then $(a + d)(b + c)$ equals

    (a) 64   (b) –64

    (c) 0   (d) None of the above

Solution: Adding each of the four equations in the expression we get: $16(a + d) + 20(b + c) = -32$.

Also, by adding the second and the third equations we get: $a + b + c + d = 0$, which means that $(a + d) = -(b + c)$.

Then from: $16(a + d) + 20(b + c) = -32$, we have: $-16(b + c) + 20(b + c) = -32 \rightarrow 4(b + c) = -32$. Hence, $(b + c) = -8$ and $(a + d) = 8$. Hence, the multiplication of $(a + d)(b + c) = -64$

5. For any real number x, the function $I(x)$ denotes the integer part of x – i.e., the largest integer less than or equal to x. At the same time the function $D(x)$

denotes the fractional part of x. For arbitrary real numbers x, y and z, only one of the following statements is correct. Which one is it?

(a) $I(x + y) = I(x) + I(y)$

(b) $I(x + y + z) = I(x + y) + I(z) = I(x) + I(y + z) = I(x + z) + I(y)$

(c) $I(x + y + z) = I(x + y) + I(z + D(y + x))$

(d) $D(x + y + z) = y + z - I(y + z) + D(x)$

Solution: There are three principle themes you need to understand in order to answer such questions.

1. **Thinking in language**. The above question is garnished with a plethora of mathematical symbols. Unless you are able to convert each of the situations given in the options into clear logical language, your mind cannot make sense of what is written in the options. The best mathematical brains work this way. Absolutely nobody has the mathematical vision to solve such problems by simply reading the notations in the problem and/or the options.

2. While thinking in language terms in the case of a question such as this, in order to understand and grasp the mathematical situation confronting us, the best thing to do is to put values into the situation. This is very critical in such problems because as you can yourself see – if you are thinking about say $I(x + y + z)$ and you keep the same notation to think through the problem, you would need to carry $I(x + y + z)$ throughout the thinking inside the problem. On the other hand if you replace the $I(x + y + z)$ situation by replacing values for x, y and z, the expression would change to a single number. Thus, if you take $I(4.3 + 2.8 + 5.3) = I(12.4) = 12$. Obviously thinking further in the next steps with 12, as the handle, would be much easier than trying to think with $I(x + y + z)$.

3. Since the question here is asking us to identify the correct option which always gives us LHS = RHS, we can proceed further in the problem using the options given to us. While doing this, when you are testing an option, the approach has to be to try to think of values for the variables such that the option is rejected, i.e., we need to think of values such that LHS ≠ RHS. In this fashion, the idea is to eliminate 3 options and identify the one option that cannot be eliminated because it cannot be disproved.

Keeping these principles in mind, if we try to look at the options in this problem we have to look for the one correct statement.

Let us check Option (a) to begin with:

The LHS can be interpreted as: $I(x + y)$ means the integer part of $x + y$. Suppose we use x as 4.3 and y as 4.2 we would get $I(x + y) = I(4.3 + 4.2) = I(8.5) = 8$

The RHS in this case would be $I(4.3) + I(4.2) = 4 + 4 = 8$. This gives us LHS = RHS.

However, if you use $x = 4.3$ and $y = 4.8$ you would see that LHS = $I(4.3 + 4.8) = I(9.1) = 9$, while the RHS would

be $I(4.3) + I(4.8) = 4 + 4 = 8$. This would clearly gives us LHS ≠ RHS and hence this option is incorrect.

The point to note here is that whenever you are solving a function based question through the rejection of the options route, the vision about what kind of numbers would reject the case becomes critical. My advise to you is that as you start solving questions through this route, you would need to improve your vision of what values to assume while rejecting an option. This is one key skill that differentiates the minds and the capacities of the top people from the average aspirants. Hence, if you want to compete against the best you should develop this numerical vision. To illustrate what I mean by numerical vision, think of a situation where you are faced with the expression $(a + b) > (a \times b)$. Normally this does not happen, except when you are multiplying with numbers between 0 and 1.)

Moving on with our problem. Let us look at Option (b).

$I(x + y + z) = I(x + y) + I(z) = I(x) + I(y + z) = I(x + z) + I(y)$]

In order to reject this option, the following values would be used:

$x = 4.3$, $y = 5.1$, and $z = 6.7$

LHS = $I(4.3 + 5.1 + 6.7) = I(16.1) = 16$

When we try to see whether the first expression on the RHS satisfies this we can clearly see it does not because:

$I(x + y) + I(z)$ would give us $I(4.3 + 5.1) + I(6.7) = I(9.4) + I(6.7) = 9 + 6 = 15$ in this case.

Thus, $I(x + y + z) = I(x + y) + I(z)$ is disproved and this option can be rejected at this point.

We thus move onto Option (c), which states:

$I(x + y + z) = I(x + y) + I(z + D(y + x))$

Let us try this in the case of the values we previous took, i.e., $x = 4.3$, $y = 5.1$, and $z = 6.7$

We get:

$I(4.3 + 5.1 + 6.7) = I(4.3 + 5.1) + I(6.7 + D(4.3 + 5.1))$

$\rightarrow I(16.1) = I(9.4) + I(6.7 + D(9.4))$

$\rightarrow I(16.1) = I(9.4) + I(6.7 + 0.4)$

$\rightarrow I(16.1) = I(9.4) + I(7.1)$

$\rightarrow 16 = 9 + 7.$

Suppose we try 4.3, 4.9 and 5.9 we get:

$I(4.3 + 4.9 + 5.9) = I(4.3 + 4.9) + I(5.9 + D(4.3 + 4.9))$

$\rightarrow I(15.1) = I(9.2) + I(5.9 + D(9.2))$

$\rightarrow I(15.1) = I(9.4) + I(5.9 + 0.2)$

$\rightarrow I(15.1) = I(9.4) + I(6.1)$

$\rightarrow 15 = 9 + 6.$

We can see that this option is proving to be difficult to shake off as a possible answer. However, this logic is not enough to select this as the correct answer. In order to make sure that you never err when you solve a question this way, you would need to either do one of two things at this point in the problem solving approach.

Approach 1: Try to understand and explain to yourself the mathematical reason as to why this option should be correct.

Approach 2: Try to eliminate the remaining option/s at this point of time.

Amongst these, my recommendation would be to go for Approach 2 because that is likely to be easier than Approach 1. Approach 1 is only to be used in case you have seen and understood during your checking of the option as to why the particular option is always guaranteed to be true. In case, you have not seen the mathematical logic for the same during your checking of the option, you typically should not try to search for the logic while trying to solve the problem. The quicker way to the correct answer would be to eliminate the remaining option/s.

(Of course, once you are done with solving the question, during your review of the question, you should ideally try to explain to yourself as to why one particular option worked – because that might become critical mathematical logic inside your mind for the next time you face a similar mathematical situation.)

In this case, let us try to do both. To freeze Option (c) as the correct answer, you would need to look at Option (d) and try to reject it.

Option (d) says:

$D(x + y + z) = y + z - I(y + z) + D(x)$

Say we take $x = 4.3$, $y = 5.1$, and $z = 6.7$ we can see that:

$D(4.3 + 5.1 + 6.7) = 4.3 + 5.1 - I(4.3 + 5.1) + D(4.3) \rightarrow$

$D(16.1) = 9.4 - I(9.4) + D(4.3) \rightarrow$

$0.1 = 9.4 - 9 + 0.3 \rightarrow$

$0.1 = 0.7$, which is clearly incorrect.

Hence, Option (c) is the correct answer.

If we were to look at the mathematical logic for Option (c) (for our future reference) we can think of why Option (c) would always be true as follows:

One of the problems in these greatest integer problems is what can be described as the loss of value due to the greatest integer function.

Thus $I(4.3 + 4.8) > I(4.3) + I(4.8)$ since the LHS is 9 and the RHS is only 8. What happens here is that the LHS gains by 1 unit because the .3 and the .8 in the two numbers add up to 1.1 and help the sum of the two numbers to cross 9. On the other hand if you were to look at the RHS in this situation, you would realise that the decimal values of 4.3 and 4.8 are individually both lost.

In this context, when you look at the LHS of the equation given in Option (c), you see that the value of the LHS would retain the integer values of x, y and z while the sum of the decimal values of x, y and z would get aggregated and combined into 1 number. This gives us three cases:

Case 1: When the addition of the decimal values of x, y and z is less than 1;

Case 2: When the addition of the decimal values of x, y and z is more than 1 but less than 2;

Case 3: When the addition of the decimal values of x, y and z is more than 2 but less than 3.

Each of these three cases would be further having a two way fork – viz:

Case A: When the addition of the decimal values of x and y add up to less than 1;

Case B: When the addition of the decimal values of x and y add up to more than 1 but less than 2.

I would encourage the reader to take this case from this point and move it to a point where you can explore each of these cases six situations and see that for all these situations, the value of the LHS of the expression is equal to the value of the RHS of the equation.

6. During the reign of the great government in the country of Riposta, the government forms committees of ministers whenever it is faced with a problem. One particular year, there are x ministers in the government and they are organised into 4 committees such that:
   (i) Each minister belongs to exactly two committees.
   (ii) Each pair of committees has exactly one minister in common.
   Then
   (a) $x = 4$
   (b) $x = 6$
   (c) $x = 8$
   (d) x cannot be determined from the given information

Solution: In order to think about this situation, you need to think of the number of unique people you would need in order to make up the committees as defined in the problem. However, before you start to do this, a problem you need to solve is—how many members do you put in each committee?

Given the options for x, when we look at the options, it is clear that the number is unlikely to be larger than 4. Hence, suppose we try to think of committees with 4 members, we will get the following thought process:

First, we create the first two committees with exactly 1 member common between the two committees. We would get the following table at this point of time:

Committee 1	Committee 2	Committee 3	Committee 4
1	4		
2	5		
3	6		
4	7		

Here we have taken the individual members of the committees as 1, 2, 3, 4, 5, 6 and 7. We have obeyed the second rule for committee formation (i.e. each pair of committees has exactly one member in common) by taking only the member 4 as the common member.

From this point in the table, we need to try to fill in the remaining committees obeying the twin rules given in the problem.

So, each member should belong to exactly two committees and each pair of committees should have only 1 member in common.

When we try to do that in this table we reach the following point.

Committee 1	Committee 2	Committee 3	Committee 4
1	4	7	
2	5	1	
3	6	8	
4	7	9	

Here we have taken 7 common between the Committees 2 and 3, while 1 is common between Committees 1 and 3. This point freezes the individuals 1, 4 and 7 as they have been used twice (as required). However, this leaves us with 2, 3, 5, 6, 8 and 9 to be used once more and only Committee 4 left to fill in into the table. This is obviously impossible to do and hence, we are sure that each committee would not have had 4 members.

Obviously, if 4 members are too many, we cannot move to trying 5 members per committee. Thus, we should move trying to form committees with 3 members each.

When we do so, the following thought process unfolds:

We first fill in the first two committees by keeping exactly one person common between these committees. By taking the person '3' as a common member between Committees 1 and 2, we reach the following table:

Committee 1	Committee 2	Committee 3	Committee 4
1	3		
2	4		
3	5		

We now need to fill in Committee 3 with exactly 1 member from Committee 1 and exactly 1 member from Committee 2. Also, we cannot use the member number '3' as he has already been used twice. Thus, by repeating '5' from Committee 2 and '1' from Committee 1 we can reach the following table.

Committee 1	Committee 2	Committee 3	Committee 4
1	3	5	
2	4	1	
3	5		

Since the remaining person in Committee 3 would have to be unique from members of Committees 1 and 2, we would need to introduce a new member (say 6) in order to complete Committee 3. Thus, our table evolves to the following situation.

Committee 1	Committee 2	Committee 3	Committee 4
1	3	5	
2	4	1	
3	5	6	

At this point, the members 2, 4 and 6 have not been used a second time. Also, the committee 4 has to have its 3 members filled such that it has exactly 1 member common with committees 1, 2 and 3 respectively.

This is easily achieved using the following structure.

Committee 1	Committee 2	Committee 3	Committee 4
1	3	5	2
2	4	1	4
3	5	6	6

Hence, we can clearly see that the value of x is 6, i.e., the government had 6 ministers.

7. During the IPL Season 14, the Mumbai Indians captained by a certain Sachin Tendulkar who emerged out of retirement, played 60 games in the season. The team never lost three games consecutively and never won five games consecutively in that season. If N is the number of games the team won in that season, then N satisfies
   (a) $24 \le N \le 48$ (b) $20 \le N \le 48$
   (c) $12 \le N \le 48$ (d) $20 \le N \le 42$

Solution: In order to solve this question, we need to see the limit of the minimum and maximum number of matches that the team could have won. Let us first think about the maximum number of matches the team could have won. Since the team 'never won five games consecutively' that season, we would get the value for the maximum number of wins by trying to make the team win 4 games consecutively—as many times as we can. This can be thought of as follows:

WWWWLWWWWLWWWWL... and so on.

From the above sequence, we can clearly see that with 4 wins consecutively, we are forming a block of 5 matches in which the team has won 4 and lost 1. Since, there are a total of 60 matches in all, there would be 12 such blocks of 5 matches each. The total number of wins in this case would amount to $12 \times 4 = 48$ (this is the highest number possible).

This eliminates Option 4 as the possible answer.

If we think about the minimum number of wins, we would need to maximise the number of losses. In order to do so, we get the following thought process:

Since the team never lost three games consecutively, for the maximum number of losses the pattern followed would be—

LLWLLWLLWLLW... and so on

Thus, there are two losses and 1 win in every block of 3 matches. Since, there would be a total of 20 such blocks, it would mean that there would be a total of $20 \times 1 = 20$ wins. This number would represent the minimum possible number of wins for the team.

Thus, N has to be between 20 and 48. Thus, Option (b) is correct.

8. If the roots of the equation $x^3 - ax^2 + bx - c = 0$ are three consecutive integers, then what is the smallest possible value of b?
   (a) $-1/\sqrt{3}$ (b) -1
   (c) 0 (d) 1
   (e) $1/\sqrt{3}$

Solution: Since the question represents a cubic expression, and we want the smallest possible value of b—keeping the constraint of their roots being three consecutive values—a little bit of guesstimation would lead you to think of –1, 0 and 1 as the three roots for minimising the value of b.

Thus, the expression would be $(x + 1)(x)(x - 1) = (x^2 + x)$ $(x - 1) = x^3 - x$. This gives us the value of b as –1.

It can be seen that changing the values of the roots from –1, 0 and 1 would result in increasing the coefficient of x– which is not what we want. Hence, the correct answer should be that the minimum value of b would be –1.

Note: that for trial purposes if you were to take the values of the three roots as 0, 1, and 2, the expressions would become $x(x - 1)(x - 2) = (x^2 - x)(x - 2)$ which would lead to the coefficient of x being 2. This would obviously increase the value of the coefficient of x above –1.

You could also go for changing the three consecutive integral roots in the other direction to –2, –1 and 0. In such a case the expression would become: $x(x + 2)(x + 1) = (x2 + 2x)(x + 1) \rightarrow$ which would again give us the coefficient of x as + 2.

The total solving time for this question would be 30 seconds if you were to hit on the right logic for taking the roots as –1, 0 and 1. In case you had to check for the value of b in different situations by altering the values of the roots (as explained above) the time would still be under 2 minutes.

9. A shop stores x kg of rice. The first customer buys half this amount plus half a kg of rice. The second customer buys half the remaining amount plus half a kg of rice. Then the third customer buys half the remaining amount plus half a kg of rice. Thereafter, no rice is left in the shop. Which of the following best describes the value of x?
   (a) $2 \leq x \leq 6$ (b) $5 \leq x \leq 8$
   (c) $9 \leq x \leq 12$ (d) $11 \leq x \leq 14$
   (e) $13 \leq x \leq 18$

Solution: This question is based on odd numbers as only with an odd value of x would you keep getting integers if you halved the value of rice and took out another half a kg from the shop store.

From the options, let us start from the second option. (**Note**: In such questions, one should make it a rule to start from one of the middle options only as the normal realisation we would get from checking one option would have been that more than one option gets removed if we have not picked up the correct option—as we would normally know whether the correct answer needs to be increased from the value we just checked or should be decreased.)

Thus trying for $x = 7$ according to the second option, you would get

$7 \rightarrow 3 \rightarrow 1 \rightarrow 0$ (after three customers).

This means that $5 \leq x \leq 8$ is a valid option for this question. Also, since the question is definitive about the correct range,

there cannot be two ranges. Hence, we can conclude that Option 2 is correct.

Note: The total solving time for this question should not be more than 30 seconds. Even if you are not such an experienced solver through options, and you had to check 2–3 options in order to reach the correct option, you would still need a maximum of 90 seconds.

Directions for Questions 10 and 11: Let $f(x) = ax^2 + bx + c$, where a, b and c are certain constants and $a \neq 0$. it is known that $f(5) = -3 f(2)$ and that 3 is a root of $f(x) = 0$.

10. What is the other root of $f(x) = 0$?
    (a) –7   (b) –4
    (c) 2   (d) 6
    (e) Can not be determined

11. What is the value of $a + b + c$?
    (a) 9   (b) 14
    (c) 13   (d) 37
    (e) Can not be determined

Solution: Since, 3 is a root of the equation, we have $9a + 3b + c = 0$ (**Theory point**—A root of any equation $f(x) = 0$ has the property that if it is used to replace 'x' in every part of the equation, then the equation $f(x) = 0$ should be satisfied.)

Also $f(5) = -3f(2)$ gives us that $25a + 5b + c = -3(4a + 2b + c) \rightarrow 37a + 11b + 4c = 0$

Combining both equations we can see that $37a + 11b + 4c = 4(9a + 3b + c) \rightarrow a - b = 0$. i.e., $a = b$

Now, we know that the sum of roots of a quadratic equation is given by $-b/a$. Hence, the sum of roots has to be equal to –1. Since one of the roots is 3, the other must be –4.

The answer to Question 10 would be Option (2).

For Question 11 we need the sum of $a + b + c$. We know that $a + b = 0$. Also, product of roots is –12. One of the possible equations could be $(x - 3)(x + 4) = 0 \rightarrow x^2 + x - 12 = 0$, which gives us the value of $a + b + c$ as –10. However, –10 is not in the options. This should make us realise that there is a possibility of another equation as: $(2x - 6)(2x + 8) = 0 \rightarrow 4x^2 + 4x - 48 = 0$ in which case the value of $a + b + c$ changes. Hence, the correct answer is 'cannot be determined'.

12. Suppose, the seed of any positive integer n is defined as follows:

    Seed(n) = n, if $n < 10$

              = seed$(s(n))$, otherwise,

    Where $s(n)$ indicates the sum of digits of n. For example, Seed(7) = 7, seed (248) = seed(2 + 4 + 8) = seed (14) = seed (1 + 4) = seed (5) = 5 etc. How many positive integers n, such that $n < 500$, will have seed $(n) = 9$?
    (a) 39   (b) 72
    (c) 81   (d) 108
    (e) 55

Solution: The first number to have a seed of 9 would be the number 9 itself.

The next number whose seed would be 9 would be 18, then 27 and you should recognise that we are talking about numbers which are multiples of 9. Hence, the number of such numbers would be the number of numbers in the Arithmetic Progression:

9, 18, 27, 36, 45, ...495 = [(495 – 9)/9] + 1 = 55 such numbers.

13. Find the sum of $\sqrt{1+\dfrac{1}{1^2}+\dfrac{1}{2^2}}+\sqrt{1+\dfrac{1}{2^2}+\dfrac{1}{3^2}}+\dots$

$\qquad +\sqrt{1+\dfrac{1}{2007^2}+\dfrac{1}{2008^2}}$

(a) $2008-\dfrac{1}{2008}$ (b) $2007-\dfrac{1}{2007}$

(c) $2007-\dfrac{1}{2008}$ (d) $2008-\dfrac{1}{2007}$

(e) $2008-\dfrac{1}{2009}$

Solution: Such questions are again solved through logical processes. If you were to try this problem by going through mathematical processes you would end up with a messy solution which is not going to yield any answer in any reasonable time frame.

Instead, look at the following process.

The first thing you should notice is that the value in the answer has got something to do with the number 2008. Suppose we were to look at only the first term of the expression, by analogy the value of the sum should have something to do with the number 2. Accordingly by looking at the value obtained we can decide on which of the options fits the given answer.

So, for the first term, we see that the value is equal to the square root of 2.25 = 1.5

By analogy that in this case the value of 2008 is 2, the value of 2007 would be 1 and 2009 would be 3. Replacing these values the options become:

(a) $2-\dfrac{1}{2}$ (b) $1-\dfrac{1}{1}$

(c) $1-\dfrac{1}{2}$ (d) $2-\dfrac{1}{1}$

(e) $2-\dfrac{1}{3}$

It can be easily verified that only Option 1 gives a value of 1.5. Hence, that is the only possible answer as all other values are different. In case you need greater confirmation and surety, you can solve this for the first two terms too.

14. A function $f(x)$ satisfies $f(1) = 3600$, and $f(1) + f(2) +...+ f(n) = n^2 f(n)$, for all positive integers $n > 1$. What is the value of $f(9)$?

(a) 80   (b) 240
(c) 200   (d) 100
(e) 120

Solution: This question is based on chain functions where the value of the function at a particular point depends on the previous values.

$f(1) + f(2) = 4 f(2) \to f(1) = 3 f(2) \to f(2) = 1200$

Similarly, for $f(3)$ we have the following expression:

$f(1) + f(2) + f(3) = 9 f(3) \to f(3) = 4800/8 = 600$

Further $f(1) + f(2) + f(3) = 15 f(4) \to f(4) = 5400/15 = 360$

Further $f(1) + f(2) + f(3) + f(4) = 24 f(5) \to 5760/24 = f(5) = 240$

If you were to pause a while at this point and try to look at the pattern of the numerical outcomes in the series we are getting we get:

3600, 1200, 600, 360, 240, 1200/7

A little bit of perceptive analysis about the fractions used as multipliers to convert $f(1)$ to $f(2)$ and $f(2)$ to $f(3)$ and so on will tell us that the respective multipliers themselves are following a pattern viz:

$f(1) \times 1/3 = f(2)$;

$f(2) \times 2/4 = f(3)$;

$f(3) \times 3/5 = f(4)$ and $f(4) \times 4/6 = f(5)$

Using this logic string we can move onto the next values as follows:

$f(6) = 240 \times 5/7 = 1200/7$;

$f(7) = 1200/7 \times 6/8 = 900/7$;

$f(8) = 900/7 \times 7/9 = 100$ and

$f(9) = 100 \times 8/10 = 80$.

Thus, Option (a) is the correct answer.

Directions for Questions 15 and 16: Let S be the set of all pairs (i, j) where $1 \le i \le j < n$, and $n \ge 4$. Any two distinct members of S are called "friends" if they have one constituent of the pairs in common and "enemies" otherwise. For example, if $n = 4$, then $S = \{(1, 2), (1, 3), (1, 4), (2, 3), (2, 4), (3, 4)\}$. Here, $(1, 2)$ and $(1, 3)$ are friends, $(1, 2)$ and $(2, 3)$ are also friends, but $(1, 4)$ and $(2, 3)$ are enemies.

15. For general n, how many enemies will each member of S have?

(a) $n-3$ (b) $(n^2 - 3n - 2)/2$

(c) $2n - 7$ (d) $(n^2 - 5n + 6)/2$

(e) $(n^2 - 7n + 14)/2$

Solution: Solve by putting values: Suppose we have $n = 5$; The members would be $\{(1,2), (1,3), (1,4), (1,5), (2,3), (2,4), (2,5), (3,4), (3,5), (4,5)\}$

In this case any member can be found to have 3 enemies.

Thus the answer to the above question should give us a value of 3 with $n = 5$.

Option (a): $n-3 = 5-3 = 2$. Hence, cannot be the answer.

Option (b): $8/2 = 4$. Hence, cannot be the answer.

Option (c): $10 - 7 = 3$. To be considered.

Option (d): $6/2 = 3$. To be considered.

Option (e): $4/2 = 2$. Hence, cannot be the answer.

We still need to choose one answer between Options (c) and (d).

It can be seen that for $n = 6$, the values of Options (c) and (d) will differ. Hence, we need to visualise how many enemies each member would have for $n = 6$.

The members would be $\{(1,2), (1,3), (1,4), (1,5), (1,6), (2,3),(2,4), (2,5), (2,6), (3,4), (3,5), (3,6), (4,5), (4,6), (5,6)\}$. It can be clearly seen that the member $(1,2)$ will have 6 enemies. Option (c) gives us a value of 5 and hence can be eliminated while Option (d) gives us a value of 6 leaving it as the only possible answer.

16. For general n, consider any two members of S that are friends. How many other members of S will be common friends of both these members?

(a) $(n^2 - 5n + 8)/2$ (b) $2n - 6$

(c) $n(n-3)/2$ (d) $n - 2$

(e) $(n^2 - 7n + 16)/2$

Solution: Again for this question consider the following situation where $n = 6$.

The members would be $\{(1,2), (1,3), (1,4), (1,5), (1,6), (2,3),(2,4), (2,5), (2,6), (3,4), (3,5), (3,6), (4,5), (4,6), (5,6)\}$.

Suppose we consider the pair $(1,2)$ and $(1,3)$. Their common friends would be $(1,4)$, $(1,5)$, $(1,6)$ and $(2,3)$.

Thus there are 4 common friends for any pair of friendly members. (You can verify this by taking any other pair of friend members.)

Thus for $n = 6$, the answer should be 4.

Checking the options it is clear that only option 4 gives us a value of 4.

Maximum Solving time: 60 – 90 seconds

17. In a tournament, there are n teams $T_1, T_2, ..., T_n$, with $n > 5$. Each team consists of k players, $k > 3$. The following pairs of teams have one players in common:

T_1 & T_2, T_2 & T_3, ..., T_{n-1} & T_n, and T_n & T_1.

No other pair of teams has any player in common. How many players are participating in the tournament, considering all the h teams together?

(a) $n(k - 2)$ (b) $k(n - 2)$

(b) $(n - 1)(k - 1)$ (d) $n(k - 1)$

(e) $k(n - 1)$

Thought process:

If we take 6 teams and 4 players per team, we would get 4 players in T_1 (each one of them unique), 3 more players in T_2 (since 1 player of T_2 would be shared with T_1), 3 more players in T_3 (since 1 player of T_3 would be shared with T_2), 3 more players in T_4 (since 1 player of T_4 would be shared with T_3), 3 more players in T_5 (since 1 player of T_5 would be shared with T_4) and 2 more players in T_6 (since 1 player of T_6 would be shared with T_5 and one with T_1). Hence, there would be a total of 18 $(4 + 3 + 3 + 3 + 3 + 2)$ players with $n = 6$ and $k = 4$. Checking from the options we see that only Option (d) gives us 18 as the solution.

Maximum solution time: 60 seconds.

18. Consider four digit numbers for which the first two digits are equal and the last two digits are also equal. How many such numbers are perfect squares?

(a) 4   (b) 0

(b) 1   (d) 3

(e) 2

Thought process:

A lot of CAT takers got stuck on this question for over 5–7 minutes in the exam, since they tried to find out the squares of all two digit numbers starting from 32. However, if you are aware of the logic of finding squares of two digit numbers, you would realise that only three two-digit numbers after 32 have the last two digits in their squares equal (38, 62 and 88). Hence, you do not need to check any other number apart from these three. Checking these you would get the square of 88 as 7744. And hence, there is only one such number.

19. A confused bank teller transposed the rupees and paise when he cashed a cheque for Shailaja, giving her rupees instead of paise and paise instead of rupees. After buying a toffee for 50 paise, Shailaja noticed that she was left with exactly three times as much as the amount on the cheque. Which of the following is a valid statement about the cheque amount?

(a) Over Rupees 22 but less than Rupees 23

(b) Over Rupees 18 but less than Rupees 19

(c) Over Rupees 4 but less than Rupees 5

(d) Over Rupees 13 but less than Rupees 14

(e) Over Rupees 7 but less than Rupees 8

Thought Process:

Deduction 1: Question Interpretation: The solution language for this question requires you to think about what possible amount could be such that when its rupees and paise value are interchanged, the resultant value is 50 paise more than thrice the original amount.

Dedcution 2: Option checking process:

Armed with this logic, suppose we were to check for Option (a) i.e., the value is above ₹ 22 but below ₹ 23. This essentially means that the amount must be approximately between ₹ 22.66 and ₹ 22.69. (We get the paise amount to be between 66 and 69 based on the fact that the relationship between the Actual Amount, x and the transposed amount y is: $y - 50$ paise $= 3x$.

Hence, values below 22.66 and values above 22.70 are not possible.

→ From this point onwards we just have to check whether this relationship is satisfied by any of the values between ₹ 22.66 and ₹ 22.69.

→ Also, realise the fact that in each of these cases the paise value in the value of the transposed amount y would be 22. Thus, $3x$ should give us the paise value as 72 (since we have to subtract 50 paise from the value of 'y' in order to get the value of $3x$).

→ This also means that the unit digit of the paise value of $3x$ should be 2.

→ It can be clearly seen that none of the numbers 66, 67, 68 or 69 when being multiplied by 3 give us a units digit of 2. Hence, this is not a possible answer.

Checking for Option (b) in the same fashion:

You should realise that the outer limit for the range of values when the amount is between 18 and 19 is: 18.54 to 18.57. Also, the number of paise in the value of the transposed sum 'y' would be 18. Hence, the value of $3x$ should give us a paise value as 68 paise. Again, using the units digit principle, it is clear that the only value where the units digit would be 8 would be for a value of 18.56.

Hence, we check for the check amount to be 18.56. Transposition of the rupee and paise value would give us 56.18. When you subtract 50 paise from this you would get 55.68 which also happens to be thrice 18.56. Hence, the correct answer is Option (b).

Notice here that if you can work out this logic in your reactions, the time required to check each option would be not more than 30 seconds. Hence, the net problem solving time to get the second option as correct would not be more than 1 minute. Add the reading time and this problem should still not require more than 2 minutes.

20. How many pairs of positive integers m, n satisfy $1/m + 4/n = 1/12$ where n is an odd integer less than 60?

(a) 7   (b) 5
(c) 3   (d) 6
(e) 4

Thought Process:

Deduction 1: Since two positive fractions on the LHS equals 1/12 on the right hand side, the value of both these fractions must be less than 1/12. Hence, n can take only the values 49, 51, 53, 55, 57 and 59.

Deduction 2: We now need to check which of the possible values of n would give us an integral value of m.

The equation can be transformed to: $1/12 - 4/n = 1/m$

→ $(n - 48)/12n = 1/m$. On reading this equation you should realise that for m to be an integer the LHS must be able to give you a ratio in the form of $1/x$. It can be easily seen that this occurs for $n = 49$, $n = 51$ and $n = 57$. Hence, there are only 3 pairs.

21. The price of Darjeeling tea (in rupees per kilogram) is $100 + 0.1\ n$, on the nth day of 2007 ($n = 1, 2, ...,$ 100), and then remains constant. On the other hand, the price of Ooty tea (in rupees per kilogram) is $89 + 0.15n$, on the nth day of 2007 ($n = 1, 2, ..., 365$). On which date in 2007 will the prices of these two varieties of tea be equal?

(a) May 21   (b) April 11
(c) May 20   (d) April 10
(e) June 30

The gap between the two prices initially is of ₹11 or 1100 paise. The rate at which the gap closes down is 5 paise per day for the first hundred days. (The gap covered would be 500 paise which would leave a residual gap of 600 paise.) Then the price of Darjeeling tea stops rising and that of Ooty tea rises at 15 paise per day. Hence, the gap of 600 paise would get closed out in another 40 days. Hence, the prices of the two varieties would become equal on the 140th day of the year. $31 + 28 + 31 + 30 + 20 = 140$, means May 20th is the answer.

22. Let a, b, m, n be positive real numbers, which satisfy the two conditions that
(i) If $a > b$ then $m > n$; and
(ii) If $a > m$ then $b < n$
Then one of the statements given below is a valid conclusion. Which one is it?

(a) If $a < b$ then $m < n$ (b) If $a < m$ then $b > n$
(c) If $a > b + m$ then $m < b$
(d) If $a > b + m$ then $m > b$

The best way to think about this kind of a question is to try to work out a possibility matrix of the different possibilities that exist with respect to which of the values is at what position relative to each other. While making this kind of a figure for yourself, use the convention of keeping the higher number on top and the lower number below.

If we look at Condition (i) as stated in the problem, it states that: if $a > b$ then $m > n$

This gives us multiple possibilities for the placing of the four variables in relative order of magnitude. These relative positions of the variables can be visualised as follows for the case that $a > b$:

	Possibility 1	Possibility 2	Possibility 3
Largest number	1	a	a
2nd largest number	b	m	m
3rd largest number	m	b	n
Smallest number	n	n	b

Looking at the options, Option (a) can be rejected because, when we use the condition If X then necessarily Y, it does not mean that If Not X, then not Y.

For instance, if I make a statement like – "If the Jan Lokpal Bill is passed, corruption will be eradicated from the country; this does not mean that if the Jan Lokpal Bill is not passed then corruption would not be eradicated from the country."

Note: For this kind of reverse truth to exist the existing starting conditionality has to be of the form, only if X, then Y. In such a case the conclusion, if not X, then not Y is valid.

For instance, if I make a statement like – "Only if the Jan Lokpal Bill is passed, will corruption be eradicated from the country; this necessarily means the reverse – i.e. if the Jan Lokpal Bill is not passed then corruption would not be eradicated from the country."

This exact logic helps us eliminate the first option – which says that if $a < b$ then m should be less than n (this would obviously not happen just because if $a > b$, then m is greater than n – we would need the only if condition in order for this to work in the reverse fashion.)

Option (b) has the same structure based on the Condition (ii) in the problem – it tries to reverse a "If X, then Y conditionality" into a "If not X, then not Y" conclusion – which would only have been valid in the case of 'Only if X' as explained above.

This leaves us with Options (c) and (d) to check. If you go through these options, you realise that they are basically opposite to each other.

The following thought process would help you identify which of these is the correct answer.

When we say that $a > b + m$ where a, b and m are all positive it obviously means that a must be greater than both b and m. Thus, in this situation we have $a > b$ as well as $a > m$. In this case both the Conditions (i) and (ii) would activate themselves. It is at this point that the possibility matrix for the case of $a > b$ would become usable.

The possibility matrix that exists currently for $a > b$ is built using the following thought chain:

First think of the various positions in which 'a' and 'b' can be put, with 'a' greater than 'b' given that we have to fix up 4 numbers in decreasing order. The following possibilities emerge when we do this.

	Possibility 1	Possibility 2	Possibility 3	Possibility 4	Possibility 5	Possibility 6
Largest number	a	a	a			
2nd largest number	b			a	a	
3rd largest number		b			b	a
Smallest number			b	b		b

When we add the fact that when $a > b$, then m is also greater than n to this picture, the complete possibility matrix emerges as below:

	Possibility 1	Possibility 2	Possibility 3	Possibility 4	Possibility 5	Possibility 6
Largest number	a	a	a	m	m	m
2nd largest number	b	m	m	a	a	n
3rd largest number	m	b	n	n	b	a
Smallest number	n	n	b	b	n	b

Now, for Options (c) and (d) we know that the condition to be checked for is $a > b + m$ which means that $a > b$ and $a > m$ simultaneously. We have drawn above the possibility matrix for $a > b$. We also know from Condition (ii) in the problem above, that when $a > m$, then b should be less than n. Looking at the possibility matrix we need to search for cases where simultaneously each of the following is occurring- (i) $a > b$; (ii) $a > m$ and $b < n$. We can see that the possibilities 1, 2 and 5 will get rejected because in each of these cases b is not less than n. Similarly, Possibilities 4 and 6 both do not have $a > m$ and hence can be rejected. Only Possibility 3 remains and in that case, we can see than $m > b$.

Hence, Option (d) is correct.

---

23. A quadratic function $f(x)$ attains a maximum of 3 at $x = 1$. The value of the function at $x = 0$ is 1.
    What is the value of $f(x)$ at $x = 10$?
    (a) −119   (b) −159
    (c) −110   (d) −180
    (e) −105

Let the equation be $ax^2 + bx + c = 0$. If it gains the maximum at $x = 1$ it means that 'a' is negative.

Also $2ax + b = 0 \rightarrow x = -b/2a$. So $-b/2a$ should be 1. So the expression has to be chosen from:

$-X^2 + 2x + c$

$-2X^2 + 4x + c$

$-3X^2 + 6x + c$ ....and so on (since we have to keep the ratio of $-b/2a$ constant at 1).

Also, it is given that the value of the function at $x = 0$ is 1. This means that $c = 1$. Putting this value of c in the possible expressions we can see that at $x = 1$, the value of the function is equal to 3 in the case:

$-2X^2 + 4x + 1$

So the expression is $-2X^2 + 4x + 1$

At $x = 10$, the value would be $-200 + 40 + 1 = -159$.

Directions for Questions 24 and 25: Let $a_1 = p$ and $b_1 = q$, where p and q are positive quantities. Define

$$a_n = pb_{n-1}, \qquad b_n = qb_{n-1}, \text{ for even } n > 1,$$
$$\text{and} \qquad a_n = pa_{n-1}, \qquad b_n = qa_{n-1}, \text{ for odd } n > 1.$$

24. Which of the following best describes $a_n + b_n$ for even n?

   (a) $q(pq)^{n/2-1}(p + q)$ (b) $pq^{n/2-1}(p + q)$
   (c) $q^{(1/2)n}(p + q)$ (d) $q^{(1/2)n}(p + q)^{(1/2)n}$
   (e) $q(pq)^{n/2-1}(p + q)^{(1/2)n}$

Again to solve this question, we need to use values.
Let $a_1 = p = 5$ and $b_1 = q = 7$ (any random values.)
In such a case,
$a_2 = 5 \times 7 = 35$ and $b_2 = 7 \times 7 = 49$. So the sum of $a_2 + b_2 = 84$.
Checking the values we get:
Option a: $7 \times 1 \times (12) = 84$
Option b: $1 \times (12)$
Option c: $7 \times (12)$
Option d: $7 \times (12)$
Option e: $7 \times (12)$
Obviously apart from Option 2 all other options have to be considered. So it is obvious that the question setter wants us to go at least till the value of n as 4 to move ahead.
$a_3 = 5 \times 35 = 175$, $b_3 = 7 \times 35 = 245$
$a_4 = 7 \times 175 = 1225$, $b_4 = 7 \times 245 = 1715$
Sum of $a_4 + b_4 = 2940$.
Option a: $7 \times 35 \times 12 = 2940$,
Option c: $7 \times 7 \times 12$ eliminated
Option d: $7 \times 7 \times 12 \times 12$ eliminated
Option e: $7 \times 35 \times 12 \times 12$ eliminated
Hence, only Option (a) gives us a value of 2940 for $n = 4$. Thus it has to be correct.

25. If $p = 1/3$ and $q = 2/3$, then what is the smallest odd n such that $a_{n + b_n} < 0.01$?

   (a) 7 (b) 13
   (c) 11 (d) 9
   (e) 15

According to the question $a_1 = p = 1/3$ and $b_1 = q = 2/3$.
$a_2 = 1/3 \times 2/3 = 2/9$, $b_2 = 2/3 \times 2/3 = 4/9$
$a_3 = 1/3 \times 2/9 = 2/27$, $b_3 = 2/3 \times 2/9 = 4/27$
$a_4 = 1/3 \times 4/27 = 4/81$, $b_3 = 2/3 \times 4/27 = 12/81$
In this way, you can continue to get to the value of n at

which the required sum goes below 0.01. (It would happen at $n = 9$). However, if you are already comfortably placed in the paper, you can skip this process as it would be time consuming and also there is a high possibility of silly errors being induced under pressure.

26. The number of ordered pairs of integers (x, y) satisfying the equation $x^2 + 6x + 2y^2 = 4 + y^2$ is
   (a) 12 (b) 8
   (c) 10 (d) 14

These kinds of questions and thinking are very common in examinations and hence you need to understand how to solve such questions.

In order to think of such questions, you need to first 'read' the equation given. What do I mean by 'reading' the equation? Let me illustrate:

The first thing we do is to simplify the equation by putting all the variables on the LHS. This would give us the equation $x^2 + 6x + y^2$. When we have an equation like $x^2 + 6x + y^2 = 4$, we should realise that the value on the RHS is fixed at 4. Also, if we take a look at the LHS of the equation we realise that the terms x^2 and y^2 would always be positive integers or 0 (given that x and y are integers). $6x$ on the other hand could be positive, zero or negative depending on the value of x (if x is positive $6x$ is also positive, if x is negative $6x$ would be negative and if x is 0, $6x$ would also be zero.)

Thus, we can think of the following structures to build a value of 4 on the LHS for the equation to get satisfied:

	Value of x^2	Value of $6x$	Value of y^2
Case 1	0	0	+
Case 2	+	+	+
Case 3	+	−	+
Case 4	+	−	0

Once you have these basic structures in place, you can think of the cases one by one. Thinking in this structured fashion makes sure that you do not miss out on any possible solutions — and that, as you should realise, is critical for any situation where you have to count the number of solutions. You simply cannot get these questions correct without identifying each possible situation. Trying to do such questions without first structuring your thought process this way would lead to disastrous results in such questions!! Hence, this thinking is very critical for your development of quantitative thinking.

Let us look at **Case 1:** In Case 1, since the value of the first two components on the LHS are 0, it must mean that we are talking about the case of $x = 0$. Obviously, in this case the entire value of 4 for the LHS has to be created by using the term y^2.

Thus to make $y^2 = 4$, we can take $y = +2$ or $y = -2$. This gives us two possible solutions $(0, 2)$ and $(0, -2)$

Case 2: The minimum positive value for $6x$ would be when $x = 1$. This value for $6x$ turns out to be 6 – which has already made the LHS larger than 4. To this if we were to add two more positive integers for the values of x^2 and y^2 it would simply take the LHS further up from $+6$. Hence, in Case 2 there are no solutions.

Case 3: In this case the value of x has to be negative and y can be either positive or negative. Possible negative values of x as $-1, -2, -3, -4, -5$ etc. give us values for $6x$ as $-6, -12, -18, -24, -30,$ etc.

We then need to fill in values of x^2 and y^2 and see whether it is possible to add an exact value to any of these and get $+4$ as the final value of the LHS.

This thinking would go the following way:

If $6x = -6$: x must be -1 and hence $x^2 = 1$. Thus, $x^2 + 6x = -5$, which means for $x^2 + 6x + y^2 = 4$ we would need $-5 + y^2 = 4 \rightarrow y^2 = 9 \rightarrow y = +3$ and $y = -3$

Thus we have identified two more solutions as $(-1, 3)$ and $(-1, -3)$

If $6x = -12$: x must be -2 and hence $x^2 = 4$. Thus, $x^2 + 6x = -8$, which means for $x^2 + 6x + y^2 = 4$ we would need $-8 + y^2 = 4 \rightarrow y^2 = 12 \rightarrow y$ is not an integer in this case and hence we get no new solutions for this case.

If $6x = -18$: x must be -3 and hence $x^2 = 9$. Thus, $x^2 + 6x = -9$, which means for $x^2 + 6x + y^2 = 4$ we would need $-9 + y^2 = 4 \rightarrow y^2 = 13 \rightarrow y$ is not an integer in this case and hence we get no new solutions for this case.

If $6x = -24$: x must be -4 and hence $x^2 = 16$. Thus, $x^2 + 6x = -8$, which means for $x^2 + 6x + y^2 = 4$ we would need $-8 + y^2 = 4 \rightarrow y^2 = 12 \rightarrow y$ is not an integer in this case and hence we get no new solutions for this case.

If $6x = -30$: x must be -5 and hence $x^2 = 25$. Thus, $x^2 + 6x = -5$, which means for $x^2 + 6x + y^2 = 4$ we would need $-5 + y^2 = 4 \rightarrow y^2 = 9 \rightarrow y = +3$ and $y = -3$

Thus we have identified two more solutions as $(-5, 3)$ and $(-5, -3)$

If $6x = -36$: x must be -6 and hence $x^2 = 36$. Thus, $x^2 + 6x = 0$, which means for $x^2 + 6x + y^2 = 4$ we would need $0 + y^2 = 4 \rightarrow y^2 = 4 \rightarrow y = +2$ and $y = -2$

Thus we have identified two more solutions as $(-6, 2)$ and $(-6, -2)$

If $6x = -42$: x must be -7 and hence $x^2 = 49$. Thus, $x^2 + 6x = 7$, which means that $x^2 + 6x$ itself is crossing the value of 4 for the LHS. There is no scope to add any value of y^2 as a positive integer to get the LHS of the equation equal to 4. Thus, we can stop at this point.

Notice that we did not need to check for the Case 4 because if there were a solution for Case 4, we would have been able to identify it while checking for Case 3 itself.

Thus, the equation has 8 solutions.

27. The number of ordered pairs of integral solutions (m, n) which satisfy the equation $m \times n - 6(m + n) = 0$ with $m \leq n$ is:
    (a) 5   (b) 10
    (c) 12   (d) 9

In order to solve a question of this nature, you again first need to 'read' the equation:

The equation $m \times n - 6(m + n) = 0$ can be restructured as: $m \times n = 6(m + n)$

When we read an equation of this form, we should be able to read this as:

The LHS is the product of two numbers, while the RHS is always going to be a multiple of 6. Further, we also know that the value of $m \times n$ would normally always be higher than the value of $m + n$. Thus, we are trying to look for situations where the product of two integers is six times their sum.

While looking for such solutions, we need to look for situations where either:

The RHS is non negative – hence = 0, 6, 12, 18, 24, 30, 36…

The RHS is negative – hence = $-6, -12, -18…$

We would now need to use individual values of $m + n$ in order to check for whether $m \times n = 6(m + n)$

For $m + n = 0$; $6(m + n) = 0$. If we use m and n both as 0, we would get $0 = 0$ in the two sides of the equation. So this is obviously one solution to this equation.

For the RHS = -6, we can visualise the product of $m \times n$ as -6, if we use m as -3 and n as 2 or vice versa. Thus, we will get two solutions as $(2, -3)$ and $(-3, 2)$

For the RHS = -12, $m + n = -2$, which means that m and n would take values like $(-4,2)$; $(-5,3)$; $(-6,4)$. If you look inside the factor pairs of -12, there is no factor pair which has an addition of -2.

For RHS = -18, $m + n = -3$. Looking into the factor pairs of 18 (viz: 1×18, 2×9, 3×6) we can easily see -6 and 3 as a pair of factors of -18 which would add up to -3 as required. Thus, we get two ordered solutions for (m,n) viz: $(-6,3)$; $(3,-6)$

For RHS = -24, $m + n = -4$. If we look for factors of -24, which would give us a difference of -4, we can easily see that within the factor pairs of 24 (viz: 1×24, 2×12, 3×8 and 4×6) there is no opportunity to create a sum of $m + n = -4$.

For RHS = -30, $m + n = -5 \rightarrow$ factors of 30 are 2×15, 5×6; there is no opportunity to create a $m + n = -5$ and $m \times n = -30$ simultaneously. Hence, there are no solutions in this case.

For RHS = -36, $m + n = -6 \rightarrow$ factors of 36 are 2×18, 3×12, 4×9 and we can stop looking further; there is no opportunity to create $m + n = -6$ and $m \times n = -36$ simultaneously. Hence, there are no solutions in this case.

For RHS = -42, $m + n = -7 \rightarrow$ factors of 42 are 2×21, 3×14, 6×7 and we can stop looking further; there is no opportunity to create $m + n = -42$ and $m \times n = -7$ simultaneously. Hence, there are no solutions in this case.

For RHS = -48, $m + n = -8 \rightarrow$ factors of 48 are 2×24, 3×16, 4×12… 4×12 gives us the opportunity to create $m + n = -8$ and $m \times n = -48$ simultaneously. Hence, there are two solutions in this case viz: $(4, -12)$ and $(-12, 4)$

Note: While this process seems to be extremely long and excruciating, it is important to note that there are a lot of refinements you can make in order to do this fast. The 'searching inside the factors' shown above is itself a hugely effective short cut in this case. Further, when you are looking for pairs of factors for any number, you need not look at the first few pairs because their difference would be very large. This point is illustrated below:

For RHS = -54, $m + n = -9 \rightarrow$ factors of 54 are 3×18, 6×9 and we can stop looking further; (Notice here that we did not need to start with 1×54 and 2×27 because they are what can be called as 'too far apart' from each other). There is no opportunity to create $m + n = -6$ and $m \times n = -36$ simultaneously. Hence, there are no solutions in this case.

For RHS = -60, $m + n = -10 \rightarrow$ relevant factor search for 60 are 4×15, 5×12 and we can stop looking further; there is no opportunity to create $m + n = -10$ and $m \times n = -60$ simultaneously. Hence, there are no solutions in this case.

For RHS = -66, $m + n = -11 \rightarrow$ relevant factor search for 66 is 6×11 and we can stop looking further; there is no opportunity to create $m + n = -11$ and $m \times n = -66$ simultaneously. Hence, there are no solutions in this case.

Note: While solving through this route each value check should take not more than 5 seconds at the maximum. The question that starts coming into one's mind is, how far does one need to go in order to check for values?? Luckily, the answer is not too far.

As you move to the next values beyond -66, -72 (needs $m + n = -12$, while the factors of 72 do not present this opportunity), -78 (needs $m + n = -13$, which does not happen again).

To move further you need to start working out the logic when $6(m + n)$ is positive. In such a case, the value of m and n would both need to be positive for $m \times n$ also to be positive. If $m + n = 1$, we cannot get two positive values of m and n such that their product is 6. If $m + n = 2$, $m \times n = 12$ would not happen.

A little bit of logical thought would give you that the first point at which this situation would get satisfied. That would be when $6(m + n) = 144$ which means that $m + n = 24$ and for $m \times n$ to be equal to 144, the value of each of m and n would be 12 each.

(A brief note about why it is not possible to get a value before this:

If we try $6(m + n) = 132$ (for instance), we would realise that $m + n = 22$. The highest product $m \times n$ with a limit of $m + n = 22$ would occur when each of m and n is equal and hence individually equal to 11 each. However, the value of 11 for m and n gives us a product of 121 only, which is lower than the required product of 132. This would happen in all cases where $6(m + n)$ is smaller than 144.)

Checking subsequent values of $6(m + n)$ we would get the following additional solutions to this situation:

$6(m + n)$	$(m + n)$	Relevant Factor pairs for the value of $6(m + n)$	Solutions??
150	25	10,15	10,15; 15,10
156	26	None	None
162	27	9,18	9,18; 18,9
168,174	28,29	None	None
180,186	30,31	None	None
192	32	8,24	8,24; 24,8
198,204	33,34	None	None
210,216	35,36		

Break-down of the above thought process:

Note that while checking the factor pairs for a number like 216, if you were to list the entire set of factors along with the sum of the individual factors within the pairs, you would get a list as follows:

Factor Pairs for 216:

Pair	Sum of Factors in the Pair
1×216	217
2×108	110
3×72	75
4×54	58
6×36	42
8×27	35
9×24	33
12×18	30

However, a little bit of introspection in the correct direction would show you that this entire exercise was not required in order to do what we were doing in this question – i.e., trying to solve for $m + n = 36$ and $m \times n = 216$.

The first five pairs where the larger number itself was greater than or equal to 36 were irrelevant as far as searching for the correct pair of factors is concerned for this question. When we saw the sixth pair of 8×27, we should have realised that since the sum of $8 + 27 = 35$, which is < 36, the subsequent pairs would also have a sum smaller than 36. Hence, you can stop looking for more factors for 216.

Thus, effectively to check whether a solution exists for $6(m + n) = 216$, in this question, all we needed to identify was the $8 \times 27 = 216$ pair and we can reject this value for $6(m + n)$ giving us an integral solution in this case.

This entire exercise can be completed in one '5 second thought' as follows:

If $6(m + n) = 216 \rightarrow m + n = 36$ then one factor pair is 6×36 itself whose sum obviously is more than 36. So, looking for the next factor pair where the smaller number is > 6, we see that 8×27 gives us a factor pair sum of $8 + 27 = 35 < 36$ and hence we reject this possibility.

Also, you should realise that we do not need to look further than 216 – as for values after 216, when we go to the next factor pair after $6 \times (m + n)$, we would realise that the sum of the factor pair would be lower than the required value for the immediately next factor pair.

Hence, the following solutions exist for this question: 0,0; 2,–3; –3,2; 3,–6; –6,3; 4,–12; –12,4; 12,12; 15,10; 10,15; 9,18; 18,9; 8,24; 24,8

A total of 14 solutions

Author's note: Doubtless this question is very long, but if you are able to understand the thought process to adopt in such situations, you would do yourself a big favor in the commonly asked questions of finding number of integral solutions.

28. How many positive integral solutions exist for the expression $a^2 - b^2 = 666$?

    In order to solve this question, we need to think of the expression $(a - b)(a + b) = 666$ Obviously, the question is based on factor pairs of 666. If we look at the list of factor pairs of 666 we get:

1	666
2	333
3	222
6	111
9	74
18	37

    Since, 37 is a prime number, we will get no more factor pairs.

    Now, if we look at trying to fit in the expression $(a - b)(a + b)$ for any of these values, we see the following occurring:

    Example: $(a - b) = 9$ and $(a + b) = 74$. If we try to solve for a and b we get: $2a = 83$ (by adding the equations) and 'a' would not be an integer. Consequently, b would also not be an integer and we can reject this possibility as giving us a solution of $a^2 - b^2 = 666$.

    Armed with this logic if we were to go back to each of the factor pairs in the table above, we realise that the sum of the two factors within a factor pair is always odd and hence none of these factor pairs would give us a solution for the equation.

    Thus, the correct answer would be 0.

29. How many positive integral solutions exist for the expression $a^2 - b^2 = 672$?

    In order to solve this question, we need to think of the expression $(a - b)(a + b) = 672$ Obviously, the question is based on factor pairs of 672. If we look at the list of factor pairs of 672 we get:

		Sum of factors
1	672	Odd
2	336	Even
3	224	Odd
4	168	Even
6	112	Even
8	84	Even
12	56	Even
16	42	Even
21	32	Odd
24	28	Even

    Based on our understanding of the logic in the previous question, we should realise that this works for all situations where the sum of factors is even. Hence, there are 7 positive integral solutions to the equation $a^2 - b^2 = 672$.

30. The function a_n is defined as $a_n - a_{n-1} = 2n$ for all $n \geq 2$. $a_1 = 2$.

    Find the value of $a_1 + a_2 + a_3 + \dots a_{12}$

    In order to solve such questions, the key is to be able to identify the pattern of the series. A little bit of thought would give you the following structure:

    $a_1 = 2$

    $a_2 - a_1 = 4 \rightarrow a_2 = 6$

    $a_3 - a_2 = 6 \rightarrow a_3 = 12$

    $a_4 - a_3 = 8 \rightarrow a_4 = 20$

    $a_5 - a_4 = 10 \rightarrow a_5 = 30$

    If we look for the pattern in these numbers we should be able to see the following:

    $2 + 6 + 12 + 20 + 30\dots$
    $= 2(1 + 3 + 6 + 10 + 15 + \dots)$

    Looking at it this way shows us that the numbers in the brackets are consecutive triangular numbers.

    Hence, for the sum till a_{12} we can do the following:

    $2(1 + 3 + 6 + 10 + 15 + 21 + 28 + 36 + 45 + 55 + 66 + 78) = 728$.

31. The brothers Binnu and Kinnu have been challenged by their father to solve a mathematical puzzle before they are allowed to go out to play. Their father has asked them "Imagine two integers a and b such that $1 \leq b \leq a \leq 10$. Can you correctly find out the value of the expression $\sum ab$?" Can you help them identify the correct value of the foregoing expression?

    (a) 1155   (b) 1050
    (c) 1135   (d) None of these

    This question is again based on a pattern recognition principle. The best way to approach the search of the pattern is to start by working out a few values of the given expression. The following pattern would start emerging:

Value of a	Possible values of b	Value of the sum of the possible products 'a × b'	Explanation
1	1	1	With 'a' as 1, the only value for b is 1 itself.
2	1, 2	$2 \times 1 + 2 \times 2 = 2 \times 3$	With 'a' as 2, b can take the values of 1 and 2 – and $2 \times 1 + 2 \times 2$ can be written as 2×3
3	1, 2, 3	$3 \times 1 + 3 \times 2 + 3 \times 3 = 3 \times 6$	With 'a' as 3, b can take the values of 1, 2 and 3 – and $3 \times 1 + 3 \times 2 + 3 \times 3$ can be written as 3×6
4	1, 2, 3, 4	$4 \times 1 + 4 \times 2 + 4 \times 3 + 4 \times 4 = 4 \times 10$	

At this point you should realise that the values are following a certain pattern – the series of values for 'a' are multiplied by a series of consecutive triangular numbers (1, 3, 6, 10 and so on.) Thus, we can expect the subsequent numbers to be got by multiplying 5 × 15, 6 × 21, 7 × 28, 8 × 36 and 9 × 45.

Hence, the answer can be got by:
$1 \times 1 + 2 \times 3 + 3 \times 6 + 4 \times 10 + 5 \times 15 + 6 \times 21 + 7 \times 28 + 8 \times 36 + 9 \times 45 =$
$1 + 6 + 18 + 40 + 75 + 126 + 196 + 288 + 405 = 1155$

32. For the above question, what would be the answer in case the inequality is expressed as: $1 \le b < a \le 10$?

In this case the solution would change as follows:

Value of a	Possible values of b	Value of the sum of the possible products 'a × b'	Explanation
1	No possible values for 'b', since b'' has to be greater than or equal to 1 but less than 'a' at the same time	0	With 'a' as 1, the only value for b is 1 itself.
2	1	2×1	With 'a' as 2, b can only take the value of 1.
3	1, 2	$3 \times 1 + 3 \times 2 = 3 \times 3$	With 'a' as 3, b can take the values of 1 and 2 – and $3 \times 1 + 3 \times 2$ can be written as 3×3
4	1, 2, 3	$4 \times 1 + 4 \times 2 + 4 \times 3 = 4 \times 6$	With 'a' as 4, b can take the values of 1,2 and 3 – and $4 \times 1 + 4 \times 2 + 4 \times 3$ can be written as 4×6

At this point you should realise that the values are following a certain pattern (just like in the previous question) – the series of values for 'a' are multiplied by a series of consecutive triangular numbers (1, 3, 6, 10 and so on). The only difference in this case is that the multiplication is what can be described as 'one removed', i.e., it starts from the value of 'a' as 2. Thus, we can expect the subsequent numbers to be got by multiplying 5 × 10, 6 × 15, 7 × 21, 8 × 28 and 9 × 36 and 10 × 45. Notice here that the values of 'a' can go all the way till 10 in this case as the inequality on the rightmost side of the expression is $a \le 10$.

Hence, the answer can be got by:
$1 \times 0 + 2 \times 1 + 3 \times 3 + 4 \times 6 + 5 \times 10 + 6 \times 15 + 7 \times 21 + 8 \times 28 + 9 \times 36 + 10 \times 45 =$
$0 + 2 + 9 + 24 + 50 + 90 + 147 + 224 + 324 + 450 = 1320.$

33. Consider the equation of the form $x^2 + bx + c = 0$. The number of such equations that have real roots and have coefficients b and c in the set {1, 2, 3, 4, 5, 6,7), is
(a) 20 (b) 25
(c) 27 (d) 29

We know that in order to have the roots of an equation to be real, we should have the values of the discriminant of the quadratic equation (defined as the value $b^2 - 4ac$ for a standard quadratic equation $ax^2 + bx + c = 0$) to be non-negative.

In the context of the given equation in this problem, since the value of the coefficient of x^2 is 1, it means that we need to have $b^2 - 4c$ to be positive or 0.

The only thing to be done from this point is to look for possible values of a and b which fit this requirement. In order to do this, assume a value for 'b' from the set {1, 2, 3, 4, 5, 6} and try to see which values of b and c satisfy $b^2 - 4c \ge 0$.

When $b = 1$, c can take none of the values between 1 and 6, since "$b^2 - 4c$" would end up being negative

When $b = 2$, c can be 1;
When $b = 3$, c can be 1 or 2;
When $b = 4$, c can be 1 or 2 or 3 or 4;

When $b = 5$, c can take any value between 1 and 6;
When $b = 6$, c can take any value between 1 and 7;
When $b = 7$, c can take any value between 1 and 7
Thus, there are a total of 27 such equations with real roots.

34. The number of polynomials of the form $x^3 + ax^2 + bx + c$ which are divisible by $x^2 + 1$ and where a, b and c belong to $\{1, 2, ..., 8)$, is

(a) 1   (b) 8
(c) 9   (d) 10

For a polynomial $P(x)$ to be divisible by another polynomial $D(x)$, there needs to be a third polynomial $Q(x)$ which would represent the quotient of the expression $P(x)/D(x)$. In other words, this also means that the product of the polynomials $D(x) \times Q(x)$ should equal the polynomial $P(x)$.

In simpler words, we are looking for polynomials that would multiply $(x^2 + 1)$ and give us a polynomial in the form of $x^3 + ax^2 + bx + c$. The key point in this situation is that the expression that would multiply $(x^2 + 1)$ to give an expression of the form $x^3 + ...$ Would necessarily be of the form $(x + \text{constant})$. It is only in such a case that we would get an expanded polynomial starting with x^3. Further, the value of the constant has to be such that the product of $1 \times$ constant would give a value for 'c' that would belong to the set $\{1, 2, 3, 4, 5, 6, 7, \text{ or } 8)$. Clearly, there are only 10 such values possible for the constant – viz 1, 2, 3,...8 and hence the required polynomials that would be divisible by $x^2 + 1$ would be got by the expansion of the following expressions: $(x^2 + 1)(x + 1)$; $(x^2 + 1)(x + 2)$; $(x^2 + 1)(x + 3)$;... ; $(x^2 + 1)(x + 8)$. Thus, there would be a total of eight such expressions which would be divisible by $x^2 + 1$. Hence, Option (b) is the correct answer.

35. A point P with coordinates (x, y) is such that the product of the coordinates $xy = 144$. How many possible points exist on the X–Y plane such that both x and y are integers?

(a) 15   (b) 16
(c) 30   (d) 32

The number of values for (x, y) such that both are integers and their product is equal to 144 is dependent on the number of factors of 144. Every factor pair would gives us 4 possible solutions for the ordered pair (x, y). For instance, if we were to consider 1×144 as one ordered pair, the possible values for (x, y) would be $(1,144)$; $(144,1)$; $(-1,-144)$; $(-144,-1)$. This would be true for all factor pairs except the factor pair 12×12. In this case, the possible pairs of (x, y) would be $(12,12)$ and $(-12,-12)$.

If we find out the factor pairs of 144 we will get the following list:

Factor Pair	Number of solutions for (x, y)
1×144	4 solutions – as explained above
2×72	4 solutions
3×48	4 solutions

Factor Pair	Number of solutions for (x, y)
4×36	4 solutions
6×24	4 solutions
8×18	4 solutions
9×16	4 solutions
12×12	2 solutions

Thus, there are a total of 30 solutions in this case.

36. Let $x_1, x_2, ..., x_{40}$ be fifty nonzero numbers such that $x_i + x_{i+1} = k$ for all i, $1 \leq i \leq \infty$. If $x_{14} = a$, $x_{27} = b$, then $x_{30} + x_{39}$ equals

(a) $3(a + b) - 2k$
(b) $k + a$
(c) $k + b$
(d) None of the foregoing expressions

Since, $x_{14} = a$, x_{15} would equal $(k - a)$ [we get this by equating $x_{14} + x_{15} = k \rightarrow a + x_{15} = k \rightarrow x_{15} = (k - a)$]. By using the same logic on the equation $x_{15} + x_{16} = k$, we would get $x_{16} = a$. Consequently $x_{17} = k - a$, $x_{18} = a$, $x_{19} = k - a$, $x_{20} = a$. Thus, we see that every odd term is equal to '$k - a$' and every even term is equal to 'a'. Further, we can develop a similar logic for x_i in the context of 'b'. Since, $x27 = b$, $x28 = k - b$, $x29 = b$ and so on. This series also follows a similar logic with x_i being equal to b when 'i' is odd and being equal to $k - b$ when 'i' is even.

Thus, for every value of x_i, we have two ways of looking at its value—viz either in terms of a or in terms of b. Thus, for any x_{even}, we have for instance $x_{20} = a = k - b$.

Solving $a = k - b$ we get $a + b = k$.

Further, when we look at trying to solve for the specific value of what the question has asked us, i.e., the value of $x_{30} + x_{39}$ we realise that we can either solve it in terms of 'a' or in terms of 'b'. If we try to solve it in terms of 'a' we would see the following happening:

$X_{30} + x_{39} = a + k - a = k$

Similarly, in terms of 'b' $x_{30} + x_{39} = k - b + b = k$. Since we know that $k = a + b$ (deduced above), we can conclude $x_{30} + x_{39} = a + b$. However, if we look at the options, none of the options is directly saying that.

Options (b) and (c) can be rejected because their values are not equal to $a + b$. A closer inspection of Option (a), gives us an expression: $3(a + b) - 2k$. This expression can be expressed as $3(a + b) - 2(a + b) = (a + b)$ and hence this is the correct answer.

37. The great mathematician Ramanujam, once was asked a puzzle in order to test his mathematical prowess. He was given two sets of numbers as follows:

Set X is the set of all numbers of the form: $4^n - 3n - 1$, where $n = 1, 2, 3, ...$

Set Y is the set of all numbers of the form $9n$, where $n = 0, 1, 2, 3, ...$

Based on these two definitions of the set, can you help Ramanujam identify the correct statement from amongst the following options:

(a) Each number in Y is also in X
(b) Each number in X is also in Y
(c) Every number in X is in Y and every number in Y is in X.
(d) There are numbers in X that are not in Y and vice versa.

In order to solve such questions conveniently, you would need to first create a language representation for yourself with respect to the two sets.

Set X can be mentally thought of as:

A positive integral power of 4 – a multiple of 3 (with the multiplier being equal to the power of 4 used) – a constant value '1'.

Thus, the set of values in X can be calculated as (0, 9, 54, 243 and so on)

Similarly, Set Y can be thought of as multiples of 9, starting from $9 \times 0 = 0$.

The numbers that would belong to the set Y would be: (0, 9, 18, 27, 36 and pretty much all multiples of 9)

It can be clearly seen that while all values in X are also in Y, the reverse is not true. Hence, the statement in Option (b) is correct.

38. The number of real roots of the equation

$$\log_{2x}\left(\frac{2}{x}\right)(\log_2(x))^2 + (\log_2(x))^4 = 1, \text{ for values}$$

of $x > 1$, is

(a) 0   (b) 1
(c) 2   (d) 27

The only way to handle such questions is to try to get a 'feel' of the equation by inserting a few values for x and trying to see the behaviour of the various terms in the equation.

Towards this end, let us start by trying to insert values for x in the given equation.

Because the problem tells us that $x > 1$, the first value of x which comes to mind is $x = 2$. At $x = 2$, the value of the LHS would become equal to 1. This can be thought of as follows:

$$\text{LHS} = \log_{2x}(1)(\log_2(2))^2 + (\log_2(2))^4 = 0 + 1 = 1.$$

As we try to take higher values of x as 3, 4, 5 and so on we realise first that for values like 3, 5 we will get terms like

$\text{Log}_6 (2/3)(\log_2 (3))^2 + (\log_2 (3))^4$ which is clearly not going to be an integral value, because terms like $\log_2 3$, $\log_6 2$ and $\log_6 3$ would have irrational decimal values by themselves. In fact, we can see that for numbers of x that are not powers of 2, we would never get an integral value to the LHS of the expression.

Thus, we need to see the behaviour of the expression only for values of x like 4, 8 and so on before we can conclude about the number of real roots of the equation.

At $x = 4$, the expression becomes:

$\text{Log}_8 (2/4)(\log_2(4))^2 + (\log_2(4))^4$

By thinking about this expression it is again clear that there are going to be decimals in the first part of the

expression—although they are going to be rational numbers and not irrational—and hence we cannot summarily rule out the possibility of an integral value of this expression—without doing a couple of more calculations. However, there is another thought which can help us confirm that the equation will not get satisfied in this case because the LHS is much bigger than the RHS.

This thought goes as follows:

The LHS has two parts: The first part is $\text{Log}_8 (2/4)$ $(\log_2(4))^2$ while the second part is $(\log_2(4))^4$; The value of the second part is 16 while the value of the first part (though it is negative) is much smaller than the required –15 which will make the LHS = 1.

Hence, we can reject this value.

39. The number of points at which the curve $y = x^6 + x^3 - 2$ cuts the x-axis is

(a) 1   (b) 2
(c) 4   (d) 6

By replacing $x^3 = m$, the equation given in the question, can be written in the form:

$y = m^2 + m - 2 \rightarrow$
$y = (m + 2)(m - 1) \rightarrow m = -2$ and $m = 1$.

This gives $x^3 = -2$ and $x^3 = 1$. This gives us two clear values of x (these would be the roots of the equation) and hence x, the curve would cut the 'x' axis at two points exactly.

40. Number of real roots of the equation $8x^3 - 6x + 1 = 0$ lying between -1 and 1, is

(a) 0   (b) 1
(c) 2   (d) 3

In order to trace the number of real roots for any equation (cubic or larger) the only feasible way to look at it is to try to visualise how many times the graph of the parallel function (in this case: $8x^3 - 6x + 1$) cuts the X-axis.

The following thought process would help you do this:

Since the question is asking us to find out the number of real roots of $8x^3 - 6x + 1 = 0$ between the range -1 and $+1$, we will need to investigate only the behaviour of the curve for the function $y = 8x^3 - 6x + 1$ between the values -1 and $+1$

The first thing we do is to look at the values of the function at -1, 0 and $+1$.

At $x = -1$; the value of the function is $-8 + 6 + 1 = -1$.

At $x = 0$; the value of the function is 1.

At $x = 1$: the value of the function is 3.

If plotted on a graph, we can visualise the three points as given here.

From this visualisation it is clear that the value of the function is -1 at $x = -1$ and $+1$ at $x = 0$ and $+3$ at $x = 1$. It is clear that somewhere between -1 and $+1$, the function would cut the x-axis at least once as it transits from a negative value to a positive value. Hence, the equation would necessarily have at least one root between -1 to 0. What we need to investigate in order to solve this question is specifically— does the function cut the x-axis more than once during this range of values on the x-axis? Also, we should realise that in case the graph will cut the X–axis more than once, it would cut it thrice—since if it goes from negative to positive once, and comes back from positive to negative, it would need to become positive again to go above the x-axis.

This can be visualised as the following possible shapes:

If the graph cuts the x-axis once (and it has one real root in this range)

If the graph cuts the x-axis thrice (and it has three real roots in this range)

Of course the graph can technically also cut the x-Axis twice between the values of $x = 0$ and $x = 1$. In such a case, the graph would look something like below:

Which of these graphs would be followed would depend on our analysis of the behaviour of the values of $8x^3 - 6x + 1$ between the values of x between -1 and 0 first and then between 0 and 1.

Between -1 and 0:

The value of $8x^3$ would remain negative, while $-6x$ would be positive and $+1$ would always remain constant. If we look that the values of $8x^3$ as we increase the value of x from -1 to -0.9 to -0.8 to -0.7 to ... -0.1, the negative impact of $8x^3$ reduces as its magnitude reduces. (Please understand the difference between magnitude and value when we are talking about a negative number. For instance when we talk about increasing a negative number its magnitude is decreased).

At the same time the positive magnitude of $-6x$ also reduces but the rapidity with which the value of $-6x$ would decrease will be smaller than the rapidity with which the value of $8x^3$ would decrease. Hence, the positive parts of the expression would become 'more powerful' than the negative part of the expression – and hence the graph would not cut the x-axis more than once between -1 and 0.

The last part of our investigation, then would focus on the behaviour of the graph between the values of $x = 0$ and $x = 1$. When x moves into the positive direction (i.e., when we take $x > 0$) we realise that of the three terms $8x^3$ and $+1$ would be positive, while the value of $-6x$ would be negative.

It can be easily visualised that at $x = 1/4$, the value of the expression on the LHS of the equation becomes: $8/64 - 6/4 + 1$, which is clearly negative. Thus, after $x = 0$, when we move to the positive values of x, the value of the expression $8x^3 - 6x + 1$ becomes negative once more. Thus the correct graph would look as below:

Thus, the equation has three real roots between -1 and $+1$.

REVIEW TEST 1

1. Consider the following two curves in the x-y plane:
   $$y = x^3 + x^2 + 7$$
   $$y = x^2 + x + 7$$
   Which of the following statements is true for $-4 \leq x \leq 4$?
   (a) The two curves intersect once
   (b) The two curves intersect twice
   (c) The two curves do not intersect
   (d) The two curves intersect thrice

2. Given that $-1 \leq v \leq 1$ and $-2 \leq u \leq -0.5$ and $-2 \leq z \leq 0.5$ and $x = vz /u$, then which of the following is necessarily true?
   (a) $-0.5 \leq x \leq 2$ (b) $-4 \leq x \leq 4$
   (c) $-4 \leq x \leq 0$ (d) $-2 \leq x \leq 0$

3. Let $g(x) = \max (7 - x, x + 3)$. The smallest possible value of $g(x)$ is:
   (a) 4   (b) 4.5
   (c) 1.5   (d) None of the above

4. p, q, r are real numbers such that $p + q + r \neq 0$. Of the conditions given in the options, which one must p, q and r satisfy so that the following system of linear simultaneous equations has at least one solution?
   $$x + 2y - 3z = p$$
   $$2x + 6y - 11z = q$$
   $$x - 2y + 17z = r$$
   (a) $5p - 2q - r = 0$ (b) $5p + 2q + r = 0$
   (c) $5p + 2q - r = 0$ (d) $5p - 2q + r = 0$

5. A leather factory produces two kinds of bags, standard and deluxe. The profit margin is ₹20 on a standard bag and ₹30 on a deluxe bag. Every bag must be processed on Machine A and on Machine B. The processing times per bag on the two machines are as follows:

   Time required (Hours/bag)

	Machine A	Machine B
Standard Bag	4	6
Deluxe Bag	5	10

   The total time available on machine A is 1400 hours and on machine B is 2500 hours. Among the following production plans, which one meets the machine availability constraints and maximizes the profit?
   (a) Standard 150 bags, Deluxe 160 bags
   (b) Standard 200 bags, Deluxe 120 bags
   (c) Standard 100 bags, Deluxe 200 bags
   (d) Standard 120 bags, Deluxe 180 bags

6. The function $f(x) = |x - 2| + |2.5 - x| + |3.6 - x|$, where x is a real number, attains a minimum at:
   (a) $x = 2.3$ (b) $x = 2.5$
   (c) $x = 2.7$ (d) None of the above

7. When the curves $y = \log_{10} x$ and $y = x^{-1}$ are drawn in the x-y plane, how many times do they intersect for positive values of x?
   (a) Never   (b) Once
   (c) Twice   (d) More than twice

8. In a coastal village, every year floods destroy exactly half of the huts. After the flood water recedes, twice, the number of huts destroyed are rebuilt. The floods occurred consecutively in the last three years namely 2001, 2002 and 2003. If floods are again expected in 2004, the number of huts expected to be destroyed is:
   1. less than the number of huts existing at the beginning of 2001.
   2. less than the total number of huts destroyed by floods in 2001 and 2003.
   3. less than the total number of huts destroyed by floods in 2002 and 2003.
   4. more than the total number of huts built in 2001 and 2002.

9. If x and y are integers then the equation $5x + 19y = 64$ has:
   (a) no solution for $x < 300$ and $y < 0$
   (b) no solution for $x > 250$ and $y > -100$
   (c) a solution for $250 < x < 300$
   (d) a solution for $-59 < y < -56$

Directions for Questions 10 and 11: The graph given below represents a quadratic expression, $f(x) = ax^2 + bx + c$. The minimum value of $f(x)$ is -2 and it occurs at $x = 2$

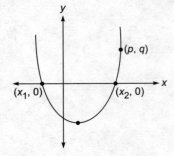

x_1 and x_2 are such that $x_1 + x_2 + 2x_1x_2 = 0$.

10. What is the nature of the roots of the equation $f(x) = 0$?
    (a) Complex conjugates
    (b) Rational
    (c) Irrational
    (d) Cannot be determined

11. Find the value of the function at $x = 3$
    (a) 2
    (b) – 1
    (c) 5
    (d) none of these

12. Let S denote the infinite sum $2 + 5x + 9x^2 + 14x^3 + 20 x^4 + $ ......, where $|x| < 1$ and the coefficient of x^{n-1} is $\frac{1}{2}\{n (n + 3)\}$, $(n = 1, 2,……)$. Then S equals:
    (a) $(2 - x)/(1 - x)^3$
    (b) $(2 - x)/(1 + x)^2$
    (c) $(2 + x)/(1 - x)^2$
    (d) $(2 + x)/(1 + x)^3$

13. Safdar was asked to calculate the arithmetic mean of ten positive integers each of which had two digits. By mistake he interchanged the two digits in one of the ten integers. As a result, his answer for the arithmetic mean became 1.8 more than what it should have been. Based on this information, find the value of $b - a$:
    (a) 1
    (b) 2
    (c) 3
    (d) 4

14. Suppose for any real number x, $[x]$ denotes the greater integer less than or equal to x, Let $L(x, y) = [x] + [y] + [x + y]$ and $R (x, y) = [2x] + [2y]$. Then it's impossible to find any two positive real numbers x and y for which.
    (a) $L (x, y) = R (x, y)$
    (b) $L (x, y) \neq R (x, y)$
    (c) $L (x, y) < R (x, y)$
    (d) $L (x, y) > R (x, y)$

15. If u, v, w and m are natural numbers such that $u^m + v^m = w^m$, then which one of the following is true:
    (a) $m \geq \min (u, v, w)$
    (b) $m \geq \max (u, v, w)$
    (c) $m < \min (u, v, w)$
    (d) None of these

16. If $pqr = 1$, the value of the expression $1/(1 + p + q^{-1}) + 1/(1 + q + r^{-1}) + 1/(1 + r + p^{-1}) =$
    (a) $p + q + r$
    (b) $1/(p + q + r)$
    (c) 1
    (d) $p^{-1} + q^{-1} + r^{-1}$

17. Sanjay's shop sells samosas of different sizes. Each samosa is sold at the price of ₹ 2 per samosa up to 200 samosas. Beyond 200, for every 20 additional samosas, the price of the whole lot goes down by 10 paise per. samosa. What should be the maximum size of the lot in order to maximize revenue:
    (a) 240
    (b) 300
    (c) 400
    (d) None of these

18. Let x, y and z be distinct integers x and y are odd and positive, and z is even and positive. Which one of the following statements cannot be true?
    (a) $(x - z)^2 y$ is even
    (b) $(x - z) y^2$ is odd
    (c) $(x - z) y$ is odd
    (d) $(x - y)^2 z$ is even

Directions for Questions 19 to 21: Answer these questions on the basis of the information given below.
x, y and z are three real numbers satisfying the following conditions.
$$x + y + z = 10$$
$$x^2 + y^2 + z^2 = 62$$
$$x^3 + y^3 + z^3 = 340$$

19. Find the value of $(xy + yz + xz)$.
    (a) 21
    (b) 37
    (c) 19
    (d) 20

20. Find the value of xyz.
    (a) 30
    (b) 15
    (c) – 15
    (d) – 30

21. Find the value of $x^4 + y^4 + z^4$.
    (a) 1925
    (b) 1922
    (c) 1920
    (d) None of these

22. Every ten years, the Indian government counts all the people living in the country. Suppose that the director of the census has reported the following data on two neighbouring villages Chota Hazri and Mota Hazri:

    Chota Hazri has 4,522 fewer males than Mota-Hazri.
    Mota Hazri has 4,020 more females than males.
    Chota Hazri has twice as many females as males.
    Chota Hazri has 2,910 fewer females than Mota Hazri.

    What is the total number of males in Chota Hazri?
    (a) 11264
    (b) 14174
    (c) 5632
    (d) 10154

23. At a certain fast food restaurant, Brian can buy 3 burgers, 7 shakes, and one order of fries for ₹ 120 exactly. At the same place, it would cost ₹ 164.50 for 4 burgers, 10 shakes, and one order of fries. How much would it cost for an ordinary meal of one burger, one shake, and one order of fries?
    (a) ₹ 31
    (b) ₹ 41
    (c) ₹ 21
    (d) Cannot be determined

24. If $x > 7$ and $y < -2$, then which of the following statements is true?
    (a) $(x + 4y) > 1$
    (b) $x > -4y$
    (c) $-4x < 5y$
    (d) None of these

25. For a Fibonacci sequence, from the third term onwards, each term in the sequence is the sum of the previous two terms in that sequence. If the difference in squares of seventh and sixth terms of this sequence is 517, what is tenth term of this sequence?
    (a) 147
    (b) 76
    (c) 123
    (d) Cannot be determined

REVIEW TEST 2

1. Let x, y be two positive numbers such that $x + y = 1$.

    Then, the minimum value of $\left(x + \dfrac{1}{x}\right)^2 + \left(y + \dfrac{1}{y}\right)^2$

    is

    (a) 12   (b) 20
    (c) 12.5   (d) 13.3

2. Ujakar and Keshab attempted to solve a quadratic equation. Ujakar made a mistake in writing down the constant term. He ended up with the roots (4, 3). Keshab made a mistake in writing down the co-efficient of x. He roots as (3, 2). What will be the exact roots of the original quadratic equation?

    (a) (6,1)   (b) (−3,−4)
    (c) (4,3)   (d) (−4,−3)

3. A change making machine contains 1 rupee, 2 rupee and 5 rupee coins. The total number of coins is 300. The amount is ₹ 960. If the number of 1 rupee coins and the number of 2 rupee coins are interchanged, the value comes down by ₹ 40. The total number of 5 rupee coins is:

    (a) 100   (b) 140
    (c) 60   (d) 150

4. If $x > 2$ and $y > -1$, then which of the following statements is necessarily true?

    (a) $xy > -2$ (b) $-x < 2y$
    (c) $xy < -2$ (d) $-x > 2y$

Directions for Questions 5 to 7: A, B, C and D collected one rupee coins following the given pattern.
Together they collected 100 coins.
Each one of them collected an even number of coins.
Each one of them collected at least 10 coins.
No two of them collected the same number of coins.

5. The maximum number of coins collected by any one of them cannot exceed :

    (a) 64   (b) 36
    (c) 54   (d) None of these

6. If A collected 54 coins, then the difference in the number of coins between the one who collected maximum number of coins and the one who collected the second highest number of coins must be at least:

    (a) 12   (b) 24
    (c) 30   (d) None of these

7. If A collected 54 coins and B collected two more coins than twice the number of coins collected by C, then the number of coins collected by B could be:

    (a) 28   (b) 20
    (c) 26   (d) 22

Directions for Questions 8 and 9: A, B and C are three numbers. Let
@ (A, B) = Average of A and B,

$/ (A, B)$ = Product of A and B, and
$x (A, B)$ = The result of dividing A by B.

8. The sum of A and B is given by:

    (a) $/(@ (A, B), 2)$ (b) $x(@(A, B), 2)$
    (c) $@(/(A, B), 2)$ (d) $@ (x(A, B), 2)$

9. Average of A, B and C is given by:

    (a) $@(/@(/(B, A), 2), C), 3$
    (b) $x(@(/@(B, A), 3), C), 2)$
    (c) $/((x(@ (B, A), 2), C), 3)$
    (d) $/(x(@(/@(B, A), 2), C), 3), 2)$

Directions for Questions 10 and 11: For real numbers x and y, let $f (x, y)$ = Positive square root of $(x + y)$, if $(x + y)^{0.5}$ is real $= (x + y)^2$, otherwise $g (x, y) = (x + y)^2$, if $(x + y)^{0.5}$ is real $= - (x + y)$ otherwise

10. Which of the following expressions yields a positive value for every pair of non-zero real numbers (x, y)?

    (a) $f(x, y) - g(x, y)$ (b) $f(x, y) - (g(x, y))^2$
    (c) $g(x, y) - (f(x, y))^2$ (d) $f(x, y) + g(x, y)$

11. Under which of the following conditions is $f(x, y)$ necessarily greater than $g(x, y)$?

    (a) Both x and y are less than−1
    (b) Both x and y are positive
    (c) Both x and y are negative
    (d) $y > x$

Directions for Questions 12 to 14: For three distinct real numbers x, y and z, let
$f(x, y, z) = \min (\max (x, y), \max (y, z), \max (z, x))$
$g(x, y, z) = \max (\min (x, y), \min (y, z), \min (z, x))$
$h(x, y, z) = \max (\max (x, y), \max (y, z), \max (z, x))$
$j(x, y, z) = \min (\min (x, y), \min (y, z), \min (z, x))$
$m(x, y, z) = \max (x, y, z)$
$n(x, y, z) = \min (x, y, z)$

12. Which of the following is necessarily greater than 1?

    (a) $[h(x, y, z) - f(x, y, z)]/j(x, y, z)$
    (b) $j(x, y, z)/h(x, y, z)$
    (c) $f(x, y, z)/g(x, y, z)$
    (d) $[f(x, y, z) + h(x, y, z) - g(x, y, z)]/j(x, y, z)$

13. Which of the following expressions is necessarily equal to 1?

    (a) $[f(x, y, z) - m(x, y, z)]/[g(x, y, z) - h(x, y, z)]$
    (b) $m(x, y, z) - f(x, y, z) - f(x, y, z)]/[g(x, y, z) - n(x, y, z)]$
    (c) $[j(x, y, z) - g(x, y, z)]/h(x, y, z)$
    (d) $[f(x, y, z) - h(x, y, z)]/f(x, y, z)$

14. Which of the following expressions is in determinate?

    (a) $[f(x, y, z) - h(x, y, z)]/[g(x, y, z) - j(x, y, z)]$
    (b) $f(x, y, z) - h(x, y, z) + g(x, y, z) + j(x, y, z)]/[j(x, y, z) + h(x, y, z) - m(x, y, z) - n(x, y, z)]$
    (c) $[g(x, y, z) - j(x, y, z)]/[f(x, y, z) - h(x, y, z)]$
    (d) $[h(x, y, z) - f(x, y, z)]/[n(x, y, z) - g(x, y, z)]$

15.

x	1	2	3	4	5	6
y	4	8	16	28	44	64

In the above table, for suitable chosen constants a, b and c, which one of the following best describes the relation between y and x?

(a) $y = a + bx$
(b) $y = a + bx + cx^2$
(c) $y = e^{a+bx}$
(d) None of these

16. If $a_1 = 1$ and $a_{n+1} = 2a_n + 5$; $n = 1, 2\ldots\ldots$, then a_{100} is equal to:

(a) $(5 \times 2^{99} - 6)$
(b) $(5 \times 2^{99} + 6)$
(c) $(6 \times 2^{99} + 5)$
(d) $(6 \times 2^{99} - 5)$

17. Let x, y and z be distinct integers that are odd and positive. Which one of the following statements cannot be true?

(a) xyz^2 is odd
(b) $(x - y)^2 z$ is even
(c) $(x + y - z)^2 (x + y)$ is even
(d) $(x - y)(y + z)(x + y - z)$ is odd

18. Let S be the set of prime numbers greater than or equal to 2 and less than 100. Multiply all elements of S. With how many consecutive zeros will the product end?

(a) 1
(b) 4
(c) 5
(d) 10

19. Each of the numbers $x_1, x_2, \ldots\ldots\ldots, x_n$; $n \geq 4$, is equal to 1 or -1. Suppose

$x_1 x_2 x_3 x_4 + x_2 x_3 x_4 x_5 + x_3 x_4 x_5 x_6 + \ldots\ldots\ldots\ldots + x_{n-2} x_{n-1} x_n x_1 + x_{n-1} x_n x_1 x_2 + x_n x_1 x_2 x_3 = 0$, then,

(a) n is even
(b) n is odd
(c) n is an odd multiple of 3
(d) n is prime

For a real number x, let $f(x) = 1/(1 + x)$, if x is non-negative $= 1 + x$, if x is negative $f^n(x) = f(f^{n-1}(x))$; $n = 2, 3\ldots\ldots$

20. What is the value of the product $f(2) f^2(2) f^3(2) f^4(2) f^5(2)$?

(a) $1/13$
(b) 3
(c) $1/18$
(d) None of these

21. r is an integer ≥ 2. Then, what is the value of $f^{r-1}(-r) + f^r(-r) + f^{r+1}(-r)$?

(a) -1
(b) 0
(c) 1
(d) None of these

22. The set of all positive integers is the union of two disjoint subsets:

$\{f(1), f(2), \ldots\ldots, f(n), \ldots..\}$ and $\{g(1), g(2), \ldots\ldots g(n), \ldots\ldots\}$, where $f(1) < f(2) < \ldots\ldots < f(n) \ldots..$, and $g(1) < g(2) < \ldots\ldots < g(n) \ldots\ldots$, and $g(n) = (f(n)) + 1$ for all $n \geq 1$.

What is the value of $g(1)$?

(a) 0
(b) 2
(c) 1
(d) Cannot be determined

Directions for Questions 23 to 25: There are three bottles of water, A, B, C, whose capacities are $10L$, $6L$, and $4L$ respectively. For transferring water from one bottle to another and to drain out the bottles, there exists a piping system. The flow through these pipes is computer–controlled. The computer that controls the flow through these pipes can be fed with three types of instructions, as explained below.

Instruction type	Explanation of the instruction
Fill (X, Y)	Fill bottle labeled X from the water in bottle labeled Y where the remaining capacity of X is less than or equals to the amount of water in Y.
Empty (X, Y)	Empty out the water in bottle labeled X into bottle labeled Y, where the amount of water in X is less than or equals to remaining capacity of Y.
Drain (X)	Drain out all the water contained in bottle labeled X.

Initially, A is full with water, and B and C are empty.

23. After executing a sequence of three instructions, bottle A contains two liters of water. The first and the third of these instructions are shown below.

First instruction: FILL (C, A)

Third instruction: FILL (C, A)

Then, which of the following statements about the instructions is true?

(a) The second instruction is FILL(B, A)
(b) The second instruction is EMPTY(C, B)
(c) The second instruction transfers water from B to C
(d) Cannot be determined

24. Consider the same sequence of three instructions and the same initial state mentioned above. Three more instructions are added at the end of the above sequence to have A contain $8L$ of water. In this total sequence of six instructions, the fourth one is DRAIN (A). This is the only DRAIN instruction in the entire sequence. At the end of the execution of the above sequence, how much water is contained in C?

(a) $2L$
(b) $4L$
(c) 0
(d) None of these

25. For the question above, what is the amount of water contained in B?

(a) $2L$
(b) $4L$
(c) 0
(d) None of these

REVIEW TEST 3

Directions for Questions 1 to 3: These are based on the functions defined below

$$Q(a, b) = \text{Quotient when } a \text{ is divided by } b$$
$$R^2(a, b) = \text{Remainder when } a \text{ is divided by } b$$
$$R(a, b) = a^2/b^2$$
$$SQ(a, b) = \sqrt{(a-1)/(b-1)}$$

1. $SQ(5, 10) - ? > 0$
   (a) $(8/3) R(5, 10)$
   (b) $R^2(5, 10) + Q(5, 10)$
   (c) $R^2(5, 10)/2$
   (d) $\frac{1}{2}\{R(2,3) + SQ(17,26)\}$

2. $SQ(a, b)$ is same as
   (a) $bQ(a, b) + R^2(a)$
   (b) $\sqrt{R(a,b) - 1}$
   (c) $[R\{(a-1), (b-1)\}$
   (d) $\sqrt{R(a,1) - 1}/\sqrt{R(b,1)}$

3. Which of the following relations cannot be false?
   (a) $R(a, b) = R^2(a, b) \cdot Q(a, b)$
   (b) $a^2 \cdot Q(a, b) = b^2 \cdot R^2(a, b)$
   (c) $a = R^2(a, b) + y \cdot Q(a, b)$
   (d) $SQ(a, b) = R(a, b) \cdot R^2(a, b)$

Directions for Questions 4 to 7: *Answer the questions based on the following information:*

$$W(a, b) = \text{least of } a \text{ and } b$$
$$M(a, b) = \text{greatest of } a \text{ and } b$$
$$N(a) = \text{absolute value of } a$$

4. Find the value of $1 + M[y + N\{-W(x, y)\}, N\{y + W(M(x, y), N(y))\}]$ given that $x = 2$ and $y = -3$.
   (a) 0
   (b) 1
   (c) 2
   (d) 3

5. Given that $a > b$, then the relation $M\{N(x), W(x, y)\} = W[x, N\{M(x, y)\}]$ does not hold if
   (a) $x > 0, y < 0, |x| > |y|$
   (b) $x > 0, y < 0, |y| > |x|$
   (c) $x > 0, y > 0$
   (d) $x < 0, y < 0$

6. Which of the following must be correct for $x, y < 0$
   (a) $N(W(x, y)) \leq W(N(x), N(y))$
   (b) $N(M(x, y)) > W(N(x), N(y))$
   (c) $N(M(x, y)) = W(N(x), N(y))$
   (d) $N(M(x, y)) < M(N(x), N(y))$

7. For what value of x is $W(x^2 + 2x, x + 2) < 0$?
   (a) $-2 < x < 2$
   (b) $-2 < x < 0$
   (c) $x < -2$
   (d) Both (2) and (3)

8. It is given that, $(a^{n-3} + a^{n-5} b^2 + \ldots + b^{n-3}) pq = 0$, where p and $q \neq 0$ and n is odd then $\dfrac{(a^n - b^n)(a + b)}{(a^n + b^n)(a - b)}$ =?
   (a) 1
   (b) -1

(c) 3/2
(d) 0

9. If $f = \dfrac{1}{\log_2 \pi} + \dfrac{1}{\log_{4.5} \pi}$, which of the following is true?
   (a) $f > 4$
   (b) $2 < f < 4$
   (c) $1 < f < 2$
   (d) $0 < f < 1$

10. If $px + qy > rx + sy$, and $y, x, p, q, r, s > 0$ and if $x < y$, then which of the following must be true?
    (a) $\dfrac{p}{q} > \dfrac{q}{r}$
    (b) $p - q > r - s$
    (c) $p + q > r + s$
    (d) $p + q < r + s$

Directions for Questions 11 to 13: $f(x)$ and $g(x)$ are defined by the graphs shown below:

Each of the following questions has a graph of function $h(x)$ with the answer choices expressing $h(x)$ in terms of a relationship of $f(x)$ or/and $g(x)$. Choose the alternative that could represents the relationship appropriately.

11.

   (a) $6f(x) + 6g(x)$
   (b) $-1.5f(x) + 1.5g(x)$
   (c) $1.5f(x) + 1.5g(x)$
   (d) None of these

12.

   (a) $9 - f(x) g(x)$
   (b) $[f(x) + g(x) + 4]^2 + [f(x) - 2]^2 + [g(x)]$
   (c) $[f(x) - g(x) + 4]^2 - 2$
   (d) $f(x)g(x) - 9$

13. (a) $2 f(x) + g(x)$
    (b) $f(x) + 2g(x) - 9$
    (c) $\dfrac{3}{2} f(x) + \dfrac{g(x)}{2}$
    (d) None of these

14. If $p^a = q^b = r^c$ and $\dfrac{p}{q} = \dfrac{q}{r}$, $\left(\dfrac{1}{a} + \dfrac{1}{c}\right) b = ?$

(a) 1

(b) 1/2

(c) 3/4

(d) 2

15. What could be the equation of the following curve?

(a) $(a^2 + b^2)^2 = m^2(a^2 + b^2)$

(b) $(a^2 + b^2 - mb)^2 = m^2(a^2 + b^2)$

(c) $a^2 + b^2 - mb = m^2(a^2 + b^2)$

(d) None of these

Directions for Questions 16 to 18: It is given that $f(x) = p^x$, $g(x) = (-p)^x$; $h(x) = (1/p)^x$, $k(x) = (-1/p)^x$

16. Think of a situation where a function is odd or even, if the function is odd it is given a weightage of 1; otherwise, it is given a weightage of 0. What is the result if the weightages of four functions are added?

(a) 2

(b) 0

(c) 1

(d) −1

17. If 'p' and 'x' are both whole numbers other than 0 and 1, which of the functions must have the highest value?

(a) $g(x)$ only

(b) $f(x)$ only

(c) $g(x)$ and $h(x)$ both

(d) $h(x)$ and $k(x)$ both

18. Which of the following is true if 'p' is a positive number and x is a real number?

(a) $\{f(x) - h(x)\} / \{g(x) - k(x)\}$ is always positive

(b) $f(x) \cdot g(x)$ is always negative

(c) $f(x) \cdot h(x)$ is always greater than one

(d) $g(x) \cdot h(x)$ could exist outside the real domain

19. If x, and $y \geq 1$ and belong to set of integers then which of the following is true about the function $(xy)^n$?

(a) The function is odd if 'x' is even and 'y' is odd.

(b) The function is odd if 'x' is odd and 'y' is even.

(c) The function is odd if 'x' and 'y' both are odd.

(d) The function is even if 'x' and 'y' both are even.

20. If $f(a,b)$ = remainder left upon division of b by a, then the maximum value for $f(f(a, b), f(a + 1, b + 1)) \times f(f(a, b), 0)$ is ..... (b and a are co-primes)

(a) $a - 1$

(b) a

(c) 0

(d) 1

Space for Rough Work

REVIEW TEST 4

1. The number of solutions of $\dfrac{\log 5 + \log(y^2 + 1)}{\log(y - 2)} = 2$ is:

   (a) 3 (b) 2
   (c) 1 (d) None of these

Information for Questions 2 and 3: Given below are two graphs labeled $F(x)$ and $G(x)$. Compare the graphs and give the answer in accordance to the options given below:

   (a) $F(-x) = G(x) + x/3$
   (b) $F(-x) = -G(x) - x/2$
   (c) $F(-x) = -G(x) + x/2$
   (d) $2F(-x) = +G(x) - x/3$

2.

3.

4. If a is a natural number which of the following statements is always true?

   (a) $(a + 1)(a^2 + 1)$ is odd
   (b) $9a^2 + 6a + 6$ is even
   (c) $a^2 - 2a$ is even
   (d) $a^2(a^2 + a) + 1$ is odd

5. In the figure below, equation of the line PQ is

   (a) $x + y = 120$ (b) $2x + y = 120$
   (c) $x + 2y = 120$ (d) $2x + y = 180$

6. For which of the following functions is $\dfrac{f(a) - f(b)}{a - b}$ constant for all the numbers 'a' and 'b', where $a \neq b$?

   (a) $f(y) = 4y + 7$ (b) $f(y) = y + y^2$
   (c) $f(y) = \cos y$ (d) $f(y) = \log_e y$

7. Given that $f(a, b, c) = \dfrac{a + b + c}{3}$ then

   (a) $f(a, b, c) \geq \dfrac{|a| + |b| + |c|}{3}$

   (b) $f(a, b, c) \geq \max(a, b, c)$

   (c) $|f(a, b, c)| \geq \dfrac{|a + b + c|}{3}$

   (d) $|f(a, b, c)| \leq \dfrac{|a| + |b| + |c|}{3}$

8. We are given two variables x and y. The values of the variables are $x = \dfrac{1}{a + b}$ and $y = \dfrac{3}{c + x}$. Find the value of the expression $\dfrac{7y}{x}$

   (a) $\dfrac{21(a + b)^2}{ca + cb + 1}$ (b) $\dfrac{3(a + b)}{7\,ab + ac}$

   (c) $\dfrac{7}{3(ca + cb + 1)}$ (d) None of these

9. If $p = \dfrac{12 - |x - 3|}{12 + |x - 3|}$ the maximum value that 'p' can attain is:

   (a) 1 (b) 2
   (c) 21 (d) 12

10.

   Refer to the graph. What does the shaded portion represent?

   (a) $x + y \leq 0$ (b) $x \geq y$
   (c) $x + 1 \geq y + 1$ (d) $x + y \geq 0$

11. If a, b, c are positive numbers and it is known that $a^2 + b^2 + c^2 = 8$ then:

   (a) $a^3 + b^3 + c^3 \leq 16\sqrt{\dfrac{2}{3}}$

   (b) $a^3 + b^3 + c^3 \geq 64$

   (c) $a^3 + b^3 + c^3 \geq 16\sqrt{\dfrac{2}{3}}$

   (d) $a^3 + b^3 + c^3 \leq 64$

12. Find the value of the expression given in terms of variables 'x' and 'y'.

$$\frac{(x^2 + (a-c)x - ac)(x^2 - ax - bx + ab)(x+c)}{(x^2 - a^2)(x^2 - bx^2 - c^2x + bc^2)}$$

(a) $\dfrac{(x-b)(x-c)}{(x-a)}$

(b) $\dfrac{(x+a)(x+c)}{(x-b)}$

(c) $\dfrac{(x+a)(x-b)}{(x-c)}$

(d) None of these

Directions for Questions 13 and 14: These questions are based on the relation given below:

$f^a(y) = f^{a-1}(y-1)$ where $a > 1$ (integer values only) and $f^1(y) = 2/y$ if 'y' is positive or $f^1(y) = 1/(y^2 + 1)$ otherwise.

13. What is $f^a(a-1)$?
   (a) 0
   (b) 1
   (c) 2
   (d) Indeterminate.

14. What is the value of $f^a(a+1)$?
   (a) 1
   (b) a
   (c) 2a
   (d) 2

15. Raman derived an equation to denote distance of a Haley's comet (x) in the form of a quadratic equation. Distance is given by solution of quadratic $x^2 + Bx + c = 0$. To determine constants of the above equation for Haley's Comet, two separate series of experiments were conducted by Raman. Based on the data of first series, value of x obtained is (1, 8) and based on the second series of data, value of x obtained is (2, 10). Later on it is discovered that first series of data gave incorrect value of constant C while second series of data gave incorrect value of constant B. What is the set of actual distance of Haley's Comet found by Raman?
   (a) (11, 3)
   (b) (6, 3)
   (c) (4, 5)
   (d) (3,11)

Space for Rough Work

16. 'a', 'b' and 'c' are three real numbers. Which of the following statements is/are always true?
   (A) $(a-1)(b-1)(c-1) < abc$.
   (B) $(a^2 + b^2 + c^2)/2 \geq ca + cb - ab$
   (C) $a^2 b \sqrt{c}$ is a real number
   (a) Only A is true
   (b) Only B and C are true
   (c) Only B is true
   (d) None is true

17. If we have f[g(y)] = g[f(y)], then which of the following is true?
   (a) [f[f [g[g[g[g(y)]]]]]] = [f[g[g[f[f[g(y)]]]]]]
   (b) [f[f[f[g[f[g(y)]]]]]] = f[f[g[g[g[f(y)]]]]]
   (c) [g[f[g[g[g[f(y)]]]]]] = [f [g[g[f [f[f(y)]]]]]]
   (d) [g[f[g[g[f[g[f(y)]]]]]]] = [f[g[g[g[g[g[f(y)]]]]]]]

18. $f(a) = \dfrac{a^8 - 1}{a^2 + 1}$ and $g(a) = \dfrac{a^4 - 3}{(a+1)^2}$, what is $f\left(\dfrac{1}{g(2)}\right)$?
   (a) 0.652
   (b) $\dfrac{1468}{2250}$
   (c) $-\dfrac{734}{1625}$
   (d) 0

19. Dev was solving a question from his mathematics book when he encountered the expression $\dfrac{\log a}{b - c} = \dfrac{\log b}{c - a} = \dfrac{\log c}{a - b}$ then $a^a\, b^b\, c^c$ is
   (a) –1
   (b) 1
   (c) 0.5
   (d) 2

20. The number of solutions of $\dfrac{\log 5 + \log(a^2 + 1)}{\log(a-2)} = 2$ is:
   (a) 1/2
   (b) 2
   (c) 1
   (d) None of these

REVIEW TEST 5

Directions for the Questions 1 to 3: Refer to the data given below and answer the questions.

Given $\frac{a}{b} = \frac{1}{2}$, $\frac{c}{d} = \frac{1}{3}$ and $z = \frac{a+c}{b+d}$, answer the questions below on limits of z.

1. If $y \geq 0$ and $p \geq 0$ then the limits of 'z' are:

   (a) $z \leq 0$ or $z \geq 1$
   (b) $\frac{1}{3} \leq z \leq \frac{1}{2}$
   (c) $z \geq \frac{1}{2}$ or $z \leq \frac{1}{3}$
   (d) $0 \leq z \leq 1$

2. $c \leq 0$ and $1/3 \leq z \leq 1/2$ only if:

   (a) $a > 1.5c$
   (b) $c > -1$
   (c) $a \leq 0$
   (d) $a > -1.5c$

3. If $a = -31$, which of the following value of 'd' gives the highest value of 'z'?

   (a) $d = 72$
   (b) $d = 721$
   (c) $d = -31$
   (d) $d = 0$

4. Find the integral solution of: $5y - 1 < (y + 1)^2 < (7y - 3)$

   (a) 2
   (b) $2 < y < 4$
   (c) $1 < y < 4$
   (d) 3

5. If $f(a) = \frac{a-1}{a+1}$, $x \geq 0$ and if $y = f\left(\frac{1}{a}\right)$ then

   (a) As 'a' decreases, 'y' decreases
   (b) As 'a' increases, 'y' decreases
   (c) As 'x' increases, 'y' increases
   (d) As 'x' increases, 'y' remains unchanged

6. If f and g are real functions defined by $f(a) = a + 2$ and $g(a) = 2a^2 + 5$, then fog is equal to

   (a) $2a^2 + 7$
   (b) $2a^2 + 5$
   (c) $2(a+2)^2 + 5$
   (d) $2a + 5$

7. If 'p' and 'q' are the roots of the equation $x^2 - 10x + 16 = 0$, the value of $(1 - p)(1 - q)$ is

   (a) -7
   (b) 7
   (c) 16
   (d) -16

8. Given that 'a' and 'b' are positive real numbers such that $a + b = 1$, then what is the minimum value of

   $$\sqrt{12 + \frac{1}{a^2}} + \sqrt{12 + \frac{1}{b^2}} ?$$

   (a) 8
   (b) 16
   (c) 24
   (d) 4

9. Let p, q and r be distinct positive integers satisfying $p < q < r$ and $p + q + r = k$. What is the smallest value of k that does *not* determine p, q, r uniquely?

   (a) 9
   (b) 6
   (c) 7
   (d) 8

10. Given odd positive integers p, q and r which of the following is not necessarily true?

    (a) $p^2 q^2 r^2$ is odd
    (b) $3(p^2 + q^3)r^2$ is even
    (c) $5p + q + r^4$ is odd
    (d) $r^2 (p^4 + q^4)/2$ is even

11. $f(a) = (a^2 + 1)(a^2 - 1)$ where $a = 1, 2, 3...$ which of the following statement is not correct about $f(a)$?

    (a) $f(a)$ is always divisible by 5
    (b) $f(a)$ is always divisible by 3
    (c) $f(a)$ is always divisible by 30
    (d) None of these

Directions for Questions 12 and 13: The following questions are based on the graph of parabola plotted on $x - y$ axes. Answer the questions according to given conditions if applicable and deductions from the graph.

12.

The above graph represent the equations

    (a) $y^2 = kx, k > 0$
    (b) $y^2 = kx, k < 0$
    (c) $x^2 = ky - 1, k < 0$
    (d) $x^2 = ky - 1, k > 0$

13.

The above graph represents the equation

    (a) $x^2 = ky, k < 0$
    (b) $y^2 = kx + 1, k > 0$
    (c) $y^2 = kx + 1, k < 0$
    (d) None of these

14. Mala while teaching her class on functions gives her students a question.

    According to the question the functions are $f(x) = -x$, $g(x) = x$. She also provides her students with following functions also.

    $$f(x, y) = x - y \text{ and } g(x, y) = x + y$$

    Since she wants to test the grasp of her students on functions she asks them a simple question "which of the following is not true?" and provides her students with the following options. None of her students were able to answer the question in single attempt. Can you answer her question?

    (a) $f[f(g(x, y))] = g(x, y)$
    (b) $g[f[g[f(x, y)]]] = f(x, y)$
    (c) $f(x) + g(x) + f(x, y) + g(x, y) = g(x) - f(x)$
    (d) None of these

Directions for Questions 15 and 16: We are given that $f(x) = f(y)$ and $f(x, y) = x + y$, if $x, y > 0$

$f(x, y) = xy$, if $x, y = 0$

$f(x, y) = x - y$, if $x, y < 0$

$f(x, y) = 0$, otherwise

15. Find the value of the following function: $f[f(2, 0),$ $f(-3, 2)] + f[f(-6, -3), f(2, 3)]$.

(a) 0

(b) 2

(c) -8

(d) None of these

16. Find the value of the following function:

$\{f[f(1, 2), f(2, 3)]\} \times \{f[f(1.6, 2.9), f(-1, -3)]\}$

(a) 12

(b) 36

(c) 48

(d) 52

17. Given that $f(a) = a(a + 1)(a + 2)$ where $a = 1, 2,$ $3, \ldots$ Then find $S = f(1) + f(2) + f(3) + \ldots + f(10)$?

(a) 4200

(b) 4290

(c) 4400

(d) None of these

18. We have three inequalities as:

(i) $2^a > a$

(ii) $2^a > 2a + 1$

(iii) $2^a > a^2$

For what natural numbers n are all the three inequalities satisfied?

(a) $a \geq 3$

(b) $a \geq 4$

(c) $a \geq 5$

(d) $a \geq 6$

19. For the curve $p^3 - 3pq + 2 = 0$, the set A of points on the curve at which the tangent to the curve is horizontal and the set B of points on the curve at which the tangent to the curve is vertical are respectively:

(a) (1, 1) and (0, 0)

(b) (0, 0) and (1, 1)

(c) (1, 1) and null set

(d) None of these

20. If $f(a) = a^2 - \dfrac{1}{a^2}$ and $g(a) = \dfrac{1}{\sqrt{f(a) - 4}}$, then the real domain for all values of 'a' such that $f(a)$ and $g(a)$ are both real and defined is represented by the inequality:

(a) $a^2 - a - 1 > 0$

(b) $a^4 - 4a^2 - 1 > 0$

(c) $a^2 - 4a - 1 > 0$

(d) None of these

ANSWER KEY

Review Test 1

1. (d)	2. (b)	3. (d)	4. (a)
5. (a)	6. (b)	7. (b)	8. (c)
9. (c)	10. (c)	11. (b)	12. (a)
13. (b)	14. (d)	15. (d)	16. (a)
17. (b)	18. (a)	19. (c)	20. (d)
21. (b)	22. (d)	23. (a)	24. (d)
25. (c)			

Review Test 2

1. (c)	2. (a)	3. (b)	4. (b)
5. (a)	6. (c)	7. (d)	8. (a)
9. (d)	10. (d)	11. (a)	12. (d)
13. (a)	14. (b)	15. (c)	16. (d)
17. (d)	18. (a)	19. (a)	20. (a)
21. (b)	22. (b)	23. (b)	24. (c)
25. (c)			

Review Test 3

1. (d)	2. (c)	3. (c)	4. (c)
5. (d)	6. (c)	7. (d)	8. (a)
9. (c)	10. (c)	11. (c)	12. (a)
13. (d)	14. (d)	15. (b)	16. (b)
17. (b)	18. (d)	19. (b)	20. (c)

Review Test 4

1. (d)	2. (c)	3. (b)	4. (d)
5. (a)	6. (a)	7. (d)	8. (a)
9. (a)	10. (a)	11. (c)	12. (d)
13. (b)	14. (a)	15. (c)	16. (c)
17. (c)	18. (d)	19. (b)	20. (c)

Review Test 5

1. (b)	2. (c)	3. (d)	4. (b)
5. (b)	6. (a)	7. (d)	8. (a)
9. (d)	10. (d)	11. (d)	12. (b)
13. (d)	14. (b)	15. (a)	16. (d)
17. (b)	18. (c)	19. (c)	20. (b)

BLOCK VI

COUNTING

Chapter 17
Permutations and Combinations

Chapter 18
Probability

Chapter 19
Set Theory

...BACK TO SCHOOL

In my experience, students can be divided into two broad categories on the basis of their ability in solving chapters of this block.

Category 1:   Students who are comfortable in solving questions of this block, since they understand the underlying concepts well.

Category 2:   Students who are not able to tackle questions of this block of chapters since they are not conversant with the counting tools and methods in this block.

If you belong to the second category of students, the main thing you would need to do is to familiarise yourself with the counting methods and techniques of Permutations and Combinations. Once you are through with the same, you would find yourself relatively comfortable at both Permutations & Combinations (P&C) and Probability—the chapters in this block which create the maximum problems for students. Set Theory being a relatively easier chapter, the Back to School section of this block concentrates mostly on P & C and Probability. However, before we start looking at these counting methods, right at the outset, I would want you to remove any negative experiences you might have had while trying to study P& C and Probability. So if you belong to the second category of students, you are advised to read on:

Look at the following table:

Suppose, I were to ask you to count the number of cells in the table above, how would you do it??

$$5 \times 5 = 25!!$$

I guess, all of you realise the fact that the number of cells in this table is given by the product of the number of rows and columns. However, if you ask a 5 year old child to count the same, he would be counting the number of cells physically. In fact, when you were 5 years old, you would also have required to do a physical count of the number of cells in the table. However, there must have come a point where you must have understood that in all such situations (no. of cells in a table, no. of students in a class, etc.) the total count is got by simply multiplying the number of rows and the number of columns. What I am interested in pointing out to you, is that the discovery of this process for this specific counting situation surely made your counting easier!! What used to take you much longer started taking you shorter times. Not only that, in situations where the count was too large (e.g. 100 rows × 48 columns) an infeasible count became extremely easy. So why am I telling you this??

Simply because just as the rows into columns tool for counting had the effect of making your count easier, so also the tools for counting which P& C describe will also have the effect of making counting easier for you in the specific situations of counting that you will encounter. My experience of training students shows that the only reason students have problems in this block is because it has not been explained properly to them in their +2 classes.

Contd

If you try to approach these chapters with the approach that it is not meant to complicate your life but to simplify it, you might end up finding out that there is nothing much to fear in this chapter.

THE TOOL BOX APPROACH TO P&C

While studying P&C, your primary objective should be to familiarise yourself with each and every counting situation. You also need to realise that there are a limited number of counting situations which you need to tackle. You can look at this as the process of the creation of what can be described as a counting tool box.

Once this tool box is created, you would be able to understand the basic situations for counting. Then solving tough questions becomes a matter of simplifying the language of the question into the language of the answer—a matter I would come back to later.

Let us now proceed to list out the specific counting situations which you need to get a hold on. You need to know and understand the following twelve situations of counting and the tools that are used in these situations. Please take note that these tools are explained in detail in various parts of the text on the Permutations and Combinations chapter. You are required to keep these in mind along with the specific situations in which these apply. Look at these as a kind of comprehensive list of situations in which you should know how to count using mathematical tools for your convenience.

The Twelve Counting Situations and Their Tools

Tool No. 1: The ^nC_r tool—This tool is used for the specific situation of counting the number of ways of selecting r things out of n **distinct** things.

Example: Selecting a team of 11 cricketers out of a team of 16 distinct players will be $^{16}C_{11}$.

Tool No. 2: The tool for counting the number of selections of r things out of n **identical** things. (Always 1)

Example: The number of ways of selecting 3 letters out of five A's. Note that in such cases there will only be one way of selecting them.

Tool No. 3: The 2^n tool—The tool for selecting any number (including 0) of things from n **distinct** things $(^nC_0 + {}^nC_1 + {}^nC_2 ..... + {}^nC_n = 2^n)$. Example the number of ways you can or cannot eat sweets at a party if there are ten sweets and you have the option of eating one piece of as many sweets as you like or even of not eating any sweet. Will be given by 2^{10}.

Corollary: The $2^n - 1$ tool—Used when zero selections are not allowed. For instance in the above situation if you are asked to eat at least one sweet and rejecting all sweets is not an option.

Tool No. 4: The $n + 1$ tool—The tool for selecting any number (including 0) of things from n **identical** things. For instance, if you have to select any number of letters from A, A, A, A and A then you can do it in six ways.

Tool No. 5: The $^{n+r-1}C_{r-1}$ tool—The tool for distributing n identical things amongst r people/groups such that any person/group might get any number (including 0). For instance, if you have to distribute 7 identical gifts amongst 5 children in a party then it can be done in $^{(7+5-1)}C_{(5-1)}$ ways. i.e. $^{11}C_4$ ways.

Tool No. 6: The $^{n-1}C_{r-1}$ tool—The tool for distributing n identical things amongst r people/groups such that any person/group might get any number (except 0).

Suppose in the above case you have to give at least one gift to each child it can be done in: $^6C_4$ ways.

Tool No. 7: The mnp rule tool—The tool for counting the number of ways of doing three things when each of them has to be done and there are m ways of doing the first thing, n ways of doing the second thing and p ways of doing the last thing. Suppose you have to go from Lucknow to Varanasi to Patna to Ranchi to Jamshedpur and there are 5 trains from Lucknow to Varanasi & there are 4 trains from Varanasi to Patna, six from Patna to Ranchi and 3 from Ranchi to Jamshedpur, then the number of ways of going from Lucknow to Jamshedpur through Varanasi, Patna & Ranchi is $5 \times 4 \times 6 \times 3 = 360$.

Note that this tool is extremely crucial and is used to form numbers and words.

For example how many 4 digit numbers can you form using the digits 0, 1, 2, 3, 4, 5 & 6 only without repeating any digits. In this situation the work outline is to choose a digit for the first place (=6, any one out of 1, 2, 3, 4, 5 & 6 as zero cannot be used there), then choosing a digit for the second place (=6, select any one out of 5 remaining digits plus 0), then a digit for the third place (5 ways) and a digit for the fourth place (4 ways).

Tool No 8: The r! tool for arrangement—This tool is used for counting the number of ways in which you can arrange r things in r places. Notice that this can be derived out of the mnp rule tool.

Tool No 9: The AND rule tool—Whenever you describe the counting situation and connect two different parts of the count by using the conjunction 'AND', you will always replace the 'AND' with a multiplication sign between the two parts of the count. This is also used for solving Probability questions. For instance, suppose you have to choose a vowel '**AND**' a consonant from the letters of the word PERMIT, you can do it in $^4C_1 \times {}^2C_1$ ways.

Tool No 10: The OR rule tool—Whenever you describe the counting situation and connect two different parts of the count by using the conjunction '**OR**, you will always replace the '**OR**' with an Addition sign between the two parts of the count. This is also used for solving Probability questions. For instance, suppose you have to select either 2 vowels or a consonant from the letters of the word PERMIT, you can do it in $^4C_2 + {}^2C_1$ ways.

Tool No 11: The Circular Permutation Tool [(n – 1)! Tool]—This gives the number of ways in which n distinct things can be placed around a circle. The need to reduce the value of the factorial by 1 is due to the fact that in a circle there is no defined starting point.

Tool No 12: The Circular Permutation Tool when there is no distinction between clockwise and anti clockwise arrangements [(n – 1)!/2 Tool]—This gives the number of ways in which n distinct things can be placed around a circle when there is no distinction between clockwise and anti clockwise arrangements. In such a case the number of circular permutations are just divided by 2.

Two More Issues

(1) What about the ^nP_r tool? The ^nP_r tool is used to arrange r things amongst n. However, my experience shows that the introduction of this tool just adds to the confusion for most students. A little bit of smart thinking gets rid of all the problems that the ^nP_r tool creates in your mind. For this let us consider the difference between the ^nP_r and the ^nC_r tools.

$$^nC_r = n!/[r! \times (n-r)!] \text{ while } {}^nP_r = n!/[(n-r)!].$$

A closer look would reveal that the relationship between the ^nP_r and the ^nC_r tools can be summarised as:

$$^nP_r = {}^nC_r \times r!$$

Read this as: If you have to arrange r things amongst n things, then simply select r things amongst n things and use the $r!$ tool for the arrangement of the selected r

items amongst themselves. This will result in the same answer as the ^nP_r tool.

In fact, for all questions involving arrangements always solve the question in two parts—First finish the selection within the question and then arrange the selected items amongst themselves. This will remove a lot of confusions in questions of this chapter.

(2) Treat Both Permutations and Combinations and Probability as English language chapters rather than Maths chapters: One of the key discoveries in getting stronger at this block is that after knowing the basic twelve counting situations and their tools (as explained above) you need to stop treating the questions in this chapter as questions in Mathematics and rather treat them as questions in English. Thus, while solving a question in these chapters your main concentration and effort should be on converting the question language into the answer language.

What do I mean by this?

Consider this:

Question Language: What is the number of ways of forming 4 letter words from 5 vowels and 6 consonants such that the word contains one vowel and three consonants?

To solve this question, first create the answer language in your mind:

Answer Language: Select one vowel out of 5 **AND** select three consonants out of 6 **AND** arrange the four selected letters amongst themselves.

Once you have this language the remaining part of the answer is just a matter of using the correct tools. Thus, the answer is $^5C_1 \times {}^6C_3 \times 4!$

As you can see, the main issue in getting the solution to this question was working out the language by connecting the various parts of the solution using the conjunction AND (In this case, the conjunction OR was not required.). Once, you had the language all you had to do was use the correct tools to count.

The most difficult of questions are solved this way. This is why I advise you to treat this chapter as a language chapter and not as a chapter in Mathematics!!

Pre-assessment Test

1. How many words of 11 letters could be formed with all the vowels present in even places, using all the letters of the alphabet? (without repetitions)
   (a) $^{21}P_6.5!$
   (b) $21!$
   (c) $^{21}P_5(5!)$
   (d) $^{26}P_s$

2. A candidate is required to answer 6 out of 10 questions, which are divided into two groups each containing 5 questions, and he is not permitted to attempt more than 4 from each group. In how many ways can he make up his choice?
   (a) 300
   (b) 200
   (c) 400
   (d) 100

3. m men and n women are to be seated in a row so that no two women sit together. If $m > n$, then find the number of ways in which they can be seated.
   (a) $m! \times {}^{m+1}P_n$
   (b) $m! \times {}^{m+1}C_n$
   (c) $m! \times {}^mP_n$
   (d) $m! \times {}^mC_n$

4. How many different 4-digit numbers can be made from the first 4 whole numbers, using each digit only once?
   (a) 20
   (b) 18
   (c) 24
   (d) 20

5. How many different 4-digit numbers can be made from the first 4 natural numbers, if repetition is allowed?
   (a) 128
   (b) 512
   (c) 256
   (d) None of these

6. How many six-lettered words starting with the letter T can be made from all the letters of the word TRAVEL?
   (a) 5
   (b) 5!
   (c) 124
   (d) None of these

7. In the question above, how many words can be made with T and L at the end positions?
   (a) 24
   (b) 5!
   (c) 6!
   (d) None of these

8. If the letters of the word ATTEMPT are written down at random, find the probability that all the T's are together.
   (a) 2/7
   (b) 1/7
   (c) 4/7
   (d) 3/7

9. A bag contains 3 white and 2 red balls. One by one, two balls are drawn without replacing them. Find the probability that the second ball is red.
   (a) 2/5
   (b) 1/10
   (c) 2/10
   (d) 3/5

10. Three different numbers are selected from the set $X = \{1,2,3,4,\ldots,10\}$. What is the probability that the product of two of the numbers is equal to the third?
    (a) 3/10
    (b) 1/40
    (c) 1/20
    (d) 4/5

Directions for Questions 11 and 12: Read the passage below and solve the questions based on it.

India plays two matches each with New Zealand and South Africa. In any match, the probability of different outcomes for India is given below:

Outcome	Win	Loss	Draw
Probability	0.5	0.45	0.05
Points	2	0	1

Outcome of all the matches are independent of each other.

11. What is the probability of India getting at least 7 points in the contest? Assume South Africa & New Zealand Play 2 matches.
    (a) 0.025
    (b) 0.0875
    (c) 0.0625
    (d) 0.975

12. What is the probability of South Africa getting at least 4 points? Assume South Africa and New Zealand play 2 matches.
    (a) 0.2025
    (b) 0.0625
    (c) 0.0425
    (d) Can't be determined

13. If $^nC_4 = 126$, then $^nP_4 = ?$
    (a) 126
    (b) 126 * 2!
    (c) 126 * 4!
    (d) None of these

14. The number of ways, in which a student can choose 5 courses out of 9 courses, if 2 courses are compulsory, is
    (a) 53
    (b) 35
    (c) 34
    (d) 32

15. What is the value of $^{18}C_{16}$?
    (a) 5!
    (b) 6!
    (c) 153
    (d) Can't be determined

16. How many triangles can be drawn from N given points on a circle?
    (a) N!
    (b) 3!
    (c) N! / 3!
    (d) $(N-1)N(N-2)/6$

17. Following are the alphabets for which the alphabet and its mirror image are same. $A, H, I, M, 0, T, U, V, W, Y, X$. These alphabets are called as symmetrical. Other are called as unsymmetrical. A password containing 4 alphabets (without repetitions) is to be formed using symmetrical alphabets. How many such passwords can be formed?
    (a) 720
    (b) 330
    (c) 7920
    (d) Can't be determined

18. How many 5 letter words can be formed out of 10 consonants and 4 vowels, such that each contains 3 consonants and 2 vowels?
    (a) $^{10}P_3 \times {}^4P_2 \times 5!$ (b) $^{10}C_3 \times {}^4C_2 \times 5!$
    (c) $^{10}P_3 \times {}^4C_2 \times 5!$ (d) $^{10}C_2 \times {}^4P_2 \times 5!$

19. A question paper consists of two sections A and B having respectively 3 and 4 questions. Four questions are to be solved to qualify in that paper. It is compulsory to solve at least one question from Section A and two questions from Section B. In how many ways can a candidate select the questions to qualify in that paper?
    (a) 30   (b) 18
    (c) 48   (d) 60

20. A student is allowed to select at most n books from a collection of $(2n + 1)$ books. If the total number of ways in which he can select at least one book is 63, find the value of n.
    (a) 4   (b) 3
    (c) 5   (d) 6

21. A man and a woman appear in an interview for two vacancies for the same post. The probability of a man's selection is 1/4 and that of a woman's selection is 1/3. What is the probability that both of them will be selected?
    (a) 1/12   (b) 1/3
    (c) 2/5   (d) 3/7

22. In Question 21, what will be the probability that only one of them will be selected?
    (a) 11/12   (b) 1/2
    (c) 7/12   (d) 5/12

23. In Question 21, what will be the probability that none of them will be selected?
    (a) 1/2   (b) 1/3
    (c) 2/5   (d) 3/7

24. How many different signals can be made by hoisting 5 different coloured flags one above the other, when any number of them may be hoisted a time?
    (a) 2^5 (b) $^5P_5$
    (c) 325   (d) None of these

25. Find the number of ways in which the letters of the word MACHINE can be arranged so that the vowels may occupy only odd positions.
    (a) $4! \times 4!$ (b) $^7P_3 \times 4!$
    (c) $^7P_4 \times 3!$ (d) None of these

ANSWER KEY

1. (a)	2. (b)	3. (a)	4. (b)
5. (c)	6. (b)	7. (d)	8. (b)
9. (a)	10. (b)	11. (b)	12. (d)
13. (c)	14. (b)	15. (c)	16. (d)
17. (c)	18. (b)	19. (a)	20. (b)
21. (a)	22. (d)	23. (a)	24. (c)
25. (a)			

17 Chapter

Permutations and Combinations

STANDARD THEORY

Factorial Notation! Or $\lfloor$

$$\lfloor n = n(n-1)(n-2)\ldots3.2.1$$

$$n! = \underline{n}(n-1)(n-2)\ldots3.2.1$$

= Product of n consecutive integers starting from 1.

1. $0! = 1$

2. Factorials of only Natural numbers are defined.

   $n!$ is defined only for $n \geq 0$

   $n!$ is not defined for $n < 0$

4. $^nC_r = 1$ when $n = r$.

5. Combinations (represented by ^nC_r) can be defined as the number of ways in which r things at a time can be **SELECTED** from amongst n things available for selection.

   The key word here is **SELECTION**. Please understand here that the order in which the r things are selected has no importance in the counting of combinations.

   ^nC_r = Number of combinations (selections) of n things taken r at a time.

   $^nC_r = n! /[r! \, (n-r)!]$; where $n \geq r$ (n is greater than or equal to r).

   Some typical situations where selection/combination is used:

   (a) Selection of people for a team, a party, a job, an office etc. (e.g. Selection of a cricket team of 11 from 16 members)

   (b) Selection of a set of objects (like letters, hats, points pants, shirts, etc) from amongst another set available for selection.

In other words any selection in which the order of selection holds no importance is counted by using combinations.

6. Permutations (represented by ^nP_r) can be defined as the number of ways in which r things at a time can be **SELECTED & ARRANGED** at a time from amongst n things.

The key word here is **ARRANGEMENT**. Hence please understand here that the order in which the r things are arranged has critical importance in the counting of permutations.

In other words permutations can also be referred to as an **ORDERED SELECTION**.

^nP_r = number of permutations (arrangements) of n things taken r at a time.

$^nP_r = n!/ (n-r)!; \; n \geq r$

Some typical situations where **ordered selection/ permutations** are used:

(a) Making words and numbers from a set of available letters and digits respectively

(b) Filling posts with people

(c) Selection of batting order of a cricket team of 11 from 16 members

(d) Putting distinct objects/people in distinct places, e.g. making people sit, putting letters in envelopes, finishing order in horse race, etc.)

The exact difference between selection and arrangement can be seen through the illustration below:

Selection

Suppose we have three men A, B and C out of which 2 men have to be selected to two posts.

This can be done in the following ways: AB, AC or BC (These three represent the basic selections of 2 people out of three which are possible. Physically they can be counted as 3 distinct selections. This value can also be got by using $3C_2$.

Note here that we are counting AB and BA as one single selection. So also AC and CA and BC and CB are considered to be the same instances of selection since the order of selection is not important.

Arrangement

Suppose we have three men A, B and C out of which 2 men have to be selected to the post of captain and vice captain of a team.

In this case we have to take AB and BA as two different instances since the order of the arrangement makes a difference in who is the captain and who is the vice captain.

Similarly, we have BC and CB and AC and CA as 4 more instances. Thus in all there could be 6 arrangements of 2 things out of three.

This is given by $^3P_2 = 6$.

7. **The Relationship Between Permutation & Combination:**

   When we look at the formulae for Permutations and Combinations and compare the two we see that,

   $$^nP_r = r! \times {}^nC_r$$
   $$= {}^nC_r \times {}^rP_r$$

   This in words can be said as:

   The permutation or arrangement of r things out of n is nothing but the selection of r things out of n followed by the arrangement of the r selected things amongst themselves.

8. **MNP Rule:** If there are three things to do and there are M ways of doing the first thing, N ways of doing the second thing and P ways of doing the third thing then there will be **M × N × P** ways of doing all the three things together. The works are mutually inclusive.

   This is used to for situations like:

   The numbers 1, 2, 3, 4 and 5 are to be used for forming 3 digit numbers without repetition. In how many ways can this be done?

   Using the MNP rule you can visualise this as: There are three things to do→ The first digit can be selected in 5 distinct ways, the second can be selected in 4 ways and the third can be selected in 3 different ways. Hence, the total number of 3 digit numbers that can be formed are $5 \times 4 \times 3 = 60$

9. When the pieces of work are mutually exclusive, there are M+N+P ways of doing the complete work.

Important Results

The following results are important as they help in problem solving.

1. Number of permutations (or arrangements) of n different things taken all at a time = $n!$

2. Number of permutations of n things out of which P_1 are alike and are of one type, P_2 are alike and are of a second type and P_3 are alike and are of a third type and the rest are all different = $n! / P_1! P_2! P_3!$

   Illustration: The number of words formed with the letters of the word Allahabad.

   Solution: Total number of Letters = 9 of which A occurs four times, L occurs twice and the rest are all different.

   Total number of words formed = $9! / (4! 2! 1!)$

3. Number of permutations of n different things taken r at a time when repetition is allowed = $n \times n \times n \times ... (r$ times$) = n^r$.

   Illustration: In how many ways can 4 rings be worn in the index, ring finger and middle finger if there is no restriction of the number of rings to be worn on any finger?

   Solution: Each of the 4 rings could be worn in 3 ways either on the index, ring or middle finger. So, four rings could be worn in $3 \times 3 \times 3 \times 3 = 3^4$ ways.

4. Number of selections of r things out of n identical things = 1

   Illustration: In how many ways 5 marbles can be chosen out of 100 identical marbles?

   Solution: Since, all the 100 marbles are identical Hence, Number of ways to select 5 marbles = 1

5. Total number of selections of zero or more things out of k identical things = $k + 1$.

   This includes the case when zero articles are selected.

6. Total number of selections of zero or more things out of n different things =
   $$^nC_o + {}^nC_1 + {}^nC_2 + ... + {}^nC_n$$
   $$^nC_o + {}^nC_1 + {}^nC_2 + ... + {}^nC_n = 2^n$$
   Corollary: The number of selections of 1 or more things out of n different things = $^nC_1 + {}^nC_2 + ... + {}^nC_n = 2^n - 1$

7. Number of ways of distributing n identical things among r persons when each person may get any number of things = $^{n+r-1}C_{r-1}$

   Imagine a situation where 27 marbles have to be distributed amongst 4 people such that each one of them can get any number of marbles (including zero marbles). Then for this situation we have, $n = 27$ (no. of identical objects), $r = 4$ (no. of people) and the answer of the number of ways this can be achieved is given by:
   $$^{n+r-1}C_{r-1} = {}^{30}C_3.$$

8. Corollary: No. of ways of dividing n non distinct things to r distinct groups are:
   $$^{n-1}C_{r-1} \rightarrow \text{For non-empty groups only}$$

Also, the number of ways in which n distinct things can be distributed to r different persons:
$$= r^n$$

9. Number of ways of dividing $m + n$ different things in two groups containing m and n things respectively $=$
$$^{m+n}C_n \times {}^mC_m =$$
$$= (m + n)! \ /m! \ n!$$
Or, $^{m+n}C_m \times {}^nC_n = (m + n)! \ / \ n! \ m!$

10. Number of ways of dividing $2n$ different things in two groups containing n things $= 2n! \ / \ n! \ n! \ 2!$

11. $^nC_r + {}^nC_{r-1} = {}^{n+1}C_r$

12. $^nC_x = {}^nC_y \Rightarrow x = y$ or $x + y = n$

13. $^nC_r = {}^nC_{n-r}$

14. $r \cdot {}^nC_r = n \cdot {}^{n-1}C_{r-1}$

15. $^nC_r \ / \ (r + 1) = {}^{n+1}C_{r+1} \ /(\ n + 1)$

16. For ^nC_r to be greatest,
    (a) if n is even, $r = n/2$
    (b) if n is odd, $r = (n + 1)/2$ or $(n - 1)/2$

17. Number of selections of r things out of n different things
    (a) When k particular things are always included
    $$= {}^{n-k}C_{r-k}$$
    (b) When k particular things are excluded $= {}^{n-k}C_r$
    (c) When all the k particular things are not together in any selection
    $$= {}^nC_r - {}^{n-k}C_{r-k}$$
    No. of ways of doing a work with given restriction $=$ total no. of ways of doing it — no. of ways of doing the same work with opposite restriction.

18. The total number of ways in which 0 to n things can be selected out of n things such that p are of one type, q are of another type and the balance r of different types is given by: $(p + 1)(q + 1)(2^r - 1)$.

19. Total number of ways of taking some or all out of $p + q + r$ things such that p are of one type and q are of another type and r of a third type
    $$= (p + 1)(q + 1)(r + 1) - 1$$
    [Only non-empty sets]

20. $\dfrac{^nC_r}{^nC_{r-1}} = \dfrac{n - r + 1}{r}$

21. Number of selections of k consecutive things out of n things in a row $= n - k + 1$

Circular Permutations

Consider two situations:
There are three A, B and C. In the first case, they are arranged linearly and in the other, around a circular table –

Linear arrangement $\Rightarrow$ ABC BCA and CAB

ABC
ACB
BCA
BAC
CAB
CBA

Circular A

$\Rightarrow$ ACB CBA and BAC

For the linear arrangement, each arrangement is a totally new way. For circular arrangements, three linear arrangements are represented by one and the same circular arrangement.

So, for six linear arrangements, there correspond only 2 circular arrangements. This happens because there is no concept of a starting point on a circular arrangement. (i.e., the starting point is not defined.)

Generalising the whole process, for $n!$, there corresponds to be $(1/n) \ n!$ ways.

Important Results

1. Number of ways of arranging n people on a circular track (circular arrangement) $= (n - 1)!$

2. When clockwise and anti-clockwise observation are not different then number of circular arrangements of n different things $= (n - 1)! \ /2$
   e.g. the case of a necklace with different beads, the same arrangement when looked at from the opposite side becomes anti-clockwise.

3. Number of selections of k consecutive things out of n things in a circle
   $$= n \text{ when } k < n$$
   $$= 1 \text{ when } k = n$$

Some More Results

1. Number of terms in $(a_1 + a_2 + ... + a_n)^m$ is $^{m+n-1}C_{n-1}$

   Illustration: Find the number of terms in $(a + b + c)^2$.

   Solution: $n = 3$, $m = 2$
   $^{m+n-1}C_{n-1} = {}^4C_2 = 6$
   Corollary: Number of terms in
   $(1 + x + x^2 + ... x^n)^m$ is $mn + 1$

2. Number of zeroes ending the number represented by
   $n! = [n \ /5] + [n \ /5^2] + [n \ /5^3] + ... [n \ /5^x]$
   [] Shows greatest integer function where $5^x \le n$

   Illustration: Find the number of zeroes at the end of 1000!

   Solution: $[1000/5] + [1000/5^2] + [1000/5^3] + [1000/5^4]$
   $200 + 40 + 8 + 1 = 249$

   Corollary: Exponent of 3 in $n! = [n!/3] + [n!/32] + [n!/3^3] + ... [n!/3^x]$ where $3^x \le n$
   [] Shows greatest integer fn.

   Illustration: Find how many exponents of 3 will be there in 24!.

   Solution: $[24/3] + [24/3^2] = 8 + 2 = 10$

3. Number of squares in a square of $n \times n$ side $= 1^2 + 2^2 + 3^2 + 4^2 + \dots n^2$

   Number of rectangles in a square of $n \times n$ side $= 1^3 + 2^3 + 3^3 + 4^3 + \dots n^3$. (This includes the number of squares.)

   Thus the number of squares and rectangles in the following figure are given by:

Number of squares $= 1^2 + 2^2 + 3^2 = 14 = \in n^2$

Number of rectangles $= 1^3 + 2^3 + 3^3 = 36$ $(\in n)^2 = \in n^3$ for the rectangle.

A rectangle having m rows and n columns:

The number of squares is given by: $m.n + (m - 1)(n - 1) + (m - 2)(n - 2) + \dots$ until any of $(m - x)$ or $(n - x)$ comes to 1.

The number of rectangles is given by: $(1 + 2 + \dots + m)(1 + 2 + \dots + n)$

Space for Notes

WORKED-OUT PROBLEMS

In the following examples the solution is given upto the point of writing down the formula that will apply for the particular question. The student is expected to calculate the values after understanding the solution.

Problem 17.1 Find the number of permutations of 6 things taken 4 at a time.

Solution The answer will be given by $^6P_4$.

Problem 17.2 How many 3-digit numbers can be formed out of the digits 1, 2, 3, 4 and 5?

Solution Forming numbers requires an ordered selection. Hence, the answer will be $^5P_3$.

Problem 17.3 In how many ways can the 7 letters M, N, O, P, Q, R, S be arranged so that P and Q occupy continuous positions?

Solution For arranging the 7 letters keeping P and Q always together we have to view P and Q as one letter. Let this be denoted by $\underline{PQ}$.

Then, we have to arrange the letters M, N, O, $\underline{PQ}$, R and S in a linear arrangement. Here, it is like arranging 6 letters in 6 places (since 2 letters are counted as one). This can be done in 6! ways.

However, the solution is not complete at this point of time since in the count of 6! the internal arrangement between P and Q is neglected. This can be done in 2! ways. Hence, the required answer is 6! × 2!.

Task for the student: What would happen if the letters P, Q and R are to be together? (Ans: 5! × 3!)

What if P and Q are never together? (Answer will be given by the formula: Total number of ways − Number of ways they are always together)

Problem 17.4 Of the different words that can be formed from the letters of the words BEGINS how many begin with B and end with S?

Solution B & S are fixed at the start and the end positions. Hence, we have to arrange E, G, I and N amongst themselves. This can be done in 4! ways.

Task for the student: What will be the number of words that can be formed with the letters of the word BEGINS which have B and S at the extreme positions? (Ans: 4! × 2!)

Problem 17.5 In how many ways can the letters of the word VALEDICTORY be arranged, so that all the vowels are adjacent to each other?

Solution There are 4 vowels and 7 consonants in Valedictory. If these vowels have to be kept together, we have to consider AEIO as one letter. Then the problem transforms itself into arranging 8 letters amongst themselves (8! ways). Besides, we have to look at the internal arrangement of the 4 vowels amongst themselves. (4! ways)

Hence Answer = 8! × 4!.

Problem 17.6 If there are two kinds of hats, red and blue and at least 5 of each kind, in how many ways can the hats be put in each of 5 different boxes?

Solution The significance of at least 5 hats of each kind is that while putting a hat in each box, we have the option of putting either a red or a blue hat. (If this was not given, there would have been an uncertainty in the number of possibilities of putting a hat in a box.)

Thus in this question for every task of putting a hat in a box we have the possibility of either putting a red hat or a blue hat. The solution can then be looked at as: there are 5 tasks each of which can be done in 2 ways. Through the MNP rule we have the total number of ways = 2^5 (Answer).

Problem 17.7 In how many ways can 4 Indians and 4 Nepalese people be seated around a round table so that no two Indians are in adjacent positions?

Solution If we first put 4 Indians around the round table, we can do this in 3! ways.

Once the 4 Indians are placed around the round table, we have to place the four Nepalese around the same round table. Now, since the Indians are already placed we can do this in 4! ways (as the starting point is defined when we put the Indians. Try to visualize this around a circle for placing 2 Indians and 2 Nepalese.)

Hence, Answer = 3! × 4!

Problem 17.8 How many numbers greater than a million can be formed from the digits 1, 2, 3, 0, 4, 2, 3?

Solution In order to form a number greater than a million we should have a 7 digit number. Since we have only seven digits with us we cannot take 0 in the starting position. View this as 7 positions to fill:

— _ — _ — _ —

To solve this question we first assume that the digits are all different. Then the first position can be filled in 6 ways (0 cannot be taken), the second in 6 ways (one of the 6 digits available for the first position was selected. Hence, we have 5 of those 6 digits available. Besides, we also have the zero as an additional digit), the third in 5 ways (6 available for the 2nd position − 1 taken for the second position.) and so on. Mathematically this can be written as:

$$6 \times 6 \times 5 \times 4 \times 3 \times 2 \times 1 = 6 \times 6!$$

This would have been the answer had all the digits been distinct. But in this particular example we have two 2's and two 3's which are identical to each other. This complication is resolved as follows to get the answer:

$$\frac{6 \times 6}{2! \times 2!}$$

Problem 17.9 If there are 11 players to be selected from a team of 16, in how many ways can this be done?

Solution $^{16}C_{11}$.

Problem 17.10 In how many ways can 18 identical white and 16 identical black balls be arranged in a row so that no two black balls are together?

Solution When 18 identical white balls are put in a straight line, there will be 19 spaces created. Thus 16 black balls will have 19 places to fill in. This will give an answer of: $^{19}C_{16}$. (Since, the balls are identical the arrangement is not important.)

Problem 17.11 A mother with 7 children takes three at a time to a cinema. She goes with every group of three that she can form. How many times can she go to the cinema with distinct groups of three children?

Solution She will be able to do this as many times as she can form a set of three distinct children from amongst the seven children. This essentially means that the answer is the number of selections of 3 people out of 7 that can be done.

Hence, Answer = $^{7}C_{3}$.

Problem 17.12 For the above question, how many times will an individual child go to the cinema with her before a group is repeated?

Solution This can be viewed as: The child for whom we are trying to calculate the number of ways is already selected. Then, we have to select 2 more children from amongst the remaining 6 to complete the group. This can be done in $^{6}C_{2}$ ways.

Problem 17.13 How many different sums can be formed with the following coins:
5 rupee, 1 rupee, 50 paisa, 25 paisa, 10 paisa and 1 paisa?

Solution A distinct sum will be formed by selecting either 1 or 2 or 3 or 4 or 5 or all 6 coins.

But from the formula we have the answer to this as :
$2^6 - 1$.

[Task for the student: How many different sums can be formed with the following coins:

5 rupee, 1 rupee, 50 paisa, 25 paisa, 10 paisa, 3 paisa, 2 paisa and 1 paisa?

Hint: You will have to subtract some values for double counted sums.]

Problem 17.14 A train is going from Mumbai to Pune and makes 5 stops on the way. 3 persons enter the train during the journey with 3 different tickets. How many different sets of tickets may they have had?

Solution Since the 3 persons are entering during the journey they could have entered at the:

1st station (from where they could have bought tickets for the 2nd, 3rd, 4th or 5th stations or for Pune → total of 5 tickets.)

2nd station (from where they could have bought tickets for the 3rd, 4th or 5th stations or for Pune → total of 4 tickets.)

3rd station (from where they could have bought tickets for the 4th or 5th stations or for Pune → total of 3 tickets.)

4th station (from where they could have bought tickets for the 5th station or for Pune → total of 2 tickets.)

5th station (from where they could have bought a ticket for Pune → total of 1 ticket.)

Thus, we can see that there are a total of 5 + 4 + 3 + 2 + 1 = 15 tickets available out of which 3 tickets were selected. This can be done in $^{15}C_{3}$ ways (Answer).

Problem 17.15 Find the number of diagonals and triangles formed in a decagon.

Solution A decagon has 10 vertices. A line is formed by selecting any two of the ten vertices. This can be done in $^{10}C_{2}$ ways. However, these $^{10}C_{2}$ lines also count the sides of the decagon.

Thus, the number of diagonals in a decagon is given by: $^{10}C_{2} - 10$ (Answer)

Triangles are formed by selecting any three of the ten vertices of the decagon. This can be done in $^{10}C_{3}$ ways (Answer).

Problem 17.16 Out of 18 points in a plane, no three are in a straight line except 5 which are collinear. How many straight lines can be formed?

Solution If all 18 points were non-collinear then the answer would have been $^{18}C_{2}$. However, in this case $^{18}C_{2}$ has double counting since the 5 collinear points are also amongst the 18. These would have been counted as $^{5}C_{2}$ whereas they should have been counted as 1. Thus, to remove the double counting and get the correct answer we need to adjust by reducing the count by ($^{5}C_{2} - 1$).

Hence, Answer = $^{18}C_{2} - (^{5}C_{2} - 1) = {}^{18}C_{2} - {}^{5}C_{2} + 1$

Problem 17.17 For the above situation, how many triangles can be formed?

Solution The triangles will be given by $^{18}C_{3} - {}^{5}C_{3}$.

Problem 17.18 A question paper had ten questions. Each question could only be answered as True (T) or False (F). Each candidate answered all the questions. Yet, no two candidates wrote the answers in an identical sequence. How many different sequences of answers are possible?

(a) 20   (b) 40

(c) 512   (d) 1024

Solution $2^{10} = 1024$ unique sequences are possible. Option (d) is correct.

Problem 17.19 When ten persons shake hands with one another, in how many ways is it possible?

(a) 20   (b) 25
(c) 40   (d) 45

Solution For n people there are always $^nC_2$ shake hands. Thus, for 10 people shaking hands with each other the number of ways would be $^{10}C_2 = 45$.

Problem 17.20 In how many ways can four children be made to stand in a line such that two of them, A and B are always together?

(a) 6   (b) 12
(c) 18   (d) 24

Solution If the children are A, B, C, D we have to consider A & B as one child. This, would give us 3! ways of arranging AB, C and D. However, for every arrangement with AB, there would be a parallel arrangement with BA. Thus, the correct answer would be $3! \times 2! = 12$ ways. Option (b) is correct.

Problem 17.21 Each person's performance compared with all other persons is to be done to rank them subjectively. How many comparisons are needed to total, if there are 11 persons?

(a) 66   (b) 55
(c) 54   (d) 45

Solution There would be $^{11}C_2$ combinations of 2 people taken 2 at a time for comparison. $^{11}C_2 = 55$.

Problem 17.22 A person X has four notes of Rupee 1, 2, 5 and 10 denomination. The number of different sums of money she can form from them is

(a) 16   (b) 15
(c) 12   (d) 8

Solution $2^4 - 1 = 15$ sums of money can be formed. Option (b) is correct.

Problem 17.23 A person has 4 coins each of different denomination. What is the number of different sums of money the person can form (using one or more coins at a time)?

(a) 16   (b) 15
(c) 12   (d) 11

Solution $2^4 - 1 = 15$. Hence, option (b) is correct.

Problem 17.24 How many three-digit numbers can be generated from 1, 2, 3, 4, 5, 6, 7, 8, 9, such that the digits are in ascending order?

(a) 80   (b) 81
(c) 83   (d) 84

Solution Numbers starting with 12 – 7 numbers

Numbers starting with 13 – 6 numbers; 14 – 5, 15 – 4, 16 – 3, 17 – 2, 18 – 1. Thus total number of numbers starting from 1 is given by the sum of 1 to 7 = 28.

Number of numbers starting from 2- would be given by the sum of 1 to 6 = 21

Number of numbers starting from 3- sum of 1 to 5 = 15

Number of numbers starting from 4 – sum of 1 to 4 = 10

Number of numbers starting from 5 – sum of 1 to 3 = 6

Number of numbers starting from 6 = 1 + 2 = 3

Number of numbers starting from 7 = 1

Thus a total of: $28 + 21 + 15 + 10 + 6 + 3 + 1 = 84$ such numbers. Option (d) is correct.

Problem 17.25 In a carrom board game competition, m boys n girls ($m > n > 1$) of a school participate in which every student has to play exactly one game with every other student. Out of the total games played, it was found that in 221 games one player was a boy and the other player was a girl.

Consider the following statements:

I. The total number of students that participated in the competition is 30.

II. The number of games in which both players were girls is 78.

Which of the statements given above is/are correct?

(a) I only   (b) II only
(c) Both I and II   (d) Neither I nor II.

Solution The given condition can get achieved if we were to use 17 boys and 13 girls. In such a case both statement I and II are correct. Hence, option (c) is correct.

Problem 17.26

In how many different ways can all of 5 identical balls be placed in the cells shown above such that each row contains at least 1 ball?

(a) 64   (b) 81
(c) 84   (d) 108

Solution The placement of balls can be 3, 1, 1 and 2, 2, 1. For 3, 1, 1- If we place 3 balls in the top row, there would be $^3C_1$ ways of choosing a place for the ball in the second row and $^3C_1$ ways of choosing a place for the ball in the third row. Thus, $^3C_1 \times {}^3C_1 = 9$ ways. Similarly there would be 9 ways each if we were to place 3 balls in the second row and 3 balls in the third row. Thus, with the 3, 1, 1 distribution of 5 balls we would get $9 + 9 + 9 = 27$ ways of placing the balls.

We now need to look at the 2, 2, 1 arrangement of balls. If we place 1 ball in the first row, we would need to place 2 balls each in the second and the third rows. In such a case, the number of ways of arranging the balls would be $^3C_1 \times {}^3C_2 \times {}^3C_2 = 27$ ways. (choosing 1 place out of 3 in the first row, 2 places out of 3 in the second row and 2 places out of 3 in the third row).

Similarly if we were to place 1 ball in the second row and 2 balls each in the first and third rows we would get 27 ways of placing the balls and another 27 ways of placing the balls if we place 1 ball in the third row and 2 balls each in the other two rows.

Thus with a 2, 2, 1 distribution of the 5 balls we would get 27 + 27 + 27 = 81 ways of placing the balls.

Hence, total number of ways = Number of ways of placing the balls with a 3,1,1 distribution of balls + number of ways of placing the balls with a 2, 2, 1 distribution of balls = 27 + 81 = 108.

Hence, option (d) is correct.

Problem 17.27 There are 6 different letter and 6 correspondingly addressed envelopes. If the letters are randomly put in the envelopes, what is the probability that exactly 5 letters go into the correctly addressed envelopes?

    (a) Zero   (b) 1/6
    (c) 1/2   (d) 5/6

Solution If 5 letters go into the correct envelopes the sixth would automatically go into it's correct envelope. Thus, there is no possibility when exactly 5 letters are correct and 1 is wrong. Hence, option (a) is correct.

Problem 17.28

There are two identical red, two identical black and two identical white balls. In how many different ways can the balls be placed in the cells (each cell to contain one ball) shown above such that balls of the same colour do not occupy any two consecutive cells?

    (a) 15   (b) 18
    (c) 24   (d) 30

Solution In the first cell, we have 3 options of placing a ball. Suppose we were to place a red ball in the first cell- then the second cell can only be filled with either black or white – so 2 ways. Subsequently there would be 2 ways each of filling each of the cells (because we cannot put the colour we have already used in the previous cell).

Thus, the required number of ways would be 3 × 2 × 2 × 2 = 24 ways.

Hence, option (c) is correct.

Problem 17.29

How many different triangles are there in the figure shown above?

    (a) 28   (b) 24
    (c) 20   (d) 16

Solution Look for the smallest triangles first—there are 12 of them.

Then, look for the triangles which are equal to half the rectangle—there are 12 of them.

Besides, there are 4 bigger triangles (spanning across 2 rectangles).

Thus a total of 28 triangles can be seen in the figure. Hence, option (a) is correct.

Problem 17.30 A teacher has to choose the maximum different groups of three students from a total of six students. Of these groups, in how many groups there will be included a particular student?

    (a) 6   (b) 8
    (c) 10   (d) 12

Solution If the students are A, B, C, D, E and F- we can have $^6C_3$ groups in all. However, if we have to count groups in which a particular student (say A) is always selected- we would get $^5C_2 = 10$ ways of doing it. Hence, option (c) is correct.

Problem 17.31 Three dice (each having six faces with each face having one number from 1 to 6) are rolled. What is the number of possible outcomes such that at least one dice shows the number 2?

    (a) 36   (b) 81
    (c) 91   (d) 116

Solution **All 3 dice have twos** – 1 case.

Two dice have twos:

This can principally occur in 3 ways which can be broken into:

If the first two dice have 2- the third dice can have 1, 3, 4, 5 or 6 = 5 ways.

Similarly, if the first and third dice have 2, the second dice can have 5 outcomes → 5 ways and if the second and third dice have a 2, there would be another 5 ways. Thus a total of 15 outcomes if 2 dice have a 2.

With only 1 dice having a two- If the first dice has 2, the other two can have 5 × 5 = 25 outcomes.

Similarly 25 outcomes if the second dice has 2 and 25 outcomes if the third dice has 2. A total of 75 outcomes. Thus, a total of 1 + 15 + 75 = 91 possible outcomes with at least.

Hence, option (c) is correct.

Problem 17.32 All the six letters of the name SACHIN are arranged to form different words without repeating any letter in any one word. The words so formed are then arranged as in a dictionary. What will be the position of the word SACHIN in that sequence?

    (a) 436   (b) 590
    (c) 601   (d) 751

Solution All words staring with A, C, H, I and N would be before words starting with S. So we would have 5! Words (= 120 words) each starting with A, C, H, I and N. Thus, a total of 600 words would get completed before we start off with S. SACHIN would be the first word starting with S, because A, C, H, I, N in that order is the correct alphabetical sequence. Hence, Sachin would be the 601st word. Hence, option (c) is correct.

Problem 17.33 Five balls of different colours are to be placed in three different boxes such that any box contains at least one 1 ball. What is the maximum number of different ways in which this can be done?

    (a) 90   (b) 120
    (c) 150   (d) 180

Solution The arrangements can be [3 & 1 & 1 or 1 & 3 & 1 or 1 & 1 & 3] or 2 & 2 & 1 or 2 & 1 & 2 or 1 & 2 and 2.

Total number of ways = $3 \times {}^5C_3 \times {}^2C_1 \times {}^1C_1 + 3 \times {}^5C_2 \times {}^3C_2 \times {}^1C_1 = 60 + 90 = 150$ ways

Hence, option (c) is correct.

Problem 17.34 Amit has five friends: 3 girls and 2 boys. Amit's wife also has 5 friends : 3 boys and 2 girls. In how many maximum number of different ways can they invite 2 boys and 2 girls such that two of them are Amit's friends and two are his wife's?

(a) 24   (b) 38
(c) 46   (d) 58

Solution The selection can be done in the following ways:

2 boys from Amit's friends and 2 girls from his wife's friends OR 1 boy & 1 girl from Amit's friends and 1 boy and 1 girl from his wife's friends OR 2 girls from Amit's friends and 2 boys from his wife's friends.

The number of ways would be:

${}^2C_2 \times {}^2C_2 + {}^3C_1 \times {}^2C_1 \times {}^3C_1 \times {}^2C_1 + {}^3C_2 \times {}^3C_2 = 1 + 36 + 9 = 46$ ways.

Problem 17.35

In the given figure, what is the maximum number of different ways in which 8 identical balls can be placed in the small triangles 1, 2, 3 and 4 such that each triangle contains at least one ball?

(a) 32   (b) 35
(c) 44   (d) 56

Solution The ways of placing the balls would be 5, 1, 1, 1 (4!/3! = 4 ways); 4, 2, 1 & 1 (4!/2! = 12 ways); 3, 3, 1, 1 (4!/2! × 2! = 6 ways); 3, 2, 2, 1 (4!/2! = 12 ways) and 2, 2, 2, 2 (1 way). Total number of ways = 4 + 12 + 6 + 12 + 1 = 35 ways. Hence, option (b) is correct.

Problem 17.36 6 equidistant vertical lines are drawn on a board. 6 equidistant horizontal lines are also drawn on the board cutting the 6 vertical lines, and the distance between any two consecutive horizontal lines is equal to that between any two consecutive vertical lines. What is the maximum number of squares thus formed?

(a) 37   (b) 55
(c) 91   (d) 225

Solution The number of squares would be $1^2 + 2^2 + 3^2 + 4^2 + 5^2 + 6^2 = 91$. Hence, option (c) is correct.

Problem 1.37 Groups each containing 3 boys are to be formed out of 5 boys—A, B, C, D and E such that no group contains both C and D together. What is the maximum number of such different groups?

(a) 5   (b) 6
(c) 7   (d) 8

Solution All groups – groups with C and D together = ${}^5C_3 - {}^3C_1 = 10 - 3 = 7$

Problem 17.38

In how many maximum different ways can 3 identical balls be placed in the 12 squares (each ball to be placed in the exact centre of the squares and only one ball is to be placed in one square) shown in the figure given above such that they do not lie along the same straight line ?

(a) 144   (b) 200
(c) 204   (d) 216

Solution The thought process for this question would be:

All arrangements $({}^{12}C_3)$ – Arrangements where all 3 balls are in the same row $(3 \times {}^4C_3)$– arrangements where all 3 balls are in the same straight line diagonally (4 arrangements) – arrangements where all 3 balls are in the same column (4 arrangements) = ${}^{12}C_3 - 3 \times {}^4C_3 - 4 - 4 = 220 - 12 - 4 - 4 = 200$ ways.

Hence, option (b) is correct.

Problem 17.39 How many numbers are there in all from 6000 to 6999 (Both 6000 and 6999 included) having at least one of their digits repeated?

(a) 216   (b) 356
(c) 496   (d) 504

Solution All numbers – numbers having no numbers repeated = $1000 - 9 \times 8 \times 7 = 1000 - 504 = 496$ numbers. Hence, option (c) is correct.

Problem 17.40 Each of two women and three men is to occupy one chair out of eight chairs, each of which is numbered from one to eight. First, women are to occupy any two chairs from\those numbered one to four; and then the three men would occupy any three chairs out of the remaining six chairs. What is the maximum number of different ways in which this can be done?

(a) 40   (b) 132
(c) 1440   (d) 3660

Solution ${}^4C_2 \times 2! \times {}^6C_3 \times 3! = 6 \times 2 \times 20 \times 6 = 1440$. Hence, option (c) is correct.

Problem 17.41 A box contains five set of balls while there are three balls in each set. Each set of balls has one colour which is different from every other set. What is the least number of balls that must be removed from the box in order to claim with certainty that a pair of balls of the same colour has been removed?

(a) 6   (b) 7
(c) 9   (d) 11

Solution Let $C1, C2, C3, C4$ and $C5$ be the 5 distinct colours which have no repetition. For being definitely sure that we have picked up 2 balls of the same colour we need to consider the worst case situation.

Consider the following scenario:

Set 1	Set 2	Set 3	Set 4	Set 5
C1	C2	C3	C4	C5
C6	C8	C7	C9	C9
C7	C6	C10	C10	C8

In the above distribution of balls each set has exactly 1 ball which is unique in it's colour while the colours of the other two balls are shared at least once in one of the other sets. In such a case, the worst scenario would be if we pick up the first 10 balls and they all turn out to be of different colours. The 11th ball has to be of a colour which has already been taken. Thus, if we were to pick out 11 balls we would be sure of having at least 2 balls of the same colour. Hence, option (d) is correct.

Problem 17.42 In a question paper, there are four multiple-choice questions. Each question has five choices with only one choice as the correct answer. What is the total number of ways in which a candidate will not get all the four answers correct?

(a) 19 (b) 120
(c) 624 (d) 1024

Solution 5^4 would be the total number of ways in which the questions can be answered. Out of these there would be only 1 way of getting all 4 correct. Thus, there would be 624 ways of not getting all answers correct.

Problem 17.43

Each of 8 identical balls is to be placed in the squares shown in the figure given in a horizontal direction such that one horizontal row contains 6 balls and the other horizontal row contains 2 balls. In how many maximum different ways can this be done?

(a) 38 (b) 28
(c) 16 (d) 14

Solution The 6 balls must be on either of the middle rows. This can be done in 2 ways. Once, we put the 6 balls in their single horizontal row- it becomes evident that for placing the 2 remaining balls on a straight line there are 2 principal options:

1. Placing the two balls in one of the four rows with two squares. In this case the number of ways of placing the balls in any particular row would be 1 way (since once you were to choose one of the 4 rows, the balls would automatically get placed as there are only two squares in each row.) Thus the total number of ways would be $2 \times 4 \times 1 = 8$ ways.

2. Placing the two balls in the other row with six squares. In this case the number of ways of placing the 2 balls in that row would be $^6C_2$. This would give us $^2C_1 \times 1 \times {}^6C_2 = 30$ ways. Total is $30 + 8 = 38$ ways.

Hence, option (a) is correct.

Problem 17.44 In a tournament each of the participants was to play one match against each of the other participants. 3 players fell ill after each of them had played three matches and had to leave the tournament. What was the total number of participants at the beginning, if the total number of matches played was 75?

(a) 8 (b) 10
(c) 12 (d) 15

Solution The number of players at the start of the tournament cannot be 8, 10 or 12 because in each of these cases the total number of matches would be less than 75 (as $^8C_2$, $^{10}C_2$ and $^{12}C_2$ are all less than 75.) This only leaves 15 participants in the tournament as the only possibility.

Hence, option (d) is correct.

Problem 17.45 There are three parallel straight lines. Two points A and B are marked on the first line, points C and D are marked on the second line and points E and F are marked on the third line. Each of these six points can move to any position on its respective straight line.

Consider the following statements:

I. The maximum number of triangles that can be drawn by joining these points is 18.

II. The minimum number of triangles that can be drawn by joining these points is zero.

Which of the statements given above is/are correct?

(a) I only (b) II only
(c) Both I and II (d) Neither I nor II

Solution The maximum triangles would be in case all these 6 points are non-collinear. In such a case the number of triangles is $^6C_3 = 20$. Statement I is incorrect.

Statement II is correct because if we take the position that A and B coincide on the first line, C & D coincide on the second line, E & F coincide on the third line and all these coincidences happen at 3 points which are on the same straight line- in such a case there would be 0 triangles formed. Hence, option (b) is correct.

Problem 17.46 A mixed doubles tennis game is to be played between two teams (each team consists of one male and one female). There are four married couples. No team is to consist of a husband and his wife. What is the maximum number of games that can be played?

(a) 12 (b) 21
(c) 36 (d) 42

Solution First select the two men. This can be done in $^4C_2$ ways. Let us say the men are A, B, C and D and their respective wives are a, b, c and d.

If we select A and B as the two men then while selecting the women there would be two cases as seen below:

Case 1:

A	If b is selected to partner A
B	There will be 3 choices for choosing B's partner – viz a, c and d

Thus, total number of ways in this case = ${}^4C_2 \times 1 \times {}^3C_1 = 18$ ways.

Case 2:

A	If either c or d is selected to partner A
B	There will be 2 choices for choosing B's partner – viz a and any one of c and d

Total number of ways of doing this = ${}^4C_2 \times 2 \times {}^2C_1 = 24$ ways.

Hence, the required answer is $18 + 24 = 42$ ways.

Hence, option (d) is correct.

Space for Rough Work

LEVEL OF DIFFICULTY (I)

1. How many numbers of 3-digits can be formed with the digits 1, 2, 3, 4, 5 (repetition of digits not allowed)?
   - (a) 125
   - (b) 120
   - (c) 60
   - (d) 150

2. How many numbers between 2000 and 3000 can be formed with the digits 0, 1, 2, 3, 4, 5, 6, 7 (repetition of digits not allowed?
   - (a) 42
   - (b) 210
   - (c) 336
   - (d) 440

3. In how many ways can a person send invitation cards to 6 of his friends if he has four servants to distribute the cards?
   - (a) 6^4
   - (b) 4^6
   - (c) 24
   - (d) 120

4. In how many ways can 5 prizes be distributed to 8 students if each student can get any number of prizes?
   - (a) 40
   - (b) 5^8
   - (c) 8^5
   - (d) 120

5. In how many ways can 7 Indians, 5 Pakistanis and 6 Dutch be seated in a row so that all persons of the same nationality sit together?
   - (a) 3!
   - (b) 7!5!6!
   - (c) 3!.7!.5!.6!
   - (d) 182

6. There are 5 routes to go from Allahabad to Patna & 4 ways to go from Patna to Kolkata, then how many ways are possible for going from Allahabad to Kolkata via Patna?
   - (a) 20
   - (b) 5^4
   - (c) 4^5
   - (d) $5^4 + 4^5$

7. There are 4 qualifying examinations to enter into Oxford University: RAT, BAT, SAT, and PAT. An Engineer cannot go to Oxford University through BAT or SAT. A CA on the other hand can go to the Oxford University through the RAT, BAT & PAT but not through SAT. Further there are 3 ways to become a CA(viz., Foundation, Inter & Final). Find the ratio of number of ways in which an Engineer can make it to Oxford University to the number of ways a CA can make it to Oxford University.
   - (a) 3:2
   - (b) 2:3
   - (c) 2:9
   - (d) 9:2

8. How many straight lines can be formed from 8 non-collinear points on the X-Y plane?
   - (a) 28
   - (b) 56
   - (c) 18
   - (d) 19860

9. If $^nC_3 = {}^nC_8$, find n.
   - (a) 11
   - (b) 12
   - (c) 14
   - (d) 10

10. In how many ways can the letters of the word DELHI be arranged?
   - (a) 119
   - (b) 120
   - (c) 60
   - (d) 24

11. In how many ways can the letters of the word PATNA be rearranged?
   - (a) 60
   - (b) 120
   - (c) 119
   - (d) 59

12. For the arrangements of the letters of the word PATNA, how many words would start with the letter P?
   - (a) 24
   - (b) 12
   - (c) 60
   - (d) 120

13. In Question no.11, how many words will start with P and end with T?
   - (a) 3
   - (b) 6
   - (c) 11
   - (d) 12

14. If $^nC_4 = 70$, find n.
   - (a) 5
   - (b) 8
   - (c) 4
   - (d) 7

15. If $^{10}P_r = 720$, find r.
   - (a) 4
   - (b) 5
   - (c) 3
   - (d) 6

16. How many numbers of four digits can be formed with the digits 0, 1, 2, 3 (repetition of digits is not allowed?
   - (a) 18
   - (b) 24
   - (c) 64
   - (d) 192

17. How many numbers of four digits can be formed with the digits 0, 1, 2, 3 (repetition of digits being allowed?
   - (a) 12
   - (b) 108
   - (c) 256
   - (d) 192

18. How many numbers between 200 and 1200 can be formed with the digits 0, 1, 2, 3 (repetition of digits not allowed?
   - (a) 6
   - (b) 6
   - (c) 2
   - (d) 14

19. For the above question, how many numbers can be formed with the same digits if repetition of digits is allowed?
   - (a) 48
   - (b) 63
   - (c) 32
   - (d) 14

20. If $(2n + 1)P_{(n-1)} : (2n - 1)P_n = 7:10$ find n
    (a) 4   (b) 6
    (c) 3   (d) 7

21. If $(^{28}C_{2r} : {}^{24}C_{2r-4}) = 225:11$ Find the value of r.
    (a) 10   (b) 11
    (c) 7   (d) 9

22. Arjit being a party animal wants to hold as many parties as possible amongst his 20 friends. However, his father has warned him that he will be financing his parties under the following conditions only:
    (a) The invitees have to be amongst his 20 best friends.
    (b) He cannot call the same set of friends to a party more than once.
    (c) The number of invitees to every party have to be the same.
    Given these constraints Arjit wants to hold the maximum number of parties. How many friends should he invite to each party?
    (a) 11   (b) 8
    (c) 10   (d) 12

23. In how many ways can 10 identical presents be distributed among 6 children so that each child gets at least one present?
    (a) $^{15}C_5$ (b) $^{16}C_6$
    (c) $^9C_5$ (d) 6^{10}

24. How many four digit numbers are possible, criteria being that all the four digits are odd?
    (a) 125   (b) 625
    (c) 45   (d) none of these

25. A captain and a vice-captain are to be chosen out of a team having eleven players. How many ways are there to achieve this?
    (a) 10.9   (b) $^{11}C_2$
    (c) 110   (d) 10.9!

26. There are five types of envelopes and four types of stamps in a post office. How many ways are there to buy an envelope and a stamp?
    (a) 20   (b) 45
    (c) 54   (d) 9

27. In how many ways can Ram choose a vowel and a consonant from the letters of the word ALLAHABAD?
    (a) 4   (b) 6
    (c) 9   (d) 5

28. There are three rooms in a motel: one single, one double and one for four persons. How many ways are there to house seven persons in these rooms?
    (a) 7!/1!2!4!   (b) 7!
    (c) 7!/3   (d) 7!/3!

29. How many ways are there to choose four cards of different suits and different values from a deck of 52 cards?

(a) 13.12.11.10   (b) $^{52}C_4$
(c) 134   (d) 52.36.22.10

30. How many new words are possible from the letters of the word PERMUTATION?
    (a) 11!/2!   (b) (11!/2!) − 1
    (c) 11! − 1   (d) None of these

31. A set of 15 different words are given. In how many ways is it possible to choose a subset of not more than 5 words?
    (a) 4944   (b) 4^{15}
    (c) 15^4 (d) 4943

32. In how many ways can 12 papers be arranged if the best and the worst paper never come together?
    (a) 12!/2!   (b) 12! − 11!
    (c) (12! − 11!)/2   (d) 12! − 2.11!

33. In how many ways can the letters of the word 'EQUATION' be arranged so that all the vowels come together?
    (a) $^9C_4 \cdot {}^9C_5$ (b) 4!.5!
    (c) 9!/5!   (d) 9! − 4!5!

34. A man has 3 shirts, 4 trousers and 6 ties. What are the number of ways in which he can dress himself with a combination of all the three?
    (a) 13   (b) 72
    (c) 13!/3!.4!.6!   (d) 3!.4!.6!

35. How many motor vehicle registration number of 4 digits can be formed with the digits 0, 1, 2, 3, 4, 5? (No digit being repeated.)
    (a) 1080   (b) 120
    (c) 300   (d) 360

36. How many motor vehicle registration number plates can be formed with the digits 1, 2, 3, 4, 5 (No digits being repeated) if it is given that registration number can have 1 to 5 digits?
    (a) 100   (b) 120
    (c) 325   (d) 205

Directions for Question 37 to 39: There are 25 points on a plane of which 7 are collinear. Now solve the following:

37. How many straight lines can be formed?
    (a) 7   (b) 300
    (c) 280   (d) none of these

38. How many triangles can be formed from these points?
    (a) 453   (b) 2265
    (c) 755   (d) none of these

39. How many quadrilaterals can be formed from these points?
    (a) 5206   (b) 2603
    (c) 13015   (d) None of these

40. There are ten subjects in the school day at St. Vincent's High School but the sixth standard students have only 5 periods in a day. In how many ways can we form a time table for the day for the sixth standard students if no subject is repeated?
    (a) 510
    (b) 105
    (c) 252
    (d) 30240

41. There are 8 consonants and 5 vowels in a word jumble. In how many ways can we form 5-letter words having three consonants and 2 vowels?
    (a) 67200
    (b) 8540
    (c) 720
    (d) None of these

42. How many batting orders are possible for the Indian cricket team if there is a squad of 15 to choose from such that Sachin Tendulkar is always chosen?
    (a) 1001.11!
    (b) 364.11!
    (c) 11!
    (d) 15.11!

43. There are 5 blue socks, 4 red socks and 3 green socks in Debu's wardrobe. He has to select 4 socks from this set. In how many ways can he do so?
    (a) 245
    (b) 120
    (c) 495
    (d) 60

44. A class prefect goes to meet the principal every week. His class has 30 people apart from him. If he has to take groups of three every time he goes to the principal, in how many weeks will he be able to go to the principal without repeating the group of same three which accompanies him?
    (a) $^{30}P_3$
    (b) $^{30}C_3$
    (c) 30!/3
    (d) None of these

45. For the above question if on the very first visit the principal appoints one of the boys accompanying him as the head boy of the school and lays down the condition that the class prefect has to be accompanied by the head boy every time he comes then for a maximum of how many weeks (including the first week) can the class prefect ensure that the principal sees a fresh group of three accompanying him?
    (a) $^{30}C_2$
    (b) $^{29}C_2$
    (c) $^{29}C_3$
    (d) None of these

46. How many distinct words can be formed out of the word PROWLING which start with R & end with W?
    (a) 8!/2!
    (b) 6!2!
    (c) 6!
    (d) None of these

47. How many 7-digit numbers are there having the digit 3 three times & the digit 5 four times?
    (a) 7!/(3!)(5!)
    (b) $3^3 \times 5^5$
    (c) 77
    (d) 35

48. How many 7-digit numbers are there having the digit 3 three times & the digit 0 four times?
    (a) 15
    (b) $3^3 \times 4^4$
    (c) 18
    (d) None of these

49. From a set of three capital consonants, five small consonants and 4 small vowels how many words can be made each starting with a capital consonant and containing 3 small consonants and two small vowels.
    (a) 3600
    (b) 7200
    (c) 21600
    (d) 28800

50. Several teams take part in a competition, each of which must play one game with all the other teams. How many teams took part in the competition if they played 45 games in all?
    (a) 5
    (b) 10
    (c) 15
    (d) 20

51. In how many ways a selection can be made of at least one fruit out of 5 bananas, 4 mangoes and 4 almonds?
    (a) 129
    (b) 149
    (c) 139
    (d) 109

52. There are 5 different Jeffrey Archer books, 3 different Sidney Sheldon books and 6 different John Grisham books. The number of ways in which at least one book can be given away is
    (a) $2^{10} - 1$
    (b) $2^{11} - 1$
    (c) $2^{12} - 1$
    (d) $2^{14} - 1$

53. In the above problem, find the number of ways in which at least one book of each author can be given.
    (a) $(2^5 - 1)(2^3 - 1)(2^8 - 1)$
    (b) $(2^5 - 1)(2^3 - 1)(2^3 - 1)$
    (c) $(2^5 - 1)(2^3 - 1)(2^3 - 1)$
    (d) $(2^5 - 1)(2^3 - 1)(2^6 - 1)$

54. There is a question paper consisting of 15 questions. Each question has an internal choice of 2 options. In how many ways can a student attempt one or more questions of the given fifteen questions in the paper?
    (a) 3^7
    (b) 3^8
    (c) 3^{15}
    (d) $3^{15} - 1$

55. How many numbers can be formed with the digits 1, 6, 7, 8, 7, 6, 1 so that the odd digits always occupy the odd places?
    (a) 15
    (b) 12
    (c) 18
    (d) 20

56. There are five boys of McGraw-Hill Mindworkzz and three girls of I.I.M Lucknow who are sitting together to discuss a management problem at a round table. In how many ways can they sit around the table so that no two girls are together?
    (a) 1220
    (b) 1400
    (c) 1420
    (d) 1440

57. Amita has three library cards and seven books of her interest in the library of Mindworkzz. Of these books she would not like to borrow the D.I. book, unless the Quants book is also borrowed. In how

many ways can she take the three books to be borrowed?

(a) 15   (b) 20
(c) 25   (d) 30

58. From a group of 12 dancers, five have to be taken for a stage show. Among them Radha and Mohan decide either both of them would join or none of them would join. In how many ways can the 5 dancers be chosen?

(a) 190   (b) 210
(c) 278   (d) 372

59. Find the number of 6-digit numbers that can be found using the digits 1, 2, 3, 4, 5, 6 once such that the 6-digit number is divisible by its unit digit. (The unit digit is not 1.)

(a) 620   (b) 456
(c) 520   (d) 528

60. An urn contains 5 boxes. Each box contains 5 balls of different colours red, yellow, white, blue and black. Rangeela wants to pick up 5 balls of different colours, a different coloured ball from each box. If from the first box in the first draw, he has drawn a red ball and from the second box he has drawn a black ball, find the maximum number of trials that are needed to be made by Rangeela to accomplish his task if a ball picked is not replaced.

(a) 12   (b) 11
(c) 20   (d) 60

61. How many rounds of matches does a knock-out tennis tournament have if it starts with 64 players and every player needs to win 1 match to move at the next round?

(a) 5   (b) 6
(c) 7   (d) 64

62. There are N men sitting around a circular table at N distinct points. Every possible pair of men except the ones sitting adjacent to each other sings a 2 minute song one pair after other. If the total time taken is 88 minutes, then what is the value of N?

(a) 8   (b) 9
(c) 10   (d) 11

63. In a class with boys and girls a chess competition was played wherein every student had to play 1 game with every other student. It was observed that in 36 matches both the players were boys and in 66 matches both were girls. What is the number of matches in which 1 boy and 1 girl play against each other?

(a) 108   (b) 189
(c) 210   (d) 54

64. Zada has to distribute 15 chocolates among 5 of her children Sana, Ada, Jiya, Amir and Farhan. She has to make sure that Sana gets at least 3 and at most 6 chocolates. In how many ways can this be done?

(a) 495   (b) 77
(c) 417   (d) 435

65. Mr Shah has to divide his assets worth ₹ 30 crores in 3 parts to be given to three of his songs Ajay, Vijay and Arun ensuring that every son gets assets atleast worth ₹ 5 crores. In how many ways can this be done if it is given that the three sons should get their shares in multiples of ₹ 1 crore?

(a) 136   (b) 152
(c) 176   (d) 98

66. Three variables x, y, z have a sum of 30. All three of them are non-negative integers. If any two variables don't have the same value and exactly one variable has a value less than or equal to three, then find the number of possible solutions for the variables.

(a) 98   (b) 285
(c) 68   (d) 294

67. The letters of the word ALLAHABAD are rearranged to form new words and put in a dictionary. If the dictionary has only these words and one word on every page in alphabetical order then what is the page number on which the word LABADALAH comes?

(a) 6089   (b) 6088
(c) 6087   (d) 6086

68. If x, y and z can only take the values 1, 2, 3, 4, 5, 6, 7 then find the number of solutions of the equation $x + y + z = 12$.

(a) 36   (b) 37
(c) 38   (d) 31

69. There are nine points in a plane such that no three are collinear. Find the number of triangles that can be formed using these points as vertices.

(a) 81   (b) 90
(c) 9   (d) 84

70. There are nine points in a plane such that exactly three points out of them are collinear. Find the number of triangles that can be formed using these points as vertices.

(a) 81   (b) 90
(c) 9   (d) 83

71. If xy is a 2-digit number and u, v, x, y are digits, then find the number of solutions of the equation: $(xy)^2 = u! + v$

(a) 2   (b) 3
(c) 0   (d) 5

72. Ten points are marked on a straight line and eleven points are marked on another straight line. How many triangles can be constructed with vertices from among the above points?

(a) 495   (b) 550
(c) 1045   (d) 2475

73. For a scholarship, at the most *n* candidates out of 2*n* + 1 can be selected. If the number of different ways of selection of at least one candidate is 63, the maximum number of candidates that can be selected for the scholarship is
    (a) 3
    (b) 4
    (c) 2
    (d) 5

74. One red flag, three white flags and two blue flags are arranged in a line such that,
    (a) no two adjacent flags are of the same colour
    (b) the flags at the two ends of the line are of different colours.
    In how many different ways can the flags be arranged?
    (a) 6
    (b) 4
    (c) 10
    (d) 2

75. Sam has forgotten his friend's seven-digit telephone number. He remembers the following: the first three digits are either 635 or 674, the number is odd, and the number nine appears once. If Sam were to use a trial and error process to reach his friend, what is the minimum number of trials he has to make before he can be certain to succeed?
    (a) 1000
    (b) 2430
    (c) 3402
    (d) 3006

76. There are three cities *A*, *B* and *C*. Each of these cities is connected with the other two cities by at least one direct road. If a traveler wants to go from one city (origin) to another city (destination), she can do so either by traversing a road connecting the two cities directly, or by traversing two roads, the first connecting the origin to the third city and the second connecting the third city to the destination. In all there are 33 routes from *A* to *B* (including those via *C*). Similarly there are 23 routes from *B* to *C* (including those via *A*). How many roads are there from *A* to *C* directly?
    (a) 6
    (b) 3
    (c) 5
    (d) 10

77. Let *n* be the number of different 5-digit numbers, divisible by 4 that can be formed with the digits 1, 2, 3, 4, 5 and 6, with no digit being repeated. What is the value of *n*?
    (a) 144
    (b) 168
    (c) 192
    (d) none of these

78. How many numbers greater than 0 and less than a million can be formed with the digits 0, 7 and 8?
    (a) 486
    (b) 1086
    (c) 728
    (d) none of these

79. In how many ways is it possible to choose a white square and a black square on a chess board so that the squares must not lie in the same row or column?
    (a) 56
    (b) 896
    (c) 60
    (d) 768

Directions for Questions 80 and 81: Answer these questions based on the information given below.

Each of the 11 letters *A*, *H*, *I*, *M*, *O*, *T*, *U*, *V*, *W*, *X* and *Z* appear same when looked at in a mirror. They are called symmetric letters. Other letters in the alphabet are asymmetric letters.

80. How many four-letter computer passwords can be formed using only the symmetric letters (no repetition allowed)?
    (a) 7920
    (b) 330
    (c) 14640
    (d) 419430

81. How many three-letter computer passwords can be formed (no repetition allowed) with at least one symmetric letter?
    (a) 990
    (b) 2730
    (c) 12870
    (d) 15600

82. Twenty seven persons attend a party. Which one of the following statements can never be true?
    (a) There is a person in the party who is acquainted with all the twenty six others.
    (b) Each person in the party has a different number of acquaintances.
    (c) There is a person in the party who has an odd number of acquaintances.
    (d) In the party, there is no set of three mutual acquaintances.

83. There are 6 boxes numbered 1, 2, ...6. Each box is to be filled up either with a red or a green ball in such a way that at least 1 box contains a green ball and the boxes containing green balls are consecutively numbered. The total number of ways in which this can be done is
    (a) 5
    (b) 21
    (c) 33
    (d) 60

84. How many numbers can be formed with odd digits 1, 3, 5, 7, 9 without repetition?
    (a) 275
    (b) 325
    (c) 375
    (d) 235

85. In how many ways five chocolates can be chosen from an unlimited number of Cadbury, Five-star, and Perk chocolates?
    (a) 81
    (b) 243
    (c) 21
    (d) 31

86. How many even numbers of four digits can be formed with the digits 1, 2, 3, 4, 5, 6 (repetitions of digits are allowed)?
    (a) 648
    (b) 180
    (c) 1296
    (d) 540

Directions for Questions 87 and 88: In a chess tournament there were two women participating and every participant played two games with the other participants. The number of games that the men played among themselves exceeded the number of games that the men played with the women by 66.

87. The number of participants in the tournament were?

   (a) 12   (b) 13

   (c) 15   (d) 11

88. The total number of games played in the tournament were?

   (a) 132   (b) 110

   (c) 156   (d) 210

Space for Rough Work

LEVEL OF DIFFICULTY (II)

1. How many even numbers of four digits can be formed with the digits 1, 2, 3, 4, 5, 6 (repetitions of digits are allowed)?
   - (a) 648
   - (b) 180
   - (c) 1296
   - (d) 600

2. How many 4 digit numbers divisible by 5 can be formed with the digits 0, 1, 2, 3, 4, 5, 6 and 6?
   - (a) 220
   - (b) 249
   - (c) 432
   - (d) 288

3. There are 6 pups and 4 cats. In how many ways can they be seated in a row so that no cats sit together?
   - (a) 6^4
   - (b) $10!/(4!).(6!)$
   - (c) $6! \times {}^7P_4$
   - (d) None of these

4. How many new words can be formed with the word MANAGEMENT all ending in G?
   - (a) $10!/(2!)^4 - 1$
   - (b) $9!/(2!)^4$
   - (c) $10!/(2!)^4$
   - (d) None of these

5. Find the total numbers of 9-digit numbers that can be formed all having different digits.
   - (a) ${}^{10}P_9$
   - (b) $9!$
   - (c) $10! - 9!$
   - (d) $9.9!$

6. There are V lines parallel to the x-axis and 'W' lines parallel to y-axis. How many rectangles can be formed with the intersection of these lines?
   - (a) ${}^vP_2.{}^wP_2$
   - (b) ${}^vC_2.{}^wC_2$
   - (c) ${}^{v-2}C_2.{}^{w-2}C_2$
   - (d) None of these

7. From 4 gentlemen and 4 ladies a committee of 5 is to be formed. Find the number of ways of doing so if the committee consists of a president, a vice-president and three secretaries?
   - (a) ${}^8P_5$
   - (b) 1120
   - (c) ${}^4C_2 \times {}^4C_3$
   - (d) None of these

8. In the above question, what will be the number of ways of selecting the committee with at least 3 women such that at least one woman holds the post of either a president or a vice-president?
   - (a) 420
   - (b) 610
   - (c) 256
   - (d) None of these

9. Find the number of ways of selecting the committee with a maximum of 2 women and having at the maximum one woman holding one of the two posts on the committee.
   - (a) 16
   - (b) 512
   - (c) 608
   - (d) 324

10. The crew of an 8 member rowing team is to be chosen from 12 men, of which 3 must row on one side only and 2 must row on the other side only. Find the number of ways of arranging the crew with 4 members on each side.
    - (a) 40,320
    - (b) 30,240
    - (c) 60,480
    - (d) None of these

11. In how many ways 5 MBA students and 6 Law students can be arranged together so that no two MBA students are side by side?
    - (a) $\dfrac{7!6!}{2!}$
    - (b) $6!.6!$
    - (c) $5!.6!$
    - (d) ${}^{11}C_5$

12. The latest registration number issued by the Delhi Motor Vehicle Registration Authority is DL-5S 2234. If all the numbers and alphabets before this have been used up, then find how many vehicles have a registration number starting with DL-5?
    - (a) 1,92,234
    - (b) 1,92,225
    - (c) 1,72,227
    - (d) None of these

13. There are 100 balls numbered $n_1, n_2, n_3, n_4, \ldots n_{100}$. They are arranged in all possible ways. How many arrangements would be there in which n_{28} ball will always be before n_{29} ball and the two of them will be adjacent to each other?
    - (a) $99!/2!$
    - (b) $99!.2!$
    - (c) $99!$
    - (d) None of these

14. Find the sum of the number of sides and number of diagonals of a hexagon.
    - (a) 210
    - (b) 15
    - (c) 6
    - (d) 9

15. A tea party is arranged for $2M$ people along two sides of a long table with M chairs on each side. R men wish to sit on one particular side and S on the other. In how many ways can they be seated (provided R, $S \le M$)
    - (a) ${}^MP_R.{}^MP_S$
    - (b) ${}^MP_R.{}^MP_S\left({}^{2M-R-S}P_{2M-R-S}\right)$
    - (c) ${}^{2M}P_R.{}^{2M-R}P_S$
    - (d) None of these

16. In how many ways can 'mn' things be distributed equally among n groups?
    - (a) ${}^{mn}P_m.{}^{mn}P_n$
    - (b) ${}^{mn}C_m.{}^{mn}C_n$
    - (c) $(mn)!/(m!)(.n!)$
    - (d) None of these

17. In how many ways can a selection be made of 5 letters out of 5As, 4Bs, 3Cs, 2Ds and 1E?
    - (a) 70
    - (b) 71
    - (c) ${}^{15}C_5$
    - (d) None of these

18. Find the number of ways of selecting 'n' articles out of $3n + 1$, out of which n are identical.
    (a) 2^{2n-1}
    (b) $^{3n+1}C_n/n!$
    (c) $^{3n+1}P_n/n!$
    (d) None of these

19. The number of positive numbers of not more than 10 digits formed by using 0, 1, 2, 3 is
    (a) $4^{10} - 1$
    (b) 4^{10}
    (c) $4^9 - 1$
    (d) None of these

20. There is a number lock with four rings. How many attempts at the maximum would have to be made before getting the right number?
    (a) 10^4
    (b) 255
    (c) $10^4 - 1$
    (d) None of these

21. Find the number of numbers that can be formed using all the digits 1, 2, 3, 4, 3, 2, 1 only once so that the odd digits occupy odd places only.
    (a) $4!/(2!)^2$
    (b) $7!/(2!)^3$
    (c) $1!.3!.5!.7!$
    (d) None of these

22. There is a 7-digit telephone number with all different digits. If the digit at extreme right and extreme left are 5 and 6 respectively, find how many such telephone numbers are possible.
    (a) 120
    (b) 1,00,000
    (c) 6720
    (d) None of these

23. If a team of four persons is to be selected from 8 males and 8 females, then in how many ways can the selections be made to include at least one male.
    (a) 3500
    (b) 875
    (c) 1200
    (d) None of these

24. In the above question, in how many ways can the selections be made if it has to contain at the maximum three women?
    (a) 1750
    (b) 1200
    (c) 875
    (d) None of thes

25. How many figures are required to number a book containing 150 pages?
    (a) 450
    (b) 360
    (c) 262
    (d) None of these

26. There are 8 orators A, B, C, D, E, F, G and H. In how many ways can the arrangements be made so that A always comes before B and B always comes before C.
    (a) $8!/3!$
    (b) $8!/6!$
    (c) $5!.3!$
    (d) $8!/(5!.3!)$

27. There are 4 letters and 4 envelopes. In how many ways can wrong choices be made?
    (a) 4^3
    (b) $4! - 1$
    (c) 16
    (d) $4^4 - 1$

28. In the question above, find the number of ways in which only one letter goes in the wrong envelope?
    (a) 4^3
    (b) $^4C_1 + {}^4C_2 + {}^4C_3 + {}^4C_4$

29. In question 27, find the number of ways in which only two letters go in the wrong envelopes?
    (a) 4
    (b) 5
    (c) 6
    (d) 3

(c) $^4C_0 + {}^4C_1 + {}^4C_2 + {}^4C_3$
(d) 0

30. A train is running between Patna to Howrah. Seven people enter the train somewhere between Patna and Howrah. It is given that nine stops are there in between Patna and Howrah. In how many ways can the tickets be purchased if no restriction is there with respect to the number of tickets at any station? 2 people do not buy the same ticket.
    (a) $^{45}C_7$
    (b) $^{63}C_7$
    (c) $^{56}C_7$
    (d) $^{52}C_7$

31. There are seven pairs of black shoes and five pairs of white shoes. They all are put into a box and shoes are drawn one at a time. To ensure that at least one pair of black shoes are taken out, what is the number of shoes required to be drawn out?
    (a) 12
    (b) 13
    (c) 7
    (d) 18

32. In the above question, what is the minimum number of shoes required to be drawn out to get at least 1 pair of correct shoes (either white or black)?
    (a) 12
    (b) 7
    (c) 13
    (d) 18

33. In how many ways one white and one black rook can be placed on a chessboard so that they are never in an attacking position?
    (a) 64×50
    (b) 64×49
    (c) 63×49
    (d) None of these

34. How many 6-digit numbers have all their digits either all odd or all even?
    (a) 31,250
    (b) 28,125
    (c) 15,625
    (d) None of these

35. How many 6-digit numbers have at least 1 even digit?
    (a) 884375
    (b) 3600
    (c) 880775
    (d) 15624

36. How many 10-digit numbers have at least 2 equal digits?
    (a) $9 \times {}^{10}C_2 \times 8!$
    (b) $9.10^9 - 9.9!$
    (c) $9 \times 9!$
    (d) None of these

37. On a triangle ABC, on the side AB, 5 points are marked, 6 points are marked on the side BC and 3 points are marked on the side AC (none of the points being the vertex of the triangle). How many triangles can be made by using these points?
    (a) 90
    (b) 333
    (c) 328
    (d) None of these

38. If we have to make 7 boys sit with 7 girls around a round table, then the number of different relative arrangements of boys and girls that we can make so that so that there are no two boys nor any two girls sitting next to each other is

(a) $2 \times (7!)^2$ (b) $7! \times 6!$

(c) $7! \times 7!$ (d) None of these

39. If we have to make 7 boys sit alternately with 7 girls around a round table which is numbered, then the number of ways in which this can be done is

(a) $2 \times (7!)^2$ (b) $7! \times 6!$

(c) $7! \times 7!$ (d) None of these

40. In the Suniti Building in Mumbai there are 12 floors plus the ground floor. 9 people get into the lift of the building on the ground floor. The lift does not stop on the first floor. If 2, 3 and 4 people alight from the lift on its upward journey, then in how many ways can they do so? (Assume they alight on different floors.)

(a) $^{11}C_3 \times {}^3P_3$ (b) $^{11}P_3 \times {}^9C_4 \times {}^5C_3$

(c) $^{10}P_3 \times {}^9C_4 \times {}^5C_3$ (d) $^{12}C_3$

Directions for Questions 41 and 42. There are 40 doctors in the surgical department of the AIIMS. In how many ways can they be arranged to form a team with:

41. 1 surgeon and an assistant

(a) 1260   (b) 1320

(c) 1440   (d) 1560

42. 1 surgeon and 4 assistants

(a) $40 \times {}^{39}C_4$ (b) $41 \times {}^{39}C_4$

(c) $41 \times {}^{40}C_4$ (d) None of these

43. In how many ways can 10 identical marbles be distributed among 6 children so that each child gets at least 1 marble?

(a) $^{15}C_5$ (b) $^{15}C_9$

(c) $^{10}C_5$ (d) $^9C_5$

44. Seven different objects must be divided among three people. In how many ways can this be done if one or two of them can get no objects?

(a) 15120   (b) 2187

(c) 3003   (d) 792

45. How many 6-digit even numbers can be formed from the digits 1, 2, 3, 4, 5, 6 and 7 so that the digits should not repeat?

(a) 720   (b) 1440

(c) 2160   (d) 6480

46. How many 6-digit even numbers can be formed from the digits 1, 2, 3, 4, 5, 6 and 7 so that the digits should not repeat and the second last digit is even?

(a) 720   (b) 320

(c) 2160   (d) 1440

47. How many 5-digit numbers that do not contain identical digits can be written by means of the digits 1, 2, 3, 4, 5, 6, 7, 8 and 9?

(a) 6048   (b) 7560

(c) 5040   (d) 15,120

48. How many different 4-digit numbers are there which have the digits 1, 2, 3, 4, 5, 6, 7 and 8 such that the digit 1 appears exactly once.

(a) $7 \cdot {}^8P_4$ (b) $^8P_4$

(c) $4 \cdot 7^3$ (d) 7^3

49. How many different 7-digit numbers can be written using only three digits 1, 2 and 3 such that the digit 3 occurs twice in each number?

(a) $^7C_2 \cdot 2^5$ (b) $7!/(2!)$

(c) $7!/(2!)^3$ (d) None of these

50. How many different 4-digit numbers can be written using the digits 1, 2, 3, 4, 5, 6, 7 and 8 only once such that the number 2 is contained once.

(a) 360   (b) 840

(c) 760   (d) 1260

Space for Rough Work

LEVEL OF DIFFICULTY (III)

1. The number of ways in which four particular persons A, B, C, D and six more persons can stand in a queue so that A always stands before B, B always before C and C always before D is
   - (a) $10!/4!$
   - (b) $^{10}P_4$
   - (c) $^{10}C_4$
   - (d) None of these

2. The number of circles that can be drawn out of 10 points of which 7 are collinear is
   - (a) 130
   - (b) 85
   - (c) 45
   - (d) Cannot be determined

3. How many different 9-digit numbers can be formed from the number 223355888 by rearranging its digits so that the odd digits occupy even positions?
   - (a) 120
   - (b) $9!/(2!)^3.3!$
   - (c) $(4!)(2!)^3.3!$
   - (d) None of these

4. How many diagonals are there in an n-sided polygon $(n > 3)$?
   - (a) $(^nC_2 - n)$
   - (b) $^nC_2$
   - (c) $n(n-1)/2$
   - (d) None of these

5. A polygon has 54 diagonals. Find the number of sides.
   - (a) 10
   - (b) 14
   - (c) 12
   - (d) 9

6. The number of natural numbers of two or more than two digits in which digits from left to right are in increasing order is
   - (a) 127
   - (b) 128
   - (c) 502
   - (d) 512

7. In how many ways a cricketer can score 200 runs with fours and sixes only?
   - (a) 13
   - (b) 17
   - (c) 19
   - (d) 16

8. A dices is rolled six times. One, two, three, four, five and six appears on consecutive throws of dices. How many ways are possible of having 1 before 6?
   - (a) 120
   - (b) 360
   - (c) 240
   - (d) 280

9. The number of permutations of the letters a, b, c, d, e, f, g such that neither the pattern 'beg' nor 'acd' occurs is
   - (a) 4806
   - (b) 420
   - (c) 2408
   - (d) None of these

10. In how many ways can the letters of the English alphabet be arranged so that there are seven letters between the letters A and B?
    - (a) $31!.2!$
    - (b) $^{24}P_7.18!.2$
    - (c) $36.24!$
    - (d) None of these

11. There are 20 people among whom two are sisters. Find the number of ways in which we can arrange them around a circle so that there is exactly one person between the two sisters?
    - (a) 18!
    - (b) $2!.19!$
    - (c) 19!
    - (d) None of these

12. There are 10 points on a straight line AB and 8 on another straight line, AC none of them being A. How many triangles can be formed with these points as vertices?
    - (a) 720
    - (b) 640
    - (c) 816
    - (d) None of these

13. In an examination, the maximum marks for each of the three papers is 50 each. The maximum marks for the fourth paper is 100. Find the number of ways with which a student can score 60% marks in aggregate.
    - (a) 3,30,850
    - (b) 2,33,551
    - (c) 1,10,551
    - (d) None of these

14. How many rectangles can be formed out of a chess-board?
    - (a) 204
    - (b) 1230
    - (c) 1740
    - (d) None of these

15. On a board having 18 rows and 16 columns, find the number of squares.
    - (a) $^{18}C_2.^{16}C_2$
    - (b) $^{18}P_2.^{16}P_2$
    - (c) $18.16 + 17.15 + 16.14 + 15.13 + 14.12 + \ldots\ldots +$ $4.2 + 3.1$
    - (d) None of these

16. In the above question, find the number of rectangles.
    - (a) $^{18}C_2.^{16}C_2$
    - (b) $^{18}P_2.^{16}P_2$
    - (c) 171.136
    - (d) None of these

Directions for Questions 17 and 18: Read the passage below and answer the questions.

In the famous program *Kaun Banega Crorepati*, the host shakes hand with each participant once, while he shakes hands with each qualifier (amongst participant) twice more. Besides, the participants are required to shake hands once with each other, while the winner and the host each shake hands with all the guests once.

17. How many handshakes are there if there are 10 participants in all, 3 finalists and 60 spectators?
    - (a) 118
    - (b) 178
    - (c) 181
    - (d) 122

18. In the above question, what is the ratio of the number of handshakes involving the host to the number of handshakes not involving the host?

(a) 43 : 75   (b) 76 : 105

(c) 46 : 75   (d) None of these

19. What is the percentage increase in the total number of handshakes if all the guests are required to shake hands with each other once?

    (a) 82.2%   (b) 822%

    (c) 97.7%   (d) None of these

20. Two variants of the CAT paper are to be given to twelve students. In how many ways can the students be placed in two rows of six each so that there should be no identical variants side by side and that the students sitting one behind the other should have the same variant?

    (a) $2 \times {}^{12}C_6 \times (6!)^2$ (b) $6! \times 6!$

    (c) $7! \times 7!$ (d) None of these

21. For the above question, if there are now three variants of the test to be given to the twelve students (so that each variant is used for four students) and there should be no identical variants side by side and that the students sitting one behind the other should have the same variant. Find the number of ways this can be done.

    (a) $6!^2$ (b) $6 \times 6! \times 6!$

    (c) $6!^3$ (d) None of these

22. Five boys and three girls are sitting in a row of eight seats. In how many ways can they be seated so that not all girls sit side by side?

    (a) 36,000   (b) 45,000

    (c) 24,000   (d) None of these

23. How many natural numbers are there that are smaller than 10^4 and whose decimal notation consists only of the digits 0, 1, 2, 3 and 5, which are not repeated in any of these numbers?

    (a) 32   (b) 164

    (c) 31   (d) 212

24. Seven different objects must be divided among three people. In how many ways can this be done if one or two of them must get no objects?

    (a) 381   (b) 36

    (c) 84   (d) 180

25. Seven different objects must be divided among three people. In how many ways can this be done if at least one of them gets exactly 1 object?

    (a) 2484   (b) 1218

    (c) 729   (d) None of these

26. How many 4-digit numbers that are divisible by 4 can be formed from the digits 1, 2, 3, 4 and 5?

    (a) 36   (b) 72

    (c) 24   (d) None of these

27. How many natural numbers smaller than 10,000 are there in the decimal notation of which all the digits are different?

    (a) 2682   (b) 4474

    (c) 5274   (d) 1448

28. How many 4-digit numbers are there whose decimal notation contains not more than two distinct digits?

    (a) 672   (b) 576

    (c) 360   (d) 448

29. How many different 7-digit numbers are there the sum of whose digits are odd?

    (a) 45.10^5 (b) 24.10^5

    (c) 224320   (d) None of these

30. How many 6-digit numbers contain exactly 4 different digits?

    (a) 4536   (b) 2,94,840

    (c) 1,91,520   (d) None of these

31. How many numbers smaller than 2.10^8 and are divisible by 3 can be written by means of the digits 0, 1 and 2 (exclude single digit and double digit numbers)?

    (a) 4369   (b) 4353

    (c) 4373   (d) 4351

32. Six white and six black balls of the same size are distributed among ten urns so that there is at least one ball in each urn. What is the number of different distributions of the balls?

    (a) 25,000   (b) 26,250

    (c) 28,250   (d) 13,125

33. A bouquet has to be formed from 18 different flowers so that it should contain not less than three flowers. How many ways are there of doing this in?

    (a) 5,24,288   (b) 2,62,144

    (c) 2,61,972   (d) None of these

34. How many different numbers which are smaller than 2.10^8 can be formed using the digits 1 and 2 only?

    (a) 766   (b) 94

    (c) 92   (d) 126

35. How many distinct 6-digit numbers are there having 3 odd and 3 even digits?

    (a) 55   (b) $(5.6)^3.(4.6)^3.3$

    (c) 281250   (d) None of these

36. How many 8-digit numbers are there the sum of whose digits is even?

    (a) 14400   (b) 4.5^5

    (c) 45.10^6 (d) None of these

Directions for Questions 37 and 38: In a chess tournament there were two women participating and every participant played two games with the other participants. The number of games that the men played among themselves exceeded the number of games that the men played with the women by 66.

37. The number of participants in the tournament were:

    (a) 12   (b) 13

    (c) 15   (d) 11

38. The total number of games played in the tournament were:

(a) 132   (b) 110

(c) 156   (d) 210

39. There are 5 bottles of sherry and each have their respective caps. If you are asked to put the correct cap to the correct bottle then how many ways are there so that not a single cap is on the correct bottle?

(a) 44   (b) $5^5 - 1$

(c) 5^5 (d) None of these

40. Amartya Banerjee has forgotten the telephone number of his best friend Abhijit Roy. All he remembers is that the number had 8-digits and ended with an odd number and had exactly one 9. How many possible numbers does Amartya have to try to be sure that he gets the correct number?

(a) 104.9^5 (b) 113.9^5

(c) 300.9^5 (d) $764.9^5.6!$

41. In Question 40, if Amartya is reminded by his friend Sharma that apart from what he remembered there was the additional fact that the last digit of the number was not repeated under any circumstance then how many possible numbers does Amartya have to try to be sure that he gets the correct number?

(a) $200.8^5 + 72.9^5$ (b) 8.9^6

(c) $36.8^5 + 7.9^6$ (d) $36.8^5 + 8.9^6$

42. How many natural numbers not more than 4300 can be formed with the digits 0,1, 2, 3, 4 (if repetitions are allowed)?

(a) 574   (b) 570

(c) 575   (d) 569

43. How many natural numbers less than 4300 can be formed with the digits 0, 1, 2, 3, 4 (if repetitions are not allowed)?

(a) 113   (b) 158

(c) 154   (d) 119

44. How many even natural numbers divisible by 5 can be formed with the digits 0, 1, 2, 3, 4, 5, 6 (if repetitions of digits not allowed)?

(a) 1957   (b) 1956

(c) 1236   (d) 1235

45. There are 100 articles numbered $n_1, n_2, n_3, n_4, \ldots n_{100}$. They are arranged in all possible ways. How many arrangements would be there in which n_{28} will always be before n_{29}.

(a) $5050 \times 99!$ (b) $5050 \times 98!$

(c) $4950 \times 98!$ (d) $4950 \times 99!$

46. The letters of the word PASTE are written in all possible orders and these words are written out as in a dictionary. Then the rank of the word SPATE is

(a) 432   (b) 86

(c) 59   (d) 446

47. The straight lines S_1, S_2, S_3 are in a parallel and lie in the same plane. A total number of A points on S_1; B points on S_2 and C points on S_3 are used to produce triangles. What is the maximum number of triangles formed?

(a) $^{A+B+C}C_3 - {}^A C_3 - {}^B C_3 - {}^C C_3 + 1$

(b) $^{A+B+C}C_3$

(c) $^{A+B+C}C_3 + 1$

(d) $\left({}^{A+B+C}C_3 - {}^A C_3 - {}^B C_3 - {}^C C_3\right)$

48. The sides AB, BC, CA of a triangle ABC have 3, 4 and 5 interior points respectively on them. The total number of triangles that can be constructed by using these points as vertices are

(a) 212   (b) 210

(c) 205   (d) 190

49. A library has 20 copies of CAGE; 12 copies each of RAGE Part1 and Part 2 ; 5 copies of PAGE Part 1, Part 2 and Part 3 and single copy of SAGE, DAGE and MAGE. In how many ways can these books be distributed?

(a) $62!/(20!)(12!)(5!)$ (b) $62!$

(c) $62!/ (37)^3$ (d) $62!/(20!)(12!)^2(5!)^3$

50. The AMS MOCK CAT test CATALYST 19 consists of four sections. Each section has a maximum of 45 marks. Find the number of ways in which a student can qualify in the AMS MOCK CAT if the qualifying marks is 90.

(a) 36,546   (b) 6296

(c) 64906   (d) None of these

Space for Rough Work

ANSWER KEY

Level of Difficulty (I)

1. (c)	2. (b)	3. (b)	4. (c)
5. (c)	6. (a)	7. (b)	8. (a)
9. (a)	10. (b)	11. (d)	12. (b)
13. (a)	14. (b)	15. (c)	16. (a)
17. (d)	18. (d)	19. (b)	20. (c)
21. (c)	22. (c)	23. (c)	24. (b)
25. (c)	26. (a)	27. (a)	28. (a)
29. (a)	30. (b)	31. (a)	32. (d)
33. (b)	34. (b)	35. (d)	36. (c)
37. (c)	38. (b)	39. (d)	40. (d)
41. (a)	42. (a)	43. (c)	44. (b)
45. (b)	46. (c)	47. (d)	48. (a)
49. (c)	50. (b)	51. (b)	52. (d)
53. (d)	54. (d)	55. (c)	56. (d)
57. (c)	58. (d)	59. (d)	60. (a)
61. (b)	62. (d)	63. (a)	64. (d)
65. (a)	66. (d)	67. (a)	68. (b)
69. (d)	70. (d)	71. (b)	72. (c)
73. (a)	74. (a)	75. (c)	76. (a)
77. (c)	78. (c)	79. (d)	80. (a)
81. (c)	82. (b)	83. (b)	84. (b)
85. (b)	86. (a)	87. (b)	88. (d)

Level of Difficulty (II)

1. (a)	2. (b)	3. (b)	4. (b)
5. (d)	6. (b)	7. (b)	8. (d)
9. (b)	10. (c)	11. (a)	12. (d)
13. (c)	14. (b)	15. (b)	16. (d)
17. (b)	18. (d)	19. (a)	20. (c)
21. (d)	22. (c)	23. (d)	24. (a)
25. (d)	26. (a)	27. (b)	28. (d)
29. (c)	30. (a)	31. (d)	32. (c)
33. (b)	34. (b)	35. (a)	36. (b)
37. (b)	38. (b)	39. (a)	40. (b)
41. (d)	42. (a)	43. (d)	44. (b)
45. (c)	46. (a)	47. (d)	48. (c)
49. (a)	50. (b)		

Level of Difficulty (III)

1. (a)	2. (b)	3. (d)	4. (a)
5. (c)	6. (c)	7. (b)	8. (b)
9. (a)	10. (c)	11. (d)	12. (b)
13. (c)	14. (d)	15. (c)	16. (c)
17. (c)	18. (b)	19. (d)	20. (a)
21. (d)	22. (a)	23. (b)	24. (a)
25. (b)	26. (c)	27. (c)	28. (b)
29. (a)	30. (b)	31. (c)	32. (b)
33. (d)	34. (a)	35. (c)	36. (c)
37. (b)	38. (c)	39. (a)	40. (c)
41. (a)	42. (c)	43. (b)	44. (b)
45. (c)	46. (b)	47. (d)	48. (c)
49. (d)	50. (c)		

Hints

Level of Difficulty (III)

1. $^{10}C_4 \times 6! = 10!/4!$

2. For drawing a circle we need 3 non collinear points. This can be done in:

$$^3C_3 + {}^3C_2 \times {}^7C_1 + {}^3C_1 \times {}^7C_2 = 1 + 21 + 63 = 85$$

3. The odd digits have to occupy even positions. This

   can be done in $\dfrac{4!}{2!2!} = 6$ ways.

   The other digits have to occupy the other positions.

   This can be done in $\dfrac{5!}{3!2!} = 10$ ways.

   Hence total number of rearrangements possible = 6 × 10 = 60.

4. The number of straight lines is $^nC_2$ out of which there are n sides. Hence, the number of diagonals is $^nC_2 - n$.

5. $^nC_2 - n = 54$.

6. We cannot take '0' since the smallest digit must be placed at the left most place. We have only 9 digits from which to select the numbers. First select any number of digits. Then for any selection there is only one possible arrangement where the required condition is met. This can be done in $^9C_1 + {}^9C_2 + {}^9C_3 + ... + {}^9C_9$ ways = $2^9 - 1 = 511$ ways.

   But we can't take numbers which have only one digit, hence the required answer is 511 − 9.

7. 200 runs can be scored by scoring only fours or through a combination of fours and sixes.

   Possibilities are 50 × 4, 47 × 4 + 2 × 6, 44 × 4 + 4 × 6 … A total of 17 ways.

8. Of the total arrangements possible (6!) exactly half would have 1 before 6. Thus, 6!/2 = 360.

9. Total number of permutations without any restrictions − Number of permutations having the 'acd' pattern − Number of permutations having the 'beg' pattern + Number of permutations having both the 'beg' and 'acd' patterns.

10. *A* and *B* can occupy the first and the ninth places, the second and the tenth places, the third and the eleventh place and so on… This can be done in 18 ways.

    A and *B* can be arranged in 2 ways.

    All the other 24 alphabets can be arranged in 24! ways.

    Hence the required answer = 2 × 18 × 24!

11. First arrange the two sisters around a circle in such a way that there will be one seat vacant between them. [This can be done in 2! ways since the arrangement of the sisters is not circular.]

    Then, the other 18 people can be arranged on 18 seats in 18! ways.

12. $^{10}C_2 \times {}^8C_1 + {}^{10}C_1 \times {}^8C_2 = 360 + 280 = 640$

14. A chess board consists 9 parallel lines × 9 parallel lines. For a rectangle we need to select 2 parallel lines and two other parallel lines that are perpendicular to the first set. Hence, $^9C_2 \times {}^9C_2$.

15-16. Based on direct formulae.

15. This is a direct result based question. Option (c) is correct. Refer to result no. 6 in Important Results 2.

16. $(1 + 2 + 3 + \ldots + 18)(1 + 2 + 3 + \ldots + 16)$

17-19. Based on simple counting according to the conditions given in the passage

17. $^{10}C_1 + 3 \times 2 + {}^{10}C_2 + 60 + 60 = 181$

18. Handshakes involving host = 76
Hence, the required ratio is 76 : 105.

19. The guests (Spectators) would shake hands $^{60}C_2$ times = 1770.
Required percentage increase = 977.9%.

20. First select six people out of 12 for the first row. The other six automatically get selected for the second row. Arrange the two rows of people amongst themselves. Besides, the papers can be given in the pattern of 121212 or 212121. Hence the answer is $2 \times ({}^{12}C_6 \times 6! \times 6!)$.

21. The difference in this question from the previous question is the number of ways in which the papers can be distributed. This can be done by either distributing three different variants in the first three places of each row or by repeating the same variant in the first and the third places.

22. Required permutations = Total permutations with no condition − permutations with the conditions which we do not have to count.

23. We have to count natural numbers which have a maximum of 4 digits. The required answer will be given by:
Number of single digit numbers + Number of two digit numbers + Number of three digit numbers + Number of four digit numbers.

24. Let the three people be A, B and C.
If 1 person gets no objects, the 7 objects must be distributed such that each of the other two get 1 object at least.
This can be done as 6 & 1, 5 & 2, 4 & 3 and their rearrangements.
The answer would be
$$({}^7C_6 + {}^7C_5 + {}^7C_4) \times 3! = 378$$
Also, two people getting no objects can be done in 3 ways.
Thus, the answer is 378 + 3 = 381

25. If only one gets 1 object
The remaining can be distributed as: (6,0), (4, 2), (3, 3).

$$({}^7C_1 \times {}^6C_6 \times 3! + {}^7C_1 \times {}^6C_4 \times 3! + {}^7C_1 \times {}^6C_3 \times 3!/2!)$$
$$= 42 + 630 + 420 + 1092.$$
If 2 people get 1 object each:
$$^7C_1 \times {}^6C_1 \times {}^5C_5 \times 3!/2! = 126.$$
Thus, a total of 1218.

26. Natural numbers which consist of the digits 1, 2, 3, 4. and 5 and are divisible by 4 must have either 12, 24, 32 or 52 in the last two places. For the other two places we have to arrange three digits in two places.

27. No. of 1 digit nos = 9
No. of 2 digit nos = 81
No. of 3 digit nos = $9 \times 9 \times 8 = 648$
No. of 4 digit nos = $9 \times 9 \times 8 \times 7 = 4536$
Total nos = 9 + 81 + 648 + 4536 = 5274

28. If the two digits are a and b then 4 digit numbers can be formed in the following patterns.
$aabb$; $aaab$ or $aaaa$.
You will have to take two situations in each of the cases- first when the two digits are non zero digits and second when the two digits are zero.

29. For the total of the digits to be odd one of the following has to be true:
The number should contain 1 odd + 6 even or 3 odd + 4 even or 5 odd + 2 even or 7 odd digits. Count each case separately.

33. $^{18}C_4 + {}^{18}C_5 + {}^{18}C_6 + \ldots + {}^{18}C_{17} + {}^{18}C_{18}$
$= [{}^{18}C_0 + {}^{18}C_4 + \ldots + {}^{18}C_{18}] - [{}^{18}C_0 + {}^{18}C_1 + {}^{18}C_2 + {}^{18}C_3]$
$= 2^{18} - [1 + 18 + 153 + 816]$
$= 261158$

35. Total number of 6 digit numbers having 3 odd and 3 even digits (including zero in the left most place) $= 5^3 \times 5^3$.
From this subtract the number of 5 digit numbers with 2 even digits and 3 odd digits (to take care of the extra counting due to zero)

36. There will be 5 types of numbers, viz. numbers which have
All eight digits even or six even and two odd digits or four even and four odd digits or two even and six odd digits or all eight odd digits. This will be further solved as below:
Eight even digits → $5^8 - 5^7 = 4 \times 5^7$
Six even and two odd digits →
when the left most digit is even → $4 \times {}^7C_5 \times 5^5 \times 5^5$
when the left most digit is odd → $5 \times {}^7C_6 \times 5^6 \times 5^1$
Four even and four odd digits →
when the left most digit is even → $4 \times {}^7C_5 \times 5^5 \times 5^4$
when the left most digit is odd → $5 \times {}^7C_4 \times 5^4 \times 5^3$
Two even and six odd digits →
when the left most digit is even → $4 \times {}^7C_1 \times 5 \times 5^6$

when the left most digit is odd → $5 \times {}^7C_2 \times 5^2 \times 5^5$

Eight odd digits → 5^8

37–38. Solve through options.

39. This question is based on a formula: The condition is that 'n' things (each thing belonging to a particular place) have to be distributed in 'n' places such that no particular thing is arranged in its correct place.

$n! - \dfrac{n!}{1!} + \dfrac{n!}{2!} - \dfrac{n!}{3!}$ sign of the terms will be alternate

and the last term will be $\dfrac{n!}{n!}$.

However, this can also be solved through logic.

40. The possible cases for counting are:

Number of numbers when the units digit is nine + the number of numbers when neither the units digit nor the left most is nine + number of numbers when the left most digit is nine.

42. The condition is that we have to count the number of natural numbers not more than 4300.

The total possible numbers with the given digits = $5 \times 5 \times 5 \times 5 = 625 - 1 = 624$.

Subtract form this the number of natural number greater than 4300 which can be formed from the given digits = $1 \times 2 \times 5 \times 5 - 1 = 49$.

Hence, the required number of numbers = $624 - 49 = 575$.

43. The required answer will be given by

The number of one digit natural number + number of two digit natural numbers + the number of three digit natural numbers + the number of four digit natural number starting with 1, 2, or 3 + the number of four digit natural numbers starting with 4.

46. The following words will appear before SPATE. All words starting with A + All words starting with E + All words starting with P + All words starting with SA + All words starting with SE + SPAET

47. For the maximum possibility assume that no three points other than given in the question are in a straight line.

Hence, the total number of Δ's = ${}^{A+B+C}C_3 - {}^AC_3 - {}^BC_3 - {}^CC_3$

48. Use the formula $\dfrac{n!}{p!q!r!}$.

$n(E) = 7 \times 6 \times 5 \times 4 \times 3 \times 2 \times {}^7C_2$

$n(S) = 7^7$

$n(E) = 8 \times 7 + 8 \times 7 = 112$

$n(S) = 64C_2 = \dfrac{2 \times 8 \times 7 \times 2}{64 \times 63} = \dfrac{1}{18}$

49. Use the formula $\dfrac{n!}{p!q!r!}$

Solutions and Shortcuts

Level of Difficulty (I)

1. The number of numbers formed would be given by $5 \times 4 \times 3$ (given that the first digit can be filled in 5 ways, the second in 4 ways and the third in 3 ways – MNP rule).

2. The first digit can only be 2 (1 way), the second digit can be filled in 7 ways, the third in 6 ways and the fourth in 5 ways. A total of $1 \times 7 \times 6 \times 5 = 210$ ways.

3. Each invitation card can be sent in 4 ways. Thus, $4 \times 4 \times 4 \times 4 \times 4 \times 4 = 4^6$.

4. In this case since nothing is mentioned about whether the prizes are identical or distinct we can take the prizes to be distinct (the most logical thought given the situation). Thus, each prize can be given in 8 ways — thus a total of 8^5 ways.

5. We need to assume that the 7 Indians are 1 person, so also for the 6 Dutch and the 5 Pakistanis. These 3 groups of people can be arranged amongst themselves in 3! ways. Also, within themselves the 7 Indians the 6 Dutch and the 5 Pakistanis can be arranged in 7!, 6! And 5! ways respectively. Thus, the answer is $3! \times 7! \times 6! \times 5!$.

6. Use the MNP rule to get the answer as $5 \times 4 = 20$.

7. An IITian can make it to IIMs in 2 ways, while a CA can make it through in 3 ways. Required ratio is 2:3. Option (b) is correct.

8. For a straight line we just need to select 2 points out of the 8 points available. ${}^8C_2$ would be the number of ways of doing this.

9. Use the property ${}^nC_r = {}^nC_{n-r}$ to see that the two values would be equal at $n = 11$ since ${}^{11}C_3 = {}^{11}C_8$.

10. There would be 5! ways of arranging the 5 letters. Thus, $5! = 120$ ways.

11. Rearrangements do not count the original arrangements. Thus, $5!/2! - 1 = 59$ ways of rearranging the letters of PATNA.

12. We need to count words starting with P. These words would be represented by P _ _ _ _.
The letters ATNA can be arranged in $4!/2!$ ways in the 4 places. A total of 12 ways.

13. P _ _ _ T. Missing letters have to be filled with A,N,A. $3!/2! = 3$ ways.

14. Trial and error would give us ${}^8C_4$ as the answer. ${}^8C_4 = 8 \times 7 \times 6 \times 5/4 \times 3 \times 2 \times 1 = 70$.

15. ${}^{10}P_3$ would satisfy the value given as ${}^{10}P_3 = 10 \times 9 \times 8 = 720$.

16. $3 \times 3 \times 2 \times 1 = 18$

17. $3 \times 4 \times 4 \times 4 = 192$

18. Divide the numbers into three-digit numbers and 4- digit numbers— Number of 3 digit numbers = 2

$\times 3 \times 2 = 12$. Number of 4-digit numbers starting with 10 = $2 \times 1 = 2$. Total = 14 numbers.

19. 3-digit numbers = $2 \times 4 \times 4 - 1 = 31$ (-1 is because the number 200 cannot be counted) ; 4-digit numbers starting with 10 = $4 \times 4 = 16$, Number of 4 digit numbers starting with 11 = $4 \times 4 = 16$. Total numbers = $31 + 16 + 16 = 63$.

20. At $n = 3$, the values convert to $^7P_2$ and $^5P_3$ whose values respectively are 42 & 60 giving us the required ratio.

21. At $r = 7$, the value becomes $(28!/14! \times 14!)/(24!/10! \times 14!) \rightarrow 225{:}11$.

22. The maximum value of ^nC_r for a given value of n, happens when r is equal to the half of n. So if he wants to maximise the number of parties given that he has 20 friends, he should invite 10 to each party.

23. This is a typical case for the use of the formula $^{n-1}C_{r-1}$ with $n = 10$ and $r = 6$. So the answer would be given $^9C_5$.

24. For each digit there would be 5 options (viz 1, 3, 5, 7, 9). Hence, the total number of numbers would be $5 \times 5 \times 5 \times 5 = 625$.

25. $^{11}C_1 \times {}^{10}C_1 = 110$. Alternately, $^{11}C_2 \times 2!$

26. $5 \times 4 = 20$.

27. In the letters of the word ALLAHABAD there is only 1 vowel available for selection (A). Note that the fact that A is available 4 times has no impact on this fact. Also, there are 4 consonants available — viz: L, H, B and D. Thus, the number of ways of selecting a vowel and a consonant would be $1 \times {}^4C_1 = 4$.

28. Choose 1 person for the single room & from the remaining choose 2 people for the double room & from the remaining choose 4 people for the 4 persons room $\rightarrow {}^7C_1 \times {}^6C_2 \times {}^4C_4$.

29. From the first suit there would be 13 options of selecting a card. From the second suite there would be 12 options, from the third suite there would be 11 options and from the fourth suite there would be 10 options for selecting a card. Thus, $13 \times 12 \times 11 \times 10$.

30. Number of 11 letter words formed from the letters P, E, R, M, U, T, A, T, I, O, N = $11!/2!$.
Number of new words formed = total words -1 = $11!/2! - 1$.

31. $^{15}C_0 + {}^{15}C_1 + {}^{15}C_2 + {}^{15}C_3 + {}^{15}C_4 + {}^{15}C_5 = 1 + 15 + 105 + 455 + 1365 + 3003 = 4944$

32. All arrangements – Arrangements with best and worst paper together = $12! - 2! \times 11!$.

33. The vowels EUAIO need to be considered as 1 letter to solve this. Thus, there would be 4! ways of arranging Q, T and N and the 5 vowels taken together. Also, there would be 5! ways of arranging the vowels amongst themselves. Thus, we have $4! \times 5!$.

34. $^3C_1 \times {}^4C_1 \times {}^6C_1 = 72$.

35. 4-digit Motor vehicle registration numbers can have 0 in the first digit. Thus, we have $6 \times 5 \times 4 \times 3 = 360$ ways.

36. Single digit numbers = 5
Two digit numbers = $5 \times 4 = 20$
Three digit numbers = $5 \times 4 \times 3 = 60$
Four digit numbers = $5 \times 4 \times 3 \times 2 = 120$
Five digit numbers = $5 \times 4 \times 3 \times 2 \times 1 = 120$
Total = $5 + 20 + 60 + 120 + 120 = 325$

37. $^{25}C_2 - {}^7C_2 + 1 = 280$

38. $^{25}C_3 - {}^7C_3 = 2265$

39. $^{25}C_4 - {}^7C_4 - {}^7C_3 \times {}^{18}C_1 = 11985$

40. $^{10}C_5 \times 5! = 30240$

41. $^8C_3 \times {}^5C_2 \times 5! = 67200$

42. The selection of the 11 player team can be done in $^{14}C_{10}$ ways. This results in the team of 11 players being completely chosen. The arrangements of these 11 players can be done in 11!.
Total batting orders = $^{14}C_{10} \times 11! = 1001 \times 11!$
(**Note:** Arrangement is required here because we are talking about forming batting orders).

43. $^{12}C_4 = 495$

44. $^{30}C_3$

45. $^{29}C_2$

46. R _ _ _ _ _ W. The letters to go into the spaces are P, O, L, I, N, G. Since all these letters are distinct the number of ways of arranging them would be 6!.

47. $7!/3! \times 4! = 35$

48. The number has to start with a 3 and then in the remaining 6 digits it should have two 3's and four 0's. This can be done in $6!/2! \times 4! = 15$ ways.

49. $^3C_1 \times {}^5C_3 \times {}^4C_2 \times 5! = 21600$

50. If the number of teams is n, then $^nC_2$ should be equal to 45. Trial and error gives us the value of n as 10.

51. From 5 bananas we have 6 choices available (0, 1, 2, 3, 4 or 5). Similarly 4 mangoes and 4 almonds can be chosen in 5 ways each.
So total ways = $6 \times 5 \times 5 = 150$ possible selections. But in this 150, there is one selection where no fruit is chosen.
So required no. of ways = $150 - 1 = 149$
Hence Option (b) is correct.

52. For each book we have two options, give or not give. Thus, we have a total of 2^{14} ways in which the 14 books can be decided upon. Out of this, there would be 1 way in which no book would be given. Thus, the number of ways is $2^{14} - 1$.
Hence, Option (d) is correct.

53. The number of ways in which at least 1 Archer book is given is $(2^5 - 1)$. Similarly, for Sheldon and Grisham we have $(2^3 - 1)$ and $(2^6 - 1)$. Thus required answer would be the multiplication of the three. Hence, Option (d) is the correct answer.

54. For each question we have 3 choices of answering the question (2 internal choices + 1 non-attempt). Thus, there are a total of 3^{15} ways of answering the question paper. Out of this there is exactly one way in which the student does not answer any question. Thus there are a total of $3^{15} - 1$ ways in which at least one question is answered.

Hence, Option (d) is correct.

55. The digits are 1, 6, 7, 8, 7, 6, 1. In this seven-digit no. there are four add places and three even places— OEOEOEO. The four odd digits 1, 7, 7, 1 can be arranged in four odd places in $[4!/2! \times 2] = 6$ ways [as 1 and 7 are both occurring twice].

The even digits 6, 8, 6 can be arranged in three even places in $3!/2! = 3$ ways.

Total no. of ways = $6 \times 3 = 18$.

Hence, Option (c) is correct.

56. We have no girls together, let us first arrange the 5 boys and after that we can arrange the girls in the spaces between the boys.

Number of ways of arranging the boys around a circle = $[5 - 1]! = 24$.

Number of ways of arranging the girls would be by placing them in the 5 spaces that are formed between the boys. This can be done in $^5P_3$ ways = 60 ways.

Total arrangements = $24 \times 60 = 1440$.

Hence, Option (d) is correct.

57. Books of interest = 7, books to be borrowed = 3

Case 1— Quants book is taken. Then D.I book can also be taken.

So Amita is to take 2 more books out of 6 which she can do in $^6C_2 = 15$ ways.

Case 2— If Quants book has not been taken, the D.I book would also not be taken.

So Amita will take three books out of 5 books. This can be done in $^5C_3 = 10$ ways.

So total ways = 15 + 10 = 25 ways.

Hence Option (c) is correct.

58. We have to select 5 out of 12.

If Radha and Mohan join- then we have to select only $5 - 2 = 3$ dancers out of $12 - 2 = 10$ which can be done in $^{10}C_3 = 120$ ways.

If Radha and Mohan do not join, then we have to select 5 out of $12 - 2 = 10 \to {}^{10}C_5 = 252$ ways.

Total number of ways = 120 + 252 = 372.

Hence, Option (d) is correct.

59. The unit digit can either be 2, 3, 4, 5 or 6.

When the unit digit is 2, the number would be even and hence will be divisible by 2. Hence all numbers with unit digit 2 will be included which is equal to 5! Or 120.

When the unit digit is 3, then in every case the sum of the digits of the number would be 21 which is a multiple of 3. Hence all numbers with unit digit 3 will be divisible by 3 and hence will be included. Total number of such numbers is 5! or 120.

Similarly for unit digit 5 and 6, the number of required numbers is 120 each.

When the unit digit is 4, then the number would be divisible by 4 only if the ten's digit is 2 or 6. Total number of such numbers is $2 \times 4!$ or 48.

Hence total number of required numbers is $(4 \times 120) + 48 = 528$.

Hence, Option (d) is the answer.

60. As we need to find the maximum number of trials, so we have to assume that the required ball in every box is picked as late as possible. So in the third box, first two balls will be red and black. Hence third trial will give him the required ball. Similarly, in fourth box, he will get the required ball in fourth trial and in the fifth box, he will get the required ball in fifth trial. Hence maximum total number of trials required is 3 + 4 + 5 = 12.

Hence, Option (a) is the answer.

61. Since every player needs to win only 1 match to move to the next round, therefore the 1st round would have 32 matches between 64 players out of which 32 will be knocked out of the tournament and 32 will be moved to the next round. Similarly in 2nd round 16 matches will be played, in the 3rd round 8 matches will be played, in 4th round 4 matches, in 5th round 2 matches and the 6th round will be the final match. Hence total number of rounds will be 6 ($2^6 = 64$).

Hence, option (b) is the answer.

62. Total number of pairs of men that can be selected if the adjacent ones are also selected is $^NC_2$. Total number of pairs of men selected if only the adjacent ones are selected is N. Hence total number of pairs of men selected if the adjacent ones are not selected is $^NC_2 - N$.

Since the total time taken is 88 min, hence the number of pairs is 44.

Hence, $^NC_2 - N = 44 \to N = 11$.

Hence, Option (d) is the answer.

63. Let the number of boys be B. Then $^BC_3 = 36 \to B = 9$
Let the number of girls be G. Then $^GC_2 = 66 \to G = 12$. Therefore total number of students in the class = 12 + 9 = 21. Hence total number of matches = $^{21}C_2 = 210$. Hence, number of matches between 1 boy and 1 girl = $210 - (36 + 66) = 108$.

Hence, Option (a) is the answer.

64. We will first give 3 chocolates to Sana and 1 each to the other 4. So we have already distributed 7 chocolates. Now we are left with 8 chocolates that have to be distributed among 5 people. So number of ways possible is $12!/8!4! = 495$. Out of these we have to eliminate cases in which Sana gets

more than 6 chocolates. As we have already given her 3 chocolates that means we have to eliminate cases in which she gets 7 or 8 or 9 or 10 or 11 chocolates out of 495 cases. She would get 11 chocolates in one case, 10 chocolates in $^4C_1$ cases, 9 chocolates in $^5C_1$ cases, 8 chocolates in $^6C_2$ cases and 7 chocolates in $^7C_3$ cases. So, total number of cases that need to be eliminated is 60. So the required number of ways is 495 − 60 = 435.

Hence, Option (d) is the answer.

65. Firstly we will give 5 crores each to the three sons. That will cover 15 crores out of 30 crores leaving behind 15 crores. Now 15 crores can be distributed in three people in 17!15!2! ways or 136 ways.

Hence, Option (a) is the answer.

66. Let $x = 3$. Then $y + z = 27$. For the conditions given in the question, no. of solutions is 20.

Similarly for $x = 2$ there will be 23 solutions, for $x = 1$ there will be 26 solutions and for $x = 0$, there will be 29 solutions. Therefore total 98 solutions are possible.

Similarly for $y = 3$ to 0, there will be 98 solutions and for $z = 3$ to 0, there will be 98 solutions.

Hence there will be total of 294 solutions. Hence, Option (d) is the answer.

67. No. of words starting with A = 8!/ 2!3! = 3360.
No. of words starting with B = 8!/ 2!4! = 840
No. of words starting with D = 8!/2!4! = 840
No. of words starting with H = 8!/2!4! = 840
Now words with L start.
No. of words starting with LAA = 6!/2! = 180
Now LAB starts and first word starts with LABA.
No. of words starting with LABAA = 4! = 24
After this the next words will be LABADAAHL, LABADAALH, LABADAHAL, LABADAHLA and hence, Option (a) is the answer.

68. We will consider $x = 7$ to $x = 1$.
For $x = 7$, $y + z = 5$. No. of solutions = 4
For $x = 6$, $y + z = 6$. No. of solution = 5
For $x = 5$, $y + z = 7$. No. of solution = 6
For $x = 4$, $y + z = 8$. No. of solution = 7
For $x = 3$, $y = z = 9$. No. of solutions = 6
For $x = 2$, $y + z = 10$. No. of solutions = 5
For $x = 1$, $y + z = 11$. No. of solutions = 4
Hence number of solutions = 37
Hence, Option (b) is the answer.

69. As no three points are collinear, therefore every combination of 3 points out of the nine points will give us a triangle. Hence, the answer is $^9C_3$ or 84.

Hence, Option (d) is correct.

70. The number of combinations of three points picked from the nine given points is $^9C_3$ or 84. All these combinations will result in a triangle except the combination of the three collinear points. Hence number of triangles formed will be 84 − 1 = 83.

Hence, Option (d) is the answer.

71. $(xy)^2 = u! + v$

Here xy is a two-digit number and maximum value of its square is 9801. 8! is a five-digit number => u is less than 8 and 4! is 24 which when added to a single digit will never give the square of a two-digit number. Hence u is greater than 4. So, possible values of u can be 5, 6 and 7.

If $u = 5$, $u! = 120$ => $(xy)^2 = u! + v$ => $(xy)^2 = 120 + v = 120 + 1 = 121 = 11^2$

If $u = 6$, $u! = 720$ => $(xy)^2 = u! + v$ => $(xy)^2 = 720 + v = 720 + 9 = 729 = 27^2$

If $u = 7$, $u! = 5040$ => $(xy)^2 = u! + v$ => $(xy)^2 = 5040 + v = 5040 + 1 = 5041 = 71^2$

So there are three cases possible. Hence, 3 solutions exist for the given equation.

Hence, Option (b) is the correct answer.

72. In order to form triangles from the given points, we can either select 2 points from the first line and 1 point from the second OR select one point from the first line and 2 from the second.

This can be done in:

$^{10}C_2 \times {}^{11}C_1 + {}^{10}C_1 \times {}^{11}C_2 = 495 + 550 = 1045$

73. If we have 'n' candidates who can be selected at the maximum, naturally, the answer to the question would also represent 'n'.

Hence we check for the first option. If $n = 3$, then $2n + 1 = 7$ and it means that there are 7 candidates to be chosen from. Since it is given that the number of ways of selection of at least 1 candidate is 63, we should try to see, whether selecting 1, 2 or 3 candidates from 7 indeed adds up to 63 ways. If it does this would be the correct answer.

$^7C_1 + {}^7C_2 + {}^7C_3 = 7 + 21 + 35 = 63$. Thus, the first Option fits the situation and is hence correct.

74. This problem can be approached by putting the white flags in their possible positions. There are essentially 4 possibilities for placing the 3 white flags based on the condition that two flags of the same color cannot be together:

1, 3, 5; 1, 3, 6; 1, 4, 6 and 2, 4, 6.

Out of these 4 possible arrangements for the 3 white flags we cannot use 1, 3, 6 and 1, 4, 6 as these have the same color of flag at both ends- something which is not allowed according to the question. Thus there are only 2 possible ways of placing the white flags— 1, 3, 5 OR 2, 4, 6. In each of these 2 ways, there are a further 3 ways of placing the 1 red flag and the 2 blue flags. Thus we get a total of 6 ways. Option (a) is correct.

75. The possible numbers are:

635 _ _ _ 9	9 in the units place	$9 \times 9 \times 9 = 729$ numbers
635 _ _ _ _	9 used before the units place	$3 \times 9 \times 9 \times 4 = 972$ numbers
674 _ _ _ 9	9 in the units place	$9 \times 9 \times 9 = 729$ numbers
674 _ _ _ _	9 used before the units place	$3 \times 9 \times 9 \times 4 = 972$ numbers
Total		3402 numbers

76. We need to go through the options and use the MNP rule tool relating to Permutations and Combinations. We can draw up the following possibilities table for the number of routes between each of the three towns. If the first option is true, i.e., there are 6 routes between A to C:

A-C	Possibilities for C-B	Possibilities for total routes A-C-B (Say X)	Possibilities for Total routes A–B (Y)
6	5, 4, 3, 2, 1	30, 24, 18, 12, 6	3, 9, 15, 21, 27
			Note: these values are derived based on the logic that X + Y = 33

We further know that there are 23 routes between B to C.

From the above combinations the possibilities for the routes between B to C are:

B–A (Y in the table above)	A–C	B–A–C	B–C	Total
3	6	18	5	23
9	6	54 not possible	4	
15	6	90 not possible	3	
21	6	126 not possible	2	
27	6	162 not possible	1	

It is obvious that the first possibility in the table above satisfies all conditions of the given situation. Option (a) is correct.

77. With the digits 1, 2, 3, 4, 5 and 6 the numbers divisible by 4 that can be formed are numbers ending in: 12, 16, 24, 32, 36, 52, 56 and 64.

Number of numbers ending in 12 are: $4 \times 3 \times 2 = 24$

Thus the number of numbers is $24 \times 8 = 192$

Option (c) is correct.

78. A million is 1000000 (i.e. the first seven digit number). So we need to find how many numbers of less than 7 digits can be formed using the digits 0,7 and 8.

Number of 1 digit numbers = 2

Number of 2 digit numbers = $2 \times 3 = 6$

Number of 3 digit numbers = $2 \times 3 \times 3 = 18$

Number of 4 digit numbers = $2 \times 3 \times 3 \times 3 = 54$

Number of 5 digit numbers = $2 \times 3 \times 3 \times 3 \times 3 = 162$

Number of 6 digit numbers = $2 \times 3 \times 3 \times 3 \times 3 \times 3 = 486$

Total number of numbers = 728. Option (c) is correct.

79. The white square can be selected in 32 ways and once the white square is selected 8 black squares become ineligible for selection. Hence, the black square can be selected in 24 ways. $32 \times 24 = 768$. Option (d) is correct.

80. Since there are 11 symmetric letters, the number of passwords that can be formed would be $11 \times 10 \times 9 \times 8 = 7920$. Option (a) is correct.

81. This would be given by the number of passwords having:

1 symmetric and 2 asymmetric letters + 2 symmetric and 1 asymmetric letter + 3 symmetric and 0 asymmetric letters

$^{11}C_1 \times {}^{15}C_2 \times 3! + {}^{11}C_2 \times {}^{15}C_1 \times 3! + {}^{11}C_3 \times 3! = 11 \times 105 \times 6 + 55 \times 15 \times 6 + 11 \times 10 \times 9 = 6930 + 4950 + 990 = 12870$. Option (c) is correct.

82. Each of the first, third and fourth options can be obviously seen to be true— no mathematics needed there. Only the second option can never be true.

In order to think about this mathematically and numerically— think of a party of 3 persons say A, B and C. In order for the second condition to be possible, each person must know a different number of persons. In a party with 3 persons this is possible only if the numbers are 0, 1 and 2. If A knows both B and C (2), B and C both would know at least 1 person— hence it would not be possible to create the person knowing 0 people. The same can be verified with a group of 4 persons i.e., the minute you were to make 1 person know 3 persons it would not be possible for anyone in the group to know 0 persons and hence you would not be able to meet the condition that every person knows a different number of persons. Option (b) is correct.

83. With one green ball there would be six ways of doing this. With 2 green balls 5 ways, with 3 green balls 4 ways, with 4 green balls 3 ways, with 5 green balls 2 ways and with 6 green balls 1 way. So a total of $1 + 2 + 3 + 4 + 5 + 6 = 21$ ways. Option (b) is correct.

84. One digit no. = 5; Two digit nos = $5 \times 4 = 20$; Three digit no = $5 \times 4 \times 3 = 60$; four digit no = $5 \times 4 \times 3 \times 2 = 120$; Five digit no.= $5 \times 4 \times 3 \times 2 \times 1 = 120$ Total number of nos = 325. Hence Option (b) is correct.

85. For each selection there are 3 ways of doing it. Thus, there are a total of $3 \times 3 \times 3 \times 3 \times 3 = 243$. Hence, Option (b) is correct.

86. Number of even numbers = $6 \times 6 \times 6 \times 3$

87. Solve this one through options. If you pick up option (a) it gives you 12 participants in the tournament.

This means that there are 10 men and 2 women. In this case there would be $2 \times {}^{10}C_2 = 90$ matches amongst the men and $2 \times {}^{10}C_1 \times {}^2C_1 = 40$ matches between 1 man and 1 woman. The difference between number of matches where both participants are men and the number of matches where 1 participant is a man and one is a woman is $90 - 40 = 50$ – which is not what is given in the problem.

With 15 participants → 11 men and 2 women.

In this case there would be $2 \times {}^{11}C_2 = 110$ matches amongst the men and $2 \times {}^{11}C_1 \times {}^2C_1 = 44$ matches between 1 man and 1 woman. The difference between number of matches where both participants are men and the number of matches where 1 participant is a man and one is a woman is $110 - 44 = 66$ – which is the required value as given in the problem. Thus, option (b) is correct.

88. Based on the above thinking we get that since there are 15 players and each player plays each of the others twice, the number of games would be $2 \times {}^{15}C_2 = 2 \times 105 = 210$

Level of Difficulty (II)

1. Number of even numbers $= 6 \times 6 \times 6 \times 3$

2. We need to think of this as: Number with two sixes or numbers with one six or number with no six.

   0, 1, 2, 3, 4, 5, 6

   Numbers with 2 sixes:

   Numbers ending n zero ${}^5C_1 \times 3!/2! = 15$

   Numbers Ending in 5 and

   (a) Starting with 6 ${}^5C_1 \times 2! = 10$

   (b) Not starting with 6 ${}^4C_1$ (as zero is not allowed) $= 4$

   Number with 1 six or no sixes.

   Numbers ending in 0 ${}^6C_3 \times 3! = 120$

   Numbers ending in 5 ${}^5C_1 \times {}^5C_2 \times 2! = 100$

   Thus a total of 249 numbers.

3. First arrange 6 pups in 6 places in 6! ways.

   This will leave us with 7 places for 4 cats. Answer $= 6! \times 7p_4$.

4. Arrangement of M, A, N, A, E, M, E, N, T is

   $$\frac{9!}{2! \times 2! \times 2! \times 2!}.$$

5. For nine places we have following number of arrangements.

   $9 \times 9 \times 8 \times 7 \times 6 \times 5 \times 4 \times 3 \times 2$

6. For a rectangle, we need two pair of parallel lines which are perpendicular to each other. We need to select two parallel lines from 'v' lines and 2 parallel lines from 'w' lines. Hence required number of parallel lines is ${}^vC_2 \times {}^wC_2$.

7. From 8 people we have to *arrange* a group of 5 in which three are similar $\dfrac{8P_5}{3!}$ or $\dfrac{8C_5 \times 5!}{3!}$.

8. $\dfrac{4C_4 \times 4C_1 \times 5!}{3!} + \dfrac{4C_2 \times 4C_3 \times 5!}{3!} - 4C_2 \times 4C_3 \times 2C_2$
   $\times 2!$

9. Since the number of men and women in the question is the same, there is no difference in solving this question and solving the previous one (question number 8) as committees having a maximum of 2 women would mean committees having a minimum of 3 men and committees having at maximum one woman holding the post of either president or vice president would mean at least 1 man holding one of the two posts. Thus, the answer would be:

   Number of committees with 4 men and 1 woman (including all arrangements of the committees) + Number of committees with 3 men and 2 women (including all arrangements of the committees)–Number of committees with 3 men and 2 women where both the women are occupying the two posts.

   $= ({}^4C_4 \times {}^4C_1 \times 5!)/3! + ({}^4C_3 \times {}^4C_2 \times 5!)/3! - ({}^4C_3 \times {}^4C_2 \times {}^2C_2 \times 2!) = 80 + 480 - 48 = 512$

10. ${}^7C_1 \times {}^6C_2 \times 4! \times 4! = 60480$

11. First make the six law students sit in a row. This can be done in 6! Ways. Then, there would be 7 places for the MBA students. We need to select 5 of these 7 places for 5 MBA students and then arrange these 5 students in those 5 places. This can be done in ${}^7C_5 \times 5!$ Ways.

    Thus, the answer is:

    $6! \times {}^7C_5 \times 5! = 7! \times 6!/2!$

12. The required answer will be given by counting the total number of registration numbers starting with DL-5A to DL-5R and the number of registration numbers starting with DL-5S that have to be counted.

13. Out of 100 balls arrange 99 balls (except n_{28}) amongst themselves. Now put n_{28} just before n_{29} in the above arrangement.

14. ${}^6C_2 = 15$.

15. We need to arrange R people on M chairs, S people on another set of M chairs and the remaining people on the remaining chairs. ${}^MP_R \times {}^MP_S \times {}^{2M-R-S}P_{2M-R-S}$.

16. Each group will consists of m things. This can be done in: ${}^{mn}C_m \cdot {}^{mn-m}C_m \cdot {}^{mn-2m}C_m {}_{......} {}^mC_m$

    $$= \frac{mn!}{(mn-m)!m!} \cdot \frac{(mn-m)!}{(mn-2m)!m!} \cdots \frac{m!}{0!m!} = \frac{mn!}{(m!)^n}$$

    Divide this by $n!$ since arrangements of the n groups amongst themselves is not required.

    Required number of ways $= \dfrac{mn!}{(m!)^n \cdot n!}$

17. Number of ways of selecting 5 different letters $= {}^5C_5 = 1$

Number of ways of selecting 2 similar and 3 different letters = $^4C_1 \times {}^4C_3 = 16$

Number of ways of selecting 2 similar letters + 2 more similar letters and 1 different letter = $^4C_2 \times {}^3C_1 = 18$

Number of ways of selecting 3 similar letters and 2 different letters = $^3C_1 \times {}^4C_2 = 18$

Number of ways of selecting 3 similar letters and another 2 other similar letters = $^3C_1 \times {}^3C_1 = 9$

Number of ways of selecting 4 similar letters and 1 different letter = $^2C_1 \times {}^4C_1 = 8$

Number of ways of selecting 5 similar letters = $^1C_1$ = 1

Total number of ways = 1 + 16 + 18 + 18 + 9 + 8 + 1 = 71.

18. Divide $3n + 1$ articles in two groups.
   (i) n identical articles and the remaining
   (ii) $2n + 1$ non-identical articles

   We will select articles in two steps. Some from the first group and the rest from the second group.

Number of articles from first group	Number of articles from second group	Number of ways.
0	n	$1 \times {}^{2n+1}C_n$
1	$n - 1$	$1 \times {}^{2n+1}C_{n-1}$
2	$n - 2$	$1 \times {}^{2n+1}C_{n-2}$
3	$n - 3$	$1 \times {}^{2n+1}C_{n-3}$
..	..	....
$n - 1$	1	$1 \times {}^{2n+1}C_1$
n	0	$1 \times {}^{2n+1}C_0$

Total number of ways = $^{2n+1}C_n + {}^{2n+1}C_{n-1} + {}^{2n+1}C_{n-2}$

$+ .... {}^{2n+1}C_1 + {}^{2n+1}C_0 = \dfrac{2^{2n+1}}{2} = 2^{2n}$.

19. We have four options for every place including the left most.

   So the total number of numbers = $4 \times 4 \times 4 \times ... = 4^{10}$.

   We have to consider only positive numbers, so we don't consider one number in which all ten digits are zeroes.

20. Total number of attempts = 10^4 out of which one is correct.

21. For odd places, the number of arrangements = $\dfrac{4!}{2!2!}$

   For even places, the number of arrangements = $\dfrac{3!}{2!}$

   Hence the total number of arrangements = $\dfrac{4! \times 3!}{2! \times 2! \times 2!}$

22. The number would be of the form 6 ____ 5

The 5 missing digits have to be formed using the digits 0, 1, 2, 3, 4, 7, 8, 9 without repetition.

   Thus, $^8C_5 \times 5! = 6720$

23. $1m + 3f = {}^8C_1 \times {}^8C_3 = 8 \times 56 = 448$

   $2m + 2f = {}^8C_2 \times {}^8C_2 = 28 \times 28 = 784$

   $3m + 1f \; {}^8C_3 \times {}^8C_1 = 56 \times 8 = 448$

   $4m + 0f = {}^8C_4 \times {}^8C_0 = 70 \times 1 = 70$

   Total = 1750

24. Solve this by dividing the solution into,

   3 women and 1 man or
   2 women and 2 men or
   1 woman and 3 men or
   0 woman and 4 men.

   This will give us:

   $^8C_3 \times {}^8C_1 + {}^8C_2 \times {}^8C_2 + {}^8C_1 \times {}^8C_3 + {}^8C_0 \times {}^8C_4$
   $= 448 + 784 + 448 + 70 = 1750$

25. For 1 to 9 we require 9 digits
   For 10 to 99 we require 90×2 digits
   For 100 to 150 we require 51×3 digits

26. Select any three places for A, B and C. They need no arrangement amongst themselves as A would always come before B and B would come before C.

   The remaining 5 people have to be arranged in 5 places.

   Thus, $^8C_3 \times 5! = 56 \times 120 = 67200$

   Or

   $\dfrac{8 :}{3 : \times 5 :} \times 5! = 8!/3!$

27. Total number of choices = 4! out of which only one will be right.

28. At least two letters have to interchange their places for a wrong choice.

29. Select any two letters and interchange them $({}^4C_2)$.

30. $^{45}C_7$ (refer to solved example 16.14).

31. For one pair of black shoes we require one left black and one right black. Consider the worst case situation:

   $7LB + 5LW + 5RW + 1RB$ or
   $7RB + 5LW + 5RW + 1LB = 18$ shoes

32. For one pair of correct shoes one of the possible combinations is $7LB + 5LW + 1R$ (B or W) = 13

   Some other cases are also possible with at least 13 shoes.

33. The first rook can be placed in any of the 64 squares and the second rook will then have only 49 places so that they are not attacking each other.

34. When all digits are odd.

   $5 \times 5 \times 5 \times 5 \times 5 \times 5 = 5^6$

   When all digits are even

   $4 \times 5 \times 5 \times 5 \times 5 \times 5 = 4 \times 5^5$
   $5^6 + 4 \times 5^5 = 28125$

35. All six digit numbers – Six digit numbers with only odd digits.

$= 900000 - 5 \times 5 \times 5 \times 5 \times 5 \times 5 = 884375.$

36. "Total number of all 10-digits numbers – Total number of all 10-digits numbers with no digit repeated" will give the required answer.

$$= 9 \times 10^9 - 9 \times {}^9P_8$$

37. There will be two types of triangles

    The first type will have its vertices on the three sides of the ΔABC.

    The second type will have two of it's vertices on the same side and the third vertex on any of the other two sides.

    Hence, the required number of triangles

    $= 6 \times 5 \times 3 + {}^6C_2 \times 8 + {}^5C_2 \times 9 + {}^3C_2 \times 11$

    $= 90 + 120 + 90 + 33$

    $= 333$

38. First step – arrange 7 boys around the table according to the circular permutations rule. i.e. in 6! ways.

    Second step – now we have 7 places and have to arrange 7 girls on these places. This can be done in ${}^7P_7$ ways. Hence, the total number of ways = 6! × 7!

39. 2 × 7! × 7! (Note: we do not need to use circular arrangements here because the seats are numbered.)

40. We just need to select the floors and the people who get down at each floor.

    The floors selection can be done in ${}^{11}C_3$ ways.

    The people selection is ${}^9C_4 \times {}^5C_3$.

    Also, the floors need to be arranged using 3!

    Thus, ${}^{11}C_3 \times {}^9C_4 \times {}^5C_3 \times 3!$ or ${}^{11}P_3 \times {}^9C_4 \times {}^5C_3$

41. To arrange a surgeon and an assistant we have ${}^{40}P_2$ ways.

42. To arrange a surgeon and 4 assistants we have or $40 \times {}^{39}C_4$ ways.

43. Give one marble to each of the six children. Then, the remaining 4 identical marbles can be distributed amongst the six children in ${}^{(4+6-1)}C_{(6-1)}$ ways.

44. Since it is possible to give no objects to one or two of them we would have 3 choices for giving each item. Thus, $3 \times 3 \times 3 \times 3 \times 3 \times 3 = 2187$.

45. For an even number the units digit should be either 2, 4 or 6. For the other five places we have six digits. Hence, the number of six digit numbers = ${}^6P_5 \times 3 = 2160$.

46. Visualize the number as:

    $- - - - - - - -$

    This number has to have the last two digits even. Thus, ${}^3C_2 \times 2!$ will fill the last 2 digits.

    For the remaining places : ${}^5C_4 \times 4!$

    Thus, we have ${}^5C_4 \times 4! \times {}^3C_2 \times 2! = 720$

47. ${}^9C_5 \times 5! = 15120$

48. ${}^4C_1 \times 7 \times 7 \times 7 = {}^4C_1 \times 7^3$

49. Select the two positions for the two 3's. After that the remaining 5 places have to be filled using either 1 or 2.

    Thus, ${}^7C_2 \times 2^5$

50. ${}^4C_1 \times {}^7C_3 \times 3! = 840$

18 Chapter

Probability

CONCEPT AND IMPORTANCE OF PROBABILITY

Probability is one of the most important mathematical concepts that we use/come across in our day-to-day life. Particularly important in business and economic situations, probability is also used by us in our personal lives. For a lot of students who are not in touch with Mathematics after their Xth/XIIth classes, this chapter, along with permutations and combinations, is seen as an indication that XIIth standard Mathematics appear in the MBA entrance exams. This leads to students taking negative approach while tacking/preparing for the Mathematics section. Students are advised to remember that the Math asked in MBA entrance is mainly logical while studying the chapter.

As I set out to explain the basics of this chapter, I intend to improve your concepts of probability to such an extent that you feel in total control of this topic.

For those who are reasonably strong, my advice would be to use this chapter both for revisiting the basic concepts as well as for extensive practice.

Probability means the chance of the occurrence of an event. In layman terms, we can say that it is the likelihood that something—that is defined as the event—will or will not occur. Thus probabilities can be estimated for each of the following events in our personal lives:

(a) the probability that an individual student of B.Com will clear the CAT,

(b) The chance that a candidate chosen at random will clear an interview,

(c) The chance that you will win a game of flush in cards if you have a trio of twos in a game where four people are playing,

(d) The likelihood of India's winning the football World Cup in 2014.

(e) The probability that a bulb will fuse in it's first day of operation, and so on.

The knowledge of these estimations helps individuals decide on the course of action they will take in their day-to-day life. For instance, your estimation/ judgement of the probability of your chances of winning the card game in Event c above will influence your decision about the amount of money you will be ready to invest in the stakes for the particular game. The application of probability to personal life helps in improving our decision making.

However, the use of probability is much more varied and has far reaching influence on the world of economics and business. Some instances of these are:

(a) the estimation of the probability of the success of a business project,

(b) the estimation of the probability of the success of an advertising campaign in boosting the profits of a company,

(c) the estimation of the probability of the death of a 25-year old man in the next 10 years and that of the death of a 55-year old man in the next 10 years leading to the calculation of the premiums for life insurance,

(d) the estimation of the probability of the increase in the market price of the share of a company, and so on.

UNDERLYING FACTORS FOR REAL-LIFE ESTIMATION OF PROBABILITY

The factors underlying an event often affect the probability of that event's occurrence. For instance, if we estimate the probability of India winning the 2015 World Cup as 0.14 based on certain expectations of outcomes, then this probability will definitely improve if we know that Sachin Tendulkar will score 800 runs in that particular World Cup.

As we now move towards the mathematical aspects of the chapter, one underlying factor that recurs in every question of probability is that whenever one is asked the question, what is the probability? the immediate question that arises/should arise in one's mind is the probability of what?

The answer to this question is the probability of the EVENT.

The EVENT is the cornerstone or the bottomline of probability. Hence, the first objective while trying to solve any question in probability is to define the event.

The event whose probability is to be found out is described in the question and the task of the student in trying to solve the problem is to define it.

In general, the student can either define the event narrowly or broadly. Narrow definitions of events are the building blocks of any probability problem and whenever there is a doubt about a problem, the student is advised to get into the narrowest form of the event definition.

The *difference* between the narrow and broad definition of event can be explained through an example:

Example: What is the probability of getting a number greater than 2, in a throw of a normal unbiased dice having 6 faces?

The broad definition of the event here is getting a number greater than 2 and this probability is given by 4/6. However, this event can also be broken down into its more basic definitions as:

The event is defined as getting 3 or 4 or 5 or 6. The individual probabilities of each of these are 1/6,1/6,1/6 and 1/6 respectively.

Hence, the required probability is 1/6 + 1/6 + 1/6 + 1/6 = 4/6 = 2/3.

Although in this example it seems highly trivial, the narrow event-definition approach is very effective in solving difficult problems on probability.

In general, event definition means breaking up the event to the most basic building blocks, which have to be connected together through the two English conjunctions—AND and OR.

The Use of the Conjunction AND (Tool No. 9)

Refer *Back to school* section. Whenever we use AND as the natural conjunction joining two separate parts of the event definition, we replace the AND by the multiplication sign.

Thus, if A AND B have to occur, and if the probability of their occurrence are $P(A)$ and $P(B)$ respectively, then the probability that A AND B occur is got by connecting $P(A)$ AND $P(B)$. Replacing the AND by multiplication sign we get the required probability as:

$$P(A) \times P(B)$$

Example: If we have the probability of A hitting a target as 1/3 and that of B hitting the target as 1/2, then the probability that both hit the target if one shot is taken by both of them is got by

Event Definition: A hits the target AND B hits the target.

$$\rightarrow P(A) \times P(B) = 1/3 \times 1/2 = 1/6$$

(Note that since we use the conjunction AND in the definition of the event here, we multiply the individual probabilities that are connected through the conjunction AND.)

The Use of the Conjunction OR (Tool No. 10)

Refer Back to school section. Whenever we use OR as the natural conjunction joining two separate parts of the event definition, we replace the OR by the addition sign.

Thus, if A OR B have to occur, and if the probability of their occurrence are $P(A)$ and $P(B)$ respectively, then the probability that A OR B occur is got by connecting

$P(A)$ OR $P(B)$. Replacing the OR by addition sign, we get the required probability as

$$P(A) + P(B)$$

Example: If we have the probability of A winning a race as 1/3 and that of B winning the race as 1/2, then the probability that either A or B win a race is got by

Event Definition: A wins OR B wins.

$$\rightarrow P(A) + P(B) = 1/3 + 1/2 = 5/6$$

(Note that since we use the conjunction OR in the definition of the event here, we add the individual probabilities that are connected through the conjunction OR.)

Combination of AND and OR

If two dice are thrown, what is the chance that the sum of the numbers is not less than 10.

Event Definition: The sum of the numbers is not less than 10 if it is either 10 OR 11 OR 12.

Which can be done by
(6 AND 4) OR (4 AND 6) OR (5 AND 5) OR (6 AND 5) OR (5 AND 6) OR (6 AND 6)
that is, 1/6 × 1/6 + 1/6 × 1/6 + 1/6 × 1/6 + 1/6 × 1/6 + 1/6 × 1/6 + 1/6 × 1/6 = 6/36 = 1/6

The bottomline is that no matter how complicated the problem on probability is, it can be broken up into its narrower parts, which can be connected by ANDs and ORs to get the event definition.

Once the event is defined, the probability of each narrow event within the broad event is calculated and all the narrow events are connected by Multiplication (for AND) or by Addition (for OR) to get the final solution.

Example: In a four game match between Kasporov and Anand, the probability that Anand wins a particular game is 2/5 and that of Kasporov winning a game is 3/5. Assuming that there is no probability of a draw in an individual game, what is the chance that the match is drawn (Score is 2–2).

For the match to be drawn, 2 games have to be won by each of the players. If 'A' represents the event that Anand won a game and K represents the event that Kasporov won a game, the event definition for the match to end in a draw can be described as: [The student is advised to look at the use of narrow event definition.]

(A&A&K&K) OR (A&K&A&K) OR (A&K&K&A)
  OR (K&K&A&A) OR (K&A&K&A) OR
              (K&A&A&K)

This further translates into

$$(2/5)^2(3/5)^2 + (2/5)^2(3/5)^2 + (2/5)^2(3/5)^2 + (2/5)^2(3/5)^2$$
$$+ (2/5)^2(3/5)^2 + (2/5)^2(3/5)^2$$

$$= (36/625) \times 6 = 216/625$$

After a little bit of practice, you can also think about this directly as:

$${}^4C_2 \times (2/5)^2 \times {}^2C_2 \times (3/5)^2 = 6 \times 1 \times 36/625 = 216/625$$

Where, $4C_2$ gives us the number of ways in which Anand can win two games and $2C_2$ gives us the number of ways in which Kasporov can win the remaining 2 games (obviously, only one).

BASIC FACTS ABOUT PROBABILITY

For every event that can be defined, there is a corresponding non-event, which is the opposite of the event. The relationship between the event and the non-event is that they are mutually exclusive, that is, if the event occurs then the non-event does not occur and vice versa.

The event is denoted by E; the number of ways in which the event can occur is defined as $n(E)$ and the probability of the occurrence of the event is $P(E)$.

The non-event is denoted by E'; the number of ways in which the non-event can occur is defined as $n(E')$ while the probability of the occurrence of the event is $P(E')$.

The following relationships hold true with respect to the event and the non-event.

$n(E) + n(E') =$ sample space representing all the possible events that can occur related to the activity.

$$P(E) + P(E') = 1$$

This means that if the event does not occur, then the non-event occurs.

$$\rightarrow P(E) = 1 - P(E')$$

This is often very useful for the calculation of probabilities of events where it is easier to describe and count the non-event rather than the event.

Illustration

The probability that you get a total more than 3 in a throw of 2 dice.

Here, the event definition will be a long and tedious task, which will involve long counting. Hence, it would be more convenient to define the non-event and count the same.

Therefore, here the non-event will be defined as

A total not more than $3 \rightarrow 2$ or $3 \rightarrow (1\&1)$ OR (1&2) OR (2&1) = 1/36 + 1/36 + 1/36 = 3/36 = 1/12. However, a word of caution especially for students not comfortable at mathematics: Take care while defining the non-event. Beware of a trap like → event definition: Total > 10 in two throws of a dice does not translate into a non-event of < 10 but instead into the non-event of ≤ 10.

SOME IMPORTANT CONSIDERATIONS WHILE DEFINING EVENT

Random Experiment An experiment whose outcome has to be among a set of events that are completely known but whose exact outcome is unknown is a random experiment (e.g. Throwing of a dice, tossing of a coin). Most questions on probability are based on random experiments.

Sample Space This is defined in the context of a random experiment and denotes the set representing all the possible outcomes of the random experiment. [e.g. Sample space when a coin is tossed is (Head, Tail). Sample space when a dice is thrown is (1, 2, 3, 4, 5, 6).]

Event The set representing the desired outcome of a random experiment is called the event. Note that the event is a subset of the sample space.

Non-event The outcome that is opposite the desired outcome is the non-event. Note that if the event occurs, the non-event does not occur and vice versa.

Impossible Event An event that can never occur is an impossible event. The probability of an impossible event is 0. e.g. (Probability of the occurrence of 7 when a dice with 6 faces numbered 1–6 is thrown).

Mutually Exclusive Events A set of events is mutually exclusive when the occurrence of any one of them means that the other events cannot occur. (If head appears on a coin, tail will not appear and vice versa.)

Equally Likely Events If two events have the same probability or chance of occurrence they are called equally likely events. (In a throw of a dice, the chance of 1 showing on the dice is equal to 2 is equal to 3 is equal to 4 is equal to 5 is equal to 6 appearing on the dice.)

Exhaustive Set of Events A set of events that includes all the possibilities of the sample space is said to be an exhaustive set of events. (e.g. In a throw of a dice the number is less than three or more than or equal to three.)

Independent Events An event is described as such if the occurrence of an event has no effect on the probability of the occurrence of another event. (If the first child of a couple is a boy, there is no effect on the chances of the second child being a boy.)

Conditional Probability It is the probability of the occurrence of an event A given that the event B has already occurred. This is denoted by $P(A|B)$. (E.g. The probability that in two throws of a dices we get a total of 7 or more, given that in the first throw of the dices the number 5 had occurred.)

The Concept of Odds For and Odds Against

Sometimes, probability is also viewed in terms of *odds* for and *odds against* an event.

Odds in favour of an event E is defined as: $\dfrac{P(E)}{P(E)'}$

Odds against an event is defined as: $\dfrac{P(E)'}{P(E)}$

Expectation: The expectation of an individual is defined as Probability of winning × Reward of winning

Illustration: A man holds 20 out of the 500 tickets to a lottery. If the reward for the winning ticket is ₹ 1000, find the expectation of the man.

Space for Notes

Solution: Expectation = Probability of winning × Reward of winning = $\dfrac{20}{500} \times 1000 = ₹\ 40$.

ANOTHER APPROACH TO LOOK AT THE PROBABILITY PROBLEMS

The probability of an event is defined as

$$\dfrac{\text{Number of ways in which the event occurs}}{\text{Total number of outcomes possible}}$$

This means that the probability of any event can be got by counting the numerator and the denominator independently.

Hence, from this approach, the concentration shifts to counting the numerator and the denominator.

Thus for the example used above, the probability of a number > 2 appearing on a dice is:

$$\dfrac{\text{Number of ways in which the event occurs}}{\text{Total number of outcomes possible}} = \dfrac{4}{6}$$

The counting is done through any of
(a) The physical counting as illustrated above,
(b) The use of the concept of permutations,
(c) The use of the concept of combinations,
(d) The use of the MNP rule.
[*Refer to the chapter on Permutations and Combinations to understand b, c and d above.*]

🎯 WORKED-OUT PROBLEMS

Problem 18.1 In a throw of two dice, find the probability of getting one prime and one composite number.

Solution The probability of getting a prime number when a dices is thrown is 3/6 = 1/2. (This occurs when we get 2, 3 or 5 out of a possibility of getting 1, 2, 3, 4, 5 or 6.)

Similarly, in a throw of a dice, there are only 2 possibilities of getting composite numbers viz : 4 or 6 and this gives a probability of 1/3 for getting a composite number.

Now, let us look at defining the event. The event is—getting one prime and one composite number.

This can be got as:

The first number is prime and the second is composite OR the first number is composite and the second is prime.

$$= (1/2) \times (1/3) + (1/3) \times (1/2) = 1/3$$

Problem 18.2 Find the probability that a leap year chosen at random will have 53 Sundays.

Solution A leap year has 366 days. 52 complete weeks will have 364 days. The 365th day can be a Sunday (Probability = 1/7) OR the 366th day can be a Sunday (Probability = 1/7). Answer = 1/7 + 1/7 = 2/7.

Alternatively, you can think of this as: The favourable events will occur when we have Saturday and Sunday or Sunday and Monday as the 365th and 366th days respectively. (i.e. 2 possibilities of the event occurring). Besides, the total number of ways that can happen are Sunday and Monday OR Monday and Tuesday … OR Friday and Saturday OR Saturday and Sunday.

Problem 18.3 There are two bags containing white and black balls. In the first bag, there are 8 white and 6 black balls and in the second bag, there are 4 white and 7 black balls. One ball is drawn at random from any of these two bags. Find the probability of this ball being black.

Solution The event definition here is: 1st bag and black ball OR 2nd Bag and Black Ball. The chances of picking up either the 1st OR the 2nd Bag are 1/2 each.

Besides, the chance of picking up a black ball from the first bag is 6/14 and the chance of picking up a black ball from the second bag is 7/11.

Thus, using these values and the ANDs and ORs we get:

$$(1/2) \times (6/14) + (1/2) \times (7/11) = (3/14) + (7/22) = (66 + 98)/$$
$$(308) = 164/308 = 41/77$$

Problem 18.4 The letters of the word LUCKNOW are arranged among themselves. Find the probability of always having NOW in the word.

Solution The required probability will be given by the equation

= No. of words having NOW/Total no. of words

= 5!/7! = 1/42 [See the chapter of Permutations and Combinations to understand the logic behind these values.]

Problem 18.5 A person has 3 children with at least one boy. Find the probability of having at least 2 boys among the children.

Solution The event is occurring under the following situations:

(a) Second is a boy and third is a girl OR

(b) Second is a girl and third is a boy OR

(c) Second is a boy and third is a boy

This will be represented by: $(1/2) \times (1/2) + (1/2) \times (1/2) + (1/2) \times (1/2) = 3/4$

Problem 18.6 Out of 13 applicants for a job, there are 5 women and 8 men. Two persons are to be selected for the job. The probability that at least one of the selected persons will be a woman is:

Solution The required probability will be given by

First is a woman and Second is a man   OR

First is a man and Second is a woman   OR

First is a woman and Second is a woman

i.e. $(5/13) \times (8/12) + (8/13) \times (5/12) + (5/13) \times (4/12)$
$$= 100/156 = 25/39$$

Alternatively, we can define the non-event as: There are two men and no women. Then, probability of the non-event is

$$(8/13) \times (7/12) = 56/156$$

Hence, $P(E) = (1 - 56/156) = 100/156 = 25/39$

[*Note:* This is a case of probability calculation where repetition is not allowed.]

Problem 18.7 The probability that A can solve the problem is 2/3 and B can solve it is 3/4. If both of them attempt the problem, then what is the probability that the problem gets solved.

Solution The event is defined as:

A solves the problem   AND B does not solve the problem

OR

A doesn't solve the problem   AND B solves the problem

OR

A solves the problem   AND B solves the problem.

Numerically, this is equivalent to:

$$(2/3) \times (1/4) + (1/3) \times (3/4) + (2/3) \times (3/4)$$
$$= (2/12) + (3/12) + (6/12) = 11/12$$

Problem 18.8 Six positive numbers are taken at random and are multiplied together. Then what is the probability that the product ends in an odd digit other than 5.

Solution The event will occurs when all the numbers selected are ending in 1, 3, 7 or 9.

If we take numbers between 1 to 10 (both inclusive), we will have a positive occurrence if each of the six numbers selected are either 1, 3, 7 or 9.

The probability of any number selected being either of these 4 is 4/10 (4 positive events out of 10 possibilities) [*Note:* If we try to take numbers between 1 to 20, we will have a probability of 8/20 = 4/10. Hence, we can extrapolate up to infinity and say that the probability of any number selected ending in 1, 3, 7 or 9 so as to fulfill the requirement is 4/10.]

Hence, answer = $(0.4)^6$

Problem 18.9 The probability that Arjit will solve a problem is 1/5. What is the probability that he solves at least one problem out of ten problems?

Solution The non-event is defined as:

He solves no problems i.e. he doesn't solve the first problem and he doesn't solve the second problem ... and he doesn't solve the tenth problem.

Probability of non-event = $(4/5)^{10}$
Hence, probability of the event is $1-(4/5)^{10}$

Problem 18.10 A carton contains 25 bulbs, 8 of which are defective. What is the probability that if a sample of 4 bulbs is chosen, exactly 2 of them will be defective?

Solution The probability that exactly two balls are defective and exactly two are not defective will be given by $(4C_2) \times (8/25) \times (7/24) \times (17/23) \times (16/22)$

Problem 18.11 Out of 40 consecutive integers, two are chosen at random. Find the probability that their sum is odd.

Solution Forty consecutive integers will have 20 odd and 20 even integers. The sum of 2 chosen integers will be odd, only if
(a) First is even and Second is odd OR
(b) First is odd and Second is even
Mathematically, the probability will be given by:

P(First is even) $\times P$(Second is odd) + P(First is odd) $\times P$(second is even)

Space for Rough Work

= $(20/40) \times (20/39) + (20/40) \times (20/39)$
= $(2 \times 20^2/40 \times 39) = 20/39$

Problem 18.12 An integer is chosen at random from the first 100 integers. What is the probability that this number will not be divisible by 5 or 8?

Solution For a number from 1 to 100 not be divisible by 5 or 8, we need to remove all the numbers that are divisible by 5 or 8.

Thus, we remove 5, 8, 10, 15, 16, 20, 24, 25, 30, 32, 35, 40, 45, 48, 50, 55, 56, 60, 64, 65, 70, 72, 75, 80, 85, 88, 90, 95, 96, and 100.
i.e. 30 numbers from the 100 are removed.
Hence, answer is 70/100 = 7/10 (required probability)

Alternatively, we could have counted the numbers as number of numbers divisible by 5 + number of numbers divisible by 8 − number of numbers divisible by both 5 or 8.

$$= 20 + 12 - 2 = 30$$

Problem 18.13 From a bag containing 8 green and 5 red balls, three are drawn one after the other. Find the probability of all three balls being green if
(a) the balls drawn are replaced before the next ball is picked
(b) the balls drawn are not replaced.

Solution
(a) When the balls drawn are replaced, we can see that the number of balls available for drawing out will be the same for every draw. This means that the probability of a green ball appearing in the first draw and a green ball appearing in the second draw as well as one appearing in the third draw are equal to each other.
Hence answer to the question above will be:

Required probability = $\dfrac{8}{13} \times \dfrac{8}{13} \times \dfrac{8}{13} = (8^3/13^3)$

(b) When the balls are not replaced, the probability of drawing any color of ball for every fresh draw changes. Hence, the answer here will be:

Required probability = $\dfrac{8}{13} \times \dfrac{7}{12} \times \dfrac{6}{11}$

LEVEL OF DIFFICULTY (I)

1. In throwing a fair dice, what is the probability of getting the number '3'?

   (a) $\dfrac{1}{3}$ (b) $\dfrac{1}{6}$

   (c) $\dfrac{1}{9}$ (d) $\dfrac{1}{12}$

2. What is the chance of throwing a number greater than 4 with an ordinary dice whose faces are numbered from 1 to 6?

   (a) $\dfrac{1}{3}$ (b) $\dfrac{1}{6}$

   (c) $\dfrac{1}{9}$ (d) $\dfrac{1}{8}$

3. Find the chance of throwing at least one ace in a simple throw with two dice.

   (a) $\dfrac{1}{12}$ (b) $\dfrac{1}{3}$

   (c) $\dfrac{1}{4}$ (d) $\dfrac{11}{36}$

4. Find the chance of drawing 2 blue balls in succession from a bag containing 5 red and 7 blue balls, if the balls are not being replaced.

   (a) $\dfrac{3}{13}$ (b) $\dfrac{21}{64}$

   (c) $\dfrac{7}{22}$ (d) $\dfrac{21}{61}$

5. From a pack of 52 cards, two are drawn at random. Find the chance that one is a knave and the other a queen.

   (a) $\dfrac{8}{663}$ (b) $\dfrac{1}{6}$

   (c) $\dfrac{1}{9}$ (d) $\dfrac{1}{12}$

6. If a card is picked up at random from a pack of 52 cards. Find the probability that it is
   (i) a spade.

   (a) $\dfrac{1}{9}$ (b) $\dfrac{1}{6}$

   (c) $\dfrac{1}{4}$ (d) $\dfrac{1}{4}$

   (ii) a king or queen.

   (a) $\dfrac{3}{13}$ (b) $\dfrac{2}{13}$

   (c) $\dfrac{7}{52}$ (d) $\dfrac{1}{169}$

   (iii) 'a spade' or 'a king' or 'a queen'

   (a) $\dfrac{21}{52}$ (b) $\dfrac{5}{13}$

   (c) $\dfrac{19}{52}$ (d) $\dfrac{15}{52}$

7. Three coins are tossed. What is the probability of getting
   (i) 2 Tails and 1 Head

   (a) $\dfrac{1}{4}$ (b) $\dfrac{3}{8}$

   (c) $\dfrac{2}{3}$ (d) $\dfrac{1}{8}$

   (ii) 1 Tail and 2 Heads

   (a) $\dfrac{3}{8}$ (b) 1

   (c) $\dfrac{2}{3}$ (d) $\dfrac{3}{4}$

8. Three coins are tossed. What is the probability of getting
   (i) neither 3 Heads nor 3 Tails?

   (a) $\dfrac{1}{2}$ (b) $\dfrac{1}{3}$

   (c) $\dfrac{2}{3}$ (d) $\dfrac{3}{4}$

   (ii) three heads

   (a) $\dfrac{1}{8}$ (b) $\dfrac{1}{4}$

   (c) $\dfrac{1}{2}$ (d) $\dfrac{2}{3}$

9. For the above question, the probability that there is at least one tail is:

   (a) $\dfrac{2}{3}$ (b) $\dfrac{7}{8}$

   (c) $\dfrac{3}{8}$ (d) $\dfrac{1}{2}$

10. Two fair dice are thrown. Find the probability of getting

(i) a number divisible by 2 or 4.

(a) $\dfrac{1}{2}$ (b) $\dfrac{3}{4}$

(c) $\dfrac{1}{3}$ (d) $\dfrac{2}{3}$

(ii) a number divisible by 2 and 4.

(a) $\dfrac{1}{3}$ (b) $\dfrac{1}{4}$

(c) $\dfrac{3}{4}$ (d) $\dfrac{5}{7}$

(iii) a prime number less than 8.

(a) $\dfrac{11}{13}$ (b) $\dfrac{1}{13}$

(c) $\dfrac{1}{4}$ (d) $\dfrac{13}{36}$

11. A bag contains 3 green and 7 white balls. Two balls are drawn from the bag in succession without replacement. What is the probability that
 (i) both are white?

(a) $\dfrac{1}{7}$ (b) $\dfrac{5}{11}$

(c) $\dfrac{7}{11}$ (d) $\dfrac{7}{15}$

(ii) they are of different colour?

(a) $\dfrac{7}{15}$ (b) $\dfrac{7}{9}$

(c) $\dfrac{5}{11}$ (d) $\dfrac{7}{11}$

12. 100 students appeared for two examinations. 60 passed the first, 50 passed the second and 30 passed both. Find the probability that a student selected at random has failed in both the examinations?

(a) $\dfrac{1}{5}$ (b) $\dfrac{1}{7}$

(c) $\dfrac{5}{7}$ (d) $\dfrac{5}{6}$

13. What is the probability of throwing a number greater than 2 with a fair dice?

(a) $\dfrac{2}{3}$ (b) $\dfrac{2}{5}$

(c) 1   (d) $\dfrac{3}{5}$

14. Three cards numbered 2, 4 and 8 are put into a box. If a card is drawn at random, what is the probability that the card drawn is

(i) a prime number?

(a) 1   (b) $\dfrac{1}{3}$

(c) $\dfrac{4}{5}$ (d) $\dfrac{5}{7}$

(ii) an even number?

(a) 1   (b) $\dfrac{2}{3}$

(c) $\dfrac{1}{2}$ (d) $\dfrac{3}{5}$

(iii) an odd number?

(a) 1   (b) 0

(c) $\dfrac{1}{3}$ (d) $\dfrac{2}{3}$

15. Two fair coins are tossed. Find the probability of obtaining
 (i) 2 Heads

(a) 1   (b) $\dfrac{2}{3}$

(c) $\dfrac{1}{2}$ (d) $\dfrac{1}{4}$

(ii) 1 Head and 1 Tail

(a) $\dfrac{1}{2}$ (b) 1

(c) $\dfrac{1}{3}$ (d) $\dfrac{2}{3}$

(iii) 2 Tails

(a) 1   (b) $\dfrac{1}{4}$

(c) $\dfrac{2}{3}$ (d) $\dfrac{1}{2}$

16. In rolling two dices, find the probability that
 (i) there is at least one '6'

(a) $\dfrac{11}{36}$ (b) $\dfrac{22}{36}$

(c) $\dfrac{15}{36}$ (d) $\dfrac{29}{36}$

(ii) the sum is 5

(a) $\dfrac{1}{4}$ (b) $\dfrac{1}{9}$

(c) $\dfrac{1}{2}$ (d) $\dfrac{1}{6}$

17. From a bag containing 4 white and 5 black balls a man draws 3 at random. What are the odds against these being all black?

(a) $\dfrac{5}{37}$ (b) $\dfrac{37}{5}$

(c) $\dfrac{11}{13}$ (d) $\dfrac{13}{37}$

18. Amit throws three dice in a special game of Ludo. If it is known that he needs 15 or higher in this throw to win then find the chance of his winning the game.

(a) $\dfrac{5}{54}$ (b) $\dfrac{17}{216}$

(c) $\dfrac{13}{216}$ (d) $\dfrac{15}{216}$

19. Find out the probability of forming 187 or 215 with the digits 1, 2, 3, 4, 5, 6, 7, 8, 9 when only numbers of three digits are formed and when
(i) repetitions are not allowed

(a) $\dfrac{12}{504}$ (b) $\dfrac{18}{504}$

(c) $\dfrac{2}{504}$ (d) $\dfrac{24}{504}$

(ii) repetitions are allowed

(a) $\dfrac{2}{729}$ (b) $\dfrac{6}{729}$

(c) $\dfrac{11}{729}$ (d) $\dfrac{4}{729}$

20. In a horse race there were 18 horses numbered 1–18. The probability that horse 1 would win is 1/6, that 2 would win is 1/10 and that 3 would win is 1/8. Assuming that a tie is impossible, find the chance that one of the three will win.

(a) $\dfrac{47}{120}$ (b) $\dfrac{119}{120}$

(c) $\dfrac{11}{129}$ (d) $\dfrac{1}{5}$

21. Two balls are to be drawn from a bag containing 8 grey and 3 blue balls. Find the chance that they will both be blue.

(a) $\dfrac{1}{5}$ (b) $\dfrac{3}{55}$

(c) $\dfrac{11}{15}$ (d) $\dfrac{14}{45}$

22. Two fair dice are thrown. What is the probability of
(i) throwing a double?

(a) $\dfrac{1}{6}$ (b) 1

(c) $\dfrac{2}{3}$ (d) $\dfrac{1}{2}$

(ii) the sum is greater than 10

(a) $\dfrac{2}{3}$ (b) $\dfrac{2}{5}$

(c) $\dfrac{1}{6}$ (d) $\dfrac{1}{12}$

(iii) the sum is less than 10?

(a) $\dfrac{5}{6}$ (b) $\dfrac{2}{5}$

(c) $\dfrac{3}{5}$ (d) $\dfrac{2}{3}$

23. In a certain lottery the prize is ₹ 1 crore and 5000 tickets have been sold. What is the expectation of a man who holds 10 tickets?
(a) ₹ 20,000   (b) ₹ 25,000
(c) ₹ 30,000   (d) ₹ 15,000

24. Two letters are randomly chosen from the word LIME. Find the probability that the letters are *L* and *M*.

(a) $\dfrac{1}{2}$ (b) $\dfrac{1}{4}$

(c) $\dfrac{1}{3}$ (d) $\dfrac{1}{6}$

Directions for Questions 25 to 27: Read the following passage and answer the questions based on it.

The Bangalore office of Infosys has 1200 executives. Of these, 880 subscribe to the *Time* magazine and 650 subscribe to the *Economist*. Each executive may subscribe to either the *Time* or the *Economist* or both. If an executive is picked at random, answer questions 25–27.

25. What is the probability that
(i) he has subscribed to the *Time* magazine.

(a) $\dfrac{11}{15}$ (b) $\dfrac{11}{12}$

(c) $\dfrac{7}{15}$ (d) $\dfrac{7}{11}$

(ii) he has subscribed to the *Economist*.

(a) $\dfrac{13}{21}$ (b) $\dfrac{13}{20}$

(c) $\dfrac{13}{24}$ (d) $\dfrac{12}{30}$

26. He has subscribed to both magazines.

(a) $\dfrac{22}{40}$ (b) $\dfrac{11}{40}$

(c) $\dfrac{12}{20}$ (d) $\dfrac{4}{20}$

27. If among the executives who have subscribed to the *Time* magazine, an executive is picked at random.

What is the probability that he has also subscribed to the *Economist*?

(a) $\dfrac{3}{8}$ (b) $\dfrac{5}{8}$

(c) $\dfrac{2}{3}$ (d) $\dfrac{1}{8}$

28. A bag contains four black and five red balls. If three balls from the bag are chosen at random, what is the chance that they are all black?

(a) $\dfrac{1}{21}$ (b) $\dfrac{1}{20}$

(c) $\dfrac{2}{23}$ (d) $\dfrac{1}{9}$

29. If a number of two digits is formed with the digits 2, 3, 5, 7, 9 without repetition of digits, what is the probability that the number formed is 35?

(a) $\dfrac{1}{10}$ (b) $\dfrac{1}{20}$

(c) $\dfrac{2}{11}$ (d) $\dfrac{1}{11}$

30. From a pack of 52 playing cards, three cards are drawn at random. Find the probability of drawing a king, a queen and jack.

(a) $\dfrac{16}{5525}$ (b) $\dfrac{1}{13^3}$

(c) $\dfrac{1}{14^3}$ (d) $\dfrac{1}{15^3}$

31. A bag contains 20 balls marked 1 to 20. One ball is drawn at random. Find the probability that it is marked with a number multiple of 5 or 7.

(a) $\dfrac{3}{10}$ (b) $\dfrac{7}{10}$

(c) $\dfrac{1}{11}$ (d) $\dfrac{2}{3}$

32. A group of investigators took a fair sample of 1972 children from the general population and found that there are 1000 boys and 972 girls. If the investigators claim that their research is so accurate that the sex of a new born child can be predicted based on the ratio of the sample of the population, then what is the expectation in terms of the probability that a new child born will be a girl?

(a) $\dfrac{243}{250}$ (b) $\dfrac{250}{257}$

(c) $\dfrac{9}{10}$ (d) $\dfrac{243}{493}$

33. A bag contains 3 red, 6 white and 7 black balls. Two balls are drawn at random. What is the probability that both are black?

(a) $\dfrac{1}{8}$ (b) $\dfrac{7}{40}$

(c) $\dfrac{12}{40}$ (d) $\dfrac{13}{40}$

34. A bag contains 6 red, 4 white and 8 blue balls. If three balls are drawn at random, find the probability that

(i) all the three balls are of the same colour.

(a) $\dfrac{17}{240}$ (b) $\dfrac{5}{51}$

(c) $\dfrac{31}{204}$ (d) None of these

(ii) all the three balls are blue.

(a) $\dfrac{8}{51}$ (b) $\dfrac{50}{51}$

(c) $\dfrac{7}{102}$ (d) $\dfrac{13}{51}$

35. If $P(A) = 1/3$, $P(B) = 1/2$, $P(A \cap B) = 1/4$ then find $P(A' \cup B')$

(a) $\dfrac{1}{3}$ (b) $\dfrac{2}{5}$

(c) $\dfrac{2}{3}$ (d) $\dfrac{3}{4}$

36. A and B are two candidates seeking admission to the IIMs. The probability that A is selected is 0.5 and the probability that both A and B are selected is at most 0.3. Is it possible that the probability of B getting selected is 0.9.

(a) No   (b) Yes
(c) Either (a) or (b)   (d) Can't say

37. The probability that a student will pass in Mathematics is 3/5 and the probability that he will pass in English is 1/3. If the probability that he will pass in both Mathematics and English is 1/8, what is the probability that he will pass in at least one subject?

(a) $\dfrac{97}{120}$ (b) $\dfrac{87}{120}$

(c) $\dfrac{53}{120}$ (d) $\dfrac{120}{297}$

38. The odds in favour of standing first of three students Amit, Vikas and Vivek appearing at an examination are 1 : 2. 2 : 5 and 1 : 7 respectively. What is the probability that either of them will stand first (assume that a tie for the first place is not possible).

(a) $\dfrac{168}{178}$ (b) $\dfrac{122}{168}$

(c) $\dfrac{5}{168}$ (d) $\dfrac{125}{168}$

39. A, B, C are three mutually exclusive and exhaustive events associated with a random experiment. Find $P(A)$ if it is given that $P(B) = 3/2 \, P(A)$ and $P(C) = 1/2 \, P(B)$.

(a) $\dfrac{4}{13}$ (b) $\dfrac{2}{13}$

(c) $\dfrac{12}{13}$ (d) $\dfrac{1}{13}$

40. A and B are two mutually exclusive events of an experiment. If $P(A') = 0.65$, $P(A \cup B) = 0.65$ and $P(B) = p$, find the value of p.

(a) 0.25   (b) 0.3
(c) 0.1   (d) 0.2

41. A bag contains 4 white and 2 black balls. Another contains 3 white and 5 black balls. If one ball is drawn from each bag, find the probability that
 (i) both are white.

(a) $\dfrac{1}{3}$ (b) $\dfrac{2}{3}$

(c) $\dfrac{1}{4}$ (d) $\dfrac{3}{4}$

 (ii) both are black.

(a) $\dfrac{3}{24}$ (b) $\dfrac{1}{24}$

(c) $\dfrac{3}{12}$ (d) $\dfrac{5}{24}$

 (iii) one is white and one is black.

(a) $\dfrac{13}{24}$ (b) $\dfrac{15}{24}$

(c) $\dfrac{11}{21}$ (d) $\dfrac{1}{2}$

42. The odds against an event is 5 : 3 and the odds in favour of another independent event is 7 : 5. Find the probability that at least one of the two events will occur.

(a) $\dfrac{52}{96}$ (b) $\dfrac{69}{96}$

(c) $\dfrac{71}{96}$ (d) $\dfrac{13}{96}$

43. Kamal and Monica appeared for an interview for two vacancies. The probability of Kamal's selection is 1/3 and that of Monica's selection is 1/5. Find the probability that only one of them will be selected.

(a) $\dfrac{2}{5}$ (b) $\dfrac{1}{5}$

(c) $\dfrac{5}{9}$ (d) $\dfrac{2}{3}$

44. A husband and a wife appear in an interview for two vacancies for the same post. The probability of husband's selection is $(1/7)$ and that of the wife's selection is 1/5. What is the probability that
 (i) both of them will be selected?

(a) $\dfrac{1}{35}$ (b) $\dfrac{2}{35}$

(c) $\dfrac{3}{35}$ (d) $\dfrac{1}{7}$

 (ii) one of them will be selected?

(a) $\dfrac{1}{7}$ (b) $\dfrac{3}{7}$

(c) $\dfrac{2}{7}$ (d) None of these

 (iii) none of them will be selected?

(a) $\dfrac{24}{35}$ (b) $\dfrac{20}{35}$

(c) $\dfrac{21}{35}$ (d) $\dfrac{2}{7}$

 (iv) at least one of them will be selected?

(a) $\dfrac{12}{35}$ (b) $\dfrac{11}{35}$

(c) $\dfrac{16}{35}$ (d) $\dfrac{1}{5}$

Space for Rough Work

LEVEL OF DIFFICULTY (II)

1. Two fair dices are thrown. Given that the sum of the dice is less than or equal to 4, find the probability that only one dice shows two.
   (a) $\dfrac{1}{4}$
   (b) $\dfrac{1}{2}$
   (c) $\dfrac{2}{3}$
   (d) $\dfrac{1}{3}$

2. A can hit the target 3 times in 6 shots, B 2 times in 6 shots and C 4 times in 6 shots. They fire a volley. What is the probability that at least 2 shots hit?
   (a) $\dfrac{1}{2}$
   (b) $\dfrac{1}{3}$
   (c) $\dfrac{2}{3}$
   (d) $\dfrac{3}{4}$

3. There are two bags, one of them contains 5 red and 7 white balls and the other 3 red and 12 white balls, and a ball is to be drawn from one or the other of the two bags. Find the chance of drawing a red ball.
   (a) $\dfrac{37}{120}$
   (b) $\dfrac{30}{120}$
   (c) $\dfrac{11}{120}$
   (d) None of these

4. In two bags there are to be put altogether 5 red and 12 white balls, neither bag being empty. How must the balls be divided so as to give a person who draws one ball from either bag
   (i) the least chance of drawing a red ball?
   (a) $\dfrac{3}{35}$
   (b) $\dfrac{5}{32}$
   (c) $\dfrac{7}{32}$
   (d) $\dfrac{1}{16}$
   (ii) the greatest chance of drawing a red ball?
   (a) $\dfrac{3}{4}$
   (b) $\dfrac{2}{3}$
   (c) $\dfrac{5}{8}$
   (d) $\dfrac{5}{7}$

5. If 8 coins are tossed, what is the chance that one and only one will turn up Head?
   (a) $\dfrac{1}{16}$
   (b) $\dfrac{3}{35}$
   (c) $\dfrac{3}{32}$
   (d) $\dfrac{1}{32}$

6. What is the chance that a leap year, selected at random, will contain 53 Sundays?
   (a) $\dfrac{2}{7}$
   (b) $\dfrac{3}{7}$

7. Out of all the 2-digit integers between 1 to 200, a 2-digit number has to be selected at random. What is the probability that the selected number is not divisible by 7?
   (a) $\dfrac{11}{90}$
   (b) $\dfrac{33}{90}$
   (c) $\dfrac{55}{90}$
   (d) $\dfrac{77}{90}$

8. A child is asked to pick up 2 balloons from a box containing 10 blue and 15 red balloons. What is the probability of the child picking, at random, 2 balloons of different colours?
   (a) $\dfrac{1}{2}$
   (b) $\dfrac{2}{3}$
   (c) $\dfrac{1}{3}$
   (d) $\dfrac{3}{5}$

9. Tom and Dick are running in the same race; the probability of their winning are 1/5 and 1/2 respectively. Find the probability that
   (i) either of them will win the race.
   (a) $\dfrac{7}{10}$
   (b) $\dfrac{3}{10}$
   (c) $\dfrac{1}{5}$
   (d) $\dfrac{7}{9}$
   (ii) neither of them will win the race.
   (a) $\dfrac{7}{10}$
   (b) $\dfrac{3}{10}$
   (c) $\dfrac{2}{5}$
   (d) $\dfrac{4}{5}$

10. Two dice are thrown. If the total on the faces of the two dices are 6, find the probability that there are two odd numbers on the faces?
   (a) $\dfrac{2}{5}$
   (b) $\dfrac{1}{5}$
   (c) $\dfrac{5}{9}$
   (d) $\dfrac{3}{5}$

11. Amarnath appears in an exam that has 4 subjects. The chance he passes an individual subject's test is 0.8. What is the probability that he will
   (i) pass in all the subjects?
   (a) 0.8^4
   (b) 0.3^4
   (c) 0.7^3
   (d) None of these

(ii) fail in all the subjects?
(a) 0.4^2 (b) 0.2^4
(c) 0.3^4 (d) None of these

(iii) pass in at least one of the subjects?
(a) 0.99984   (b) 0.9984
(c) 0.0016   (d) None of these

12. A box contains 2 tennis, 3 cricket and 4 squash balls. Three balls are drawn in succession with replacement. Find the probability that
(i) all are cricket balls.
(a) $\dfrac{1}{27}$ (b) $\dfrac{2}{27}$
(c) $\dfrac{25}{27}$ (d) $\dfrac{1}{8}$

(ii) the first is a tennis ball, the second is a cricket ball, the third is a squash ball.
(a) $\dfrac{8}{243}$ (b) $\dfrac{5}{243}$
(c) $\dfrac{4}{243}$ (d) $\dfrac{11}{243}$

(iii) all three are of the same type.
(a) $\dfrac{11}{81}$ (b) $\dfrac{1}{9}$
(c) $\dfrac{13}{81}$ (d) $\dfrac{17}{81}$

13. With the data in the above question, answer the questions when the balls are drawn in succession without replacement.
(i)
(a) $\dfrac{3}{84}$ (b) $\dfrac{1}{84}$
(c) $\dfrac{5}{84}$ (d) None of these

(ii)
(a) $\dfrac{2}{21}$ (b) $\dfrac{4}{21}$
(c) $\dfrac{1}{21}$ (d) $\dfrac{1}{9}$

(iii)
(a) $\dfrac{3}{84}$ (b) $\dfrac{1}{84}$
(c) $\dfrac{5}{84}$ (d) $\dfrac{11}{84}$

14. In the Mindworkzz library, there are 8 books by Stephen Covey and 1 book by Vinay Singh in shelf A. At the same time, there are 5 books by Stephen Covey in shelf B. One book is moved from shelf A to shelf B. A student picks up a book from shelf B. Find the probability that the book by Vinay Singh.

(i) is still in shelf A.
(a) $\dfrac{1}{3}$ (b) $\dfrac{8}{9}$
(c) $\dfrac{3}{4}$ (d) None of these

(ii) is in shelf B.
(a) $\dfrac{3}{54}$ (b) $\dfrac{4}{54}$
(c) $\dfrac{5}{54}$ (d) None of these

(iii) is taken by the student.
(a) $\dfrac{3}{54}$ (b) $\dfrac{1}{54}$
(c) $\dfrac{2}{27}$ (d) None of these

15. The ratio of number of officers and ladies in the Scorpion Squadron and in the Gunners Squadron are 3 : 1 and 2 : 5 respectively. An individual is selected to be the chairperson of their association. The chance that this individual is selected from the Scorpions is 2/3. Find the probability that the chairperson will be an officer.
(a) $\dfrac{25}{42}$ (b) $\dfrac{13}{43}$
(c) $\dfrac{11}{43}$ (d) $\dfrac{7}{42}$

16. A batch of 50 transistors contains 3 defective ones. Two transistors are selected at random from the batch and put into a radio set. What is the probability that
(i) both the transistors selected are defective?
(a) $\dfrac{4}{1225}$ (b) $\dfrac{3}{1225}$
(c) $\dfrac{124}{1224}$ (d) None of these

(ii) only one is defective?
(a) $\dfrac{141}{1225}$ (b) $\dfrac{121}{1225}$
(c) $\dfrac{123}{1224}$ (d) None of these

(iii) neither is defective?
(a) $\dfrac{1082}{1224}$ (b) $\dfrac{1081}{1225}$
(c) $\dfrac{1081}{1224}$ (d) None of these

17. The probability that a man will be alive in 35 years is $\dfrac{3}{5}$ and the probability that his wife will be alive is $\dfrac{3}{7}$. Find the probability that after 35 years.

(i) both will be alive.

(a) $\dfrac{2}{35}$ (b) $\dfrac{9}{35}$

(c) $\dfrac{6}{35}$ (d) $\dfrac{3}{35}$

(ii) only the man will be alive.

(a) $\dfrac{12}{35}$ (b) $\dfrac{11}{35}$

(c) $\dfrac{13}{35}$ (d) $\dfrac{8}{35}$

(iii) only the wife will be alive.

(a) $\dfrac{2}{35}$ (b) $\dfrac{3}{35}$

(c) $\dfrac{6}{35}$ (d) $\dfrac{11}{35}$

(iv) at least one will be alive.

(a) $\dfrac{27}{35}$ (b) $\dfrac{12}{35}$

(c) $\dfrac{11}{35}$ (d) $\dfrac{7}{35}$

18. *A* speaks the truth 3 out of 4 times, and *B* 5 out of 6 times. What is the probability that they will contradict each other in stating the same fact?

(a) $\dfrac{2}{3}$ (b) $\dfrac{1}{3}$

(c) $\dfrac{5}{6}$ (d) None of these

19. A party of *n* persons sit at a round table. Find the odds against two specified persons sitting next to each other.

(a) $\dfrac{n+1}{2}$ (b) $\dfrac{n-3}{2}$

(c) $\dfrac{n+3}{2}$ (d) None of these

20. If 4 whole numbers are taken at random and multiplied together, what is the chance that the last digit in the product is 1, 3, 7 or 9?

(a) $\dfrac{15}{653}$ (b) $\dfrac{12}{542}$

(c) $\dfrac{16}{625}$ (d) $\dfrac{17}{625}$

21. In four throws with a pair of dices what is the chance of throwing a double twice?

(a) $\dfrac{11}{216}$ (b) $\dfrac{25}{216}$

(c) $\dfrac{35}{126}$ (d) $\dfrac{41}{216}$

22. A life insurance company insured 25,000 young boys, 14,000 young girls and 16,000 young adults. The probability of death within 10 years of a young boy, young girl and a young adult are 0.02, 0.03 and

0.15 respectively. One of the insured persons dice. What is the probability that the dead person is a young boy?

(a) $\dfrac{36}{165}$ (b) $\dfrac{25}{166}$

(c) $\dfrac{26}{165}$ (d) $\dfrac{32}{165}$

23. Three groups of children contain 3 girls and 1 boy, 2 girls and 2 boys, and 1 girl and 2 boys respectively. One child is selected at random from each group. The probability that the three selected consist of 1 girl and 2 boys is

(a) $\dfrac{3}{8}$ (b) $\dfrac{1}{5}$

(c) $\dfrac{5}{8}$ (d) $\dfrac{3}{5}$

24. A locker at the world famous WTC building can be opened by dialing a fixed three-digit code (between 000 and 999). Don, a terrorist, only knows that the number is a three-digit number and has only one six. Using this information he tries to open the locker by dialing three digits at random. The probability that he succeeds in his endeavour is

(a) $\dfrac{1}{243}$ (b) $\dfrac{1}{900}$

(c) $\dfrac{1}{1000}$ (d) $\dfrac{3}{216}$

25. In a bag there are 12 black and 6 white balls. Two balls are chosen at random and the first one is found to be black. The probability that the second one is also black is:

(a) $\dfrac{11}{17}$ (b) $\dfrac{12}{17}$

(c) $\dfrac{13}{18}$ (d) None of these

26. In the above question, what is the probability that the second one is white?

(a) $\dfrac{3}{17}$ (b) $\dfrac{6}{17}$

(c) $\dfrac{5}{17}$ (d) $\dfrac{1}{17}$

27. A fair dice is tossed six times. Find the probability of getting a third six on the sixth throw.

(a) $\dfrac{{}^5C_2 \, 5^2}{6^2}$ (b) $\dfrac{{}^5C_2 \, 5^3}{6^6}$

(c) $\dfrac{{}^5C_3 \, 5^2}{6^3}$ (d) $\dfrac{{}^5C_3 \, 5^2}{6^6}$

28. In shuffling a pack of cards, four are accidentally dropped. Find the chance that the dropped cards should be one from each suit.

(a) $\dfrac{13^4}{^{52}C_4}$ (b) $\dfrac{12^4}{^{52}C_2}$

(c) $\dfrac{13^2}{^{34}C_2}$ (d) $\dfrac{12^2}{^{22}C_3}$

29. Three of the six vertices of a regular hexagon are chosen at random. The probability that the triangle with these vertices is equilateral is

(a) $\dfrac{1}{10}$ (b) $\dfrac{3}{10}$

(c) $\dfrac{1}{5}$ (d) $\dfrac{4}{10}$

30. There are 5 red shoes and 4 black shoes in a sale. They have got all mixed up with each other. What is the probability of getting a matched shoe if two shoes are drawn at random?

(a) $\dfrac{6}{9}$ (b) $\dfrac{4}{9}$

(c) $\dfrac{2}{9}$ (d) $\dfrac{5}{9}$

31. A person draws a card from a pack of 52, replaces it and shuffles it. He continues doing it until he draws a heart. What is the probability that he has to make 3 trials?

(a) $\dfrac{9}{64}$ (b) $\dfrac{3}{64}$

(c) $\dfrac{5}{64}$ (d) $\dfrac{1}{64}$

32. For the above problem, what is the probability if he does not replace the cards?

(a) $\dfrac{274}{1700}$ (b) $\dfrac{123}{1720}$

(c) $\dfrac{247}{1700}$ (d) $\dfrac{234}{1500}$

33. An event X can happen with probability P, and event Y can happen with probability P'. What is the probability that exactly one of them happens?

(a) $P + P' - 2PP'$ (b) $2PP' - P' + P$
(c) $P - P' + 2PP'$ (d) $2P'P - P' + P$

34. In the above question, what is the probability that at least one of them happens?

(a) $P + P' + PP'$ (b) $P + P' - PP'$
(c) $2PP' - P' - P$ (d) $P + P' - 2PP'$

35. Find the probability that a year chosen at random has 53 Mondays.

(a) $\dfrac{2}{7}$ (b) $\dfrac{5}{28}$

(c) $\dfrac{1}{28}$ (d) $\dfrac{3}{28}$

36. There are four machines and it is known that exactly two of them are faulty. They are tested one by one in a random order till both the faulty machines are

identified. Then the probability that only two tests are needed is

(a) $\dfrac{2}{3}$ (b) $\dfrac{1}{6}$

(c) $\dfrac{1}{3}$ (d) $\dfrac{5}{6}$

37. For the above question, the probability that exactly 3 tests will be required to identify the 2 faulty machines is

(a) $\dfrac{1}{2}$ (b) 1

(c) $\dfrac{1}{3}$ (d) $\dfrac{2}{3}$

38. Seven white balls and three black balls are randomly placed in a row. Find the probability that no two black balls are placed adjacent to each other.

(a) $\dfrac{7}{15}$ (b) $\dfrac{2}{15}$

(c) $\dfrac{3}{7}$ (d) $\dfrac{2}{7}$

39. A fair coin is tossed repeatedly. If Head appears on the first four tosses then the probability of appearance of tail on the fifth toss is

(a) $\dfrac{1}{7}$ (b) $\dfrac{1}{2}$

(c) $\dfrac{3}{7}$ (d) $\dfrac{2}{3}$

40. The letters of the word 'article' are arranged at random. Find the probability that the vowels may occupy the even places.

(a) $\dfrac{2}{35}$ (b) $\dfrac{1}{35}$

(c) $\dfrac{3}{36}$ (d) $\dfrac{2}{34}$

41. What is the probability that four Ss come consecutively in the word MISSISSIPPI?

(a) $\dfrac{4}{165}$ (b) $\dfrac{2}{165}$

(c) $\dfrac{3}{165}$ (d) $\dfrac{1}{165}$

42. Eleven books, consisting of five Engineering books, four Mathematics books and two Physics books, are arranged in a shelf at random. What is the probability that the books of each kind are all together?

(a) $\dfrac{5}{1155}$ (b) $\dfrac{2}{1155}$

(c) $\dfrac{3}{1155}$ (d) $\dfrac{1}{1155}$

43. Three students appear at an examination of Mathematics. The probability of their success are 1/3, 1/4,

1/5 respectively. Find the probability of success of at least two.

(a) $\dfrac{1}{6}$ (b) $\dfrac{2}{5}$

(c) $\dfrac{3}{4}$ (d) $\dfrac{3}{5}$

44. A bag contains 8 white and 4 red balls. Five balls are drawn at random. What is the probability that two of them are red and 3 are white?

(a) $\dfrac{12}{44}$ (b) $\dfrac{14}{33}$

(c) $\dfrac{14}{34}$ (d) $\dfrac{15}{34}$

45. A team of 4 is to be constituted out of 5 girls and 6 boys. Find the probability that the team may have 3 girls.

(a) $\dfrac{4}{11}$ (b) $\dfrac{3}{11}$

(c) $\dfrac{5}{11}$ (d) $\dfrac{2}{11}$

46. 12 persons are seated around a round table. What is the probability that two particular persons sit together?

(a) $\dfrac{2}{11}$ (b) $\dfrac{1}{6}$

(c) $\dfrac{3}{11}$ (d) $\dfrac{3}{15}$

47. Six boys and six girls sit in a row randomly. Find the probability that all the six girls sit together.

48. From a group of 7 men and 4 women a committee of 6 persons is formed. What is the probability that the committee will consist of exactly 2 women?

(a) $\dfrac{5}{11}$ (b) $\dfrac{3}{11}$

(c) $\dfrac{4}{11}$ (d) $\dfrac{2}{11}$

49. A bag contains 5 red, 4 green and 3 black balls. If three balls are drawn out of it at random, find the probability of drawing exactly 2 red balls.

(a) $\dfrac{7}{22}$ (b) $\dfrac{10}{33}$

(c) $\dfrac{7}{12}$ (d) $\dfrac{7}{11}$

50. A bag contains 100 tickets numbered 1, 2, 3, …, 100. If a ticket is drawn out of it at random, what is the probability that the ticket drawn has the digit 2 appearing on it?

(a) $\dfrac{19}{100}$ (b) $\dfrac{21}{100}$

(c) $\dfrac{32}{100}$ (d) $\dfrac{23}{100}$

(a) $\dfrac{3}{22}$ (b) $\dfrac{1}{132}$

(c) $\dfrac{1}{1584}$ (d) $\dfrac{1}{66}$

Space for Rough Work

LEVEL OF DIFFICULTY (III)

1. Out of a pack of 52 cards one is lost; from the remainder of the pack, two cards are drawn and are found to be spades. Find the chance that the missing card is a spade.
   (a) $\frac{11}{50}$ (b) $\frac{11}{49}$
   (c) $\frac{10}{49}$ (d) $\frac{10}{50}$

2. A and B throw one dice for a stake of ₹ 11, which is to be won by the player who first throws a six. The game ends when the stake is won by A or B. If A has the first throw, what are their respective expectations?
   (a) 5 and 6   (b) 6 and 5
   (c) 11 and 0   (d) 9 and 2

3. Counters marked 1, 2, 3 are placed in a bag and one of them is withdrawn and replaced. The operation being repeated three times, what is the chance of obtaining a total of 6 in these three operations?
   (a) $\frac{11}{27}$ (b) $\frac{7}{27}$
   (c) $\frac{1}{27}$ (d) $\frac{5}{14}$

4. A speaks the truth 3 times out of 4, B 7 times out of 10. They both assert that a white ball is drawn from a bag containing 6 balls, all of different colours. Find the probability of the truth of the assertion.
   (a) $\frac{12}{49}$ (b) $\frac{3}{10}$
   (c) $\frac{21}{40}$ (d) None of these

5. In a shirt factory, processes A, B and C respectively manufacture 25%, 35% and 40% of the total shirts. Of their respective productions, 5%, 4% and 2% of the shirts are defective. A shirt is selected at random from the production of a particular day. If it is found to be defective, what is the probability that it is manufactured by the process C ?
   (a) $\frac{16}{69}$ (b) $\frac{25}{69}$
   (c) $\frac{28}{69}$ (d) $\frac{27}{44}$

6. A pair of fair dice are rolled together till a sum of either 5 or 7 is obtained. The probability that 5 comes before 7 is
   (a) 0.45   (b) 0.4
   (c) 0.5   (d) 0.7

7. For the above problem, the probability of 7 coming before 5 is:
   (a) $\frac{3}{5}$ (b) 0.55
   (c) 0.4   (d) 0.7

8. For the above problem, the probability of 4 coming before either 5 or 7 is:
   (a) $\frac{3}{13}$ (b) $\frac{7}{13}$
   (c) $\frac{11}{13}$ (d) $\frac{10}{13}$

9. The probability of a bomb hitting a bridge is 1/2 and two direct hits are needed to destroy it. The least number of bombs required so that the probability of the bridge being destroyed is greater than 0.9 is:
   (a) 7 bombs   (b) 3 bombs
   (c) 8 bombs   (d) 9 bombs

10. What is the probability of the destruction of the bridge if only 5 bombs are dropped?
    (a) 62.32%   (b) 81.25%
    (c) 45.23%   (d) 31.32%

11. Sanjay writes a letter to his friend from IIT, Kanpur. It is known that one out of 'n' letters that are posted does not reach its destination. If Sanjay does not receive the reply to his letter, then what is the probability that Kesari did not receive Sanjay's letter? It is certain that Kesari will definitely reply to Sanjay's letter if he receives it.
    (a) $\frac{n}{(2n-1)}$ (b) $\frac{n-1}{n}$
    (c) $\frac{1}{n}$ (d) None of these

12. A word of 6 letters is formed from a set of 16 different letters of the English alphabet (with replacement). Find out the probability that exactly 2 letters are repeated.
    (a) $\frac{225 \times 224 \times 156}{16^6}$ (b) $\frac{18080}{16^6}$
    (c) $\frac{15 \times 224 \times 156}{16^6}$ (d) None of these

13. A number is chosen at random from the numbers 10 to 99. By seeing the number, a man will sing if the product of the digits is 12. If he chooses three numbers with replacement, then the probability that he will sing at least once is:
    (a) $1-\left(\frac{43}{45}\right)^3$ (b) $\left(\frac{43}{45}\right)^3$

(c) $1 - \dfrac{48 \times 86}{90^3}$ (d) None of these

14. In a bag, there are ten black, eight white and five red balls. Three balls are chosen at random and one is found to be black. The probability that the rest two are white is. Find the probability that the remaining two balls are white.

    (a) $\dfrac{8}{23}$ (b) $\dfrac{4}{33}$

    (c) $\dfrac{10 \times 8 \times 7}{23 \times 22 \times 21}$ (d) $\dfrac{5}{23}$

15. In the above question, find the probability that the remaining two balls are red.

    (a) $\dfrac{10}{231}$ (b) $\dfrac{12}{231}$

    (c) $\dfrac{12}{363}$ (d) None of these

16. Ten tickets are numbered 1, 2, 3…, 10. Six tickets are selected at random one at a time with replacement. The probability that the largest number appearing on the selected ticket is 7 is:

    (a) $\dfrac{(7^6 - 1)}{10^6}$ (b) $\dfrac{7^6 - 6^6}{10^6}$

    (c) $\dfrac{6^6}{10^6}$ (d) None of these

17. A bag contains 15 tickets numbered 1 to 15. A ticket is drawn and replaced. Then one more ticket is drawn and replaced. The probability that first number drawn is even and second is odd is

    (a) $\dfrac{56}{225}$ (b) $\dfrac{26}{578}$

    (c) $\dfrac{57}{289}$ (d) None of these

18. Six blue balls are put in three boxes. The probability of putting balls in the boxes in equal numbers is

    (a) $\dfrac{1}{21}$ (b) $\dfrac{1}{8}$

    (c) $\dfrac{1}{28}$ (d) $\dfrac{1}{7}$

19. AMS employs 8 professors on their staff. Their respective probability of remaining in employment for 10 years are 0.2, 0.3, 0.4, 0.5, 0.6, 0.7, 0.8, 0.9. The probability that after 10 years at least 6 of them still work in AMS is

    (a) 0.19   (b) 1.22

    (c) 0.1   (d) None of these

20. A person draws a card from a pack of 52, replaces it and shuffles it. He continues doing so until he draws a heart. What is the probability that he has to make at least 3 trials?

21. Hilips, the largest white goods producer in India, uses a quality check scheme on produced items before they are sent into the market. The plan is as follows: A set of 20 articles is readied and 4 of them are chosen at random. If any one of them is found to be defective then the whole set is put under 100% screening again. If no defectives are found, the whole set is sent into the market. Find the probability that a box containing 4 defective articles will be sent into the market.

    (a) $\dfrac{364}{969}$ (b) $\dfrac{364}{963}$

    (c) $\dfrac{96}{969}$ (d) $\dfrac{343}{969}$

22. In the above question, what is the probability that a box containing only one defective will be sent back for screening?

    (a) $\dfrac{2}{3}$ (b) $\dfrac{1}{5}$

    (c) $\dfrac{2}{5}$ (d) $\dfrac{4}{5}$

23. If the integers m and n are chosen at random from 1 to 100, then the probability that a number of the form $7^m + 7^n$ is divisible by 5 is

    (a) $\dfrac{1}{4}$ (b) $\dfrac{1}{2}$

    (c) $\dfrac{1}{16}$ (d) $\dfrac{1}{6}$

24. Three numbers are chosen at random without replacement from (1, 2, 3 …, 10). The probability that the minimum number is 3 or the maximum number is 7 is

    (a) $\dfrac{12}{37}$ (b) $\dfrac{11}{40}$

    (c) $\dfrac{13}{35}$ (d) $\dfrac{14}{35}$

25. An unbiased dice with face values 1, 2, 3, 4, 5 and 6 is rolled four times. Out of the 4 face values obtained, find the probability that the minimum face value is not less than 2 and the maximum face value is not greater than 5.

    (a) $\dfrac{16}{81}$ (b) $\dfrac{14}{6^4}$

    (c) $\dfrac{16}{80}$ (d) None of these

26. Three faces of a dice are yellow, two faces are red and one face is blue. The dice is tossed three times.

(top right, answers for question 20:)

    (a) $\dfrac{3}{17}$ (b) $\dfrac{8}{19}$

    (c) $\dfrac{2}{17}$ (d) $\dfrac{11}{16}$

Find the probability that the colours yellow, red and blue appear in the first, second and the third toss respectively.

(a) $\dfrac{1}{18}$ (b) $\dfrac{1}{12}$

(c) $\dfrac{1}{9}$ (d) $\dfrac{1}{36}$

27. If from each of three boxes containing 3 white and 1 black, 2 white and 2 black, 1 white and 3 black balls, one ball is drawn at random, then the probability that 2 white and 1 black ball will be drawn is

(a) $\dfrac{13}{32}$ (b) $\dfrac{12}{14}$

(c) $\dfrac{12}{25}$ (d) $\dfrac{3}{13}$

28. Probabilities that Rajesh passes in Math, Physics and Chemistry are m, p and c respectively. Of these subjects, Rajesh has a 75% chance of passing in at least one, 50% chance of passing in at least two and 40% chance of passing in exactly two. Find which of the following is true.

(a) $p + m + c = \dfrac{19}{20}$ (b) $p + m + c = \dfrac{27}{20}$

c) $pmc = \dfrac{1}{20}$ (d) $pmc = \dfrac{1}{8}$

29. There are 5 envelopes corresponding to 5 letters. If the letters are placed in the envelopes at random, what is the probability that all the letters are not placed in the right envelopes?

(a) $\dfrac{119}{120}$ (b) $\dfrac{59}{60}$

(c) $\dfrac{23}{24}$ (d) $\dfrac{4^5}{5^5}$

30. For the above question what is the probability that no single letter is placed in the right envelope.

(a) $\dfrac{12}{35}$ (b) $\dfrac{11}{30}$

(c) $\dfrac{12}{25}$ (d) $\dfrac{3}{12}$

31. An urn contains four tickets having numbers 112, 121, 211, 222 written on them. If one ticket is drawn at random and Ai ($i = 1, 2, 3$) be the event that the ith digit from left of the number on ticket drawn is 1, which of these can be said about the events A_1, A_2 and A_3?
(a) They are mutually exclusive
(b) A_1 and A_3 are not mutually exclusive to A_2
(c) A_1 and A_3 are mutually exclusive
(d) Both b and c

32. The probability that a contractor will get a plumbing contract is 2/3 and the probability that he will get an electric contract is 5/9. If the probability of getting at least one contract is 4/5, what is the probability that he will get both the contracts?

(a) $\dfrac{19}{45}$ (b) $\dfrac{13}{45}$

(c) $\dfrac{12}{35}$ (d) $\dfrac{11}{23}$

33. If $P(A) = 3/7$, $P(B) = 1/2$ and $P(A' \cap B') = 1/14$, then are A and B are mutually exclusive events?
(a) No (b) Yes
(c) Either yes or no (d) Cannot be determined

34. Six boys and six girls sit in a row at random. Find the probability that the boys and girls sit alternately.

(a) $\dfrac{1}{132}$ (b) $\dfrac{1}{462}$

(c) $\dfrac{1}{623}$ (d) $\dfrac{1}{231}$

35. A problem on mathematics is given to three students whose chances of solving it are 1/2, 1/3 and 1/4 respectively. What is the chance that the problem will be solved?

(a) $\dfrac{2}{3}$ (b) $\dfrac{3}{4}$

(c) $\dfrac{1}{3}$ (d) $\dfrac{1}{2}$

36. A and B throw a pair of dice alternately. A wins if he throws 6 before B throws 5 and B wins if he throws 5 before A throws 6. Find B's chance of winning if A makes the first throw.

(a) $\dfrac{1}{2}$ (b) $\dfrac{5}{12}$

(c) $\dfrac{1}{3}$ (d) $\dfrac{5}{11}$

37. Two persons A and B toss a coin alternately till one of them gets Head and wins the game. Find B's chance of winning if A tosses the coin first.

(a) $\dfrac{1}{3}$ (b) $\dfrac{2}{3}$

(c) $\dfrac{1}{2}$ (d) None of these

38. A bag contains 3 red and 4 white balls and another bag contains 4 red and 3 white balls. A dice is cast and if the face 1 or 3 turns up, a ball is taken from the first bag and if any other face turns up, a ball is taken from the second bag. Find the probability of drawing a red ball.

(a) $\dfrac{11}{20}$ (b) $\dfrac{12}{21}$

(c) $\dfrac{2}{11}$ (d) $\dfrac{11}{21}$

39. Three groups of children contain respectively 3 girls and 1 boy, 2 girls and 2 boys, and 1 girl and 3 boys. One child is selected at random from each group.

The probability that the three selected consists of 1 girl and 2 boys is:

(a) $\dfrac{13}{32}$

(b) $\dfrac{12}{32}$

(c) $\dfrac{15}{32}$

(d) $\dfrac{11}{32}$

40. The probabilities of A, B and C solving a problem are $\dfrac{1}{3}$, $\dfrac{2}{7}$ and $\dfrac{3}{8}$ respectively. If all the three try to solve the problem simultaneously, find the probability that exactly one of them will solve it.

(a) $\dfrac{26}{65}$

(b) $\dfrac{25}{56}$

(c) $\dfrac{52}{65}$

(d) $\dfrac{25}{52}$

41. A bag contains 5 black and 3 red balls. A ball is taken out of the bag and is not returned to it. If this process is repeated three times, then what is the probability of drawing a black ball in the next draw of a ball?

(a) 0.7

(b) 0.625

(c) 0.1

(d) None of these

42. For question 41, what is the probability of drawing a red ball?

(a) 0.375

(b) 0.9

(c) 0.3

(d) 0.79

43. One bag contains 5 white and 4 black balls. Another bag contains 7 white and 9 black balls. A ball is transferred from the first bag to the second and then a ball is drawn from the second bag. Find the probability that the ball drawn is white.

(a) $\dfrac{7}{18}$

(b) $\dfrac{5}{9}$

(c) $\dfrac{4}{9}$

(d) $\dfrac{11}{18}$

44. V Anand and Gary Kasparov play a series of 5 chess games. The probability that V Anand wins a game is 2/5 and the probability of Kasparov winning a game is 3/5. There is no probability of a draw. The series will be won by the person who wins 3 matches. Find the probability that Anand wins the series. (The series ends the moment when any of the two wins 3 matches.)

(a) $\dfrac{992}{3125}$

(b) $\dfrac{273}{625}$

(c) $\dfrac{1021}{3125}$

(d) $\dfrac{1081}{3125}$

45. There are 10 pairs of socks in a cupboard from which 4 individual socks are picked at random. The probability that there is at least one pair is.

(a) $\dfrac{195}{323}$

(b) $\dfrac{99}{323}$

(c) $\dfrac{198}{323}$

(d) $\dfrac{185}{323}$

46. A fair coin is tossed 10 times. Find the probability that two Heads do not occur consecutively.

(a) $\dfrac{1}{2^4}$

(b) $\dfrac{1}{2^3}$

(c) $\dfrac{1}{2^5}$

(d) None of these

47. In a room there are 7 persons. The chance that two of them were born on the same day of the week is

(a) $\dfrac{1080}{7^5}$

(b) $\dfrac{2160}{7^5}$

(c) $\dfrac{540}{7^4}$

(d) None of these

48. In a hand at a game of bridge what is the chance that the 4 kings are held by a specified player?

(a) $\dfrac{10}{4165}$

(b) $\dfrac{11}{4165}$

(c) $\dfrac{110}{4165}$

(d) None of these

49. One hundred identical coins each with probability P of showing up Heads are tossed once. If $0 < P < 1$ and the probability of Heads showing on 50 coins is equal to that of Heads showing on 51 coins, then value of P is

(a) $\dfrac{1}{21}$

(b) $\dfrac{49}{101}$

(c) $\dfrac{50}{101}$

(d) $\dfrac{51}{101}$

50. Two small squares on a chess board are chosen at random. Find the probability that they have a common side:

(a) $\dfrac{1}{12}$

(b) $\dfrac{1}{18}$

(c) $\dfrac{2}{15}$

(d) $\dfrac{3}{14}$

Space for Rough Work

ANSWER KEY

Level of Difficulty (I)

1. (b)	2. (a)	3. (d)	4. (c)
5. (a)	6(i). (c)	6(ii). (b)	6(iii). (c)
7(i). (b)	7(ii). (a)	8(i). (d)	8(ii). (a)
9. (b)	10(i). (a)	10(ii). (b)	10(iii). (d)
11(i). (d)	11(ii). (a)	12. (a)	13. (a)
14(i). (b)	14(ii). (a)	14(iii). (b)	15(i). (d)
15(ii). (a)	15(iii). (b)	16(i). (a)	16(ii). (b)
17. (b)	18. (a)	19(i). (c)	19(ii). (a)
20. (a)	21. (b)	22(i). (a)	22(ii). (d)
22(iii). (a)	23. (a)	24. (d)	25(i). (a)
25(ii). (c)	26. (b)	27. (a)	28. (a)
29. (b)	30. (a)	31. (a)	32. (d)
33. (b)	34(i). (b)	34(ii). (c)	35. (d)
36. (a)	37. (a)	38. (d)	39. (a)
40. (b)	41(i). (c)	41(ii). (d)	41(iii). (a)
42. (c)	43. (a)	44(i). (a)	44(ii). (c)
44(iii). (a)	44(iv). (b)		

Level of Difficulty (II)

1. (d)	2. (a)	3. (a)	4(i) (b)
4(ii) (c)	5. (d)	6. (a)	7. (d)
8. (a)	9(i) (a)	9(ii) (b)	10. (d)
11(i) (a)	11(ii) (b)	11(iii) (b)	12(i) (a)
12(ii) (a)	12(iii) (a)	13(i) (b)	13(ii) (c)
13(iii) (c)	14(i) (b)	14(ii) (c)	14(iii) (b)
15. (a)	16(i) (b)	16(ii) (a)	16(iii) (b)
17(i) (b)	17(ii) (a)	17(iii) (c)	17(iv) (a)
18. (b)	19. (b)	20. (c)	21. (b)
22. (b)	23. (a)	24. (a)	25. (a)
26. (b)	27. (b)	28. (a)	29. (a)
30. (b)	31. (a)	32. (c)	33. (a)
34. (b)	35. (a)	36. (b)	37. (c)
38. (a)	39. (b)	40. (b)	41. (a)
42. (d)	43. (a)	44. (b)	45. (d)
46. (a)	47. (b)	48. (a)	49. (a)
50. (a)			

Level of Difficulty (III)

1. (a)	2. (b)	3. (b)	4. (c)
5. (a)	6. (b)	7. (a)	8. (a)
9. (a)	10. (b)	11. (a)	12. (a)
13. (a)	14. (b)	15. (a)	16. (b)
17. (a)	18. (c)	19. (a)	20. (d)
21. (a)	22. (b)	23. (a)	24. (b)
25. (a)	26. (d)	27. (a)	28. (b)
29. (a)	30. (b)	31. (b)	32. (a)
33. (b)	34. (b)	35. (b)	36. (d)
37. (a)	38. (d)	39. (b)	40. (b)
41. (a)	42. (a)	43. (c)	44. (a)
45. (b)	46. (b)	47. (b)	48. (b)
49. (d)	50. (b)		

Solutions and Shortcuts

Level of Difficulty (I)

1. Out of a total of 6 occurrences, 3 is one possibility $= 1/6$.

2. 5 or 6 out of a sample space of
   1, 2, 3, 4, 5 or 6 $= 2/6 = 1/3$

3. Event definition is:
   (1 and 1) or (1 and 2) or (1 and 3) or (1 and 4) or
   (1 and 5) or (1 and 6) or (2 and 1) or (3 and 1) or
   (4 and 1) or (5 and 1) or (6 and 1)
   Total 11 out of 36 possibilities $= 11/36$

4. Event definition: First is blue and second is blue
   $= 7/12 \times 6/11 = 7/22$.

5. Knave and queen or Queen and Knave $\rightarrow$
   $4/52 \times 4/51 + 4/52 \times 4/51 = 8/663$

6. (i) $13/52 = 1/4$
   (ii) 4 kings and 4 queens out of 52 cards.
   Thus, $8/52 = 2/13$.
   (iii) 13 spades + 3 kings $\rightarrow 19/52$.

7. (i) Event definition is: T and T and H or T and H
   and T or H and T and $T = 3 \times 1/8 = 3/8$.
   (ii) Same as above $= 3/8$.

8. (i) Probability of 3 heads $= 1/8$
   Also, Probability of 3 tails $= 1/8$.
   Required probability $= 1 - (1/8 + 1/8) = 6/8$
   $= 3/4$.
   (ii) H and H and $H = 1/8$.

9. At least one tail is the non-event for all heads.
   Thus, P (at least 1 tail) $= 1 - P$(all heads)
   $= 1 - 1/8 = 7/8$.

10. (i) Positive outcomes are 2(1 way), 4(3 ways),
    6(5 ways) 8(5 ways), 10 (3 ways), 12 (1way).
    Thus, $18/36 = 1/2$
    (ii) Positive outcomes are: 4, 8 and 12
    4 (3 ways), 8(5 ways) and 12(1 way)
    Gives us $9/36 = 1/4$.
    (iii) Positive outcomes are 2(1 way), 3(2 ways),
    5(4 ways), 7(6 ways). Total of 13 positive out-
    comes out of 36.
    Thus, $13/36$.

11. (i) First is white and second is white $7/10 \times 6/9 =$
    $7/15$.
    (ii) White and Green or Green and White
    $7/10 \times 39 + 3/10 \times 7/9$
    $42/90 = 7/15$.

12.

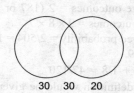

30   30   20

From the figure it is evident that 80 students passed at least 1 exam. Thus, 20 failed both and the required probability is 20/100 = 1/5.

13. 3 or 4 or 5 or 6 = 4/6 = 2/3

14. (i) Since 2 is the only prime number out of the three numbers, the answer would be 1/3

    (ii) Since all the numbers are even, it is sure that the number drawn out is an even number. Hence, the required probability is 1.

    (iii) Since there are no odd numbers amongst 2, 4 and 8, the required probability is 0.

15. (i) The event would be Head and Head $\rightarrow \frac{1}{2} \times \frac{1}{2} = \frac{1}{4}$

    (ii) The event would be Head and Tail OR Tail and Head $\rightarrow = \frac{1}{2} \times \frac{1}{2} + \frac{1}{2} \times \frac{1}{2} = 1/8$

    (iii) The event would be Tail and Tail $\rightarrow \frac{1}{2} \times \frac{1}{2} = \frac{1}{4}$

16. (i) With a six on the first dice, there are 6 possibilities of outcomes that can appear on the other dice (viz. 6 & 1, 6 & 2, 6 & 3, 6 & 4, 6 & 5 and 6 & 6). At the same time with 6 on the second dice there are 5 more possibilities for outcomes on the first dice: (1 & 6, 2 & 6, 3 & 6, 4 & 6, 5 & 6)

    Also, the total outcomes are 36. Hence, the required probability is 11/36.

    (ii) Out of 36 outcomes, 5 can come in the following ways – 1 + 4; 2 + 3; 3 + 2 or 4 + 1 $\rightarrow$ 4/36 = 1/9.

17. Odds against an event = $\dfrac{p(E^2)}{p(E)}$

    In this case, the event is: All black, i.e., First is black and second is black and third is black.

    $P(E) = 5/9 \times 4/8 \times 3/7 = 60/504 = 5/42$.

    Odds against the event = 37/5.

18. Event definition is: 15 or 16 or 17 or 18.

    15 can be got as: 5 and 5 and 5 (one way)

    Or

    6 and 5 and 4 (Six ways)

    Or

    6 and 6 and 3 (3 ways)

    Total 10 ways.

    16 can be got as: 6 and 6 and 4 (3 ways)

    Or

    6 and 5 and 5 (3 ways)

    Total 6 ways.

    17 has 3 ways and 18 has 1 way of appearing.

    Thus, the required probability is: (10 + 6 + 3 + 1)/216 = 20/216 = 5/54.

19. (i) Positive outcomes = 2 (187 or 215)

    Total outcomes = 9 × 8 × 7

    Required probability = 2/504 = 1/252

    (ii) = 2/729.

20. 1/6 + 1/10 + 1/8 = 47/120

21. The event definition would be given by:

First is blue and second is blue = 3/11 × 2/10 = 3/55

22. (i) There are six doubles (1, 1; 2 & 2; 3 & 3; 4 & 4; 5 & 5; 6 & 6) out of a total of 36 outcomes $\rightarrow$ 6/36 = 1/6

    (ii) Sum greater than 10 means 11 or 12 $\rightarrow$ 3/36 = 1/12

    (iii) Sum less than 10 is the non event for the case sum is 10 or 11 or 12. There are 3 ways of getting 10, 2 ways of getting 11 and 1 way of getting a sum of 12 in the throw of two dice. Thus, the required probability would be 1 – 6/36 = 5/6.

23. Expectation = Probability of winning × Reward of winning = (10/5000) × 1 crore = (1 crore/500) = 20000.

24. $1/^4C_2 = 1/6$.

25.

550   330   320

    (i) 880/1200 = 11/15

    (ii) 650/1200 = 13/24

26. 330/1200 = 11/40

27. 330/880 = 3/8

28. Black and Black and Black = 4/9 × 3/8 × 2/7 = 23/504 = 1/21.

29. $1/^5P_2 = 1/20$.

30. 6 × (4/52) × (4/51) × (4/50) = 16/5525.

31. Positive Outcomes are: 5, 7, 10, 14, 15 or 20 Thus, 6/20 = 3/10.

32. 972/1972 = 243/493.

33. Black and black = (7/16) × 6/15 = 7/40

34. (i) The required probability would be given by:

    All are Red OR All are white OR All are Blue

    = (6/18) × (5/17) × (4/16) + (4/18) × (3/17) × (2/16) + (8/18) × (7/17) × (6/16)

    = 480/(18 × 17 × 16) 5/51

    (ii) All blue = (8 × 7 × 6)/(18 × 17 × 16) = 7/102

35. The required value of the union of the two non events (of A and B) would be 1 – 1/4 = 3/4

36. P (Both are selected) = P(A) × P(B)

    Since P(A) = 0.5, we get

    0.3 = 0.5 × 0.6.

    The maximum value of P(B) = 0.6.

    Thus P(B) = 0.9 is not possible.

37.

19/40   1/8   5/24

We have: $19/40 + 1/8 + 5/24 = 97/120$

38. P (Amit) = 1/3

P (Vikas) = 2/7

P (Vivek) = 1/8.

Required Probability = $1/3 + 2/7 + 1/8 = 125/168$.

39. $P(A) + P(B) + P(C) = 1 \rightarrow 2P(B)/3 + P(B) + P(B)/2 = 1 \rightarrow 13P(B)/6 = 1 \rightarrow P(B) = 6/13$. Hence, $P(A) = 4/13$

40. $P(A) = 1 - 0.65 = 0.35$.

Hence, $P(B) = 0.65 - 0.35 = 0.3$

41. (i) The required probability would be given by the event:

White from first bag and white from second bag $= (4/6) \times (3/8) = ¼$

(ii) The required probability would be given by the event:

Black from first bag and black from second bag $= (2/6) \times (5/8) = 10/48 = 5/24$

(iii) This would be the non event for the event [both are white OR both are black).

Thus, the required probability would be:

$¼ - 5/24 = 13/24$.

42. P (E_1) 3/8

P (E_2) = 7/12.

Event definition is: E_1 occurs and E_2 does not occur or E_1 occurs and E_2 occurs or E_2 occurs and E_1 does not occur.

$(3/8) \times (5/12) + (3/8) \times (7/12) + (5/8) \times (7/12) = 71/96$.

43. Kamal is selected and Monica is not selected or Kamal is not selected and Monica is selected $\rightarrow (1/3) \times (4/5) \leftarrow (2/3) \times (1/5) = (6/15) = (2/5)$.

44. (i) $1/5 \times 1/7 = 1/35$

(ii) $(1/5) \times (6/7) + (4/5) \times (1/7) = 10/35 = 2/7$.

(iii) $(4/5) \times (6/7) = 24/35$

(iv) Both selected or 1 selected = $1/35 + 2/7 = 11/35$.

Level of Difficulty (II)

1. The possible outcomes are:

$(1, 1); (1, 2); (2, 1), (2, 2); (3, 1); (1, 3)$.

Out of six cases, in two cases there is exactly one '2'

Thus, the correct answer is $2/6 = 1/3$.

2. Event definition is A hits, B hits and C hits OR any two of the three hits.

3. The event can be defined as:

First bag is selected and red ball is drawn.

$1/2 \times 5/12 + ½ \times 3/15 = (5/24) + (3/30) = 37/120$

4. (a) For the least chance of drawing a red ball the distribution has to be 5 Red + 11 white in one bag and 1 white in the second bag. This gives us

$$\frac{1}{2} \times \frac{5}{16} + \frac{1}{2} \times 0 = \frac{5}{32}$$

(b) For the greatest chance of drawing a red ball the distribution has to be 1 Red in the first bag and 4 red + 12 white balls in the second bag. This gives us

$$\frac{1}{2} \times 1 + \frac{1}{2} \times \frac{4}{16} = \frac{5}{8}$$

5. One head and seven tails would have eight positions where the head can come.

Thus, $8 \times (1/2)^8 = (1/32)$

6. A leap year has 366 days – which means 52 completed weeks and 2 more days. The last two days can be (Sunday, Monday) or (Monday, Tuesday) or .... (Saturday, Sunday).

2 scenarios out of 7 have a 53rd Sunday.

Thus, 2/7 is the required answer.

7. The count of the event will be given by:

The number of all 2 digit integers – the number of all 2 digit integers divisible by 7

8. Blue and Red or Red and Blue

$= (10/25) \times (15/24) + (15/25) \times (10/24) = (1/2)$.

9. (i) $1/5 + ½ = 7/10$.

(ii) $1 - (7/10) = (3/10)$

10. A total of six can be made in any of the following ways $(1 + 5, 2 + 4, 3 + 3, 4 + 2, 5 + 1)$

11. The event definitions are:

(a) Passes the first AND Passes the second AND Passes the third AND Passes the fourth

(b) Fails the first AND Fails the second AND Fails the third AND Fails the fourth

(c) Fails all is the non-event.

12. (i) First is cricket and second is cricket and third is cricket $\rightarrow (3/9) \times (3/9) \times (3/9) = (1/27)$

(ii) $(2/9) \times (3/9) \times (4/9) = (8/243)$

(iii) All are cricket or all are tennis or all are squash. $(3/9)^3 + (2/9)^3 + (4/9)^3 = (99/729) = (11/81)$

13. (i) $(3/9) \times (2/8) \times (1/7) = (1/84)$

(ii) $(2/9) \times (3/8) \times (4/7) = (1/21)$

(iii) $(3/9) \times (2/8) \times (1/7) + 0 + (4/9) \times (3/8) \times (2/7)$ $30/504 = 5/84$

14. The event definitions are

(i) The book transferred is by Stephen Covey

(ii) The book transferred is by Stephen Covey AND The book picked up is by Stephen Covey

(iii) The book transferred is by Stephen Covey AND The book picked up is by Vinay Singh.

15. $(2/3) \times (3/4) + (1/3) \times (2/7) = (1/2) + (2/21) = (25/42)$

16. (i) $(3/50) \times (2/49) = (3/1225)$

(ii) $(3/50) \times (47/49) + 47/50 \times (3/49) = (141/1225)$

(iii) $(47/50) \times (46/49) = (1081/1225)$

17. (i) $(3/5) \times (3/7) = (9/35)$

(ii) $(3/5) \times 4/7 = (12/35)$

(iii) $(2/5) \times (3/7) = (6/35)$

(iv) $(3/5) \times (4/7) + (2/5) \times (3/7) + (3/5) \times (3/7) = 27/35$

18. They will contradict each other if: A is true and B is false or A is false and B is true.

$$(3/4) \times (1/6) + (1/4) \times (5/6) = 1/3.$$

19. For the counting of the number of events, think of it as a circular arrangement with $n - 1$ people (by considering the two specified persons as one). This will give you $n(E) = (n - 2)! \times (2)!$

20. The whole numbers selected can only be 1, 3, 7 or 9 and cannot contain 2, 4, 6, 8, 0 or 5.

21. $^4C_2 \times (6/36)^2 \times (30/36)^2 = 6 \times (1/36) \times (25/36) = 25/216.$

22. The required probability will be given by the expression:

$$\frac{\text{The number of young boys who will die}}{\text{The total number of people who will die}}$$

23. Girl and Boy and Boy or Boy and Girl and Boy

Or

Boy and Boy and Girl

$= (3/4) \times (2/4) \times (2/3) + (1/4) \times (2/4) \times 2/3$
$\qquad + (1/4) \times (2/4) \times (1/3) = 18/48 = 3/8.$

24. $n(E) = 1$

$n(S) = {}^3C_1 \times 9 \times 9 = 243$

25. 11/17 (if the first one is black, there will be 11 black balls left out of 17)

26. 6/17

27. There must have been two sixes in the first five throws. Thus, the answer is given by:

$${}^5C_2 \times \frac{1}{6} \times \frac{1}{6} \times \frac{1}{6} \times \frac{5}{6} \times \frac{5}{6} \times \frac{5}{6}$$

28. $\dfrac{{}^{13}C_1 \times {}^{13}C_1 \times {}^{13}C_1 \times {}^{13}C_1}{{}^{52}C_4}$

29. There will be $^6C_3$ triangles formed overall. Out of these visualise the number of equilateral triangles.

30. $(5/9) \times (4/8) + (4/9) \times (3/8) = 32/72 = 4/9$

As matched shoes means both red or both black.

31. The event definition here is that first is not a heart and second is not a heart and third is a heart $= (3/4) \times (3/4) \times (1/4) = 9/64.$

32. $(39/52) \times (38/51) \times (13/50) = 247/1700.$

33. The event definition will be: Event X happens and Y doesn't happen Or Y happens and X does not happen.

34. X happens and Y does not happen or X doesn't happen and Y happens or X happens and Y happens

$$P \times (1 - P) + (1 - P) \times P' + P \times P' = P + P' - PP'$$

35. Same logic as question 6.

36. $(2/4) \times (1/3) = 1/6.$ (Faulty and faulty)

37. Faulty and not Faulty and Faulty or Not Faulty and Faulty and Faulty $= (2/4) \times (2/3) \times (1/2) + (2/4) \times (2/3) \times (1/2) = 1/3.$

38. When you put the 7 balls with a gap between them in a row, you will have 8 spaces.

39. The appearance of head or tail on a toss is independent of previous occurrences.

Hence, 1/2.

40. $\dfrac{3! \times 4!}{7!} = 1/35.$

41. $P = \dfrac{\text{No. of arrangements with four 5s together}}{\text{Total No. of arrangements}}$

$$= \frac{[8! / (4! \times 2!)]}{[11! / (4! \times 4! \times 2!)]}$$

$$= 8! \times 4!/11! = 24/990 = 4/165.$$

42. $\dfrac{(5! \times 4! \times 2! \times 3!)}{11!} = \dfrac{24 \times 2 \times 6}{11 \times 10 \times 9 \times 8 \times 7 \times 6} = 1/1155.$

43. $(1/3) \times (1/4) \times (4/5) + (1/3) \times (3/4) \times (1/5) + (2/3) \times (1/4) \times (1/5) + (1/3) \times (1/4) \times (1/5)$

$= 10/60 = 1/6.$

44. $^5C_3 \times [\, (8/12) \times (7/11) \times (6/10) \times (4/9) \times (3/8)] = 14/33.$

45. There can be three girls and one boy.

46.

$$P = \frac{\text{Total no of ways in which two people sit together}}{\text{Total No. of ways}}$$

$$= (10! \times 2!)/11!$$

47. Consider the 6 girls to be one person. Then the number of arrangements satisfying the condition is given by $n(E) = 7! \times 6!$

48. $^6C_2 \times [\, (7/11) \times (6/10) \times (5/9) \times (4/8) \times (4/7) \times (3/6)]$
$\qquad\qquad\qquad\qquad\qquad\qquad = 5/11.$

49. The event definition is Red AND Red AND Not Red OR Red AND Not Red AND Red OR Not Red AND Red AND Red.

50. The numbers having 2 in them are: 2, 12, 22, 32....92 and 21, 23, 24, 25....29. Hence, $n(E) = 19.$

Level of Difficulty (III)

1. This problem has to be treated as if we are selecting the third card out of the 50 remaining cards.

11 of these are spades.

Hence, 11/50.

2.

	Chance that A will win	Chance that B will win
First throw	$\dfrac{1}{6}$	$\dfrac{5}{6} \times \dfrac{1}{6}$
Second throw	$\dfrac{5}{6} \times \dfrac{5}{6} \times \dfrac{1}{6}$	$\dfrac{5}{6} \times \dfrac{5}{6} \times \dfrac{5}{6} \times \dfrac{1}{6}$
Third throw	$\dfrac{5}{6} \times \dfrac{5}{6} \times \dfrac{5}{6} \times \dfrac{5}{6} \times \dfrac{1}{6}$	$\dfrac{5}{6} \times \dfrac{5}{6} \times \dfrac{5}{6} \times \dfrac{5}{6} \times \dfrac{5}{6} \times \dfrac{1}{6}$

The chance that A will win is an infinite GP with a $= \dfrac{1}{6}$ and $r = \dfrac{25}{36}$

Similarly, the chance that B will win is an infinite GP with $a = \dfrac{5}{36}$ and $r = \dfrac{25}{36}$.

3. A total of 6 can be obtained by either $(1 + 2 + 3)$ or by $(2 + 2 + 2)$.

4. A is true and B is true = $(3/4) \times (7/10) = (21/40)$.

5. The required probability will be given by:

$$\frac{\text{Percentage of defective from } C}{\text{Percentage of defectives from } A, B \text{ and } C}$$

6. and 7.

We do not have to consider any sum other than 5 or 7 occurring.

A sum of 5 can be obtained by any of $[4 + 1, 3 + 2, 2 + 3, 1 + 4]$

Similarly a sum of 7 can be obtained by any of $[6 + 1, 5 + 2, 4 + 3, 3 + 4, 2 + 5, 1 + 6]$

For 6: $n(E) = 4$, $n(S) = 6 + 4$
$P = 0.4$

For 7: $n(E) = 6$
$n(S) = 6 + 4$ $P = 0.6$

8. The number of ways for a sum of 4 = 3 i.e. $[3 + 1, 2 + 2, 1 + 3]$

9. Try to find the number of ways in which 0 or 1 bomb hits the bridge if n bombs are thrown.

The required value of the number of bombs will be such that the probability of 0 or 1 bomb hitting the bridge should be less than 0.1.

10. The required probability will be given by: $1 - [^nC_0 + {}^nC_1]\left(\dfrac{1}{2}\right)^n$ for $n = 5$.

11. The required answer will be given by:

$$\frac{\text{P (Kesari does not receive the letter)}}{\begin{array}{l}\text{P (Kesari does not receive the letter)} + \\ \text{P (Kesari replied and Sanjay did not} \\ \text{receive the reply)}\end{array}}$$

12. $n(E) = {}^6C_2 \times 16 \times 15 \times 14 \times 13 \times 12$
$n(S) = 16^6$

13. The number of events for the condition that he will sing = 4. $[34, 43, 26, 62]$
The number of events in the sample = 90.
Probability that he will sing at least once
= 1 − Probability that he will not sing.

14. The required probability would be given by the event definition:
First is white and second is white = $8/22 \times 7/21 = 4/33$

15. The required probability would be given by the event definition:
First is red and second is red = $5/22 \times 4/21 = 10/231$

16. The number of ways in which 6 tickets can be selected from 10 tickets is 10^6.
The number of ways in which the selection can be done so that the condition is satisfied = $7^6 − 6^6$.

17. In the first draw, we have 7 even tickets out of 15 and in the second we have 8 odd tickets out of 15.
Thus, $(7/15) \times (8/15) = 56/225$.

18. The total number of ways in which the 6 identical balls can be distributed amongst the three boxes such that each box can get 0, 1, 2, 3, 4, 5 or 6 balls is given by the formula: $^{n+r-1}C_r$ where n is the number of identical balls and r is the number of boxes. This will give the sample space.

19. Event definition:
Any six of them work AND four leave OR any seven work AND three leave OR any eight work AND two leave OR any nine work AND one leaves OR All ten work.

20. "To make at least 3 trials to draw a heart" implies that he didn't get a heart in the first two trials.

21. A box containing 4 defectives would get sent to the market if all the 4 articles selected are not defective.
Thus, $^{16}C_4/^{20}C_4 = 364/969$

22. If the box contains only 1 defective, it would be sent back if the defective is one amongst the 4 selected for testing.

To ensure one of the 4 is selected, the no. of ways is $^{19}C_3$, while the total no. of selections of 4 out of 20 is $^{20}C_4$.
Thus, $^{19}C_3/^{20}C_4 = 1/5$.

23. For divisibility by 5 we need the units digit to be either 0 or 5.
The units digit in the powers of 7 follow the pattern – 7, 9, 3, 1, 7, 9, 3, 1, 7, 9.......
Hence, divide 1 to 100 into four groups of 25 elements each as follows.

     $A = 1, 5, 9, \text{------} \rightarrow 25$ elements
     $B = 2, 6, 10, \text{------} \rightarrow 25$ elements
     $C = 3, 7, 11, \text{------} \rightarrow 25$ elements
     $D = 4, 8, 12, \text{------} \rightarrow 25$ elements

Check the combination values of m and n so that $7^m + 7^n$ is divisible by 5.

24. P(minimum 3) or P (maximum 7)
   P(minimum 3) = $^7C_2/^{10}C_3$ = 21/120
   P(max 7) = $^6C_2/^{10}C_2$ = 15/120

   Note: The logic for this can be explained for minimum 3 conditions as: Since the minimum value has to be 3, the remaining 2 numbers have to be selected from 4 to 10. This can be done in $^7C_2$ ways.

25. For the event to occur, the dice should show values from 2, 3, 4 or 5. This is similar to selection with repetition.

26. Yellow and Red and Blue = (3/6) × (2/6) × (1/6)
   = (6/216) = 1/36.

27. Two white and one black can be obtained only through the following three sequences:
   Ball drawn from A and B are white and the ball drawn from C is Black. or
   Ball drawn from A and C are white and the ball drawn from B is Black. or
   Ball drawn from B and C are white and the ball drawn from A is Black.

28. At least one means (exactly one + exactly two + exactly three)
   At least two means (exactly two + exactly three)
   The problem gives the probabilities for passing in at least one, at least two and exactly two.

29. All four are not in the correct envelopes means that at least one of them is in a wrong envelope. A little consideration will show that one letter being placed in a wrong envelope is not possible, since it will have to be interchanged with some other letter.
   Since, there is only one way to put all the letters in the correct envelopes, we can say that the event of not all four letters going into the correct envelopes will be given by
   5! – 1 = 119

30. $n(E)$ = 44
   $n(S)$ = 120

31. A_1 = (112 or 121)
   A_2 = (112 or 211)
   A_3 = (121 or 211)
   Option (b) is correct.

32.
   2/3   5/9
   X

   From the venn diagram we get:
   (2/3) + (5/9) – x = 4/5 → x = (2/3) + (5/9) – (4/5)
   = 19/45

33.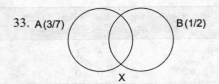
   A(3/7)   B(1/2)
   X

   Also $P(A \cup B) = 1 - P(A' \cap B')$
   (3/7) + (1/2) – x = 13/14 → x = 0
   Thus, there is no interference between A and B as $P(A \cap B) = x = 0$. Hence, A and B are mutually exclusive.

34. The required probability will be given by $\dfrac{2 \times 6! \times 6!}{12!}$.

35. The non-event in this case is that the problem is not solved.

36-37. Are similar to Question No. 2 of LOD III.

38. The event definition will be:
   The first bag is selected AND a red ball is selected. OR
   The second bag is selected AND a red ball is selected.

39. The event definition is:
   A girl is selected from the first group and one boy each are selected from the second and third groups. OR A girl is selected from the second group and one boy each are selected from the first and third groups. OR A girl is selected from the third group and one boy each are selected from the first and second groups.

40. The event definition will be:
   A solves the problem and B and C do not solve the problem. OR B solves the problem and A and C do not solve the problem. OR C solves the problem and A and B do not solve the problem.

41. The three balls that are taken out can be either 3 black balls or 2 black and 1 red ball or 1 black and 2 red ball or 3 red balls.
   Each of these will give their own probabilities of drawing a black ball.

42. 3 Blacks and 4th is Red or 2 Blacks and 1 Red and 4th is Red or 1 Black and 2 Reds and 4th is Red
   = (5/8) × (4/7) × (3/6) × (3/5) + $^3C_1$ × (5/8) × (4/7) × (3/6) × (2/5) + $^3C_1$ × (5/8) × (3/7) × (2/6) × (1/5)
   = $\dfrac{180 + 360 + 90}{1680}$ = 630/1680 = 3/8 = 0.375

43. The event definition would be: Ball transferred is white and white ball drawn
   Or
   Ball transferred is black and white ball is drawn.
   The answer will be given by:
   (5/9) × (8/17) + (4/9) × (7/17) = 68/153 = 4/9

44. Solve this on a similar pattern to the example given in the theory of this chapter.

45. Required probability = 1 – probability that no pair is selected

46. We can have a maximum of 5 heads.

   For 0 heads → $P(E) = (1/2^{10}) \times 1$

   For 1 heads → $P(E) = (1/2^{10}) \times 1$

   For 2 heads and for them not to occur consecutively we will need to see the possible distribution of 8 tails and 2 heads.

   Since the 2 heads do not need to occur consecutively, this would be given by (All – 2heads together)

   $\rightarrow (^{10}C_8 - 9)$

   $P(E) = \dfrac{(^{10}C_8 - 9)}{2^{10}}$

   Solving in this fashion, we would get $1/2^3$.

47. This can be got by taking the number of ways in which exactly two people are born on the same day divided by the total number of ways in which 7 people can be born in 7 days of a week. For the first part select two people from 7 in $^7C_2$ ways & select a day from the week on which they have to be born in $^7C_1$ ways & for the remaining 5 people select 5 days out of the remaining six days of the week & then the number of arrangements of these 5 people in 5 days-thus a total of $^7C_2 \times ^7C_1 \times ^6C_5 \times 5!$ ways. Also, the number of ways in which seven people can be born on 7 days would be given by 7^7. Hence, the answer is given by: $(^7C_2 \times ^7C_1 \times ^6C_5 \times 5!/7^7) = 21 \times 7 \times 6 \times 120/7^7 = 3 \times 6 \times 120/7^5 = 2160/7^5$.

48. This can be got by defining the number of ways in which the player can get a deal of 13 cards if he gets all four kings divided by the number of ways in which the player can get a deal of 13 cards without any constraints from 52 cards:

   The requisite value would be given by: $^{48}C_9/^{52}C_{13} =$ [48!/39! × 9!] × [13! × 39!/52!] = (48! × 13! × 39!)/ (39! × 9! × 52!) = 13 × 12 × 11 × 10/52 × 51 × 50 × 49 = 1 × 11/17 × 17 × 5 × 49 = 11/4165

49. P of heads showing on 50 coins = $^{100}C_{50} \times P^{50}(1 - p)^{50}$

   P of heads showing on 51 coins = $^{100}C_{51} \times P^{51}(1 - p)^{49}$

   Both are equal

   $^{100}C_{50} \times P^{50}(1 - P)^{50} = ^{100}C_{51} \times P^{51}(1 - P)^{49}$

   or $\dfrac{100 \times 49 \times ... \times 52 \times 51}{1 \times 2 \times ... \times 49 \times 50} \times (1 - P)$

   $= \dfrac{100 \times 99 \times ... \times 53 \times 52}{1 \times 2 \times ... \times 48 \times 49} \times P$

   or $\dfrac{51}{50} \times (1 - P) = P$

   or $51 \times (1 - P) = 50\, P$

   or $51 - 51\, P = 50\, P$

   or $51 = 101\, P$

   $\therefore P = \dfrac{51}{101}$

50. The common side could be horizontal or vertical. Accordingly, the number of ways the event can occur is.

   $n(E) = 8 \times 7 + 8 \times 7 = 112$

   $n(S) = 64C_2$

   $= \dfrac{2 \times 8 \times 7 \times 2}{64 \times 63} = \dfrac{1}{18}$

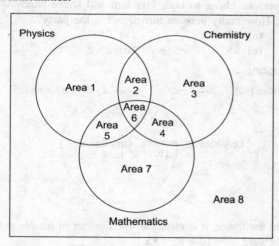

Figure 2: Refers to the situation where there are three attributes being measured. In the figure below, we are talking about people who passed Physics, Chemistry and/or Mathematics.

19

Chapter

Set Theory

Set Theory is an important concept of mathematics which is often asked in aptitude exams. There are two types of questions in this chapter:

(i) Numerical questions on set theory based on venn diagrams

(ii) Logical questions based on set theory

Let us first take a look at some standard theoretical inputs related to set theory.

⌥ SET THEORY

Look at the following diagrams:

Figure 1: Refers to the situation where there are two attributes A and B. (Let's say A refers to people who passed in Physics and B refers to people who passed in Chemistry.) Then the shaded area shows the people who passed both in Physics and Chemistry.

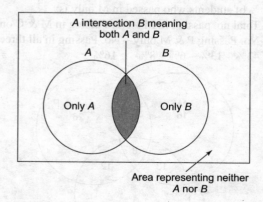

In mathematical terms, the situation is represented as:
Total number of people who passed at least 1 subject =
$A + B - A \cap B$

In the above figure, the following explain the respective areas:

Area 1: People who passed in Physics only

Area 2: People who passed in Physics and Chemistry only (in other words—people who passed Physics and Chemistry but not Mathematics)

Area 3: People who passed Chemistry only

Area 4: People who passed Chemistry and Mathematics only (also, can be described as people who passed Chemistry and Mathematics but not Physics)

Area 5: People who passed Physics and Mathematics only (also, can be described as people who passed Physics and Mathematics but not Chemistry)

Area 6: People who passed Physics, Chemistry and Mathematics

Area 7: People who passed Mathematics only

Area 8: People who passed in no subjects

Also take note of the following language which there is normally confusion about:

People passing Physics and Chemistry—Represented by the sum of areas 2 and 6

People passing Physics and Maths—Represented by the sum of areas 5 and 6

People passing Chemistry and Maths—Represented by the sum of areas 4 and 6

People passing Physics—Represented by the sum of the areas 1, 2, 5 and 6

In mathematical terms, this means:

Total number of people who passed at least 1 subject =
$P + C + M - P \cap C - P \cap M - C \cap M + P \cap C \cap M$

Let us consider the following questions and see how these figures work in terms of real time problem solving:

Illustration 1

At the birthday party of Sherry, a baby boy, 40 persons chose to kiss him and 25 chose to shake hands with him. 10 persons chose to both kiss him and shake hands with him. How many persons turned out at the party?

    (a) 35   (b) 75

    (c) 55   (d) 25

Solution:

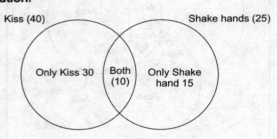

From the figure, it is clear that the number of people at the party were 30 + 10 + 15 = 55.

We can of course solve this mathematically as below:

Let $n(A)$ = No. of persons who kissed Sherry = 40

$n(B)$ = No. of persons who shake hands with Sherry = 25

and $n(A \cap B)$ = No. of persons who shook hands with Sherry and kissed him both = 10

Then using the formula, $n(A \cup B) = n(A) + n(B) - n(A \cap B)$

$n(A \cup B) = 40 + 25 - 10 = 55$

Illustration 2

Directions for Questions 1 to 4: Refer to the data below and answer the questions that follow:

In an examination 43% passed in Math, 52% passed in Physics and 52% passed in Chemistry. Only 8% students passed in all the three. 14% passed in Math and Physics

and 21% passed in Math and Chemistry and 20% passed in Physics and Chemistry. Number of students who took the exam is 200.

Let Set P, Set C and Set M denotes the students who passed in Physics, Chemistry and Math respectively. Then

1. How many students passed in Math only?
     (a) 16   (b) 32
     (c) 48   (d) 80

2. Find the ratio of students passing in Math only to the students passing in Chemistry only?
     (a) 16:37   (b) 29:32
     (c) 16:19   (d) 31:49

3. What is the ratio of the number of students passing in Physics only to the students passing in either Physics or Chemistry or both?
     (a) 34/46   (b) 26/84
     (c) 49/32   (d) None of these

4. A student is declared pass in the exam only if he/she clears at least two subjects. The number of students who were declared passed in this exam is?
     (a) 33   (b) 66
     (c) 39   (d) 78

Sol. Let P denote Physics, C denote Chemistry and M denote Maths.

% of students who passed in P and C only is given by % of students who passed in P and C - % of students who passed all three = 20% – 8% = 12%

% of students who passed in P and M only is given by % of students who passed in P and M - % of students who passed all three = 14% – 8% = 6%

% of students who passed in M and C only is:

% of students who passed in C and M - % of students who passed all three = 21% – 8% = 13%

So, % of students who passed in P only is given by:

Total no. passing in P – No. Passing in P & C only – No. Passing P & M only – No. Passing in all three→

52% – 12% – 6% – 8% = 26%

% of students who passed in M only is:

Total no. passing in M – No. Passing in M & C only – No. Passing P & M only – No. Passing in all three→

43% – 13% – 6% – 8% = 16%

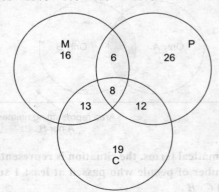

% of students who passed in Chemistry only is
Total no. passing in C – No. Passing in P & C only – No.
Passing C & M only – No. Passing in all three →
52% – 12% – 13% – 8% – = 19%

The answers are:

1. Only Math = 16% = 32 people. Option (b) is correct.
2. Ratio of Only Math to Only Chemistry = 16:19. Option (c) is correct.
3. 26:84 is the required ratio. Option (b) is correct.
4. 39 % or 78 people. Option (d) is correct.

Illustration 3

In the Mindworkzz club all the members participate either in the Tambola or the Fete. 320 participate in the Fete, 350 participate in the Tambola and 220 participate in both. How many members does the club have?

(a) 410
(b) 550
(c) 440
(d) None of these

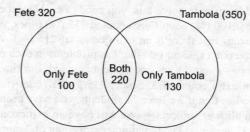

The total number of people = 100 + 220 + 130 = 450
Option (d) is correct.

Illustration 4

There are 20000 people living in Defence Colony, Gurgaon. Out of them 9000 subscribe to Star TV Network and 12000 to Zee TV Network. If 4000 subscribe to both, how many do not subscribe to any of the two?

(a) 3000
(b) 2000
(c) 1000
(d) 4000

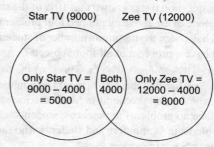

The required answer would be 20000 – 5000 – 4000 – 8000 = 3000.

Illustration 5

Directions for Questions 1 to 3: Refer to the data below and answer the questions that follow.

Last year, there were 3 sections in the Catalyst, a mock CAT paper. Out of them 33 students cleared the cut-off in Section 1, 34 students cleared the cut-off in Section 2 and 32 cleared the cut-off in Section 3. 10 students cleared the cut-off in Section 1 and Section 2, 9 cleared the cut-off in Section 2 and Section 3, 8 cleared the cut-off in Section 1 and Section 3. The number of people who cleared each section alone was equal and was 21 for each section.

1. How many cleared all the three sections?
   (a) 3
   (b) 6
   (c) 5
   (d) 7
2. How many cleared only one of the three sections?
   (a) 21
   (b) 63
   (c) 42
   (d) 52
3. The ratio of the number of students clearing the cut-off in one or more of the sections to the number of students clearing the cutoff in Section 1 alone is?
   (a) 78/21
   (b) 3
   (c) 73/21
   (d) None of these

Since, $x = 6$, the figure becomes:

The answers would be:

1. 6. Option (b) is correct.
2. 21+21+21=63. Option (b) is correct.
3. (21+21+21+6+4+3+2)/21 = 78/21. Option (a) is correct.

Illustration 6

In a locality having 1500 households, 1000 watch Zee TV, 300 watch NDTV and 750 watch Star Plus. Based on this information answer the questions that follow:

1. The minimum number of households watching Zee TV and Star Plus is:

   Logic: If we try to consider each of the households watching Zee TV and Star Plus as independent of each other, we would get a total of $1000 + 750 = 1750$ households. However, we have a total of only 1500 households in the locality and hence, there has to be a minimum interference of at least 250 households who would be watching both Zee TV and Star Plus. Hence, the answer to this question is 250.

2. The minimum number of households watching both Zee TV and NDTV is:

   In this case, the number of households watching Zee TV and NDTV can be separate from each other since there is no interference required between the households watching Zee TV and the households watching NDTV as their individual sum $(1000 + 300)$ is smaller than the 1500 available households in the locality. Hence, the answer in this question is 0.

3. The maximum number of households who watch neither of the the three channels is:

   For this to occur the following situation would give us the required solution:

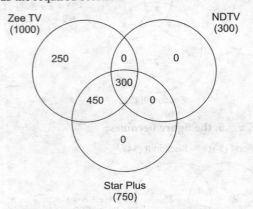

   As you can clearly see from the figure, all the requirements of each category of viewers is fulfilled by the given allocation of 1000 households. In this situation, the maximum number of households who do not watch any of the three channels is visible as $1500 - 1000 = 500$.

Illustration 7

1. In a school, 90% of the students faced problems in Mathematics, 80% of the students faced problems in Computers, 75% of the students faced problems in Sciences, and 70% of the students faced problems in Social Sciences. Find the minimum percent of the students who faced problems in all four subjects.

   Solution: In order to think about the minimum number of students who faced problems in all four subjects you would need to think of keeping the students who did not face a problem in any of the subjects separate from each other. We know that 30% of the students did not face problems in Social Sciences, 25% of the students did not face problems in Sciences, 20% students did not face problems in computers and 10% students did not face problems in Mathematics. If each of these were separate from each other, we would have $30+25+20+10=85\%$ people who did not face a problem in one of the four subjects. Naturally, the remaining 15% would be students who faced problems in all four subjects. This represents the minimum percentage of students who faced problems in all the four subjects.

2. For the above question, find the maximum possible percentage of students who could have problems in all 4 subjects.

   In order to solve this, you need to consider the fact that 100 (%) people are counted 315 (%) times, which means that there is an extra count of 215 (%). When you put a student into the 'has problems in each of the four subjects' he is one student counted four times — an extra count of 3. Since, $215/3 = 71$ (quotient) we realise that if we have 71 students who have problems in all four subjects — we will have an extra count of 213 students. The remaining extra count of 2 more can be matched by putting 1 student in 'has problems in 3 subjects' or by putting 2 students in 'has problems in 2 subjects'. Thus, from the extra count angle, we have a limit of 71% students in the 'have problems in all four categories.'

   However, in this problem there is a constraint from another angle — i.e. there are only 70% students who have a problem in Social Sciences — and hence it is not possible for 71% students to have problems in all the four subjects. Hence, the maximum possible percentage of people who have a problem in all four subjects would be 70%.

3. In the above question if it is known that 10% of the students faced none of the above mentioned four problems, what would have been the minimum number of students who would have a problem in all four subjects?

   If there are 10% students who face none of the four problems, we realise that these 10% would be common to students who face no problems in Mathematics, students who face no problems in Sciences, students who face no problems in Computers and students who face no problems in Social Sciences.

   Now, we also know that overall there are 10% students who did not face a problem in Mathematics; 20%

students who did not face a problem in computers; 25% students who did not face a problem in Sciences and 30% students who did not face a problem in Social Sciences. The 10% students who did not face a problem in any of the subjects would be common to each of these 4 counts. Out of the remaining 90% students, if we want to identify the minimum number of students who had a problem in all four subjects we will take the same approach as we took in the first question of this set — i.e. we try to keep the students having problems in the individual subjects separate from each other. This would result in: 0% additional students having no problem in Mathematics; 10% additional students having no problem in Computers; 15% additional students having no problem in Sciences and 20% additional students having no problem in Social Sciences. Thus, we would get a total of 45% (0+10+15+20=45) students who would have no problem in one of the four subjects. Thus, the minimum percentage of students who had a problem in all four subjects would be 90 – 45 = 45%.

Illustration 8

In a class of 80 students, each of them studies at least one language—English, Hindi and Sanskrit. It was found that 65 studied English, 60 studied Hindi and 55 studied Sanskrit.

1. Find the maximum number of people who study all three languages.

   This question again has to be dealt with from the perspective of extra counting. In this question, 80 students in the class are counted 65 + 60 + 55 = 180 times — an extra count of 100. If we put 50 people in the all three categories as shown below, we would get the maximum number of students who study all three languages.

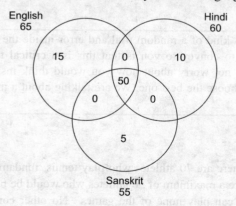

2. Find the minimum number of people who study all three languages.

   In order to think about how many students are necessarily in the 'study all three languages' area of the figure (this thinking would lead us to the answer to

the minimum number of people who study all three languages) we need to think about how many people we can shift out of the 'study all three category' for the previous question. When we try to do that, the following thought process emerges:

Step 1: Let's take a random value for the all three categories (less than 50 of course) and see whether the numbers can be achieved. For this purpose we try to start with the value as 40 and see what happens. Before we move on, realise the basic situation in the question remains the same — 80 students have been counted 180 times — which means that there is an extra count of 100 students & also realise that when you put an individual student in the all three categories, you get an extra count of 2, while at the same time when you put an individual student into the 'exactly two languages category', he/she is counted twice — hence an extra count of 1. The starting figure we get looks something like this:

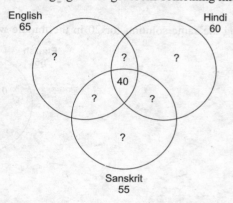

At this point, since we have placed 40 people in the all three categories, we have taken care of an extra count of $40 \times 2 = 80$. This leaves us with an extra count of 20 more to manage and as we can see in the above figure we have a lot of what can be described as 'slack' to achieve the required numbers. For instance, one solution we can think of from this point is as below:

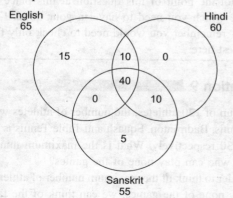

One look at this figure should tell you that the solution can be further optimised by reducing the middle value in the figure since there is still a lot of 'slack' in the figure — in the form of the number of students in the 'exactly one language category'. Also, you can easily see that there are many ways in which this solution could have been achieved with 40 in the middle. Hence, we go in search of a lower value in the middle.

So, we try to take an arbitrary value of 30 to see whether this is still achievable.

In this case we see the following as one of the possible ways to achieve this (again there is a lot of slack in this solution as the 'only Hindi' or the 'only Sanskrit' areas can be reallocated):

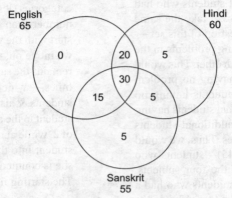

Trying the same solution for 20 in the middle we get the optimum solution:

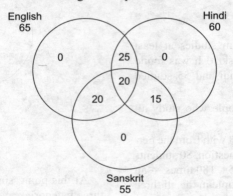

We realise that this is the optimum solution since there is no 'slack' in this solution and hence, there is no scope for re-allocating numbers from one area to another.

Author's note: You might be justifiably thinking how do you do this kind of a random trial and error inside the exam? That's not the point of this question at this place. What I am trying to convey to you is that this is a critical thought structure which you need to have in your mind. Learn it here and do not worry about how you would think inside the exam — remember you would need to check only the four options to choose the best one. We are talking about a multiple choice test here.

Illustration 9

In a group of 120 athletes, the number of athletes who can play Tennis, Badminton, Squash and Table Tennis is 70, 50, 60 and 30 respectively. What is the maximum number of athletes who can play none of the games?

In order to think of the maximum number of athletes who can play none of the games, we can think of the fact that

since there are 70 athletes who play tennis, fundamentally there are a maximum of 50 athletes who would be possibly in the 'can play none of the games'. No other constraint in the problem necessitates a reduction of this number and hence the answer to this question is 50.

LEVEL OF DIFFICULTY (I)

Directions for Questions 1 and 2: Refer to the data below and answer the questions that follow:

In the Indian athletic squad sent to the Olympics, 21 athletes were in the triathlon team; 26 were in the pentathlon team; and 29 were in the marathon team. 14 athletes can take part in triathlon and pentathlon; 12 can take part in marathon and triathlon; 15 can take part in pentathlon and marathon; and 8 can take part in all the three games.

1. How many players are there in all?
   - (a) 35
   - (b) 43
   - (c) 49
   - (d) none of these
2. How many were in the marathon team only?
   - (a) 10
   - (b) 14
   - (c) 18
   - (d) 15

Directions for Questions 3 and 4: Refer to the data below and answer the questions that follow.

In a test in which 120 students appeared, 90 passed in History, 65 passed in Sociology and 75 passed in Political Science. 30 students passed in only one subject and 55 students in only two. 5 students passed no subjects.

3. How many students passed in all the three subjects?
   - (a) 25
   - (b) 30
   - (c) 35
   - (d) Data insufficient
4. Find the number of students who passed in at least two subjects.
   - (a) 85
   - (b) 95
   - (c) 90
   - (d) Data insufficient

Directions for Questions 5 to 8: Refer to the data below and answer the questions that follow.

5% of the passengers who boarded Guwahati- New Delhi Rajdhani Express on 20th February, 2002 do not like coffee, tea and ice cream and 10% like all the three. 20% like coffee and tea, 25% like ice cream and coffee and 25% like ice cream and tea. 55% like coffee, 50% like tea and 50 % like ice cream.

5. The number of passengers who like only coffee is greater than the passengers who like only ice cream by
   - (a) 50%
   - (b) 100%
   - (c) 25%
   - (d) 0
6. The percentage of passengers who like both tea and ice cream but not coffee is
   - (a) 15
   - (b) 5
   - (c) 10
   - (d) 25
7. The percentage of passengers who like at least 2 of the 3 products is
   - (a) 40
   - (b) 45
   - (c) 50
   - (d) 60
8. If the number of passengers is 180, then the number of passengers who like ice cream only is

   - (a) 10
   - (b) 18
   - (c) 27
   - (d) 36

Directions for Questions 9 to 15: Refer to the data below and answer the questions that follow.

In a survey among students at all the IIMs, it was found that 48% preferred coffee, 54% liked tea and 64% smoked. Of the total, 28% liked coffee and tea, 32% smoked and drank tea and 30% smoked and drank coffee. Only 6% did none of these. If the total number of students is 2000 then find

9. The ratio of the number of students who like only coffee to the number who like only tea is
   - (a) 5:3
   - (b) 8:9
   - (c) 2:3
   - (d) 3:2
10. Number of students who like coffee and smoking but not tea is
    - (a) 600
    - (b) 240
    - (c) 280
    - (d) 360
11. The percentage of those who like coffee or tea but not smoking among those who like at least one of these is
    - (a) more than 30
    - (b) less than 30
    - (c) less than 25
    - (d) None of these
12. The percentage of those who like at least one of these is
    - (a) 100
    - (b) 90
    - (c) Nil
    - (d) 94
13. The two items having the ratio 1:2 are
    - (a) Tea only and tea and smoking only.
    - (b) Coffee and smoking only and tea only.
    - (c) Coffee and tea but not smoking and smoking but not coffee and tea.
    - (d) None of these
14. The number of persons who like coffee and smoking only and the number who like tea only bear a ratio
    - (a) 1:2
    - (b) 1:1
    - (c) 5:1
    - (d) 2:1
15. Percentage of those who like tea and smoking but not coffee is
    - (a) 14
    - (b) 14.9
    - (c) less than 14
    - (d) more than 15
16. 30 monkeys went to a picnic. 25 monkeys chose to irritate cows while 20 chose to irritate buffaloes. How many chose to irritate both buffaloes and cows?
    - (a) 10
    - (b) 15
    - (c) 5
    - (d) 20

Directions for Questions 17 to 20: Refer to the data below and answer the questions that follow.

In the CBSE Board Exams last year, 53% passed in Biology, 61% passed in English, 60% in Social Studies, 24% in Biology & English, 35% in English & Social

Studies, 27% in Biology and Social Studies and 5% in none.

17. Percentage of passes in all subjects is
    (a) Nil   (b) 12
    (c) 7   (d) 10
18. If the number of students in the class is 200, how many passed in only one subject?
    (a) 48   (b) 46
    (c) more than 50   (d) less than 40
19. If the number of students in the class is 300, what will be the % change in the number of passes in only two subjects, if the original number of students is 200?
    (a) more than 50%   (b) less than 50%
    (c) 50%   (d) None of these
20. What is the ratio of percentage of passes in Biology and Social Studies but not English in relation to the percentage of passes in Social Studies and English but not Biology?
    (a) 5:7   (b) 7:5
    (c) 4:5   (d) None of these

Directions for Questions 21 to 25: Refer to the data below and answer the questions that follow.

In the McGraw-Hill Mindworkzz Quiz held last year, participants were free to choose their respective areas from which they were asked questions. Out of 880 participants, 224 chose Mythology, 240 chose Science and 336 chose Sports, 64 chose both Sports and Science, 80 chose Mythology and Sports, 40 chose Mythology and Science and 24 chose all the three areas.

21. The percentage of participants who did not choose any area is
    (a) 23.59%   (b) 30.25%
    (c) 37.46%   (d) 27.27%
22. Of those participating, the percentage who choose only one area is
    (a) 60%   (b) more than 60%
    (c) less than 60%   (d) more than 75%
23. Number of participants who chose at least two areas is
    (a) 112   (b) 24
    (c) 136   (d) None of these
24. Which of the following areas shows a ratio of 1:8?
    (a) Mythology & Science but not Sports: Mythology only
    (b) Mythology & Sports but not Science: Science only
    (c) Science: Sports
    (d) None of these
25. The ratio of students choosing Sports & Science but not Mythology to Science but not Mythology & Sports is
    (a) 2:5   (b) 1:4
    (c) 1:5   (d) 1:2

Directions for Questions 26 to 30: Refer to the data below and answer the questions that follow.

The table here gives the distribution of students according to professional courses.

| Courses | STUDENTS | | | |
| | English | | Maths | |
	MALES	FEMALES	MALES	FEMALES
Part-time MBA	30	10	50	10
Full-time MBA only	150	8	16	6
CA only	90	10	37	3
Full time MBA & CA	70	2	7	1

26. What is the percentage of Math students over English students?
    (a) 50.4   (b) 61.4
    (c) 49.4   (d) None of these
27. The average number of females in all the courses is (count people doing full-time MBA and CA as a separate course)
    (a) less than 12   (b) greater than 12
    (c) 12   (d) None of these
28. The ratio of the number of girls to the number of boys is
    (a) 5:36   (b) 1:9
    (c) 1:7.2   (d) None of these
29. The percentage increase in students of full-time MBA only over CA only is
    (a) less than 20   (b) less than 25
    (c) less than 30   (d) more than 30
30. The number of students doing full-time MBA or CA is
    (a) 320   (b) 80
    (c) 160   (d) None of these.

Directions for Questions 31 to 34: Refer to the data below and answer the questions that follow:

A newspaper agent sells The TOI, HT and IN in equal numbers to 302 persons. Seven get HT & IN, twelve get The TOI & IN, nine get The TOI & HT and three get all the three newspapers. The details are given in the Venn diagram:

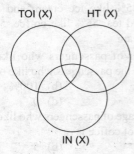

31. How many get only one paper?
    (a) 280   (b) 327
    (c) 109   (d) None of these
32. What percent get The TOI and The HT but not The IN
    (a) more than 65%   (b) less than 60%
    (c) ≅ 64%   (d) None of these.

33. The number of persons buying The TOI and The HT only, The TOI and The IN only and The HT and The IN only are in the ratio of
    (a) 6:4:9
    (b) 6:9:4
    (c) 4:9:6
    (d) None of these
34. The difference between the number reading The HT and The IN only and HT only is
    (a) 77
    (b) 78
    (c) 83
    (d) None of these.
35. A group of 78 people watch Zee TV, Star Plus or Sony. Of these, 36 watch Zee TV, 48 watch Star Plus and 32 watch Sony. If 14 people watch both Zee TV and Star Plus, 20 people watch both Star Plus and Sony, and 12 people watch both Sony and Zee TV find the ratio of the number of people who watch only Zee TV to the number of people who watch only Sony.
    (a) 9:4
    (b) 3:2
    (c) 5:3
    (d) 7:4

Directions for Questions 36 and 37: Answer the questions based on the following information.

The following data was observed from a study of car complaints received from 180 respondents at Colonel Verma's car care workshop, viz., engine problem, transmission problem or mileage problem. Of those surveyed, there was no one who faced exactly two of these problems. There were 90 respondents who faced engine problems, 120 who faced transmission problems and 150 who faced mileage problems.

36. How many of them faced all the three problems?
    (a) 45
    (b) 60
    (c) 90
    (d) 20
37. How many of them faced either transmission problems or engine problems?

Space for Rough Work

(a) 30
(b) 60
(c) 90
(d) 40

Directions for Questions 38 to 42: given below are five diagrams one of which describes the relationship among the three classes given in each of the five questions that follow. You have to decide which of the diagrams is the most suitable for a particular set of classes.

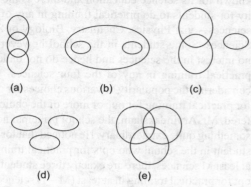

(a)   (b)   (c)

(d)   (e)

38. Elephants, tigers, animals
39. Administrators, Doctors, Authors
40. Platinum, Copper, Gold
41. Gold, Platinum, Ornaments
42. Television, Radio, Mediums of Entertainment
43. Seventy percent of the employees in a multinational corporation have VCD players, 75 percent have microwave ovens, 80 percent have ACs and 85 percent have washing machines. At least what percentage of employees has all four gadgets?
    (a) 15
    (b) 5
    (c) 10
    (d) Cannot be determined

LEVEL OF DIFFICULTY (II)

1. At the Rosary Public School, there are 870 students in the senior secondary classes. The school is widely known for its science education and there is the facility for students to do practical training in any of the 4 sciences – viz: Physics, Chemistry, Biology or Social Sciences. Some students in the school however have no interest in the sciences and hence do not undertake practical training in any of the four sciences. While considering the popularity of various choices for opting for practical training for one or more of the choices offered, Mr. Arvindaksham, the school principal noticed something quite extraordinary. He noticed that for every student in the school who opts for practical training in at least M sciences, there are exactly three students who opt for practical training in at least (M – 1) sciences, for M = 2, 3 and 4. He also found that the number of students who opt for all four sciences was half the number of students who opt for none. Can you help him with the answer to "How many students in the school opt for exactly three sciences?"
   - (a) 30
   - (b) 60
   - (c) 90
   - (d) None of these

2. A bakery sells three kinds of pastries—pineappple, chocolate and black forest. On a particular day, the bakery owner sold the following number of pastries: 90 pineapple, 120 chocolate and 150 black forest. If none of the customers bought more than two pastries of each type, what is the minimum number of customers that must have visited the bakery that day?
   - (a) 80
   - (b) 75
   - (c) 60
   - (d) 90

3. Gauri Apartment housing society organised annual games, consisting of three games – viz: snooker, badminton and tennis. In all, 510 people were members in the apartments' society and they were invited to participate in the games — each person participating in as many games as he/she feels like. While viewing the statistics of the performance. Mr Capoor realised the following acts. The number of people who participated in at least two games was 52% more than those who participated in exactly one game. The number of people participating in 1, 2 or 3 games respectively was at least equal to 1. Being a numerically inclined person, he further noticed an interesting thing — the number of people who did not participate in any of the three games was the minimum possible integral value with these conditions. What was the maximum number of people who participated in exactly three games?
   - (a) 298
   - (b) 300
   - (c) 303
   - (d) 304

4. A school has 180 students in its senior section where foreign languages are offered to students as part of their syllabus. The foreign languages offered are: French, German and Chinese and the numbers of people studying each of these subjects are 80, 90 and 100 respectively. The number of students who study more than one of the three subjects is 50% more than the number of students who study all the three subjects. There are no students in the school who study none of the three subjects. Then how many students study all three foreign languages?
   - (a) 18
   - (b) 24
   - (c) 36
   - (d) 40

Directions for Questions 5 and 6: Answer the questions on the basis of the information given below.

In the second year, the Hampard Business School students are offered a choice of the specialisations they wish to study from amongst only three specialisations —Marketing, Finance and HR. The number of students who have specialised in only Marketing, only Finance and only HR are all numbers in an Arithmetic Progression—in no particular order. Similarly, the number of students specialising in exactly two of the three types of subjects are also numbers that form an Arithmetic Progression.

The number of students specialising in all three subjects is one-twentieth of the number of students specialising in only Finance which in turn is half of the number of students studying only HR. The number of students studying both Marketing and Finance is 15, whereas the number of students studying both Finance and HR is 19. The number of students studying HR is 120, which is more than the number of students studying Marketing (which is a 2 digit number above 50). It is known that there are exactly 4 students who opt for none of these specialisations and opt only for general subjects.

5. What is the total number of students in the batch?
   - (a) 223
   - (b) 233
   - (c) 237
   - (d) Cannot be determined

6. What is the number of students specialising in both Marketing and HR?
   - (a) 11
   - (b) 21
   - (c) 23
   - (d) Cannot be determined

Directions for Questions 7 to 9: In the Stafford Public School, students had an option to study none or one or more of three foreign languages viz: French, Spanish and German. The total student strength in the school was 2116 students out of which 1320 students studied French and 408 students studied both French and Spanish. The number of people who studied German was found to be 180 higher than the number of students who studied Spanish. It was also observed that 108 students studied all three subjects.

7. What is the maximum possible number of students who did not study any of the three languages?
   (a) 890   (b) 796
   (c) 720   (d) None of these

8. What is the minimum possible number of students who did not study any of the three languages?
   (a) 316   (b) 0
   (c) 158   (d) None of these

9. If the number of students who used to speak only French was 1 more than the number of people who used to speak only German, then what could be the maximum number of people who used to speak only Spanish?
   (a) 413   (b) 398
   (c) 403   (d) 431

Directions for Questions 10 to 13: In the Vijayant-khand sports stadium, athletes choose from four different racquet games (apart from athletics which is compulsory for all). These are Tennis, Table Tennis, Squash and Badminton. It is known that 20% of the athletes practising there are not choosing any of the racquet sports. The four games given here are played by 460, 360, 360 and 440 students respectively. The number of athletes playing exactly 2 racquet games for any combination of two racquet games is 40. There are 60 athletes who play all the four games but in a strange coincidence, it was noticed that the number of people playing exactly 3 games was also equal to 20 for each combination of 3 games.

10. What is the number of athletes in the stadium?
    (a) 1140   (b) 1040
    (c) 1200   (d) 1300

11. What is the number of athletes in the stadium who play either only squash or only Tennis?
    (a) 120   (b) 220
    (c) 340   (d) 440

12. How many athletes in the stadium participate in only athletics?
    (a) 160   (b) 1040
    (c) 260   (d) 220

13. If all the athletes were compulsorily asked to add one game to their existing list (except those who were already playing all the four games) — then what will be the number of athletes who would be playing all 4 games after this change?
    (a) 80   (b) 100
    (c) 120   (d) 140

Directions for Questions 14 and 15: Answer the questions on the basis of the following information.

In the Pattbhiraman family, a clan of 192 individuals, each person has at least one of the three Pattabhiraman characteristics—Blue eyes, Blonde hair, and sharp mind. It is also known that:

(i) The number of family members who have only blue eyes is equal to the number of family members who have only sharp minds and this number is also equal to twice the number of family members who have blue eyes and sharp minds but not blonde hair.

(ii) The number of family members who have exactly two of the three features is 50.

(iii) The number of family members who have blonde hair is 62.

(iv) Among those who have blonde hair, 26 family members have at least two of the three characteristics.

14. If the number of family members who have blue eyes is the maximum amongst the three characteristics, then what is the maximum possible number of family members who have both sharp minds and blonde hair but do not have blue eyes?
    (a) 11   (b) 10
    (c) 12   (d) Cannot be determined

15. Which additional piece of information is required to find the exact number of family members who have blonde hair and blue eyes but not sharp minds?
    (a) The number of family members who have exactly one of the three characterisitcs is 140.
    (b) Only two family members have all three characteristics.
    (c) The number of family members who have sharp minds is 89.
    (d) The number of family members who have only sharp minds is 52.

16. In a class of 97 students, each student plays at least one of the three games – Hockey, Cricket and Football. If 47 play Hockey, 53 play Cricket, 72 play Football and 15 play all the three games, what is the number of students who play exactly two games?
    (a) 38   (b) 40
    (c) 42   (d) 45

Directions for Questions 17 to 19: Answer the questions on the basis of the information given below.

In the ancient towns of Mohenjo Daro, a survey found that students were fond of three kinds of cold drinks (Pep, Cok and Thum). It was also found that there were three kinds of beverages that they liked (Tea, Cof and ColdCof).

The popluation of these towns was found to be 400000 people in all—and the survey was conducted on 10% of the population. Mr. Yadav, a data analyst observed the following things about the survey:

(i) The number of people in the survey who like exactly two cold drinks is five times the number of people who like all the three cold drinks.

(ii) The sum of the number of people in the survey who like Pep and 42% of those who like Cok but not Pep is equal to the number of people who like Tea.

(iii) The number of people in the survey who like Cof is equal to the sum of 3/8th of those who like Cok and ½ of those who like Thum. This number is also equal to the number who like ColdCof.

(iv) 18500 people surveyed like Pep;

(v) 15000 like all the beverages and 3500 like all the cold drinks;

(vi) 14000 do not like Pep but like Thum;

(vii) 11000 like Pep and exactly one more cold drink;

(viii) 6000 like only Cok and the same number of people like Pep and Thum but not Cok.

17. The number of people in the survey who do like at least one of the three cold drinks?

(a) 38500   (b) 31500
(c) 32500   (d) 39500

18. What is the maximum number of people in the survey who like none of the three beverages?
(a) 24000   (b) 16000
(c) 12000   (d) Cannot be determined

19. What is the maximum number of people in the survey who like at least one of the three beverages?
(a) 7000   (b) 32,000
(c) 33000   (d) Cannot be determined

20. In a certain class of students, the number of students who drink only tea, only coffee, both tea and coffee and neither tea nor coffee are x, $2x$, $\dfrac{57}{x}$ and $\dfrac{57}{3x}$ respectively. The number of people who drink coffee can be
(a) 41   (b) 40
(c) 59   (d) Both a and c.

Space for Rough Work

ANSWER KEY

Level of Difficulty (I)

1. (b)	2. (a)	3. (b)	4. (a)
5. (b)	6. (a)	7. (c)	8. (b)
9. (c)	10. (b)	11. (a)	12. (d)
13. (c)	14. (b)	15. (a)	16. (b)
17. (c)	18. (c)	19. (c)	20. (a)
21. (d)	22. (c)	23. (c)	24. (a)
25. (b)	26. (d)	27. (b)	28. (b)
29. (c)	30. (a)	31. (a)	32. (c)
33. (b)	34. (d)	35. (a)	36. (c)
37. (b)	38. (b)	39. (e)	40. (d)
41. (a)	42. (b)	43. (c)	

Level of Difficulty (II)

1. (b)	2. (b)	3. (c)	4. (c)
5. (d)	6. (c)	7. (b)	8. (b)
9. (d)	10. (d)	11. (c)	12. (c)
13. (d)	14. (a)	15. (c)	16. (d)
17. (a)	18. (b)	19. (c)	20. (d)

Solutions and Shortcuts

Level of Difficulty (I)

Solutions for Questions 1 and 2: Since there are 14 players who are in triathlon and pentathlon, and there are 8 who take part in all three games, there will be 6 who take part in only triathlon and pentathlon. Similarly,

Only triathlon and marathon = 12 – 8=4 & Only Pentathlon and Marathon = 15 – 8 = 7.

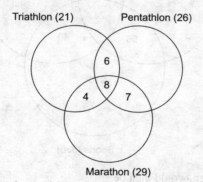

Triathlon (21)   Pentathlon (26)

Marathon (29)

The figure above can be completed with values for each sport (only) plugged in:

The answers would be:

3 + 6 + 8 + 4 + 5 + 7 + 10 = 43. Option (b) is correct.

Option (a) is correct.

Solutions for Questions 3 and 4:

History (90)   Sociology (65)

Political Science (75)

The given situation can be read as follows:

115 students are being counted 75+65+90= 230 times.

This means that there is an extra count of 115. This extra count of 115 can be created in 2 ways.

A. By putting people in the 'passed exactly two subjects' category. In such a case each person would get counted 2 times (double counted), i.e., an extra count of 1.

B. By putting people in the 'all three' category, each person put there would be triple counted. 1 person counted 3 times – meaning an extra count of 2 per person.

The problem tells us that there are 55 students who passed exactly two subjects. This means an extra count of 55 would be accounted for. This would leave an extra count of 115 – 55 = 60 more to be accounted for by 'passed all three' category. This can be done by using 30 people in the 'all 3' category.

Hence, the answers are:

3. Option (b)
4. Option (a)

Solutions for Questions 5 to 8:
Based on the information provided we would get the following figure:

Coffee (55)   Tea (50)

Ice cream (50)

The answers could be read off the figure as:

5. [(20 – 10)/10] * 100 = 100%. Option (b) is correct.
6. 15% (from the figure). Option (a) is correct.
7. 10+10+15+15=50%. Option (c) is correct.
8. Only ice cream is 10% of the total. Hence, 10% of 180 =18. Option (b) is correct.

Solutions for Questions 9 to 15: If you try to draw a figure for this question, the figure would be something like:

Coffee (48) Tea (54)

Smoking (64)

We can then solve this as:
$$x - 10 + 28 - x + x + 30 - x + x + 2 + 32 - x + x - 6 = 94 \rightarrow$$
$$x + 76 = 94 \rightarrow x = 18.$$

Note: In this question, since all the values for the use of the set theory formula are given, we can find the missing value of students who liked all three as follows:
$$94 = 48 + 54 + 64 - 28 - 32 - 30 + \text{All three} \rightarrow \text{All three} = 18$$

As you can see this is a much more convenient way of solving this question, and the learning you take away for the 3 circle situation is that whenever you have all the values known and the only unknown value is the center value – it is wiser and more efficient to solve for the unknown using the formula rather than trying to solve through a venn diagram.

Based on this value of x we get the diagram completed as:

Coffee (48) Tea (54)

Smoking (64)

The answers then are:
9. $8:12 = 2:3 \rightarrow$ Option (c) is correct.
10. 12 % of 2000 = 240. Option (b) is correct.
11. $30/94 \rightarrow$ more than 30%. Option (a) is correct.
12. 94%. Option (d) is correct.
13. Option (c) is correct as the ratio turns out to be 10:20 in that case.
14. $12:12 = 1:1 \rightarrow$ Option (b) is correct.
15. 14%. Option (a) is correct.
16. $30 = 25 + 20 - x \rightarrow x = 15$. Option (b) is correct.

Solutions for Questions 17 to 20:
Let people who passed all three be x. Then:
$$53 + 61 + 60 - 24 - 35 - 27 + x = 95$$
$$\rightarrow x = 7.$$

The venn diagram in this case would become:

Biology 53% English 61%

Social Studies 60%

17. Option (c) is correct.
18. 33% of 200 = more than 50. Option (c) is correct.
19. If the number of students is increased by 50%, the number of students in each category would also be increased by 50%. Option (c) is correct.
20. $20:28 = 5:7$. Option (a) is correct.

Solutions for Questions 21 to 25: The following figure would emerge on using all the information in the question:

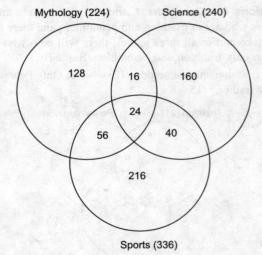

Mythology (224) Science (240)

Sports (336)

The answers would then be:
21. 240/880 = 27.27%. Option (d) is correct.
22. 504/880 = 57.27%. Hence, less than 60. Option (c) is correct.
23. $40 + 16 + 56 + 24 = 136$. Option (c) is correct.
24. Option a gives us 16:128 = 1:8. Option (a) is hence correct.
25. $40:160 \rightarrow 1:4$. Option (b) is correct.

Solutions for Questions 26 to 30: The following Venn diagrams would emerge:

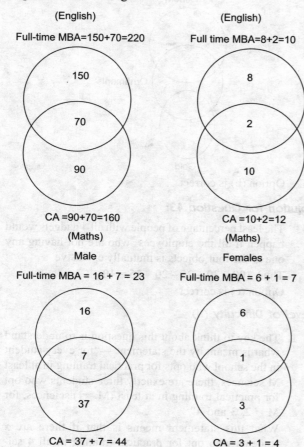

(English)
Full-time MBA=150+70=220

150

70

90

CA =90+70=160
(Maths)
Male

Full-time MBA = 16 + 7 = 23

16

7

37

CA = 37 + 7 = 44

(English)
Full time MBA=8+2=10

8

2

10

CA =10+2=12
(Maths)
Females

Full-time MBA = 6 + 1 = 7

6

1

3

CA = 3 + 1 = 4

26. Math Students = 130. English Students =370
130/370 = 35.13%. Option (d) is correct.

27. Number of Female Students = 10 + 8 + 10 + 2 + 10 + 6 + 3 + 1 = 50. Average number of females per course = 50/3 = 16.66. Option (b) is correct.

28. 50:450 = 1:9. Option (b) is correct.

29. 40/140 → 28.57%. Option (c) is correct.

30. From the figures, this value would be 150+8+ 90 + 10 + 16+6+37+3= 320. Option (a) is correct.

Solutions for Questions 31 to 34: The following figure would emerge-

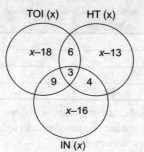

TOI (x)   HT (x)

x–18   6 x–13

9   3   4

IN (x)

x–16

Based on this figure we have:

$x + x - 13 + 4 + x - 16 = 302 \rightarrow 3x - 25 = 302 \rightarrow x = 327$. Hence, $x = 109$.

Consequently the figure becomes:

TOI (109)   HT (109)

91   6   96

3

9   4

93

IN (109)

The answers are:

31. 91 + 93 + 96 = 280. Option (a) is correct.

32. 193/302 ≅ 64%

33. 6:9:4 is the required ratio. Option (b) is correct.

34. 96 – 4 = 92. Options (d) is correct.

35. 78 = 36 + 48 + 32 – 14 – 20 – 12 + x → x = 8.

The figure for this question would become:

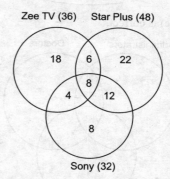

Zee TV (36)   Star Plus (48)

18   6   22

8

4   12

8

Sony (32)

Required ratio is 18:8 → 9:4. Option (a) is correct.

36. Option (c)

Engine (90)   Transmission (120)

0   0   30

90

0   0

60

Mileage (150)

37. There are 30 such people. Option (b) is correct.

Engine (90) Transmission (120)

0   0   30

90

0   0

60

Mileage (150)

Solutions for Questions 38 to 42:

38. Option (b) is correct

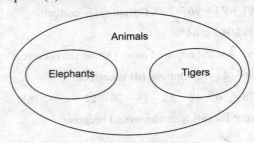

Animals

Elephants   Tigers

39. Option (e) is correct.

Administrators   Doctors

Authors

40. Option (d) is correct.

Platinum   Copper

Gold

41. Option (a) is correct.

Platinum

Ornaments

Gold

42. Option (b) is correct

Solution for Question 43:

43. The least percentage of people with all 4 gadgets would happen if all the employees who are not having any one of the four objects is mutually exclusive.

Thus, $100 - 30 - 25 - 20 - 15 = 10$

Option (c) is correct

Level of Difficulty (II)

1. The key to think about this question is to understand what is meant by the statement —"for every student in the school who opts for practical training in at least M sciences, there are exactly three students who opt for practical training in at least (M − 1) sciences, for M = 2, 3 and 4"

What this statement means is that if there are x students who opt for practical training in all 4 sciences, there would be $3x$ students who would opt for practical training in at least 3 sciences. Since opting for at least 3 sciences includes those who opted for exactly 3 sciences and those who opted for exactly 4 sciences—we can conclude from this that:

The number of students who opted for exaclty 3 sciences = Number of students who opted for at least 3 sciences – Number of students who opted for all 4 sciences = $3x - x = 2x$

Thus, the number of students who opted for various number of science practicals can be summarised as below:

	Number of students who opted for at least n subjects	Number of students who opted for exactly n subjects
n = 4	x	x
n = 3	3x	2x
n = 2	9x	6x
n = 1	27x	18x

Also, number of students who opt for none of the sciences = twice the number of students who opt for exactly 4 sciences = $2x$.

Based on these deductions we can clearly identify that the number of students in the school would be: $x + 2x + 6x + 18x + 2x = 29x = 870 \rightarrow x = 30$.
Hence, number of students who opted for exactly three sciences = $2x = 60$.

2. (b) In order to estimate the minimum number of customers we need to assume that each customer must have bought the maximum number of pastries possible for him to purchase.
Since, the maximum number of pastries an individual could purchase is constrained by the information that no one bought more than two pastries of any one kind—this would occur under the following situation—First 45 people would buy 2 pastries of all three kinds, which would completely exhaust the 90 pineapple pastries and leave the bakery with 30 chocolate and 60 black forest pastries. The next 15 people would buy 2 pastries each of the available kinds and after this we would be left with 30 black forest pastries. 15 people would buy these pastries, each person buying 2 pastries each.
Thus, the total number of people (minimum) would be: $45 + 15 + 15 = 75$.

3. (c) Let the number of people who participated in 0, 1, 2 and 3 games be A, B, C, D respectively. Then from the information we have:
$C + D = 1.52 \times B$ (Number of people who participate in at least 2 games is 52% higher than the number of people who participate in exactly one game)
$A + B + C + D = 510$ (Number of people invited to participate in the games is 510)
This gives us: $A + 2.52B = 510 \rightarrow B = \dfrac{25}{63}(510 - A)$
For A to be minimum, $510 - A$ should give us the largest multiple of 63. Since, $63 \times 8 = 504$ we have $A = 6$.
Also, $2.52B = 504$, so $B = 200$ and $C + D = 1.52B = 304$.
For number of people participating in exactly 3 games to be maximum, the number of people participating in exactly 2 games has to be minimised and made equal to 1. Thus, the required answer = $304 - 1 = 303$.

4. (c) In order to think about this question, the best way is to use the process of slack thinking. In this question, we have 180 students counted 270 times. This means that there is an extra count of 90 students. In a three circle venn diagram, extra counting can occur only due to exactly two regions (where 1 individual student would be counted in two subjects leading to an extra count of 1) and the exactly three region (where 1 individual student would be counted in 3 subjects leading to an extra count of 2).
This can be visualised in the figure below:

A student placed in the all three area will be counted three times when you count the number of students studying French, the number of students studying German and the number of students studying Chinese independently. Hence, HE/SHE would be counted three times—leading to an extra count of 2 for each individual places here.
A person placed in any of the three 'Exactly two' areas would be counted two times when we count the number of students studying French, the number of students studying German and the number of students studying Chinese independently. Hence, HE/SHE would be counted two times—leading to an extra count of 1 for each individual placed in any of these three areas.
The thought chain leading to the solution would go as follows:
(i) 180 students are counted $80 + 90 + 100 = 270$ times.
(ii) This means that there is an extra count of 90 students.
(iii) Extra counts can fundamentally occur only from the 'exaclty two' areas or the all three area in the figure.
(iv) We also know that 'The number of students who study more than one of the three subjects is 50% more than the number of students who study all the three subjects' hence we know that if there are a total of 'n' students studying all three subjects, there would be $1.5n$ students studying more than one subject. This in turn means that there must be $0.5n$ students who study two subjects.
(Since, number of students studying more than 1 subject = number of students studying two subjects + number of students studying three subjects.
i.e. $1.5n = n +$ number of students studying 2 subjects $\rightarrow$ number of students studying 2 subjects = $1.5n - n = 0.5n$)
(v) The extra counts from the n students studying 3 subjects would amount to $n \times 2 = 2n$ – since each student is counted twice extra when he/she studies all three subjects.
(vi) The extra counts from the $0.5n$ students who study exactly two subjects would be equal to $0.5n \times 1 = 0.5\ n$.

(vii) Thus extra count = $90 = 2n + 0.5n \rightarrow n = 90/2.5 = 36$.

(viii) Hence, there must be 36 people studying all three subjects.

Solutions 5 and 6: The following would be the starting Venn diagram encapsulating the basic information:

HR (120)

From this figure we get the following equation:

$40x + (19 - x) + x + y = 120$. This gives us $40x + y = 101$

Thinking about this equation, we can see that the value of x can be either 1 or 2. In case we put x as 1, we get $y = 61$ and then we have to also meet the additional condition that $15-x$, $19-x$ and y should form an AP which is obviously not possible (since it is not possible practically to build an AP having two positive terms below 19 and the third term being 61. Hence, this option is rejected.

Moving forward, the other possible value of x from the equation is $x = 2$ in which case we get, $y = 21$ and $15 - x = 13$ and $19 - x = 17$. Thus, we get the AP 13, 17, 21 which satisfies the given conditions. Putting $x = 2$ and $y = 21$ in the figure, the venn diagram evolves to:

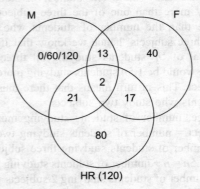

HR (120)

In this figure the value that only Marketing takes can either be 0, 60 or 120 (to satisfy the AP condition). However, since the total number of students in Marketing is a two digit number above 50, the number of people studying only marketing would be narrowed down to the only possibility which remains – viz 60.

Thus, the number of students studying in the batch = $120 + 40 + 60 + 13 + 4 = 237$.

The number of students specialising in both Marketing and HR is $21 + 2 = 23$

5. (d) The total number of students is either 113 or 128.

6. (c) The number of students studying both Marketing and HR is 23.

Solutions 7 to 9:

7 & 8: In order to think about the possibility of the maximum and/or the minimum number of people who could be studying none of the three languages, you need to first think of the basic information in the question. The basic information in the question can be encapsulated by the following Venn diagram:

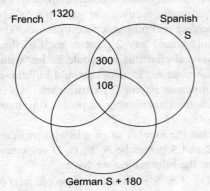

German S + 180

At this point we have the flexibility to try to put the remaining numbers into this Venn diagram while maintaining the constraints the question has placed on the relative numbers in the figure. In order to do this, we need to think of the objective with which we have to fill in the remaining numbers in the figure. At this stage you have to keep two constraints in mind while filling the remaining numbers:

(a) The remaining part of the French circle has to total $1320 - 408 = 912$;

(b) The German circle has to be 180 more than the Spanish circle.

When we try to fill in the figure for making the number of students who did not study any of the three subjects maximum:

You can think of first filling the French circle by trying to think of how you would want to distribute the remaining 912 in that circle. When we want to maximise the number of students who study none of the three, we would need to use the minimum number of people inside the three circles—while making sure that all the constraints are met.

Since we have to forcefully fit in 912 into the remaining areas of the French circle, we need to see whether while doing the same we can also meet the second constraint.

This thinking would lead you to see the following solution possibility:

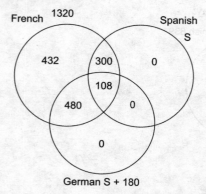

French 1320   Spanish
                       S
432   300   0
    108
480   0

0

German S + 180

In this case we have ensured that the German total is 180 more than the Spanish total (as required) and at the same time the French circle has also reached the desired 1320. Hence, the number of students who study none of the three can be 2116–1320 = 796 (at maximum).

When minimising the number of students who have studied none of the three subjects, the objective would be to use the maximum number of students who can be used in order to meet the basic constraints. The answer in this case can be taken to as low as zero in the following case:

French 1320   Spanish
                       S
912   300   316/2 = 158
    108
0

300+180+316/2
= 638

German S + 180

Note: While thinking about the numbers in this case, we first use the 912 in the 'only French' area. At this point we have 796 students left to be allocated. We first make the German circle 180 more than the Spanish circle (by taking the only German as 300 +180 to start with, this is accomplished). At this point, we are left with 316 more students, who can be allocated equally as 316 ÷ 2 for both the 'only German' and the 'only Spanish' areas.

Thus, the minimum number of students who study none of the three is 0.

Solution 9:
In order to think about this question, let us first see the situation we had in order to maintain all constraints.

If we try to fit in the remaining constraints in this situation we would get:

French 1320   Spanish
432   300
    108
480

German

This leaves us with a slack of 796 people which would need to be divided equally since we cannot disturb the equilibrium of German being exactly 180 more than Spanish.

This gives us the following figure:

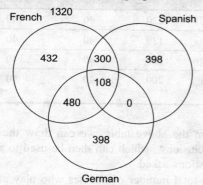

French 1320   Spanish
432   300   398
    108
480   0

398

German

When you think about this situation, you realise that it is quite possible to increase Spanish if we reduce the only French area and reallocate the reduction into the 'only French' and German area. A reduction of 10 from the 'only French' area can be visualised as follows:

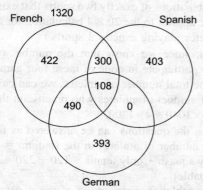

French 1320   Spanish
422   300   403
    108
490   0

393

German

In this case, as you can see from the figure above, the number of students who study only Spanish has gone up by 5 (which is half of 10).

Since, there is still some gap between the 'only German' and the 'only French' areas in the figure, we should close that gap by reducing the 'only French' area as much as possible.

The following solution figure would emerge when we think that way:

French 1320   Spanish 839

366   300   431

108

546   0

365

German 1019

Hence, the maximum possible for the only Spanish area is 431.

Solutions 10 to 13: The information given in the question can be encapsulated in the following way:

Game	Only that game	2 games combination 1	2 games combination 2	2 games combination 3	3 games combination 1	3 games combination 2	3 games combination 3	All 4 games
Tennis (460)	220	40	40	40	20	20	20	60
TT (360)	120	40	40	40	20	20	20	60
Squash (360)	120	40	40	40	20	20	20	60
Badminton (440)	200	40	40	40	20	20	20	60

From the above table, we can draw the following conclusions,, which can then be used to answer the questions asked.

The total number of athletes who play at least one of the four games = $220 + 120 + 120 + 200 + 40 \times 6 + 20 \times 4 + 60 = 1040$

(Note : that in doing this calculation, we have used 40×6 for calculating how many unique people would be playing exactly two games—where 40 for each combination is given and there are $^4C_2 = 6$ combinations of exactly two sports that exist. Similar logic applies to the 20×4 calculation for number of athletes playing exactly 3 sports.)

Also, since we know that the number of athletes who participate in none of these four games is 20% of the total number of athletes, we can calculate the total number of athletes who practise in the stadium as $5 \times 1040 \div 4 = 1300$.

Thus, the questions can be answered as follows:

10. The number of athletes in the stadium = 1300.
11. Only squash + only tennis = $120 + 220 = 340$ (from the table)
12. Only athletics means none of the 4 games = total number of athletes – number of athletes who play at least one game = $1300 - 1040 = 260$.

13. In case all the three game athletes would add one more game they would become 4 game athletes. Hence, the number of athletes who play all four games would be: Athletes playing 3 games earlier + athletes playing all 4 games earlier = $80 + 60 = 140$

Solutions 14 and 15: The starting figure based on the information given in the question would look something as below:

Blue eyes   Blonde hair 62

2x   z

a

x   y

2x

Sharp Minds

From this figure we see a few equations:
$x + y + z = 50$; $a + y + z = 26 \rightarrow x - 24 = a$.
Also, since $5x + 62 = 192$, we get the value of x as 26. The figure would evolve as follows.

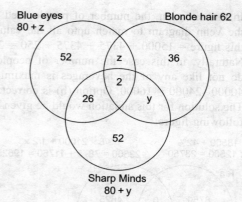

Blue eyes
80 + z

Blonde hair 62

52   z   36

2

26   y

52

Sharp Minds
80 + y

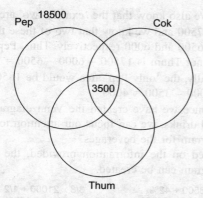

Pep 18500   Cok

3500

Thum

Based on this we can deduce the answer to the two questions as:

14. For the number of family members with blue eyes to be maximum, the family members with both sharp minds and blonde hair, but not blue eyes (represented by '*y*' in the figure), would be at maximum 11 because we would need to keep $z > y$. Hence, Option (a) is the correct answer.

15. If we are given the information in Option (c) we know the value of *y* would be 9 and hence, the value of *z* would be determined as 15. Hence, Option (c) provides us the information to determine the exact number of family members who have blonde hair and blue eyes but not sharp minds. Notice here that the information in each of the other options is already known to us.

16. Solve this again using slack thinking by using the following thought process:

97 students are counted 47 + 53 + 72 = 172 times—which means that there is an extra count of 75 students (172 – 97 = 75). Now, since there are 15 students who are playing all the three games, they would be counted 45 times—hence they take care of an extra count of 15 × 2 = 30. (**Note:** in a 3 circle venn diagram situation, any person placed in the all three areas is counted thrice—hence he/she is counted two extra times).

This leaves us with an extra count of 45 to be managed—and the only way to do so is to place people in the exactly two areas. A person placed in the 'exactly two games area' would be counted once extra. Hence, with each student who goes into the 'exactly two games' areas it would be counted once extra. Thus, to manage an extra count of 45, we need to put 45 people in the 'exactly two' area. Option (d) is correct.

Solutions 17 to 19: When you draw a Venn diagram for the three cold drinks, you realise as given here.

Once you fill in the basic information into the Venn diagram, you reach the following position:

At this point we know that since the 'all three area' is 3500, the value of the 'exactly two areas' would be 5 × 3500 = 17500. Also, we know that "11000 like Pep and exactly one more cold drink" which means that the area for Cok and Thum but not Pep is equal to 17500 – 11000 = 6500. Further, when you start adding the information: "6000 like only Cok and the same number of people like Pep and Thum but not Cok," the Venn Diagram transforms to the following:

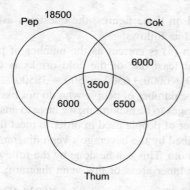

Pep 18500   Cok

6000

3500

6000   6500

Thum

Filling in the remaining gaps in the picture we get:

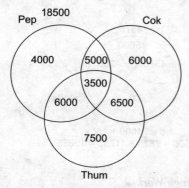

Pep 18500   Cok

4000   5000   6000

3500

6000   6500

7500

Thum

Note, we have used the following info here:
Thum but not Pep is 14000 and since we already know that Thum and Cok but not Pep is 6500, the value of 'only Thum' would be 14000 – 6500 = 7500.

We also know that the 'exactly two' areas add up to 17500 and we know that two of these three areas are 6500 and 6000 respectively. Thus, Pep and Cok but not Thum is 17500 – 6000 – 6500 = 5000. Finally, the 'only Pep' area would be 18500 – 5000 – 6000 – 3500 = 4000.

Once we have created the Venn diagram for the cold drinks, we can focus our attention to the Venn diagram for the beverages.

Based on the information provided, the following diagram can be created.

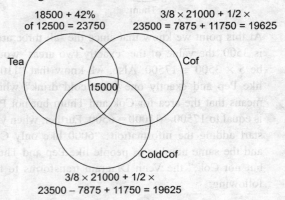

18500 + 42% of 12500 = 23750

3/8 × 21000 + 1/2 × 23500 = 7875 + 11750 = 19625

3/8 × 21000 + 1/2 × 23500 – 7875 + 11750 = 19625

Based on these figures, the questions asked can be solved as follows:

17. Option (a) is correct as the number of people who like at least one of the cold drinks is the sum of 18500 + 6000 + 6500 + 7500 = 38500.

18. For the number of people who do not like any of the beverages to be maximum, we have to ensure that the number of people used in order to meet the situation described by the beverage's venn diagram should be minimum. This can be done by the following values in the inner areas of this venn diagram:

18500 + 42% of 12500 = 23750

3/8 × 21000 + 1/2 × 23500 = 7875 + 11750 = 19625

3/8 × 21000 + 1/2 × 23500 = 7875 + 11750 = 19625

In this situation, the number of people used inside the Venn diagram to match upto all the values for this figure = 15000 + 4375 + 4375 + 250 = 24000. Naturally, in this case the number of people who do not like any of the beverages is maximised at 40000 – 24000 = 16000. Option (b) is correct.

19. The solution for this situation would be given by the following figure:

18500 + 42% of 12500 = 23750

3/8 × 21000 + 1/2 × 23500 = 7875 + 11750 = 19625

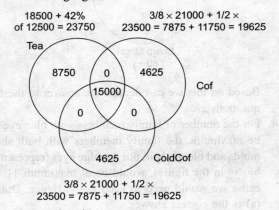

3/8 × 21000 + 1/2 × 23500 = 7875 + 11750 = 19625

The number of people who like at least one of the three beverages is:

15000 + 8750 + 4625 + 4625 = 33000. Option (c) is correct.

20. The number of people cannot be a fraction in any situation. We can deduce that the values of x and $3x$ have to be factors of 57. This gives us that the values of x can only be either 1 or 19 (for both x and $3x$ to be a factor of 57).

So, the number of people who drink tea is equal to $2x + 57/x$ which can be 59 (if $x = 1$) or 41 (if $x = 19$).

Hence, Option (d) is correct.

TRAINING GROUND FOR BLOCK VI

HOW TO THINK IN PROBLEMS ON BLOCK VI

1. The probability that a randomly chosen positive divisor of 10^{29} is an integer multiple of 10^{23} is : $a2/b2$, then '$b - a$' would be: **(XAT 2014)**
   - (a) 8
   - (b) 15
   - (c) 21
   - (d) 23
   - (e) 45

Solution: This question appeared in the XAT 2014 exam. The number $10^{29} = 2^{29} \times 5^{29}$.

Factors or divisors of such a number would be of the form: $2^a \times 5^b$ where the values of a and b can be represented as $0 \leq a, b \leq 29$, i.e., there are $30 \times 30 = 900$ possibilities when we talk about randomly selecting a positive divisor of 10^{29}.

Next, we need to think of numbers which are integral multiples of 10^{23}. Such numbers would be of the form $2^x \times 5^y$ such that $x, y \geq 23$.

Hence, the number of values possible when the chosen divisor would also be an integer multiple of 10^{23} would be when $23 \leq x, y \leq 29$. There would be $7 \times 7 = 49$ such combinations.

Thus, the required probability is $49 \div 900$. In the context of $a^2 \div b^2$, the values of a and b would come out as 7 and 30 respectively. The required difference between a and b is 23. Hence, Option (d) is correct.

2. Aditya has a total of 18 red and blue marbles in two bags (each bag has marbles of both colors). A marble is randomly drawn from the first bag followed by another randomly drawn from the second bag, the probability of both being red is 5/16. What is the probability of both marbles being blue? **(XAT 2014)**
   - (a) 1/16
   - (b) 2/16
   - (c) 3/16
   - (d) 4/16
   - (e) None of the above

Solution: This problem has again appeared in XAT 2014. The problem most students face in such situations is to understand how to place how many balls of each colour in each bag. Since there is no directive given in the question that tells us how many balls are there and/or how many balls are placed in any bag the next thing that a mathematically oriented mind would do would be to try to assume some variables to represent the number of balls in each bag. However, if you try to do so on your own you would realise that that would be the wrong way to solve this quesiton as it would lead to extreme complexity while solving the problem. So how can we think alternately? Is there a smarter way to think about this question?

Yes indeed there is. Let me explain it to you here. In order to think about this problem, you would need to first think about how a fraction like 5/16 would emerge. The value of $5/16 = 10/32 = 15/48 = 20/64 = 25/80 = 30/96$ and so on. Next, you need to understand that there are a total of 18 balls and this 18 has to be broken into two parts such that their product is one of the above denominators. Scanning the denominators we see the opportunity that the number $80 = 10 \times 8$ and hence we realise that the probability of both balls being red would happen in a situation where the structure of the calculation would look something like: $(r_1/10) \times (r_2/8)$. Next, to get 25 as the corresponding numerator with 80 as the denominator the values of r_1 and r_2 should both be 5. This means that there are 5 red balls out of ten in the first bag and 5 red balls out of 8 in the second bag. This further means that the number of blue balls would be 5 out of 8 and 3 out of 8. Thus, the correct answer would be: $(5/10) \times (3/8) = 25/80 = 5/16$. Hence, Option (c) is the correct answer.

3. The scheduling officer for a local police department is trying to schedule additional patrol units in each of two neighbourhoods – southern and northern. She knows that on any given day, the probabilities of major crimes and minor crimes being committed in the northern neighbourhood were 0.418 and 0.612, respectively, and that the corresponding probabilities in the southern neighbourhood were 0.355 and 0.520. Assuming that all crimes occur independent of each other and likewise that crime in the two neighbourhoods are independent of each other, what is the probability that no crime of either type is committed in either neighbourhood on any given day? **(XAT 2011)**
   - (a) 0.069
   - (b) 0.225
   - (c) 0.690
   - (d) 0.775
   - (e) None of the above

Solution: This question appeared in XAT 2011, and the key to solving this correctly is to look at the event definition. A major crime not occurring in the northern neighbourhood is the non-event for a major crime occurring in the nothern neighbourhood on any given day. Its probability would be $(1-0.418) = 0.582$.

The values of minor crime not occurring in the northern neighbourhood and a major crime not occurring in the southern neighbourhood and a minor crime not occurring in the northern neighbourhood would be $(1-0.612)$; $(1-0.355)$ and $(1-0.520)$ respectively. The value of the required probability would be the probability of the event:

Major crime does not occur in the northern neighbourhood and minor crime does not occur in the northern neighbourhood and major crime does not occur in the southern neighbourhood and minor crime does not occur in the northern neighbourhood =

$(1-0.418) \times (1-0.612) \times (1-0.355) \times (1-0.520)$. Option (a) is the closest answer.

4. There are four machines in a factory. At exactly 8 pm, when the mechanic is about to leave the factory, he is informed that two of the four machines are not working properly. The mechanic is in a hurry, and decides that he will identify the two faulty machines before going home, and repair them next morning. It takes him twenty minutes to walk to the bus stop. The last bus leaves at 8 :32 pm. If it takes six minutes to identify whether a machine is defective or not, and if he decides to check the machines at random, what is the probability that the mechanic will be able to catch the last bus?

(a) 0   (b) 1/6
(c) 1/4   (d) 1/3
(e) 1

Solution: The first thing you look for in this question, is that obviously the mechanic has only 12 minutes to check the machines before he leaves to catch the bus. In 12 minutes, he can at best check two machines. He will be able to identify the two faulty machines under the following cases:

(The first machine checked is faulty AND the second machine checked is also faulty) OR (The first machine checked is working fine AND the second machine checked is also working fine)

Required probability = $\frac{2}{4} \times \frac{1}{3} + \frac{2}{4} \times \frac{1}{3} = \frac{1}{3}$

5. Little Pika who is five and half years old has just learnt addition. However, he does not know how to carry. For example, he can add 14 and 5, but he does not know how to add 14 and 7. How many pairs of consecutive integers between 1000 and 2000 (both 1000 and 2000 included) can Little Pika add?

(a) 150   (b) 155
(c) 156   (d) 258
(e) None of the above

Solution: This question again appeared in the XAT 2011 exam. If you try to observe the situations under which the addition of two consecutive four-digit numbers between 1000 and 2000 would come through without having a carry over value in the answer you would be able to identify the following situations – each of which differs from the other due to the way it is structured with respect to the values of the individual digits:

Category 1: 1000 + 1001; 1004 +1005, 1104 + 1105 and so on. A little bit of introspection should show you that in this case, the two numbers are 1abc and 1abd where $d = c + 1$. Also, for the sum to come out without any carry-overs, the values of a, b and c should be between 0 and 4 (including both). Thus, each of a, b and c gives us 5 values each – giving us a total of $5 \times 5 \times 5 = 125$ **such situations.**

Category 2: 1009 + 1010; 1019 + 1020; 1029 + 1030; 1409 + 1410. The general form of the first number here would be 1ab9 with the values of a and b being between 0 and 4 (including both). Thus, each of a, b and c gives us 5 values each – giving us a total of $5 \times 5 = 25$ **such situations.**

Category 3: 1099 + 1100; 1199 + 1200; 1299 + 1300; 1399 + 1400 and 1499 + 1500. There are only **5 such pairs.** Note that 1599 + 1600 would not work in this case as the addition of the hundreds' digit would become more than 10 and lead to a carry-over.

Category 4: 1999 + 2000 is the only other situation where the addition would not lead to a carry-over calculation. Hence, **1 more situation.**

The required answer = 125 + 25 + 5 + 1 = 156. Option (c) is the correct answer.

6. In the country of Twenty, there are exactly twenty cities, and there is exactly one direct road between any two cities. No two direct roads have an overlapping road segment. After the election dates are announced, candidates from their respective cities start visiting the other cities. The following are the rules that the election commission has laid down for the candidates:

- Each candidate must visit each of the other cities exactly once.
- Each candidate must use only the direct roads between two cities for going from one city to another.
- The candidate must return to his own city at the end of the campaign.
- No direct road between two cities would be used by more than one candidate.

The maximum possible number of candidates is
(a) 5   (b) 6
(c) 7   (d) 8
(e) 9

Solution: Again an XAT 2011 question. Although this question carried a very high weightage (it had 5 marks where 'normal questions' had 1 to 3 marks) it is not so difficult once you understand the logic of the question. The key to understanding this question is from two points.

(a) Since there is exactly one direct road between any pair of two cities – there would be a toal of $20C_2$ roads = 190 roads.

(b) The other key condition in this question is the one which talks about each candidate must visit each of the other cities exactly once and 'No direct road between two cities would be used by more than one candidate.' This means two things. i) Since each candidate visits each city exactly once, if there are 'c' candidates, there would be a total of 20c roads used and since no road is repeated it means that the 20 roads Candidate A uses will be different from the 20 roads Candidate B uses and so on. Thus, the value of $20c \leq$ 190 should be an inequality that must be satisfied. This gives us a maximum possible value of c as 9. Hence, Option (e) is correct.

7. In a bank the account numbers are all 8 digit numbers, and they all start with the digit 2. So, an account number can be represented as $2x_1x_2x_3x_4x_5x_6x_7$. An

account number is considered to be a 'magic' number if $x_1x_2x_3$ is exactly the same as $x_4x_5x_6$ or $x_5x_6x_7$ or both, x_i can take values from 0 to 9, but 2 followed by seven 0s is not a valid account number. What is the maximum possible number of customers having a 'magic' account number?

(a) 9989   (b) 19980
(c) 19989   (d) 19999
(e) 19990

Solution: This question appeared in XAT 2011. In order to solve this question, we need to think of the kinds of numbers which would qualify as magic numbers. Given the definition of a magic number in the question, a number of form 2mnpmnpq would be a magic number while at the same time a number of the form 2mnpqmnp would also qualify as a magic number. In this situation, each of m,n and p can take any of the ten digit values from 0 to 9. Also, q would also have ten different possibilities from 0 to 9. Thus, the total number of numbers of the form 2mnpmnpq would be $10^4 = 10000$. Similarly, the total number of numbers of the form 2mnpqmnp would also be $10^4 = 10000$. This gives us a total of 20000 numbers. However, in this count the numbers like 21111111, 22222222, 23333333, 24444444 etc have been counted under both the categories. Hence we need to remove these numbers once each (a total of 9 reductions). Also, the number 20000000 is not a valid number according to the question. This number needs to be removed from both the counts.

Hence, the final answer = $20000 - 9 - 2 = 19989$.

8. If all letters of the word "CHCJL" be arranged in an English dictionary, what will be the 50th word?

(a) HCCLJ   (b) LCCHJ
(c) LCCJH   (d) JHCLC
(e) None of the above

Solution: A Xat 2010 question. In the English dictionary the ordering of the words would be in alphabetical order. Thus, words starting with C would be followed by words starting with H, followed by words starting with J and finally words starting with L. Words starting with C = 4! = 24; Words starting with H = 4! ÷ 2! = 12 words. Words starting with J = 4! ÷ 2! = 12 words. This gives us a total of 48 words. The 49th and the 50th words would start with L. The 49th word would be the first word starting with L (=LCCHJ) and the 50th word would be the 2nd word starting with L – which would be LCCJH. Option (c) is correct.

9. The supervisor of a packaging unit of a milk plant is being pressurised to finish the job closer to the distribution time, thus giving the production staff more leeway to cater to last minute demand. He has the option of running the unit at normal speed or at 110% of normal – "fast speed". He estimates that he will be able to run at the higher speed 60% of time. The packet is twice as likely to be damaged at the higher speed which would mean temporarily stop-

ping the process. If a packet on a randomly selected packaging runs has probability of 0.112 of damage, what is the probability that the packet will not be damaged at normal speed?

(a) 0.81   (b) 0.93
(c) 0.75   (d) 0.60
(e) None of the above

Solution: Again a XAT 2013 question. Let the probability of the package being damaged at normal speed be 'p'. This means that the probability of the damage of a package when the unit is running at a fast speed is '$2p$'. Since, he is under pressure to complete the production quickly, we would need to assume that he runs the unit at fast speed for the maximum possible time (60% of the time).

Then, we have

Probability of damaged packet in all packaging runs
$= 0.6 \times 2p + 0.4 \times p = 0.112$.
$\Rightarrow p = 0.07$

Probability of non damaged packets at normal speed
$= 1 - p = 1 - 0.07 = 0.93$. Option (b) is correct.

10. Let X be a four-digit positive integer such that the unit digit of X is prime and the product of all digits of X is also prime. How many such integers are possible?

(a) 4   (b) 8
(b) 12   (d) 24
(e) None of these

Solution: This one is an easy question as all you need to do is understand that given the unit digit is a prime number, it would mean that the number can only be of the form $abc2$; $abc3$ or $abc5$ or $abc7$. Further, for each of these, the product of the four digits $a \times b \times c \times$ units digit has to be prime. This can occur only if $a = b = c = 1$. Thus, there are only 4 such numbers viz: 1112, 1113, 1115 and 1117. Hence, Option (a) is correct.

11. The chance of India winning a cricket match against Australia is 1/6. What is the minimum number of matches India should play against Australia so that there is a fair chance of winning at least one match?

(a) 3   (b) 4
(c) 5   (d) 6
(e) None of the above

Solution: This is another question from the XAT 2009 test paper. A fair chance is defined when the probability of an event goes to above 0.5. If India plays 3 matches, the probability of at least one win will be given by the non-event of losing all matches. This would be:
$1 - (5/6)^3 = 1 - 125/216 = 91/216$ which is less than 0.5. Hence, Option (a) is rejected.

For four matches, the probability of winning at least 1 match would be:
$1 - (5/6)^4 = 1 - 625/1296 = 671/216$ which is more than 0.5. Hence, Option (b) is correct.

12. Two teams *Arrogant* and *Overconfident* are participating in a cricket tournament. The odds that team *Arrogant* will be champion is 5 to 3, and the odds that team *Overconfident* will be the champion is 1 to 4. What are the odds that either *Arrogant* or team *Overconfident* will become the champion?
(a) 3 to 2   (b) 5 to 2
(c) 6 to 1   (d) 7 to 1
(e) 33 to 7

Solution: You need to be clear about what odds for an event mean in order to solve this. Odds for team *Arrogant* to be champion being 5 to 3 means that the probability of team *Arrogant* being champion is 5/8. Similarly, the probability of team *Overconfident* being champion is 1/5 (based on odds of team *Overconfident* being champion being 1 to 4). Thus, the probability that either of the teams would be the champion would be

$$= \frac{5}{8} + \frac{1}{5} = \frac{33}{40}$$

This means that in 40 times, 33 times the event of one of the teams being champion would occur. Hence, the odds for one of the two given teams to be the chamion would be 33 to 7.

So required odds will be 33 to 7. Option (e) is correct.

13. Let X be a four-digit number with exactly three consecutive digits being same and is a multiple of 9. How many such X's are possible?
(a) 12   (b) 16
(c) 19   (d) 21
(e) None of the above

Solution: Since the number has to be a multiple of 9, the sum of the digits would be either 9 or 18 or 27. Also, the number would either be in the form aaab or baaa. For the sum of the digits to be 9, we would have the following cases:

$a = 1$ and $b = 6$ for the numbers 1116 and 6111;

$a = 2$ and $b = 3$ for the numbers 2223 and 3222;

$a = 3$ and $b = 0$ for the number 3330 and

$b = 9$ and $a = 0$ for the number 9000. We get a total of 6 such numbers.

Similarly for the sum of the digits to be 18 we will get: 3339, 9333; 4446, 6444; 5553, 3555; 6660. We get a total of 7 such numbers.

For the sum of the digits to be 27 we will get the numbers: 6669, 9666; 7776, 6777; 8883, 3888 and 9990. Thus, we get a total of 7 such numbers. Hence, the total number of numbers is 20. Option (e) is correct.

14. A shop sells two kinds of rolls—egg roll and mutton roll. Onion, tomato, carrot, chilli sauce and tomato sauce are the additional ingredients. You can have any combination of additional ingredients, or have standard rolls without any additional ingredients subject to the following constraints:

(a) You can have tomato sauce if you have an egg roll, but not if you have a mutton roll.
(b) If you have onion or tomato or both you can have chilli sauce, but not otherwise.

How many different rolls can be ordered according to these rules?
(a) 21   (b) 33
(c) 40   (d) 42
(e) None of the above.

Solution: Let the 5 additional ingredients onion, tomato, carrot, chilli sauce and tomato sauce are denoted by O, T, C, CS, TS respectively.

Number of ways of ordering the egg roll:

For the egg roll there are a total of 32 possibilities (with each ingredient being either present or not present – there being 5 ingredients the total number of possibilities of the combinations of the egg rolls would be equal to $2 \times 2 \times 2 \times 2 \times 2 = 32$ ways).

However, out of these 32 instances, the following combinations are not possible due to the constraint given in Statement (b) which tells us that to have CS in the roll either of onion or tomato must be present (or both should be present). The combinations which are not possible are:

(CS) (CS, TS) (CS, C) (CS, C, TS)

Total number of ways egg roll can be ordered
= 32 – 4 = 28.

Number of ways of ordering the mutton roll:

Total number of cases for mutton roll without any constraints = $2 \times 2 \times 2 \times 2 = 16$ ways. Cases rejected due to constraint given in statement (b): (CS); (CS,C) → 16 – 2 = 14 cases.

Total number of ways or ordering a roll = 28 + 14 = 42. Option (d) is correct.

15. Steel Express stops at six stations between Howrah and Jamshedpur. Five passengers board at Howrah. Each passenger can get down at any station till Jamshedpur. The probability that all five persons will get down at different stations is:

(a) $\dfrac{^6P_5}{6^5}$ (b) $\dfrac{^6C_5}{6^5}$

(c) $\dfrac{^7P_5}{7^5}$ (d) $\dfrac{^6C_5}{7^5}$

(e) None of the above.

Solution: The required probability would be given by:

$$\frac{\left(\begin{array}{c}\text{Total number of ways in which 5 people can get down} \\ \text{at 5 different stations from amongst 7 stations}\end{array}\right)}{\left(\begin{array}{c}\text{Total number of ways in which 5 people can get down} \\ \text{at 7 stations}\end{array}\right)}$$

The value of the numerator would be $^7P_5$, while the value of the denominator would be 7^5. The correct answer would be Option (c).

16. In how many ways can 53 identical chocolates be distributed amongst 3 children– C_1, C_2 and C_3 – such that C_1 gets more chocolates than C_2 and C_2 gets more chocolates than C_3?

(a) 468
(b) 344
(c) 1404
(d) 234

Solution: 53 identical chocolates can be distributed amongst 3 children in $^{55}C_2$ ways =1485 ways ($^{n+r-1}C_{r-1}$ formula). Out of these ways of distributing 53 chocolates, the following distributions methods are not possible as they would have two values equal to each other– (0, 0, 53); (1, 1, 51); (2, 2, 49)….(26, 26, 1).

There are 27 such distributions, but when allocated to C_1, C_2 and C_3 respectively, each of these distributions can be allocated in 3 ways amongst them. Thus, C_1= 0, C_2 = 0 and C_3= 53 is counted differently from C_1 = 0, C_2 = 53 and C_3 = 0 and also from C_1 = 53, C_2 = 0 and C_3 = 0. This will remove $27 \times 3 = 81$ distributions from 1485, leaving us with 1404 distributions. These 1404 distributions are those where all three numbers are different from each other. However, whenever we have three different values allocated to three children, there can be 3! = 6 ways of allocating the three different values amongst the three people. For instance, the distribution of 10, 15 and 48 can be seen as follows:

C_1	C_2	C_3	
48	15	10	Only case which meets the problems' requirement.
48	10	15	
15	48	10	
15	10	48	
10	15	48	
10	48	15	

Hence, out of every six distributions counted in the 1404 distributions we currently have, we need to count only one. The answer can be arrived at by dividing $1404 \div 6 = 234$. Option (d) is correct.

17. In a chess tournament at the ancient Olympic Games of Reposia, it was found that the number of European participants was twice the number of non-European participants. In a round robin format, each player played every other player exactly once. The tournament rules were such that no match ended in a draw – any conventional draws in chess were resolved in favour of the player who had used up the lower time. While analysing the results of the tournament, K.Gopal the tournament referee observed that the number of matches won by the non-European players was equal to the number of matches won by the European players. Which of the following can be the total number of matches in which a European player defeated a non-European player?

(a) 57
(b) 58
(c) 59
(d) 60

Solution: If we assume the number of non-European players to be n, the number of European players would be 2n. Then there would be three kinds of matches played –

Matches between two Europan players – a total of $^{2n}C_2$ matches – which would yield a European winner.

Matches between two non-European players – a total of $^nC_2$ matches, – which would yield a non-European winner.

Matches, between a European and a non-European player = $2n^2$. These matches would have some European wins and some non-European wins. Let the number of European wins amongst these matches be x, then the number of non-European wins = $2n^2 - x$.

Now, the problem clearly states that the number of European wins = Number of non-European wins

$$\Rightarrow \frac{2n(2n-1)}{2} + x = \frac{n(n-1)}{2} + 2n^2 - x$$
$$\Rightarrow n(n+1) = 4x$$

This means that the value of 4 times the number of wins for a European player over a non-European player should be a product of two consecutive natural numbers (since n has to be a natural number).

Among the options, $n = 60$ is the only possible value as the value of $4 \times 60 = 15 \times 16$.

Hence, Option (d) is correct.

18. A man, starting from a point M in a park, takes exactly eight equal steps. Each step is in one of the four directions – East, West, North and South. What is the total number of ways in which the man ends up at point M after the eight steps?

(a) 4200
(b) 2520
(c) 4900
(d) 5120

Solution: For the man to reach back to his original point, the number of steps North should be equal to the number of steps South. Similarly, the number of steps East should be equal to the number of steps West.

The following cases would exist:

4 steps north and 4 steps south = $8!/(4! \times 4!) = 70$ ways;

3 steps north, 3 steps south, 1 step east and 1 step west = $8!/(3! \times 3!) = 1120$ ways;

2 steps north, 2 steps south, 2 steps east and 2 steps west = $8!/(2! \times 2! \times 2! \times 2!) = 2520$ ways;

1 step north, 1 step south, 3 steps east and 3 steps west = $8!/(3! \times 3!) = 1120$ ways;

4 Steps east and 4 steps west = $8!/(4! \times 4!) = 70$ ways;

Thus, the total number of ways = $70 \times 2 + 1120 \times 2 + 2520 = 140 + 2240 + 2520 = 4900$ ways.

Option (c) is correct.

🎯 BLOCK REVIEW TESTS

REVIEW TEST 1

1. 18 guests have to be seated, half on each side of a long table. 4 particular guests desire to sit on one particular side and 3 others on the other side. Determine the number of ways in which the sitting arrangements can be made
   (a) $^{11}P_n \times (9!)^2$
   (b) $^{11}C_5 \times (9!)^2$
   (c) $^{11}P_6 \times (9!)^2$
   (d) None of these

2. If m parallel lines in a plane are intersected by a family of n parallel lines, find the number of parallelograms that can be formed.
   (a) $m^2 \times n^2$
   (b) $m^{(m+1)} n^{(n+1)}/4$
   (c) $^mC_2 \times {}^nC_2$
   (d) None of these

3. A father with eight children takes three at a time to the zoological garden, as often as he can without taking the same three children together more than once. How often will he go and how often will each child go?
   (a) $^8C_3, {}^7C_3$
   (b) $^8C_3, {}^7C_2$
   (c) $^8P_3, {}^7C_3$
   (d) $^8P_3, {}^7C_2$

4. A candidate is required to answer 7 questions out of 2 questions which are divided into two groups, each containing 6 questions. He is not permitted to attempt more than 5 questions from either group. In how many different ways can he choose the 7 questions?
   (a) 390
   (b) 520
   (c) 780
   (d) None of these

5. Find the sum of all 5 digit numbers formed by the digits 1, 3, 5, 7, 9 when no digit is being repeated.
   (a) 4444400
   (b) 8888800
   (c) 13333200
   (d) 6666600

6. Consider a polygon of n sides. Find the number of triangles, none of whose sides is the side of the polygon.
   (a) $nC_3 - 2n - n \times (n-4)C_1$
   (b) $n(n-4)(n-5)/3$
   (c) $n(n-4)(n-5)/6$
   (d) $n(n-11(n-2)/3$

7. The number of 4 digit numbers that can be formed using the digits 0, 2, 3, 5 without repetition is
   (a) 18
   (b) 20
   (c) 24
   (d) 20

8. Find the total number of words that can be made by using all the letters from the word MACHINE, using them only once.
   (a) 7!
   (b) 5020
   (c) 6040
   (d) 7!/2

9. What is the total number of words that can be made by using all the letters of the word REKHA, using each letter only once?
   (a) 240
   (b) 4!
   (c) 124
   (d) 5!

10. How many different 5-digit numbers can be made from the first 5 natural numbers, using each digit only once?
    (a) 240
    (b) 4!
    (c) 124
    (d) 5!

11. There are 7 seats in a row. Three persons take seats at random. What is the probability that the middle seat is always occupied and no two persons are sitting on consecutive seats?
    (a) 7/70
    (b) 14/35
    (c) 8/70
    (d) 4/35

12. Let $N = 33^x$. where x is any natural no. What is the probability that the unit digit of N is 3?
    (a) 1/4
    (b) 1/3
    (c) 1/5
    (d) 1/2

13. Find the probability of drawing one ace in a single draw of one card out of 52 cards.
    (a) $1/(52 \times 4)$
    (b) 1/4
    (c) 1/52
    (d) 1/13

14. In how many ways can a committee of 4 persons be made from a group of 10 people?
    (a) 10! / 4!
    (b) 210
    (c) 10! / 6!
    (d) None of these

15. In Question 14, what is the number of ways of forming the committee, if a particular member must be there in the committee?
    (a) 12
    (b) 84
    (c) 9!/ 3!
    (d) None of these

16. A polygon has 54 diagonals. The numbers of sides of this polygon are
    (a) 12
    (b) 84
    (c) 3. 3!
    (d) 4. 4!

17. An anti-aircraft gun can take a maximum of 4 shots at an enemy plane moving away from it, the probabilities of hitting the plane at first, second, third and fourth shots are 0.4, 0.3, 0.2 and 0.1 respectively. What is the probability that the gun hits the plane?
    (a) 0.7654
    (b) 0.6976
    (c) 0.3024
    (d) 0.2346

18. 7 white balls and 3 black balls are placed in a row at random. Find the probability that no two black balls are adjacent.
    (a) 2/15
    (b) 7/15
    (c) 8/15
    (d) 4/15

19. The probability that A can solve a problem is 3/10 and that B can solve is 5/7. If both of them attempt to solve the problem, what is the probability that the problem can be solved?
    - (a) 3/5
    - (b) 1/4
    - (c) 2/3
    - (d) 4/5

20. The sides *AB*, *BC*, *CA* of a triangle *ABC* have 3, 4 and 5 interior points respectively on them. Find the number of triangles that can be constructed using these points as vertices.
    - (a) 180
    - (b) 105
    - (c) 205
    - (d) 280

21. From 6 gentlemen and 4 ladies, a committee of 5 is to be formed. In how many ways can this be done if there is no restriction in its formation?
    - (a) 256
    - (b) 246
    - (c) 252
    - (d) 260

22. From 4 officers and 8 jawans in how many ways can 6 be chosen to include exactly one officer?

23. From 4 officers and 8 jawans in how many ways can 6 be chosen to include atleast one officer?
    - (a) ${}^{12}C_6$
    - (b) 1296
    - (c) 1344
    - (d) 224

24. From 4 officers and 8 jawans in how many ways can 6 be chosen to include atleast one officer?
    - (a) 868
    - (b) 924
    - (c) 896
    - (d) none of these

24. Two cards are drawn one after another from a pack of 52 ordinary cards. Find the probability that the first card is an ace and the second drawn is an honour card if the first card is not replaced while drawing the second.
    - (a) 12/13
    - (b) 12/51
    - (c) 1/663
    - (d) None of these

25. The probability that Andrews will be alive 15 years from now is 7/15 and that Bill will be alive 15 years from now is 7/10. What is the probability that both Andrews and Bill will be dead 15 years from now?
    - (a) 12/150
    - (b) 24/150
    - (c) 49/150
    - (d) 74/150

Space for Rough Work

REVIEW TEST 2

1. A group consists of 100 people; 25 of them are women and 75 men; 20 of them are rich and the remaining poor; 40 of them are employed. The probability of selecting an employed rich woman is:
   (a) 0.05   (b) 0.04
   (c) 0.02   (d) 0.08

2. Out of 13 job applicants, there are 5 boys and 8 men. It is desired to choose 2 applicants for the job. The probability that at least one of the selected applicant will be a boy is:
   (a) 5/13   (b) 14/39
   (c) 25/39   (d) 10/13

3. Fours dogs and three pups stand in a queue. The probability that they will stand in alternate positions is:
   (a) 1/34   (b) 1/35
   (c) 1/17   (d) 1/68

4. Asha and Vinay play a number game where each is asked to select a number from 1 to 5. If the two numbers match, both of them win a prize. The probability that they will not win a prize in a single trial is:
   (a) 1/25   (b) 24/25
   (c) 2/25   (d) None of these

5. The number of ways in which 6 British and 5 French can dine at a round table if no two French are to sit together is given by:
   (a) $6! \times 5!$ (b) $5! \times 4!$
   (c) 30   (d) $7! \times 5!$

6. A cricket team of 11 players is to be formed from 20 players including 6 bowlers and 3 wicketkeepers. Find the number of ways in which a team can be formed having exactly 4 bowlers and 2 wicketkeepers:
   (a) 20790   (b) 6930
   (c) 10790   (d) 360

7. Three boys and three girls are to be seated around a circular table. Among them one particular boy Rohit does not want any girl neighbour and one particular girl Shaivya does not want any boy neighbour. How many such arrangements are possible?
   (a) 5   (b) 6
   (c) 4   (d) 2

8. Words with five letters are formed from ten different letters of an alphabet. Then the number of words which have at least one letter repeated is
   (a) 19670   (b) 39758
   (c) 69760   (d) 99748

9. Sunil and Kapil toss a coin alternatively till one of them gets a head and wins the game. If Sunil starts the game, the probability that he (Sunil) will win is:

10. The number of pallelograms that can be formed if 7 parallel horizontal lines intersect 6 parallel vertical lines, is:
    (a) 42   (b) 294
    (c) 315   (d) None of these

11. $1.3.5...(2n-1)/2.4.6...(2n)$ is equal to:
    (a) $(2n)! \div 2^n(n!))^2$ (b) $(2n)! \div n!$
    (c) $(2n-1) \div) n-1)!$ (d) 2^n

12. How many four-digit numbers, each divisible by 4 can be formed using the digits 1, 2, 3, 4 and 5 (repetitions allowed)?
    (a) 100   (b) 150
    (c) 125   (d) 75

13. A student is to answer 10 out of 13 questions in a test such that he/she must choose at least 4 from the first five questions. The number of choices available to him is:
    (a) 140   (b) 280
    (c) 196   (d) 346

14. The number of ways in which a committee of 3 ladies and 4 gentlemen can be appointed from a meeting consisting of 8 ladies and 7 gentlemen, if Mrs. Pushkar refuses to serve in a committee if Mr.Modi is its member, is
    (a) 1960   (b) 3240
    (c) 1540   (d) None of these

15. A room has 3 lamps. From a collection of 10 light bulbs of which 6 are not good, a person selects 3 at random and puts them in a socket. The probability that he will have light, is:
    (a) 5/6   (b) 1/2
    (c) 1/6   (d) None of these

16. Two different series of a question booklet for an aptitude test are to be given to twelve students. In how many ways can the students be placed in two rows of six each so that there should be no identical series side by side and that the students sitting one behind the other should have the same series?
    (a) $2 \times {}^{12}C_6 \times (6!)^2$ (b) $6! \times 6!$
    (c) $7! \times 7 \times$ (d) None of these

17. The letters of the word PROMISE are arranged so that no two of the vowels should come together. The total number of arrangements is:
    (a) 49   (b) 1440
    (c) 7   (d) 1898

18. Find the remainder left after dividing 1! + 2! + 3! + ... + 1000! by 7.
    (a) 0   (b) 5
    (c) 21   (d) 14

19. In the McGraw-Hill Mindworkzz mock test paper, there are two sections, each containing 4 questions. A candidate is required to attempt 5 questions but

not more than 3 questions from any section. In how many ways can 5 questions be selected?

(a) 24   (b) 48
(c) 72   (d) 96

20. A bag contains 10 balls out of which 3 are pink and rest are orange. In how many ways can a random

sample of 6 balls be drawn from the bag so that at the most 2 pink balls are included in the sample and no sample has all the 6 balls of the same colour?

(a) 105   (b) 168
(c) 189   (d) 120

Space for Rough Work

REVIEW TEST 3

1. There is one grandfather, 5 sons and daughters and 8 grandchildren in a family. They are to be seated in a row for dinner. The grandchildren wish to occupy the 4 seats at each end and the grandfather refuses to have a grandchild on either side of him. Find the number of ways in which the family can be made to sit :
   (a) 11360
   (b) 11520
   (c) 21530
   (d) None of these

2. A bag of 200 electric switches contains 16 defective switches. One switch is taken out at random from the bag. Find the probability that the switch drawn is (i) defective (ii) non-defective?
   (a) (i) 2/25   (ii) 23/25
   (b) (i) 4/25   (ii) 21/25
   (c) (i) 3/25   (ii) 22/25
   (d) (i) 1/25   (ii) 20/25

3. In a group photograph at the Patna Women's College, all the seven teachers should sit in the first row and all the twenty students should sit in the second row. The two corners of the second row are reserved for the two tallest students, interchangeable only between them and if the middle seat of the front row is reserved for the principal. Find the number of possible arrangements:
   (a) $720 \times 18!$
   (b) $1440 \times 18!$
   (c) $1370 \times 18!$
   (d) None of these

4. In a certain town, all telephone numbers have six digits, the first two digits always being 53 or 54 or 56 or 82 or 84. The number of telephone numbers having all the six digits distinct is:
   (a) 8400
   (b) 9200
   (c) 7200
   (d) None of these

5. Three groups X, Y and Z are contesting for a position on the Board of Directors of a company. The probabilities of their winning are 0.5, 0.3 and 0.2 respectively. If the group X wins, then the probability of introducing a new product is 0.7 and the corresponding probabilities for group Y and Z are 0.6 and 0.5 respectively. The probability that the new product will be introduced is:
   (a) 0.52
   (b) 0.74
   (c) 0.63
   (d) None of these

6. A computer hardware firm manufactures two parts of the computer—CPU and Monitor. In the process of manufacture of the CPU, 9 out of 100 are likely to be defective. Similarly 5 out of 100 are likely to be defective in the process of manufacture of Monitor. The probability that the assembled part will not be defective is:
   (a) 0.8645
   (b) 0.9645
   (c) 0.6243
   (d) None of these

7. There are 4 applicants for the post of the Indian cricket captain and one of them is to be selected by the votes of the 5 wise men (also called as the selectors). The number of ways in which the votes can be given is:
   (a) 1048
   (b) 1072
   (c) 1024
   (d) None of these

8. In a Football Tournament, there were 171 matches played. Every two teams played one match with each other. The number of teams participating in the Tournament is:
   (a) 19
   (b) 18
   (c) 17
   (d) 16

9. Seven points lie on a circle. How many chords can be drawn by joining these points?
   (a) 22
   (b) 21
   (c) 23
   (d) 24

10. Ten different letters of an alphabet are given. Words with 5 letters are formed from these given letters. Find the number of words which have at least one letter repeated:
   (a) 69760
   (b) 30240
   (c) 99748
   (d) None of these

11. There are eight chairs marked A to H. Two girls and three boys wish to occupy one chair each. First, the girls chose the chairs from amongst the chairs marked A to D, then the boys selected the chairs from amongst the remaining, marked E to H. The number of possible arrangements is:
   (a) $6C_3 \times 4C_3$
   (b) $^4P_2 \times {}^4P_3$
   (c) $^4C_3 \times {}^4P_3$
   (d) $^4C_2 \times {}^4C_3$

12. Prabhjeet a fan of poker, wants to play poker every night for the maximum number of nights possible. The key constraint for him is that he has only 8 friends who are willing to play with him and he wants to hold poker games with distinct groups of friends. His mother has put the condition that in case the same group is repeated on any day, she would stop his poker games and make him study—something that he should be doing anyway. Being a mathematically-oriented person, Prabhjeet calculates the maximum number of nights on which he can play poker without violating his mother's condition. What is the value that he has calculated?
   (a) 70
   (b) 105
   (c) 140
   (d) 120

13. A five digit number divisible by 3 is to be formed using the numerals 0, 1, 2, 3, 4 and 5 without repetition. The total number of ways this can be done is:
   (a) 216
   (b) 240
   (c) 3125
   (d) 600

14. There are 6 equi-distant points A, B, C, D, E and F marked on a circle with radius M. How many convex

pentagons of distinctly different areas can be drawn using these points as vertices?

(a) $^6P_5$ (b) 1

(c) 55^5 (d) None of these

15. Five men *A*, *B*, *C*, *D* and *E* occupy seats in a row such that *C* and *D* sit next to each other. In how many possible ways can these five men sit?

(a) 24   (b) 48

(c) 72   (d) None of these

16. The number of zero at the end of 60! is

(a) 12   (b) 14

(c) 16   (d) 18

17. A department had 8 male and female employees each. A project team involving 3 male and 3 female members needs to be selected from the department employees. How many different project teams can be formed?

(a) 112896   (b) 3136

(c) 720   (d) 112

18. From a group of 7 men and 6 women, 5 persons are to be chosen to form a committee so that at least 3 men are there on the committee. In how many ways can it be done?

(a) 756   (b) 735

(c) 564   (d) None of these

19. The number of different ways that the letters of the word STALLION can be arranged so that the vowels always come together, is:

(a) 2160   (b) 720

(c) 4320   (d) 880

20. If a polygon has 54 diagonals, then find the number of its sides.

(a) 13   (b) 12

(c) 11   (d) 10

Space for Rough Work

ANSWER KEY

Review Test 1

1. (b)	2. (c)	3. (b)	4. (c)
5. (d)	6. (a)	7. (a)	8. (a)
9. (d)	10. (d)	11. (d)	12. (a)
13. (d)	14. (b)	15. (b)	16. (a)
17. (b)	18. (b)	19. (d)	20. (c)
21. (c)	22. (d)	23. (c)	24. (d)
25. (b)			

Review Test 2

1. (c)	2. (c)	3. (b)	4. (b)
5. (b)	6. (a)	7. (c)	8. (c)

Review Test 3

9. (c)	10. (c)	11. (a)	12. (c)
13. (a)	14. (d)	15. (d)	16. (b)
17. (b)	18. (b)	19. (b)	20. (b)

1. (d)	2. (a)	3. (b)	4. (a)
5. (c)	6. (a)	7. (d)	8. (a)
9. (b)	10. (b)	11. (b)	12. (a)
13. (a)	14. (b)	15. (b)	16. (b)
17. (b)	18. (a)	19. (a)	20. (b)

MOCK TEST PAPERS

The following section contains 3 mock tests based on the CAT 2011 pattern of QA. As mentioned elsewhere in the book, the papers varied greatly in difficulty levels—from the ridiculously easy to the tough. However, one thing common about the trend of difficulty in the papers was that after the initial few days, the quality of questions in the tests became more and more difficult—and became quite like the CAT papers of the past years. In the coming years, the CAT is expected to retain the degree of difficulty normally associated with the exam over the past decade and more and hence the tests I am providing are on the tougher side.

- You should take these tests only after you are through with your preparations of the entire book.
- Each question in these tests carries a weightage of +4 and −1.
- Take each of these tests in a limited time frame of 45 minutes (adhere strictly to the time limits).
- A net score of anywhere above 40 (with a maximum of 2 errors) in these tests would give you a high 99+ percentile in the exam. Note that in case you score more than 40 but have made 5–6 errors in doing so, your percentile would drop to around 90. Hence, the higher your percentage accuracy, the more the exam is going to reward you.
- Similarly:
  30+ with 100% accuracy can expect a percentile of 95+.
  30+ with 4-5 errors would give around 80 percentile.

For more practice and mock tests log on to www.mindworkzz.in.

1. Works W1 and W2 are done by Priyanka and Sanjana. Priyanka takes 80% more time to do the work W1 alone than she takes to do it together with Sanjana. How much percent more time Sanjana will take to do the work W2 alone than she takes to do it together with Priyanka?
   (1) 125% (2) 180%
   (3) 20% (4) 80%

2. The value of the expression $(x^2 - x + 1)/(x - 1)$ cannot lie between?
   (1) (1, 3) (2) (−1, −3)
   (3) (−1, 3) (4) (−1, 2)

3. What is the maximum value of the function $y = \min(12 - x, 8 + x)$?
   (1) 12 (2) 10
   (3) 11 (4) 8

4. How many integral values for the set (x, y) would exist for the expression $|x - 4| + |y - 2| + = 5$?
   (1) 16 (2) 14
   (3) 12 (4) 20

5. A book contains 20 chapters. Each chapter has a different number of pages (each under 21). The first chapter starts on page 1 and each chapter starts on a new page. What is the largest possible number of chapters that can begin on odd page numbers?
   (1) 19 (2) 15
   (3) 10 (4) 11

6. How many even three-digit integers have the property that their digits, read left to right, are not in a strictly increasing order?
   (1) 420 (2) 416
   (3) 412 (4) 422

7. An unlimited number of coupons bearing the digits 1, 2 and 3 are available. What is the possible number of ways of choosing 4 of these coupons so that they can not be used to make the number 123?

   (1) 15 (2) 18
   (3) 21 (4) 24

8. How many real solutions exist for the equation $3^x - 2x - 1 = 0$?
   (1) 2 (2) 3
   (3) 5 (4) 1

9. The number of rational points $x = p/5$ satisfying $\log(2x - 3/4)/\log x > 2$, where p is an integer and $gcd(p, 5) = 1$ is/are
   (1) 2 (2) 3
   (3) 5 (4) 1

10. Two schools play against each other in a grass court tennis tournament. Each school is represented by 8 students. Every game is a doubles game, and every possible pair from the first school must play one game against every possible pair from the second school. How many games will each student play?
    (1) 196 (2) 180
    (3) 192 (4) 164

11. Consider the set $T_x = \{x, x + 1, x + 2, x + 3, x + 4, x + 5\}$. For $x = 1, 2, 3, 4 \ldots 999$. How many of these sets do not contain any 7 or any integral multiple of 7?
    (1) 121 (2) 143
    (3) 144 (4) 145

12. In the figure below you can see points A, B, C, D on a circle. Chord AB is a diameter of this circle. The measure of angle ABC is 35°. The measure of angle BDC is:

(1) 35°   (2) 45°
(3) 55°   (4) 60°

13. There are two arithmetic progressions, A_1 and A_2, whose first terms are 3 and 5 respectively and whose common differences are 6 and 8 respectively. How many terms of the series are common in the first n terms of A_1 and A_2, if the sum of the nth terms of A_1 and A_2 is equal to 6000?

(1) 101   (2) 105
(3) 107   (4) 111

14. Shaurya Sharma travels from Delhi to Lucknow at a speed of 100 Kmph and returns to Delhi at a speed of 50 Kmph. He again leaves for Lucknow immediately at a speed of 30 Kmph and goes back to Delhi at a speed of 60 Kmph. What is his average speed for the entire journey?

(1) 54 kmph   (2) 48 kmph
(3) 56 kmph   (4) 50 kmph

15. At 9 PM, Divya is driving her car at 100 km/h. At this velocity she has enough petrol to cover a distance of 80 km. Unfortunately the nearest petrol pump is 100 km away. The amount of petrol her car uses per km is proportional to the velocity of the car. What is the earliest time that Divya can arrive at the petrol pump?

(1) 10:12 pm   (2) 10:15 pm
(3) 10:20 pm   (4) 10:25 pm

16. The number y is defined as the sum of the digits of the number x, and z as the sum of the digits of the number y. Let 'A' be defined as the number of natural numbers x which satisfy the equation $x + y + z = 60$ and let 'B' be defined as the number of natural numbers x which satisfy the equation $x + y + z = 84$. Which of the following statements about A and B is/are correct?

 (i) $A > B$ (ii) $A < B$
(iii) $A = B$ (iv) $A + B = 6$

(1) i & iv only   (2) ii & iv only
(3) iii only   (4) iii & iv only

17. The letters of the word HASTE are written in all possible orders and these words are written out as in dictionary. Then the dictionary rank of the word HEATS is:

(1) 52   (2) 54
(3) 56   (4) 58

18. Problems A, B and C were posed in a mathematical contest. 25 competitors solved at least one of the three. Amongst those who did not solve A, twice as many solved B as C. The number solving only A was one more than the number solving A and at least one other. The number solving just A equalled the number solving just B plus the number solving just C. How many solved just C?

(1) 2   (2) 4
(3) 6   (4) can not be determined

19. x, y are integers belonging to $\{1, 2, 3, 4, 5, 6, 7, 8, 9 \dots 15\}$. How many possible ratios of x/y can you get such that x/y is an integer?

(1) 22   (2) 40
(3) 42   (4) 44

20. Five friends Amit, Arun, Abhishek, Aishwarya and Azad buy lottery tickets having numbers 2, 4, 6, 8 and 10 respectively. Arun exchanges his ticket with Abhishek, Abhishek with Aishwarya, Aishwarya with Azad and Azad with Arun. Amit does not exchange his ticket. For three consecutive exchanges, the difference between the ticket numbers of two particular persons is constant at 2. After the fourth exchange, the difference in their ticket numbers will be

(1) 1   (2) 2
(3) 4   (4) Cannot be determined

Space for Rough Work

ANSWER KEY

1. (1)	2. (3)	3. (2)	4. (4)
5. (2)	6. (2)	7. (3)	8. (1)
9. (2)	10. (1)	11. (2)	12. (3)
13. (3)	14. (4)	15. (2)	16. (4)
17. (3)	18. (1)	19. (4)	20. (2)

Solutions and Shortcuts

Solution 1: Level of Difficulty (2)

Let p be the amount of work Priyanka can do per day and s be amount of work Sanjana can do per day. According to the given statement ... $((w1/p) - (w1/(p + s)))/(w1/(p + s))$ $= 0.8$ this gives $s = 0.8p$, what we were asked is, $((w2/s) - (w2/(p + s)))/(w2/(p + s))$ substituting $s = 0.8p$, we get the required value as 1.25 i.e. 125%. Hence, choice (1) is the right answer.

Solution 2: Level of Difficulty (3)

The expression needs to be evaluated at different values of x and we can easily see that at $x = 0$, the value of the function becomes -1. Further at $x = 0.5$ we can find that the value is $-3/2$. So we can understand that the value of the function is reducing when we move to the right of 0. It can also be seen that to the left of 0 also there will be a drop in the value of the function. For instance at $x = -0.1$ also the value of the function will be less than -1. So obviously the function is reaching a kind of a maximum at -1 and is not going beyond that when the range of values are in this range.

It can be observed that after $x = 1$, the function will become positive. At $x = 1.1$ it can be seen that the value of the function would become around 10-11. As you would increase the value of x beyond 1, 1 the function would reduce in value. Also, it can be seen that after $x = 1$, the funtion would achieve its minimum value at $x = 2 \rightarrow$ where its value would be 3. After 2 the value would start increasing. Hence, the value of the function cannot be between -1 to $+3$. Hence, option 3 is the correct answer.

Solution 3: Level of Difficulty (1)

Equate $12 - x = 8 + x$ to give you the intersection point between the two lines $12 - x$ and $8 + x$. The intersection occurs at a value of x as 2. It can be visualized by plotting both these lines that the maximum value of the given function would occur at $x = 2$. Hence, the correct answer would be 10.

Solution 4: Level of Difficulty (2)

Solutions would exist for the following structures of making the value of 5: $0 + 5 \rightarrow$ This would happen if we take the value of x as 4 and y can take the values of 7 or -3. Hence, there would be 2 sets of integral (x, y) values giving us $0 + 5 = 5$
$1 + 4 \rightarrow (5, 6), (5, -2), (3, 6), (3, -2) \rightarrow$ four solutions
$2 + 3 \rightarrow$ four possibilities again
$3 + 2 \rightarrow$ four possibilities again

$4 + 1 \rightarrow$ four possibilities again
$5 + 0 \rightarrow$ 2 possibilities

Solution to Question 5: Level of Difficulty (2)

There would be 10 chapters with even number of pages. Place them to start with—each of them would start on an odd numbered page. After that start to place the chapters with an odd number of pages—the first one would start on an odd numbered page, the second on an even numbered page, the third on an odd numbered page and so on. Thus there would be $10 + 5 = 15$ chapters out of 20 which can at the maximum start on an odd numbered page. Hence, option 2 is correct.

Solution to Question 6: Level of Difficulty (2)

For this question, you would have to count the actual number of numbers. In the hundreds, the first numbers you would find would be in the 120s. The first numbers are 124, 126, 128, 134, 136, 138, 146, 148, 156, 158, 168, 178.

In the 200s, the values would be 234, 236, 238, 246, 248, 256, 258, 268, 278

In the 300s the values would be 346, 348, 356, 358, 368, 378

In the 400s the values would be 456, 458, 468, 478

In the 500s there would be only 2 values.

1 value in the 600s and no value after that. Hence 34 values. But in all there are 450 even three digit numbers starting from 100, 102, 104 …998. Hence, the required answer is $450 - 34 = 416$.

Solution 7: Level of Difficulty (2)

Each of the 3 places can take 3 letters $\Rightarrow 27$. But we don't want the combination $(1, 2, 3) \Rightarrow 3! = 6$ are out $\Rightarrow 27 - 6 = 21$.

Solution 8: Level of Difficulty (3)

It can be seen by plotting the graph of this expression that the function $y = 3^x - 2x - 1$ would cut the x axis twice. Hence, the equation would have 2 real solutions.

Solution 9: Level of Difficulty (3)

$\log (2x - 3/4) > 2 \log x$ solving we get 2 cases:

Case 1: When $x > 1 \Rightarrow (2x - 3/4) > x^2$.

Case 2: When $x < 1 \Rightarrow (2x - 3/4) < x^2$

Solving these inequalities we get: x lies in $(3/8, 1/2) \cup (1, 3/2)$ viz. $(0.375, 0.5) \cup (1, 1.5)$

In these ranges we have two independent values which could be expressed as $p/5$ viz. $0.4 = 2/5$ and $1.2 = 6/5$. Since in both the cases, p is co prime with 5, we can say that both these cases satisfy the conditional requirements. Hence, choice (2) is the right answer.

Solution 10: Level of Difficulty (2)

Total matches being played $= 8C2 * 8C2 = 28^2 = 784$. Thus, a total of $784 \times 4 = 3136$ people are part of these 784 matches. Each of the 16 players would play in the same number of matches $= 3136/16 = 196$.

Hence, choice (1) is the right answer.

Solution 11: Level of Difficulty (2)

In this case you would get the sets like: {1, 2, 3, 4, 5, 6}, {8, 9, 10, 11, 12, 13}, {15, 16, 17, 18, 19, 20}…. As we can see the starting digits for each of these sets consists of an Arithmetic Progression as 1, 8, 15…. The next step is to find the number of terms in this series before 999. This can be done as: Series is 1, 8, 15, 22 … 995 …. And this series would have $[(995 - 1)/7] + 1 = 143$ terms.

Solution 12: Level of Difficulty (1)

Join $AC \Rightarrow < ACB = 90° \Rightarrow < CAB = 55°$. But $< BDC = < CAB$ as they are subscribed by the same arc. Hence, choice (3) is the right answer.

Solution 13: Level of Difficulty (2)

Use
$$t_n = a + (n-1)d$$
$$6000 = a_1 + a_2 + (n-1)(d_1 + d_2)$$
or, $\quad n = 429$
so, we have two A.P. series
$\quad$ 3, 9, 15, 21, ———, 2571 (Calculate t_n)
$\quad$ 5, 13, 21, ———, 3429 (Calculate t_n)
so, common series is 21, 45 ———, x where $x £ 2571$
$\quad$ On solving, x comes for $n = 107$. Hence, choice (3) is the right answer.

Solution 14:

Let the distance between Delhi and Lucknow be 300 kms. The total time taken would be $3 + 6 + 10 + 5 = 24$ hours. The total distance would be 1200 kms. Hence, the average speed is given by
$\quad$ Average speed = (total distance/total time)
$\quad$ = 1200/24 = 50 kmph
Hence, choice (4) is the right answer.

Solution 15: Level of Difficulty (2)

Divya needs to travel 100 km @ 80 km/h $\Rightarrow$ Time taken = 5/4 hours. Hence, choice (2) is the right answer.

Solution 16: Level of Difficulty (3)

Go through trial and error for both situations.
$\quad$ We can see that $x + y + z = 60$ is satisfied for $z = 44, 47$ and 50. Hence, $A = 3$.
$\quad$ We can see that $x + y + z = 84$ is satisfied for $z = 73, 70$ and 67. Hence, $B = 3$.
$\quad$ Hence, choice (4) is the right answer.

Solution 17: Level of Difficulty (2)

The letters available to us are: A, E H, S and T in their alphabetical order. When we form 5 letter words out of these, the following order of appearing in the dictionary would hold…

Words starting with A___ 4! = 24
Words starting with E___ 4! = 24
Words starting with HA___ 3! = 6
Words starting with HE … complete description:
First word: HEAST, Second word = HEATS…
Hence, the 56th word in the list would be HEATS. Option 3 is correct.

Solution 18: Level of Difficulty (2)

Let a solve just A, b solve just B, c solve just C, and d solve B and C but not A. Then $25 - a - b - c - d$ solve A and at least one of B or C. The conditions give: $b + d = 2(c + d)$; $a = 1 + 25 - a - b - c - d$; $a = b + c$. Eliminating a and d, we get: $4b + c = 26$. But $d = b - 2c >= 0$, so $b = 6$, $c = 2$. Hence, choice (1) is the right answer.

Solution 19: Level of Difficulty (2)

If we take x as 2, we will get 2 integers,
With x as 3 we will get 2 integers,
With x as 4 we have 3 integers,
With x as 5 we have 2 integers,
With x as 6 we have 4 integers,
With x as 7, we have 2 integers,
With x as 8 we have 4 integers,
With x as 9 we have 3 integers,
With x as 10 we have 4 integers,
With x as 11 we have 2 integers,
With x as 12 we have 6 integers,
With x as 13 we have 2 integers
With x as 14 we have 4 integers,
With x as 15 we have 4 integers.
$\quad$ Thus there would be a total of 44 such integral ratios. Hence, the option 4 is correct.

Solution 20: Level of Difficulty (1)

Name	Amit	Arun	Abhishek	Aishwarya	Azad
Initial	2	4	6	8	10
1st exchange	2	10	4	6	8
2nd exchange	2	8	10	4	6
3rd exchange	2	6	8	10	4
4th exchange	2	4	6	8	10

From the table, it is clear that the difference between Arun and Aishwarya's lottery ticket value is constant upto the 3rd exchange and equal to 2. After the 4th exchange also it equals 2.

1. In the diagram, all triangles are equilateral. If $AB = 16$, then the total area of all the black triangles is

(1) $25\sqrt{3}$ (2) $27\sqrt{3}$
(3) $35\sqrt{3}$ (4) $37\sqrt{3}$

2. In the figure below $DC = AC = 1$ and $CB = CE = 4$. If the area of triangle ABC is equal to S then the area of the quadrilateral $AFDC$ is equal to:

(1) $\dfrac{S}{2}$ (2) $\dfrac{S}{4}$

(3) $\dfrac{S}{5}$ (4) $\dfrac{2S}{5}$

3. Find the number of zeroes in $100^1 * 99^2 * 98^3 * 97^4 * 96^5 * \underline{\qquad} * 1^{100}$
(1) 970 (2) 1070
(3) 1120 (4) 1124

4. The crew of an 8-member rowing team is to be chosen from 12 men (M_1, M_2 ..., M_{12}) and 8 women (W_1, W_2 ..., W_8). There have to be 4 people on each side with at least one woman on each side. Further it is also known that on the right side of the boat (while going forward) W_1 and M_7 must be selected while on the left side of the boat M_2, M_3 and M_{10} must be selected. What is the number of ways in which the rowing team can be arranged?
(1) $1368 \times 4! \times 4!$ (2) $1200 \times 4! \times 4!$
(3) $1120 \times 4! \times 4!$ (4) $728 \times 4! \times 4!$

5. In a community of 20 families, every family is expected to have the number of offsprings in an Arithmetic Progression with a common difference of 2, starting with 2 offsprings in the first family. Further for every child in the family every family is expected to deposit the same number of gold coins as there are children in the family towards a community contribution) for each child the family has. What will be the total number of gold coins collected in the community?
(1) 11480 (2) 11280
(3) 10880 (4) 10280

6. A boy plays a mathematical game wherein he tries to write the number 1998 into the sum of 2 or more consecutive positive even numbers (e.g. 1998 = 998 + 1000). In how many different ways can he do so?
(1) 5 (2) 6
(3) 7 (4) 8

7. Find the remainder when 2^{650} is divided by 224.
(1) 124 (2) 66
(3) 32 (4) 28

8. How many numbers are there between 100 and 1000, which have exactly one of their digits as 8?
(1) 300 (2) 1444
(3) 225 (4) 729

9. $f(n)$ is a function which is defined in three different domains as

$$f(n) = \begin{cases} 2n + 4 \text{ if } n < -1 \\ 3n + 5 \text{ if } -1 \le x < 1 \\ 2n - 5 \text{ if } x \ge 1 \end{cases}$$

Find the value of (–5)?
(1) –20   (2) –12
(3) –32   (4) –36

10. Aman while getting bored in his school starts to draw lines on a fixed pattern. First, he draws a line 10 mm long. Then he constructs a square with this line as its diagonal. He then draws another square with a side of the first square as its diagonal. This process is repeated 'x' times, until the perimeter of the xth square is less than $\frac{1}{12.5}$ mm. What is the least value of 'n'?
(1) 16   (2) 18
(3) 20   (4) 22

11. In the world championship of table tennis, players play best of 5 game matches. In every game the first player who scores 21 points wins. Service changes alternately between the 2 players after every five points. A player can score points both during his service and his opponent's service. Raman beat Ching Mai by 21-16 in a game. 24 of the 37 points played were won by the player serving. Who served first?
(1) Raman   (2) Ching Mai
(3) Either could have served first
(4) Indeterminate

12. A square of side 12 m is drawn and a circle is inscribed in it. Now with

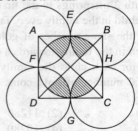

Now with each vertex as center, a circle is drawn passing through the midpoints of the two sides of the square, which meet at the vertex. Find the area of the shaded portion. (in m²)
(1) $18\pi - 36$ (2) $36\pi - 72$
(3) $9\pi - 72$ (4) $18\pi - 72$

13. In a bombing of the Nathula pass, the Indian troops have to destroy a bridge on the pass. The bridge is such that it is destroyed when exactly 2 bombs hit it. A MIG-27 is dispatched in order to do the bombing. Flt Lt. Rakesh Sharma needs to ensure that there is at least 97% probability for the bridge to be destroyed. He knows that when he drops a bomb on the bridge the probability of the bomb hitting the bridge is 90%. Weather conditions and visibility being poor he is unable to see the bridge from his plane. How many bombs does he need to drop to be 95% sure that the bridge will be destroyed?
(1) 3   (2) 4
(3) 5   (4) 6

14. In a bombing of the Nathula pass, the Indian troops have to destroy a bridge on the pass. The bridge is such that it is destroyed when exactly 3 bombs hit it.

Flt Lt. Rakesh Sharma for his extraordinary skills is given the responsibility to drop the bombs again. If he drops a maximum of 5 bombs and he knows that when he drops a bomb on the bridge the probability of the bomb hitting the bridge is 90%. What will be the probability that the bridge would have been destroyed? (assume the bridge is visible to Flt Lt Sharma this time).
(1) 0.98348   (2) 0.98724
(3) 0.99144   (4) 0.99348

15. In a peculiar chessboard containing 12×12 squares, what is the greatest number of 5×5 squares that can be traced?
(1) 8   (2) 16
(3) 64   (4) 32

16. In the following figure (not drawn to scale) $\angle DEF = 42°$. Find the other two angles of ΔDEF if DE and DF are the angle bisectors of $\angle ADB$ and $\angle ADC$ respectively.

(1) 28° and 11°0   (2) 65° and 73°
(3) 67° and 71°   (4) 48° and 90°

17. The sides of a triangle have 4, 5 and 6 interior points marked on them respectively. The total number of triangles that can be formed using any of these points
(1) 371   (2) 415
(3) 286   (4) 421

18. The sides of a triangle have 4, 5 and 6 interior points marked on them respectively. The total number of triangles that can be formed using any of these points and/or the vertices would be?
(1) 704   (2) 415
(3) 684   (4) 421

19. The number of digits lying between 2000 and 7000 (including 2000 and 7000) which have at least two digits equal but at most 3 digits equal is:
(1) 2476   (2) 2474
(3) 2475   (4) 2473

20. The number of ways in which three distinct numbers in AP can be selected from 1, 2, 3, …, 24 is
(1) 144   (2) 276
(3) 572   (4) 132

ANSWER KEY

1. (4)	2. (4)	3. (4)	4. (1)
5. (1)	6. (3)	7. (3)	8. (3)
9. (4)	10. (2)	11. (1)	12. (2)
13. (1)	14. (3)	15. (3)	16. (4)
17. (4)	18. (1)	19. (1)	20. (4)

Solutions and Shortcuts

Solution 1: Level of Difficulty (1)

In the diagram, there are 27 black triangles. If the entire diagram was divided into the smallest size equilateral triangles, there would be $1 + 3 + 5 + 7 + 9 + 11 + 13 + 15 = 64$ equilateral triangles). Thus, 27/64 of D ABC is coloured black, so 37/64 is unshaded.

Area of triangle $ABC = \{\sqrt{(3)/4}\} \times 16 \times 16 = 64\sqrt{3}$. Hence, the area of the unshaded portion is $37\sqrt{3}$. Drop a perpendicular from A, meeting BC at D. Since D ABC is equilateral and $AB = 16$, then $BD = DC = 8$. Hence, Option 4 is correct.

Solution 2: Level of Difficulty (3)

The best way to solve problems like these is to assume specific case: Assume ACB and ECB to be right angled. Also assume that the point C is at the origin (0, 0). Then by the information we can conclude that E would be (4, 0), B(0, 4), A(1, 0) and D(0, 1).

Then the equations of the lines AB and ED would be $4x + y = 4$ and $x + 4y = 4$ respectively.

The intersection point would be got by equating these lines: $F = (4/5, 4/5)$.

Area of CFA is 2/5. Hence, area of $CAFD = 2*2/5 = 4/5$. But area of $ABC = S = 2$. Hence, choice (4) is the right answer.

Solution 3: Level of Difficulty (2)

$= (1 + 6 + 11 + 16 + 26 + 31\_\_\_ + 96) + (1 + 26 + 51 + 76)$
$= 20*48.5 + 4*38.5$
$= 970 + 154 = 1124$

Solution 4: Level of Difficulty (3)

In this question you will first have to complete the selection of 4 people for either side and then arrange the rowers on each side (which would be done by using 4!)

The solution would depend on the following structure—the structure would vary based on whether you select 2 more men for the right side or you select 1 man and 1 woman for the right side or you select 2 women for the right side.

The solution would be given by:
$^{12}C_2 \times 4! \times ^8C_1 \times 4! + ^{12}C_1 \times ^8C_1 \times 4! \times ^7C_1 \times 4!$
$+ ^8C_2 \times 4! \times ^6C_1 \times 4! = 1368 \times 4! \times 4!$
Hence, Option 1 is the correct answer.

Solution 5: Level of Difficulty (3)

The number of children in the family would be: 2, 4, 6, 8, 10, 12, 14, 16, 18, 20, 22, 24, 26, 28, 30, 32 ,34, 36, 38, 40.

Hence, the number of gold coins selected would be:
$2 \times 2 + 4 \times 4 + 6 \times 6 + \ldots 40 \times 40 = 4 + 16 + 36 + 64 + 100 + 144 + 196 + 256 + 324 + 400 + 484 + 576 + 676 + 784 + 900 + 1024 + 1156 + 1296 + 1444 + 1600 = 11480$

Solution 6: Level of Difficulty (3)

For answering this question we need to plan the use of the factors of 1998.
$1998 = 2 \times 3^3 \times 37 \to 16$ factors viz. $1 \times 1998, 2 \times 999, 3 \times 666, 6 \times 333, 9 \times 222, 18 \times 111, 27 \times 74, 54 \times 37$.

Thus we could form 7 APs as follows:
(1) An AP with 2 terms and average 999
(2) An AP with 3 terms and average 666 and so on $\to$ 7 ways.

Solution 7: Level of Difficulty (1)

$$2^{650} = 25 \cdot (2^3)^{215} = 32 \times 8^{215}/224 = 8^{215}/7$$

gives us a remainder of 1. Since we have cut the numerator and denominator by 32 in the process, the actual remainder must be 32.

Solution 8: Level of Difficulty (2)

There are exactly 72 numbers in which 8 comes at the units place. Given by $8 \times 9 \times 1$

Similarly at the tens place there are $8 \times 1 \times 9$ ways Also at the hundred's place there are $1 \times 9 \times 9 = 81$ ways So, there are $72 + 72 + 81 = 225$ numbers between 100 and 1000 which have exactly one of their digits as 8.

Solution 9: Level of Difficulty (1)

$$f(-3) = 2(-5) + 4 = -6$$
$$f(-6) = 2(-6) + 4 = -8$$
$$f(-8) = 2(-8) + 4 = -12$$
$$f(-12) = -20$$
$$f(-20) = -36$$

Solution 10: Level of Difficulty (2)

(3) Diagonal of first square = 10 mm.
Side of first square = $10/\sqrt{2}$
Side of second square = $10 \times 1/(\sqrt{2})^2 \ldots$
Side of xth square = $10 \times 1/(\sqrt{2})^x$
$\Rightarrow 4 \times 10 \times 1/(\sqrt{2})^x < 0.08 \Rightarrow 1/(\sqrt{2})^x < 0.002$
$\Rightarrow (1/2)^{x/2} < 2/1000 \Rightarrow x$ should be at least 18.

Solution 11: Level of Difficulty (3)

In all 37 services are made. Two cases are possible.
(a) Raman has served 20 times and Ching Mai has served 17 times.
(b) Ching Mai has served 20 times and Raman has served 17 times.

We would need to see what occurs in each case to understand which of these situations holds true.

Case (a): In this case Raman starts serving. Let X be the score obtained by Raman in his services and Y be the score obtained by Raman when Ching Mai serves. The following table would emerge:

Player who serves	No. of balls serves	Scores of Raman	Scores of Ching Mai
R	C		
R	20	X	20 – X
C	17	Y	17 – Y

Now, $X + Y = 21$, $X + 17 - Y = 24$.

$\Rightarrow X = 14 \Rightarrow$ we get an acceptable solution.

Case (b): In this case Ching Mai starts serving.

Player who serves	No. of balls serves	Scores of Raman	Scores of Ching Mai
R	C		
C	20	X	20 – X
R	17	Y	17 – Y

$\Rightarrow \qquad X + Y = 21$
$\Rightarrow \qquad 20 - X + Y = 24$
$\Rightarrow \qquad Y = 12.5$ (inadmissible)

Hence Raman started first.

Solution 12: Level of Difficulty (2)

In order to solve the question you need to find the difference between the area of the quarter circle (inside the square) and the right angled triangle at the center of the inner circle having base and height equal to 6 m each. The required area would be 4 times this value.

Hence, the required answer would be given by:

$$4x\,[36\pi/4 - 18] = 36\pi - 72$$

Solution 13: Level of Difficulty (3)

The probability if he drops 3 bombs will be given by: Hit and Hit OR Miss and Hit and Hit OR Hit and Miss and Miss
$= 0.9 \times 0.9 + 0.1 \times 0.9 \times 0.9 + 0.9 \times 0.1 \times 0.9 = 0.81 + 0.081 + 0.081 = 0.972 > 0.97$.

Hence, 3 bombs would give him a probability of higher than 97% for the bridge to be destroyed.

Solution 14: Level of Difficulty (3)

The bridge would be destroyed under the following conditions: In 3 bombs OR In 4 Bombs Or In 5 Bombs Hit, Hit and Hit OR One miss and 3 hits (3 ways) OR 2 misses and 3 hits ($4C_2 = 6$ ways)

$= (0.9)^3 + 3 \times (0.9)^3 \times (0.1)^1 + 6 \times (0.9)^3 \times (0.1)^2$
$= 0.729 + 3 \times 0.0729 + 6 \times 0.00729 = 0.99144$.

Solution 15: Level of Difficulty (2)

The required answer would be given by $8 \times 8 = 64$ (Because if you take the top side of the square on the top side of the chess board, you would be able to trace out 8 squares. Similarly you would get exactly 8 squares in each row when you move to the next row of the chess board. This would continue till the 8th row of the chess board is taken as the top

row of the 5×5 square. Hence, $8 \times 8 = 64$).

Solution 16: Level of Difficulty (2)

The measure of the angle EDF has to be 90° since it should be half of the 180° angle. Hence, the required answer has to be option 4.

Solution 17: Level of Difficulty (3)

You can form triangles by taking 1 point from each side, or by taking 2 points from any 1 side and the third point from either of the other two sides.

This can be done in: $4 \times 5 \times 6 + {}^4C_2 \times {}^{11}C_1 + {}^5C_2 \times {}^{10}C_1 + {}^6C_2 \times {}^9C_1 = 120 + 66 + 100 + 135 = 421$

Solution 18: Level of Difficulty (3)

In order to solve this question, you will first need to solve assuming that neither of the three vertices (say A, B or C) are used. For this we can solve the following way: You can form triangles by taking 1 point from each side, or by taking 2 points from any 1 side and the third point from either of the other two sides.

This can be done in: $4 \times 5 \times 6 + {}^4C_2 \times {}^{11}C_1 + {}^5C_2 \times {}^{10}C_1 + {}^6C_2 \times {}^9C_1 = 120 + 66 + 100 + 135 = 421$

Then, you need to consider situations where you are either taking one of the vertices of the triangle ABC or taking two vertices from the triangle. Thus assuming 6 points on AB, 4 on AC and 5 on BC the following possibilities emerge:

Taking $A - 5C_2 + 6 \times 5 + 6 \times 4 + 5 \times 4 = 10 + 30 + 24 + 20 = 84$

Taking $B - 4C_2 + 4 \times 5 + 4 \times 6 + 5 \times 6 = 80$

Taking $C - 6C_2 + 6 \times 4 + 6 \times 5 + 5 \times 4 = 89$

Taking $AB - 9$

Taking $AC - 11$

Taking $BC - 10$

Thus the total number of ways is: $421 + 84 + 80 + 89 + 9 + 11 + 10 = 704$

Solution 19: Level of Difficulty (3)

Numbers having 3 digits equal—Starting with 2: Numbers with 3 twos-222_ → 9 numbers (and 3 such cases so a total of 27 such numbers) Numbers with 3 digits other than twos → like 2000, 2111, 2333 … 2999 = 9 numbers

Total of 36 numbers

Similarly, numbers starting with 3 and having 3 digits common would be 36

numbers starting with 4 and having 3 digits common would be 36

numbers starting with 5 and having 3 digits common would be 36

numbers starting with 6 and having 3 digits common would be 36

Total numbers having 3 digits equal = 180.

Numbers having 2 digits equal—Again we first count number of numbers that are starting with 2 and having 2 digits equal and then multiply the same by 5 to get the answer: In order to find the number of numbers starting with

2 and having 2 digits equal we need to divide the same into:

(a) Numbers starting with 2 and having 2 twos and two more digits equal $3C_1 \times 9 = 27$

OR

(b) Numbers starting with 2 and having 2 twos and two more digits which are not equal to one another-

$$3C_1 \times 9C_1 \times 8C_1 = 216$$

OR

(c) Number of numbers starting with 2 and having two digits which are same and a fourth digit which is other than 2 as well as different from the other digit which has been used for 2 digits same.

$$9C_1 \times 3C_1 \times 8C_1 = 216$$

Thus, the total number of such numbers is 459.
Totally, $459 \times 5 + 180 + 1$ (for 7000) = 2476

Solution 20: Level of Difficulty (2)

If we take common difference = 1, then (1, 2, 3), (2, 3, 4) … (22, 23, 24). There will be 22 combinations.

If we take common difference = 2, then total 20 combinations are possible i.e. (1, 3, 5), (2, 4, 6), (3, 5, 7), …, (20 , 22, 24).
If we take c.d. = 3, 18 combinations are possible
If we take c.d. = 4, 16 combinations are possible
(There will be two combinations in last i.e. (1, 12, 23) & (2, 13, 24) with c.d. = 11
So total no. of combinations

$$= 22 + 20 + 18 + 16 + \ldots + 4 + 2$$
$$= 2 \times (1 + 2 + 3 + \ldots + 11)$$
$$= 2 \times \frac{11 \times 12}{2} = 132$$

1. Find the number of solutions for x if $50 \leq x \leq 120$ such that $\left[\dfrac{x}{6}\right] + \left[\dfrac{x}{5}\right] + \left[\dfrac{x}{10}\right] = \dfrac{7x}{15}$, where $[y]$ indicates the greatest integer less than or equal to y.
   (1) 0
   (2) 1
   (3) 2
   (4) 3

2. The number of ordered pairs of positive integers (m, n) such that $\dfrac{1}{m} + \dfrac{1}{n} = \dfrac{1}{15}$ is:
   (1) 10
   (2) 2
   (3) 4
   (4) 9

3. Let 'f' be a function such that for real x & y, $f(x) \times f(y) = f(x + y)$ & $\dfrac{f(x)}{f(y)} = f(x - y)$ for all $f(y) \neq 0$.
   Given that $f(0) = 1$ and $f(1) = 3$, then $f(x - 1) + f(-x - 1)$
   (1) cannot be negative.
   (2) has minimum value 2/3.
   (3) lies between 0 and 2/3.
   (4) none of these.

4. Let $a = \dfrac{1^2}{1} + \dfrac{2^2}{3} + \dfrac{3^2}{5} + \ldots + \dfrac{1001^2}{2001}$ and $b = \dfrac{1^2}{3} + \dfrac{2^2}{5} + \dfrac{3^2}{7} + \ldots + \dfrac{1001^2}{2003}$. The integer closest to $a - b$ is
   (1) 500
   (2) 501
   (3) 1000
   (4) 1001

5. Which of the following statements is false?
   (1) The product of three consecutive even numbers must be divisible by 48.
   (2) $x\%$ of $y\%$ of z is same as $z\%$ of $x\%$ of y.
   (3) The factorial of any natural number greater than 1 cannot be a perfect square.

   (4) The numbers $(100)_2, (100)_3, (100)_4, (100)_5 \ldots$ and so on, when converted to decimal system are all in an arithmetic progression.

6. Find the length of the string wound on a cylinder of height 48 cm and a base diameter of $5\dfrac{1}{11}$ cm. The string makes exactly four complete turns round the cylinder while its two ends touch the cylinder's top and bottom.
   (1) 192 cm
   (2) 80 cm
   (3) 64 cm
   (4) Cannot be determined

7. In Coorg, the production of tea is three times the production of coffee. If a percent more tea and b percent more coffee were produced, the aggregate amount would be $5c$ percent more. But if b percent more tea and a percent more coffee were produced, the aggregate amount produced would be $3c$ percent more. What is the ratio $a : b$?
   (1) $1 : 3$
   (2) $1 : 2$
   (3) $2 : 1$
   (4) $3 : 1$

8. A girl wished to purchase m roses for n rupees. (m and n are integers). The shopkeeper offered to give the remaining 10 flowers also if she paid him a total of ₹ 2. This would have resulted in a saving of 80 paise per dozen for her. How many flowers did she wish to buy initially?
   (1) 4
   (2) 5
   (3) 6
   (4) 7

9. Samit went to the market with ₹ 100. If he buys three pens and six pencils he uses up all his money. On the other hand if he buys three pencils and six pens he would fall short by 20%. If he wants to buy equal number of pens & pencils, how many pencils can he buy?
   (1) 4
   (2) 5
   (3) 6
   (4) 7

Directions for Questions 10 and 11: The graph given below represents a quadratic expression, $f(x) = ax^2 + bx + c$. The minimum value of $f(x)$ is -2 and it occurs at $x = 2$

x_1 and x_2 are such that $x_1 + x_2 + 2x_1x_2 = 0$.

10. What is the nature of the roots of the equation $f(x) = 0$?
    (1) Complex conjugates
    (2) Rational
    (3) Irrational
    (4) Cannot be determined

11. Find the value of the function at $x = 3$
    (1) 2   (2) -1
    (3) 5   (4) none of these

12. How many numbers are there between 100 and 1000, which have exactly one of their digits as 7?
    (1) 300   (2) 1444
    (3) 225   (4) 729

13. A group of men was employed to shift 545 crates. Every day after the first, 6 more men than the previous day were put on the job. Also, every day after the first, each man working, shifted 5 fewer crates than the number of crates moved by each man the previous day. The result was that during the latter part of the period, the number of crates shifted per day began to go down. 5 days were required to finish the work.

    What was the number of crates shifted on the third day?
    (1) 137   (2) 169
    (3) 26   (4) 152

14. A group of men was employed to shift 545 crates. Every day after the first, 6 more men than the previous day were put on the job. Also, every day after the first, each man working, shifted 5 fewer crates than the number of crates moved by each man the previous day. The result was that during the latter part of the period, the number of crates shifted per day began to go down. 5 days were required to finish the work.

    What was the number of men working on the fifth day?
    (1) 13   (2) 25
    (3) 19   (4) 75

15. In the figure given, the radius of the smaller circle is $\sqrt{2} - 1$ cm. Then the area of shaded region will be

    (1) $3 - \sqrt{2}$ cm²
    (2) $\dfrac{3}{4}(4 - \pi) + \sqrt{2}(4 - \sqrt{2}\,\pi)$ cm²
    (3) $\dfrac{3}{4}(4 - 5\pi) + \dfrac{1}{\sqrt{2}}(4 - 3\pi)$ cm²
    (4) Data insufficient

16. Two sisters go up 40-step escalators. The older sister rides the up escalator, but can only take 10 steps up during the ride since it is quite crowded. The younger sister runs up the empty down escalator, arriving at the top at the same time as her sister. How many steps does the younger sister take?
    (1) 70   (2) 60
    (3) 80   (4) 70

17. In how many ways may the numbers {1, 2, 3, 4, 5, 6} be ordered such that no two consecutive terms have a sum which is divisible by 2 or 3?
    (1) 6   (2) 12
    (3) 15   (4) 14

18. Let $f(n)$ denote the square of the sum of the digits of n. Let $f^2(n)$ denote $f(f(n))$, $f^3(n)$ denote $f(f(f(n)))$ and so on. Then $f^{1998}(11) =$
    (1) 49   (2) 56
    (3) 169   (4) 16

19. A biologist catches a random sample of 60 fish from a lake, tags them and releases them. Six months later she catches a random sample of 70 fish and finds 3 are tagged. She assumes 25% of the fish in the lake on the earlier date have died or moved away and that 40% of the fish on the later date have arrived (or been born) since. What does she estimate as the number of fish in the lake on the earlier date?
    (1) 840   (2) 280
    (3) 560   (4) 750

20. Michael Jordan's probability of hitting any basketball shot is three times than mine, which never exceeds a third. To beat him in a game, I need to hit a shot myself and have Jordan miss the same shot. If I pick my shot optimally, what is the maximum probability of winning which I can attain?
    (1) $\dfrac{1}{16}$ (2) $\dfrac{1}{12}$
    (3) $\dfrac{5}{6}$ (4) 1/14

ANSWER KEY

1. (4)	2. (4)	3. (2)	4. (2)
5. (4)	6. (2)	7. (4)	8. (2)
9. (1)	10. (3)	11. (2)	12. (3)
13. (2)	14. (2)	15. (3)	16. (1)
17. (2)	18. (3)	19. (1)	20. (2)

Solutions and Shortcuts

Solution 1: Level of Difficulty (2)

Since a greatest integer function always delivers an integer value, $\dfrac{7x}{15}$ must be an integer.

So possible values of x lying in the given domain would be 60, 75, 90, 105 and 120. Out of these 60, 90 and 120 satisfy the given equation.

Solution 2: Level of Difficulty (2)

$$\frac{1}{m}+\frac{1}{n}=\frac{1}{15} \Rightarrow \frac{m+n}{mn}=\frac{1}{15} \Rightarrow mn-15(m+n)=0$$

Adding 225 to both sides we get, $mn - 15(m + n) + 225 = 225 \Rightarrow (m - 15)(n - 15) = 225.$

Now we have to consider all the factors of 225 which are 1, 3, 5, 9, 15, 25, 45, 75 and 225. Hence 9 possible ordered pairs of (m, n) satisfy the given condition.

Solution 3: Level of Difficulty (2)

The given properties lead us to an exponential function, i.e. $f(x) = a^x$. Given that $f(1) = 3 \Rightarrow a = 3$. So the given function is $f(x) = a^x$.

$$f(x - 1) + f(-x - 1) = 3^{x-1} + 3^{-x-1}$$
$$= \frac{1}{3}(3^x + 3^{-x}) \ge \frac{1}{3} \cdot 2\sqrt{3^x \cdot 3^{-x}}$$

$$[\because \text{A.M} \ge \text{G.M.}]$$

$\Rightarrow 3^{x-1} + 3^{-x-1} \ge 2/3.$

Hence the minimum value of $3^{x-1} + 3^{-x-1} = 2/3.$

Solution 4: Level of Difficulty (2)

$$a - b = \frac{1^2}{1} + \frac{2^2 - 1^2}{3} + \frac{3^2 - 2^2}{5} + \frac{4^2 - 3^2}{7} + \dots$$

$$+ \frac{1001^2 - 1000^2}{2001} - \frac{1001^2}{2003}$$

Since $=\;\;=1$ for all $k \ge 0$, it follows that

$a - b = \;\; - \;\; \approx 1001 - 500.25 \approx 500.75$

Hence, $a - b \approx 501.$

Solution 5: Level of Difficulty (2)

The numbers in option (4) can be written as $2^2, 3^2, 4^2, 5^2 \dots$ so on, which are not in an arithmetic progression. All the other statements always hold true.

Solution 6: Level of Difficulty (2)

The base circumference $= \dfrac{22}{7} \times \dfrac{56}{11} = 16$ cm. The length of one complete turn $= \sqrt{16^2 + 12^2} = 20$ cm. Hence, total length = 80 cm.

Solution 7: Level of Difficulty (2)

Let x be the production of tea and y be the production of coffee. It is given that $x = 3y$.

Also, $x(100 + a) + y(100 + b) = (x + y)(100 + 5c)$

$\rightarrow \quad\quad x(a - 5c) = y(5c - b)$

i.e. $\quad\quad 3a - 15c = 5c - b$

i.e. $\quad\quad 3a + b = 20c$ (i)

Also, $x(100 + b) + y(100 + a) = (x + y)(100 + 3c)$

$\rightarrow \quad\quad x(b - 3c) = y(3c - a)$

i.e. $\quad\quad 3b - 9c = 3c - a$

i.e. $\quad\quad a + 3b = 12c$ (ii)

Eqn. (i) $- 3 \times$ Eqn. (ii) given,

$$\begin{array}{r} 3a + b = 20c \\ a + 3b = 12c \\ \hline -8b = -16c \end{array}$$

i.e. $\quad\quad b = 2c$

$\therefore \quad\quad 3a = 18c \rightarrow a = 6c$

$\therefore \quad\quad \dfrac{a}{b} = \dfrac{6c}{2c} = \dfrac{3}{1}$

Hence (4).

Solution 8: Level of Difficulty (2)

$n = 1$; since n is an integer < 2.

$\therefore \quad\quad \dfrac{100}{m} - \dfrac{200}{m + 10} = \dfrac{80}{12}$

$\therefore \quad\quad m = 5.$

Hence [2].

Solution 9: Level of Difficulty (1)

9 pens + 9 pencils would cost him ₹ 225. Hence, he can buy 4 pens and 4 pencils for ₹100.

Solution 10: Level of Difficulty (2)

The differentiation of the function would give:

$2ax + b = 0 \rightarrow x = -b/2a = 2 \rightarrow -b = 4a \rightarrow b = -4a.$

Hence, the expression would become: $x^2 - 4x + c$. At $x = 2$, it becomes $4 - 8 + c = -2 \rightarrow c = 2$. Hence, the equation is $x^2 - 4x + 2$.

10. 3

It can be seen for this equation that the roots are irrational.

Solution 11: Level of Difficulty (1)

→ $b = -4a$.

Hence, the expression would become: $x^2 - 4x + c$. At $x = 2$, it becomes $4 - 8 + c = -2 \rightarrow c = 2$

Hence, the equation is $x^2 - 4x + 2$.

At $x = 3$, the function becomes $11 - 12 = -1$.

Solution 12: Level of Difficulty (2)

Solution 13: Level of Difficulty (2)

Consider a three digit number in which 7 comes exactly once i.e. from 107 to 997.

If you fix seven at the units place and use the other digits for filling in the other 2 places you will get 72 numbers in which 7 comes at unit place i.e. $\underline{8} \times \underline{9} \times {}_7$

Similarly, at the ten's place there would be i.e. $\underline{8} \times {}_7 \times 9 = 72$ ways

And also at the hundred's place there would be ${}_7 \times \underline{9} \times \underline{9} = 81$ ways

So, the total numbers from 100 to 1000, there are $72 + 72 + 81 = 225$ numbers in which they have exactly one of their digit is 7.

Solution 13: Level of Difficulty (2)

Solve through trial and error (2)

Solution 14: Level of Difficulty (2)

Solve through trial and error (2)

Solution 15: Level of Difficulty (3)

Let radius of bigger circle be R.

∴ $OC = R\sqrt{2}$ cm.

If 'r' be the radius of smaller circle. Then $R\sqrt{2} = R + r + r\sqrt{2}$ (By Fig.)

$$R(\sqrt{2} - 1) = r(\sqrt{2} + 1)$$
$$R(\sqrt{2} - 1) = (\sqrt{2} - 1)(\sqrt{2} + 1) \quad (\because r = \sqrt{2} - 1)$$
$$\Rightarrow \qquad R = (\sqrt{2} + 1)\,\text{cm}.$$

Area of shaded part $= R^2 - \dfrac{\pi R^2}{4} - \pi r^2$

$$= (\sqrt{2} + 1)^2 - \frac{\pi}{6}(\sqrt{2} + 1)^2 - \pi(\sqrt{2} - 1)^2$$

$$= 2 + 1 + 2\sqrt{2} - \pi \left(\frac{2 + 1 + 2\sqrt{2}}{4} + 2 + 1 - 2\sqrt{2} \right)$$

$$= 3 + 2\sqrt{2} - \frac{\pi}{4}(3 + 2\sqrt{2} + 12 - 8\sqrt{2})$$

$$= 3 + 2\sqrt{2} - \frac{\pi}{4}(15 - 6\sqrt{2})$$

$$= 3\left(1 - 5\frac{\pi}{4}\right) + 2\sqrt{2}\left(1 - 3\frac{\pi}{4}\right)$$

$$= \frac{3}{4}(4 - 5\pi) + \frac{1}{\sqrt{2}}(4 - 3\pi)$$

Solution 16: Level of Difficulty (2)

In the time it takes the older sister to reach the top, the up escalator has carried her forward 30 steps, because the total length of the escalator is 40 steps and she took 10 steps herself. Therefore, in the same time the down escalator pushes the younger sister back 30 steps. To make up this set-back and cover the original 40 steps separating her from the top the younger sister must make a total of 70 steps.

Solution 17: Level of Difficulty (2)

Each of the numbers from 1 to 6 can only have two possible neighbours to avoid sums divisible by 2 or 3. For example, 5 may neighbour only 2 or 6. If we write the numbers 1, 4, 3, 2, 5, and 6 in that order in a ring then each number will be next to its two possible neighbors. Therefore, to order the six numbers successfully we need only start at any point along the ring (6 choices) and list the numbers as they appear around the ring in either direction (2 choices) for a total of 12 possible orderings.

Solution 18: Level of Difficulty (1)

We find $f^4(11) = 169$, $f^6(11) = 169$ ∴ $f^{1998}(11) = 169$.

Solution 19: Level of Difficulty (2)

Suppose there are N fishes initially. Then after 6 months, $N \times 75\%/60\% = 5N/4$ fishes, and $60 \times 75\% = 45$ tagged. Estimate $45/(5N/4) = 3/70$, or $N = 840$

Solution 20: Level of Difficulty (2)

If I choose a shot that I will make with probability p (where p is between 0 and 1/3), then Michael Jordan will make the same shot with probability $3p$. Hence, the probability that I make a shot that Jordan subsequently misses is $p(1 - 3p)$. The graph of this function is a parabola which equals zero when $p = 0$ and $p = \dfrac{1}{3}$. By symmetry the vertex (maximum) is midway between the two, at $p = \dfrac{1}{6}$.

Hence, the best chance I have of winning the game is $\dfrac{1}{12}$.

MODEL TEST PAPER
(base on the Latest Online Pattern)

Instructions:

Time: 70 mins in each section

This section contains 1 model test paper. The paper has 2 sections having 20 questions each. In order to reach the qualifying score, you would need to solve at least 36 questions at 100% accuracy. However at an accuracy of 90%, you would need around 45 attempts with at least 40 correct questions.

While taking the test you have to ensure that you have to spend the entire 70 mins allocated for a section within the section itself. You are not allowed to move between the sections while solving a section.

MODEL TEST PAPER
(base on the Latest Online Pattern)

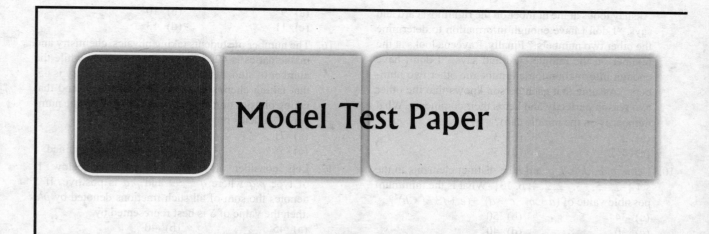

Model Test Paper

Section I: Quantitative Aptitude and Data Interpretation

1. I bought 7 apples, 9 oranges and 5 guavas. Rajan bought 11 apples, 10 guavas and 18 oranges for an amount which was three-fourth more than what I had paid. What per cent of the total amount paid by me was paid for the apples?
   (a) 37.5%   (b) 62.5%
   (c) 58.3%   (d) 45%

2. Find the sum of all the roots of the given function:
   $F(x) = |x - 2|^2 + |x - 2| - 2$
   (a) 4   (b) 3
   (c) 5   (d) not possible to find

3. The equation $(x + 1)^{0.5} - (x - 1)^{0.5} = (4x - 1)^{0.5}$ has:
   (a) no solutions   (b) one solution
   (c) two solutions   (d) more than two solution

4. A man has 7 friends comprising 4 ladies and 3 gentlemen. His wife also has 7 friends comprising 4 gentlemen and 3 ladies. Find the no. of ways in which 6 people can be invited by man and his wife such that among them 3 are ladies , 3 are gentlemen, 3 are man's friends and 3 are wife's friends.
   (a) 324   (b) 400
   (c) 475   (d) 485

5. Five balls of different colours are to be placed in three boxes of different sizes. Each box can hold all 5 balls. In how many different ways we can place balls so that no box remains empty?
   (a) 60   (b) 150
   (c) 300   (d) 600

6. Find the sum of the series
   $1/(1 + 1^2 + 1^4) + 2/(1 + 2^2 + 2^4) + 3/(1 + 3^2 + 3^4)$
   +...............till infinity
   (a) 1/3   (b) 1/2

   (c) 2/3   (d) 3/4

7. Ishant and Ganguly were warming up for a match practice. So both of them were taking a round of the cricket stadium which had a circumference of 1000 m. If they both maintain a uniform speed throughout the run and Ishant crosses Ganguly for the first time in 3.5 mins., then what is the time taken by Ishant to cover 4 laps of the ground? Both have the same starting speed and as per coach's orders both have to complete 4 laps of the ground. Also Ishant being a fast bowler runs at twice the speed of Ganguly.
   (a) 20 min   (b) 15 min
   (c) 10 min   (d) 7 min

8. The college auditorium is to be painted. But due to lack of funds it couldn't be done. So a sincere student took the initiative and decided to paint the audi. Seeing his enthusiasm other students joined him. He is the only person doing the job on the first day. On the second day 2 more boys join him. On the third day 3 more boys join the group of the previous day and so on.....In this manner, the job is finished in exactly 25 days. How many days would 15 workers take to do the same job, given that one man is twice as efficient as a boy.
   (a) 142   (b) 143
   (c) 145   (d) 147

9. Three cards, each with a positive integer written on it, are lying face-down on a table. Twinkle, Raveena, and Akshay are told that
   (a) the numbers are all different,
   (b) they sum to 13, and
   (c) they are in increasing order, left to right

   First, Twinkle looks at the number on the left-most card and says, "I don't have enough information to determine the other two numbers." Then

Akshay looks at the number on the rightmost card and says, "I don't have enough information to determine the other two numbers." Finally, Raveena looks at the number on the middle card and says, "I don't have enough information to determine the other two numbers." Assume that each person knows that the other two reason perfectly and hears their comments. What number is on the middle card?

(a) 2   (b) 3
(c) 4   (d) 5

10. Let a, b, c, d, e, f, g and h be distinct elements in the set $\{-7, -5, -3, -2, 2, 4, 6, 13\}$. What is the minimum possible value of $(a + b + c + d)^2 + (e + f + g + h)^2$?

(a) 34   (b) 50
(c) 30   (d) 40

11. A sum of money gets doubled in little over 4 years at X % SI. Had the rate been Y % the sum would have been thrice in little less than 7 years. Then the least possible value of (Y-X), given that it is an integer will be

(a) 4   (b) 5
(c) 2   (d) 6

Directions for Questions 12 and 13: A, B, and C are three persons on a circular track in random order. They start moving simultaneously with constant speeds such that after some time t, A, B, C are at the initial positions of B, C and A respectively (none of them having completed a full revolution during the time).

12. If A, B and C can complete a full rotation of a circular track in 4, 6 and 12 minutes respectively, then t (in seconds) can be:

(a) 60   (b) 240
(c) 120   (d) both 120 and 240 seconds are possible

13. If A, B and C come again to their initial positions simultaneously next time after 1 hour; then t can not be equal to

(a) 10 minutes   (b) 12 minutes
(c) 15 minutes   (d) 18 minutes

14. For each real number x, let $f(x)$ be the minimum of the numbers $4x + 1$, $x + 2$, and $-2x + 4$. Then the maximum value of $f(x)$ is

(a) 1/3   (b) 1/2
(c) 2/3   (d) 8/3

Questions (15 and 16): A group of students are asked to take at least one subject from Physics, Chemistry, and Mathematics for their courses.

15. The number of students taking exclusively one subject is 50 while the number of students taking exclusively two subjects is 30. The number of students taking physics, chemistry, and mathematics is 45, 44, and 48 respectively. The number of students taking all subjects is

(a) 9   (b) 10
(c) 11   (d) 13

16. The number of students taking physics, chemistry and mathematics is 42, 45 and 49 respectively while the number of students taking physics or chemistry is 65, that taking chemistry or mathematics is 70 and that taking physics or mathematics is 72. What is the number of students not taking all 3 subjects?

(a) 71   (b) 77
(c) 58   (d) cannot be determined

17. Lets consider all irreducible fractions below 1, of type p/q where $q = 99$ and p/q is positive. If S denotes the sum of all such fractions denoted by p/q, then the value of S is best represented by

(a) 45   (b) 40
(c) 50   (d) 44

18. 900 distinct 'n' digit numbers are to be formed by using only 3 digits 2,5,7. Find the smallest value of 'n' for which this is possible.

(a) 5   (b) 6
(c) 7   (d) 8

19. Let $g(x) = 1 + x - [x]$ and $f(x) = -1$ for $x < 0$, 0 for $x = 0$, 1 for $x > 0$. Find $f(g(x))$.

(a) x (b) 0
(c) 1   (d) $f(x)$

20. 301! is divisible by $(30!)^n$. What is the max. possible integral value of n?

(a) 13   (b) 16
(c) 9   (d) 10

Directions for Questions 21 to 23: Answer the questions on the basis of data given in the table:

The table below shows the sales and expenditure of three companies—KESARI foods, KASTURI foods and KABULI foods for the financial year 2004-2005. These companies are located in the different parts of the world. Expenditure break-ups are in percentage. Closely analyse the data and answer the questions.

Particulars	Kesari foods (Sales ₹ 7.5)	Kasturi foods (Sales ₹ 1.9)	Kabuli foods (Sales ₹ 6.9)
Operating Profit	7	9	9
Interest paid	10	11	12
Rental	21	19	18
Taxes	8	8	11
Salaries	12	9	12
Raw material cost	25	18	19
Power and Electricity	5	10	7
Labour cost	5	6	4
Transportation	3	2	3

Contd

Particulars	Kesari foods (Sales ₹ 7.5)	Kasturi foods (Sales ₹ 1.9)	Kabuli foods (Sales ₹ 6.9)
Maintenance	2	5	2
Miscellaneous	2	3	3
Total	**100**	**100**	100

* Sales to be read as ₹ million/month

* Sales break ups are in percentages (%)

21. What can be concluded about the expenditure in salaries, raw material, transportation and rental of all the three companies listed above in the table?
    (a) Percentage wise Kabuli food is spending more than each of the other two.
    (b) Revenue wise Kesari foods is spending more than Kasturi and Kabuli together.
    (c) Revenue wise Kasturi and Kabuli are spending less then Kesari foods.
    (d) Percentage wise Kasturi spends more than Kesari, which in turn spends more than Kabuli.

22. If the interest paid by KESARI FOODS is reduced by 1%, and everything else remains the same, its operating profit will:
    (a) increase by 1% per cent.
    (b) not change.
    (c) increase by 0.0075 million
    (d) increase by 2% per cent

23. If the average monthly salary in Kabuli FOODS is ₹ 9,517.24, then how many employees does Kabuli have?
    (a) 28   (b) 48
    (c) 81   (d) 87

Directions for Questions 24 to 27: Performance study of various brands of soap is given below with their cost/100 gm.

Brand	% increase in skin softness S_1	% increase in natural fairness S_2	% reduction in skin diseases S_3	% reduction in foul smell S_4	% reduction in dry skin S_5	Cost C
B_1	55	49	35	30	30	100
B_2	20	25	40	35	32	50
B_3	69	63	45	20	15	50
B_4	51	48	55	40	38	25
B_5	38	30	25	22	24	100

Benefit/Rupee spent for a soap is measured by a variable known as 'R' where

$R_1 = S_1/C$, $R_2 = S_2/C$, $R_3 = S_3/C$ and so on.

24. "Soap Effectiveness Index" = $(R_1 + R_2 + R_3 + R_4 + R_5)/100$. With respect to the "Soap Effectiveness Index" if the soap brands are arranged in the increasing order, then which of the options, satisfy?
    (a) B_1, B_2, B_3, B_4 (b) B_2, B_1, B_3, B_4
    (c) B_2, B_1, B_3, B_5 (d) B_1, B_3, B_4, B_5

25. A family wants to purchase 3 different kinds of soaps for different requirements. They want to make a choice of 3 soaps according to the following condition that any of the three soaps selected should have the highest value among all the brands in any quality criteria excluding cost. Which of the following option satisfies their requirement?
    (a) B_3, B_1, B_5 (b) B_4, B_2, B_1
    (c) B_3, B_4, B_1 (d) None of these

26. In the case of Brand "B3", the company starts a scheme under which the customers get 1 soap free for every 4 purchased. After the change has come into effect, in how many cases for the Brand 'B3', the value of the quantities $S_1, S_2, S_3, S_4, S_5, R_1, R_2, R_3, R_4$ and R_5 is higher in comparison to Brand "B4"?
    (a) 4   (b) 3
    (c) 2   (d) 1

27. A family would like to change the soap brand that they are using. The condition the family members make is that the new brand should have the highest value in at least 3 out the first four quality parameters (S_1, S_2, S_3, S_4) and for the fifth column (S_5), the value of R should be at least greater than 80% of the 'R' value of the old brand. If they are using brand B_2 now, then which brand can they replace it with ?
    (a) B_3 (b) B_1
    (c) B_4 (d) No brand satisfies the above criteria

Directions for Questions 28 to 30: Given below is table indicating the individual scores of ten players of two different basketball teams in single match between them. Each had 5 players and all the scoring shots carried either two or three points. The team scoring the maximum points won. Players scored for their own teams only.

Player	Points
Arun	15
Birender	17
Chiranjeev	23
Dhruv	18
Eleswarappu	13

Contd

Player	Points
Fardeen	16
Geetam	19
Hasan	24
Ishwar	15
Jeetu	20

The difference between the lowest and the highest individual scores in both the teams is the same.

The highest individual scores from the teams had the same number of scoring shots.

Arun, Dhruv, Fardeen and Geetam had an even number of scoring shots comprising both 2 and 3 –pointers.

Birender, Eleswarappu, and Ishwar had an odd number of scoring shots comprising both 2 and 3 –pointers.

Chiranjeev was another player in his team to score 8 points in 4 shots.

28. What is the difference between the numbers of 3 – pointer shots scored by both the teams?
    (a) 4   (b) 5
    (c) 6   (d) 7

29. Which of the following could be a difference between the total 2 –pointer and 3 –pointer shots scored by both the teams together?
    (a) 7   (b) 8
    (c) 11   (d) 10

30. Who among the given players had the highest ratio of points scored to number of scoring shots?
    (a) Arun   (b) Chiranjeev
    (c) Eleswarappu   (d) Fardeen

Section II: Verbal Ability and Logical Reasoning

Passage I

In this passage from a novel, the narrator has been reading letters of his grandmother. Susan Ward was a young woman—a writer and a mother—whose husband Oliver was working as a mining engineer in Leadville, in the West. Here, the narrator imagines Susan Ward as she spends the winter with her family in Milton, New York, before rejoining her husband in the spring.

From the parental burrow, Leadville seemed so far away that it was only half-real. Unwrapping her apple-cheeked son after a sleigh ride down the lane, she had difficulty in believing that she had ever lived anywhere but here in Milton.

She felt how the placid industry of her days matched the placid industry of all the days that had passed over that farm through six generations. Present and past were less continuous than synonymous. She did not have to come at her grandparents through a time machine. Her own life and that of the grandfather she was writing about showed her similar figures in an identical landscape. At the milldam where she had learned to skate she pulled her little boy on his sled, and they watched a weasel snow-white for winter flirt his black-tripped tail in and out of the mill's timbers. She might have been watching with her grandfather's eyes.

Watching a wintry sky die out beyond black elms, she could not make her mind restore the sight of the western mountains at sunset from her cabin door, or the cabin itself, or Oliver, or their friends. Who were those glittering people intent on raiding the continent for money or for scientific knowledge? What illusion was it that she bridged between this world and that? She paused sometimes; cleaning the room she had always called Grandma's Room, and thought with astonishment of the memory of Oliver's great revolver lying on the dresser when he, already a thoroughing Westerner, had come to the house to court her.

The town of Milton was dim and gentle, molded by gentle lives, the current of change as slow through it, as the seep of water through a bog. More than once she thought how wrong those women in San Francisco had been, convinced that their old homes did not welcome them on their return. Last year when Oliver's professional future was uncertain, she would have agreed. Now, with the future assured in the form of Oliver's appointment as manager of the Adelaide mine in Leadville, the comfortable past asserted itself unchanged. Need for her husband, like worry over him, was turned low. Absorbed in her child and in the writing of her book, she was sunk in her affection for home. Even the signs of mutability that sometimes jolted her—the whiteness of her mother's hair, the worn patience of her sister's face, the morose silences of her brothers-in-law, now so long and black that the women worried about him in low voices—could not more than briefly interrupt the deep security and peace.

I wonder if ever again Americans can have that experience of returning to a home place so intimately known, profoundly felt, deeply loved, and absolutely submitted to. It is not quite true that you can't go home again. But it gets less likely. We have had too many divorces, we have consumed too much transpiration, we have lived too shallowly in too many places. I doubt that any one of my son's generation could comprehend the home feelings of someone like Susan Ward. Despite her unwillingness to live separately from her husband, she could probably have stayed on indefinitely in Milton, visited only occasionally by an asteroid husband. Or she would have picked up the old home and remade it into a new place. What she resisted was being a woman with no real home.

When frontier historians theorize about the uprooted, the lawless, the purseless, and the socially cut-off who emigrated to the West, they are not talking about people like my grandmother, so much that was cherished and loved, women like her had to give up; and the more they gave it up, the more they carried it helplessly with them. It was a process like ionization: what was subtracted from one pole was added to the other. For that sort of pioneer, the west was not a new country being created, but an old one being reproduced; in that sense our pioneer women were always more realistic than our pioneer men. The moderns, carrying little baggage of the cultural kind, not even living in traditional air, but breathing in to their space helmets, a scientific mixture of synthetic gases (and polluted at that) are the true pioneers. Their circuitry seems to include no domestic sentiment; they have had their empathy removed. Their computers have no ghostly feedback of home, Sweet Home. How marvelously free they are! How unutterably deprived!

31. In the beginning of the first paragraph, the phrase "parental burrow" suggests
    (a) a lack of luxurious accommodations
    (b) an atmosphere of peaceful security
    (c) the work required to sustain a home
    (d) the loss of privacy

32. It can be said that Ward "did not have to come at her grandparents through machine" because
    (a) she was deeply immersed in the history and literature of the period of their lives.
    (b) her life in Milton closely resembled theirs
    (c) as a writer she could intuitively sense their lives
    (d) she possessed written accounts of their lives

33. The reference to the grandfather's eyes at the end of the second paragraph indicates that Ward
    (a) longed to see nature as her ancestors did
    (b) felt that her grandfather would approve of her life choices
    (c) was seeing something her grandfather himself might well have seen
    (d) longed to let her grandfather know what she was experiencing

34. The reference to a bog in the first part of the fifth paragraph serves to convey a sense of the
    (a) natural setting of the town of Milton
    (b) deliberate pace of life in Milton
    (c) confinement that Ward first felt in Milton
    (d) vague foreboding that permeated Milton

35. Ward came to feel differently from "those women in San Francisco" because
    (a) the rigors of life in West made life in East seem more pleasant
    (b) the problems in her sister's life made her more content with the situation in her own life
    (c) her own career as a writer had become more important to her
    (d) she was free to enjoy her surroundings as she was confident about her ancestral home always welcoming her.

36. The word "sunk" (Paragraph 5) in the passage conveys the degree to which Ward
    (a) is depressed about being separated from her husband

    (b) is concerned about her son's social development
    (c) allows herself to be totally engrossed in what she is doing
    (d) lets down her defenses to free her creativity

Passage II

When one company acquires another, the larger firm usually takes over the smaller one. There are exceptions to the rule, however, such as the Good—Value Mart merger.

Once the leading chain of supermarkets in New England, Good Food Stores has been steadily declining for twenty years. Their sales fell from 25 per cent to 5 per cent of the market. During the same period (1958-1978), earning plunged from over 8 million to a loss of 23 million. With such a track record, Good Food stores hardly seemed a likely candidate for acquisition.

But the Midwest-based Value Mart chain acquired Good Food earlier this year with high hopes of turning around the New England chain. Value Mart is a privately owned chain of supermarkets, with approximately sixty stores throughout the Midwest. The average sales for last year ran a little over 6 million per store. On the other hand, Good Food is a publicly held company that averaged sales of 4 million in each of its 230 stores. In the last five years, Value Mart's earnings reached nearly 15 million, while Good Food lost 40 million during that same period.

The chairman of Value Mart, Harold Brown, is an old hand at putting ailing supermarkets back on their feet. In 1963, Mr. Brown helped turn around an old Cincinnati chain; he changed it from an unprofitable, out of date store to a market leader with a profit of 7 million in just six years. After leaving the Cincinnati chain, Brown, along with thirty other investors, bought Value Mart and turned it around, so that in the past year it has surpassed even the Cincinnati chain in sales. Brown's two success stories now account for 60 percent of the supermarket business in the Cincinnati area.

Although Brown's track record has been good (and was, In fact, the reason Value Mart was able to obtain the necessary funds to acquire Good Food), there has been some speculation on whether Value Mart has undertaken more than it can handle. A powerful New England trade member wonders whether Value Mart has the know-how and strength to take on the leading established New England chains.

Good Food's problems started in the late 1950's and early 1960's, when they failed to follow their competitors move to the suburbs and large shopping centers. This put Good Food behind in market share.

Good Food then made another bad move in 1962 in an attempt to regain some of its lost market share. They acquired a wavering division of supermarkets in the New York area and tried to establish themselves there, while maintaining a policy of low investment and high prices back home in New England. The strategy did not work, and consequently Good Food had to pull to out of New York. In addition, Good Food has lost customers in New England.

688 How to Prepare for Quantitative Aptitude for the CAT

Good Food's woes were increased by mismanagement. Complacent task forces were formed to "study" problems instead of dealing with them immediately. Coupled with this was a group of directors who were, for the most part, not industry experts but bankers and lawyers.

The choices facing Good Food in 1976 were as follows: sell, if possible; liquidate; or push onwards. The decision was made to seek a merger partner, and Value Mart was contacted through Good Food's investment counselor. Given Good Food's unpromising situation, it seems surprising that Value Mart was interested. Mr. Brown, however, fresh out of a Cincinnati price war, realized that his home market was saturated and that acquisition or territorial expansion was the necessary means for growth.

Value Mart took charge of the situation and began to reorganise even before the merger was completed. Their top executives took over key positions in the Good Food organisation, a move that included ousting Good Food's president. In an attempt to drastically cut down on administrative expenses, over two hundred jobs at the management level were abolished. (it is expected that this alone will result in savings of over 3 million).

Another change was placing control of grocery merchandising and buying in the hands of those at the corporate level, rather than dividing this function amongst Good Food's store managers and executives. This facilitated the introduction of Value Mart's tried-and-true policy of "deal buying," or taking advantage of cut-rate prices to buy huge quantities of canned or packaged goods. Because "buying" in such quantity necessitates ample inventory space, construction was begun the day after the merger, to increase Good Food's warehousing facilities to the tune of 7 million. The new warehouse will be the largest supermarket warehouse in the United States, and it is expected to save in cost and avoid out-of-stock problems.

The Value Mart strategy for turning around the New England chain also involves deemphasizing nonfood items and hence attracting customers by placing emphasis on the quality of its produce (fruits and vegetables) and meats. Problems at the store level are being corrected by extending work hours at individual stores, cleaning up dirty premises(Good Food had reduced personnel in its stores in an attempt to cut labor costs, resulting in dirty stores and low morale among the employees), and teaching store managers how to repackage and maintain their fresh produce.

Visits to each Good Food store by a Value Mart senior vice-president of operations resulted in control and, equally as important, a demonstrated and direct interest by top management in individual store operations.

This top-level involvement in daily store routine is a far cry from the old Good Food "hands off" approach. The Midwestern senior vice-president not only visits each store to make suggestions, but also comes back unannounced to check on the implementations of changes.

Mr. Brown's immediate objective is to increase business from present customers. He estimates an increase in volume of over 100 million if sales per customer can be improved by only 10 percent. Once sales are up and stores are operating smoothly, Brown plans to renovate about sixty-five of Good Food's largest stores, a move that should bring in an additional 6- 7 million in weekly sales.

Finally, the older and smaller Good Food stores will be given a facelift with the increased revenue from the redone larger stores. Value Mart intends to feed its profits back into the entire operation to keep it going and constantly moving ahead.

37. What was the principal reason for Value Mart's interest in the declining Good Food chain?
    (a) Value Mart wanted to establish a foothold in the east.
    (b) Brown was tempted by the challenge offered by Good Food.
    (c) Brown saw Good Food as a means for growth.
    (d) The acquisition price was very low.

38. What was Good Food's first bad move that led to eventual decline?
    (a) Over expansion
    (b) Failure to maintain good relations with suppliers
    (c) failure to follow the trend to the suburbs
    (d) failure to maintain quality merchandise

39. In the early 1960s Good Food tried to enter the New York area. Why was their strategy unsuccessful?
    A. because of low investment in their home territory
    B. because of high prices in their home territory
    C. because of lack of prior knowledge about the New York market
    (a) A only
    (b) B only
    (c) A and B only
    (d) B and C only

40. What was Value Mart's initial move in reorganising Good Food?
    (a) placing Value Mart's top executives in key Good Food positions.
    (b) cutting expenses
    (c) making buying and merchandising corporate-level functions
    (d) improving produce quality

41. According to the passage, what is "deal buying"?
    (a) buying packaged goods in the huge quantities from wholesalers
    (b) buying packaged goods in huge quantities at cut-rate prices
    (c) buying packaged goods from small dealers at reduced prices
    (d) buying produce from big, out –of-town farmers at reduced prices

42. One of the most important and constructive reforms in National Politics is the abolition of the post of the State Ministers in the various departments.

Each of the following, if true, would strengthen the above argument, except

(a) There are few, if any, specific duties or responsibilities assigned to the State Minister in any department.

(b) A historian claimed that the post was "superfluous."

(c) People of Cabinet minister caliber normally refuse the post if offered a ministership in the guise of a state minister.

(d) The office is used as a means of appeasing regional parties, by giving their MPs ministerial status and perks without giving the many significant responsibilities.

43. Jaya and Devika are both successful women who are also members of a socially disadvantaged section of the society. Jaya has a firm belief in positive discrimination. By positive discrimination she believes that the negative discrimination that society has subjected her section of the society to can only be offset through reverse discrimination. She believes that if positions of economic, social and political eminence, power and honor are offered principally to historically disadvantaged sections of society, then these groups will begin to play a more significant role in society today. Devika, on the other hand, feels that she has succeeded in her chosen field of work on her hard work and on her own merits. She thinks that the principle of positive discrimination is flawed since it will result in the lowering of standards and decreases competition between similarly qualified personnel who will expect to achieve positions because of their factors other than rather than their suitability for the particular position.

Which of the following best sums up Jaya's argument?

(a) Positive discrimination will encourage more people to apply for jobs, previously unavailable to them.

(b) Positive discrimination will give extra opportunities to socially disadvantaged sections of the society.

(c) Quality and professionalism will improve because of the greater number of positions held by members of minority groups.

(d) Positive discrimination will remove deep rooted prejudices against the weaker sections of society from the work arena.

Directions for Questions 44 to 46: The sentences given in each question, when properly sequenced, form a coherent paragraph. Each sentence is labelled with a letter. Choose the most logical order of sentences from among the given choices to construct a coherent paragraph.

44.

1. In the twentieth century, John Maynard Keynes has been the most important scholar working in the tradition of the classical political economists.

A. But his interest, like theirs, was in the analysis of the great issues of his day, the greatest of which in the inter-war period was not growth but unemployment, a problem so acute at the time that in desperation the Germans turned to Hitler and to fascism.

B. The very future of Western democracies was placed at risk.

C. Keynes was concerned not just to understand unemployment intellectually, but to put forward practical suggestions as to how the problem could be solved.

D. This does not mean that he agreed with everything they wrote.

6. He believed fervently that, for all its faults, Western liberal democracy offered the best hope for the world, and he saw himself working to save it.

(a) DCBA   (b) BACD

(c) BCDA   (d) DABC

45.

1. For centuries philosophers have dealt with aspects of humanness, of humanity. But, surprisingly, there is no agreed-upon definition of the quality of humanness.

A. It is my conviction that we are beginning to identify these components, that we can see the gradual emergence of humanness in our evolutionary history.

B. But if this sense of humanity came into being in the course of evolutionary history, then it must have component parts, and they in turn must be identifiable.

C. Those who tried to define humanness found themselves molding Jell-O.: it kept slipping through the fingers.

D. It hardly seemed necessary, partly because it appeared so obvious: humanness is what we feel about ourselves.

6. I am therefore perplexed by, and impatient with, a popular alternative view that is championed by several scholars.

(a) ABCD   (b) DCBA

(c) BCDA   (d) CBDA

46.

A. Economists see the world as a machine.

B. A very complicated one perhaps, but nevertheless a machine, whose workings can be understood by putting together carefully and meticulously its component parts.

C. A lever pulled in a certain part of the machine with certain strength will have regular and predictable outcomes elsewhere in the machine.

D. The behaviour of the system as a whole can be deducted from a simple aggregation of these components.

(a) ABDC   (b) ABCD

(c) ACBD   (d) ADBC

Directions for Questions 47 to 50: Fill in the blanks with the appropriate words from the options given below.

47. The King has ---------- to a proposal to enhance the powers of the council of ministers.
    (a) coincided   (b) allied
    (c) assented   (d) opined

48. The disciplinary committee has --------- the use of detention after classes as a punishment for bad behaviour.
    (a) extended   (b) authorized
    (c) clamped   (d) embargo

49. The judge ---------- the use of capital punishment for serious crimes.
    (a) franchised   (b) endorse
    (c) agreed   (d) condoned

50. The committee were in favour of the proposal but the president -------- it.
    (a) vetoed   (b) countenance
    (c) sanctioned   (d) condoned

For Questions 51 to 55 read the following instructions: Sunday morning, local pediatrician Dr. Raju Sarma had appointments with five infants scheduled at 9:00, 9:30, 10:00, 10:30, and 11:00. Each of the five, including the Oke baby, is a different number--1, 2, 3, 4, or 5--of months old. The following notes are available.

1. Immediately after seeing infant Bimal, Dr. Sarma examined the Michaels infant, who is 2 months younger than Bimal.
2. Eshwarya isn't the one of the five who is 1 month old.
3. The doctor saw Dhruv later in the morning than the 1-month-old.
4. The 9:30 appointment was with the 3-month-old baby.
5. The Lavande infant isn't the one who is 5 months of age.
6. Dr. Sarma saw the Nalini infant, then examined Amar, who is 2 months older than the Nalini baby.
7. The pediatrician's 10:00 appointment was with Charu, who isn't the Michaels or the Nalini baby.
8. The Pattabhiraman baby isn't the 1-month-old and wasn't the doctor's 9:00 examinee.

51. How old (in months) is infant Bimal?
    (a) 2   (b) 3
    (c) 4   (d) 5

52. At what time did infant Eshwarya meet the doctor?
    (a) 9   (b) 9:30
    (c) 10   (d) 10:30

53. Whose baby is infant Charu?
    (a) Oke   (b) Michaels
    (c) Lavande   (d) Nalini

54. Which of the following is not correct with respect to infant Dhruv?

(a) He is Nalini's baby.
(b) He is 2 months old.
(c) His appointment was at 11.00.
(d) He is not the Oke baby.

55. Who was the last infant to meet the doctor?
    (a) Amar   (b) Dhruv
    (c) Charu   (d) Eshwarya

Directions for Questions 56 to 58: Read the information given below and answer the questions that follow.

Four men - Amar, Bijay, Chetan and Derek and four women - Preeti, Queen, Raveena and Surabhi are sitting for a formal get together, in such a way that they face the centre and form a circle. No two women and no two men are next to each other, Amar is to the immediate left of Raveena, who is opposite to Queen. Preeti and Queen have only Chetan dancing between them. Preeti is sitting opposite to Surabhi, who is sitting to the immediate right of Bijay.

56. If Bijay is the only person sitting between Queen and Surabhi, then who is opposite to him?
    (a) Amar   (b) Queen
    (c) Chetan   (d) Derek

57. Which of the following is an acceptable arrangement of the invitees in clock\vise direction (names of individuals are only represented by their first letters in the options given below)?
    (a) C, Q, P, D, S, B, A and R
    (b) Q, C, P, D, R, A, S and B.
    (c) A, R, D , P, C, Q, B and S
    (d) D, R, A, S, B, Q, P and C.

58. Which of the following pairs are opposite to each other?
    (a) Queen and Raveena
    (b) Surabhi and Preeti
    (c) Chetan and Derek
    (d) both options (a) and (b) are correct

Directions for Questions 59 and 60: Six persons-Akshay, Bobby, Celina, Dimple, Esha, and Faisal took up a job with XYZ Consultants in a week from Monday to Saturday. Each of them joined for different posts on different days. The posts were of-Clerk, Officer, Technician, Manager, Supervisor and Sales Executive though not in the same order.

Faisal joined as a Manager on the first day. Bobby joined as a Supervisor but neither on Wednesday nor Friday. Dimple joined as a Technician on Thursday. The officer joined the firm on Wednesday. Esha joined as a clerk on Tuesday. Akshay joined as a Sales Executive.

59. Who joined the firm on Wednesday?
    (a) Bobby   (b) Celina
    (c) Esha   (d) Data inadequate

60. Who was the last to join the firm?
    (a) Esha   (b) Faisal
    (c) Bobby   (d) Akshay

ANSWER KEY

1. (c)	2. (a)	3. (a)	4. (d)
5. (c)	6. (b)	7. (d)	8. (d)
9. (c)	10. (a)	11. (b)	12. (d)
13. (d)	14. (d)	15. (a)	16. (d)
17. (b)	18. (c)	19. (c)	20. (d)
21. (b)	22. (c)	23. (d)	24. (a)
25. (d)	26. (c)	27. (d)	28. (c)
29. (d)	30. (d)	31. (b)	32. (b)
33. (c)	34. (b)	35. (d)	36. (c)
37. (c)	38. (c)	39. (c)	40. (a)
41. (b)	42. (b)	43. (b)	44. (d)
45. (b)	46. (a)	47. (c)	48. (b)
49. (d)	50. (a)	51. (d)	52. (b)
53. (c)	54. (c)	55. (a)	56. (d)
57. (b)	58. (d)	59. (b)	60. (c)

Solutions

Section I

1. Let us look at the two equations. Let (7 apples + 9 oranges + 5 guavas) cost ₹ x … (1). Hence, (11 apples + 18 oranges + 10 guavas) will cost ₹ 1.75x … (2). Had, in the second case, Rajan decided to buy 14 apples instead of 11, the quantity of each one of them would have doubled over the first case and hence it would have cost me ₹ 2x. So (14 apples + 18 oranges + 10 guavas) = ₹ 2x … (3)

   Now subtracting the second equation from the third, we get 3 apples cost ₹ 0.25x. Since 3 apples cost Re 0.25x, 7 of them will cost Re 0.583x. This is the amount that I spent on apples. Hence, fraction of the total amount paid = 0.583 = 58.3%.

   Hence, Option (c) is correct.

2. Let $|x - 2| = y$
$$y^2 + y - 2 = 0$$
$$y = -2, 1$$
$$|x - 2| = 1$$
$$x - 2 = 1, \ x - 2 = -1$$
$$x = 3, 1$$
   sum of roots = 4

   Hence, Option(a) is correct.

3. Squaring the given equation
$$x + 1 + x - 1 - 2(x^2 - 1)^{0.5} = 4x - 1$$
$$4(x^2 - 1) = 4x^2 + 1 - 4x$$
$$x = 5/4$$
   but this value of x does not satisfy the given equation

   Hence, Option (a) is correct.

4. case 1: $^4C_3 \, ^4C_3 = 16$
   case 2: $(^4C_2 \, ^3C_1)(^3C_1 \, ^4C_2) = 324$
   case 3: $(^4C_1 \, ^3C_2)(^3C_2 \, ^4C_1) = 144$

5. case4: $^3C_3 \, ^3C_3 = 1$
   total = 485

   Hence, Option (d) is correct.

5. Since no box remains empty possible balls can be distributed in manner(2, 2, 1) or (3, 1, 1)
   i.e. $(^5C_2 \, ^3C_2 \, ^1C_1 + \, ^5C_3 \, ^2C_1 \, ^1C_1)3! = 300$

   Hence, Option (c) is correct.

6. solution nth term = $n/(1 + n^2 + n^4) = n/((n^2 + 1)^2 - n^2) = n/(n^2 - n + 1)(n^2 + n + 1)$
$$\tfrac{1}{2}(1/(n^2 - n + 1) - 1/(n^2 + n + 1))$$
   sum = 1/2

   Hence, Option (b) is correct.

   You can also solve this question using values.

7. The ratio of the speeds of Ishant and Ganguly is 2 : 1. Hence they should meet at only

   one point on the circumference i.e. the starting point (As the difference in the ratio in reduced form is 1). For the two of them to meet for the first time, Ishant should have completed one complete round over Ganguly. Since the two of them meet for the first time after 3.5 mins, Ishant should have completed 2 rounds (i.e. 2000 m) and Ganguly should have completed 1 round. (i.e. 1000 m) in this time. Thus, Ishant would complete the race (i.e. 4000 m) in 7 min. Hence, Option (d) is correct.

8. Lets say one boy can do the x part of the work in 1 day.. On the first day only 1 boy works, he can do xth part of the work. On the second day 2 more join him...together the boys can do $x(1 + 2)$ of the work on second day. On third day 3 more boys join the group...they can do $x(1 + 2 + 3)$ part o the work on 3rd day....and so on...Hence we have the sum $x(1) + x(1 + 2) + x(1 + 2 + 3)$.....so on till 25 terms = 1 (as the work is completed in 25 days) now this is nothing but the summation $x * \text{sigma}[n(n + 1)/2]$ from $n = 1$ to $n = 25$ this can be spit into $x/2*(\text{sigma } (n^2) + \text{sigma}(n))$ $n = 1$ to $n = 25$ applying formula for sigma$(n^2) = n(n + 1)(2n + 1)/6$ and sigma$(n) = n(n + 1)/2$ and substituting $n = 25$, we get $x*2925 = 1$ or $x = 1/2925$. Hence one boy can do the work in 2925 days. One man can do it in half the no. of days, ie 1462.5 = 1463 days. and so 10 men can do it in 146.3 = 147 days.

   Hence, Option (d) is correct.

9. The possibilities are:
   1,2,10
   1,3,9
   1,4,8
   1,5,7
   2,3,8
   2,4,7
   2,5,6

3,4,6

When Twinkle is not able to respond after seeing the left most card, we can assume that 3, 4, 6 was not the correct order. Akshay knows this when he sees his card, and hence he must not have seen any of 10,9 or 6. This leaves us with the possible combinations 1, 4, 8; 1, 5, 7; 2, 3, 8 and 2, 4, 7. If Raveena had seen a 3 or 5 she would have known all the cards. Since she does not answer, she must have seen a 4 on the middle card.

Hence, Option (c) is correct.

10. The sum of the positives is 25 and the negatives is 17. The best way to distribute the +8 is 5 and 3 by taking 13, 2, –5 and –7 in the first bracket and the remaining values 4, 6, –2 and –3 in the second bracket. The required answer would be 34.

Hence, Option (a) is correct.

11. The values at which this would occur would be $X = 24\%$ and $Y = 29\%$.

Hence, Option (b) is correct

12. This question is based on the concept that the net distance travelled by all three of them (added up) together is going to be either 1 full round (For the circular order ABC) or 2 full rounds (For the circular order ACB). It can be seen that with the given times for completing a round, if $t = 120$, then the net distance covered by them is equal to 1 complete round. For $t = 240$ seconds it becomes two complete rounds.

Hence, Option (d) is correct.

13. Using the logic that the net distance traveled by all three of them (added up) together is going to be either 1 full round (For the circular order ABC) or 2 full rounds (For the circular order ACB). Since, all three of them are at their respective starting points after an hour, the times required by each of them must be a factor of 60 minutes. (& Can only be 1, 2, 3, 4, 5, 6, 10, 12, 15, 20, 30 or 60 minutes). With these values, we can see that for t equal to 10,12 or 15 minutes it is possible to have either 1 complete round or 2 complete rounds as the total distance traveled by all three of them. Only 18 minutes gives no possibility of creating a total of 1 complete round or 2 complete rounds. Option (d) is correct.

14. Plot the graph of the three lines and realize the maximum point for $f(x)$ would be at the intersection of $x + 2$ and $-2x + 4$. This occurs at $x = 2/3$, and $f(x)$ is 8/3 at that point. Hence, Option (d) is correct.

15. Solve using options. If you put 9 in the middle (all three) you get 36 for only Physics & Physics+ 1 more subject. Similarly, 35 for only Chemistry & Chemistry+ one more subject, 39 for Mathematics & Mathematics + 1 more subject.

The sum of these numbers should be equal to [number of students taking only 1 subject + 2 times number of students taking exactly two subjects] = 50 + 30 + 30 = 110.

Since, 36 + 35 + 39 is also 110, this is the correct answer. The other options won't work here.

Hence, Option (a) is correct.

16. If you were to plot a venn diagram for this question you would realize that we do not know the number of students having only Physics and Chemistry, Only Chemistry and Mathematics and also only Physics and Mathematics. Also, we do not know the value of the total number of students. Hence, we cannot determine the answer to this question. Hence, Option (d) is correct.

17. The required sum would be given by: (1/99 + 2/99 +….+ 98/99) – (11/99 + 22/99 +…+ 88/99)– (9/99 + 18/99 + … 90/99) = 40. Option (b) is correct.

18. We have to find the value of n for which $3^n > 900$ $\rightarrow n > 7$

Hence, Option(c) is correct.

19. $g(x) > 1$ for all x
$$f(g(x)) = 1$$
Option(c) is correct.

20. When we expand 30!...we get $1 \times 2 \times 3 \ldots 30$. $2^{26} \times 3^{14} \times 5^7 \times 7^4 \times 11^2 \times 13^2 \times 17^1 \times 19^1 \times 23^1 \times 29^1$

From this list it is clear that the constraint for the maximum value of n would be either due to the 2's, the 3's, the 5's or the 29's.

301! has $150 + 75 + 37 + 18 + 9 + 4 + 2 + 1 = 296$ twos and hence has [296/26]=11 instances of 2^{26}.

301! has $100 + 33 + 11 + 3 + 1 = 148$ threes and hence has [148/14]=10 instances of 3^{14}.

301! has $60 + 12 + 2 = 74$ fives and hence has [74/7] = 10 instances of 5^7.

301! has 10 instances of 29^1.

Hence, the correct answer would be 10. Hence, Option (d) is correct.

21. It can be seen that Option (b) is correct, as the expenditure of Kesari Foods on these 4 categories are 4.575 while the combined expenditure of Kasturi and Kabuli is lower than that. Hence, Option (b) is correct.

22. If there is a 1% reduction in interest, there would be an increment of 0.0075 million in the operating profit. Hence, Option (c) is correct.

23. $0.12 \times 6900000/9517.24 = 87$. Hence, Option (d) is correct.

24. Soap Effectiveness Index for B_1 is (199/100)/100 = 0.0199

Soap Effectiveness Index for B2 is (152/50)/100 = 0.0304

Soap Effectiveness Index for B3 is (212/50)/100 = =0.0424

Soap Effectiveness Index for B4 is (232/25)/100 = =0.0928

Soap Effectiveness Index for B5 is (139/100)/100 = =0.0139

Hence, B_1, B_2, B_3, B_4 is the correct order.

Option (a) is correct.

25. Quality wise the value of R_1, R_2, R_3, R_4 and R_5 are all maximum only for B4. Hence, the correct option is None of these. Option (d) is correct.

26. B3 is better than B_4 in S_1 and S_2 only. For all other values, B_4 has a higher value (in spite of the scheme which has the effect of B_4's cost coming down to 40.) Option (c) is correct.

27. Only Brand B_3 satisfies the first condition (of having the highest value in at least 3 of the first four categories- however, the brand does not satisfy the other criteria. Hence, Option (d) is correct.

28. The only way to divide the teams would be given by the following table:

WINNING TEAM			LOSING TEAM		
Player Name	Points	Scoring shots break up	Player Name	Points	Scoring shots break up
Hasan	24		Jeetu	20	
Chiranjeev	23	5-4	Fardeen (Even)	16	4-2
Geetam (Even)	19	3-5	Arun (Even)	15	3-3
Dhruv (Even)	18	2-6	Ishwar (Odd)	15	1-6
Birender (Odd)	17	3-4	Eleswarappu (Odd)	13	3-2

Further, Hasan and Jeetu having the same number of scoring shots means three possibilities for them:

	Hasan (24 points)	Jeetu (20 points)
Possibility 1	8-0	4-4
Possibility 2	6-3	2-7
Possibility 3	4-6	0-10

Based on the above tables we can conclude that the difference between the number of 3 pointers would always be 6. Hence, Option (c) is correct.

29. The only way to divide the teams would be given by the following table:

WINNING TEAM			LOSING TEAM		
Player Name	Points	Scoring shots break up	Player Name	Points	Scoring shots break up
Hasan	24		Jeetu	20	
Chiranjeev	23	5-4	Fardeen (Even)	16	4-2
Geetam (Even)	19	3-5	Arun (Even)	15	3-3
Dhruv (Even)	18	2-6	Ishwar (Odd)	15	1-6
Birender (Odd)	17	3-4	Eleswarappu (Odd)	13	3-2

Further, Hasan and Jeetu having the same number of scoring shots means three possibilities for them:

	Hasan (24 points)	Jeetu (20 points)
Possibility 1	8-0	4-4
Possibility 2	6-3	2-7
Possibility 3	4-6	0-10

Based on the above tables we can conclude that the difference between the number of 2 pointers and 3 pointers for the teams could be either 0, 10 or 20. Only option (d) gives a possible value of this difference.

30. The only way to divide the teams would be given by the following table:

WINNING TEAM			LOSING TEAM		
Player Name	Points	Scoring shots break up	Player Name	Points	Scoring shots break up
Hasan	24		Jeetu	20	
Chiranjeev	23	5-4	Fardeen (Even)	16	4-2
Geetam (Even)	19	3-5	Arun (Even)	15	3-3
Dhruv (Even)	18	2-6	Ishwar (Odd)	15	1-6
Birender (Odd)	17	3-4	Eleswarappu (Odd)	13	3-2

From the above table, it is clear that Fardeen has the highest ratio of 2.66.

Option (d) is correct.

Section II

31. Option (b);The phrase is used in order to suggest the peaceful atmosphere.

32. Option (b); Third paragraph, second line clearly suggests that the writer's life resembled his grandparents'

33. Option (c); She was imitating her grandfather.

34. Option (b); In the whole fifth paragraph, the reference is being given to the peace in milton.

35. Option (d); As per the paragraph 5th, the Ward was free to enjoy her life.

36. Option (c);[clearly mentioned in the passage]

37. Option (c) This is an indirect question and the answer lies in the 8th and 9th paragraph.

38. Option (c) Given in sixth paragraph

39. Option (c) This is also gives in the seventh paragraph

40. Option (a) This is given in the tenth paragraph

41. Option (b)This is given in the eleventh paragraph

42. The correct answer is option (b). [This is clearly an irrelevant option]

43. The correct answer is (b).[this is the summary which covers the main idea.]

44. In the above paragraph, the starting sentence is already defined. The sentence sequence 1DA is using a double contrast- A kind of flip flop argument. Statement D opposes(contrasts) the idea of 1, while statement A again contrasts the opposition of D. In this question, recognizing this structure is sufficient to get to the correct answer. Option (d) is correct.

45. In the above question, the key sentence sequence is the BA sequence, which is in the form of an idea transformation since, B introduces the concept of the component parts, while A refers to these components in a different context altogether. Hence, the correct answer is option (b).

46. The sentence sequence AB is in the form of an idea elaboration, while the sentence sequence DC is in the form of generic to specific. Hence, the correct answer is (a).

47. Option (c) [assented in the sense of agreed]

48. Option (b) [given permission, thus authorised is the answer]

49. Option (d) [in the sense of - to forgive]

50. Option (a) [in the sense of disagree/not allow]

51. Option (d) is correct.

52. Option (b) is correct.

53. Option (c) is correct.

54. Option (c) is correct.

55. Option (a) is correct.

Solutions for 56 to 58:

The two possible distributions of the eight in clockwise fashion are:

Possibility 1: APCQDSBR

Possibility 2: ASBQCPDR

Based on these arrangements the answers are:

56. This case is referring to possibility 2. Derek would be opposite Bijay (gap of 3 people between any 2 opposite persons on the table). Option (d) is correct.

57. Possibility 2 is reflected in Option (b). Hence, Option (b) is correct.

58. Preeti and Surabhi are always opposite each other as are Queen and Raveena (in both cases). Hence, Option (d) is correct.

Solutions for 59 to 60:

Six persons A, B, C, D, E & F on six days, Monday to Saturday, six posts –Clerk (C), Officer (O), Technician (T), Manager (M), Supervisor (S) and Sales Executive (SE).

The second paragraph gives the clues directly to fit in the following table:

A → Sales Executive	
B →	X Wed, X Friday
C →	
D → Technician	Thursday
E → Clerk	Tuesday
F → Manager	Monday

We also know that the officer joined on Wednesday. It can only be Celina (C). Thus, the table will look like:

A → Sales Executive	Friday
B → Supervisor	Saturday
C → Officer	Wednesday
D → Technician	Thursday
E → Clerk	Tuesday
F → Manager	Monday

Thus, the answers are:

59. Celina. Option (b) is correct.
60. Bobby. Option (c) is correct.

SOLVED PAPERS

IIFT 2013

SNAP 2011

XAT 2014

Solved Quantitative Aptitude Questions from Other
Competitive Examinations (IIFT, SNAP and XAT)

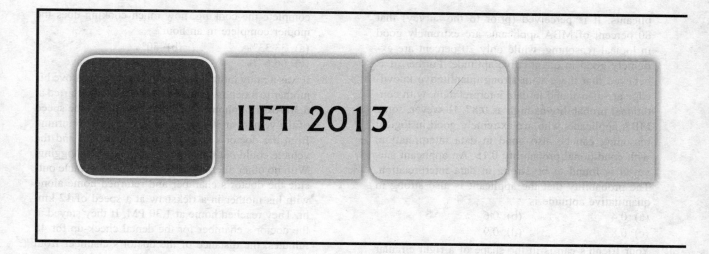

1. Suppose there are 4 bags. Bag 1 contains 1 black and $a^2 - 6a + 9$ red balls, bag 2 contains 3 black and $a^2 - 6a + 7$ red balls, bag 3 contains 5 black and $a^2 - 6a + 5$ red balls and bag 4 contains 7 black and $a^2 - 6a + 3$ red balls. A ball is drawn at random from a randomly chosen bag. The maximum value of probability that the selected ball is black, is
   (a) $16/a^2 - 6a + 10$
   (b) $20/ a^2 - 6a + 10$
   (c) 1/16
   (d) None of the above

2. If the product of the integers a, b, c and d is 3094 and if $1 < a < b < c < d$, what is the product of b and c?
   (a) 26
   (b) 91
   (c) 133
   (d) 221

3. Mrs. Sonia buys ₹249.00 worth of candies for the children of a school. For each girl she gets a strawberry flavoured candy priced at ₹3.30 per candy; each boy receives a chocolate flavoured candy priced at ₹ 2.90 per candy. How many candies of each type did she buy?
   (a) 21, 57
   (b) 57, 21
   (c) 37, 51
   (d) 27, 51

4. There is a triangular building (ABC) located in the heart of Jaipur, the Pink City. The length of the wall in east (BC) direction is 397 feet. If the length of south wall (AB) is perfect cube, the length of southwest wall (AC) is a power of three, and the length of wall in southwest (AC) is thrice the length of side AB, determine the perimeter of this triangular building.
   (a) 3209 feet
   (b) 3213 feet
   (c) 3773 feet
   (d) 3313 feet

5. Out of 8 consonants and 5 vowels how many words can be made, each containing 4 consonants and 3 vowels?
   (a) 700
   (b) 504000

   (c) 3528000
   (d) 7056000

6. If $x^2 + 3x - 10$ is a factor of $3x^4 + 2x^3 - ax^2 + bx - a + b - 4$, then the closest approximate values of a and b are
   (a) 25, 43
   (b) 52, 43
   (c) 52, 67
   (d) None of the above

7. If the product of n positive integers is n^n, then their sum is
   (a) A negative integer
   (b) Equal to n
   (c) Equal to $n + 1/n$
   (d) Never less than n^2

8. A tennis ball is initially dropped from a height of 180 m. After striking the ground, it rebounds (3/5)th of the height from which it has fallen. The total distance that the ball travels before it comes to rest is
   (a) 540 m
   (b) 600 m
   (c) 720 m
   (d) 900 m

9. In a sports meet for senior citizens organised by the Rotary Club in Kolkata, 9 married couples participated in table tennis mixed double event. The number of ways in which the mixed double team can be made, so that no husband and wife play in the same set, is
   (a) 1512
   (b) 1240
   (c) 960
   (d) 640

10. Two trains P and Q are scheduled to reach New Delhi railway station at 10.00 AM. The probability that train P and train Q will be late is 7/9 and 11/27 respectively. The probability that train Q will be late, given that train P is late, is 8/9. Then the probability that neither train will be late on a particular day is
    (a) 40/81
    (b) 41/81
    (c) 77/81
    (d) 77/243

11. A survey was conducted to test relative aptitudes in quantitative and logical reasoning of MBA ap-

plicants. It is perceived (prior to the survey) that 80 percent of MBA applicants are extremely good in logical reasoning, while only 20 percent are extremely good in quantitative aptitude. Further, it is believed that those with strong quantitative knowledge are also sound in data interpretation, with conditional probability as high as 0.87. However, some MBA applicants who are extremely good in logical reasoning can be also good in data interpretation, with conditional probability 0.15. An applicant surveyed is found to be strong in data interpretation. The probability that the applicant is also strong in quantitative aptitude is

(a) 0.4   (b) 0.6
(c) 0.8   (d) 0.9

12. Your friend's cap is in the shape of a right circular cone of base radius 14 cm and height 26.5 cm. The approximate area of the sheet required to make 7 such caps is

(a) 6750 sq cm   (b) 7280 sq cm
(c) 8860 sq cm   (d) 9240 sq cm

13. In an engineering college there is a rectangular garden of dimensions 34 m by 21 m. Two mutually perpendicular walking corridors of 4 m width have been made in the central part and flowers have been grown in the rest of the garden. The area under the flowers is

(a) 320 sq m   (b) 400 sq m
(c) 510 sq m   (d) 630 sq m

14. If decreasing 70 by X percent yields the same result as increasing 60 by X percent, then X percent of 50 is

(a) 3.84
(b) 4.82
(c) 7.10
(d) The data is insufficient to answer the question

15. A rod is cut into 3 equal parts. The resulting portions are then cut into 12, 18 and 32 equal parts, respectively. If each of the resulting portions have integer length, the minimum length of the rod is

(a) 6912 units   (b) 864 units
(c) 288 units   (d) 240 units

16. If $\log_{10} x - \log_{10} \sqrt[3]{x} = 6 \log_x 10$ then the value of x is

(a) 10   (b) 30
(c) 100   (d) 1000

17. A mother along with her two sons is entrusted with the task of cooking *biryani* for a family get-together. It takes 30 minutes for all three of them cooking together to complete 50 percent of the task. The cooking can also be completed if the two sons start cooking together and the elder son leaves after 1 hour and the younger son cooks for further 3 hours. If the mother needs 1 hour less than the elder son to

complete the cooking, how much cooking does the mother complete in an hour?

(a) 33.33%   (b) 50%
(c) 66.67%   (d) None of the above

18. It was a rainy morning in Delhi when Rohit drove his mother to a dentist in his Maruti Alto. They started at 8.30 AM from home and Rohit maintained the speed of the vehicle at 30 km/hr. However, while returning from the doctor's chamber, rain intensified and the vehicle could not move due to severe water logging. With no other alternative, Rohit kept the vehicle outside the doctor's chamber and returned home along with his mother in a rickshaw at a speed of 12 km/hr. They reached home at 1.30 PM. If they stayed at the doctor's chamber for the dental check-up for 48 minutes, the distance of the doctor's chamber from Rohit's house is

(a) 15 km   (b) 30 km
(c) 36 km   (d) 45 km

19. Two alloys of aluminium have different percentages of aluminium in them. The first one weighs 8 kg and the second one weighs 16 kg. One piece each of equal weight was cut off from both the alloys and first piece was alloyed with the second alloy and the second piece alloyed with the first one. As a result, the percentage of aluminium became the same in the resulting two new alloys. What was the weight of each cut-off piece?

(a) 3.33 kg   (b) 4.67 kg
(c) 5.33 kg   (d) None of the above

20. Three years ago, your close friend had won a lottery of ₹ 1 crore. He purchased a flat for ₹ 40 lakhs, a car for ₹ 20 lakhs and shares worth ₹ 10 lakhs. He put the remaining money in a bank deposit that pays compound interest @ 12 percent per annum. If today, he sells off the flat, the car and the shares at certain percentage of their original value and withdraws his entire money from the bank, the total gain in his assets is 5%. The closest approximate percentage of the original value at which he sold off the three items is

(a) 60 percent   (b) 75 percent
(c) 90 percent   (d) 105 percent

21. If $\log_{13} \log_{21} \{\sqrt{x+21} + \sqrt{x}\} = 0$, then the value of x is

(a) 21   (b) 13
(c) 81   (d) None of the above

22. If x is real, the smallest value of the expression $3x^2 - 4x + 7$ is :

(a) 2/3   (b) 3/4
(c) 7/9   (d) None of the above

23. The average of 7 consecutive numbers is P. If the next three numbers are also added, the average shall

(a) Remain unchanged   (b) Increase by 1

(c) Increase by 1.5   (d) Increase by 2

24. The duration of the journey from your home to the College in the local train varies directly as the distance and inversely as the velocity. The velocity varies directly as the square root of the diesel used per km., and inversely as the number of carriages in the train. If, in a journey of 70 km. in 45 minutes with 15 carriages, 10 litres of diesel is required, then the diesel that will be consumed in a journey of 50 km. in half an hour with 18 carriages is

(a) 2.9 litres   (b) 11.8 litres
(c) 15.7 litres   (d) None of the above

25. The capacity of tap Y is 60% more than that of X. If both the taps are opened simultaneously, they take 40 hours to fill the rank. The time taken by Y alone to fill the tank is

(a) 60 hours   (b) 65 hours
(c) 70 hours   (d) 75 hours

ANSWER KEY

1. (d)	2. (b)	3. (b)	4. (d)
5. (c)	6. (c)	7. (d)	8. (c)
9. (a)	10. (b)	11. (b)	12. (d)
13. (c)	14. (d)	15. (c)	16. (d)
17. (b)	18. (c)	19. (c)	20. (c)
21. (d)	22. (d)	23. (c)	24. (b)
25. (b)			

Solutions

1. The number of balls every bag is $a^2 - 6a + 10$. The probability of picking up a black ball would be defined as:

   Probability of picking up bag 1 × Probability of picking up a black ball + Probability of picking up bag 2 × Probability of picking up a black ball + Probability of picking up bag 3 × Probability of picking up a black ball + Probability of picking up bag 4 × Probability of picking up a black ball
   $= \frac{1}{4} \times [1/(a^2 - 6a + 10)] + \frac{1}{4} \times [3/(a^2 - 6a + 10)] + \frac{1}{4} \times [5/(a^2 - 6a + 10)] + \frac{1}{4} \times [7/(a^2 - 6a + 10)] = \frac{1}{4} [16/(a^2 - 6a + 10)] = [4/(a^2 - 6a + 10)]$.
   Hence, Option (d) is correct.

2. The key in this question is to look for factor pairs of 3094. If we do a prime factor search of 3094, we get $3094 = 2 \times 7 \times 13 \times 17$. These are clearly the values of a, b, c and d in that order. Thus, the value of the product of b and c is $13 \times 7 = 91$. Hence, Option (b) is correct.

3. Solve this one through options. If you use Option (a) you get:
   $21 \times 3.3 + 57 \times 2.9 = 234.6 \neq 249$.
   Option (b) gives us: $57 \times 3.3 + 21 \times 2.9 = 249$.
   Hence, Option (b) is correct.

4. The perimeter $P = AB + BC + AC$.
   Of these $BC = 397$, $AC = 3^n$ and $AB = a^3$.
   Thus, $P = 397 + 3^n + a^3$
   We also know that $AC = 3 \times AB$
   $3^n = 3 \times a^3 \rightarrow$
   $3^{n-1} = a^3$.
   So, $P = 397 + 3^n + 3^{n-1}$
   $\rightarrow (P - 397) = 3^{n-1} \times (3 + 1) = 3^{n-1} \times 4$
   This means that $(P - 397)$ should be a multiple of 3 and 4 simultaneously.

   Checking the options, only Option (d) meets the criteria because if we put $P = 3313$ we get $P - 397 = 2916$ which is a multiple of 3 and 4. The other options do not satisfy this requirement and hence Option (d) is the correct answer.

5. We would need to select 4 consonants and 3 vowels and arrange them. This can be done in ${}^8C_4 \times {}^5C_3 \times 7!$ $= 70 \times 10 \times 5040 = 3528000$ words.

6. The equation $x^2 + 3x - 10$ has two factors 2 and -5. Putting $x = 2$ in the expression $3x^4 + 2x^3 - ax^2 + bx - a + b - 4$, we get: $48 + 16 - 4a + 2b - a + b - 4 = 0 \rightarrow$
   $5a - 3b = 0$ ...(i)
   We also have: $x = -5$.
   Putting $x = 2$ in the expression $3x^4 + 2x^3 - ax^2 + bx - a + b - 4$, we get: $26a + 4b = 1621$ ...(ii)
   Solving (i) and (ii) simultaneously we get $a = 52$ and $b = 67$. Option (c) is correct.

7. Since we are talking about the calculation of the sum of n positive integers, it cannot be negative or a fraction. Thus, Options (a) and (c) are ruled out. Further, Option (b) can be rejected by taking a sample value of n as 4 – it gives us n^n as 256. A possible value of the 4 integers could be: 1, 2, 16 and 8. Obviously their sum is not equal to the value of n and hence we can also reject Option (b). This leaves us only with Option (d) as a possible answer. Hence, Option (d) is correct.

8. The total distance traveled would be the infinite sum of the 'falling down' distance plus the infinite sum of the 'bouncing up' distance traveled by the ball. The answer would be got by:
   $180 \div (1 - 3/5) + 108 \div (1 - 3/5) = 450 + 270 = 720$. Hence, Option (c) is correct.

9. The number of ways of selecting 2 men and 2 women (such that there would be no husband wife pair in the same set) would be ${}^9C_2 \times {}^7C_2$. Further, there are two ways in which we can form the two teams for the same set of players. Thus, the correct answer would be: ${}^9C_2 \times {}^7C_2 \times 2 = 36 \times 21 \times 2 = 1512$. Hence, Option (a) is correct.

10. Let the probability of P coming late $= P(P)$; the probability of Q coming late $= P(Q)$. Then:
    $P(P \cup Q) = P(P) + P(Q) - P(P \cap Q)$

Where $P(P \cup Q)$ means the situation where at least one of the two trains P and Q is late and $P(P \cap Q)$ means the situation where both the trains P and Q are late.

The value of $P(P \cap Q) = 7/9 \times 8/9 = 56/81$.

This gives us:

$P(P \cup Q) = 7/9 + 11/27 - 56/81 = (63 + 33 - 56)/81 = 40/81$.

Thus, the probability that none of the two trains is late = 1 – Probability that at least 1 train is late.

The required answer = 1– 40/81 = 41/81.

Hence, Option (b) is correct.

11. Out of every 100 applicants, 80 are extremely good at Logical Reasoning while 20 are extremely good at Quantitative Aptitude. Further, since the probability of someone who is extremely good at Quantitative Aptitude also being strong at Data Interpretation is 0.87, we can expect $20 \times 0.87 = 17.4$ people out of 20 to be strong at DI.

Also, since the related probability for someone being strong at DI if he/she is strong at LR is 0.15, we get $80 \times 0.15 = 12$ people who would be expected to be strong at DI (from the 80 who are strong at LR).

Thus, we get a total of 29.4 people in every 100 who would be strong at DI. Naturally, if we find someone who is strong at DI, the probability he/she would also be strong at QA = $17.4/29.4 \approx 0.6$. Hence, Option (b) is correct.

12. The surface area of the sheet required to make the cap would be equal to the lateral surface area of the cap which is given by the formula $\pi \times r \times l$. Since the base radius is 14 cm and height is 26.5 cm, the value of 'l' can be calculated using $r^2 + h^2 = l^2 \to l = 29.97 \approx 30$. Thus, 7 caps would require $7 \times \pi \times 14 \times 30 = 9240$ cm^2. Hence, Option (d) is correct.

13. The area of the garden is $34 \times 21 = 714$ sq. m. Out of this the area covered by the paths $= 4 \times 34 + 4 \times 21 - 4 \times 4 = 204$ sq. m. The remaining area being covered by flowers would be equal to: $714 - 204 = 510$ sq.m.

14. Solve this one through options. One reading of the question sentence should tell you clearly that there would be a value of 'X' that would satisfy this – and hence Option (d) can be rejected. This leaves us to check the first three options. Rather than trying to solve the question by creating complex mathematical processes, it is better to solve this using the options. The following process would help you identify whether an option is correct or not.

For Option (c): X % of 50 = 7.10 implies that the value of X must be 14.2%.

If we now visualise the equation 70 – 14.2% of 70 = 60 + 14.2% of 60, we can clearly realise that the LHS

and the RHS of the above equation do not match. Hence, this option can be rejected.

For Option (b): X % of 50 = 4.82 implies that the value of X must be 9.64 %.

If we now visualise the equation 70 – 9.64 % of 70 = 60 + 9.64 % of 60, we can clearly realise that the LHS and the RHS of the above equation do not match. Hence, this option can be rejected.

15. Solve this question using options. The correct option would be the smallest number amongst the given options, whose 1/3rd value would be divisible by 12, 18 as well as by 32. If we try the lowest option first our thought process would go as follows:

Option (d): If rod length = 240, then 1/3rd of the rod length = 80. But 80 is not divisible by 12. Hence, option (d) is wrong.

Option (c): If rod length = 288, then 1/3rd of the rod length = 96. But 96 is not divisible by 18. Hence, option (c) is wrong.

For Option (b), rod length = 864, we get 1/3rd of the rod length = 288 which is a multiple of 12, 18 and 32 simultaneously. Hence, Option (c) is correct.

16. $\log_{10} x - \log_{10} \sqrt[3]{x} = 6 \log_x 10 \to \log_{10} x - 1/3 \times \log_{10} x = 6/(\log_{10} x)$;

Put $\log_{10} x = m$, gives us:

$m - 1/3 \times m = 6/m \to m^2 - 1/3 \times m^2 = 6 \to m^2 = 9 \to m = \pm 3$.

We can reject the value of $m = -3$ because that would involve x to be a decimal value between 0 and 1 (which is ruled out from the options).

Thus, $m = 3$, which means that $\log_{10} x = 3 \to x = 10^3 = 1000$.

Hence, Option (d) is correct.

17. The total work for them is 100% per hour. If we try to go through the options and try Option (b) which is the easiest to check – we get: The mother's work per hour = 50%. This would mean that the mother requires 2 hours to complete the task. Since it is given that the elder son takes one hour more than his mother to complete the task, it would imply that the elder son's time taken for the task = 3 hours $\to$ elder son's work per hour = 33.33%. Then the younger son's work per hour would be 100–50–33.33= 16.66% per hour.

With these working rates, we need to confirm whether the last condition mentioned in the problem matches with these working rates for the two sons. The condition states that – "The cooking can also be completed if the two sons start cooking together and the elder son leaves after 1 hour and the younger son cooks for further 3 hours." If we go by this – we will get that the elder son would do 33.33% of the work in the first hour, while the younger son would cook for 4 hours and do 66.66% of the work – thus completing 100% of the work together (since 33.333% + 66.666% = 100%).

Thus, Option (b) is the correct option.

18. The equation that one needs to solve for this question is:

$d/30 + d/12 = 4.2$. (4.2 here, means that the total time taken for the travel is 4 hours 12 minutes – since he comes home in exactly 5 hours, which includes the 48 minutes at the doctor's chamber.)

The value of 'd' can then be checked from the options – the best option which fits the value of $d = 36$. Hence, Option (c) is correct.

19. The main focus in this problem should be on understanding that the cut off piece's weight should be such that the alloyed pieces that are created should have the same ratio weight wise for each of the two alloys.

Thus, if the weight of the cut off pieces is 'w' each, then:

$(8-w)/w = w/(16-w)$.

Again to solve this, it is better to try to use the options given in the question to see which one fits the above equation.

Using Option (c), we can see that if we take $w = 5.33$, we get:

$2.66/5.33 = 5.33/10.66 = ½$.

Hence, Option (c) is correct.

20. 30 lakh invested @ 12% per annum compounded, would approximately become 42 lakh in three years. Since, he gets back 1.05 crore – his return on his remaining 70 lakh would be equal to 1.05 crore – 42 lakh ≈ 63 lakh – which is around 90% of the value of his investment of 70 lakh. Thus, Option (c) is the correct answer.

21. $\log_{13}\log_{21}\{\sqrt{x+21} + \sqrt{x}\} = 0$ implies:

$\log_{21}\{\sqrt{x+21} + \sqrt{x}\} = 13^0 = 1$ implies:

$\{\sqrt{x+21} + \sqrt{x}\} = 21^1$

The value of x can be visualised to be 100 because at $x = 100$, LHS = RHS.

Hence, Option (d) is correct.

22. The given expression would have its minima at the value of x got by differentiating the quadratic expression with respect to x and equating the resultant linear expression to 0. We get $6x-4 = 0$, which means that the minima would occur at $x = 2/3$.

The minimum value would be got by putting $x = 2/3$ in the given expression.

We get, minimum value = $12/9 – 8/3 + 7 = 17/3$.

Hence, Option (d) is correct.

23. It can be experimentally verified by taking the values of the 7 integers as 1, 2, 3, 4, 5, 6 and 7 to get an average of 4, while the average of the group if the next three numbers are included would become 5.5 (the group of numbers would be 1, 2, 3, 4, 5, 6, 7, 8, 9 and 10).

Thus, the average increases by 1.5.

Hence, Option (c) is correct.

24. Let Distance of the journey = D, Diesel used per km = A and the number of carriages = N. Then we have

Time, $T = \dfrac{K \times D \times N}{\sqrt{A}}$

From the first set of values given in the question, we have $T = 45$, $D = 70$, $N = 15$ and $A = 1/7$. Putting these values in the equation we get: $K = \dfrac{3}{70\sqrt{7}}$

The equation then becomes, $T = \dfrac{3 \times D \times N}{70\sqrt{7} \times \sqrt{A}}$.

In the second case, $D = 50$ km, $N = 18$ and $T = 30$ minutes.

Solving for A, we get the value of $A = 11.8$.

Hence, Option (b) is correct.

25. Let the work done by Tap X in an hour be w. Then the work done by Tap Y in an hour would be $1.6\,w$. Together, they would do $2.6\,w$ work in an hour. Thus, the total work in 40 hours = $40 \times 2.6\,w$.

This amount of work would be done by Y alone in $\dfrac{40 \times 2.6\,w}{1.6\,w}$ hours = 65 hours.

Hence, Option (b) is correct.

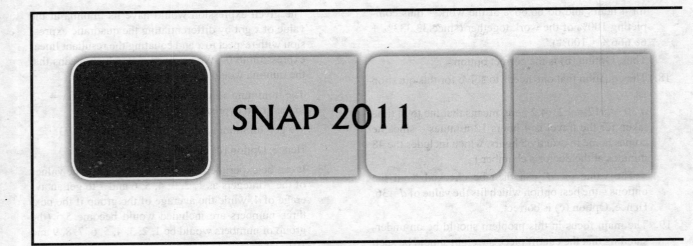

SNAP 2011

Note: The SNAP 2011 paper had 40 questions on the **Quantitative Aptitude and Data Interpretation** section. Apart from the solutions to the 31 questions in Quantitative Aptitude given here, the solutions to the 9 questions of data interpretation are available in my book—*How to Prepare for Data Interpretation for the CAT* also published by McGraw Hill.

1. A train travelling at 36 kmph crosses a platform in 20 seconds and a man standing on the platform in 10 seconds. What is the length of the platform in meters?
   (a) 240 meters   (b) 100 meters
   (c) 200 meters   (d) 300 meters

2. By walking at 4/5th of his usual speed, a man reaches office 10 minutes later than usual. What is his usual time?
   (a) 20 min   (b) 40 min
   (c) 30 min   (d) 50 min

3. A man and a woman 81 miles apart from each other, start travelling towards each other at the same time. If the man covers 5 miles per hour to the women's 4 mile per hour, how far will the woman have travelled when they meet?
   (a) 27   (b) 36
   (c) 45   (d) None of these

4. Two people were walking in opposite directions. Both of them walked 6 miles forward then took right and walked 8 miles. How far is each from starting positions?
   (a) 14 miles and 14 miles
   (b) 10 miles and 10 miles
   (c) 6 miles and 6 miles
   (d) 12 miles and 12 miles

5. Four men and three women can do a job in 6 days. When 5 men and 6 women work on the same job,

the work gets completed in 4 days. How long will 2 women and 3 men take to do the job?
   (a) 18   (b) 10
   (c) 8.3   (d) 12

6. Ram completes 60% of a task in 15 days and then takes the help of Rahim and Rachel. Rahim is 50% as efficient as Ram is and Rachel is 50% as efficient as Rahim is. In how many more days will they complete the work?
   (a) $\dfrac{121}{3}$ (b) $\dfrac{51}{7}$
   (c) $\dfrac{40}{7}$ (d) $\dfrac{65}{7}$

7. A and B can do a piece of work in 21 and 24 days respectively. They start the work together and after some days A leaves the work and B completes the remaining work in 9 days. After how many days did A leave?
   (a) 5   (b) 7
   (c) 8   (d) 6

8. A trader makes a profit equal to the selling price of 75 articles when he sells 100 of the articles. What % profit does he make in the transaction?
   (a) 33.33%   (b) 75%
   (c) 300%   (d) 150%

9. In a 100 m race, if A gives B a start of 20 meters, then A wins the race by 5 seconds. Alternatively, if A gives B a start of 40 meters the race ends in a dead heat. How long does A take to run 200 m?
   (a) 10 seconds   (b) 20 seconds
   (c) 30 seconds   (d) 40 seconds

10. A 4 cm cube is cut into 1cm cubes. What is the percentage increase in the surface area after such cutting?

(a) 4% (b) 300%

(c) 75% (d) 400%

11. A number G236G0 can be divided by 36 if G is:
    (a) 8
    (b) 6
    (c) 1
    (d) More than one values are possible

12. Amit can do a work in 12 days and Sagar in 15 days. If they work on it together for 4 days, then the fraction of the work that is left is:
    (a) 3/20 (b) 3/5
    (c) 2/5 (d) 2/20

13. A rectangular park 60 m long and 40 m wide has two concrete crossroads running in the middle of the park and rest of the park has been used as a lawn. If the area of the lawn is 2109 sq. m, then what is the width of the road?
    (a) 2.91 m (b) 3 m
    (c) 5.82 m (d) None of these

14. A bag contains 5 white and 3 black balls; another bag contains 4 white and 5 black balls. From any one of these bags a single draw of two balls is made. Find the probability that one of them would be white and other black.
    (a) 275/504 (b) 5/18
    (c) 5/9 (d) None of these

15. Three parallel lines are cut by two transversals as shown in the given figure. If AB = 2 cm, BC = 4 cm and DE = 1.5 cm, then the length of EF is:

    (a) 2 cm (b) 3 cm
    (c) 3.5 cm (d) 4 cm

16. $\log_{10}10 + \log_{10}10^2 + \ldots + \log_{10}10^n$
    (a) $n^2 + 1$ (b) $n^2 - 1$
    (c) $\dfrac{n^2 + n}{2} \cdot \dfrac{n(n+1)}{3}$ (d) $\dfrac{(n^2 + n)}{2}$

17. The sum of a number and its reciprocal is thrice the difference of the number and its reciprocal. The number is:
    (a) $\pm\sqrt{2}$ (b) $\pm\dfrac{1}{\sqrt{2}}$
    (c) $\pm\dfrac{1}{\sqrt{3}}$ (d) $\pm\sqrt{3}$

18. The total number of natural numbers that lie between 10 and 300 and are divisible by 9 is

19. If $^nC_x = 56$ and $^nP_x = 336$, find n and x.
    (a) 7, 3 (b) 8, 4
    (c) 8, 3 (d) 9, 6

20. One side of an equilateral triangle is 24 cm. The midpoints of its sides are joined to form another triangle whose midpoints are in turn joined to form still another triangle. This process continues indefinitely. Find the sum of the perimeters of all the triangles.
    (a) 144 cm (b) 72 cm
    (c) 536 cm (d) 676 cm

21. The probability that a leap year selected at random contains either 53 Sundays or 53 Mondays, is:
    (a) 17/53 (b) 1/53
    (c) 3/7 (d) None of these

22. Find the intercepts made by the line $3x + 4y - 12 = 0$ on the axes:
    (a) 2 and 3 (b) 4 and 3
    (c) 3 and 5 (d) None of these

23. The average of 4 distinct prime numbers a, b, c, d is 35, where $a < b < c < d$. a and d are equidistant from 36 and b and c are equidistant from 34 and a, b are equidistant from 30 and c and d are equidistant from 40. The difference between a and d is:
    (a) 30 (b) 14
    (c) 21 (d) Cannot be determined

24. Ramsukh bhai sells *rasgulla* (a favourite Indian sweets) at ₹ 15 per kg. A *rasgulla* is made up of flour and sugar in the ratio 5 : 3. The ratio of price of sugar and flour is 7 : 3 (per kg). Thus he earns $66\dfrac{2}{3}\%$ profit. What is the cost price of sugar?
    (a) ₹ 10/kg (b) ₹ 9/kg
    (c) ₹ 18/kg (d) ₹ 14/kg

25. A reduction of 20% in the price of sugar enables a person to purchase 6 kg more for ₹ 240. What is the original price per kg of sugar?
    (a) ₹ 10/kg (b) ₹ 8/kg
    (c) ₹ 6/kg (d) ₹ 5/kg

26. A solid sphere is melted and recast into a right circular cone with a base radius equal to the radius of the sphere. What is the ratio of the height and radius of the cone so formed?
    (a) 4 : 3 (b) 2 : 3
    (c) 3 : 4 (d) None of these

27. The speed of scooter, car and train are in the ratio of 1 : 4 : 16. If all of them cover equal distance then the ratio of time taken/velocity for each of the vehicle is:
    (a) 256 : 16 : 1 (b) 1 : 4 : 16
    (c) 16 : 4 : 1 (d) 16 : 1 : 4

28. B is twice efficient as A and A can do a piece of work in 15 days. A started the work and after a few days B joined him. They completed the work in 11

days, from the starting. For how many days did they work together?

(a) 1 day
(b) 2 days
(c) 6 days
(d) 5 days

29. A, B, C and D purchased a restaurant for ₹ 56 lakhs. The contribution of B, C and D together is 460% that of A, alone. The contribution of A, C and D together is 366.66% that of B's contribution and the contribution of C is 40% that of A, B and D together. The amount contributed by D is:

(a) 10 lakhs
(b) 12 lakhs
(c) 16 lakhs
(d) 18 lakhs

30. The salary of Raju and Ram is 20% and 30% less than the salary of Saroj respectively. By what percent is the salary of Raju more than the salary of Ram?

(a) 33.33%
(b) 50%
(c) 15.18%
(d) 14.28%

31. The radius of a wire is decreased to one-third and its volume remains the same. The new length is how many times the original length?

(a) 2 times
(b) 4 times
(c) 5 times
(d) 9 times

ANSWER KEY

1. (b)	2. (b)	3. (b)	4. (b)
5. (c)	6. (c)	7. (b)	8. (b)
9. (c)	10. (b)	11. (a)	12. (c)
13. (b)	14. (a)	15. (b)	16. (d)
17. (a)	18. (a)	19. (c)	20. (a)
21. (c)	22. (b)	23. (b)	24. (d)
25. (a)	26. (d)	27. (a)	28. (b)
29. (d)	30. (d)	31. (d)	

Solutions

1. The speed of the train in m/s would be $36 \times 5 \div 18 = 10$ m/s. If the train takes 10 seconds to cross a man on the platform, it means that the length of the train = $10 \times 10 = 100$ m.

   Also, while crossing the platform, the distance traveled by the train is equal to: Length of Train + Length of Platform.

   Hence, Length of Platform + 100 = $20 \times 10 \rightarrow$ Length of Platform = 100 meters. Option (b) is the correct answer.

2. As the distance is constant, the speed and time are inversely proportional to each other. Walking at $4/5^{th}$ of his usual speed would mean that the man would take $5/4^{th}$ of his usual time. Thus, the extra time taken = $5/4^{th}$ of $t - t = 1/4^{th}$ of t (where t = normal time taken).

   But the extra time taken is given as 10 minutes. Hence, $t/4 = 100 \rightarrow t = 40$ minutes.

   Hence, Option (b) is correct.

3. Their relative speed would be equal to 9 miles per hour (as they are approaching each other). Thus, they would meet in $81 \div 9 = 9$ hours. The woman would travel $9 \times 4 = 36$ miles in that time. Hence, Option (b) is correct.

4. Since both have them have taken a 90° turn, it clearly implies that 6 miles and 8 miles (the distances they have walked) would be the base and height of a right-angled triangle. Their distance from the starting point would be calculated by the hypotenuse of each right-angled triangle. The appropriate Pythagoras triplet would be 6, 8, 10 and hence their distance from the start would be 10 miles each.

   Hence, Option (b) is correct.

5. 24 man days + 18 woman days = 20 man days + 24 woman days → 1 man-day = 1.5 woman days.

   In terms of woman days the total work would be:

   24 man days + 18 woman days = 36 woman days + 18 woman days = 54 woman days.

   2 women and 3 men would be equivalent to 2 women + 4.5 women = 6.5 women.

   The number of days required would be:

   54/6.5 = 8.3 days. Hence, Option (c) is correct.

6. Since Ram has completed 60% of the task in 15 days – this gives us two pieces of information –

   (i) That 40% of the task is left;
   (ii) Ram's rate of work is 4% per hour.

   Then, from the information in the problem we can see that Rahim's work rate would be 2% per annum, while Rachel's work rate would be 1% per annum. Thus, their combined rate of work would be 7% per hour giving us 40/7 as the required answer.

   Option (c) is correct.

7. In the 9 days that he works alone, B would do $\frac{9}{24}$ of the work. This means that A and B together have done $\frac{15}{24}$ of the work. Thus, $\frac{d}{24} + \frac{d}{21} = \frac{15}{24}$

   Solving the above equation we get $d = 7$.

   Hence, Option (b) is correct.

8. The profit percent = $\frac{75}{100} \times 100 = 75$. Hence, Option (b) is correct.

9. From the second statement, we have that in the time A runs 100 m, B would run 60 m. Thus, their ratio of speeds is 5:3. From this point you can start checking with the options in order to get to the correct answer.

   If we check for Option (a) we see that, A's speed = 20m/s, B's speed = 12 m/s. This would satisfy the second condition – i.e., if A gives B a start of 40 meters the race ends in a dead heat.

We need to see whether these values satisfy the first condition too – i.e., if A gives B a start of 20 meters, then A wins the race by 5 seconds.

A would complete the race in 5 seconds and B at that time would have reached from 20 m to 80 m (as he would simultaneously have traveled 60 m in 5 seconds @ 12 m/s). To cover the remaining 20 m, A would not be taking 5 seconds. Hence, we can reject this option.

The same thinking can be applied to the other options to get the correct answer.

For Option (c): A's speed = 6.666 m/s, B's speed = 4 m/s

We need to see whether these values satisfy the first condition too – i.e., if A gives B a start of 20 meters, then A wins the race by 5 seconds.

A would complete the race in 15 seconds and B at that time would have reached from 20 m to 80 m (as he would simultaneously have traveled 60 m in 15 seconds @ 4 m/s). To cover the remaining 20 m, A would be taking 5 seconds. Hence, this option is correct.

Option (c) is the correct answer.

10. The initial surface area = $6 \times 4 \times 4 = 96$ sq. cm. The new surface area = $64 \times 6 \times 1 \times 1 = 384$ sq. cm. The surface area is becoming 4 times the original, which means that there is a 300% increase in the surface area. Hence, Option (b) is correct.

11. With $G = 8$, divisibility can be verified. Hence, Option (a) is correct.

12. Amit's work per day = 8.33%, Sagar's work per day = 6.66%. Combined work per day = 15%. In 4 days they would complete $15 \times 4 = 60\%$ work. Fraction of work left = 40 out of 100 or 2 out of 5. Hence, Option (c) is correct.

13. The total area of the field is 2400 sq. m. If we try to keep the width of the road as 3 m, we can see that the total area of the roads = $3 \times 60 + 3 \times 40 - 3 \times 3 = 291$ sq. m. – leaving 2109 sq. m for the lawn. Hence, Option (b) is correct.

14. The event definition would be:

First bag & white ball & black ball OR First bag & black ball & white ball

OR

Second bag & white ball & black ball OR Second bag & black ball & white ball

$$= \frac{1}{2} \times \frac{5}{8} \times \frac{3}{7} + \frac{1}{2} \times \frac{3}{8} \times \frac{5}{7} + \frac{1}{2} \times \frac{4}{9} \times \frac{5}{8} + \frac{1}{2} \times \frac{5}{9} \times \frac{4}{8}$$

$$= \frac{30}{112} + \frac{40}{144} = \frac{275}{504}$$

15. The ratio of AB to BC would be equal to the ratio of DE to EF. Since, BC is twice the value of AB, EF

would also be twice the value of DE and hence, EF = 3 cm. Hence, Option (b) is correct.

16. The value of the expression = $1 + 2 + 3 + \dots n$ = sum of the first n natural numbers $\frac{n \times (n+1)}{2} = \frac{n^2 + n}{2}$. Hence, Option (d) is correct.

17. Solve through options by checking for the given conditions. The value of $\pm\sqrt{2}$ fits the conditions. Hence, Option (a) is the correct answer.

18. We need to find the number of terms in the series: 18, 27, 36, … 297

There are 32 terms in this series since it starts with 9×2 and ends with 9×33.

Hence, Option (a) is correct.

19. We know that the value of ${}^nC_x \times r! = {}^nP_x$

Since, the value of ${}^nP_x$ is 6 times the value of ${}^nC_x$, we know that $r = 3$. Checking the options, we can see that $n = 8$ and $r = 3$ fits the given values. Hence, Option (c) is the correct answer.

20. The second perimeter would be half the first perimeter. In order to get the answer to this question, we need the infinite sum of the geometric progression: $72 + 36 + 18 + 9 + \dots$ This is a GP with $a = 72$ and $r = \frac{1}{2}$. The infinite sum of the given series = 144. Hence, Option (a) is correct.

21. A leap year has 366 days, which means that it has 52 completed weeks + 2 extra days. Thus, if 1st January is a Saturday, 30th December would also be a Saturday. For a 53rd Sunday or Monday, the year should start either from a Saturday, Sunday or a Monday in which case, the last two days of the year would be (Saturday, Sunday) or (Sunday, Monday) or (Monday, Tuesday) respectively. The required probability is 3/7. Hence, Option (c) is correct.

22. For the x-intercept $y = 0$ and hence the x-intercept = 4. Similarly, for the y-intercept, the value of $x = 0$ and hence the y-intercept = 3. Hence, Option (b) is correct.

23. A quick look at the various prime numbers between the 20s to the 40s gives us the following list: 23, 29, 31, 37, 39, 41, 43, 47. The given conditions are satisfied by the set of numbers: 29, 31, 37 and 43. Thus, $a = 29$ and $d = 43$ and hence the required difference between and d is 14. Hence, Option (b) is correct.

24. 8 kg of *rasgulla* would give a revenue of ₹120 and a cost of ₹72. (Note: Cost should be 3/5 of the revenue for a profit of 66.66%.) 8 kg of the sweet would also require 5 kg of flour and 3 kg of sugar. Thus, the cost of 5 kg flour + 3 kg sugar = ₹72. The price of sugar that satisfies this condition in association with the additional condition that the ratio of the price of sugar to flour is 7:3 is ₹14/kg.

Hence, Option (d) is correct.

25. Reduction of 20% in the price of sugar would increase the quantity by 25% = increase of 6 kg (for the same cost). Thus, the original quantity = 24 kg and the new quantity = 30 kg. The price of sugar (original) = 240 ÷ 24 = ₹10/ kg.

26. The volume of the sphere = $\dfrac{4\pi r^3}{3}$. The volume of a right circular cone = $\dfrac{\pi r^3 h}{3}$.

   Since the radii of the sphere and the cone are equal, when we equate the two volumes we get $4r = h$. Hence, the ratio of height to radius for the right circular cone is 4:1. Hence, Option (d) is correct.

27. If the speeds are 1 kmph, 4 kmph and 16 kmph respectively, they would cover a distance of (say 16 km) in 16 hours, 4 hours and 1 hour respectively. The ratio of time taken to velocity would be (16/1): (4/4) : (1/16) = 16:1:1/16 = 256:16:1. Hence, Option (a) is correct.

28. A's work = 6.66% per hour. Thus, B's work = 13.33% per hour. Combined work = 20% per hour. Checking the options: Option (a) does not work because 10 × 6.66 + 20 × 1 ≠ 100.

   For Option (b) we get: 9×6.66 + 2×20 = 60 +40 = 100%.
   Hence, Option (b) is correct.

29. From the given statements we can work out the values of the individual investments as follows:

   Statement: The contribution of B, C and D together is 460% that of A, alone means that A's investment = 56 ÷ 5.6 = 10 lakhs.

   Statement: The contribution of A, C and D together is 366.66% that of B's contribution means that B's investment = 56 ÷ 4.6666 = 12 lakhs.

   Statement: The contribution of C is 40% that of A, B and D together implies that C's investment = 56 × 40 ÷ 140 (unitary method) = 16 lakhs

   Hence, D's investment = 56 −10 − 12 − 16 = 18 lakhs.
   Hence, Option (d) is correct.

30. If Saroj is taken as 100, Raju would be 80 and Ram would be 70. The salary of Raju would be 14.28% more than the salary of Ram. Hence, Option (d) is correct.

31. If the wire is 1/3rd in terms of the radius, per unit length the volume of material required would be 1/9th. Thus, the length of the wire—if the volume has to be kept the same—would be 9 times the original length. Hence, Option (d) is correct.

XAT 2014

Note: XAT 2014 had 31 questions on the **Quantitative Aptitude** section. Of these there were 21 questions directly on Quantitative Aptitude and 9 questions were on Data Interpretation. In this book, the paper consists of the 22 questions from QA part. The 9 question on DI for XAT 2014 can be found in my book—*How to Prepare for Data Interpretation for the CAT* also published by McGraw Hill.

1. x, 17, $3x - y^2 - 2$, and $3x + y^2 - 30$, are four consecutive terms of an increasing arithmetic sequence. The sum of the four numbers is divisible by:
   (a) 2
   (b) 3
   (c) 5
   (d) 7
   (e) 11

2. In quadrilateral PQRS, PQ = 5 units, QR = 17 units, RS = 5 units, and PS = 9 units. The length of the diagonal QS can be:
   (a) > 10 and < 12
   (b) > 12 and < 14
   (c) > 14 and < 16
   (d) > 16 and < 18
   (e) Cannot be determined

3. Consider the formula,

   $$S = \frac{\alpha \times \omega}{\tau + \rho \times \omega}$$, where all the parameters are positive

   integers. If ω is increased and α, τ and ρ are kept constant, then S:
   (a) increases
   (b) decreases
   (c) increases and then decreases
   (d) decreases and then increases
   (e) Cannot be determined

4. Prof. Suman takes a number of quizzes for a course. All the quizzes are out of 100. A student can get an A grade in the course if the average of her scores is more than or equal to 90. Grade B is awarded to a student if the average of her scores is between 87 and 89 (both included). If the average is below 87, the student gets a C grade.

   Ramesh is preparing for the last quiz and he realises that he will score a minimum of 97 to get an A grade. After the quiz, he realises that he will score 70, and he will just manage a B. How many quizzes did Prof. Suman take?
   (a) 6
   (b) 7
   (c) 8
   (d) 9
   (e) None of these

5. A polynomial "$ax^3 + bx^2 + cx + d$" intersects x-axis at 1 and −1, and y-axis at 2. The value of b is:
   (a) −2
   (b) 0
   (c) 1
   (d) 2
   (e) Cannot be determined

6. The sum of the possible values of X in the equation $|X + 7| + |X - 8| = 16$ is:
   (a) 0
   (b) 1
   (c) 2
   (d) 3
   (e) None of the above

7. There are two windows on the wall of a building that need repairs. A ladder 30 m long is placed against a wall such that it just reaches the first window which is 26 m high. The foot of the ladder is at Point A. After the first window is fixed, the foot of the ladder is pushed backwards to Point B so that the ladder can reach the second window. The angle made by the ladder with the ground is reduced by half, as a result of pushing the ladder. The distance between points A and B is
   (a) < 9 m
   (b) ≥ 9 m and < 9.5 m
   (c) ≥ 9.5 m and < 10 m
   (d) ≥ 10 m and < 10.5 m
   (e) ≥ 10.5 m

8. Amitabh picks a random integer between 1 and 999, doubles it and gives the result to Sashi. Each time Sashi gets a number from Amitabh, he adds 50 to the number, and gives the result back to Amitabh, who doubles the number again. The first person, whose result is more than 1000, loses the game. Let 'x' be the smallest initial number that results in a win for Amitabh. The sum of the digits of 'x' is:
   (a) 3
   (b) 5
   (c) 7
   (d) 9
   (e) None of these

9. Consider four natural numbers: $x, y, x + y,$ and $x - y$. Two statements are provided below:
   I. All four numbers are prime numbers.
   II. The arithmetic mean of the numbers is greater than 4.
   Which of the following statements would be sufficient to determine the sum of the four numbers?
   (a) Statement I
   (b) Statement II
   (c) Statement I and Statement II
   (d) Neither Statement I nor Statement II
   (e) Either Statement I or Statement II

10. Triangle ABC is a right-angled triangle. D and E are mid points of AB and BC respectively. Read the following statements.
    I. $AE = 19$
    II. $CD = 22$
    III. Angle B is a right angle.
    Which of the following statements would be sufficient to determine the length of AC?
    (a) Statement I and Statement II
    (b) Statement I and Statement III
    (c) Statement II and III
    (d) Statement III alone
    (e) All three statements

11. There are two circles C_1 and C_2 of radii 3 and 8 units respectively. The common internal tangent, T, touches the circles at Points P_1 and P_2 respectively. The line joining the centers of the circles intersects T at X. The distance of X from the center of the smaller circle is 5 units. What is the length of the line segment P_1P_2?
    (a) ≤ 13
    (b) > 13 and ≤ 14
    (c) > 14 and ≤ 15
    (d) > 15 and ≤ 16
    (e) > 16

12. The probability that a randomly chosen positive divisor of 10^{29} is an integer multiple of 10^{23} is: a^2/b^2, then '$b - a$' would be:
    (a) 8
    (b) 15
    (c) 21
    (d) 23
    (e) 45

13. Circle C_1 has a radius of 3 units. The line segment PQ is the only diameter of the circle which is parallel to the X-axis. P and Q are points on curves given by the equations $y = a^x$ and $y = 2a^x$ respectively, where $a < 1$. The value of a is:
    (a) $1/\sqrt[6]{2}$
    (b) $1/\sqrt[6]{3}$
    (c) $1/\sqrt[3]{6}$
    (d) $1/\sqrt{6}$
    (e) None of these

14. There are two squares S_1 and S_2 with areas 8 and 9 units, respectively. S_1 is inscribed within S_2, with one corner of S_1 on each side of S_2. The corners of the smaller square divides the sides of the bigger square into two segments, one of length 'a' and the other of length 'b', where, $b > a$. A possible value of 'b/a', is:
    (a) ≥ 5 and < 8
    (b) ≥ 8 and < 11
    (c) ≥ 11 and < 14
    (d) ≥ 14 and < 17
    (e) > 17

15. Diameter of the base of a water-filled inverted right circular cone is 26 cm. A cylindrical pipe, 5 mm in radius, is attached to the surface of the cone at a point. The perpendicular distance between the point and the base (the top) is 15 cm. The distance from the edge of the base to the point is 17 cm, along the surface. If water flows at the rate of 10 meters per minute through the pipe, how much time would elapse before water stops coming out of the pipe?
    (a) < 4.5 minutes
    (b) ≥ 4.5 minutes but < 4.8 minutes
    (c) ≥ 4.8 minutes but < 5 minutes
    (d) ≥ 5 minutes but < 5.2 minutes
    (e) ≥ 5.2 minutes

16. Aditya has a total of 18 red and blue marbles in two bags (each bag has marbles of both colors). A marble is randomly drawn from the first bag followed by another randomly drawn from the second bag, the probability of both being red is 5/16. What is the probability of both marbles being blue?
    (a) 1/16
    (b) 2/16
    (c) 3/16
    (d) 4/16
    (e) None of these

17. Consider a rectangle $ABCD$ of area 90 units. The points P and Q trisect AB, and R bisects CD. The diagonal AC intersects the line segments PR and QR at M and N respectively. What is the area of the quadrilateral $PQMN$?
    (a) > 9.5 and ≤ 10
    (b) > 10 and ≤ 10.5
    (c) > 10.5 and ≤ 11
    (d) > 11 and ≤ 11.5
    (e) > 11.5

18. Two numbers, $297B$ and $792B$, belong to base B number system. If the first number is a factor of the second number then the value of B is:
    (a) 11
    (b) 12
    (c) 15
    (d) 17
    (e) 19

19. A teacher noticed a strange distribution of marks in the exam. There were only three distinct scores: 6, 8 and 20. The mode of the distribution was 8. The sum of the scores of all the students was 504. The number of students in the most populated category was equal to the sum of the number of students with lowest score and twice the number of students with the highest score. The total number of students in the class was:

    (a) 50   (b) 51
    (c) 53   (d) 56
    (e) 57

20. Read the following instruction carefully and answer the question that follows:

    Expression $\sum_{n=1}^{13} \frac{1}{n}$ can also be written as $\frac{x}{13!}$

    What would be the remainder if x is divided by 11?

    (a) 2   (b) 4
    (c) 7   (d) 9
    (e) None of the above

21. A rectangular swimming pool is 48 m long and 20 m wide. The shallow edge of the pool is 1 m deep. For every 2.6 m that one walks up the inclined base of the swimming pool, one gains an elevation of 1 m. What is the volume of water (in cubic meters), in the swimming pool? Assume that the pool is filled up to the brim.

    (a) 528   (b) 960
    (c) 6790   (d) 10560
    (e) 12960

22. The value of the expression:

    $\sum_{i=2}^{100} \frac{1}{\log_i 100!}$ is:

    (a) 0.01   (b) 0.1
    (c) 1   (d) 10
    (e) 100

ANSWER KEY

1. (a)	2. (b)	3. (a)	4. (d)
5. (a)	6. (b)	7. (e)	8. (c)
9. (a)	10. (e)	11. (c)	12. (d)
13. (a)	14. (d)	15. (d)	16. (c)
17. (d)	18. (e)	19. (e)	20. (d)
21. (d)	22. (c)		

Solutions

1. Given that one of the terms of the AP is 17, we can identify that the AP would either have all four odd numbers or have two odd and two even numbers.

    Either ways the sum of the AP for four numbers would be even and hence would be divisible by 2.

Note: we can safely assume here that since the terms of the AP are based on values of the variables x and y, all the four terms of the AP would be integers and there would be no possibility of some of the terms having decimal values.

Hence, Option (a) is correct.

2. Since, PQ, QR, RS and PS are consecutive sides in the quadrilateral, we would get a figure for the quadrilateral as:

In this figure we have two relationships for the range of the value of SQ (based on the fact that the sum of two sides of a triangle would always be greater than the third side).

From Triangle SRQ: $5 + QS > 17 \rightarrow 5 + x > 17 \rightarrow x > 12$

From Triangle PQS: $x < 5 + 9 \rightarrow x < 14$.

Hence, $12 < x < 14$. Hence, Option (b) is correct.

3. The expression can be modified to:

    $$\frac{1}{S} = \frac{\tau + \rho \times \omega}{\alpha\omega} = \frac{\tau}{\alpha\omega} + \frac{\rho}{\alpha} = \frac{K_1}{\omega} + K_2$$

    It can be clearly seen that when ω is increased, $\frac{1}{S}$ would decrease. Hence, S would increase if we increase ω.

    Hence, Option (a) is correct.

4. The difference between just getting an A grade and just getting a B grade would be equal to (number of quizzes × 3). The difference between the required score to manage an A grade and the score achieved to just manage a B grade as given in the problem's information is equal to $97 - 70 = 27$.

    Thus, number of quizzes × 3 = 27. Hence, number of quizzes is 9.

    Hence, Option (d) is correct.

5. When a polynomial intersects the x-axis, the value of $y = 0$. When a polynomial intersects the y-axis, the value of $x = 0$.

    If we take the polynomial as $y = ax^3 + bx^2 + cx + d$, we get:

    Intersects x-axis at $x = 1$ implies: $a + b + c + d = 0$;

    Intersects x-axis at $x = -1$ implies: $-a + b - c + d = 0$.

    Hence, $2(b + d) = 0$ or simply put $(b + d) = 0$.

    Intersects y-axis at $y = 2$ implies: $0 + d = 2 \rightarrow d = 2$.

    Hence, $b = -2$. Hence, Option (a) is correct.

6. You need to consider the value of the expression for three ranges of values of X.

If $X \geq 8$, $|X + 7|$ and $|X - 8|$ are both non-negative.

If $-7 \leq X < 8$, $|X + 7|$ is positive and $|X - 8|$ is negative.

& If $X < -7$, $|X + 7|$ and $|X - 8|$ are both negative.

For the first case:

If $X \geq 8$, $|X + 7|$ and $|X - 8|$ are both non-negative.

$|X + 7| = X + 7$ and $|X - 8| = X - 8$.

Hence, $|X + 7| + |X - 8| = 16$;

Implies $X + 7 + X - 8 = 16$

$\rightarrow 2X - 1 = 16$

$\therefore x = 8.5.$

For the second case:

If $-7 \leq X < 8$, $|X + 7|$ is positive and $|X - 8|$ is negative.

$|X + 7| = X + 7$ and $|X - 8| = 8 - X$.

Hence, $X + 7 + 8 - X = 16$. This leads to the ridiculous outcome $15 = 16$.

Of course this is not possible and hence we can rule out this range – i.e. there would be no value of X between $-7 \leq x < 8$ that would satisfy this equation.

For the third case:

If $X < -7$, $|X + 7|$ and $|X - 8|$ are both negative.

$|X + 7| = -7 - X$ and $|X - 8| = 8 - X$.

Thus, we get:

$-7 - X + 8 - X = 16 \rightarrow 2X = -15 \rightarrow X = -7.5.$

Thus, we have two possible values of X: i.e. 8.5 and -7.5 and their sum $= 8.5 - 7.5 = 1$.

Hence Option (b) is correct.

7.

From the figure we have:

$\cos \theta = y/30$ and $\cos 2\theta = x/30$.

Solving using Pyhtagoras theorem we get:

$x = \sqrt{30^2 - 26^2} = \sqrt{224} \approx 15$. Thus, the value of the angle 2θ is approximately equal to $60°$. Hence, $\theta \approx 30°$.

Solving $\cos 30 = y/30$, we get $y = 15\sqrt{3}$ m.

The distance between A and B would be $15\sqrt{3} - 15$
$= 15 \times 0.73 \approx 10.95$.

Hence, Option (e) is correct.

8. Let the number chosen by Amitabh be X. Then the flow of the numbers would go as follows:

	Amitabh	Sashi
Round 1	2X	2X + 50
Round 2	4X + 100	4X + 150
Round 3	8X + 300	8X + 350
Round 4	16X + 700	16X + 750
Round 5	32X + 1500 (Obviously the game cannot continue beyond this point as the value would definitely have crossed 1000 by this time.)	

The latest that Amitabh can win is when Sashi gets a value of 16X +750. For 16X +750 > 1000, the smallest possible value of X = 16. Hence, sum of the digits of X = 1 + 6 = 7. Hence, Option (c) is correct.

9. If we take only Statement I, for all four numbers to be prime one of them must be even and hence equal to 2. Only in such an event do we get $x + y$ and $x–y$ as odd numbers and only if they are odd can all the four numbers be prime. A little bit of trial and error then gives us we get $x = 5$, $y = 2$, $x + y = 7$ and $x – y = 3$. There is not other case of $x–y$, x and $x+y$ being prime as if we take y as 2, these numbers become $x–2$, x and $x+2$ and hence represent three consecutive odd numbers. (After 3, 5, 7 there is no situation where three consecutive odd numbers are all prime.)

Hence, Statement I is sufficient.

Statement II can be easily rejected as all it is giving us is that the sum of the four numbers is greater than 16. As we can easily imagine there are infinite sets of four such numbers, which have a sum greater than 16.

Hence, Option (a) is correct.

10. First things first while solving this. If we do not include Statement III, we do not know which angle is a right angle and hence cannot uniquely calculate the value of the Side AC.

Also, Statement III alone does not give us anything. Hence, we can reject Options (a) and (d). Options (b) and (c) give us similar set of information – i.e., the value of 1 median and the fact that B is the right angle in the triangle. This is also clearly not sufficient to answer the question.

For Option (e): We have 2 medians of a right-angled triangle, and we know B is the right angle. Hence, we can find AC.

Hence, Option (e) is the correct answer.

11. Let A, B be the centre of the two circles with radius 3 cm and 8 cm respectively.

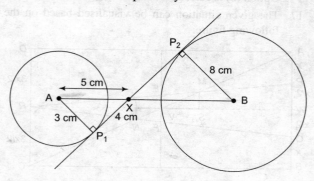

The use of the Pythagoras triplet 3, 4, 5 is self evident from the figure.

In order to find P_1P_2 we need to find the value of XP_2. The similarity between triangles AP_1X and BP_2X implies that $\dfrac{AP_1}{BP_2} = \dfrac{P_1X}{P_2X}$.

Since, we know three of the lengths in the above equation we get:

$\dfrac{3}{8} = \dfrac{4}{P_2X} \rightarrow P_2X = 4 \times 2.66 = 10.66$.

Thus, the length of $T = 4 + 10.66 = 14.66$

Hence, Option (c) is correct.

12. $10^{29} = 5^{29} \times 2^{29}$. Thus, the number of divisors of $10^{29} = (29 + 1)(29 + 1) = 30 \times 30$.

Now, if we look at divisors of 10^{29}, which satisfy the given condition, we need to get divisors of the form: as $N \times 10^{23}$. The number of such divisors can be traced based on the number of divisors of N, such that $10^{29} = N \times 10^{23}$.

$N = 10^6 = 5^6 \times 2^6$ which would have $7 \times 7 = 49$ divisors. Hence, 10^{29} would have 49 divisors that are also divisible by 10^{23}.

The probability that a randomly chosen divisor of 10^{29} is divisible by 10^{23} is $49/900 = a^2/b^2$.

Thus, $a = 7$ and $b = 30$ and consequently $b - a = 23$.

Hence, Option (d) is correct.

13. The crux of the solution to this problem lies in understanding the fact that the Points P and Q would have the same Y-coordinates (since the diameter PQ is parallel to the X-axis) while their X co-ordinates would differ by 6 (since the diameter of the circle is 6).

We thus have two possible cases:

Case 1: If P lies on the curve $y = a^x$ and Q lies on the curve $y = 2a^x$

Then, the difference between the x-coordinates of being 6, we get:

$y = 2a^x - a^{(x + 6)}$. We get $a = 2^{1/6}$

Case 2: If Q lies on the curve $y = a^x$ and P lies on the curve $y = 2a^x$

Then, the difference between the x-coordinates of being 6, we get:

$y = a^x - 2a^{(x + 6)}$. We get $a = (1/2)^{1/6}$

Since, we are given that $a < 1$, only Case 2 is possible and hence Option (a) is correct.

14. If you visualise a figure for this situation, you would be able to see something as follows:

Solving through Pythagoras theorem, we will get $a = 0.18$ and $b = 3 - 0.18 = 2.82$.

Hence, the value of $b/a = 2.82/0.18 = 15.666$. Hence, Option (d) is correct.

15. The following figure would exemplify the situation, with the pipe attached at a height of h from the apex (bottom) of the cone.

In the above figure the cones with height h and the cone with height $h + 15$ are similar to each other. Hence using similarity we will get:

$\dfrac{10}{26} = \dfrac{h}{h+15}$

$\rightarrow 10h + 150 = 26h \rightarrow 16h = 150 \rightarrow = 9.375$ cm.

Based on this information we can then calculate the volume of water that would flow out from the pipe as: Total volume of the cone with height $(h + 15)$ – Volume of cone with height h.

$$= \frac{1}{3}\pi\left[\left(13^2 \times (15+9.375)\right) - \left(5^2 \times 9.375\right)\right]$$

Calculating this we get the volume of water that over-flows $= 1295\pi$ cm^3

Further, the rate at which the water flows out of the hole per minute is given by: $\pi \times (0.5^2 \times 1000)$ cm^3

Hence, the required time can be given as,

$$\frac{1295\pi}{\pi \times (0.5^2 \times 1000)} = 5.18 \text{ min}$$

Hence, Option (d) is the correct answer.

16. Let there be 'r' red marbles in the first bag and 'R' red marbles in the second bag.

Also, let there be 'b' blue marbles in the first bag and 'B' blue marbles in the second bag.

Then $(r + b) + (R + B) = 18$

The number of ways of selecting 1 marble from the first bag and one marble from the second bag $= (r + b) \times (R + B)$.

Also, the number of ways of selecting a red marble from the first bag and a red marble from the second bag $= r \times R$.

Hence, the probability of selecting two red marbles would be given by:

$$\frac{r \times R}{(r+b) \times (R+B)} = \frac{5}{16}.$$

This equation shows us that the value of $(r + b) \times (R + B)$ must be a multiple of 16 while the value of $r \times R$ must be a multiple of 5.

We now know that $(r + b) + (R + B) = 18$ and $(r + b) \times (R + B) =$ a multiple of 16.

If we try to break down 18 into two parts, such that their product is a multiple of 16, we get two cases:

Case I: $16 \times 2 = 32$ and Case II: $10 \times 8 = 80$.

Analysing Case I:

If $(r + b) \times (R + B) = 32$, then $r \times R = 10$ (in order to maintain the ratio of 5/16 between the two).

There would be 16 balls in one bag and 2 balls in the second bag.

The second bag must contain 1 red and 1 blue ball. i.e., $R = 1$ and $B = 1$

Since $r \times R = 10$ we get $r = 10$ and $b = 6$.

The probability of both balls being blue in this case would turn out as:

$$\frac{1}{2} \times \frac{6}{16} = \frac{3}{16}.$$

If we try to solve the other case in the same way, we get $r = 5$, $R = 5$ and $b = 3$ and $B = 5$ and the probability of both balls being blue becomes $\frac{1}{2} \times \frac{3}{8} = \frac{3}{16}$.

We get the same answer in both the cases. Hence, Option (c) is correct.

17. The given situation can be visualised based on the following figure:

The area of the quadrilateral $PQNM =$ Area of $PQFE$ − Area Triangle MVS + Area Triangle VFN.

So our focus to find the area of the required quadrilateral should shift to the area of the three individual components on the right hand side of the above equation.

Finding the area of quadrilateral PQFE: Being a parallelogram, the required area would be given by: $\frac{1}{2} \times$ *sum of parallel sides* $\times$ *perpendicular distance between the parallel sides*.

In the figure, let side $AB = 3x$ and side $BC = y$. Then, for the quadrilateral $PQFE$, the perpendicular distance between the parallel sides would be $y/2$.

Further, the sum of parallel sides would be equal to

$$PQ + EF = x + \frac{x}{2} = \frac{3x}{2}$$

Area of $PQFE = \frac{1}{2} \times \frac{3x}{2} \times \frac{y}{2}$

We know that the area of the rectangle is $3x \times y = 90$. Hence, area of $PQFE = 90 \div 8 = 11.25$.

Finding the area of the triangle MSV = Finding the area of the triangle MEV.

$$\frac{1}{2} \times \text{base} \times \text{height} = \frac{1}{2} \times EV \times \text{height}$$

Using similarity between APM and VEM, we can see that since $AP = x$ and $EV = x/4$, the ratios of the lengths of APM and VEM would be 4:1.

Thus, if the height of $APM = 4h$, the height of $VEM = h$ and also $4h + h = y/2 \rightarrow h =$ height of VEM with base $VE = y/10$.

Hence, area triangle $MEV = \frac{1}{2} \times EV \times \text{height} = \frac{xy}{80}$ $= 0.375$.

Similarly, the area of triangle $VFN \approx 0.27$.

Thus, the required area $= 11.25 - 0.375 + 0.27$ ≈ 11.145.

Hence, Option (d) is correct.